CLASSICAL TOWN HISTORIES

GENERAL EDITOR: W. B. STEPHENS

ACADEMIA TERTIA ANGLICANA

ACADEMIA TERTIA ANGLICANA;

OR, THE

ANTIQUARIAN ANNALS

OF

STANFORD

BY

FRANCIS PECK

With a new introduction by
A. ROGERS AND J. S. HARTLEY

This edition originally printed by
James Bettenham for the Author, London, 1727
Republished EP Publishing Limited, 1979

PUBLISHER'S NOTES

The parts which comprise this work, the main text, Books I–XIV, the Chronological Table of Contents, and the following additions to the text are all separately paginated. The revised manuscript of Richard Butcher's *The Survey and Antiquitie of the Towne of Stamford* and William Forster's Letters to Dr. Tanner and Mr. John Stevens with Francis Peck's own notes, are added at the end of Peck's text. No index was prepared for the original work; but an index compiled by members of the Stamford Survey Group is included at the end of the text in this reprint.

───────────

The text and plates for this reprint have been reproduced from the Lincolnshire Library Service copy No. 57355 and the Stamford Town Council copy No. 166. Full details of these are deposited with the Lincolnshire Library Service and with the Joseph Phillips Collection in the Town Hall, Stamford.

───────────

The plates have been inserted in the text in the order printed on each plate and a list of these is included in the new introductory material. In Book XI the page numbers 7 and 8 are always wanting, though the sequence of the text is correct. The note on this error of pagination in the author's Errata is also incorrect, since the word 'no' has been left out of his correction.

───────────

The text and most of the plates are reproduced in this volume at 88% of the original size. Plates 27, 28 and 29 are reproduced at 83% and plate 6 at 77%.

───────────

───────────

ISBN 0 7158 1300 5

───────────

British Library Cataloguing in Publication Data
Peck, Francis
    Academia tertia anglicana, or, The antiquarian
    annals of Stanford. – (Classical town histories).
    1. Stamford, Eng. – History
    I. Title   II. Series
    942.5'38   DA690.S8
    ISBN 0–7158–1300–5

Printed in Great Britain by Redwood Burn Limited, Trowbridge & Esher

INTRODUCTION

'who built, demolish'd and re-edified this famous towne'

The town of Stamford, built on the banks of the river Welland on the borders of the counties of Lincoln, Northampton and Rutland, seems to have developed an antiquarian frame of mind very early indeed. Leland, visiting the town in the second quarter of the sixteenth century, reported at least two incidents which reputedly occurred in the town some two hundred years earlier – the establishment of a quasi-university there in the early years of the reign of Edward III, and a sack of the town which local tradition asserted had taken place during the reign of 'one of the three Edwards'. Significantly, both of these events had left their mark on the fabric of the town, the former in the shape of 'halls' (allegedly scholastic) which were still standing when Leland came to Stamford, and the latter in the form of derelict buildings as yet unrepaired.[1]

In the light of this double trend, a long-term collective memory and a willingness to read history into the fabric of the town around them, it is no wonder that the community of Stamford threw up one of the earliest of all urban historians, Richard Butcher in 1646. Entitled *The Survey and Antiquitie of the town of Stamford*, his short book was as much a description of the contemporary town, its monuments and traditions, as a straightforward account of the town's annals. The book was reprinted (with new orthography) in 1717, along with a description of Tottenham High Cross, compiled by the Revd. Wilhelm Bedwell in 1631.

'had not the troubles of these times hindered my intended speed'

Of Butcher, little is known, but that little is intriguing. He was of course writing in stirring times, and Stamford, royalist to the core, was destined to play a not inconsiderable part in the events of the 1640s. But it had its own local political activities; from the late sixteenth century, the town had experienced a number of disputes involving the neighbouring county gentry. In 1588–94, there was a *fracas* known as the 'Stamford turmoil' involving among others the Heron and the Irby families of Lincolnshire; and Butcher himself reports a local quarrel in 1594 between the gentry families of Molyneux of Nottinghamshire, Tyrwhit (or perhaps Thorold) of Lincolnshire, and Rookwood of Suffolk.[2] Riots took place in the town over borough elections, and the Earl of Exeter and his deputy recorder frequently asserted that they had been at pains to 'suppress disorders in the town'.[3] Plague too struck the town frequently between 1600 and 1660. The borough council of what was described as 'this poor decayed town' spent much time and effort on attempting to make the river Welland below Stamford navigable; and in 1631, new trade ordinances were drawn up.[4] Then there was the problem of puritanism: the development of radical preaching in the town was accompanied from the early sixteenth century by a measure of hostility which on occasion erupted into violence.[5] All of the parish clergy of the town were ejected by the Earl of

Manchester in 1645–6; and one of the town's two M.P.s (Geoffrey Palmer, lawyer) played a major part in the trial of Strafford, and later was sent to the Tower and replaced because he was 'the first man that desired to have his protestation against the Remonstrance entered in the name of all the rest'.[6] The corporation and the Earl of Exeter were locked in dispute over several matters (renewing the town's charters and the leases of the town mills among them) and, perhaps most significant for Richard Butcher, a proposal by Henry, Lord Grey of Groby (newly entitled Earl of Stamford), for a monopoly of brewing in the town provoked a storm.[7]

'Then Stamford, love the man that honours thee'

Richard Butcher was caught up in most of these great matters, both as town clerk and as an innkeeper and victualler. Described as 'gentleman', he was admitted to the freedom of the town in June 1626 on payment of the large fine of £3 – despite the fact that in his *Survey* he describes Stamford as his native town. Four months later, he was elected town clerk and soon after was involved in a dispute over a newly introduced fee for his office of £2 per annum, which he took from admission fines.[8] Of his period of office, we know nothing; but in March 1634, at the order and direction of the privy council, he was dismissed. The circumstances are obscure, for he used his later tenure of the office to score through the dismissal entry so that most of it is illegible; but it apparently referred to the proposal by the Earl of Stamford to erect and administer a common town brewery at the expense of the town's innkeepers and victuallers. Involved in the issue were the Earl of Exeter and his agent, John Balguy, who had been elected recorder for the borough 'at the request of the Earl of Exeter by letter'. Butcher's tenure of the office of clerk of the peace may well have resulted in other causes of friction with Balguy. Balguy instituted the proceedings, alleging that Butcher had preferred various false accusations and spoken abusive words against the king and the recorder (the Earl of Stamford's brewhouse had been granted by royal monopoly in 1632); and he seems to have resented royal infringements on the town's liberties, appealing behind the town's charters to Magna Carta. In his submission to the Council, he acknowledged that he had carried himself very offensively against the Earl of Exeter and his deputy because they had endeavoured to suppress some disorders in the town. But the most important reason was clearly his opposition to the common brewhouse; his dismissal described him as innkeeper, and he seems to have resented particularly the extension of the Earl's monopoly 'to all brewers dwelling outside Stamford nearby, for all drinks that they sell in the town'.[9]

His book reveals him as a vitriolic person, bitter against members of the town council. But when it appeared, in 1646, he had recovered some of his local standing: 'now forasmuch as the Alderman, Comburgesses and Capitall Burgesses of this Towne or Borough have now upon good and deliberate consideracion thought the aforesaid Mr. Butcher [and several others dismissed at other times] to be men well deservinge to beare office in the Towne . . .', the dismissal order was deleted. He was not however restored as town clerk.[10] He was elected one of the twenty-four Capital Burgesses (the 'second chamber' of the town's council) at the same time (October 1644) and he remained in office until February 1648 when, on orders from the Committee of Parliament for Indemnity he and eight other councillors were summoned to Lincoln and there resigned; the offence this time seems to have been alleged royalist sympathies (at least two of those dismissed had served in arms against parliament).[11] Stamford was a centre of royalist resistance, and it is not surprising that altogether some fourteen councillors were removed from office between February and October 1648.

Troubles continued: in April 1651, Butcher with others was brought before the quarter sessions for 'selling lesse than a full quarte of his best ale for ijd contrary to the statute'; and in 1652, he tried to negotiate a lease of the Welland navigation from the council on behalf of an unnamed contractor. At the same time, he became entangled in the sequestration of William Dobbin, innholder of Stamford Baron, and a costly lawsuit resulted.[12] In 1656, when Major General Whaley, 'being in the town' (and incidentally issuing orders concerning the town plate for which the annual races had not been run), limited the number of alehouses in Stamford – 'I cannot but take notice that Alehouses are too numerous in all places, especially in Market townes' – Richard Butcher, innkeeper, was one of thirty-eight licensees, although his relation (perhaps his son) Robert Butcher 'innholder' only obtained a temporary licence.[13]

In August 1660, Richard Butcher promptly secured a writ to ensure his restoration to the office of capital burgess, but it was not until early in 1663 that he was 'againe restored to the office of Clarke of the Peace in the sayd Liberty of Stamford and sworn before the Alderman', as he triumphantly wrote.[14] In the new charter obtained early in 1664, Butcher was named as town clerk ('that virtuous and discreet man') and given the new office of clerk of recognizances, but he did not live long after seeing the inauguration of the long coveted privileges; in September 1664, his successor as town clerk was appointed '*super mortem* of Richard Butcher gent'. Butcher was buried in All Saints parish on 25 September 1664.[15]

'Hath made old Stamford young again'

Richard Butcher's *Survey* is no mean achievement, and its real nature is best gauged in its first (1646) edition. It is full of a lively sense of civic dignity and bitter criticism of some of his council colleagues whom he accused of (among other things) plundering the town's records and appropriating its property, especially that of the town charities. His history and antiquity is highly imaginative, but in spite of its shortcomings the book gives a most valuable insight into the working of a town in the middle of the seventeenth century. As the town clerk, Butcher had a particular opportunity to record the organisation of the borough and to give details of contemporary practice.

He clearly intended a second and enlarged edition, and to this end collected a good deal of extra material. His death ended these plans, although his son continued to cherish hopes of a new version. The reprint of the *Survey* in London in 1717 along with an earlier account of Tottenham must have doomed these hopes; but at the same time it reflects the increase in antiquarian interest of the last years of the seventeenth and the first quarter of the eighteenth centuries. In Stamford itself several writers were at work. The Revd. William Forster, who served several cures in Stamford and was Warden of Browne's Hospital, was one of these: it was recorded of him in 1704 that 'Mr. Foster has made large Collections towards the Antiquities of this place.'[16] Another writer was Francis Howgrave, apothecary and publisher in Stamford, who from 1732 became printer of the *Stamford Mercury* (one of the country's earliest provincial newspapers); impatient with the delays to the long-promised and authoritative account of Francis Peck, Howgrave published in 1726 an *Essay on the Ancient and Present State of Stamford*. Francis Peck, when he came to publish his great work, *Academia Tertia Anglicana: Antiquarian Annals of Stanford* in 1727, printed in an Appendix both an enlarged version of Butcher (indicating the extra material by italics and correcting and annotating the whole work with extensive footnotes) and Forster's material which he published in the form of two letters, the one to Dr. Thomas Tanner, author of *Notitia Anglicanum*, and the other to John Stevens, editor of part of *Monasticon Anglicanum*.

'the dear-loved place of my nativity . . .'

Francis Peck had been born in Stamford on 4 May 1692, the son of Robert and Elizabeth Peck.[17] Although the *Dictionary of National Biography* suggests that his father was a prosperous farmer, on his son's admission to St. John's College, Cambridge, in 1709, it was stated that he was the son of a merchant or tradesman (*mercatoris*).[18] However William

Stukeley made a note in his own copy of the *Annals of Stanford* that Peck was 'the son of a barber who play'd on the violin.'[19] Among the freeman entries in the borough records of the late seventeenth century is the name of only one Robert Peck, a musician, who was made free of the town in 1680.[20] Stukeley's note is further supported by the comment of one of Peck's severest critics, Francis Howgrave, that 'one would think that the Author [i.e. Peck] had never conversed with any one above a Barber or a Fiddler'.[21] Of Peck's mother, even less is known. According to Browne Willis, another eighteenth-century antiquarian for whom Francis acted as scribe for a short time, Elizabeth Peck was a 'poor Woman that work'd for her Bread, being a sort of Semstress'.[22]

Most writers have assumed that Peck was at Radcliffe's, the local grammar school (now Stamford School), and this may have been the case for a short time, but when admitted to Cambridge it was stated that he had been at Charterhouse.[23] He graduated B.A. in 1715, and after being ordained in 1716 he seems to have spent some time as helper to Browne Willis at Whaddon Hall (Bucks.) but was discharged when he was discovered, according to Thomas Hearne, 'to be a Villain, for he not only preached without being in orders, but betrayed the family concerns of Mr. Willis'.[24]

Details of the later part of Peck's life are very hard to trace, and he is primarily known from the comments of his contemporaries rather than any biographical source. In 1719 he became curate of Kings Cliffe (Northants) about six miles from Stamford, and four years later rector of Goadby Marwood, near Belvoir in Leicestershire. Apart from becoming a prebendary of Lincoln Cathedral in 1738, this was all the preferment he could achieve within the Church, though not for lack of trying.[25] Likewise Peck never achieved any position of importance in the academic world. He offered himself as librarian to the Earl of Oxford in 1735 but without success.[26] It would appear that his disagreement with Willis prejudiced his chances of academic recognition, and his only distinction in his chosen field of historical study was election as a Fellow of the Society of Antiquaries in 1732.

He married Anne Curtis, almost certainly closely related to a well known Stamford family of that name before 1720,[27] by whom he had a son and a daughter, Francis and Anne.[28] A second son, Thomas, died young. Peck died at his rectory of Goadby on 9 July 1743.[29]

'this learned and industrious antiquary'

Peck never seems to have been admitted to the inner circle of antiquaries, though well known to most of them. He corresponded with Maurice Johnson, founder-secretary of the Spalding Gentleman's Society, to which all the leading lights belonged, but he was never made a member. Although admitted to a similar society at Peterborough, he played no active part in it.[30] With William Stukeley, vicar of All Saints in Stamford, he helped found similar small societies in Stamford itself and in some nearby villages.[31] But his friendship with Stukeley was never close and Stukeley seems gradually to have tired of his companionship. Certainly the letters that passed between Stukeley and William Warburton, a future bishop of Gloucester, were highly critical of Peck; as Warburton wrote,[32]

> Of all the dabblers in the blind creeks of the Ocean of Immortality, commend me to Clarissimus [Peck] who launches out folio after folio, and makes every year a good trading voyage though he takes in nothing but ballast ... yet this is poured out on a necessitous world under the name of riches.

Perhaps Warburton, 'a bad scholar, a literary bully and a man of untrustworthy character', according to the *Oxford Companion to English Literature*, is not the best witness to Peck's academic character. Yet Stukeley, the Gales, Hearne and Browne Willis were all critical of him, while only a few of the lesser known antiquarians had much good to say of him.

As Warburton suggests, his literary output was prolific. In 1717, he published *An Exercise upon the Creation*, a collection of biblical verses arranged according to themes, and two years later, his first book of verses was published, in which appear the earliest references to Stamford:

FRANCIS PECK, M.A. Rector of GODEBY, *p.200.*

There are two slightly different engravings of this portrait. One version without the coats of arms is used as the frontispiece to Volume I of both the 1732 and 1779 editions of Francis Peck's *Desiderata Curiosa*; and the one reproduced here, with coats of arms, is used in John Nichols's *History and Antiquities of the County of Leicester*, Volume II, Part I, 1795.

I. Highmore pinx 1735.　　　　I. Faber fecit.

Francis Peck M.A.

This portrait was used as the frontispiece to Francis Peck's *Memoirs of the Life and Actions of Oliver Cromwell*, 1740.

> Of Oxford's once divided sons thence made
> The new, tho' short, Abode ...

a reference to the short-lived secession of northern scholars from Oxford to Stamford in the early years of the reign of Edward III. Other works followed: in 1720, a piece on the Book of Ecclesiastes; a long poem on the beauties and antiquities of the Vale of Belvoir, probably written after he had moved to a living under the shadow of the castle there; page upon page of couplets about Lincoln, which were never published; and many other verses. Sermons, too, brought together at the very end of his life in his *Four Discourses* (1742); and a first excursus into the history of Stamford, his *History of Bullrunning*, published anonymously in Stamford about 1723. But neither the scale of his writing, nor its content, endeared him to his contemporary antiquarians.

'... very conceited ...'

One of the causes for this hostility was apparently a lack of tact; Peck often seems to have given offence. Johnson, who was compiling a history of Lincolnshire, can scarcely have been pleased to be told by Peck that he too was intending to publish a history of the county.[33] Equally when Peck preached, he appears to have been rather too pointed in criticism of his hearers. He made matters worse in 1720 by printing a sermon which had already given offence, 'to let the world see how much I was wronged'.[34] This arrogance appeared also in his approach to his academic work. He was always ready to press his contemporaries to subscribe to his many publications, even suggesting that Hearne should send him some of his publications and collect the money from an Oxford bookseller who was selling Peck's books. Hearne took this to mean that he was expected to act as debt collector for Peck and wrote back in a suitably offended tone.[35] Moreover Peck's opinion of the value of his collections was clearly greater than that of others.

At times, particularly when Peck published his *New Memoirs of the Life and Poetical Works of Mr John Milton*, he faced more extreme academic criticism. Warburton believed that Peck was the author of a poem in the volume which Peck ascribed to Milton.[36] Others questioned whether the portrait which Peck published really was of Milton.[37] Moreover Peck was known to be a strong supporter of the royalist cause, and his publication of volumes about Cromwell and Milton was in direct contrast to his extravagent writings about Charles I's death in his verses *Sighs upon the never enough lamented Death of Queen Anne*, published in 1719. Though he never explained openly why he should have written volumes on Milton and Cromwell, he stated in a letter to Grey: 'For my part I do not see how Westminster Abbey is profaned by a cenotaph in honour of Milton considered only as a poet; his politics I have nothing to say to. You or I may write of Milton and Cromwell and still think as we please.'[38] Though often he attempted to write verse, his efforts are generally very poor and are best forgotten![39]

'... may be seen when another man speaks and when I do ...'

There was yet another side to Peck's literary work which aroused the scorn of his contemporaries. By the very nature of much of his work he was relying upon help from others. He sought notes from many different sources[40] and collected any manuscripts he could, laying himself open to the accusation that he 'hath got some good papers of other men's'.[41] The range of his historical interests was very wide; apart from his published works, he projected, planned and in some cases wrote histories of Lincolnshire, Leicestershire and the town of Grantham.[42] In such work as the two volumes of *Desiderata Curiosa* and the appendix to his *Memoirs of the Life and Actions of Oliver Cromwell*, 'a collection of divers curious historical pieces' as he titled it, he presented collections of historical documents supplied by others, to which he added footnotes. The range of subjects covered in these collections is considerable and there is little or no sense of unity among the documents.[43] While his contemporaries acknowledged the value of some of the documents, they rightly criticised this lack of unity.

In spite of all these failings there is nevertheless much for which Peck deserves credit. One of his works which never reached publication, though completed, was a study of the life and work of Nicholas Ferrar. The manuscript was later lost by Ferrar's relation Peckard, a loss regretted by most modern biographers of Ferrar.[44] Such a loss only serves to illustrate Peck's achievements. Since much of his work was in editing rather than historical writing, he has left transcripts of many documents for modern historians to use. His aims in collecting his materials were set out in an advertisement sheet at the end of his *Cromwell*. In this he sought contributions towards a new history of Leicestershire,[45] asking questions about the natural history and antiquities of the county. As an outline for a local study, these queries have a modern ring. He asks of the history of the parish church, its dedication; how many chapels there are and where they are situated; whether it is a rectory or vicarage; who is patron and incumbent; about financial matters; whether there are manuscripts surviving, and many other questions relating to the furnishings.

Another side of Peck was his interest in bibliography. He had a very fine library, including at least four works printed before 1500. In about 1790 it was stated that: 'in modern times it would not be an easy task for a Clergyman in a retired Country village, with a very moderate income, to amass such a store of early printed books.'[46] His *Complete Catalogue of all the Discourses written both for and against Popery in the time of King James II*, published in 1735, formed the basis of the Chetham Society catalogue.[47] In addition he was in correspondence with Joseph Ames, the bibliographer, and supplied him with many references.[48] When Peck died his son inherited his books, with the instruction that none was to be sold until he reached the age of thirty. But after the son's death in 1749, his collection was sold by a London bookseller, together with other libraries, so it is impossible to estimate the full extent of his father's collection.[49]

'I thought I should have despatched it much sooner'

From early in his life there is evidence that Peck intended to publish some account of the history of Stamford. When he was about seventeen, he copied out Butcher's *Survey of Stamford*, making alterations when necessary and leaving spaces for notes and emendations. In a series of appendices to this, he collected information about the many medieval religious institutions of the town. It appears that he added to this manuscript at various times but it was eventually abandoned. In his own introduction to his manuscript of Butcher, he mentions that he had 'many times wished some one or other would have reprinted Mr. Butcher's excellent book'.[50] But the 1717 edition is identical with that of 1646, with none of the improvements made in Peck's manuscript.

In January and February 1720 Peck told Thomas Hearne, with whom he carried on a lengthy correspondence, that he was 'preparing for the press the Antiquities of the Place of my Nativity' and asked that Hearne should obtain copies of '2 little Papers' about St. Michael's Priory which Peck thought were in the Bodleian. At this time he planned to publish the work in '5 little Octavos'.[51] A month later he wrote to Maurice Johnson, asking whether he had any materials relating to Stamford.[52] At this stage Peck wrote that 'I shall publish the first, of 5 small volumes I intend, in 3 months time'. These planned volumes were to cover 'first the Annals . . .'. By the start of 1721 he was thinking of extending his work to seven volumes and including information on other parts of Lincolnshire; later in the year he printed proposals for a six volume work which was also to include the antiquities of 'several Parochial, Conventual and Cathedral Churches' in various parts of the country.[53] Yet another proposal for publication of a history of Stamford appeared in January 1723. By this time Peck was clearly well on the way with his collections, and he apologised for delay in its publication owing to the discovery of many new items. He was still intending to print a companion volume about Lincolnshire.[54] In 1726, he claimed that he had been working on his volume for 'above these ten years last past'.

We hear nothing more of Peck's proposals for publishing a history of his own town until 1726 when he issued a folio sheet announcing that 'there is now printing in folio &c. *Academia Tertia Anglicana*'. A letter of Peck's dated 3 November, sent to Browne Willis, announced that over a hundred sheets were already printed.[55] In August of 1726 Peck had learned that there was 'printing at Stamford a sorry Piece of one Mr Butcher's most of which, tho' it never deserved it, hath been twice printed already',[56] a reference to Howgrave's *Essay* which appeared in that year. According to the Revd. Michael Tyson writing to Richard Gough in 1771,[57] this work was actually written by Tyson's grandfather, Edward Curtis, formerly Steward of Browne's Hospital in Stamford. It was published, so Tyson claimed, 'only to plague Peck'. The title was directly based on Peck's printed proposals; and Howgrave wrote the preface, remarkable for its personal attack upon Peck.[58] The Preface is sprinkled with quotations from Peck's minor works, usually sneeringly presented, and a private letter from Peck to Howgrave warning him not to issue his volume is apparently quoted in full. In this Peck 'begs to remind' Howgrave

> that as Reputation is a most valuable Flower I will not suffer mine to be blasted by any Body, much less such a child in Antiquities as you are. Therefore look well to yourself; I am yet only on the defensive; But if you begin the war, I thank God, I have both Money to sue, and a pen to answer him who bespatters.

'. . . to put all into an order of time . . .'

These taunts caused Peck to rush his work into print. By the end of August he was announcing that his work would be 'committed to several Presses, for its more speedy despatch'. Early in 1727 the *Academia Tertia Anglicana, or Antiquarian Annals of Stanford* was finally published. Stukeley's comment written in his own copy of the work was to the point.[59]

> Mr Peck brought his memoirs here printed to the Antiquarian society, while I was secretary there, every parish, church, college, religious house, &c was handled in a distinct chapter. Some persuaded him to turn the book into the form of Annals. He put it to the press in 1726, . . . and by there [*sic*] advice, spoil'd the book.

Roger Gale felt that 'it is no hard matter, beside the labour, to compose such a great [i.e. *voluminous*] work by writing everybody's life that has any relation to it'.[60]

Certainly, until this present reprint, Peck's *Annals* has been cumbersome and difficult to use, with no index and a table of contents which does little more than give an outline of the major chronological events. The work is split into fourteen 'books', most of them devoted to the reign of one of the medieval kings; in addition, there are two letters and a reprint of Butcher's *Survey*, with extensive additions and footnotes. Each chapter and each Appendix is separately paginated. In following this arrangement, Peck averred that he was following the example of Bishop Kennett of Peterborough whose *Parochial Antiquities* provided him with a model.[61] Although some subjects are dealt with in only one place in the volume, most are scattered, lending weight to the judgements of Stukeley and Gale. Cole, the mid-eighteenth-century antiquary, was only one to point this out; commenting upon the way in which Peck had 'so disjointed, mangled and new sentenced' all his documents, he wrote, 'and what with detatched Books, Chapters, and Heads of Chapters, that endeavouring to be more than ordinarily clear he is become many times quite obscure'.[62] It was this fragmentation which earned Peck much of his contemporary scorn.

However, there is much that is of great value to the local historian, and much that is unobtainable elsewhere. For Peck was thorough in his search for materials relevant to his subject, pressing correspondents in London, Oxford and Cambridge, and antiquarian acquaintances in many parts of the country, for 'any Minutes in your Reading of any Thing that happened here, or any ways relates to Stamford'.[63] While the originals of most of the manuscripts which Peck quotes from outside Stamford still survive, most of those that he found in the town have now disappeared. He occasioned much ill-feeling by his purchase of the surviving records of Browne's Hospital in 1722,[64] but it would appear that many other records belonging to the Hospital had already been lost.[65] Of Peck's own manuscript collections relating to Stamford, very little has been traced. Sir Thomas Cave of Stanford Hall on the borders of Northamptonshire and Leicestershire purchased all Peck's manuscripts for 'a trifle, twenty pounds or less'.[66] A fire at Stanford at the end of the eighteenth century seems to have destroyed those relating to Stamford. Thus the *Annals* is a vital source for original material about the town, from its origins up to the end of the reign of Henry VI (1461).

'. . . nothing but the Antiquities of Stamford . . .'

As a collector of information Peck can have had few rivals. On page after page of the *Annals* there are footnotes meticulously acknowledging the sources of his statements and quotations, reflecting also the breadth of his reading. On occasions he appears to get carried away with his quotations from other writers but the reasons may be seen in the first five pages of the work. Here he presents the story of Bladud in detail, leaving his readers to draw their own conclusions about the reliability of the information, having guided them through the various versions of the tale. This approach is typical of Peck's attitude towards his historical collections; whenever he can he allows the documents to speak for themselves, rarely taking a partisan viewpoint. It is an attitude which appears in most of his historical works, and one which shows best in his two volumes of *Desiderata Curiosa* first published in 1732 and 1735 and reprinted in one volume in 1779.

But although Peck's creative contribution to the history of Stamford is limited, there are some aspects of the book which merit attention. In the best tradition of the early eighteenth-century antiquarians he was not only concerned with collecting documents about Stamford. He noted what was being discovered during excavations in the town and asked workmen what they had observed when buildings were demolished.[67] He watched while alterations were being made to buildings in the neighbourhood[68] and recorded the appearance of medieval stained glass destroyed in his own lifetime.[69] Descriptions like that of the house of Boniface Bywater in St. Mary's Street[70] are invaluable. While documentary information in the *Annals* is far more abundant than observation of physical remains, there is much of great importance to the present day historian.

Nevertheless Peck's weaknesses mar the book seriously. He has his favourite themes, constantly recurring. In 1812 Thomas Blore, the historian of Stamford's charities, wrote 'If we are to believe with Peck that all the houses in the town which bear marks of antiquity, are remnants of Colleges and Halls for education, the whole town must have been full of them.'[71] It is to Peck, basically, that we owe the report of seventeen parish churches (rather than fourteen), as well as the large number of 'colleges'.[72] If his comments about Roman antiquities are often confusing and inaccurate and his quotations from other authors overlong and at times irrelevant, it is because he was anxious to provide his readers with all the information which they might need to further their understanding of every subject he covered.

'. . . what I have here done must stand as it is . . .'

It was always Francis Peck's intention to publish at least one more volume of collections relating to Stamford, and he sought contributors of documents for this on a number of occasions. He hoped to continue his account of the town to his own time, but his attention was diverted into his other publishing projects. In addition copies of his 'first volume' of the *Annals*, which he printed at his own cost, were still available in 1740[73.] and some would appear still to have been unsold at his death in 1743.[74] His son had little interest in his father's collection of books and manuscripts and all were sold. Thus the materials for a continuation of the *Annals* passed to Sir Thomas Cave. These manuscripts have been scattered. Those that survived the fire and remain at Stanford Hall include volumes of notes relating to Leicestershire, Lincolnshire, General Topography and an important collection of copies of documents relating to Grantham. In addition there are the Mordaunt Manuscripts calendared by the Historical Manuscripts Commission in their Tenth Report (Appendix VI, Abergavenny, 1887). Others which have found their way to the British Museum include the important Premonstratensian register copied from the Belvoir Muniments.[75] The copy of Butcher's *Survey of Stamford* which Peck made as a student has found its way back to Stamford where it is among the Town Hall collections. How much has been lost cannot be estimated, but it would appear, from promises Peck made for the printing of further volumes of documents, as well as references to *Mss penes me* in footnotes in published volumes, that much valuable documentary material has gone.

In 1785 William Harrod, a Stamford printer and newspaper publisher, issued two duodecimo volumes *The Antiquities of Stamford and St. Martin's* based unashamedly on Peck, quoting extensively from him, with footnotes and some contemporary information. Apparently hurriedly printed it adds nothing to Peck's account of medieval Stamford. Thomas Blore's *Account of the Public Schools, Hospitals and other Charitable Foundations . . . of Stamford* published in 1812 and the *History of Stamford* (1822) (until recently thought to be the work of John Drakard, another newspaper publisher) both add little to Peck's account of early and medieval Stamford, though both have much more value for the later period. Burton's *Chronology of Stamford* (1846) and the various guide books to the town of the nineteenth and twentieth centuries repeat Peck's account as interpreted by Blore. The later nineteenth-century writers Mackenzie Walcott and Nevinson added some new material, mainly by putting together Peck's descriptions and their own observations; but it is only in the last few years, with the publication of the Quincentenary lectures of 1961, and the work of the Stamford Survey Group and the Royal Commission on Historical Monuments, that much new material has come to light to be placed alongside Peck's *magnum opus*.[76]

Peck's *Annals* has then been the source to which all later historians and writers of guide books of Stamford have turned. His influence can be seen through to the present day and there are few books which deal with the topography and medieval history of Stamford which do not draw much of their information from this volume. While later writers have referred to the *Annals* as 'costly' or 'cumbersome', it cannot be ignored. With the new index provided in this edition, it becomes possible for the first time to make real use of the *Antiquarian Annals of Stanford* in the way Peck would have wished.

A. ROGERS
JOHN S. HARTLEY

NOTES

1. J. Leland, *Itinerary*, ed. L. Toulmin Smith (1909) iv, pp. 89–90.
2. An article on the 'Stamford turmoils' will shortly be published in the new journal, the *Stamford Historian*. See also Butcher, p. 12 (references to Butcher here are to the pages in Peck's edition printed in this volume).
3. Butcher, p. 28; *Cal. S. P. Dom., 1634–5*, p. 15 etc.
4. Butcher, pp. 8–9, 28–9; A. Rogers (ed.), *Making of Stamford* (1965), pp. 58–76; *Cal. S. P. Dom., 1635*, p. 61.
5. *Cal. L. P. Hen. VIII*, I, pp. 206–7; XIII 2, p. 215; Butcher, p. 24. The case of John Vicars, rector of St. Mary's church, Stamford, who established a conventicle in the town for praying and preaching and who was temporarily defrocked by the Court of High Commission, occupies several pages of *Cal. S. P. Dom.* and *Acts of the Privy Council*.
6. A. G. Matthews (ed.), *Walker Revised* (1948), *sub nom.*; W. E. Foster, *Plundered Ministers of Lincolnshire* (c. 1910), pp.99–105. On Palmer, see *Cal. S. P. Dom., 1641–3*, p. 189.
7. The Town Hall Books (H.B.), Stamford Borough Records (S.B.R.), Town Hall, Stamford, are full of these matters, and *Cal. S. P. Dom.* also record several occasions of disputes.
8. H.B., I, 345d, 346d, 349–50. Two daughters were baptised (1630, 1632), and his son Richard in October 1633 in St. Mary's parish.
9. H.B., I, 373d, 374; *Cal. S. P. Dom., 1633–4*, pp. 300, 467. Butcher's submission was made on 19 February, his dismissal on 25 March 1634, H.B., I, 416. His name was not recorded as town clerk in the elections of October 1633, and his successor Mathew Bunworth was elected in April 1634; a new hand records events from October 1633. It is important to realise that the Hall Books have a confusing method of recording the dates, holding over the regnal year in which a year's office of alderman began until the end of that year of office.
10. H.B., I, 416, 416d. Butcher calls himself 'sometime towne-clerke' in 1646.
11. H.B., I, 427d.
12. H.B., I, 439d; *Cal. Committee for Advance of Money*, 1338, 1376; Stamford Borough Sessions Rolls (now in Lincolnshire Archives Office).
13. H.B., I, 448. There were at least three later Butchers, Robert and Henry (both clerks) and John (upholsterer), H.B., II, list of freemen; II, 22d, 81d. Robert Butcher innholder seems to have lived in St. Mary's parish, with an inn in St. Mary's Street.
14. H.B., II, 7, 16d.
15. H.B., II, 23d; Book of Charters (S.B.R.), fols. 315–8; All Saints parish registers. His son Robert, in the later edition of the *Survey*, says he died in 1665. His will and inventory have not been found. Dorothy his wife was buried in St. George's parish in Sept. 1664, and a Richard Butcher in that same parish in Sept. 1667.
16. R. E. G. Cole (ed.), *Speculum Dioeceseos Lincolniensis* pt. i, *Lincoln Record Society* 4 (1913), p. 114; he is here called 'Thomas' Foster. See also Peck, Preface, p. xii.
17. There is no full biography of Peck, and most information about his career is based on the account, sometimes inaccurate, given by J. Nichols in *Literary Anecdotes of the Eighteenth Century* (1812 edn.) i, pp. 507–21. He was baptised in St. John's parish, Stamford, on 12 May 1692: parish registers.
18. J. E. B. Mayor, *Admissions to the College of St. John, Cambridge* Pt. II (1893), p. 196, and notes, p. lxxxiv.
19. In photocopy of *Designs of Stamford Antiquities* in Phillips Collection, Town Hall, Stamford.
20. H.B., II, 89.
21. F. Howgrave, *An Essay of the Ancient and Present State of Stamford* (1726), Preface, pp. vi–vii.
22. H. E. Salter (ed.), *Remarks and Collections of Thomas Hearne*, vol. ix, *Oxford Historical Society* 65 (1914), p. 217.
23. J. and J. A. Venn, *Alumni Cantabrigienses* Pt. I iii (1924), p. 333. There was another Francis Peck at Trinity College at this time.

24. Salter (ed.), *Oxf. Hist. Soc.* 65, *op. cit.*, p. 218.

25. W. C. Lukis (ed.), *The Family Memoirs of the Rev. William Stukeley* . . . ii, *Surtees Society* 76 (1883), p. 248. See also H. P. Wright, *The Story of the Domus Dei of Stamford* (1890), p. 163 and J. Nichols, *Illustrations of the Literary History of the Eighteenth Century* ii (1828), p. 13, where it is clear that Peck and Stukeley were trying to obtain the wardenship of Browne's Hospital at Stamford for Peck. See also Bodl. Eng. Misc. e.121 f.34 where Stukeley records this attempt in his diary.

26. H.M.C., *Report on the manuscripts of the Duke of Portland* VI (1901), p. 60.

27. Stamford Court Rolls (S.B.R.) I fol. 111d (5 May 1720).

28. Probate Copy of Will of Francis Peck dated 17 July 1742 in Phillips Collection.

29. *Dictionary of National Biography.*

30. Minute Book of Peterborough Gentlemen's Society I, in Peterborough Reference Library.

31. W. C. Lukis (ed.), *The Family Memoirs of the Rev. William Stukeley* . . . i, *Surtees Soc.* 73 (1882), p. 123.

32. Nichols, *Literary Illustrations*, *op. cit.*, ii, p. 30, where many letters of Warburton to Stukeley may be seen, most of which are far more critical of Peck than this.

33. Spalding Gentlemen's Soc. Library, Spalding, 2/66, 20 Oct. 1722.

34. F. Peck, *Ad Magistratum: A Sermon* . . . *Oct. 6 1720* [?1720], preached and printed at Stamford.

35. Bodleian MS, Rawlinson letters, 9–10, fol. 9.

36. Nichols, *Lit. Illus.*, *op. cit.*, ii, p. 119, *Lit. Anec.*, *op. cit.*, v, p. 645.

37. See Nichols, *Lit. Anec.*, *op. cit.*, i, pp. 514–15.

38. Nichols, *Lit. Illus.*, *op. cit.*, v, p. 355.

39. Cf., for example, the lines in J. Nichols, *The History and Antiquities of the County of Leicester* II pt. 1 (1785; reprinted by EP Publishing, 1971), Appendix pp. 61–6, about the Vale of Belvoir; or among the Braye MSS (Lincolnshire) at Stanford Hall, about Lincoln:
    'The ancient Town some make quinquipartite
    Where ev'n five cities into one unite'.

40. E.g., Dr. Zachary Grey of Cambridge, see Nichols, *Lit. Illus.*, *op. cit.*, v, p. 353, and *Lit. Anec.*, *op. cit.*, ii, pp. 543–4n; and William Warren, Leicestershire Records Office, Braye MSS, 23D57/2049.

41. Salter (ed.), *Oxford Hist. Soc.* 65, *op. cit.*, p. 218.

42. For Lincolnshire, Spalding Gentlemen's Soc. 2/66; for Leicestershire, see note 45; for Grantham, see G. H. Martin, *The Royal Charters of Grantham* (1963), pp. 234–9, and Braye MSS.

43. F. Peck, in *Memoirs of . . . Cromwell, Historical Pieces* (1740), pp. 105–13.

44. E.g., A. L. Maycock, *Nicholas Farrer of Little Gidding* (1938), p. 314, and *Chronicles of Little Gidding* (1954), pp. 1–2.

45. Peck's notes on the area around Belvoir are acknowledged to have been a major source for Nichols's *History and Antiquities of the County of Leicester*, II, pt. 1, p. 203, *sub* Godeby (Goadby Marwood) in Framland Hundred.

46. Nichols, *Lit. Illus.*, *op. cit.*, v, p. 361n. The following pages contain a list of some of the early volumes in Peck's collection.

47. T. Jones (ed.), *A Catalogue of the Collection of Tracts for and against Popery* . . ., *Chetham Soc.* 48 (1859) and 64 (1865).

48. Nichols, *Lit. Illus.*, *op. cit.*, v, pp. 356–70.

49. Nichols, *Lit. Anec.*, *op. cit.*, i, p. 521; B.L., Sale Catalogue of Thomas Payne, Bookseller, London 1758.

50. MS in Phillips Collection Room, Town Hall, Stamford.

51. Bodl. MS., Rawl. Letters 9–10, fol. 5.

52. Spalding Gentlemen's Society MSS 2/66.

53. Bodl. MS., Rawl. 9–10, fols. 5, 6, 7.

54. Bodl. MS., Top. Northants c.17, fol. 179.

55. B.L., Add. MS. 5833, fols. 176–7.

56. Advertisement in *Northampton Mercury*, 22 August 1726.

57. *Old Lincolnshire* i (1883–5), pp. 174–5.

58. Nichols, *Lit. Anec.*, *op. cit.*, viii, p. 573.

59. Photocopy in Phillips Collection.

60. Lukis (ed.), *Surtees Soc.* 73, *op. cit.*, pp. 200–1.

61. Preface, p. ix.

62. B.L., Add. MS 5833, fol. 177.

63. Letter to M. Johnson, 29 March 1720, Spalding Gentlemen's Soc. 2/66.

64. See Wright, *Story of the Domus Dei*, *op. cit.*, pp. 135–6; Howgrave, *op. cit.*, p. 99.

65. *Annals*, Preface, p. x.

66. Nichols, *Lit. Illus.*, *op. cit.*, vii, p. 426.

67. *Annals* I, p. 11; XI, p. 24.

68. W. C. Lukis (ed.), *The Family Memoirs of the Rev. William Stukeley* . . . iii *Surtees Soc.* 80 (1887), p. 72.

69. *Annals* XIV, pp. 23, 36–7.

70. *Annals* XI, p. 26.

71. T. Blore, *Stamford Charities* (1812), p. 27.

72. See Stamford Survey Group, *Report 2, The Religious Foundations of Medieval Stamford*, 1974 for a critical assessment of this subject.

73. See advertisement in Peck, *Memoirs of . . . Cromwell, op. cit.*

74. Will (S.B.R.).

75. B.L., Birch MSS. 4934–8; see F. A. Gasquet (ed.), *Collectanea Anglo-Premonstratensia, Camden Soc.* 3rd Series vi, x, xii (1904–6); H. M. Colvin, 'The *Registrum Premonstratense*: A Lost MS. rediscovered', *Journal of Ecclesiastical History* viii, (1957).

76. Rogers (ed.), *op. cit.*; R.C.H.M., *The Town of Stamford* (1977); Stamford Survey Group, *Reports 1 and 2* (1970, 1974).

LIST OF PLATES

LIST OF PLATES

Illustrations in the Text

Academia tertia Anglicana;

OR, THE

ANTIQUARIAN ANNALS

OF

STANFORD

IN

Lincoln, Rutland, *and* Northampton *Shires.*

CONTAINING

The Hiſtory of the Univerſity, Monaſteries, Gilds, Churches, Chapels, Hoſpitals
& Schools there; with Memoirs of the Lords, Magiſtrates, Founders, Benefactors, Clergy, & other antient Inhabitants: interſperſed with many new & curious
Particulars touching the Britons, Romans, Saxons, Danes, French, Jews, Church
Hiſtory, Parliaments, Councils, Pleadings, Occurrences in the Barons wars, & the
wars between the two Houſes of York & Lancaſter; as alſo the Acts & Anceſtry
of divers Lord Chancellors, Knights of the Garter, Knights of the Bath, Abbats
of Peterborough, Priors of Durham, Biſhops of Lincoln, & ſundry other famous
Perſons & antient Families.

Being not only a particular Hiſtory of Stanford & ſeveral other old Towns, but an
uncommon Series of Civil & Eccleſiaſtical Affairs under each Reign: Gathered
from the beſt Accounts Print & MS. with a large Chronological Table of Contents, & Variety of Sculpture:

In XIV. BOOKS.

Compiled by F R A N C I S P E C K, Rector of Godeby by Melton in
Leiceſterſhire.

Ex fumo dare lucem. Hor.

London: Printed for the AUTHOR by JAMES BETTENHAM
in the Year M,DCC,XXVII.

TO THE

Moſt High, Puiſſant, and Noble PRINCE,

HIS GRACE

JOHN

Duke and Earl of RUTLAND;

Marquis of GRANBY;

Baron Roos of HAMLAKE, TRUSBUT, & BELVOIR;

AND

Baron MANNERS of HADDON.

May it pleaſe YOUR GRACE,

THERE are ſome ſuch peculiar Circumſtances, both in the Acts & Fortunes of Your Anceſtors, & in Your own very Titles, ſo analogous to this Work, & ſo adapted to beſtow a Brightneſs upon it; that were I to chuſe a Patron where-ever I would, I can really think of none ſo proper for it as Your Grace.

One

One of the former Owners of Belvoir Caftel (fo famous for its lofty Situation, ftately Structure, & moft beautiful Profpects) was William de Albini the third, a great Baron in King John & King Henry the thirds time, who founded the Priory & Hofpital of Newfted by Stanford, & whofe Life is here new wrote more largely than it was ever yet done; whereby will appear, that, as a Soldier, he was a perfon of as much Valor & Generofity; as a Chriftian, of as much Charity & Piety; as any of the Age he lived in.

William de Albini the fourth his fon, another of the former Owners of Belvoir Caftel, & alfo a kind Benefactor to the fame Priory & Hofpital of Newfted, was likewife a Baron of great Worth & Virtue. I had formerly the Honor to fhew Your Grace a Copy of his remarkable Seal, & now prefent it afrefh, with fome new Memoirs of his Life & Actions.

Of all the Kings of England the greateft Friend the Town of Stanford ever had was King Edward the fourth. And he gave the Burgeffes of that place the Royal Arms of England, to be impaled & born with their own. This he did for their eminent fervice to him at the Battel of Loofe-Coat-field, & becaufe he could hardly do them a greater Honor.

Thus King Henry the eighth gave Thomas Earl of Rutland (Your Graces Anceftor) by reafon of his defcent from a Sifter of the fame King Edward the fourth, part of the Royal Arms of France & England, to be added to his former right honorable Shield, as a Teftimony of his Lordfhips high Rank & princely Lineage.

What an happy Parallel then do we here find, as in the near Relation of thefe things to the renowned King Edward the fourth, fo in that Augmentation of Honor thereby conferred both on this antient Borough & Your Graces moft noble Family!

Likewife a good part of the Town of Stanford it felf, is a part of that County whofe Name is fo honored by being Your Graces Title.

As therefore Travellers, Antiquaries, Foreigners, and the Nobility themfelves throng to vifit Your Grace, to fee Your magnificent & delightful Dwelling, & to behold the Country from it; As the great Leland himfelf was formerly there, & went thence to Stanford[a]: So, from Stanford, I, the meaneft of Your Servants, now moft humbly wait on Your Grace, to lay this Collection at Your Feet.

And here, my Lord, I cannot but look, with Surprife, at the Country; with Admiration, at You! For Belvoir Views are indeed the Fineft I ever faw. But there is one View, & that infinitely the Fineft of all, which You fee hence, & yet no man living befides can difcern from this, or any other, place: I mean, Two & Twenty Mannors[b] of his own, all lying within fight of his own Caftel.

Thus emphatically are You Lord of Belvoir; & moft eminently, as Your very Name imports, a DOMINUS *de* MANERIIS.

And as Your Tenents of all thefe, & a great many other Mannors, grow old & rich in Your Farms; as the Son fucceeds the Father, & fo on, from one generation to another, 'till what they fo eafily rent looks more like a Freehold than an Eftate held of another; You appear more like a Father, than a Mafter, of them; & are truly a PRINCE at the Head of a numerous People.

From Belvoir Your Grace likewife fees Croxton Park Houfe, that elegant Retirement of Your own Choice & Building.

From the fame rich Profpect You alfo behold two other curious Seats[c], & four other goodly Mannors[d], all, by Your moft happy Marriage, now added to thofe above.

a Vide Lib. I. p. 17.
b Belvoir, Croxton, Befcaby, Saltby, Sproxton, Waltham, Eaton, Braunftone, Knipton, Harby, Hofe, Plungar, Barkfton, Redmile, Granby, Sutton, Bottsford, Normington, Eafthorpe, Mufton, Wolftrope, & Eagle.
c Averham, & Kelham.
d Averham, Kelham, Rollfton, & Syerfton.

And

And thus Fortune, who never permitted any man even to vie with Your Anceſtors in the great number of their Mannors to be ſeen from their own Caſtel, at length raiſed You thence to behold a yet greater number of your own than ever any of Your Predeceſſors did.

The King too, as if His Majeſty & Fortune contended who ſhould do moſt for Your Glory, hath alſo graciouſly appointed You Lord Lieutenant & *Cuſtos Rotulorum* of the County of Lei-ceſter, Knight of the moſt noble Order of the Garter, & one of the Lords of His Bed-Chamber.

What are yet, if any thing can be, more valuable than all theſe things, in Your Family, Your Grace is bleſt with a moſt accompliſhed Lady, & a beautifully blooming Offspring; In Your Self with a moſt lively, agreeable Perſon, Good Senſe, & a Sweet Demeanor.

What therefore to wiſh Your Grace more, I know not; un-leſs it be, that as You ſo well adorn what You now are, ſo You may long & happily enjoy what You now have; &, if it be poſſible for Nature, or Fortune, to do any thing more for one whom they have already done ſo much for, as You riſe in Years may You grow in Riches, in Honor, in Virtue, in every great Endowment, & moſt deſirable Bleſſing.

And This, my Lord, ſhall always be my ſincere Prayer, not only for Your Individual Self, but every Branch of Your moſt Illuſtrious Houſe.   I am,

May it pleaſe Your Grace,

Your Graces moſt obliged,

moſt devoted, &

moſt obedient

humble ſervant,

FRANCIS PECK.

PREFACE.

AS to the Compaſs of this work, in general, it is a brief Chronicle of every Reign; in particular, it is the Antiquarian Annals of the town of Stanford.

If we conſider it as a brief chronicle of every reign, there were ſo many important affairs of ſo many of our kings themſelves tranſacted here, that the reader will be ſurpriſed to find this one place ſhould be the ſcene of ſo many great & curious occurrences.

If, to what regards our kings, we put the acts & anceſtry of all thoſe great perſonages who lived in thoſe reigns, & were, ſome way or other, related, as to this kingdom in general, ſo alſo, to this town in particular; and to thoſe memorable things which all theſe tranſacted here, only add thoſe other which have a collateral relation to them, & which laſt therefore muſt needs be a little opened, that the other may be the better underſtood; few people can then hardly imagine what an infinite variety of the moſt memorable accidents in the general hiſtory of England, have a near relation to the particular hiſtory of this place.

In the main however, I have taken in nothing but the Antiquities of Stanford, all (except a very few things) which I have any where ſaid, being wrote purely to illuſtrate the hiſtory of that borough, or the lives of them who founded any houſe of religion there, or were benefactors to any ſuch foundations; or were lords & owners of the town, or buried there; or by ſome other ſuch like material circumſtance related to it. So much was neceſſary with regard to men.

And, as to things, beſides a bare minute of facts done here, ſometimes ſomething of the reaſon & occaſion of them was required to be ſaid; for, without that, & occaſional touches of the antient topography of this place & neighbourhood, it would be impoſſible to give much life to mere local antiquities, & conſequently the reader would ſoon grow tired with having nothing elſe but an heap of fragments & old deeds to keep him awake. Whereas, by following the courſe I have here taken, there are few, if any, reigns, eſpecially the nearer we deſcend to our own times, but the accounts thereof may be ſomewhat improved from theſe collections, whenever any perſon ſhall take the pains to write them anew. And, according to my notion, the beſt way of writing the particular Antiquities of any place is, whenever they will admit of it, to write them in ſuch a method as may render them the moſt ſerviceable to the general hiſtory of that county, or kingdom, they relate to: This then is what I have here attempted.

As to the particular books, in the firſt I have indulged my ſelf the liberty of enquiring both for a Britiſh & a Roman Town where Stanford now ſtands, & think I have met with ſome hints, what from Hiſtory, & what from evidences on the ſpot, for a Roman ſtation, if not a Britiſh Town, there.

2

there. However, in matters of so much uncertainty, I have contented my self to let the beam rest in æquilibrio, without pretending to weigh it down with any assertions of my own.

The second contains the life of S. Vilfrid the elder bishop of York, & founder of the Benedictin priory of S. Leonard by Stanford; in whose story, as there now & then occur some things a little legendary, it must be remembred that Bede & other monkish writers deal much in miracles, a great many whereof it is like were fables; but, if we reject all of them, we shall lose a good deal of history. For, with the learned bishop Nicholson, [a] ' *I dare promise that the English historian shall frequently discover* ' *some hidden treasure, even in the midst of the most drossy miracles.*

The third is mostly taken up with the wars between the Saxons & Danes, intermixed with some few remarks upon the state of Christianity hereabouts, in those most pious times, if we consider the Saxons; most barbarous, if we consider the Danes.

The fourth contains all such matters relating to Stanford as fall under the reigns of the four Norman intruders; & introduces with the conqueror, first a swarm of French, & soon after another of Jews; neither I dare say at all desired by the former inhabitants of this nation. By what little I have said of the brave Hereward de Wake it may be seen, that, if the rest of his countrymen had preserved the courage of their ancestors, the Normans would have found it very difficult, if not impossible, to have made good their settlement so long as they did: a business the conqueror himself discovered was a work of so much care, that he let in the Jews purely to strengthen himself, being thereby assured of so many spies as they were individuals, without ever being obliged to give them any thing but his protection for their intelligence. Here you have also an account of the prodigious dole which William Rufus made, as he pretended, for the Rest of his fathers soul; a circumstance which, according to the notion of those times, might have passed for a very pious act, if wise men had not discerned that he did it more to engage the peoples affections to himself, & to keep out his elder brother, than through any respect for his father. But, I forget my self; such Criticisms as these are, now, but of little use; & will make this preface a great deal longer than I intend it.

In the other ten books matters are continued to the end of the reign of K. Henry the sixth; where, in the pursuit of any story already treated of by our English Historians, I have compared all the authors I had by me upon every affair which I write of, & copied an expression of one, & an observation of another, adding withall my own translation, or remarks, just as occasion offered, or my design required.

My first purpose was to have printed only twelve books in all; which, being drawn up a great deal more concise, were not done, as here in a chronological order, but reduced under particular heads, briefly treating of the university, monasteries, Athenæ, churches, hospitals, &c. but when I

[a] Hist. Lib. fol. edit. p. 107.

2   *had*

had almoſt compleated them in that method, my ſecond thoughts were, that to put all into an order of time would be the moſt uſeful management of a piece of hiſtory. For ſo doing I had likewiſe the learned biſhop Kennets example in the conduct of his parochial Antiquities. I reſolved therefore to compoſe my book anew after the ſame form with his Lordſhips. And thus I ſet about doing the whole over again in the ſame manner I have here publiſhed it; & this is the reaſon it hath been ſo long delayed after it was firſt promiſed. I thought indeed I ſhould have diſpatched it much ſooner, but it took up a great deal more time than I was at firſt aware of.

Beſides this was not all. For, whilſt I thought I was only putting what I had before collected into a new method, ſo many new things almoſt every day fell into my way, that before I dreamt any thing of the danger of having too much (a fancy which I believe few Antiquaries are ſeldom troubled with) my collections were inſenſibly grown too big for me ever to think of publiſhing the whole at the price I had at firſt propoſed. In this ſtraight I reſolved to prefer Antiquities before modern Hiſtory, & to end this book with the end of K. Henry the ſixths reign. An ill-natur'd man may perhaps ſay, the book is imperfect, becauſe not brought down to theſe times; to which I ſhall only anſwer, I never heard that fault objected to my Lord of Peterboroughs parochial Antiquities, who ends his book where I end mine. However if I meet with encouragement, the continuation may ſoon come forth; for from the firſt of Edward the fourth to this time I have a collection almoſt wholly from MSS. If not, what I have here done muſt ſtand as it is. And indeed, if the materials be good, it would be pity to throw any of them out to make room for modern hiſtory; if bad, it were needleſs to trouble the world with any more of them. In ſuch a caſe my misfortune, not my fault, is, that I have taken too much pains in an unprofitable ſearch. Be that as it will, when a man is once got ſo deep into a buſineſs, he is willing if he can to ſee the whole of it. And truly I have run thro' ſo many books & papers in this enquiry, that I have often thought of one in Spencer,

     ' ª *Whoſe chamber all was hang'd about with Rolls,*

     ' *Some made in Books, ſome in long Parchment Scrolls,*

  ' *That were all wormeaten, & full of Cankerholes;*

     ' *Amidſt them all he in a chair was ſet,*

     ' *Toſſing & turning them withouten end.*

For verily,

     ' ᵇ *Beguiled with delight of novelties,*

      ' *And natural deſire of countrys ſtate,*

    ' *So long I read in theſe Antiquities,*

      ' *That how the time was fled I quite forgat.*

But to proceed. When I firſt thought of publiſhing this work, I likewiſe propoſed to have added at the bottom of the page the Latin of all thoſe paſſages tranſlated from our old hiſtorians, & inſerted into the body of it.

a Fairy Queen Lib. 2. Cant. 9. Stanza, 57. 58. p. 308. ⎫
b id. Lib. 2. Cant. 10. Stanza, 67. p. 328. ⎬ Mr. Hughs edition.

                                                But

But that I found would make the book near one third bigger than it now is. I next proposed to insert only the Latin of what charters & other principal materials I took from printed books, omitting the Latin of matters of less curiosity. But this I perceived would make it yet a deal to big. I was therefore forced to strike out the Latin of almost every thing taken from printed books, & when I had given the translation, content my self with referring the reader to the books & pages themselves where he might find the Latin. But all this would not do. To bring matters into a narrower compass still, I was likewise obliged to strike out the Latin of many original papers, of all which I have given the translation, & directed to the proper offices & places where the originals themselves are to be met with. The most curious things of this kind are however given at large at the bottom of the page. In the translation of all which things the reader will sometimes, I doubt, find the expression very low, & sometimes again very obscure. For many printed copies of our old monkish historians are in divers places not sense. And again many of the MSS. I have been favored with, were either transcribed by unskilful copiers, or in divers places so worn & mutilated, that men of better judgment than I am could, in several places, not make out the meaning. Whereas had we all these things fair, & exact, & uncorrupted as they should be, it is well known there is nothing fine & elegant to be drawn out of them; the plainness & truth they carry in them is all they have to recommend them. Where therefore the account is taken from the best copies, the reader must expect no more; where it is taken from bad, I hope he will be content, because it is the best I could give him.

Again. In sundry places are inserted Extracts from several old deeds, which Extracts are marked B. H. as relating to Mr. Browns Hospital, for all which we are obliged to the late Reverend Mr. William Forster, sometime warden of that house. Those Extracts indeed are very brief, but they are here of some use, & may hereafter perhaps be of more. The originals I am told are now all destroyed; I was unwilling therefore to lose what was left, & so have given them just as I found them. The smallest hints sometimes clear up the greatest difficulties, & the knowledge of one little incident as often brightens a whole story.

At the end of the fourteenth book I have added twelve Plates & a brief account entitled the Close, relating to some Antiquities & Curiosities of a later date. After all follows a chronological table, whereby the reader, as he may occasionally want them, is assisted to find the most material matters in the whole book, there being few things unminuted there, save only those brief Extracts I just now mentioned, which being so very short & imperfect, & relating almost wholly to the hospital, I thought it even needless to take any farther notice of.

' ᵃ As for what concerns the impression it self [of my own part] in order
' to make it more beautiful, I have been obliged to recede, in several respects,
' from our usual way of printing; which, if I am allowed to speak freely,

---

ᵃ Mr. P. dez Maizeauxs dedication of Mr. Locks remains to Mr. Wrottesley.

' *is extremely vicious. It is matter of wonder, that in such a country as*
' *this, where there is so much encouragement for printing, there should pre-*
' *vail a sort of Gothic taste, which deforms our English Impressions, &*
' *makes them not a little ridiculous. For can any thing be more absurd than*
' *so many capital letters, that are not only prefixed to all nouns substantives,*
' *but also often to adjectives, pronouns, particles, & even to verbs? And*
' *what shall we say of that odd mixture of Italic, which instead of help-*
' *ing the Reader to distinguish matters more clearly, does only perplex him, &*
' *breeds a confusion shocking to the eye?——Surely, if the authors on the one*
' *hand, & the readers on the other, would oppose this Barbarism, it would be*
' *no difficult matter to restore a just taste, & a beautiful way of printing.*

*Again. Whenever any old printed Historians are quoted in their own
words, tho' almost all transcribers & printers make use of dipthongs in what
they have hitherto been pleased to give us from them, I have not thought
good to follow their examples, since, in so doing, I should infallibly depart
from the original text of my several authors. A modern, who writes his
own sense of things in the Latin tongue, may justly enough be allowed the
use of them, but it is a jest to use them in copying Hen. Hunt. Mat.
Paris, or any other antient Historian, & yet alledge we have kept up to
the text. For this reason, wherever any modern, who writes his own
sentiments in Latin, is transcribed, there dipthongs are allowed; but where
they are forced by former transcribers into the body & text of any old
Historian, & that old Historian is here quoted, there they are thrown out
again, & single vowels substituted in their places, that the copy may look
more true & accurate & like the original.*

*For the same reason as dipthongs are thrown out, the old way of spelling
the names of persons & places is retained. Thus, instead of Wilfrid, Penda,
Oswi & an hundred more; when I give any thing from Bede, where those
names occur, I always chuse to write Vilfrid, Pendan, Osuiu, &c. because
Mr. Smith assures us* [a], *that way of writing agrees best with the most antient copies of that author. However, where other authors spell those, or
any other, names otherwise, I always do so too. My constant method (except
where the slips of my pen, or of the press, have prevented me) being always
to keep close to my author, & to spell as he does.*

*Again. Sometimes where I speak my own sentiments, & have justly that
liberty; & sometimes when I copy others, & that liberty is not so allowable
(for, what thro' the inadvertency of my own thoughts, or the carelesness of the
press, or both, I see it is gone so) I have departed from the common orthography, to that, which, by observing the root & etymology of words, is I think
apparently more just. Thus, instead of abbot, market, perswade, publick,
extream, forrest, castle, honour, & the like (seeing those words are derived
from* abbas, mercatura, suadeo, publicus, extremus, foresta, castellum, honor) *I have chose to write* abbat, mercat, persuade, public, extreme, forest,
castel, honor, &c. *Wherever therefore any word is differently spelled from
the common usage, it is either in compliance with the author from whom I
transcribe, or, if casually altered, this is my apology for so doing.*

a Præfat. ad Bedæ opera Ecclesiastica.

At

At the end of all I have added Mr. Butchers MS. & two letters by Mr. Forster, none of which I at first intended to publish, but at length being persuaded that a correct copy of them, with what I have added at the bottom of the page, might not be unacceptable to the curious, I altered my mind, &, tho' my own book is indeed big enough, have nevertheless subjoined them.

The survey and antiquity of the town of Stanford was first published by Mr. Butcher, in 1646. in seven sheets, in quarto. A little before the restoration he revised it, & made several additions, with an intent to publish a new impression. But, when he had finished, delaying, or not meeting with sufficient encouragement to print the same, his death soon after put an end to that design; till at last his son succeeded to his intentions, & promised to publish it, but went no farther: whereby the same has ever since continued in MS. whereof it being my fortune to meet with several copies, I have thence published this impression.

About the year 1706. Mr. Forster, sometime rector of S. Michaels in Stanford, afterwards of S. Clement Danes Lond. (a Gent. of much better abilities for such a work than Mr. Butcher) began at first to review Mr. Butchers book, but afterwards to meditate an entire new work; & went on with his resolution by starts for some years, reading a good deal, but, what is much to be regretted, thro' an inveterate palsie in his head, digesting very little; all I could find among his papers any ways compleated being only these two letters, the greatest part of both which were formerly published by Mr. John Stevens in his two additional volumes to the Monasticon.

In his letter to Dr. Tanner Mr. Forster undertakes to prove there was neither a British nor a Roman Town where Stanford now stands. His arguments are long, & he bestowed great pains upon them. How I differ from him about those matters, & my reasons for so doing, may be seen by what I have wrote. Having proved, as he thinks, that there was neither a British nor a Roman Town where Stanford now stands, he next labours to shew that Stanford was first built by the Saxons about the year 501.

In his letter to Mr. Stevens he carries it a little higher, & fancies it was first erected by Hengist, in memory of his defeating the Picts & Scots here about the year 449. That Letter may be divided into six sections, in the first whereof he treats of the Saxon inhabitants of Stanford; in the second, of the churches; in the third, of the monasteries; in the fourth, of the hospitals; in the fifth, of the university & monasteries; in the sixth & last of the miraculous cure of one Samuel Wallis of a consumption; which being a sort of a protestant miracle, the author of the additions to the Monasticon thought it not agreeable to his religion, or undertaking, or both, to take any notice of.

In fine, throughout the whole I have produced my vouchers, whereby may be seen when another speaks, & when I do. As therefore I arrogate no merit to my self from other mens labors, I have only this to desire, that I may not be charged with other mens errors. My own I am ready to answer for & to correct, when I am civilly shewn them; but all the notice I shall take of any rude animadversions will be only to despise the writers of them.

4

THE

The SUBSCRIBERS NAMES.

Those with this mark ‡ before their names subscribed for large paper.

A

HIS Grace Hugh Lord Primate of Ireland.
‡ The Right Honourable William Earl of Albemarle.
The Society of Antiquaries, London.
John Anstis, Esq; garter king of arms.
Edward Alexander, Esq; of Doctors Commons.
Mr. Daniel Austen.
Mr. Stephen Austen, bookseller, three books.
Mr. Thomas Astley, bookseller, three books.

B

‡ The Right Hon. Charles Lord Bruce.
The Right Reverend George Lord Bishop of Bath and Wells.
‡ Sir Charles Buck of Hanby, Bar.
‡ The Hon. James Brudenell, Esq; master of the King's jewel office.
‡‡ John Bridges, Esq; two books.
The Rev. Ralph Bridges, D. D. vicar of South-Weald in Essex.
The Rev. Nathaniel Bridges, A.M. rector of Orlingbury and Wadenhoe in Northamptonshire.
‡‡ Charles Bertie, Esq; one of the members of parliament for the borough of Stanford, two books.
‡ Beverly Butler of Stanford, Esq;
The Rev. Thomas Baker, B. D. of St. John's college, Cambridge.
Thomas Bacon of Catley near Linton in Cambridgeshire, Esq;
‡ Joshua Blackwell of Stanford, Esq;
The Rev. Thomas Blackwell, A. M. rector of St. Clement Danes.
Mr. John Buckby of Kibworth in Leicestershire.
John Browne of Leysthorp in Leicestershire, Esq;
Francis Browne of Gretford, Esq;
‡ John Browne, Esq;
Thomas Burrel of Stanford, Esq;
Mr. Edward Benet of Stanford
The Rev. John Burman, A.M. rector of Denton in Lincolnshire.
John Boulter of Gawthorp in Yorkshire, Esq;
Walter Boulter, Esq;
John Bowes, Esq;
‡ Charles Bale, M. D. physician to the Charter-house.
Mr. Samuel Brougham, one of the clerks in chancery.
Mr. William Bristow, one of the clerks in chancery.
Mr. Francis Bedwell.
Joseph Bowles, A. M fellow of Oriel, and keeper of the Bodleian library, in Oxford.
The Rev. Charles Bertie, A. M. rector of Uffington.
Brazennose college, Oxford; for the library.
Samuel Boroughs of Greys Inne, Esq;
The Rev. James Banks.
Henry Bradshaw of Marple in Cheshire, Esq;
‡ William Benson, Esq;

Mr. John Brindley, bookbinder, six books.
Mr. Jonah Bowyer, bookseller, three books.
Mr. James Bettenham, printer.

C

‡ His Grace William Lord Archbishop of Canterbury, two books.
‡ His Grace James Duke of Chandos.
‡ The Right Hon. George Earl of Cardigan.
The Right Hon. Philip Earl of Chesterfield.
The Right Hon. Hugh Earl of Cholmondely.
‡ The Right Hon. John Lord Carteret.
‡ The Right Hon. William Lord Craven.
The Right Hon. Henry Lord Colerane.
‡ The Hon. William Cecil, Esq, Mayor of Stanford.
Thomas Cartwright of Aynhoe, Esq; one of the knights of the shire for the county of Northampton.
Dixon Colby, M. D. of Stanford.
‡ Saville Cust of Stanford, Esq;
‡ Mr. Edward Curtis of Stanford.
The Rev. Samuel Carte, A. M. vicar of St. Martins, Leicester.
Samuel Carte, LL. B.
George Clive, Esq; bencher of Lincolns Inne.
Robert Cholmondely of Holford in Cheshire, Esq;
John Campbell of Stackpole Court in the county of Pembroke, Esq;
‡ Humphrey Chetham's library.
James Chetham, Esq;
Mr. Matthew Colborne, one of the clerks in chancery.
‡ Mr. Samuel Cranmer, banker in Fleetstreet.
‡ Mr. Colley Cibber.
Clavering, Esq;

D

‡ Henry Dove, of Upton in Northamptonshire, Esq;
‡ Simon Degge, Esq; F. R. S.
The Rev. John Davies, D. D. master of Queens college, Cambridge.
‡ Mr. George Denshire of Stanford.
The Rev. Edward Dunn, LL. D.
The Rev. Joseph Disney, A. M.

E

‡ The Right Hon. Brownlowe Earl of Exeter.
‡ Sir William Ellis of Nocton in Lincolnshire, Bar.
Sir John Eden, Bar.
‡ The Rev. William Edmunson, D. D. president of St. John's college, Cambridge.
Vigerus Edwards, Esq; secretary of the bankrupts.
Walter Edwards, Esq; one of the clerks in chancery.
Mr. Thomas Edlin, bookseller, three books.

F

The Right Hon. the Lord Viscount Fermanagh.
‡ Sir Andrew Fontaine, Bar. vice-chamberlain to Her Royal Highness the Princess.

c   ‡ Richard

‡ Richard Foley, Efq; prothonotary of the court of common-pleas.

The Rev. Robert Felton, D. D. principal of Edmund hall, Oxon.

George Fothergill of Lincolns Inne, Efq;

Ralph Freman, Efq;

William Freeman, Efq; fecretary of the appeals.

‡ Henry Furnes, Efq;

John Freind, M. D.

The Rev. William Freeman, A. B. two books.

Mr. John Forfter.

Mr. Giles Fletcher, bookfeller, three books.

G

‡ The Right Hon. John Lord Gower.

Roger Gale, Efq; F. R. S. and one of the commiffioners of excife.

Samuel Gale, Efq;

‡ William Goodhall of Holywell, Efq;

‡ Thomas Granger, Efq:

John Green, M. D. of Grantham.

Mr. Edward Gee, one of the clerks in chancery.

Mr. Thomas Gibbs.

The Rev. Thomas Gibfon, A. M. rector of Pafton and Polebroke in Northamptonfhire.

Mr. Fletcher Gyles, bookfeller, fix books.

Mr. Thomas Greene, bookfeller, fix books.

Mr. John Goudge, bookfeller, fix books.

H

The Right Rev. and Hon. the Lord Bifhop of Hereford.

‡ The Right Hon. Emanuel Scroop, Lord Vifcount How, one of the knights of the fhire for the county of Nottingham.

Sir Charles Hotham, Bar.

‡ The Reverend James Holcot, A. M. vicar of Fotheringhay in Northamptonfhire.

Humphrey Hyde of Dowfeby in Lincolnfhire, Efq;

Mr. George Hill of Doctors Commons.

Samuel Hartup of Little Dalby in Leicefterfhire, Efq;

The Rev. David Humphreys, A. M.

Samuel Hetherington of the Middle Temple, Efq; receiver of the fines.

William Hamilton of Lincolns Inne, Efq;

Mr. John Hamilton, one of the clerks in chancery.

Mr. Edward Halfted, of Clements Inne.

Mr. Harper of Lincolns Inne.

Mr. Timothy Hutchinfon, one of the clerks in chancery.

Mr. Barrington Horfmanden, one of the clerks in chancery.

Mr. Benjamin Hall of Cliffords Inne.

The Rev. Michael Hutchinfon, D. D.

The Rev. John Hotchkin, A. M.

I

The Right Hon. Sir Jofeph Jekyll, Kt. mafter of the rolls, and one of his Majefty's moft honourable Privy Council.

‡ St. John's college, Cambridge; for the library.

‡ The Rev. Robert Jenkin, D. D. mafter of St. John's college, and Lady Margaret's profeffor of divinity, in Cambridge.

James Joye of Duke-ftreet in Weftminfter, Efq;

Maurice Johnfon, jun. Efq; of Spalding in Lincolnfhire.

John Idle, Efq;

‡ Francis Jephfon, Efq; ferjeant at arms.

Thomas Jett, Efq; auditor of the imprefs.

The Rev. Hannes, A. M. mafter of the free-fchool in Stanford.

‡ Theodore Janfen, Efq;

Henry Johnfon, Efq;

The Rev. John Ifaac, A. M. rector of Whitwell in Rutland.

Meffieurs William and John Innys, bookfellers; fix books.

Mr. John Jackfon, bookfeller, three books.

K

Abel Kettelbey of the Inner-Temple, Efq;

James Kendal, Efq;

Alexander Keilet, Efq; one of the proprietors of the New River water, and one of the clerks in chancery.

Mr. John Knight, one of the clerks in chancery.

Dr. King of Stanford.

John Kynafton, Efq; one of the knights of the fhire for the county of Salop.

Mr. Charles King, bookfeller; fix copies.

Meffrs. John and James Knapton, bookfellers.

L

‡ Right Hon. John Lord Vifcount Lymington.

‡‡ The Right Rev. Edmund Lord Bifhop of London, two books.

The Right Rev. Richard Lord Bifhop of Lincoln, two books.

Peter Leneve, Efq; norroy king of arms.

‡ Samuel Lowe, Efq; one of the members of parliament for the borough of Alborough.

George Lynn of Southwick, Efq;

Richard Langley, Efq;

Stephen Martin Leake, Efq;

Lincoln college, Oxon; for the library.

‡ Francis Lewis of Stanford hall in the county of Nottingham, Efq;

The Rev. Charles La Motte, A. M.

Mr.   Lewis, bookfeller.

Mr. Bernard Lintot, bookfeller.

M

‡ His Grace John Duke of Montagu.

The Right Hon. Thomas Earl of Macclesfield.

The Right Hon. Henry Lord Vifcount Morpeth, one of the members of parliament for the borough of Morpeth.

The Hon. and Rev. John Montagu, D. D. dean of Durham.

‡ Sir Thomas Mackworth, Bar.

‡ Richard Mead, M. D.

Samuel Mead, Efq; bencher of Lincolns Inne.

Dr. John Burchard Menckenius, counfellor and hiftoriographer to the King of Poland.

The Rev. Thomas Mangy, D. D. prebendary of Durham; fix books.

Thomas Martin, Efq;

Edward Mills, Efq;

Mr. John Merriman of Uppingham.

The Rev. John Maxwell, A. M.

‡ Mr. William Morland of the Inner Temple.

‡ Mr. Nathaniel May, Druggift.

Mr. Hugh Morgan.

Francis Cudworth Mafham, Efq; one of the mafters, and accomptant general in the court of chancery.

St. Mary Magdalen college, Oxon; for the library.

Mr. Benjamin Motte, bookfeller, fix copies.

Mr. Randal Minfhull, bookfeller, three copies.

N

The Right Rev. John Lord Bifhop of Norwich.

‡ Sir

‡ Sir Isaac Newton, Kt. president of the Royal Society.

The Hon. General Francis Nicholson.

‡ John Noel of Walcot, Esq;

‡ William Nicholas, Esq;

The Rev. William North, rector of Braunston in Leicestershire.

George Nevil of Holt, Esq;

William Noel, Esq; one of the members of Parliament for the borough of Stanford.

Mr. Harmen Noerthouck, bookseller; six books.

O

‡ The Right Hon. Edward Earl of Oxford, and Earl Mortimer.

The Right Rev. John Lord Bishop of Oxford.

Thomas Owen, Esq; bencher of Lincolns Inne.

Mr. John Owen of Aldersgate-street.

Mr. Thomas Osborn, bookseller, ten books.

P

‡ The Right Hon. Thomas Earl of Pomfret.

The Right Hon. John Lord Viscount Percivall.

‡‡ The Right Rev. White Lord Bishop of Peterborough, two books.

The Hon. Rob. Price, Esq; one of His Majesty's justices of the court of common pleas.

The Hon. William Phipps, Esq;

‡ Thomas Palmer of Fairfield, Esq; one of the members of parliament for Bridgwater.

The Rev. Robert Palmer, D.D.

The Rev. Zachary Pearce, D.D. F.R.S. rector of St. Martins in the fields.

Tracey Pauncefort, Esq;

Thomas Parker of the Inner Temple, Esq;

John Prat, Esq;

Mr. Thomas Powel, one of the clerks in chancery.

The Rev. Squire Payne, A.M. rector of Bernack.

The Rev. John Peak, A.M. rector of St. John Baptists, Stanford.

St. Peter's college, Cambridge, for the library.

‡ The Right Hon. William Pulteney, Esq; one of the members of parliament for the borough of Heydon in Yorkshire.

The Rev. William Pymont, A.M. rector of King's Cliffe in Northamptonshire.

John Plumtree, Esq; one of the members of parliament for the town of Nottingham.

Mr. John Parker, bookseller; three books.

Mr. William Pepper, bookseller; three books.

Mr. John Pemberton, bookseller; three books.

Mr. Edmund Palmer, bookseller in Stanford.

Q

Queen's college, Oxon; for the library.

R

‡ His Grace John Duke of Rutland.

‡ His Grace Charles Duke of Richmond.

‡ Richard Rawlison, LL.D.

‡ Mr. Thomas Richardson.

‡ Mr. Pelsant Reeves, one of the clerks in chancery.

Mr. Richard Rowlandson, of the Inner Temple.

Dudley Ryder, Esq;

Mr. Joseph Radcliff.

Mr. John Racquet, gentleman usher of the court of exchequer.

‡ Mr. John Rowell of Peterborough, merchant.

The Rev. Samuel Rogers, A.M. rector of St. Peters, Stanford.

Mr. William Richards of St. Martins, Stanford.

Mr. Charles Rivington, bookseller; six copies.

S

‡ The Right Hon. Talbot Earl of Suffex.

The Right Rev. Benjamin Lord Bishop of Sarum.

‡ Sir Thomas Saunders Sebright, Bar. one of the knights of the shire for the county of Hertford.

The Right Hon. Edward Southwell, Esq; one of His Majesty's principal secretaries of state for the kingdom of Ireland.

Sir John Shephard, Bar.

‡ Benjamin Haskins Styles, Esq; one of the members of parliament for the Devizes.

‡ The corporation of Stanford.

Robert Stephens of the Middle Temple, Esq;

William Spycer of the Middle Temple, Esq; secretary of the presentations.

Thomas Salisbury of Hampstead, Esq;

John Strange, Esq;

Edward Staples, Esq; clerk of the house of Commons.

Thomas Slater of Lincolns Inne, Esq;

Edmund Sawyer of Lincolns Inne, Esq;

Samuel Strode, Esq;

William Sanderson, Esq; deputy usher of the black rod.

Mr. Samuel Scot, merchant.

Mr. George Smith of Durham.

The Rev. Francis Storer, A.M. vicar of Stapleford in Leicestershire.

The Rev. Standish, A.M. rector of Uppingham in Rutland.

The Rev. Philip Stubs, A.M. archdeacon of St. Albans.

Thomas Strangeways Robinson, of Pickering in the county of York, Esq;

The Rev. Joseph Smith, D.D. rector of St. Dyonis, Back-church.

Mr. Joseph Smith, bookseller, twelve books.

‡ Mr. John Sturt, engraver.

Mr. George Strahan, bookseller, six books.

Mr. Edward Symon, bookseller, three kooks.

Mess. B. and J. Sprint, booksellers, three books.

Mr. J. Stephens, bookseller.

T

The Rev. Thomas Tanner, D.D. chancellor of Norwich.

‡ The Rev. Culpepper Tanner, A.M. late rector of Easton.

The Rev. Styan Thirlby, A.M. fellow of Jesus college, Cambridge.

Mark Thurstan, Esq; one of the masters in chancery.

Mr. Ralph Thoresby, of Leeds.

Cholmondely Turner, Esq;

‡ Trinity College, Cambridge; for the library.

The Rev. Joseph Trapp, A.M. rector of Christ's Church.

‡ The governor of Mr. Truesdale's hospital in Stanford, for the hospital.

Mr. Jacob Tonson, bookseller.

V

Mr. Gerard Vandergutcht, engraver.

W

The Right Rev. Thomas Lord Bishop of Waterford.

Sir

Sir Anthony Weftcombe, Bar.
‡ John Wingfield of Tickencoat, Efq;
Browne Willis of Whaddon hall in the county
　of Bucks, Efq;
‡ Hugh Wrottefley of Lincolns Inne, Efq;
The Rev. Daniel Wilkins, LL. D. archdeacon
　of Suffolk.
The Rev. Godfrey Wafhington, A. M. fellow
　of St. Peter's college, Cambridge.
The Rev. Chriftopher Wardel, A. M. rector of
　Stathern in Leiceftershire.
　　　Wills, Efq; one of His Majefty's learn-
　ed counfel in the law.
John Wood of Lincolns Inne, Efq;
Thomas Woodford, Efq; fecretary to the Right
　Hon. the Lord High Chancellor.
‡ James Weft, A. M. of Baliol college, Oxon.
The Rev. Miles Weft, A. M. minifter of Put-
　ney.

Henry Wefton, Efq; purfe-bearer to the Right
　Hon. the Lord High Chancellor.
Mr. John Waller of Lincolns Inne.
The Rev. Mofes Williams, A. M.
Mr. William Wall.
The Rev. Nathaniel Wefton, A. M. vicar of
　Exton and Enpingham.
‡ William Wardour, Efq;
The Rev. John Wood, A. M. rector of Cofloc
　in the county of Nottingham.
Mr. James Woodman, bookfeller, fix books.
Mr. Richard Williamfon, bookfeller, three
　books.
Mr. Thomas Wotton, bookfeller, three books.
Mr. Thomas Worrall, bookfeller, three books.
Mr. John Worrall, bookfeller, three books.

Y

Robert Yard, Efq;

ADVERTISEMENT.

THE fubfcribers books may be had either of Mr. John Brindley, bookbinder
in Town-Ditch by Little-Britain, London; or of Mr. Edward Holcot, in
Stanford; or of the Author, at his houfe in Godeby by Melton in Leiceftershire, for
whom any letters fo directed will come to hand.

This book is alfo fold by the following bookfellers in London.

Mr. Stephen Auften, at the Angel over againft
　the North door of St. Pauls.
Mr. Thomas Aftley, at the Dolphin and Crown
　in St. Pauls Churchyard.
Mr. Jonah Bowyer, in Pater-nofter Row.
Mr. Thomas Edlin, at the Princes Feathers in the
　Strand.
Mr. Fletcher Gyles, over againft Grays Inne
　Gate, Holborn.
Mr. Thomas Greene, by Charing-crofs.
Mr. John Goudge, in Weftminfter Hall.
Meffieurs William and John Innys, in St. Pauls
　Churchyard.
Mr. John Jackfon, at St. James's.
Mr. Charles King, in Weftminfter Hall.
Meffieurs James and John Knapton, at the
　Crown in St. Pauls Churchyard.
Mr.　　Lewis, in Ruffel-ftreet, Covent Garden.
Mr. Bernard Lintot, between the Temple Gates.
Mr. Benjamin Motte, at the Middle Temple
　Gate.
Mr. Randal Minfhul, in Ship-yard by Temple Bar.
Mr. Harmen Noerthouck, at Cicero's Head in
　Taviftock-ftreet.
Mr. Thomas Osborn in Grays Inne.
Mr. John Parker, near the Cocoa-tree Choco-
　late Houfe in Pall Mall.

Mr. William Pepper, at the Crown in Maiden-
　lane, Covent Garden.
Mr. John Pemberton, in Fleetftreet.
Mr. Charles Rivington, at the Bible and Crown
　in St. Pauls Churchyard.
Mr. Jofeph Smith, at Inigo Jones's Head in the
　Strand.
Mr. George Strahan, at the Golden Ball in
　Cornhill.
Mr. Edward Symon, in Cornhill.
Meff. B. and J. Sprint, in Little Britain.
Mr. J. Stephens, at the Bible in the Butcher-Row,
　near St. Clements Church in the Strand.
Mr. Jacob Tonfon, at Shakefpear's Head in
　the Strand.
Meffieurs James Woodman and David Lyon, at
　Camden's Head in Ruffel-ftreet, Covent Gar-
　den.
Mr. Richard Williamfon, near Grays Inne Gate,
　Holborn.
Mr. Thomas Wotton, at the three Daggers in
　Fleetftreet.
Mr. Thomas Worral, at the Judge's Head over
　againft St. Dunftan's Church, Fleetftreet.
Mr. John Worral, at the Bible and Dove in
　Bell-yard, near Temple Bar.

Academia

St. Maries.

All Saints.

St. John's.

N.º 1.

To y.º Worshipfull y.º Mayor, Aldermen, Town Clerk, & Capital Burgeſses of Stamford.
This Plate, representing their Comon Hall, in Acknowledgm.ᵗ of their Favour, is gratefully Inscribed
by F. P.

Academia tertia Anglicana;

OR, THE

ANTIQUARIAN ANNALS

of the TOWN of

STANFORD

IN

Lincoln, Rutland, *and* Northampton *Shires.*

BOOK I.

From the fuppofed Foundation of a Britifh Univerfity there, *Anno mundi* MMMC. *ante Chriftum* DCCCLXIII. to the fuppofed diffolution of the fame about the DCV. year after the Incarnation.

———*Ex fumo dare lucem.* Hor.

I. THE Age is dark which I begin with, but every hint, tho' never fo obfcure, the purfuit whereof, may at laft yield any thing for my purpofe, demands a fearch. If I hate fables then, yet I muft fpeak to fome traditions. The firft Tradition which prefents itfelf in our ftory is that of Bladuds Univerfity. I believe it would be reckoned a flight extravagant enough, fhould I pretend to carry up the antiquity of this place as high as the time he is fuppofed to live in; much more to talk of fchools here, when the reader will perhaps fay, the Britons had hardly houfes, lefs probably a town, & far more unlikely an academy, either here, or in any other part of the ifle. And yet fome (as you will fee prefently) contend for all thefe. And indeed that feveral places do yet preferve their Britifh names, is no argument that Stanford never had one: many other towns may be with it, in this cafe, equally unfortunate. And they, who, from the name, will allow it to be no more than a Saxon town, are foon anfwered by obferving to them, how eafily the old Britifh name might be loft, when the Saxons had given it a new one

B   fo

fo many ages ago, and driven the native inhabitants, with their Language, into one of the remoteft corners of the Ifland.

II. For the favor of making Stanford a Britifh Univerfity (before I began to fearch more particularly into thefe matters) I thought we had been obliged to Geoffry of Monmouth; & (as I imagined the ftory came from no body but him) was (thro' the lownefs of his credit) for rejecting it as a fable. However, tho', for this reafon, I accounted it no more than a fable, yet I had a curiofity to fee (if I could) exactly after what manner he related it. At laft I met with Mr. Thompfons tranflation of that author, & (not being able to procure a copy of the Original) read it over with great fatisfaction; but, to my furprife, got to the end of the book, without meeting with fo much as the name of Stanford, or any other I could take for it. Under the reign of Bladud I thought I fhould be fure to find fomething about Stanford, but not a tittle does he there, or any where elfe, mention, concerning the univerfity that prince is faid to have founded here. This was fome fort of a difappointment; &, when I had run over Mr. Thompfons Apology for his writings, I was the more forry for it; becaufe, had I found fuch an account there, the good opinion that Gentleman hath poffeffed me with for Geoffry (compared to what I had of him before) would have inclined me to receive it with a belief of its being fomething more than a fable. And tho', from him alone, I would not have affirmed, that, in fo early an age, there was an Univerfity where Stanford now ftands; yet would I at leaft have begged leave to demur on the premifes, & fubmitted the being of it to better judges.

III. But, if Geoffry be filent, whom have we then to fpeak for us? I anfwer. ' In the time of the Britons (faith Rous the Warwic An-
' tiquary, as quoted by Leland [1]) there were many univerfities; Grece-
' lade, Stawnford, Cambridge, Oxford, Lechlade, & Caerleon in
' Wales.' Except Rous, moft, if not all, of thofe authors, who fay any thing of a Britifh Univerfity at Stanford, quote Harding for their firft authority, as he quotes Merlin for his. Now there were two Merlins: Ambrofe Merlin, & Merlin of Caledonia. ' [2]Ambrofe Merlin lived,
' *anno Chrifti* 480. & Merlin of Caledonia, *anno Chrifti,* 570. Geof-
' fry of Monmouth (faith Leland [3]) met with the works of one or other
' of thefe authors, &, delighted with the novelty of the thing, tranf-
' lated it into Latin verfe.' Geoffry of Monmouth lived under K. Stephen, about the year 1150. But the faid Geoffry, as I have noted, (& confequently the Merlin whom he tranflates) fays nothing about Stanford. Whence it follows, I. that the Merlin whom Geoffry met with was certainly Ambrofe. And II. that it muft be Merlin of Caledonia whom Harding refers to, as fpeaking of the Britifh Univerfity in this place. Granting therefore both Ambrofe Merlin & Geoffry

---

1 Itin. vol. 4. p. 144.   3 Comment. p. 48.
2 Hiftorical Libra. part 1. 8°. p. 80.

of

of Monmouth to be, either fabulous authors, or silent in the case; those Concessions do not any ways invalidate the Being of a British University at Stanford. But, whatever is determined, this may be said for it; that they, who would set that aside, must first set aside the credit of Merlin of Caledonia: An author whose reputation, I suppose, is at least one form higher than his name-sakes. As to the Merlins, I know bishop Nicholson affirms [1] they were both one; but Mr. Leland[2] makes them two. And truly as Ambrose is silent, & Merlin of Caledonia speaks of a British university at Stanford, I am of Lelands side, & believe they were distinct. Merlin of Caledonia's book indeed I have never seen; but, that he actually speaks of such an university here, since Harding affirms it, so many copy, & none contradict him, I think we may very readily admit. Now then let Harding himself speak.

'   [3]When at Athenes he had studied clere,
'   Hee brought withe hym iiij philosophiers wise,
'   Schole to hold in Britayn and exercyse.
'   [4]Staforde he made, that [4]Sanforde hight this day,
'   In whiche he made an universitee.
'   His Philosophiers, as Merlyn doth saye,
'   Had scholers [5]fele of great habilitee,
'   Studying ever alway in unitee,
'   In all the seven liberal science,
'   For to purchace wysedome and sapience?

So far Harding. I shall next set down what some other writers (tho', as I intimated, I believe they only copy him) are pleased to discourse upon this subject. I am led to do so from a presumption that even those of my readers, who believe it all a fable, may one time or another, be diverted with running over what others more fond of the fancy have said upon it. Leland I know, speaking of ' Bladud & his ' philosophers that tawght at Staunford,' very frankly says, [6] ' this is like ' a Dreme.' But be it a dreme, here is another poetical Gentleman who tells it so well, that I persuade my self the reader will not be tired with his amplification of it. The person I mean is John Higgins, who wrote the history of our British kings, and by a pretty prosopopoeia, makes the supposed ghost of each prince relate his own story. Among the rest Bladud speaks thus.

'   Then was I chose king of this lande,
'   And had the crowne as had the reste;
'   I bare the scepter in my hande,
'   And sworde, that all our foes oppresse.

[1] Hist. library fol. p. 31.
[2] Comment. *ut supra.*
[3] Fol. 22.

[4] Sic.
[5] Saxon, for *many.*
[6] Collect. vol. III. p. 425.

Eke

' Eke for becaufe the Greekes did ufe
  ' Me well in Greece at Athens late,
' I bad thofe foure I brought to chufe
  ' A place that I might dedicate
' To all the mufes and their artes,
  ' To learnings ufe for evermore.
' Which when they fought in divers partes,
  ' At laft they found a place therefore.
' Amidft the realme it lies welnighe,
  ' As they by arte and skill did prove:
' An healthful place, not lowe nor highe,
  ' An holfome foyle for their behove:
' With water ftreames, and fpringes for welles,
  ' And medowes fweete, & valeyes grene:
' And woodes, groaves, quaries, all things elfe,
  ' For ftudentes weale or pleafure bene.
' When they reported this to me,
  ' They prayde my grace, that I would builde
' Them there an univerfitie
  ' The fruites of learnyng for to yelde.
' I buylte the fcholes, like Aticks then,
  ' And gave them landes to maintayne thofe
' Which were accounted learned men,
  ' And could the groundes of artes difclofe.'
' The towne is called Stamforde yet,
  ' There ftande the walles untill this daye:
' Foundations eke of fcholes I fett,
  ' Bide yet, not maintainde, in decaye.
' Wherby the lande receavid ftore
  ' Of learned clearkes long after that [1] &c.

IV. Bale[2], Pits[3], & Stow[4], have all the fame ftory, with little variation. But we muft not omit here the celebrated Drayton, who, fpeaking of Brute & Bladud, fings[5],

' Britain had thofe were learn'd, endu'd with nobler parts:
' As he, from learned Greece, that, by the liberal arts,
' To Stanford in this ifle feem'd Athens to transfer;
' Wife Bladud, of her kings, that great philofopher, &c.

[1] Fol. 43. b. fol. 44. a. The only one of Higgins books I ever faw is in 4°. it was once my own, but I gave it to my good friend the reverend & learned Mr. Tho. Baker, B. D. of S. Johns Coll. Camb. Mr. Baker writes, —— ' The book is imperfect begin-' ning & end, fo I can fay nothing of the ' edition; I know of no other: nor dare I ' pretend to judge of the author. He was ' well efteemed in the age he wrote.' Letter to me Jan. 1725-6.

[2] P. 10. 11.
[3] *In vita* Blad.
[4] P. 15.
[5] Polyolb. p. 112. 113.

Upon

Upon which his excellent Commentator Selden.[1] 'Some testimony is [Merlin *apud* Harding *cap.* 5. *ex iisdem &* Balæo].' that he went to Athens, 'brought thence with him four philosophers, & instituted by them an 'university at Stanford. But of any persuading credit I find none.'

V. These are all I shall at present take notice of, who speak of a British university in Bladuds time at Stanford, or, whatever it was called, at that place, we may suppose, which then stood where Stanford now does. The Age is dark, & therefore the best accounts of it must needs be short. For those few imperfect relations we have now left us concerning the Britons, if we take away the fables & uncertainties they are made up with, all lie in a very little room. But then it requires great judgment to distinguish & part out what is truth, when it is bewrapt & clouded with such an heap of fictions. Where therefore the truth is so very hard to be discovered, I shall be extreme cautious of asserting any thing; for I never had a fancy to trouble people with mere guesses & conjectures. In such cases it is enough to set down things as I find them; not to affirm, or to deny a matter, because others think, or say, or would have it so; but rather to leave it to time, & more judicious persons than I am, to enquire it out. The chief inducement which led me to this search, was, because I thought, altho' the present name of Stanford be purely Saxon, yet, whether there ever was a British university there in Bladuds days or not, there must have been a British town here, if not in his, yet in very early times, since Merlin of Caledonia would scarce fix a British university where there never was a British town; that being the way to make one falsity bewray another: a blunder which no writer of any tolerable capacity would ever be guilty of.——When the first sheet of this book was printed off, I had never seen Rous, any farther than as there quoted from Leland. But, by a sight of his book (which is exceeding scarce) I since find, that when he speaks of Bladuds university at Stanford, he does not write from any new authority of his own; but copies Harding. So that instead of, *except Rous, most, if not all*, &c. as p. 2. above, I should rather have said, *not only Rous, but all those writers who say any thing of a British university at Stanford, quote Harding for their authority, as he quotes Merlin for his.* What is here offer'd the reader is desired to accept, as the best account I can yet meet with, of the foundation & beginning of this British university (if there ever was any such) at Stanford.

VI. Having done with Bladud, now a little of the Romans, those Circa An. 86. masters of the world, who scattered their medals, urns, pavements, instruments of war & sacrifice, & many other curious antiquities, in every province where they extended their conquests. Of these the first monument I have met with in this neighbourhood is the remains of Ermingstreet, one of their great roads. 'Ermingstreet, 'saith Selden [2], being of English idiom, seems to have its name from

---

1 id. p. 123.   2 Notes on polyolb. p. 256.

C   ' Inmunrull,

‘ Iɲmunɟull, in that fignification whereby it interprets an univerſal
‘ pillar worſhipt for Mercury prefident of waies.’ But faith another,
‘ ¹ our chronicles generally call it Ermyn-ſtreet, of the Britiſh word
‘ Armyinth; becauſe it croſſes mountains & wayleſs places for the
‘ better direction of travellers. And this laſt derivation, faith biſhop
‘ Kennet ², feems more natural than what Mr. Selden, & from him
‘ Mr. Burton ³, would affix to it.

VII. It is, I think, agreed by all who underſtand antiquities, that
the four great Roman roads in Britain were made when Agricola was
lieutenant here. And, as Domitian recalled Agricola in the 86 year
of Chriſt, ſo thoſe great roads (admitting they were made by him)
muſt have been compleated then, if not ſome years before. ‘ As to the
‘ common opinion of Ermingſtreet, that it went from W. N. W. to
‘ E. S. E. from S. Davids to Southampton ⁴ [I believe] as Mr. More-
‘ ton fays, ⁵ it deferves no great credit; there being (as he adds) no ſure
‘ authority for it. In Henry of Huntingdon ’tis faid to go from ſouth
‘ to north. Accordingly we find it to do ſo here. And whether there
‘ be another Ermingſtreet, or not, this I take to be the very Erming-
‘ ſtreet, which is uſually reckoned one of the four great ways; this
‘ being, in many places, as ſignal & confiderable for its breadth &
‘ height as Watlingſtreet, & alſo paved as that is in ſome places. It
‘ comes out of Eſſex into Cambridgſhire, where there are yet ſome
‘ remains of the name. It runs along the weſt ſide of Cambridg-
‘ ſhire, & carries us directly by Royſton, & thro’ Caxton, to Godman-
‘ cheſter & Huntingdon. A little above Stilton, fays Camden ⁶, it
‘ appears with an high bank. Thence a Roman portway leads ſtraight
‘ to Cheſterton.’ Upon the Nen, between Cheſterton & Caſter, the
ſaid Mr. Camden & others who follow him, ſometimes place Dornford. ‘ ⁷ Henry of Huntingdon, in his recenſion of Britiſh cities, adds
‘ ſix to Ninnius catalogue, whereof this is one. Caer Dorm, fays
‘ he, that is Dormeceaſtre, which being in Huntingdonſhire is now ut-
‘ terly deſtroyed. What is left of it, faith Burton ⁸, at this day is
‘ called Dornford near unto Walmesford. Dornford, fays Camden ⁹,
‘ befides the finding of old coins, has the apparent marks of a ruin-
‘ ous city. For here the Roman portway runs thro’ the middle of a
‘ ſquare fort, defended on the north ſide with walls, on the reſt
‘ with ramparts of earth. Undoubtedly, continues he, this is the Du-
‘ robrivæ of Antonine, that is the river paſs: And now for the ſame
‘ reaſon called Dornford nigh Cheſterton.’ In another place he fays,
‘ ¹⁰ as to that termination Briva, which is an adjunct to the names of
‘ very many places, it ſignifies (as I ſuppoſe) among the antient Bri-
‘ tons & Gauls, a bridge, or the paſſage over a river; ſince we find
‘ it no where uſed but at rivers. In this iſland there were one or

1 Author of the antiquities of Allcheſter
cited in Bp. Kennets par. ant. p. 15.
  2 par. antiq. p. 16.
  3 Comment. on Ant. p. 95.
  4 id. ib.
  5 Northamptonſhire, p. 502.

6 In Hunt.
7 Burton, p. 203.
8 id. ib.
9 in Hunt.
10 in Hertf. p. 301.

' two Durobrivæ, that is, unlefs I am much deceived, paffages over
' the water. In Gaul there was Briva Ifariæ, now Pontoife, where
' was the paffage over the Ifara, or Yfore; Briva Oderæ, over the
' Odera; & Samarobriva, for that is the right name, over the river
' Soain.

VIII. Mr. Burton, by his manner of quoting him, feems to concur
with Cambden; for fpeaking of Dornford, ' this, fays he, ₁ in Camb-
' dens judgment is Antoninus his Durobrivæ here, which he interprets,
' *fluminis trajectus,* a ferry or paffage over the river.' Now Cambden himfelf fays, ₂ *Briva, trajectum vel vadum, Britannis prifcis &*
' *Gallis fignificaffe exiftimo, cum ad flumina folummodo reperiatur.*'
Which is well tranflated by bifhop Gibfon, when he fays above, ' *it*
' *fignifies as I fuppofe,* &c.' But this expreffion neverthelefs *fignificaffe*
exiftimo feems to intimate that Cambden himfelf did not underftand
Welch, & for that reafon fpeaks with fo much diffidence. What
confirms my conjecture is, Mr. Talbot fays, ³ ' Durobrivias or Doore-
' briff, in Welch fignifies fharp ftreme, *fluctus rapidus.* Now this account of Doorebriff is widely different from Mr. Cambdens notion
of Briva above recited; & yet, if he be right in the other part of
his affertion that Briva only occurs where there is a river, as well fuit-
ed to a river as his.

IX. And now we are fpeaking of rivers, give me leave before I go
on to remark, that the prefent name of the river whereon the town
of Stanford is fituate, is Welland. Now Ueallan in Saxon fignifies
furere, æftuare, ebullire, to rage, to boil, to bubble; & Ueallano the
very name, *furens, æftuans, ebulliens,* raging, boiling bubbling. A name
fo well agreeing with the nature of a fharp ftreme, or *fluctus rapidus,*
that it looks as much like a tranflation of the Britifh Doorebriff into
the Saxon Welland, as it is the juft etymology of the latter.

X. Mr. Lloyd, & Mr. Bohun, in their geographical dictionaries, affert Stanford is the Durobrivæ of Antonine in thefe parts. I fay, in
thefe parts, becaufe, as Mr. Cambden hath told us above, there are
two places of this name mentioned in the Itinerary. Alfo Mr. Talbot, fpeaking of the Durobriviæ hereabouts, places it about Stanford.
' *Puto effe Stanford, aut fimile,* ₄ (fays he) I take it to be Stanford,
' or the like.' After which he goes on very remarkably upon
the name it felf. ' We have Durobrivæ [mentioned in the Itinerary] twice
' between London & Canterbury, which, I told you, I thought
' to be Rochefter. And indeed I think the fame name [Durobriviæ,
' or Durobrivæ] ought to be ufed both here [at Stanford] & there
' [at Rochefter.] As we often fee that one & the fame name, as far
' as a word only extends, from fome common propriety, is impofed

1 p. 203.   J. Lelandi Itin. vol. 3. p. 145.
2 In Hertf.   4 in loco fupra citato.
3 annotat. in Ant. Itin. impreff. in calce

' on two places very remote from one another. For whereas thefe
' two local appellations have been wrefted from the language of that
' people who then inhabited this ifland, the laft fyllables being changed
' & handfomely turned into a Latin termination, it is like either the
' difference muft have been greater, or certainly that [fuch as it is]
' more remote from the laft final fyllable.

XI. ' Rochefter, faith Mr. Lambard, [1] is called in Latine, Durobre-
' vum, Dorobrevum, Dorubernia, & Durobrivis; in Brittifhe, Dourbryf,
' that is to fay, a fwift ftream: in Saxon Hꞃoꝼeꞃceaꞃtꞃe that is, Rofi-
' civitas, Rofes city, in fome old charters, Rofibrevi.' And how
well does all this agree with what goes before! Perhaps then, altho' the prefent name of Stanford be Saxon, we are now not fo much
to feek either for the Britifh, or Roman name of that place, as fome
may imagine. For fhould I, with Talbot, Lloyd, & Bohun, call Stanford the Britifh Doorebriff, & the Roman Durobrivæ in thefe parts, almoft fo much I think emerges from what has been already offered. However if we contend for Stanford, as others may contend for Chefterton,
others for Dornford, & others for Caftre to be the Durobrivæ in thefe
parts mentioned in the Itinerary, I fhall for the prefent leave it un-
determined; & now I am arrived where fome place Dornford, travel
on with Ermingftreet towards Stanford: repeating, as I pafs, fuch remarks as I find other authors have made upon it, & adding withal my own.

XII. ' Some think, faith Cambden, [2] that this city [Dormceaftre]
' ftood upon both banks of the river.' Here alfo his difciple Burton copies him. 'It feems that the old city poffeffed both banks of
' the river.' [3] Others of their opinion I meet with none. Indeed that
there may be a fquare fort at Dornford, thro' which the Port-way
runs, tho' I never faw it, with Cambden, I yet admit. But that the
grand ftation of thefe parts, was fituate by the water, on both or
either fide the very river banks, having often had a view of the country in my road from Cliffe to Peterborough, I cannot at all allow.
For the meadow on either fide is a low flat, & particularly on the
fouth very broad & fpacious as well as low, & confequently, upon
every flood, liable to great inundations; fo that this fituation lays it
open to fuch inconveniencies, as the wifdom of the Romans, I perfuade my felf, would hardly ever permit any ftation of theirs (efpecially
when they might have higher ground fo near as Caftre) to be endan-
gered with. Sure I am that their laft ftation by being placed at Chefterton, (except we make Chefterton, Dornford & Caftre all one, &
then it will be the biggeft that ever was heard of) looks as if they did
not care for coming too near the banks of fuch an angry water as the
Nene. But to proceed.

XIII. ' Having croffed the Nyne below Caftre, faith Mr. Moreton,

---

[1] Perambulation of Kent. p. 293.   [2] In Hunt.   [3] p. 203.

' Erming-

'[1] Erming-ftreet paffes their meadow & field, where 'tis now only a
'private field-way, in a ftrait raifed bank.' A little way off, on the
right hand of this bank, lies Caftre. Mr. Cambden, fpeaking yet of
Dormeceaftre, goes on. [2]'Others are of opinion that the little village
'Caftre, on the other fide was part of it. And truly this opinion is
'well backed by an antient Hiftorian that fays, there was a place cal-
'led Durmundceaftre by Nene, where Kinneburga founded a little nun-
'nery, firft called Kinneburg-ceaftre, & afterwards for fhortnefs Caftre.'
And again. [3]'This City, as I faid before, took up a great deal of ground
'on each fide the river in both counties. For the little village Caftre,
'which ftands a mile from the river, feems to have been a part of it,
'by the inlaid chequer pavements found there. And doubtlefs it was
'a place of more than ordinary note, for in the adjoining fields (which
'inftead of Dormanton, they call Normanton, fields) fuch quantities
'of Roman coin are thrown up, that a man would really think
'they had been fown.' Thefe are good evidences to prove that Caftre was infallibly a Roman ftation, but not that the Roman town
there was a mile long & reached quite down to the river, much lefs
that it took in Dornford & Chefterton on the other fide, which would
make it above a mile longer yet: A length fo unconfcionable for one
ftation, that I cannot but fmile at them who contend for it.

XIV. As to the Chequer pavements abovementioned, any one who
paffes this way may now fee a good part of one, in the cellar of a little houfe, on the fouth fide of Caftre church, known at prefent 1723.
by the fign of the boot; in which houfe I having lately fome property, in right of my wife, was once minded to have taken up the faid
pavement, & difpofed of it in fome other place. But, on fecond
thoughts, refolved to leave it there, as being unwilling to deprive the
town of fo fair a mark of its Antiquity. The faid pavement runs a
good way up the yard belonging to the faid houfe, & beyond it (if I
may believe fome of the inhabitants) croffes the church-yard at the weft
end of the Church. The medals dug & plowed up in this neighbourhood, are, as I read, [4]'the coins of many emperors, all from
'Trajan to Valens. Some pieces of urns & other antique veffels of
'earth have alfo been found here; as alfo ftones of foundations
'& ruin'd walls; little tiles, ridge tiles, & bricks.' 'At Caftre, as
'Mr. Morton adds, [5]Ermingftreet has the name of Norman gate, &
'fometimes of forty foot way, as being formerly fo broad. This
'way, fays another, [6]is alfo called by the inhabitants the lady Cony-
'burrows way, for Kyneburgs way, which, from all conjectures ap-
'pears to be nothing but a Roman paved way, leading from a fortrefs
'on the other fide of the river Nyne to the caftle, or principal fort

1 P. 502.
2 In Hunt.
3 In Northampt.

4 Britan. ant. & nova in Northampt. p.471:
5 P. 502.
6 Brit. ant. & nova ut fupra.

'upon

' upon the hill, where now the church ſtands, which was the reſidence
' then of the Roman Governor or chief commander.'   Here my author (in complaiſance to Mr. Cambden & his followers, who place the
city of Dormeceaſtre on either ſide the river in both counties) allows
of a fortreſs on the other ſide of the ſame, but for all that very judi-
ciouſly places the principal fort upon the hill : a much ſafer place for
his Roman governor or chief commander to reſide at.

XV. ' On the weſt ſide of Caſtre, ſaith Mr. Moreton, 'Ermingſtreet
' advances towards Upton.   Nigh Upton it branches.   The leſſer
' branch of it runs north eaſt-ward by the name of Long-dike, as hav-
' ing been trenched on the ſides thereof; whereof are ſtill ſome foot-
' ſteps, & particularly in that part of it ſouthward of Hillow brook:
As I once rode this way with the late John Bridges Eſq; when we
came to ſurvey Helpſtone church, we found a good part of the upper
end of the floor of the ſouth iſle there, had been repaired with ſmall
Roman bricks brought thither from ſome place in the neighbourhood.
' This branch of Ermingſtreet, ſaith Camden[2], is ſometimes called
' Long-ditch, & ſometimes High-ſtreet.'   But Mr. Moreton is wrong
when he ſays[3], ' it croſſes the Welland into Lincolnſhire over Lol-
' ham bridges.'   For Lolham bridges are not laid over the Welland,
& beſides, it muſt not only croſs Lolham, but Weſt Deping bridge,
before it can be ſaid to paſs into that county.   ' Lolham bridges, as
' he adds[4], are now ſix in number, & have together 14 arches :
' bridges, as Mr. Cambden rightly obſerves, of great antiquity.'   But of
theſe bridges, ſaith another[5], ' but eleven arches are ſtill to be ſeen,
' tho' cleft and ruinous with age.'   How many arches there are I can't
tell (having never counted them) but there are ſix ſeveral bridges, a
ſmall diſtance from each other : all having ſeveral arches, tho' none
of them (as far as I can ſee) of any great antiquity, or cleft or ruinous
with age.   However the great pit, over which the biggeſt bridge is
now erected, in my judgment ſeems formerly to have communicated
with ſome other pits both above & below it, but particularly that towards Stanford, now called Pilſgate haven.   And for this reaſon, &
becauſe this branch of Ermingſtreet runs directly acroſs thoſe pits at
Lolham, we may well enough admit the original bridges there firſt
erected, to have been very antient.

XVI. Return we now to the other branch of Ermingſtreet.   ' From
' Upton the principal branch or main part of it, as Mr. Moreton calls
' it[6], retaining ſtill the name of forty foot way', advances northward.
Particularly on the weſt of Bernack I have ſeen it again, whence it
runs on the north ſide of Pilſgate 'till it comes up to Burghley park
wall, which, without any gate near to let in the curious traveller to
trace & purſue it, runs directly acroſs it.   So that Mr. Moreton is

1 P. 502.
2 In Northampt.
3 P. 502.
4 Id. ib.
5 Brit. ant. & nova, ut ſupra.
6 Northamptonſhire, p. 502.

                                                           miſtaken.

mistaken when he says it only went by [1] Burghley park, since its evident it runs immediately thro' it.   However, I believe that Gentleman is right when he afterwards says [1], ' a great part of it has been digged ' away to gravel walks at Burghley.'   On the north side of Burghley park it appears again, whence it may be tracked to S. Michaels priory, formerly a nunnery of the Benedictin order, by Stanford.   But they are mistaken who would bring that road down the nuns lane, on the east side of that priory, & so across the Welland', ' at a place where ' 'tis most likely was the *stony ford* that gave name to the town,' since it is evident it crossed the river on the west, not east, side of that religious house, & so ran directly athwart Bradecroft.   But now we are got to S. Michaels priory, let us stop a little, & here take an account of another piece of antiquity.

XVII. In summer, 1723. in the Water-street was dug up a Roman urn, a vessel as described to me by good judges, who saw several large pieces of it, narrow at the top and bottom, widening very much & bellying out in the midst.   It was made of a bright glased earth, the inner shell very thin, no thicker than a modern sixpence, crusted over with sand on the outside, & then cased with another shell of the same thickness and color.   So that it was like an urn within an urn, or one pot wrought over another, & divided only by a little sand; which seems to have been cast over the inner vessel immediately after it came out of the furnace, and then another coat or vessel was immediately cast over that.   It is generally believed the same was full of treasure; but the mason who dug it up, could neither be persuaded, or frighted, to tell what he found in it.

XVIII. Return we now to Ermingstreet, which, having crossed the river, as above; runs all along the east end of the meadow called Bradecroft, forming a short, but pleasant, gravel walk, parted by a dike from Mr. Burmans close, called the crown-close, formerly belonging to Sempringham abby.   At the end of this meadow is a bridge of one arch over a small branch of the Welland, whose stream (being stopped by a cataract, or wash as it is called, about half way between Stanford & Tinwell) is part of it by this channel conveyed to a mill of great antiquity, called the kings-mill.   Much about half way between the foresaid little bridge & wash, stood Bredcroft hall, a place where formerly the sessions, as tradition says, were kept for Rutland. The foundations of this old structure may yet be plainly discovered on the northern bank of this water course.   Being passed the foresaid little bridge Ermingstreet appears again very conspicuously; & runs all the way up the hill along the west end of the Austin friers wall, 'till it arrives at the great road from Stanford to Uppingham.   So that it appears, that Ermingstreet, tho' it did not pass thro' the very heart,

---

1 Northamptonshire, p. 602.

or midſt, of Stanford, yet ran directly acroſs this weſtern ſuburb belonging to it, called Bredcroft.

XIX. The learned Roger Gale Eſq; ſpeaking of this Ermingſtreet, is pleaſed to ſay, [1] ' it croſſes the Nen at Dornford, from whence it turns ' to the weſt of Upton, & ſo to Tinwel in Rutland about a mile ' above Stanford on the Welland.' But I dont find Ermingſtreet comes any nearer Tinwel than the place above, juſt without Stanford, at the northweſt corner of the Auſtin friers wall, where (as I obſerved) it croſſes the Uppingham road. However this mentioning of Tinwell reminds me of an offer once made me by one Mr. Parry a ſurgeon (who then ſojourned in Stanford, but now dwelling in London) to ſhew me a military trench or encampment (whether Roman or no indeed I cannot ſay) ſomewhere in the fields between Stanford & Tinwel. But he left Stanford ſoon after on a ſudden, & ſo I miſſed the opportunity of his company to the place, which, where it is, for want of his directions, I am yet to ſeek. As to Encampments I ſhall only obſerve, firſt, [2] ' the Britons made their fortifications with great ſtones, ' or earth, caſt up into high banks with intrenchments round them.' Secondly, all the Roman Encampments I ever read of, or ſaw, were ſquare; & that ſquare generally oblong: as that at Vernometum or Burrow on the hill, in this neighbourhood where I now live. Thirdly, the Gothic manner of fortifying was by a wide circular ditch. Fourthly, [3] ' The Saxons made their Foſſe circular, but then it was more nar- ' row, leſs deep, & generally of greater circumference than the Gothic. ' [4] Sometimes quinquangular.' Laſtly, [5] ' the Danes made their Foſſe ' large & round:' but not ſo large as the Gothic.

XX. But to proceed. Within the walls of the Auſtin friers abovementioned on the 22. of Feb. 17$\frac{11}{12}$. (as I was informed by the late Mr. Richard Walburg, my ſelf being then at Cambridge) ' were dug up a ' large parcel of glaſed tiles of different colors, two inches thick, ' twelve inches long and nine inches broad; a whole load of them was ' found as they lay a paved floor, & more might have been taken up, ' but that they were ſpoiled, & ſo it was not thought worth the while.' A good many of them were carried by the ſaid Mr. Walburg (whoſe words I juſt now uſed) to an houſe of his at Pilſgate, & there employed as before, in flooring a room. Theſe I have ſince ſeen, & am ſatisfied are Roman. But whether firſt laid down here by the Romans, or afterwards brought hither from ſome other place in the neighbourhood by the fathers of that ſociety, may be equally queſtioned. However as they might dig good free-ſtone juſt by their own doors, far it is certain they would not fetch them. And now to go on again. Croſſing the road leading from Stanford to Uppingham, at the north-

---

1 Eſſay on the Roman ways in Brit. at the end of Lelands Itin. vol. 6.
2 Plots Staffordſhire, p. 395.
3 Additions to Camb. on Norfolk, p. 400.
4 Plots Oxfords. Firſt edition, p. 334.
5 Id. ib.

                                                              weſt

weſt corner of the Auſtin friers wall as above, Ermingſtreet immediately appears again, with a broad raiſed bank, which forms a pleaſant walk of a good length. For the London road being carried thro' Stanford for the convenience of paſſengers to lodge there, part of this old Roman way hath been long diſuſed; which part ſo forſaken is now diſtinguiſhed from the reſt of High-Dike (ſo they here call Ermingſtreet) by the name of Green-Bank: this piece of it being ſo little travelled, that it is always green. About half way between Stanford & great Caſtreton (that is, a mile from either place) the road from London to York comes in again & joins with Ermingſtreet; after which, all the reſt of Ermingſtreet, between the ſaid towns of Stanford and great Caſtreton, is very diſcernable by its high bank; but, being much frequented, looks now not near ſo green as it did before, but, like other great roads, worn & footed by man & horſe.

XXI. Before I proceed to trace Ermingſtreet any farther north, I here beg leave to turn back a while to Stanford, & obſerve that the common road thro' Stanford into the north (viz. into York, or Scotland) has always, time out of mind, lain under the town gate, ſometimes called S. Clements, ſometimes Skof-gate, ſometimes Scot-gate, & now, for ſhortneſs, Sco-gate. Now it is a mile from this gate to the half way place between Stanford & great Caſtreton abovementioned, where this north road from Stanford comes in to, & joyns, with the great Roman way above, called Ermingſtreet. And yet Cambden ſpeaks of a [1] ' *via militaris Romanorum, quæ* STATIM *te ex oppido in boream pro-* ' *ficiſcentem excipit* —— a military way of the Romans which IMME- ' DIATELY receives you as you go out of the town into the north. He can never mean ſure by the words STATIM, IMMEDIATELY, &c. that part of Ermingſtreet, which, when you are got out of Sco-gate (except you there ſtrike out of your way & the ſaid north road to come at it) is yet a mile off! ' STATIM, ſays Dr. Littleton, [2] *prima brevi, a* ' *ſtando itidem, cum quid ita ſit*; *ut, qui facit, ſtet*; *non moveat e loco.*' I am apt to think therefore there were here two Roman ways, to wit, that great road already in part traced as above, made very direct & ſtraight to paſs on with more expedition, when no ſtay here could be conveniently allowed; & another, ſhort, ' vicinal way, or *minor che-* ' *minus,* as Dr. Plot calls them [3], ' turned off I ſuppoſe from the great road into the town, for the ſoldiers to bait or reſt here on occaſion, when their march did not require ſo much haſt. Agreeable to this notion, the learned doctor abovementioned, in his account of Oxfordſhire, ſpeaks, [4] ' of a little crooked Roman way laid purpoſely from a great ' one to take in Oxford.' And again tells us, [5] ' that the Romans ' where the way was not well laid out, or was longer than needed,

[1] In Coritanis.
[2] In verbo.
[3] Oxf. firſt edit. p. 316.

[4] Id. p. 318.
[5] Id. p. 321.

E

' did

' did commonly (to keep the people from idlenefs, & the foldiers from
' mutinies) lay them ftraiter & better.' It appears then that the Roman
roads, like other ways, were fometimes crooked, and fometimes ftraight ;
& turned fometimes this, & fometimes that way, as they faw, or fancied, moft for their convenience.

XXII. fome old deeds hereafter quoted, in the courfe of thefe antiquities, fpeak of the *magnus chiminus*, & *magnum foffatum*, in this
neighbourhood. And the word *magnus* or *magnum*, for ought we
know ; may there be ufed by way of diftinction, & not by way of
eminence. Be that as it will, certain I am that the deep, hollow
way, *quæ* STATIM *te ex oppido in boream proficifcentem excipit*, looks
very much like a work of the Romans ; and, whether it be or not,
I believe Cambden took it for fuch ; or elfe, I don't know how he
could write, or any body can tranflate, his words above, as they fhould
do. Now admitting this cut to be a work of the Romans, there were
then certainly two Roman ways here, & as certainly there was a town,
where Stanford now ftands, in the times of the Romans ; fince this
laft way could be made for no other end, but, as hath been intimated, for the convenience of the foldiery to turn in there to reft or re-
frefh themfelves. I fhould here end my obfervations upon Ermingftreet, being now got to the end of my bounds, out of which I indeed began fo long ago (as any one, who cares not for remarks of
this fort, may fay) when I took up the account of Ermingftreet fo far
fouth, before I brought it to Stanford ; but there are others, of a different
tafte, who will perhaps be as much pleafed with my difcourfing a little
farther upon it ; for which reafon, &, as I am allured on by the veftigia
of the road which I have fo often travelled, I fhall e'en proceed, without
any more ceremony, to fay what I have read, or obferved, about it.

XXIII. It may be remembred, I have already followed this road as
far as Great Caftreton on the Guafh, fo called to diftinguifh it from
Little Caftreton, another village, about a mile off, to the right, on the
fame river. Now, ' the hither part of Lincolnfhire, faith Talbot, ' is
' commonly called Caifeven, or Caifteven. In it probably was fome
' town called Caufennæ, or Caftennæ, which hath given name to the
' adjacent fields & parts about it.' Cambden, fpeaking of Stanford,
fays, ² ' tho' there may be here fome remains of antiquity, & the military
' way of the Romans (which immediately receives you as you go out of
' the town into the north) fufficiently declares there has been once a
' ferry here ; yet they do not prove that this was that Gaufennæ, which
' Antoninus hath placed not far hence. But fince the little village Brig-
' Caftreton, in which name appears a note of Antiquity, is but a mile
' off [he fhould have faid two] where the river Gwafh, or Wafh, cuts
' the military way acrofs, the affinity of the name Gwafh with Gau-
' fennæ, & the diftance being not inconfiftent, make me apt to believe,

1 In loco fupra citato.   2 In Corit.

'till

' 'till time fhall bring the truth to light, that Gaufennæ is at prefent
' called Brig-Caftreton.   And if I fhould think Stanford to have fprang
' from the ruins of this town, & that this part of the country is cal-
' led Kefteven from Gaufennæ (as the other part is named Lindfey
' from the city of Lindum) I would have the reader take it as my bare
' opinion, & pafs what judgment he pleafes.'   What Mr. Cambden here
fays, about Stanford arifing out of the ruins of Bridge-Caftreton, fhall
be confidered elfewhere [1].   At prefent give me leave to note, that upon
thefe two laft paffages of Talbot & Cambden, Mr. Burton well obferves, [2] ' it is Talbots conjecture that Gaufennes, or Gaufennis, gave
' name to the hithermoft part of Lincolnfhire, now called Cafteven; even
' as Lindfey, another part thereof, hath its name from Lindum.   But
' Cambden calls it his opinion! who yet pretends to no certainty of
' place, except it be at Bridge-Caftreton upon Wafh, or Gwafh; fo mak-
' ing fome affinity between the old name of the ftation, & that of the
' river at this day.

XXIV. After all it is very odd that Brig-Caftreton in Rutland, fhould
give name to Kefteven one of the hundreds of Lincolnfhire.   For my
part I fhould rather think that Stanford, which is in Kefteven, if it be
not the Durobrivæ, is the Gaufennæ, of Antonine; or, at leaft, if
Cambden will have Caftre, to be Durobrivæ; & Brig-Caftreton, Gaufennæ; yet that there was a Roman town near Stanford as well as at
both thofe places.   Likewife, what if I fhould go a little farther &
fay, Caftre was called Dorme or Dorn-ceafter, whence alfo Dornford;
& that Stanford was named Doorebriff, or Durobrivæ, from the rapidity
or roughnefs of the Welland; & again that Brig-Caftreton was called Gaufennæ.   For my part I fee no abfurdity in all this.   However my readers
will pleafe to take me right: I only furmife what I fometimes think;
the matters I write of are too uncertain for me to affirm any thing
in.   But admitting there was a Roman town at Stanford, & another at
Brig-Caftreton (tho' but two miles from it) the nearnefs of thefe places
is no objection to the contrary.   Dr. Plot indeed fays, ' [3] upon thefe
' confular, prætorian, or military ways, the Romans eftablifhed their
' Itineraries, ftations, or manfions at certain diftances, which feem to
' have been the extent of the daily marches of their foldiers; the length
' whereof, as they were feldom under ten, fo they as rarely exceeded
' thirty Italian miles.'   But this is no rule.   For here we find it is but
feven miles from Caftre to Stanford; but fix from Bridge-Caftreton to
Margidunum or Margidoverton; & again, but as many from Stretton
(the town on the Roman ftreet or way) ad Pontem, to Ponton.   Nay
it is but four from Bridge-Caftreton to Stretton; but two from Chefterton to Caftre; but one from Chefterton, or Caftre, to Dornford;
& no more from Bridge-Caftreton to little Caftreton; all in the neighbourhood of Stanford.

1 Anno 449. infra;   2 P. 203.   3 Staff. p. 400.

XXV. By the way, Sir William Dugdale fays, [1] 'the gaining of
' Marfhland in Norfolk ; and Holland in Lincolnfhire, was a work
' very antient, as by many circumftances may be gathered ; & there-
' fore confidering the induftry, & skill of the Romans, he conceives it
' moft likely to have been performed by them. Mr. Cambden, faith
' he, in his Britannia, fpeaking of the Romans in Britain, hath an
' obfervation out of Tacitus in the life of Agricola; which Dr. Hol-
' land (who tranflated Cambden) delivers thus. The Romans wore
' out & confumed the bodies of the Britons, in clearing of woods,
' & paving the fenns. But the words of Tacitus are, *paludibus emu-*
' *niendis,* of which Sir William queries, whether the word *emuniendis,*
' do not mean walling or banking.' Be that as it will, if the fenns
were firft drained by the Romans, as Sir William furmifes, perhaps
this may be the reafon why we find the Roman ftations fo thick hereabouts. The attempt only of fuch a work requiring an almoft incredible number of hands ; & thofe hands that laboured, near as many
more to furnifh them with proper fubfiftence & other neceffaries.

XXVI. Before I leave Bridge-Caftreton, a word or two concerning
a coin found there. In the parfonage houfe about the year 1708, was
found a remarkable Roman coin (what emperor I could not learn)
with a Britannia, (very like that on our modern Half-pence) on the
reverfe. It was prefented by Mr. Jonathan Clough, then (& now)
rector of that place, to the late Mr. William Forfter, then rector of
S. Michaels Stanford, as a curiofity worthy of his particular regard.
Mr. Forfter himfelf, from whom I had this account, told me with fome
concern, that leaving this coin one day in his parlor window, fome
of his children met with it, & taking it for an halfpenny or farthing,
difpofed of it fo as he could never hear of it again. The learned bifhop Kennet mentions two coins, one of Caraufius, & the other of
Allectus, both which had on the reverfe, [2] ' the picture of Pallas with
' an olive leaf in her right-hand, reaching it out, in token of peace
' offered ; & a fpear in her left hand, that, if peace was refufed, then
' wars fhould enfue :' the fame with one of which might probably be
the coin above. Which coin, if it belonged to either of thofe princes,
was minted before the year of Chrift 294, when Allectus, the laft of
them, was flain by Afclepiodotus. [3] Whereof I have nothing more to
add, but that meeting lately with Mr. Clough, after acquainting him
with what Mr. Forfter told me as above, all that he pleafed to anfwer
was, it was fo long ago he could not remember whether he ever gave
Mr. Forfter fuch a coin, much lefs what emperor it was, or whether
dug up, or only found dropped in his houfe.

XXVII. Being paffed Bridge-Caftreton, Ermingftreet appears again
very plainly juft beyond the place where a track, on the left, turns

---

1 Letter to Sir Thomas Brown, dated   2 Paroch. Antiq. p. 11.
Oct. 4. 1658. printed among Sir Thomas's   3 Videfis Speed. p. 161.
pofthumous works, 8vo. Lond. 1712.

out of the great road to Tickencoat. Thence it carries you almoſt
to Horn-lane with a very high bank. A little before you enter that
lane, & 'till you are got thro' it, the bank, being much worn by frequent travelling, is but diſcernable, but immediately beyond it, riſes
again with a greater eminence. For ' at five miles croſs, as Mr. Gale
' obſerves¹, it is very apparent, where it divides it ſelf, & ſends out
' one branch towards Nottingham, & another [by Stretton, Ponton,
' Ancaſtre] towards Lincoln ; from which laſt place we ſcarce ever
' loſe the tract of a great Roman way, 'till it hath brought us as far as
' Carliſle, where ſome end this Ermingſtreet.' But, now we are got
ſo far north from Stanford, it is time we haſt back. For variety however let us return by Belvoir, where an antiquary will find good entertainment in viewing thoſe curious family pieces, the pictures of all the
earls of Rutland at length, as big as the life ; reaching, in a moſt a-
greeable order, from one end of a long gallery to the other ; which
terminates with the laſt earl. From Belvoir (ſo named from its fine
views) to guide us the reſt of the way back, let us take Mr. Leland.
' From Beauvoire caſtelle, ſays he², to Croxton two miles ; & from
' Croxton I rood a ſix miles farther into a little through-fare caullid
' . . . . . . by good paſture & corn grounde, but . . . . . . &
' little woode, ... Then I rode a ſix miles farther by . . . . .
' grounde, & there I enterid to the cawſey of Wathelingſtreet, that
' there goith betwixt Ankeſter & Staunforde. And thens a three miles
' to Caſtelleford bridge ſtill upon the great creſte of Wathelingſtreate
' by champaine grounde, corn, & gras, but little or no wode. Un-
' der Caſtelleforde bridge of three arches of ſtone rennith a praty broke.
' I can take it to be no other broke but Waſch that cummith out of
' Ruthelandſhire, & not far beneth Staunford goith into Weland ry-
' ver. From Caſtelforde bridge to Stanford ſtill on the creſt of Wa-
' thelingſtreate a mile.' Note Mr. Leland, in theſe paſſages, miſtakes
Ermingſtreet for Watlingſtreet, & writes (why I know not) Caſtelford
bridge for Bridge Caſtreton bridge. I cannot forbear obſerving here
alſo, that, by what he ſays above, he ſeems to think he had not loſt
the track of Ermingſtreet 'till he got to Stanford ; whereas, if he
kept the common road out of the north ; he quitted Ermingſtreet or
the great Roman road, half way betwixt us & Caſtreton, & then rode
into Stanford thro' that deep hollow way without Scogate which (as
I have hinted) it is reaſonable to imagine Cambden himſelf took for
Ermingſtreet, or elſe could never write as he did : & I believe Mr.
Leland, when he rode this way, was of the ſame mind : both of them
right in thinking that hollow way was a work & road of the Romans,
& both of them wrong in fancying it was Ermingſtreet it ſelf ; ſince it
was indeed, as has been touched, only a *minor cheminus* or ſhort vi-

¹ Eſſay, as above.　　　² Itinerary Vol. 1. p. 98, 99.

E　　　　　　　　cinal

cinal way for the conveniency of the foldiers, upon their marches, to take in the town. But to go on with him.[1] 'After that I paffid 'out of Stanford, I could not well find the creft of Wathelingftreate.' Now the reafon why he could not find the creft of Ermingftreet after he paffed out of Stanford fouth, was, becaufe (as I have fhewn) the main bank of that great road did not run thro' the town, but aflant the weft fide of it. He adds,[1] 'but it went thens to Wedon in the ftreate, Toucefter, & as I take to Stratford, Dunftable & S. Albans.' Here he confounds the two courfes of Erming & Watling, Streets. Ermingftreet went (as has been fhewn) by Stanford, Stilton, Huntingdon, Caxton, &c. but never came near any of thofe places laft named by Leland; whereas Watlingftreet went by all thofe places, but never came near Stanford. And fo much of the Romans.

XXVIII. 'Lucius, the firft chriftian king that ever was (faith Dr. 'Cave[2]) a potent & confiderable prince in this ifland, who embraced 'the chriftian religion about the year CLXXXVI. fent a folemn em- 'baffie to Eleutherius bifhop of Rome for fome who might farther 'inftruct him & his people in the faith; who accordingly difpatched 'Faganus & Derwianus hither upon that errand.' As glib as this ftory goes down with Dr. Cave it will not pafs with bifhop Nicholfon. 'Lucius, fays that prelate,[3] wanted fome body it feems to inftruct 'him in the firft rudiments of chriftianity; & thereupon fent a letter to 'pope Eleutherius, defiring fome perfons in holy orders might be fent 'hither to baptife him & his people. There is not any copy of this 'epiftle now extant, & yet I dare not fay the original is loft. Not to 'mention the inconfiftences that are among the feveral authors upon 'whofe credit this whole ftory refts, 'tis obfervable that the pretended 'epiftle, in return, from Eleutherius, feems to intimate that Lucius's 'requeft was quite of another nature; & that his enquiry was after 'the imperial civil law, & not after the precepts of the gofpel. But 'in fhort, the popes letter has fo many undeniable marks of forgery 'upon it, that we cannot think it worth our while to be very inquifi- 'tive after the kings; & tho' a genuine piece of this kind were highly 'to be prized, we do not defire to build upon fhadow & fable.' This ftory of Lucius (which all our old chronicles are full of, but we may not, for the reafons above, allow to be true) our old antiquary Mr. Butcher (without any manner of authority for what he fays) has improv- ed with many unaccountable additions, relating to Stanford & the Britifh univerfity there. 'For thofe fchools, as he would perfuade us, '[4] flourifhed with all manner of heathenifh learning 'till the time of this 'Lucius. And, as before it was famous throughout the world for the 'proficiency of Ethnic learning, fo in that bleffed time (fays he) when 'England was firft enlightened with the glorious beams of the gofpel,

---

1 id. ib.   3 Hift. Lib. 2d. Edit. p. 90.
2 Preface to his Apoftolici. p. 8, 9.   4 MS. penes me, p. 2, 3.

' it much more flourished with learned & religious men, who de-
' voutly taught the knowledge of Christ, in so much that in a short
' time according to the devotion of those days, there were in &
' about Stanford eight houses of religion, thirteen parish churches, &
' three chapels erected; the same being furnished with the learnedst
' & gravest men of that age that were to be found in the world, the
' fame of whose piety & learning caused many christian princes & o-
' ther great men which neighboured upon the isles of Britain, to send
' their sons & friends hither to be taught by those pious masters :
' whereby Stanford attained the name & honour of an university.'

XXIX. This fine stuff shews that Mr. Butcher (tho' he must needs
be trying his knack that way) was but a bungler at invention. He
meets with some vouchers for an university begun here in Bladuds time,
& somewhere perhaps, said to be in being in the reign of Lucius.
He therefore takes care to make his professors christians as soon as ever
that prince is said to be converted. But he should have first proved
Lucius's own conversion, & then perhaps we might have indulged
him the rest. But now, when he talks of such a number of monasteries, churches, & chapels erected, when it is more probable there
were yet none at all built here, all this must be charged to his own
score, who, having met with the names of so many afterwards (as indeed there were more of each sort) & being ignorant where to fix
their foundations, here therefore whips them all down together, & so
makes short work with what he knew not how to give a better account of. But I pass on from such trifling, & as to universities shall
only now observe, that as Dr. Stillingfleet relates, ₁ ' there is extant in the
' Theodosian code, ² an edict of Gratian, requiring all the chief ci-
' ties of these parts of the Roman Empire to settle & maintain in
' them professors of learning, both of the Greek & Roman Languages.
' By virtue of which edict we are to search for the antient schools of
' learning among the Britons, in the chief cities of the provinces at
' that time; especially at London, which was the *caput gentis*, being
' Augusta, or the imperial city; & so at York, & Caerleon. So that
' the British Churches, as long as the Roman power continued here,
' had the same advantages for learning which they had in other pro-
' vinces.

XXX. Now of the Saxons. The same Dr. Stillingfleet says, ₃ ' the
' Saxons not improbably had their name at first from the short swords
' they did commonly wear, called Sachs; as the Quirites, had their
' name from Quiris, a sort of spear ; & the Scythians from Scytten,
' to shoot with a bow. The Angles or Saxons, as Bede tells us, ⁴ were
' invited by Vortigern to defend his country [against the Picts & Scots]
' but more truly, as it happened, to conquer it themselves.' They

1 Origines Brit. p. 215.
2 C. 13. Tit. 3. Lib. 11.
3 Orig. Brit. p. 305.
4 Hist. Eccl. p. 52.

arrived

Anno arrived in the year of Chrift, 449. & the very firft battle which ever
449. they fought was at our Stanford, and proved, for the prefent, an entire defeat of thofe ravaging barbarians.   The circumftances of the
Rencounter were remarkable, as well on account of their victory, as
their making ufe of long, not fhort, fwords to obtain it : a particular
which does not at all fuit with Dr. Stillingfleets hypothefis.   Henry of
Huntingdon (a good old Hiftorian) gives us the relation thus.   "[1] The
' enemy was advanced as far as Stanford in Lincolnfhire, a town ftand-
' ing forty [now we reckon it but thirty fix] miles fouth on this fide
' the city of that name.   The Picts & Scots fought with fpears & lances,
' but when the Saxons moft furioufly fell on with their axes & long
' fwords, they immediately fled, unable to refift the weight of fo fierce
' an attac.'   Huntingdon, in this account, is followed by Ranulf Higden, who copies him almoft to a word.   Trevifa thus tranflates his author
Higden.   [2]' 𝕿𝖍𝖊 𝖊𝖓𝖊𝖒𝖞𝖘 𝖜𝖊𝖗𝖊 𝖈𝖔𝖒𝖊 𝖚𝖓𝖙𝖔 𝕾𝖙𝖆𝖓𝖋𝖔𝖗𝖉 : 𝖜𝖍𝖊𝖗𝖊 𝖜𝖍𝖊𝖓 𝖙𝖍𝖊
' 𝕻𝖞𝖈𝖙𝖊𝖘 𝖆𝖓𝖉 𝖙𝖍𝖊 𝕾𝖈𝖔𝖙𝖙𝖊𝖘 𝖚𝖘𝖊𝖉 𝖑𝖔𝖓𝖌 𝖘𝖆𝖋𝖙𝖘 𝖆𝖓𝖉 𝖘𝖕𝖊𝖗𝖊𝖘, 𝖙𝖍𝖊 𝕾𝖆𝖗𝖔𝖓𝖘
' 𝖋𝖆𝖚𝖌𝖍𝖙𝖊 𝖜𝖎𝖙𝖍 𝖑𝖔𝖓𝖌𝖊 𝖘𝖜𝖊𝖗𝖉𝖊𝖘 𝖆𝖓𝖉 𝖆𝖗𝖊𝖘 ?

XXXI. Mr. Cambden fays, [3] ' it is thought Gaufennæ [the Roman
' town at Bridge-Caftreton, as he will have it] was deftroyed, when,
' as Huntingdon relates above, the Picts & Scots had laid wafte all the
' country as far as Stanford.'   And adds, [3] ' if I fhould think that
' Stanford fprang from the ruins of this town, I would have the rea-
' der take it as my bare opinion, & pafs what judgment he pleafes.'
Here, as Mr. Cambden pretends no other authority for his opinion, but
meerly his own judgment, I beg leave to invert the queftion, & inftead of, why might not Stanford rife out of the ruins of Caftreton?
ask, why might not Caftreton as well arife out of the ruins of Stanford? or rather, why might not there be then towns at both places,
& both thofe places be deftroyed by the incurfions of thefe barbarians ? 'Tis certain there was then a town at Stanford; for (as Huntingdon above informs us) Hengift met the enemy there, & not at Caftreton.   And as there was a town then at Stanford, that town was then
probably deftroyed.   For the Picts & Scots came, not to fettle in the
country, but to wafte & deftroy it.   It is certain then, if they got thither before Hengift, they deftroyed Stanford (as undoubtedly they already had Caftreton, if there was then a town there) whereas it is
uncertain whether Hengift arrived foon enough to prevent them.   All
that we know of the matter is, not that he faved Stanford, but that
he there ftopped them from advancing any farther.

XXXII. ' [4] And fo Vortigerus hadde the vyctory by helpe of the
' Saxons, & gave to Egyftus londe in Lyndefaye.'   So Higden, to which
Huntingdon adds, ' [5] when the news of this victory [at Stanford] was
' carried over into Saxony, with a relation of the fruitfulnefs of the

---

1 P. 309.
2 Fol. 183. b. col. b.
3 In Corit.

4 Polychron. fol. 183. b. col. b.
5 P. 309, 310.

2   ' ifle,

' ifle, & the flothfulnefs of the Britons, prefently there was a larger
' fleet fent thither, carrying a ftronger force of foldiers, which, joyn-
' ing them who went over before, made their army now invincible.
' Thefe therefore, who came over laft, undertook to compleat the
' bufinefs, provided the Britons would allow them a place among
' them to live in, which was agreed to, with this condition, that the
' Saxons fhould always fight the enemy, & the Britons always pay
' their forces.' What made this agreement the more fpeedy, was,
becaufe, as Higden tells us, [1] ' at thys feconde tyme the Saxons brought
' with them Engyftus doughter, a fayre mayde, merveylle of kynde
' & wonder of fyghte for men to beholde. The kynge, Vortygerus,
' behelde her often, & badde that fhe fholde ferve hym inftede of
' his boteler. And the kynge asked her to wyfe, & egged her fader
' thereto; as though it were agaynfte his wyll; & gave Kente inftede
' of a gyfte to hym, & confented that Engiftus fholde fende for his
' fone.' And thus Hengift & his Saxons had two fettlements, one in
Lindfey & the other in Kent.

XXXIII. Now it is obfervable we have yet at Stanford a cuftom,
which, as my author fays, [2] ' Littleton, the famous Englifh lawyer,
' calls Burrough-Englifh, viz. that the younger fons inherit what lands
' and tenements their fathers dying inteftate have poffeffed in this
' manor.' The learned Dr. Plot gives this account of the rife & progrefs of this cuftom. [3] ' That the younger fon, or brother, fhould thus
' inherit lands of any fort, may feem indeed not a little unnatural.
' But the famous Littleton renders this reafon, why, in fome places,
' they enjoy this privilege, for that in law they are prefumed the leaft
' able to fhift for themfelves. Upon which account, in Kent, where
' the youngeft fometimes enjoys the benefit of Gavelkind, tho' not the
' whole inheritance, they have the privilege of the Aftre, or herth
' for fire, in the manfion houfe, in their divifion; becaufe the young-
' eft being the tendereft have the greateft reafon to be kept warm at
' home. Thefe are reafons, faith the doctor, which appear plaufible
' enough, but I guefs the more fubftantial caufe of this cuftom may
' rather be, that the places where now Burrow Englifh obtains, were
' antiently liable to the fame ungodly cuftom, granted to the lords of
' manors in Scotland by K. Evenus or Eugenius, whereby they had
' the privilege of enjoying the firft nights lodging with their tenants
' brides, fo that the eldeft fon being prefumed to be the lords, they
' ufually fettled their lands (& not without reafon) upon the youngeft
' fon whom they thought their own: which being practifed a long
' time, grew at length to a cuftom.

XXXIV. By the way, admitting this to be a good reafon why the
fecond fon fhould be preferred before the eldeft; yet, in cafe this was

---

1 Polychron. ut fupra.
2 Britan. antiq. & nova in Linc. p. 1424. b.

3 Staff. p. 277, 278.

G

the cuftom, if a mans wife had any more children than two, it is no reafon at all why the youngeft fhould be preferred (as the doctors words feem to imply) before the fecond, third, fourth, or any other but the eldeft. For my part I rather take the reafon of Borough-Englifh here to be this. The town of Stanford being a trading place, & confequently inhabited moftly by tradefmen, their eldeft fons, it was prefumed, were fet up, or had their portions given them in their fathers life-time; when therefore the father died inteftate, the remainder of what he was at his death poffeffed of, was by this cuftom given up to the youngeft, as being yet unprovided for. But to go on with the doctors notion & account.

XXXV. ' Now that this cuftom, faith he, ' obtained as well in ' England as Scotland, we may rationally conclude from the *marcheta* ' *mulierum* (which K. Malcolm ordered their tenants to give their lords ' in lieu of it when he took it away) that was antiently paid here as ' well as there. For which we have the exprefs teftimony of Bracton. ' *Tranavit*, says he, *totam Angliam marcheti hujus pecuniarii confuetudo* ' *in mancipiorum filiabus maritandis*; that is, this cuftom was fpread ' all over the nation, &c. whereof I have feen a particular record of ' one Maynard of Berks, in thefe words. William Maynard, who ' holds lands in Heurft, acknowledges himfelf to be the abbat of Ab- ' bendons villane, & to hold of him in villenage & by villenary cuf- ' toms, to wit, by the fervice of xviij. d. a year, & paying *maritagium* ' & *marchetum*, for his daughter & fifter, at the will of the abbat.' Here then we fee the meaning of Gerfon & Ourlop, fines, which, as you will hereafter find, [2] the inhabitants of Wirthorp, by Stanford, paid the abbat of Croyland, on their daughters marriage, or in cafe they were ftolen. And, as Borough-Englifh does yet prevail in Stanford, & as Gerfon & Ourlop did formerly prevail at Writhorp, I queftion not but all thefe cuftoms (being fo nearly related) prevailed formerly in both thofe places, & likewife in Stanford beyond the bridge. As for Borough-Englifh, the doctor adds, [3] ' nor did it only prevail in Eng- ' land & Scotland, but, as I have read, in the ifle of Guernfey, & the ' kingdom of Ireland too, where it is called Lohempy.' Now Borough-Englifh being a Saxon ufage, it is probable it came in with Hengift him-felf. For Vortigern, as you may remember, gave Hengift lands firft in Lindfey, it is like about Stanford (as he firft beat the Picts & Scots there) where we now find Borough-Englifh; and afterwards in Kent, where we now find Gavelkind: So apparent then are yet the remains of that gallant man & his refpective fettlements, both at Stanford & in Kent above other places.

Anno 449. XXXVI. How the Saxons made a conqueft of the Britons whom they came to defend, belongs rather to a general Hiftorian, one who treats of the whole kingdom; than me, who write only of a particu-

---

1 In loco fupra citato.   2 Anno 1109. infra.   3 Ib. ut fupra.

lar fpot, to infift upon: A word or two then of Hengifts death, &
away to other matters. ' In the year of Chrift 489. faith Matthew of
' Weftminfter (as tranflated by Sir William Dugdale) [1] when Aurelius
' Ambrofius king of the Britons fent to raife all the power of the na-
' tion to extirpate thefe pagans [the Saxons] unto whom he gave bat-
' tle near the river Don in the north; Eldol earl of Gloucefter, hav-
' ing an earneft defire to encounter perfonally with Hengift, rufht thro'
' the thickeft of them with that troop which he commanded, & pull'd
' him out by the nofe of his helmet; whereupon the Saxons fled, &
' the Britons had the victory. Which being, by the admirable cou-
' rage of Eldol, thus obtain'd, & a meeting had of the principal com-
' manders of the Britifh army, to confider how to difpofe of Hengift;
' up ftood Eldad bifhop of Gloucefter (brother to the earl) & faid in
' great wrath, that if all would have him faved, he himfelf would cut
' him in pieces; asking, why they fhould be fo effeminate as to ftick
' at it? whereupon Eldol, taking him out of the town, drew his fword,
' & cut off his head.' Here I cannot fay but Hengift, for his treacherous murder of fo many Britons at Ambresbury, Anno 461. deferved
no better ufage than what he now met with. However (as this laft
battle was fought no lefs than forty years after he beat the Picts & Scots
at Stanford, that action being in 449. at which time he had a daughter
marriageable, whom he foon after gave to Vortigern) Hengift muft now
be pretty near, if not all out, fourfcore years of age. So that for my
part I cannot fee quite fuch a deal of valor in Eldol, as my author does,
when he magnifies his admirable courage in taking fuch a decrepit old
fellow by the nofe.

XXXVII. I return now to our Britifh univerfity. According to Bede
& the Saxon chronicle, Auftin the monk arrived in Britain, *anno Chrifti*
597. & as the fame vouchers affirm, in 601. had the pall fent him, as
archbifhop of Canterbury, by pope Gregory the great. When Auftin
came over, if we may believe Rous, & Harding, & their followers (whom
I fhall prefently cite in their own words) the Britifh & Saxon chriftians, mixing together in this univerfity, were infected with the Arrian &
Pelagian herefies; & befides maintained fome cuftoms & opinions contrary to the practice & doctrine of the then Roman church: the reafon whereof, if I miftake not, was this. The Britons had been long
ago converted by the apoftles, or ' at leaft, as bifhop Lloyd fays, [2] by
' fome others who liv'd foon after their times.' When the Saxons
arriv'd, and were fettled here, fome of them I reckon were converted
by the fucceffors of thofe Britons; fome of the defcendents of which Britons and Saxons, it feems now lived here together mix'd. The reft of
the Saxons not yet converted, were converted moftly now by Auftin
and his companions. They therefore who received their Chriftianity
from Auftin, of courfe agreed with the then Roman church in every

Anno 597.
Anno 601.

---

1 Baronage, vol. I. p. 1.   2 Hiftorical account of church government, p. 48.

thing; whereas they, who had received their Christianity another way, would agree with it, in nothing but just what they pleased.   However all the matters in dispute betwixt these two parties, (the Arrian & Pelagian heresies abovementioned excepted) I think may be reduced to these three particulars.   First. ' the Britons, as Bede says, [1] performed the ' office of baptism, different [but wherein that difference consisted he ' does not say] from the manner of the Roman church.'   Secondly, ' the canonical tonsure of their clergy, as Pits tells us, [2] was four- ' square, like that of the eastern, and not round, like that of the ' western, church.'   Now Austin, maintained it should be round, ' shaped as Mr. Smith says, [3] like the crown of thorns which our ' blessed lord wore in his passion.'   But the Britons insisted, as the same learned Gentleman acquaints us, [4] ' that it should be cut after ' their fashion [the fashion of the eastern church] from ear to ear. Thirdly, ' the Britons kept Easter Sunday, as archbishop Usher tells us, ' [5] upon the lords day falling between the fourteenth & twentieth days ' of the paschal moon.'   ' Nay, as Mr. Smith adds, [6] on the fourteenth ' day of the moon it self, if it chanced to be Sunday.'   Whereas, Austin, with his companions & converts, maintain'd, [7] ' that the Easter ' lords day should be kept according to the computation of the Aposto- ' lic see, from the fifteenth to the twenty first [day of the moon.]

XXXVIII. The inconvenience of following these different accounts was, as Bede rightly observes, [8] ' that Easter day was sometimes kept ' twice in one year.'   For when they who followed the British cycle had made an end of fasting (passion week, according to their calculation, being over) & proceeded to keep the lords day following as the festival of Easter Sunday; it sometimes happened that others (who observed the now Roman cycle, which, sometimes computed Easter a week later than the British) persisting yet in fasting, kept their palm sunday, when the first kept their Easter sunday.   Now, thro' following one cycle, all the offence given to weak christians by such inconsistent fasting & feasting would at once be avoided.   But then the question was, whose cycle was the truest?   And here the Britons contended as stifly for their way, as Austin did for his.   And this was called the Quartadeciman controversie; a controversie wherein almost all the rest of the christian world as well as Britain, was, at one time or another, involv'd.   But I shall hereafter have occasion to speak largely of it, under the years of Christ 662. and 663. when (so far as regards this nation) it was both revived & determined, so shall wave any farther discourse of it now.   As for the Canonical tonsure, the difference about it is too frivolous to deserve any more notice.   And as to their disagreement about the manner of administring baptism, I meet with no particulars of it.

1 Lib. 2. cap. 2.
2 P. 18, 19.
3 Appendicis ad Bedæ opera Hist. p. 705.
4 Ib.

5 Primord. p. 931.
6 Appendicis, ut supra, p. 698.
7 Primord. ut supra.
8 Hist. Eccl. p. 131

XXXIX. Now, admitting there was a British univerſity at Stanford when Auſtin arrived in this iſland, & that the hereſies & opinions above-mentioned were then maintained here, & that, after his arrival, there were great debates & canvaſſing of the ſaid matters between him and his followers in oppoſition to the Britons & Saxons, who ſtudied here together; as far as they regard our Stanford Antiquities, the iſſue of all theſe diſputes ſeems to have been this. When Auſtin could not pre-vail with thoſe ſtudents to renounce their opinions, he wrote to his friend pope Gregory to give him an account of the affair, & in the end, procured from him, in caſe they perſiſted in their errors, a full power to diſſolve thoſe ſeminaries (as he ſoon after did) for their ob-ſtinacy & heretical depravity. Rous (as quoted by Leland) ſpeaking of the ſchools in Britain, (without naming Stanford, or any other parti-cular place) ſays, [1] ' pope Gregory [who, by the way, died in the year ' of Chriſt, 606.] interdicted the public ſchools of the Engliſh upon ' account of the Pelagian hereſie & other errors of the Britons con-' trary to the catholic faith.' Harding is more particular in point of place, & names Stanford, & no other ſchools. ' This univerſitie of ' Stanford, ſays he, [2] dured to the comyng of Saynt Auguſtyne, & ' the byſhoppe of Roome interdyted it for hereſyes that fell among ' the Saxons & the Britonnes together mixte.' Stow copies him ex-actly. ' This univerſity at Stanford, ſays he, [3] dured to the comming ' of S. Auſtin, at which time the biſhop of Rome interdicted it for he-' reſies, that fell among the Saxons & Brytaines together mixt. So ' ſaith Harding.' Harding it may be obſerved, in his own words (as they are exactly copied above) ſpeaks only of hereſies in general; & yet Grafton makes him mention the Arrian & Pelagian hereſies in particular, and ſtill would be thought to copy him as exactly as any body elſe. ' John ' Harding in the firſt book and twenty fifth chapter of his ſtory ſhew-' eth, ſaith he, [4] that the ſchool or univerſity of Stanford was forbid-' den by Auſtin the monk, like as other univerſities of this realme ' were, under pretence that they maintained the Arrian and Pelagian ' hereſies. The which his prohibition was the cauſe of the decay of ' the ſame univerſities; and therefore long after his time there was ' no common profeſſing of learning, but in great monaſteries and ab-' bies.' Our old antiquary Mr. Butcher concludes his account of this Britiſh univerſity, (after his detail of the monaſteries, churches, and cha-pels then founded, as he imagines) thus——[5] ' but as no glory is perma-' nent in this tranſitory life, ſo in time the luſtre of this bright ſhining ' taper of fame began to wax dimme and decline by the foggy and pe-' ſtiferous miſts of hereſie and errors, like mortal diſeaſes breeding in ' a body long enur'd with peace, health, and quietneſs; which cauſed ' this Stamfordian univerſity to be diſſolved by the decree and power ' of Gregory the firſt of that name biſhop of Rome.

[1] Itin. vol. 4. p. 144.   [2] Cap. 25. fol. 22.   [3] P. 15.   [4] P. 46.   [5] MS. penes me, p. 3.

H

XL. To conclude. For a Britifh Univerfity at Stanford, I as yet find no farther proof than what hath been advanced above. Surmifes they are a pretty many indeed, but not enow to be admitted as a fatisfactory evidence. And truly, if I may fpeak, Cambridge muft quit her Cantaber, and we our Bladud, and defcend to later times for the beginning of our univerfities. For this is not the univerfity I contend for at this place, but one of a later date. So much however touching the Britifh univerfity at Stanford; *where* (if we may believe any of the abovementioned authors, or, to add the words of one more)

———[1] *' Learning, 'till Saint Auftin came,*
' Flourifht with memorable fame;
' But, buried in her ruins now,
' Small light of fuch fair lamp can fhow.

1 Slatyers palæalbion, p. 99.

The end of the firft book.

3

Academia tertia Anglicana;

OR, THE

ANTIQUARIAN ANNALS

of the TOWN of

STANFORD

IN

Lincoln, Rutland, *and* Northampton *Shires.*

BOOK II.

From the fuppofed diffolution of the Britifh univerfity about the year of Chrift 605. to the death of Vilfrid (bifhop of York, and founder of the Benedictin priory of S. Leonard by Stanford) who deceafed in 709.

I. IN 634, was born the famous Vilfrid, afterwards bifhop (never archbifhop) of York, and at length canonized for a faint. He was founder of S. Leonards cell by Stanford, as fhall be related in its proper place more largely. At prefent, as the fame S. Leonards is the firft monaftery we read of erected here, or indeed in all thefe parts (being, as fhall be hereafter proved, finifhed before Medefhamftede, or Peterborough, it felf) it feems neceffary, from the relation which that action gives Vilfrid to this undertaking, to begin here fome account of fo celebrated a perfon.

II. Authors differ about his parentage, fome affirming that he was nobly, others meanly, defcended. Of the firft and I believe trueft opinion is Eadmerus, who (as Mr. Smith tells us) fays, [a] 'he was born 'of a renowned ftock of the Angles.' Of the fecond is bifhop Godwin, who affirms, [b] 'he was born in the north countrey of mean pa- 'rentage.' The fame bifhop adds, [c] 'the time of his childhood he loft 'in his fathers houfe, being untaught 'till he was fourteen years of 'age, at what time not fuftayning the frowardnefs of his ftepmother, 'he went abroad to feek his fortune. And firft he light upon cer-

Anno 634.

---

a Serie: Vilfridianæ, in appendicis ad Bedæ opera hift. a cl. Smitho, p. 730.

b Catalogue of bifhops. p. 436.
c Ib.

B

' tain

'tain courtiers, that had been beholding to his father for divers cour-
'tesies. By them he was presented to the queene, as a child for wit
'and beauty not unfit to do her service. She, by questioning, found
'the inclination of the boy, that he was desirous to become a Schol-
'lar.' As for Vilfrids father what his particular degree of honour or
fortune was, I find not. But sure it was far from mean. For how
could a mean man, as bishop Godwin says he was, confer divers courtesies on courtiers or persons of the first rank? I rather think therefore
that he had some place at court, or at least lived honorably near it.

Anno
648.

III. 'When he came to be fourteen, Vilfrid, as Bede acquaints
'us, [a] began to fancy a monastic, above a secular life. Wherewith
'informing his father (his mother being then dead) he readily consent-
'ed to his desires, and wished him to pursue his resolutions.' Upon
this [b] 'Eanfleda, wife of Osuiu K. of the Northumbers, greatly en-
'couraged this towardliness in the child, & sent him to the monks
'of Lindisfarne to be taught & educated. [c] For this purpose she parti-
'cularly recommended him to one Cudda, a noble person, then going
'to make his entry in that monastery. To him therefore Vilfrid
'joyned himself, & thus accompanied, [d] came to Lindisfarne, & there
'devoted himself to the service of the monks.

Anno
652.

IV. '[e] After he had some years attended Gods service in that mo-
'nastery, the youth, being a person of good judgment, began to think
'that way of discipline which had been taught by the Scots very
'imperfect, & resolved therefore in himself to go to Rome, & see
'how the ecclesiastic, or monastic, rites were observed there. Where-
'with when he acquainted his brethren [the monks] they, commend-
'ing his intention, wished him to go thro' with what he proposed.
'Upon this, waiting soon after on queen Eanfleda, he likewise
'made his desires known to her. She, delighted with his proposal,
'sent him to Erconberct (K. of Kent) her own uncles son, requesting
'he would send him over honorably to Rome. At that time Hono-
'rius one of pope Gregory's disciples, was archbishop of Canterbu-
'ry; where, when Vilfrid had tarried some time, diligently applying
'himself to learn those things whereon he was now so intent, there
'came thither another youth called Benedict Biscop, a Saxon noble,
'desiring also to go to Rome.

Anno
653.

V. '[e] To his company, in 653, the king joyned Vilfrid, & order-
'ed him to take him along with him to Rome. But, when they came
'to Lions, Vilfrid was detained there by Dalfin bishop of that see;
'whilest Benedict went forward on his journey. For that prelate was
'so charmed with Vilfrids behaviour, together with the comeliness of
'his person, the readiness of his address, & the constancy & ripeness of
'his thoughts; that, as long as Vilfrid & his companions staid with

a Hist. Ecclesiasticæ, p. 205.   d Bedæ Hist. Ecclef. ut supra.
b Leland. loco supra.   e Id. p. 205.
c Serici de vita Vilf. ut supra.

'him

' him, he supplied them with every thing they wanted ; & moreover
' offered, if he would accept of it, to commit a good part of France
' to his government [as a bishop, I suppose] & to give him his own
' brothers daughter, a virgin, to wife ; & always to receive him as his
' own adopted child. But Vilfrid, returning him thanks for the kind-
' ness which he was pleased to express towards a stranger, replied, he
' rather approved a monastic life, & for the sake of it had left his own
' country to travel to Rome.' However leave we now Vilfrid a while
with the good bishop of Lions, & returning into England, let us relate what happened in Mercia (that province of the Heptarchy wherein Stanford is scituate) as being things which will help to illustrate
some other matters we shall hereafter have occasion to speak of.

VI. It hath been surmised above, that there were British & Saxon
Christians at Stanford when Austin arrived here, & that he got that
university put down for the heresies & opinions before spoken of,
which it is said they maintained. But, after all, whether there were
really any such Christians at Stanford, may yet be made a question.
For, if there were, 'tis almost certain they disappeared, soon after the
supposed interdict of those schools by Pope Gregory, & paganism again
prevailed in these parts 'till the reign of Pendan, whose son Peada was
this very year converted to the Roman faith upon this occasion. [a]
' Repairing to Osuiu K. of the Northumbers, Peada requested he
' would give him his daughter Alchfleda to wife ; but it seems could not
' obtain what he desired, without he & his people (for, by the way,
' [b] Peada in the daies of his father, & with his permission, governed
' the middle Angles) would receive baptism.' Upon this repulse Pea-
' da took time to consider of the proposal, & inform himself what
' Christianity was. [c] ' But at last when he had heard the preaching of
' the gospel, the promise of a heavenly kingdom with the hope of a
' resurrection & a future immortality, he freely declared that he would
' be made a Christian, tho' he should not succeed in his court to the
' virgin ; being most of all persuaded to embrace the faith, by a son
' of Osuiu's named Alchfrid, who was his brother in law & particu-
' lar friend, having before married his sister Cyniburga. He was bap-
' tized therefore by bishop Finan, with all the nobles and captians and
' their attendants who came with him, in a famous town of the kings
' named *ad murum* [Walls-end near Newcastle.] Thence, taking with
' him four priests, who, by their lives & doctrine, seemed fit to teach
' & baptize his own nation, he returned joyfully home. Those fore-
' mentioned priests going therefore, along with the prince himself,
' into his province, preached the word, & were freely heard ; every
' day many, both nobles & commons, renouncing their wretched ido-

a Id. 125.
b Bede Lib. 3. cap. 21. instead of middle
Angles, Speed, p. 253. reads middle part
of Mercia, which is a mistake.
c Beda. ut supra.

C

' latry,

' latry, & receiving baptifm. Nor did K. Penda himfelf forbid the
' preaching of the gofpel, but, in his own Mercian territory, who
' would might hear. He rather hated & defpifed thofe in whom,
' being inftructed in the faith of Chrift, he did not difcern works
' anfwerable to their belief; faying, they were forry wretches, &
' deferved heartily to be contemned, who would not obey that God
' in whom they profeffed themfelves to believe.'

VII. Return we now to Vilfrid, whom (after he had refufed the bifhop of Lions obliging offers, as above related) [a] 'that prelate fent to
' Rome, giving him a guide to conduct him thither, & a large fupply
' of every thing which he might any ways have occafion for in his
' travels; earneftly defiring, that when he returned home, he would
' come that way back, & call on him. Being arrived at Rome, &
' daily giving himfelf up to prayer, & a meditation of fuch eccle-
' fiaftical matters as (before he went thither) he propofed to confider,
' he was received into the friendfhip of a very learned man, one Boni-
' face, an archdeacon & one of the popes council [of whom we fhall
' elfewhere have occafion to fpeak] by whofe direction he learned an
' exact Cycle when to keep eafter, & many other things, which he
' knew would be of ufe for ecclefiaftical difcipline in his own coun-
' try.' Leave we him then making the beft ufe of his time at Rome,
to obferve, in this part of his abfence, what other matters happened
in England, relating to a farther illuftration of thefe antiquities.

Anno
655.

VIII. [b] 'In 655. Pendan K. of the Mercians, at the command of
' Cadwaline K. of the Britons, gathering an innumerable army [not-
' withftanding the double marriage of their children, as before relat-
' ed] invaded Northumbria, the province of K. Ofuiu. [c] Ofuiu, when
' he found what cruel work he made, his own brother being killed
' by him, to buy peace offered him an incredible number of royal
' gifts & jewels, fo he would return home, & give over ravaging the
' provinces of his kingdom with fuch an univerfal carneage. But
' when that perfidious king, who had decreed to kill & extirpate Of-
' uiu's whole people root & branch, would, by no entreaties, agree to
' his propofal, he implored the help of the divine mercy to refcue him
' from his barbarous impiety, & binding himfelf in a vow, faid, if
' this pagan does not know how to accept of our prefents, let us offer
' them to our God, who does. He vowed therefore, if he obtained
' the victory, that he would give his daughter to be dedicated to God
' in holy virginity, together with twelve whole manors [alluding, I
' fuppofe, to the number of the twelve apoftles] to erect monafteries;
' & thus, attended by a very fmall company, fet readily upon his ene-
' mies. [d] It is faid the pagans had an army thirty times bigger, & eve-
' ry one of thofe thirty parts commanded by very noble & well ex-

---

a Id. p. 205.   c Beda. p. 129.
b Matt. Weftmon. p. 120.   d Beda & M. Weft. locis fupra.

' perienced

'perienced leaders. [a]Againſt all which appeared K. Oſuiu with his
'ſon Alchfrid, having, as I ſaid, but a very little army, yet truſting in
'their captain Chriſt Jeſus. Battle being joyned the pagans were put
'to flight, and ſlain, as were in ſhort almoſt all the thirty great cap-
'tains, who came to aſſiſt them. [b]Among the reſt fell alſo the
'moſt wicked K. Penda himſelf, who had before deprived ſo many
'noble perſonages of their lives. [c]Thus K. Oſuiu made an end of
'this war *in regione Loidis* [at Oſuinthorpe near Rippon in Yorkſhire]
'in the thirteenth year of his reign, upon the 15. day of November,
'to the great advantage of both people. For he delivered his own
'country from the ravages of the pagans, & converted all the people
'of Mercia, & and of the neighbouring provinces, after he had ſlain
'their faithleſs governor, to the chriſtian religion.

IX. Now what an abſolute victory this was may be gathered from
what is ſaid by good authors upon Oſuiu & his ſon Alchfrids farther
actions immediately conſequent thereupon. The uſe I am to make of
theſe obſervations is very great, & will ſoon diſcover it ſelf. Firſt then,
Pendan being ſlain as above, Oſuiu immediately poſſeſſed himſelf of
the kingdom of that wicked prince, & governed it, as you will preſently
find, for the firſt three years, by Northumbrian lieutenants, at the end
of which he made Peada his ſon-in-law deputy of the South Mercians. By the way, ' the ſouth Mercians, as Bede tells us, [d]then con-
'ſiſted of five thouſand families parted by the Trent from the North
'Mercians whoſe country contained ſeven thouſand families.' Secondly, after the battle of Oſuinthorpe, Oſuiu was not only K. of the
Northumbers & North Mercians, & governor of the South Mercians
by his lieutenants or deputies, but ruled the whole Heptarchy, being,
as Speed tells us, [e]' the tenth Monarch, or ſole governor of all the Eng-
'liſhmen.

X. Oſuiu's victory & other proſperities following it being thus prodigious, it were almoſt needleſs to obſerve here, that he was as good
as his word in performing the vow he made before he defeated Pendan; however, as this part of my collections may perhaps look a little defective without a word or two more about that matter, take
therefore this ſhort account of it from Bede. Immediately after the engagement, [f]' K. Oſuiu, according as he had vowed, returning thanks to
'God for the victory, gave Elfleda his daughter (then ſcarce a year
'old) to be conſecrated to him in perpetual virginity; aſſigning like-
'wiſe twelve portions of lands, ſix in Deira province, & ſix in Berni-
'cia, to endow a monaſtery. All which poſſeſſions ſufficed to main-
'tain [g]ten families, that is, altogether, one hundred & twenty perſons.

a Beda ib.
b Matt. Weſtm. quo ſupra.
c Bedæ p. 130.
d Ib.
e P. 305. b.
f P. 129, 130.
g Here I reckon it ſhould be twelve, &

not ten families. For he vowed to give
twelve manors; & we here find he did give
twelve portions, & that thoſe twelve portions ſufficed to maintain one hundred & twenty perſons, which is juſt twelve families,
reckoning each family to conſiſt of ten perſons.

' Then

' Then the forenamed daughter of K. Ofuiu went to a monaftery cal-
' led Heruteu [Hartlepool in the bifhoprick of Durham] where the
' abbefs Hilda at that time prefided, to be made a votarefs; which ab-
' befs having, two years after, procured lands fufficient to maintain ten
' families, at Streanfhalch [Whitby in Yorkfhire] erected a monaftery
' there, wherein the faid daughter of the king, firft lived as a nun, &
' afterwards prefided as an abbefs.

XI. But to proceed. Whilft South Mercia was governed by Northumbrian lieutenants, the firft & chief of thofe lieutenants it is probable was Alchfrid fon of Ofuiu. For whom could he fo well, either in gratitude or juftice, appoint firft & chief in that lieutenancy,

Anno
658. as him who had fo valiantly affifted in the defeat of Pendan. ' Three
' years after Pendan was flain, K. Ofuiu, as Bede himfelf tells us, ª gave
' to Peada (K. Pendans fon) becaufe he was his own fon - in - law,
' the kingdoom of the South-Mercians.' Thus then we find Ofuiu
reftored Peada to the government of a part of his father Pendans province, but ftill admitted him to rule over that part, not in the capacity of a free fovereign & rightful fucceffor, but as a vaffal by conqueft
& his own deputy. For this reafon Speed concludes his account of
Peada in thefe words. ᵇ' This Peada, reigning as fubftitute to K. Ofwi,
' by fome is not accounted a Mercian king, his regimen refting under
' the command of another.' Nor had he reigned at all, had it not
been for the reafon before alledged. Now, from what I have faid
above, I think it is beyond all contradiction apparent, that K. Ofuiu
& his fon Alchfrid had, at this time, as much power in the province
of Mercia, fouth or north, as they had before & after this time in their
own Northumbrian territories. Take this conclufion then along with
you, & you will prefently fee the ufe of it.

XII. It may be remembred we left Vilfrid fet down clofe to his ftudies, under the care of his mafter Boniface the archdeacon, at Rome;
it is time now that we refume his ftory. ' When he had fpent fome
' months there, fays Bede, ᶜbufied in his happy ftudies, he returned to
' his friend Dalfin bifhop of Lions in France, & tarrying with him
' three years, was by him fhorn a monk & withall had in fo great efti-
' mation, that he intended to make him his heir. But, before he could
' accomplifh his defire, that prelate was fnatched away by a cruel death;
' & fo Vilfrid was referved for a bifhopric in his own country. For
' queen Baldhild, ordered the bifhop [who had reproved her a little
' too freely for her incontinency] to be murdered, whom his clerc
' Vilfrid followed to the very place where they chopt off his head, defir-
' ing, tho' Dalfin greatly oppofed it, to die with him. But when thofe
' ruffians found Vilfrid was a ftranger, born in England, they fpared,
' & would not kill him with his bifhop.' This was done in this 658.
year of Chrift, Vilfrid being then in the four, or five & twentieth year
of his age. Upon which difafter ' he returned to Britain, as the fame

a P.   b P. 253. a.   c P. 206.

3

' Bede

' Bede tells us, ᵃ& was there received into prince Alchfrids friendſhip
' who had learned to follow the rules of holy church [according to
' the Roman uſage] & finding Vilfrid a perſon exactly of his own
' perſuaſion, ſoon after gave him lands at a place called Stanford, ſuf-
' ficient to maintain [a whole monaſtery of] ten families.' By the
way, this monaſtery of ten families, if I take it right, reckoning each
family to conſiſt of ten monks, would in the whole make up a ſociety
of one hundred perſons. It may alſo be obſerved, the learned Dr. Gale,
ᵇ agrees with venerable Bede as above, that Alchfrid gave Vilfrid lands
at a place called Stanford to found a monaſtery in, but then they neither ſet down any other tokens or particulars, whereby the Stanford
they are ſpeaking of, may be diſtinguiſhed from other towns of that
name.

XIII. Leland relates theſe matters thus. After the murder of his
good friend the biſhop of Lions, Vilfrid ' ᶜ returned home, perfectly
' accompliſhed in eloquence, prudence, & apoſtolic learning; where
' he devoted himſelf entirely to Alfrid, ſon of Oſwi, king of the Nor-
' thumbers; which royal youth, with his fathers conſent, gave him a
' place at Stanford in Yorkſhire, whereon to erect a monaſtery.' Here
Mr. Leland is right in every thing but the Stanford he makes choice
of for the ſituation of his monaſtery. For it was not at Stanford in
Yorkſhire, but our Stanford in Lincolnſhire, where Alchfrid gave lands
& Vilfrid erected that religious houſe. But, before I proceed to prove
this, I muſt firſt take notice of another Gentleman, who contends for
Stanford in Yorkſhire. For at length the learned Mr. Smith compleats
a new edition of Bede (a work deſigned, & long time with great ac-
curacy carried on, by his excellent father) wherein, under the above
tranſlated paſſage of his author, he puts down the following notes, as
enquiring what Stanford is there meant.

XIV. ' ᵈ There is a town called Stanford in the ſouth part of Lin-
' colnſhire, but there ſeems to be good reaſon to queſtion whether
' this be the place which Bede means. The town indeed, if we may
' believe Henry of Huntingdon, is very antient. For in the ſecond
' book of his hiſtory, the Saxons are ſaid to have defeated the Picts &
' Scots there, about the year 449. And truly Weſſingtons ᵉ M S. p. 38.
' a. has theſe particulars —— In Stanforth is a cell in honor of S. Leo-
' nard, founded firſt of all by S. Vilfrid; & afterwards by K. William
' the conqueror & William [Kairliph] biſhop of Durham, given to the
' prior & convent of Durham to make a cell for the monks of that
' houſe —— But the cell erected by S. Vilfrid was not founded here,
' & that for this reaſon; becauſe this Stanford ſtands in Lincolnſhire,

a Ib.
b Script. To. I. p. 55.
c Comment. p. 104.
d Ad imum p. 206.
e John Weſſington (who died prior of

Durham, A. D. 1446.) wrote a book, *de juribus & poſſeſſionibus Eccleſie Dunelm.* This
book is now in the Cotton Library, Vitel-
lius, A. 9. Biſhop Nicholſons Engliſh Hiſtorical Library, p. 128, 129. fol. edit.

' which

' which, when prince Alchfrid gave lands at that place to Vilfrid, was
' not under the power of the Northumbrian, but the Mercian, fcep-
' tre.   We muft look therefore for fome place of this name in the
' kingdom of the Northumbers ; & *perhaps* Stanford upon the river
' Deruent in Yorkfhire is the place we are in fearch of.'   Here Mr.
Smith concludes with a *forfan,* perhaps ; but in another place deter-
mines pofitively againft us.   Thefe are his words——[a] ' *ab illo accepit*
' *terram decem familiarum in agro Ebor.*'   That is, ' had lands given
' him by Alchfrid fufficient for [a monaftery of] ten families in York-
' fhire.'   Thus then, in the circumftance of the place, Mr. Smith joyns
with Leland, tho' indeed he takes no notice of the paffage I have
quoted from him.   I fuppofe therefore when he wrote thefe notes he
had either not feen that paffage or forgot that he had.   For had he
remembred that Stanford in Yorkfhire, was, by that author fixed for the
place, where Vilfrid founded his monaftery, he is I know a Gentleman
fo ingenuous as well as learned, that I am fatisfied he would have told
us, Mr. Leland alfo had faid fo.

XV.   Neverthelefs, after all that Mr. Leland & Mr. Smith have faid
for Stanford in Yorkfhire, the Stanford Bede mentions could be no
other than Stanford in Lincolnfhire.   Mr. Smiths objection that Stanford in Lincolnfhire was not, Anno 658. under the power of the Northumbers, is the only one that can be made againft us ; & that I have
already confuted above from his own author Bede.   From what has
been faid upon this head already, we may therefore fafely pronounce,
that Alchfrid did give lands, & Vilfrid did found this monaftery at
Stanford in Lincolnfhire in the year of Chrift 658. king Ofuiu being
yet alive, &, that, as it is was a work of piety, the father concurred
with the fon to bring it to perfection.   This affertion may be farther
illuftrated by a confideration of the following particulars.   Firft, K.
Ofuiu having Peada K. of the fouth Mercians, as I have related, under his own power & fubjection ; as by right of conqueft he did what
he lift with that prince (keeping him three years from the crown, &
then giving him but half a kingdom, inftead of a whole one) had an
equal power to difpofe of any lands in the country which he left him,
but above all others thofe which belonged to the crown (as Stanford
in Lincolnfhire always did, it being a royal borough) juft as his own
pleafure inclined him.   Secondly, When Peada was made king of the
fouth Mercians (which, by the way, was this very year 658. three
years after the defeat of his father Pendan ; as Bede the oldeft of all
our Saxon writers, & the trueft, fays above : & not *anno* 655. or 656.
as the Saxon chronicle & other Peterborough accounts affirm) ' he &
' his father-in-law Ofwi, as the faid Saxon chronicle obferves[b], had a
' meeting & difcourfe about founding a monaftery in honor of Chrift
' & S. Peter ; which they did ; & called it Medefhamftede.'   Which

a Seriei Vilfridianæ, p· 751   b Sub anno 655.

2

                                                      paffage

paſſage ſerves alſo farther to ſhew, that the power of Oſuiu prevailing abſolutely as above related, Peada himſelf found his ſaid father-in-law & conquerors conſent neceſſary to confirm the grants even of his own donations to monaſteries in his own Mercian territories. For Peada is by all writers allowed to be the founder of the church & monaſtery of Medeſhamſtede, &, I think we never read of any particular gift of Oſuiu's own to that place; which ſhews that he only confirmed what Peada gave, & that Peada found his conſent neceſſary. Thirdly, as Vilfrid had his education in their monaſtery, the monks of Lindisfarne had a juſt title to his favor. Fourthly, Vilfrid, as I conceive, inſtructed Alchfrid before he went to Rome in the chief principles of the chriſtian religion; &, it is probable, undertook that very journey, as much to ſatisfie Alchfrid, as himſelf, when Eaſter ought to be kept, &c. For immediately upon his return we find him devoting himſelf entirely to that prince, when they certainly had ſome conference about thoſe matters, it appearing from Bede himſelf (as hereafter quoted[a]) that, on his return he inſtructed Alchfrid more perfectly in the chriſtian literature. Vilfrid deſerved well therefore of Oſuiu for the great pains he had taken with his ſon Alchfrid. *Fifthly,* K. Alchfrid himſelf thought ſo. And all this happening juſt after his fathers vanquiſhing Pendan (when, upon account of his late victory Oſuiu was diſpoſed to give any thing to the church, & his power alſo being equal to his will) Alchfrid therefore took occaſion to remind him of Vilfrids ſervices to himſelf as a good preceptor in the chriſtian inſtitutes, & thereupon requeſted ſome lands of him at Stanford in the province of Lindſey which he had ſo lately conquered; intimating, that he intended to make his chriſtian tutor Vilfrid a preſent of them, & ſo deſired they might be ſuch as would yield a ſufficient maintenance for a religious ſociety of ten families, or one hundred perſons. *Sixthly,* this the father who had a kindneſs for Vilfrid equal to his ſons, & in the late battle had been greatly aſſiſted by Alchfrids valor (as it was alſo a work of piety in thoſe days, whatever ſenſe we have of it now, reckoned highly meritorious) immediately conſented to. And thus Alchfrid, as Leland expreſſes it, [b] ‘ *annuente patre, curavit ut Steno-* ‘ *fordiæ* [*Coritanorum quippe, non*] *Brigantum, locum condendo coenobio* ‘ *aptum acciperet Wilfridus.*' That is, ‘ with his fathers aſſiſtance, took ‘ care to provide Vilfrid a fit place at Stanford in [Lincoln, not in] ‘ Yorkſhire, whereon to erect a monaſtery.' *Seventhly,* Peada, as he was Oſuiu's vaſſal, could not; as he was a chriſtian & his ſon-in-law, would not oppoſe him in giving what lands in Mercia himſelf thought proper to erect, or endow, monaſteries. On the contrary, his own great gifts to Medeſhamſtede ſufficiently ſhew, that, far from oppoſing, he would rather concur in any ſuch deſign. Beſides, in any thing of this kind, Oſuiu, conſidered either as a father-in-law or a conqueror,

a Anno 664. infra.   b Comment. p. 104.

might

might prevail on Peada as easily by entreaty as command. Or again, if Peadas consent was at all thought necessary, he might give it at the request of Alchfrid, for whom he had always an especial friendship, on account of the many good offices (such as converting him to the christian faith, assisting to make up the match between him & his own sister, &c.) he had done for him. Eighthly, Upon Alchfrids making this acknowledgment to Vilfrid for his christian instructions, Vilfrid remembers his own obligations to the monks of Lindisfarne, for his education; & therefore makes them a present for their reward of what K. Alchfrid, with K. Osuiu's good liking, had given him in part for his. By which act of his this monastery of S. Leonards by Stanford became a cell to Lindisfarne, & afterwards to Durham. Ninthly, Some indeed imagine there was a cell belonging to the monks of Durham at a place called Stanford in that Bishopric. For instance. The ca-' talogue of monasteries in the *Monasticon Anglicanum,* [a] under the ' title *Dunelm* mentions *Stamford cella,* but adds indeed in *Com. Linc.*' The learned Dr. Thomas Tanner, in his *Notitia Monastica,* places it also among the monasteries of the bishopbric of Durham, & not, as it should be, among the monasteries of Lincolnshire. Mr. Burtons catalogue, in Speeds chronicle, mentions such a cell, first at Stanford in Durham diocese, [b] valued at 36. l. 17. s. & then at S. Leonards by Stanford in Lincolnshire, [c] valued at 30. l. & so makes two of one. Reyner follows Burton, & so runs into the same error. Mr. Stephens, in his first additional volume to the Monasticon, very honestly says, [d] ' he can-' not find the valuation of S. Leonards cell by Stanford, Lincolnshire, ' in the Monasticon.' Now the reason is, not that it is not there, but (as I observed before) because it is there wrong placed. He looked for it, as any body else would, among the monasteries of Lincolnshire, where it ought to have been put down; whereas it is set among the monasteries of the bishopbric of Durham. However, if Mr. Stevens could not find the value of it in the Monasticon, he may if he pleases see the valuation of it twice in his own book last cited, [e] but, in both places, falsely reckoned as above, not at Stanford in Lincolnshire, but at Stanford in the bishopbric of Durham, as if it stood some where in that county. Whereas, let any person shew me any town, or monastery, of this name in that bishop-bric; or that the registers of that church, or any other authentic evidence, mention such a place; or any prior, or other religious person belonging to it; & I will immediately give up all that is asserted in this article for error. Tenthly, As there was really no place in the bishopbric of Durham called Stanford, so, tho' there is a town called Stanford-bridge upon the river Derwent in Yorkshire, yet was there never (as far as I can learn from what books I have seen) any monastery there, founded either by Vilfrid, or any body else; much less one

a Vol. I. p. 1039.   d P. 229.
b P. 1071. b.   e P. 27, & p. 173.
c P. 1077. b.

                                                              belonging

belonging to Durham. Mr. Smith is very well acquainted with the regifters of that church, which, I fuppofe, are as filent about Stanford in Yorkfhire as they are about Stanford in the bifhopbric; or elfe, I prefume, he would have hinted fomething from them in his notes above cited, relating to Stanford in Bede. And, if they be filent, what? in the name of wonder! became of this royal foundation if it was not at Stanford in Lincolnfhire; & how was it thus unaccountably loft & fwallowed up? But eleventhly, as inevident as thefe laft matters are, it is certain the priory of S. Leonard by Stanford, & the diftinct rectories & churches of S. Mary Bennewerk & S. Maries by the bridge in Stanford Lincolnfhire, all belonged to the monaftery of Durham; & that the priors of that cell, & the rectors of thofe churches, were always prefented by the prior & convent of Durham for the time being. This Mr. Smith well knows. For it is to him I am obliged for an extract of the regifters of that place, touching the admiffions of divers perfons to all thofe places. Twelfthly, tho' Mr. Smith may perhaps not know it, it is as certain that the prior & convent of Durham had antiently very large poffeffions at Stanford in Lincolnfhire; the whole whereof made up a diftinct manor within the manor of Stanford, &, as it belonged to the church of Durham, was, & is to this day, called the manor of S. Cuthberts Fee. Thirteenthly, The abbat of Croyland had antiently a large penfion out of this priory, the occafion whereof, as Leland obferves, was this. [a] ' Coldingham of old ' tyme was a celle gyven by a kynge of Scottes to Croylande, & they ' receyed oftentyme rentes thens. But at laft Dirham compounded ' to gyve Croylande eight poundes by yere for it, out of their ' celle of S. Leonards by Staunforde.' Laftly, prior Weffingtons MS. above quoted by Mr. Smith, fays, ' the cell founded by S. Vilfrid, in ' honor of S. Leonard, was at Stainforth.' Unlefs therefore any one can fhew me another Benedictine monaftery (the monks of this houfe being of the fame order with their patrons of Durham) dedicated to S. Leonard (a name which their cell here retains to this day) at fome other place called Stanford, under the patronage of the prior & chapter of Durham; I think we have abundant reafon to conclude this to be the place where Alchfrid gave lands & Vilfrid founded his cell.

XVI. The premifes above, are I conceive fairly drawn, & full to the purpofe I contend for. Let any one then judge, whether, with Mr. Smith, we muft look for Vilfrids monaftery at Stanford in Yorkfhire upon the river Deruent? Or, with me, at Stanford in Lincolnfhire, upon the river Welland? And indeed (had Ofuiu never fubdued Mercia) why might not Alchfrid, (tho' in fact no more than bare prince of the Northumbers) as well erect a monaftery at Stanford in Lindfey, as his own wife Kiniburga erect a nunnery at Caftre (afterwards from her called Kiniburgceaftre) in the fame province of Mercia, & within feven miles of that place, where fhe was her felf

[a] Itin. vol. 4. p. 128.

E

firft

firſt abbeſs, and at length buried, 'till, for her ſanctity, her bones were removed to Medeſhamſtede, now S. Peters burg, three miles farther from us ?

XVII. I juſt touched above how a diſcourſe paſſed between Peada K. of the South Mercians & his father-in-law Oſuiu K. of the Northumbers, about founding a monaſtery in honor of S. Peter at Medeſhamſtede, ſometime this preſent year 658. ' After which, the Saxon chro-' nicle ſays, [a]K. Peada lived not long, being murdered by the treaſon ' of his own wife the Eaſter following.' But Speed ſays, & he quotes Swaſam for it, that [b]' Peada was brought to his end by the practice of his mother, & not of his wife.' I cannot find any ſuch account in the Peterborough writers publiſhed 1724. by Mr Sparke. There Hugo Candidus ſays, [c]' it was his wife.' But Speed will have it other-wiſe, ' whereby, ſays he, [d]this blot is taken from this chriſtian lady ' [Peada's wife] & brands the face of her [his mother, a pagan] who ' moſt deſerves it.' Be that as it will, as Peada came not to the king-dom of South Mercia till this preſent year 658. (three years after the death of his father Pendan, whoſe death happened in 655.) & as the ſame Peada was himſelf murdered the very next year after he began his foundation at Medeſhamſtede; our monaſtery of S. Leonard by Stan-ford is apparently as old as S. Peters at Medeſhamſtede; & (as all matters, upon the ſaid Peada's murder, were at a ſtand there till the year 664. when K. Vulfere reſumed his brother Peada's undertaking) was certainly finiſhed before it. And therefore, as I have pronounced above (at the beginning of the life of Vilfrid the founder) may be juſtly ſaid to be the firſt monaſtery we read of erected here, or indeed in all theſe parts.

XVIII. This monaſtery of S. Leonard by Stanford being a cell be-longing to the cathedral priory of Durham, it may not be impertinent to obſerve here, that cells were generally made uſe of by thoſe greater houſes, either for places of nurſery for young monks, whither they were ſent to ſtudy, and perform their novitiate under the inſpec-tion of ſome grave and learned ſeniors ; or for puniſhment of offen-ders, who were baniſhed thither from the pomps & pleaſures of their principal houſes; or laſtly, for receſs of great & faultleſs men, who ſometimes being elected to abbies or biſhopbric's, & afterwards, by the intriegues of the king, pope, or their own monaſteries, put by; choſe rather to end their days in ſuch diſtant places as theſe, than live any longer in the houſe with ſuch perſons as themſelves had been elected to govern : Such a retirement making their diſappointments more ea-ſie & ſupportable. Thus, as I ſhall elſewhere ſhew at large, [e]Henry of Stanford, prior of Finchale, & biſhop of Durham elect, but after-

a Videſis ſub annis 655, 656.   d Ut ſupra.
b P. 253. a.   e Anno XI. E. III. infra:
c P. 4.

wards set aside by the intriegues of K. Edward the 2. & the pope, withdrew to our S. Leonards, and died here.

XIX. Milton, gives a beautiful description of a monastic life & such places as these are, in the following verses.

' *But let my due feet never fail*
' *To walk the studious cloysters Pale,*
' *And love the high embowed roof*
' *With antique pillars, massie proof,*
' *And storied windows, richly dight,*
' *Casting a dim, religious, light.*
' *There let the pealing organ blow*
' *To the full-voic'd choir below,*
' *In service high, & anthemns clear,*
' *As may, with sweetness thro' mine ear,*
' *Dissolve me into extasies,*
' *And bring all heav'n at once before my eyes.*
' *And may, at last, my weary age*
' *Find out the peaceful hermitage,*
' *The hairy gown, & mossie cell,*
' *Where I may sit & rightly spell*
' *Of ev'ry star that heav'n doth shew,*
' *And ev'ry herb that sips the dew;*
' *'Till old experience do attain*
' *To something, like prophetic strein!*

As to our S. Leonards I shall at present only add, there is now a good part of the nave of the priory church yet standing, a beautiful, antient piece. But, as the Saxons had scarce any thing but wooden buildings, I cannot think that which now remains can have been any part of the very church built here by Vilfrid, but rather part of a new church erected where that stood, at the joynt expence of William Kairliph bishop of Durham & K. William the conqueror: of which church, & the curious remains of it more below [a].

XX. Having above, beyond all possible contradiction, proved Vilfrid to be the founder of S. Leonards by Stanford, I shall without any farther stop, pursue the history of his life, as well as I have been able to gather the particulars of it from Bede & other authors of good credit; observing, by the way, all such collateral hints & notices as will in any sort help farther to illustrate the antiquities of Stanford. The next passage I meet with relating to Vilfrid is indeed a little upon the legend, on which account I should here not have taken any notice of it; but, as it helps to explain other matters which will hereafter occur, must beg leave to mention it. The fact I mean is Vilfrids attestation of the princess Edilthryda's chastity, who, having been twice married, particularly the last time to K. Ecgfrid, & living with him

[a] Anno 1082.

twelve years; remained a pure virgin to the laſt, & then went into a monaſtery. This K. Ecgfrid was the eldeſt ſon of K. Oſuiu, & I now call him King becauſe Bede himſelf does ſo (as he often does his brother Alchfrid) for all their father K. Oſuiu was yet alive. The matter I was ſpeaking of ſtands thus. 'In 660 K. Ecgfrid, ſays Bede, [a] eſ-
'pouſed a wife named Edilthryda, daughter of Anna K. of the Eaſt
'Angles, which lady was the widow of one Tondberct, prince of the
'South Gyrvii [or, fen folks] but her firſt husband dying ſoon after
'they were married, ſhe was now given to the forenamed K. Ecgfrid,
'with whom after ſhe had conſorted twelve years, ſhe nevertheleſs
'remained an unſpotted maid to the laſt, as, (when ſome doubted it)
'on my enquiry biſhop Vilfrid told me, affirming himſelf to be
'moſt certainly informed of her integrity; that K. Ecgfrid promiſed
'to give him divers lands & a great ſum of mony, if he could pre-
'vail with her to admit of the kings embraces, becauſe he knew ſhe
'eſteemed no body more than the biſhop.' But Vilfrid, inſtead of ſoliciting her to gratifie her ſpouſe, as you will hereafter find, privately (thinking it no doubt more piety to do ſo) put her upon asking leave to withdraw & go into a monaſtery; which, the king at length conſented to; but could never after endure Vilfrid, who, as he thought & well might, was the occaſion of her acting ſo. However note here, Ecgfrid & Edilthryda were now only married; her retiring into a nunnery & Ecgfrids reſentment thereupon you will meet with at large hereafter.

XXI. The next affair wherein I find Vilfrid engaged is diſputing with the Scots about the Quartadeciman controverſy, or time of keeping Eaſter ſunday. Biſhop Lloyd gives us the occaſion from whence this difference aroſe. 'Anciently, ſays that prelate, [b] they found Ea-
'ſter by a Cycle of eighty four years, which was called the Roman
'account ſo lately as in pope Leo's time. The Scots & South Picts
'uſed the ſame Cycle from the time of their converſion, & ſo did
'the Britains without any manner of alteration. But about eighty
'years after the rending of the Roman empire, the Romans having
'left off the uſe of that Cycle, took up another of nineteen years:
'[being that which we now follow] which, tho' it was better in many
'reſpects, yet was new in theſe parts, & made a great difference from
'the former. And when the Romans had uſed this new Cycle ano-
'ther eighty years, coming then to have to do with theſe northern na-
'tions, they would needs have impoſed the uſe of it upon them [as,
if there be any truth in it, I have noted Auſtin & his monks would have done upon the Britiſh & Saxon ſtudents in our univerſity of Stanford] 'as a condition of their communion. They did indeed face
'them down with two things, tho' both probably falſe. One was,
'that the Romans had received their Cycle by tradition from S. Peter;

Anno 660.

Anno 662.

[a] p. 162.   [b] Hiſtorical account of church governm. p. 67.

2

'the

' the other, that it was made ufe of every where, except in thefe iflands.
' To the firft of thefe affertions the Scots (for want of knowing bet-
' ter) oppofed only the authority of S. John for their Cycle ; as to
' the other, they could not tell what to fay. Whereas, in trúth (tho'
' they did not know it) the [new] Roman account came, but an age
' or two before, from Alexandria, & was not yet received in all the
' weftern church, not in fome part of France in particular ; but that
' in ufe among the Scots was the fame Cycle that they & the Britons
' had ever ufed fince their converfion, & it was the fame that was
' antiently ufed in the Roman church. We that live fo many ages
' from thefe times, (fays an author [a] whom I fhall by & by give
' fome account of) may think it ftrange that great affemblies fhould
' be held, hot difputes maintained, & at laft a great divifion made,
' becaufe thefe matters could not be adjufted to every ones liking ; for
' after the heat is over, we may think there was no fufficient caufe to
' make fo great a ftir. It is neceffary therefore to premife here [that
it was not when we fhould keep Eafter, but a] [b] ' fubjection to the pope,
' [c] that was at the bottom of the controverfy. And fince at this time
' it gave the great turn, by which the Romanifts prevailed over the
' Britons, it may be worth the while to give the relation of it out
' of Bede, tho' fomething longer than to deferve our confideration, if
' the weight of the caufe, rather than of the reafons there alledged,
' did not require it.

XXII. ' In 662. when Colman, who was fent out of Scotland, fucceed-
' ed to the bifhopric of Lindisfarne, faith he, [e] the controverfy about
' the obfervation of Eafter, as alfo other points of ecclefiaftical difci_
' pline, ran high : So that many of the more timorous, not without
' reafon, began to be heartily concerned, leaft haply having received the
' word of Chriftianity, they fhould, or might have, run in vain. This came
' at laft to the ears of the princes, King Ofuiu & his fon Alchfrid ;
' for Ofuiu had been inftructed & baptized by the Scots ; he was alfo
' fingularly well fkilled in their language, & thought whatever they
' taught to be the beft. Alchfrid had for his tutor in the chriftian
' literature, our Vilfrid, a very great fcholar ; whofe learning he juftly
' efteemed preferable to all the traditions of the Scots : infomuch that
[befides lands to endow S. Leonards at Stanford] ' he had given him
' a monaftery of forty families at Rippon [Inhrypum] in Yorkfhire,
' which he had a little before beftowed upon thofe who followed the
' Scots for the fame purpofe. But, when they chofe rather to give it
' up, than change their cuftoms ; he gave it to him, who, both for
' his learning & way of life, was very worthy of fuch a place.

XXIII. ' In 664. faith the fame Bede, Agilberct, bifhop of the Weft

Anno
664.

a Hiftorical collections of the Saxons, &c.
p. 269.
  b Id. p. 268.

c Id. p. 269.
d Hift. Ecclef. p. 131. &c.

F

' Saxons,

' Saxons, a friend of KING Alchfrid & the abbat Vilfrid, came to the
' province of the Northumbers, & ftaid with them fome time. He,
' at the requeſt of Alchfrid, ordained Vilfrid [now thirty years old]
' a prieſt in his own monaſtery at Rippon. The diſpute about Eaſter,
' the tonſure, & other eccleſiaſtic rites being then debated, it was re-
' ſolved a ſynod ſhould be called at [Strenaeſhalch] Whitby, for de-
' termining this queſtion. Accordingly, both the KINGS, father & ſon,
' came thither; as alſo both the biſhops, to wit, Colman & his cler-
' gy which were from Scotland; & Agilberĉt with the presbyters Aga-
' tho & Vilfrid: James alſo & Romanus, who ſided with the laſt. The
' Abbeſs Hilda ᵃ with her people was of the Scotch party, as was alſo
' the venerable biſhop Cedd, who had been ordained by them long
' before, & was, in this council, a moſt careful interpreter for both
' parties. Firſt of all K. Oſuiu premiſed, that it was the duty of thoſe
' who ſerve one God, to have one rule of life, nor ſhould they diſ-
' agree in the adminiſtration of the heavenly ſacraments, who all
' expeĉted one & the ſame kingdom in heaven. They ſhould en-
' quire rather which was the trueſt tradition, & that this was to
' be followed by all. In the firſt place therefore he command-
' ed his biſhop Colman to declare what was the cuſtom he maintain-
' ed, & whence it had its original. Then Coleman ſaid, this Eaſter
' which I am wont to keep I had from my anceſtors, who ſent me
' biſhop hither; which all our fathers, men beloved of God, are known
' to have obſerved after the ſame manner. That this may not be deſpiſed
' or condemned by any, 'tis the very ſame Eaſter which we read S. John
' the evangeliſt, the diſciple more eſpecially beloved by our lord, with
' all the churches which he governed, did obſerve. Who, having
' ſpoke theſe & ſuch like things, the king commanded Agilberĉt to de-
' clare before them the manner of his obſervation; whence it had
' its beginning, & upon what authority he relied. Agilberĉt anſwered,
' pray let my diſciple Vilfrid the presbyter ſpeak in my ſtead, becauſe
' we two, and all the reſt who ſit here with us, are obſervers of the
' ſame eccleſiaſtical tradition, & becauſe he can better and more ma-
' nifeſtly explain our ſentiments in the Engliſh tongue, than I can do
' by an interpreter. Then Vilfrid, the King commanding him to ſpeak,
' thus began. The Eaſter, ſaid he, which we keep we have ſeen at
' Rome (where the bleſſed apoſtles SS. Peter & Paul lived, taught, ſuf-
' fered, and were buried) to be kept by all. This we have beheld uni-
' verſally obſerved in Italy & in Gaul, where we have travelled either
' for learning or devotion. This we find to be kept in one & the
' ſame, not a different order of time, thro' Afric, Aſia, Egypt, Greece,

---

ᵃ ' This Hilda was great grandchild to
' K. Edwin. Bede ſaith ſhe ſo held her ſub-
' jeĉts to the reading of Scripture & doing
' works of righteouſneſs, that many among
' them were fit to be churchmen, and to
' ſerve at the altar: ſo that we afterwards
' ſaw five biſhops out of her monaſtery — &

' Tatfrith a ſixth, ſaith my author, was eleĉt-
' ed biſhop, but died before he could be or-
' dained. Being ſo well ſtored with learned
' men as ſhe was, & having ſuch a power
' over them as ſhe had, it is no wonder that
' we here read of her being preſent at the
' ſynod. Bp. Lloyd. p. 170, 171.

' &

' & all the world wherever the church of Chrift is fpread ; throughout
' divers nations & languages, except thefe only, & the accomplices of their
' obftinacy, the Picts & Britons ; with whom, & not with all thefe nei-
' ther, they contend againft the whole world in a very foolifh attempt.
' When he had faid this, Colman anfwered, 'tis very ftrange that you
' fhould call our attempt foolifh, wherein we follow the example of fo
' great an apoftle, who feemed worthy to lean upon the breaft of our
' lord : when all the world knows with what wifdom he lived.   Vilfrid
' replied, far be it from us that we fhould accufe S. John of folly, for
' obferving the law of Mofes according to the letter, the church then
' judaizing in many things, nor could the apoftles of a fudden caft off
' all the obfervance of that law which had been inftituted by God.
' In like manner it hath been thought neceffary, that all they who are
' converted to the faith, fhould lay afide images, which where invented
' by devils ; that they might give no fcandal to thofe Jews which were
' left among the nations.   Thus Paul circumcifed Timothy, offered
' facrifices in the temples, & with Aquila & Prifcilla fhaved his head
' at Corinth.   There was nothing in all this but to avoid offending the
' Jews.   Upon this account James faid to Paul, thou feeft, brother, how
' many thoufands there are of the Jews that believe ? And they are all
' zealous of the law, Acts xxi. 21.   But at this time of the day, now the
' gofpel fhines with fuch brightnefs thro' the world, it is not neceffary,
' nay it is not lawful, for thofe that believe, to be circumcifed, & make
' their offerings of carnal facrifices unto God.   Therefore it was that John
' kept his Eafter according to the cuftom of the law, upon the four-
' teenth day of the month at even, not regarding whether it was the
' fabath, or any other day.   But Peter, when he preached at Rome,
' being mindful that our lord rofe from the dead on the firft day of the
' week, & fo gave the world hope of the refurrection, underftood that
' Eafter was to be obferved after fuch a manner, as according to the
' cuftom & precept of the law, he might always expect the rifing
' of the moon upon the fourteenth day of the firft month , 'till
' the evening, as well as John.   And, when it was rifen, if the
' lords day (which was then called the prime of the fabath) fell next
' morning, he began to keep the Eafter of our lord upon the very
' fame evening, as at this day we are all wont to do.   But if the lords
' day did not follow the next morning after the fourteenth day of the
' moon, but was to happen on the fixteenth, feventeenth, or any other
' day of the moon till the twenty firft ; then he waited for it, & in
' the even of the Saturday before it, began to obferve the holy folem-
' nities of Eafter.   Thus it fell out that the Eafter lords day could be
' kept only from the fifteenth day of the moon to the twenty firft.
' Neither does this evangelic and apoftolic tradition deftroy, but rather
' fulfil the law, in which it is commanded that Eafter fhall be obferv-
' ed from the fourteenth day of the firft month at even, to the twenty
' firft day of the fame month at even.   To imitate which manner of

' obfervation

' obfervation all the fucceffors of S. John in Afia after his death, &
' the church all over the world, is now enclined.   And that this is
' the true Eafter, and that none but this ought to be obferved by the
' faithful, as we learn from ecclefiaftic hiftory, was not newly decreed,
' but confirm'd, by the council of Nice.   Whence it appears, Col-
' man, that ye do not, as ye imagine, follow the example of John,
' nor yet of Peter, whofe tradition ye knowingly gainfay; neither do
' ye agree either with law or gofpel in the obfervation of your Eafter.
' For John obferving the pafchal time according to the decrees of the
' mofaic law, took no notice of the prime of the fabath [or firft day of
' the week] which you do not follow, who do not celebrate Eafter
' but on the prime of the fabath.   Peter kept the Eafter lords day from
' the fifteenth to the twenty firft day of the moon, which you do not,
' who will have it from the fourteenth to the twentieth; fo that your
' Eafter often begins upon the thirteenth day at even, which neither
' the law makes any mention of; nor yet did the lord the author &
' giver of the gofpel, in it, but on the fourteenth day at even, both
' eat the old pafs-over & deliver the facraments of the new teftament
' to be obferved by the church in remembrance of his paffion.   Nay
' & farther you utterly difcard the twenty firft day of the moon, which
' the law chiefly recommends to be obferved, from your celebration
' of Eafter.   And thus, as I have faid, in keeping this moft high fef-
' tival, ye neither agree with John, nor Peter, nor with the law, nor
' yet with the gofpel.   To thefe things Colman replied, 'tis not cre-
' dible that holy man Anatolius, fo highly recommended in ecclefia-
' ftical hiftory, did judge contrary to the law & the gofpel, who wrote
' that Eafter was to be kept from the fourteenth to the twentieth; or
' that our moft reverend father Columba & his fucceffors, men belov-
' ed of God, who kept Eafter as we do, either did not underftand, or
' act contrary to the divine pages; fince there were many of them to
' whofe fanctity heavenly figns & the miracles they did bore witnefs:
' whom I, not doubting to be holy men, their life, manners, & dif-
' cipline, always defift not to follow.   'Tis evident, fays Vilfrid, that
' Anatolius was a man moft holy, moft learned, moft deferving of the
' higheft efteem.   But what have you to do with him, when you do
' not keep his decrees neither?   For he in obferving his Eafter, fol-
' lowing altogether the rule of truth, laid down a cycle of nineteen
' years, of which you are either ignorant, or (being known & obferv-
' ed by all the church of Chrift) make nothing of.   He fo computed
' the fourteenth day of the moon, as to the lords day of Eafter, that
' it might be confeffed, after the manner of the Egyptians, [a] at even
' to be the fifteenth day.   He alfo fo obferved the twentieth for

a The Egyptians computed the natural day
to confift (not as we do, of a day & a night,
but) as truth itfelf teaches, of a night & a

day. So Mofes, who was skilful in all the
learning of the Egyptians —— the evening
& the morning were the firft day.

                                                      ' the

‘ the lords day of Eaſter, that the ſame day declining, you might take
‘ it for the twenty firſt.   The rule of which diſtinction this is enough
‘ to prove you ignorant of, that oftentimes you moſt manifeſtly keep
‘ Eaſter before the full moon, that is, upon the thirteenth day [a].   As
‘ to your father Columba & his followers, whoſe holineſs you declare
‘ you will imitate, and whoſe rules & precepts confirm’d by heavenly
‘ ſigns you will follow, I might return this anſwer.   Many will ſay
‘ to the lord in the day of judgment, have we not propheſied caſt out
‘ devils, & done many mighty works in thy name? The lord ſhall
‘ anſwer, I never knew you.   But far be it from me that I ſhould
‘ ſpeak this of your fathers; ’tis much more juſt to believe well, than
‘ ill, of thoſe that are unknown to us.   So that I do not deny them
‘ to have been the ſervants & beloved of God, who loved him with a
‘ ruſtical ſimplicity, but pious intention.   Nor do I think that ſuch an
‘ obſervation of Eaſter was very prejudicial to them, ſo long as none
‘ came amongſt them to acquaint them with the decrees of a more
‘ perfect inſtitution which they might have followed.   And I do be-
‘ lieve that if any catholic calculator had come among them, they would
‘ have followed his admonitions, as they did approve of thoſe things
‘ which they had learned and knew to be the commandments of God.
‘ But as for you & your companions, now you have heard, if you re-
‘ fuſe to follow the decrees of the apoſtolic ſee, nay and which are
‘ the decrees alſo of the univerſal church, & are confirmed by the holy
‘ Scriptures, without all doubt you ſin.   For tho’ your fathers were
‘ holy men, ſhall their paucity, from a corner of the moſt remote
‘ iſland, be preferred before the church of Chriſt, which is ſpread over
‘ the whole world? And tho’ your Columba was a holy man, & pow-
‘ erful in his gifts (& indeed our Columba, if he was Chriſts) yet can
‘ he be preferr’d before the moſt bleſſed prince of the apoſtles, to whom
‘ the lord ſaid, thou art Peter, & upon this rock I will build my chucrh,
‘ & the gates of hell ſhall not prevail againſt it: & I will give
‘ unto thee the keys of the kingdom of heaven? Vilfrid urging theſe
‘ things, the king ſaid, was this, Colman, truly ſpoken by our lord to
‘ Peter? Who anſwered, yes, Sir.   The king replied, can you ſet
‘ forth any thing of ſo great power committed to your Columba?
‘ Nothing, ſays Colman.   The king asked them again, are you both
‘ agreed as to this without any controverſie, that theſe things were
‘ principally ſpoken to Peter, and that to him the keys of the kingdom of
‘ heaven were given by our lord? They both anſwered, yes.   Where-
‘ upon he thus concluded, then I ſay to you, becauſe he is the door-
‘ keeper I will not contradict him.   But, ſo far as I know & am able,
‘ I deſire to be obedient to all his appointments; leaſt when I come
‘ to the gates of the kingdom of heaven, there ſhould be none to un-

---

[a] This laſt argument of Vilfrids, as is well   pend. p. 703. is unanſwerable.
obſerved by the learned editor of Bede, Ap-

' lock them for me, if he be againſt me, who is prov'd to have the
' keys.   The king declaring this, [almoſt] all the aſſembly aſſented
' to it, both thoſe of higher & meaner quality : ſo that caſting off the
' leſs perfeᴄt inſtitution, they made haſt to embrace thoſe things which
' they knew to be better.   For the diſputation being ended, & the
' aſſembly diſſolved, Agilberᴄt returned home; & Colman ſeeing his
' doᴄtrine ſet at nought & his party deſpiſed, taking thoſe that were
' willing to follow him, to wit, thoſe who would not receive the Ro-
' man Eaſter & canonical tonſure (for concerning the laſt there was no
' ſmall diſpute) return'd into Scotland to conſult, with his friends
' there, what was to be done.   Cedd, leaving the ways of the Scotch,
' went home to his own ſee, approving the Roman Eaſter.   This diſ-
' pute was held in the year of Chriſt 664. which was the 22ᵈ of K. Oſ-
' uiu's reign.'   So far Bede.

XXIV. Before I proceed I beg leave to obſerve here, that this account of the council of Whitby, & ſome other paſſages of Bede may
be found tranſlated into Engliſh, in a book entitled, ' Hiſtorical Col-
' leᴄtions, relating the originals, converſions, & revolutions of the in-
' habitants of Great Britain to the Norman conqueſt : 8ᵛᵒ London print-
' ed for John Wyat, 1706.'   Where the compiler ſays in his title,
' the Engliſh authors are cited in their own words, & the reſt careful-
' ly tranſlated.'   An aſſertion which it would have been well if he had
made good.   But let any one compare his tranſlation of theſe debates
about Eaſter, as it ſtands there in his own book, beginning p. 269. &
as I have here correᴄted it, with our author Bede, and he will find
that writer is not at all to be depended upon, when he comes to tranſ-
late.   For ſome other things however inſerted in the courſe of this
work, I thank, & acknowledge my ſelf obliged to, him; nor can I
yet paſs on, without adding his remark upon K. Oſuiu's determination at the council of Whitby, with the quotation which follows it
from Biſhop Patrick.

XXV. ' Many a diſputation, ſays he [a], is turn'd off the hinges by
' that which is very little to the purpoſe; for when the judgment is
' tired, then any thing that ſtrikes the fancy prevails.   Thus K. Oſuiu was
' carried away with a notion that S. Peter was literally a porter, &
' that he lay at his mercy whether he ſhould ever be able to enter into
' heaven.   Becauſe this gave ſo great a turn to the Engliſh nation that
' it was thereby entirely brought to a ſubjeᴄtion to Rome, & many
' are not ſtill able to ſee thro' the miſt, I will therefore give an ac-
' count of S. Peters keys from biſhop Patrick [b].   The power which
' theſe words, I will give thee the keys of heaven, import, was not
' beſtowed upon S. Peter alone, as they of the Roman church ima-
' gine; but what Chriſt here ſpake to him, as the prime apoſtle, he
' intended to all the reſt.   This is manifeſt by comparing three places
' in the goſpel together, which ſpeak of this power.   For what is

a P. 278.   b Dignity of the chriſtian prieſthood, p. 4.
2
                                                                    ' here

'here faid of it by way of prediction or promife, that he would con-
'fer it; is, a little after, fpoken of by way of defcription & explica-
'tion of the nature of this power & the manner of ufing it, as you
'may fee Matt. xviii. 15. to 21. where verfe the 18. he fpeaks in the
'plural number, whatfoever ye fhall bind on earth, fhall be bound in
'heaven; & whatfoever ye fhall loofe on earth, fhall be loofed in
'heaven.   Which is the very fame power & in the very fame words
'promifed here to S. Peter, I will give thee the keys of the kingdom
'of heaven, & whatfoever thou fhalt bind on earth, fhall be bound
'in heaven; & whatfoever thou fhalt loofe on earth, fhall be loofed
'in heaven.   And then in a third place, when this power is actually
'conferr'd upon them, they are all invefted with it, after our Saviours
'refurrection but before his afcenfion, John xx. 22, 23. when he
'does not fay, λάβε, receive thou, as if he had fpoke to one alone,
'but λάβετε, receive ye the holy ghoft.   Whofoever fins ye remit,
'they are remitted to them; & whofoever fins ye retain, they are re-
'tained: which it is evident was fpoken to every one of them.'

XXVI. After the murder of Peada K. of the South Mercians, as before related; his brother & fucceffor K. Vulfere (tho' at firft an idola-
ter, yet at length a zealous chriftian) finifhed the church & monaftery
of Medefhamftede, the foundations whereof, as I have already touched,
were laid in 658. by the good, but unfortunate, Peada.   In his charter (tho' by the way, I am fatisfied it is fpurious) K. Vulfere defcribes
the jurifdiction of that church while it was yet an abby, & ' makes,
' as Mr. Forfter obferves ᵃ, Stanford one of the boundaries of the lands
' which he gave to it.'   I fhall here give fo much of that piece as is
neceffary to underftand what I fhall afterwards fay upon it: The Latin
you have elfewhere ᵇ, the Englifh whereof is this.   ' Vulfere by the
' favor of God K. of the Mercians, to all who reverence Chrift, &
' his holy church, greeting.   Infomuch as I defire by my authority,
' not only to confirm to the church of Medefhamftede, all that my
' predeceffor & brother Peada, or Ofuiu my brother in the chriftian
' faith & fellow-king, before granted; but alfo to add fomewhat of
' my own: I therefore grant to the bleffed Peter thefe marfhes, fens,
' lakes, and fifheries, with all the lands therein lying, from Medefham-
' ftede it felf to Northburc; & thence as far as the place which they call
' Folies; & thence the whole fen in a ftraight line as far as Efendic; &
' from Efendic to the place which they call Fethermuthe; & from thence
' in a ftraight line to the place ten miles farther, which they, who live
' thereabouts, call Cuggedic; & from thence to Raggewilh; & from
' Raggewilh five miles to the main river which leads to Elm & to Wyfe-
' berch; & thence, as you go, three miles againft the courfe of the main
' river to Throkenholt; & from Throkenholt in a ftraight line over the

a Letter to Dr. Tanner, MS. penes me,   b Monaft. Ang. I. p. 64. b. Gunton, p. 119.
p. 6.   Lel. Collect. I. p. 5. Saxon. Chron. p. 38.

' great

' great fen to Dereforde twenty miles endways; & thence to Grates-crofs,
' by a fair ftream called Bardane, fix miles to Paccelade; And fo dividing
' all thofe marfhes & great fens with the inhabitants of Huntingdonfhire;
' together with the marfhes & lakes of Scalfremere & Witlefmere, &
' fundry other meres belonging to the fame, with the lands alfo &
' tenements which lie on the fouth-fide of Scalfremere; & with all
' the inclofed fen every where as far as to Medefhamftede; & fo from
' Medefhamftede to Walmisford; & from Walmisford as far as to
' Clive; & thence to Eftune; and from Eftune to Stanford; & from
' Stanford, following the courfe of the river, to the bovefaid Nort-
' burc. Within thefe bounds therefore let all things be under the ju-
' rifdiction of this apoftolic monaftery. All which, tho' fmall indeed,
' I fo grant, as I my felf have royally held them, free from all fervice,
' & let this moft free church enjoy them free as a queen & not as a
' fervant, &c. I Vulfere the king have confirmed it. I Ofwi, king
' of the Northumbers, have praifed it. I Kyneburg, the kings [Vul-
' feres] fifter embrace it. I Kynefuith, the Kings [Vulferes] fifter alfo,
' have favoured it. I Vilfrid, the prieft, fervant of the churches, &
' carrier of the gofpel among the nations have affected it, &c. This
' privilege was confirmed, *anno* 664.' Here I beg leave to note if
Vulferes charter be genuine, & was granted as above, then Ofuiu's concurrence with Vulfere fhews that prince yet retained fome power in
Mercia. Be that as it will, in this charter are well defcribed the liberties of that famous monaftery now called the foke or fee of Burg,
containing divers towns & lordfhips, among which fo much of Stanford as lies on the South fide of the Welland was always reckoned
a part; & all together yet enjoy fome of the many privileges formerly
granted to that church & monaftery. But what proves this charter beyond
all contradiction fpurious, is, that our Vilfrid is here called carrier of
the gofpel among the nations, (a circumftance alluding to his converting the Frieflanders) for as that matter happened not 'till *anno* 678.
the bare anticipating of it in 664. detects the forgery of the whole
piece; which had it been genuine would have been a farther demonftration of the great refpect which both K. Ofuiu & K. Vulfere had for
Vilfrid, in calling him to be a witnefs of this their joynt tranfaction;
& again, from Vilfrids particular fubfcription thereto, that tho' it was
reckoned very honourable to be an abbat, yet that in thefe times it
was accounted ftill more honourable to be a prieft.

XXVII. Vilfrid, as I before related, was made prieft in his own monaftery by Agilberct bifhop of the Weft Saxons. ' To that office he
' was ordained at the command of K. Alchfrid, that prince it feems
' defiring, as Bede fays [a], that a perfon of Vilfrids great learning &
' piety might be his own particular prieft & doctor.' But as honourable as it was to be a prieft & a kings conftant companion, K. Alch-

frid was not fatisfied 'till he had the fame year procured Vilfrid to be confecrated a bifhop.   For ' foon after he had detected & put down ' the Scots, fays the fame Bede, [a] with advice & confent of his ' father Ofuiu, K. Alchfrid fent Vilfrid into France [b] to the king there, ' to get him confecrated bifhop for him & his people.   For after Colmans ' departure, faith Heddius as quoted by bifhop Lloyd, [c] the kings [Of-' uiu and Alchfrid] would have Vilfrid be their bifhop in his ftead.   So ' Vilfrid being elected into the place, defir'd the king to give him leave ' to go into France for his ordination.   His words were thefe; it is ' to be confidered how I may come by the epifcopal degree without ' the offence of any catholic man.   For there are here in Britain many ' bifhops, of whom I would not accufe any one; tho' in truth I know ' that they are either *Quartadecimani* (as the Britons and Scots) or they ' are fuch as have been ordained by them; & that the apoftolic fee ' hath neither received them into communion, nor them that confent ' to fchifmatic's.   And therefore I defire you to fend me into France, ' where there live many catholic bifhops, that I may be made bifhop ' without any offence to the apoftolic fee.'   Upon his arrival in France, ' the French King fent him to Agilbert (the fame who ordained Vil-' frid prieft, & having left Britain, was now made bifhop of Paris) ' by him he was confecrated with great honor, [d] eleven bifhops affi-' fting [e] in a royal town called Compeigne.'   But faith another, [f] ' whilft ' Vilfrid delayed his return, fome envying that victory which he ob-' tained over Colman, perfuaded K. Ofuiu to get another confecrat-' ed in his place ; By whofe council the king being infatuated called ' Cedd, abbat of Leftingham, & fent him to Kent for ordination.' ' Hereby, adds another, [g] it is evident that after the victorious difpute, ' there remained fo great a party diffatisfied, that they prevailed even ' upon the converted Ofuiu to forfake his Vilfrid.   But this ordina-' tion of Cedd, faith Mr. Smith, [h] was againft the Canons for a two-' fold reafon.   Firft, becaufe, tho' Cedd was a good man, yet he was ' thruft into a fee that was already full.   And fecondly, becaufe he ' was ordained by Quartadeciman fchifmatic's.'   For as Bede tells us, [i] ' when Cedd arrived in Kent, he found archbifhop Deufdedit dead, ' & as yet no other appointed in his place.   So he went thence into ' Weft Saxony, where Vine was bifhop, & by him was he confecrat-' ed, who to affift him in the ordination took two Britifh bifhops, who ' kept the lords day of Eafter, as we have often faid, contrary to ca-' nonical cuftom, from the fourteenth to the twentieth day of the ' moon.   For, except Vine himfelf, there was not one bifhop in Bri-' tain canonically ordained.   However Vilfrid returning the fame year,

a Ib. 206.
b Id. p. 137.
c Hift. Britifh churches, p. 128.
d Beda. p. 206.
e Id. p. 137.
f Rich. Haguft. de epif. Hag. cap. 6. as

quoted by the author of the Hiftor. Collections. p. 281.
  g Hift. Collect. p. 281:
  h Serieri Vilf. p. 751. ;
  i p. 138.

H   ' by

' by his doctrine promoted divers catholic obfervations in the churches
' of the Englifh.   Whereby it came to pafs that the Roman inftitution
' every day increafing, all the Scots who remained among the Englifh,
' either joined him, or withdrew into their own country.

XXVIII. Vilfrid neverthelefs being for the prefent kept out of his
fee by Cedd, ' lived, as Mr. Smith obferves, [a] retired in his own
' monaftery at Rippon, fave that he was frequently invited by K.
' Vulfere to exercife his epifcopal function in Mercia.   Likewife
' Ecgbert K. of Kent fent for him thither, where he ordained many
' priefts & not a few deacons. [b] For returning out of France before
' Theodore the new Archbifhop came over [who was a Grecian, &
put in by the Pope] ' he thus, for a time fupplied the want of him.'

Anno   Thus matters refted, till [c] ' in 669. Theodore himfelf came over,
669.   ' who ordered Cedd to be depofed from the fee of York which he
' had ufurped, & replaced Vilfrid there, who had a better title to it.
' [d] Cedd then leading a quiet life in a monaftery, Vilfrid held the bi-
' fhopbric of York, as alfo not only of all the Northumbers, but of
' the Picts as far as ever K. Ofuiu had extended his empire.   And be-
' caufe, as my author Bede continues, it was the manner of this moft
' reverend prelate, rather to walk on foot to preach the gofpel, than
' ride about his diocefe; archbifhop Theodore ordered him to ride
' where he had a longer journey than ordinary to go, & out of meer
' refpect & veneration for his pious labors, with his own hand would
' needs lift him on horfeback; thus, as he found him an holy man,
' compelling him to ride where it was neceffary.' Now about this laft
paffage the author of the Hiftorical collections abovementioned, blunders egregioufly, & backs his blunder with a very fcurrilous reflection.   Thefe are his words. [e] 'Venerable Bede thinks he may honeft-
' ly conceal the faults of fo great a man, & therefore only tells us
' that after his advancement, K. Ofuiu was fo charmed with his con-
' verfation that he would lift him up on horfeback with his own hand,
' when Theodore had advifed him to ride about for the vifitation of
' his diocefe, which was fo large.' Now Vilfrids fault which our author would here make venerable Bede conceal, muft be his pride in
fuffering K. Ofuiu to lend an hand to help him up on horfeback;
whereas it appears from Bede himfelf, in the paffage laft tranflated,
whofe own very words you may alfo read below; [f] that it was only
the archbifhop & not the king who fhewed him this great refpect in
helping him on horfeback the firft time; & that riding, as a matter both
of conveniency & decency, was what the archbifhop, as his metropolitan, exprefly enjoyned Vilfrid, & that Vilfrid, far from priding him-

a Seriei, ut fupra.
b Beda. p. 143.
c Seriei, loco quo prius.
d Beda. p. 143, 144.
e p. 281, 282.
f Et quia moris erat eidem reverentiffi-

mo antiftiti opus evangelii magis ambulan-
do per loca, quam equitando perficere; juffit eum Theodorus, ubicunq; longius iter
inftaret, equitare, multumq; renitentem, ftu-
dio & amore pii laboris, ipfe eum manu fua
levavit in equum. in loco fupra citato.

felf on that occafion, very much oppofed it.   If therefore people will throw dirt at this rate, they muft have a care fome of it does not in the end ftick upon their own backs.

XXIX. But to return. Vilfrid being reftored, as above, to his epif-copal chair, ' the fame year, as Mr. Smith fays, a rebuilt the church ' of York erected by Paulinus. The next year K. Ofuiu, as Bede ' obferves, b fell fick of a diftemper whereof he at laft died in the ' fifty eight year of his age; who, at that time, was grown fo fond ' of the Roman inftitution, that he intended if he could have got cur-' ed of his infirmity, to have gone to Rome, & ended his days there, ' & withal to have intreated bifhop Vilfrid to be his guide in his tra-' vels thither, promifing to give him a great fum of mony for fo do-' ing. But deceafing the 15th of February [there was an end of that ' defign, &] he left his fon Ecgfrid heir of his kingdom.' After the death of Ofuiu, ' K. Vulfere, as Mr. Speed writes, c tranflated the ' monarchy [or firft throne of the heptarchy] from the kings & coun-' try of the Northumbers, unto himfelf & his fucceffors the Mercians, ' who wore the imperial diadem without reverfement, until fuch time ' as great Egbert fet it upon the Weft Saxons head.' Concerning Vulfere I beg leave to add, that if, whilft he was a pagan, he at firft with-held from the monks of Lindisfarne, the ufe of their cell & lands, at Stanford in Lincolnfhire (a fuggeftion which any one may advance, yet no body can prove) no doubt, but on his converfion to the chri-ftian faith, he made them amends, by reftoring them whole at leaft, if not with addition.   After which it was eafie, both in his & many of his fucceffors days, for them or their fucceffors at length removed to Durham, to procure new charters to make good their title.   And foon after the Norman conqueft we fee therefore, in prior Wefling-tons MS. quoted by Mr. Smith, d K. William granted them a confir-mation fo ftrong, that he was ever after reckoned one of the founders of their cell of S. Leonard : But of that confirmation more hereafter. e

XXX. f ' This year likewife Vilfrid rebuilt the church of Rippon ' from the ground for monks, & defigning to confecrate the place ' with great ftate, prevailed with the kings Ecgfrid & his brother El-' fuin, to honor the folemnity with their prefence. This year alfo, ' or the next, the Picts making incurfions into the kingdom of the ' Northumbers [if you will believe my author] were driven back by ' the prayers of Vilfrid. In 671. as Bede tells g us, K. Ecgfrids queen ' Edilthryda abovementioned, having a long time earneftly defired him ' to grant her leave to withdraw into a monaftery, when fhe had in ' fome fort brought him, tho' very unwillingly, to comply with her ' requeft, entered the monaftery of the abbefs Ebba, K. Ecgfrids own

Anno
670.

Anno
671.

a Seriei Vilf. p. 751.
b p. 147.
c p. 307. a.
d Ad imum p. 206.

e Anno 1082. infra.
f Seriei Vilf. quo fupra.
g p. 162.

' aunt,

' aunt, fituate in a place called Cell-dingham [from the multitude of
' cells there, now Coldingham in Scotland] receiving the veil of a
' nuns habit from bifhop Vilfrid.   Soon after, as the Ely hiftorian ac-
' quaints us, [a] K. Ecgfrid had a mind to have her again, & being fo
' perfuaded by them who were about him, attempted to take her out
' of the monaftery.   Upon the news of whofe coming, the abbefs told
' her there was no efcaping but by flight.   At this Edilthryda, depart-
' ed & fled out of the precincts of the monaftery, & with two other
' nuns climbed up an high hill in that neighbourhood, where God
' poured down fuch prodigious fhowers of rain, & fo furrounded the
' mountain with water, that, as it is received by the inhabitants of
' that place, he hid them there feven days together, all which time they
' remained without either meat or drink, occupied in prayer ; 'till at
' length the king, ftroke with amazement, departed to York.' Hitherto the fortunes of our great prelate Vilfrid ran fmooth & happily, but
his white days began now to be mixt with clouds, & as a fad earneft
of more to follow, the firft ftorm which befel him was the lofs of
K. Ecgfrids favor.   For that prince, when he found himfelf utterly
difappointed of ever having his wife again, ' never after, as my laft
' author informs us, [b] loved Vilfrid with the fame affection as before,
' but, tho' he diffembled the matter inwardly hated him for a long
' time, & waiting an opportunity for this reafon at laft expelled him
' from his fee.'   As for Edilthryda, fhe, in 673. got farther from
her husband, & ' built a monaftery, as the fame hiftorian relates, [c] at
' Ely, where fhe affembled a great number of both fexes under a
' monaftic habit, & was by Vilfrid himfelf made the firft abbefs over
' them.'

XXXI. The fame year was held the council of Herutford [Hertford]
where were prefent Theodore archbifhop of Canterbury, Bifi bifhop of the
Eaft-Angles, Vilfrid bifhop of the Northumbers by his proxies (he appeared not in perfon I fuppofe becaufe he fufpected the archbifhop would
there attempt, as he afterwards, but elfewhere, actually did ; to decree fomething to his prejudice) Putta bifhop of Rochefter, Leutherius
bifhop of the Eaft-Saxons, & Vynfrid bifhop of the Mercians.   When
they were met, archbifhop Theodore produced a book of canons,
& fhewed them ten articles in it, which he faid were neceffary for
them, & defired might be obferved with more than ordinary diligence,
& the infringers of any one of them, *ipfo facto*, fufpended.   All which
was agreed to, & recorded.   Thofe articles, as Bede tells us, [d] were,
' I. that we all alike obferve the holy lords days of Eafter after [not
' on] the fourteenth [day of the] moon of the firft month.   II. That

a In Mon. Ang. Vol. I. p. 89. b.
  b Ib. Mr. Smith has the fame paffage, in his
appendix to Bede, Number XVIII. & for it
quotes Mabillons life of S. Ethildrit, Sæc. II.
p. 750. but the words *Vilfridum non eo af-*

fectu, &c. which he takes for Mabillons, are
not his, but the Ely Hiftorians here quoted,
as may be feen by comparing them.
  c Id. p. 87. b.
  d p. 149.

' no

' no bishop invade anothers diocese, but be content with the govern-
' ment of the people committed to him.   III. That whatsoever mona-
' steries are consecrated to God, it be lawful for no bishop to disturb
' them in any manner, or violently to take away from them any of
' their effects.   IV. That monks themselves shift not from place to
' place, that is, from monastery to monastery, without leave of their
' proper abbat; but remain in that obedience which they promised at
' the time of their conversion.   V. That no clere leaving his proper
' bishop, run wandring about at pleasure, or coming to any other, be
' received without the testimonial letters of his own bishop.   And if he
' has been once so received, & when invited will not return, both the
' receiver & he who was so received shall be liable to excommunication.
' VI. That stranger bishops & clerc's be content [in places out of their
' own cure or diocese] with what is out of hospitality offer'd
' them; & that it be lawful for none of them to exercise any priestly
' office without the the consent of the bishop of the diocese where
' they abide.   VII. That a synod be assembled twice every year.   But
' [says Theodore] because divers occasions hinder, it pleased us one
' & all to meet once a year, on the first of August at Clofeshoch [Cliffe
' by Rochester.]   VIII. That no bishop, out of ambition, set himself
' before another, but that all acknowledge the time & order of their
' consecration.   IX. That more bishops be made, as the number of the
' faithful increase.   But on this article [says Theodore] we were for the
' present silent.   X. That none be allowed to marry, but accord-
' ing to law. That none commit incest; none leave his proper wife, save
' as the gospel teaches, by reason of fornication.   That if any one hath
' put away his proper wife wedded to him by lawful marriage, if he
' would be truly a christian, let him be wedded to no other; but ei-
' ther remain single, or be reconciled to his wife.'   All which being
agreed to, Theodore shut up the council with this short prayer[a], ' the
' divine grace keep us, all our lives long, in the unity of his church.'

XXXII. [b] ' Not long after, archbishop Theodore being offended at
' Vynfrid bishop of the Mercians for his disobedience in a certain af-
' fair, deposed him from his bishopbric.   [c] What affair Vynfrid was
' disobedient in, Bede saith not.   But if any man, continues Mr. Smith,
' consider the affairs & counsels of this time, he will find it was done
' for no other reason than that he would not let his see be divided
' into more dioceses.   For tho' in the council Theodore was for the
' present silent in the article concerning the number of bishopbric's
' being encreased, yet, that he was so in his own mind resolv'd, both
' the ninth article about that matter, and the necessity of the church
' sufficiently demonstrate.'   Thus Vynfrid was dealt with; nor was Vilfrid (upon whose account this passage was inserted, as a preamble to
what presently follows) used a jot better. But first note. ' About 675.

a Beda. loco supra.   b Id. ib.   c In nota ad imum paginæ predict.

I   Vulferre,

‘ Vulfere, who died that year, fought & was vanquiſh'd by K. Ecgfrid,
‘ & (as my author adds[a]) the prayers of our great biſhop Vilfrid
[Tho' granting Vilfrids prayers were able to work miracles, except
Vulfere took Vilfrids monaſtery at Stanford away from his monks of
Lindisfarne, I find no reaſon why he ſhould ſo employ them againſt
Vulfere] ‘ who now loſt the greateſt part of the province of Lindiſſe.
‘ At the ſame time likewiſe Vilfrid dedicated a church at Hexham, in
‘ honor of the bleſſed apoſtle S. Andrew.

Anno
678.

XXXIII. I have before obſerved [b] how extreamly K. Ecgfrid was ſet
againſt biſhop Vilfrid, & for what reaſon.   Mr. Smith has the ſame
paſſage & proceeds[c].   ‘ From this beginning roſe the kings hatred
‘ againſt Vilfrid; which Ermenburga, whom he afterwards married,
‘ diſcovering, ſhe more inflamed with the fancies which ſhe put into
‘ his head.   For ſhe, becauſe Vilfrid had often taken notice of her le-
‘ vity, pride, oppreſſions and other faults; bore him alſo a ſecret grutch.
‘ Wherefore perceiving the King began to ſtagger in his affections to-
‘ wards him, ſhe began with treacherous inſinuations (under a pretence
‘ of admiring it) to relate his glory to the King.   For ſetting before
‘ him the abundance of his riches, the multitude of his monaſteries,
‘ the ſtatelineſs of his buildings, & the number of his princely atten-
‘ dance, what have you more for your ſelf, ſays ſhe, than what you
‘ have given him ? All your kingdom is but his biſhopbric.   Greatly
‘ moved by theſe & the like ſuggeſtions, &, as if he thereby conſult-
‘ ed nothing but his own ſafety, hearkening to little elſe, the King
‘ thought hardly any thing could poſſibly be more for his own advan-
‘ tage, than to get Vilfrid deprived of all that he had, & his biſhopbric
‘ divided into more dioceſes.'   Being thus reſolved to depoſe Vilfrid,
‘ becauſe, as the ſame Mr. Smith elſewhere tells us[d], he could by
‘ no means effect it without the archbiſhops conſent, the king ordered
‘ letters of a very foul charge againſt him to Theodore, &, as Aedius
‘ relates, by preſents brought him over to comply.   Theodore came
‘ therefore to the kings court, & by his authority fulfilled Ecgfrids de-
‘ ſire.   For immediately, Vilfrid being abſent, he conſecrated three
‘ biſhops into his place, to wit Eata for the church of Hexham or Lin-
‘ disfarne, Boſa for York, & Eadhed for the province of Lindiſſe.'   Now
here Mr. Smith makes Hexham & Lindisfarne but one biſhopbric, but
Mr. Wharton ſays[e], ‘ in 678. archbiſhop Theodore, who had often,
‘ but in vain, demanded of Vilfrid to appoint more biſhops in the great
‘ kingdom of the Northumbers; with K. Ecgfrids leave, by his own
‘ authority now appointed & ordained three biſhops (to wit, Boſa of
‘ York, Eata of Hexham, & Eadhed of Lindiſſe, which then by right
‘ of conqueſt belonged to the Northumbers) leaving Wilfrid Lindis-

a Seriei Vilfrid. p. 751.
b Paragr. XXX. ſupra.
c Num. XVIII. appendicis ad Bedæ opera

d Seriei Vilf. p. 751.
e Angliæ ſacræ I. p. 693.

‘ farne,

' farne, the old see of the Northumbrian bishops:' And so makes two
of Hexham & Lindisfarne.   Malmsbury says[a], ' they pretended there
' was good cause for what they did, since the revenue was so large
' that three bishops might be maintain'd with that which made one so
' proud; & besides the circuit of the diocese was sufficient for four.'
' And indeed this charge, as Mr. Smith says[b], might seem right, if
' they had either not utterly plundered him, who got all this by his
' own industry, or but acted with his consent.   Nor will the ninth
' article of the synod of Hertford give Theodore any color for doing
' thus.   For altho' it was discoursed among them, that more bishops
' should be made as the number of the faithful increased; yet was there
' nothing then diffined concerning the division of their dioceses, but
' touching this article [says Theodore] we were for the present silent.
' However when Vilfrid was thus depriv'd of [three parts of] his see
' by Theodore, tho' he was not himself with them, the matter could
' not be long concealed from him.   Whereupon, in the greatest sur-
' prise, he goes to the kings palace, to enquire, for what reason they
' had so acted?   And, asking both the king & the archbishop, why?
' without any fault of his, they pretended, like highwaymen, to rob
' him of the substance given him by princes for God? They answer'd
' before all the people, we charge you with no crime at all against any
' man, but, for all that, change not the sentence we have passed about
' you.   Whereupon, not satisfied with such answer, by advice of his
' fellow-bishops, as Heddius informs us[c], he appealed to the apostolic see.
' After which, as Mr. Smith proceeds[d], turning from the kings tribu-
' nal, he said to them, who flattered their master by laughing at his
' misfortunes, you who now laugh at my condemnation thro' envy, to
' your own confusion shall this day twelvemonth weep bitterly.   And,
' as he foretold, so it came to pass.   For on that very day twelve-
' month, *anno* 679. there being a sharp battle fought betwixt Ecgfrid
' & Edilred, was slain Elfuin K. Ecgfrids brother, on account of whose
' death the king & court were stroke with great sorrow: & thus all
' the mockery that they made about Vilfrids expulsion was turned into
' bitterness.——It is observable Vilfrid appealed to the pope by advice
' of his fellow-bishops; whence it is manifest, that some bishops stood
' up for him, & that Theodore turned this prelate out of his see, by
' his own, & not any synodical, authority.'   Now these his fellow bishops, had their own sees divided, (as I take it) & so stood up for
themselves as much as for Vilfrid.

XXXIV. Before Vilfrids second journey to Rome, ' he lived some-
' time at Ely, as the Historian of that church relates[e], with [K. Ecg-
' frids divorced queen] ' Etheldred now abbess of that place; where
' he then, & as oft as need required, administred the rights of his

a Gest. Pontif. Lib. 3. de Archiep. Ebor.   d Loco supra.
b Seriei Vilf. p. 751.   c Mon. Ang. I. p. 89. b.
c Cap. 23.

' episcopal

' episcopal office.' At length, as Bede himself informs us [a], setting out
' for Rome to acquaint the pope with this affair, Vilfrid, when he had
' taken ship, was, by a west wind, driven into Friesland, & being ho-
' norably received by those barbarians & their king Aldgils, preached
' Christ to them, & instructing many thousands of them in the word
' of truth, washed them in the font of baptism from the uncleanness
' of their sins. And thus he began the evangelic work there, which
' afterwards the most reverend prelate Vilbrod, compleated with great
' devotion.' After Vilfrid, as Mr. Smith tells us [b], had stayed all the
' whole winter among the Frieslanders, he again set forward on his
' journey for Rome, & went into France to K. Dagobert, who re-
' ceived him hospitably with much gladness, & earnestly desired him to
' accept of Streisburg, the biggest bishopric in his kingdom; &, when
' he would not comply with his royal pleasure, sent him, with many
' presents & great gifts, accompanied by his own bishop Deodate for
' a guide, to the apostolic see. From France Vilfrid went forwards to
' the K. of Lombardy, & was by him likewise nobly received.

Anno XXXV. ' In 679. Vilfrid arrived at Rome, saith Mr. Smith [c], by
679. ' which time, Cenwald, a religious monk, bringing letters from
' Theodore was got thither, whereby this dissension was not unknown
' to pope Agatho. Wherefore, in October the same year, he called
' a synod of above fifty priests & bishops in the church of our Savior
' erected by Constantine, where Vilfrids affair was debated before his
' accusers, & he, by the judgment of all, pronounced worthy of his
' bishopric, & to have been accused without any fault. Now this synod
' was assembled before Vilfrid reached Rome, to take cognizance of
' the state of the British church then disturbed by the dissension be-
' tween Theodore the archbishop, & the rest of the prelates of that
' province; &, among other things, decreed, that every kingdom erect-
' ed within the isle of Britain, should have, according to the ex-
' tent of its empire, bishops of provinces so appointed, that, reckoned
' all together with the archbishop, they should make up the number
' of twelve prelacies, whom the archbishop should promote & conse-
' crate according to Canon.——Now this difinition of the Roman sy-
' nod seems to have favored Theodores removing Vilfrid from his
' see, & consecrating three other bishops into his place. But if it be
' considered, that Theodore did this, Vilfrid being absent & knowing
' nothing of the matter, & against the consent of his fellow bishops;
' as also, that Vilfrid never opposed the division of his own bishopbric,
' provided such bishops might be promoted with whom he could una-
' nimously serve God, & such others be elected out of the clergy of
' the church as the bishops assembled in council should appoint; it
' will then be certainly confessed, that this council did not confirm by
' its authority, what Theodore undertook by force, without advising,

a P. 206, 207.   b Seriei Vilfridianæ p. 752.   c Id. ib.
1
' either

‘ either with his collegues, or Vilfrid himself, to perform.   Wherefore
‘ the Roman synod, saving whole its own disinition touching the above
‘ division of sees, decreed, that Vilfrid should be restored to the bishop-
‘ bric which he lately held; & with advise of a council for that pur-
‘ pose to be assembled, should elect those suffragans to himself, with
‘ whom he could peaceably converse; & who, being so promoted,
‘ should be consecrated by the archbishop; setting aside, no doubt, all
‘ those who, in his absence, were, without all reason, thrust into his
‘ bishopbric.   Lastly, that all, who shall attempt to violate or infringe
‘ this decree, should be liable to an eternal Anathema.

XXXVI. ‘ In 680. the same pope Agatho, as Bede relates[a], assem-   Anno
‘ bling a synod at Rome consisting of one hundred & twenty five bi-   680,
‘ shops against certain hereticks, who maintained that there was but
‘ one will & operation in our blessed Lord and Savior; commanded
‘ Vilfrid also to be called, &, sitting among the bishops, to relate
‘ what his faith & that of the province, or island, whence he came,
‘ was, touching the question in debate: And when he & his people
‘ were found catholic in their belief, was pleased to order this article
‘ (among the rest) to be inserted in the acts of that synod, & it was
‘ accordingly thus recorded.   Vilfrid, beloved of God, bishop of the
‘ city of York, appealing to the apostolic see about his own business,
‘ & by authority of the same concerning matters certain & uncertain
‘ absolved, & set in the seat of judgment, with one hundred & twen-
‘ ty five other bishops assembled in synod, professed, &, with his sub-
‘ scription, confirm’d the true and catholic faith, for all the north part
‘ or islands of Britain & Ireland, which are inhabited by the nations
‘ of the English and Britons together with the Scots & Picts.

XXXVII. Whilst he now stayed at Rome, solliciting to be restored
to his bishopbric, which, as has been shewn, he very honorably effected; Vilfrid (if it be not one forgery upon the back of another)
procured a Bull to confirm the lands & privileges of the church of Medeshamstede.   For it seems ‘ K. Ethelred, as the Saxon chronicle ac-
‘ quaints us[b], informed the pope by letters & the mouth of Vilfrid, that
‘ his brothers Peada & Vulfere had erected a certain monastery called
‘ Medeshamstede, & discharged it from all service due either to king
‘ or bishop; & desired that he would confirm it with his Bull & bles-
‘ sing.   Whereupon the pope sent over his bull to this purpose.   To
‘ Ethelred the worthy king of the Mercians, Theodore archbishop of
‘ Canterbury, &c.   I Agatho the Roman pope send greeting.   I have
‘ heard the petition of K. Ethelred, archbishop Theodore, &c. & will
‘ that it be done in every particular as ye have desired.   I forbid there-
‘ fore on the grace of God & S. Peter, also of all saints & all conse-
‘ crated heads, either king, bishop, earl, or any other person, to re-

a p. 207.   b p. 41, 42, 43.

K   ‘ ceive

' ceive any tribute, cuftom, tax, farthing, or demand any fervice
' from that abby of Medefhamftede. The bifhop of the diocefe I
' alfo forbid, that he never prefume to celebrate either ordination
' or confecration in this abby, fave when he fhall be thereunto re-
' quefted by the abbat; & that he demand no epifcopal mulct, or fy-
' nodal, or take tribute of any manner of thing there. I will alfo,
' that throughout that whole ifland, the abbat be efteemed a Roman
' legate; & that whofoever fhall be elected abbat there by the monks,
' be confecrated by the archbifhop of Canterbury. I will alfo & con-
' firm, that if any perfon hath vowed a pilgrimage to Rome, & can-
' not perform it (hindred whether by ficknefs, poverty, or any other
' affair whatfoever) that repairing to that monaftery in Medefhamftede,
' he have the fame remiffion from Chrift, S. Peter, the abbat, & monks,
' as he would have had in cafe he had actually gone to Rome, &c.   In
' a word I pronounce, that whoever fhall obferve thefe letters & this man-
' date, fhall live for ever with almighty God in the kingdom of heaven;
' & whofoever fhall violate the fame, fhall, without he repent, be ex-
' communicated & damned with Judas & all the devils in hell.' This was
the fubftance of the Bull: the whole may be feen in the Monafticon[a].

XXXVIII. To proceed. ' Vilfrid, as Mr. Smith fays[b], being thus
' reftored to his bifhopric by the decrees of the pope & fynod, & re-
' ceiving with him a bull from Agatho directed to K. Ecgfrid & arch-
' bifhop Theodore, returned into England; & carried the bull to the
' king, who neverthelefs received it with prodigious fcorn, & caft Vil-
' frid into prifon, his queen Ermenburga perfuading him fo to do,
' who alfo rudely took away from him a little cafket of reliques, as
' it hung about his neck; but as all hiftorians witnefs, fhe paid very
' feverely for fo doing. For [if you will believe my author] being
' poffeffed with an evil fpirit, fhe could never be reftored to health
' before Vilfrid was difcharged out of prifon, & had his liberty to
' depart where he pleafed.   Flying his country therefore he went thence
' to the Mercians.'   Upon his arrival there K. Ethelred commanded
' archbifhop Theodore, as the Saxon chronicle relates[c], to call a coun-
' cil of all the prelates at Bifhops Hatfield. When they were there
' affembled, he ordered the bull to be read which the pope had fent
' him [relating to Medefhamftede] & then they all confirmed & ftrength-
' ened it.   Then faid the king, all that my brother Peada & my bro-
' ther Vulfere, & my fifters Cyneburga & Kynefwitha, gave & confirmed
' to S. Peter & the abbat, I will that they remain good, &c. I alfo
' this day give to S. Peter, thefe lands & all the appurtenances, that
' is, Bredune, Hrepingas, Cedenac, Swinefhefed, Heanbyrig, Lodefhac,
' Scuffenhalch, Coftesford, Stretford, Waetelleburne, Lufgeard, Ethel-
' huniglond, Barthanig. Thefe lands (that none of my fucceffors may
' retract any thing therefrom) I give to S. Peter as freely as I my felf
' have poffeffed them; if any one does therefore retract from them,

a I. p. 67. b.   b Seriei Vilf. p. 753, 754.   c p. 43.

3

                                                                    ' let

' let him be liable to the curſe of the pope of Rome, & the curſe of
' all biſhops, & of all who are now witneſſes : And this I confirm with
' the ſign of the ✠ of Chriſt.'   But what makes this inſtrument likewiſe appear no better than another piece of forgery (not to mention other reaſons) is, that in the Saxon chronicle our Vilfrids name
is ſubſcribed thus[a], ' I Vilfrid, archbiſhop of York, am witneſs of this
' charter, & confirm the ſaid curſe, ✠.'   But in the Monaſticon thus [b].
' I Vilfrid by apoſtolic favor regaining the ſee of York, a witneſs &
' bringer of this confirmation aſſent to it ✠.'   For firſt, Vilfrid never
was an archbiſhop ; and ſecondly, if he had, would never have ſubſcribed one & the ſame inſtrument thus variouſly.   One of theſe copies
therefore was certainly forged, & it is well if the other was not ſo
too.

XXXIX. To paſs on. ' At firſt Vilfrid, as Mr. Smith tells us[c] ; being
' well received among the Mercians by Beorhtuald. K. Ethelreds nephew
[& one would have thought he ſhould had the ſame reception from
K. Ethelred himſelf] ' was afterwards, by command of that king &
' Oſthryd his wife (K. Ecgfrids ſiſter) expelled Mercia ; & went thence
' to Centuin K. of the Weſt Saxons. But there alſo the queen being
' [his enemy as ſhe was queen] Ermenburgas ſiſter, could not endure
' him & forced him to depart that country likewiſe.'   ' Being   Anno
' thus baniſhed from his biſhopbric, as Bede relates[d], & wandring about   681.
' a long while from place to place, altho' (by reaſon of the forenamed
' K. Ecgfrids hatred) he could not be received into his own country
' or dioceſe ; Vilfrid however was not to be reſtrain'd from preach-
' ing the goſpel. Wherefore, turning aſide to the South Saxons, who
' hitherto were wholly enſlaved by idolatry, he miniſtred the word of
' faith & chriſtian baptiſm to that people. Edilualch was then King of
' that country, who, a little before, had been baptiſed in Mercia.
' Vilfrid therefore with that princes conſent, nay to his great joy, bap-
' tiſed the chief commanders & captains of that country ; & the preſ-
' byters Eappa & Padda, Burghelm & Oiddi, the reſt of the people :
' ſome then & ſome afterwards. [And now my author preſents you
with a whole cluſter of miracles. For he proceeds] ' It is alſo re-
' markable that preaching the goſpel to this nation, Vilfrid reſcued it,
' not only from the miſery of eternal damnation, but alſo from the
' dreadful danger of preſent death. For it ſeems that for three whole
' years before he came into this province, there had been no rain in
' all thoſe parts, whereby a moſt terrible famine invading the com-
' monalty, they were many of them ſtarved to death. Nay they re-
' late that oftentimes forty or fifty people at once, overcome with
' hunger, have gone to a precipice or ſea bank, &, in their diſtreſs,
' taking hold of one anothers hands, all thrown themſelves down head-

a Ib.
b loco ſupra citato.

c Seriei Vilfridianæ, p. 754.
d p. 156, 157.

' long

' long together, to perish by the fall, or be swallowed up by the waves.
' But, on that very day wherein this nation was converted, there fell
' a gentle, but plenteous rain, the earth reviv'd, & there followed a
' glad & fruitful year in the fields which now looked as fresh as they
' used to do.   And thus their old superstition being quite removed
' & idolatry cast out, the hearts & flesh of all men rejoyced in the
' living God, finding he was the true God, & that he had enriched
' them both with internal & external blessings.   For the bishop when
' he came first into the province, & saw what sad havoc the famine
' made among them, taught them to get their livelihood by fishing.
' For their sea & rivers abounded with fish, but no body among them
' understood how to catch any thing but eels.   Wherefore getting all
' their eel-nets, from all parts, together, they sent the bishops men into the
' sea, who with Gods assistance presently took three hundred fishes of
' divers sorts, which being divided into three parts, they gave one
' hundred to the poor, another hundred to them whom they borrow-
' ed the nets of, & one hundred they kept for themselves: By which
' kindness the bishop much turned the hearts of them all to love him,
' & they began more freely to hope for heavenly blessings on his preach-
' ing, by whose ministry they had already received those that were
' temporal.   At the same time K. Edilualch gave the most reverend
' prelate Vilfrid lands sufficient to maintain eighty seven families,
' where he might receive his people who wander'd about with him in
' banishment.   [This last is a passage which truly shews the number
of our Vilfrids attendants! For reckoning every one of his eighty seven
families to consist of ten persons, the whole makes up eight hundred
& seventy people ; a retinue so prodigious, that, except cardinal Wool-
sey, all the English prelates I ever read of, were private men to him!]
' The place [where he had these lands given him] was called Selaeseu,
' which signifies the island of the seal, or sea-calf [not Chichester it
self, as Mr. Smith thinks[a], but that place some miles distance from
thence, where Vilfrid erected the first bishopbric of the South-Saxons,
tho' afterwards removed thither.]   ' When bishop Vilfrid therefore had
' obtained this place, he erected a monastery there for regulars, con-
' sisting chiefly of those brethren whom he brought with him.   Thus
' he exercised the office of a bishop, both as a preacher & a prelate,
' in those parts for five years, (that is, 'till the death of K. Ecgfrid)
' deservedly honored by all.   And because the king, with possession
' of the forenamed place, gave him, together with fields & people,
' every kind of thing else there besides; instructing them in the chri-
' stian faith, he baptised all the people, among which were two hun-
' dred & fifty servants & maidens; all which, as he, by baptism, de-
' livered from the bondage of Satan; he also, by giving them freedom,
' released from the yoke of human servitude.

a In nota ad imum p. 156, vel 157.

XL. ' In

XL. 'In 685. King Ecgfrid, as the Saxon chronicle says,[a] was slain
' just by the north sea & a great army with him, on the twentieth
' day of May; & Alchfrid his brother entered upon the kingdom.
' And now archbishop Theodore, as Mr. Smith relates, [b] minding to
' redress the wrong which he had formerly committed against Vilfrid
' (the said archbishop, being in his advanced age troubled with fre-
' quent sickness) invited Vilfrid & Erconuold his bishops to come to him
' at London, where, confessing his fault, he was reconciled to Vilfrid,
' whom he also intreated to succeed him in the archbishopbric, but
' Vilfrid would not be prevailed on to accept of that see, without
' the decree of a greater council. Theodore moreover wrote to K. Alch-
' frid (who succeeded Ecgfrid) adjuring him, to be heartily friends with
' Vilfrid. [What Vilfrid had done to disoblige his old friend K. Alchfrid I find not; but as Ecgfrid & his queen Ermenburga set almost
every body else against him, it is very probable it was either one or
both of them who brought even Alchfrid himself at last to be one of
the number] 'He wrote likewise to Elbfleda abbess of Whitby & Ethel-
' red king of the Mercians [who also were greatly exasperated against
' him] to be reconciled to Vilfrid. Whereupon Ethelred restored to
' him many monasteries & districts in his territory. [Of these it is like
the priory of S. Leonard by Stanford, together with the province &
monastery of Oundle in Northamptonshire (of which last hereafter [c])
were part.] 'And in 686. King Alchfrid, according to the archbishops
' precept, invited him worshipfully to him, & first (John bishop of Hex-
' ham either being deposed, or freely resigning) gave him that bishop-
' bric & monastery, with the appurtenances belonging to it, in the
' parts of Hexham.   The same year, says Bede,[d] Cedwall king of the
' West Saxons took the isle of Wight, hitherto wholly given up to
' idolatry; who proposing to put all the natives to the sword & plant
' people of his own province there, vowed (tho' himself as they say
' was not yet baptised) if he should take it, to give a fourth part of
' all the island, & of the spoil to God.   Which he so made good,
' that he would needs offer it to bishop Vilfrid (who then happened
' to be in his country) for Gods service.   The measure of the island,
' according to English computation, is sufficient to maintain twelve
' hundred families, out of which the bishop had lands given him suf-
' ficient to serve for three hundred.   But he commended his share to
' one of his clerc's named Bernuin (who was his own sisters son) giv-
' ing him a priest named Hiddil to administer the word & baptism
' of life to all who would be saved.

XLI. In 687. K. Alchfrid, as Mr. Smith writes[e], restored to Vil-
' frid his proper episcopal See in York city, & the monastery of Rip-
' pon, with their revenues; expelling, as Heddius sets down, those

a Sub eo anno.   d p. 261.
b Seriei Vilf. p. 754.   e Seriei Vilf. p. 754.
c Anno 709. infra.

                    L   ' other

' other bifhops [who had ufurped his province] or more truly Cud-
' berct of Lindisfarne, John of Hexham, & Bofa of York refigning for
' peace-fake: Bede witnefling, that Cudberct, being fo admonifhed by
' a divine oracle, returned this very year to Farne ifland. ' Cuthbert
dying the fame year in Farne ifland, the fee of Lindisfarne remained
a year without a bifhop of its own, ' and, as the fame Bede tells us, [a]
' the venerable prelate Vilfrid held the government of that church for
' a year, 'till Eadberct was elected & confecrated in the ftead of Cud-
' berct. Vilfrid being thus reftored to his proper fee, as Mr. Smith
' obferves, [b] remained neverthelefs but five years in the dignity of his

Anno
691.

' eftate. For, in 691. the exciters of the former differences again fet
' the king againft the bifhop, fo that at laft a great quarrel breaking
' out, the holy man of God being expelled by the king, withdrew
' from the territory of the Northumbers. The firft occafion of the
' difference was, that the king would needs take away the revenues
' from the monaftery of Rippon, defigning to erect a bifhops fee there.
' And this diffenfion took its rife, according to Heddius, from an old
' original; to wit, becaufe King Ecgfrid long before, or rather archbi-
' fhop Theodore at his inftigation, had made Eadhed bifhop of that
' church. Another matter about which they jarred was, that Vil-
' frid would not confent to the decrees of the archbifhop; not thofe
' promulged towards the beginning & end of his government, but
' thofe which fprung, in the middle part of the time which he prefid-
' ed, out of the faid difcord between them. Neverthelefs the enemies
' of this prelate were not ignorant that Theodore was afterwards much
' troubled in his own mind for what he had done. However by the
' kings authority, & that the thing might not feem to be done with-
' out fome color of reafon, Vilfrid was expelled under a pretext of a
' decree of the late archbifhop Theodore. Upon this he ftraightway
' fled to his moft faithful friend Ethelred king of the Mercians, who
' received him with great honor; in whofe kingdom this banifhed pre-
' late governed the fee of Lichfield then vacant by the death of Sexu-
' ulph. ' Here inftead of Lichfield Mr. Carte, who follows Mr. Wharton, fays [c] ' Vilfrid had then the diocefe of Leicefter committed to
' him. ' And this account I believe is trueft. I know indeed bifhop
' Nicholfon, fpeaking of Lichfield, fays, [d] in the perufal of the hifto-
' ry of this diocefe, one great miftake (which has been unanimoufly
' fwallowed by all our church hiftorians) is to be obferved to our reader.
' And that is, we are told, that (upon the fubdivifion of Mercia into
' three diocefes, about 740) there was a bifhop placed at Leicefter.
' We do indeed meet with one Totta, who is faid to have been *epif-*
' *copus Legecestrie*, about that time; but *Legercestria* is the old name
' of Leicefter, as *Legecester* is of Chefter. It was therefore in truth

a p. 179.   liæ p. 3. vide etiam Angliæ facræ I. p. 424.
b Seriei Vil. quo fupra.   d Hift. Library, Fol. edit. p. 131.
c In Tabularum fuarum de epifcopis Ang-

' at

' at Weſt-Cheſter that the new diocefe was erected, & not at Leiceſter:
' which is too near to Lichfield were there no other argument againſt
' it.' Now tho' biſhop Nicholſon thus cautions his readers againſt falling into the fame miſtake with Mr. Wharton, he is I doubt under a
miſtake himſelf. I allow with his lordſhip that Legerceſtre was the
old name of Leiceſter, & Legeceſtre the old name of Cheſter. But
for all that there wants only one letter, to wit an [r] (which might eaſily
be dropped by a careleſs tranſcriber, or omitted by an ignorant one
who knew not the difference between Legerceſtre & Legeceſtre.
This was a fault even of H. Hunt & Matt. of Weſtm. themſelves. For
if you turn to the notes under Paragraphs the XIII. and XIV. of the III.
Book of theſe collections, you will there find a remarkable inſtance
where they both do ſo : nor indeed was it their fault alone, but common to almoſt all our monkiſh writers) to make not only Vilfrid &
Totta, but likewiſe Cuthwin, as they all truly were, biſhops of Leiceſter. Alſo that there was once a biſhopbric there, that preſent diſtinct juriſdiction of the biſhops fee at Leiceſter, is moreover a good
argument. But what proves there was an epiſcopal feat there, is, that
the paſſages told of Cuthwin, Vilfrid, & Totta, ſuit not ſo well (as any
one upon due conſideration of them will ſoon perceive) with Cheſter
as Leiceſter. But to go on with Mr. Smith.ᵃ ' This year alſo
' Oftfor biſhop of Worceſter, was confecrated by Vilfrid, for that
' Theodore the archbiſhop being dead, there was, as yet, no other me-
' tropolitan appointed.

XLII. I have before briefly touched how Vilfrid converted the Frie-
ſlanders, upon his being as it ſeemed accidentally, but more truly as
it afterwards appeared providentially, driven amongſt them.   There he
left ſeveral monks to carry on the work of the goſpel.   And in 692.   Anno
' thoſe brethren, as Bede relates, ᵇ elected Suidberct one of their own   692.
' number, a perſon of a modeſt carriage & gentle diſpoſition, to be
' ordained their biſhop, whom, being ſent into Britain, the moſt reve-
' rend biſhop Vilfrid confecrated at their requeſt ; himſelf now reſiding
' among the Mercians in baniſhment : there being yet alſo no new arch-
' biſhop in the room of Theodore.' From 692. to 703. (when Vilfrid continued yet in exile) I find no particular account of him, ſave
that in 695. the body of the famous queen Edilthryda (ſometime ab- Anno
beſs of Ely) being taken up, ſixteen years after her burial, by Sexburga   695.
her ſiſter & ſucceſſor as abbeſs of that place, Vilfrid was one of thoſe
who atteſted the miracle of its being found uncorrupt. ' A certain ſign,
' as Bede would perſuade,ᶜ that in her life time ſhe kept herſelf un-
' corrupt & never knew man. '   But in my opinion, a more certain
ſign that ſhe was well embalmed.   Our Leiceſterſhire antiquary tells
us,ᵈ ' that in 1608. his ſelf was preſent at the opening of the marquiſs of

a p. 754. ut ſupra.   c p. 162.
b p. 193, 194.   d Burton, p. 51, 52.

' Dorſet

' Dorfet [Thomas Greys] cofin, whofe body having lyen in the vault
' of Aftley in Warwickfhire by the fpace of 78 years, was at the cut-
' ting open of the cerecloth viewed perfect, & found nothing corrupt-
' ed, the flefh of the body nothing perifhed or hardned, but in color,
' proportion, & foftnefs alike to any ordinary corps newly interr'd.'
And yet this man was no virgin, but the father of feveral children.
However queen Edilthryda was afterwards canonized, & known by the
name of S. Audry[a].

Anno
703.

XLIII. As for Vilfrid, fays my author[b], ' after he had now a long
' time exercifed his office of a bifhop up and down Mercia, in 703.
' at the defire of king Alchfrid, Berctuald the archbifhop called a ge-
' neral council of the bifhops of all Britain to meet at Neftrefield
' five miles north of Rippon, at which council Vilfrid was ordered
' to appear, & affurance given him, that if he could prove he was
' really injured, he fhould have all imaginable reparation made for the
' wrong that he complained was done him. Well: He came, but met
' with none of the juftice they promifed him. For fome bifhops, in-
' dulging the kings humor, began prefently to exafperate Vilfrid with
' falfe calumnies, & to provoke him with all the contradictions they
' were able. And when they could not prove what they objected
' with any fhew of reafon, they at laft added to their objections,
' that he would not fubmit a tittle to the decrees of archbifhop Theo-
' dore. To whom anfwering, I did fubmit, faid he, to thofe decrees
' of Theodore which he promulged in peace & with a canonical au-
' thority, & will in every particular obey them. Neverthelefs pray
' tell me how it is, that for two & twenty years ye can be difobedi-
' ent to the letters fent from the apoftolic fee, & fo vehemently ac-
' cufe me becaufe I dont receive thofe inftitutions of Theodore which
' he did not compofe by a canonical authority, but, as you your felves
' very well know, by the dictates of difcord? ——Vilfrid then did not
' reckon they did him fuch an injury by dividing his bifhopbric into
' more fees, as that thofe prelates, to wit, Bofa & John, fhould ex-
' ercife the epifcopal function, who according to Theodores decree in-
' deed, but againft Vilfrids confent (he being then unjuftly banifht)
' were promoted to that high honor. For the Roman bifhops decreed,
' that that diocefe, being fo large & wide, fhould be parted into more
' fees; but that neverthelefs was not to be done by meer archiepifco-
' pal authority, but a council folemnly affembled, they being firft de-
' pofed, who in Vilfrids abfence, were, contrary to the canons, ordain-
' ed bifhops. This council therefore oppofed it felf to the apoftolic
' fee, not for that it would part the diocefe of York, but would it
' felf confirm it to thofe bifhops, who held it by a violent & unjuft
' intrufion. Mean time a great many high words without any reafon in
' them being retorted among them with a noife confufed enough, a
' young man, belonging to the court & well known to Vilfrid, thruft

a Smith ad imum p. 163. Bedæ fuæ.   b Seriei Vilf. p. 755. & fequentibus.

4

himfelf

‘ himſelf into the croud, & coming up to him acquainted him with
‘ the meaning of the councils being in ſuch a tumult. They deſign
‘ nothing, ſaid he, but to couſen you, by getting you firſt of all to ſet
‘ your own hand to ſtand to their judgments, whatever they decree:
‘ ſo that when you are once tied down by that band of confinement,
‘ you may never be able to alter any thing afterwards; for as much as
‘ the reſult of their decree will be this. That you forfeit all that you
‘ at any time held in lands, biſhopbric, monaſteries, or any other qua-
‘ lity, in the kingdom of the Northumbers; & if you have procured
‘ any thing in Mercia under K. Ethelred, that you be forced to relin-
‘ quiſh all that, by ſurrendring the whole to the archbiſhop, to be
‘ collated by him on whom he pleaſes. And laſtly, that, by your
‘ own ſubſcription, you be degraded from the honor of a biſhop.
‘ Underſtanding all this, when the biſhops urged him to ſubſcribe,
‘ Vilfrid ſtoutly & conſtantly refuſed to do ſo. But whom they could
‘ not trick by cunning, they preſently attempted to oppreſs by force.
‘ Wherefore they paſſed ſentence, that he ſhould be diveſted of all that
‘ he had, & not hold ſo much as the ſmalleſt portion of any one lit-
‘ tle houſe or monaſtery, either in the kingdom of the Northumbers
‘ or of the Mercians. Nevertheleſs when this reſolution was divulged,
‘ his very enemies were ſeized with horror at the ſame, ſaying, it was
‘ an impious thing, that a perſon every way honorable, ſhould, with-
‘ out any certain crime being fixed on him, be ſtripped of all that he
‘ had. Whereupon the king & the archbiſhop, being deſired by ſome
‘ about them, granted him the monaſtery which he had erected at
‘ Rippon, but on this condition, that he ſhould there quietly ſit down,
‘ & without the kings licenſe never go out of the bounds of that houſe,
‘ or any longer adminiſter the office of a biſhop, but that of himſelf
‘ he ſhould renounce his rank of honor, & confirm it with the teſti-
‘ mony of his own ſubſcription. But the ſynod now demanding of
‘ him to give up his right, he acted like a moſt reſolute prelate. For
‘ he would not, with one word ſpoil the labors of many years, &
‘ condemn the doctrine & rites, which, by his teaching, the province
‘ had received. Wherefore, proteſting his innocence, he again appealed
‘ to the Roman pontif. Whereat, the king & archbiſhop being highly
‘ incenſed, ſaid, now ſure we ſee he is guilty, & let him be condemn’d,
‘ ſince he would rather be judged by them than us. The king alſo,
‘ by the violence of his army, would have forced him to ſubmit to
‘ the decree, if he could have got the archbiſhops conſent for ſo do-
‘ ing. After theſe things & this diſcourſe paſſed, Vilfrid returned to
‘ K. Ethelred & related to him the whole affair; who, ſurpriſed at ſo
‘ great an injuſtice & violence, heartily condol’d with him for the injury that was done him, & promiſed he would himſelf keep for
‘ him what monaſteries he had in Mercia, in the ſame condition they
‘ were then in; ’till he ſhould ſend either particular meſſengers or let-
‘ ters with him to Rome, to underſtand what he ſhould do in theſe

M

‘ weighty

' weighty affairs.   But the enemies of Vilfrid, who had ufurped his
' right, pronounced that he & all they who took part with him, were
' excommunicate ; & fo ftifly rejected all communion with him, that
' if any abbat or prieft of his, invited by any faithful of the common-
' alty, did but blefs the food which was fet before him with the fign
' of the crofs ; they ordered it to be thrown out of doors, as if it had
' been offer'd to idols ; commanding likewife Gods veffels, which
' Vilfrids companions eat out of, to be wafhed, as if they had been
' polluted, before any body elfe fhould make ufe of them.

Anno   XLIV. ' About the end of the year 703. our bifhop got to Rome.
704.   ' Thither alfo were reached meffengers from Berctuald the archbifhop
' with his letters of accufation, humbly requefting audience to be given
' them from that moft glorious fee, concerning the meffage whereon
' they were employed.   But when pope John the VI. with his bifhops
' affembled from all parts were come to the place where fynods were
' then wont to be held, Vilfrid firft prefented a fchedule of his petition
' to the fynod, praying, that the pontif would vouchfafe to requeft
' Ethelred K. of the Mercians (by the fame inftance of authority where-
' with his predeceffors Agatho, Benedict, & Sergius required it before)
' that no man might prefume, thro' envy or wicked covetoufnefs,
' to invade or take from him thofe monafteries with their appurtenan-
' ces, which were given him by K. Ethelred himfelf, his brother Vul-
' fere, or any other perfons whatfoever, for the redemption of their
' fouls.   Likewife that he would intreat K. Alchfrid to fulfil all thofe
' things which his own predeceffor Agatho had decreed.   But if this
' fhould perchance feem hard to the king, that the bifhopbric of the
' city of York, with the monafteries which he held & were very many,
' might be beftowed at the popes pleafure on whom he fhould think
' would beft govern them ; & that only two monafteries, Rippon &
' Hexham with all their lands & poffeffions, be reftored to him.   Pope
' John, when he heard thefe things, thought neceffary to examine
' what his predeceffors had decreed in this affair.

    XLV. ' What helped to acquit Vilfrid at this time, as Bede him-
' felf tells us[a], was a reading of the acts of the fynod of pope Aga-
' tho, held when Vilfrid was the fecond time at Rome, & fitting in
' council among the bifhops there.   For when, (as the caufe required)
' the acts of that fynod were on fome certain days read before the
' nobles & a multitude of others at the popes command, they came
' at laft to the place where it was wrote, ' Vilfrid, beloved of God,
' bifhop of the city of York, appealing to the apoftolic fee about his
' own bufinefs, & by authority of the fame concerning matters cer-
' tain and uncertain abfolved, & fet in the feat of judgment, with CXXV.
' other bifhops affembled in fynod, profeffed, & with his fubfcription
' confirm'd the true & catholic faith, for all the north part or iflands

a p. 207.

1

' of Britain & Ireland, which are inhabited by the nations of the Eng-
' lifh & Britons, together with the Picts & Scots.' As above *anno* 680.
' Which when it was read, a great furprife feifed the audience, & the
' reader ftopping fhort, they began to enquire of one another, who
' that bifhop Vilfrid was. Then Boniface a counfellor of the popes
' and a many others, who had feen him there in pope Agatho's time,
' faid, that he was the bifhop, who being lately accufed by his coun-
' trymen, was again come thither to be judged by the apoftolic fee;
' who being accufed before, faid they, & repairing hither (the caufe &
' controverfie of both parties being prefently after heard & adjudged)
' was pronounced by pope Agatho to have been driven from his bi-
' fhopbric contrary to right, & had in fo great efteem by him, that
' he would needs command him to take his place in a council of
' bifhops which he affembled, as a perfon of an uncorrupt faith
' & an upright life. Which being heard, they all, together with the
' pontif himfelf, faid, a man of fo great authority, who had been a
' bifhop near forty years, ought by no means to be condemn'd, but
' being abfolv'd entirely from the crimes whereof he was accufed,
' fhould be return'd home with honor.

XLVI. ' Afterwards one day, fays Mr. Smith[a], the fynod being
' affembled, they commanded Vilfrids party & his accufers, who came
' from the archbifhop to appear. Whereupon his accufers firft faid, that
' bifhop Vilfrid contumacioufly oppofing the canons of Berctuald arch-
' bifhop of Canterbury & all Britain, (altho' thofe canons were de-
' creed before a fynod) refufed to fubmit to the fame. To the fub-
' ftance of which accufation Vilfrid thus replied. I humbly & ear-
' neftly befeech your moft excellent Holinefs, that, condefcending to
' fo mean a perfon as I am, you will be pleafed to hear the truth of
' this matter from me. For I was fitting in council with my own
' abbats, priefts, & deacons [a paffage by the way worth noting, as it
fhews that bifhops formerly called their diocefan fynods, as, (under the
king) the archbifhop fometimes now does his provincial council] ' when
' they fent to me one of the bifhops there affembled to ask me in the
' kings name, as alfo in the archbifhops, if I would fubmit to the fole de-
' termination of the archbifhop himfelf, & was ready to comply with
' every particular he had decreed in his own private judgment, or not? To
' this I anfwer'd the bifhop who asked me, it were fitting we fhould firft
' know what the fentence of his judgment is, before we can declare
' whether we are ready or no to fubmit to it. He then affirmed, he
' did not know what it was himfelf; nor would the archbifhop, he
' faid, by revealing it to any of us after any other manner, be wil-
' ling to make known the full of his refolution, without we firft, in
' open council, with our own hands would freely fubfcribe, that re-
' folving to obey his fole judgment in all things, and no ways declin-

a in loco ult. citato.

' ing

‘ ing it, we will not depart a jot therefrom.   I said, I never before
‘ now heard that a fubfcription fo ftrict & full of confinement as this,
‘ was infifted upon by any man whatever : that being bound as ftrong-
‘ ly as by an oath, he fhould promife to perform the decrees made,
‘ tho’ requiring impoffibilities ; & all this before he might know what
‘ they contain’d.   Neverthelefs I replied there, before the affembly, that
‘ in all things wherein the archbifhops judgment appeared agreeable
‘ to the decrees of the holy fathers, and to prefidents & canonical
‘ difinitions, & in no wife differing from the fynod of S. Agatho &
‘ the reft of his orthodox fucceffors, we fhall be found heartily ready
‘ to fubmit to it.

XLVII. ‘ This tractable anfwer, having produced in the Romans a
‘ joyful applaufe, his accufers were ordered to return home, the bifhops
‘ faying, that tho’ it was provided by the canons, that every accufer,
‘ who was found faulty in the firft article of his charge fhould be heard
‘ no farther, they neverthelefs, out of reverence for archbifhop Berc-
‘ tuald, would not be wanting, but difcufs every thing in order tho-
‘ roughly.   Whereupon it came to pafs, that within four months af-
‘ ter there being held feventy little councils, folely, or chiefly, upon
‘ this account ; they had all an end as glorious for Vilfrid, as igno-
‘ minious for his accufers.   In 704. therefore the pope wrote to
‘ the kings Ethelred & Alchfrid, and to the archbifhop Berctuald, to
‘ reftore him to his fee.   The bull which he fent to thofe kings, ran
‘ thus.   To the moft eminent lords, Ethelred K. of the Mercians, &
‘ Alchfrid K. of the provinces of Deira & Bernicia, John the Pope :
‘ We rejoice at the acceffions, thro’ Gods working grace, of your
‘ excellent religion ; difcerning the fervor of the faith in you,
‘ which, the lord enlightening your fouls, you received by the
‘ preaching of the prince of the apoftles & now effectually retain,
‘ that a yet better acceffion may fulfil our joy.   But the inex-
‘ tricable diffenfion of fome hath afflicted our foul, & made fad the
‘ ears of our fellow priefts & the whole church, which alfo, with
‘ the Lords affiftance, it behoves us to bring to correction, that
‘ not being defpifers of the pontifical decrees, but obedient fons,
‘ ye may together be approved keepers of the pontifical decrees before
‘ the lord, the judge of all men.   For long ago, when, under our
‘ predeceffor pope Agatho of apoftolic memory, bifhop Vilfrid, com-
‘ ing hither, appealed to the apoftolic fee ; his adverfaries, who then
‘ came hither, from Theodore of venerable memory archbifhop of the
‘ church of Canterbury, & from the abbefs Hilda of religious memory,
‘ to accufe him being prefent ; the bifhops from divers provinces being
‘ with the bovenamed faid holy pope here likewife affembled, regular-
‘ ly enquired into the allegations of both parties, & fententially de-
‘ creed between them : which fame fentence his fucceffors, the holy
‘ popes our predeceffors, thought good to follow.   Neither was the
‘ prelate Theodore of venerable memory (who was fent from this

‘ apoftolic

' apoftolic fee) ever known afterwards to contradict what was done,
' or fend any farther accufation, to this apoftolic fee; but rather, as
' hath appeared, both from what he declared, & by the pontific decrees,
' fubmitted to that fentence. It were therefore, with Gods affiftance,
' to be prevented, that no diffenfion be upheld in one place, whilft
' every where elfe there is a perfect unanimity both of fellow-priefts
' & people. So much we have thought good to premife concerning
' affairs paft. Touching prefent matters alfo we have judg'd proper
' to make known to your excellent chriftianity, that thofe who have
' come hither from the faid ifle of Britain & brought accufations againft
' bifhop Vilfrid, he afterwards arriving here with his brethren, they
' have retorted upon his accufers, the very things which they accufed
' him of; whofe differences we have for fome days procured to be
' heard before a convention of bifhops & priefts, who happened to
' be at prefent here; before whom all the particulars whatever, which
' the parties have either in former or frefh writings brought in charge,
' or they could here find, or was verbally alledged by them, being
' carefully difcuffed, have been brought to our cognition; 'till they
' the principal perfons, among whom the contention hath arifen, fhall
' meet together, who, to put an end to all difputes, ought to affem-
' ble & fit in council. And therefore we admonifh Berctuald, pre-
' late of the holy church of Canterbury, our moft reverend brother,
' (whom, by authority of the prince of the apoftles, we have confirm-
' ed archbifhop there) to call a fynod, together with bifhop Vilfrid;
' & a council being regularly celebrated, that he caufe the bifhops,
' Bofa & John, to come into the fynod; & that he hear what both
' parties have to fay; & confider what they are, among themfelves,
' willing to agree to; And if fo be, that, by his management, he fhall
' be able to determine this regularly at the fynod, he does a grateful
' thing to us & the parties. But, if it otherwife fall out, let him fy-
' nodically admonifh them, that upon his admonitions each party may
' confider what things will be moft convenient for themfelves; & then
' let them come together to this apoftolic fee, that what hath not hi-
' therto been determined, may be debated & decided in a fuller coun-
' cil; & fo they who come in difcord, may, by the grace of the holy
' fpirit, return in peace. Likewife let every one of them who fhall
' refufe, or, what is to be execrated, defpife to come, know, that he
' ought to fubmit himfelf to a dejection, & be thrown hence, & not
' received there by any of the prelates or faithful. For he, who hath
' lived difobedient to Chrift his author, cannot be received among his
' minifters & difciples. Moreover let your chriftian & royal fublimi-
' ty, for the fear of God & reverence & peace of the chriftian faith,
' which the Lord Jefus Chrift gave to his difciples, caufe a fpeedy
' meeting & concurrence in this affair; that thefe things, of which,
' by Gods infpiration, we have a thorough infight, may take effect.
' That for your religious endeavours of this fort there may be laid up

N   ' for

' for you a reward in heaven, & that Chrift being your protector, ye
' may in this world reign fafely & at length enjoy the bleffed fociety
' of his eternal kingdom.   Wherefore, my moft dear fons, remember
' what the moft bleffed Agatho & the reft of the prelates of the Roman
' church after him, together with us, in one voice, by apoftolic au-
' thority, have ordained in this fame affair.   For be who he will who
' with audacious rafhnefs fhall defpife what we have done, he fhall not
' go unpunifhed by God, or being debarred from heaven efcape with-
' out lofs.   The moft high grace keep fafe your eminence.

XLVIII. ' ᵃ Having tarried divers months at Rome, & defeated all
' his adverfaries, Vilfrid being now minded to ftay at the apoftolic fee
' & end his days there, the pope & Roman fynod commanded him to
' return home.   Wherefore being enriched with many reliques of the
' faints, coming back for Britain, when he got into the parts of France, ᵇ
' he was taken with a fudden illnefs, &, that increafing upon him, fo
' hard put to it, that he could not bear to ride on horfeback, but
' was carried in a bed by the hands of his fervants.   Being thus
' brought into Meaulx a city of France, he lay, for four days & nights,
' like one dead, fhewing that he was alive only by his breath which
' was but juft perceiveable.   When he had continued thus, without
' either eating or drinking, fpeaking or hearing any thing, the fpace
' of four days ; at laft when the fifth day began to dawn, rifing as if
' he had waked out of a found fleep, he fat down again, & opening
' his eyes, beheld the choirs of his brethren finging & weeping round
' about him.   Whereupon beginning to breathe fomewhat more free-
' ly, he afked where Acca the prieft was ? Who, being immediately
' called, came in, & feeing him much better, & now able to fpeak ;
' falling on his knees, gave thanks to God, with all the brethren there
' prefent.   Afterwards when they had fat down a while, & tremb-
' ling began to fpeak of the divine judgments ; the prelate order-
' ed the reft to leave the room for an hour, & then began to dif-
' courfe thus to the prieft Acca.   There but now appeared to me a
' tremendous vifion, which I would have you hear & wrap up in fi-
' lence, 'till I know how God pleafes to difpofe of me.   For there ftood
' by me a certain goodly perfon in white raiment, faying, that he was
' Michael the archangel : and for this, faid he, am I fent, that I may
' call you back from death ; for the Lord hath granted you your life,
' thro' the prayers & tears of your difciples & brethren, & the intercef-
' fion of his mother the ever bleffed virgin Mary.   Wherefore I fay to
' you, as you will now prefently recover of this infirmity, be fure you be
' ready, for after four years I will revifit you.   Mean while arriving
' at your own country, you fhall recover the greateft part of your pof-
' feffions which have been taken away from you, & end your life in
' perfect peace.   The bifhop therefore recovered, & they all rejoycing

a Seriei Vilfridianæ, p. 757, 758.   b Bedæ p. 207, 208.

' & giving

' & giving thanks to God, he set forward on his journey & came to
' Britain.

XLIX. ' There, ᵃ the letters which he had received from the Roman
' pontif being read in a convention of nobles, Berctuald the archbi-
' shop, & Ethelred late king of the Mercians (now an abbat) very wil-
' lingly favoured them.   Which Ethelred sending for K. Cenred
' (whom he had appointed to reign after himself) to come to him ;
' exhorted him always to respect Vilfrid heartily & to become to him
' an unwearied champion against all his adversaries : who promised he
' would.   But Alchfrid would not submit to the apostolic injunction.
' However not long after he was seized with so grievous a disease,
' that he in a manner lost the use of all his limbs, & finding him-
' self about to die, confessed his sin against Vilfrid, & then said in the hear-
' ing of the abbesses Elfleda & Edilburga & divers other witnesses, if
' Vilfrid could have come soon enough to me on my sending for him,
' I would immediately have made amends for my offence.   For I had
' vowed to God & S. Peter, if I had got well of this infirmity, to
' observe all things according to the holy Vilfrids mind, & the judg-
' ment of the apostolic see.   But, as it pleases God, I shall die; I
' require, in the name of God, whoever succeeds me, to make peace
' & agreement with bishop Vilfrid, for the peace of mine & his own
' soul.   The king died in 705. & after him Eaduulf reigned a short   Anno
' space.   To whom our prelate, repairing out of banishment, sent   705.
' messengers as to a friend, whom he austerely answered, I swear by
' my life if he does not depart my kingdom in six days time, as many
' of his companions as I find, shall be put to death.   But he, after
' these barbarous words, was expelled the kingdom, which he held but
' two months ; & Osred, a royal youth, son of king Alchfrid succeed-
' ed him.   In the first year of whose reign Berctuald assembled Osred,
' with his princes & three bishops (to wit, Bosa of York, John of Hex-
' ham, & Eadfrid of Lindisfarne) at a place where he held a synod on
' the river Nid, & laid before them the decrees of the Roman coun-
' cil ; which those three bishops opposing, said, how can any one
' pretend to alter what our predecessors archbishop Theodore & king
' Ecgfrid formerly thought good ; & what the archbishop & almost
' all the bishops of all Britain, together with us, at Estrefield after-
' wards judged meet ? However the issue of this council was at last,
' that all the bishops with the king & his nobles should make peace
' with Vilfrid by restoring him the two monasteries of Hexham &
' Rippon.

L. ' In 707. as Vilfrid was travelling from Hexham, he was taken   Anno
' with a malady like that he was formerly troubled with at Meaulx ;   707.
' but recovering his health again, a year & an half after this, & not   Anno
' long before the time of his death, being at Rippon with two ab-   708.

ᵃ Seriei Vilf. p. 759.

3   ' bats

‘ bats & other brethren in number eight, he ordered him who had the
‘ keys to open his treasury, & commanded him to divide his wealth
‘ into four shares; one part whereof he gave, for the good of his
‘ soul, to the churches of S. Mary & S. Paul at Rome; another to the
‘ poor; a third to the heads of the two often-mentioned monasteries
‘ of Hexham & Rippon, to be divided between them; & a fourth to
‘ them who underwent tedious exiles along with him: In the last place
‘ he made Tadberct abbat of Rippon. After these things relinquish-
‘ ing the kingdom of the Northumbers, he withdrew into Mercia to
‘ K. Celred.’ The reasons why Vilfrid retired into Mercia were the
great friendships which he received from good king Cenred, & his
desire to be near his successor K. Celred, who he no doubt hoped
would as much favor him. Besides which it is probable he fancied
the mild air & amoenitie of these southern parts, would be more a-
greeable to his old age (he being now almost seventy six years old, five
& forty whereof he was a bishop) than the cold bleak winds of the
north. When therefore he had almost finished the four last years of
his life (which, if he did not dream so, S. Michael foretold him
should be his last) we find him retiring, & at last ᵃ ‘April the 24th.

Anno 709. ‘ A. D. 709 dying at a little monastery in this neighbourhood, ᵇ some
‘ say his own, ᶜ others borrowed of Cuduald abbat of Medeshamstede, ᵈ
‘ at Oundle that is by Stanford.’ My author here speaks of Oundle
as an obscure place, & directs his reader to look for it by Stanford as
a town of more eminence & note. As I rode thro’ Oundle in April
1723. I saw there a very antient chappel, now converted to a barn
or workhouse, which I am persuaded by the great antiquity of its structure (and seeing I read of no other house of religion there) belonged heretofore to that very monastery, wherein Vilfrid, our founder died.
Had Mr. Bridges lived, who spared for no expence to illustrate the antiquities of Northamptonshire, no doubt he would have obliged us
both with a draught, & a full account of that place. Soon after Vilfrids decease, ᵉ ‘ his body was set on a bier, ᶠ & carried by the assistance
‘ of the brethren [of Oundle monastery, aided no question by them of
‘ Stanford] to his own first monastery at Rippon in Yorkshire, ᵍ where
‘ it was buried in the church of the blessed apostle S. Peter, ʰ on the

a Seriei sæpedictæ p. 759.
b Bedæ Hist. Eccl. p. 208.
c Petroburgenses, inquit Cl. Smithus,
aiunt hoc monasterium [Undalense] semper
ad se pertinuisse, nec fuisse unquam Vilfridi
monasterium, sed Hæddius, & ex eo Beda aliter. Galeus conjicit primo fuisse Vilfridi,
postea ad Petroburgenses spectasse. Ex nota
ad imum paginæ 204. Bedæ Hist. eccl.
    d Defunctus est in monasterio suo apud
Undalum quod est juxta Stanford. Ex chron.
ecclesiæ Ebor. authore Thoma Stubbs. Here
Stubbs calls Oundle Vilfrids monastery,
‘ which, saith bishop Patrick, as appears by

‘ all our [Peterborough] records was only
‘ part of the possession of the monastery of
‘ Medeshamstede. So Hugo Candidus, com-
‘ monly called Swapham, *in hujus abbatis*
‘ [i. e. Cudbaldi] tempore S. Vilfridus epis-
‘ copus in possessione ipsius monasterii ad
‘ Undalum, transivit ad dominum? Supple-
‘ ment to Mr. Gunton, p. 239, 240.
    e Bedæ, p. 204.
    f ejusdem p. 208.
    g idem p. 204.
    h id. p. 208.

‘ south

' fouth fide of the high altar, [i] with all the honor befitting fo great a
' prelate, [h] & this epitaph wrote upon his tomb.

> *Vilfridus hic magnus requiefcit corpore preful,*
> *Hanc domino qui aulam, ductus pietatis amore,*
> *Fecit, & eximio facravit nomine Petri*
> *(Cui claves celi Chriftus dedit arbiter orbis)*
> *Atq; auro ac Tyrio devotus veftiit oftro.*
> *Quin etiam fublime crucis radiante metallo*
> *Hic pofuit tropheum, nec non & quatuor auro*
> *Scribi evangelii precepit in ordine libros;*
> *Ac thecam e rutilo his condignam condidit auro.*
> *Pafchalis qui etiam folemnia tempora curfus*
> *Catholici ad juftum correxit dogma canonis,*
> *Quem ftatuere patres, dubioq; errore remoto,*
> *Certa fue genti oftendit moderamina ritus :*
> *Inq; locis iftis monachorum examina crebra*
> *Colligit, ac monitis cavit que regula patrum*
> *Sedulus inftituit : multifq; domiq; forifq;*
> *Jactatus nimium per tempora longa periclis,*
> *Quindecies ternos poftquam egit epifcopus annos,*
> *Tranfiit, & gaudens celeftia regna petivit :*
> *Dona, Jefu, ut grex paftoris calle fequatur.*

Which epitaph, containing a good epitome of his life, as near as I
can render it, may be thus tranflated.

> *Here the great prelate Vilfrids body refts,*
> *Who, mov'd with love of piety, for God*
> *This temple made, & confecrated it*
> *To Peters princely name (on whom the worlds*
> *Great ruler, Chrift, conferr'd the keys of heaven)*
> *With gold & purple vefts of Tyrian dye*
> *Enriching it devout : as pious where*
> *He fixt the fublime trophy of the crofs*
> *With jewels radiant, & the gofpels four*
> *With golden letters fhining in four books*
> *Commanded to be wrote, & for them fram'd*
> *A goodly fhrine compos'd of glittring gold.*
> *The folemn courfes of the pafcal feaft*
> *He made correct, as will'd the juft decree*
> *Of Canon catholic, fix'd by the fathers,*
> *And, doubtful error fet apart, declar'd*
> *The rites true guidance to his countrymen.*
> *Here of religious monks he numbers great*
> *Affembled, & all orders, which the rule*
> *Of fathers fet, induftroufly obey'd.*

a id. p. 204.   b id. p. 208.

O

Thus when he had for three times fifteen years
A bishop liv'd, at home, abroad, long time
With many dangers sadly tost, he died,
And joying reach'd the heavenly kingdom : Grant,
O Christ, his flock may tread their pastors steps.

LI. Nevertheless tho' Vilfrid was, as hath been related, thus solemnly buried & entombed at Rippon, yet his body did not rest there much above two centuries,ᵃ 'for in the time of Odo archbishop of 'Canterbury it was translated to Canterbury, & placed in the high 'altar, which was dedicated to the honor of our Lord. After which 'the church of Canterbury being burnt, Lanfranc took up the re- 'liques of S. Vilfrid, & placed them in a shrine. But when several 'years after the monks had a mind that they should be put into a more 'fixed place, there was a sepulchre made for them on the north side 'of the altar, & they were, as Eadmerus witnesses, reverently inclosed 'therein on the 12th day of October' [what year my author saith not.] Matthew of Westminster,ᵇ says, Vilfrid died the twelfth day of October at Oundle. But Mr. Smith, as I have observed, puts down the 24th of April for the day of the death of that prelate ; a difference I know not how to reconcile, unless we should say that Matthew of Westminster by mistake sets down the day whereon he was last buried at Canterbury, for the day whereon he died at Rippon. Be that as it will, certain it is that the festival of this S. Vilfrid, called Vilfrid the elder bishop of York, is now celebrated in the Roman church, on the twelfth day of October.ᶜ

a Seriei p. 759, 760.   b p. 129.   c Kalend. Roman.

The end of the second book.

Academia tertia Anglicana;

OR, THE

ANTIQUARIAN ANNALS

of the TOWN of

STANFORD

IN

Lincoln, Rutland, *and* Northampton *Shires.*

BOOK III.

From the death of bishop Vilfrid, *anno* 709. to the coming in
of William the conqueror, *anno* 1066.

I. FROM the death of bishop Vilfrid, in 709. to the devastations of the Danes in 870 (being no less than one hundred
and sixty one years) there is a casm, or gap, in these antiquities, which, after much reading & reflection bestowed in searching and
thinking on a supply for it, I am not yet able to fill up with any
thing very satisfactory: And conjectures I am at best not very fond of. I
shall pass over this dark space therefore, & proceed directly to speak of the
Danes. ‘ Now[a], of five great plagues or scourges wherewith they re-
‘ member this island to have been afflicted (that is to say, the Romans;
‘ Picts and Scots; Saxons; Danes; and Normans) this of the Danes is
‘ judged to have been beyond all comparison the most miserable[b]. For
‘ when they once arrived where they hoped to speed, their manner
‘ was to fortifie some place; or, if they could, surprise some town or
‘ city for their rendezvous [as you will hereafter find they did Stanford]
‘ and, when they had devoured it, & all that was about it; they made
‘ excursions wheresoe’er new hopes invited them, ’till all being wast with-
‘ in the reach of their inroads, they quitted that place, and made a new &
‘ unexpected seisure of another; divers bands of them at the same time
‘ using in several places the same, or such like course of rapine that some of
‘ them did in others. Nor was the wealth and plenty only of the land thus
‘ made a prey unto them, but the people themselves without regard of sex
‘ or condition, their cities, towns, and houses, went all to sword, to fire,
‘ & to ruin.

a Life of Alfrid, p. 3.　　　　b id. p. 11.

B　　　　　　　II. How

II. How thefe barbarians came firft into England, or what havoc they made in other parts, is not my bufinefs to relate; but Ingulf being very particular in his account of their cruelties in this neighbourhood in 870. and finding moft of it tranflated to my hand by the learned Mr. Hearne[a]. I fhall here tranfcribe it, with the addition of what he omitted, not doubting but my reader will be highly pleafed with fo full & curious a narration of fo diftant an affair. ‘ Winter being end-
‘ ed, fays Ingulf[b], the Danes took fhipping & went into Lindiffe in
‘ Lincolnfhire, and landing at Humberftan, fpoiled all that country.
‘ At which time the famous & antient monaftery of Bardney was de-
‘ ftroyed; the monks being all maffacred in the church without mer-
‘ cy. And when they had ftayed there all fummer, wafting the coun-
‘ try with fire and fword, about Michaelmas they came into Kefteven
‘ in the fame county, where they committed the like murders and de-
‘ folations. At length in September 870. count Algar & two knights
‘ his fenefchals call’d Wibert & Leofric (from whofe names the people
‘ thereabouts have fince given appellations to the villages where they
‘ lived, calling them Wiberton & Leofrington) drew together all the
‘ youth of Holland, with a brave body of two hundred men belong-
‘ ing to Croyland abby, who were led by one Toly, a famous foldier
‘ among the Mercians before his converfion, but now a converted
‘ monk of the fame monaftery. Thefe, taking with them about three
‘ hundred more ftout & warlike men from Deping, Langtoft, & Ba-
‘ fton; to whom alfo joyned Morchar lord of Brunne, with his ftrong
‘ & numerous family; & being met by the fheriff of Lincoln named
‘ Ofgot, a valiant and antient foldier, with the Lincolnfhire forces in
‘ number five hundred more; muftered together in Kefteven on S. Mau-
‘ rices day, gave the pagans battel, & by Gods affiftance vanquifhed
‘ them, with the flaughter of three of their kings and a great number
‘ of common foldiers; the chriftians purfuing the barbarians to their
‘ very camp, where finding a very ftout refiftance, night at laft parted
‘ them, and the earl drew back his army. But it feems the fame
‘ night there returned to the Danifh camp all the reft of the princes of
‘ that nation, who, dividing the country among them, had marched
‘ out to plunder. Their names were Godrum, Baffeg, Ofketel, Half-
‘ den, and Hamond; and as many earls, to wit Frena, Unguar, Ubba,
‘ and both the Sidroc’s, with great forces, a multitude of captives, and
‘ a great deal of fpoil. Their return being known, the greateft part
‘ of the Chriftians, ftroke with terror, fled away by night; whilft thofe
‘ that were left with the forefaid earl and his captains (being fcarce
‘ two hundred out of eight) early in the morning, after hearing divine
‘ fervice and receiving the Sacrament, being refolved to die for Chrift,
‘ & in defence of their country, marched into the field againft their
‘ enemies: but the earl perceiving his forces to be too much weaken-

---

a Notes upon the fame Life, p. 35, &c.   b p. 20, &c.

I   ‘ ed,

' ed, appointed brother Toly with his five hundred men to fight in
' the right wing, becaufe they were the ftrongeft; affigning him like-
' wife a very ftout fecond, the brave Morchar, with thofe that follow-
' ed him.   As for the renowned Sherif of Lincolnfhire Ofgot with
' his five hundred men, he fet him in the left wing; giving him alfo
' a moft valiant fecond, to wit the ftout knight Harding of Rihale,
' with all the Stanfordians, becaufe they were all brave fellows & fit
' for fharp fervice, refolving himfelf with his fenefchals to keep the
' main body, as being moft convenient for affifting either wing if there
' were occafion.   The Danes being now exafperated at the flaughter, of
' their men, having buried their three kings early in the morning at a
' place then called Launden, but afterwards from this burial Trekingham;
' four of their kings and eight counts marched out, whilft two kings and
' four counts guarded the camp and captives.   But the Chriftians, becaufe
' of the fmallnefs of their number, drawing themfelves up in one body,
' made with their fhields a ftrong teftudo againft the force of their enemies
' arrows, and kept off the horfe with their pikes.   And thus, being well
' ordered by their commanders, they kept the ground all day.   But night
' coming on, notwithftanding 'till then they had remained unbroken, and
' had withftood the force of their enemies arrows; whofe horfes, being
' tired, began to flag; yet they very imprudently left an entire victory to
' the pagans.   For the pagans, feigning a flight, began to quit the field.
' Which the Chriftians had no fooner perceived (however their com-
' manders forbad and oppofed it) than they broke their ranks, and
' purfuing the pagans were all difperfed thro' the plain without any
' order or command.   So that the pagans returning, like lions among
' a flock of fheep, made a moft prodigious flaughter among them; whilft
' the ftout Count Algar, and brother Toly with fome of the beft foldiers,
' getting on a rifing ground, and being drawn up into a round body,
' did for a long time endure their infults; 'till at laft the faid valiant
' and ever memorable earl, with his fornam'd fix brave captains feeing
' the ftouteft men of their fmall army flain, got upon the thickeft
' heaps of the Chriftians dead bodies, and being refolved to fell their
' lives as dear as they could, after having received many wounds, died
' honourably in the field, upon the dead bodies of their brethren.
' There now only remain'd a few young men of Sutton and Gedney;
' but thefe, flinging away their arms, fled into a neighbouring wood;
' and, by that means efcaping, came the night following, to the mo-
' naftery of Croyland, where they related the flaughter of the chrifti-
' ans and brother Toly, and the lofs of the whole company, which
' they told at the church door with great lamentation, whilft abbat
' Theodore and his convent were celebrating their matin vigils a. The
' abbat and monks being extremely confounded at this ill news, re-
' folved to keep with them only the elder monks and fome few fmall
' children, thinking perhaps their helplefnefs would provoke the bar-

a matutinas vigilias. Ing.

C   ' barians

' barians to compaſſion; and ſo ſent away all the younger and ſtouter
' men, together with the reliques of the monaſtery (to wit, the re-
' mains of S. Guthlac's body, the whip wherewith he uſed to diſci-
' pline himſelf, and his pſalter; together with other principal jewels
' and muniments of the houſe, that is to ſay, the charters of the foun-
' dation by king Ethelbald, with the confirmations of divers other
' princes and certain donations of king Witlaf) commanding them to
' fly into the neighbouring fenns and marſhes, and there expect the
' iſſue of the war. Who, with heavy hearts ſubmitting to what was
' ordered, having loaded a ſmall veſſel with the foreſaid reliques and
' royal muniments, threw the table of the high altar, covered with
' gold plates and formerly given them by king Witlaf, and ten cha-
' lices, with the lavars for their feet, pots, platters, and other veſſels
' of braſs, into the abby well, which, when they were caſt in, ſtill
' the end of the altar-table, which was very long, do what they could,
' always appeared above water. Whereupon, drawing it out again,
' and ſeeing the blaze of the towns in Keſteven which were ſet on
' fire by the Danes grow by degrees nearer and nearer, & fearing that
' the pagans would ſoon be with them; they left it with the abbat
' and old monks aforeſaid, & ſo going aboard their veſſel fled to the
' wood of Ancaryg, adjoyning to the ſouth ſide of their iſland, where
' they ſtaid with one brother Toret an anchoret and other brethren
' four days, being thirty in number, whereof ten were prieſts, the reſt
' of lower orders. But abbat Theodore taking with him two old per-
' ſons, hid the foreſaid altar table without the church on the north
' ſide, but where to this day could never be known. Afterwards the
' abbat and all the reſt, putting on their ſacred veſtments, and aſſem-
' bling in the choir, celebrated the regular hours of devotion, & then
' went thro' the whole pſalter of David; which done the abbat him-
' ſelf ſaid high maſs, and brother Elfget a deacon, brother Savin a ſub-
' deacon, and brother Egelred and brother Ulric two boys, who car-
' ried the wax-lights, aſſiſted. When maſs was ended, and the abbat
' and his foreſaid attendants had juſt communicated; the pagans break-
' ing into the church, the venerable Theodore, like a true martyr and
' the hoſt of Chriſt, was ſacrificed upon the very altar, by the hands of
' their moſt cruel king Oſketul; and all his aſſiſtants, who ſtood round
' about him had their heads hewed and chopt off by the barbarians; where-
' upon the old folks and children beginning to run out of the choir,
' were apprehended, examined, and put to death with moſt cruel tor-
' ments, to make them diſcover where the treaſures of the church
' were concealed; Sir Aſker the prior being tortured in the veſtry;
' Sir Lethwyn the ſub-prior in the hall, whom brother Turgar, a boy
' of ten years of age, of a moſt beautiful aſpect and perſon, would not
' be parted from, but following of him into the hall, when he ſaw his dear
' old man murdered there, begged heartily to die and be killed with
' him; but was ſaved by Count Sidroc the younger, who took pity

' on

'   on his childhood, ftript him of his habit, put on him a Danifh coat,
'   and ordered him to follow him wherever he went : fo that he on-
'   ly, of all both old and young who were left in the monaftery, efcaped;
'   going in and out among the Danes all the time of their ftay like
'   one of themfelves, by the favor and protection of the forefaid earl.
'   All the monks being thus flain by their barbarous inquifitors, and
'   but little of the wealth belonging to the monaftery yet difcover-
'   ed; they then broke open the tombs of the faints (who were
'   inclofed in large marble chefts fet up a great height round about
'   S. Guthlac's own monument) with axes and hammers. On the right
'   hand fide of which faint, ftood the tomb of S. Ciffa the prieft and
'   anchoret; the tomb of S. Bettelm, who in his life miniftred to S. Guth-
'   lac; and the tomb of lord abbat Siward of pious memory. On the
'   left hand of S. Guthlac ftood the tomb of S. Egbert his counfellor
'   and confeffor; the tomb of S. Tatwin, the guide and pilot of the
'   veffel which brought S. Guthlac to Croyland; the tomb of the moft
'   holy virgin Etheldritha; as alfo the tombs of queen Celfreda, and
'   of Wymund fon of king Witlaf. But finding a far more inconfider-
'   able plunder than they expected, being mad at the difappointment,
'   they bafely threw together all the bodies of the faints on an heap,
'   and fetting fire to it on the third day after their coming, to wit on
'   the feventh of the kalends of September [Aug. 26.] in a moft violent
'   rage burnt it with the church and all the other buildings of the
'   whole monaftery. At length on the fourth day they fet forwards
'   towards Medefhamftede, with innumerable droves of cattel before
'   them; where finding the gates of the monaftery locked, & being en-
'   raged thereat; they began to make an affault upon it with bows,
'   arrows, and other inftruments. And breaking in at the fecond onfet,
'   Tuba, brother of count Hubba, was knocked down with a ftone
'   juft at the very gate, and carried off for dead by his fervants, into his
'   brother Hubba's tent. Whereat Hubba was fo provoked, and efpe-
'   cially againft the monks, that he flew every man of them who had
'   a religious habit on him with his own hands; whilft the reft of them
'   deftroyed the others, 'till at laft they all perifh'd; both the venerable
'   father Hedda the lord abbat, and all his monks, with all their neigh-
'   bours, being flain. At the fame time brother Turgar was admonifh-
'   ed by his mafter Sidroc to keep out of the way, and have a care
'   how he came near count Hubba, for fear he fhould meet with the
'   fame fate. And now having dug up the altars, broke down all the
'   monuments, burnt a noble library of books, tore in pieces a prodi-
'   gious quantity of charters belonging to the monaftery, kicked about
'   the pretious remains of the holy virgins S. Kyneburga, S. Kynefwita,
'   and S. Tibba[a], demolifhed the walls, and fired the church with all

'   the

a Here Ingulf, when he fays they kick'd
about the remains of S. Kyneburga, S. Kynefwita, & S. Tibba; tells a thumping ftory.

For the bones of S. Kyneburga & S. Kynefwita, were buried at Kyneburgceaftre, now
Caftre; and S. Tibba's at Ryhal; at which
places

' the offices belonging to it, it continued burning for fifteen days after.
' When they had stayed here the space of four days, they got together
' all the spoil they could out of the whole country round about, and
' marched towards Huntyngdoun. But in their way thither as the two
' Sidroc's, who always marched last to cover the retreat, brought up
' the rear of their army which had now safely pass'd the river Nene;
' they at length going over themselves, two waggon loads of rich
' moveables happened to be sunk in a deep eddy on the left of the
' *stone* bridge, as also the beasts that drew them, which were drown'd
' before they could be got out. In the getting out whereof whilst
' the younger Sidroc and his men were busied, & putting their plun-
' der into other carriages; brother Turgar slipt away into the next
' wood, and, walking all night, about break of day, he got to Croy-
' land. Where he found his brethren the monks return'd again the
' day before from Ancaryg, & very active in quenching the fire (which
' yet burnt in many places among the ruins of the monastery) as well
' as they could. Whom when they beheld safe and found, they were
' a little comforted; but understanding from him where the abbat and
' the rest of their brethren lay murdered, and how all the monuments
' and tombs of the saints were broken down, and their holy books
' burnt with their bodies, they were all stroke with an inexpressible
' concern and grief, & for a long time made sad lamentations. At
' length when they had wept their fill, they return'd to put out the
' fire; and casting out the ruins of the church roof, just by the high
' altar they found the body of their venerable father abbat Theodore,
' with the head cut off, stript of all his cloaths, and half burnt; squeez-
' ed also by the fall of the rafters and mashed to the ground, eight
' days after his murder, lying, among the wood which had been quench'd
' from any farther burning, a little way off from the place where he
' was killed; with all the rest of his attendants, who fell with him,
' except Ulric the taper bearer, likewise close crushed to the floor
' with the weight of the rubbish fallen in upon them. However they
' were not all found at once, but at several times. For the bodies of
' some of the monks were found half a year after the day of their
' martyrdom, in other places than those where they suffer'd. Thus
' Sir Paulin and Sir Herbert, both very old and decrepit persons, who
' had their heads lopt off and were tortured to death in the choir, af-
' ter being strictly sought for there, were at length found in the chap-
' ter-house. And Sir Grimketul and Sir Agamund, who were both
' above an hundred years of age, and were run thro' with swords in
' the cloyster, were found in the parlor. All the rest, both old and

places they all yet lay quiet in their respective
sepulchres. But as they were all, sometime
between the years 1006. and 1013. taken up
by Elfius, and removed to Burg; Ingulf,
who lived in the conquerors time, and knew
they had all of them their respective shrines
then at Burg, thought they were there when

the Danes now plundered Medeshamstede,
& consequently concluded their remains
could then fare no better than he thus by
mistake relates they did. See an account of
these saints being translated to Burg, in this
third book, paragraph the XX.

' young,

' young, after they had been fought for in divers places and at divers
' times, brother Turgar relating the particular circumftances of their
' feveral deaths, only one, the abovementioned Ulric excepted, were
' found with great forrow and many a tear. Sir Briftan, fometime
' chanter of the monaftery, an excellent mufitian and eloquent poet,
' being one of the chief perfons now left, wrote then a threnody or
' lamentation upon the burning of Croyland, which they have in many
' places. Having therefore with great pains cleared the monaftery from
' rubbifh and other filth as well as their time would allow; they now
' began to talk among themfelves about chufing an abbat, and fo pro-
' ceeding to an election, the venerable father Godric, was, tho' much
' againft his own confent, elected by all their fuffrages. To whom af-
' terwards came that venerable antient perfon prior Toret of Ancarig,
' and Sir Tifa his fub-prior, both very holy and devout anchorets, and
' moft humbly intreated, that taking with him fome brethren, he would
' pleafe to make a ftep to Medefhamftede, and, in his charity, com-
' mit the bodies of that abbat and his brethren, which as yet lay un-
' buried and expofed to wild beafts and birds of prey, to chriftian
' burial. The venerable abbat Godric condefcending therefore to their
' requeft, with many brethren (among whom Turgar was one) and be-
' ing met there by all the brethren of Ancarig, went to Mede-
' fhamftede, and with great induftry collecting together all the bodies
' of the monks, being fourfcore and four in number, buried them on
' S. Cecilia's day, in the middle churchyard of that monaftery, over
' againft that part of the church which was once the eaft front, in one
' large vault made on purpofe for this occafion; and fet over the body
' of the abbat, whom he buried in the middle of his monks, a pyra-
' midal ftone, three feet high, as many in length, and one in breadth;
' which had infculped on it, the effigies of the abbat and his monks,
' ftanding round about him[a]. This, in memory of the ruin'd mona-
' ftery, he ordered to be called Medefhamftede; and vifiting it once every
' year as long as he lived, and pitching his tent over the ftone, faid
' mafs for the fouls of them who were there buried, on two days to-
' gether, with great devotion. The kings highway running alfo thro'
' the middle of the churchyard, had the faid ftone on the right hand
' of them who came up from the forefaid ftone bridge towards Croy-
' land, and a ftone crofs with the figure of our Saviour likewife in-
' fculped on it, which the forefaid abbat Godric then fet up on the

---

a The ftone here mentioned is now 1726.
to be feen, but removed (as a monument of
fo great antiquity deferved) out of the churchyard into the church it felf. There is a cut
of it in Mr. Guntons hiftory of that place,
but whoever carefully infpects either that
draught, or the ftone it felf (as I have done)
will foon difcern that the figures on the ftone,
are not, as Ingulf affirms, the effigies of the
abbat and his monks; but more truly (as I
think Mr. Stephens obferves) reprefentations of Chrift and his apoftles. The faid
ftone when in the churchyard, as I remember, ftood a little way off from a garden
wall & paffage, almoft oppofite to the fouth
eaft point of the fouth crofs of the prefent
church, but rather above, tho' not full eaft of
it by a good deal: which fhews the church of
Burg is longer now than it was when it was
firft deftroyed, and alfo that, when it was
afterwards rebuilt, it was fet back and removed more northward.

' left; that all such as passed by, remembering the said holy monastery,
' might offer up their prayers for the souls of the faithful buried in that
' churchyard; &, in reverence of Christ, refrain from committing such
' wickednesses and robberies within the bounds of that monastery for
' the future.

III. When the whole neighbourhood was thus miserably ravaged, and
the town of Stanford had actually sent out a party to resist the invaders,
doubtless, tho' we now find not the particular circumstances of that
tragedy, this place suffered the same sad fortune with those above. But
some will perhaps say, where all this while was [a] ' Burdred the Mercian
' king, he who was thereunto deputed by Ethelwolph the West-Saxon
' monarch as a shield of defence against the raging Danes, that made
' desolations wherever they came! He who in continual employments
' against them spent his time, and that with such noble resolutions
' and manhood, that Ethelwolph held him worthy of his alliance, and
' made him his son-in-law?' I answer. ' Beorrhed, as Ingulf relates [b],
' all that space was engaging the Britons, who disturbed the western
' parts of his kingdom with frequent irruptions; but when he heard
Anno ' what lamentable havoc the Danes had made in the eastern quarters
871. ' of his country, he came to London, and assembling a great army,
' marched into those parts, and seising the whole island of Ely into
' his own hands, marched thence into the country of the Gyrvii.'
' Gyr, says Hugo Candidus [c], signifies a deep pool, or meer; and they
' are called Gyrvii, who live near, or within, any marsh, pool, or fen.'
' There, continues Ingulf [d], he took into his possession all the lands like-
' wise belonging to Medeshamstede monastery, to wit, whatever lying
' between Stanford, Huntyngdoun, and Wysebeck, before then belong-
' ed to that abby.' Part of these lands K. Beorrhed kept himself and
part, such as lay more remote, he gave to his soldiers. Ingulf sets
down besides a particular of many lordships, which he, at the same
time, took away from Croyland, and that monastery could never after
recover. The pretence for his doing so was, I suppose, the better to
enable himself to withstand the Danes, or perhaps to buy a truce of
them. But the true cause, as Ingulf would persuade, was his own sor-
did avarice. Here nevertheless it may be necessary to reflect, how far
Ingulfs private resentment for the hardships his own monastery underwent by the loss of those lands may affect his writing; and again, what
allowance, considering the great necessities of the times, may be indulged a prince, otherwise very just, but at present so embarrassed. For
certain it is, that ' in 874. [e] the Danes drove him beyond sea, af-
' ter he had enjoyed the crown about two and twenty years. Where-
' upon he went to Rome, and stayed there 'till he died. His body was
' buried in our ladies church belonging to the English school [now the

a Speed. p. 256.   d loco quo supra.
b p. 25.   e Chron. Sax. sub anno 874.
c p. 2.

                                                                Jesuits

Jefuits college] ' there. The fame year alfo they committed the go-
' vernment of Mercia to one Ceolwolph, a forry earl or thane of the
' kings, making him fwear, and give hoftages, to furrender it when-
' ever they required him; moreover that he fhould be always ready to
' help them on occafion, and likewife furnifh them with all neceffaries
' for their army.

IV. All the country being thus fallen into the hands, or power,
of the Danes; and the town of Stanford (as I fhall hereafter fhew)
being always reckoned one of the five great cities held by that people,
as fo many places of retreat againft any fudden Excurfions of the Saxons; whatever that place fuffered in the late war for oppofing the Danes,
I think (now it fell into their hands, and was employed for the purpofe I have faid) we may fafely conclude, was, about this time, repaired, and made up again by its new mafters; who, we may prefume,
now built the walls and towers upon them, and, I believe, the caftle
it felf. What fomewhat confirms this, is, that we find there was certainly now, or very foon after, a caftle at Stanford. Likewife Henry
of Huntingdon and the Saxon chronicle, fpeaking of Stanford being
taken from the Danes in 942. fay, it had been then, *diu*, a *long time*,
in their hands; in which *long time*, we may fuppofe, they erected all
thefe fortifications about it, and fo held it for a garrifon. Indeed
Mr. Butcher tells us (tho' when thofe things were done, as to the particular year; or where he learned them, as to his authors, he fays not)
that[a] ' Stanford being ruin'd by the Danes, was reedified by Alured
[or Alfred the great] ' and a bridge of ftone built over the Welland.'
Now that Stanford was actually deftroyed by thofe barbarians, is pretty evident from what hath been already faid. And that the town was
rebuilt, and a bridge erected over the Welland by K. Alfred, if we
had not Mr. Butchers word for it, might be admitted, if we obferve
what a multitude of towns, caftles, cities, and other buildings, after
they had been ruined by the Danes, that prince reftored in other places[b].
But what deftroys all probability of K. Alfreds doing any thing, for
the ornament or defence of Stanford, is that it cannot be proved he
ever recovered thefe parts, much lefs this place, from the Danes. But,
tho' he kept them pretty quiet from making excurfions abroad as they
did formerly, yet, either by force or agreement with him, they held
this place to themfelves all the reft of his time. However Mr. Butcher
finding perhaps fomewhere (tho', for the reafon above, I believe, very
untruly) that K. Alfred erected a bridge at Stanford; becaufe the bridge
we had, when he wrote his book, was of ftone: concluded, I fuppofe,
that K. Alfreds bridge was alfo made of the fame materials. But therein (could we admit that K. Alfred built a bridge here) we muft not
altogether follow him. Ingulf it is true fays, not once, but twice, in
what I have already taken from him, that in 870. there was a ftone

a MS. penes me, p. 3.   b See Spelmans life of Alfred, p. 161, & 163.

I

bridge over the Nene at Medeſhamſtede. But then that bridge, if it had ſtone ſupporters, had only a timber floor, and was not arched with ſtone. For, ſaith Stow [a], ' Matilde, K. Henry the firſts queen, ' built the firſt arched bridge, at Stratford now called Bow, becauſe ' the bridge was arched like unto a bow, a rare piece of worke, for ' before that time the like had never been ſeene in England.' As for any bridge at Stanford, I believe there was none yet built there, nor indeed 'till the Danes were quite expelled thence; for when the Danes kept garriſon at Stanford on the north ſide of the Welland, and the Saxons at the ſame time kept garriſon at Stanford on the ſouth ſide of the Welland (as you will by and by find they did) it is improbable that there was then any bridge there, or if either party attempted to build one, that the other would ſuffer it. Farther to ſhew the miſery of theſe days, I ſhall only add, that the orderly, quiet, ſubject had not only the Danes to diſtreſs him upon every occaſion, ' but [b], ' by example of the Danes, & ſometimes pretending that they were ' Danes, many Engliſh themſelves began entirely to apply themſelves ' to robbery and plunderings.

Anno 901. V. K. Alfred died in 901. and was ſucceeded by his ſon Edward, ſirnamed the elder. ' In 907. [c] the Danes again ravaging Mercia,

Anno 907. ' were gloriouſly vanquiſhed at Welmesford field.' Here Welmesford, as we may learn from Florence of Worceſter [d] and Stow [e]; ſeems to be a miſtake for Wodnesfield, a mile north from Wolverhampton in Staffordſhire.

Anno 911. The Saxon chronicle places this action in 911. but does not name the place. The words of that chronicle, may be thus render'd. ' [f] This year the army of the Danes which dwelt in the kingdom of ' the Northumbers, broke the peace, and deſpiſing the agreement which ' K. Edward and his ſon had made with them, waſted the country of ' the Mercians. Mean time the king being in Kent, got about an ' hundred ſhips together, which ſailed towards the ſouth-eaſt to meet ' him. The pagans fancying the greateſt part of his forces to be on ' board, thought they might ramble where they pleaſed without com-' ing to a battel. But as ſoon as the king heard that they were gone ' out to plunder, he ſent his army both out of the Weſt Saxon parts ' and Mercia, which followed them at the heels whilſt they return'd ' home; then they fought, and were routed, many thouſands of them ' being ſlain.' Let it be fought when or where it would, this, as another rightly obſerves [g], ' ſeems to have been the deciſive battel, ' whereby the Danes [tho' they not long after recruited] were [for the ' preſent] brought under the power of the Saxons.' And at this time I reckon it was that the Danes at Stanford, finding that they could not long keep that place from falling into the ſaid K. Edwards hands, over-

a p. 197.
b See the paſſage from Ingulf as quoted in a collection of curious diſcourſes publiſhed by Mr. Hearne, p. 36.
c Lel. Collect. Vol. I. p. 218.

d in campo Wodnesfield.
e p. 106.
f ſub anno 911.
g Hiſtorical Collections, p. 320.

I   ' threw

threw the caftle there, and retreated to fome other garrifon. For we find that prefently after this victory K. Edward was not wanting to himfelf, but taking the advantage of fo good an opportunity, immediately fet himfelf to rebuild what thefe ravagers had deftroyed, and efpecially fuch caftles, forts, and other places as might be of ufe and fervice to him in fuppreffing their farther inroads and devaftations. In that work, faith Ingulf, [a] ' he was much affifted by his fifter Ethelfleda, ' a moft prudent virago, furpaffing the antient Amazons.

VI. Among other places therefore, ' in 914. [b] fhe rebuilt the caftle Anno
' of Staunford, near the river Welland.' So Matthew of Weftmin-914.
fter. [c] ' In 914. Elfleda, countefs of the Mercians, rebuilt Thameworth. ' Afterwards proceeding to Stanford, fhe rebuilt the caftle on the north-' ern bank of the river Weiloand.' Now that there was a caftle at Stanford before Elfleda's time (altho' this is the firft time I meet with the direct mention of it in any antient authors) is plain from the words of both thofe already quoted here. Both which ufe the fame word *reftauravit*, fignifying, that fhe reftored, rebuilt, or repaired the caftle before erected at Stanford, after, as it fhould feem, it had been firft demolifhed by the Danes. Here neverthelefs I may not conceal that the Saxon chronicle, [d] Florence of Worcefter, [e] and Simeon of Durham [f], fpeaking of a caftle erected about this time by the countefs Elfleda, inftead of faying fhe erected that caftle at Stanford on the north fide of the Welland, read Stafford on the north fide of the Stowe. It may alfo be obferved, that thofe authors above who mention the caftle fhe built at Stanford, fpeak nothing of any caftle fhe erected at Stafford. And fo *vice verfa*. This difference notwithftanding, both parties are I believe in the right : it being my opinion fhe built a caftle at both places. ' The caftle of Stanford, faith Mr. Butch-' er, [g] whilft it ftood, was fituate upon the fide of an hill (as indeed ' all the town ftands upon the rifing of an hill) but the caftle hill ap-' pears fomewhat artificial, being caft up round, and higher than the ' ordinary degree, ftanding well towards the midft of the town, and ' fomewhat fouth-weft : facing the town with a very pleafant profpect.'

VII. The faid countefs of the Mercians had fcarce finifhed this new building at Stanford, and turned her back to do the fame at other places ; when her old adverfaries the Danes came and retook it. And now (having other defigns than what they had before when they overthew it) again made it a garrifon for themfelves, fortifying it more ftrongly than before. The very time when they took it appears not. But that the caftle here was, foon after it was rebuilt by Elfleda, held by them as a fort to retire to upon occafion, appears by her brother king Edward

a p. 28.

b Anno 914. Elfleda reftauravit caftrum de Staunford juxta Weland fluvium. Lel. Collect. Vol. 3. p. 389.

c Anno 914. Elfleda, Merciorum domina, Thameworth reftauravit. Deinde ad Stan-

fordiam progrediens, in aquilonari plaga fluminis Weiloand turrem reftauravit. p. 183.

d Sub anno 913.

e p. 600.

f p. 153.

g MS. penes me, p. 5.

E the

the elders erecting another castle here, on the south side of the river Welland in 922. at what time the Danes, then in actual possession of the castle on the north side of the river, finding their progress into the south stopped by that new castle, were at length forced to yield it up; and so, their fortress being surrendred, themselves were quickly after driven out of the country. Mr. Moreton, whose natural history of Northamptonshire deserves great commendation (tho' many people, who have not understanding enough to judge of it, pretend to run it down) describes K. Edwards progress hither, together with some remarks on a defeat which he gave the Danes on the south side of Burghley park, thus. [a] ' As to the battel upon Wittering heath, a
' spacious plain about three miles to the south of Stanford, wherein
' according to a tradition rife in Mr. Cambdens time, and now no less,
' the Danes received a memorable overthrow: we meet with no re-
' mains of it, nor any thing relating to it, except, perhaps, that part
' of an entrenchment in a heathy common, on the south side of Burgh-
' ley park wall. There I was shewn a pretty high bank, with a trench
' about eighty yards in length running down to the Southrope rill,
' which has Wittering heath to the west side of it. That this is real-
' ly part of a military entrenchment, I do not affirm. But it has the
' face of some of our rampires that are assuredly such, and is higher
' considerably than the ordinary partition banks of the rest of the com-
' mon. Add to this what I have from Mr. Gibbon, a Gent. of very
' good credit, that he has seen three or four Saxon coins in Major
' Cambridges collection, that were found nigh this entrenchment in
' some earth wrought up by a mole. Neither have we any better
' light, as to the time of that traditionary engagement between the Saxons
' and Danes. The likeliest conjecture I can offer of the time of the
' battel is, that it was fought by K. Edward the elder, the same year
Anno   ' that he took Stanford. The year before K. Edward was at Colchester;
921.   ' his next expedition, so far as we can learn, was towards Stanford:
' his way thither was by Cambridge. And we find the army of Cam-
' bridge-Danes submitting to him, in the latter end of 921. In
Anno   ' 922, he advances, as we have observed, to Stanford, in order to
922.   ' reduce it. His way thither, 'tis very probable, was over Witter-
' ing heath; for that was the direct road from Colchester and Cam-
' bridge: And there he might meet with opposition from an army
' of Danes. For Stanford, which was their head quarter in that
' part of the country, was not yet surrendred. But that prince,
' wheresoever he went, had success attending him. And having de-
' feated the Danes upon Wittering heath, the memory of which
' overthrow tradition has preserved, he pursued his intended expedi-
' tion against the Danish garrison at Stanford, who yielded them-
' selves without great difficulty.'

a Northamptonshire, p. 544, 545

VIII. But

VIII. But let us hear what our old writers fay about thefe matters. ' In 922. between proceffion week & midfummer faith the Saxon ' chronicle,[a] K. Edward went with his army to Stanford, & com- ' manded a fort to be built on the fouth fide of the river. Upon ' this all the people who belonged to the city on the north fide of ' the water, yielded themfelves to him and chofe him for their prince.' Again. 'In 941. faith Marianus Scotus as quoted by Leland[b] [who, ' by the way, miftakes the year] after rogation-tide Edward the elder ' with his army went to Stanford, and built a ftout fort on the fouth ' fide of the river Welund; and forced not only the Danes who held ' the caftle on the northern bank, but likewife all who belonged to it, ' to furrender to him.' Florence of Worcefter, who (as I think Mr. Hearne fomewhere obferves) is little elfe than a bare copier of Maria- nus, hath almoft the fame words. ' In 941. faith he[c] [but he fhould ' alfo fay, as the Saxon chronicle does, 922.] the moft victorious K. ' Edward the elder, after the rogation feafon, went with his army to ' Stanford, and built a ftout fort on the fouth fide of the river We- ' lund; and compelled not only the Danes who kept the caftle on ' the north fide of the fame river, but likewife all them who belong- ' ed to it, to a furrendry.'

IX. Upon thefe paffages, before I proceed, a few remarks. Firft then, it may be obferved the Saxon chronicle does not fay the town on the north fide of the river, but what feems to imply yet fomething more, all the people who belonged to the city on the north fide of the water, yielded themfelves to him, and chofe him for their prince. Marianus and Florentius are ftill more particular, mentioning both the garrifon or Danes who kept the caftle, and likewife other people who belonged to it. Who thofe other people were fhall be enquired here- after. At prefent it may fuffice to obferve, that, by what may be ga- thered from the concurrent teftimonies of thefe authors, K. Edward made not only the Danes who kept the caftle, but alfo the whole town and country which belonged to it, fubmit to his arms and acknowledge him for their fovereign. Secondly. None of thefe au- thors it may be noted, tho' they all three mention a caftle or fort which K. Edward built on the fouth fide of the Welland, make ufe of the name Stanford-Baron, to diftinguifh the town on that fide the water, from the town of Stanford on the other fide. Yet Mr. Cambden fays,[d] ' when Edward the elder fortifyed the fouthern banks of the river

---

a Inter ambervalia & mediam æftatem, ivit Eadweardus rex cum exercitu ad Stan- fordam, et juffit extrui munitionem in au- ftrali parte fluminis. Omnis item populus qui ad feptentrionalem urbem pertinebant ei fefe dederunt, & petebant eum ipfis in dominum. Sub anno 922.

b Anno 941. poft rogationes cum exerci- tu Stanfordiam profectus eft Edwardus fe- nior, firmamq; in auftrali parte amnis We- lund arcem munivit; & non folum Danos,

qui in feptentrionali plaga arcem tenebant, fed & omnes qui ad illam pertinebant, in de- ditione accepit. Collect. Vol. 3. p. 284.

c Anno 941. Rex Eadwardus invictiffimus fenior, poft rogationes, Stanfordam profec- tus eft, firmamque in auftrali plaga amnis Welund arcem munivit; & non folum Danos qui in feptentrionali plaga ejus amnis arcem tenebant, fed & omnes qui ad illam pertinebant, in deditionem accepit. p. 601.

d In Coritan.

' to

' to hinder the Danish inroads from the north, as Marianus informs
' us, he built also on the south bank (which is now called Stanford-
' Baron) a very strong castle.' Here any body who hath not seen Marianus's words, would almost be led to think Mr. Cambden met with
the name of Stanford-Baron in that author: But we find he did not.
That name being indeed abundantly more modern than the age we
are now writing of. The first time I meet with it is the 34. H. 6.
under which year see more of it. Thirdly. By the word *munivit*, made
use of by Marianus and Florentius in the passages above quoted, some
may perhaps think that strictly speaking those authors do not mean
that K. Edward did now at first erect, but only fortifie or garrison a
fort or castle there standing before. But what at once silences this
fancy, are the words of the Saxon chronicle, as inserted immediately
before those of Marianus and Florentius.

X. Mr. Butcher, speaking of this last castle, and the situation thereof, writes thus[a]. ' Mr. Cambden makes mention of a castle in Stan-
' ford-Baron —— but the very ruins thereof are come to ruin.
' Only the book of Peterborough [what book he says not] relates,
' that Eleanor, wife of K. Edward the first, in the place where the said
' castle stood, erected an house of nuns, and endowed the same with
' fair possessions: which being dissolved amongst many others in the
' time of Henry the eight, the same came in the days of queen Eli-
' sabeth into the possession of William lord Burghley, and at this day
' is turned into a farm, and part of the inheritance of his posterity
' in the house of Exeter.' Now this account of Mr. Butchers is a mixture of truth and falshood. As to queen Eleanors nunnery at Stanford,
see *anno* 1290. 19. E. 1. below. The nunnery whose situation Mr. Butcher
here describes, and the site whereof belongs to the earl of Exeter; was
founded by William Waterville abbat of Burg, in 1156. However
I certainly believe the castle of Stanford on the south side the river,
while it stood, was built somewhere within those very walls where
William Waterville afterwards founded his said nunnery. In building whereof it is probable he made use of the ruins of this castle for
part of his materials. Certain it is this castel is never spoken of as
standing, by any author who wrote after, or indeed a good while before his foundation of that nunnery. What became of the said castle
I shall hereafter offer some conjecture of. As for the area thereof, Mr.
Cambden sought it in vain[b]. ' But, Mr. Moreton says[c], the ground-
' plot of this fortress or castle is still visible on the west side of Stan-
' ford-Baron, or the southern city, a little above the 'spital: tho' it
' seems it escaped Mr. Cambden when he sought it.' Thus Mr. Moreton fancies he has found it: But he errs. For what he takes for the
foundations of a castle, are indeed the vestigia of the 'spital it self,
called, as you will hereafter find, sometimes S. Leonards, sometimes

a MS. penes me, p. 5.   c Northamp. p. 544.
b Nusquam tamen hodie apparet. ubi supra.

S. Giles hofpital, fometimes the houfe of lepers, and fometimes the Hermitage. Befides, the place Mr. Moreton makes choice of for his fortrefs to ftand upon, is fo much out of the way, that it would there have had little, or no, influence upon the river, and lefs upon the caftle on the other fide of the water; the very purpofes for which it is faid to have been erected. Whereas fet it where the nunnery ftood, it will then ftand upon the edge of Ermingftreet, on the very brink of the Stony-ford whence Stanford takes its prefent name, where the water is fhalloweft, and where the Danes would therefore moft probably attempt a paffage into the fouth, and confequently where the moft care was required to ftop them from fo doing. Add to all this, this fituation is much nearer to the caftle on the north, than that which Mr. Moreton affigns, and of courfe better placed to watch and curb any fudden attempt or invafion from thence; being an eminent fpot, and fronting, tho' not directly, yet well towards the other. Nor is, I think, the very area it felf undifcernable. For at the north-weft point of the nuns inclofure, we fee a round bank artificially caft up, with a deep well in the middle of it; which I take, by the circular foundations yet vifible, to have been no part of the nunnery (tho' afterwards inclofed within its walls) but the remains of this caftle. Return we now to the founder of it, K. Edward the elder. ' Thus he ' went on[a], fettling England, fecuring the habitations of the natives, ' and left his fortifications in fuch opportune places, that his conquefts ' were in no danger of a relapfe; but efpecially it was his care, that ' if a town ftood on the north fide of a river, he would clap another ' over againft it on the fouth fide, that he might be every where able ' to put a ftop to the excurfions of the enemy.' And this we find he did at Stanford.

XI. ' But whilft K. Edward tarried at Stanford, faith the Saxon chro- ' nicle[b], his fifter Ethelfleda departed this life at Tameweorthige.' So Florence of Worcefter[c]. ' Whilft thefe things were doing his fifter ' Egelfleda, countefs of the Mercians, a lady of remarkable juftice, pru- ' dence, and moft renowned valor, died the 19. of the Kalends of ' July [June 13.] in the eighth year of her government of the Mer- ' cians.' Her rebuilding Stanford caftle, with the many other celebrated actions of this extraordinary lady, have prevailed with me, before I pafs on, to add here a fhort account of her. ' At her riper ' years, fays Leland[d], fhe married Ethelred, the equally learned and ' powerful earl of the Mercians; by whom fhe had only one daughter, ' in bearing whereof fhe underwent fuch vehement pains and travel, that ' fhe ever after refufed the marriage bed.' So Fabian[e]. ' Of her it is ' tolde, that when fhe had ones affayed the woe and forow that wo-

a Hiftor. collections, p. 321.
b Sub anno 922.
c p. 601.

d Comment. p. 157.
e Chron. part 1. p. 225. a.

F   ' men

' men feele and fuffer in bearinge of a childe, fhe hated the embra-
' finge of her husbande ever after, and tooke witnefs of God, and
' fayde, that it was not convenient or femeli to a kinges doughter to
' ufe fuch flefhlie likinge, whereof fuch forow fhould enfue.' Or as
Sir Richard Baker has it[a], ' that it was a foolifh pleafure which brought
' with it fo exceffive pains.' As for what relates to the greatnefs of
' her mind, faith Leland[b], it was fo prodigious, that it will fooner
' merit our admiration than belief. For whilft her brother was king,
' fhe, as well as that prince, had always a numerous army in the field,
' affifted by whofe valor fhe often routed the Danes, erected new towns,
' and fortifyed them with walls and ditches.' ' For feven years together,
' fays Huntingdon[c], fhe every year built a town or two.' ' We cannot
' therefore[d], pafs over how much in that age England was indebted
' to a Woman.' No body I know of has ever yet reckoned up the
towns fhe built. Some indeed have mentioned one, fome another,
and fome more; whilft of any fingle writer the author of the Saxon
chronicle, I think, obferves the moft: tho' not all. For once then,
tho' I don't pretend to mention all my felf, I will here fet down as
many as the notes I have at prefent collected fpeak of. And firft.
' In 912. as the Saxon chronicle fays[e], fhe built the caftle of Scer-
' geate.' I know not where it is; but this, I fuppofe, is what the author of the chronicle of Mailrofs fpeaks of, when he fays[f], fhe built
Scoriate. II. The fame year, as the Saxon chronicle adds[g], ' fhe built
' another caftle at Bricge [Bridgnorth.] III. ' In 913. as the fame
' chronicle adds[h], fhe built Tamaweorthige [Tamworth] caftle.' This
Matthew of Weftminfter fays[i], was in 914. IV. The fame year, 913.
fays the Saxon chronicle[k], fhe built Stafford caftle. This Florence of
Worcefter fays[l], was in 914. V. In 914. fhe built the caftle on the
north fide of the Welland at Stanford. VI. The fame year fhe built
another, as the Saxon chronicle relates[m], at Eadesbyrig [Edisbury in
Chefhire[n].] VII. And another at Werenwic[o] [Warwick.] VIII. And
in 915. another at Cyricbyrig[p] [Chirbury.] IX. And another at We-
ardbyrig[q]; [Wedsborow in Staffordfhire.] X. And another at Rum-
cof[r] [Runckhorne in Chefhire.] XI. In 916. fays the fame Saxon
chronicle[s], fhe took Brecenanmere [Brecnock.] Marianus, as quoted
by Cambden[f], fays fhe took it in 913. XII. In 918. as the Saxon
chronicle adds[t], fhe took Deoraby [Derby.] XIII. And in 920. fhe
took Legraceafter[u], [Leicefter.] XIV. Cambden fays[x], fhe alfo repair-

a Chron. p. 9.
b ubi fupra.
c Lib. 5.
d Hift. coll. p. 225.
e p. 103.
f p. 146.
g p. 103.
h p. 103.
i p. 183.
k p. 104.
l p. 600.

m p. 105.
n notes on Camb. Brit. in Chefhire.
o p. 104.
p ib. 12.
q ib.
r ib.
f p. 590. bifhop Gibfons 1ft. edition.
t p. 196.
u ib.
x p. 558.

ed Chefter.   XV. And built Finburrow[a].   XVI. Fabian likewife affirms[b], fhe built Shrowsbury.   XVII. And a bridge over the Severn
called Brimsbiri bridge[c].   Laftly, ' She and her husband, as Leland tells
' us[d], founded the priory of Ofwald (it ftood north, north-weft, from
' Gloucefter abby, upon Severn ripe) inftituting prebendaries in it;
' and thither tranflated the body of S. Ofwald K. of Northumberland,
' & there richly entombed it.'   To conclude.   This lady, as the fame
' Leland obferves[e], to her immortal honor, is thus celebrated by the
' fprightly mufe of Huntendune.

> *O Elfleda potens ! O terror virgo virorum !*
> > *Victrix nature, nomine digna viri !*
> *Te quoq; fplendidior fecit natura puellam,*
> > *Te probitas fecit nomen habere viri.*
> *Te mutare decet, fed folum nomina, fexus;*
> > *Tu regina potens, rexque trophea parens.*
> *Jam nec Cefarei tantum meruere triumphi;*
> > *Cefare fplendidior, virgo, virago, vale !*

Which I thus tranflate.

> *O potent Elfleda ! Maid mens terror !*
> *You, who did conquer natures felf, worthy*
> *The name of man ! more beauteous nature form'd*
> *A woman : but your valor fhall fecure*
> *Mans higher name.   For name you only need,*
> *Not fex, to change ; unconquerable queen,*
> *King rather, who fuch trophies have obtain'd !*
> *O virgin, and virago both, farewel !*
> *No Cæfar yet fuch triumphs hath deferv'd*
> *As you, than any, all the Cæfars more renown'd !*

XII. King Edward the elder died in 924. and was fucceeded by his fon
Athelftan.   ' John Stow in his chronicle reports, faith our old antiquary
' Mr. Butcher[f], that in the time of K. Athelftan there was a mint for
' coyning of mony in Stanford-Baron.   So that no doubt, continues
' Mr. Butcher, the limits of the jurifdiction and liberties of Stanford,
' have been beyond what they are now.'   Stows own words are thefe[g].
' He made feven coining mints at Canterburie, foure for the kinge,
' two for the archbyfhop, and one for the abbat.   At Rochefter three,
' two for the king, and one for the bifhop.   Befides thefe, in London, eight;
' in Winchefter, fix; in Lewes, two; in Haftinges, two; in Chichefter,
' one; in Hampton, two; in Warham, two; in Excefter, two; in
' Shaftsburie, two; and in every good towne, one coiner.'   Here Stow we
fee does not particularly mention either Stanford or Stanford-Baron.
But that there was a mint in Stanford on the fouth fide of the river,

a p. 560.
b p. 224.
c ib.
d Itin. vol. 4. p. 63.

e Comment. p. 158.
f MS. penes me, p. 9.
g p. 107.

if not now, yet in K. Edgars time, is certain. But then the being of such a coinage there, is not to be taken as any mark of the kings favor to the place, or an inftance that the jurifdiction of Stanford on the north fide of the river was then larger, as Mr. Butcher would furmife; but more truly as a royalty granted to the abbat of Medefhamftede then lord of Stanford beyond the bridge.

Anno
939.

XIII. In 939. died K. Athelftan, ' to whom, as Simeon of Durham ' relates[a], his brother [or, as others affirm, fon] Edmund fucceeded in ' the kingdom. In which year Onlaf [the Dane] firft came to York, ' then marching fouth befieged Hampton : But not prevailing there he ' led his army to Tamworth, where he wafted all the country ; and, ' as he return'd to Leicefter, K. Edmund and his army met him. There ' was no matter of a fight, for the two archbifhops Odo and Wulftan, ' reconciled the two kings. The peace was fo made, that Watling- ' ftreet fhould be the boundary of each kingdom. Edmunds part lay ' on the fouth fide, and Onlafs on the north.' To underftand this divifion note Watlingftreet ran acrofs the kingdom from Dover to Cardigan ; obferving which courfe, you will perceive, by looking up- on any map of England, that the town of Stanford, and a good deal of this neighbourhood yet more towards the fouth, were part of the territory by this agreement affigned to Onlaf. Which obfervation remembred, will much help to fhew why this, or that, Danifh or Saxon, king (as hereafter, in the courfe of this hiftory to the conqueft of the whole kingdom by Cnute the Dane, fhall be particularly related) ei- ther fpared, or plundered, this place. Immediately after this divifion of the kingdom between Onlaf and K. Edmund, Stanford and all the country round about it, which had, as I have fhewn, been taken from the Danes by K. Edward the elder, in purfuance of this new contract, was again furrendred to them. We find indeed no particular relation of any fuch matter in any of our old hiftorians, but what proves it is, that the very firft time they mention it afterwards is in 942. when, they all agree, it was again taken from the Danes, by Edmund the now king of the Saxons. All the country north of Watlingftreet being thus furrendred to Onlaf, my opinion is, that prince immediately after divided his part or fhare of the kingdom into five great Danifh provinces, and made Lincoln, Leicefter, Nottingham, Derby, and Stanford, the capitals, or chief towns of thofe feveral diftricts. My reafons for this affertion are, Firft, Dane-lage, Mercian-lage, and Weft-Saxon-lage, as we are affur- ed by the learned bifhop Nicholfon, do not fignifie Dane-law, Mer- cian-law, and Weft-Saxon-law, as commonly fuppofed ; but the pro- vince, or precinct, of the Danifh, Mercian, or Weft-Saxon, govern- ment here. But take it in his lordfhips own words[b]. ' By the way, ' I am not fatisfied with the opinion of Cambden, Lambard, Spel- ' man (and generally all our Englifh antiquaries and hiftorians who have

a p. 134.   b Hift. Lib. part 1. p. 113. 8° edition.

I

' treated

' treated of thefe matters) that there were in this kingdom before the
' conqueft, three codes or digefts of laws: which, from the feveral
' countries where they firft prevailed, were rightly named the Weft-
' Saxon, Mercian, and Danifh, laws. This conceit is deriv'd down
' without contradiction or due examination, from the moft early tranf-
' lators of our Saxon records; who took it for granted, that Laga
' (in Weft-Saxena-laga, Myrcena-laga, and Dene-laga) was a word of
' the fame import and fignification with the Norman Ley. Whereas
' in truth Laga or Lage, is properly a country or diftrict; and fo, 'tis
' very evident, it ought to have been tranflated in the laws of Ethel-
' bert, Cnute, and Edward the confeffor; even in thofe very parts of
' them, which have occafioned all thefe miftakes.' Secondly. That there
was, long before the Norman conqueft, fuch a Diftrict as Stanford-fhire,
the book of Bury puts beyond all contradiction: the words of which
book be thefe[a]. ' There are two and thirty fhires in England. In
' thefe two and thirty fhires are ufed three forts of laws; the one cal-
' led Weft-Saxon law; another Danifh law; and a third, Mercian law.
' To Weft-Saxon law belonged, Kent, Suffex, Surrey, Berks, Wilts,
' Southampton, Somerfet, Dorfet, Devon: nine fhires. To Dane law
' belonged, York, Nottingham, Derby, Leicefter, Lincoln, Northamp-
' ton, Bedford, Bucks, Hertford, Effex, Middlefex, Norfolk, Suffolk;
' Cambridge, Stamford: fifteen fhires. To Mercian law belonged,
' Gloucefter, Worcefter, Hereford, Warwic, Oxford, Chefter, Stan-
' ford, [Salop [b],] eight fhires.' Now had not both Stamford and
Stanford fhires been mentioned in this account, the whole would have
been of no authority as to our Stanford; becaufe either of thofe names
would have been thought a miftake of the tranfcriber for Stafford.
Whereas allowing one of them for that county, the other can ftand
for no other but our Stamford, or Stanford-fhire. Selden [c], from
Malmsbury, has the fame number of fhires, diftributed under the fame
divifions; except that, as I muft confefs, inftead of Stamford, he reads
Huntingdon. However this alteration makes not much againft us, becaufe his author Malmsbury, for ought we know to the contrary, might
as well miftake as our author, the book of Bury. Here note likewife,
that tho' the Danifh diftrict is, in the book of Bury, as alfo in Malmf-
bury, faid to contain fifteen fhires, yet that diftrict was not always fo
large; but frequently contracted, or extended, juft as their fortunes in
England were profperous or unlucky. Before this time, I think, they
had no certain bounds, or, if they had, the compafs of them was much
narrower. Thofe fifteen fhires, as may be gathered from any map of Saxon
Britain, are indeed the whole territory which was now affign'd to Onlaf, and what were afterwards always claimed by virtue of this agree-

---

a See the fame, in Mr. Thyns difcourfe upon the antiquities of fhires, as publifhed by Mr. Hearne in his collection of curious dif-courfes, p. 40.

b Salop, omitted by an overfight of Mr. Thyne, or Mr. Hearn, is here fupplied from Selden.

c Notes on polyolbion, p. 194.

ment as their right by his fucceffors; tho' they could not always get,
or when they had got, maintain poffeffion of them.   But whenever
they did fo hold them, thofe fifteen Saxon fhires were comprehended
firft in the five forefaid great provinces of the Danes, and afterwards
in their feven diftricts hereafter mentioned.   Thirdly, Stafford being in
the Mercian lage, or diftrict, could not be one of thefe five great cities
of the Danes; but Stamford or Stanford was, & is therefore rightly fet
down under Dane-lage.   Fourthly, Lincoln, Leicefter, Nottingham,
Derby, and Stanford, immediately after, but never before this agreement between Onlaf and Edmund, are in all writers by way of eminence, called, the five cities; and their inhabitants Fifburgingi, and
Fifburgenfes.   Which appellations thofe places and their inhabitants retain'd as long as the Danes kept any footing in England. Laftly, all the divifions we find the Danes ever parted England, or their
fhare of it, into, were three.   Firft, that of the five cities above fpoken
of.   Secondly, that of the feven Cities, when they added York and
Chefter to the other five.   And thirdly, that of Cnute, when he fplit
the whole kingdom into four provinces, under four deputies of his
own : of which laft hereafter.   From the premifes it appears, that the
five provinces Onlaf now divided his kingdom into were very large,
every one of them taking in two, three, or more counties, if we confider England as divided into fhires by the Saxons.   Moreover that
all, or at leaft the beft part of, the fhires mentioned in any authors
under Dane law, or the Danifh diftrict, as they fhould rather fay, were
now comprehended in the territories of thefe five cities : Thofe being only Saxon accounts relating how many of their fhires made up
the five provinces of the Danifh Kingdom.   Likewife that what we
here call Danifh jurifdictions or diftricts, the Saxons, in their way of
fpeaking, called fhires.   For inftance, what the Danes called the jurifdiction, diftrict, or province of Stanford, the Saxons (who no doubt
often difcourfed among themfelves about this new divifion made by the
Danes, having alfo fhires of their own long before) called Stanford-fhire.
I fhall only add, when K. Edward the elder in 922. took Stanford
from the Danes, it may be remembred that he forced not only the
Danes who kept the caftle on the north fide of the Welland there,
but likewife all the people who belonged to it, to fubmit to his arms,
and acknowledge him for their fovereign.   From which paffage, as
enlightned by what hath been here faid, I think we may gather, that the
Danes had even then made Stanford a fort of a capital or head-town
over all the leffer places lying about it in their hands.   And that the
inhabitants of thofe places and of Stanford were the people who then
fubmitted to K. Edward by a furrendry of the caftel there.

    XIV. Wherever the Danes prevailed, Chriftianity difappear'd; but where-
ever the Saxon arms were victorious, it reviv'd again.   Thus did it
at Stanford in 942. when the Danes (altho' they had fo lately got near
half the kingdom affign'd to themfelves) edging and elbowing for more

Anno
942.

room,

room, were defeated by K. Edmund, who came upon them and over-ran their country; taking from them all their five cities with so much expedition, that all our historians who mention his recovering, speak of his subduing, them, with a *veni, vidi, vici*; all as one action. However as some of them say Lincoln, Leicester, Nottingham, Derby and Stanford, were those five cities; whereas others instead of Stanford read Stafford, but agree in every particular about the rest: I must here beg leave to put down as many of these authors, as my notes afford, in their own words at length; this course I think being the best way to finish the dispute, and make that easie to other enquirers, which at first was the occasion of some doubt and trouble to my self. First then I shall set down the advocates for Stanford. Secondly, those for Stafford (so many I mean of both sides as I have yet had opportunity to examine) And thirdly, sum up the evidence.

XV. First then, for Stanford. First let Florence of Worcester speak. ' In 942. says he,[a] the magnificent Eadmund king of the English, ut-' terly wrested the five cities Lincoln, Snotingham, Deorbei, Leo-' gereceastre, and Stanford out of the Danes hands; and reduced all ' Mercia to his own subjection.' Secondly. 'King Edmund, says ' Henry of Huntingdon,[b] leading his army into that part of Mercia, ' which had been *diu* long before subdued by the pagans, as far as the ' very broad river Humber, overthrew the Danes in battel, and victo-' riously took the five cities, Lincoln, Legeceftre, Stanford, Snoting-' ham, and Derebi. Whereupon he utterly extirpated the Danes ' (who at that time were also called Normans) and removing paganism ' from the cities aforesaid, by the grace of God restored the splendor ' of the faith.' Thirdly. ' K. Eadmund, says the Saxon chronicle,[c] ' lord of the English, protector of his friends, and undertaker of great ' enterprises, invaded Mercia, where the way of the white fountain, ' and the river Humber, a spacious water, bound the country. The ' five cities Ligoraceftre, Lindcylne, Snotingaham, Stanford, and Deo-' raby before this belonged to the Danes, and being forced to be sub-' ject to those [Normans or] northern men, were *diu* long tormented ' under the pagan dominion and bondage, 'till at length the warlike ' heir of Eadweard, to his great honor, set them free.' Fourthly, Ro-' ger Hoveden,[d] hath exactly the same words as Florence of Worcester. ' Fifthly, ' K. Eadmund, says Matthew of Westminster,[e] wresting ' Lincoln, Notingham, Derebi, Legeceftre, and Stanford out of the ' Danes hands, reduced them all, with all Mercia, under his own au-' thority.' Sixthly, ' K. Edmund, saith the abbat of Dundrainand,[f]

a p. 603.
b Edmundus rex ducens exercitum in il-lam partem Merce, que paganis diu subdi-ta fuerat usque ad latissimum flumen Hum-bre, belli forte Dacos vicit, & quinque ur-bes victoriosus cepit, Lincolniam, Legece-striam, & Stanfordiam, & Snotingham & Derebi. Dacos igitur (qui etiam eo tempore Normanni sunt vocati) penitus extirpavit,

& ab urbibus predictis, infidelitate remota, Dei gratia fidei fulgorem restituit. p. 355.
c Sub anno 942.
d p. 423.
e Rex Eadmundus Lincolniam, Noting-ham, Derebi, Legeceftriam & Stanfordiam de manibus Danorum eripiens, cum Mercia tota omnia sub pottestate sua redegit. p. 187.
f p. 148.

' wrested

' wrefted the five cities, Lincoln, Snotingaham, Deorbei, Legaceftre,
' Stanford, quite out of the hands of the Danes.' Seventhly, 'Ed-
' mund the brother of Adelftane, fays Mr. Stow,[a] took out of the
' Danes hands the towns of Lincolne, Nottingham, Darbie, Leicefter,
' and Stanford; and brought all Mercia to his dominion.' Between thefe
who are for Stanford, and thofe who are for Stafford, to keep the
peace I will here clap a neutral, who fpeaks of K. Edmunds reduc-
ing the five cities, but yet, as if he was aware of a difpute, does not
name them. 'Edmund fon of Athelftan, fays he as quoted by Leland,[b]
' reigned fix years and an half. He victoriously took the five cities
' from the Danes, and when he had fubdued them, kept Northum-
' berland in his own fubjection.'

XVI. Now hear thofe who contend for Stafford. And firft let Ranulph Higden fpeak. 'Edmonde, kynge of Englonde, faith his tranfla-
' tor Trevifa,[c] toke and wan out of the Danes hondes that were
' paynyms fyve noble cytees, Lyncolne, Notyngam, Derby, Stafforde,
' and Legecefter. He toke fro' them thofe cytees in that they were
' paynyms, and caufed thofe cytees to be of ryghte byleve.' Secondly, 'As teftifieth Henry archdeacon of Huntingdon, faith Fabian,[d] thys
' Edmunde had ofte warre wyth the Danes, the whiche as he [Hunt]
' affirmeth, held then manie good townes in myddle Englande, as Lin-
' colne, Notingham, Derby, Stafforde, and Laycetour; the whiche by
' his knightly manhoode he wan from them.' This quotation from
' Huntingdon is different from the text of that author as printed by
Sir Henry Savile. There Huntingdon, reads Stanford, not Stafford.
Either therefore Sir Henry altered the word Stafford in his copy for
Stanford; or Fabian met with one where he read Stafford. Thirdly, 'K. Edmond, fays Holingfhed,[e] affembling an army, firft fubdued
' thofe Danes which had got into their poffeffion the cities and towns
' of Lincolne, Lecefter, Derby, Stafford, and Notingham; conftreyn-
' ing them to receyve the chriftian faith, and reduced all the coun-
' tries even unto Humber under his fubjection.' Fourthly, 'Edmund
' the fifth fon of K. Edward, fays Speed,[f] fubdued as he went into the
' north, thofe towns where the Danes kept, and got from them Lin-
' colne, Leicefter, Darby, Stafford, and Nottingham; compelling
' them to receive baptifm and to become his fubjects: fo that the
' country was wholly his unto Humber.' Fifthly. 'After the death of
' Athelftan, fays Sir Richard Baker,[g] his brother Edmund, the fifth
' fon of his father, fucceeded. But no fooner was the crown upon
' his head, but the Danes were upon his back; and in Northum-
' berland made infurrections; whom he not only fuppreffed in that
' part but took from them the towns of Lincoln, Leicefter, Darby,
' Stafford, and Nottingham; compelling them withall to receive

a p. 108.   e Vol. 1. p. 227.
b Collect. I. p. 195.   f P. 399. b.
c Fol. 235. pag. 2. b.   g p. 10. b.
d fol. 242. b.

2

' baptifm,

' baptifm, and to become his fubjects: fo as the country was wholly
' his as far as Humber.' And thefe are all that I have yet met with,
who read Stafford.

XVII. To fum up the matter.   'The Fifburgenfes, faith Mr. Hearne,[a]
' were the inhabitants of Lincoln, Leicefter, Nottingham, Derby, and
' Stanford.' So bifhop Gibfon, [b] 'The Fifburgingi (or Fifburhingan,
' as the Saxons called them) were the Danifh inhabitants of the five
' towns of Leicefter, Lincoln, Nottingham, Stanford, and Derby.
' To thefe were afterwards added the cities of York and Chefter.   And
' then the fame people, and for the like reafon, were called Seofenburgen-
' fes.' Now befides all thofe for Stanford, whofe words have been
recited, many others I doubt not might be produced for the fame opinion, had I their books at hand to confult. But thefe above are, I
think, enow (as they are moft in number, and, which weighs moft,
the oldeft writers) to put the matter now out of difpute. Befides,
Mr. Hearne and my lord of London, tho' they did not perhaps mufter
up the forces on either fide fo very particularly as I have done, yet
no doubt had confidered the cafe, when they pronounced as hath
been faid: And, from the premifes, I think we may agree with them.
I fhall only add, that 'in 946, as bifhop Kennet obferves, [c] to Edmund
' fucceeded his brother Edred, who kept the whole Scene of action
' on the other fide of the Humber.' So that you will hear of the
Danes in thefe parts no more yet a good while.

XVIII. The pagan Danes being driven out of thefe parts, the Saxon
chriftians fet themfelves to reftore what monafteries and churches the
Danes had deftroyed. Particularly in 947. Turketil, K. Edreds lord
chancellor, became a great benefactor to the monks of Croyland, giving them, among other lands, the manor of Writhorp. This Writhorp, as Mr. Leland tells us, [d] was Writhorp in Northamptonfhire by
Staunford.

Anno
947.

XIX. Nor was it very long before Medefhamfted, that other neighbouring monaftery, met with a like generous and great benefactor (another lord chancellor) to reftore it likewife from its ruins. [e]   'For in
' 970. Adelwold, afterwards bifhop of Winchefter, began that work,
' it being then juft an hundred years after it was deftroyed by the Danes.'
Alfo that bifhop, as the Saxon chronicle hath it, [f] 'built a wall about
' that monaftery, and then gave it the name of Burch, it being before
' called Medefhamftede. When Adelwold came thither, as the fame
' author relates, [g] he found there nothing but old walls and defert
' woods. At laft however he light upon the charter which the abbat Head-
' da had formerly wrote (whence it appeared, that K. Vulfere and his
' brother Ethelred built that monaftery) hid in an old wall. Where-

Anno
970.

a Notes on Lelands Collect. p. 866.
b Additions to Cambd. p 865.
c paroch. antiq. p. 43.
d Itin. Vol. 4. p. 128.

e Monaft. Ang. I. 70. a
f p. 120.
g ib.

H   ' upon

' upon he repaired to K. Eadgar, and fhewed him the charter which he
' had found at Medefhamftede. To whom that prince [by a new char-
' ter of his own] replied thus. [a] We Eadger, under the celeftial king,
Anno ' prefident of the kingdom of Great Britain —— [*inter cætera*] do
972. ' grant to the monaftery of Medefhamftede the perpetual privilege of
' a mint in Stanford. [b] We do alfo appoint a particular mercat in
' Burch, to wit, that no other be had between Stanford and Hunten-
' dune. And to that we give, and there command to be paid the
' whole toll without any contradiction; that is to fay, firft from all Witlef-
' mere to the kings [c] Tolbooth which lies at the hundred of Nor-
' mans-crofs [d]; and from Witlefmere as Merelode comes to the river
' Nen; and thence, according to the courfe of the fame water, to
' Walmesforde; and from Walmesforde to Stanforde; and from Stan-
' forde, following the courfe of the [Welland] river to Crulond; and
' from Crulond as far as Muft; and from Muft as far as Kingesdelf;
' and thence as far as the forefaid Witlefmere —— [e] Thefe lands, and
' all other which belong to [Burch] monaftery, I pronounce a fhire,
' to wit [privileged] with fac and foc, tol and team, and infangthef.
' And thefe rights, and all other whatfoever [thereunto belonging] I
' call the fhire of Chrift and S. Peter [f]. This privilege I Edgar, king
' of all Albion, have confirmed with the fign of the holy ✠.' The
mint at Stanford here granted to the abbat of Burg, was, I fuppofe,
only a confirmation of that coinage before granted by K. Athelftan.
' It appears by this charter of K. Edgar, as Mr. Forfter thinks [g], that
' there was now a market at Stanford. For, fays he, when he orders
' that there fhall not be any other market between Stanford and
' Huntingdon, it implies there was a market then at both thofe places.'
And he might have added, this was a good way to make the mercat
at Burg more frequented. And indeed as for Stanford, it was now
(and how long before we cant tell, but we may fuppofe, a good
while) not only a mercat town, but a royal borough. ' For, fays Mr.
' Leland [h], Staunford was privilegyd but in kynge Edwards [i] days for
' a borowe, as concernyng a place in the parliament howfe; yet it
' was a borow toune in kynge Edgares, and then, and fyns it hathe
' allway longyd to the croune.' What K. Edgar calls the fhire of Chrift
and S. Peter, is now called the foke of Burg [k]. ' This charter of
' K. Edgar was granted in 972. the fixteenth of that princes reign.'
And thus, with thefe, and many other privileges, recited at large in
his faid charter; ' the pacific Edgar, as Henry of Huntingdon ftiles him [l],
' confirmed Burgh abby by Stanford.' Here Huntingdon makes Burg

a Gunton, p. 137. Mon. Ang. I. 66. b.
b Stanforth, Sax. chron.
c Theolneum.
d The Danes were now often called Normans, and from them the crofs here mentioned was fo named.
  e Chron. Sax.
f Gunton & Mon. Ang. in locis fupra

citatis.
  g Letter to Dr. Tanner, MS. in my hands,
p. 6.
  h Itin. Vol. 7. p. 10.
i Edward the firfts.
k Monaft. Ang. ut fupra.
l p. 356.

a fort

a fort of an obfcure place, and directs you to look for it by a more noted town called Stanford.

XX. Before I pafs to other matters, a word or two here, if it may not be thought impertinent to mention fuch things; of the tranflation of S. Kyneburga, and S. Cynefuitha from Caftre (within feven miles) and of S. Tibba from Rihal (within two miles of Stanford) to Burg: fince, for want of knowing when the fame happened, Ingulf, as I have fhewn, was led into a very great miftake. In 1006. upon the re- moval of Ethelwold abovementioned from being abbat of Burg to be bifhop of Winchefter, he was fucceeded at Burg by a monk of that monaftery named Elfius. This Elfius (fometime between 1006. and 1013.) [a] ' dug up S. Kyneburga and S. Cynefuitha, who lay in Caftre; ' and S. Tibba, who lay in Rihal; and carried them to Burch, and con- ' fecrated them all to S. Peter. 'Who Kyneburga was hath been elfewhere faid; I fhall only add therefore, that Cynefuitha was her fifter[b], ' and ' Tibba their cofen.' Mr. Cambden fpeaks of ' Rihal[c], where, (when ' fuperftition had fo infatuated our anceftors, that with the multitude ' of faints it had in a manner taken away the knowledge of the true ' God) Tibba, fays he, a little fort of a goddefs, was worfhipt like ano- ' ther Diana or patronefs of hawking and fowling, by the lovers of thofe ' diverfions.' Hugo Candidus tells us very gravely [d], ' that when S. ' Tibba was brought to Burg, fhe fhewed, by the great miracles fhe ' wrought, fhe liked mightily to have her bones reft among the good ' monks of that houfe.' And fo much for the prefent of Burg.

XXI. Now again of the Danes. ' In July 1013. fays Florence of ' Worcefter[e], Suane K. of the Danes, with a ftrong fleet, arrived at Sandic; ' but, after ftaying only a few days there, foon left that place; and ' failing round the country of the Eaft Angles, entred the mouth of ' the river Humber, out of which he went up the Trent, and failed ' to Geainefburch, where he came on fhore, and encamped his army. ' To whom without delay Earl Uhtred and the Northumbers, and then ' firft the people of Lindiffe, next the inhabitants of the five cities, ' and foon after all the people north of Watlingftreet, offered to be- ' come fubject, and making peace with him, and giving hoftages, fwore ' fealty to him: upon which he ordered them to provide horfes and ' provifion for his army.' The town of Stanford being one of the five cities here fpoken of, it may be remembred thofe five cities were in 939. reftored to the Danes, when K. Edmund (who fucceeded Athel- ftan) and Onlaf the Dane divided the country betwixt them. I have already related how in 942. K. Edmund retook thofe five cities; ever fince which time (notwithftanding the Danes almoft conftantly infefted fome or other parts of England) thofe cities remained fubject to the Saxons. But here it may be obferved, that, by thofe five places being

a Chron. Sax. p. 120.
b Hugonis Candidi p. 38.
c In Coritan.

d p. 34.
e p. 614.

formerly

formerly fo often in the hands of the Danes, the prefent inhabitants were many of them not improbably (for all K. Ethelreds maffacre in 1002.) of Danifh original, but now indeed, like one and the fame people, converted, intermarried, and living quietly with the Saxons. However, not without fome inclination to be fure towards their own countrymen the Danes; and this I take to be the reafon why the faid five cities fo readily fubmitted to Suane. The Saxon chronicle, dif-courfihg of what now happened, inftead of people, fays[a], ' all the ' army north of Watlingftreet fubmitted to Suane.' Whence it is not unlike, but that K. Ethelred, being apprehenfive of an invafion, or a revolt, or both, hereabouts; kept therefore fome ftanding forces ready to oppofe any fuch attempt. Now thofe forces with fome of the peo-ple of thefe parts at firft it is probable made what refiftance they could; enough however to provoke Suane (who, by the havoc which you will find Ingulf relates he made in this neighbourhood, had certainly met with fome oppofition in it) yet not enough, as you will fee afterwards, to fatisfie Ethelred. What in fome part confirms thefe things, Mat-thew Weftminfter fays[b], ' the Northumbers, and the inhabitants of ' Lindfey, and of the five cities fubmitted firft; and that foon after ' all the people on the north fide of Watlingftreet, when they had ' no body left to defend them [king Ethelreds forces being, as I have faid, defeated] ' were conftreined to furrender, make peace, and after ' giving hoftages, fwear fealty to him.

XXII. All the five cities however, by making their fubmiffion; or poffibly for the fake of fome old Danes yet left among their inhabi-tants; or becaufe they who now arrived, if they could not conquer the whole kingdom, meant at leaft to infift upon a furrendry of thofe places back again to themfelves; I reckon efcaped being plunder'd. The Hoftages given Suane, as we may learn from the Saxon chroni-cle[c], ' were gathered out of every province.' Some of them it is like were Stanford men: what became of them I fhall fhew by & by. But now, if the faid five cities did efcape, to fee what an efcape in-deed this town of Stanford then had, and what other places then fuf-fered (fome of them not above two or three miles from the fame) hear Ingulf. ' In 1013. faith he[d], K. Swane landing with a frefh fleet ' and a moft cruel army, deftroyed all the whole country before him. ' For pouring out of Lyndefey, he burnt the towns, pluckt out the ' peoples bowels, and murdered all the Religious with divers torments. ' Then Bafton and Langtoft were burnt, and the monaftery of S. Pega ' [Peakirk] with all its adjoyning manors, Glynton, Northumburth ' [Norborough] Makefey, Etton, Badyngton, and Bernak were alto-' ther confumed, and all the people belonging to them either mur-' dered, or carried into captivity. In like fort the monaftery of Burg

a fub anno 1013.
b p. 201.

c ut fupra.
d p. 56.

' and

' and the neighbouring villages, and alſo its manors of Eye, Thorp,
' Walton, Wytheryngton, Paſton, Dodiſthorpe, and Caſtre, were all
' firſt plundered, and then given up to the flames. The abbat, with the
' greater part of his convent, taking with them the reliques of SS.
' Kyneburga, Kyneſuitha, and Tilba, fled to Thorney. Whilſt the
' prior with ſome other brethren, taking with him the arm of S. Oſ-
' wald the king, ſought the like ſhelter in the iſle of Ely.' As for
' Suane, the Saxon chronicle ſays[a], ' having paſſed Watlingſtreet, he
' did as much miſchief as lay in the power of an army. But it may
be obſerved all that is here related from Ingulf, was done long before
he came to Watlingſtreet. So that it ſeems he began at leaſt in our
neighbourhood, if not before he got hither; and gave all before him
to fire and ſword. It is not my province to purſue the reſt of his
actions; let it ſuffice then only to obſerve, that the other affairs of
this year were in ſhort, that Suane drove firſt K. Ethelreds queen and
children, and afterwards K. Ethelred himſelf, into Normandy. Laſt of
all that Suane died on the third of February, and his army (then got
back again to Gainsborough) choſe his ſon Cnute king.

XXIII. On Suanes death the Engliſh thought now was the time
to be rid of the Danes, and ſent for K. Ethelred out of Normandy.
' He return'd in Lent, ſays the Saxon chronicle[b], and was chearfully
' received by all his people. Cnute in the mean while tarried at Geg-
' nesburch with his army 'till Eaſter, and then agreed with the peo-
' ple of Lindeſige, that they ſhould find horſes for his army, and then
' all together march out to plunder.' By the way theſe people of
Lindſey, were not only thoſe who lived about Gainsborough, as ſome
may think; but all thoſe inhabitants of the five cities and other parts
north of Watlingſtreet, who, as hath been ſaid, had given hoſtages
and ſworn fealty to K. Suane. All theſe, what with the hopes of
prey; and of Cnutes protection; and alſo by virtue of their oaths and
hoſtages; were eaſily drawn over to joyn him: but ſee what they got
by it. ' Before they were ready, continues the Saxon chronicle[c],
' K. Ethelred came upon them in Lindeſige with a ſtout army, where
' he waſted and burnt the country, and killed as many people as he
' could lay hands on.' Thus K. Ethelred puniſhed them for ſubmitting
firſt to Suane, & then to his ſon Cnute. How the town of Stanford
in particular fared at this time I cannot ſay; but ſuppoſe, like the reſt
of its neighbours. Upon this defeat in Lindſey, ' Cnute, as the Saxon
' chronicle adds[d], fled thence with his fleet (thus were that miſerable
' people deluded by the covenant he had made with them!) and ſail-
' ed to the ſouth 'till he came to Sandwic.' Cnute being thus fled,
whilſt Ethelred ſtayed here, all theſe parts ſubmitted to him. The
news whereof was ſoon carried to Cnute; or rather Cnute himſelf

Anno
1014.

a ſub anno 1013.
b ſub anno 1014.

c ib.
d ib.

I

carried it with him to Sandwic. For, after he once left them, what else could he think would be the issue? Neverthelefs, to be reveng'd of them for so doing, when he got to that place, ' there, as the above ' chronicle proceeds[a], he set ashore the hostages which had been given ' to his father, after he had first cut off their hands and noses.' This he thought they deserv'd for their friends deserting him; not considering that, *with his assistance*, they could not at this time stand before Ethelred, much less *without* it.

XXIV. It was some time before tidings of this barbarity, committed by Cnute upon their hostages, reached these parts; the people whereof, for their sakes I guess, would not have submitted to Ethelred, if they could possibly have avoided it. Nor did they at last submit to him as fully as they should; but, when his back was turn'd (not yet knowing how Cnute had used their pledges) they seem to Anno have been disposed to revolt again to the Danes. Upon this in 1015.
1015. Ethelreds son Edward came into this country of the five cities, and reduced them more perfectly, by military execution, or fine, or both, to his fathers obedience. The Saxon chronicle, among other matters, touches some of these things thus. ' In 1015. says the writer of that ' history[b], there was a great council at Oxnaford, and there duke Eadric ' betrayed Sigeferth and Morcar, the noblest thanes among all the in- ' habitants of the seven cities: for he wheedled them both into his ' chamber, where they were basely murdered.' [By the way, Morcar I believe lived at Brunne by Stanford, and was descended from Morcar lord of that place, who was slain, as above related, in 870. fighting valiantly against the Danes. But to go on with my author.] ' K. Ethelred immediately [after they were murdered] seised all the ' [c] effects belonging to both those thanes, and at the same time order- ' ed the relict of Sigeferth to be apprehended and brought to Mealdel- ' mesbyrig [Malmsbury.] After a short space the clito Eadmund com- ' ing thither, took that lady, without the kings leave, and married her. ' Thence after the feast of our lady's nativity [Sept. 8.] that Clito ' marched northwards, and reduced all that people under his own sub- ' jection.' All England being thus again reduced to Ethelred, never- theless did not long continue so. However, after his cruelty acted up- on the hostages as above, [d] ' Cnute sailed to Denmark, as hopelesse of ' any good issue in England. But Turkil a Dane, retained in K. Ethel- ' reds pay [to fight against his own Danish countrymen] seeing success ' so suddenly altered, sore repented him of his revolte from the Danes, ' and knowing now was the time to recover his reputation, with nine ' of his ships sailed into Denmark, instantly importuning Canute to ' addrefs again for England —— Canute therefore, with the aid of his ' brother Harold, rigged forth a navie of two hundred saile, all furnished ' with souldiers and abiliments of warre; whose terror landed in Eng-

a ib.   b sub eo anno.   c facultates.   d Speed p. 421. a.

' land

' land before him.' ' All that time [a], K. Ethelred lay fick at Cofham
' [in Wilts.] But duke Eadric had raifed one army, and the clito
' Eadmund another in the north.' ' This Edmund [b], whether it were
' for the great ftrength of his body, or for that he always ufed to go
' in armor; was firnamed Ironfide.' ' When they came to join [c], the
' duke [another traytor like Turkil] would needs with his treachery
' feduce the clito Eadmund [from his own father] which when he
' could not do, they parted, and, without any battle quitted the coun-
' try to their enemies. Eadric however enticed away forty of the
' kings fhips, and joined them to Cnute,' [who was then upon the
fea, and failing for England.]

XXV. ' In 1016. Cnute [d], came with his fleet of one hundred and
' fixty fail, and with him duke Eadric, crofs the Thames among the Mer-
' cians to Greeklade. Thence, about Chriftmafs, they turned into
' Waeringfcire [Warwicfhire] where they plundered, and burnt the vil-
' lages, and killed every body they met with. Hereupon the clito
' Eadmund began [again] to affemble an army, but when he had raifed
' what men he could, they fignified little, for want of the kings prefence
' among them, and of the Londoners to come and joyn them. The
' expedition was therefore put off for the prefent, and every body
' return'd home. But, after Chriftmafs, there was a more general
' fummons, requiring every one, tho' he lived never fo far off, to ap-
' pear under a great penalty. And a meffenger was fent to the king
' at London, entreating him to come and meet the Clito's army with
' all the forces he could get. But when they both met in one body,
' it was to no more purpofe than it had often been before. For it
' was told the king that fome, who were to aid him, had treache-
' rous defigns againft him. He therefore difmiffed his army, and re-
' turn'd to London. As for the clito Eadmund, he rode down to
' earl Uhtred, among the Northumbers.' ' There a many, thought,
' fays Florence of Worcefter [e], that Edmund and Uhtred would affem-
' ble a yet bigger army againft Cnute.' And perhaps they might attempt it, but, when they found the country would not joyn with
them; they gave it over. Then, inftead of that, ' juft as Cnute and
' Edric in one part of the kingdom [e], fo Edmund and Uhtred in ano-
' ther part of it, fell to plundering of whole provinces together.' The
reafon why Edmund and Uhtred fell upon fome provinces in this manner, was, ' becaufe, as Roger Hoveden fays [f], they would not go out
' with them to fight againft the Danes.' This proves, as I intimated,
that Edmund and Uhtred would have got together a greater army for
that purpofe if they could. Alfo we may infer, that as Edmund and
Uhtred fell upon fome provinces, becaufe they would not go out
with them to fight againft the Danes; fo thofe other provinces which

a Sax. Chron. anno 1015.   d Chron. Sax. fub eo anno.
b Stow p. 117.   e p. 616.
c Chron. Sax. quo fupra.   f P. 434.

Cnute

Cnute and Edric fell upon, were thofe which would not go out with them to fight againſt the Saxons. If then we obſerve whom Edmund and Uhtred fell upon, we may ſee what parts were for the Danes; if we mind whom Cnute and Edric fell upon, what were for the Saxons.

XXVI. Now then to be particular. ' The clito Eadmund and Uhtred ' went into Stafford, Salop, and Leiceſter-ſhires, ſaith the Saxon chro- ' nicle[a], ſpoiling the parts that were for Cnute; whilſt Cnute, on the ' other hand, ravaged the parts which were for them.' Agreeable to the ſame chronicle, Florence of Worceſter[b], Henry of Huntingdon[c], Matthew of Weſtminſter[d], Holingſhed[e], and Speed[f], read Staffordſhire; and ſo, I believe, ſhould Roger Hoveden. But he is ſingular, and in- ſtead of that, reads Staenfordſhire[g]. However, tho' he is wrong in writing Staenford, inſtead of Stafford, ſhire; he by the way is the author; and his the book of Croyland, ' which, as Mr. Butcher ſays[h], ' makes mention of Stanford, and Stanford-ſhire, before the conqueſt: And this the paſſage. Now one reaſon why the people of Stafford, Salop, and Leiceſter-ſhires, would not go out to fight the Danes, was, probably becauſe their inclinations were moſt diſpoſed to ſide with the Danes; another, becauſe they underſtood they were ſtronger than Edmund and Uhtred; and ſo were afraid, both of a defeat, and that they ſhould afterwards ſuffer for joyning with them. Another per- haps was, that, in theſe fickle times, they thought it wiſeſt, if poſſible, to ſtand neuter. This I reckon they at laſt did, and probably ſuffer- ed leſs, tho' plunder'd by Edmund and Uhtred, than if they had been plunder'd by Cnute and Edric: Ones own countrymen being gene- rally more merciful than foreigners upon any ſuch occaſion. How- ever Mr. Holingſhed (and he is followed by Speed) ſays[i], ' Edmund & ' Utred ſpared not to exerciſe great cruelty upon the inhabitants [of the three bovementioned counties] ' as a puniſhment for their revolt- ' ing, that other might take enſample thereof.' Here, tho' it is ſaid, they were revolted; I rather fancy they had not yet done ſo: becauſe Cnute had not yet got down to them. That they were ready enough to do ſo as ſoon as he arriv'd among them, I believe was very pro- bable. But to proceed. When Cnute heard what Edmund and Uhtred were doing in Stafford, Salop, and Leiceſter-ſhires, to be even with them, he did the ſame where he was. For knowing all thoſe parts were now diſaffected to him, probably for uſing the hoſtages ſo baſe- ly which they gave his father; ' he and Edric Streon, ſays Roger ' Hoveden[k], waſted firſt Buccingahamſhire, then Beadafordſhire, Hun- ' tandunſhire, Northamptunſhire, Lincolnſhire, Nottinghamſhire, and

a ſub anno 1016.
b p. 616.
c p. 362.
d p. 203.
e Vol. I. p. 252.
f p. 422. a.

g prius Staenfordenſem, deinde Scrobesbe- rienſem et Legaceſtrenſem provincias deva- ſtare,——p. 434.
h MS. penes me, p. 9.
i Vol. I. p. 252.
k p. 434.

' at laft the country of the Northumbers.'   Here Hoveden, having
mentioned Staenfordſhire above, ſays nothing of Stanford.   But the
Saxon chronicle deſcribes the march of Cnute more at large, to wit [a],
' thro' Buccinghamſhire, into Beadfordſhire; and thence to Huntan-
' dunſhire; and ſo thro' the fens to Stanford; thence into Lincoln-
' ſhire; atferwards into Snotingahamſhire; and at laft into the province
' of the Northumbers towards York.'   So Henry of Huntingdon [b],
' thro' Buckinghamſhire, into Bedfordſhire; and ſo into Huntendune-
' ſhire; and ſo near the fens to Stanford; and ſo into Lincolnſhire,
' and thence into Snotinghamſhire; and ſo into Nordhumbre towards
' Everwic' [York.]   By the way both the Saxon chronicle and Henry
of Huntingdon, tho' they do not ſay Stanfordſhire; yet ſay that he
went firſt to Stanford; thence into Lincolnſhire——which I think looks a
little diſtinct, and as if Stanford was not at this time reckoned a part
of that county.   Be that as it will.   ' Thus, ſaith Speed [c], Cnute made
' ſpoil of all, ſo that the miſerable Engliſh went to wracke, on all ſides.'
And again [d].   ' Theſe were the daies of Englands mourning, ſhee be-
' ing unable to maintaine her defenders, and yet forced to cheriſh
' her devourers.'   The end of all this plundering on both ſides was,
that when Uhtred underſtood what ſad work Cnute made in all thoſe
places where he came, ' he gave over his devaſtations in the north, and,
' as the Saxon chronicle relates [e], driven by neceſſity to do ſo, ſub-
' mitted himſelf, as did all the Northymbers with him.   He alſo gave
' hoſtages, but for all that was murdered.   After which Cnute made
' Yric earl of the Northymbers in the room of Uhtred.'

XXVII. Before we proceed to other matters, let us here look back
a little, and take a ſhort ſurvey of the condition of this town for the
four laſt years.   In 1013. this place ſubmitted to Suane with the reſt
of the five cities, gave hoſtages, and ſo eſcaped being plundered.   What
an eſcape that was hath been ſhewn.   In 1014. Ethelred plundered
the five cities for ſubmitting to Suane & Cnute: to add to which miſ-
fortune Cnute ſlit the noſes and cut off the hands of the hoſtages
they gave his father.   In 1015. Edward, ſon of Ethelred, thinking they
had not yet ſuffered enough, came, and what by fire, and military execution, reduced all the five cities more perfectly to his fathers obedience.   In 1016. to make Uhtred deſiſt from plundering the north,
Cnute came into theſe parts, and particularly *thro'* or *near* the fens
to Stanford (but juſt before reduced to Ethelred) and fell upon it, and
all places where he paſſed, in a moſt outragious manner.   And thus
in the ſpace of three years only, Stanford was plunder'd (ſo hard was
its fortune!) three ſeveral times over; if not more.   The actions of
theſe four laſt years are, in all our Engliſh hiſtorians which I have yet ſeen,
huddled together and related with great confuſion.   I have here there-

a ſub anno 1016.   d p. 420. b.
b p. 362.   e ut ſupra.
c p. 422. a.

K   fore

fore endeavoured to set them in a clearer light (all those I mean relating to the course of my present undertaking) and explain them at large.
This I have at last done to my own satisfaction, and hope it may be
to my readers.

XXVIII. Affairs being in this melancholy situation, K. Ethelred died
on S. Georges day, and was succeeded by his son Edmund. ' Stanford, saith
' Mr. Butcher[a], remained without a castle or walls 'till the time of Edmund
' Ironside a Saxon king about two hundred years before the conquest.
[Here now is an achronism, or gross mistake in point of time. For
Edmund Ironside reigned in all but from S. Georges to S. Andrews
day of this very year 1016. which far from being two hundred, is
barely fifty years, before the conquest] ' who built the castle' [And
again, if he means there was no castle here before now, as gross a
mistake in point of fact] ' and compassed the towne with a wall of
' stone of an indifferent height, for its better defence against the Danes ;
' garnishing the same with *five* strong and stately watchtowers, two
' towards the water - side, for discovery and defence against the
' enemy on the south, the one called Beesfort, the other Holme-tower.
' The other three bulwarks or watch-towers are towards the east, north,
' and west, for discovery and defence against the enemy on those
' parts, called Carpe-tower, white-tower, and north-bulwark.' In some
of the devastations made here within the course of the four last years,
it is not indeed improbable but the castle and walls might be again
demolish'd either by the Danes, or Saxons; who both plunder'd this
place. And so Edmund Ironside (who reigned only one week above
six months, and in that short space fought five several pitched battels
with the Danes, none of them as good luck would have it in this
neighbourhood; and in the end, as some say, died a natural death ;
or as others relate, was murdered by Edric Streon) might (tho' he
never lived to see either of them finished) give orders for the castle
to be once more rebuilt, and (as the troubles of the times called for all
the defence which could be given either this, or any other great place)
for new walls (if it had none before, which is improbable ; for would
the Danes let Stanford, the most southerly, and perhaps most exposed
of all their five, nay seven, great cities, remain thus long without them?)
to be added around the town it self. His mistakes thus corrected, it
is time now however to observe, that we are beholden to the said
Mr. Butcher, for the above names (none of which I ever yet met with
any where else) of five bulwarks or watch-towers, erected upon the
walls of Stanford. Nevertheless, if we may believe Leland, Mr. Butcher is out in the number. For says that excellent antiquary[b], ' there
' were *seven principal* towers or wards in the wauls of Staunford, to
' eche of the whiche were certeyne of the freeholders in the towne
' allotid to wache and warde in tyme of neede.' Besides these *seven*

a MS. penes me, p. 3, 4.   b Itin. vol. 7. p. 10.

                                                        principal

The Common Seal

Indorsed with the Common Seal

The Arms of the Town or Borough of STAMFORD as antiently carved upon the South and North Gates of the Town from a Book in the Heralds Office touching the Visitation of Lincoln Shire Anno 1634. marked C. 23. 1.ˢᵗ Index Fol. 3. b.

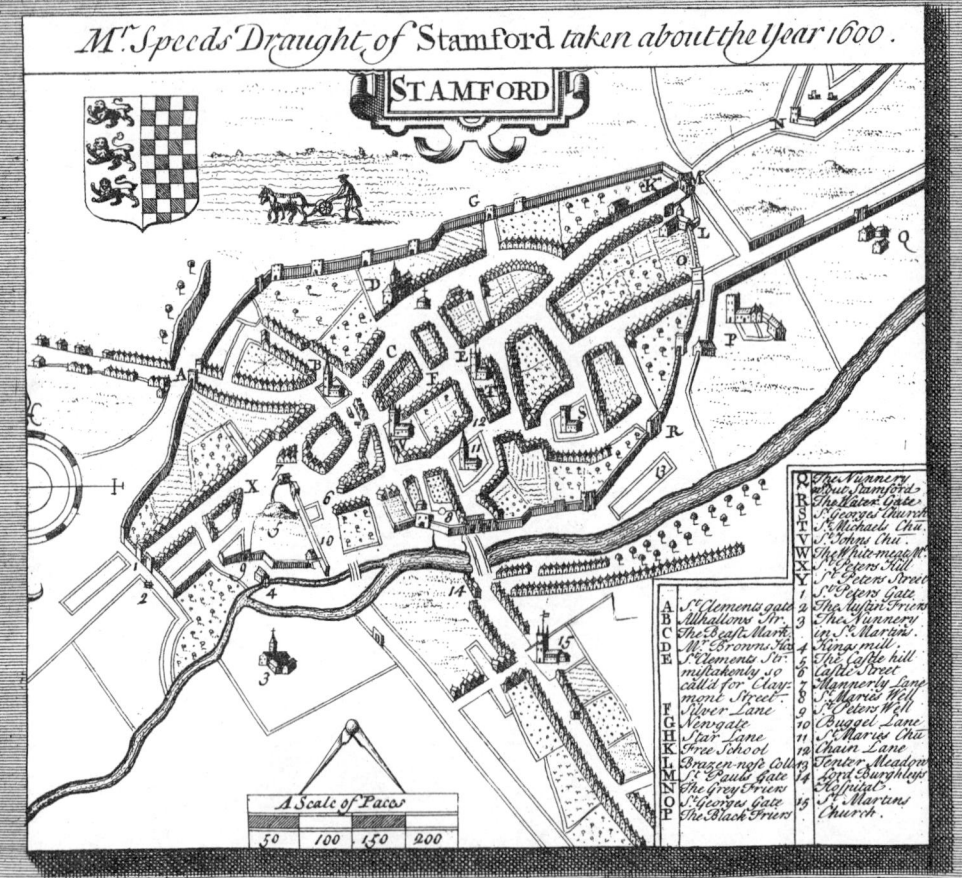

Mr. Speeds Draught of Stamford taken about the Year 1600.

STAMFORD

	A Scale of Paces			
	50	100	150	200

A	St Clements gate	Q	The Nunnery
B	Alhallows Str.		but Stamford
C	The Beast Mark	R	The Water Gate
D	Mr Browns Sta	S	St Georges Church
E	St Clements Str.	T	St Michaels Chu.
	mistakenly so	W	St Johns Chu.
	call'd for Clay-	X	The White-meat-mt.
	mont Street	Y	St Pegns Hill
F	Silver Lane	Z	St Peters Street
G	Newgate	1	St Peters Gate
H	Star Lane	2	The Austin Friers
K	Free School	3	The Nunnery
L	Brazen-nose Colledg		in St Martins
M	St Pauls Gate	4	Kings mill
N	The Grey Friers	5	The Castle hill
O	St Georges Gate	6	Castle Street
P	The Black Friers	7	Mannerly Lane
		8	St Maries Well
		9	St Peters Well
		10	Buggel Lane
		11	St Maries Chu.
		12	Shairt Lane
		13	Tenter Meadow
		14	Lord Burghleys Hospital
		15	St Martins Church

To the honoured Sr. Thomas Saunders Sebright Bart. (one of ye kind Encouragers of this Work) This Plate is most thankfully Inscrib'd by F. P.

I. Harris Sculp.ᵗ

principal towers, according to Mr. Speeds map (which is very accurate) there were four other leſſer forts erected for the ſame purpoſe, upon the walls of Stanford : which make the number in all *eleven.* More-over ' the walls, as Mr. Butcher adds[a], have in them five principal ' gates or entries ; S. Peters gate, on the weſt ; S. Clements, on the ' north ; S. Pauls and S. Georges, on the eaſt, and the bridge-gate, ' towards the ſouth. To theſe may be added a ſixth, ſtanding north ' eaſt, called the new gate ; as being made long ſince the former gates ' were erected : all the reſt appearing to have ſlips of ſtrong portculli-' ſes, which the new gate wanteth. Beſides, here are towards the ' ſouth, two antient poſtern gates which ſeem as antient as the walls ' themſelves : the one ajoyning to the bridge-gate : the other, not far from S. Georges lane, leading into the Tenter meadows.' Old and new, poſtern and great, gates ; Mr. Butcher here makes the num-ber in all to be eight. But he forgets to reckon another, called Gled-gate. By the way, ſome of theſe gates are now (and I believe all of them were formerly) embattelled ; and had alſo ſtrong towers upon them. Having fixed the number of them, taking Mr. Speeds map for our guide, let us now walk round Stanford, and, as the pſalm-iſt ſays[b], ' mark well her bulwarks and gates, that ye may tell them ' who come after.

XXIX. Beginning then at the eaſt end of Mr. Speeds map, the firſt eminence at the upper end of the wall, as there delineated and mark-ed with the letter M. is S. Pauls gate. So called becauſe it ſtood near S. Pauls church. This gate is embattelled, and hath yet a tower or lodge upon it. The next eminence ſtanding directly in the wall is another gate marked O, called now from the church of that name, S. Georges gate ; but formerly Cornſtal gate ; from the church of S. Michael Cornſtal ſtanding once not far from it. This gate likewiſe is embattelled, and hath yet a tower or lodge upon it. The next emi-nence, being without any mark in the map, by the remains yet to be ſeen in the walls over againſt the black friers, appears to have been one of the ſeven principal bulwarks or watch-towers before ſpoken of. The next eminence is another gate marked R. Mr. Butcher knew not any name it had. But Mr. Speed calls it, the water gate. By what hath been ſaid it appears then, that the eaſt end of Stanford, was defended by S. Pauls gate, S. Georges gate, one principal bulwark, and the water gate.

XXX. Come we now to the ſouth ſide, where the firſt eminence, ſtanding directly in the wall, but without a mark, was another of the ſeven principal towers. The next eminence, likewiſe without a mark, and drawn ſomewhat leſs, was one of the four ſmaller forts. The next eminence alſo without any mark, is the poſtern adjoyning to the bridge gate, thro' which coals and other goods being landed from the

---

a MS. penes me, p. 4.   b Pſ. 48. 12.

water

water are brought up into the town. The next eminence, adjoyning to the laſt, needs no mark, and therefore has none; its ſituation ſhewing it to be the bridge gate: over which is now erected the townhall. The next eminence, likewiſe without a mark, was another of the ſeven principal bulwarks, ſtanding ſomewhere about S. Maries well. It appears then, that (without reckoning the river or caſtle) the ſouth ſide of Stanford was guarded by one principal bulwark, one ſmaller fort, the poſtern near the bridge gate, bridge gate, and one other principal bulwark.

XXXI. Paſs we on to the weſt end, where the firſt eminence, ſtanding directly in the wall, but without any mark, is Gledgate: ſo called I conceive from the Engliſh *glade,* a ſtraight open paſſage or thoroughfare. The next eminence, marked with the figure 1. is S. Peters gate: ſo called from S. Peters church ſtanding formerly not far from it, exactly in the place marked with the letter X. This gate is likewiſe embattelled, and hath yet a tower, or lodge, upon it. The next eminence, a little above S. Peters gate, without any mark, was another of the ſeven principal bulwarks. The remains of it are yet very apparent in the walls; at the top whereof are ſeveral loop-holes to ſhoot arrows thro'. The next eminence marked with the letter A. is S. Clements gate. So called from S. Clements church ſtanding formerly not far from it, in a place now part of Mr. Noels garden. This gate is likewiſe embattelled, and hath yet a tower or lodge upon it. The next eminence, without any mark, was one of the four ſmaller forts. It appears then, that the weſt end of Stanford was defended by Gledgate, S. Peters gate, one principal bulwark, S. Clements gate, and one ſmall fort.

XXXII. Proceed we laſtly to the north ſide, where the three firſt eminences, ſtanding directly in the wall, as I take it, were the other three principal bulwarks. The next eminence, being (as all the three laſt) without any mark, as I conceive, was another of the four ſmaller forts. The next eminence, marked with the letter G. is newgate. The laſt eminence, without any mark, was the other of the four ſmall forts. It appears then that the north ſide of Stanford (as being moſt expoſed to any aſſaults) was defended by three principal bulwarks, one ſmall fort, new gate, and another ſmall fort. And ſo much of the bulwarks and gates belonging to the walls of Stanford on the north ſide of the Welland.

XXXIII. As to the ſouthern city, tho' I do not find that was ever walled, yet I perceive it was defended, I. by a gate in the ſtreet called eaſt-by-the-water, or the water ſtreet; not at the end of that ſtreet, but, as I conceive, at the end of that part of it where the houſes are double-rowed: this gate was called Webſteres gate. II. By another gate at the paſs called th'abutts, leading to Burghley. III. By another gate between S. Giles Hoſpital and the great ſtreet pointing north and ſouth; which gate ſtanding in the higheſt part of the town, was called High-gate; and from it the ſaid ſtreet is yet called High-gate, or High-

gate-ſtreet,

gate-ſtreet, and High-ſtreet. IV. By another gate, over againſt S. Martins church, leading to little Wirthorp. V. By the caſtle ſtanding
within the nunnery walls. And laſtly, by a gate adjoyning to S. Thomas's hoſpital, at the ſouth end of the bridge, over which I conceive
ſtood afterwards a ſmall chappel. Return we now to proſecute our
hiſtory.

XXXIV. In 1017. (ſoon after the death of Edmund Ironſide) King
' Cnute, ſays the Saxon-chronicle [a], took upon him the government
' of the whole Engliſh nation, and divided it into four parts; reſerv-
' ing the country of the Weſt-Saxons for himſelf; that of the Eaſt
' Angles he gave to Thurcyll; Mercia, to Eadric; and the province
' of the Northumbers, to Yric.' By this diviſion, Stanford (formerly
reckoned a part of Mercia) was for a ſhort time, together with many
other places, added to the country of the Eaſt Angles, under the juriſdiction of Thurcyl. For had not Stanford and a good part of Mercia been added to the province of the Eaſt-Angles under Thurcyl, the
ſaid Thurcyl, or as Hugo Candidus calls him [b], ' Turkil Hoche [could
not, as the ſame Hugo ſays he did] ' give to the church of Burg a
' mint in Stanford, and the land there on that ſide the water.' On that
ſide the water, that is, in Northamptonſhire, on that ſide of the Welland whereon the church of Burgh ſtands. K. Vulfere, as I have ſhewn,
was the firſt who gave thoſe lands to the church of Burg, then called
Medeſhamſtede. Turkil Hoche therefore only confirmed what lands
were before given by that prince. In the ſame manner his grant of
a mint was no more than a confirmation of what K. Athelſtan granted in 924. and K. Edgar confirm'd in 972. to the then abbats and
monks of that church. However this paſſage confirms, as I elſewhere
ſaid, that the abbat of Burgs mint here was kept, *ex iſta parte aquæ*,
on that part of Stanford which lies on the ſouth ſide of the water, and
is yet within the particular juriſdiction or fee of the ſoke of Burg.
As for the reign or viceroyſhip of this little king, Thurcyl, it was
but ſhort; for, as the Saxon chronicle tells us [c], ' at Martinmaſs 1021.
' king Cnute outlawed earl Thurkil.

XXXV. ' In 1063. ſaith Mr. Gunton [d], Leofric [then abbat of Burg]
' redeemed of K. Edward [the confeſſor] certain lands belonging to
' his monaſtery.' And in particular, ' gave the king, ſays Hugo
' Candidus [e], eight marcs of gold for Burchle by Stanford, which was
' in demeſne and leaſed out, to a certain capellan of the queens
' called Elfgar, for term of his life. But when he was dead, the K.
' & Q. would have taken it away from the church.' Mr. Leland, in
his collectanea from my laſt author ſays [f], ' Leuin of London, a no-
' ble matron, gave to the monaſtery of Bůrch, Fiskerton, Flectune,
' and Burchle.' But he is miſtaken, ſhe only gave Fiskerton and Flec-

Anno 1017.

Anno 1021.

Anno 1063.

a Sub eo anno.
b p. 44.
c ut ſupra.

d p. 15.
e in loco ſupra citato.
f Vol. I. p. 11.

2   L   tune,

tune, not Burchle, to that church. For Candidus fays[a], ' Leofric re-
' deemed Fiskertune, which she gave; and in like manner, Flectune
' which she gave:' then adds, ' he redeemed Burchle &c.' which Mr.
Leland, writing faft, might think she also gave; but there his hand was
too nimble for his eye. In this K. Edward the confeffors time[b], the
town of Stanford was governed by twelve liege-men, who, for that
purpofe, had great privileges there. They are fo called, becaufe they
were of old judges of the laws in the faid town; the magiftracy whereof they continued to hold till the 3. of E. 1. and after. But by whom
they were firft inftituted is yet a queftion. However they are the firft
magiftrates of Stanford I hitherto find any account of.

XXXVI. I shall now only fet right Mr. Butchers miftake about the
battel between the two Harolds, and fo pafs to matters after the conqueft. ' Huntingdon, fays he[c], makes mention of a fight that was
' held between Harold K. of Norway, and Harold K. of England, when,
' as the Englifh K. moft valiantly at Stamford-bridge gave battel to the
' Norwegians, there being a fierce fight, which continued from morning
' to noon on both fides; when as a certain valiant Norwegian, who
' had almoft foil'd the Englifh throughout the whole battel, returning
' to go into his ship was ftroaken with a dart, fo that he forthwith
' dyed, whereby the Norwegians were difcomfited.' Now this battel
was not fought here, but at Stanford-bridge in Yorkfhire. Mr. Leland
gives us a few circumftances of it, which take as follow[d]. Harold
' K. of Norway was killed at Stanforde by York (where Olave, funne
' to the K. of Norway & Paule of Orkeney fled to theyr fhippes) and
' Harold brother to Sir Olave was flayne, and Coftina K. Haroldes of
' England brother. At this battaile of Stanford, ther was a Dane
' faught manfully and kyllid many, ontyl he, under the bridge, was
' privily fmitten to death. K. Harold toke fo much of the fpoile
' of Stanford bridg battel to his owne ufe, that many of his foldiers
' depertid, and many had but faint hertes.' Of this gallant Dane (or
Norwegian as he calls him) give me leave to add from Marianus[e],
' one Norwegian deferves an everlafting remembrance, who, ftanding
' by himfelf on Steinesforthe-brigge, and having killed above forty
' of the Englifh with his battel-ax, ftopped their whole army 'till the
' ninth hour of the day; 'till at laft one of the Englifh getting aboard
' a fmall veffel in the river, run him thro' with his lance, at one of the
' holes of the bridge.

a loco quo fupra.
b Videfis fub annis 20. W. 1. et 3. E. 1.
infra.
c MS. penes me, p. 29.
d Itin. Vol.
e fub anno 1066.

The end of the third book.

1. Worthorpe house.
2. St Peters Gate.
3. Kings Mill.
4. St Peters Hill.
5. Mr Noels house.
6. The Nunnery.
7. All Saints Church.
8. St Johns Church.
9. Broms Hospital.
10. St Maries Church.
11. St Michaels Church.
12. Rihal Steeple.
13. St Martins Church.
14. St Georges Church.
15. Brazen Nose College.
16. The Grey Fryers.
17. The White Fryers.

Prospect of the Town of STANFORD from a Corner of Worthorp Warren

Lib IV.

To Mr Roger Willmott Esqr.
Mayor of Stanford this present
Year 1726. One of the kind
incouragers of this Work. This
Plate is most thankfully
Inscribed.

Therman Sculp

Academia tertia Anglicana;

OR, THE

ANTIQUARIAN ANNALS

of the TOWN of

STANFORD

IN

Lincoln, Rutland, *and* Northampton *Shires.*

BOOK IV.

From the coming in of K. William the conqueror in 1066.
to the Death of K. Stephen in 1154.

WILLIAM the firſt.

I. **M**UCH about the time when the battel of Haſtings was Anno
fought between Harold and William the conqueror, died 1066.
Leofric abovementioned, lord abbat of Burg; ‘ a perſon,
‘ as the Saxon chronicle relates [a], who ſo enriched that monaſtery with
‘ lands, and gold, and ſilver; that Burg was now called [by way of
‘ eminence, the rich or] golden city.’ Upon his death, ‘ the monks,
‘ as the ſame chronicle adds [b], made choice of one Brand their prior, a
‘ very wiſe and good man, for their abbat, and ſent him to Edgar A-
‘ theling, for [what is very obſervable, tho’ Harold was ſlain] ‘ the
‘ people of theſe parts [had no notion of the conqueror, but] ‘ thought
‘ Edgar ſhould be king; who [when Brand came to him] ‘ very civilly
‘ confirm’d the election. But afterwards when K. William heard of it,
‘ he took ſnuff at it, and ſaid the abbat had put an affront upon him.
‘ Whereupon the abbat was forced to give him forty marks to be
‘ friends.’ Among others who came in with the conqueror, I find the
names of Albini, Bohun, Camville, Colville, Dive, Diſpencer, de la
Laurd, Delaund, Lacy, Lutterel, Malherbe, Peche, Ros, Roſcel, Truſ-
but, Valence, Verdun, Warenn, Waterville, &c. of whoſe deſcendents
the courſe of theſe collections will lead me to ſpeak much hereafter.

---

[a] p. 168.   [b] Sub hoc anno.

Circa
1068.

II. About 1068. K. William firſt gave leave for the Jews to tranſplant themſelves from Roan into England. Whereupon in a ſhort ſpace that people ſo ſpread themſelves, that in all cities and other the beſt ſort of towns in the kingdom, they planted their Synagogues and openly taught the doctrine of their Rabbins with great exactneſs. Particularly divers of them ſettled at Stanford, where they had a Library, Schools, and a Synagogue: of all which hereafter.[a] Now alſo Hereward de Wake, lord of Brunne or Burn in this neighbourhood, ' being, as Mr. ' Stow ſays, [b] in Flanders, and hearing that the realm was ſubdued by ' ſtrangers, and that his inheritance (his father Leofric being dead) was ' given to a Norman [[c] Ivo Talbois, the conqueror's ſiſter's ſon] and that ' his mother, a widow, was much injured, cometh with ſpeed into ' England with his wife Thurfride, and gathering together a company of ' his kindred, chaſed the Normans out of his father's inheritance. Then ' goeth to his uncle by his fathers ſide [the foreſaid Brand lord] abbat ' of Burg, and firſt making confeſſion of his ſinnes and abſolution re- ' ceived, watched all night in the Church in prayers and faſting; and the ' next day offer'd his ſword upon the altar, and, after the goſpel, the ' abbat put the ſame hallowed ſword about his neck, with a benedi- ' ction; and communicating the holy myſteries of Chriſt he remained ' a lawful ſoldier or knight.' Here then we have the Saxon manner of making knights. But, as my author adds, [d] ' this conſecration of a ſol- ' dier the Normans abhorred, and not onely this cuſtome, but many o- ' thers did they alter.' As for Hereward he was a very gallant man, who could not endure the thoughts of ſubmitting to the Normans, ſome ex- ploits which he perform'd againſt them will be ſeen preſently: but,

Nov. 27.
Anno
1069.

what leads to them, we muſt firſt obſerve, that ' Nov. 27. 1069. as the ' Saxon chronicle tells us, [e] died Brand lord abbat of Burh, Herewards ' uncle; to whom, ſaith the chronicle of Burg, [f] by collation from the ' king, ſucceeded Turold.' This Turold, you will find, lived much at Stan- ford. ' In lent [10$\frac{69}{70}$. 4. W. 1.] the king, as the Saxon chronicle adds, ' [g] ſuffered [and what is that in a prince but in a manner to command?] ' all the monaſteries in England to be rifled.' The only monaſtery I can aſſuredly affirm we had then at Stanford, was that of S. Leonard. But how the monks of that houſe fared, when thoſe of other places were plunder'd, I know not; however I believe not very hardly, becauſe, as you will afterwards find, K. William himſelf was a benefactor to it. Be that as it will, ſome monaſteries it is certain eſcaped, and Burg in particular was immediately after this very time rich enough to invite a whole army to the plunder of it. For, to go on with the Saxon chro- nicle, where I laſt broke off: [g] ' afterwards the ſame year, K. Swane ' [another Daniſh king] came up the Humber, from Denmark. Where-

---

[a] 1290. 18. E. 1. infra.
[b] p. 144.
[c] Supplement to Gunton p. 264.
[d] Stow, ut ſupra.

[e] Sub hoc anno.
[f] Chron. Joh. abb. de Burgo, p. 47.
[g] Sub anno dicto.

' upon

'upon the people of thofe parts went out to meet, & made a league
'with, him; thinking he intended to ravage their country.   It was then
'told the monks of Burg that certain perfons of their own neighbour-
'hood intended to ranfac that monaftery.   Thofe were Hereward and his
'relations, who joyning with the Danes, faith an author cited by Le-
'land, [a] invited them to plunder Burg, becaufe he underftood that
'Brande the abbat (his uncle) was dead, & that the king had given the
'abby to a certain Norman monk called Turold, who lay then at Stan-
'ford with his foldiers' (who were probably fent to guard him on the road,
and put him in poffeffion.)   For thofe foldiers, as the Saxon chronicle
adds [b], were Normans, and Turold himfelf a very fevere man.   Here-
'upon, as the fame chronicle proceeds, [2] the prior of that church named
'Ywar, by night carried off the books, cowls, veftments, and all that
'he could lay Hands on, and before day withdrew to abbat Turold at
'Stanford, begged his protection, told him the outlaws would certainly
'be at Burg, and that he acted thus (in bringing away what he was able)
'by his brethrens direction.   Accordingly at break of day all thofe out-
'laws came thither with abundance of veffels, and attempted to get
'into the monaftery; but the monks made an head, and fhut the doors
'againft them.   Then they fired and burnt all the monks lodgings, and
'all the whole town but one houfe.   For when the fire had made way
'for them, they broke in by the Bull-dyke-gate, where the monks ran
'to meet, and begged them to forbear thefe outrages.   But not mind-
'ing what any of them faid, they went into the church, got up to the
'rood, and took away the crown from our lords head, a crown entirely
'made of gold.   They took away likewife the golden pedeftal on which
'the rood ftood.   Moreover climbing up into the fteeple, they carried
'off the abbats mitre which was hid there, made all of gold and filver.
'Thence alfo they took two fhrines overlaid with gold, and nine fil-
'ver ones.   Likewife fifteen great crucifixes, part gold and part filver;
'& in a word fuch abundance of jewels, heaps of mony, variety of
'books and veftments as were innumerable.   And all this, they faid,
'they did out of refpect for the monaftery [that the Normans might
'not have thofe things.]   After they got to their Ships, they went to
'Ely, & there laid up their fpoil.   Then came abbat Turold, and an
'hundred and fixty men with him, all well armed, from Stanford.
'But at his arrival, he found every thing, both within and without the
'monaftery, except the church, burnt.   Mean time the outlaws, hav-
'ing notice of his coming, were all got on board: This happened the
'fecond of June.   Then the two kings, William and Swane, were re-   June 2.
'conciled; whereupon the Danes left Ely, and failed homewards with   1070.
'the 'bovefaid treafure.   But when they got into the middle of the
'main ocean, there rofe a violent ftorm, which difperfed all thofe fhips
'in which the treafure was, fo that fome were drove into Norway,

[a] Collect. Vol. 1. p. 13.   [b] 3. ut fup.

' fome

' fome into Ireland, and fome into Denmark. All that they made a
' fhift to carry over (confifting of cloaks, fome fhrines, croffes, and
' many other forts of treafure) they conveyed to one of the kings bo-
' roughs and put into the church. But afterwards, by their careleſ-
' nefs and being drunk one night, that church was fet on fire and
' every thing confumed which was left in it: Thus was the monafte-
' ry of Burg burnt and plundered. When thefe things were over, ab-
' bat Turold arrived at Burg; thither alfo the monks returned, and ce-
' lebrated divine fervice, after that church had now lain deftitute a
' whole week, without any religious rites being perform'd in it. When
' this was told bifhop Egelric, he excommunicated all thofe who had
' been concern'd in this naughty action.' ' This Egelric, faith bifhop
' Godwin, [a] was firft a monk of Burg, then bifhop of Durham. He built a
' church at Chefter on the ftreet in the bifhopbric of Durham where,
' in digging the foundation, he found fuch an infinite deal of mony,
' as, after that, not caring for the revenues of his bifhopbric, he re-
' figned the fame to Egelwyn his brother, and returned himfelf to
' Burg. There he beftowed great coft in building and repairing that
' church and monaftery, as alfo in making a cawfie with timber, lime,
' and fand thro' the fenns between Deping and Spalding; a work verie
' neceffarie and of infinite charge. This cawfie was called, after the
' name of the maker, Elrich-rode.' But to return. Hereward growing every day more formidable to abbat Turold, ' that prelate, as the
' chronicle of John abbat of Burg obferves, [b] granted threefcore and
' two whole hides of the lands belonging to that church to certain fti-
' pendiary knights to protect him againft Hereward. Many fkirmifhes,
' as bifhop Patrick notes [c], were afterwards fought between them. All
' which notwithftanding, as the forefaid chronicle of abbat John con-
' tinues [d], the abbat with divers other great perfonages was taken prifo-
' ner by Hereward, and with many of his mercenaries detained in cufto-
' dy, 'till thirty thoufand marks of filver were paid for his ranfom.
' After this, fays bifhop Patrick [e], forgetting the promife he had made
' to Hereward at his releafe, never to difturb him, the abbat made
' war upon him again. Upon which Hereward, finding himfelf like
' to fuffer for his kindnefs, returned, and again burnt the monaftery
Anno ' and town which they were rebuilding. In 1071. faith the abovemen-
1071. ' tioned abbat of Burg [f], Hereward, with divers other exiled Englifh,
' made war upon the king in Ely fens. The king, fays Speed [g], leaft
' delay fhould give them advantage, and the ifle harbour more of fuch
' his unbridled fubjects, with a great power hafted thitherwards, and
' ftopping up the eaft paffage from all flight or relief, drew a caufey on
' the weft fide thro' the deepe fennes, even two miles of lengthe, where

---

[a] Cat. of bifhops. p. 500. 501.   [e] in loco fupra citato.
[b] p. 47.   [f] ut prius.
[c] Supplement to Gunton, p. 264.   [g] p. 441. b.
[d] quo fupra.

' likewife

' likewife he then built the caftel of Wyfebech ; againft which they in
' the ifle raifed another of timber and turfes, and called it, according
' to the name of their captain, Hereward ; at which place, many af-
' faults and bickerings being made, but yet no entrance gotten, Morcar
[one of thofe exiles, who, as Sir William Dugdale acquaints us [a], was
earl of Northumberland, and, among other places, lord of Caftreton by
Stanford] ' by boat efcaped out of the ifle, and in Scotland obtained
' by price, what thefe diftreffed could not by prayer. Hereward alfo
' went out of the ifle, and got a gallant crew of choice and youth-
' ful foldiers, which ftood moft ftoutly for the defence of their liber-
' ties. Afterwards, as bifhop Patrick adds [b], he took Ivo Talbois [the
' conquerors nephew, earl of Anjou, and lord of Spalding and all Hol-
' land] prifoner ; and for his ranfom had his own lands reftored him by
' the conqueror, and lived many years after in peace.

III. ' William the conqueror, as Mr. Holland obferves [c], ordained
' the terms for determining matters of law to be kept but four times
' of the year, according as is ufed at this day.' Which terms, as I take
it, were not yet fixed at any certain place, but were always kept at
the kings court, where he himfelf was. Agreeable to which notion
Ingulf acquaints us he was to have had a hearing at Stanford before
the kings juftices about a caufe between his own monaftery and
one Afhford of Helpftone their bailif ; which being to be heard at
Stanford fhews that the kings juftices then fat there, and inclines
me to think that the king himfelf alfo was then likewife there. But let
Ingulf himfelf fpeak, the paffage is remarkable, and thus he relates it.
' In 1076. fays he [d], when I was invefted abbat of Croyland, I found   Anno
' in that monaftery threefcore and twelve monks, but all of them in   1076.
' want, and thro' that variety of misfortunes which had befallen the
' houfe, left in a manner to fhift for themfelves. Whereupon I enqui-
' red of all who knew the circumftances of the monaftery, both lay-
' men and clergy, by what incomes & revenues they had feen it in
' former days fupported ; and of what particulars the fubftance belong-
' ing to it was wont to confift ? Conjuring them, in the moft earneft
' manner, that they would deal truly and openly with me, and conceal
' nothing from me in this affair with which it was proper for me to
' be acquainted. They replied, that one Afhford of Helpefton (who
' had been bailif to abbat Wlketule my immediate predeceffor) had,
' for many years, had the management of the whole eftate belonging to
' the monaftery ; that he had always let out their lands and houfes to
' their tenants ; that he received all the rents and profits ; paid the
' fervants of the monaftery juft what he pleas'd ; was grown prodigious
' rich, having feldom or never repaired any of the ruins of the houfe ;

a Baron. Vol. 1. p. 6. b.
b ut fupra.
c Collect, curious difcourfes, pub. by Mr.

Hearne, p. 52.
d p. 76, 77.

'And, as he only knew the state of the monastery, of course he
'only was able to relieve it. As soon as I understood this, I caused
'the said Ashford to be sent for, gave him plainly to understand the
'naked condition of the monastery, to what want it was reduced by his
'means and management, and took all imaginable pains both by pray-
'ers and promises to move his compassion. I shewed him moreover
'at large how unacquainted I my self was with these matters, being so
'lately come to be abbat; and the extreme want and misery we must
'all necessarily be reduced to, unless he lent his helping hand to re-
'lieve us. But none of these things would move him; they made no
'more impression on him than if he had been a rock of adamant; on
'the contrary, like the deaf adder which stoppeth her ears, he slighted
'my prayers, laughed at my promises, and, as if he had conceived a joy
'in our distresses, made a jest of all that I could say to him. When
'I saw this, I begged of him that he would only give me the rolls of
'our lands and other estates, and particularly laboured with repeated
'intreaties to move him but to inform me what rents we had in our own
'neighbourhood and the towns about us. At length he was somewhat
'persuaded by the great promises I made him to comply. But, after
'he had shewed me what possessions the monastery had in other
'towns, when he came to speak of Helpeston, he not only concealed
'what rents we had there, but said that our houses were his, and, a-
'vouching them to be his own by inheritance, with his many oaths
'almost persuaded me to believe so. However this being stoutly de-
'nied by the seniors of our house, and they producing sufficient deeds
'and charters to make good what they asserted, he, after a great deal
'of squabling, cried, a fig for your rights; those houses are my own,
'and I will prove it before the kings justices —— And so flung out of
'the monastery. [a] We therefore commencing a suit for the said tene-
'ments, a day of hearing was appointed before the kings justices at Stan-
'ford; on which day, after I had commended my self to the prayers of
'my brethren (as being to go before the kings justices about the buisi-
'ness of the house) trusting in God, I took horse, and set out for
'Stanford. He likewise, but depending on the multitude of his riches
'and placing all his confidence in his wealth, stubbornly rode forth to
'meet us, against the cause of God. But see! mounting at this rock of
'offence, when he was got about half way, his horse threw him, and so
'broke his neck; which being presently told the kings court at Stanford,
'and us expecting judgment there: we, not giving entire credit to the
'relation [upon his not appearing] had another day ordered for the
'hearing. But on the morrow as his neighbours and relations were
'carrying him towards Burg (in which monastery he had before ap-
'pointed himself to be buried) and bearing his body on a bier over ten

a Nobis itaque in dictis tenementis coram   juridicus apud Stanford datus est, &c.
regis ministris calumpniam ponentibus, dies

'; acres

' acres of meadow belonging to us, which he, when living, affirmed
' to be his; on a ſudden an extraordinary black cloud drawing over
' the ſun, brought on a darkneſs like the night, and the heavens pour-
' ed down ſuch a flood of rain, that, from the abundance of it, any
' one might have taken this for one of Noahs days; moreover the
' bier was in a moment unaccountably broke aſunder, and the corps of
' the dead man tumbling down, immediately rolled into the midſt of
' the dirt; which, when the bearers beheld, diſcerning it to be the hand
' of God, they openly confeſſed the wrong he had done; and his re-
' lations and neighbours running to meet us, who at this very inſtant
' were coming from Stanford [Helpeſton being in the road between
' Stanford and Croyland] falling on their Knees at our feet, begged
' pardon for ſo baſe an injury which was by God himſelf thus pub-
' lickly reveng'd. We, on the other hand, giving God thanks, for-
' gave the injury, and received our meadow, with all the other mat-
' ters for which we went to law, by them utterly diſclaimed, and to
' this day peaceably enjoy them.'

IV. William the conqueror and William Kairliph biſhop of Durham, Anno
as I have already touched, ᵃ refounded S. Leonards cell by Stanford, 1082.
and gave it to the prior and convent of Durham to make a cell for the
monks of that houſe. The preciſe time when they did ſo was in
1082. for then I find ᵇ biſhop Kairliph gave new lands, and K. William,
after beſtowing a great many other lands, towns, and Churches himſelf;
confirmed all the lands new and old, granted to the church of Durham. Indeed S. Leonards monaſtery and S. Cuthberts fee at Stanford
(tho' both of them belonged to Durham) are neither of them particularly mentioned in the tenor of biſhop Kairliphs charter to that church,
or in the account of the conquerors own benefactions: both in the
monaſticon. ᵇ But thoſe pieces in Dugdale are but abridgments, and ſo
they might be omitted. For I queſtion not but John Weſſington (as
his MS. quoted by Mr. Smith ᶜ intimates) had either ſeen biſhop Kairliphs and K. Williams charters more at large, or ſome other equally
good authority for theſe things when he ſaid, ' in Stainforth is a cell in
' honor of S. Leonard, founded firſt by S. Vilfrid, afterwards by K. Willi-
' am the conqueror and William biſhop of Durham; and by them given
' to the prior and convent of Durham for the monks to reſide in.' From
a conſideration of which paſſage, as alſo becauſe there were few ſtone
churches in England before the conquerors time; and likewiſe upon a
view of the preſent remains of the priory church of S. Leonard (now
a farmers barn without Stanford) which are exceeding antient; I venture to fix this for the time when that church, the remains whereof we
now ſee, was firſt erected. The front of the nave, which carries a venerable air of beauty and antiquity, ſhews it was a ſumptuous fabric.

ᵃ Book II. Par. XIV.　　　　　　　　ᶜ See Book II. Par. XIV. above.
ᵇ Monaſt. Ang. Tom. I. p. 43. b. &c.

The

The fide ifles are now both down, which (when ftanding) made the prefent front above as broad again; and being, no doubt, like it, fet out with archings and carvings, we can hardly imagine any thing more ftately. Beyond the nave, which, the very method of building conventual churches affures us, was above as long again as what is now left of it, ftood the fteeple wherein hung the bells, and, on each fide of that, the crofs ifles. Beyond the fteeple, which (only to anfwer what we now fee left of the church) muft needs be very fine, was built the choir; fo that what is now left is not near one fifth part of this once moft beautiful church: Correfpondent whereto we may be pretty well affured was the monaftery it felf. The windows of the church, as we may obferve by the draught of the remains, were fo narrow, that (being alfo, according to the fafhion of the times, glafed with painted glafs) the infide muft neceffarily be exceeding dark; but that was what the age affected. The great number of lamps which they kept continually burning in fuch places fet off their altars and veftments to a better advantage, and brightened by the luftre of the many jewels which they were always adorned with, diffufed a light more glorious than the day it felf —— Now I have been fpeaking of bifhop Kairliphs charter to the church of Durham, I cant forbear taking notice of what bifhop Kennet is pleafed to obferve upon a part of it. ' In ' 1082. fays that excellent antiquary, [a] an artifice was contriv'd to ob- ' tain indulgence from the pope, that whatever churches the church of ' Durham had in advoufon, they fhould from thenceforth commit ' them to be ferved by honeft clerks, who, as to the cure of fouls, ' fhould be refponfible to the bifhop in whofe diocefe they were; but ' as to the benefits and all accruing profits, fhould be always account- ' able to the prior and his brethren. And this, as his lordfhip juftly ' notes, was effectual appropriation.' I have before obferved, [a] that, befides being patrons of S. Leonards priory, the prior and convent of Durham were alfo patrons of the diftinct rectories and parifh churches of S. Mary at the Bridge, and S. Mary Benne-werk, in Stanford. The rectors of both which churches, as well as of many others in this neighbourhood under their prefentation, now felt the hardfhip of this indulgence granted, as above, to their patrons: Both the faid churches, tho' only the firft of them is now left, being thus early in being; if not much fooner. For Benne-werk is compounded of two Saxon words, and fignifies *within* the *werks* or walls. Agreeable to which etymology S. Mary Benne-werk church, ftood in the Gannoc (a ftreet formerly fo called) at the weft end of the town, juft within S. Peters gate, which gate, whilft the faid church ftood, was not called S. Peters, but Weft-gate. This church then was of Saxon erection, and undoubtedly called S. Mary Benne-werk, to diftinguifh it from fome other church of S.

a Cafe of impropriations, p. 24.

Mary

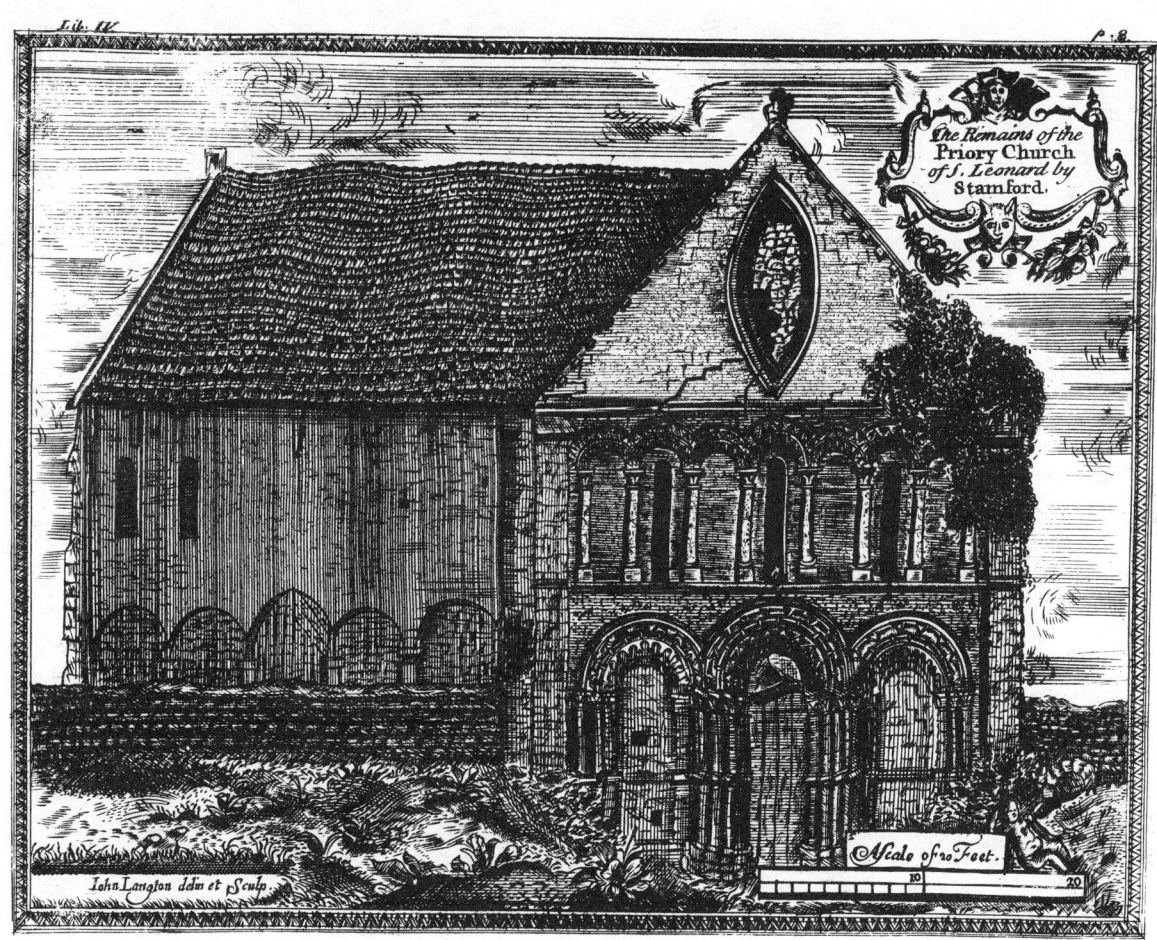

The Remains of the Priory Church of S. Leonard by Stamford.

A Scale of 20 Feet.

Iohn Langton delin et Sculp.

Mary then likewise in being, which, as we read of no other here dedicated to that faint, muſt be S. Maries at the bridge. At preſent I ſhall only add there is now a church at Stanford, called S. Maries, ſtanding not far from the bridge; but the preſent fabric thereof I think is not old enough for the times we are diſcourſing of (the ſame having been rebuilt as I take it about the latter end of the reign of K. Henry the third; ſo ſhall defer my account of it to that time.)

V. In 1086. was finiſhed the general ſurvey of all England; called Domeboc, or Doomſday-book ſurvey. ' The itinerant commiſſioners ' for theſe parts, as appears by the lieger book of Worceſter quoted by ' Sir William Dugdale [a] were Wulſtan biſhop of Worceſter, Remigius ' biſhop of Lincoln, Walter Giffard E. of Buckingham, Henry de Fer- ' rers, and Adam brother of Eudo, &c. Theſe inquiſitors, ſaith biſhop ' Kennet [b], upon the oaths of the ſhirives, the lords of each manor, ' the presbyters of every church, the reves of every hundred, and ſix ' villanes of every village, were to enquire into the name of the place, ' who held in K. Edward [the confeſſors] time, who the preſent poſſeſ- ' ſor, how many hides in the manor, how many carucates in demeſne, ' how many freemen, how many tenants in ſoccage, how many in ville- ' nage, how much in wood, meadow and paſture, how many mills and ' fiſhponds, how much added or taken away, what the value, and how ' much taxed for in K. Edwards time, what now, and what advance ' could be made of it? Beſides which the king took an account, ſays ' Simeon of Durham [c], of all the caſh or ready mony which every man ' had in his hands. Nay he was ſo very particular, ſays the Saxon ' chronicle [d], that, what is a ſhame to be ſpoke, tho' the king thought ' it no ſhame to be done; there was not an Ox, Cow, or Hog, but ' what he had brought into this appraiſement.   Yet is it not for all ' that, ſaith Mr. Tyrrel [e], ſo exact a ſurvey as our monkiſh hiſtorians ' repreſent it, who ſuppoſe there was not an hyde, or yard land; a ' lake, or fiſh-pool; any town or place that is not ſet down in it.   For ' ſince, as Dr. Brady well obſerves [f], this ſurvey was chiefly intended to ' give the king a true account of his own lands or demeſnes, as alſo ' what were held by his tenants in capite [chief or head tenants] it is ' not to be admired if many of thoſe towns and villages, which were ' then held by their feudataries or under tenants, are quite omitted in it : ' And I my ſelf (ſaith he) have obſerved ſome cities and towns of note ' which are not mentioned; as any one may find, that will but take the ' pains to compare it with an exact catalogue of the antient towns and ' villages in England, the greateſt part of which he will not be able to ' find there.' And indeed where they did take an account of any place, the kings commiſſioners were not ſo ſtrict as his commands were

a Baron. Vol. I. p. 257. b.
b Paro. Antiq. p. 63. 64.
c ――― immo quantum vive pecunie quiſ-
quam poſſidebat in omni regno ſuo. p. 213.

d p. 186, 187.
e Hiſt. Eng. Vol. 2. p. 54.
f So cited by Mr. Tyrrel. Vol. 2. p. 54.

rigid.   On the contrary they were fometimes partial on the good-na-
tur'd fide, and in this neighbourhood, the monks of Croyland in particular partook of that favour.   ' For they weighed not our eftate to
' the full price, fays Ingulf [a], thus kindly providing, thro' their zealous
' affections towards us, a relief for us againft the kings future taxes and
' other burthens which might afterwards be charged upon the houfe.'
And no doubt but feveral other monafteries likewife found the fame
favor.   ' This Inquifition, faith bifhop Kennet [b], was regiftred in two
' books, now kept in the treafury of the Exchequer, in the leffer of
' which is the defcription of Effex, Norfolk, and Suffolk, and at the
' end of it this fhort note.   In 1086. the 20. of W. 1. was made this
' defcription, not only thro' thefe three counties, but the others alfo.'
So much then touching the conquerors furvey in general.   Let us
now fee how Stanford is furveyed there in general; then how Stanford in Lincolnfhire, Stanford in Rutland, Stanford, Burghley, and
great & little Wirthorp in Northamptonfhire are particularly defcribed
in it.

VI. And firft, how Stanford is furveyed there in general; for which
we are obliged to the learned Dr. Gale [c].

Stanford burgum regis dedit gel-dum T. R. E. pro xij. hundret et dimidio, in exercitu, et in navigio, et in Dane-geld.	The kings borough of Stanford paid tax in K. Edwards time for twelve hundrets and an half; towards paying the army, navy, and Dane-geld.
Ibi funt fex cuftodie; quinque in Lyncolefcire, et fexta in Hantune-fcire que eft ultra pontem; et tamen ipfa reddebat omnem confuetudinem cum aliis, preter gablum et thelo-neum, quod abb. de Burg habebat et habet.	There are fix wards there. Five in Lyncolefcire, and the fixth in Hantunefcire, which is beyond the bridge. But neverthelefs that ward paid all cuftoms or dues with the reft, except gabel and

toll, which the abb. of Burg had and hath.

Here it is faid Stanford paid geld for twelve hundreds and an half,
and afterwards that it was divided into fix wards; which paffages fuggeft
that Stanford was, tho' not now, yet in K. Edwards time, and before then,
a fhire town; and that, as the town of Stanford contained fix wards, fo
the fhire of Stanford, contained twelve hundreds and an half.   I know the
word fhire in old monkifh writers does not always denote a county, as it
now does with us; but rather the precincts or lordfhip of fome place; as
Allerton-fhire, the diftrict or townfhip of North-Allerton; but here both
hundreds and wards being mentioned, it is abfurd to think the town was
diveded into both.   ' Many places, faith Dr. Brady [d], are either called
' Burghs in the conquerors furvey, or there are Burgeffes mentioned in

a p. 79.
b par. Antiq. p. 64

c. Decem Script. p. 775, 776.
d Hift. of Boroughs Vol. 1. preface, p. 2.

' the

' the defcription of them; feveral of which are not now efteemed Burghs,
' nor is there any light or information to be had from them, what
' Burghs, or Burgeffes then were, as Torchfey, Louth, and Stanford in
' Lincolnfhire, &c.' However the common notion of a Burgh, as Mr.
Somner in his Saxon dictionary tells us [a], is, that it fignifies a city, fort,
' fortrefs, tower, caftle, borough, free-borough, or town corporate.'
' And as to the burgeffes, Dr. Brady himfelf tells us [b], ' they were
' tradefmen.' The army and navy above mentioned were the army and
navy almoft always kept up by our latter Saxon kings to keep out the
Danes. The Dane-geld was a tribute paid by the faid princes to the Danes
to keep them quiet, when they were afraid they would be too many
both for their army and navy likewife.

VII. Let us now fee how that part of Stanford which lies in Lincolnfhire is more particularly defcribed; for which we are alfo obliged
to the fame learned Gent. who gave us that of Stanford in general.

[c] *In his V. cuftodiis T. R. E. fuerunt C.XL. et I manfiones.*

In Stanford T. R. E. erant XII. lagemanni, qui habebant infra domos fuas facam, et focam, et fuper homines fuos; preter geld, et heriote, et forisfacturam corporum fuorum de XL. oris argenti, et preter latronem. Hoc idem modo habent. [d] *Si non funt nifi novem. Unus eorum habet XVII. manfiones.*

In thefe five wards, in the time of K. Edward were one hundred, forty, and one manfions.

In Stanford, in the time of K. Edward, were twelve lagemen, who had within their own houfes fac & foc, and over their own men; except the tax, and heriots, and the forfeiture of their bodies when it amounted to forty ounces of filver; and except fe-lons goods. They have the fame privilege ftill. But there are but nine of them left. One of them has feventeen manfions belonging to his jurifdiction.

What thefe lagemen were, I have already touched [e]. ' Sac, faith Dr.
' Brady [f], fignifies a liberty or power granted by the king to try and judge
' caufes, and of receiving the forfeitures arifing from them, within
' fuch and fuch limits, dominions, or jurifdictions.' Soc, as the fame
' Gent. obferves [g], is the place, territory, or precinct wherein Sac or liber-
' ty of court was alfo exercifed; the circuit of the place of franchife; or
' the liberty, privilege, or franchife it felf.' Manfio comprehends more
than a houfe. For in Domefday it is faid, ' Roger de Bufli had in Snot-
' ingham three manfions in which were feated eleven houfes.'

VIII. Let us next fee how that part of Stanford which lies in Rutland is more particularly defcribed. [h] [c] In the Northamptonfhire part
' of Doomfday-book, (as the learned Mr. Moreton was pleafed to in

a in voce.
b Hift. Boroughs, Vol. 1. p. 16.
c Decem Script. in loco quo fupra.
d Si! rectius ut opinor, fed.
e Lib. III. Parag. XXXV.

f Appendix to his 1. Vol. of Boroughs, p. 8.
g ib.
h Thorotons Nott. p. 488.

' form me [a]) at the end of the firſt ſet of Rutland towns, is inſerted
' thus.

Rex habet in dominio de Port-land II. carrucatas, et duas partes tertie carrucate; et XII. acras pra-ti. Ad eccleſiam S. Petri jacet una carrucata terre; et ad eccleſiam omnium SS. dimidiam carrucatam.

The king has in the demeſne of Portland two carrucates, and two parts of a third carrucate; and twelve acres of meadow. One carrucate of the land lies in S. Peters, and half a carrucate in All-Saints pariſh.

Portland cum prato T. R. E. red-didit XLVIII. et X. ſol. pro fel-tris ſummariorum regis. Inſupher debet rex habere IX. libras et XII. ſolidos, pro aliis exitibus Burgi.

The Portland, with the meadow, in K. Edwards time paid XLVIII. and X. ſhillings to provide coarſe ſtrong cloth coverings for the

kings ſumpter horſes. Moreover the king ſhould have IX. pounds XII. ſhillings for the other charges of the borough.

Likewiſe, as Mr. Wright acquaints us [b], ' Albertus Clericus, or Aubrey
' the clerk, held, at the time of Doomſday ſurvey, the churches of Oche-
' ham and Hameldun, and S. Peters in Stanford, which belongs to
' Hameldun, together with the lands adjoyning to the ſaid churches;
' viz. ſeven bovates; all which the ſaid Albert held by the kings grant
' and favor. And he held in demeſne four carrucates and eighteen vil-
' lanes, and ſix bordarii having five carrucates, which laſt mentioned
' eſtate was valued, in the time of K. Edward, at VIII. l. but at the
' conquerors ſurvey at X. l.'

Upon which paſſages I beg leave to note. Port was antiently a name for almoſt any corporation: As appears by Port-mote-court, that is, the borough court: Port-way, the road leading to the Borough: Port-meadow at Huntington, that is the borough-meadow. Portland there-fore is nothing elſe but Borough-land. And we muſt not read as above, Portland, but the king has in the demeſne of the Borough-land, two carrucates, &c. ' A carrucate, as biſhop Kennet obſerves [c], is a plough
' land, or as much arable ground as in one year could be till'd with
' one plough. Computed ſometimes at ſixty, eighty, an hundred, an
' hundred and twelve, eight-ſcore, or nineſcore acres; different accord-
' ing to time and place.' Mr. Moreton is pleaſed to add [d], tho' North-
' ampton had two churches of the names abovementioned as well Stan-
' ford, yet I think this article [as ſet down above from his letter] be-
' longs to Stanford, firſt becauſe it comes at the cloſe of a company
' of Rutland towns, the laſt of them Caſtreton, which is very near S.
' Peters and All Saints in Stanford; ſecondly, Northampton is before
' accounted for in page the firſt of that ſurvey' [the ſame ſurvey, to wit, as publiſhed by the ſaid Mr. Moreton, at the end of his natural

---

a By a letter wrote to my worthy friend the Revd. Mr. Payne Rector of Bernack for my uſe, dated at Oxenden Dec. 28. 1722.

b Ant. Rutland. p. 95. a.

c Gloſſary, at the end of his lordſhips paroch. Ant.

d Letter, as above.

history.] Rutland, I know, was never a diſtinct county 'till K. Henry the third made it ſo, and then gave it to his brother Richard the K. of the Romans. Before which time what we now call the county of Rutland, belonged part to Northampton, and part to Nottingham, ſhire. However what is here above tranſcribed from Doomſday, ſhews, I think, evidently that S. Peters pariſh at Stanford is not in Lincolnſhire. And if not in Lincolnſhire, it muſt be either in Northamptonſhire, ſince what we now call Rutland was once a part of that county [a]; or elſe in Nottinghamſhire, ſince a good part of what we now call Rutland, and particularly Hameldune chercheſoch, to which S. Peters church in *Stanford* formerly belonged, was once likewiſe a part of that county [b]. And if S. Peters pariſh at Stanford is not in Lincolnſhire, then S. Mary Benne-werk pariſh, and Bredcroft, and Broadheng (all which lie between S. Peters pariſh and the reſt of Rutland) cannot be in that county of Lincoln neither. Broadheng, is a fair, beautiful meadow on the ſouth ſide of the Welland, ſo called from its ſmooth, broad area, and the *henging*, for ſo the Saxons expreſs hanging, of its banks over the river: This meadow is now reckoned a part of the united pariſhes of *All Saints* and *S. Peter.* And thus the old town of Stanford (I mean Stanford on both ſides of the river) certainly ſtands in three counties. A Bovate is the ſame as an Oxgang; that is, as much land as one ox can plow in one ſeaſon. ' Skene, as quoted by Minſheu [c], ſays, an oxen-gate of land ſhould ' always contain thirteen acres.' Villanes, ſaith biſhop Kennet [d], as ' ſome pretend derive from the Fr. Vilain, Lat. *vilis,* baſe and vile. But ' rather, ſaith his lordſhip, from *villa,* a country farm (as *ruſtici, coloni, &c.*) where theſe men of low and ſervile condition had ſome ' ſmall portion of cottages and ſervices allotted to them, for which ' they were depending on the lord, and bound to certain works and ' other corporal ſervices. They were of two ſorts, firſt, villanes in ' groſs, who, as to their perſons, their iſſue, and their ſtock, were a ' ſort of abſolute ſlaves, the ſole property of their lord, moveable and ' alienable at pleaſure. Secondly, Villanes regardant or appendant to a ' manor, who were aſcrib'd as members of ſuch a fee, and, as a perti- ' nence of it, deſcended to the heir, or paſt along to every new lord. ' For their ſervice they held ſome ſmall portion of houſe and land in ' villenage —— The villanes over and above their operations or cuſtoma- ' ry labors, paid an annual rent in mony. The *Bordarii,* often men- ' tioned in the Doomſday inquiſition, were diſtinct, as the ſame learned ' prelate tells us [e], from the *ſervi* and *villani,* and ſeem to be thoſe of ' a leſs ſervil condition, who had a boņþ or cottage with a ſmall parcel ' of land allow'd to them, on condition they ſhould ſupply the lord

a See 4. E. 1. infra.
b See 51. H. 3. infra.
c in voce Oxgang.

d in voce.
e On the word.

' with

‘ with poultry and eggs, and other small provisions for his *board* and
‘ entertainment.’ Tenants in demesne, as we may learn from Dr. Bra-
‘ dy [a], were such as lived *in dominio regis vel aliorum,* under the power
‘ of the king, or other lords —— And such tenants, as he adds [b], re-
‘ ceived justice from their lords, and were judg'd by them in most
‘ cases.’

IX. Let us next see how that part of Stanford which lies in Northamptonshire is more particularly described in the book of Doomsday;
which is thus set down by Mr. Moreton [c].

Idem Willielmus tenet duas hidas et dimidiam virgatam minus in Stanford; et abbas Benedictus emit ab eo. Terra est quinque carrucatarum. Ibi sunt XVII. villani cum presbytero; et quatuor bordarii habentes quatuor carrucatas. Ibi octo acre prati. Valuit XX. solidos. Modo XL. solidos. Leuric libere tenuit T. R. E.

‘ The same William holds two
‘ hides and half a virgate, more
‘ or less, in Stanford. And ab-
‘ bat Benedict purchased of him.
‘ The land, in all, is five carru-
‘ cates. There are here seventeen
‘ villanes with a presbyter; and
‘ four bordarii, who have four
‘ carrucates. There are eight
‘ acres of meadow. Formerly
‘ let for XX. shillings. Now for forty. Leuric held them free in King
‘ Edwards time.

Who this William was, by turning to the former part of Mr. Moretons printed copy, I cannot find. But Mr. Tyrrel tells us from Dr.
Brady [d], ‘ that the manner of making this survey was, always in every
‘ county setting down the kings name first, and after him all his great
‘ men in order that held of him in chief, with numbers placed before
‘ them, for the better finding them in the book.’ If so, it is strange,
that this William, who was certainly one of those chief men who held
under the king in Northamptonshire, is no better accounted for by Mr.
Moreton. ‘ A hide of land, as bishop Kennet says [e], is as much as is
‘ sufficient to the cultivation of one plough. The quantity never expresly
‘ determin'd; but varied according to different places: Some making
‘ it sixty four, some ninety six, some an hundred acres. A virgate,
‘ as his lordship adds [e], was likewise uncertain, according to the dif-
‘ ference of place and custom: They reckon'd in some parts fourty,
‘ in other thirty, twenty, and but fifteen acres.’ Who this abbat Benedict was I find not, there being no abbat of Burg, Croyland, or Thorney, of the name of Benedict, before the conquest, or at this time.
Leuric, as I have shewn [f], was abbat of Burg in 1063. ‘ The said Leo-
‘ fric, as Mr. Willis observes [g], being a Person of the blood royal, and
‘ very much in favor with K. Edward, held four other abbies in his

a Hist. Bor. Vol. I. p. 16.
b ib.
c Printed copy of Doomsday, at the end of his natural History of Northampt.

d Hist. of England, Vol. II. p. 53.
e On the word.
f Lib. III. Par. XXXV.
g Hist. abbies. Vol. I. p. 144.

‘ hands

' hands at once, viz. Burton, Coventry, Croyland, and Thorney; to
' gether with that of Burg;' by virtue of which laft he held fome; but
as it fhould feem not thefe lands at Stanford free.

X. Let us next fee how Burghley in Northamptonfhire is particularly
defcribed in Doomfday book; for which we are obliged to Mr.
Stevens[a].

In Burglea tenet Goisfridus tres virgatas terre de abbate. Terra eft II. carrucatarum. In dominio eft una; et III. fervi, et VII. villani, cum I. bordario: habent I. carrucatam. Ibi fex acre prati, et III. acre filve. Valuit X. folidos; modo XL. folidos.

In Burgle Goisfrid holds three virgates of land of the abbat. All the land amounts to two carrucates. One is in demefne; and three fervants, and feven villanes, with one bordarius: they have one carrucate. There are fix acres of meadow and ten acres of wood; formerly let for X. s. now XL. s.

This paffage is well explain'd by another in Hugo candidus, where we read [b],

Burlee. Primus Galfridus de Wintone. Willielmus de Burglee tenet tres hidas et unam virgatam et dimidiam in Norhamptonfcire, fcilicet, in Burgelee et Armiftone.

In Burlee, the chief tenant is Geoffry de Winton [or Winter.] William of Burglee holds three hides and one virgate and an half in Norhamptonfcire, to wit, in Burgelee and Armiftone.

XI. Let us fee how great Wirthorp in Northamptonfhire is defcribed in the fame inquifition; for which we are beholden to Ingulf[c].

In Wridthorp S. Guthlacus habuit, habetq; unam hidam et dimidiam ad geld. Terra eft II. Carrucat. In dominio eft una carrucata, et XI. villani, et XI. bordarii, cum duabus carrucatis. Ibi tres acre prati, et unum molendinum de quinque folidis; valent XL. folidos.

In Wridthorp S. Guthlac had, and hath, one hide and an half towards paying the tax. The whole is two carrucates. One carrucate is in demefne, and XI. villanes, and XI. bordarii, with two carrucates. There are three acres of meadow, and one mill, which are let for five, but are worth XL. fhillings.

The abbat of Croyland was antiently lord of the manor of great Wirthorp by Stanford. That manor, it may be remembred, was given to the abbat and monks of Croyland by Turketil, king Edreds lord chancellor[d].

XII. Laftly, as to little Wirthorp, the abbat of Burg was antiently lord of the manor of little Wirthorp by Stanford. That manor, as

a Additions to his 2d addit. Vol. 166. a.
videfis etiam Joh. Lel. collect. To. I. p. 16.
b p. 57.

c p. 81. Videfis etiam predicti ad monaft.
Angl. Supplem. p. 74. a.
d See Lib. III. Par. XVIII.

we

we may learn from the forefaid Mr. Stephens [a], is thus defcribed in the book of Doomfday.

In Writorp tenet Aluvinus de abbatia III. virgatas terre, que pertinent ad Witeringham; ibi funt III. fochamanni cum una carruca-ta, et dimid. et IV. acre prati; valet VIII. folidos.

In Writorp Aluvin holds of the abby three virgates of land, which belong to Witeringham; there are III Sochmen, with one car-rucate & an half, and four acres of meadow; worth VIII. fhillings.

To which I fhall only add from bifhop Kennet [b], ' Socmen were the ' foccage tenants within the extent of fuch an honour or mannor.' King William the conqueror died the 9. of Sept. 1087. and was fuc-ceeded by his fecond fon king

WILLIAM the fecond.

Anno 1087. I. W 2.

XIII. After his coronation, ' King William went to Winchefter, and, ' as the Saxon chronicle relates [c], opened the exchequer there, and the ' treafures which his father had amaffed of gold and filver, and of veffels, ' veftments, jewels, and divers other things of great value, difficult to be ' enumerated: Then (as his father, before he died, commanded) divided ' thofe riches, to every church in England a part; particularly, to fome ' principal churches ten marcs of gold; to others, fix; and to every ' rural church, five fhillings. Befides which, an hundred pounds were ' fent to every county, to be diftributed among the poor of the fame; ' and all for the health and good of his fathers foul.' This, whether we confider it as the fathers, or the fons gift, was a truly royal and prodigious benefaction. And yet, if we may believe Stow, was ftill larger than here reprefented. For, inftead of every county, he fays [d], ' to every borough towne he gave an hundred pounds to be dealt to ' the poor.' Now admitting this benefaction to be fact in every cir-cumftance, to fee the greatnefs of it we need only reflect on the number of counties, boroughs, cathedral, conventual, collegiate, and parifh churches in this nation, the laft of which only at this time, as Ranulf Higden tells us [e], amounted to 45002. As to Stanford, this is the firft benefaction, I read of, confer'd on the poor of this borough. The churches which here partook of it, were S. Leonards, S. Peters, both the S. Maries, and both the All-Saints; and perhaps fome others: but thefe are all I can affuredly affert were yet in being. Every one of which had at the leaft five fhillings a piece, over and above the hun-dred pounds which were appointed for the poor. King William the 2. was flain the firft of Auguft 1100. and fucceeded by his youngeft brother, King

a Suppl. ut fupra. p. 166. a.
b in verbo Soka.
c Sub anno 1086.

d p. 178.
e Chron. p. 201.

HENRY the firſt.

XIV. [a] ' In the feaſte of S. Michael 1103. Anſelme the archbiſhop   Sep.29.
' held a councel at Weſtminſter, where divers conſtitutions were made,   1103.
' namely, that prieſts ſhould no more be ſuffered to have wives, who   3. H. 1.
' were never abſolutely forbidden matrimony in this land before.
' Whiche decree, ſayeth Huntington, ſeemed to ſome very pure, but
' to ſome againe very dangerous, leaſte whileſt divers of thoſe that co-
' veted to profeſſe ſuche a puritie as paſſed their powers, myght haply
' fall into moſte horrible uncleanneſs, to the high diſhonour of the
' chriſtian name & offence of the almightie.' What married clergy we
had at Stanford at this time I find not but cannot but obſerve, that,
for this decree, Anſelm, a very pious, good man, was the principal
ſtickler; who himſelf indeed, as far as I can perceive, was never married. However we yet ſee among the works of that prelate, a little
piece, wrote with exquiſit touches, entitled *deploratio S. Anſelmi pro
amiſſa virginitate.* By his own confeſſion he himſelf fell then into a
worſe crime than marriage; & it is a great pity therefore but a conſideration of his own frailty, had taught him not to perſecute others, who,
to avoid the like falling, entered into wedloc. But I forbear. His aſhes
are ſacred. He meant well perhaps in contending for celibacy as the pu-
rer ſtate; & we cannot but commiſerate the ſin of his youth, ſince, in
his riper years, his ſorrow for it is expreſſed with ſo pathetic a ſtrain,
that ſure his eyes wept with his pen, & his heart grieved as much as
his tongue. There is joy in heaven, we are aſſured, when a ſinner is
converted; & the church therefore forgetting the fault of his youth,
called Anſelm, firſt to be an abbat, then an archbiſhop, & then a ſaint.
I ſhall only add, that, notwithſtanding all his attempts to part the
clergy & their wives, tho' it was effected afterwards, yet was it a matter too hard for Anſelm to accompliſh. At the ſame councel it was
decreed [b], ' that abbats ſhould not make any more knights or men of
' warre.' The manner how they formerly did ſo, I have before related [c]. Item [d], ' that there ſhould be no more buying & ſelling of men
' uſed in England, which was hitherto accuſtomed as if they had been
' kyne or oxen.' Whence (Stanford being a mercat town) it ſeems
that to this time we had Turkiſh traffic in the midſt of a chriſtian
country.

XV. In 1109. Joffred abbat of Croyland ſent ſome brethren of that   Anno
houſe to Cotenham, whence they went often to Cambridge, and (as   1109.
is ſaid by them who will allow that univerſity to be no older) firſt ſettled Schools there, where they taught philoſophy and the liberal arts,
and at the ſame preached againſt Judaiſm, and ſollicited ſubſcriptions
from their auditors, towards rebuilding their church and monaſtery,

a Holingſhed, p. 340. a. b.   c Anno 1129. ſupra.
b 3. id. p. 341. a.   d Hol. ut prius.

         both

both which had been lately confumed by fire. For all, or at leaft moft
of, which purpofes he fent likewife fome brethren to Stanford, where
chriftianity it felf was in fome danger thro' the boldnefs, number, and
infinuations of the Jews. ' For the faid abbat, as Peter of Blefens relates [a],
' fent to his manor of Wridthorp by Stanford brother Elfin, Brother
' Fregift, and brother Harold, (all of them his fellow-monks, but of
' Englifh extraction) of whom Sir Elfin was made prior, being a man of
' excellent wit and profoundly learned. Thefe, preaching often to the
' Stanfordians, exceedingly profpered in their miniftry, and ftrengthened
' the chriftian faith againft the Jewifh depravity; and alfo fully open-
' ing the condition of their monaftery fo lately burnt and then going to
' be rebuilt, procured a great many contributions from the merchants
' and other good chriftians in all the neighbourhood thereabouts. Where-
' upon, as their collections came in, they often vifited their defolate
' mother, with a very plentiful hand; but not with the fame plenty as
' that wherewith they at Cambridge comforted their faid parent; be-
' caufe they had there a richer country, a beter place, a more gene-
' rous and virtuous people, and Gods grace anfwer'd all more abundant-
' ly. However the venerable abbat Joffrid (feeing his Sons who abode
' at Wridthorp, often, as their ability gave leave, mindful of their
' common mother, and with all their power folliciting the neighbour-
' hood for her relief, and, tho' they were divers times thro' their ex-
' ceeding kindnefs in fending all that they could rap and rend towards
' the repair of the abby, in great want of neceffaries themfelves, yet
' fo far from being negligent that they were even ftrict in the obedience
' enjoyned them, and bearing all with the utmoft patience) granted them
' leave to hear the confeffions both of the neighbours and all other
' good chriftians, as well as of their fifters the nuns of that place; and
' to abfolve, and enjoyn them canonical and wholfom penances for
' their fins fo confeffed; as alfo licenfe to receive the alms given them,
' and to convert them to their own neceffary occafions; it being very
' reafonable that he fhould live of the altar, whom God had called to
' ferve at it. He alfo affigned them for their fupport his whole vil-
' lage of Wridthorp aforefaid, that is to fay, three virgates of land in
' demefne, and four acres of meadow, with three holms being as much
' as two acres, and one water mill, with the fifhery of the pool and
' of his whole river, together with fourteen natives in the fame vil-
' lage, of which every one holds a virgate of land (to wit, eight and
' twenty acres of arable, and eleven acres of meadow) and pays
' for his land fourteen fhillings, befides carriage of corn and hay;
' and pays alfo Gerfon [b] to the lord for his daughters marriage,
' and Ourlop [b] in cafe they be ftolen, and Stoth and other fervices
' and aids as in the monaftery charters are more fully defcribed. All
' which the forefaid venerable abbat Joffrid affigned to his forefaid

[a] p. 115, 116. [b] About Gerfon and Ourlop, fee Book I. Par. XXXV.

' monks

' monks, with the whole court of the forefaid village, and all its rents
' and profits whatfoever.   He gave them likewife all other the
' emoluments of the forefaid village or of his court whatfoever,
' in the town or its fields arifing; to wit, wafts, hirns, forebalks
' of arable land, foredol of meadow, foredikes about his mill
' and the damns belonging to it.   They alfo the forefaid monks, in
' the following years which happened to be more plentiful and abun-
' dant, went on vigoroufly with the bufinefs which was enjoyned them,
' and always preferving their own and the confciences of their fifters
' the neighbouring holy nuns pure and unfpotted from the world,
' tranfmitted a great many very fair prefents of the faithful to their
' monaftery, and what by their own induftry, and what thro' the ob-
' lations of good people which by the favor of Chrift they procured,
' greatly affifted the forenamed abbat and their brethren in rebuilding
' their church.'   By this account of Peter Blefens it looks as if abbat
Joffrid did not fend thofe three monks only to tarry a while at Wridthorp, but, as he gave them the whole manor and made Elfin prior,
that he founded a little monaftery or college there ; which monaftery
or college, being made a cell to Croyland, was afterwards always filled
with novices belonging to that abby, who were fent to ftudy there, under the three faid monks, or others who fucceeded them.   Which practice, if it was not begun in the time of prior Elfin, yet I believe was
afterwards certainly put in execution, when the Carmes and other religious began to read lectures and fet up their Schools at Stanford. And
perhaps All-Saints college which Mr. Burton [a] places at Withorpe, &
at the fuppreffion of religious was valued only at 1. 19. 4. was the very cell thus founded : for I find no other account of it.

XVI. Here I beg leave farther to note, that, as appears by the forefaid Blefens, when the monks of Croyland came to gather collections
towards rebuilding their monaftery, they found here a multitude of Jews,
which is one fign; and a multitude of chriftian merchants, which is
another fign ; and of thefe laft obtained much alms, which is a proof
of the then flourifhing condition of this town and neighbourhood. Befides which, the many fair prefents which they collected here in after
years, points equally at the farther growth of the riches and devotion
of the inhabitants of Stanford, fhewing, as a teftimony of both, that a
good part of Croyland abby was rebuilt by their contributions.   In
the fame account we read of nuns at Wridthorp ; but by whom founded I cannot yet difcover : this being the firft time I meet with any mention of them.   To which I fhall here only add, that all the nuns of
this houfe, except the priorefs & one more, dyed in the great peftilence,
which raged in 1349. at what time the revenues of the faid houfe were
much exhaufted.   And that the faid nunnery, of the order of S. Be-

---

[a] Valuation of Monaft. in Speed, under the title Northamptonfhire.

net, in 1354. was united to the nunnery of S. Michael at little Wrid
thorp by Stanford, of the same order [a].

July 5.   XVII. Upon the fifth day of July, 1110. K. Henry the firſt being at
1110.   Stanford, confirmed there the charters of Manaſſer Arſic an Engliſh ba
10.H.1. ron and his lady, to the priory of Cogges in Oxfordſhire, a Benedictine
cell belonging to the abby of Feſcamp in Normandy. Thoſe charters
may be ſeen at large in the monaſticon [b]. Some of the great perſons who attended the king during his ſtay at Stanfort (as it is there
called) were witneſſes to the ſaid confirmation, to wit, Robert biſhop
of Lincoln, Gilbert of Aquila, William of Tanquerville, and Lewis ſon

Anno   of Hubert the ſteward. ' In 1118. one Leofwine, ſaith biſhop Patrick,
1118.   ' requiring from the abbat of Burg five ſhillings for the houſes he had
    ' beyond the river of Stanphord, which he pretended to have a grant
    ' of from abbat Ernulph and other abbats; it was adjudged in court

Anno   ' that he ſhould loſe the ſaid five ſhillings. In 1125. as I find in ſome
1125.   ' MS. collections lent me by the Right Reverend White lord biſhop
    ' of Burg [d], when Walter the archdeacon ſieſed the lands of that church
    ' into the kings hands upon the death of abbat John, it was found
    ' that the ſaid abbat had in Stanford two and forty men, having houſes
    ' belonging to the land adjacent not meaſured; and ſeventeen men not
    ' having any land, but only the houſes which they live in; theſe are
    ' in Hamptonſcire. There are alſo in the ſame ſhire fifteen underſeles,
    ' who do no ſervice but in thoſe bounds where their lands lie, &c.'

Anno   After the abby of Burg had been void about two years, and K. Henry
112⅞.   had all that time received the revenues, ' he gave that monaſtery
    ' as the Saxon chronicle relates [e], to a certain abbat named Henry Pei-
    ' tow, then abbat of S. John de Angeli in Normandy. But all the
    ' archbiſhops and biſhops ſaid that was not fairly done by the king,
    ' neither was it lawful for the abbat himſelf to hold two abbies at once.
    ' But he made the king believe he had reſigned his abby in Normandy
    ' by reaſon of the great diviſions in that country, and that he did ſo
    ' by the counſel and leave of the pope and of the abbat of Cluni; as
    ' alſo becauſe he was ſent legate from the holy ſee to gather the Rome-
    ' ſcot: But all this was but a ſtory. The truth was he had a mind
    ' to hold both abbies; and ſo he did, as long as God thought fit. This
    ' man was in Clerc's orders, biſhop of Sceſſcuns, afterwards made a
    ' monk of Cluni, then prior of that monaſtery, at length prior of Sa-
    ' venni, and after all, becauſe he was related to the king of England
    ' and the earl of Peitow, the earl gave him the abby of S. John de

---

a See more annis 1349. 1354. infra.
b To. I. p. 574. a.
c Supplement to Gunton, p. 73.
d Hec eſt deſcriptio maneriorum abbatie
de Burch, cum Walterus Archidiaconus
eam recepit & ſeiſivit in manus R. Henrici
poſt obitum Johannis abbatis. —— In Stanford ſunt XLII. homines habentes domos

ad terram adjacentem non menſuratam, &
XVII. homines non habentes terras preter
manſuras; & hii ſunt in Hamptonaſcira.
Sunt item in eadem ſcira XV. Underſeles
qui nullum ſervitium faciunt, niſi hiis bondis
in quorum terre ſedent, &c. Swaph.
  e Sub anno 1127.

2

' Angeli.

‘ Angeli. After this, by his great cunning, he got the archbishop-
‘ bric of Befencun, which he held three days. When he had loft
‘ this defervedly, becaufe he got it unjuftly, he afterwards obtained
‘ the bifhopbrick of Seintes, five miles off his abby, and held it near
‘ feven days. But then the abbat of Cluni deprived him of that, as
‘ he had before of his archbifhopbric. Then he thought with himfelf
‘ that if he could but get into England, he might live as he pleas’d.
‘ Whereupon appealing thence to the king, he faid, that he was an
‘ old, infirm man, and unable to bear the great injuftice and diftracti-
‘ ons then reigning in his own country, and therefore begged, that he
‘ would for his own fake, and the fakes of all his friends, confer on
‘ him the church of Burch; which the king granted, becaufe he was
‘ his kinfman, and one of the chief of thofe who made oath and at-
‘ tefted the proceedings when the earl of Normandys fon and the earl
‘ of Anjou’s daughter were divorced for confanguinity. After this
‘ manner was this abby unhappily beftowed on him this year fometime
‘ between the feaft of the nativity and Candlemafs, at London; whence
‘ he went with the king to Wincefter, and thence to Burg, where he
‘ lived like a drone in a bee-hive. For as a drone devours and carries
‘ away every thing which is brought into a hive, fo he fent beyond
‘ fea whatever he could lay hands on, no matter whether he found it
‘ within or without the houfe, or took it from clerks or lay-men:
‘ nor did he ever there do, or leave behind him any thing that was
‘ good. And let no body think we tell an untruth, for it was well
‘ known all over the kingdom, that, after he was come thither (to wit,
‘ on the funday when they fing, *exurge quare*, O. D. [a]) prefently there
‘ were feen and heard a great many hunters, which hunters were all
‘ great, black, deformed creatures; having with them black, fawcer-
‘ eyed, fierce dogs; and rode upon black horfes and black ftags. This
‘ was feen in the park at Burch; and in all the woods between that
‘ town and Stanford: And the monks themfelves heard the found of
‘ the horns which they blew in the night. This was feen and heard
‘ from the time he came thither, all Lent until Eafter. Such was his
‘ coming. As for his departure (faith my author, who wrote this be-
‘ fore Peitow refign’d) we can yet fay nothing of that: God only
‘ knows.’ Many I fear will be difpleafed with me for inferting here
fuch an old monkifh tale as this. But Mr. Cambden [b], Mr. Gunton [c],
and bifhop Patrick [d] all take notice of it, which are authorities enow to
juftifie me for fo doing. And Hugo Candidus very gravely tells us [e], ‘ for a
‘ great many perfons of unqueftionable veracity, both faw thefe hunters,
‘ and heard them.’ However, for all that, I would not have my readers confider it as fact, but a piece of humor. For admitting the devil was an hunting,

---

a Sexagefima funday.
b In Northamptonfhire.
c Hift. of the church of Burg, p. 22.
d Supplement, p. 275
e p. 74.

G I

I dont fee any relation that has to the abbat of Burgs plundering that monaſtery, unleſs, like the fiend himſelf, the abbat had blown his horn and
ſet his dogs upon the monks (which I find not) as the Goblins (my
author would perſuade us) did on the deer. ' This abbat, as Mr. Willis
' tells us [a], reſigned in 1133 and theſame year was ſucceeded by Martin
' de Bec, or Vecti.'

Circa
ann.
1133.

XVIII. The ſaid Martin de Vecti, as I gather from divers collateral
notices, ſometime between 1133. and 1147. firſt erected the church of
S. Martin, beyond Stanford bridge.   My hints are, I. ' the ſaid Martin
' de Vecti, as Hugo Candidus affirms [b], [tho' he ſets down no year
' when he did ſo] aſſigned, *inter alia*, ten ſhillings a year out of the
' profits of S. Martins church at Stanford, to the uſe of the ſacriſty of
' Burg.'   II. I conceive the ſaid Martin de Vecti was the firſt who
gave that penſion to the church of Burg; this being the firſt time I
meet with the mention either of that penſion, or of S. Martins church;
tho' both occur frequently afterwards.   III. It is obſervable, both the
name of the church and of the abbat, is Martin.   IV. We read above,
in the deſcription of that part of Stanford which lies in Northamptonſhire as ſet down in the book of Doomſday, *there are here ſeventeen
villanes with a presbyter:* which almoſt evidently ſhews there was then
but one church here.   V. The abbat of Burg was then and long before
lord of the manor of Stanford on that ſide the bridge.   Laſtly, a bull
of pope Eugenius the third, confirming the lands and privileges of the
church of Burg in 1146. ſpeaks in the plural, of churches, &c. at
Stanford on that ſide the bridge under the juriſdiction of Burg [c].
Whence I conclude firſt, that the old church of All-Saints in the water
ſtreet was, 'till the ſaid Martin de Vecti erected the church of S. Martin,
the only pariſh church of Stanford beyond the bridge.   And ſecondly,
that about this time the town on that ſide the water beginning to grow
more populous, the then lord of that manor Martin de Vecti firſt built
and endowed the old church of S. Martin (I call it old in oppoſition
to that now ſtanding) and gave it his own name; reſerving the patronage, & the foreſaid penſion out of the profits thereof to his own
monaſtery of Burg.   And thus All-Saints pariſh there was divided into
two.   All that I have farther to add under this reign, is, that the town
of Stanford on the north ſide of the river, as I find [d], was in the demeſne of this K. Henry the firſt.   And that ' in 1135. as ſaith the chro-
' nicle of John abbat of Burg [e], was founded Stanford abby.'   What
Stanford I know not; but if ours, an abby of Ciſtercians, ſince we
certainly had ſuch a monaſtery, but by whom founded, or where ſituate,

Anno
1135.

a Hiſt. Abbies Vol. I. p. 146.
b p. 87.
c See an extract of that bull, ſo far as it
concerns Stanford, under that year below.

d See the inquiſition, under the 5. of H.
3. below.
e p. 72.

to me remains yet a ſecret —— K. Henry the firſt died on the ſecond day
of December 1135. and was ſucceeded by king

STEPHEN.

XIX. In 1140. was a great meeting at Stanford to conclude a peace   Anno
between K. Stephen and Ranulph earl of Cheſter, who both came hither   1140.
for that purpoſe. If we may believe the Saxon chronicle, matters
ſtood thus between them. ' In 1140. ſays the author of that work [a],
' began a ſmart war between the king and Ralph E. of Cheſter ; not be-
' cauſe the king would not give him, as he did every body elſe, what-
' ever he thought fit to ask ; but becauſe the more he gave them, they
' were but the more inveterate againſt him.   The earl now held Lincoln
' againſt the king, and there ſieſed every thing which belonged to him.
' Whereupon the king repairing thither, beſieged him and his brother
' William de Romare in the caſtle.   But the earl ſlipt out privately,
' and went to Robert earl of Glouceſter [his father in law] whom he
' brought thither with a great army ; where, on Candlemaſs day, they
' fought a ſharp battle againſt their maſter, and took him priſoner
' (for his men betrayed him and ran away) and brought him to Briſtow,
' where they clapt him in priſon.   Speed ſays [b], the earl, with his coun-
' teſſe and brother coming to Lincolne [only] to keepe their Chriſt-
' maſs ; the citizens, knowing the kings jealouſies, and deſirous to cur-
' ry favor with him, ſent ſecret intelligence, that if he would ſurpriſe
' both thoſe brethren, he had now the fitteſt advantage.'   Accordingly the king came, but, inſtead of catching the two brothers, was, as
you have heard, tho' he firſt faught bravely for it, in the end ſnapt up
himſelf.   ' Then, ſays my former author [c], was all England in a greater
' commotion than was ever known, and all ſort of calamities abound-
' ed in it.   After theſe things K. Henries daughter, who had been em-
' preſs of Almaine and was now counteſs of Anjou, came to London ;
' but, when the Londoners attempted to ſieſe her, ſhe got away, tho'
' not without the loſs of many of her followers.   After this Henry
' biſhop of Winceſter, king Stephens brother, had a conference with
' earl Robert, and with the empreſs, and gave them his oath that he
' would never again eſpouſe the king his brothers cauſe, and excommu-
' nicated all thoſe who now ſtood up for him.   He promiſed alſo to
' ſurrender Winceſter to them, and was the occaſion of their going
' thither.   But ſoon after their arrival there King Stephens Queen fol-
' lowed them with her forces, and beſieged them, 'till there aroſe a
' great famine in the town.   Whereupon, when they were no longer
' able to bear with the famine they got away privately and fled for
' it ; whereof when the beſiegers were advertiſed, they purſued them,
' and took Robert earl of Glouceſter, whom they brought to Rouceſter

---

a Sub 20 anno.   b p. 489. b.   c Sax. chron. ut ſupra.

' and

' and there threw into prifon : As for the empref fhe took refuge in
' a monaftery. Then prudent men, fome the kings and fome the earls
' friends, interceded ; and fo managed the bufinefs that the king fhould
' be exchanged for the earl, and the earl for the king : which was done.
' After this a peace was concluded between the king and earl Ralph at
' Stanford, each of them taking an oath and plighting his faith that he
' would not betray the other. But all this was to very little purpofe.
' For, guided by ill counfel, the king afterwards arrefted him at North-
' ampton, and flung him into prifon ; not long after which, govern'd
' by yet worfe advife, he fet him at liberty, conditionally that he fhould
' fwear upon the holy crofs, and give hoftages, to furrender all his
' caftles to the king. Some of them he yielded accordingly, but fome
' he kept, and befides did more ill things than he need.' Our monk
we may perceive is all along very fparing of K. Stephen, and concludes with a fcurvy reflection upon the earl of Chefter. But other
hiftorians give a different account of that earl, and fay, that all his
fault was only too much affection for his relations and rightful fovereign the emprefs and her fon duke Henry.

Dec. 17.   XX. ' Pope Eugenius the 3d, as Hugo Candidus relates [a], by his bull
1145.   ' bearing date the 17. of Decemb. 1145. confirmed to the church of
' Burg, *inter alia*, Burg with the mint there —— Alfo in Stanford nine
' and fifty manfures of land, with the lands, mills, churches, toll, coi-
' nage of mony ; [all thefe in Northamptonfhire.] Likewife in the
' fame town in Lincolnfhire, feven manfures.' The faid pope, as the
' fame author obferves [b], by another bull, bearing date three days after
Dec. 20.   ' the former (viz. Dec. 20. 1145.) remarking what lands were then held
1145.   ' in fee by the ftipendiary knights of the church of Burg, mentions, *in-*
' *ter alia*, the fee of Roger the infant or minor of Torpel, to wit Ufford
' and Pilton with their appurtenances and the lands which he hath in
' Makefei —— The fee of Afceline of Waterville, to wit Torp [Water-
' ville,] Marham, and Upton, with their appurtenances —— The fee of
' Geoffry of Winchefter, to wit, Armeftun and Burchle, &c.' By this brief
extract it appears, that the abbat of Burg had a mint both at Burg and Stanford.   Alfo that there was now, as I obferv'd, more than one parifh church
in that part of Stanford which lies in Northamptonfhire. Roger de Torpel and Afceline de Waterville aforefaid were both of them benefactors to the priory of S. Michael at Stanford, founded in 1156 by William Waterville then abbat of Burg.   Now the charters of the faid
Roger and Afceline being without date, meeting with their names
here fixes the time when they both lived, and fhews that their donations were conferr'd on the faid priory at, or very foon after, its firft
erection. ' The fame pope Eugenius, as my author faith [c] from the
Aug. 17. ' original in the Cotton library, upon the 17. of Aug. 1147. con-
1147.

    a p. 78, &c.   b p. 82. &c.   c Mon. Ang Tomi 2. p. 26. b.

                                 3   ' firmed

' firmed to Robert prior of Huntendune and his brethren, *inter alia*,
' the tythe of Stanford mills.'

    XXI. ' In 1149. King Stephen directed his mandate to Robert de   Anno
' Chilvey bifhop of Lincoln [a], ordering him to fee the monks of Thor- 1149.
' ney reſtored to their land of Weng, which Robert de Mans gave
' them in free alms, and that he ſhould maintain them in as peace-
' able poſſeſſion of the ſame, as it appears by the earl of Warwic's char-
' ter, they were thereto admitted; and all this, that there might not be
' any injury or hardſhip put upon them. Witneſs Robert de Ver, at
' Stanford. At the ſame time the ſaid K. Stephen certified [b], that the
' abbat and monks of Burg had before him made a dereinment or proof
' againſt the canons of Lincoln at Lincoln of their right to their land
' at Nortop. Witneſs Ralph the ſon of Gilbert at Stanford. At the
' ſame time the ſaid king Stephen, ſaith Peter Bleſens [c], here confirm-
' ed to the church of Croyland all the lands and privileges of the ſaid
' church. Witneſs himſelf, the queen, earl Simon [of Northampton
' I ſuppoſe] and others, at Stanford. In 1152. as near as I can gather   Anno
' from Holingſhed [d], that noble and valiant erle of Cheſter called Ranulf 1152.
' departed this life, a man of ſuch ſtoutneſſe of ſtomacke, that uneth [i. e.
' hardly] might death make him to yield or ſhewe any token of feare.
' He was poiſoned, as was thought, by William Peverell. The ſame
' author adds [e], altho' erle Ranulf favored the part of duke Henrie, yet
' in theſe late yeares hee did but little for him, and therefore it was
' thought that the death of this erle was not ſo great a loſſe to the
' duke, as the deathes of Euſtace, erle Simon, and other the kings
' friends deceaſing about the ſame time ſeemed to further him; ſo that
' hys part became dayly ſtronger, and the kings to decay. About the
' ſame time alſo the caſtels of Reeding and Beertwel were delivered to
' duke Henrie; and the lady Gundreda counteſſe of Warwike did drive
' out of the caſtel there the ſouldiers that helde it for K. Stephen, and
' delivered the towne to the duke. And thus things came to paſſe in
' ſundry places with ſo good ſucceſſe as duke Henry could wiſh.
' Whereupon meaning to follow the ſteps of proſperous fortune, he
' marched forth unto Stanford.' Hither he came, ſays William of Neuberry [f], ' *cum inſtructo exercitu*, with a well inſtructed army.' For he
had twice before it ſeems attempted either the town, or caſtle, or both,
and met with as many repulſes. But he was reſolved now to carry it,

---

a Stephanus rex Anglie, &c. Roberto epiſ. Linc. ſal. Mando tibi quod facias monachos de Thornei reſarciri de terra de Wenga, quam Robertus de Mans eis in eleemoſyna dedit; & facias eos ita in pace tenere, ſicut in carta comitis Warwici teſtatur quod eis data fuerit, ne ſuper hoc fiat eis injuria vel contumelia. Teſte Roberto de Ver, apud Stanford. Ex cartul. eccleſiæ de Thorney penes Com. de Weſtmoreland.

b Stephanus rex Anglie, &c. Sciatis quod abbas & monachi de Burgo dirationaverunt coram me verſus canonicos Lincolnienſes apud Linc. terram ſuam de Nortop. Teſte Radulfo filio Gilberti apud Stanford. Suapham. fol. 41.
c p. 451.
d p. 387. b.
e ib.
f Vol. 1. p. 100.

and, as Henry of Huntington says[a], ‘ *tertiam igitur obſidionem congeſſit*
‘ *circa caſtellum de Stanford,* ſat down therefore a third time to beſiege
‘ it. *Capta ſtatim urbe, &c.* the town he preſently took, but the re-
‘ bels who kept the caſtle, ſent meſſengers to the king, requiring
‘ him to come to their reſcue. But he at the ſame time had laid ſiege
‘ to Gipeſwig caſtel, held againſt him by Hugh Bigot. From the

Anno   ‘ leaguer of which place when he would neither deſiſt, nor ſpare any
1153.   ‘ ſupplies for his friends who were beſieged at Stanford, the caſtel there
‘ was ſurrendred to the great prince Henry; as, after ſome time, was
‘ that of Gipeſwig to K. Stephen. Departing from Stanford the duke
‘ of Normandy went to Nottingham, and preſently took the town; for
‘ they who kept the caſtel, had ſet it on fire.’ The end of all theſe
‘ ſieges and combuſtions, as Mr. Stow acquaints us [b], was this. ‘ At
‘ length thorough the great labour of the archbiſhop of Canterbury and
‘ the other biſhops, the king commanded the nobles to meet at Win-
‘ cheſter, where the duke being received with great joie, the king, in
‘ ſight of all men adopted him his ſonne, and confirmed to him the
‘ principalitie of England. The duke received him in place of a father,
‘ granting to him all the daies of his life to enjoie the name and ſeat
‘ of the kings preeminence.’ —— K. Stephen died the 2. of Oct. 1154.
and was ſucceeded by the ſaid duke.

a Edit. Franc. p. 397. edit. Lond. fol. 227. b. 40.   b p. 214.

The end of the fourth book.

Academia tertia Anglicana;

OR, THE

ANTIQUARIAN ANNALS

of the TOWN of

STANFORD

IN

Lincoln, Rutland, *and* Northampton *Shires.*

BOOK V.

Containing the reign of K. Henry the second.

I. ' UPON the second of January 115⁴⁄₇. died Martin [de ⟨Jan. 2.
' Vecti aforesaid] abbat of Burg, and the same day, 115⁴⁄₇.
' says the Saxon chronicle ᵃ, the monks of their own ⟨I. H. 2
' accord chose another abbat, his name William of Walteville.' This
William of Walteville, or Walterville (as my author should rather call
him) founded (as shall be by and by related) the priory conventual of
S. Michael, an house of Benedictine nuns at little Wirthorp by Stanford.
It is then in me but a piéce of Antiquarian justice to begin here some
account of him. His election to the church of Burg is thus related by
Hugo Candidus ᵇ. ' The same day that abbat Martin died, all the
' monks met together that they might chuse one of their own body to
' be their father, pastor, and guardian; fearing least, thro' delay, some
' stranger might get in by mony, and domineer over them; and so
' the last end be worse than the first. Wherefore, because it was very
' hard for a multitude to agree in one person, they chose out of their
' own number twelve old monks of good understanding to make an e-
' lection for them, as God should direct, in private. The manner of
' the election was thus. They made them swear upon the holy gospels
' and the holy reliques, that they would not be moved in their choice,
' either by love or hatred: but, that as God and the spirit of wisdom
' advised, would chuse one who was well qualified to govern the
' abby, in every circumstance; this they all did: Hugo the eldest
' beginning to take the oath and all the rest following. After which

a Sub anno 1154.   b p. 89. &c.

B

' the

' the prior got up, and made oath for himfelf and the whole convent,
' that they would all chufe him in whom thofe twelve fhould agree.
' This being done, the twelve went out of the chapterhoufe into the
' abbats chamber; and the prior, with the reft who remained there, fang
' the feven Pfalms, and prayed God to direct them by the grace of his
' holy fpirit; which the twelve alfo begged by finging prayers & *ve-*
' *ni creator fpiritus:* after which they fell to conference. When fome
' of them propofed that the eldeft fhould before all the reft fay whom
' they were for, but that was refufed. At laft, on more mature conful-
' tation it was agreed, to elect one difcreet, wife, perfon, the fenior
' of the reft, being the forefaid Hugh, to hear every one of them con-
' fefs and tell what God had put in their hearts. Which being done,
' he asked them, if they would know what every mans opinion was
' fingly? They faid, no: but he fhould declare in whom the major part
' of them were agreed. To which he replied, that they were all in a
' manner agreed in one man, to wit, William Waterville; and, if any
' one of them were againft it, he had ftill liberty to contradict it.
' But they were fo far from oppofing it, that they all confented. And
' fo entring into the chapterhoufe, and declaring what they had done,
' the whole company praifed God. And the day after having performed
' the obfequies of the deceafed abbat, Reinald the [other] prior and Hugh
' the fpirit [a], went to the king then at Oxford, together with archbi-
' fhop Theobald and divers barons; and there laid before him and the
' archbifhop the death of abbat Martin; at which news the king and
' the archbifhop and all the reft both rich and poor were much con-
' cerned. After this the monks defired the kings leave for them to elect
' another abbat. But the king demanded, if they had elected no body
' already? Whereupon the monks immediately prefented William of
' Waterville to him, formerly his own clerc, humbly befeeching his
' grace to admit of him to be their abbat. Whereupon the king order-
' ed the archbifhop to examine well whether the brethren had unani-
' moufly agreed to the election, or how they had oppofed it? But
' they all declaring and protefting that the election was made by the
' whole convent; the king confirmed what they had done, and then by
' his own charter granted the abby to the forefaid elect. After this
' *Te Deum* being fung and prayers made, the abbat did homage and
' legality [b] to the king. Then repaired to Robert bifhop of Lincoln for
' his benediction, who, appointing him a day and place, accordingly
' gave it him. And thereupon he was inftalled at Burg on the funday
' called Sexagefima [c], with a folemn proceffion of abbats, monks, clercs,

---

a Albus, candidus, fpiritus, ab amiffo fanguine nuncupatus, quafi fpiritui quam ho-mini fimilior.

b Legalitas.

c Inftead of Sexagefima Mr. Sparke in his text of candidus, p. 91. writes Quadra-gefima. But that cannot be the true reading, becaufe prefently after follows, *in proximo capite jejunii.* Suapham and Wittlefea, were aware of this, and fo read, as I do, Sexagefima. That they fo read Mr. Sparke himfelf notes, *ad imum paginæ prædict.*

4

'   ' and

' and laymen.   There moreover was prefent W. archdeacon of Nor-
' thampton from the bifhop, with other clerc's, who commended the
' cure of fouls to him; and then fpent the day in great rejoycing and
' gladnefs.   In the beginning of the enfuing lent the abbat finding a
' great want of provifion in the monaftery, prefently began to buy and
' continued fo to do, both wheat, malt, oats, beans, cheefe, wine,
' and all other neceffaries 'till the feaft of S. Bartholomew.   This was a
' very great expence; and yet he likewife difcharged all the debts of his
' predeceffor, which were three hundred marc's of filver, befides three-
' fcore more owing for intereft, which, thro' his induftry, the king
' ordered to be remitted.   He recovered alfo the fee and fervice of
' Geoffry de la Mare the conftable, for an hundred marc's which he gave
' the king.   To whom alfo he gave an hundred more for the confir-
' mation of nine knights fee's, which had been held by earl Simon'
[of Northampton.]   Leave we now our good abbat a while at Burg,
and proceed to other matters.   ' In this 1. of H. the 2. [a] when the
' fherif of Northampton and Leicefterfhire gave up his accompts, Geof-
' fry de Clinton owed the king fourfcore marcs of filver for the ward-
' fhip of William de Diva's fon, with his land.'   The Diva's took their
names I fuppofe from the river Dive in Normandy, mentioned in Dugdale [b], near the banks whereof I guefs they formerly dwelt.   Some of
this family were benefactors to the nunnery of S. Michael by Stanford,
for which reafon thus much is here faid of them.

II. ' In the 2. of H. 2. Richard lord Humet being then conftable of 2. H. 2.
' Normandy, faith the fame Dugdale [c], in confideration of his fervices
' obtained from that king, a grant of the lordfhip of Stanford in Lin-
' colnfhire, with all its appurtenances, both of the caftel & borough;
' excepting the fervices of the abbat of Burg and William Lanvalei.'
This gift another writer [d] expreffes thus.   ' When Henry of Anjou, by
' the name of Henry the fecond, came to the crown, he gave the whole
' village of Stanford, being his demefne, excepting the fees of the ba-
' rons and knights of the faid village, to Richard Humez or Humetz,
' to hold of him by homage and other fervice.'   This Richard Humet
is the firft old lord of Stanford, to whom that lordfhip was granted
from the crown, of any I yet read of.   I have alfo read (I think in
fome part of Doomfday as publifhed by Mr. Moreton [e]) ' that the abbat
' of Burg held in Writtorp two hides of the fee of Croyland.   And
' there Richard de Humez held half an hide.   The faid Richard Hu-
' met, faith the forefaid Dugdale [f], had likewife by the gift of K.
' Henry the 2. at the fame time, the lordfhips of Ketene in Rutland,

a Ex MS. collect. Johannis Philipot arm.
fecialis fomerfet. penes peritifs. antiquarium
Johannem Anftis arm. Garter. principalem
regem armorum.
    b Baronage, Tome I. p. 27. a.
    c id. p. 631. a.

d Britannia ant. & nova. Vol. 2. p. 1422. a.
    e Abbas de Burgo S. Petri tenet in Writ-
torp duas hidas de feodo de Croyland. Inde tenet Richardus de Humez dimidiam hidam.
    f Ut fupra in loco ult. citato.

' and

' and **Dudinton** in Northamptonſhire ; as alſo Kiſinberge and Siringeham
' in Bucks ; which were of the fee of Walter Giffard, late earl of Buck-
' ingham :   As alſo the lordſhip of Meiſe and Haie of Lutenore,
' both lying in Normandy.'

Anno   III. ' In the latter end of 1156. William Waterville abovementioned
1156.   ' lord abbat of Burg, in honor of God [as Candidus relates [a]] began a
' priory of holy nuns without Stanford, and founded and built the
' church of the bleſſed Michael the archangel there ; in which he aſ-
' ſembled no leſs than forty holy virgins, living regularly in religion
' and pure virginity.' Forty was the number at firſt, but doubtleſs, as
other benefactions came in, it was afterwards much encreaſed. To
this nunnery the ſaid William Waterville and the convent of Burg
gave, firſt, the church of S. Michael without Stanford, erected purely
for the ſaid nuns, and ſo made conventual. Conditionally nevertheleſs that the prior, prioreſs, and nuns ſhould be put in by the abbat
and convent of Burg ; that the ſaid houſe ſhould be wholly under the
ſubjection of that of Burg ; and acknowledge its ſubjection to the ſame
by the annual penſion of a noble. For ſays the firſt charter, ' Be
' it known to all the ſons of the church, that I William by the grace
' of God abbat of Burg, and the whole chapter, have given, and being
' corroborated with the authority of theſe preſents granted, to the re-
' ligion of the holy nuns abiding at Stanford, the church of the bleſ-
' ſed Michael in perpetual alms, with all things to the ſame church be-
' longing, well, and in peace, freely, and honorably to be poſſeſſed, for
' the relief and health of our ſouls, to be ordered, in every circum-
' ſtance, under our ſubjection, and by our advice. Particularly, that
' the prelate appointed to overſee the buſineſs of the ſame, be either
' placed, or diſplaced, at the pleaſure of the lord abbat with advice of
' his chapter. In like ſort that the nomination of a prioreſs, to preſide
' over the reſt, ſhall be at the diſpoſal of the abbat with advice of his
' chapter. And in like manner that the admiſſion of the holy nuns,
' who ſhall there ſerve God, ſhall depend on the abbats pleaſure and
' advice of his chapter. And that they alſo the holy nuns, and the
' diſpoſal of all their affairs, ſhall in all caſes be at the ordering of
' the lord abbat and his chapter ; ſo, to wit, that for advantage of this
' monaſtery the monaſtery of Burg may not ſuffer detriment. Moreover
' that this monaſtery ſhall recogniſe its ſubjection to the monaſte-
' ry of Burg, by an annual penſion of half a marc of ſilver, to be paid
' to the Almnerer, towards mending the books, the morrow after the
' feaſt of S. Michael.' Secondly, with the conſent of the convent of
Burg, the ſaid William Waterville gave the ſaid nuns the revenues of
the church of S. Martin at Stanford (built by his immediate predeceſſor)
conditionally nevertheleſs, that, for this ſecond benefaction, after the
death of Peter the prieſt (then incumbent of the ſaid church of S.

a p. 92.

Martin)

Martin) they fhould likewife every Michaelmas acknowledge their fubjection to the monaftery of Burg, by the payment of ten fhillings to
the fame.   Candidus indeed fays[a], ' he obliged the faid nuns to pay
' yearly ten fhillings out of the faid church of S. Martin which he had
' purchafed, to the facrifty of Burg.'   But his purchafing the faid church
feems to be a miftake.   For, as I have fhewn, his own predeceffor Martin de Vecti firft built the faid church, and firft affigned the penfion of ten
fhillings out of the revenues of that church to the facrifty of Burg.   William Waterville then had no occafion to purchafe that church, which
was built by his own immediate predeceffor, and the patronage whereof
he undoubtedly referved to himfelf and fucceffors, the abbats and monks
of Burg; or to affign that penfion which was before affign'd.   The
faid William Waterville firft indeed appropriated that church, with the
confent of his convent, to the faid nunnery.   But the penfion of ten
fhillings referved in his fecond charter, feems to be, for thefe reafons,
only a new refervation of the penfion before charged upon it by Martin de Vecti: However let the charter it felf fpeak[b].   ' Be it known
' to all men, both future as well as prefent, that I William, by the
' grace of God, abbat of Burg, with affent of the convent, before a
' multitude of men and women, have given, and, being fortified with
' the authority of thefe prefents, confirmed to the holy nuns who
' ferve God in the monaftery of the bleffed Michael the archangel by
' Staunforde, in our fubjection and cuftody, the church of the bleffed
' Martin of Staunforde, into free and perpetual alms, with all things
' to the fame church belonging, for the love of God and for the re-
' lief of our fouls; to the end that the fame nuns may always have,
' and poffefs, the fame church, unto their proper ufes; nor fhall it be
' lawful for them to give it to any one, nor to alienate it into other
' hands; becaufe we have decreed, by witnefs of this prefent inftrument,
' that, out of the profits of this church, together with the other alms,
' which we have affigned to the fame to ferve God, they be, for the
' future, more plentifully fuftained; they therefore recognifing the
' church of Burg with an annual penfion of ten fhillings at the feaft of
' S. Michael, after it [the church of S. Martin] fhall be clear of Peter
' the Prieft.   This donation was made in the church of the bleffed
' Michael the archangel at Stanforde, before a great many perfons.'
By virtue of this charter the faid nuns of S. Michael ever after prefented a vicar to the faid church of S. Martin till the 30. of H. 8. when
their houfe was diffolved.   Thirdly, with the confent of his convent,
the faid William Waterville, gave likewife to this nunnery, by a third
charter, the revenues of the church of S. Firmin at Thirlby in Lin-

a Ex regiftri Ecclefiæ de Burgo olim penes Cl. Seldenum, folio 63. a. citati in Monaft. Ang. Tomi I. p. 488. b.   Et ex regiftri de Suapham folio 51.   Ac etiam ex regiftri alii ejufdem ecclefiæ de Burgo, in bib.
Cotton. Vefp. E. XXII. fol. 39. b.

b p. 29.
c Ex regiftri prioratus S. Michaelis juxta
Stanford, anno 1657. penes Galf. Minfhul
generofum; fol. 4. b. citato in Mon. Ang.
Tomi II. p. 881. a.

colnfhire,

colnſhire, within ſeven miles of Stanford.   Theſe two laſt benefactions he gave them for their future ſubſiſtence; upon the demiſe, or remove, of the two incumbents there.   However, for this laſt gift of the
church of Thirlby, he likewiſe obliged them to acknowledge their
ſubjection to Burg, with a noble of ſilver annually; to be paid, half at
Eaſter and half at Michaelmas, to the almnerer of that church, and the
firſt payment to commence immediately after the remove or death of
Geoffry the capellan, then incumbent there : in which third charter he
thus expreſſes himſelf[a].   ' Be it known to all men, both future as well
' as preſent, that I William, by the grace of God, abbat of Burg, and
' the whole convent, have given, and being fortifyed with the autho-
' rity of theſe preſents confirmed to the holy nuns who ſerve God in
' the monaſtery of the B. Michael the archangell by Staunforde, in our
' ſubjection and cuſtody, the church of the bleſſed martyr Firmin of
' Thurleby, into free & perpetual alms, with all things to the ſame
' church belonging, for the love of God and for the relief of our
' ſouls; ſo that the ſame holy nuns may always have and poſſeſs the
' ſame church, unto their proper uſes; nor ſhall it be lawful for them
' to give it to any one, or to alienate it into other hands; becauſe we
' have decreed, by witneſs of this preſent inſtrument, that, out of the
' profits of this church, together with the other alms which we have
' aſſigned to the ſame to ſerve God, they be for the future more plen-
' tifully ſuſteined; they therefore recogniſing our church with the an-
' nual penſion of half a marc of ſilver, to be paid at the two terms of
' Eaſter and Michaelmas to our almnerer, when it [the church of
' Thurleby] ſhall be clear of Geoffry the capellan.'   By virtue of this
charter the ſaid nuns always preſented a vicar to the ſaid church of
Thurleby 'till the 30. of H. 8. when their houſe was diſſolved: ſince
which time the provoſt and fellows of the college of K. Henry the 6.
at Eaton by Windſor, are become patrons of the ſaid vicarage.   As to
our nunnery of S. Michael, theſe are all the donations of the founders own immediate gift which I have yet met with.   Nothing of the
monaſtery or church is now ſtanding, but the ſituation is well known,
and at this day called the nuns in S. Martins.   There are divers traditions both of the beauty of the church, and the ſtately remains pulled
down in the memory of man; theſe laſt not without the loſs of his
life who threw down the firſt ſtone, and the leg of another labourer
then miſerably broken.

   IV. It was an annual cuſtom of this priory on the morrow after the
feaſt of S. Michael (when the nuns paid any of the abovementioned
penſions to the lord abbat and monks of Burg) that the lady prioreſs and
ſome of her ſiſters, in the names of themſelves and of the whole convent, made, either by word of mouth at Burg, or ſent in writing thi-

---

a Ex regiſtri prioratus S. Michaelis ſupradicti folio 7. a citato in Mon. Ang. Tomi II. p. 882.

ther

ther under the convent feal, a recognition, that is an acknowledgment
& recital of the fubjection of the church of the nuns of S. Michael at
Stanford, to the abbat and convent of Burg.   For example, that under
the convent feal generally ran thus [a].   'A. the priorefs, and the convent
' of the holy nuns of the monaftery of S. Michael of Staunford, to all
' whom thefe prefent letters fhall come, greeting.   Unto your know-
' ledge we defire it may come, that we, and all our goods, within
' our priory and without, wherefoever being, in our manors & churches,
' by confent of the lord abbat of Burg, and the convent of the
' fame place, to us appropriated; in whofe fee our church is founded,
' and our priory; and by whofe bounties we are fupported; are in the
' difpofal of the fame, for our profit and utility, and of our church,
' as it fhall feem to them under God to be more wholfomely expedient.
' And that our prior, who fhall have the care of feeing the bufinefs
' of our monaftery, both incomes & disburfements, duly managed,
' fhall be placed or difplaced, at the will of the lord abbat, with ad-
' vice of his chapter.   And that when the priorefs of the faid mona-
' ftery of ours fhall chance to depart this life, no election of a future
' priorefs may be made, without fpecial licence of the faid lord
' abbat firft asked and obtained.   Likewife that during the vacancy of
' the priory, the fame lord abbat, as it is meet, fhall freely difpofe of
' our capital houfe, by affigning, at the expences of our houfe, a war-
' den in his name, over us and our poffeffions, 'till we fhall have
' lawfully elected, and, for the time of that vacancy, made an end with
' the fame.   Moreover, we the holy nuns, and the ordinations of all
' our affairs, in all cafes, as aforefaid, are at the difpofal of the faid
' lord abbat & his chapter, fo to wit, that, for advantage of our
' monaftery, the monaftery of Burg may not fuffer any detriment.
' Wherefore we faithfully and firmly before God profefs, by thefe pre-
' fents, for us and our fucceffors, for ever inviolably to obferve the
' conditions aforefaid, and regularly yield to the faid lord abbat, for
' the time being, in all obedience.   Our monaftery fhall alfo recognife
' the monaftery of Burg with the annual penfion of a marc of filver,
' the morrow after the feaft of S. Michael, towards mending the books,
' to be paid into the treafury.   In witnefs whereof we have caufed
' thefe prefent letters to be figned with the feal of our chapter.' The faid
Recognition was fometimes expreffed a great deal more concife, thus [b].

a Ex regiftri Petriburg. in bibl. Cott. par. 2. fol. 130. citati in Monaft. Ang. Tomi I. p. 489. a.
  b A. prioriffa & conventus fanctimoniali-um S. Michaelis de Staunford, fidelibus ad quos litere prefentes pervenerint falutem. Ad notitiam veftram volumus pervenire, nos & omnia noftra, in difpofitione D. abbatis & conventus de Burgo effe, in quorum feo-do fundata eft ecclefia noftra, & de quorum beneficiis fuftentamur.   Unde prefenti fcrip-

to figillo capituli noftri fignato, atteftamur eos liberam habuiffe & habere difpofitionem de omnibus rebus & poffeffionibus noftris, fecundum quod viderint, & eis & nobis, ex-pedire.   Unde fideliter promittimus, coram Deo, quod nunquam ab corum confilio & difpofitione refiliemus, fed per omnia eis eri-mus obedientes.   Ex regiftri ecclefiæ de Bur-go, in Bib. Cott. fub imagine Vefp. E. XXII. fol 39. b.

'A. the priorels & convent of the holy nuns of S. Michael of Staun-
'ford, to the faithful unto whom thefe prefent letters fhall come,
'greeting.   Unto your knowledge we defire it may come, that we and
'all that we have, are in the difpofal of the lord abbat and convent of
'Burg, in whofe fee our church is founded, & by whofe favors we are
'fupported.   Wherefore, by this prefent writing, figned with the feal
'of our chapter, we atteft them to have had, and have, the free dif-
'pofal, of all our effects & poffeffions, according to what they fhall
'fee convenient for themfelves & us.   Wherefore we faithfully pro-
'mife before God, that we will never deviate from their counfel &
'difpofal but in all things be to them obedient.'   Some fhort time after
the foundation of this nunnery (but the exact year when I find not) K.
Henry the 2. by his charter confirmed the donations of the founder thus [a].
'Henry, by the grace of God, king of England, duke of Norman-
'dy and Aquitain, and earl of Anjou, to his archbifhops, bifhops, ab-
'bats, earls, barons, judges, fherifs, officers, & all his faithful, French
'& Englifh, of all England, greeting.   Know ye that I have granted,
'& by this prefent charter confirmed, to the nuns of S. Michael of
'Staunford, all the donations which have been juftly made them, and
'for which they have the charters of their donors, according as the charters
'of the fame donors witnefs.   Wherefore I will & firmly command, that
'the forefaid church of S. Michael & the nuns there ferving God, may
'have & hold all thofe donations (& what elfe fhall be fairly made them)
'well & in peace, freely & quietly, wholly, fully, & honorably, in
'churches & tithes, & lands & rents, in wood & in plain, in meadows
'& paftures, in waters & mills, in parks, fifheries, & marfhes, in ways
'& roads, & in all other places & other things; & with all their li-
'berties & free cuftoms, as the charters of their donors do, or fhall ho-
'neftly witnefs.   Witneffes R. archbifhop of Roan, Jordan dean of Sarum,
'Roger the capellan, mafter Osbert of the chamber, Roger le Bigod,
'Hugh de Creiffacre, Roger of the fhield, William de Stutevill, &
'Roger de Pavilli; at Clarendon.'

a Henricus D. G. rex Anglie, dux Normannie & Aquitanie, & comes Andegavie,
archiepifcopis, epifcopis, abbatibus, comitibus,
baronibus, juftitiariis, vicecomitibus, miniftris, & omnibus fidelibus fuis, Francis &
Anglis, totius Anglie, falutem.   Sciatis me
conceffiffe, et prefenti carta confirmaffe,
monialibus S. Michaelis de Staunford, omnes donationes que rationabiliter eis facte
funt, & unde cartas donatorum fuorum habent, fecundum quod eorundem donatorum
carte teftantur.   Quare volo & firmiter pre-
cipio quod predicta ecclefia S. Michaelis &
moniales ibidem Deo fervientes, omnes donationes illas, & que rationabiliter eis fient,
habeant & teneant, bene & in pace, libere
& quiete, integre & plenarie & honorifice,
in ecclefiis, & decimis, & terris, & redditibus, in bofco & plano, in pratis & pafturis,
in aquis & molendinis, in vivariis & pifca-
riis, & marifcis, in viis & femitis, & in omnibus aliis locis & aliis rebus; & cum omnibus libertatibus, & liberis confuetudinibus
fuis ficut carte donatorum teftantur, vel rationabiliter teftabuntur.   Teftibus R. archie-
pifcopo Rothom.   Jordano decano Sarum,
Rogero capellano, magiftro Ofberto de ca-
mera, Rogero le Bigod, Hugone de Creiffacre, Rogero de Scuto, Willielmo de Stutevill, Rogero de Pavilli; apud Clarendo-
nam.   Ex rotulo patenti de anno 3°. E. 4.
ut in exemplari penes per honorabilem ac
D. D. Brownlow Comitem Exoniæ.

V. ' ᵃ In the 5. H. 2. Richard de Humez, lord of Stanford, ac- 5. H. 2.
' compted for ten pounds part of the laſt years profits of the ſhriefalty of
' Rutland.   ᵇ In the 7. H. 2. the ſaid Richard accompted for ten pounds 7. H. 2.
' more, part of the rent of the ſixth, or then laſt, years profits of the
' ſaid ſhriefalty of Rutland.   ᶜ Upon the 9. of Jan. 116⅗. pope Alex- Jan. 9.
' ander the ſecond confirmed to the abbat & monks of Thorney, *inter* 116⅗
' *alia*, what land they had at Stanford.   ᵈ In 1163. 9. H. 2. Richard 116⅗
' Humet, getting together the barons of Normandy & Brittany, in the 9. H. 2
' month of Auguſt, took the caſtle of Combert in Brittany, on the be- Aug
' half of K. Henry the 2. which caſtle Raphe de Fulgers poſſeſſed, af-
' ter the death of John de Dol.   ᵉ The ſaid Richard was ſherif of Rut- 1164
' land from 1164. to 1180.   ᶠ In the 10. of H. 2. William Lanvalei 10. H. 2.
' was one of the witneſſes to a recognition then made by the king touch-
' ing the peoples rights and liberties.   ᵍ In the 11. of H. 2. in the 11. H. 2
' aſſieging of Briges [ʰ Bridgnorth in Wales] the king was in no ſmall
' danger of his life; for one of the enemies ſhooting directly at him,
' had perced him through the bodie, if Hubert de ſaint Clere, cone-
' ſtable of Colcheſter, perceyving the arrowe comming, had not thruſt
' himſelfe betwixt the king & the ſame, & ſo, preſerving his maſter,
' receyved the ſtrype hymſelfe, whereof he dyed preſently after, be-
' ſeeching the king to be good lorde to one only daughter which he
' had, whom the king beſtowed in marriage upon William Langvalee,
' togither with her fathers inheritance, which William begat of hir a
' ſonne that bare both his name & ſurname.'   This William the father was that William Lanvalei, whoſe ſervice or fee at Stanford was ex-
preſly excepted out of the grant of that manor by the preſent K. H. 2.
to Richard Humet ⁱ.   ' Wakerly ᵏ [in Northamptonſhire within five
' miles of Stanford] was antiently [a part of] the eſtate of this Wil-
' liam, who was alſo governor of Colcheſter caſtle [in right of his wife,
' daughter of the above Hubert de ſaint Clere] & warden of the foreſt
' of Eſſex as far as Chelmsford bridge.'   He was a baron of England, and
as ſuch Sir William Dugdale ˡ mentions him.   But tho' his marriage
was thus remarkable, that great antiquary ſays nothing of it; & little of
his wife, any farther than that her chriſtian name was Hawyſe ᵐ.   Stow
ſays ⁿ, the ſon of this William Lanvalei, bore the name & ſurname of
his grandfather [meaning, I ſuppoſe, Hubert de ſaint Clere] but that
ſeems to be a miſtake; for I find no account of any ſuch perſon.   Whereas William, ſon of William Lanvalei, as you will hereafter find º, was
a benefactor to the nuns of S. Michael by Stanford.

a Ex MS. collectionibus Johannis Philipot fecialis antedicti.
  b Id. ib.
  c Mon. Ang. Tom. I. p. 250. b. where ſee his confirmation.
    d Baron. Vol. I. p. 631. b.
    e Wrights Rutland, p. 9.
    f Baron. Vol. I. p. 633. b.

g Holingſhed, Vol. II. p. 408. a.
h Stow, p. 222.
i 2. H 2. ſupra.
k Brit. ant. & nova, Vol. III. p. 451. a
l Baron. To. I. p. 633. a. b.
m Id. p. 633. b.
n Ut ſupra.
o Anno 1215. infra.

VI. Upon

Feb. 3.   **VI. Upon** the 3. of Feb. 117⁷⁄. Richard Humet, lord of Stanford, at
117¹· the requeſt of William de Colville, baron of Bitam, a perſon highly
reſpected by him, gave S. Andrews church in Stanford (whereof he was
patron) to be appropriated to the nuns of S. Michael; but that donation
not to take place 'till after the death of Peter the then incumbent. For
ſaith his charter ᵃ, ' be it known, to preſent & future people, that I Ri-
' chard de Humet, conſtable of [Normandy to] Henry K. of England, in
' an intuition of the high piety, and for remiſſion of my ſins, &
' at the petition of our beloved William de Coleville, have given &
' granted, & by this preſent charter confirmed to the abby of S. Mi-
' chael of Staunforde, & to the nuns there ſerving God, the church
' of S. Andrew at Staunforde, which Peter the Dean has, to be held in
' alms for ever; ſaving, ſo long as he ſhall live, the right of the fore-
' named Peter. Done in the year of the word incarnate 1170. on S.
' Blaſes day, in the hall at Staunforde. Preſent Bertram de Verdun,
' Girold de Normanville, Walter de Cardonville, Walter the Briton,
' Robert de Kernelle, Walter de Amundeville, Helte de Boſcoale,
' & divers others.' Sir William Dugdale ſays ᵇ, ' this Richard Humet
' beſtowed alſo on the foreſaid nuns of S. Michael, a yearly rent of
' ten marcs payable out of his lordſhip of Stanford.' But the ſame is a
miſtake. For the ſaid rent of ten marcs was not the gift of the ſaid
Richard Humet, but of William his ſon. And if Sir William Dugdale had not been too haſty in looking over the charter of K. John, confirming the ſaid grant of the ſaid William (printed in his own Monaſticon ᶜ, & to which he refers in his Baronage ᵈ) he would have eaſily ſeen
it was as I ſay. By virtue of the above grant of Richard Humet, the
ſaid nuns of S. Michael, after the death of Peter the dean, preſented a
vicar to the foreſaid church of S. Andrew 'till the 30. of H. 8. when
their houſe was diſſolved. The ſaid Peter, as I conceive, was dean of
Stanford; &, if ſo, the firſt that I meet with. He was alſo the ſame perſon, as I gueſs, who, as appears by the charter of William Waterville
above ᵉ, was the laſt rector of S. Martins. And, as that church was built by
Martin de Vecti & given by his next ſucceſſor to the nuns aforeſaid, was
not only the laſt, but probably the firſt & only rector thereof. His being
alive now ſhews that he muſt be a pretty elderly man, and conſequently that it was not long before the appropriations of the ſaid churches
took place by his death. As to the place where this inſtrument was
executed, it may be queſtioned whether by the hall at Staunforde was
meant, ſome gild-hall, belonging to the burgeſſes; or the hall houſe,
or caſtel, which Richard lord Humet had now there. Bertram de Verdun,
was a young nobleman who had ſome lands at Stanford, & now lived
there with his guardian Richard Humet.

a Ex regiſtri prioratus S. Michaelis penes   c To. I. p. 488. b.
Galf. Minſhul gen. 1657. folio 4. b. citato   d In loco ſupra citato.
in Monaſt. Ang. Tomi II. p. 880.   e Anno 1156.
   b Baron. To. I. p. 631. b.

VII. [a] ' In 1174. 21. H. 2. Richard Humet, lord of Stanford, was one
' of the witnesses to that instrument made between K. Henry the 2. &
' William K. of Scotland, whereby that king acknowledged subjection
' to K. Henry, & accordingly did homage to him for that realm.
' This Richard married Maud one of the daughters and coheirs of
' Maud de la Hay. By her he had issue William de Humet his son &
' heir.' About this time one Brand de Fossato, a person of great piety,
sold all his estate, and built an hospital & chappel to the honor of God,
& the blessed S. John the baptist, & the glorious S. Thomas of Canterbury (murdered Dec. 28. 1170.) which hospital & chappel he erected at
the head of Stanford bridge, on the south side of the river (where the
lord Burghleys hospital now stands) for reception of poor strangers,
where by his care, & the bounty of one Siward (who it seems joined
with him in this pious undertaking) they were relieved with bread,
beer, meat, lodging, and other refreshments, as they passed by; whilst
at the same time some monks & other poor were constantly subsisted
there. To which hospital, [b] ' Richard Humet & Bertram de Verdun
' abovementioned, gave also the land whereon their church & church-
' yard were placed. [c] Anketill de Mallory & William de Dive, con-
' stables to the earl of Leycester, now yeelded to the king the castels of
' Leycester, Groby, & Mountsorrel, to the intente that he shoulde deale
' more courteously with the earl their master,' who had been in arms
against the king. This Anketill de Mallory, or some other person of
his name, as I conceive, had lands at Stanford, & gave name to the
lane there called Mallory lane, now corruptly mannerly lane. Matildis wife of William de Dive was a benefactress to the nuns of S. Michael by Stanford; of which hereafter. [d] ' This year also, while the
' king was detained in Normandy by the rebellion of his sons, Jeoffry
' his base son by Rosamund, bishop elect of Lincoln, rais'd an im-
' mense sum of mony, thro' this whole diocese; but either from an ho-
' nourable sense that the king had no occasion for it, or for a pru-
' dent fear of exposing himself to danger by illegal exactions, he had the
' mony refunded to the rural deans, who were to distribute it to those
' persons of whom it had been levied in their respective districts. [e] In
' the feast of Candlemass K. Henry the sonne [who, by his fathers great
indulgence, had been crowned, and made partner with him in the kingdom; but afterward rebelled against him, & was now reconciled] ' to
' put his father out of all doubt & mystrust of any evil meaning in
' him, sware fealtie to him at Mauns in Normandy against all persons
' in presence of Richard de Humez his constable & many others.'

VIII. About this time William Waterville lord abbat of Burg & founder
of S. Michaels priory by Stanford [f], ' settled a yearly maintenance upon

a Baron. ut supra.
b Id. ib.
c Holingshed, Vol. II. p. 436. a.
d Bp. Kennets par. antiq. p. 130.
e Holing. Vol. II. p. 439. b.
f Gunton.

E　　　　　　　　　　　　　' the

' the church of S. John Baptiſt in Burg, enacting, that the chaplain
' ſhould yearly upon Michaelmaſs day bring his church key to the ſa-
' criſt of the monaſtery, as an acknowledgment of his dependance on it.
' He was alſo very induſtrious in perfecting the buildings of his monaſte-
' ry [there] & erecting new ones. He built the cloyſter there, & co-
' vered it with lead. He ordered & diſpoſed the choir of that church
' in that manner it ſtood in the great rebellion, & in ſome ſort conti-
' nues now. He founded the chappel of Thomas Becket there, which
' was finiſhed by his ſucceſſor, & is now ſtanding in the middle arch
' of the minſter as you enter it. He built alſo a chappel in his own
' houſe & other neceſſary offices.   It would be too long to mention
' particularly all the land, rents, & penſions, which this abbat bought
' at London, Irtlingborough, Hargrave, Eaſton, Warmington, Paſton,
' Walton, Cambridge, & ſeveral other places.   I will name only one.
' ᵃ He purchaſed all the village on the ſouth ſide the bridge of Stan-
' ford, & redeemed for a ſum of mony fourteen houſes with the ground
' belonging to them beyond the bridge there, which a certain knight claim-
' ed as his inheritance.   ᵇ He likewiſe increaſed the rents of the market
' & town of Burg, & built uſeful offices in all the mannors belonging to
' the church, & did a great many other good things (beſides thoſe alrea-
' dy mentioned) & had done more, & greater, if he had not been hin-
' dered by great misfortunes & diſturbances which were given him both
' by falſe domeſtics & other rich men; who accuſed him to the king,
' & to the archbiſhops Theobald, Thomas a Becket, and Richard (who
Anno ' ſucceeded them) ſo that at laſt he was [in 1175.] by the anger of the
1175. ' king, depoſed in the chapter-houſe of Burg, before a multitude of ab-
' bats & monks; being neither convicted of any crimes, nor confeſſing
' any, but privily accuſed to the archbiſhop by ſome monks, when he
' had held his abby twenty years. And altho the Burg writers are ſi-
' lent in the cauſe of his depoſition, yet others have taken notice of
' it. John Brompton relates it thus.   Richard archbiſhop of Canter-
' bury came to the abby of Burg, & depoſed William of Waterville the
' abbat there, for that he, againſt the will of the monks, entred with
' a band of armed men into the church, & took from thence ſome re-
' liques, & the arm of S. Oſwald, *pro denariis ad Judeos invadendis;*
' the monks ſtanding in defence of their reliques, many of them were
' grievouſly wounded.' Roger Hoveden is more particular. ' Richard
' archbiſhop of Canterbury, ſays he ᶜ, depoſed William of Walterville,
' abbat of Burg, becauſe that he had broke into his own cloyſter, with a
' violent & armed force, & would have carried away the reliques of
' the ſaints, together with the arm of S. Oſwald the king & martyr;
' in defence whereof the monks & ſervants of the church were
' ſome wounded & ſome ſlain. But the true & principal reaſon of his

a Id. & Hugonis Cand. p. 92.
b Hiſt. church of Burg, p.

c Sub anno 1175. chronici ſui edit. 1596.
fol. 313. a. 30.

depoſition

' deposition was, that he was fallen into the kings displeasure for his
' brothers sake, one Walter of Walterville [in the parish of Achirch in
' Northamptonshire, where antiently was his castle] whom abbat Willi-
' am received, with others of that party, being then in arms against the
' king.   These reasons, saith Mr. Gunton, I cannot contradict, tho' to
' me it seems strange that a man, who was brought in abbat with such
' an universal kindness of the society as hath been related [a], & did such
' abundance of good, should be guilty of such violence & sacrilege also
' as is scarce credible.   And it is less credible that he, who inriched the
' monastery of Burg so vastly as hath been already said, should impove-
' rish & oppress it, as he is accused to have done, in the account they
' gave the pope of this business.   For I must let the reader know that
' William thinking himself wronged by this sentence, appealed to pope
' Alexander, who upon mature hearing of the cause, enjoyned him si-
' lence for ever.   So we are told in a bull of his successor pope Urban
' (still exstant in Suapham) & directed to Benedict (who succeeded
' this William) confirming the foresaid deposition of William Walter-
' ville, by whose malignity the monastery of Burg (saith the bull) was
' much *attritum & gravatum*, & he himself also *de prava conversatione*
' *graviter infamatus*.   Which damage done to the monastery, if he was
' truly accused, arose its likely from borrowing of mony, to carry on
' all those great works which he did, & attempted.   For, in the said
' bull it is said, that William Norman procurator for the abbat, having
' taken up great sums of mony in the abbats name, for which he stood
' bound, desired satisfaction.   But the mony appearing to have been bor-
' rowed, *non pro utilitate, sed pro gravamine monasterii*, pope Lucius
' absolved the monastery, *ab impetitione tam creditorum quam fidejusso-*
' *rum*, freeing them from all obligation to pay the mony so borrowed
' [either to the creditors or sureties] as appears, the bull saith, by the
' writing of pope Lucius.   Whereupon Urban, being induced by these
' reasons, & moved by the desire of K. Henry, again confirmed the de-
' position, as Alexander had done; & again absolved them from that
' debt, of which they had been acquitted in the judgment of his prede-
' cessor Lucius.   Thinking it but reasonable that a debt which was
' remitted them, *communis juris equitate*, should be relaxed also, *spe-*
' *ciali apostolice sedis indulgentia*.   But whatever his crimes were, for
' which the king was incensed against him, he had been once (as I
' shewed before) very much in his favour, & procured from him a con-
' firmation of all the privileges granted by the kings grandfather to the
' church of Burg.   As for his deposition, all agree that it was decreed
' in 1175. notwithstanding which he was always commemorated among
' the benefactors to the church of Burg on the last day of November.'
And so much concerning the founder of the priory of S. Michael by
Stanford.

a Anno 1156. supra.

IX. [a] ' In

Anno IX. [a] ' In 1176. Bertram de Verdun founded the abby of Croxden
1176. ' in Staffordfhire.   This Crokefden, as Leland calls it [b], was an abby
' of Bernardine monks.   Bertram de Verdun, as he adds, was fome-
' tyme lord of Staunford.'   The faid Bertram, I believe, had a confiderable eftate at Stanford & Caftreton in this neighbourhood, all which
(except what he before gave to the hofpital of S. John Baptift at Stanford bridge [c]) he now gave to his faid abby of Croxden.   But I no
where find, except in Mr. Leland, that the faid Bertram was now, or at
any other time, lord of Stanford; neither will the times wherein Richard Humet (guardian of the faid Bertram) & William Humet his fon
& heir were actually lords of that manor, admit of his ever being fo;
unlefs we fhould fay, that in the town of Stanford were divers manors,
as indeed there were (to wit, the manor of Stanford, the manor of
Clipfhill, S. Cuthberts fee, Barke fee, &c.) & that the manor of Stanford properly fo called was held by Richard Humet, whilft one of the
other, probably Clipfhill, was at the fame time held by the faid Bertram de Verdun.   Be that as it will, what lands the faid Bertram had
now at Stanford will, in fome fort, appear, by a brief extract of his
grant to the monks of Croxden, which take as follows.   [d] ' Bertram
' de Verdun, to all &c. Know ye that I have given & granted to God,
' & to the bleffed Mary, & to the abby of the vale of S. Mary of
' Crokefdene which I have founded, & to the monks there ferving
' God, into pure & perpetual alms, for the fouls of Norman de Verdun
' my father, & Leceline my mother, & of Richard de Humez my guar-
' dian [e], & for my health, & of Roehais my wife, all my land of Crokef-
' dene, &c. & the whole fervice which Achard of Stanfort & his heirs
' did owe me for their tenement which they did hold of me in the
' town of Stanfort, & in the town of Caftretone; and my mill of Stan-
' fort, which is between the bridge & the caftel, with all its appurte-
' nances; & the whole land which I had in the fame town of Stanfort,
' &c.'   Soon after K. Henry the 2. confirmed to the faid monks of
Crokefdene, *inter alia* [f], ' of the faid Bertrams gift one mill in Stan-
' ford, which is between the bridge & the caftel, with the whole tene-
' ment which belongs to that mill, & the whole tenement which Akard
' of Stanford holds of the fame Bertram, &c.   By the way, [g] ' Lefceline,
' Bertram de Verduns mother, was daughter of Geoffry de Clinton,
' lord chamberlain & treafurer to K. Henry the firft. Bertrams father had
' with her in marriage, as it feems, the lordfhip of Brandon in War-
' wickfhire, where was antiently a caftel, built, as it is probable, by the
' fame Norman.'   But to return.   [h] ' This year alfo (viz. 1176.)
' the king by common confente of his nobles & other eftates, di-

a Bp. Kennets parochial Ant. p. 131.
b Collect. To. I. p. 31.
c See Par. VII. above.
d Ex Mon. Ang. Tomi III. partis I.
pag. 40.

e Qui me nutrivit.
f Mon. Ang. To. I. p. 914. a.
g Baronage, Vol. I. p. 471. b.
h Holingfhed, Vol. II. p. 443. b.

' vided

' vided this realme into fix parts, appointing three juftices itinerantes
' in every one of them, of which juftices Berthran de Verdun was one.'
Berthran, I fuppofe, was the fame as Bertram; which fhews that his
guardian Richard Humet, lord of Stanford, gave him a very liberal Education, & that his genius leading him more particularly to a ftudy of
the laws, he was, for his great knowledge therein, appointed one of the
juftices itinerantes.   Achard of Stanford abovementioned, but when I
find not, on the death of Gwido his fon & heir, gave the nuns of S. Michael the church of All-Saints in Staunford, Nicolfcire (fo called to
diftinguifh it from the church of All-Saints in Staunford, Hantunfcire)
to be appropriated to their monaftery, he being then patron of the
faid church; for which purpofe his charter is thus expreffed. a ' Be it
' known to all that I Achard of Staunford, on the death of Gwido my
' fon & heir, granted & gave, & now do grant & by this prefent
' charter confirm, the church of All-Saints of Staunford in Nicolfcire,
' to the church of S. Michael the archangel, & the fervants of God
' there, into perpetual & pure alms; for the foul of the fame Gwido,
' & for the fouls of my father and mother, and all my anceftors, &
' for redemption of my fins.   Witneffes, Gilebert abbat of Swine-
' fhefed, Thomas the monk, &c.'   By virtue of this charter the faid nuns
of S. Michael prefented a vicar to the faid church of All-Saints 'till the
30. of H. the 8. when their priory was diffolved.

X. b ' In 1177. there being [at Stanford &] through all England a Anno
' great multitude of Jewes, bycaufe they had no place appoynted them 1177.
' where to bury thofe that died, but only at London; they were con-
' ftreyned to bring all their dead corpfes thither from all parts of the
' realme.   To eafe them therefore of that inconvenience, they obteyn-
' ed of K. Henry a grant to have a place affigned them in every quarter
' where they dwelled, to bury their dead bodies.'   I have before related how Brand de Foffato & one Siward about 1174. firft erected the
hofpital of S. John the Baptift & S. Thomas of Canterbury, at the head
of Stanford bridge on the fouth fide of the Welland, for relief of travellers & other poor.   There they appointed a warden to overfee the
houfe & fome monks to celebrate divine fervice; whereof they made
the abbat of Burg, for the time being, patron; the faid abbat to prefent a warden, or other brethren, as any fuch place or places became
vacant.   And much about this time, as I gather, pope Alexander the
third received the faid hofpital into the protection of S. Peter, for
which purpofe he promulged the following bull, directed to one of the
founders. c ' Alexander the bifhop, fervant of the fervants of God, to
' his beloved fon Brand de Foffato, greeting & apoftolical benediction.

a Ex regiftri dicti prioratus S. Michaelis   ton fol. 41. citato in Mon. Ang. Tomi II.
penes Galf. Minfhul gen. 1657. fol. 3. b.   p. 403. b. Aliud autem extat exemplar in
citato in Mon. Ang. Tomi II. p. 880. b.   regiftri cartarum ecclefiæ de Burgo in bib.
  b Hollingfhed, Vol. II. p. 450. b.   Cott. fub imagine Vefp. E. XXII. folio
  c Ex regiftri cujufdam ad C. nobil. de   30. b.
Heterborough fpectantis, penes Chr. D. Hat-

F

'It is both worthy & agreeable to reason, that we should encourage
'their just desires, who, forsaking worldly pomps, apply themselves to
'works of charity, and have chose to serve almighty God with a con-
'stant devotion. Now we having been given to understand, by your
'intimation transmitted to us, that you, guided by divine inspiration,
'having sold all you did possess, have erected a certain hospital &
'chappel, to the honor of God, & of the blessed John, & of the glo-
'rious martyr Thomas late archbishop of Canterbury, at the head of
'the bridge of Stanford, on the south part, for reception of stran-
'gers & poor people frequently passing by that place, where you have
'chose to exhibit a perpetual offering to your creator; thence is it that
'we, in reverence of God, & of the aforesaid saints, & the devo-
'tion which you discover you entertain for them, to your reasonable
'request the more freely consenting, receive the forewritten hospital
'& chappel, with all which the same hospital at present rightfully pos-
'sesses, or hereafter, by the bounty of popes, oblations of the faith-
'ful, or any other just ways, by Gods favor, shall be able to procure,
'under the blessed Peters & our own protection, & do together enclose
'the same with the defence of the present instrument; appointing, that
'the foresaid chappel have power to retain a proper capellan, chan-
'try, churchyard, & free burial in the same churchyard, without con-
'tradiction of any sort. We decree therefore that it be lawful for no
'man whatsoever, rashly to disturb, or with any manner of vexations
'annoy the foresaid hospital; or to infringe this letter of our protecti-
'on & constitution, or to gainsay it in any part. And if any person
'shall presume to attempt it, he shall find that he goes about to in-
'cur the displeasure of almighty God, & of the blessed Peter & Paul
'his apostles. Given at Anagnia, the fifth of Feb. in the year . . .
In this bull it is observable pope Alexander takes no notice of Siward,
the joynt founder of this hospital, as I conceive, with Brand de Fossato. But that omission shall be made amends for hereafter [a].

24.H.2.   XI. [b] 'In the 24. H. 2. Bertram de Verdun, being with the king at
'Marleberg, was thence sent to those ambassadors of the king of Spain
'(to whom the king, in his great council held at London a little be-
'fore, had given dispatch) with his letters upon sundry concerns, where-
'of one was the kings safe conduct in that pilgrimage which he
'had designed to S. James in Galicia, in regard that city lay within
'his dominions.' I dont know exactly when Richard Humet, constable of Normandy & lord of Stanford, died; but find, that upon
his death (which, as near as I can guess, was about this time) K. Henry
the second confirmed to William Humet, son & heir of the said Richard, the constableship of Normandy, to him & his heirs, to hold
in fee; so that this family were hereditary constables of that dutchy.
By the same grant he confirmed also, to the said William & his heirs,

a See 20. apr. 1. R. 1. below.   b Baron. Vol. I. p. 471. b.

the

the manor of Stanford, with the appurtenances of the castle & borough. So much of the said grant as I have seen, runs thus. [a] ' Henry, by the ' grace of God, K. of England, duke of Normandy & Aquitain, &c. ' Know ye that I have granted & by the present charter confirmed to ' William de Humets my constableship, which Richard de Humez ' his father had of me, to him & his heirs, to hold, of me & my ' heirs, in fee & inheritance. Moreover I grant & confirm to the ' same William all the underwritten particulars, which, to his fore- ' named father I granted & gave for his service, & by my charter ' confirmed to him & his heirs, to be held in fee & inheritance : ' to wit, Stanford with all the appurtenances of the castel & bo- ' rough, &c.' The other particulars, at the same time confirmed to the same William, were, [b] ' the inheritance of the lordships of Ke- ' tene, Dudington, & Siringham ; as also of Waddon & Winchendon ' in Norfolk. Likewise that grant of the lordship of Meisy, & Hay of ' Luteneire, with the land of Appoghard in Normandy ; an incre- ' ment which he himself had added thereto.' The witnesses to this charter, which is without date, were, [c] ' Richard bishop of Winton, ' H. bishop of Bayonne ; Nicholas the capellan, Walter son of Ro- ' bert, Ralph de Glanville, Hugh de Cressy, Fulc Paynell, Bertram de ' Verdun, Richard Giff, Robert de Stutevill, and Gilbert Pipard ; given ' at Caen.'

XII. [d] ' Whereas there had been a dispute for some time depending May 2. ' between lord Akarius abbat of Burg & the convent of the same place, 1182. ' of the one part ; & lord William de Humez, the kings constable & 28.H.2. ' lord of Stanford beyond the bridge in Lincolnshire, of the other ' part ; touching certain liberties the foresaid abbat & convent & their ' tenants in Stanford, as well beyond the bridge in Lincolnshire, as on ' this side the bridge in Northamptonshire, concerning ; it was now ' thus agreed : To wit, that the foresaid lord William hath granted,

a Henricus D. G. rex Anglie, dux Normannie & Aquitanie, &c. Sciatis me concessisse & presenti carta confirmasse W. de Humetz constabulariam meam, quam Richardus de Humez pater suus habebat de me, sibi & heredibus suis, tenendum, de me & heredibus meis, in feodo & hereditate. Concedo etiam eidem Willielmo & confirmo omnia subscripta, que prefato patri suo concessi & dedi pro servicio, & cartis meis confirmavi, sibi & heredibus suis, in feodo & hereditate tenenda, viz. Stanford, cum omnibus pertinentiis castelli & Burgi, &c.

b Baronage Vol. I. p. 631. b.

c Testibus, R. Winton. & H. Baiocensi episcopis, Nicholao capellano, Waltero filio Roberti, Ranulpho de Glanville, Hugone de Cressy, Fulcone Paynell, Bertramo de Verduno, Richardo Giff, Roberto de Stutevilla, Gilberto Pipard ; apud Cadomum. Ex MS. collect. antiquarii peritissimi Petri le Neve arm. Norroy regis armorum.

d Cum, inter D. Akarium abbatem de Burgo S. Petri & ejusdem loci conventum, & D. Willielmum de Humez constabularium D. regis & D. de Stanford ultra pontem in Com. Linc. super quibusdam libertatibus predictos abbatem & conventum & tenentes eorundem in Stanford tam ultra pontem in com. Linc. quam citra pontem in com. Northamp. tangentibus, materia fuisset exorta, in hunc modum conquievit ; viz. quod predictus D. Willielmus concessit, pro se & heredibus suis, quod abbas de Burgo S. Petri & ejusdem loci conventus habeant in tenura sua citra pontem in Com. Northamp. & infra villam Stanford in Com. Linc. soc & sake, tol & tem, infangthef, utfangthef, tictores & textores ad vendendum in domibus & curiis suis, laniatores, piscatores, fullones & cujuslibet officii negotiatores. Factum est hoc anno incarnationis verbi MCLXXXII. secundo die SS. Philippi & Jacobi apostolorum apud Stanford. Testibus Radulpho filio Roberti, Radulpho de Meishenden, &c. Ex registri de Suapham fol. 237.

3

' for him & his heirs, that the abbat of Burg & the convent of the
' fame place may have in their tenure on this fide the bridge in
' Northamptonfhire, & within the town of Stanford in Lincolnfhire,
' foc & fake, tol & tem, infangthef, utfangthef, tictors & textors,
' butchers, fifhermen, & fullers, & agents of every trade, to fell in
' their houfes & courts.   This agreemant was made in the year of
' the incarnation of the word, 1182. the fecond day of SS. Philip
' & James the apoftles at Stanford.   Witneffes Ralph fon of Robert,
' Ralph de Meifhenden, &c.'   In the Saxon charters, bifhop Kennet
fays [a], ' Thol was the liberty of buying & felling, or keeping a mar-
' ket in fuch a mannor; in later times it fignified the cuftomary dues
' or rent paid to the lord of a mannor for his profits of the fair
' or market, called the Toling-pence.   Hence the Tol-booth, Tol-
' fey, or place where fuch cuftom was paid.   This Toll at publick
' fairs & markets was paid at the found of a bell, as we have now
' a market bell, which poffibly might give name to the *tolling* of
' a bell.   Team, faith Minfhæu, is an old Saxon word [a], & fignifies a
' royaltie; a power to have fervants & flaves, called *nativi, bondi,*
' *villani*; & all baronies infeoffed with Theam, have the fame pow-
' er, for unto them all their bondmen, children, goods, & chattels
' properly appertain.   Infangthef, faith bifhop Kennet [a], is a liberty
' granted from the king to fome lords of a mannor to try all
' thieves their tenants within their own court; as outfangthef was
' a liberty of trying foreiners or ftrangers apprehended for theft
' within their own fee.'   The fecond day of the feaft of SS. Philip
& James the apoftles being mentioned above fhews, that befides the
day appointed in the Calendar for celebration of the feftival of any
faint or faints, fometimes one or more days following were antiently kept in honor of fome particular, firft-rate faints, as perhaps, the
12 apoftles, SS. Mark, Luke, George, &c.

30.H.2.   XIII. [b] ' In the 30. of H. 2. William Humet, lord of Stanford,
' had fifty pounds land, formerly blanc ferm, in Stanford; which he
' held during the kings pleafure; of which mony William Baffet
' high fherif of Lincoln had an allowance in his accompt.   Bertram
' de Verdun, it is very like, faith Sir William Dugdale [c], had his re-
' fidence for the greateft part of this kings reign at his caftle of Brandon
' in Warwickfhire, for it is evident that he was fherif of that coun-
' ty & Leicefterfhire, from the fixteenth, until the thirtieth of K Hen-
' ry the 2d. inclufive.   In the 31. of H. 2. he had the cuftody of the
' honor of Chefter, Hugh Kevelioc earl of Chefter being then dead,
' & Ranulph his fon, within age, as it is like.'   Henry the 2d. died
the 9. day of July 1189. and was fucceeded by his fon K. Richard
the firft.

a In voce.   b Madoxs Hift. of the excheq. p. 225.   c Bar. Vol. II. p. 471. b.

The end of the fifth book.   3

Academia tertia Anglicana;

OR, THE

ANTIQUARIAN ANNALS

of the TOWN of

STANFORD

IN

Lincoln, Rutland, *and* Northampton *Shires*,

BOOK VI.

Containing the reign of K. Richard the firft.

I. ª ' ON the day of K. Richards coronation, the Jews that Sept. 3.
' dwelt in London & other pattes, meaning to honor 1189.
' the fame with their prefence, & to prefent him fome I. R. 1.
' honourable gift, whereby they might procure his friendfhip; K. Ri-
' chard, out of a zealous minde to Chriftes religion, abhorring their
' nation, and doubting fome forcerie; commaunded they fhould not
' come within the church when he fhould receyve the crown, nor
' within the palace whileft he was at dinner. But, at dinner time, a-
' mong other that preffed in at the palace gate, divers Jews were a-
' bout to thruft in, 'till one of them was ftriken by a Chriftian, who,
' alledging the kings commaundment, kept them back; which fome
' of the unruly people perceyving, falling upon the Jews with ftaves,
' bats, & ftones, chafed them home. Herewith rofe a rumor, that the
' king had commaunded the Jews to be deftroyed; & thereupon the
' people came running to affault them in their houfes; whiche, when
' they could not eafily brake up nor enter, by reafon the fame were
' ftrongly builded, they fet fire on, fo that divers houfes were confu-
' med, not only of the Jews, but alfo of their neighbours; fo hide-
' ous was the rage of the fire. The king being advertifed of this, fent
' fome of his officers to appeafe the tumult. But their authority was no-
' thing regarded, nor their perfuafions any thing heeded, but their threat-
' nings rather brought themfelves in daunger of lyfe among the rude
' fort of thofe that were about to fpoyle the houfes & fhoppes of the

a Holing. Vol. II. p. 477, 478.

6 B

Jewes,

' Jewes, to the better accomplifhment of which, the light that the
' fire of thofe houfes that brenned gave, after it was once night, did
' minifter no fmall help.   The Jewes in thofe houfes were either fmol-
' dred & brenned to death, or at their comminge foorthe moft cruelly
' received on the poyntes of fpeares, billes, fwordes, & gleaves of their
' adverfaries that watched them.   This wood rage continued from the
' midft of one day 'till two of the clocke of the other, the commons
' all that while never ceafing their fury, but ftill killing them in moft
' rafh & unreafonable manner.   At length, rather wearied than fatisfi-
' ed, they withdrew from their riotous enterprife, after they had exe-
' cuted many horrible enormities.   Finally, after the tumult was ceaf-
' ed, the king commaunded that no man fhould hurte any of the
' Jewes, & fo they were reftored to peace.   So great a riot well de-
' ferved punifhment, but yet it paffed over without correction in re-
' fpect of the great number of tranfgreffors.'   However, notwithftanding the kings command, what thefe wretched people underwent at
London, was but a prelude to their misfortunes in the reft of the kingdom. For a period began now to draw on, near, but yet wrapt in darknefs,
at what time following the black example which London the capital
of the nation had fet them, almoft all at once the inhabitants of fundry other populous places fell upon that unfortunate & wandring fect
of unbelievers.   Dreadful was the butchery; & (whether for their infidelity, ufury, or any other fins, God was pleafed to bring this diftrefs upon them) a many thoufands found, by the lofs of their lives, what a
misfortune it was then to be a Jew in England: whereof prefently.
But firft note, foon after his coronation, K. Richard intending to fet out
for the holy land, [a] ' for men & foldiers, the prelates ftirred up innu-
' merable, by their manifold exhortations (the archbifhop of Canterbury
' having travelled thro' Wales in perfon for that purpofe, going after-
' wards with the king to Palestine where he died) in pulpits, & pri-
' vate conferences founding nothing but the croffe & paffion of Chrift,
' calling the world to revenge his caufe upon the pagans, & fetting
' fouls on fire with vehement geftures & perfuafions.'   As alfo that

Dec. 5.   II. On the 5. of December K. Richard confirmed to the lord abbat of
1189.   Burg, all his poffeffions at Stanford, &, *inter alia*, right of patronage
1. R. 1. to a religious houfe there called S. Pulchers, as alfo to S. Giles hofpital: which is the firft time I meet with the mention of either of
thofe places.   As for S. Pulchers, where it was fituate, any farther
than that it ftood on the fouth fide of the river, I am yet not able to
fix; & likewife as much to feek about the founder.   By the name
however it appears that it was an houfe of canons regular, of the order of the holy fepulcher; whofe bufinefs was here to receive & entertain all fuch pilgrims & knights of the holy fepulcher as paffed by

a Speed, p. 531. a.

out

out of the north, on their journey towards Jerufalem; the pilgrims to vifit the holy fepulcher of Chrift there, & the knights to guard them, &, at all fitting opportunities, fight for recovery of that holy place from the keeping of the Saracens. S. Giles Hofpital ftood where now the 'fpital houfe ftands at the upper end of S. Martins, & had formerly a fair chappel belonging to it, with lands to maintain a capellan, & feveral poor lepers; but who was the founder I cannot learn. A gentleman [a], on my fpeaking of this hofpital once in his company, was pleafed to ask, if I had not obferved, that all churches & hofpitals dedicated to S. Giles, ftood, as this did, very near, or quite, out of the town? and inftanced in S. Giles in the fields, S. Giles Cripplegate, & feveral others I now forget. We could not then think why it fhould be fo, but, admitting it to be fact, perhaps this may be reafon. S. Giles was the patron of cripples & lepers; a thing fo well known that a lame perfon is fometimes proverbially & in derifion called after the name of his protector, lame Giles. Houfes dedicated to that faint were all founded then, like this at Stanford, for reception of fuch perfons; & ftood, like this, at firft without the town, tho' afterwards by acceffion of new buildings in divers places, fuch houfes might at length be furrounded & brought within a town. Where alfo there is now only a church dedicated to S. Giles, it is probable there was formerly likewife an hofpital ftanding by it. The reafon why fuch hofpitals were fet without the town, was, becaufe generally fuch lame & leprous people were very nafty & not fit to live within the town. A cuftom borrowed of the Jews. For [b] ' the lord fpake unto Mofes fay-
' ing, command the children of Ifrael that they put out of the camp
' every leper, & every one that hath an iffue, & whofoever is defiled by
' the dead. Both male & female fhall ye put out, without the camp
' fhall ye put them, that they defile not their camps in the midft where-
' of I dwell. And the children of Ifrael did fo, & they put them with-
' out the camp.' Thus again we read [c], ' Miriam became leprous, as
' white as fnow —— [d] And Miriam was fhut out from the camp.' And
again, [e] ' this fhall be the law of the leper —— the prieft fhall go forth
' out of the camp, and the prieft fhall look & behold if the plague of
' leprofie be healed in the leper, &c.' So that it feems they were not to come into the camp 'till they were recovered, & the prieft had pronounced them perfectly clean. To all which I will venture to add one more conjecture. England, as I have faid, ever fince the conqueft, fwarmed with Jews, & the town of Stanford was now full of them; it is not at all improbable then, that it was not by reading of the bible, but rather perfonal converfe with the Jews, that the Englifh (who had now a great many leprous people among them) learnt to put

a Mr. Edward Benet of Stanford.   d Numb. xii. 15.
b Numb. v. 1, 2, 3, 4.   e Levit. xiv. 2, 3.
c Numb. xii. 10.

                                                            them

them without the camp, & to build hospitals, a softer name than a
pest house, without the town for such persons to dwell in, to prevent
the infection spreading. I shall now give here so much of K. Richards
charter to the church of Burg as relates to the foresaid matters belonging to the said monastery at Stanford.   [a] ' Richard, by the grace of
' God, &c. know ye that we have granted, &c. to the monastery of
' Burg, at Stanford, all that part of the town which lies towards Burg
' on this side the bridge, with the lands & mills to the same part ad-
' jacent, & with the church of S. Martin & with the church of All-
' Saints; the monastery also of S. Michael, with all things to the same
' monastery pertaining, & the hospital of S. John & the blessed Tho-
' mas the martyr, the house of the holy sepulchre, & the hospital of S.
' Giles. Given by the hand of William de Longcamp our chancellor
' & bishop of Ely, the 5. of December, in the first year of our reign.'
' [b] The same day the king took ship for Normandy.

III. Return we now to the Jews, who, in the spring of the year, were
massacred in many cities & great towns, as Norwich, Bury, & divers
others. The circumstances of those cruel proceedings at three several
places, to wit, Lyn, Stanford, & York, shall be here related at large,
because there are three different causes assigned for the beginning of
those proceedings at those three places. The tumult at Lyn happened
on this occasion.   [c] ' It fortuned that one of the Jews there was be-
' come a Christian; wherewith those of his nation were so moved, that
' they determined to kill hym wheresoever they might find him; & here-
' uppon they sette uppon him one day as he came by through the
' streates. He, to escape their handes, fled to the nexte churche [the
churches in those times being always open] ' but his countrymen were
' so desirous to execute their malicious purpose, that they followed him
' still, & enforced themselves to breake into the church upon him
[the doors whereof either himself, or some christian friends, had
shut for him.] ' Herewith the noyse being raysed by the Christians that
' soughte to save the converted Jewe, a number of mariners beeing
' forreyners that were arryved there with their vessels out of sundrye
' partes, & dyverse also of the townesmen came to the reskue, & set-
' ting upon the Jews, caused them to flee into their houses. The
' townesmen were not very earnest in pursuing of them, because of the
' kings proclamation before made in favour of the Jewes. But the
' maryners followed them to their houses, slew divers of them, robbed
' & sacked their goods, & finally set their dwellings on fire, & so

a Richardus, D. G. &c. Sciatis nos concessisse, &c. monasterio de Burgo apud Stanfordiam, totam partem ville que est versus
Burgum citra pontem, cum terris & molendinis eidem parti adjacentibus, & cum
ecclesia S. Martini, & cum ecclesia omnium
SS. monasterium item S. Michaelis cum
omnibus ad idem monasterium pertinentibus,

& hospitale S. Johannis & B. Thome martyris, domum S. Sepulchri, & hospitale S.
Egidii, &c. Datum per manum Willielmi
de Longocampo cancellarii nostri & Elyen-
sis episcopi, quinto Decembris, anno regni
primo. Ex registri de Suapham folio 20.
  b Holing. Vol. II. p. 482.
  c Holing. Vol. II. p. 483.

' brente

‘ brente them up altogither. Thefe marriners beeing enriched wyth
‘ the fpoyle, & fearyng to be called to accompte by the kinges offi-
‘ cers, gotte them foorthwithe to fhipboorde, & hoyfting up fayles, de-
‘ parted, & fo efcaped the danger of that whiche might have bene other-
‘ wyfe layde to their charge. The townefmen beeing called to accompt
‘ excufed themfelves by the marriners, burdening them with all the
‘ faulte.’ This murder of the Jews at Lyn, I fuppofe was at the great
fair or mart there; which mart is always held juft before midlent fair
at Stanford; & it is now cuftomary with the Londoners & other
tradefmen who frequent thofe meetings to go from one to the other, &
fo onward to Grantham, Lincoln, Gainfborough, Hull, Beverly, York,
Rotheram, & Newcaftle; at which laft place they fhip their goods, &
return to London. And it is worth obferving that at almoft every one
of thefe places the Jews then met with a frefh affault. Before thefe
things happened at Lyn, the king being, as I intimated, fet fail for
Normandy, to meet the French king, with whom, & their united
forces, he was fhortly to fet forward to the relief of Jerufalem, [a] ‘ af-
‘ ter he was gone over, & the foldiers (whiche prepared themfelves to
‘ follow) beganne to affemble in routes, the heades of the common
‘ people began to waxe wylde, & fayne would they have had fome
‘ occafion of rayfing a newe tumulte againft the Jews.’ And this
brings me to their perfecutions here.

IV. For fay my authors [b], ‘ after thefe things a new tumult was raifed
‘ againft the Jews at Stanford. For affembling there, in mid-lent
‘ fair time, a multitude of young fellows out of divers parts, who had
‘ inlifted themfelves in the Croifade for Jerufalem, & who difdained that
‘ the enemies of the crofs who dwelt here fhould live in fuch afflu-
‘ ence, when themfelves had not monies fufficient to defray the neceffary
‘ expences of fo great a journey; they e’en made no fcruple at all to
‘ take away from fuch unjuft poffeffors, as they thought, that wealth
‘ which was fo much wanted to bear their own charges in the pilgri-
‘ mage they had undertaken. Thinking therefore they fhould do God a
‘ fervice by falling upon his enemies, whofe goods they had fuch a mind
‘ to, they fet boldly upon them; none either of the townfmen, or of
‘ them who came to the fair, oppofing themfelves in this mad enter-
‘ prife; but, on the contrary, fome of them joyning with them. Upon
‘ this feveral of the Jews were killed, whilft the reft got into the
‘ caftel, & with much ado efcaped. However they pillaged their houfes,
‘ got a prodigious deal of mony, & away they went; none of them being
‘ ever called to an account for it. There was indeed a certain Chriftian,
‘ one John, one of the moft impudent & bufie fellows in this affair,
‘ who, ftriking off to Northampton, lodged part of his mony in the
‘ hands of his landlord there, by whom he was afterwards fecretly made

a Id. p. 482.   Knyghton, col. 2402. Gul. Neub. lib. 4.
b Walt. Hemingford, lib. 2. cap. 43. cap. 8. p. 369. edit. Hearne.

' away with for lucre of it, & that done, his body thrown out of the
' town in the dark; which being found next morning, and some
' knowing it again, the greedy homicide immediately flipped away
' & withdrew himself.' Let Higden, as translated by Trevisa, tell
the rest. ' Thenne, says he [a], olde wyves mette, & there were
' seene wonders; false syghts of false tokens. And the meschaunt
' men [a meschaunt man is a chaunter of the mass, *qui miffam*
' *canit*] ' bare on honde that it was for the holyneffe of that man
' that they heelde a very marter, & also worfhypped the fepulcre of
' the dede man with folempne watches & grete gyftes. But wyfe men
' loughe them too fcorne. But clerkes of the places were ryghte well
' apayed therewith, for they had prouffyte therby. This was told the
' byfhoppe, and anone he forbade the doynge of fymple men upon
' payne of curfynge [or excommunication; & fo put an end to] ' the
' grete boofte of covetuous men & theyr fals marter.' But to return.
How many Jews were thus flain at Stanford, I know not; but
guefs they were a great many. For William of Neuberry, fpeaking in general of thofe flain at York, Lincoln, Stanford, and other
great places, fays the multitude was ineftimable or not to be number'd. One of the chief abettors of this riot, or, if not of this riot,
of a robbery much of the fame kind, & about the fame time, done
at Stanford, was Gerard de Camville, a great Baron & at this very time
high fheriff of the county: So that he ought rather to have protected
the Jews from any injury, than have joyned with the mob to do them
violence. Walter Hemingford & William of Neuberry are pleafed to
fay no body was called to an accompt for all this mifchief; but for
all that the faid Gerard de Camville, as he well deferved, was afterwards brought to a reckoning for this, or fomething, as I faid, very
like it; whereof hereafter [b]. Let us next fee how their fellow Jews
fared at York.

Mar. 16.
$11\frac{89}{90}$.
1. R. 1.
V. ' The fame year, fays Hoveden [c], on the 16. of March, the Jews
' of York, to the number of five hundred, befides women & children,
' fhut themfelves up into the caftel there, with confent & leave both
' of the conftable of the caftle & of the fheriff of the county. How-
' ever, fays Mr. Tirrel [d], the conftable happening to go out of the caftle
' about fome buifinefs, was fhut out by thofe Jews that were within,
' fearing leaft by fome means or other he might be fet againft them; &
' they could not be prevailed on to readmit him.' This exafperated
both the conftable & fherif. ' Whereupon, as Hoveden goes on, the
' citizens & ftrangers who came to the county court, by their encou-
' ragement, unanimoufly made an attac upon the Jews, who, when
' they carried on the affault night & day, offer'd a great fum for liber-
' ty to depart with their lives only; but the people would not accept

a Polychron. fol. 292. p. 2. col. b.   379. a. n. 1.
b 5. R. 1. infra.   d Hift. Eng. Vol. II. p. 480.
c Franc. edit. p. 665. Lond. edit. fol.

' it.

‘ it. Then a certain doctor of the law ſtood up, & ſaid, Ye men of
‘ Iſrael, hear me.   We our ſelves had better cut our own throats, than
‘ fall into the hands of the enemies of our law.   [Almoſt] all there-
‘ fore, both men & women, conſented to what he [thus deſpairing]
‘ adviſed; & every maſter of a family falling to work immediately, &
‘ beginning with the chief perſons of his own houſe, with a ſharp
‘ raſor firſt cut his wifes throat, then his ſons, daughters, ſervants, &
‘ in the laſt place his own.’   Fabian ſays ᵃ, ‘ they cut their maſter
‘ veines, & ſo bled to death.’   ‘ This done, continues Hoveden, ſome
‘ of them [that were yet left alive] threw the dead bodies of their
‘ ſlain over the wall upon the peoples heads.   The reſt, ſays Holing-
‘ ſhed ᵇ, perceyving what theſe & their great Rabbi had done, ſet fire
‘ upon all their goods & ſubſtance which they had got into the tower
‘ with them, & ſo conſuming the ſame, woulde have brente alſo the
‘ reſidue of their fellows which would not agree to the Rabbies coun-
‘ ſel in the cruel murthering of themſelves; if they had not taken a
‘ ſtrong turret hard by within the tower & defended themſelves both
‘ from the fyre & crueltie of their brethren , who had made away
‘ themſelves.   On the morowe, thoſe that were ſaved, called out to
‘ the people, & not only ſhewed after what ſort their fellowes were
‘ diſpatched; but alſo offred to be baptiſed if they might have their
‘ lives : which thyng was graunted; & they came foorth; howbeit
‘ they were no ſooner entred into the preaſe, but they were all ſlaine.
‘ After this the people ranne to the cathedral, & broke into thoſe places,
‘ where theyr bondes & oblygations laye, by the whyche they hadde
‘ dyvers of the kinges ſubjects bounde unto them in moſte unconſcio-
‘ nable ſorte & for ſuch deteſtable uſurye, as (if the authors that write
‘ thereof, were not of credite) would hardly be beleeved.   All whyche
‘ evydences or bondes they ſolemnly burned in the myddeſt of the
‘ churche.   After whyche eche went his way, the ſouldiours to the
‘ king, & the commons to their houſes : and ſo was the citie quieted.
‘ But, ſays my author, tho’ they of Lynne were excuſed, yet they of
‘ Yorke eſcaped not ſo eaſily.   For the kyng beyng advertyſed of ſuche
‘ outrage, done contrarie to the order of his lawes, wrote over to the
‘ biſhoppe of Ely his chauncellor, commaunding him to take cruel pu-
‘ niſhment of the offenders.   The biſhop with an army went to Yorke,
‘ but the chiefe authors of the ryot, hearing of his comming, fledde in-
‘ to Scotlande; yet the biſhoppe cauſed earneſt enquiry to bee made of
‘ the whole matter.   The citizens excuſed themſelves & offred to
‘ prove, that they were not of counſell with them that had committed
‘ the ryot; neither had they ayded nor comforted them therein in
‘ any manner of wiſe.   And indeede the moſt parte of them that were
‘ the offenders, were of the country & townes neere the citie, with
‘ ſuch as were croſſed into the holie land & now gone over to the

a Part. 2. p. 8. a.   b Holing. p. 482, 483.

‘ kyng;

' kyng; so that verie few, or none, of the substantial men of the citie
' were founde to have joined with them.   Howbeit this would not
' excuse the citizens, but that they were put to their fine by the stoute
' bishop, every one paying his portion according to his abilitye; the
' common sorte being pardoned, sith the ringleaders were gone out of
' the way.   I have been the more particular, says Mr. Tyrrel [a] (who
relates a good deal of these proceedings) ' that so the reader may see,
' how highly the people were now incensed against the Jews for their usu-
' ry & extortion, albeit they were maintained & protected by the govern-
' ment to peel the people, that so themselves might be squeez'd, &
' their riches taken from them, whenever the king had occasion; &
' likewise that he may observe how violent the common people (or
mob as we now call them) ' have been in former ages against those
' whose religion they had in abhorrence.'   As to the Jews at Stanford
I shall at present only add, this slaughter of them was not so very de-
structive, but that we shall afterward find them here in as numerous a
sort almost as before.

21. Ap.   VI. On the 21. of April, 1190. K. Richard, being at Samur in Nor-
1190.   mandy, confirmed to the master & brethren of the hospital of S. John
1. R. 1.   the baptist & S. Thomas of Canterbury at Stanford, first, the site or
ground whereon the hospital it self was built.   Secondly, the house
& chappel founded by Siward.   Thirdly, the lands, possessions, &
other matters given by Brand de Fossato.   And lastly, the meadow
given by the lords Richard de Humet & Bertram de Verdun, to build
a church on, & make a churchyard of.   The charter of the said K. Richard is thus express'd.   [b] ' Richard, by the grace of God, king of
' England, duke of Normandy, &c. to his archbishops, &c. greeting.
' Know ye that we have granted, & by this our present charter con-
' firmed to God & the hospital of S. John the Baptist & the blessed Tho-
' mas the martyr at Stanford, & to the master & brethren there serving
' God, the place in which the hospital it self is founded, with its ap-
' purtenances, & all the lands & possessions, & all the achats which
' Brand de Fossato, or any other gave to the same hospital; & that part
' of the meadow which lies by the bridge towards the north, the which
' lord Richard de Humez the constable & Bertrann de Verdun gave to
' the foresaid hospital, to make in it a church & a churchyard.   And
' therefore we will, &c.   Given at Samur, the 21. of April, in the
' first year of our reign.'   In the bull of pope Alexander the 2. (insert-
' ed anno 1177. above) it is said Brand de Fossato built the hospital &
chappel of S. John & S. Thomas at Stanford, & no notice is there
taken of Siward or any chappel by him erected here.   Whereas here
no mention at all is made of any chappel built by Brand de Fossato:
tho', being alledged by unquestionable evidences, both must be true.

a In loco quo supra.   citata in Monast. Ang. Vol. II. p. 403. b.
b Ex carta 33. H. 3. m. 3. per inspex.

From the words of that bull, & what is here faid in the charter of K. Richard the firft. I conclude then, that the chappel of this hofpital, being at firft but fmall, & built at the head, & perhaps overthwart the fouth end of Stanford bridge, by Brand de Foffato; upon that large piece of meadow being given as above by Richard de Humet & Bertram de Verdun (containing all that ground which is now the fite of the lord Burghleys hofpital, the orchat belonging to it, & the George inne in S. Martins High ftreet; in the churchyard whereof, as appears by the faid bull, they had privilege of free burial) was now built, at the expence of Siward, an handfome church, fufficient to receive the mafter, brethren, & fervants of the hofpital, with the pilgrims, knights, & all other occafional comers.

VII. Sir William Dugdale in his monafticon, places this hofpital of S. John the Baptift & S. Thomas of Canterbury at Stanford, among the houfes of the friers hofpitalers of the order of S. Auftin; and yet produces no authority I can any where find, why we fhould follow him. On the contrary, its being under the patronage of the abbat & convent of Burg who were Benedictines, & fometimes prefented a fellow-monk, fometimes a fecular, parifh prieft, to this mafterfhip; fhews, it was more truly an hofpital under the government of monks or fecular parifh priefts (for canons I find none admitted to it) juft as the abbat & monks of Burg thought fit to prefent. What led Sir William into the forefaid error was perhaps the corporation of this houfe being called *magifter & fratres*, & *frater* being commonly tranflated a frier. But thereby are frequently committed great errors. For when the word *frater* is applied to a monk, it ought not to be tranflated frier, but brother. And again, applied to a mendicant, it ought not to be tranflated brother, but frier. For want of obferving this diftinction, monks are frequently called friers, & friers monks: a miftake which a great many good writers are often guilty of, but may eafily be avoided by obferving the true diftinction which I have here fuggefted. If any one is pleafed to think this not worth minding, I hope he will not blame me, who think otherwife, for obferving it. I fhall only add *magifter & fratres*, in regard to fome foundations may alfo not fignifie either monks or friers, but only the mafter & poor of fuch an houfe; the poor of fuch places, tho' meer laymen, being often called the mafters brethren, in regard he is expected to ufe them as fuch.

VIII. [a] [c] On the 25. of June, K. Richard, being at Turon in Nor-
[c] mandy, confirmed to lord William Humet the conftablefhip of Nor-

25. June
1190.
I. R. I.

---

[a] Richardus primus rex Anglie, confirmavit donationem patris fui Willielmo de Humez, filio Richardi de Humez, &c. Hiis teftibus, Godefrido epifcopo Winton, Hugone epifcopo Ceftrie, Willielmo filio Radulphi fenefchallo Normannie, Pagano de Rochefs fenefchallo Andegavie, Willielmo comite Surrie, Roberto de Harecurt, Willielmo de Fors, Philippo de Columbariis, Roges de Saceio, Galfrido de Lafceles, &c. Datum per manum Johannis de Alenfun l' Exonienfis archidiaconi, vicecancellarii noftri apud Turonis, xxvº. die Junii, anno regni noftri primo. Ex MS. collect. Petri le Neve arm. Norroy regis armorum.

[c] mandy

'mandy to him & his heirs, to hold in fee.   As also the manor of Stan-
' ford with the appurtenances of the castel & borough, together with all
' those other lands confirmed to the said William by the charter of K.
' Henry the 2. his father.   The witnesses to K. Richards confirmation
' were, Godefry bishop of Winton, Hugh bishop of Chester, William
' (son of Ralph) steward of Normandy, Pagan de Rochess steward of
' Anjou, William [Warenn] earl of Surry, Robert de Harecurt, Wil-
' liam de Fors, Philip de Columbers, Roges de Sacey, Geoffry de Laf-
' celes, &c.   Given by the hand of John d' Alensun archdeacon of
' Exon, our *vicechancellor*, at Turon, the 25. day of June, in the first

Oct. ' year of our reign.'   (In Oct. the 2. R. 1.) K. Richard being in Sicily,
1190. on his way to the holy land, there concluded an agreement with Tan-
2. R. 1. cred king of that island, concerning repayment of the dowry given
formerly with Joan K. Richards sister, upon her marriage with William
late K. of Sicily, brother of Tancred; & divers other matters; & there
ᵃ ' put in upon their oaths for his sureties, two archbishops & two bi-
' shops of his owne there present, & twenty great lords & principal
' men of his subjects, among whom were, Jordanus de Humez his con-
' stable & Bertram de Verdun.'   What relation this Jordan de Humez
the constable had to William de Humez the constable of Normandy
& lord of Stanford, I know not; Sir William Dugdale, in his account
of the Humets, mentions no such person; however I conceive he was
one of the admirals of K. Richards fleet, for (tho' he does not name
Jordan de Humez there as one of the said admirals) yet Hoveden says ᵇ,
' when K. Richard was at Chinon in Anjou [on his way to the holy land]
' he appointed Gerard archbishop of Auxe, Bernard bishop of Bayeux,
' Robert de Sabul, Richard de Canvil, & William de Forz [*constabula-*
' *rios*] admirals of his fleet.'   And the same Hoveden ᶜ, speaking of
Jordan de Humez being, as above, one of K. Richards sureties, calls
him, Jordanus de Humez *constabularius noster*, but without any adjunct
of *classis*, *Normannie*, or the like, to shew whereof his constableship
sisted ᵈ.

IX. About this time lord Hamon Peche the elder gave the nuns of S.
Michael without Stanford, part of the tythes belonging to the church
of S. John the evangelist at Corebi in Lincolnshire.   The charter
whereby he made the said donation is now lost, but the same was afterwards confirmed by Hugh Wells bishop of Lincoln ᵉ.   This Hamon
Peche married Alice daughter of Pain Peverel.   ᶠ ' Pain Peverel an
' eminent soldier, & highly fam'd for his martial enterprises, was stan-
' dard bearer to Robert Curthose [eldest son of K. William the con-
' queror] in the holy land; & afterward obtained from K. Henry the
' first the barony of Brunne in Cambridgeshire.   The said Pain Peverell

a Speed, p. 533. b.   d Of this Jordan see more 16. John below.
b Ed. Lond. fol. 379. b.   e See that confirmation anno 1226. infra.
c Id. fol. 385. a. 40.   f Baron. Vol. I. p. 438. a.

' died

‘ died about 1112; & was fucceeded by William his fon ; which Wil-
‘ liam went to Jerufalem & there died without iffue. So that his four fifters
‘ became his heirs, betwixt whom his barony was divided. Of thefe, Maud
‘ Dover died without iffue.   Alice married to Hamon Peche.   Roefe
‘ to [a] . . . . Harcourt.   And Afceline to [Geoffry] Waterville.’ William
fon of Pain Peverell died before the end of the year 1166. For [b] ‘ in
‘ the 10. H. 2. Hamon Peche [who, as hath been faid, married his fifter
Alice] ‘ being fherif of Cambridgefhire, fo continued ’till half of the
‘ twelfth year; at which time, upon affefment of an aid for mar-
‘ rying the kings daughter, he certified his knights fees in Suffolk to be
‘ eleven & an half, & two fourthe parts; & in Cambridgefhire feven &
‘ a twelfth part *de veteri feoffamento* [c]; as alfo an half, third, & fourth
‘ part *de novo*.   Which fees in Cambridgefhire were of his wifes inheri-
‘ tance, viz. Alice daughter to Pain Peverell [not William Peverell,
as printed in Dugdale] ‘ one of the coheirs of William Peverell, [not
Pain Peverell, as printed in Dugdale] ‘ her brother. For all which fees
‘ in the 14. of H. the 2. he paid a mark each, as part of the honor of
‘ Brunne.   And in the 2. R. 1. [being the prefent year] upon collecti-
‘ on of the fcutage of Wales ix. l. x. s. ix. d.’   I have been more par-
‘ ticular in my account of this family, by reafon of the feveral benefactions which, as you will find, were given by feveral defcendants of the
perfons here named to the forefaid nuns of S. Michael by Stanford.

X. [d] ‘ On the 21. of Aug. 3. R. 1. when K. Richard had taken the
‘ city of Acon (wherein the Queens of England & Sicily, as alfo the
‘ daughter of the emperor of Cyprus, were then refident) he commit-
‘ ted it to the cuftody of Bertram de Verdun : ‘ Which Bertram de-
‘ parting this life in 1192. 4. R. 1. at Joppa in the holy land, was buried
‘ at Acon aforefaid.’   About this time the Jews of Stanford had got
fuch faft hold, it fhould feem, of one William de Burghels eftate there,
that if his patrons the abbat & convent of Burg had not fupplied him
with mony upon a leafe (another eftate of his at Stanford) they would
have entred upon his lands.   But hear the man. [f] ‘ Be it known to
‘ all men, prefent as well as future, that I William de Burghel, have
‘ mortgaged to my lord Benedict lord abbat of Burg & to the convent of
‘ the fame place, my whole tenement at Stanford, which I held of them

(right margin:) 21. Aug. 1191. 3. R. 1.
1192. 4. R. 1.

---

a Perhaps Robert Harecurt mentioned in the laft paragraph.
b Baron. To. I. p. 676. a.
c ‘ *De veteri feoffamento*, that is to fay,
‘ whereof his anceftor had been enfeoffed
‘ in the time of K. Hen. the 1.’ Bar. To. II. p. 457. a.
d Hoveden edit. Lon. fol. 397. b. Baron. To. I. p. 471. b.
e Bar. To. I. p. 472. a.
f Notum fit omnibus, tam prefentibus quam futuris, quod ego Willielmus de Burghel, invadiavi D. meo Benedicto D. abbati de Burgo & conventui ejufdem, totum tenementum meum de Stanford, quod de

eis tenui ad firmam, pro quindecim marcis per annum, cum omnibus pertinentiis ejuf-dem tenementi, citra pontem & ultra. Et predicti abbas & conventus commodaverunt mihi fuper predictum tenementum & omnia ejus pertinentia XL. marcas argenti, ad ac-quietandum me verfus Judeos de Stanford, pro quibus effem exhereditatus, nifi in pre-dicta pecunia mihi fuccurriffent ——— Hiis teftibus, Roberto de Nevil, magiftro amico Willielmo de Huntendon, Rogero Bacon, clericis; Adamo archidiacono, Gaufrido de Mara, &c. Ex regiftri Swapham nuncupati folio 248.

‘ at

‘ at farm for fifteen marcs a year, with all the appurtenances of the
‘ fame tenement, on this fide the bridge & beyond. And the forefaid
‘ abbat & convent have lent me upon the forefaid tenement & all its
‘ appurtenances forty marcs of filver, to difcharge me towards the Jews
‘ of Stanford, for which I had been turned out of my eftate, if they
‘ had not fupplied me with the forefaid mony. Witneffes, Robert Ne-
‘ vill, mafter William de Huntendon my friend, & Roger Bacon, clercs;
‘ Adam the archdeacon, & Geoffry de Mara.’ The name of Roger Bacon occurring here as a witnefs (tho’ whether this was the fame Roger,
fo famous for his great knowledge in the mathematics, fince Leland [a]
fays he died not ’till 1248. I affert not) reminds me of the tradition
which the common people of Stanford divert themfelves with about
that celebrated fcholar. Every one knows the famous ftory of his
brafen-head; that, fome great thing being to be done in a critical moment, his man was fet to watch when it fpoke; which at laft did fo, &
then flew in pieces. This fine tale, with fome fmall alteration,
they would have relate to Stanford. For when Stanford was an univerfity, we had then a college called Brafen-nofe; the gate whereof is
yet ftanding, in the middle of the door belonging to which is affixed a face
of brafs, holding an iron ring in the mouth. Now this is the very head
which, they would have it, frier Bacon made, & fpake; &, at the opening of whofe mouth, if the friers man had but taken the iron ring out
of it which now hangs there, all Stanford had inftantly been walled
round with brafs! —— And I have feen fome wifeacres, when others
told this, fhake their heads merely out of a concern, that the man
fhould be fo carelefs as to mifs the opportunity! —— But, to put away
childifh things —— ‘ The ftory of frier Bacons head, fays the great Sir
‘ Thomas Brown [b], is furely too literally received, & was but a myfti-
‘ cal fable concerning the philofophers great work, wherein he emi-
‘ nently excelled. Implying no more by the copper head, than the
‘ veffel wherein it was wrought; & by the words it fpake, the op-
‘ portunity to be watched, about the *tempus ortus*, or birth of the my-
‘ ftical child, or philofophical king of Lullius: the rifing of the *terra*
‘ *foliata* of Arnoldus, when the earth fufficiently impregnated with the
‘ water, afcendeth white & fplendent; which not obferved the work is
‘ irrecoverably loft. Now letting flip this critical opportunity, he mif-
‘ fed the intended treafure. Which had he obtained, he might have
‘ made out the tradition of making a brazen wall about [Stanford or]
‘ England; that is, the moft powerful defence & ftrongeft fortification
‘ which gold could have effected.’

XI. Having before related how the Jews were robbed & murdered at Lyn, Stanford, & York; & how the offenders were proceeded
againft at the laft of thofe places; I fhall now briefly touch how Gerard

a Comment de Scriptoribus Brit. p. 259.   b Vulgar errors, Lond. 1658. 4°. p. 461.

de Camville was likewife proceeded againft, for being too buifie in that Anno
affair, or fomething very like it, at Stanford.   And of him I find, that ᵃ 1194.
' about the fecond of April, the king being at Nottingham, by advice 2. April.
' & contrivance of the bifhop of Ely the chancellor (as it was faid)
' he was accufed for receiving of certain thieves, who had fpoiled fome
' merchants of their goods as they were going to Stanford fair ; & that
' they came from his houfe when they committed the robbery, & re-
' turned thither after they had done it.   Alfo they appealed him of
' treafon, becaufe he would not appear upon the fummons of the
' kings juftitiary, nor ftand to law concerning the receiving of thofe rob-
' bers, nor bring them to juftice.   But he anfwered that he was earl
' Johns man [that is, his tenent or feudatory] & would ftand to the
' law of his court.   He was alfo accufed that he was with force of
' arms in the affiftance of earl John, & other the kings enemies, when
' the kings caftels of Nottingham & Tickhil were furprifed : all which
' Gerard denied ; whereupon his accufers gave fecurity for profecuting
' their accufation ; as he did alfo of defending himfelf by one of his
' free men or tenents, who was his furety.   And I fuppofe it was for
' thefe offences, fays Mr. Tyrrel ᵇ, that this Gerard was by the king dif-
' feifed of the caftle & fherifwick of Lincoln.'   And in the end the faid
Gerard de Camville, as Sir William Dugdale relates ᶜ, ' was con-
' ftrained to give two thoufand marks to be repoffeffed of his own eftate,
' & to obtain the kings favour.   And Nichola his wife a fine of three
' hundred marks, for liberty to marry her daughter to whom fhe pleafed,
' fo that he were not an enemy to the king.'

XII. Next of the jufts & torneaments at Stanford.   ᵈ ' Tho' tornea-
' ments had been already forbidden by three general councils, & that
' the bodies of thofe that were killed in fuch unlawful rencounters,
' fhould be deprived of Chriftian burial ; & tho' there had not been
' torneaments here fince the reign of K. Stephen, yet the king now order'd
' that there fhould be torneaments, that is tiltings (or feats of arms) per-
' formed in England.   ᵉ The occafion of them was pretended to make
' Englifh fubjects more expert in arms, & that they might not be inful-
' ted by the French, who, in thefe feats, did much excell them. One more
' ingenuous reafon was no doubt to advance the kyngs revenue.   For
' in the chart that grants them, rates were impos'd for licenfe of tilt-
' ing.   ᶠ The charter of the faid graunte was delyvered by the king
' unto William earl of Salisbury, to have the keeping thereof : but
' Huberte Walter archbifhop of Caunterbury & lorde chiefe juftice,
' made his brother Theobald Walter collector of the money.   The te-
' nor of the charter was, ᵍ Richard, by the grace of God, king of
' England, duke of Normandy & Aquitain, earl of Anjou.   Know

a Hoveden. edit. Lond. fol. 419. b. n. 10.
b Vol. II. p. 531.
c Baron. To. II. p. 627. b.
d Tyrrel, p. 543.

e Bp. Kennets paroc. antiq. p. 153.
f Holingfhed, Vol. 2 p. 523.
g Ex Cl. Hearnii ad Gul. Neub. hift.
præfationis, p. 49, &c.

' ye

' ye that we have granted that there be torneaments in England in five
' places; between Sarum & Wilton; between Warewicke & Kencling-
' wrthe; between Stanforde & Warineford; between Brackelye &
' Mixebr; between Blie & Tykehill.   So that the peace of our land be
' not broken; nor shall the justitiary power be diminished; nor any da-
' mage done to our forests.   And an earl who will torney there, shall
' give us twenty marcs; & a baron, ten marcs; & a knight who hath
' lands, four marcs; & a knight who hath no lands, two marcs.   More-
' over no stranger shall torney there.   Wherefore to you we command
' that at the day of tourneying ye have there two clercs & two knights
' of your own to take the oaths of the earls & barons that they shall
' pay us the aforesaid mony before the torneament begins, & cause to
' be entred how much, & of whom, they have received.   And ye shall
' take ten marcs for this charter to our use; whereof the earl of Sarum,
' & the earl of Clare, & the earl of Warenn, are pledges.   Witness my
Aug. 22. ' self at Ville l'Evesche, the 22. of August.'   The manner how the
1194.   peace was to be kept by them who went to torney.   a ' From the time
6. R. 1. ' when a knight, or earl, or baron, or any other torneyer, shall depart
' from his own house towards the torneament, & [from the torneament]
' towards his own house, he shall take nothing unjustly in the way with-
' out license [or paying for it] whether meat, drink, or any other ne-
' cessaries.   Moreover he shall in any case do injury to none on the
' road, whether by himself, or servants; nor to the best of his power, by
' himself or attendants, suffer any one to be unjustly molested.   And
' if he shall find any person so offending, & is able, himself or his at-
' tendants, to cause reparation to be made, he shall accordingly see it
' be done.   And if he is not able to cause such reparation to be made,
' let him therewith acquaint the barons who have sworn to see the
' peace of the lord the king kept by the torneyers; & their judgment
' shall set it right.'   The form of the oath.   a ' It must be sworn by
' all the earls & barons of England, & by all who have a mind to tor-
' ney, that they will be accountable to the lord the king, & to the
' chief justice of the lord the king; & that they will preserve the peace
' of the lord the king entire & unhurt, both in their journeyings to-
' wards the torneaments, & from the torneaments, to the utmost of
' their power; & particularly, throughout the forests of the lord the king,
' & throughout his mercats.   And that none shall do any thing amiss,
' nor may permit any of his attendants to transgress the law.   And, if
' ought be unjustly acted, let him make it known to the barons who
' have taken this oath; &, whatsoever that transgression, is let it be
' amended by their decree.   And if any torneyer, or any servant, or
' whoever he be, should owe the truce to another; he shall give him
' lawful truce in the torneament, & in going to, & coming from, the

a Id. ib.

' torneament.

‘ torneament.   And if he will not give him truce, let him be compelled
‘ to it, or not be permitted to torney.   Moreover it muſt be ſworn by
‘ all that they will not torney, before they ſhall have given full ſatis-
‘ faction to the lord the king for their mony, according to the rate
‘ of the lord the king therefore made.   And, if they ſhall find any tor-
‘ neying who hath not accordingly given ſatisfaction, that they will
‘ arreſt his body, & deliver him to the bailif of the lord the king to be
‘ tranſmitted to the chief juſtitiar.’   I have not yet read of any knights,
tho’ doubtleſs there were many, who tilted here upon this permiſſion.

XIII. ª In this 6. R. 1. William de Albini the 3d. [who afterwards
founded the hoſpital & priory of S. Mary at Newſted by Stanford, & was]
‘ ſon of William de Albini the ſecond (called Brito & alſo Meſchines)
‘ ſon of William de Albini the firſt, ſon of Robert de Todenei, a noble
‘ Norman (which Robert built Belvoir caſtle) was with K. Richard the
‘ firſt in his army in Normandy.’   About this time the abbat & convent
of Burg granted to one maſter Reiner of Stanford clerc (for what con-
ſiderations I know not) the tythes of the demeſnes of four perſons in
the pariſh of Bernac, to be held of them for ever at the yearly rent of
twenty ſhillings.   In return for which kindneſs the ſaid Reiner (finding no doubt he had a good bargain on’t) engaged to pay the ſaid abbat
& convent a penſion of ten ſhillings yearly, over & above the ſaid rent.
To theſe proceedings Hubert archbiſhop of Canterbury was made privy,
who, in his charter to the abbat & convent of Burg, applauds the ſaid
Reiner for ſo doing : wherein he thus writes, ᵇ ‘ Hubert by the grace of
‘ God archbiſhop of Canterbury, to the abbat & convent of Burg, grace,
‘ &c.   Whereas ye have piouſly & liberally granted to our beloved
‘ ſon & clerc, maſter Reiner of Stanford, the tythes of the demeſnes of
‘ four men of the pariſh of Bernake ; to wit, of Geoffry ſon of Geof-
‘ fry, Hugh Fannel, Gilbert ſon of Hugh, & Geoffry Hok ; to be held
‘ of you for ever at the yearly rent of twenty ſhillings.   And where-
‘ as the ſame maſter Reiner, thro’ the devotion which he bears unto
‘ your church, deſirous to be aſſiſting to its profit, & to augment its
‘ rent, hath added ten ſhillings thereto —— we, by the preſent writing,
‘ commend that [donation.]   Farewel.’   This Reiner, as appears by
two charters (the one of Aſcelina de Waterville, the other of Matildis
de Diva her ſiſter) which I ſhall preſently ſet down, was, ſomewhat
about this time, dean of Stanford.

XIV. Aſcelina, the youngeſt ſiſter & coheireſs of William ſon of
Pain Peverell, married, as I before obſerved, Geoffry de Waterville.

a Baron. To. I. p. 113. b.

b Hubertus, D. G. Cant. arch. &c. abbati & conventui S. Petri de Burgo gratiam,
&c. Cum dilecto filio & clerico noſtro
magiſtro Reinero de Stanford, decimas do-
miniorum quatuor hominum de parochia de
Bernake, ſcil. Gaufridi filii Gaufridi, Hugonis Fannel, Gilberti filii Hugonis, & Gaufridi Hok; de vobis ſub annuo cenſu xx.

ſolidorum in perpetuum tenendas, pie & li-
beraliter conceſſeritis; Idem magiſter Rei-
nerus, ob devotionem quam ad eccleſiam
veſtram gerit, ejus utilitati cupiens adeſſe, &
ejus redditum augmentare, decem ſolidos ad-
jecit ---- eam [donationem] preſenti ſcripto
commendamus. Valete. Ex regiſtri Suapham nuncupati folio 40.

4   ᵃ ‘ The

[a] ' The said Geoffry & Ascelina de Waterville had issue two daughters,
' Ascelina de Waterville & Matildis de Diva.   From Ascelina descend-
' ed Roger de Torpel; & from Matildis, Hugh de Diva.'   These two
sisters Ascelina de Waterville & Matildis de Diva were great benefactresses
to the nuns of S. Michael by Stanford; of which benefactions I shall now
give an account.   Ascelina, the eldest of these two ladies, was twice married; divers of her benefactions being given for the souls of her husbands
& children: but what the names of those her husbands were I find not.
However she had two sons, Geoffry & Thomas, besides her other son
Roger de Torpel abovementioned.   The said Ascelina de Waterville
gave the nuns aforesaid, first, one moiety or half of Upton chappel in
Northamptonshire, the profits whereof she assigned to the kitchen of
the said nuns.   In making of which donation she thus words it.   [b] ' To
' all unto whom the present writing shall come, Ascelina de Waterville,
' eternal greeting in the lord.   Your universality shall understand that I
' have given & granted to God & the church of S. Michael of Staun-
' forde, & to the nuns there serving God, unto their proper uses, the
' moiety of the chappel of Uptone, which unto us is known to belong,
' into pure & perpetual alms, for their kitchen; for love of God, & for
' the health of my soul, & for the souls of Geoffry & Thomas my sons,
' & for the souls of all my predecessors and successors.   Witnesses,
' Ricard dean of Norburi, &c.'   Secondly, with consent of her heirs,
she gave the said nuns two shares of one third part of the church of
Corebi before mentioned; the profits whereof she assigned to buy cloaths
for them: upon which account she thus expresses her self.   [c] ' To all
' the children of holy mother church unto whom the present writing
' shall come, Acelina de Waterville, greeting in the lord.   Your uni-
' versality shall understand that I, with consent of my heirs, have given
' & granted, & by this my present charter confirmed, to God & the
' church of S. Michael the archangel of Stanford, & to the holy nuns
' there serving God, two parts of a third part of the church of Corebi,
' of which the right of advouson belongs unto me, with all their ap-

a Mon. Ang. To. II. p. 30. a.
b Ex registri prioratus S. Michaelis juxta Stanford penes Galf. Minshul, gen. 1657. folio 7. b. citato in Mon. Ang. To. II. p. 882. b.
c Universis S. matris ecclesie filiis, Acelina de Watervilla in domino salutem. Noverit universitas vestra me, consensu heredum meorum, dedisse & concessisse, Deo & ecclesie S. Michaelis archiangeli de Stanford, & sanctis monialibus ibidem Deo servientibus, duas partes tertie partis ecclesie de Corebi, quarum jus advocationis ad me spectat, cum omnibus pertinentiis suis, libere & quiete, in puram & perpetuam eleemosynam, possidendas; ad vestimenta sanctarum monialium ibidem Deo servientium. Pro animabus patris mei & matris mee, & pro animabus dominorum meorum & liberorum meorum, & omnium antecessorum meorum, & pro salute anime mee.   Ut autem hec mea donatio tractu temporis rata & inconcussa permaneat, presens scriptum sigilli mei appositione roboravi. His testibus, Reinero tunc temporis decano Stanford, Roberto vicario omnium SS. Hugone capellano, Rogero de Torpell, Radulpho de Diva, Radulpho de mortuo mari, Thoma de Colewill, Philippo de Colewill, Galfrido de Colewill, Willielmo de Colewill, Roberto de Colewill, Radulpho de Colewill, Willielmo de S. Laurentio, Thoma Patric, & multis aliis. Descripta fuit hec charta, cum plurimis aliis eidem prioratui spectantibus, e codice MS. penes Joh. Langley arm. 1649. per Cl. Dodsworth, in ejusdem collectaneorum acervum Vol. 59. fol. 165. &c.

' purtenances,

' purtenances, freely & quietly, into pure & perpetual alms, to be pof-
' fefled; towards cloathing of the holy nuns there ferving God.   For
' the fouls of my father & my mother, & for the fouls of my lords &
' children, & of all my anceftors, & for the health of my foul.   More-
' over that this my donation in tract of time may remain firm & un-
' fhaken, I have corroborated the prefent writing with the putting to
' of my feal.   Witnefles, Reiner then dean of Stanford, Robert vicar
' of all faints [in the mercat] Hugh the capellan, Roger de Torpell,
' Ralph de Diva, Ralph Mortimer, Thomas de Colewill, Philip de
' Colewill, Geoffry de Colewill, William de Colewill, Robert de
' Colewill, Ralph de Colewill, William of S. Laurence, Thomas Pa-
' tric, and many others.'   Thirdly, not fatisfied with giving the faid
nuns thefe two fhares of her faid third part of the church of Corebi,
fhe foon after gave them that other remaining third part thereof which
fhe had before referved.   Upon which occafion her charter runs thus.
a ' To all the children of holy mother church, unto whom the
' prefent writing fhall come, Acelina de Waterville, greeting in the
' lord.   Your univerfality fhall underftand, that I have given & granted,
' & by this my prefent charter confirmed, to God & the church of S.
' Michael the archangel of Stanford, & to the holy nuns there ferving
' God, the third part of the church of Corebi, of which the right of
' advoufon belongs unto me, & with the affent of the parfon who
' then was (to wit, Robert de Burton) with all its appurtenances, free-
' ly & quietly, into pure & perpetual alms, to poffefs it, towards cloath-
' ing the holy nuns there ferving God.   For the fouls of my father &
' my mother, & for the fouls of my lords & children, & all my an-
' ceftors, & for the health of my foul.   And that this my donation
' may be firm, & remain unfhaken, I have confirmed the prefent writ-
' ing with the putting to of my feal.   Witnefles, Hugh the capellan,
' lord Thomas de Colevill, Geoffry de Colevill, Ralph de Colevill, &
' Philip de Colevill, Geoffry de Colevill & William of S. Laurence, &
' mafter Sampfon, Thomas Patric, & many others.   Farewel.'   Fourthly, fhe gave the faid nuns of S. Michael four bovates of arable land
with the appurtenances, in old Stokehanc fields at Corebi aforefaid; the
profits whereof fhe does not by her deed of gift appropriate to any par-

---

a Univerfis S. matris ecclefie filiis ad quos
prefens fcriptum pervenerit, Acelina de Watervilla falutem in Domino.   Noverit univerfitas veftra me dediffe & conceffiffe, &
hac prefenti carta mea confirmaffe, Deo &
ecclefie S. Michaelis archi-angeli de Stanford, & fanctimonialibus ibidem Deo fervientibus, tertiam partem ecclefie de Corebi, cujus jus advocationis ad me fpectat, & affenfu perfone qui tunc temporis erat (fcilicet,
Roberti de Burton) cum omnibus pertinentiis fuis, libere & quiete, in putam & perpetuam eleemofynam, poffidere eam, ad vef-
timenta fanctarum monialium ibidem Deo
fervientium.   Pro animabus patris & matris
mee, & pro animabus dominorum meorum
& liberorum meorum, & omnium antecefforum meorum, & pro falute anime mee.
Et, ut hec mea donatio firma fit, & inconcuffa permaneat, figilli mei appofitione confirmavi.   Hiis teftibus, Hugone capellano,
domino Thoma de Colevilla, Galfrido de
Colevill, Radulpho de Colevill, & Philippo
de Colevill, Galfrido de Colevill, & Willielmo de S. Laurentio, & magiftro Samp-
fone, Thoma Patric, & multis aliis. Valete.
Ex eodem codice MS. Cl. Dodfw.

ticular ufe, but only thus gives it to that fifterhood in general. a ' To
' all the children of holy mother church unto whom the prefent writing
' fhall come, Acelina de Waterville, mother of Roger de Torpell, greet-
' ing in the lord. Your univerfality fhall underftand that I, in an intuiti-
' on of divine piety, & for the health of my foul, & of my ance-
' ftors & fuccefTors, have given, & granted, & by this my prefent char-
' ter confirmed, to God & the church of S. Michael of Staunford, & to
' the nuns there ferving God, into free & pure & perpetual alms, fout
' bovates of arable land in the fields of Corebi, with all the appurte-
' nances & eafements within & without; to wit, which lie in old
' Stokehane, between the land of Hamund Peche [her uncle in law]
' eaft, & the land of Ralph de Diva [her nephew] weft, & bound up-
' on the wood of Swafeld, to have & to hold, well & in peace, freely
' & quietly, & clear of all fecular cuftom, & exaction, & fervice. And
' I Afcelina & my heirs will warant the forefaid bovats of land belong-
' ing to the nuns againft all men & women for ever. And that this
' conceffion, & charitable donation may be firm & for ever remain un-
' fhaken, I Acelina, in my full power [fhe being now a widow & free
to do fo] ' have corroborated the prefent writing with the muniment of
' my feal. Witneffes, Hillary capellan of Corebi, Walter capellan of
' Bertune [Coggles] William capellan of Swafeld, Herebert capel-
' lan of Crewill, Ralph de Diva, William the chamberlain, John his
' fon, Geoffry the chamberlain, Robert de Diva of Swafield, William
' de Coleville, Ralph de Coleville, Richard de Coleville, & many
' others.' Laftly, fhe gave the faid nuns one other bovate of land lying
in Corebi field aforefaid, the profits whereof fhe ordered to be expended in a pittance, or entertainment on the day of her anniverfary; which
the faid nuns obliged themfelves to keep & celebrate. The charter
whereby fhe gave this laft mentioned bovate is now loft; but that fhe
did actually give them fo much land for an allowance to be fpent on
her year day, is evident from one of her fon Roger de Torpells confirmations which you will hereafter meet with in the courfe of thefe

a Omnibus S. matris ecclefie filiis, ad
quos prefens fcriptum pervenerit, Afcelina de
Watervilla, mater Rogeri de Torpell, falutem in Domino. Noverit univerfitas veftra
me, divine pietatis intuitu, & pro falute anime
mee, & anteceforum & fuccefforum meorum, conceffiffe & dediffe, & hac prefenti
carta mea confirmaffe, Deo & ecclefie S.
Michaelis de Staunford, & monialibus ibidem
Deo fervientibus, in liberam & puram & perpetuam eleemofynam, quatuor bovatas terre
arabilis in campis de Corebi, cum omnibus
pertinentiis & arfiamentis intra & extra,
viz. que jacent in Stokehane antiqua, inter
terram Hamundi Peche apud orientem, &
terram Radulphi de Diva apud occidentem,
& capiant fuper nemus de Swafeld, tenendas & habendas, bene & in pace, libere &

quiete & folute ab omni feculari confuetudine & exactione & fervitio. Et ego Afcelina & heredes mei warantizabimus predictas
bovatas terre pertinentis monialibus contra
omnes homines & feminas in perpetuum.
Et ut ifta conceffio & caritativa donatio rata
fit & in pofterum inconcuffa permaneat, prefens fcriptum, ego Acelina, in plena pote-
ftate mea, figilli mei munimine corroboravi.
Hiis teftibus, Hillario capellano de Corebi,
Waltero capellano de Bertune [Coggles]
Willielmo capellano de Swafeld, Hereber-
to capellano de Crewill, Radulpho de Diva, Willielmo camerario, Johanne filio ejus,
Galfrido camerario, Roberto de Diva de
Swafield, Willielmo de Coleville, Radulpho de Coleville, Richardo de Coleville, &
multis aliis. Ex eodem codice MS. Dodfw.

collections.

collections. At prefent I fhall only add, tho' all thefe donations were undoubtedly made at different times, yet none of them being dated to fix the certain year when they were fo given, I have here placed them all together, to render the beams of her many charities the more bright & ftarry.

XV. Having thus given an account of Afcelina de Waterville, & her benefactions to the nuns of S. Michael, I fhall now do the like of her fifter Matildis de Diva & her donations to the fame convent. Matildis the youngeft daughter of Geoffry & Afcelina de Waterville married William de Diva. By him fhe had iffue two fons, Hugh & Ralph; & a daughter named after her felf Matildis. The faid Matildis de Diva gave the faid nuns, firft, one third part of the forefaid church of Corebi. For which purpofe fhe thus fpeaks. [a] ' Be it known to all men, prefent & future, that I Matildis de Diva, daughter of Geoffry de Walterville, thro' an intuition of high piety, & for the fouls of my ' father & my mother, & by name of my aunt Matildis de Dovere, & ' of my husband William; & for my own health, & of my children; ' have given & granted, & by this my prefent charter confirmed, to ' God & the church of the nuns of S. Michael of Staunforde, a third ' part in the church of Corby, of which third part the right of advoufon ' unto me belonged, freely & quietly in perpetual alms to be poffeffed, ' with all its appurtenances. Witneffes, Reiner dean of Staunforde, ' Alexander the parfon, &c.' Secondly, fhe gave the faid nuns part of the chappel of Upton. The charter whereby fhe made that donation is now loft; but, as you will find, was confirmed by her fon Ralph. Thirdly, fhe gave the faid nuns the tythe of all fuch wood as was, or fhould be, grubbed up in the lands belonging to her & her heirs. The charter whereby fhe made that donation is now likewife loft; but, as you will elfewhere fee, was firft confirmed by her fon Ralph, & afterwards by Hugh Wells bifhop of Lincoln.

XVI. And now I am fpeaking of this lady, fomething alfo muft be faid of a fervant of hers, who, like her felf, had a great refpect for the forefaid nuns of S. Michael. Her I mean was one Adelicia de Capeni, a perfon it feems who had been fo faithful to her miftrefs, that, for a reward of her fervices, fhe was pleafed to give her a bovate of land with fome houfes & their appurtenances at Corby; all which fhe gave her, not only for her own life, but for ever, with liberty to beftow the fame on whom fhe thought fit. And for this her charter runs thus. [b] ' Matildis ' de Diva, to all her men & friends, French & Englifh, as well prefent ' as future, greeting. Your univerfality fhall underftand that I have ' given, granted, & by this my charter confirmed, to Adelicia de Capeni, for her fervice, one bovate of land in the town of Corebi, that to ' wit,

a Ex regiftri prioratus S. Michaelis penes Galf. Minfhul, gen. 1657. folio 6. a. citato in Mon. Ang. tomi II. p. 881. b.

b Matildis de Diva, omnibus hominibus & amicis fuis, Francis & Anglis, tam prefentibus quam futuris, falutem. Noverit univerfitas veftra quod ego dedi, conceffi, & hac mea carta confirmavi, Adelicie de Capeni, pro fervicio fuo, unam bovatam terre in villa de Corebi, illam fcilicet, quam Willielmus

' wit, which William fon of Toche held, with all the appurtenances, with.
' in the town & without.   This forefaid land I have given to Adelicia,
' & to whomfoever fhe will give it, to hold of me & my heirs, in
' fee & inheritance, freely, quietly & honorably, for half a pound of
' cumin to be paid thence yearly in Eafter, for all fervice & cuftom
' unto me, or unto my heirs, belonging; faving the fervice of the lord
' the king. Witneffes, Richard canon of Bernewell, Robert dean of
' Birtun, Alan de Birtun, Peter de Swafeld, Geoffry de Aumenill,
' William the chamberlain, Robert de Diva, Reynald de Truffavile.'
The feal reprefents a lady with a branch in her hand, arrayed after the
fafhion of the times, whereof (as near as I could draw it from the imprefs affixed to the original, now in the hands of the right honorable
Brownlow earl of Exeter) I fhall here give the fculpture.

Sigillum Matildis de Diva.

How long Adelicia de Capeni held this donation her felf I know not ;
but at length perceive fhe gave it to the forefaid nuns of S. Michael ;
at what time (either at requeft of the faid nuns, or of the faid
Adelicia de Capeni, or both) her miftrefs, the faid Matildis de Diva, in
order to corroborate their title to the fame, by another inftrument
gave, as fhe is pleafed to exprefs it, the faid bovate of land to the faid
nuns.   But that gift of hers (as will hereafter appear by the confirma-

mus filius Toche tenuit, cum omnibus per- des meos, pertinente; falvo fervicio D. Re-
tinentiis, infra villam & extra. Hanc pre- gis. Hiis teftibus, Richardo canonico de
dictam terram dedi Adelicie, & cuicunq; vo- Bernewell, Roberto decano de Birtun, &
luerit illam dare, tenendam de me & heredi- Hugone de Swafeld, Waltero capellano de
bus meis, in feudo & hereditate, libere, quiete, Birtun, Alano de Birtun, Petro de Swafeld,
& honorifice, pro dimidia libra cimini, red- Galfrido de Aumenill, Willielmo camera-
denda inde annuatim in pafcha, pro omni rio, Roberto de Diva, Reginaldo de Truf-
fervicio & confuetudine ad me, vel ad here- favile.

_____tion

tion of her son Ralph) was but a mere confirmation of what Adelicia de Capeni first gave. However take it in her own words, which (the original being now likewise in the hands of the same right honorable peer) run thus. [a] ' Matildis de Diva, to all her men, French & English, pre-
' sent & future, greeting. Your universality shall understand that I have
' given & granted, & by this my charter confirmed, to God & the nuns
' of S. Michael of Stanford there serving God, one bovate of land in
' the town of Corebi, with all the houses & with all the appurtenances,
' within the town & without the town; to wit, that bovate which I
' had before given to Adelicia de Capeni for her service, as the charter
' of the same Adelicia, which she therefore had of me, attests; to hold
' & have to the foresaid nuns, of me, & of my heirs, freely, quietly &
' honorably; paying therefore to me & my heirs yearly, for all service &
' for all exaction, & for all custom, unto me or unto my heirs belonging,
' half a pound of cumin at Easter. And the foresaid bovate, with all its
' appurtenances, I & my heirs will warant to the bovesaid nuns, against
' all men & all women. Witnesses, Roger de Torpel, Gervase de Ber-
' nake, Geoffry de Lehulm, Richard canon of Bernewell, Thomas de
' Taletorp, William the chamberlain of Corebi, Walter the parson of
' Stokes, Thomas the clerc of Stanford.' I shall only add, Matildis abovementioned, daughter of this Matildis de Diva, married William Otom [b].

XVII. [c] ' In the 7. R. 1. William de Albini the third [who after- 7. R. 1.
' wards founded Newsted] had the shriefalty of the counties of Warwic
' & Leicester for the last half of that year, so also of Roteland in the
' 8 & 9. & again of Warwic & Leicester for the last half of the 9 year.
' [d] Which 9. of R. 1. it was commanded, that after the feast of the   1197.
' purification, no man in any county, should sell any thing but by the 9. R. 1.
' measure prescribed, for the measure of the same quantity. And that
' after midlent fair at Stanford, no man should sell any cloth of less
' width than two ells within the lists. [e] The foresaid William de Al-
' bini the third had the sheriffalty of Roteland in the 10. R. 1. for the 10. R. 1.
' last half year. He was likewise sherif of Bucks & Bedfordshire, in

a Matildis de Diva, omnibus hominibus & amicis suis, Francis & Anglis, presentibus & futuris, salutem. Noverit universitas vestra me dedisse, & concessisse, & hac carta mea confirmasse, Deo & monialibus de S. Michaele de Stanford ibidem Deo servientibus, unam bovatam terre in villa de Corebi, cum omnibus domibus & cum omnibus pertinentiis, intra villam & extra villam; illam scilicet bovatam quam antea dederam Adelicie de Capeni pro servicio suo, sicut carte ipsius Adelicie, quam ipsa inde habuit de me, testatur; tenendam & habendam predictis monialibus, de me, & de heredibus meis, libere & quiete & honorifice; reddendo inde, mihi & heredibus meis, annuatim, pro omni servicio & pro omni exactione & pro omni consuetudine, ad me vel ad heredes meos pertinente, dimidiam libram cimini ad pascha. Predictam vero bovatam, cum omnibus pertinentiis suis, ego & heredes mei, warantizabimus supradictis monialibus, contra omnes homines & omnes feminas, His testibus, Rogero de Torpel, Gervasio de Bernake, Galfrido de Lehulmo, Richardo canonico de Bernewell, Thoma de Taletorp, Willielmo camerario de Corebi, Waltero persona de Stokes, Thoma clerico de Stanford.

b Ex cartæ citatæ in Monast. Ang. tomi II. p. 31. a.

c Bar. tome I. p. 113. a.

d Chron. Rogeri de Hoved. edit. Franc. p. 775. edit. Lond. fol. 440. b. 40. & annalium de Burton. p. 253.

e Baron. tome I. p. 113, 114.

' which

' which year he accounted to the king six hundred marks for Agatha
' Trusbut, with her inheritance, whom he afterwards took to wife.
' [a] The said Agatha, dowghter & heire to the lord Tresbur had two
' husbonds. Gul. de Albiniaco was the one. The lord Tresbur gave
' in his arms three bolts. [b] In the same 10. R. 1. William de Coleville
' gave a fine of thirty marcs for livery of his purparty of fifteen knights
' fees in Binebruc & Aburne in Lincolnshire.' Which last article is here
mentioned, to shew the time when he lived, & thereby in some measure
fix the date of an old deed (now in my hands) relating to some land
at North Witham granted by the said William de Colevill & Maud his
wife to one Q. a monk, which runs thus. ' Know present & future people
' that I William le Colevil & Matilda my wife, have given & granted,
' & for me & my heirs sold, & by this our present charter confirmed to
' Q. the monk & his heirs, for his service, one half acre of land; to
' wit, that which lies beyond the land of the church towards NorWcome
' [North-Witham] near the land of the same Q. the monk, at Walter-
' busc: paying therefore yearly he & his heirs, to me & my heirs, one
' clove of a july-flower, to wit, at Easter; for all service & exaction:
' to hold & to have, of me & my heirs, to him & his heirs, freely, quiet-
' ly, well, & in peace, as is aforesaid. And I William le Colevil & my
' heirs will warant the foresaid land to the foresaid Q. the monk &
' his heirs, & to whomsoever he shall give & sell it, against all men.
' For this selling & gift of the lands the said Q. the monk hath given
' me six shillings before hands. And that this may be firm, to the pre-
' sent charter I have put to my seal. Witnesses John le Dive, Gilbert
' de Biliggeie, Robert Bernard, Hugh le Dive, Robert le Dive, Robert
' de Witme [Witham] Thomas son of Ascelina, William the clerc,
' & o——thers.' The seal is wanting. King Richard the first died the 19.
' of October 1216. & was succeeded by his brother king John.

a Lelands itin. Vol. 7. p. 10.   b Baron. tome I. p. 626. a.

The end of the sixth book.

Academia tertia Anglicana;

OR, THE

ANTIQUARIAN ANNALS

of the TOWN of

STANFORD

IN

Lincoln, Rutland, *and* Northampton *Shires*.

BOOK VII.
Containing the reign of K. John.

I. 6 [a] IN the 1. of K. John, Ranulph the 3. E. of Chester called Anno
     ‘ Blandevil, forsook his lawful wife Constance, by reason 1. John.
     ‘ that the king haunted her company, &, being divorced
‘ from her, by his advice & example, wedded Clemencia, daughter of
‘ Raphe de Feugers, widow of Alan Dinant: William de Humet con-
‘ stable of Normandy [& lord of Stanford] giving the king two hundred
‘ pounds to be paid in England, that this his neice might marry thus.
‘ [b] William de Albini the third [who afterwards built Newsted] was
‘ this year sherif of Bucks & Bedfordshire. ‘ Upon the 18. Nov. 1200. Nov. 18.
‘ [d] deceased that pious prelate Hugh bishop of Lincoln, who was the great 1200.
‘ example of this age for piety, chastity, & all other christian virtues.’
There are several miracles which our monkish historians relate happened
on the way, as he was carried from London to be buried at Lincoln.
One of them they have been so kind as to bestow on the good town
of Stanford. I shall therefore give a brief relation of these matters; &
then, as some have more, some less, faith in such things than others,
let every man judge for himself. ‘ As they carried his body, saith
‘ Capgrave [e], from London to Lincoln, four lighted wax tapers were
‘ constantly born along with it by some children, which neither any
‘ blasts of wind or falls of rain were ever able to extinguish!’ More

a Baron. Vol. I. p. 41. b.   d Tyrrel. Vol. II, p. 712.
b Id. p. 114. a.   e Capg. ut supra.
c Capg. aurea legenda, fol. 186.

modeftly Matthew of Weftminfter [a], ' in all this journey it could never
' be once faid, tho' the weather was fometimes ftormy, that there was
' a time when fome one or other of the wax candles, which were car-
' ried about the bier, did not keep light.' Well! ' when they got to
' Bikelefwade, fays Capgrave [b], & went to fet the corps for that night
' in the church there, there was a man, as the people crouded to get
' in along with it, had his arm broke; who, being carried home, & at
' length dropt into a gentle flumber, faw, in his fleep, a bifhop handling
' & examining his arm, who, after a fhort fpace, gave him his benedicti-
' on, & fo left him. Whereupon the man, awaking, found his arm
' perfectly well again! Likewife when they came to Stanford, an harm-
' lefs honeft man, much addicted to devotion (a fhoemaker by trade)
' bowing his head under the bier, & lifting up his eyes & hands to hea-
' ven, fell a praying after this manner. I thank thee, O father of mer-
' cies & God of all confolation, that thou haft been pleafed to have pity
' on me & haft comforted me, and (which I have in this world above
' all things defired) on my attempting to fet the fhoulder of my finful
' body to the moft holy body of this thy fervant, that I have merited
' to approach him who hath fo faithfully ferved thee. I befeech thee
' therefore, almighty God, let my foul be this night with the foul of
' this thy fervant in paradife, where I queftion not but his already is.
' He had no fooner faid thus, but he went home, confeffed himfelf,
' made his will, received the facrament, & prefently after quietly ex-
' pired!'

 II. ' ' In the 2. of K. John, William de Albini the third [who after-

2. John. wards built Newfted] ' had a fpecial licenfe to make a park at Stoke
[Albini] ' in Northamptonfhire, & liberty to hunt the fox & hare, it ly-
' ing within the precinct of the foreft of Rockingham. [d] The fame year
' Hugh Bardolf & other the kings juftices going to Bofton fair with
' intent to fiefe all woolen cloaths that were not two ells within the
' lifts, according to K. Richards late affize or ftatute [which took place
after midlent fair at Stanford, 1197.] ' the merchants fo prevailed with
' the juftices, that the cloaths were not fiefed, nor the late affize far-
' ther obferved: fo that for the future they might make their cloaths
' as broad or as narrow as they pleafed. For which licenfe (tho' to the
' damage of many) the juftices procured the king a great fum of

3. John. ' mony. [e] In the 3. John, died Baldwin the firft of that name, lord
' Wac; whereupon Baldwin his fon & William Humet [lord of Stan-
ford] ' gave a fine to the king of a thoufand marks, for livery of his
' lands in England & Normandy; but with condition, that he fhould
' not marry without the confent of the king & his own friends.
' Whereupon fhortly after he took to wife Agnes daughter of the faid

---

a Non erat hora, in qua in aliquo cereo- c Baronage Vol. I. p. 114. a.
rum non effet ignis, &c. p. 263.   d Tyrrel, p. 716.
 b Ut fupra.   e Baron. Vol. I. p. 539. b.

             ' William

' William Humet, & had with her the manor of Wichendon. ᵃThe
' fame year upon that difcontent of the barons, becaufe the king would
' not reftore them their rights, which caufed their refufal to attend him
' into Normandy; he, thereupon requiring the delivery of their caftles
' into his hands, began firft with William de Albini the third [who
' afterwards built Newfted] & demanded Belvoir; who, fubmitting,
' gave up his fon in hoftage, & fo retained it ftill. ᵇ In the 4. of K.
' John, the king by his charter dated Jan. 15. at Alencon in Normandy Jan. 15.
' gave William de Albini the manor of Oskyngton (Oufton) in Not-   4. John.
' ting. & an hundred fhillings of foccage land lying in Wilberfton &
' Stoke in Northamptonfhire. ᶜThe fame year upon friday in Eafter
' week, the king [who was then in Normandy] being told that Ra-
' nulph earl of Chefter with fome others intended to defert him,
' came to the caftle of Vire, where the faid earl repaired to him, &
' fo excufed the matter, that the king, with thofe who then attended
' him, feemed well fatisfied, but would not longer truft him with the
' caftle of Simili without fufficient pledges for his fidelity; fo that he
' was neceffitated to procure his friend William de Humet conftable of
' Normandy [& lord of Stanford] & R. conftable of Chefter to be bound
' for him, upon penalty of forfeiting all the fees he held of him for his
' faithful cuftody thereof. About this time, ᵈ ' the borough of Stan-
' ford was fined twenty marcs, for making a foolifh prefentment, & for
' the mercat being removed, & alfo becaufe they chofe the meaner people
' of the town to be of the jury. Stephen de Lenne of Stanford was alfo
' fined one marc for felling wine contrary to affife meafure. And fo
' was Jordan de London of Stanford for the fame, becaufe he was a
' priefts fon. ✝Likewife the borough of Stanford paid the king a fine
' to enjoy their antient cuftoms & liberties;' whereby it fhould feem
they were now forfeited.

III. Lucy, wife of William Humet, lord of Stanford, gave, but the exact
time when I find not, with confent of the faid William her hufband &
Richard her fon, to the nuns of S. Michael by Stanford half a marc of filver
yearly out of her lands at Bredcrofd by Stanford, conditionally that
the faid nuns fhould conftantly keep her anniverfary day with an obfequy; one half of the faid half marc of filver to be expended in a pittance
upon that occafion, & the other half of the faid marc to go towards the
charge of the infirmary. Her charter, touching the faid benefaction,
runs thus. ᵉ ' To all the children of holy mother church, Lucy, wife
' of lord William de Humet, conftable of the lord the king, greeting.
' Let your univerfality know that I, with affent of William my
' lord & Ricard my fon, have given & granted by this my charter, to

a Bar. Vol. I. p. 114. a.
b id. ib.
c id. p. 41, 42.
d ex rotulo incerti anni R. Johannis, in-
fcripto E. rot. 8. dorfo amerciamenta Linc.
Ex placitis & affifis captis apud Lincoln.

craftino octab. S. trinitatis coram S. de Pat-
fhul, E. de Fauconberge, & fociis eorum,
anno regni R. Joh. 4.
e ex autographo in officio armorum, citato in Monaft. Ang. tomi I. p. 488. b.

' God

' God & S. Mary & the church of S. Michael of Stanford & to the
' holy nuns there ferving God, half a marc of filver out of my land
' of Bradecrofd; to wit, fix fhillings out of two bovates which William
' Martin holds, & eight pence out of one bovate which Leuvin holds;
' into pure & perpetual alms, free & quit from all fervice & action fe-
' cular, as any alms can be better & more freely given; for the health
' of my foul, & of William my lord, & of Richard my fon, & of my
' anceftors.   Moreover this aforenamed land I bought of Toften Bodin,
' who had it, by the gift of lord Richard Humet, for his fervice.   Like-
' wife the forenamed holy nuns, thro' an intuition of charity, have gran-
' ted me, for my life, full fellowfhip of the prayers & of all the good
' works of the forenamed place of S. Michael, & will keep the day of
' my obit for ever with an annual obfequy.   Of this forefaid half
' marc I have affigned one moiety for a pittance for the convent on
' the day of my anniverfary, & the other part for ever to the infirma-
' ry. Witneffes, Jordan de Humet, William de Sae, Henry his brother,
' Ralf de Agnis, Giflebert del Val, mafter William, Salvage [who]
' gave his daughter.'   Sir William Dugdale in his baronage takes no
notice of Richard (fon of William Humet) here mentioned.

IV. About the fame time Walter de Cardonville having given the
faid nuns of S. Michael by Stanford a virgate of land, worth half
a marc *per annum*, lying at Draiton near the monaftery of Sudwic; and
the forefaid lady Lucy de Humet, with her husbands confent, having
given the faid monaftery of Sudwic half a marc *per annum* out of
her lands at Bradecrofd abovementioned, lying juft by the faid nunnery of S. Michael; the faid monafteries, with confent of William
lord Humet aforefaid, lord of the fee in both places, made an exchange of the faid lands, & by mutual deeds delivered to each other
(each of the faid deeds being firft fealed with the feals of William lord
Humet & the convent by whom it was delivered) confirmed the fame.
I fhall here exemplifie a copy of that deed which the convent of Sudwic gave the nuns of S. Michael upon this occafion.   The original,
from whence I tranfcribed the underwritten copy, is now in the Rt.
honourable the E. of Exeters archives, & may be thus englifhed.   ᵃ ' This
' agreement made between the convent of Sudwic, & the convent of
' holy nuns of the church of S. Michael of Stanford [witneffeth,] that
' whereas the forefaid convent of nuns, by the gift of Walter de Car-
' donville, fhould have one virgate of land, which Ralf Frefel held, by
' paying half a marc yearly; which virgate is of the fee of Draiton,
' near the land of William de la Ward, & is near to the forefaid church
                                                        ' of

a Hec conventio facta inter conventum   marcam annuatim, quevirgata ÷ [fic, pro, *eft*]
ecclefie de Sudwic, & conventum fanctimo-   de feodo de Draitona, juxta terram Will- iel-
nialium ecclefie S. Michaelis . . . . . .   mi de Lawarda, & ·|· [fic, pro, *eft*] vicina
. . . . . . cet, quod cum predictus conven-   predicte ecclefie de Sudwic; Et, alia parte,
tus monialium, de dono Walteri de Cardon-   cum conventus Suwic [ita.] de dono D.
villa haberet virgatam unam terre quam Ra-   Lucie de Hum [ita.] per affenfum domini
nulphus Frefel tenuit, reddendo dimidiam   fui, haberet dimidiam marcatam redditus in
                                                                                    terra

‘ of Sudwic; And, on the other part, whereas the convent of Sudwic,
‘ by the gift of lady Lucie de Humet, with assent of her lord should
‘ have half a marc of rent in the land of Bradecroft, which is nigh to
‘ the forenamed church of nuns; by common assent of either convent,
‘ & by assent & concession of lord William de Humet (of whose fee
‘ each alms is known to be) it is thus agreed between either convent;
‘ viz. that the foresaid convent of nuns hath granted & resigned to the
‘ foresaid church & convent of Sudwic for ever, whatsoever right it had
‘ in the foresaid virgate of land of the gift of Walter de Cardonville,
‘ in exchange for the forewritten half marc of rent of the gift of the
‘ forenamed lady Lucie de Humet, in the land of Bradecroft. And the
‘ forenamed convent of Sudwic hath granted & resigned to the foresaid
‘ church of the nuns of Stanford, whatever right it had in the forewritten
‘ half marc of rent of the land of Bradecroft, in exchange for the forewrit-
‘ ten virgate of the fee of Draiton. And the foresaid convent of nuns
‘ hath resigned & delivered to the convent of Sudwic all the muniments
‘ which it had relating to the forenamed half marc of rent, to wit, of
‘ the foresaid virgate of the fee of Draiton. And the convent of Sud-
‘ wic in like manner hath resigned & delivered all the muniments which
‘ it had, touching the forenamed half marc of rent in the land of Brade-
‘ croft. And that this agreement & foresaid exchange between either
‘ convent may for ever obtain the strength of firmness & stability, let it
‘ be confirmed by attestation of the present writing, & by the seal
‘ of either convent, & also by the seal & testimony of lord William
‘ de Humet. Witnesses, Richard de Humet, Jordan de Humet, Baud.
‘ Wac, William Piro .. Ralf de Agnis, William le Moine, Bartholo-
‘ mew de Mortimer, Peter de Aupegart, William de Hasteinville, the
‘ Salvage, William de Sac, Henry de Humet his brother, Gislebert de
‘ Valle, Orace the butler, Roger de Mountchanch, Henry de Drue-
‘ valle.’ The seal of William lord Humet represents an armed knight,
mounted on his courser; a drawn sword in his right hand, & his shield

terra de Bradecroft, que vicina est prefate ecclesie monialium; ex communi assensu utriusque conventus, & assensu & concessione D. Willielmi de Hum (de cujus feodo utraq; eleemosina esse dinoscitur) ita convenit inter utrumque conventum; quod predictus conventus monialium concessit & resignavit predicte ecclesie & conventui de Sudwic imperpetuum, quicquid juris habuit in predicta virgata terre de dono Walteri de Cardonvilla, in excambium prescripte dimidie marcate redditus de dono prenominate D. Lucie de Hum in terra de Bradecroft. Et prefatus conventus [de] Suwic concessit & resignavit predicte ecclesie monialium de Stanford, quicquid juris habuit in prescripta dimidia marcata redditus de terra de Bradecroft, in excambium prescripte virgate de feudo de Draiton. Et predictus conventus monialium resignavit & tradidit conventui

Sudwic omnia munimenta que habuit de prenominata dimidia marcata, scil. de predicta virgata de feudo de Draiton. Et conventus Sudwic similiter resignavit & tradidit omnia munimenta que habuit de prenominata dimidia marcata redditus in terra de Bradecroft. Et ut hec conventio & predictum excambium inter utrumque conventum perpetuis temporibus firmitatis & stabilitatis robur obtineant, presentis scripti attestatione & utriusque conventus sigillo, necnon & D. Willielmi de Humet testimonio & sigillo sit confirmata. Testibus, Richard. de Hum, Jordano de Hum, Baud. Wac, Willielmus Piro ... Radulpho de Agnis, Petro de Aupegart, Willielmo de Hasteinvilla, Salvagio, Willielmo de Sae, Henrico de Humet fratre suo, Gisleberto de Valle, Oratio pincerna, Rogero de Monte Chanch, Henrico de Druevalle.

3

on his left arm, riding in full career, armed a cap en pied. The feal
of the convent of Sudwic reprefents a church as here depicted.

Sigillum Conventus de Sudwic

V. William Humet lord of Stanford gave the Cyftercian monks of
that place (but the exact time when I find not) the yearly fum of ten
marcs to be annually received in the town of Staunford, out of the
lands & rents which he had there: of which donation more by & by.
ᵃ ' It is reported of this William de Humet, that K. John made him
' juftice of England, & that he advifed the king to go into Normandy;
' but that when he came thither the country rofe againft him, in fo
' much that he was vanquifh'd & taken. Alfo that when he heard the
' king was returned into England, he fled.' No time is fet down in
my author when thefe things happen'd, but all this, it fhould feem,
6. John. was about the 6. of K. John. For then William earl Warenn, the
fifth of the name of William, ' ᵇ had the caftle & honour of Eye in
' Suffolk committed to his charge. Alfo a grant of the manors of
' Graham [Grantham] & Stanford in Lincolnfhire.' Upon which laft
occafion we have this record. ᶜ ' The king to the fherif of Lincoln,
' greeting. Know ye that we have committed to our beloved William
' earl of Warenn, Grantham & Stanford, with the appurtenances, to
' hold until he fhall recover his lands in Normandy, or until we fhall
' elfewhere make him a competent exchange. So neverthelefs that he
' may not talliate the men of Stanford, fave by our precept. And
' therefore to you we command, that ye caufe him to have feifin thereof
' without delay. Witnefs the king at Weftm. the 19. of April.

a Baron. Vol. I. p. 631. b.   c Bradys hift. boroughs. part II. p. 51.
b id. p. 76. a.

3   ' ᵃ By

' ᵃ By this record it feems probable, that by the original grant, Willi-
' am de Warenna might have power & licenfe to talliate Grantham,
' but could not impofe tallage upon Stanford.'

 VI. ᵇ ' In the 9. of K. John, the king refufing to admit Stephen
' Langton to be archbifhop of Canterbury, it occafioned a quarrel be-
' tween him & the pope, which by degrees was fo inflamed, that March
' 22. the bifhops ᶜ William of London, Euftace of Ely, & Malgor of
' Winchefter, executed the orders of the pope, & interdicted the whole
' kingdom.' So remarkable a circumftance as the interdict of a whole
kingdom deferves fome notice to be taken of it, & therefore as far as
Stanford fhared in the calamity, fhall be now & hereafter touched. At
this time it muft be, that, as Mr. Butcher tells us ᵈ, ' William earl
' Warenn gave & granted to this towne one place of burial, contain-
' ing five acres, without the eaft gate of Stanford to bury the dead
' bodies of excommunicated perfons, & to build there a chappel & houfe
' for poor brethren.' That hofpital was probably S. Logars, but where
fituate I find not. ᵉ ' Upon the interdict the king feifed all the lands
' & goods of thofe religious perfons who denied to perform divine fer-
' vice ; & particularly within this diocefe of Lincoln fent out this pre-
' cept. ᶠ The king to all of the diocefe of Lincoln, clercs & laity,
' greeting. Know ye that from the monday next before Eafter, we have
' committed to W. de Cornhul archdeacon of Huntingdon & Gerard
' de Camvile, all the lands & effects of the abbats, & of the priors, &
' of all the religious, & alfo of the clergy of the diocefe of Lincoln,
' who will not from after that time perform divine fervice ; & to you
' we command, that ye from thence forth look well to them, &c.'
Thus the king fequeftred ᵍ ' all abbies & priories, commanding all
' their church rents to be confifcated. But in this affair the abbats
' were fo cautious, that they would not leave their houfes & monafte-
' ries, unlefs expelled by force. Which the kings officers perceiving,
' they durft not offer them any violence, having no command from
' the king fo to do. However they converted their goods to the kings
' ufe, providing for them food & raiment, tho' very fparingly, out of
' their own eftates. Alfo the barns of clergymen were every where
' locked up by the kings command, & the corn feifed for his fervice.
' ʰ K. John, notwithftanding that the realme was thus wholy interdyted
' & vexed, fo that no priefts could be found to fay any fervice in
' churches or chapels, made yet no great account thereof as touching
' any offence towards God or the pope. ' However, by procure-
' ment of Stephen the archbifhop, licenfe was at laft granted to the con-
' ventual churches to celebrate divine fervice once every weeke.' So

a Bradys Hift. Boroughs, Vol. p. 51.   f Prynne tome II. p. 255.
b Bp. Kennets par. ant. p. 171.   g Tyrrel, p. 737.
c Stow, p. 249.   h Holings. p. 567. b.
d MS. penes me, p. 46.   i Stow, p. 250.
e Bp. Kennet, ut fupra.

           that

that altho' they had no fervice in the parifh churches at Stanford, there was neverthelefs at laft fervice once a week at St. Leonards & St. Michaels priories, & perhaps at fome other religious houfes there. But all this notwithftanding, [a] ' the king fent his fheriffs & other minifters into ' all parts of England, commanding, with terrible threats, all prelates ' & their inferior clergy, that they fhould forthwith depart the kingdom ' & repair to the pope, requiring him to do the king juftice for this ' injury.'

VII. [b] ' In this 9. of K. John, William earl Warenn [lord of Stanford] ' gave 3000 marks for the cuftody of the lands of Gilbert de

Anno 1209.

' Aquila, to the ufe of his fifter, wife of the fame Gilbert.' [c] In 1209. ' the pope beynge afcerteyned of K. Jhons obftinancy that he perfeve' red in againft holye churche, fente a new commiffion, by vertue ' whereof, the curfe of enterdytyng was newly denounced & manifefted ' in fondri places of Englande. And over that, the pope by authoritie ' of the fayd bull affoyled al the lordes of England, of all homage & ' feaultye, that thei of right owed the king, to the entente that they ' fhould arife againft him, & deprive him of all kingly honour. [d] Of the ' maner of thys enterdyction fome fay, that the land was enterdited tho' rowly, & the churches & houfes of religion clofed, that now here was ufed ' neither maffe or divine fervice: By whiche reafon none of the feven fa' craments in all thys terme fhould be miniftred, nor child chriftened, nor ' man confeffed, nor maried. But it was not fo ftrayte. Forthere were di' vers placed in England whiche were occupied wyth divine fervice al ' that feafon, by licenfe purchafed then or before. Alfo children were ' chriftened through all the land, & men houfeled [confeffed] & anea' led [abfolved] except fuch perfonnes as were excepted by name in ' the bull.' But to proceed. Upon this new interdict [e] ' the king re' quired of his nobles new oaths of allegiance, pledges of fuch as he ' moft fufpected, & homage of all freeholders even of twelve years of ' age.' Not long after, [f] ' when corne began to waxe ripe, to revenge ' himfelf of them who had refufed to go with him [to fight the Scots] ' the king caufed the pales of all the parkes & forefts which he had ' within his realme to be throwne downe, & the ditches to be made ' plain, that the deere breaking out & raunging abrode in the corne ' fields might deftroy & eat up the fame before it could be ryped. For ' which act (if it were fo indeed) many a bitter curfe proceeded from ' the poore husbandmen.' I infert this, becaufe all Stanford fouth of the Welland, was, at this time, part of the kings foreft of Rockingham, tho' afterwards disforrefted by K. John himfelf: whereof by & by.

a Tyrrel, ut fupra.
b Baron. Vol. I. p. 76. a. b.
c Fabian, part II. p. 31. a. b.
d id. p. 32. b.
e Speed. p. 571. a. b.
f Holingfhed. p. 568.

VIII. [a] ' In

VIII. ᵃ ' In 1210. the king commanded all the Jews, men & wo- | Anno
' men, to be imprifoned & grievoufly punifhed, becaufe he would have | 1210.
' all their mony. Whereupon fome gave all they had, & promifed
' more, to the end they might efcape fo many torments as he did put
' upon them. For every one of them had one eye at leaft pull'd out.
ᵇ In 1211. a peace being concluded between K. John & the French king, | Anno
' ᵇ William de Albini [the 3. who afterwards built Newfted] was one | 1211.
' of K. Johns fureties, who fwore that he fhould obferve the articles.'

IX. ᶜ ' In the 14. of K. John, Alan Baffet, baron of Wycomb, gave | 14. John.
' an hundred marks that his daughter might take to husband the fon &
' heir of William Lanvalei. ᵈ In 1213. William earl Warenn [lord of | Anno
Stanford] ' was one of thofe four great earls who obliged themfelves by | 1213.
' oath, that K. John fhould perform whatfoever the pope did determine
' for fatisfaction as to thofe particulars touching which the king was
' excommunicated. And, in the fame year, was one of the witneffes
' to the inftrument, figned by the king the 15. of May, whereby he | May 15.
' refigned his realm & crown to the pope; & at his doing homage
' thereupon. In the fame year having fatisfied the king that he was
' innocent of that confpiracy whereof he then ftood much fufpected
' (& wherein Euftace de Vefci & Robert Fitzwalter were chief) he had,
' amongft others, the cuftody of the caftles of Bambury & New Caftle
' upon Tine, with the whole bailiwic of Northumberland, committed
' to his truft.' Soon after doing homage to the pope, the king ᵉ ' fente
' his letters to all fherifes, commaunding them to fummon foure law-
' ful men of every towne belonging to the demeafne of the crowne [as
Stanford then & long after did] ' to make their appearance at S.
' Albons, upon the 4. of Auguft, to make inquifition of the loffes which | Aug. 4.
' every bifhop had fuftained, & what ought to be reftored to them, by the
' king. ᶠ On the 25. of Auguft, the archbifhop fo far indulged all | Aug. 25.
' churches, both conventual & parochial, that, tho' the interdict was
' not yet taken off, they might chant over their canonical hours with a
' low voice: which was fome favour, it being not permitted to cele-
' brate divine fervice after any other manner.'

X. ᵍ ' On the 29. of June 1214. cardinal Nicholas the popes legate | June 29.
' releafed the fentence of the interdict, after it had continued fix years, | 1214.
' three months, & fourteen days. For which *Te Deum* was folemnly
' fung by the clergy; & indeed, the whole nation highly rejoiced, that
' they were now reftored to the free & publick exercife of religious
' duties.' About this time Robert Lindfey lord abbat of Burg & the
convent of that place, with the knights & free men who had lands &
tenements in the Neffe of Burg, obliged themfelves to pay the king
1200 marcs to have part of that country, wherein all Stanford on the

---

a Stow, p. 251.   e Holing. p. 581. b.
b Holings. p. 572. b.   f Tyrrel, p. 760.
c Baron. Vol. 1. p. 383. b.   g id. p 768.
d id. p. 76. b.

south side of the Welland is situate, disforrested.   Their obligation runs
thus.   [a] ' To all the faithful of Christ, &c. Robert by the grace of
' God, abbat of Burg, & the convent of the same place, & the knights
' & freemen who have lands & tenements in the Nesse of Burg, eternal
' greeting in the Lord.   Your universality shall understand that we will
' pay to the lord K. John (for disforresting all the lands in the Nesse
' of Burg which is between the water of Nen & the water of Welande,
' as the waters meet in the town of Croyland ; & from Walmisford, as
' the great road extends it self as far as to Stupendestan without the
' town of Stanford ; & from Stupendestan, by a straight line, as far as
' to the Weland, under the wall of the nuns of Stanford, so that abby
' be within the bounds aforesaid) 1200 marcs of Esterling mony ; the
' said mony to be paid within three full years, to commence from the
' very first Easter next after the general release of the interdict of Eng-
' land.   So nevertheless that in the first year we shall pay only seven-
' ty marcs & twenty marcs ; & in the second year two hundred marcs.
[They stipulated to pay no more for the two first years, because, I suppose, the abby & all of them were yet very poor, by reason of the
mony which had been squeez'd from them by the kings officers, who,
it may be remembred, sequestred the lands of religious houses most
part of the interdict ; the rest I presume was to be paid at the full end
& term of the said three years.]   ' And unto witness hereof I Robert
' abbat of Burg, & the knights & freemen of the Nesse of Burg, to this
' writing have put to our seals.'   The king, to whom mony was always very welcome, agreed to this proposal, in pursuance whereof he
granted them his charter to disforrest the premises, an extract of which
I shall here likewise insert.   [b] ' John, by the grace of God, king of
' England, &c.   Know ye, that we have granted to the abbat of Burg,
' & to the monks & tenents who have lands or tenements in the Ness
' of Burg, within these bounds (to wit, between the water of Nen &
' the water of Welande, as they meet in Croylande ; & from Walmes-
' forde, as the great road extends as far as to Stupendestan without

a Universis Christi fidelibus, &c. Robertus D. G. abbas de Burgo & ejusdem loci
conventus, & milites & francolani qui terras & tenementa in Nasso Burgi habent,
eternam in Domino salutem. Noverit universitas vestra quod solvemus D. Regi Johanni, pro disafforestanda tota terra in Nasso Burgi que est inter aquam de Nen & a-
quam de Welande, sicut aque conveniunt
in villa de Croylande; & de Walmisford,
sicut magnum chiminum extendit se usq; ad
Stupendestan extra villam de Stanford; & de
Stupendestan, per rectam lineam, usq; ad
Weland sub curia monialium de Stanford,
ita quod abbatia illa sit infra metas predictas ;
a proximo paschate, post relaxationem generalem interdicti Anglie, in tres annos sub-
sequentes plene completos, 1200 marcas
Esterlingorum.   Ita quidem quod primo
anno solvemus 70 marcas & 20 marcas ; &

secundo anno 200 marcas. Et in hujus rei
testimonium ego R. abbas de Burgo, & milites & francolani de Nasso Burgi, huic scripto sigilla nostra apposuimus.   Ex chartul.
ecclesiæ de Burgo Swapham nuncupati folio
243.
b Johannes, D. G. rex Anglie, &c. Sciatis nos concessisse abbati de Burgo, & monachis, & tenentibus qui habent terras vel tenementa in Nasso Burgi infra has metas
(scil. inter aquam de Nen & aquam de Welande, sicut conveniunt in Croylande ; & de
Walmesford, sicut magnum chiminum extendit usque ad Stupendestan extra villam de
Stanford, & de Stupendestan extra domum
sanctimonialium S. Michaelis de Stanforde per
rectam lineam usque ad Weland, ita quod
predicta domus sit infra predictas metas) de-
aforestatam, &c. Ex ejusdem chartularii folio
52.

2   ' the

‘ the town of Stanford; & from Stupendeſtan without the houſe of
‘ the holy nuns of S. Michael of Stanford on a ſtraight line as far as
‘ the Welland, ſo that the foreſaid houſe be within the bounds afore-
‘ ſaid) to be disforreſted, &c.’   What is here meant by Stupendeſtan,
or Stupende Stan, without Stanford; is worth enquiry.

XI. William Humet, conſtable of Normandy & ſometime lord of 22. Nov.
Stanford, having formerly given the Ciſtercian monks of Stanford the 1214.
16. John.
yearly ſum of ten marcs *per annum,* K. John now confirmed that grant
by the following charter. ª ‘ John, by the grace of God, king of
‘ England, &c. to all the faithful of Chriſt, who ſhall inſpect the pre-
‘ ſent charter, greeting in the Lord.   Know ye that we have granted, &
‘ by this our charter confirmed, to God & the Cyſtercian monks, the
‘ gift of ten marcs to be annually received in the town of Staunford,
‘ which William de Humeth made & by his charter confirmed to the
‘ ſame monaſtery, into pure & perpetual alms, as the ſame charter more
‘ particularly atteſts.   Wherefore we will & firmly command that the
‘ foreſaid monks may receive & have the foreſaid ten marcs, well & in
‘ peace, freely & quietly, wholly as is aforeſaid.   Witneſſes, lord Ste-
‘ phen archbiſhop of Canterbury, William of London, Peter of Winton,
‘ Euſtace of Ely, J. of Bath, & Hugh of Lincoln, biſhops ; William
‘ earl Mareſchal, William Briewer, Thomas de Erdinton.   Given by
‘ the hands of maſter R. *de Mariſcis* our chancellor, at London, the 22.
‘ of Nov.’   This confirmation Sir William Dugdale, by a very great
overſight, places among the charters belonging to the nuns of S. Michael.   Whereas it may be obſerved there is no mention of any nuns,
or convent of S. Michael in this confirmation, as we find there expreſ-
ly is in all the charters belonging to that houſe.   Nor is there any one
hint in it to incline us to believe that this benefaction of William Humeth to the Cyſtercirn monks at Stanford, ſhould have any relation to
the ladies of the order of S. Bennet in the priory of S. Michael there.
Beſides, Sir William himſelf informs us, that he had not this confirmation of K. Johns with any evidences, or out of any chartulary belonging to the ſaid nuns, but *e cartis de anno* 16. *R. Johan. num.* 36.
Into this miſtake therefore he was perhaps led by obſerving that Richard
Humet, father of this William, gave the foreſaid nuns of S. Michael
the church of S. Andrew in Stanford, & that Lucy, wife of this William, gave them half a marc *per annum* to keep her obit, &c.   But their
giving thoſe benefactions to the nuns does not argue that the ſaid nuns
monopolized all their charitable bequeſts; on the contrary, we find,
this very William was a benefactor to the hoſpital of S. John the Baptiſt & S. Thomas of Canterbury at Stanford, as well as to the Cyſtercian monks there; & perhaps either he, or others of his family, might
be benefactors to other hoſpitals & monaſteries at Stanford, beſides the
nuns & thoſe here mentioned.

a E cartis de an. 16. R. Johan. num. 36. citat. in Monaſt. Ang. Tomi I. p. 488. b.

XII. ' ᵃ K. John, but when I find not, gave & alienated from
' the lordſhip of Stanford two carucates & an half, & five acres of
' heirable land to the hoſpital of lepers; & two acres to the monks
' of S. Michael; & one acre & half to the hoſpital of S. Logar;
' & two acres to the monks of S. Leonards in pure alms.' Alſo,
by his charter bearing date the 18. of Jan. (what year I find not)
the ſaid K. John gave the nuns of S. Michael by Stanford, a load of
thorns or dead wood yearly out of Cliff foreſt; which charter is thus
worded. ᵇ ' John, by the grace of God, king of England, lord of
' Ireland, duke of Normandy & Aquitain, earl of Anjou, to the bailifs
' of the foreſt of Clive, greeting. Know ye that we, for the health
' of our ſouls, & of all our anceſtors & ſucceſſors, have granted to the
' nuns of S. Michael of Stanford, that they may have, on any day,
' one load of thorns or dead wood, out of our foreſt of Clive. And
' therefore we will & firmly command that ye let them have the foreſaid
' load without impediment. Witneſs Hugh Bard. at Luxe. the 18. of
' Jan.' The Tradition is at Cliffe Regis, that K. John had an houſe
there. And indeed the foundations of a ſpacious building may now be
diſcerned on the ſouth ſide of the pariſh church there. The ſaid church
is antient, built cathedral-wiſe, in ſhape of a croſs, with a ſpire
ſteeple of ſtone in the middle. The ſaid K. John, or ſome of his ſucceſſors, had likewiſe great fiſhpools at Clive; ſeveral grounds there (the
pools having been long ſince drained) being yet known by the names
of the great & little Fiſh-pools. Moreover in the upper window of the
north iſle of the nave of the foreſaid church there, is yet left the figure
of a man kneeling in a religious habit, under which is wrote, *orate
pro anima Johannis Fyſchere*; which John Fyſchere, probably bought or
rented the fiſhpools there, & new glaſed that window. But theſe
things are out of the compaſs of my preſent deſign.

XIII. The foreſaid nuns had likewiſe in this reign, as I take it, tho'
I am not able to fix the exact years when, a great many other benefactions, which I ſhall now enumerate. And firſt. Lord William Langvale gave them S. Clements church at Stanford, whoſe charter, for
that purpoſe, runs thus. ᶜ ' Know preſent as well as future people, that
' I William de Langvale, ſon of William de Langvale, give & grant, &
' by this my preſent charter confirm to the holy nuns of the church of
' S. Michael of Staunforde, the church of S. Clement of the ſame town,
' with all its appurtenances, into pure & perpetual alms, freely &
' quietly, in an intuition of divine love, & for the health of the ſouls

---

a. Butchers MS. penes me, p. 10.
b Johannes D. G. rex Anglie, dominus
Hibernie, dux Normannie & Aquitanie,
comes Andegavie, ballivis foreſte de Clive,
ſalutem. Sciatis nos, pro ſalute anime noſtre
& omnium anteceſſorum & ſucceſſorum
noſtrorum, conceſſiſſe monialibus S. Michaelis de Stanford, quod habeant, quolibet
die, unam carectatam de ſpinis vel de mortuo boſco, infra foreſtam noſtram de Clive.

Et ideo volumus, & firmiter precipimus,
quod permittatis illas predictam carectatam
ſine impedimento. Teſte Hugone Bard.
apud Luxe. decimo octavo die Januarii ----
Ex exemplari quodam cujuſdam rotuli pa-
tentis de anno 3. Ed. 4.
c Ex regiſtri Prioratus S. Michaelis penes
Galf. Minſhul gen. anno 1657. folio. 3. a.
citato in Mon. Ang. tomi II. p. 880.

' of

' of my father & mother, & of all my anceftors. Witneffes, Oliver the
' Steward, William Oliver, John brother of Oliver, Ralph de Ambli,
' &c.' There are now no remains of this church of S. Clement. It
ftood near S. Clements gate, & the churchyard is now part of the
garden belonging to Mr. Noels houfe. By virtue of this charter the
nuns of S. Michael prefented a vicar to the faid church of S. Clement till the 30. of H. 8. when their houfe was diffolved.

XIV. Roger de Torpel, fon of Afcelina de Waterville, confirmed
likewife to the faid nuns of S. Michael, I. his faid mothers donation of
the third part of the church of Corby in Lincolnfhire; by the following charter. a ' To all the children of holy mother church, who fhall
' fee or hear this writing, Roger de Torpel, greeting in the Lord. Your
' univerfality fhall underftand that I have granted, & by this my pre-
' fent charter confirmed, to the church of S. Michael of Staunforde
' & to the nuns there ferving God, the gift of the church of the blef-
' fed John the evangelift of Corby, which belongs to my mother, with
' all its appurtenances, into pure & perpetual alms, for the foul of my
' father, & for the fouls of all my predeceffors. And, that this concef-
' fion may remain firm & untouched, I have corroborated it with the
' putting to of my feal. Witneffes, Roger de Huntyngfeld clerc, Tho-
' mas de Coleville, Hugh de Gretforde, William de Heddone knight,
' &c.' II. The faid Roger de Torpel confirmed his faid mother Afcelina de Watervilles donation to the faid nuns of four bovates of arable
land in old Stokehane fields at Corby aforefaid towards cloathing the
faid nuns; together with one other bovate of land there, affigned by her
for maintenance of a pittance on the day of her anniverfary; for
which purpofes he gave them this other charter. b ' To all the chil-
' dren of holy mother church unto whom the prefent writing fhall
' come, Roger de Thorpel, greeting. Your univerfality fhall under-
' ftand that I, in an intuition of charity, & for the health of my foul,
' & of my mother, & for the fouls of my anceftors, have confirmed to
' the nuns of S. Michael of Stanford the gift which my mother Ace-
' lina de Waterville made them; to wit, the four bovates of land yn
' Stokehane c in the fields of Corebi, towards cloathing the forefaid
' nuns; & the one bovate of land yn the fame fields of Corebi for a
' pittance yn the day of the anniverfary of my mother, as the charters
' of my mother witnefs. And in teftimony of this my confirmation, I

a Ex dicti regiftri folio 5. b. citato in
Mon. Ang. tomi II. p. 881. a. b.

b Univerfis S. matris ecclefie filiis ad
quos prefens fcriptum pervenerit, Rogerus de
Thorpel falutem. Noverit univerfitas veftra
me, intuitu caritatis, & pro falute anime
mee, & matris mee, & pro animabus antecefforum meorum, confirmaffe monialibus
S. Michaelis de Stanforde donum quod mater mea Acelina de Watervilla fecit eis;
fcil. quatuor bovatas terre yn Stokehane in
campis de Corebi, ad vefturam predictarum

monialium, & unam bovatam terre yn eifdem campis de Corebi ad pietanciam yn die
anniverfarii matris mee; ficut carte matris
mee teftantur. In hujus autem confirmati-
onis mee teftimonium prefenti fcripto figillum meum apponere curavi. Hiis teftibus,
Radulpho de Diva, Willielmo de Colevilla,
Roberto de Colevilla, Radulpho, & Richardo fratre ejus, Willielmo camerario, Gaufrido fratre ejus, & multis aliis. Ex MSS.
Dodfworthianorum, Vol. 59. fol. 165. &c.

c Scothawe, alio exemplari.

' have

'have caufed my feal to be put to the prefent writing. Witneffes,
'Ralph da Diva, William de Coleville, Robert de Coleville, Ralph, &
'Richard his brother, William the Chamberlain, Geoffry his brother,
'& many others.' The firft of thefe confirmations, it may be obferved,
was granted, as it fhould feem, fometime after the death of the faid Roger de Torpels father; the fecond, as it fhould feem, fometime after
the death of his mother; which fhews they were not both granted together: however being both the fame perfons grants, & both without
any date, I was unwilling to part them. There was a town called
Torpel fomewhere near Milton in Northamptonfhire, & Roger de
Torpel was one of thofe military knights who held their lands, by
knights fervice, of the church of Burg.

XV. Hugh, fon & heir of Maud de Diva, confirmed likewife his faid
mothers grant of the third part of the church of Coreby to the faid
nuns of S. Michael. There is a very unaccurate copy of this confirmation in the 59. Vol, of Mr. Dodfworths collections at Oxford, but
I fhall give it below, as I my felf tranfcribed it from the original,
now in the earl of Exeters archives; the englifh whereof is as follows.
a 'Hugh de Diva, to all his men & friends, French & Englifh, as well
'prefent as future, greeting. Your univerfality fhall underftand, that
'I have granted & by this my prefent charter confirmed, to God & to
'the church of the nuns of S. Michael of Stanford, the third part in
'the church of Corebi, which Matildis de Diva, my mother, gave to
'the forefaid nuns, & confirmed with the impreffion of her feal; for
'the fouls of my anceftors, & for the health of my own foul, into pure
'& perpetual alms, with all its appurtenances. Witneffes, Ricard of
'Burg, Hugh of Bneceftre, Geoffry dean of Stanford, Robert dean of
'Burton, Mathew the capellan, Ralph the capellan of Hengiftil,
'mafter Samfon, Ralph de Diva & Robert de Diva, Robert Cocc,
'Reginald Corfib, & many others. The Coccs, or Cocks, were a
Stanford family, & many of them buried in All-Saints church in the
mercat. I fhall only add, the feal reprefents a knight on horfeback,
armed at all points, infcribed Sigillum Hugonis de Dive.

XVI. Ralph, a younger brother of the faid Hugh, confirmed likewife
I. his mothers grants of the third part of the church of Corebi, & of
the tythe of wood then or afterwards grubbed up in the lands belonging to her & her heirs; as alfo her grant of her part of Upton chapel;

a Hugo de Diva, omnibus hominibus &
amicis fuis, Francis & Anglis, tam prefentibus quam futuris, falutem. Noverit univerfitas veftra me conceffiffe & hac prefenti
carta mea confirmaffe, Deo & ecclefie monialium de S. Michaele de Stanford, tertiam
partem in ecclefia de Corebi, quam Matildis
de Diva [Divia, Dodf.] mater mea, predictis
monialibus dedit & figilli fui impreffione
munivit; pro animabus antecefforum meorum, & pro falute anime mee, in puram &
perpetuam eleemofynam, cum omnibus pertinentiis fuis. Hiis teftibus, Ricardo de
Burgo, Hugone de Bneceftria [Barneceftria,
Dodf.] Gaufrido decano de Stanford, Roberto decano de Burton, Matheo capellano,
Radulpho capellano de Hengiftil, magiftro
Samfone, Radulpho de Diva, & Roberto de
Diva, Roberto Cocco, Reginaldo Corfib.
[hic pro Roberto Cocco, Reginaldo Corfib.
legunt exemplaria ab Oxonia mihi miffa unum
Roberto regni Eolfii, alterum Eotfii] & multis aliis.

for all which he gave them this charter.   [a] ' Ralph de Diva to all friends,
' French & Englifh, as well prefent as future, greeting.   Your univer-
' fality fhall underftand, that I have given & granted & by this my
' charter confirmed, to God & the church of S. Michael of Staunforde,
' & to the nuns there ferving God, the third part in the church of
' Corby, which Matilda de Diva my mother gave to the forefaid nuns,
' & confirmed with the impreffion of her feal; for the health of my
' foul, & of my wife, & for the fouls of my anceftors & fucceffors,
' into pure & perpetual alms, with all the appurtenances, & with [the
' tythe of] wood now grubbed, or hereafter to be grubbed, belong-
' ing to us & our heirs for ever.   Moreover I grant, & by my prefent
' charter confirm the donation & confirmation of the part of the chapel
' of Upton which is known to belong to me, with the tythes & lands,
' & with all things to the fame chapel belonging, to wit, the which
' Matilda de Diva my mother gave to the forefaid nuns, & confirm-
' ed by her charter.   And that this donation may continue ratified,
' unfhaken & for ever valid, I confirm it with the impreffion of my
' feal.   Witneffes, Alexander the capellan of Corby, William the ca-
' pellan of All Saints, &c.'   II. By another charter he confirmed his
forefaid mothers grant of that bovate of land at Corbi which fhe gave
to Adelicia de Capeni her fervant, & which the faid Adelicia gave afterwards to the forefaid nuns of S. Michael; which other charter is
thus expreffed.   [b] ' To all the children of holy mother church, prefent
' & future, to whom the prefent writing fhall come, Ralph de Diva,
' greeting.   Know ye that I have granted & by this my prefent char-
' ter confirmed, to God & the nuns of S. Michael of *Stanford*, that
' bovate of land in Corebi, with the houfes & appurtenances, within
' the town & without, which Adelicia de Capeni had, by gift of
' Mathilda de Diva my mother, for her fervice, and who gave that
' forefaid land to the forenamed nuns.   Wherefore I will that the fore-
' faid nuns may have and hold the forenamed bovate with the appur-
' tenances, freely & quietly & honorably, of me & my heirs, by pay-
' ing therefore to me & my heirs yearly for all fervice, & for all ex-
' action & cuftom to me or to my heirs belonging, half a pound of
' cumin at Eafter; faving the forinfec fervice of the lord the king.
' And I & my heirs will warant the forefaid land with the appurte-
' nances to the forefaid nuns, againft all men & all women.   Wit-
                                                                ' neffes,

a Ex regiftri prioratus S. Michaelis penes Galf. Minfhul gen. 1657. fol. 6. b. citato in Mon. Ang. tomi II. p. 882. a.

b Univerfis S. matris ecclefie filiis, prefentibus & futuris, ad quos prefens fcriptum pervenerit, Radulphus de Diva falutem. Sciatis me conceffiffe & prefenti carta mea confirmaffe, Deo & monialibus S. Michaelis de Stanford, illam bovatam terre in Corebi, cum domibus & pertinentiis infra villam & extra, quam Adelicia de Capeni habuit, ex dono Mathilde de Diva matris mee, pro fervicio fuo, & illam predictam terram dedit prefatis monialibus. Quare volo quod predicte moniales habeant & teneant prefatam bovatam cum pertinentiis, libere & quiete & honorifice, de me & heredibus meis, reddendo inde mihi & heredibus meis annuatim, pro omni fervitio & pro omni exactione & confuetudine ad me vel adheredes meos pertinentibus dimidiam libram cymini ad pafcha; falvo forinfeco D. Regis fervicio. Et ego & heredes mei warantizabimus predictam terram cum pertinentiis predictis monialibus,

contra

' neffes, Walter the parfon of Stokes, Thomas de Tholethorp, Gilbert
' de Tholethorp, William the chamberlain of Corebi, Gilbert his bro-
' ther, Peter de Swafeld, Robert de Diva, Alan de Corebi, William
' . . . . . the capellan of Corebi, Geoffry brother of William the
' chamberlain, & divers others.' The original, as below, is now in the
earl of Exeters archives; from whence I copied it. The feal reprefents a knight mounted on horfeback, armed at all points, and riding
full fpeed. Now to more public affairs.

Anno
1215.

XVII. ᵃ' In 1215. William de Albini the third [who afterwards
built Newfted] ' was joyned in commiffion with the archbifhop of
' Canterbury, William earl Warenn [lord of Stanford] & others, for
' the fafe conducting all thofe perfons who came to London in the
' terme of the Epiphany, next after the relaxation of the interdict, to
' implore the kings favor for their great offences, & thence to the
' kings court at Northampton, & fo to their own homes. ᵇ This
' year alfo the nobles of the north affembled at Stanford againft
' K. John.' The occafion they pretended for affembling thus was,
' ' that they were oftentimes called forth to ferve in the warres & to
' fight in defence of the realm, & yet notwithftanding were at home
' ftill oppreffed by the kings officers, who (upon confidence of the
' lawes) attempted all things whatfoever they conceyved. And if any
' man complayned, would anfwer by & by that they had law on theyr
' fide, to do as they had done; fo that it was no wrong but right
' which they did: & therefore, if they that were the lordes & peeres
' of the realme were men, it ftood them upon to provide that fuch
' inconvenience might be avoyded, & better lawes brought in ufe.' But
the real ground of thefe difcontents rofe from other caufes, the chief
whereof I fhall here briefly touch. ᵈ' K. John, faith Knitonᵉ, con-
' tinuing his wonted licentioufnefs, thereby provoked many of his
' nobles to wrath: For, tho' he had a modeft countenance, he was a
' moft libidinous man, exceffively lufting after women, & deriding
' their husbands on whofe wives he had taken his pleafure. Amongft
' thefe his practices hearing that Euftace de Vefci had a very beautiful
' lady, but far diftant from court, earneftly ftudying how to accom-
' plifh his defires towards her, fitting at table with her husband, &,
' feeing a ring on his finger, he laid hold on it and told him that he
' had fuch another ftone, which he refolved to fet in gold in that very
' form: & having thus got the ring, prefently fent it to her in her
' husbands name, by that token conjuring her, if ever fhe expected
' to fee him alive, to come fpeedily to him. She therefore, upon

contra omnes homines & omnes feminas.
Hiis teftibus, Waltero perfona de Stokes,
Thoma de Tholethorp, Gilleberto de Tholethorp, Willielmo camerario de Corebi,
Gilleberto fratre ejus, Petro de Swafeld,
Roberto de Diva, Alano de Corebi, Willi-
lielmo . . . . . capellano de Corebi, Gaufrido fratre Willielmi camerarii, & multis
aliis.

a Baron. Vol. I. p. 76. b. & p. 114. a.
b Ex J. Lelandi Collect. Vol. I. p. 265.
c Holingf. p. 586. b.
d Baron. Vol. I. p. 92.
e col. 2422.

2

' fight

' fight of the ring, gave credit to the meſſenger, & came with all ex-
' pedition. But ſo it happen'd, that her husband caſually riding out,
' met her on the road, & marvelling much to ſee her there, asked,
' what the matter was? And, when he underſtood how they were
' both deluded, reſolved to find out a common whore, & put her in
' apparel to perſonate his lady. All which being accordingly done, the
' king ſoon after bragged thereof, & ſaid, Euſtace, thou haſt a moſt
' lovely wife & pleaſant bedfellow. To which he anſwered, how do
' you know that? Quoth the king, I have had experience thereof. No,
' quoth Euſtace, you are miſtaken, it was not my wife, but a common
' whore. Whereat the king grew ſo enraged that he threatned to kill
' him. Euſtace therefore, apprehending the danger, fled into the north,
' & in his paſſage waſted ſome of the kings houſes, divers of the
' nobles, whoſe wives the king had vitiated accompanying him.*
The primary cauſe of theſe diſcontents is, by another writer, reported thus. a ' Robert Fitzwalter had a daughter named Maud, who was
' exceeding handſom, upon whoſe account, becauſe the king had a
' mind to debauch her, & her father would not admit of it, began
' a war all over England. For this young lady reſiding at Dunmow,
' the king firſt ſent a perſon thither to ſollicit her affections for him,
' who, when he could not prevail, afterwards, by the kings order,
' poyſoned her with a poached egg, whereof ſhe died.' b ' The chro-
' nicle of Caxton, with other, ſayen, that a greate parte of this vari-
' aunce betweene K. Jhon & his barrons was, becauſe the kyng would
' have exyled the earle of Cheſter, for ſo muche as before ſeaſons he
' had oftentimes adviſed the kyng to leave his cruelneſſe & his accuſtomed
' avowtry, the whiche he exerciſed with his brothers wife & other.
' c Others write, that the ſame diſſention aroſe by reaſon of the great
' crueltie & unreaſonable avarice which the king uſed towards all the
' eſtates & degrees of his ſubjects, as wel of the ſpiritualtie as tempo-
' raltie. d In ſhort, for that he wolde not holde the lawes of S.
' Edwarde, & alſo for diſpleaſure that he bare to divers of them, that
' thei wolde not favoure him againſte the pope, & for other cauſes
' which here be not manifeſted, the kyng fell at diſſencion with his
' lordes in ſo much that great people were rayſed on either parties.
    XVIII. ' e In Eaſter week 1215. they [Euſtace Veſcy & Robert Fitz-
walter] ' met at Stanford, with horſe & arms; whither they had now
' drawn unto them in their favor almoſt all the nobility of the whole
' kingdom, & gathered an army ineſtimable for number. f For the
' commons flocked unto them from everie part; g becauſe the king
' had rendred himſelf odious to all his ſubjects. It was reckoned that
' there was in this army two thouſand knights, beſides yeomen on

a Mon. Ang. Vol. II. p. 76. a.
b Fabian, fol. 35. a.
c Hect. Boethius as cited by Holingſ. fol.
587. b.

d Fabian, as above.
e M. Paris, ſub anno 1215.
f Holingſ. p. 588. a.
g M. Paris, ut ſupra.

' horſeback,

' horfeback, fervants, & foot men apparelled in divers forts of armor·
' ᵃ The chief ringleaders of this power were, Robert Fitzwater, Eu-
' ftace Vefcy, Richarde Percy, Robert Roos, Peter de Breufe, Nicho-
' las de Stouteville, Saer earle of Winchefter, Henry earle of Clare,
' Richard earle Bygot, William de Mombray, William de Creffy, Raufe
' Fitz-Robert, Robert de Vere, Fulke Fitz Warenn, William Mallet,
' William de Monteacute, William de Beauchamp, Simon de Kime,
' William Marfhall the yonger, William Mauduyt, Robert de Mont-
' bigonis, John Fitz-Roberte, John Fitz-Alane, G. Lavale, O. Fitz-
' Alain, W. de Hobrug, O. de Vales, G. de Gaunt, Maurice de Gaunt,
' Robert de Brakefley, Robert de Mountfichet, William de Lanvalley,
' G. de Maundeville earle of Effex, W. his brother, W. de Huntin-
' field, R. de Grefley, G. coneftable of Menton, Alexander de Panton,
' P. Fitz-John, Alexander de Sutton, Osbert de Body, John coneftable
' of Chefter, Thomas de Muleton, Conant Fitz-Hely, & many other:
' they had alfo of counfel with them as chief the archbifhop of Can-
' terburie.' All thefe now met at Stanford, fo that whether we confider the multitude of nobles, or the great number of forces, it was
certainly one of the largeft, if not the very biggeft, appearance of either fort that was ever feen at this place. From Stanford they marched to S. Edmondsbury, from S. Edmondsbury to London.

XIX. The earls & barons who had not yet joined thofe who met
at Stanford were, ᵇ ' William Marefhal earl of Pembroke, Ranulph
' earl of Chefter, William earl of Salisbury, William earl Warenn
[lord of Stanford] ' William earl of Albemarle, H. earl of Cornwall,
' William de Albiney [who afterwards built Newfted] Robert de Vi-
' pont, Peter Fitz-Hubert, Brien de Lifle, G. de Lucy, G. de Furnival,
' Thomas Baffet, H. de Braibroke, John de Baffingborne, William de
' Cantilupe, Henry de Cornhulte, John Fitz-Hugh, Hugh de Nevile,
' Philip de Albiney, John Marefchal, William Brewere.' But ᶜ ' all
' thefe, upon receipt of the barons letters, or the more part of them,
' came to London, & joyned themfelves with the barons, utterly re-
May 10.
1215.
17. John ' nouncing to ayde K. John. ᵈ Upon the 10. of May, the king pub-
' lifhed a declaration that he would not take the barons or their te-
' nants, or diffeife them, or pafs upon them by force of arms, but by
' law of the land & judgment of their peers in his court, 'till things
' fhould be determin'd by four perfons to be chofe on his part &
' four by the barons; the pope to be umpire between them. And
' for performance of this, he offered as fecurity four bifhops with
' William earl Warenn [lord of Stanford.] ᵉ The faid Willian earl
' Warenn, was [foon after] joined in commiffion with P. bifhop of
' Winchefter, William earl of Arundel & Hubert de Burg juftice of
' England, to treat with R. earl of Clare & fome other of the rebel-
' lious barons, for a peaceable compofure betwixt the king & them;

a Holing. ut fupra.   d Tyrel, p. 781.
b Tyrel, p. 774.   e Baron. Vol. I. p. 76. b.
c Holingf. p. 589.

' which

' which treaty was to be in the church of Erehey, i. e. Erith: But came
' to no effect.

XX. ª ' On the 15. of June, ᵇ when the king met the rebellious June 15.
' barons at Runnimede, William earl Warenn [aforesaid, lord of
Stanford] ' was one who most inclined to him, & by whose advice
magna carta [& the *carta de foresta*] were granted.' On the other
' hand, ᶜ ' William de Albini [who built Newsted] was one of those
' twenty five barons, who swore to the observation of *magna carta*
' & the *carta de foresta*, sealed by the king at Runnimede in the 17.
' year of his reign; & who obliged themselves by oath to compel the
' king [to observe them] in case he should recede. ᵈ Moreover there
' were eight & thirty other that were sworn to be obedient & as it
' were assistant unto those twenty five peers in such things as they
' should appoynt.' William earl Warenn [lord of Stanford] was one
of those thirty-eight; but what is somewhat remarkable ' ᵈ he was
' sworne by his attorney,' whereas all the rest took the oath in their
own persons: their names may be seen in my author ᵈ. ' ᵉ About
' the same time K. John sent his writs under the great seal into all
' parts of England, firmly enjoining all sherifs throughout the king-
' dom, to make all men within their bailiwicks, of whatsoever con-
' dition, swear, that they would observe the laws & liberties contain'd
' in *magna carta*, & to the utmost compel the king to the perform-
' ance of all things therein. Likewise June 19. the king, by letters June 19.
' patents, commanded, that twelve knights should be chosen in every
' county at the next county court, to enquire into the evil customs
' or practices of sherifs, foresters, warenners, keepers of rivers &
' river banks, & toll-gatherers towards the repairs of bridges & banks,
' to extirpate such evil customs & exactions.' Soon after this William
earl Warenn [lord of Stanford] ᶠ ' was a witness to that charter which
' the king passed in the new temple at London, unto the archbishop
' of Canterbury & others, for confirmation of the rights of the church
' & clergy.

XXI. Matters being thus agreed between the king & his barons, all
men rejoiced, & hoped there had been now an end of all their disputes: but it fell out quite otherwise. For the barons, mistrusting the
king, kept the tower of London yet in their hands; whereupon, &
being told by some Flemish soldiers about him, that he had nothing
now left him but the name of a king (the barons having assumed all
the power into their hands) the king grew very melancholy, often
walking alone, & giving other signs of inward rage & discontent. At
length he went to Windsor, then to Winchester, & thence to the isle
of Wight; whence he sent privately to the pope to absolve him from
the oath he had taken at Runnimede, & for more foreign soldiers to

a Holingf. p. 590.
b Baron. ut supra.
c Baron. Vol. I. p. 113. b.

d Holingf. ut supra.
e Tyrrel, p. 776.
f Bar. Vol. I. p. 76. b.

come

come to his affiftance. And indeed many of the northern barons were very provoking; fome of them ftill plundering the country, fome fortifying their caftles, fome building new ones, & others feifing & abufing the kings officers, who went into thofe parts about the bufi-nefs of his exchequer. Mean time fome of the barons ' ᵃ thinking ' the danger over, appointed to meet at a torneament or tryal of feats ' at arms at Stanford: whereupon Robert Fitz-walter & other great ' men wrote to William de Albini [the third, who afterwards built Newfted, & who, it fhould feem, was the chief promoter of this in-tended appearance at Stanford; his caftel of Belvoir being within fix-teen, & his manor of Offington, where alfo he had a fair manfion, within two miles of that place] ' what great conveniency it was for ' them all to keep within the city of London, which was their re-' ceptacle; & what difgrace & damage it would be to them, if by ' their negligence it fhould be loft; & therefore, by common advice, ' they deferred the jufts which were to be at Stanford on the mon-' day after the feaft of SS. Peter & Paul, to the monday after the oc-' taves of that feaft; and that they fhould be holden upon the heath ' between Staines & Hounflow. And this they did for the fecurity of ' themfelves & the city. And therefore they fent to & required them ' diligently, that they fhould come fo well provided with horfe & ' arms to the tilting, as they might receive honor; & he that be-' haved himfelf beft fhould have a bear which a certain lady fhould ' fend thither, which it feems was the prize (tho' a very homely one) ' they were then to contend for. Thus they pleafed themfelves with ' thefe idle fports, being ignorant of the fnares preparing for them.'

XXII. Mean while the kings meffengers returned, & brought with them letters from the pope, exhorting the barons to agree with the king, & threatning excommunication to all who oppofed him. ' ᵇ But ' it feems the popes letters had no effect with the barons, for they pur-' fued what they had undertaken, & fent for William de Albiny, an ' experienc'd foldier [who afterwards built Newfted] to their affiftance. ' 'Tis true, they fent to him feveral times before he came; but at ' laft, upon a chiding letter, having firft fecured the caftle of Belvoir, ' he came to London, where he was received with great joy by the ' barons; & their firft confultation with him, was, which way to fe-' cure the city from being befieged: upon which they refolved to for-' tifie all the avenues leading to it. ᶜ About Bartholomew-tide, the ' barons met with the kings commiffioners at Staines, where, not agree-' ing, the bifhops publifhed the fentence of excommunication againft ' all thofe who fhould prefume to difturb the peace of the king & ' kingdom. Yet this had little, or no, effect; moft of the barons turn-' ing this fentence upon the kings own head, who, as they affirmed, ' was the chief difturber of it. Wherefore they return'd to London

Aug.

a Tyrrel, p. 780.　　　　b Tyrrel, p. 783.　　　　c id. ib.

' with

' with great pomp, & prefently difperfed themfelves into feveral parts
' of the kingdom. The government of Effex being committed to
' Geoffry de Mandeville, that of Lincolnfhire to William de Albiny,
' &c. fo that every one was to act as a juftitiary over the province
' or county affign'd him, & to provide for the peace of the inhabi-
' tants.

XXIII. But tho' the government of Lincolnfhire was committed as
aforefaid to William de Albini (who now begins to make a greater
figure than ever) yet he went not thither, but ' ᵃ to Rochefter caftle
' (whereof he was alfo made governor by the barons) ᵇ who fwore to
' him, that, whenever that caftle fhould chance to be befieged, they
' would ufe their utmoft endeavours to relieve it.' By this means, as
appears by the fequel, he was let into a bufinefs which had very like
to have coft him his life. For ' ᶜ when he entred the caftle, & found
' neither arms, ammunition, nor victuals therein ; as alfo difcerning,
' that thofe who accompanied him thither, had no mind to ftay in it,
' he told them how difhonourable it would be to leave it, & there-
' fore fuddenly got in all the provifion that could be found in the
' town : But had not time to look out into the country for more, in
regard the king came within three days upon them with his army ᵈ.
' For, after about three months ftay in the ifle of Wight, he failed to
' Dover, where he met his meffengers whom he had fent to fetch frefh
' forces from Poictou, Gafcony, Brabant, & Flanders ; & thefe being
' now arriv'd, he prefently march'd to Rochefter, ᵉ & begirt it with
' a ftraight fiege. They [within] defended themfelves with all the va-
' lour imaginable, making divers bold fallies, with hope to have re-
' lief from the reft of the barons of their party, who were then at
' London ; ᶠ who, in purfuance of their oath, marched as far as Dart-
' ford, but then, finding themfelves too weak, retreated, becaufe the
' king had feized upon all the avenues, & caufed all the bridges to be
' broken down that led thither.

XXIV. The barons being thus retreated, the king fet ' ᵍ himfelf by
' all wayes poffible to winne this caftle, as well by battering the walles
' with engines, as by giving thereto many affaults, but the garrifon
' (confifting of ninety four knights, befides demilaunces & other fol-
' diers) ʰ fuch was their valor (tho' wearied with long watchings &
' weakened by hunger) couragioufly beat him off. ' No fiege in thofe
' dayes was more earneftly enforced, nor more obftinately defended.
' For, after that all the lymmes of the caftle had beene throwne downe,
' they kept the maifter tower 'tyll halfe thereof was alfo overthrowne ;
' & after kept the other halfe, tyll thro' famine they were conftrain-
' ed to yeelde, having nothing but horfeflefh & water to fufteyne

a Baron. Vol. I. p. 114. a.
b Tyrrel, ut fupra.
c Baron. ut fupra.
d Tyrrel, quo fupra.
e Baron. ut fupra.
f Tyrrel, ut fupra.
g Holingfhed, p. 592. b. 593. a.
h Baron. Vol. I. p. 114. b.
i Holing. p. 593. a.

' theyr

'theyr lyves. [a] It is obferved, that the king, with fome of his chief
'commanders, one day going about this caftle of Rochefter to view
'the ftrength thereof, was difcerned by an excellent bow-man, who
'thereupon asked [our] William de Albini, whether he fhould kill
'him with his arrow, that he had then in readinefs? And that he an-
'fwered, no. As alfo that the bow-man replied, he would not fpare
'us, if he had the like advantage. To whom [our] William return'd,
'Gods will be done, who will difpofe, & not he.

XXV. ' [b] At laft this hardy William, & thofe other of the nobles,
'who were then with him, accounting it moft difhonourable to perifh
'by famine, when they could not be vanquifhed by force (all their
'food being fpent) came out of the caftle, & fubmitted themfelves
Nov. 30. 'upon the feaft of S. Andrew the apoftle [c]; after it had been befieged
'the fpace of threefcore dayes, duryng which time they had beaten
'back theyr enimys at fundrie affaultes, with greate flaughter & loffe.'
Upon their furrendry [d], ' the king, by reafon of the vaft charge he had
'been at in the fiege, & [e] upon a griefe conceived for the loffe of fo
'many men, & alfo becaufe he had lien fo long about it ere he could
'wynne it [f], was fo highly enraged, that, without mercy, he command-
'ed all the noblemen fhould be hanged. Which fevere fentence was
'fo diftafted by Savaric de Maloleone (a noble Poictovin, then one of
'the chief commanders in the kings army) that he boldly told the
'king, that the war being not yet ended, he ought well to confider
'the uncertain chance thereof; adding, that if He hang'd thefe, the
'barons (his adverfaries) might, upon like advantage, deal as cruelly
'with thofe of his party; which might occafion a total defertion from
'him. Whereupon, the king, well weighing the danger, forbore the
'execution of that his fharp fentence, & inftead thereof committed
'this our William de Albini, William de Lancafter, Thomas de Mule-
'ton, Osbert Giffard, & divers other nobles, unto the cuftody of Pe-
'ter de Mauley; who fent fome of them to the caftle of Corfe, there
'to be kept under ftrict imprifonment: And fome to the caftle of
'Nottingham.' At this time alfo ' [g] the pope, on notice that the ba-
'rons ftill perfifted in the profecution of the war againft the king,
'enjoyned the archbifhop & bifhops to caufe them to be excommu-
'nicated every Lords day & holy day, & that with ringing of bells &
'lighting of candles throughout all England.' But ' [h] the barons (by-
'caufe that in the popes letter there were none of them exprefly
'named) made none account of the cenfure, reputing it as voyde, &
'not to concerne them in any maner of poynte.' From Rochefter
the king went to S. Albans, ' [i] where he received the popes letters,
'whereby he fufpended the archbifhop of Canterbury, for joyning with

a Baron. ut fupra.
b id. ib.
c Holing. quo fupra.
d Baron. ut fupra.
e Holingfhed. in loco ult. cit.

f Baron. quo fupra.
g Tyrrel, p. 784.
h Holing. ut fup.
i Tyrrel, p 785.

' the

' the barons againſt him. There he cauſed them to be publiſhed by
' that abbat; & from thence they were ſent to all cathedral & con-
' ventual churches throughout England, for the ſame purpoſe.' Thus
a great part of the ſabbath days entertainment in thoſe times was taken
up in the publication of ſuſpenſions, excommunications, & other circumſtances of this unhappy quarrel. Likewiſe at S. Albans the king [a], ' di-
' vided his army into two partes, one to remaine about London, whilſt
' he himſelf might go with the other into the north to waſte & deſtroy
' the poſſeſſions of certaine lordes there, which (as he was informed)
' went about to rayſe an armie againſt hym. The firſt night he lay
' at Dunſtable, & ſo kept on his journey till hee came to Notingham,
' where he lay in the caſtle on Chriſtmas day.   Dec. 25,

XXVI. ' [b] The morrow after Chriſtmas day he marcht to the town Dec. 26.
' of Langar; & there reſting that night, ſent a ſolemn ſummons to
' Belvoir caſtle, the next morning; requiring the ſpeedy delivery there- Dec. 27.
' of, & withall ſignifying to thoſe that held it, that if they inſiſted
' on any conditions, the lord thereof ſhould never eat more. Wher-
' upon Nicholas de Albini one of his ſons (who was a clerk in or-
' ders) taking with him Sir Hugh Charnels knight, to preſerve his fa-
' ther from that miſerable death, carried the keys of the caſtle to the
' king, & delivered them to his hands; upon condition that his father
' ſhould be mercifully dealt with, & they, with their horſe & arms,
' remain in peace. Which being promiſed, & the caſtle ſo rendred,
' the king marched forthwith thither, & committed it to the cuſtody
' of Geoffry de Butville & Oliver his brother (two Poiĉtovins) taking
' an oath of fidelity of all others he left there. Whilſt William de
' Albini was thus priſoner at Corf, his manor of Offington, being
' ſeiſed by the king, was given to William earl Warenn for the bet-
' ter defence of his caſtle of Stanford.

XXVII. Not long after ' [c] the pope, who before, at the inſtant ſute
' of K. John, had excommunicated the barons in general, excommu-
' nicated them by name. [d] Particularly William de Albini was one of
' thoſe ſo excommunicated: His ſentence bears date at Lateran the
' 17. of the kalends of June.' The king & his barons being thus
every day more & more exaſperated againſt each other, the barons at
laſt, reſolving to throw off all ſubjection to K. John, ſent for the French
kings ſon Lewis, inviting him to take upon him the crown of England, & promiſing their faithful aſſiſtance to ſecure it to him; whereupon he ſoon after levied an army, & came over to them. ' [e] By the
' 14. June 1216. the ſaid prince Lewis had got poſſeſſion of ſo much June 14.
' of the kingdom, that he ſummoned the king of Scots, & all the 1216.
' great men of England, to come & do him homage, or forthwith 13 Johπt.
' depart the nation. And, with great ſpeed, upon this his proclama-

a Holing. p. 594, 595.   d Baron. Vol. I. p. 115. a.
b Bar. Vol. I. p. 114, 115.   e Tyrrel, p. 796.
c Hol. p. 596. b.

7 H   ' tion,

' tion, there came in to him, William earl Warenn [lord of Stan-
ford] ' & many others, who deferted K. John, upon a firm belief, that
' Lewis would now obtain the kingdom of England; or (which is
' more likely) becaufe K. John was now grown odious even to his
' beft friends & neareft relations. ª K. John feeing the fidelity of
' William earl Warenn [who had hitherto been very loyal to him]
' thus doubtful, fent his precept to the faid earl, to deliver up his ca-
' ftle at Pevenfey unto Matthew Fitz-Herbert, with command to de-
' molifh it.' On the other hand, ' ᵇ William de Albini's ftout heart
' being at length humbled [by his long imprifonment at Corf] he
' gave a fine of fix thoufand marcs for his liberty; which mony was
' raifed by Agatha Trufbut his wife, out of his own lands: the king
' commanding that they fhould be delivered into her hands for that
' purpofe, with power to fell & mortgage what fhould be needful,
' fending likewife his fpecial precept to his tenants to give him effec-
Sept. ' tual aid towards the raifing of that great fum.' ᶜ In September the
' barons [who were yet in arms] perceiving that they could not make
' any great advance in the fiege of Windfor caftle, quitted it in the
' night, &, leaving their tents & engines behind them, marched, with
' all the haft they could, towards Cambridge, in order to fhut up the
' king who was then harraffing the country about the fea-coaft of
' Suffolk. ᵈ But K. John by his faithful efpials having advertifement
' of their intent, which was to get betwixt him & the places of his
' refuge; withdrewe, & was got to Stanford, ere they might reach to
' Cambridge: fo that miffing their purpofe, after they had taken fome
' fpoils, they returned to London. K. John, from Stanforde, marched
' towards Lincolne, ᵉ the caftle whereof was then befieged by Gilbert
' de Gant; but, upon his approach, he fled with all his forces as faft as
Oct.19. ' he could.' K. John lived not long after this, but died Oct. 19. not
without fufpicion of poifon, leaving his affairs in great confufion, &
his crown to his eldeft fon Henry, an infant of nine years of age.

a Baron. Vol. I. p. 76. b.   d Holing. p. 604. a. b.
b id. Vol. I. p. 115. a.   e Tyrrel, ut fupra.
c Tyrrel, p. 800, 803.
3

The end of the feventh book.

Academia tertia Anglicana;

OR, THE

ANTIQUARIAN ANNALS

of the TOWN of

STANFORD

IN

Lincoln, Rutland, *and* Northampton *Shires*.

BOOK. VIII.
Containing the reign of K. Henry the third.

I. ' KING John being dead, says Kniton [a], & Henry the third ' *elected* the 27. of Oct. the barons [who were for the said K. Henry] ' marched to fight againft Lewis ; con- ' cerning whom, when his father the king of France enquired of the ' couriers [which went between them] in what part of England his ' fon then was, they replied at Stanford.' Now what a blefling it was to have Stanford honored with the prefence of this illuftrious gentleman, will prefently appear from a character of the fine company which he afterwards brought with him into thefe parts; they being now I fuppofe much the fame as to their difpofitions, tho' not as to their numbers. But I muft firft obferve, ' [b] William de Albini the third [who afterwards built Newfted] ' having [as above] made fine to K. ' John for his redemption, now thought it his fafeft way to be quiet : ' & therefore fubmitted himfelf peaceably to K. Henry the third. But ' being not well to be trufted was conftrained to yield up his wife ' Agatha for an hoftage & afterwards his fon Nicholas the prieft.' Prince Lewis aforefaid now went into France, whereupon ' [c] his ab- ' fence was fo refented by thofe Englifh noblemen who took his part, ' that, almoft fo foon as his back was turned, William earl Warenn [lord of Stanford] ' & many other earls & barons deferting him, re- ' turned to their allegiance, & afterwards firmly adher'd to K. Henry, ' which very much weakened that French princes party.' However

Oct.27.
1.H. 3.

---

a col. 2427.
b Baron. Vol. I. p. 115. a.

c Tyrrel, p. 829.

8 B

Lewis,

Lewis, [c] [a] upon his return, minding to make a quick difpatch, fets out
' of London, his army confifting of more than 20000 foldiers, on purpofe
' not only to free Mount-forrel (then befieged by his enemies) but to
' fubdue the whole country adjoyning. Odious & grievous to the
' country was this paffage of the French, which reached as farre as Lin-
' colne, there were among them fo many ragged rafcals, the very fcum
' & filthy froth of that nation, whofe beggary was fo bafe, that they
' had not cloaths to hang on their backs; to fupply which, they made
' many go naked, in all the places where they marched. [b] For they
' left nothing untoucht that they might laye handes upon, not fparyng
' hallowed places more than prophane.'

II. ' [c] William de Albini the third, lately releafed out of captivity,
' [d] now grew into fuch efteem with K. Henry the third, that he was
' made one of the chief commanders of his army in that memorable

Anno ' battel of Lincoln, in the year 1217. (being the firft of his reign)
1217. ' where the rebellious barons, with Lovis of France (whom they had
1.H. 3. ' brought in to be made king) were totally overthrown: And after-
' wards had Muleton caftle in Lincolnfhire, & all the lands & fees of
' Thomas de Muleton (one of thofe barons) committed to his cuftody,
' which the king had feifed on as an efcheat. [e] About this time coats
' of arms began to become hereditary & defcendible, which were be-
' fore *ex placito*. Alfo menial attendants or feodaries to any noble
' perfon affumed to themfelves, for their arms, the device of the coat
' of their lord;' as my author inftances in feveral who held of the
Albini's of Belvoir.

2.H. 3.   III. ' [f] In the 2. H. 3. Hamon Peche [afterwards a benefactor to the
nuns of S. Michael by Stanford] ' upon collection of the firft fcutage
' of K. Henry the third, paid 34. marcs, 2 s. 2 d. for feventeen knights
' fees & a twelfth part, whereof his own barony did confift; & ten
' marks for five knights fees of the barony of Brunne. [g] The young
Mar. 30. ' king at Oxford on March the 30. iffued out his precept to the fherif
' of this & other counties, to take care that all Jews within their re-
' fpective liberties, fhould bear, upon their upper garments, whenever
' they went abroad, a badge of two white tablets on their breaft made
' of linen cloth or parchment, that by this token they might be diftin-
1219. ' guifht from chriftians. [h] In 1219. Mafter A. de Stanford was collated to
' the church of S. Guthlac at Deping, by the abbat & convent of Thorney.
' [i] William earl Warenn [L. of Stanford] was fherif of Surrey in the
4.H. 3. ' fourth of K. Henry the third.' At this time lived William Flemeng,
who, as I conceive, founded the college of Auftin friers here. Mr.
Leland fays, ' [k] one Fleming, a very rich man of the town of Stene-

a Speed, p. 592. b.
b Holingf. p. 612. b.
c id. p. 613. a.
d Baron. ut fupra.
e Burtons Leiceft. p. 8.
f Baron. Vol. I. p. 677. a.

g Bifhop Kennets par. antiq. p. 188.
h Ex chartulario dictæ abbatiæ penes comitem de Weftmoreland.
i Ex rotulo pipæ de eodem anno.
k Itin. Vol. 6. p. 29.

' ford

' ford in Lincolnſhire, was the firſt founder, as it is ſaid, of the Au-
' guſtyne freres in Staunford in the weſt ſuburbe, hard by S. Peters
' gate: an archi-diacon of Richemont was the performer of it.

IV. About this time the abbat & convent of Burg having a mill at
Stanford, the pool or mill-damm whereof, by keeping up the water,
was ſuppoſed to injure a meadow there called Leftheynes-croft, Ralph
ſon of Achard of Stanford granted that the pool belonging to the ſaid
mill ſhould nevertheleſs be kept banked up, ſo that the water in that
pool, before the mill ſluice, ſhould carry an ell & an half, & half a
quarter of an ell royal, in depth. And that neither he nor his heirs
might moleſt the ſaid abbat & convent, for any damage done to the
ſaid meadow by the ſaid mill-damm, he ſtipulated to the contrary by
this inſtrument. ' ª Know preſent & future people, that I Ralph, ſon
' of Achard of Staunford, have granted & by this my preſent char-
' ter confirmed, to the abbat & convent of Burg, that the damm
' of their mill in Staunford may remain banked for ever, without im-
' pediment or contradiction or vexation of me or of my heirs, as it
' was at the purification of the bleſſed Mary, in the third year of
' Henry King of England ſon of K. John; ſo, to wit, that the wa-
' ter in the pool of the foreſaid mill, before the ſluice of the ſame
' mill, may have, in depth, the length of one ell royal & an half, &
' half a quarter of an ell. And that neither I or my heirs may for
' ever be able to bring any action againſt the forenamed abbat &
' convent, touching the exaltation of the foreſaid pool above expreſſed,
' for the hurt or detriment of the meadow which is called Leftheynes-
' croft, I have given them the preſent writing corroborated with my
' ſeal, for memory of thoſe who are to come. Witneſſes, Brian
' de la Mare, Geoffry de Leham, Hugh his ſon, Richard Pekke, ma-
' ſter William de Scoter, maſter Henry of Staunford, Clement the
' vintner, William Flemeng, Henry ſon of Yſaac, Richard ſon of
' Melene. Ketel. John Bottay, Samſon ſon of Godric, & others.' At
the ſame time William ſon of William de Berc, nephew by the mothers ſide, to the ſaid Ralph ſon of Achard of Stanford (being, I ſuppoſe, his ſaid uncles next heir) confirmed the foreſaid grant, by this
other. ' ᵇ To all who ſhall ſee or hear this writing, William ſon of
' William

a Sciant preſentes & futuri, quod ego Radulphus, filius Achardi de Staunford, conceſſi & preſenti carta mea confirmavi, abbati
& conventui de Burgo, quod ſtagnum molendini ſui in Staunford permaneat exaltatum
imperpetuum, ſine impedimento vel contradictione vel vexacione mei vel heredum meorum, ſicut fuit in purificatione B. Marie, anno
tertio H. R. Anglie filii R. Johannis: ita, ſcilicet, quod aqua in ſtagno predicti molendini,
ante excluſam ejuſdem molendini, habeat, in
profundum, longitudinem unius ulne regie &
dimidie & medietatem quarte partis unius
ulne. Et ne ego vel heredes mei aliquam
controverſiam verſus prefatos abbatem & conventum movere poſſimus in poſterum, ſuper

exaltione predicti ſtagni ſuperius expreſſa, pro
nocumento vel detrimento prati quod vocatur Leftheyneſcroft, preſens ſcriptum ſigillo
meo roboratum, eis, in futurorum memo-
riam, dedi. Hiis teſtibus, Briano de la Mare,
Galfrido de Leham, Hugone filio ſuo, Richardo Pekke, magiſtro Willielmo de Scoter,
magiſtro Henrico de Staunford, Clemente
vinetario, Willielmo Flemeng, Henrico filio
Yſaac, Richardo filio Melene. Ketel. Johanne
Bottay, Sampſone filio Godrici, & aliis. Ex
regiſtri cujuſdam abbatiæ de Burgo (in bib.
Cotton. ſub imagine Veſp. E. XXII.) fol.
26. b.

b Omnibus hoc ſcriptum viſuris vel audituris, Willielmus filius Willielmi de Berc,

ſalutem,

' William de Berc, greeting.   Your univerfality fhall underftand that
' I have ratified & made good the grant & confirmation which Ralph
' (fon of Achard &) my uncle, hath made to the abbat & convent
' of Burg, concerning the pool of their mill at Staunford, which was
' faid to endamage the meadow called Leftheynefcroft.   And that
' neither I or my heirs may be able to commence any fuit againft
' the forefaid abbat & monks of Burg with relation to the now faid
' mill, contrary to the grant & confirmation of the forenamed Ralph,
' fon of Achard, my uncle, I have corroborated the prefent writing
' with the putting to of my feal.   Witneffes, Brian de la Mare, &c.
' as above.

Anno   V.   ' ª In 1220.   Hugh late bifhop of Lincoln was canonized a faint,
1220.   ' in regard of the many miracles faid to be done by him.   ᵇ His fef-
' tival is celebrated the 17. of November.   ᶜ William earl Warenn
5. H. 3.   [lord of Stanford] ' was fherif of Surrey in the 5. of K. Henry the
' third.   ᵈ And in the fame year the fame earl (having, before a grant
' of the manors of Graham & Stanford, to hold until he fhould re-
' cover his lands in Normandy, or until the king fhould make him
' an equivalent exchange for them) the fame was now done, by con-
' firming thofe lordfhips to him in lieu of them.'   There is a curious
inquifition touching the antient owners of Stanford, & other antiquities relating to that town, which may be feen in the third chapter of
Mr. Butchers MS. furvey ;   taken, as I conceive, immediately before
this confirmation.   ' ᵉ About this time William de Fortibus earl of
' Albemarle and Holdernefs, flew out into open rebellion, & coming
' to Bitam caftle [within fix miles of Stanford] ' made excurfions into
' the country adjacent, doing much fpoil, & bringing the plunder thi-
' ther.   Thence he went to Foderinghay, & furprifed that caftle.   ᶠ Upon
' his fortifying thefe caftles he had the confidence to fend his letters of
' fafe conduct to the mayors of moft of the [chief] cities of England [&
I fuppofe the lege-men of Stanford, which borough lies almoft midway
betwixt thofe caftles, had the fame complement] ' whereby he gave
' them notice that all merchants & tradefmen might have free liberty
' of paffing by his caftles, & of buying & felling at the fame.   ᵍ Thefe
' tranfactions gave fuch an alarm to the king, that he forthwith raifed
' a powerful army, marched to Bitam, & threw down the walls of that
' caftle : whereat thofe within were fo much aftonifhed, that they foon
' yielded, imploring mercy.'   This William de Fortibus the fecond,
founded, as I guefs, the black friers college at Stanford.   Be that as it

falutem.   Noverit univerfitas veftra me ra-
tam & gratam habuiffe conceffionem & confirmationem, quam Radulphus filius Achardi
& avunculus meus, fecit abbati & conventui
de Burgo, fuper ftagno molendini fui de
Staunford quod dicebatur nocumentum facere prato quod vocatur Leftheynefcroft.
Et ne ego vel heredes mei predicto abbati &
monachis de Burgo poffimus controverfiam
movere fuper jam dicto ftagno, contra conceffionem & confirmationem prefati Radul-

phi, filii Achardi, avunculi mei, prefens fcriptum figilli mei appofitione roboravi. Hiis
teftibus, Briano de la Mare, &c. ut fupra
id. ib.
   a Tyrrel, p. 840.
   b Kalend. Ecclefiæ Rom.
   c Ex rotulo pipæ de eo anno.
   d Baron. Vol. I. p. 76. a.
   e id. p. 64. a.
   f Tyrrel, p. 841.
   g Baron. Vol. I. p. 64. a.

will,

will, one, [a] if not more, of his posterity, was buried there. About this time also William de Albini the third, who afterwards built Newsted, ' [b] in consideration of a palfrey, which he gave the king then at Blithe ' in Com. Nott. obtained the wardship & marriage of Hugh, son & ' heir of Henry de Nevil (a great man in that time) then in minority.

VI. ' [c] William the fifth earl Warenn [lord of Stanford] was sherif ' of Surrey in the sixth & seventh years of K. Henry the third [d]. In ' the time of Robert Lindsey abbat of Burg [who died Oct. 22. 1222. 7. H.3. so that what I am going to relate, according to my author must happen now, if not before] ' that monastery petitioned pope Gre- ' gory the 9. [he should rather say the pope; for pope Greg. the 9. was not pope till after abbat Lindseys death] ' representing the danger they ' were in to lose some tithes, which they had held from the very foun- ' dation of that church; because some deeds concerning them were lost, ' or could not be found: & therefore desired, that he would command ' some very old men to be examined about this matter, before they ' died; least they should lose all possible proof of their right. Where- ' upon the pope sent his apostolical letters to the priors of Deping & ' S. Leonard by Stanford & to the dean of Stanford, that they should ' hear & examine such witnesses as the abbat & convent could pro- ' duce, & cause their testimony to be recorded, & to make a publick ' instrument thereof. *Datum Laterani*, 7. Kal. Apr. Pontif. 7°. This ' pope I am of opinion, was Honorius the third, not Gregory 9. for the ' 7. Kal. April. 7. Pontif. Hon. 3. answers to our Mar. 26. 1224. a lit- ' tle after abbat Lindseys death; so that the petition was probably sent ' to Rome in his time, but not return'd till then. [e] Hamon Peche [afterwards a benefactor to the nuns of S. Michael by Stanford] ' hav- ' ing been in an expedition now made into Wales, obtained the kings ' precept for levying scutage upon all his own tenants by military ser- ' vice, within the counties of Camb. Norf. Suff. Linc. Ox. Wilts, ' Dorset, & Somerset.

6. 7. H. 3.

Oct. 22. 1222.

VII. ' [f] William the 5. earl Warenn [lord of Stanford] was sherif ' of Surrey in the 8. of Henry the third. [g] In which year Martin ' de Patteshulle, Thomas de Muleton, & Henry de Braibrook, the kings ' justices itinerant, sitting at Dunstable upon pleas of novel-disseisin, no ' less than thirty verdicts were found against Faukes de Brent, in trials ' for lands unjustly taken from their owners; for which he was fined an ' hundred pounds: which he was so incensed at, that he fortified his ' castle of Bedford, & sent his brother with some armed men to take the ' justices, & bring them thither prisoners. But they having notice, ' only Henry Braibrook was taken, &, being cruelly handled, kept ' prisoner there. The king & his great council then sitting at Nor- ' thampton, being highly displeased at this insolence, resolved to lay

8. H. 3.

1224.

a See 44. H. 3. below.
b Baron. Vol. I. p. 115. a.
c Ex rotulis pipæ de iisdem annis.
d Bp. Patricks supplement to Gunton, p.

295.
e Baron. Vol. I. p. 677. a.
f Ex rotulo pipæ de eo anno.
g Tyrrel, p. 850, 851.

' aside

' afide all other bufinefs & reduce the caftle.   But firft the kings mef-
' fengers fummoned them to furrender, & were anfwered by William
' (Faukes his brother) that they did not look upon themfelves obliged
' to deliver it, unlefs they were commanded by their lord fo to do,
' becaufe they were not bound by homage or fealty to the king.   This
' fawcy anfwer fo exafperated him, that he ordered the caftle to be
' immediately befieged, & threatned (if it was taken by ftorm) not to
' fpare one man——At laft, after many attacks & the lofs of a great
' many lives on both fides, the caftle was furrendred to difcretion,
' after nine weeks fiege.   Upon this Henry de Braibrook was fet
' at liberty; but thofe that were taken prifoners, being four & twen-
' ty in all, both knights & efquires, were hanged, of whom Wil-
' liam de Brent was chief.   And then the king caufed the caftle to
' be razed.   As for Faukes's wife, the lady Margaret Rivers, fhe,
' together with her young fon Thomas, having no ways confent-
' ed to his crime, was committed to the cuftody of William earl Wa-
' renn' [lord of Stanford.]   ' ᵃ This William earl Warenn was one of
Feb.11. ' the witneffes to *magna carta*, dated at Weftminfter the 11. of Feb. in
9. H. 3. ' the 9. of K. Henry the third.   ᵇ The faid earl was fherif of Surrey the
' fame year.——ᶜ It being afterwards refolved at the earneft importunity of
' the nobility, that Falcafius de Breant (a foreigner) a perfon who [as
you have in part heard] ' had been inftrumental in divers oppreffions,
' both in K. Johns time & fince, fhould be perpetually banifht, Wil-
' liam the 5. earl Warenn [lord of Stanford] had command to con-
' duct him fafe to the fea coaft, & then leave him to the winds; which
March. ' he did accordingly in the month of March, 9. H. 3.   ᵈ Immediate-
9. H. 3. ' ly after the religious orders & all others had notice, that, if they
' would enjoy their privileges they muft renew their charters, or other-
' wife the old ones fhould be of no advantage to them.   And what
' they were to pay for their renewal was left to the difcretion of the
Mar. 17. ' juftitiary' [Hubert de Burg.   Accordingly] ' ᵉ Mar. 17. 9. H. 3. the king
9. H. 3. ' confirmed to the monaftery of Burg at Stanford, all that part of the
' town which is towards Burg on that fide the bridge, with the lands
' & mills to the fame part adjacent; & with the church of S. Martin;
' & with the church of All Saints; the monaftery of S. Michael with
' all things to the fame monaftery belonging; & the hofpital of S. John
' & the bleffed Thomas the martyr; the houfe of the holy fepulchre;
' & the hofpital of S. Giles —— And in the fame town beyond the bridge,
' fourteen manfures, with all their liberties, &c.

a Annal. de Burton. p. 276.
b Ex rot. pipæ de eo anno.
c Bar. Vol. I. p. 77. a.
d Tyrrel, p. 862.
e Henricus, &c. fciatis nos confirmaffe monafterio de Burgo S. Petri, apud Stanford, totam illam partem ville que eft verfus Burgum intra pontem, cum terris & molendinis eidem parti adjacentibus; & cum ecclefia S. Martini; & cum ecclefia omnium SS;

monafterium S. Michaelis cum omnibus ad idem monafterium pertinentibus; & hofpitale S. Johannis & B. Thome martyris; domum S. Sepulchri; & hofpitale S. Ægidii —— Et in eadem villa ultra pontem manfuras quatuordecem, cum omnibus libertatibus fuis, &c. Datum 17°. Martii, anno regni 9°. Ex regiftro ecclefiæ de Burgo Swapham nuncupato.

VIII. Lord

VIII. Lord Hamon Peche now, or before this time, gave the nuns of S. Michael by Stanford, part of the church of Corby in Lincoln-shire ;——‘ [a] William earl Warenn [lord of Stanford] was sherif of Surrey ‘ in the 10. of K. Henry the third.’ Hugh Wells bishop of Lincoln 10. H. 3. confirmed to the nuns of S. Michael by Stanford, I. a third part of the foresaid church of Corby given them by Matildis de Diva & Hugh her son & heir.   And this confirmation the said bishop granted on ac-count of the poverty of the said nuns.   On which occasion he thus expresses himself. ‘ [b] To all the faithful of Christ, unto whom the ‘ present writing shall come, Hugh by the grace of God bishop of ‘ Lincoln, eternal greeting in the lord.   Your universality shall under-‘ stand, that we, in an intuition of divine piety, & considering ‘ the poverty of the house of the blessed Michael of Stanford, by au-‘ thority episcopal, have granted & confirmed, to God, & the blessed ‘ Mary & S. Michael, & to all the nuns there serving God, the third ‘ part of the church of Corbi, with all things to the same share be-‘ longing, for sustentation of the same nuns, unto their proper ‘ uses for ever to be possessed ; the which part, by donation & ‘ presentation of dame Matildis de Diva & of Hugh her son & heir, ‘ they have fairly obtained.   Saving the episcopal dues & the dignity ‘ of the church of Lincoln.   And that it may in all times remain ‘ firm & unshaken, the present writing being corroborated with the ‘ putting to of our seal, we have joyntly confirmed.   Witnesses, ma-‘ ster Ralph archdeacon of Leiredster, master L archdeacon of Bede-‘ ford, master Richard de Swaleclive, Robert of the chapel, &c.’ II. By another instrument the said bishop confirmed to the said nuns, the churches of S. Martin, All Saints in the mercat, S. Andrews, & S. Cle-ments, all in Stanford ; & the church of S. Firmin of Thirlby, as also the foresaid third part of the church of Corby, together with tythe of all such wood as had been or was to be grubbed up in the lands belong-ing to the foresaid Matildis de Diva & her heirs ; which is thus worded. ‘ [c] To all the faithful of Christ unto whom the present writing shall ‘ come, Hugh by the grace of God bishop of Lincoln, greeting in the ‘ Lord & benediction. Altho’, by the office of the administration un-
                                                    ‘ dertaken

a Ex rotulo pipæ de eo anno.

b Omnibus Christi fidelibus, ad quos præ-sens scriptum pervenerit, Hugo D. G. Linc. episcopus, eternam in Domino salutem. Noverit universitas vestra, nos, divine pieta-tis intuitu, considerando & paupertate domus B. Michaelis de Stanford, auctoritate episco-pali, concessisse & confirmasse, Deo & B. Marie & S. Michaeli & monialibus ibidem Deo servientibus, tertiam partem ecclesie de Corbi, cum omnibus ad eandem portionem pertinentibus, ad earundem monialium susten-tationem, in usus proprios perpetuo possiden-dam ; quam quidem partem, ex donatione & presentatione D. Matildis de Diva & Hugo-nis filii & heredis ejus, rationabiliter adepte

sunt. Salvis episcopalibus consuetudinibus & Linc. ecclesie dignitate. Ut firmum & illibatum cunctis diebus permaneat, presenti scripto sigilli nostri appositione corroborato, communivimus. Hiis testibus, magistro Rad. archid. de Leiredster. magistro L. archid. de Bedeford, magistro Richardo de Swaleclive, Rob. de capella, &c. Ex MS. codicum Dodf. Vol. 59. fol. 165, &c.

c Omnibus Christi fidelibus ad quos pre-sens scriptum pervenerit, Hugo D. G. Linc. episcopus, salutem in Domino & benedictio-nem. Licet, ex suscepto administrationis of-ficio, teneamur ea que locis religionis offe-runtur beneficia nostre auctoritatis patroci-nio defendere, & contra malignantium in-
       8 D   cursus

' dertaken by us, we are bound to defend thofe benefices which are
' given to houfes of religion, with the patronage of our authority, &
' to cover them againft the facrileges of malignants with epifcopal
' protection; neverthelefs we defire it may come to the knowledge of
' your univerfality, that we hold good, & by the prefent charter con-
' firm, the donations, as they have been particularly made, to God &
' the church of S. Michael of Stanford, & to the nuns there ferving
' God, of the churches of S. Martin, & All Saints, & S. Andrew, &
' S. Clement, in the town of Stanford; & of S. Firmin of Turlebi;
' & of the third part of the church of Corbi; & of the tythes of the
' affarts of Matildis de Diva: as the charters of the donors witnefs.
' Which, that it may be for ever firm & good, by the prefent char-
' ter & my feal, we have thought good to be confirmed.   Saving the
' dignity of the church of Lincoln & the epifcopal dues.'   III. By a
third inftrument the faid bifhop confirmed to the faid nuns two third
parts of the forefaid church of Corby given them by the forefaid Matildis de Diva & Afcelina de Waterville & their heirs, & by Hamon
Peche; faving to Hugh de Oferneby his fhare there for the term of
his life; as alfo the perpetual vicarage there, with a competent manfe,
which Hilary the capellan then held, affigned to him & his fucceffors,
out of the faid fhares: which runs thus.   ' ª To all the faithful of
' Chrift, unto whom the prefent writing fhall come, Hugh by the
' grace of God bifhop of Lincoln, greeting in the Lord.   Your univer-
' fality fhall underftand that we, with the affent & free-will of our
' beloved fons in Chrift William the dean & our chapter of Lincoln,
' in an intuition of divine piety, have given & granted to our be-
' loved daughters in Chrift, the nuns of S. Michael without the bo-
' rough of Staunforde, the two parts of the church of Corbi, which
' by the gift of Matilda de Diva, & by the gift of Afcelina de Wa-
' terville, & their heirs; alfo by the gift of Hamon Peche; do belong
' to the advoufon of them the nuns; to have to the fame, & unto
' their proper ufes for ever to be held; faving the fhare of Hugh de
' Oferneby there, for the term of his life; & faving the perpetual
' vicarage, with a competent manfe, which Hilary the capellan holds
' out of the faid fhares, to him, & his fucceffors the vicars of the fame
' fhares, affigned.   Moreover the forefaid nuns fhall difcharge all dues
' epifcopal & archidiaconal, the fo-often-faid two parts befalling.   Sav-
' ing alfo in all things the epifcopal dues, & the dignity of the church

curfus epifcopali protectione communire; ad univerfitatis veftre volumus notitiam pervenire, nos ratas habere & prefenti carta confirmare, donationes, ficut rationabiliter facte funt, Deo & ecclefie S. Michaelis de Stanford & monialibus ibidem Deo fervientibus, fuper ecclefiis S. Martini, & omnium SS. & S. Andree, & S. Clementis in villa de Stanford, & S. Firmini de Turlebi; & fuper tertiam partem ecclefie de Corbi; & de

decimis de fartis Matildis de Diva: ficut carte donatorum teftantur. Quod, ut in perpetuum ratum & firmum, prefenti carta & figillo meo duximus confirmandum. Salva Linc. ecclefie dignitate & epifcopalibus confuetudinibus. Ex eodem codice MS. ut fupra.

a Ex regiftri prioratus S. Michaelis penes Galf. Minfhul gen. 1657. folio 6. a. citato in Mon. Ang. tomi II. pagina 881. b.

' of

‘ of Lincoln.   Which, that it may obtain a perpetual firmnefs, we
‘ have thought good the prefent charter fhould be fortified with our
‘ feal, together with the feal of our forefaid chapter.   Witneffes, Wil-
‘ liam the dean, John the chaunter, &c.   Given, &c. in the chapter
‘ at Lincoln the 19. of April, in the 17. year of our pontificate.’
Hugh Wells was made bifhop of Lincoln in 1209. fo that 1226. or
1227. muft be the 17. of his pontificate.

 IX. ‘ ᵃ In 1227. Richard earl of Cornwal the kings brother had
‘ feifed into his hands a certain manor, then in the tenure of one
‘ Waleran a Dutch gentleman (to whom K. John, for his good fervi-
‘ ces, had formerly given it) as parcel of his earldom of Cornwal.
‘ The king hereupon directs his letters to his brother, commanding
‘ him to come immediately, & fhew a reafon of his fact.   He doth
‘ fo, & without any pleaders help, defendeth, as juft, the feizure which
‘ he had made, concluding, among other words, that he was ready
‘ to ftand to the judgment of the kings court & peers of the realm.
‘ When the king & the chief jufticiar heard him name the peers of
‘ the realm, they (fufpecting his bent that way) were exceedingly
‘ offended; & (faid the king) either reftore the manor to Waleran,
‘ or thou fhalt depart out of the kingdom never to return.   At which
‘ peremptory fentence, the earl boldly, but too rafhly, anfwer’d, that
‘ he neither would give his right to Waleran, nor, without judgment
‘ of the peers, depart the realm.   The earl, in this heat, returns to
‘ his lodging : thence (upon furmife that Hubert the chief jufticiar had
‘ perfuaded the king to lay hold on him) he pofts to Marlborough,
‘ where finding William the young earl of Pembroke, he enters into
‘ a faft confederacy, ratified by oath ; & Ranulf earl of Chefter is ea-
‘ fily drawn to become another.   Letters thence flying about to all
‘ their friends, at Stamford there affembled unto them, the earls of
‘ Gloucefter, Warenn, Hereford, Warwick, Ferrars, many barons, &
‘ an huge multitude of armed men.   Their ftrengths being in likeli-
‘ hood able to bear out their darings, they addrefs a bold meffage to
‘ the king, by which they require him, in lofty phrafe, to make pre-
‘ fent amends to his brother for the wrong he had done; the fault
‘ whereof they imputed not to him, but to the chief jufticiar; & that
‘ if he did not without delay reftore the charter of liberties, which
‘ he had cancell’d at Oxford, they would drive him by dint of fword
‘ to give them therein competent fatisfaction.   The king feeing it no
‘ fafe time to deny their requefts, appoints to meet at Northampton
‘ in Auguft following, where the earl of Cornwal, upon his affociates
‘ refolute demand of the king, had large amends of any injury fuftain-
‘ ed, his patrimony being augmented with large poffeffions.   The mo-
‘ deration & equanimity of the king (terrified by his fathers example)
‘ peaceably finifhed this contention (the matter of the charters being,
‘ for this time, hufhed as it feemeth) which might otherwife have coft

     ª Speed, p. 601, 602.

               ‘ many

' many thoufand lives, & hazarded the ruin both of king & kingdom.
' I have feen, faith the great Selden[a], original letters of protection
' (a perfect & uncommunicable power royal) by that great prince
' Richard earl of Poictiers & Cornwal, brother to Hen. 3. fent to the fhe-
' rif of Rutland, for & in behalf of a nunnery in or about Stanford.'
Mr. Selden mentions no date of this protection, but I venture to place
it under this year, when the faid earl of Cornwal & other barons,
as above, affembled at Stanford. And it is probable the faid nuns,
afraid of fome violence from the great army which they here brought
together, for that reafon requefted the faid letters of protection. ' [b] The
' fame year Martin de Ramfey abbat of Burg paid fifty marcs into the
' kings exchequer, for disforrefting the Neffe of Burg.' This disforrefting, was, I fuppofe, only a confirmation of K. Johns abovementioned grant for that purpofe to abbat Lindfey.

18. Nov.
12. H. 3.   X. Upon the 18. of November, in the 12. year of his reign, the
king gave the nuns of S. Michael a load of thorns or dead wood to be
had yearly out of Cliffe foreft; which if not a confirmation of what
his father gave the fame ladies before[c], as I think it was not: then
they had now privilege of two loads of thorns or dead wood there,
every year. K. Henry the thirds charter is thus worded. ' [d] Henry,
' by the grace of God, king of England, lord of Ireland, duke of
' Normandy & Aquitain, earl of Anjou, to the bailifs of the foreft of
' Clive greeting. Know ye that we, for the health of our foul, & of
' the fouls of our anceftors & fucceffors, have granted to the nuns of
' S. Michael of Staunford, that they may have for ever on any day,
' one load of thorns or dead wood, in our foreft of Clive. And
' therefore we will & firmly command, that ye let the fame nuns have
' the forefaid load without impediment, as is aforefaid. Witnefs my
' felf at Staunford, the 18. day of November, in the 12. year of our
' reign.' About this time Martin de Ramfey abbat of Burg releafed
the priorefs & nuns of S. Michael aforefaid, from the yearly payment
of three fhillings, being a certain Landgavel, or rent arifing out of 24
acres of land in Stanford field. This Landgavel was however afterwards again demanded by fome of the fucceeding abbats bailifs, till,
as you will find, Robert Sutton the abbat & the convent of Burg in
1264. or thereabouts, at length gave the faid priorefs & nuns a full
difcharge from ever paying the fame.

12. Ap.
1229.   XI. The Cluniac monks of Lewes in Suffex having under them the
cell of Caftle-acre in Norfolk; & the cell of Caftle-acre having under

a Notes on Draytors Polyolb. p. 224.
b Chron. Joh. abbatis de Burgo, p. 103.
c Videfis fub anno 12. Johan. fupra.
d Henricus D. G. rex Anglie, dominus
Hibernie, dux Normannie & Aquitanie,
comes Andegavie, ballivis forefte de Clive,
falutem. Sciatis nos, pro falute anime noftre, & animarum antecefforum & fuccefo-
rum noftrorum, conceffiffe monialibus S.
Michaelis de Staunford, quod habeant im-

perpetuum quolibet die, unam carectatam de
fpinis vel de mortuo bofco, in forefta noftra
de Clive. Et ideo volumus & firmiter precipimus, quod permittatis eifdem monialibus
predictam carectatam fine impedimento habere, ficut predictum eft. Tefte meipfo apud
Staunford decimo octavo die Novembris,
anno regni noftri 12. Ex exemplari quodam (penes comitem Exoniæ) cujufdam rotuli de anno tertio Edw. 4.

it the cell of Bromholme, in the fame county: fome difputes (chiefly about electing a prior over the faid cell of Bromholme) arifing betwixt the faid monks of Bromholme, & the faid monks of Caftle-acre; there-upon the prior & convent of Lewes (as heads of both places, & in right of themfelves & the monks of Caftle-acre) complained to the pope of the difobedience of the faid monks of Bromholme. Upon which the Pontif fent his mandate, directed to the abbat of Ofulveftune & the deans of Stanford & Roteland, or any two of them, to fummon the parties before them, &, after hearing what they had for themfelves fe-verally to alledge, to decree all matters between them according to equity, from which, by his faid letters, he prohibited all future appeal. Upon receipt whereof, the abbat of Ofulveftune & the dean of Rote-land fummoned the parties to meet in S. Maries church by the bridge, at Stanford; where they accordingly appeared; & the prior of Lewes, by his proctor the prior of Caftle-acre, fet forth an account of his, & the faid prior of Caftle-acres, claim: which being heard, after many altercations, a compofition or agreement, by confent of all parties, was at laft made, & fealed with all their feals, & fo left with the abbat of Ofulveftune to fee it executed. ' Done at Stanford in the church ' of the B. Mary near the bridge, on the Wednefday next before Palm-' Sunday, in the year of our Lord 1229. Witneffes, the dean of Stan-' ford, mafter R. de Cantulupe, Sir G. Herford, mafter R. de Wrfiftede, ' mafter R. de Rokelond, mafter Walter de Suthfeld, Sir R. the capel-' lan, Walter the goldfmith, Nicholas the chamberlain, Geoffry de ' Whineberewe, Robert Wardebois, & others.' I fhall only add, thefe things, as it feems to me, were not fo much done at Stanford, becaufe the dean of Stanford was a commiffioner, as that they might be de-termined with the approbation of William earl Warenn, patron of the monks of Lewes, then I fuppofe at his caftle of Stanford.

XII. About this time Clement rector of the church of S. Michael Cornftal in Stanford, fon of Reiner Heie of the fame place, fold an houfe in the fame parifh to Hugh de Bladelawe vicar of Maxey in Nor-thamptonfhire, whereof this was the deed of fale. ' ª Know prefent ' & future people that I Clement, rector of S. Michael de Cornftal, ' fon of Reiner Heie of Stanford, have granted, fold & by this my ' prefent charter confirmed to Hugh de Bladelawe vicar of Makefey, ' for twenty marcs of filver which he hath given me, that houfe with ' the appurtenances, which is fituate in the parifh of S. Michael de ' Cornftal of Stanford, between the houfe of Ernald de Caftreton eaft, ' & the houfe of Gilbert de Clive weft.' The faid Hugh de Blade-lawe affigned the faid houfe, & as it fhould feem fome others which he bought of the faid Clement with it (for he fpeaks of houfes, in the plural) to the abbat & convent of Thorney by this inftrument. ' ᵇ Be it known to all that I Hugh de Bladelawe, vicar of Makefaye,

Circa
1230.

a Ex libri rubri abbatiæ de Thorney penes   partis 5. folio 10.
perhon. Tho. comitem de Weftmoreland,   a id. ib.

have

' have granted, given, & affigned, alfo by the prefent writing confirm-
' ed, to the lord abbat of Thornei & the convent of the fame place,
' the houfes which I bought in Stanford of Sir Clement, rector of
' the church of S. Michael in Cornftal, to have & to hold to the
' fame abbat & convent & their fucceffors for ever, by doing the fer-
' vice which from thofe houfes is due, &c. the which houfes had been
' dimifed to Geoffry the clerc, fon of Richard of Depinge, & to his
' heirs, for ten fhillings a year.' Now this is the firft time I meet
with the mention of any parifh church of S. Michael in Stanford, exprefly fo named in any antient writing. There were however two of
them, great S. Michaels (now ftanding) & this (deftroyed as I take it in
1461. when the northern men burnt the town of Stanford) which ftood
fomewhere in the ftreet called now S. Georges ftreet leading to S. Georges
gate, which gate whilft this church was ftanding, was called Cornftal
gate. But the church of S. Michael de Cornftal being as above deftroyed, the parifh of S. Michael de Cornftal is now become part of the
parifh of S. George. Having at prefent nothing farther to add about
the church of S. Michael de Cornftal, I fhall here give a brief account
of great S. Michaels church undoubtedly in being, when thefe deeds
above were executed, for why fhould not only S. Michael, but S. Michael de Cornftal be there mentioned, were it not to diftinguifh it
from fome other parifh church dedicated to the fame faint, in the
fame town, & at the fame time there ftanding?——The prefent fabric
of great S. Michaels church (being as old, if not older, than the times
we are now treating of) confifts of three ifles, & as many chancels,
all which are leaded. The north & fouth chancels are run out fomewhat wider than the north & fouth ifles, purpofely to bring the whole
into the fhape of a crofs; the fame being the only church we have now
left in Stanford erected after that figure; to me a fufficient argument
that its prefent fhell is older than any other parifh church now ftanding here. Befides which, the deep defcent into this church on all fides,
& the plainnefs of the building, are other good teftimonies of its antiquity. Likewife its being feated in the very centre of the town fhews
it muft have been built very early. For fo much ground for a church
& fo large a churchyard as belongs to it, would hardly have been
fpared from other ufes but in times of great devotion. Mounted on
the weft end of the nave is a fmall tower of wood, a deal more modern than the times we are fpeaking of, & in it four very fmall bells,
none of them above an hundred years old. About twenty years ago
the eaft end of the choir or middle chancel, being grown ruinous, was
taken down & rebuilt by the parifhioners, in the wall whereof were
found many rude pieces of fculpture & broken imagery, carelefly thrown
in as it fhould feem, & knocked on pieces, to fill up fpaces as occafion offered. Which fhews that this part of the church had been
repaired with the ruins of fome other church or religious houfe. And
indeed when S. Andrews & S. Stephens parifhes were by act of parliament

The South East Prospect of St Michaels Church in Stanford.

To Th^o Cartwright of Aynhoe Esq. one of the kind Incouragers of this work, this Plate is most thankfully inscribed.

ment united to great S. Michaels, the materials of thofe churches were ordered for the repairs of S. Michaels, or the mending of the bridges & highways about this town as the commiffioners faw occafion. In this church of S. Michael have been many infcriptions & figures of brafs cut & inlaid on feveral graveftones on the floor, but all long ago torn up. The windows likewife, antiently full of painted glafs, have now no efcutcheon or other figure left in them that I can make any thing of: fo I fhall only give here the fculpture of the church it felf, & pafs on.

XIII. ' ᵃ In the 15. of Henry the third, the advowfon of the church 15. H. 3. ' of Hamildon in Rutland, was adjudged to belong to the bifhop of ' Lincoln, together with the chapel of Brandefton, & a penfion of twenty ' fhillings from the church of S. Peter in Stanford.' About this time the nuns of S. Michael by Stanford, having employed a certain clerc, a friend of theirs, to follicit a confirmation of their privileges at Rome, he, as they afterwards alledged, againft their order, got inferted fome additional articles, to wit, one for the faid nuns to chufe their own priorefs (an act which greatly provoked the abbat & monks of Burg, in whom that right was invefted by William Waterville fometime abbat of that church & founder of this nunnery) & another to releafe them from payment of fundry penfions, referv'd to the faid abbat & monks of Burg, out of feveral churches by them heretofore given to the faid nuns. Whereupon the faid abbat & monks complaining, or at leaft threatening to complain, of all thefe matters to the pope, the nuns, confcious of their faid proctors unfair proceedings, fent their priorefs, with the charters & privileges of their houfe, to lay them before the archbifhop of Canterbury & his fuffragans, be- feeching them to reprefent their doings for them favorably to the pope, & alfo to make them & their patrons (the forefaid abbat & convent of Burg) friends, to obtain which they renounce all claim to any fuch privileges as had been thus clandeftinely procured. Their petition is thus worded. ' ᵇ To the moft beloved in Chrift the fathers ' & lords, Richard by the grace of God archbifhop of Canterbury, pri- ' mate of all England & legate of the apoftolic fee, & to his fuffra- ' gans, A. priorefs of S. Michael of Stanford & the humble convent ' of the fame place, greeting & prayers in Chrift Jhefu. To your no- ' tice we defire it may come, reverend fathers, how that a certain clerc, ' to us & our church a fpecial friend, in the Roman court fometime ' fince conftituted our proctor (for the profit of our houfe defiring ' more earneftly for the future to provide) when, for our poffeffions ca- ' nonically acquired, he ought to have craved, from the lord pope, ' only a fimple confirmation; beyond commandment & confcience, ' nay againft the common will of our chapter; in the fame letters ' of confirmation, hath caufed to be inferted a certain claufe touching ' the having a free election of a priorefs, the which to us & our church

a Wrights Rutland, p. 69.   in bib. Cotton. fub imagine Vefp. E. XXII.
b Ex regiftri cujufdam abbatiæ de Burgo   fol. 39. b.

' is

' is pernicious & hurtful, especially since it is contrary to our other
' privileges & other charters which we have relating to the foundati-
' on of our house by the founders themselves. And from hence our
' lords & founders the abbat & convent of Burg have conceived a ran-
' cor against us & an indignation, & deservedly, since (without the
' assent & free will of them, who have founded & endowed our place,
' thro' whom, after God, we live) we ought to have no election of a
' prioress or institution, as by a diligent inspection of the charter
' of the same, which we have touching the foundation of our place,
' the more evidently (if it please ye) ye shall be able to understand.
' Moreover & because there are other articles whence we have incur-
' red the indignation of our lords the abbat & convent (in as much
' as with regard to the churches which to us they have given, under
' a certain pension, them yearly to be paid; whereof we have re-
' quested confirmations from the lord pope, no mention of the pen-
' sion being had) touching this point we do confess we have erred,
' being ready, with unanimous assent, to leave both this & the other
' articles to be corrected at their pleasure. Desiring therefore, as it be-
' comes us, by such means as we are able, in humility & all kind of
' satisfaction, fully to reconcile the grace & favor of our lords &
' founders to us, we send, unto your feet, our prioress with all the
' charters & privileges of our church, earnestly beseeching, how
' that, the same charters & privileges inspected, ye may remove all
' difference, & to us, with an intuition of divine commiseration, restore
' the fulness of the former love & favor of our lords; because,
' without them, we are not able to live; without their suffrages our
' church is not able to stand, nor the order there instituted to be observed.
' As therefore there is an indignation conceived against us by our lords,
' & that all suspicion may be taken from us, we humbly & earnestly
' beg how that the truth of the business, which touching these things
' we write unto you, ye would by your letters be pleased to signifie
' to the lord pope.' There is nothing of a date either before, or after, this handsome epistle, to shew when it was wrote. But, as it is
addressed to Richard archbishop of Canterbury, the name of that prelate helps us to find out the time. The first archbishop of that name
was Richard prior of Dover, who came to that see in 1173. within
seventeen years after the nunnery of S. Michael was founded; too soon,
I cannot but think, for the nuns of that house to forget their obligations to the abbat & monks of Burg, & act as we here find they did.
The next & only archbishop of that name before the reformation was
Richardus magnus, who came in that see in 1229. & held it about two
years. This therefore is he under whose archiepiscopate these things
most probably happened; & for these reasons I have placed them here.

XIV. About this time was founded the hospital & priory of the B.
Virgin at Newsted. ' Newstede, saith Leland[a], is within less then a

---

a Itin. Vol. 6. p. 30.

' mile

‘ mile beneth Stanford, but not hard upon the ryver’ [Welland : it
being situate at the bridge of the river Guash, or Wasch, between Stanford & Offington.] ‘ Albeniacus, saith the same author ᵃ, lord of
‘ Bever castle (that of surety standeth in ᴸᵉⁱᶜᵉˢᵗʳᵉ ᵇ in the vale of
‘ Bever, was lord of Uffington by Wiland ryver, [a mile &] halfe by-
‘ nethe Stanforde on the farther side of the ripe of Lincolnshir ; &
‘ there remainid greate tokens of a manor place embateld of his, the
‘ which by the yere [heir] of Rutheland now lyving [temp. H. 8.] &
‘ having it by Rosse heir generale, hath well bene repairid.   And at
‘ such tyme as Albeneys lay communely at Uffington, one of them
‘ builded Newsteede a priory of chanons’ regular, of the order of S.
Austin.   And in another place, ‘ the third William of Albini, says he ᶜ,
‘ was the original founder, a modern one the heir of Rutland.’   The
said William de Albini the third, with consent of William his
son & heir & of other his heirs (for the health of his own, his two
wives, & all his ancestors & successors, souls) gave to Adam the first
master of this hospital & to his brethren, the place whereon their house
& chapel stood, with his mill at Offington, & divers parcels of land
in divers places situate.   Also tythe of all the bread made or used in
his family ; or, in lieu of it, the tenth quarter of all grain provided
for that purpose.   Likewise tythe of all flesh, fish, & wax in the same
manner provided for his own family, or that of his heirs.   Also pa-
sture for an hundred sheep, & for six oxen, six cows & two bulls.
All which he gave them conditionally, that the master of the said
house should be always a priest & canon regular ; that he should have
with him another canon to celebrate daily in the said chapel for the
quick & the dead, with proper persons to assist in the said administration ; that seven poor & infirm people should be constantly maintained in the said house, with necessary food, cloaths, & beds, provided at
the expence of the same ; and lastly, that upon accession of future benefactions (which were to be hoped for) the number of the
said poor & beds should be occasionally augmented : For all which
purposes the charter of his endowment is thus worded.   ‘ ᵈ To all
‘ the children of holy mother church unto whom the present writing
‘ shall come, William de Albini the third, greeting in the Lord.   Your
‘ universality shall understand that I, in an intuition of divine pie-
‘ ty, have given, granted, & by this my present charter confirmed,
‘ into pure & perpetual alms, with assent of William de Albini my
‘ eldest son & heir, & also of other my heirs, for the health of my
‘ soul, & of Agatha Trussebutt my wife, & for the soul of Margaret
‘ sometime my wife, & for the souls of all my ancestors & successors ;
‘ to God & the hospital founded in honor of the ever blessed

a id. p. 29.   c Collect. Vol. I. p. 96.
  b The castle, as Mr. Burton says, is in   d Ex vetusto exemplari penes Joh. Vincent
Lincolnshire. But he is wrong. The stables   gen. 1652. citato in Mon. Ang. tomi II. p.
are in Lincolnsh. & the castle in Leicestersh.   444. b.

8 F   ‘ Virgin

‘ Virgin Mary at the bridge of the Wafs, between Stanford & Offington,
‘ & to the brethren there about to ferve God, & to Adam mafter of the
‘ fame hofpital, & to his fucceffors (at my prefentation & of my heirs, as
‘ oft as it fhall happen to the forenamed hofpital to be void, by the
‘ diocefan of the place, for the time being, canonically inftituted)
‘ to wit, the place in which the chapel of the bleffed Mary is fituate,
‘ with the whole houfe adjacent, & my whole mill of Offington, with
‘ fuit, as well of my demefne as of the fervants of my houfe & of
‘ my tenents, & with all other things unto the faid mill belonging, fo
‘ entirely as I or any of my anceftors ever better & freelier have held the
‘ faid mill; alfo with all the land underwritten. To wit, one acre
‘ of land againft the hill of Mykelthwait eaft. And half an acre of
‘ land upon the fame hill. And three rods towards Kaudell [Cald-
‘ wel in Leicefterfhire] ‘ And two acres at . . . . . And three acres
‘ & an half in Efthawe. And half an acre at Bilnebec. And two
‘ acres in Wefthawe. And five acres in Welfiwude. And one acre
‘ without the town of Offington weft. And eight acres in Ealefhage.
‘ And one at the crofs of Tallington. And one acre in Senholing-
‘ ford. And one rod upon Clemmont [Cley-mount-hill, on the
north fide of Stanford.] ‘ And three rods in Wecelonde. And three
‘ acres at Stocwel. And three rods at Thurmodefwel. And feven
‘ acres in Mikelhawe. And one acre in the nook of Erlefhage. And
‘ half an acre at the Mere. And half an acre at Northcrofte. And
‘ half an acre at Litlebec. And half an acre by Kentelofs. And three
‘ rods at Flichegge. And one rod at Berewes fouth. And two acres
‘ beyond Stordes. And one acre in Woolfuwoode. And one acre
‘ upon Edricwonge. And one acre beyond Stongate. And half an
‘ acre in Weftmedwe. And half an acre at Edricrofte. And one
‘ acre in Atefchueit. And one acre in Witegate. And half an acre
‘ above Bemwoode. And three rods by Berwes, eaft. And three rods
‘ above Berwes. And one rod by Berwes fouth. And half an
‘ acre at Hulvergate. And half an acre by the town of Offington fouth.
‘ And one rod above Pefelond. And one acre & one rod which Be-
‘ lym gave. And one acre & one rod at Stocwell. And half an
‘ acre atte Bec. And three rods at Wetelonde. And one rod at
‘ Preftewonge. And one acre at Milneftede. And three rods under-
‘ clif. And half an acre at the crofs of Tallington. And half an
‘ acre atte Holgate. And half an acre at Gorlycrofte. And one rod
‘ atte Bec. And half an acre at little Bec. And one rod by Berwes
‘ eaft, & three rods towards Bec. And three rods by Preftwange. And
‘ half an acre at Buttingefdic. And half an acre at Holegate. And
‘ one rod at Thirlpolhill. And three rods atte Lunde. And one rod,
‘ five acres, & an half acre at Gerchefwro. And one rod in He-
‘ fortewod. And half an acre in the fame place. And two rods in
‘ Edichefwange. And half an acre in Cuttefhawe. And the whole
‘ land within Berwes which Peter the chevalier held of me. And one

2

‘ acre

' acre of meadow & an half in Lithetholm.   And two acres back Que-
' renholm.   And one rod in Mers.   And one acre in Senholm.   And
' three rods in Wrongedaites.   And half an acre in Weftmers of Ta-
' lington.   And one rod in Mikelholm of Talington.   And three
' rods in Horfholm of Talington.   And one rod in Eftmers of Ta-
' lington.   And one rod in Ofiwardeholme.   And three rods in Der-
' linge.   And half an acre in Senholme by Sitaker.   And half of the
' meadow of Baldwin Maunfell at Wrounge-Date.   And one rod in
' Mers.   And one acre in Mikelholm of Talington, which was Roger
' le Cnutes, by the meadow of the lord, & the meadow by the mill
' which is called Fourpenholm.   And one toft which Gunwara Gogel
' fometime held.   I have granted alfo & confirmed to the fame hof-
' pital & brethren, & to their fucceffors, with affent of the fame
' my heirs, the tythe of all the bread which is expended in my houfe,
' or of my heirs, wherefoever my family fhall be, or of them my
' heirs, after my deceafe; or the tenth quarter of the corn which fhall
' be expended in bread in my faid houfe, or of them my heirs, after
' my deceafe.   And the whole tythe of the meats & fifhes arifing
' out of the firft mefs which in like fort fhall be expended daily in
' my houfe, or of my heirs after my deceafe.   And moreover the
' tythe of all wax, which fhall be expended in the forenamed manner.
' Moreover I have granted to the faid hofpital & premifed brethren,
' with affent of the fame my heirs, pafture for an hundred fheep in
' the faid town, & for fix cows, & for two bulls, with my demefne oxen,
' cows, & my bulls.   And all thefe things aforefaid, I William & the
' forefaid my heirs, againft all people, to the forenamed hofpital &
' forenamed brethren & to their fucceffors, will for ever warant.   At this
' time provided (with my affent, & of William my heir then prefent, &
' the mafter aboveremembred for himfelf & for his brethren affenting;
' there acceding neverthelefs, by fpecial mandate of the venerable
' father Hugh the fecond bifhop of Lincoln, Robert archdeacon of
' Lincoln then official of the fame lord of Lincoln, & as much as in
' him lies approving the fame) that the mafter for the time being who
' fhall be appointed after the forefaid manner for the forenamed hof-
' pital, be a prieft & canon regular of fome houfe, & a man of honeft
' & approved religion; & that in like manner he have a canon with
' him refiding, & continually in the forenamed chapel celebrating for
' the quick & the dead; & that to perform it they have minifters
' neceffary & fit; the which canons fhall live according to the rule
' of S. Auftin & the fpitals; & as far as the means of the forefaid
' hofpital are able to afford, fhall chearfully & freely exhibit.   Pro-
' vided alfo particularly, that, among other the duties of the hofpital,
' feven poor weak & infirm perfons, who are of found faith & ho-
' neft life, fhall be fuftained out of the goods of the faid hofpital; to
' wit, in neceffary victuals & cloaths: unto whofe ufe feven fmall
' beds, for them to lie in, with blankets & coverlets for that purpofe

                                                    ' neceffary,

' neceſſary, in the lodging for occaſions of this ſort there deputed,
' ſhall always remain. And if by chance, by the devotion or bounty
' of the faithful, the means of the forenamed hoſpital ſhall hereafter
' increaſe, by my aſſent & of my heirs, & by the authority & or-
' dination of the dioceſan intervening, let the works of piety there
' be augmented & the number of the poor & beds increaſed.
' And that this my donation & conceſſion ſo made proviſion may
' continue ſtable in future times, it, by my preſent charter, with the
' muniment of my ſeal I have corroborated; &, for me & my heirs,
' as far as belongs to the patron, thought good to be confirmed.
' Witneſſes, Sir Robert de Heiles archdeacon of Lincoln, maſter Wil-
' liam de Watepoll official of the ſame; Alexander & Philip of Stan-
' ford, & Denes then the deans; Helyas, Alan, William, the capel-
' lans; Odonel de Albini, Philip de Waſtney, Richard de Cotes, Ro-
' ger Burun, Bartholomew de S. Hilary, William de Aldedely, knights;
' Hugh de Nevil, Hugh de Bobi, William ſon of William, the ſons
' of Roger, & others.' It ſhould ſeem by this charter, that, beſides
what William de Albini himſelf now gave to this houſe, one Be-
lym did alſo give unto the ſame one acre & a rod of land. Alexander, Philip, & Dennis, the three deans abovementioned, were deans,
the firſt of Stanford, the other two perhaps of ſome gilds there. By
another charter the foreſaid William de Albini, beſides confirming
what he had thus granted, gave to his ſaid hoſpital & priory, three
bovates of land in Uffington field, with a toft in that town, & a
rent of three ſhillings & three pence, with nine hens & three cocks
yearly. Alſo forty ſhillings a year at Chaufunt, & five ſhillings a
year at Bocceford (Botsford, as I take it, in Leiceſterſhire.) However
theſe things, he added conditionally, that, over & above the ſaid two
canons, one clerc & one deacon to ſerve them at maſs, there ſhould
be thirteen poor (alluding, I conceive, to the number of our Saviour
& his apoſtles) conſtantly maintained there; & that thoſe thirteen poor
ſhould be always choſen out of his tenents, or elſewhere, as he the
founder & they (the prior & confrater of Newſtede) ſhould agree:
which other charter is thus expreſſed. ' [a] To all the children of holy
' mother church who ſhall ſee or hear this writing, William de Al-
' bini the third, greeting alſo in the Lord. Your univerſality ſhall
' underſtand, that I, in an intuition of divine charity, & for my
' health, & of my anceſtors & ſucceſſors, have given, granted, & by
' this my preſent charter confirmed, to the hoſpital at the bridge be-
' tween Stanford & Offington (which I have founded in honor of
' the bleſſed Virgin Mary) & to the brethren there ſerving God &
' the bleſſed Mary, & to the infirm people there about to make abode,
' into pure & perpetual alms, three bovats of land in the territory of
' Offington, with the meadow & paſture, & with all the appurtenan-

a id. ib. ut ſupra.

2

' ces & liberties unto the forefaid bovates of land belonging; &
' one toft in the fame town, to wit, that which Conewara Gog-
' nel fometime held, & a rent of three fhillings & three pence,
' with nine hens, & three cocks yearly to be received; to wit, of
' the land of Richard de Middleton nine pence; of William Cok,
' twelve pence, & three hens, & one cock; of William fon of
' Thurftan, twelve pence, & three hens, & one cock; & of William
' Snell, fix pence, & three hens, & one cock; & the mill of Of-
' fington, with fuit of the whole town of Offington, as I ever had it
' better; & a rent of forty fhillings in the town of Chaufunt, of the
' land which William fon of Hamon gave me for . . . . & fer-
' vice . . . . . & a rent of five fhillings in the town of Bocceford, of
' that land which I gave to William fon of Dagun of Nouwere.
' Befides this I have granted them the whole tythe of my houfe, of
' the bread & wax, & of the firft mefs as well of the flefh as of the
' fifh daily ufed; & pafture for an hundred fheep, & for fix oxen, &
' for fix cows, & for two cattel [horfes or oxen] with my proper cat-
' tel of Offington. It is to be obferved therefore, that the number
' of the brethren ought to be this. Two priefts, to fay mafs; where-
' of one fhall daily celebrate for the dead; & the other, as occafion
' requires. And one deacon & one clerc, to ferve the faid priefts.
' There fhall alfo be there thirteen beds ready for the ufe of the in-
' firm people chofen out of my tenents or elfewhere, as to me & the
' brethren there ferving God & the bleffed Virgin Mary, fhall feem ex-
' pedient. And all thefe particulars aforefaid, with all their appurte-
' nances & liberties, I William de Albini & my heirs, to the often
' faid hofpital & brethren there ferving God & the bleffed Virgin
' Mary, againft all men will for ever warant. Witneffes, William de
' Albini junior, Odinel de Albini, Nicholas de Albini, Robert de Al-
' bini, brethren; Roger Born, William de Kafskington, mafter Simon
' de Dalington the parfon, mafter Ralph de Kotingham, Richard Mo-
' cot, Thomas de Wineb. Walter of the golden mount, Richard the
' clerc, Martin de Talington, William de Barkefton, & many others.

XV. ' [a] In 1232. died Randolph, firnamed Blundeville, earl of Chef-
' ter.' This Randolph, but when I find not, here ' [b] confirmed to
' the bleffed Mary at Thorney, all the land & the tenure which Hugh
' de Rademeld had in Pipewel, & one carucate of land in Stoke,
' with the meadow to the fame land belonging; & befides this the
' whole toft which was Robert the forefters in Stoke, as William
' de Albini [the fecond, called] Brito, granted them [to that con-
' vent.] ' Witneffes, Roger de Molbray, & Baldwin fon of Gilbert, &
' Walter de Remerville, & Geoffry fon of Geoffry, & Geoffry the
' burfar, & William the capellan, & Hugh Wake, at Stanford. ' The

Anno
1232.

a Yorks heraldry, p. 106.
b Ex regiftri abbatiæ de Thorney penes
hon. Thomam comitem de Weftmoreland

1726. 4. partis, fol. 1. cap. 4. citat. in Monaft. Ang. tomi I. p. 248. a.
c Hollingfhed, p 641. b. Tyrrel, p. 877.

' K. now

' K. now feazed into his handes a great portion of the treafure
' which Hubert de Burgh earle of Kent [& late juftice of England]
' had committed to the keping of the Templers: but whereas there
' were that travailed to have had him put to death, the K. in refpect
' of the fervice which he had done to him & to his predeceffors K.
' Richard & K. John, granted him his life, with thofe landes which
' hee had eyther by purchace or by gift of K. John; but neverthelefs
' caufed him to be kept in prifon at the caftle of the Vees [Devifes]
' under the cuftodie of foure knights belonging to the earles of Corn-
' wal, Warren, Pembroke & Ferrers, which foure earles were become
' fureties for him.   [a] William E. Warren [lord of Stanford] now gave
' CCC. marcs fine for Ifabel his daughter to marry Hugh de Albini,

Anno
1233.
' E. of Arundel.   [b] In 1233. the pope ordained a general vifitation
' of all religious houfes throughout the weftern church, & by his let-
' ters to the fuffragan bifhops of the province of Canterbury, they
' were thereby authorifed to vifit fuch houfes of monks, nuns, &
' canons regular, as lay within their refpective diocefes, & were not

Anno
1234.
' exempt from their jurifdiction.   In 1234. faith Rous [but he, or the
printer of Leland [c] fhould have rather faid in 1334.] ' a great part
' of the Oxford fcholars betook themfelves to Stanford to ftudy there,
' by reafon of certain difcords arifen among them & the townfmen

19. H. 3.
20. H. 3.
' of Oxford.   [d] In the 19. of H. 3. William earl Warenn had fifty
' pounds blanc firm in Stanford.   [e] In the 20. H. 3. at the folemn

Jan.
123⅚.
' nuptials of K. Henry with Alianor his queen (daughter to Reymond
' earl of Provence) at which time the king & queen rode in extra-
' ordinary ftate thro' London; at the fumptuous feaft then made,
' William earl Warenn [lord of Stanford] ferved the king of his royal
' cup in the earl of Arundel [his fon in laws] ftead, who being in
' minority could not perform that office, in regard he was not then
' girt with the fword of knighthood.   That the earldom of this
' earl Warenn was very great doth appear by the knights fees he held
' of the king about this time, being no lefs than fixty two in the rape
' of Lewes, befides thirty & an half in the rape of Pevenfal of the
' fee of Gilbert de Aquila.   [f] Hiftorians fpeak now of a folemn dedi-
' cation of feveral churches in this diocefe, & there is an epiftle from
' bifhop Grofthead to the archdeacon of Lincoln, wherein he warns
' him to give notice to the rectors of all churches to provide for
' confecration; fince, according to the canons of a late council held
' at London, every church unconfecrated was to have a folemn con-

Anno
1236.
' fecration within two years following.   The epiftle is undated, but
' the fubject of it feems to fix it to 1236.

XVI. And now that great lord William de Albini the third, who
founded the hofpital & priory of Newftede by Stanford, ' [g] being a

a Bar. Vol. I. p. 77. b.
b Tyrrel, p. 879.
c Itin. Vol. 4. p. 144, 145.
d Ex rotulo pipæ de eo anno.

e Baron. Vol. I. p. 77. a.
f Bp. Kennets paroch. Ant. p. 221.
g Baron. Vol. I. p. 115. b.

' ftout

' ftout & valiant foldier, moft nobly qualified, & full of days, depart-
' ed this life at Offintune the morrow preceding the nones of May   May 6.
' in the year 1236. 20. H. 3. whereupon his body was buried in that   1236.
' his hofpital at Newftede, & ª his heart handfomely depofited under 20. H. 3.
' the wall oppofit to the north fide of the high altar of Belver.   ᵇ This
' William for the health of his foul & the foul of Agatha then his wife ;
' but efpecially for the foul of Margery his former wife, gave to the
' monks of Belvoir, one fheaf of every kind of grain arifing out of
' all his lands belonging to his lordfhips of Belvoir, Wulftorp, Bote-
' lesford, Oskynton, & Stokes.   The firft of thefe his wives Margery,
' was daughter to Odonel de Vnfranville, a great baron in Northum-
' berland.   The fecond Agatha, daughter & coheir of . . . . . Trus-
' but, an eminent baron in Yorkfhire, & widow of . . . . . ᶜ She was
' alfo buried in the priory of Newftede by Stanford.   ᵈ By the firft of
' thefe wives he had iffue, William de Albini the fourth, his fon &
' heir ; Odonel, taken prifoner with him at Rochefter ; & carried to
' Corf (who lieth buried at Belvoir) as alfo Robert & Nicholas.'   He
had likewife a daughter, Alice, who married Afcelin de Waterville :
of which Alice hereafter.   Shortly after his death, ' ᵉ William de
' Beauver, paying an hundred pounds for his relief, had livery of the
' lands of William de Albini his father, the which he held of the
' king *in capite.*'   ᶠ This William was called William de Bever ' dur-
' ing his fathers life time, & afterwards William de Albini the fourth.
' ᵍ In 1237. 21. H. 3. the king exacting a thirteenth part of all his fub- Anno
' jects moveable goods, as a compenfation for confirming the great   1237.
' charter & the charter of the foreft, did accept of three great peers 21. H. 3.
' for his council, whereof William earl Warenn [lord of Stanford]
' was the chief, whom he caufed to fwear, that they would not, for
' any refpect whatfoever, give any other than good & wholfome ad-
' vice.   The faid earl was alfo one of the four, in whofe hands that
' great tax was then depofited, to the intent it might be employed
' to the fole benefit of the king & kingdom, when need fhould re-
' quire.   ʰ Otto the popes legate affembled a fynod at London, the   Nov. 20.
' morrow after the octaves of S. Martin, wherein many ordinances   1237.
' were conftituted for the ftate of the cleargie, but not altogyther very 22. H. 3.
' acceptable to divers young priefts & fcholars, infomuche, that, the
' legate afterwards comming to Oxforde & lodging in Oufney abbey,
' it chaunced as certaine fchollers preffed to the gates, thinking to
' come in & do their dutie (as they tooke the matter) unto him, the
' porter kept them backe, & gave them overthwart wordes ; where-
' upon they rufhed in upon him ; & fo began a fray betwixt them &
' the legates men, who would have beaten them back.   It fortuned

a Mon. Ang. Vol. I. p. 328. b.   e Ex rotulo pipæ de anno 20. R. H. 3.
b Baron. Vol. I. p. 115. a.   f Baron. Vol. I. p. 115.
c Lelands Itin. Vol. VII. p. 10.   g id. p. 77.
d Bar. ubi fupra.   h Holingf. p. 651, 652.

' in this hurly-burly that a poore Irifh fcholler beeyng got in neere
' to the kytchen dreffer, befought the cooke to give him fome reliefe.
' But the cooke in a great furie, tooke up a ladle full of hot broth,
' & threw it right upon his face ; whiche thyng, when another Welch
' fcoller that ftoode by behelde, he cryed out, what mean we to fuffer
' this villany ? And therewithall taketh an arrow & fettith in it his bow,
' & drawing it up to the head, let flie at the cooke [the legates bro-
ther] ' & fo flewe him.   Hereupon, againe noyfe & tumult rofe
' about the houfe ; the legat, for fear, got him into the bellfry, where
' he kept himfelf clofe 'till the dark of the night, & then ftale forth
' to Abington, & there made his complaynt to the king in fuch la-
' mentable wife, that he forthwith fent erle Warenn [lord of Stanford ' with a power of armed men, to fetch away the refidue of
' the legates fervauntes, & apprehend the chief offenders.   The erle,
' comming thither, tooke thirtie fcollers, with one mafter Odo a
' lawyer, & brought them to Wallingford caftle, & there committed
' them to prifon.   The legate alfo, in revenge, pronounced the [in-
terdict or] ' curfe againft the myfdoers, & handled the matter in
' fuche wyfe, that the regents & maifters of the univerfity, were at
' length conftreined to come unto London, & there to go barefooted
' thro' Cheapfide to St Paules, to aske him forgivneffe ; & fo; with
' much adoe, they obteyned abfolution.

Anno
1238.
23. H. 3.
XVII. ' ᵃ In 1238. one Richard of Stanford being elected abbat of
' Thorney, died within two days after his tranflation.'   From what
houfe or monaftery he was fo tranflated I find not.   ' ᵇ In the 23. of
' H. 3. there having been a great fute at law betwixt Simon de Pier-
' pont, & William earl Warenn [lord of Stanford] touching free-warenn
' in the lordfhips of the faid Simon at Herft (fince called Herft Pier-
' pont) & Godebridge in Suffex, they came to an accord.   Whereupon
' earl Warenn (in confideration of a gofhawk given to the faid Simon)
' obtained leave for himfelf & his heirs, to hunt the buck, doe, hart,
' hynd, hare, fox, goat, cat, or any other wild beaft in any of thofe
' lands. ᶜ This William earl Warenn [lord of Stanford] had two wives,
' the firft Maud, daughter to . . . earl of Arundel, who died without
' iffue, & lieth buried in the chapter-houfe at Lewes.   The fecond
' likewife called Maud, widow of Hugh Bigod earle of Norfolk &
' marfhal of England, eldeft fifter & one of the coheirs of Anfelme
' Marfhal earle of Pembroke.   The faid earl Warenn falling fick
May 27.
1240.
24. H. 3.
' at London, did there depart this life upon the fixth of the calends
' of June, 1240. & was buried in the midft of the quire in the abby
' of Lewes, before the high altar ; leaving iffue by Maud his laft wife,
' John his fon & fucceffor, & Ifabel a daughter married to Hugh de
' Albini earl of Arundel.'   This William earl Warenn, out of the
great refpect he had for Elias de Marnile, gave the nuns of S. Michael

a Ex cartul. abbatiæ de Thorney.   c Baron. Vol. I. p. 77. b.
b Baron. Vol. II. p. 457. b.

by Stanford, a rent charge of forty shillings *per annum*, arising out of the profits of his mill at Wakefield, to be spent in a pittance, or extraordinary commons, upon the 22. of April, being the anniversary of the said Elias; which anniversary the said nuns, in consideration of the said rent charge, obliged themselves for ever to observe. The earls charter upon that occasion is thus worded. ' ᵃ To ' all the children of holy mother church, unto whom the present ' writing shall come, William earl Warenn, greeting in the Lord. ' Your universality shall understand, that I, in an intuition of charity, & ' for the health of my soul, & for the souls of my father & my mo- ' ther, & of all my anceftors & my succeflors, & for the health of the ' soul of Helias de Marnile, have given, & granted, & by this my ' present charter confirmed, into pure & perpetual alms, to God & the ' church of S. Michael of Staunford, & to the nuns there ferving God, ' forty shillings of silver to the fame nuns yearly to be paid out of the rent ' of my mill of Wakefield, at the feaft of S. Michael; which I have affign- ' ed unto the kitchen of the forefaid nuns, so that the forefaid nuns ' obferve the anniverfary of the forefaid Elias yearly on the eve of S. ' George. And this conceffion & donation I William earl Warenn, & ' my heirs, will warant, to the forewritten nuns, againft all men for ever. ' And that this my conceffion & donation may be eftablifhed & re- ' main for ever unfhaken, I have corroborated my present charter with ' the putting to of my seal. Witneffes John de Bafyngburne, Ralph ' de Normanville, Ralph de Wauncy, Ralph of the white monaftery, ' Alexander dean of Staunford, the said vicar of S. Andrews, &c.' After the death of this earl, K. Henry the third seifed the town of Stanford with the appurtenances into his own hands, & held them so feifed till the 38. year of his reign.

XVIII. ' ᵇ In the 25. of H. 3. lord Hamon Peche departed this life, 25. H. 3. ' in his way to the holy land; whereupon his body was brought ' over to the priory of Barnewell near Cambridge (of the foundation of ' the Peverels his anceftors) & buried in the chapel of our lady there; ' leaving iffue, by Eve his wife (by birth an alien) Gilbert his son & ' heir, & five others, viz. Hamon, Hugh, Robert, Thomas, & Wil- ' liam.' This Hamon the father (over & above his fhare in two parts of the church of Corbi, given by him jointly with dame Matildis de Diva & dame Afcelina de Waterville, the other proprietors of the said two parts, to the nuns of S. Michael by Stanford) gave likewife, as appears by the following charter (but when I find not) the ninth part of the said church of Corbi, to the said nuns of S. Michael. ' ᶜ To ' all the children of holy mother church unto whom the present writ- ' ing shall come, Hamo Pech, son of Gilbert Pech, health in the au- ' thor

a Ex regiftri prioratus S. Michaelis penes Galf. Minihul gen. 1657. fol. 16. a. citato in Mon. Ang. tomi II. p. 882. b.
  b Baron. Vol. I. p. 677. a.

c Univerfis S. matris ecclefie filiis ad quos prefens fcriptum pervenerit, Hamo Pech, filius Gileberti Pech, falutem in auctore falutis. Noverit univerfitas veftra, me, pio

'thor of health.   Your univerſality ſhall underſtand, that I, in a pious
'intuition of charity, for the health of my ſoul, & of my anceſtors
'& ſucceſſors, have given & granted & by this my preſent charter
'confirmed, to God & the church of S. Michael of Stanford, & to the
'holy nuns there ſerving God, the ninth part of the church of Corebi,
'which belongs to me, by right of patronage, with all the appurte-
'nances, the which Hugh biſhop of Lincoln of pious memory, by
'authority of the Lateran council, conferred on Hugh the clerc of
'Oſberneby, into pure & perpetual alms to have & to hold for ever.
'And that this my donation, & conceſſion, & confirmation, may re-
'main firm & ſtable to future times, in witneſs hereof, to the pre-
'ſent writing I have put to my ſeal.   Witneſſes, William of the
'Spinny, Richard de Craudene, Yllary the capellan, Robert de Diva,
'Geoffry ſon of Brune, John Ramar, Alan le Paum. . . . Vincent,
'& many others.'   The ſeal repreſents a knight mounted on his courſer, a drawn ſword in his right hand, & his ſhield on his left arm, riding in full career, at all points armed a cap en pied; under his horſes
feet a dragon couchant, & about the verge SIGILLUM HAMONIS
PEHCHE.   Being now ſpeaking of this Hamo Pech or Pehche, I cannot omit obſerving that he alſo gave the canons of Fineſhade abby
(ſix miles from Stanford) a yearly rent of two ſhillings at Corbi aforeſaid.   His charter touching the ſaid donation having been never printed, may be acceptable to the curious, & runs thus.   ' [a] Know preſent
'& future people, that I Hamund Peche, have given, granted, & by
'this my preſent charter confirmed to God & the church of the bleſ-
'ſed Mary of Finneſheued, & to the canons there ſerving God, two
'ſhillings of rent yearly to be received at Eaſter, in the town of Corbi,
'of Geoffry (ſon of Hugh) my man & of his ſucceſſors, into pure &
'perpetual alms, for the health of my ſoul, & the ſoul of the lady
'Matilda de Lanvaley my ſiſter, & of all my anceſtors.   And I Ha-
'mund Peche & my heirs will warant & defend the foreſaid two ſhil-
'lings of yearly rent, to God & the church of the bleſſed Mary of
'Finneſheued, & to the canons there ſerving God, againſt all men for
                                                        'ever.

pio karitatis intuitu, pro ſalute anime mee, & anteceſſorum & ſucceſſorum meorum, dediſſe, & conceſſiſſe, & hac preſenti karta mea confirmaſſe, Deo & eccleſie S. Michaelis de Stanford, & ſanctimonialibus ibidem Deo ſervientibus, nonam partem eccleſie de Corebi, que ad me pertinet jure patronatus, cum omnibus pertinentiis, quam pie memorie Hugo Linc. epiſcopus, auctoritate Latronenſis concilii, Hugoni clerico de Oſbernbi contulit; in puram & perpetuam eleemoſinam tenendam & habendam imperpetuum.   Et ut hec mea donatio, & conceſſio, & confirmatio, futuris temporibus firma & ſtabilis permaneat, in hujus rci teſtimonium preſenti ſcripto ſigillum meum appoſui.   Hiis teſtibus, Willielmo de Spineto, Richardo de Craudene, Yllario capellano, Roberto de Diva, Galfrido filio Brune, Johanne Ramario, Alano le Paum . . . Vincentio, & multis aliis.

a Sciant preſentes & futuri, quod ego Hamundus Peche, dedi, conceſſi, & hac preſenti carta mea confirmavi, Deo & eccleſie B. Marie de Finneſheued, & canonicis ibidem Deo ſervientibus, duos ſolidatos redditus annuatim percipiendos ad paſcha, in villa de Corbi, de Galfrido, filio Hugonis, homine meo, & de ſucceſſoribus ſuis, in puram & perpetuam eleemoſinam, pro ſalute anime mee, & anime Domine Matilde de Lanvaley ſororis mee, & omnium anteceſſorum meorum. Et ego Hamundus Peche, & heredes mei, warantizabimus & defendemus predictos duos ſolidos annui redditus, Deo & eccleſie B. Marie de Finneſheued,

' ever. And that this my donation may remain ratified, unfhaken,
' & ftable, I have corroborated it with the munition of my feal.
' Witneffes, Sir Vitalis Engain, Sir Robert Hautein, Sir William de
' S. George, Sir William de Freiney, Richard de Glemham, Richard
' de Crouden, William Brito, John de Croudene, & others.' The originals of both thefe laft inftruments, from whence I tranfcribed them,
are now in the earl of Exeters hands.

XIX. About this time (but the very year when I find not) dame
Alice de Walterville (relict of Afcelin de Waterville, lady of Maxra,
fifter of William lord Aubeni the third who built Newftede, & aunt
of William lord Aubeni the fourth his fon) gave to the nuns of S. Michael without Stanford, a virgate of land with a toft & a croft at Afh-
ley, Affele, or Aiffele, in Northamptonfhire, then in tenure of William
the clerc there, the which virgate, &c. was given her in franc marriage
by William lord Aubeni her brother; the profits whereof, being 8 s. a
year, fhe ordered to be expended equally at her own anniverfary & the
anniverfary of Cecily her daughter; for which purpofe fhe gave them
this charter. ' ᵃ To all the faithful of Chrift, unto whom the prefent
' writing fhall come, I Alice de Walterville, lady of Maxra, fend greet-
' ing in the Lord. Your univerfality fhall underftand, that I, with
' the counfel & affent of my nephew lord William de Aubeni, have
' given, granted, & by this my prefent charter confirmed, to God &
' the church of S. Michael of Stanford, & to the nuns there ferving
' God, one virgate of land in the town of Affele, with all its appur-
' tenances, which, lord William de Aubeni my brother gave me in
' franc marriage; that, to wit, which William the clerc held in the
' fame town; into pure & perpetual alms, free & quit from all fer-
' vice & exaction fecular; for my foul, & for the foul of Cecily my
' daughter, & for the fouls of my anceftors & fucceffors: one moiety
' of the benefit of this land to be received on the day of my anni-
' verfary, & the other moiety on the day of the anniverfary of my
' daughter Cecily. And that this donation & conceffion may remain
' ratified & for ever valid, I have eftablifhed it with the muniment of
                                                              ' my

fheued, & canonicis ibidem Deo fervientibus, contra omnes homines imperpetuum.
Et ut hec mea donatio rata, & inconcuffa,
& ftabilis permaneat, figilli mei munitione
corroboravi. Hiis teftibus, Domino Vitali
Engain, D. Roberto Hautein, D. Willielmo
de S. Georgio, D. Willielmo de Freiney,
Richardo de Glemham, Richardo de Crouden, Willielmo Britone, Johanne de Croudene, & aliis.

a Univerfis Chrifti fidelibus ad quos prefens fcriptum pervenerit, ego Alicia de Walterville, domina de Maxra, falutem in Domino. Noverit univerfitas veftra, me, confilio & affenfu D. nepotis mei Willielmi de
Aubeni, dediffe, conceffiffe, & hac prefenti
carta mea confirmaffe, Deo & ecclefie S.

Michaelis de Stanford, & monialibus ibidem
Deo fervientibus, unam virgatam terre in
villa de Affele cum omnibus pertinentiis fuis,
quam D. Willielmus de Aubeni frater meus,
mihi dedit in libero maritagio; illam, fcilicet,
quam Willielmus clericus tenuit in eadem
villa; in puram & perpetuam eleemofynam,
liberam & quietam ab omni fervicio & exactione feculari; pro anima mea, & pro anima Cecilie filie mee, & pro animabus antecefforum & fucefforum meorum; ad per-
cipiendam medietatem beneficii terre illius in
die anniverfarii mei, & aliam medietatem in
die anniverfarii filie mee Cecilie. Et ut hec
donatio & conceffio rata & in pofterum va-
lida permaneat, ego eam figilli mei munimine corroboravi. Hiis teftibus, Matheo,
                                        Nicholao,

2

' my feal. Witneffes, Mathew, Nicholas, Walter, Hugh & Andrew,
' the capellans; Gilbert Scrop, Robert de Tichenis, Robert fon of
' Stephen, Richard the clerc, & many others.'   The feal as here reprefented.

Sigillum Aliciæ de Watervilla

This grant of Alice de Waterville, the faid Alice, or the forefaid nuns,
got confirmed by her nephew lord William de Aubeni the fourth abovementioned, upon the furrendry or death of William the clerc of Affele, who then held that land; which confirmation runs thus.   ' ᵃ To
' all the children of holy mother church unto whom the prefent writ-
' ing fhall come, lord William de Aubeni, greeting.   Know ye, that
' I have granted, & by this my prefent charter confirmed, to God &
' the church of S. Michael of Stanford, & to the nuns there ferving
' God, one virgate of land in the town of Affele, with all its appur-
' tenances, which William the clerc held in the fame town of my
' fee; which virgate Alice de Aubeni (who was the wife of Afcelin
' de Vaterwille) gave, & granted, & by her charter confirmed to the
' forefaid nuns.   Wherefore I will that the forefaid nuns may have
' & hold the forefaid land with its appurtenances, free & quit from
' all fecular duty which belongs unto me or unto my heirs, as pure &
                                                          ' perpetual

Nicholao, Waltero, Hugone, & Andrea,
capellanis; Gilberto Scrop, Roberto de Tichenis, Roberto filio Stephani, Richardo clerico, & multis aliis.

a Univerfis S. Matris ecclefie filiis ad
quos prefens fcriptum pervenerit, Dominus
Willielmus de Aubeni, falutem. Sciatis
me conceffiffe, & hac mea prefenti carta confirmaffe, Deo & ecclefie S. Michaelis de
Stanford, & monialibus ibidem Deo fervientibus, unam virgatam terre in villa de Affele, cum omnibus pertinentiis fuis, quam
Willielmus clericus tenuit in eadem villa de
feudo meo; quam virgatam Alicia de Albe-
ni (que fuit uxor Afcelini de Vaterwilla)
predictis monialibus dedit, & conceffit, &
fua carta confirmavit. Quare volo, ut predicte moniales, predictam terram cum pertinentiis fuis, liberam & quietam ab omni
feculari officio, quod ad me vel ad heredes
meos pertinet, habeant & teneant, ficut puram & perpetuam eleemofynam, & ficut
carta

Lib. 8.   *p. 27.*

Sigillum Willielmi de Aubèni quarti.

On the Reverse.

Forsan—*Crux Sigillum;*
Signum Salutis.

' perpetual alms, & as the charter of the forenamed Alice witneſſeth
' & doth confirm to them.   Witneſſes, Robert de Braibroch, Henry
' his ſon, Ralph ſon of Symon, Hugh de Charnel, William the ca-
' pellan, Walter the capellan, Nicholas de Aubeni the clerc, maſter
' Albin, Robert of Huntendune, William de Seint . . . ler. William
' de Oueton, & many others.'   The ſeal repreſents a boat embatteled (alluding perhaps to the height & ſtrength of the hill whereon
Belvoir caſtle ſtands, which elevates itſelf above the reſt of the earth
juſt as an high boat above the ſurface of the waves) carried above the
earth, as it were in that boat, appears a ſtrong & lofty caſtel; at
the top of the caſtel a flag diſplayed, & two mens heads facing one
another at a diſtance between the battlements.   All which as near as
I could draw it from the original impreſs is here inſculped.   Moreover, for farther ſecurity of the ſaid land to the ſaid nuns, the ſaid
Alice de Walterville, or the ſaid William de Aubeni, or the ſaid nuns,
procured an inſtrument under the ſeal of John Palmer, ſon of William the clerc abovementioned, who, upon the foreſaid ſurrendry or
death of his ſaid father, held that land, confeſſing that he the ſaid
John & his ſucceſſors were for ever obliged to pay the ſaid rent of
8 s. *per annum* to the ſaid nuns; which nuns alſo, before they accepted the ſaid inſtrument of acknowledgment, took an oath of him,
that neither he, his heirs, or aſſigns, ſhould at any time alienate the
ſaid land without a ſpecial licenſe firſt had from the prioreſs & nuns
for ſo doing; & likewiſe that the ſaid rent ſhould be conſtantly paid,
or in caſe he failed in performance of that or any other part of
his oath, then the prioreſs & nuns, or their warden, might enter upon
the premiſes, & ſeiſe the fruits of the ground, till full reparation was
made for any ſuch tranſgreſſion.   But hear the man.   ' ᵃ Know pre-
' ſent & future people, that I John Palmer, ſon of William the clerc
' of Aiſſele, & my ſucceſſors, are for ever bound to pay, to God &
' the church of S. Michael without Stanford, & to the nuns there
' ſerving God, eight ſhillings of ſilver, at two terms; to wit, at Ea-
' ſter, four ſhillings, & at the feaſt of S. Michael, four ſhillings; for
' one toft in the town of Aiſſele, with a croft & a virgate of land,
' & with all the appurtenances, within the town & without, to the
' ſaid toft belonging; to wit, for that toft with the appurtenances
' which lies between the toft of Walter ſon of William, weſt; & a
' toft of John ſon of Ralph, eaſt.   And I John, the holy goſpels be-
                                                              ' being

carta prenominate Alicie teſtatur & confir-
mat illis. Hiis teſtibus, Roberto de Braibroch, Henrico filio ejus, Radulfo filio Symo-
nis, Hugone de Charnel, Willielmo capella
no, Gualtero capellano, Nicholao de Aubeni
clerico; magiſtro Albino, Roberto de Huntendune, Willielmo de Seint . . . ler. Willielmo de Oueton, & multis aliis.

a Sciant preſentes & futuri, quod ego Jo-

hannes Palmerus, filius Willielmi clerici de
Aiſſele, & ſucceſſores mei, tenemur ſolvere
imperpetuum, Deo & eccleſie S. Michaelis
extra Stanford, & monialibus ibidem Deo ſervientibus, octo ſolidos argenti, ad duos terminos; ſcilicet, pro illo toſto cum pertinentiis, quod jacet inter toſtum Walteri filii
Willielmi, verſus occidentem; & toſtum
Johannis filii Radulphi, verſus orientem.
                                            Et
8 I

' being touched, without fraud, have faithfully fworn, for me & my
' fucceffors, that I John, & my heirs, or our affigns, will not give,
' or fell, or mortgage, or alienate, the forenamed tenement, or any
' part of the fame tenement, fave by lawful licenfe of the prio-
' refs & nuns aforefaid; & moreover the rent aforenamed at the
' appointed terms will faithfully pay; & that if we fhall do other-
' wife, or againft this oath, it may be lawful for the faid nuns, or their
' warden to feife the forenamed tenement, with the fruits of the
' ground, & to hold the fame in their hand, without all contradicti-
' on & plea, 'till we fhall make them fatisfaction touching all manner
' of tranfgreffion.   In witnefs hereof, to this writing, I have put to
' my feal.   Witneffes, Sir Reiner then dean of Stanford, mafter Pa-
' gan rector of the church of S. Clement, William de Pappele the ca-
' pellan, William le Somercotes, Adam de Ufford, Geoffry de Tur-
' lebi the clerc, Hugh Porter, & others.'   The feal is gone.   By this
laft inftrument we may obferve, that *toftum* does not always fignifie
a place where an houfe hath ftood, as fome would perfuade us; but
alfo the houfe it felf then ftanding.   I fhall only add, the originals
(from whence I copied thefe three laft deeds) are now in the earl of
Exeters poffeffion.

26. H. 3.   XX. ' [a] In the 26. of H. 3. William de Albini the fourth, having
' fummons (amongft others) to attend the king into Gafcoigne, gave
' twenty marks to be freed thereof.   [b] Alfo Maud [relict of William
late earl of Warenn & lord of Stanford] ' had then the cuftody of
' the caftle of Tuniburg committed to her.   [c] The fame year Gilbert
' fon of Hamo Peche abovementioned [which Gilbert was afterwards
a benefactor to the nuns of S. Michael by Stanford [d]] ' giving fecu-
' rity for the payment of his relief (to wit, two hundred marks) &
' doing his homage, had livery of the lands of his inheritance.   [e] About
' this time Walter of S. Edmunds abbat of Burg, augmented the rent
' of the infirmary there with feven & fifty fhillings arifing out of a
27. H. 3. ' certain rent which he bought in Stanforde.   [f] In the 27. H. 3. Wil-
' liam de Albini the fourth was with K. Henry with his army in Here-
' fordfhire, at fuch time as he advanced againft Richard Marfhal earl
' of Pembroke; who was the chief of thofe that oppofed the king,

Et ego Johannes, tactis facro-fanctis, fine dolo, fideliter juravi, pro me & fucceffori-bus meis, quod ego Johannes, & heredes mei, vel affignati noftri, non dabimus, nec vendemus, nec evadiabimus, nec alienabimus prenominatum tenementum, vel aliquam partem ejufdem tenementi, nifi per rationa-bilem licentiam prioriffe & monialium pre-dictarum; & infuper firmam prenominatam ftatutis terminis fideliter reddemus; quod fi aliter, vel contra juramentum fecerimus, li-ceat dictis monialibus, vel cuftodi earum, faifiare prenominatum tenementum cum fructibus terre, & in manu fua tenere, fine omni contradictione & placito, donec eis fatisfactionem, de qualibet tranfgreffione,

fecerimus.   In hujus rei teftimonium huic fcripto figillum meum appofui.   Hiis tefti-bus, Domino Reinero tunc decano Stan-ford, magiftro Pagano rectore ecclefie S. Clementis, Willielmo de Pappele capella-no, Willielmo de Somercotes, Adamo de Ufford, Galfrido de Turlebi clerico, Hu-gone Portero, & aliis.
a Baron. Vol. I. p. 115. b.
b id. p. 77. b.
c id. p. 677. a.
d videfis Nov. 12. 1284. 12. E. 1. infra.
e Swapham p. 118. edit. a Jo. Sparke & Patricks fupplement to Gunton, p. 302.
f Bar. Vol. I. p. 115. b.

' for

'for his taking Poictovins & other ftrangers into his council, & be-
'ftowing the principal places of profit & truft upon them, to the great
'prejudice of his native fubjects (as our hiftorians do fhew.) And
'one of thofe whofe quarters were beaten up by the enemy with the
'lofs of all their baggage, when the king lay at Grofmund caftle.'
This William de Albini the fourth (but when I find not) confirmed
the foundation & endowment of the hofpital & priory of S. Mary of
Newfted by his father William de Albini the third, as alfo all other
benefactions which any other perfons had made before, or fhould after that time, grant to the faid houfe out of his fee. He likewife
gave the canons of Newfted leave to elect their own prior, & to prefent him to the patron for his acceptance; & that in the mean time
the faid canons fhould enjoy the liberties of the houfe, & have the
cuftody of the fame: for all which purpofes he thus expreffes himfelf.
' [a] To all the children of holy mother church unto whom the pre-
'fent writing fhall come, William de Albini the fourth greeting. Ye
'fhall underftand, that I, for the health of my foul, & for the health
'of the foul of the noble man lord William de Albini my father,
'& for the fouls of Margery d'Umfranville my mother, & Albreda
'my wife, & Ifabella my wife, & of my anceftors & fucceffors, have
'granted & by this my prefent charter confirmed, to God & the church
'of S. Mary of New-Place, at the bridge of Uffintun, & to my ca-
'nons there ferving God, who are of the foundation of the faid no-
'ble man William my father, all that new-place at the bridge of Uf-
'fintun, as it is enclofed with a wall & a ditch, with the appurte-
'nances; as alfo all the donation, lands, men, poffeffions, rents, &
'liberties, with all the appurtenances & eafements, within the town
'& without, by the faid lord William my father, & by who or whom-
'foever the donors on the forefaid canons & their fucceffors collated,
'& hereafter of my fee to be conferred; to hold & have to the fore-
'faid canons & their fucceffors, freely, folely, & peaceably, wholly
'& quietly for ever, as the charters of their donors witnefs, & with
'all the profit which from thence, at any time, fhall poffibly accrue.
'Moreover, in an intuition of divine piety, I give & grant, of
'my grace & leave, for me & for Albreda my wife & Ifabella my
'wife, & for our anceftors & fucceffors, this liberty to the fore-
'named church of the bleffed Mary of Newftede, that when a
'prior fhall be wanting for the forenamed church, the canons of
'the fame place may have the free election; &, when they fhall have
'elected, that the elect may be prefented to the patron of the houfe;
'and in the mean while, 'till they can have a prior, that the
'houfe it felf, & all the rents & poffeffions of the fame houfe, with
'all the appurtenances & liberties may be in the hand & cuftody
'of the canons of the fame place; & all the rents & difburfements,

[a] Ex regiftro de Belvoir penes nob. ducem de Rutland, citato in Monaft. Ang. Vol. II. p. 446. b.

'&

' & all the goods of the forenamed houſe, freely, peaceably, &
' honorably expended by the canons themſelves, for the uſe of the
' poor & the profit of the church aforeſaid. And I William & my
' heirs, the foreſaid grant, & the confirmation of the foreſaid my
' charter, with all the bovementioned particulars & appurtenances,
' to the foreſaid canons & their ſucceſſors, as my free, pure, & per-
' petual alms, againſt all mortals, will for ever warant, maintain, &
' defend. In ſecurity whereof to this writing I have put to my ſeal.
' Witneſſes, &c.' I ſhould have before obſerved (when I firſt ſpake
of the foundation of this houſe) that there are now no remains either of the church or priory, ſave that ſome traces of the foundations & building may juſt be diſcerned above ground, & that is all.
The wall which ſurrounded the ſame is likewiſe thrown down, & the
ditch (if part of it be not taken into the cut of the new river) filled up. The bare mention of ſuch things however ſhew the danger
& inſecurity of the times both in the laſt & preſent reign. William
de Albini the fourths having no male iſſue, was the reaſon I ſuppoſe
why he gave the canons leave to elect their own prior. All the canons I yet read of were only the prior & confrater; it being a queſtion whether the deacon & clerc appointed to aſſiſt them in divine
ſervice by the 2ᵈ. charter of William de Albini the third were any
more than minor canons, if ſo much; & conſequently whether they
had any power of election. The priors being now appointed to be
elected by the canons ſhews therefore that the number of thoſe canons was increaſed, by other benefactions, the particulars whereof are
not now to be recovered. And indeed of all the loſſes that the antiquities of Stanford ever had, that of the book of doomsday, once
kept in this flouriſhing monaſtery of Newſtede, was certainly the
greateſt. It was a record that took in, non only an account of the
monaſtery of Newſteds own eſtate & endowment, but alſo as it ſhould
ſeem an account of all the particular eſtates & poſſeſſions of the neighbourhood in and about Stanford. When I come to ſpeak of the
foundation of Mr. Browns hoſpital, I ſhall exemplifie a copy (as I took
it from the original under the ſeal of the priory of Newſted) of an
extract from this celebrated book of Doomsday kept there, relating
to the title of the very ground whereon that hoſpital is built. An
inſtance ſufficient to ſhew the value of that curious book, now I
doubt utterly loſt; as many other were at the ſuppreſſion. But to
return. I ſhall only add, the ſite of this hoſpital & priory is at preſent part of the poſſeſſions of Charles Bertie Eſq; juſt by which ſtands
yet a water-mill, called after the name of the monaſtery, Newſted
mill.

29. H. 3.   XXI. ' ᵃ In the 29. H. 3. Thomas de Arches claimed, againſt the
' prioreſs of Staunford, the advouſon of the church of Sumordeby.

a Ex placitis jurat. & aſſiſ. apud Linc. 29. H. 3. rot. 12.

2   ' Gilbert

' Gilbert his anceſtor was ſeiſed [of it] who had [for his ſon] Alan,
' who had [for his ſon] Thomas the [then] claimant.   ª In the 30.   30. H. 3.
' of H. 3. Maud [reliĉt of William late earl of Warenn & lord of
Stanford] ' received livery by the king himſelf of the marſhals rod,
' ſhe being the eldeſt, who, by inheritance ought to enjoy that great
' office, by deſcent from Walter Mareſhal, ſometime earl of Pembroke.
' Whereupon the lord treaſurer & barons of the exchequer, had
' command to cauſe her to have all rights thereto belonging, & to
' admit of ſuch a deputy to ſit in the exchequer for her, as ſhe ſhould
' aſſign.   This Maud had alſo the cuſtody of Strigoil caſtle, 'till her
' death.   ᵇ In 1246. the archbyſhop of Canterbury procured a graunt   Anno
' from the pope, to recover for one year the firſt fruites of all charges   1246.
' that chaunced to be voyd within the province, duryng the tearm
' of ſeaven years then next ; till the ſumme of ten thouſand marcs
' were levied, towards the diſcharge of the ſaid archbyſhops debts.
' ᶜ Theſe parts muſt be now alſo concern'd in the ſcrutiny made by
' the biſhop of Lincoln, who, at the inſtigation of the black & grey
' friers, commanded his archdeacons & rural deans to make ſtriĉt in-
' quiſition of the lives & manners of all nobility & commonalty within
' their precinĉts ; which was thought ſuch a grievance, that, on com-
' plaint, the king ſtopped the proceedings.

   XXII. ' ᵈ In 1247. 31. H. 3. John earl of Warenn, *being then but*   1247.
' young, married Alice, ſiſter by the mothers ſide to K. Henry the   31. H. 3.
' third (for ſhe was daughter to Hugh le Brun earl of March, ſecond
' huſband to the kings mother.)   ᵉ The ſame year William de Va-
' lence [the kings brother by the mothers ſide, being ſon of her &
Hugh le Brun abovementioned] ' obtained a grant of all the lands of
' Robert de Pundelarche, excepting the dowry of Conſtance his wife,
' until the king ſhould aſſign him lands equivalent thereto.'   This Robert de Pont de l'Arche I believe either lived, or had lands, or both,
at this time in Stanford.   For I afterwards meet with this name
pretty often in theſe collecĉtions.   ' ᶠ The ſame year the archbyſhope
' of Caunterbury ſuſpended the prieſts of hys province, bycauſe they
' would not conſente (according to the graunt which he had pur-
' chaſed of the pope) that he ſhould have the firſt frutes, for one
' yeare, of every benefice that chanced to be vacant within the ſame
' province.   ᵍ The ſame year the coyne was ſo ſore clipped, that it
' was thought good to change the ſame, & make it baſer.   Where-
' upon ſtampes were graven, of a new inciſion or cut, & ſent to
' Bury, Canterbury, Develen, & other places [probably among the
reſt to Stanford, where the abbat of Burg had the privilege of a
mint] ' forbidding to uſe any other ſtampe than was uſed in the ex-
' change or minte at London, & all the old ſtampes were called in.

a Baron. Vol. I. p. 77. b.   e id. p. 774. b.
b Holingſ. p. 115. a.   f Holingſ. p. 717. b.
c Biſhop Kennets Par. Antiq. p. 238.   g Stow. p. 284.
d Baron. Vol. 1. p. 77. b.

   8 K   ' ª I have

' ᵃ I have not feen any thing farther memorable of William de Albini
' the fourth than that he had two wives, Albreda Bifeth, & Ifabel.
' Moreover that he died before the 32. of H. 3. & was buried before
' the high altar in the priory of Belvoir, & his heart at Croxton priory
' in Leicefterfhire. Laftly, that he left iffue Ifabel his daughter &
' heir, wife to Robert de Rofs (an eminent baron in Yorkfhire.) Here
' being a period to the male line of that principal branch of this no-

32. H. 3. ' ble family. ᵇ In the 32. of H. 3. died Maud, relict of William late
' earl of Warenn [& lord of Stanford.] ᶜ The fame year John earl
' of Warenn was one of the great earls who met in the parliament
' held at London, on the octaves of the purification, in which par-
' liament the king was told of his many high exactions.

35. H. 3.   XXIII. ' ᵈ About the beginning of the 35. yeare of H. 3. the bifhops
' underftanding that the archbifhop of Canterbury was about to pur-
' chafe of the pope a graunt to gather mony thro' his whole province
' of the cleargie & people for finodes & procuracies, to prevent him,
' made a collection, every one thro' hys owne dioces, of two pence
' of every marke which any beneficed man might difpende, which
' mony they ment to employ about charges in the popes court, for the
' ftay of the archbifhops fute. ᵉ The fame year Robert Grofthead bi-
' fhop of Lincoln, attended by the archdeacon of Oxford, went over
' to the pope to anfwer the appeal of the knights templars & other
' religious, who would have been exempted from his jurifdiction, & by
' their mony bought fo much of the popes favor, that the poor bifhop
' came home with difappointment. But how much the religion &
' good difcipline of thefe parts were fecured by the vigilance of this
' exemplary diocefan, appears from the declaration that he himfelf
' now made before the pope & cardinals, wherein he told them, that
' upon his firft confecration he confidered himfelf to be a bifhop &
' paftor of fouls, & therefore thought it neceffary (left the blood of
' his flock fhould in the laft judgment be required at his hands) with
' all diligence, as the fcripture advifes & commands, to vifit the fheep
' committed to him. For which reafon he began a circuit in his dio-
' cefe thro' each refpective archdeaconry, & in each of them thro' the
' feveral rural deaneries, caufing the clergy of every deanery (in or-
' der to meet at a certain time & place) to give notice to the people
' to appear on the fame day with their children to be confirmed, &
' to hear the word of God, & to confefs. In which affemblies he
' himfelf did often preach to the clergy, & a frier predicant, or minor,
' to the laity. After which four of the friers heard confeffion, &
' enjoin'd penance. And, when the children were confirm'd on that
' & the following day, then he & his clergy applied themfelves to the

1251. ' correction & reformation of abufes. ᶠ In 1251. the bifhops affembling

a Bar. Vol. I. p. 115. b.   d Hol. p. 723, 724.
b id. p. 77. b.   e Bp. Kennets paroch. antiq. p. 243.
c id. ib.   f Holing. p. 725. a.

' at

' at Dunftable, took advice how to prevent the archbifhop that he
' fhould not vifit, & concluded to fend their procurator to Rome to
' ftay the licenfe. Their procurator did fo much in the matter, that
' he might not vifit any parifh church, except the parfon required
' him. And whereas he had libertie to vifite conventual churches, yet
' might he not receive for procuracies above four markes. For this
' moderation to be had, the bifhops gave unto the pope fix thoufand
' markes. [a] The fame yeare the byfhope of Lyncolne vifited the
' religious houfes within his dioces, to underftand what rule was kept
' amongft them, ufing the matter fomewhat ftraytely (as they thought)
' for he entred into the chambers of the monkes & fearched their
' beds. And comming into the houfes of the nunnes, hee went fo
' neare as to caufe theyr breeftes to be tryed, that he might under-
' ftand of their chaft livings. [b] The faid bifhop would have enforced
' all beneficed men, within his diocefe, to bee priefts. But they
' purchafed a licenfe from Rome to remaine at the univerfities for
' certaine yeares, without taking that order upon them. [c] But the
' faid bifhop got authoritie of the pope to inftitute vicarages in churches
' impropriate to religious men, where no vicars were; & where fuch
' were as feemed too flenderly provided of fufficient maintenance,
' to augment the fame as he thought expedient. Which authoritie
' he ufed more largely than ftood with the pleafure of religious per-
' fons, bycaufe he fhewed great favor to the vicars.

 XXIV. ' [d] In the 37. of H. 3. there chaunced a great occafion of <small>37. H. 3.</small>
' ftrife betwixt the archbifhop of Canterbury & the bifhop of Win-
' chefter. For where[as] maifter Euftace de Linne, official to the
' faid archbifhop, had firft excommunicate, & after, for his contuma-
' cie, caufed to be attached a prieft, which, by authoritie of the elect
' of Winchefter as diocefane there, was entred into poffeffion of an
' hofpital in Southwark as prior, without the officials confent, who
' pretended a tytle as patrone (in his maifters name) the fayd elect of
' Winchefter caufed a ryotous fort of perfons, after the manner of warre,
' to feeke revenge, whiche, after many outrages done, came to Lam-
' beth, & there by violence tooke the fayd Euftace out of his owne
' houfe, & ledde him to Farneham, where he was kept as prifoner.
' The archbifhop, hereof advertifed, pronounced all thofe accurfed,
' whiche were authors or favorers of fuch a rafhe & prefumptuous
' deed, & farther commaunded all the bifhops in his province, by
' vertue of their obedience, to denounce the fame in their churches
' every Sunday & holyday. The bifhop of Winchefter on the other
' part, fent commaundement to the deane of Southwarke, to denounce
' his curfe to be void.' The reafon why I take notice of this affair
will be feen prefently; but I muft firft obferve, that ' [e] religion &

a Holingf. ubi fupra.   d id. p. 730, 731.
b id. p. 728. b.   e Bp. Kennets par. ant. p. 248.
c id. p. 729. a.

                  ' eccle-

Nov. 8. ' ecclefiaftical difcipline now fuffer'd much in thefe parts by the death
1253. ' of the excellent diocefan Robert Grofthead, who departed this life
Jan.14. ' at Lincoln, Nov. 8. 1253. [a] In the octaves of the Epiphany the
125¾. ' forefaid archbifhop of Canterbury & the elect of Winton were made
' friends, & thofe affoyled that were excommunicate, in which num-
' ber William de Valence & John de Warenn [both of them afterwards lords of Stanford] ' were thought to be contained, as thofe that
' fhould be prefent in ufing the force againft the official, as before ye
' have heard.

Anno   XXV. ' [b] In 1254. John earl of Warenn [afterwards lord of Stan-
1254.   ford] ' anfwered one hundred & twenty pounds for fixty knights fees,
' for which he now gave aid to the king, upon making his eldeft
' fon knight.' At this time flourifhed Henry de Hanna. ' Henry de
' Hanna, faith Pits [c], a Norwich man, & lover of a folitary life,
' embraced the order of mount Carmel (as Leland affirms) in a mo-
' naftery among the woods at Brunham in Norfolk, where he made
' his public profeffion, & fpent holily many days of his life in divine
' contemplation, preaching many learned difcourfes, moftly to his
' brethren, but fometimes to the people. This Henry de Hanna, faith
' Bale [d], was firft chofe provincial of his order in 1245. [it fhould
be 1254. the two laft figures being tranfpofed by the printer] ' &
' governed feventeen years. In 1254. faith Pits [e], he was elected pro-
' vincial mafter of his order in England, being the fecond perfon who
' ever enjoyed that poft; in difcharging of which office he vigoroufly
' employed himfelf for eighteen whole years together, with great ho-
' nor to himfelf & great advantage to his order.' Now this Henry
' de Hanna was the perfon, who, as I take it, firft began the fchools
at Stanford, fuppreffed afterwards by K. Edward the third; for which
reafon thus much is here faid of him: the reft of his life follows in
its proper place. ' [f] About the end of May, the fame year, the queen
' (notwithftanding fhe had lately received the kings commands to the
' contrary) with her two fons prince Edward & Edmund, & her uncle
' the archbifhop of Canterbury, took fhipping at Portfmouth, & arriv-
' ed at Bourdeaux the laft of the fame month; & not long after their
' landing, prince Edward was fent in great ftate to Alphonfo king of
' Caftile, where having married the faid kings fifter at Burgos, he was
' by that king honorably fent back to his father, together with his
' bride. Upon his arrival K. Henry fettled upon him & the princefs
' his wife, all Gafcoigny, Ireland, Wales, with the city & towns of
' Briftol, Stanford, & Grantham.' Herewith in fome fort agrees the
following report. ' [g] The jurats fay, that one William de Warenna,
' late earl of Surrey, held the town of Stanford, by gift of the lord

a Holing. p. 730.
b Baron. Vol. I. p. 77. b.
c in vita.
d cent. 10. p. 59.
e ubi fupra.

f Tyrrel, p. 967. Speed. p. 630. a.
g Ex placitis juris & affifæ coram Hugone
Bigod juftitiario Angliæ in diverfis comitatibus, anno regni R. H. filii R. Johannis
... rot. 22. dorfo.

' king

' the king that now is, for term of his life. Alſo, that after the
' death of the foreſaid earl, the lord the king ſeiſed the foreſaid town
' with the appurtenances into his own hand, who afterwards gave that
' town to lord Edward his ſon.' So that the fact was thus. K. Henry
gave his ſon prince Edward the manor of Stanford, & perhaps the
other places & provinces abovementioned ; & prince Edward afterwards ſettled them, or ſome of them, with ſome other places, upon his
ſpouſe, the princeſs Alianora, in dower. This appears by another
record. ' ᵃ Stanford was granted to Alianora, king [Alfonſo's] ſiſter,
' by Edward the eldeſt ſon of K. Henry the third, for her dowry, with
' the caſtles of Tikhul, Peek, & Graham.

XXVI. ' ᵇ In the 39. H. 3. John earl Warenn [afterwards lord 39. H 3.
of Stanford] ' was one of thoſe who adher'd to the king, in oppreſ-
' ſing the people, as our hiſtorians do report.' About this time, but
the certain year I find not, ' Prince Edward, ſaith Sir Richard Baker ᶜ,
' (as well as his father king Henry) being in want, was driven to
' mortgage his [wifes] towns of Stanford, Graham, & many other
' things to William de Valence a Poictovin ; whereby, adds he, ap-
' pears the diſorder of the time, when the prince was in want &
' ſtrangers had ſuch plenty.' Now it is no wonder at all that prince
Edward acted thus. For William de Valence, tho' a Poictovin by
the fathers ſide, was the kings own brother by the mothers ſide ;
& then only lent his nephew prince Edward ſome part of the
great wealth which his brother K. Henry had before given him.
' ᵈ In the 40 of H. 3. John earl Warenn [afterwards lord of Stan- 40. H. 3.
ford] ' was, with other of the chiefeſt peers in Weſtminſter-hall,
' when the archbiſhop of Canterbury, & divers other biſhops, pro-
' nounced ſolemn excommunication there, with candles lighted, againſt
' all that ſhould violate the great charter & charter of the foreſt.
' ᵈ The ſame year he had the *tertium denarium* of the county of
' Surrey yielded him by the kings precept, then ſent to the barons of
' the exchequer. ᵉ In 1256. K. Henry the 3. granted to the burgeſ- Anno
' ſes of Stanford divers exemptions & liberties, viz. I. to be free from 1256
' payment of tolls. II. to receive toll. III. their goods not to be
' arreſted, &c. ᶠ The counteſſe of Warenn, Aveſia, or Arteſia as ſome
' bookes have, ſiſter to the king by his mother, departed this life in
' hir flouriſhing youth, to the greate grief of hir brother, but ſpeci-
' ally of hir husbande John earle of Warenne, that loved hir entirely.
' ʰ In the time of Henry de Hanna abovementioned, provincial of the
' Carmes in England (to wit, in 1256.) the grey friers came firſt to
' Norwich.

a Conceſſ. Alianore ſorori regis, per Ed-
wardum primogenitum R. H. 3. pro dote,
cum caſtris de Tikhul, Peek, & Graham.
Ex rot. Vaſcon. 38. H. 3. partis 2 m. 2.
  b Baron. Vol. I. p. 77. b.
  c chron. Lond. 1684. p. 85. b.
  d Baron. ubi ſupra.

e Out of a MS. in my hands, entitled,
' an abſtract of ſeveral charters, concerning
' the borough of Stanford, dated 11. June.
' 1677. article the firſt.
  f Holingſ. p. 742. b.
  g Hujus tempore [ſcil. H. de Hanna] Nor-
divicum intrabant Carmelite, anno dom.
1256.

' Norwich.   After which were erected the Carmelite monasteries of
' Lynne, Lyncoln, Berwic, Newcastle, Sandwic, Northampton, Glou-
' cester, Stanford, & Wynton.

Anno
1257.
42. H. 3.

XXVII. ' ᵃ In 1257. 42. H. 3. the king kept his Christmass at
' London, where came to him several princes of Germany, who de-
' clared, that Richard earl of Cornwal was chosen king of Almaine.
' ᵇ Now when the said Richard earl of Cornwal, brother of K.
' Henry, was chosen emperor, Henry de Hanna abovementioned, with
' the assistance of one Nicholas Noel, begged & obtained of that earl
' the house he had at Stocwel in Oxfordshire, & turned it into a mo-
' nastery of Carmes.'   The priory of S. Leonard by Stanford being
(as I have elsewhere shewn) a cell to the cathedral priory of Durham;
if the monks of S. Leonards acted as their patrons of Durham, which
is very probable; then they were now absolved of the popes interdict which they had incurr'd, by resisting his exactors.   For I find ' ᶜ the
' monkes of Durham, the whiche onely, with the chanons of Gisborne,
' resisted the wicked proceedings of the popes exactors, & stood there-
' fore interdicted a long time, at length, after many altercations, were
' now assoyled.   Oh, sayeth Matthew Paris, if, in that theyr tribu-
' lation, they myght have had fellowes, & in theyr constant doyngs
' aydors, howe happely had the churche of Englande triumphed over
' her tormentors & oppressors!'   This is a noble speech of this honest
monks, & well agrees with the character we read of him in Speed,
' ᵈ that he was one who durst write any thing he thought.'   In Feb.
1257. John de Caleto abbat of Burg & the convent of that place de-
mised to the prioress & nuns of S. Michael without Stanford, all that
their mill at Stanford to hold of them for ever at the yearly rent of
ten marcs; & in case of non-payment the abbat & monks to distrein.
Their demise is thus expressed.   ' ᵉ To all the faithful of Christ who
' shall see or hear the present writing, John by the grace of God
' abbat of the Burg of S. Peter, & the convent of the same place, greet-
' ing in the Lord.   Your universality shall understand that we, with
' unanimous assent, have let to fee firm, & granted, to the prioress
' of S. Michael without Staunford & to the nuns of the same place,
' all our mill with its appurtenances, which we have in Staunford,
' to have & to hold, of us & our successors, to the said prioress &
' nuns & their successors, well, & in peace, freely for ever; by pay-
' ing therefore yearly to us & our successors ten marcs of silver, at
' the two terms of the year (to wit, at the feast of S. Michael five
' marcs, & at Easter five marcs) for all service, exaction, & all man-

1256. Post hec erecta sunt cenobia Lynnæ,
Lyncolniæ, Berwici, in Novo-Castro, San-
devico, Northamptona, Glouceftria, Stanfordia, & Wyntonia.   This passage & divers other notes of the like sort, were copied out of John Bales Anglorum Heliades,
a MS. in the Lord Harleys library for my
use, by the Revᵈ. & learned Mr. Thomas
Baker, B. D.

a Tyrrel, p. 981.
b Bale, p. 307.
c Holingshed. p. 747. a.
d p. 618. a.
e Ex codicis MS. in Bib. Cott. sub imagine Vesp. E. X XII. fol. 26.

' ner

' ner of other fecular demand.   And we & our fucceffors, to the faid
' priorefs & nuns & their fucceffors, the faid mill with its appurte-
' nances, againft all people, by the forefaid fervice, will for ever
' warant, acquit, & defend.   And if it fhall happen in any cafe,
' that the faid priorefs & nuns, or the fucceffors of the fame, in
' payment of the ten marcs aforefaid, at the terms aforefaid, fhall be
' wanting; then it fhall be lawful for the faid abbat & convent & their
' fucceffors, the faid priorefs & nuns, or their fucceffors, at their plea-
' fure, to diftrein, through all their lands & all their goods, in the
' county of Northampton & elfewhere, until for the forefaid ten
' marcs, to the faid abbat & convent, or their fucceffors, it fhall be
' fully fatisfied.   In witnefs whereof, to the prefent writing, made in-
' to the manner of a cyrograph, alternate feals are put, fo that to the
' counter part, remaining in the hands of the priorefs & nuns, our feals
' are put; & to the connter part, remaining with us, the feal of the ladies
' the priorefs & nuns is appendent.   Given in the year of grace, 1257. in
' the month of February.   ª When the rebellious barons came with fuch
' a power to the parliament at Oxford, as that they compelled the
' king to fubmit to thofe provifions which they made there; John
' earl Warenn ᵇ was one of the lords elected on the kings part, to
' fettle matters with other lords elected by the barons, for a mutual
' agreement.   ᶜ But the faid earl Warenn & the kings half bro-
' ther, the earl of Pembroke [William de Valence] refufed the oath
' to obferve the ordinances of that [mad] parliament.   ᵈ The fame
' year the faid John earl Warenn had fummons, with the reft of
' the great men of England, to attend the king at Chefter, thence
' to march againft Leweline prince of Wales, for reftraining his ho-
' ftile incurfions.   ᵉ July 5. 1258. 42. H. 3. the faid John was one   July 5.
' of thofe nobles who were affigned to guard & conduct the kings   1258.
' brothers [William de Valence, &c.] to the fea fide; the kings faid   42. H. 3.
' brothers having obtained his fafe conduct, of this date, for that pur-
' pofe.'   They were conftreined thus to leave the kingdom by Mountfort & the rebellious barons.   ' ᶠ In the 43. of H. 3. Hugh de Naffing-   43. H. 3.
' ton, burgefs of Staunford, mortgaged five acres of arable land lying
' in the north field of Stanford, & abutting on the land of the monks
' of S. Leonard north & above the land of the caftel;' but to whom
I find not.

XXVIII. ' ᵍ William de Fortibus the 3ᵈ. E. of Albemarle, who mar-
' ried for his fecond wife Ifabell daughter to Baldwin E. of Den; by
' her had iffue three fons, John, Thomas, & William; & two daugh-
' ters, Avice & Aveline.   This E. died in June 1260. in France, where-   June
' upon his corps was brought over into England, & interr'd in one   1260.
' of the monafteries of his anceftors foundation.   To the care & tui-

a Baron. Vol I. p. 77, 78.   e Tyrrel, p. 986.
b Annales monaft. de Burton, p. 412.   f B. H.
c Holing. p. 751. b.   g Bar. Vol. I. p. 64, 65.
d Baron. Vol. I. p. 78. a.

' tion

' tion of his widow Ifabel, were committed two of her fons before men-
' tioned, viz. Thomas & William (John being then dead, as it feems)
' but neither of them lived long after : Thomas dying firft, was buried
' in the church of the fryers preachers [or black fryers] at Stanford ;
' & William dying in Oxford, at the fryers preachers there.' This is
the firft time I find any exprefs mention of the black friers at Stanford, tho' I have before intimated [a] that I believe it was founded by
William de Fortibus the 2[d]. E. of Albemarle, grandfather of this Thomas that was now buried here. The black friers college ftood without
Stanford on the fouth-eaft part, adjoyning to the tenter meadows.
It took up a good deal of ground, & had fine gardens from the houfe
to the river fide. Part, if not all, of the church, was ftanding about
1600. when Mr. Speeds draught of Stanford was taken, whereby it
appears that the fteeple then likewife ftanding, was a ftrong quadrangular tower. But there is now nothing at all left of it. There
is a fair houfe upon the premifes, whereof the prefent proprietor is
Savil Cuft, efq ;. When Mr. Stevens fays [b], ' Speed mentions two
' houfes of Dominicans at Stanford ;' it muft be noted that Speed mentions two houfes of black monks, but none of black friers, there.
Now there is a great deal of difference between a monk & a
frier. A monk being one whofe monaftery is endowed with lands
for fupport of the religious, who belong to it ; but a frier one whofe
monaftery has very rarely any more land or eftate, than the bare fite
of the houfe & gardens ; the daily alms of the neighbourhood being
all their maintenance ; whereof if any thing remained at night, it
was diftributed among the poor, who attended for that purpofe at
the gate : Providence being always trufted by thefe latter, to provide for the morrow. ' [c] By a decree of the council of Lions it was
' from thenceforth eftablifhed that there fhould be but four orders of
' mendicants, or begging friers ; to wit, Auguftines, Carmelites, Mi-
' nors, & Dominicans.' Now all thefe four orders had each of them
their refpective monaftery at Stanford. ' [d] There be three forts of
' poverty among thefe mendicants. One is, to have nothing either
' in common or propriety ; & this is the Francifcans poverty : which
' is the greateft of all. Another is, to have nothing in propriety,
' yet fome things in common, as books, cloaths, food : this the Do-
' minicans profefs. The third & leaft is, to have fome things both
' in common & in propriety, but thofe only fuch as neceffity requires
' for food & raiment : And this is the poverty of the Carmelites &
' Auguftins. But to proceed.. One of thofe two houfes of Domi-
' nicans at Stanford, Speed, faith Mr. Stevens [e], calls the monaftery of
' S. Michael, without any mention of the founder : & gives the va-

[a] Anno 5. H. 3. fupra.
[b] 2[d]. addit. Vol. to the Monaft. Ang. p. 208. a.
[c] Brit. Ant. & nova. Vol. II. p. 214.
[d] Rofs's view of all religions. Lond. 1653. p. 329.
[e] ut fupra.

' luation

' luation of it, to wit, 72 l. 18 s. 10 d. ob. The other he names of
' S. Mary & S. Nicholas, & makes two; Talbois E. of Anjou & Wil-
' liam de Romara the founders. The valuation, 65 l. 10 s. 9 d.' Now
here is a whole cluster of mistakes, some whereof belong to Mr.
Stephens, some to Speed, & some to both. As I. Mr. Stevens says,
' Mr. Speed mentions two houses of Dominicans at Stanford.' Whereas he mentions no Dominicans, but two houses of black monks:
which, as I have noted, were very different. II. The name of the
monastery of S. Michael shews what black monks Speed meant: to
wit, Benedictins. S. Michaels is generally called a nunnery; the religious there being mostly nuns; but they had a warden, under the
prioress, who was a Benedictin, or black monk: & so Mr. Speed might
easily by mistake set down black monks, for black nuns. III. Mr.
Speed is again mistaken when he makes two houses, one valued at
72 l. 18 s. 10 d. ob. & another valued at 65 l. 19 s. 9 d. both these
valuations belonging to one & the same house, to wit, S. Michaels.
That house being in all valued at 72 l. 18 s. 10 d. ob. but when the
out-rents & other charges were paid, but at 65 l. 19 s. 9 d. IV. Mr.
Speed does not say, as Mr. Stephens affirms, that *Talbois* E. of Anjou & W. de Romara ever founded any house of religion at Stanford. But (in the same page, just above where he speaks of Stanford)
that they, & Lucy countess of Chester & Lincoln, founded a monastery
at Spalding, dedicated to S. Mary & S. Nicholas. V. Mr. Speed says
indeed one of the houses of black monks at Stanford was dedicated
also to S. Mary & S. Nicholas. It is like, instead of black monks, he
should have said, the black friers, church there was dedicated to those
saints. And so far, 'till we see proof to the contrary, we may perhaps venture to indulge him. For tho' I thought S. Mary, had been
the beloved of all orders, I find ' S. Nicholas, as bishop Kennet tells
' us [a], is the special favorite of the Dominicans.' VI. Mr. Stephens forgets himself surely, if he think that any house of Dominicans here
should have lands belonging to it, worth 65 l. 19 s. 9 d. or 72 l. 18 s.
10 d. ob. *per annum.* The bare scite could not be worth so much, &
other lands, as far as I can find, they had none.

XXIX. ' [b] Contention continuing between the schollers of Cam- Feb.
' bridge & the townsmen, many of the schollers agreed among them- 126$\frac{4}{7}$.
' selves to depart from thence, to Northampton, & there raise a new 46. H. 3.
' universitie. Whereunto the King gave his consent, & granted
' them passport. [c] The truth of this, the tradition of the town,
' & the places to this day called the college, & the college lane,
' avouch. [d] John earl Warenn [lord of Stanford] was now one of
' those, who, upon the agreement betwixt the K. & the rebellious
' barons, did, on the kings part, set his seal for confirmation of the

a par. antiq. p. 608.　　　　　　　c Moretons Northampt. p. 24.
b Stow, p. 292. where see the reason of　d Bar. Vol. I. p. 78. a.
this contention.

　　　　　　　　　　　　　' accord

47. H. 3.　' accord then made.'　In the 47. H. 3.　' ᵃ The said John E. Warenn
1263.　' had the castle of Pavenesel committed to his custody.'　In 1263.
The rebellious barons ' ᵇ elected for their chiefe captaynes, Simon de
' Mountfort E. of Leicester, Gilbert de Clare E. of Gloucester, Robert
' Ferrers E. of Derby, & John E. Warenne.'　[But the said John earl Warenn, lord of Stanford, stayed not long among them.] ' ᶜ For the K. being
' at Oxforde, there came unto him John E. Warenne, & many others.
' The Kings sonne lord Edward had procured them thus to revolte,
' promising to every one of them in reward by his charter, fiftie pound
' landes, to ayde the K. his father & him agaynst the barons.　ᵈ The
' K. now finding his party much stronger, prince Edward surprised the
' castle of Windsor, turning out the garrison put in by the barons,
' & the morning following the K. himself withdrew from Westmin-
' ster & went to the same place ; & was immediately followed by
' John E. Warenne, & such of the barons who had before secretly
' deserted the E. of Leicesters party.

Feb. 3.　　XXX. In Feb 3. 126¾. 48. H. 3. ' ᵉ The said John E. Warenn joyn-
126¾.　' ed with divers other great lords, in that submission to the award
48. H. 3. ' which Lewes K. of France, was to make betwixt the K. & his ba-
' rons, concerning those ordinances called the provisions of Oxford.
' ᶠ Friar John Stanford, died about this time at Lynne ; all that I can
' find of him is, that he was the eight minister provincial of the En-
1264.　' glish Franciscans.　ᵍ By reason of variance which chaunced this yere
' betwixt the schollers of Oxford & the townsmen, a greate number
' of the scholers withdrew, [another author ʰ says, were banished]
' to Northampton, & there studied.'　It may be remembred, the Cambridge men, as is above related, had the kings license to settle
there.　And their being now pretty well fixed at Northampton, might
be one reason perhaps, why the Oxford men went to that, before any
other place, upon this uproar at home.　But there they stayed not.
For the rebellious barons now assembling at Northampton against the
K. these Oxford scholars ' ⁱ raysed a banner to fight in defence of the
' towne agaynst him, & did more hurte to the assailants than any
' other bande, whereupon the K. threatned to hang them all.　And
' so had he done indeede, if by persuasion of his counsail he had not
' altered his purpose ; doubting to procure the hatred of their friendes.
' For there were amongst them many young gentlemen of good houses
' & noble parentage.　ᵏ Whereupon he pardoned them all.'　About
this time the abbat of Burgs bailif demanded an old rent of 3 s. a
year, for a land-gavel, out of 24. acres of land in Stanford field be-

a Bar. Vol. I. p. 78. a.
b Hol. p. 762. b.
c id. p. 764. b.
d Tyrrel, p. 1015.
e Bar. Vol. I. p. 78. a.　See that award,
dated as above in Mr. Tyrrels appendix to

his 2ᵈ. Vol. p. 30.
f Antiq. of the Eng. Francis. p. 76.
g Hol. p. 766. b.
h Tyrrel, p. 1021.
i Hol. ut supra.
k Tyrrel, ut supra.

longing to the priorefs & nuns of S. Michael; whereupon the priorefs
& fifterhood reprefenting to Robert Sutton lord abbat of Burg & the
convent there, that the faid rent had been remitted by abbat Martin
his predeceffor, & never paid, as they afferted, fince the time of that
prelate, the abbat & convent now gave them a new charter whereby
they were ever after releafed from the faid payment; which charter is
thus worded. ' [a] To all the faithful of Chrift, &c. Robert, by per-
' miffion of God, abbat of the church of S. Peter of Burg, & the con-
' vent of the fame place, greeting. Your univerfality fhall underftand
' that we, at the inftance of the beloved Amabilia priorefs of S. Mi-
' chael of Stanford, & of the holy nuns there ferving God, have re-
' leafed & quit claimed for ever, the yearly rent of 24. acres of land in
' the field of Stanford; to wit, 3 s. a year, being rent which our bailifs
' fometime demanded, in the name of Landgavel, of which they have
' been free, as they fay, from the time of Martin abbat of Burg of
' good memory. Which that it may obtain a ftrength of perpetual
' firmnefs, for memory of them who are to come, we have corrobo-
' rated this prefent writing with the appofition of our feals. Wit-
' neffes our chapter. The feal [of the abbat] exhibits a prelate in his
' habit with the coronal tonfure, in his left hand a paftoral ftaff, in
' his right a key put to his breaft.' The feal of the chapter being not
defcribed, I fuppofe is wanting. The K. & his barons continuing yet
in variance, their adherents plundered & fined the country almoft where-
ever they prevailed, & their feveral interefts led them. Thus in our
neighbourhood, the abbat of Burg being reprefented as inclining rather
to the barons fide, the bailifs of John E. Warenn [lord of Stanford]
as Walter Whytlefeye tells us, ' [b] levied forty marcs of his lands in
' Stanford to redeem the Neffe of Burg. [c] The K. kept his Eafter
' at Nottinghom, where receiving news, that the E. of Leicefter, with
' a great multitude of Londoners, had, on the paffion week, befieg-
' ed E. Warenne in the caftle of Rochefter, he refolved to raife the
' fiege & relieve it. [d] To this end, he came in Eafter week with his
' army to Stanforde. Thither the abbat of Burg fent great prefents
' to the Kings of England, & Almaine; lord Edward, & divers others.
' Who all received them kindly, fave lord Edward, who, by procure-
' ment of the lord Warine of Bafingburne utterly refufed to accept
' them; but the abbat compounded matters with lord Warine for
' fifty marcs. Moreover the abbat gave the K. a palfry worth 14.
' marcs.—[But all this fignified little.] ' The E. of Warennes bailifs
' carried away all his corn from his manors of Tinewelle & Thurle-
' by, to the value of ten marcs. Alfo 15 horfes were taken out of
' his carriages at Walmesforde, worth 24. marcs. Likewife out of his
' long carriage, as he was going towards the king, five horfes more, worth

a Ex autographo defcripfit ediditque cl.   b p. 135.
Madox, inter formularia fua Angl. form.   c Tyrrel, p. 1021.
676. p. 371.   d Whitlefey, ut fupra.

' 30 marcs.   Befides all this, the abbat gave the king, while he lay at
' Stanforde, another horfe, worth 24 marcs.   Alfo to Roger Ley-
' borne a horfe, worth 14 marcs.   Alfo to lord Berengarius le Moine
' another horfe, worth ten marcs.   Alfo in other prefents to the K.
' there made, & to the K of Almain the kings brother, & to lord
' Edward the kings eldeft fon, 114 l. 5 s. 9 d. Laftly, in maintaining divers
' horfe there for the fervice of lord Edward la Zouche, & others,
' feventy nine fhillings & ten pence.   ᵃ At Rochefter, E. Simon
' had won the bridge, & the firft gate.   ᵇ But the captain thereof John
' E. Warenne [lord of Stanford] did manfully refift the enemies, till
' the K. with the power of the marches & the north partes, ᶜ march-
' ing almoft night & day, arrived in 5. days at Rochefter.   The E. of
' Leicefter hearing of his approach, durft not ftay to give him battel,
' but went back to London, leaving only a few foldiers behind, whom
' thofe of the garrifon, in a fally they made, quickly deftroyed.'   ᵈ On

May 12.   May 12. 1264. 48. H. 3. was fought the battle of Lewes, wherein the
1264.   K. himfelf & prince Edward his fon were taken prifoners.   ' ᵉ John
48. H. 3.   ' E. Warenn [lord of Stanford] was one of the chief captains in
' the van of the kings army.   ᶠ But the faid E. with divers others,
' having with them three hundred armed men, ftraightways fled unto
' the caftle of Pemfey.   ᵍ The barons having obtained fuch a victory
' as the full fway of the whole realm was in their power, Gilbert E.
' of Clare thereupon procured a grant, under the great feal, of all the
' lands & poffeffions, lying in England of John E. Warenn (who had
' faithfully ftuck to the K. in that time of trial) excepting the caftles of
' Rigate & Lewes, to hold during the kings pleafure (*id eft*, fo long as
' he fhould be in their power.)   ʰ The faid E. Warenn finding no fecurity
' here then fled into France.   ⁱ What was of much advantage to the
' abbat & abby of Burg, all the time of this war, was, that the abbat
' caufed always as much bread, beer, & other provifions to be got ready,
' as he could poffibly procure.   So that all comers, whether of the kings,
' or barons party, finding the abby gates conftantly open, were plen-
' tifully refrefhed.   For which reafon the manors belonging to Burg
' abby, were, in many places, faved from being fet on fire & other in-
' juries.   However, fuch numbers reforting thither, it frequently hap-
' pened, that when the convent after matins, according to cuftom
' at 9 a clock, hoped to find their breakfaft ready in the hall, there
' were not fufficient neceffaries to be had for it either in the abby,
' or neighbourhood, 'till they were brought from Stanforde, & thofe
' too were fometimes taken away as they were bringing.

1265.   XXXI. In 1265. 49. H. 3. ' ᵏ Somewhat before Thurfday in Whit-
46. H. 3. ' fun-week, E. Warenn, with William de Valence E. of Pembroke

a Stow, p. 296.   f Holing. p. 769. b.
b Hol. p. 767. b.   g Baronage Vol. I. p. 213. b.
c Tyrrel, as above.   h id. p. 78. a.
d Stow, p. 297.   i Whitlefey, p. 137.
e Tyrrel, p. 1023.   k Hol. p. 772. a.

3

' the

' kings half brother & other (whiche, as ye have heard, fledde from
' the battle at Lewes) returned into the realme, landing firſt in South-
' Wales with a power of croſſe bowes & other men of warre. ᵃ Thence
' the E. ſent the prior of Monmouth unto Hereford (where Mount-
' fort E. of Leiceſter had the K. & prince in cuſtody) to move for
' reſtitution of his lands, in regard he had done nothing which might
' deſerve the forfeiture of them, as the prior then alledged. To whom
' the anſwer then returned was, that if he would come himſelf in
' perſon thither, & ſubmit to a tryal in the kings court, he ſhould
' have ſafe conduct ſo to do: which deeming not ſafe, he confede-
' rated with Clare, E. of Glouceſter (then fallen off from Mountfort)
' & other barons, who ſtood for the royal intereſt. And upon the
' eſcape of prince Edward from Hereford, out of the hands of Mount-
' fort, joyned him & his forces at Ludlow. ᵇ To prevent the ill
' conſequences of the princes eſcape, Mountfort made the king
' write letters to all his tenants, that, on the Thurſday in Whit-
' ſun-week, his ſon Edward had made his eſcape from the per-
' ſons that were his guards, & went off (as he certainly believ-
' ed) to John de Warenn [lord of Stanford] & the barons
' marchers, his rebels & diſturbers of the peace; he therefore com-
' manded them to come with horſe & arms to go with him againſt
' them. Dated at Hereford, May 30. ᶜ Afterwards Mountfort cauſed   May 30.
' other letters to be written to Simon, his own 2ᵈ. ſon, in the kings
' name, that his ſon Edward, with John de Warenn, & other rebels
' adhering to them, had ſeized ſeveral towns & caſtles, & raiſed new
' war in the kingdom, & therefore enjoined him to give him his ut-
' moſt aſſiſtance to ſuppreſs them. Dated June 28. at Monmouth.' June 28.
The ſaid John E. Warenn, [lord of Stanford] ' ᵈ had benefit of that
' glorious victory at Eveſham, on the 4. of Auguſt following; in which, Aug. 4.
' Mountfort, E. of Leiceſter, being ſlain, the K. was freed from that
' reſtraint, wherein, after the battel of Lewes, he had been ſo long
' kept by the power of thoſe rebellious barons. ᵉ After this battel
' the abbat of Burg paid the ſaid E. of Warenn an hundred pounds to
' get his manors of Caſtre, Tinewel & Thurleby, delivered out of the
' ſaid earls hands.

    XXXII. Feb. 1. 126⁴⁄₅. 50. H. 3. ' ᶠ the K. revoked his grant of the Feb. 1.
' new univerſity at Northampton, by reaſon of great diſcommoditie 126⁴⁄₅.
' thereby enſuing to the univerſitie of Oxford, whereof all the biſhops 50. H. 3.
' of the realme had given him advertiſement by their writing.' This
might be the pretended, but I believe the true, reaſon why the K. diſſolved the univerſity of Northampton was, to be revenged of the Oxford ſcholars, who, as you have heard, ſettled there, & did his men
ſo much miſchief at the ſiege of that place. I will not ſay, the K.

a Bar. Vol. I. p. 78. a.   d Baron. ut ſupra.
b Tyrrel, p. 1046, 1047.   e E chron. W. Whit. p. 138.
c Tyrrel, p. 1050.   f Stow, p. 297, 298.

likewife acted thus to encourage the Carmes fchools at Stanford; but
the white friers college there being of his own foundation, gives me
room ro put a *quære* upon it.   A word or two then of the white friers,
& of the univerfity now, if not before, begun at Stanford.   The white
friers college at Stanford was a royal foundation, as is evident by the
arms of France & England quartered, & infculped in the ftone work
of the gate, yet remaining.   It was fituate in the eaft fuburb, &, by
the out walls, which are yet ftanding, appears to have been near a mile
in circumference.   If we may believe tradition it was a very magnificent ftructure, &, in particular, famous for its beautiful church &
fteeple, which laft, they fay, was very like that fine fpire, now belonging to All Saints church in the mercat place at Stanford.   As for the
houfe, hiftory, as well as tradition, agrees, it was always made ufe of
for reception of our Englifh princes, who were lodged, & entertained
here, in their progreffes, & other journeys, into, or out of, the north.
Mr. Burton fays, ' [a] St. Marys [or the white friers college] ' was found-
' ed by K. Edw. the 3.'   But his account of the founder muft be falfe,
both by the abovementioned Henry de Hanna's being buried there in
1299. & other matters which will hereafter offer.   However, as the
arms of France & England are now to be feen quartered upon the
gate; And, as Edward the 3[d]. was the firft of all our Englifh princes,
who bore them, after that manner, quartered in his efcutcheon; probably he was a benefactor to this houfe, or at leaft that gate was erected in, or after his time; but it muft be Hen. the 3. who founded this
college of white friers at Stanford.   Since Bale having told us, ' that
' the Carmes came firft into Norfolk in 1256.' fpeaking yet of
Henry de Hanna, goes on with a ' *poft hæc,* &c. after thefe things
' were founded the monafteries of Stanford, &c.'   For K. Hen. the 3.
reigned above 16 years after the Carmelites came into Norfolk, fo
that the white friers at Stanford being certainly a royal foundation,
it is almoft as certain that it was founded by him.   For 16 years
(the remainder of his reign) is a fufficient allowance for this expreffion *poft hæc,* &c.   Efpecially when both the paffages under confideration (to wit, the coming of the Carmes into Norfolk, & the
founding their monaftery at Stanford) were done while one & the
fame man was provincial.   And indeed, 'till I fee proof to the contrary, I fhall be of opinion, that the white friers at Stanford was
50. H. 3. founded at leaft this 50. H. 3. if not fometime before the diffolution
of the new univerfity at Northampton.   And if I fhould add, that
fome both Oxford & Cambridge men when they left Northampton,
removed to Stanford, it feems not at all improbable.   I have been
the more large in endeavouring to fix the time when the monaftery
of the white friers was founded at Stanford, becaufe there are other
grounds, befides thofe already mentioned, to believe this univerfity

a Cat. Monaft. in Speeds chron. p. 1078. a.

was

was now begun, under the happy patronage of this celebrated Henry de Hanna, the 2^d provincial general of the Carmes in England : fome of which grounds I fhall here offer to the readers confideration.   The faid Henry de Hanna, as Bale tells us, ' ᵃ had his conftant refidence ' at this place.'   Now it is like he made choice of this houfe to live in, before any other of the abovementioned monafteries, founded by his own folicitation & encouragement, for thefe reafons.   I. Becaufe it ftood in a moft pleafant fituation.   Bale & Pits often call the white friers college at Stanford, *coenobium amoeniffimum*: a moft delightful monaftery.   II. Becaufe it was the kings own foundation.   Probably therefore he was warden of this houfe, as well as provincial of the order.   And III. Another & better reafon might be the great number of learned men, wherewith this fociety abounded.   There being in his time William Lidlington, John Burley, & feveral other of the beft fcholars in the kingdom members of that fraternity.   As were foon after, if not then, John Repingale, Walter Hefton, Ralf de Spalding, John Upton, & Nicholas Kenton : of all whom I fhall here-after give a particular account.   Whether thefe learned men at the white friers, were put in by the founder, or by the provincial Henry de Hanna, gathered from other monafteries of that order for the fake of their learning to this pleafant, royal, & magnificent college which he had pitched on for the place of his own refidence, I will not determine ; fince it is as probable that they joyned with & affifted one another in this agreeable work.   And certain it is, this convent was as happy in the many famous men it produced, as their fchools & houfe it felf were remarkable for the ftrictnefs of their difcipline.   Their fchool at Stanford, a large collegiate fabric in St. Georges parifh, was pulled down by the E. of Exeter in 1722. or thereabouts, & two or three new houfes built in the place where it ftood.   The great lord Burghleys mother (as appears by his own diary, a MS. in Mr. Strypes hands) was, among other things, joyntred in the white friers fchool, a place exprefly fo called, in Stanford.   Farther, as the white friers houfe at Stanford was of the kings own foundation, we may believe their fchools there were the beft furnifhed both with fcholars & ma-fters of any other belonging to that fraternity in England.   Likewife that the king fhould allow of any academical exercifes being held, or lectures read, in a monaftery of his own foundation (tho' fome-what perhaps to the prejudice of the two eftablifhed univerfities above-mentioned) will not appear furprifing, fince it is certain, this very K. Henry the 3. (as has been fhewn) confented to the Cambridge mens removing to Northampton in 126⅓. & as certain that the Carmes, who had among them many excellent tutors, were a long time permitted to read publickly, not only here, but wherever they had a monaftery. Moreover, that the Carmes fhould undertake fuch a difcipline to en-

---

a In coenobio Stanfordienfi vita functus eft.   Heliades, MS. Harley.

large the reputation of their, as yet but new order, & fo promote the increafe of it, muft be allowed a very wife courfe. There is a fhort account of this monaftery of Carmelites, or white friers at Stanford, in Mr. Stevens's 2. Vol. of addit. to the Monafticon, p. 184. which account he tells us he had of Mr. Forfter. It is there faid, ' it was ' founded by the black princes confort, who was alfo interr'd there.' Now that fhe did not found it is a miftake I have here fufficiently anfwered; neither was fhe buried there, but as you will hereafter find, at the grey friers in Stanford.

1266.
50. H 3.
XXXIII. In 1266. 50. H. 3. ' [a] Robert Ferrers E. of Derby & others [beginning a new commotion] ' beeing in Chefterfield in Derbyfhire, ' there came againft them John E. Warenn [lord of Stanford] & many ' knights; who, on Whitfun-even, met without the towne on hunt-' ing 22. knights al under one fpeare, al which they chafed & put ' to flight. Whereof when Sir John Danvil, being in the towne, ' had underftanding, hee with a fmall companie rode out, pierced ' thro' the hoft, wounding many, & efcaped. E. Warenn entring ' the towne flew manie a man, & tooke the E. Ferrers, who was ' ficke of the goute, & had that daie beene letten bloud: him they

51. H. 3.
' fent to the tower of London. [b] In the 51. of H. 3. the towns of ' Gretham, Cotefmore, Overton, Stretton, Thiftleton, Tigh, Wichen-' don, Exton, Whitwel, Alftanthorp, Burghley [on the hill] & Exwell; ' as alfo Ochcham cherchefoche, Hameldune cherchefoche, & Ridling-' ton cherchefoche, all part of the county of Nottingham, were made ' part of the county of Rutland.' Now S. Peters parifh in Stanford being part of Hameldune cherchefoche, it is, I think, evident that the faid parifh of S. Peter in Stanford, was, till then, part of the county of Nottingham. ' [c] About candlemas the K. fummoned all that owed ' him military fervice, to meet at Burg, within eight days after that ' feftival, with horfe & arms, to march againft [the rebels John Dan-' vile, & his party, abovementioned] ' who had taken & ftill held the ' ifle of Ely. All but the E. of Gloucefter [who was a fecret encou-' rager of them] ' obeyed. Whereupon John E. Warenn [lord of Stan-' ford] ' & William de Valence, were fent to admonifh him; yet they ' could not prevail with him any farther, than to obtain certain letters, ' fealed with his own feal, by which he engaged never to bear arms ' againft the K. or his fon prince Edward, unlefs in his own defence.'

52. H. 3.
June 24.
1268.
53. H. 3.
In the 52. H. 3. ' Emma, relict of Alan de Bradecroft fold two acres of ' arable land to Nicholas de Efton a burgefs of Stanford. B. H. [d] By the ' folemn preaching of Ottobon the popes legate at Northampton, prince ' Edward & his brother Edmund, as alfo Henry eldeft fon to the K. of ' the Romans, with the earls of Gloucefter, Warenn & Pembroke, & ' about cxx. other knights (being touched with the great loffes in the ' Holy Land) all received the crofs at the hands of the legate; & by

a Stow, p. 300.
b Britan. ant. & nova. in Rutl. p. 511.
c Tyrrel, p. 1070.
d Tyrrel, p. 1078.

2

' the

' the like devotion a great multitude of inferior quality likewise un-
' dertook the Crufado, in the cities & boroughs, by the preaching
' of the Francifcans. ᵃ Sir William Meynille, lord of Yevely, now
' gave to the knights of the hofpital of St. John of Jerufalem, many
' lands & tenements there.' With thefe lands & tenements, & others
given by divers other benefactors, was founded & endowed the pre-
ceptory of Yevely. Among which other benefactors, ' ᵇ Margery de
' Carun gave them many lands & tenements in Clifton, Hardwike,
' Stanford, & Langford. ᶜ One Emma de Oundel likewife gave the
' templars many good things in Stanford:' but when I find not.

XXXIV. ' ᵈ All things relating to the public being now quiet, fome
' of the great men fell at private difcord with one another; amongft
' which, it is reported, that upon a difference betwixt John earl Wa-
' renn [lord of Stanford] & Henry de Lacy afterwards E. of Lincoln,
' touching a certain pafture, they raifed what forces they could, pur-
' pofing to fight for it. Whereupon the K. (having notice thereof)
' commanded that his judges fhould, either judicially, or by an ami-
' cable agreement, compofe the fame: who, accordingly, upon enqui-
' ry by the oaths of the country, adjudged the right thereof to Lacy.'
In 1269. John earl Warenne [lord of Stanford] directed his letters 1269.
of protection in behalf of the nuns of S. Michael by Stanford, to
his bailifs there, as follows. ' ᵉ John earl of Warenne, to our bailifs
' of Eftaunford, greeting. For as much as we defire the advancement
' & profit of our dear nuns of S. Michael without Eftaunford, you
' we command, that when they fhall have need of you, that you to them
' be aiding & counfeling; &, if any do them ill, or damage, or grie-
' vance, that you him caufe to make amends to the utmoft of your power,
' according to right; & them, & their goods maintain undifturbed in
' their right, according to your power: And this fail not to do. In
' witnefs of which thing, for them we have caufed to be made our
' letters patents; given at Grettewell, without S. Nicholas, in the year
' of the incarnation of our Lord, 1269. Farewel.' The original is
now in the earl of Exeters hands. The feal (fo much of it as remains)
reprefents his fcutcheon, cheque, or & azure, on the one fide; & on the
other, the earl himfelf mounted on horfeback. His fhield (contrary to
cuftom) on his right arm, with his bearings repeated upon it. His body
without armour in a veft, or long robe, reaching down to his feet,
tyed at the wafte with a girdle. His horfe, inftead of mail, armed all
over with checque. The circumfcription broke off.

a Ex Mon. Ang. tomi 2. p. 546.
b id. p. 547. a.
c Ex codicis MS. in Bib. Cotton. fub imagine Tiberii E. IX. fol. 133. b.
d Bar. Vol. I. p. 78. a. b.
e Johan Comtte de Warenne, a nos baillifs de Eftaunford, faluz. Pur co ke nos voloms le vauncement & le profit nos. cheres no..ains de fein Michell de hors Eftaunford, [de] vous maundoms ke kaunt ils anerointt mefter de vous, ke vous lur fciez eidaunt & confcillant. Et fin ùl lur face mal, ne damage, ne greuaunce, ke vous le facez amender a voftre poer folom draiture, & eus & lur bens mainteignez enfemente en draiture a voftre poer, & co ne leffez mie. En tefmoign de que chofe lur avoms fet fare noftre lettres patentes. Donees a Grettewell de hors Nichole; l'an del' incarnacion noft. feign. mil. deus cenz. feiffaunte & nouime. Saluz.

1270.   XXXV. ' ᵃ In the beginning of ſummer 1270. 54. H. 3. the peace
54. H. 3. ' had like to have been interrupted by another fooliſh quarrel which
' then fell out between the ſaid John E. Warenn [lord of Stanford]
' & another nobleman, & might have proved of dangerous conſequence,
' if it had not been ſtopped in time. And it happened thus. There
' had been (it ſeems) a long ſuit depending between the ſaid John
' E. Warenn, & Alan lord Zouche [ᵇ of Aſhby,] concerning a cer-
' tain manor; which coming to a trial before the kings juſtices in
' Weſtminſter-hall, there happened to paſs very reproachful & unſeem-
' ly language betwixt the E. & the ſaid baron, which, at laſt, came
' to blows, inſomuch that the E. & his followers being privately
' armed, ſet upon lord Zouche & his eldeſt ſon in open court,
' & wounded them both , but the father mortally ᶜ, whereof he
' afterwards died. ᵈ As ſoon as the E. had done this raſh & wicked
' action, he, with his attendants, being too ſtrong to be apprehended,
' preſently took boats, &, paſſing over the water, fled to his caſtle of
' Rigate in Surrey. The K. & prince Edward his ſon, being highly
' provoked at this inſolence, & reſolving not to let it paſs unpuniſh-
' ed, ſent to the E. & ſummoned him to appear at court, & abide
' the law of the kingdom: but the E. fearing the impriſonment of
' himſelf & his adherents, raſhly refuſed to ſubmit. Whereupon
' prince Edward, with ſome forces, was ſent down, to bring him to
' obedience. But as ſoon as the prince arrived before the caſtle, the
' E. conſidered better of the bad conſequences of this matter; &,
' being perſuaded by the E. of Glouceſter, & lord Henry, ſon to the
' K. of the Romans ᵉ, met the prince on foot, &, with great humili-
' ty, imploring mercy ᶠ, yielded himſelf priſoner ᵍ; & afterwards made
' his peace with the K. promiſing ſatisfaction to the perſons injured.
' Which promiſe was not meerly verbal. For it appeareth, that he
54. H. 3. ' did, by a ſpecial inſtrument, dated at Creyndone in the 54. H. 3.
' oblige himſelf to come to prince Edward in the kings court, & ſtand
' to the judgment thereof, for that offence lately by him committed
' againſt Sir Alan la Zouch, & Sir Roger his ſon at Weſtminſter; &
' to perform in every point unto the K. & all others, whatſoever his
' peers ſhould deem fit, in reference to them, & likewiſe to them-
' ſelves; as alſo, whatſoever the kings juſtices ſhould judge requiſite
' to be done by him, in reference to themſelves; & not to depart
' the court till he ſhould both do & receive what was rightful & juſt,
' according to the laws & cuſtoms of this realme. And this he did
' thereby undertake to do, on penalty of forfeiting all his poſſeſſions
' in England unto the K. & his heirs; & of incurring the ſentence of
' excommunication by all or any the archbiſhops, biſhops, & prelates

a Tyrrel, p. 1087.   e Bar. Vol. I. p. 78. b.
b Bar. Vol. I. p. 689. b.   f Tyrrel, ut ſupra.
c Annal de Winton; p. 313.   g Bar. ut ſupra.
d Tyrrel, p. 1088.

' of

' of the land, as the K. fhould make choice of, to pronounce the fame
' againft him; & when, & wherefoever he fhould pleafe.   ᵃ The faid Jun. ult.
' E. Warenn [lord of Stanford] was by the prince brought up to the
' court the laft of June, where he underwent the judgment of the
' law, & was fined five thoufand pounds to the K. & two thoufand
' to lord Zouche & his fon, for the wounds & injuries they had re-
' ceived.   Another writer fays ᵇ, that he made his peace with the K.
' for 1200 marcs.   And another ᶜ, that a fine of 10000 marks was laid
' upon him, for that mifdemeanor.   Which afterwards, by the favor
' of the K. was not only reduced to eight thoufand four hundred
' marks, but an acceptance of the fame by two hundred marks *per*
' *annum* 'till it fhould be paid.   ᵈ But it was alfo farther enjoined the
' faid E. that he, with fifty of his followers, who had been all con-
' cerned in this fray, fhould walk from the new temple to Weftmin-
' fter-hall on foot, & fhould there take an oath before the kings ju-
' ftices, that they had not acted what they did out of any prepenfe
' malice, but only out of fudden heat & paffion.'   Inftead whereof, I
fuppofe, ' ᵉ the faid E. Warenn, on the Sunday after the feaft of S.
' Peter *ad vincula* [now called Lammas-day] at Winchefter, by the
' oaths of five & twenty knights there made, profeffed that he did
' not, out of premeditated malice, or contempt of the K. perpetrate the
' faid wicked deed.   ᶠ And fo this threatning tempeft was happily
' blown over.   But I muft here obferve, that lord Zouche, who was
' pretty well in years, fell into a fever by reafon of his wounds, &
' died thereof in a few days following to the great grief of all his
' friends.   Sir William Dugdale ᵍ places this fray in 1268. & Speed
' ʰ in 1269. & falfly fuppofes lord Zouche to have been chief juftice
' of England.   But, as appears by Wikes's chronicle, & the annals of
' Waverley, it fell out this very year, not long before prince Edwards
' voyage to the Holy Land.

    XXXVI. In 1271. 55. H. 3. ' ⁱ Prince Edw. had gained fo great a re-   1271.
' putation in the Holy Land, that the chief commanders of the Sara- 55. H. 3.
' cens began to fear his fuccefs, & therefore refolved, if they could,
' to difpatch him; for which end the admiral of Joppa fent privately
' to him as if he would become a chriftian, but the meffenger (un-
' known to the prince) was one of thofe affaffins bred up on pur-
' pofe to difpatch whatfoever chriftian prince was judged to be an in-
' veterate enemy to their fuperftition, on a belief that they merited
' paradife for fo doing.   So this fellow going two or three times with
' letters from his mafter to prince Edward, his fervants began to have
' lefs fufpicion of him.   However before they admitted him, they
' fearched his girdle & other places for weapons as the cuftom then

a Tyrrel, ut fupra.   f Tyrrel, ut fupra.
b Annal. de Winton, ut fupra.   g Bar. Vol. I. p. 78. b.
c Bar. ut fupra.   h Speed, p. 641. a
d Tyrrel, ut fupra.   i Tyrrel, p. 1093. Vol. II.
e Annal. Winton, ut fupra.

                                           ' was;

' was; but not fo thoroughly as they fhould : for once having deli.
' vered his letters to the prince, who was then bare headed, fitting
' near a window, with only a loofe coat about him, becaufe it was
' very hot: the prince called this fellow again to ask him fome far-
' ther queftion, who, bowing, as if in refpect, pulled out a poifon-
' ed dagger on the fudden from under his girdle, & was juft going to
' ftab the prince into the belly, but he, feeing the blow warded it off
' with his arm, & there received a dangerous wound. Yet as the
' villain was about to redouble the ftroke, the prince had no other
' way to fave himfelf, but by lifting up his foot, & ftriking him fuch
' a blow on the breaft, that he beat him down backward; then leap-
' ing up, ran in to him, & wrefted the dagger out of his hand with
' that violence, that he gave himfelf a flight hurt in the forehead, but
' however he quickly difpatched him.   Whereupon his fervants came
' running in, & one of them in a great rage & fright, took up a
' ftool & ftroke the dead mans head with that force, that he beat out
' his brains : For which the prince feverely reproved him.   So foon
' as this fad news was difperfed, all places were filled with lamentati-
' ons.   But notwithftanding all the remedies the chirurgeons could ap-
' ply, the wound in a few days began to gangreen, infomuch that
' all defpair'd of his life, except one Englifh chirurgeon, who would
' undertake to cure him, provided he might be left entirely to his
' management, & that the princefs his lady (who was then in the room)
' might be removed & not permitted to come to him, till he was paft
' danger; which being done (tho' not without great grief & reluctan-
' cy on her part) the chirurgeon prefently began to cut off the gan-
' grened flefh to the quick, which put the prince to great torment,
' but then, by application of proper remedies, the wound was fo
' well healed in 15 days time, that he was able to mount on horfe-
' back.'   The manner of the princes recovery is otherwife told by
other authors.   Particularly Speed, who fays, ' ᵃ the lady Eleanor
' gave now fo rare an example of conjugal affection, as her immor-
' tal memory doth juftly impart glory to that whole fex.   For when
' no medicine could extract the poyfon, fhe did it with her tongue,
' licking daily (while her husband flept) ᵇ *his ranckling wounds, where-*
' *by they perfectly clofed, & yet her felf received no harme; fo fove-*
' *reigne a medicine is a wives tongue, annoynted with the vertue of*
' *lovely affection.'*   Of the fame opinion is Sir Richard Baker.   For,
fays he, very gravely, ' ᶜ his wounds were thought to be mortal, &
' had perhaps been mortal, if out of unfpeakable love the lady Eleanor
' his wife had not fuckt out the poyfon with her mouth; & thereby
' effecting a cure which otherwife had been incurable. [And then merri-
ly adds,] ' it is no wonder that love fhould do wonders, which is
' it felf a wonder.'   But how miftaken thefe gentlemen are, let Mr.

a p. 646. b.   Lib. I. & Camb. in Middlefex, fol. 432.
b Here he quotes Rodericus Toletanus,   c p. 94. a.

2   Tyrrel

To his grace the very learned & most rev.d Father in God William L.d arch=bishop of Canterbury,primate and metropolitan.s of all England, one of the kind encouragers of this work ; this plate is most gratefully inscrib'd.

The South Prospect of S.t Maries Church in Stanford.

Tyrrel ſhew. ' I cannot, ſays he [a], leave this ſubject, without taking
' notice, that the vulgar ſtory of the princeſs ſucking the venom out
' of her husbands wounds, & to which he owed his recovery, is a
' meer romance; this action of hers not being mentioned by any
' antient author of, or near, that time. The firſt in whom I can find
' it being Camden, from whom it is tranſcribed by Speed, & both
' cite Roderic archbiſhop of Toledo for it. But tho' I have dili-
' gently ſearched that authors hiſtory of Spain, yet I cannot find it
' any where there, nor I believe any body elſe. For at the end of
' his work he tells his reader, that he finiſhed it A. D. 1243. *Æræ*
' *Hiſpan.* 1281. which is above 10 years before prince Edwd. married
' the princeſs Eleanor, & near 20 years before this accident of the aſ-
' ſaſſins wounding that prince.' But here it is like my readers will
ſay, what is all this to the antiquities of Stanford? why thus. Mr.
Butcher our old antiquary, ſpeaking of the croſs which the ſaid prince,
when he came to be king, erected at Stanford, in memory of the ſaid
princeſs after her death, ſwallows the fable above as glib as either
Speed or Baker, & makes this, now utterly confuted tale, the pure mo-
tive or ground of that erection.

XXXVII. Here give me leave to inſert the account I before promiſed of S. Maries church at the bridge. S. Maries church at the bridge
conſiſts of three iſles, & as many chancels anſwering them. At the
bottom of the nave or middle iſle is the ſteeple; a beautiful ſtone
ſpire, without either battlements or crockets. On the outſide, juſt
where the ſpire begins to contract it ſelf, are placed at the four corners of it the effigies of the four evangeliſts under as many ſmall ca-
nopies of ſtone. The whole is much admired by travellers, both for
its height & ſtrength, as well as beauty & antiquity. In this ſteeple
hangs a pleaſant ring of ſix bells. The tenor about 18. hundred weight.
That & the treble are remarkable for true muſical ſounds. The bells
are thus inſcribed. I. 𝖘𝖚𝖒 𝖗𝖔𝖘𝖆 𝖕𝖚𝖑𝖘𝖆𝖙𝖆, 𝖒𝖚𝖓𝖉𝖎𝖖𝖚𝖊 𝕸𝖆𝖗𝖎𝖆 𝖛𝖔𝖈𝖆𝖙𝖆. 𝕿𝖔𝖇𝖎𝖊
𝕹𝖔𝖗𝖗𝖎𝖘 𝖈𝖆𝖘𝖙 𝖒𝖊, 1621. Theſe words *Sum roſa*, &c. ſhew this was an old
bell, but recaſt in 1621. when the old inſcription was ordered to be
renewed. II. 𝕹𝖔𝖓 𝖛𝖊𝖗𝖇𝖊, 𝖘𝖊𝖉 𝖛𝖔𝖈𝖊, 𝖗𝖊𝖘𝖔𝖓𝖆𝖇𝖊, 𝖉𝖔𝖒𝖎𝖓𝖊, 𝖑𝖆𝖚𝖉𝖊𝖒. 1622. On
this bell are the arms of France & England quartered: with a ducal
coronet over the coat. Whence I reckon it was firſt given by ſome
of the dukes of York (owners of this town) & ſo ordered to be continued
when the bell was new caſt in 1622. III. 𝕺𝖒𝖓𝖎𝖆 𝖋𝖎𝖆𝖓𝖙 𝖆𝖉 𝖌𝖑𝖔𝖗𝖎𝖆𝖒 𝕯𝖊𝖎.
𝕿𝖔𝖇𝖎𝖊 𝕹𝖔𝖗𝖗𝖎𝖘 𝖈𝖆𝖘𝖙 𝖒𝖊. IV. .... 𝕮𝖍𝖗𝖎𝖘𝖙𝖊! 𝖕𝖑𝖆𝖈𝖊𝖆𝖙 .. 𝖙𝖎𝖇𝖎 𝖘𝖔𝖓𝖚𝖘 𝖎𝖘𝖙𝖊. V. On
this bell are the kings arms & the following inſcription. 𝕮𝖆𝖒𝖕𝖆𝖓𝖆
𝕭𝖚𝖗𝖌𝖊𝖓𝖘𝖎𝖇𝖚𝖘 𝖉𝖊 𝕾𝖙𝖆𝖓𝖋𝖔𝖗𝖉 𝖎𝖓𝖘𝖊𝖗𝖛𝖎𝖊𝖓𝖘. This is the town-bell, & was caſt
the 1. of K. Charles the 1. VI. 𝕱𝖊𝖆𝖗 𝕲𝖔𝖉, 𝖍𝖔𝖓𝖔𝖚𝖗 𝖙𝖍𝖊 𝖐𝖎𝖓𝖌, 1638. 𝕵. 𝕭.
𝕿. 𝕿. 𝕲𝖚𝖆𝖗𝖉𝖎𝖆𝖓𝖎. On the ſanctes bell: 𝕾𝖆𝖓𝖈𝖙𝖆 𝕸𝖆𝖗𝖎𝖆. Here I cannot
forbear obſerving that the ſaints bell, as many term it, was not ſo

---

a p. 1094.

called

called from the name of the faint that was (as here) inſcribed on it, or of the church to which it belonged; But, becauſe it was always rung out when the prieſt came to that part of the ſervice, *Sanѐte, ſanѐte, ſanѐte, Domine Deus ſabaoth*: Holy, holy, holy, Lord God of ſabaoth, or *hoſts* (for that is what *ſabaoth* ſignifies, & not *ſabath*; as too many ignorantly read it) purpoſely that they who could not come to church might underſtand what a ſolemn office the congregation were at that inſtant engaged in, & ſo, even in their abſence, be once at leaſt moved to lift up their hearts to him that made them. For this reaſon the ſanѐtes bell was generally hung where it might be heard fartheſt. Sometimes in a lantern at the top of the ſteeple; or, in a turret at one corner of it; if a tower. Sometimes thruſt out of the uppermoſt window, if a ſpire. And ſometimes in an arch, or gallows, on the outſide of the roof between the church & chancel; as we ſee at Talington by Stanford, & in many other places. This laſt ſort were ſo placed, that the rope might come down into the choir, & ſo being nearer the altar, the bell might be more readily rung out, as ſoon as ever the prieſt came to the ſacred words.

XXXVIII. Here alſo I beg leave to add a few remarks upon churches in general. The architecture of all our old churches is Gothic. Yet, notwithſtanding all the barbarouſneſs of them to whom the order owes its name, & the many rudeneſſes it is it ſelf charged with; this, I think, may be ſaid for ſome Gothic buildings, that they abound with as much variety, & ſometimes ſtrike the eye as agreeably, as the fineſt pieces of the more regular orders. Thus, if we conſider the beſt buildings we have of this kind in England, there is ſomething vaſtly great & magnificent, & ſomething alſo vaſtly beautiful in the compoſure. For inſtance. If we look upon an inſide, for a neat ſtructure with pillars, where do we ſee any finer turned than thoſe of the temple church, or Weſtminſter abby, or the cathedral of Lincoln? Some think their beautiful, taper, pillars far exceed the modern bulky ſupporters of S. Pauls, which, they ſay, have little elſe but the flutings & capitals of the Corinthian order to recommend them. For a ſtructure without pillars, nothing hardly equals Kings college chapel in Cambridge. If we look upon an outſide, Peterborough in this neighbourhood, as it now is, will ſcarce yield to any that I know of. But were it finiſhed, according to the model which we ſee in that part that is ſo; almoſt all, I think, muſt ſubmit to it. This I ſpeak of the weſt end, which, if it & the lantern were finiſhed, would ſhew five ſteeples in front. From the eaſt this church likewiſe preſents us with a view ſurpriſingly entertaining. I would mention what remains of Croyland front too, were it not abuſed with a falſe draught in the Monaſticon: a particular wherein the late indefatigable collector of the antiquities of Northamptonſhire, John Bridges eſq; (tho' it ſtood out of his immediate province) intended to have done it juſtice; & to that end long ago procured the proſpect of it to be taken afreſh by the curious hand

of

of Mr. Peter Tillemans. Our old parish churches indeed do not often present us with any thing so vastly fine, but sometimes we meet with a steeple among them, remarkably sweet & pretty. Thus S. Maries at the bridge & All Saints in the mercat, for spires; S. John Baptists, & S. Martins, for towers; all in Stanford; are very handsome. In like manner if we go west from Stanford, there are Ketton, Exton, &c. North, Great Ponton, Grantham, Newark, &c. East, Kirton, Boston, &c. South, Castre, Fotheringhay, Lowick, &c. with a multitude of other churches, which, if we consider their steeples, are exceeded, some of them by none, & the rest by few, in the kingdom. From fine things, if we turn to what is odd, the little church of Tickencoat in this neighbourhood is to be noted, for its many arches in the north wall, all the mouldings & turnings being wrought into one another, in a surprising manner; as also for a large room over the body of the chancel with a stone floor, & stone stairs up to it: which (if an anchoret, or some such sort of a religious person did not formerly live in) is alike strange in the designment. Mr. Stavely says, ' [a] the Saxons generally made their churches with descents into them, & the Normans contrarily with ascents.' Whether this be true or no I affirm not: But think it very probable. However I believe with Dr. Plot, ' [b] that in setting their churches due east & west, all the direction which people had in former times ('till the compass was invented) was from the sun it self: which rising in summer more or less northward, & in winter proportionably to the southward, of the equinoctial east: in all likelihood might occasion so many churches not to respect the due east & west points, but to decline from them more or less, according to the early or late season of the year, wherein they were founded.' An observation which seems to instruct us how to find the time of the year when any church was first laid out or erected. Again. Churches erected in every age were often built *very like*, & always *something like* one another. ' Every age, as Mr. Stavely says, ' having had something ' peculiar in the way or mode of architecture.' Possibly then by a nice examination of the different modes in the fabric of parish churches, the different ages when they were in use may be pretty nearly ascertained. Now the several modes which I have observed in parish churches, as near as I can recollect, are these. The oldest, & we must therefore reckon them first, are (such as that at Tickencoat) churches of a small extent, & low structure; with no tower or steeple, but instead of that a little arch at the west end to hang a couple of very small bells in, whose ropes are let down into the church by holes bored thro' the roof of the middle isle. Of this sort are Stretton, Whitwell, little Castreton, Esendine, Eye, & many other places hereabouts. And these, in my opinion, seem to be most antient, both as they resemble

a Hist. of churches, p. 151.   b Staffords. p. 361.   c p. 153.

Joseph

Joseph of Arimathea's church at Glaſtonbury (the Icon of which we ſee in many books) in the plainneſs of their ſtructure; & for other reaſons, too many to inſiſt upon.   As for other pariſh churches, I ſhall only mention the ſeveral ſorts of them which I have ſeen in draughts, or by a perſonal view without offering to ſay which ought to be reckoned firſt in point of antiquity.   For I do not pretend to range them.   I would only ſuggeſt a thought to better judges, & leave them to purſue the enquiry.   Some pariſh churches have their ſteeples placed cathedral-wiſe, in the midſt: as Ketton in Rutland, Kings Clive & Caſtre in Northamptonſhire; S. Mary over rees in Southwark; a multitude about Guildford in Surry, &c.   The 1ſt. of this ſort was Ed. the confeſſors abby of S. Peter at Weſtminſter.   Some have their ſteeples ſet betwixt the ſouth iſle & ſouth chancel; as Duddington in Northamptonſhire; Buckminſter in Leiceſterſhire; Godſtone in Surry, &c. but the moſt common way is at the bottom of the nave or ſide iſles. Some churches are built round like an oven, with large Dominicums or Dohms; as the round church at Cambridge, S. Pulchers at Northampton, &c.   Some churches have towers; others towers & ſpires, all of wood.   Of this laſt ſort are many in Surry & Suſſex, & thoſe able to contain many heavy bells.   Others have towers more like caſtles, than ſteeples; built of flint & pebbles incruſted together.   Of this ſort we ſee many about London.   But the moſt monſtrous I ever ſaw of this kind are at Hornſey in Middleſex, & Hitchen in Hertfordſhire.   Others have ſtone towers, & wooden ſhafts or ſpires covered with lead: of this ſort are many in Hertfordſhire, &c.   Others have ſtone towers with wooden ſhafts or ſpires covered with ſhingles, or thin pieces of wood cut out like ſlates or tiles.   Such is Lingfield in Suſſex, &c.   Other churches have huge, clumſy ſpires, built all of ſtone; as Bernac, Rihal, Croyland, & lately, Deping S. James, &c.   Others have towers & ſpires, all built of ſtone, not ſo heavy as the laſt; & differing alſo from them in that they have a ſanctes bell thruſt out under a little prominent arch at the middle, or top window of the ſpire.   Of this ſort are many between Biſhops Stafford & Cambridge.   Others have plain ſtone ſpires without either battlements or crockets.   Of this ſort Langham, Gretham, Cotiſmore, & lately Pickworth, all in Rutland, being of one model, were perhaps erected by the ſame architect.   Helpſtone in Northamptonſhire is the only hexagonal tower & ſpire I ever ſaw.   Melton Mowbray in Leiceſterſhire, Great Ponton in Lincolnſhire, Wrexam in Wales, Allhallows in Derby, &c. are beautiful towers of the quadrangular kind.   Some churches have lofty ſtone ſpires without battlements: others with battlements, but without crockets: others with battlements & crockets. Others have octangular towers; as formerly the black friers church at Norwich, &c.   Others have octangular towers upon quadrangular; as Lowic & Fotheringhay in Northamptonſhire; Boſton in Lincolnſhire, &c.   Exton in Rutland has a fine, quadrangular tower embattled; up-

on

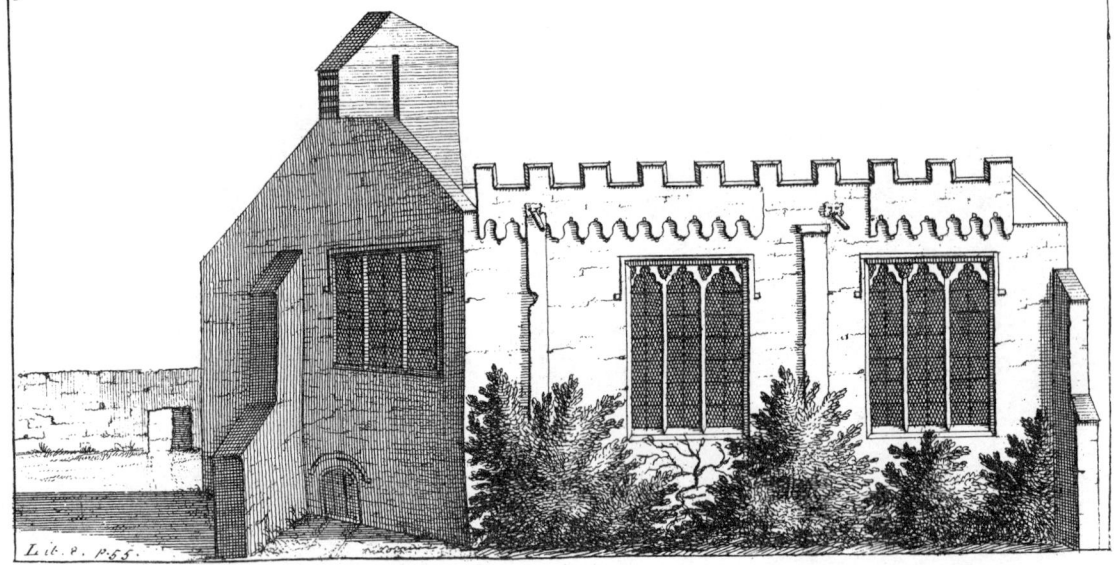

The South West Prospect of the remains of S. Pauls Church (now the Free-school) at STANFORD.

Lit. 8. p. 55.

on that an octangular tower embatteled : upon that an hexagonal spire. The laft fort of churches, I have obferved, is that multitude of curious new fabricks in & about London which have of late been raifed with vaft expence & a moft agreeable variety. This is a matter in a manner untouched. Wales, the North, Cornwall, & indeed every county in England muft be viewed by better judges in architecture than I am; before any thing in this cafe can be truly afcertained. I fhall only add, that if books of antiquity had more profpects of churches, which are feldom altered; inftead of gentlemens feats, which are altered by almoft every new proprietor, whereby the draughts are made prefently ufelefs; they would, in my opinion, come a great deal more up to the true purpofe of antiquities. But I return. As to the prefent fabric of S. Maries church by the bridge, tho' it is not older, perhaps not quite fo old, as the times we have been now writing of; yet there was a church here, dedicated to the fame faint, as early as the conqueft, & probably fome time before. And indeed the common people of this town imagine this to be the mother church of England. But they forget that the old churches of Glaftonbury, Bangor, & S. Martins in Canterbury, & perhaps fome others, have much better pleas for their antiquity. The old priory church of S. Leonard by Stanford, I believe, was the firft conventual church in all South Mercia; & if the church of S. Mary (the old church where this prefent church ftands) were as antient as that, then it was probably the firft parifh church in all the fame province. However, be that as it will, I fhall for the prefent only allow this to be the mother parifh church of Stanford; which is all that need be granted, & more than can well be proved. If we confider it as the mother parifh church of Stanford, we may, in fome fort, fay of it, as an elegant writer does of the cathedral church of Norwich. That it is a church, ' ᵃ which, in former ages, was furrounded by many ' other churches, chapels, & facred ftructures; but, in the prefent, ' mourns for fome, as Rachel did for her children, either becaufe they ' are not, or becaufe perverted to other ufes.' For of churches, chapels, & facred ftructures that are not, we had divers; & of thofe perverted to other ufes, we yet fee the remains of S. Pauls, now made the free-fchool; almoft the beft of any ufes it could be put to, except that of Gods more immediate fervice; & S. Leonards, now turned into a farmers barn.

XXXIX. About the latter end of this, or the beginning of the next reign, was founded the minorites, or grey friers college at Stanford, a large place, fituate in the eaft fuburb, on the right hand fide of the way as we go out of S. Pauls gate. The out-walls of the inclofure are yet ftanding, whereby it appears that the church, monaftery & gardens took in a great compafs of ground. The church was a very fpacious one, & the houfe an exceeding fair ftructure; but both are now de-

ᵃ Ex antiquitatum fcholæ regiæ Norwicenfis, in calce operum pofthumorum Thomæ Brown militis, pagina 3.

4   8 Q   molifhed.

molifhed.   Out of the ruins have been frequently dug many fine pieces of carving, in memory of feveral perfons yet alive.   And in the out-wall going down from S. Pauls to S. Georges gate, is yet to be feen part of a figure reprefenting a woman with difheveled hair.   Robert Glen, now (1725.) parifh clerk of S. John Baptifts church in Stanford, as he told me, faw both that & feveral other fuch figures, when they were fome years ago dug up entire out of the ruins; but what became of the reft he cannot remember.   All elfe that now remains of this once goodly fabric is a homely back gate on the fouth fide.   If I may guefs at the founder, I reckon it was K. Henry the third, who, as I find, ' ᵃ was fo taken with thefe good men (as my author calls them) ' that he was for placing them in all great towns of the nation.'   If not K. Henry, then I conceive Edmund Plantagenet afterwards earl of Kent, or fome anceftor of the faid Edmund, muft have been the perfon.   I fhall only add, ' ᵇ the fuperiors of the monafteries of ' this order were always called guardians or wardens. ᶜ The friers ' were called grey friers becaufe their cloaths were made of na-' tural wool without any die. ᵈ Whilft this order flourifhed in Eng-' land, this province was divided into feven diftricts or cuftodies, ' becaufe each of them was governed by a particular fuperior, under ' the provincial, called a *cuftos*, who had a power over all the con-' vents in his diftrict.   The feven cuftodies were London, York, Cam-' bridge, Briftol, Oxford, New-Caftle, & Worcefter. ᵉ The grey friers ' at Stanford was one of thofe monafteries accounted in Oxford cu-' ftody.'   K. H. the 3. died the 16. of Nov. 1272. & was fucceeded by his eldeft fon prince Edward.

a Hift. of the Englifh Francif. p. 25.   d id. p. 95.
b I. addit. Vol. to the monaft. p. 136.   e id. ib.
c id. p. 94.

The end of the eighth book.

Academia tertia Anglicana;

OR, THE

ANTIQUARIAN ANNALS

of the TOWN of

STANFORD

IN

Lincoln, Rutland, *and* Northampton *Shires*,

BOOK IX.

Containing the reign of K. Edward the firſt.

I. WHEN K. H. the 3. died, his ſon prince Edward was then 1272.
in the holy land. a 'That foreign expedition was politickly 1. E. 1.
' undertaken, to rid the land of many martialiſts, where-
' with the late barons wars had made it to abound. b Upon the ſolem-
' nization of K. H. the 3d's funeral, in the abbey at Weſtminſter, John
' Warenn [Lord of Stanford] and Gilbert de Clare E. of Glouceſter,
' with the clergy and people, went up to the high altar, and ſwore fealty
' to Edward his ſon, thenceforth king by the name of Edward the I.' In
1272. was born Walter Burley, afterwards a famous ſcholar, tutor to
K. Edward the 3d, and one who probably made a great figure in the
univerſity of Stanford. The time of his birth I gather from Bale, who
ſays, c 'he died in 1337. being the 63d year of his age.' Jan. 31. 1272-3. Jan. 31.
' d Humphrey de Bohun [or with the beard, ſo called in regard that his 127¾.
' anceſtor, who came in with William the Conqueror, wore a long
' beard, whereas moſt of the Normans did then totally ſhave their faces e]
' E. of Hereford, entered into a ſolemn covenant under his ſeal, with
' Henry E. of Lincoln, John E. of Warenne [lord of Stanford]
' Aymer de Valence E. of Pembroke, Robert de Clifford, and ſome
' other barons, to defend the kings perſon and the rights of his crown,
' and to redreſs what was amiſs: as by a ſpecial inſtrument, bearing
' date at Boloigne, the laſt of January in the ſame year appeareth. f The

a Fuller, p. 74.
b Bar. Vol. I. p. 78. b.
c p. 413.
d Baron. Vol. 1. p. 183. b.

e id. p. 179. b.
f Mr. Stevens additions to the Mon.
Ang. Vol. 1. p. 174.

' priory

' priory of St. Leonard without Stanford was one of those monasteries
' which had protections granted to them by K. Edward the I. when he ob-
' liged all monasteries to take such protections.   Prince Edward, saith
Mr. Butcher [a], when he came to be King, gave the castle and town of
Stanford to John E. Warenn.   But this is a mistake, for he gave it him
43. H. 3. immediately after W. de Valence was sent away by the barons.
' [b] About this time Henry Plantagenet, being by inquisition found
' to be heir to Thomas late E. of Lancaster his brother, the K. ta-
' king his homage, commanded his escheator north of Trent, that he
' should not meddle with the castles of Sandale and Coningsburgh, or
' any of the manors of Wakefield, Thorne, Soureby, Hatfield and Stain-
' ford [Stanford-bridge in Yorkshire] whereunto John E. of Surrey
' [lord of Stanford] laid claim; those being, by consent of both par-
' ties, to remain in the king's hands, to be delivered to this Henry.

Aug. 19. II. Upon the 19th of Aug. 2. E. 1. " ' at the solemnitie of K. Edw.
2. E. 1. ' the firsts coronation, were let go at libertie, catche them that catche
' might, 500 great horses by the K. of Scottes, the erles of Cornwal,
' Gloucester, Pembroke, Warenn, and others, as they were alighte be-
3. E. 1. ' side their backs."   In the 3. of E. 1. [d] ' upon K. Edwards return out
' of Gascoign, John E. of Warenn [lord of Stanford] gave him most
' honourable entertainment at his castle of Rigate, which was so accep-
' table to that king, that he pardoned him no less than a thousand marc's
' of that great sum of 10000 marc's, at which he had been fined for
' that offence in Westminster hall against Sir Alan la Zouch and his
' son.   ' [e] The same Year there was an inquisition at Stanford, before
' the Lords William de St. Omers and Warin de C. &c.'   Upon what
account this inquisition was held I find not.   But Mr. Butcher gives us
a remarkable passage from this, or another roll of the same year.   ' [f] It
' appeareth by the rolls of the hundreds of Linc. of the 3. of E. 1. in
' the tower, upon the verdict of twelve of the commons or meaner
' inhabitants of the town of Stanford, that there were twelve persons
' there called lege-men, who were so called because they were anti-
' ently judges of the law in the same town."   These lege-men were
4. E. 1. as old, or older than Edward the confessors time. [g] ' In the 4. E. 1.
' an inquisition was made to know what toll was taken by the bailiffs
' of Stanford of such persons as resorted to the mercats and fairs there.'
What verdict was returned upon this enquiry my notes say not, only another paper adds, that ' [h] in this 4. of E. 1. 'twas found by inquisition

a MS. p. 12.
b Bar. Vol. 1. p. 783. b.
c Hol. p. 786. a.
d Bar. Vol. p. 1. 78. b.
e Ex rotulis hundredorum, in turre Lond. 3. E. 1.
f Per veredictum duodecim minorum ville de Stanford, ibi fuerunt duodecim qui vocantur Lege-mani, qui sic vocabantur, quia ab antiquo fuerunt judices legum in ea-

dem villa. Ex Rot. Hund. Linc. in Turrre.
g Inquisitio de Theloneo capto per ballivos ibidem de hominibus ad mercatum & nundinas ibidem confluentibus, inter eschae-tas 4. E. 1. pro archiepiscopo Cantuar. & pat. 4. E. 1. mem. 35. in dorso.
h Out of a MS. in my hands, entitled, ' an abstract of several charters, concern- ' ing the borough of Stanford, dated 11, ' June 1677.' Article the 2d.

' that

' that the baylifs of Stanford, *ceperunt Theolonium apud Batolienses ex*
' *parte occidentali ville predicte*: took toll at the . . . . . on the
' weft part of the town aforefaid. The fame year ª John de Waren E. of
' Surrey [lord of Stanford] granted to the burgeffes of Stanford, that
' they fhould have liberty to chufe themfelves an alderman, *pur lour*
' *common governeur & jufticier, &c.* which alderman fhould be fworne
' before the E. or his ftewart, *&c.* ᵇ Licenfe was then alfo granted to
' found a chantry in the church of St. Clement at Stanford.' ᶜ Richard
' de Tynwell now occurs mafter or warden of the hofpital of St. Thomas
' of Canterbury at the bridge foot at Stanford. ᵈ By an inquifition of
' this 4. of E. 1. the jurats of the hundred of Sutton in the county of
' Northampton, fay, that the county of Rutland once belonged to that
' county, till lord Henry (father of the now lord king) gave it to the
' K. of Almaine.

III. In the 6. year of his reign K. Edward ᵉ ' ftanding in need of mo-
' ny, devifed a newe fhift to ferve his tourne, as this : whereas he was
' chiefe lorde of many lordefhips, manours, poffeffions & tenements,
' he well underftoode, that partly by length & proces of time, & part-
' ly by caufualties during the troubles of the civil wars, many mens
' evidences (as theyr charters, deedes, copies & other writings) were loft,
' wafted, and made away ; hee therefore under colour to put the fta-
' tute of *Quo Waranto* in execution, whiche was ordeyned this yere
' in the Parl. at Gloucefter in Auguft laft, as fome write, did now com-
' maunde by publicke proclamation, that all fuche as held any landes
' or tenements of hym, fhuld come and fhew by what right & title
' they held the fame, that by fuche meanes theyr poffeffions might re-
' turne unto him, by efcheate, as chief lord of the fame, and fo be fold
' or redeemed agayne at his hands. This was thought to be a fore
' proclamation that a more grevous had not lightly been herd of. Men
' in every part made complaint, and fhewed themfelves grevoufly of-
' fended, fo that the K. by meanes thereof, came into great hatred of
' his people. But the meaner fort, though they ftoode in defence of
' their right, yet it avayled them but little, bycaufe they had no evi-
' dence to fhew, fo that they were conftrayned to be quiet with lofs,
' rather than ftrive agaynft the ftreame. Many were thus called to an-
' fwere, 'till at length John E. of Surrey [& lord of Stanford] a man
' greatly beloved of the people, perceyving the K. to have cafte his
' nette for a preye, and that there was not one whych fpake a-
' gainft him, determined to ftand againft thofe fo bitter & cruel pro-
' ceedings ; and therefore being called afore the juftices aboute this
' matter, he appeared, & being asked by what right he held his landes ?

6. E. 1.

---

a idem. Article the 3.
b Ex literis Cl. Willifii mihi miffis.
c Ex antiqui regift. ecclefiæ de Burgo
penes nob. ducem de Monte-acuto, p. 297.
d Britan. antiq. & nova, in Rutl. p. 511.a.

e Holing. p. 789, 790. Sir Richard Dugdale places thefe matters under the 6. of
Edw. 1. as I have done, but Mr. Holingf-
head places them in the 8. Ed. 1. anno 1280,
but I think he is wrong as to time.

' fodenly

' fodenly drawing forth an old rufty fworde, by this inftrument (fayde
' he) doe I holde my landes, & by the fame I entende to defende
' them.   Our aunceftors coming into this realm with William [the]
' Conq. conquered theyr lands with the fworde, and wyth the fame
' will I defende me from all thofe that fhall be aboute to take them
' from me :' He did not make a conquefte of this realm alone [or
by himfelf] ' our progenitors were with him as participators & help-
' ers.   The K. underftoode into what hatred of his people by this
' means he was fallen, and therefore to avoyde civil diffention & war
' that might thereby enfue, left off his begun practice; fo that the
' thing which generally fhuld have touched & bene hurtful to all
' men, was nowe fodainly ftayed by the manhood & couragioufe ftout-
' neffe of one man, the forefaid E.'   It is true enough (as my author
obferves) that thefe enquiries were now ftayed, but they were not ended.
The Kings apprehenfions of an infurrection of the whole party thus
aggrieved, as my author hints, and not his fear of E. Warenn, or any
other particular perfon, was probably the reafon of his delay.   For it
was but a delay, and that of a twelvemonths only, before he renewed
his proceedings in this affair, and againft this very E. himfelf by name:

Anno   whereof more prefently.   In 1278. [a] ' Emma wife of Geoffry de S. Me-
1278.   ' dardo, dying about Michaelmas at Ofgoteby, William de Wodeford,
' facrift of Burg, prefented himfelf, being ready to defend the right of
' the faid church [her husband being one of the knights who held
his lands of it] ' to have the body of the faid woman buried at Burg,
' according to an agrement made long before, between the monks
' & knights of the faid church, before the B. of Lincoln.   But fhe ha-
' ving defired to be buried at Stanford, at their devout requeft, the
' forenamed facrift, out of fpecial grace and favour, condefcended for
' that time, faving the rights of the church of Burg, to let her defire
' be fulfilled.

1279.   IV.   At Eafter 1279. 7. Ed. 1. lord Roger de Coleville releafed
7. E. 1. the Nuns of St. Michael of all fervices due from a tenement of theirs
in his fee at the town of Wenton, and likewife in the field of Berk,
faving only to himfelf a yearly rent of ten fhillings, & the kings right
in the fame tenement to the K.   The charter of the faid Roger runs
thus.   [b] ' To all the faithful of Chrift, who fhall fee or hear this wri-
' ting,

a Patricks fupplement to Gunton, p. 314.
b Omnibus Chrifti fidelibus, hoc fcriptum vifuris vel audituris, Rogerus de Coleville, falutem in Domino fempiternam. No-
veritis me relaxaffe, & omnino quietum cla-
maffe imperpetuum, pro me, & heredibus
meis, five affignatis meis, monialibus S. Michaelis extra Stanford, & earum fuccefforibus,
omnimodam fervitutem, & totum jus, &
clameum, quam unquam habui, vel habere
potui, in toto illo tenemento quod dicte
moniales tenent de feodo meo in villa de
Wenton & fimiliter in campo de Berk; vi-
delicet, tam in wardis, releviis, efcaetis, quam
in fectis curiarum, & omnimodis aliis fecula-
ribus fervitiis, confuetudinibus, exactionibus,
feu demandis; ita quod ego, nec heredes mei,
nec affignati mei dictis monialibus ratione dicti
tenementi amodo & ufq; inperpetuum nic-
hil exigemus, nec exigere poterimus.   Nifi
folummodo . . . . . . odo annuum redditum decem folidorum michi, & heredibus
meis, feu affignatis meis, folvend ad duos anni terminos, viz. ad nativitatem S.
Johannis Baptifte quinq; folidorum, & ad
purificationem Marie virginis quinq; folidorum.

‘ ting, Roger de Coleville, greeting in the Lord eternal. Ye fhall
‘ underftand that I have releafed , and altogether quit claimed
‘ for ever, for me, & my heirs, or my affigns, to the Nuns of
‘ St. Michael without Stanford and their fucceffors, all manner the
‘ fervice, & the whole right & claim, which I ever had, or have
‘ been able to have, in all that tenement which the faid nuns hold of
‘ my fee in the town of Wenton, & likewife in the field of Berk, to wit,
‘ as well in wards, reliefs, efchaets, as in fuits of courts, & all man-
‘ ner the other fecular fervices, cuftoms, exactions or demands ; fo that
‘ I, nor my heirs, nor my affigns, from the faid nuns, on account of
‘ the faid tenement hence & for ever hereafter, neither will, nor fhall
‘ be able to require any thing : fave only the yearly rent of ten fhillings
‘ to me & my heirs, or my affigns, to be paid at two terms of the year,
‘ to wit, at the nativity of St. John Baptift five fhillings, and at the
‘ purification of the virgin Mary five fhillings.   Saving moreover the
‘ forinfec right of the Lord the K. unto the faid tenement belonging.
‘ And if it happen that the faid nuns fhall be wanting in payment of
‘ the faid rent at the abovefaid terms, then it fhall be lawful for me,
‘ or my heirs, or my affigns to make a diftrefs in the faid tenement,
‘ ’till it fhall be fully fatisfied to us.   And that this releafe & our quit-
‘ claim may obtain the ftrength of a perpetual firmnefs, to this writing,
‘ I have put to my feal. Witneffes, Sir William de Coleville, knight, then
‘ fteward of the faid lord Roger de Coleville, John de Burle, Richard de
‘ Rippele, Geoffry de Cottefmor, Helpa de Berk, William de Berk
‘ clerc, Ralph Maudut of Overton, & others.   Given at Berk at Eafter
‘ in the year of our Lord 1279.’   From the name of Maudut it may
be queried, whether inftead of Mercat Overton, we fhould not fay
Mauduit Overton.   The feal reprefents a knight on horfeback full
fpeed, armed a cap en pied.   The original is now in the E. of Exeters hands.   Notwithstanding E. Warenns former great words, the K.
proceeded againft him, in his enquiries upon the ftatute *de quo war-*
ranto.   ‘ For at the pleas of affifes & jurats before John de Reygate,
‘ & his affociates, the juftices itinerantes in the county of Suffex, on
‘ the morrow of St. John the Baptift, in the 7. Edw. the 1. Rot. 50. John
‘ de Warenn E. of Surrey having been fummoned to be here at this jour-
‘ ney, to fhew by what warrant he claims to have free-warenn & free-
‘ chaife, in the towns of Wurthe, Dichenyng, Clayton, Wytham,
‘ Cokefeld, Kyme, Strele, Dalecombe, Plempton, Chaggel, Her-
‘ tinglegh, Hedlegh, Lyndefend, Weftmefton, Wenham, Newyk,

rum. Salvo preterea forinfeco jure Regis ad dictum tenementum pertinente. Et fi contingat quod dicte moniales in folutione dicti redditus terminis fupradictis defecerint, bene licebit mihi vel heredibus meis, five affignatis meis, diftrictionem facere in dicto tenemento quoufq; nobis plenarie fuerit fatisfactum. Et ut ifta relaxatio & quieta clamatio noftra, perpetue firmitatis robur ob-tineant, huic fcripto figillum meum appofui. Hiis teftibus, D. Willielmo de Coleville, milite, tum fenefcallo dicti D. Rogeri de Coleville, Johanne de Burle, Richardo de Rippele, Galfrido de Cottefmor, Helpa de Berk, Willielmo de Berk Clerico, Radulfo Maudut de Overtona, & aliis. Datum apud Berk ad Pafcha, anno Domini milefimo ducentefimo feptuagefimo nono.

‘ Bertomp,

' Bertomp, Haunnes, Benham, Swambergh, Kyngeftemer, Iford, Wef-
' take, Hundefdon, Smythewyk, Holinftrode, Radmel, Pydingho, To-
' telefcombe, Suthefe, Methyng, Middleburgh, Iwenefme, Onyngden,
' Falmere, Boureme, Pecham, Brigelmefton, Slaghham, Boleyn, Herft,
' Mediam, Cranlegh, Wyndlefham, Hangleton, Adelingworth, Black-
' ington, Wyke, Wyteden, Twyny, Ponyng, Newetembre, Sadelef-
' combe, Pycomb, Pynkeden, Porteflade, Aldrington, Farncombe,
' Melefcombe, Abburton, Folking, Parkyng, Sandes, Hedefnell, Lefe-
' fend. & la fend. in that county, &c. ' And whence William de Gy-
' filham, who fues for the lord the K. fays, that William de Warenn
' father of the forefaid E. hath occupied over lord Henry, father of
' the now King, the forefaid warenn and chaife in the forefaid towns.
' And the forefaid E. holds them fo occupied to a thoufand pounds
' damage of the lord King. And the E. comes and defends the force
' & injury, when, &c. and fays, that William de Warenn, his father,
' whofe heir he is, held the barony and honor of Lewes, with the
' fee & with all the liberties, warens, chaifes, &c. & that all the fore-
' faid liberties have been annexed and conjoined to that barony &
' honor, the which barony and honor the fame William held of the lord
' K. *in capite* & in mediety, by virtue of which honor the fame K.
' therefore received his homage. And the fame William in his ho-
' mage died feifed of the waren aforefaid, & of the chace in like
' manner, with all the liberties aforefaid, to the fame barony & ho-
' nor annexed & conjoined. After whofe deceafe, the barony & ho-
' nor aforefaid came to the hand of the forefaid Henry the K. by reafon of
' the wardfhip of him John, for that he was under-age; & in all the
' time of the wardfhip aforefaid (to wit, for feventeen years & up-
' wards) was the fame K. in feifin of the warens and chaces aforefaid,
' as of them which belonged to the barony & honor aforefaid, &
' which to the fame barony & honor were annexed & conjoined.
' And faith, that, when he attained unto his age, the fame Henry the
' K. reftored to him the forefaid barony & honor, with all the liber-
' ties aforefaid, together with all the chaces & warens aforefaid, in the
' fame ftate, wherein the aforefaid William, his father, died thereof
' feifed, & as is aforefaid. And faith, that the fame Henry the K. for
' the barony and honor aforefaid, & their appurtenances aforefaid, re-
' ceived his homage, & by that warant claims himfelf to have waren &
' chace in the places where he claims to have chaces & warens; &
' thereof, as the lord the K. received the homage of the forefaid Wil-
' liam his father, who in his homage departed this life. And in like
' manner the fame Henry the K. was feifed of the homage of him John
' the E. now. And in like manner the now lord K. for the forefaid
' barony & honor, and their appurtenances aforefaid; as is aforefaid. He
' demands judgment if the forefaid lord K. Edward, in himfelf, againft
' himfelf, for the reafon aforefaid, ought not to be warant for him,
' altho' in court it be adjudged that thefe pleas may not be allowed.

' Whereupon

' Whereupon he was impleaded to anſwer afreſh thereof. ª Afterwards,
' in the Octaves of St. Martin, at Cyceſter, comes the foreſaid E. &
' ſays, that in Worth, Cokefeld, & Dychenyng, he hath his parks, &
' asks if the K. hath any claim in the ſame parks. And William de
' Gyſelingham, who ſues for the Lord K. ſaith, that for the preſent
' he claims nothing in thoſe parks. And touching the other places &
' towns where the Lord K. claims the foreſaid warens & chaces, the
' E. ſays, that all his anceſtors, always faithfully ſtuck to the ſide of the
' Kings of England; & that in the time when Normandy was loſt, his
' anceſtors were earls of Waren in Normandy, & for no loſs of
' their land in thoſe parts, would adhere to the ſide of the Kings of
' France, by reaſon whereof his anceſtors loſt their lands there; on
' which account John K. of England gave the foreſaid lands to the
' anceſtors of this E. in name of a recompenſe for their lands loſt in the
' parts of Normandy, & granted, that his anceſtors & their heirs ſhould
' have all their lands given them by the Lord K. himſelf, & all which
' they ſhould afterwards acquire to themſelves, in Warennage, becauſe
' of their ſirname a Warenna. And ſaith, that William his father, be-
' fore ever K. Henry came to the crown, had all thoſe warens & chaſes,
' where he claims to have them in the foreſaid places and town; ſo
' that William his father made no entry over the foreſaid K. Henry
' (father of the foreſaid K. that now is) nor this E. over this K. And
' that it may appear ſo, deſires it may be enquired. And William de
' Gyſelingham, who ſues for the Lord K. in like manner deſired
' there might be a jury called thereupon. And it was commanded
' the ſherif, that, parties being attached, he ſhould cauſe an election of
' jurats to be made before him. And William de Haſtinges, Richard
' de Eſſeburnham, Richard de Peveneſſe, William Manfe, John de
' Wanton, & Roger de la Hyde, knights; John & William de Hon-
' ton, Robert Trot. e .. Aumfry de Gatewyk, William Aleyn, & Ri-
' chard de Weſton, lords of towns; elected with conſent of William de
' Henere, attorney of the foreſaid K. & of the foreſaid E. ſay, upon
' their oath, That William de Waren, E. of Surrey, father of the
' now E. before ever Henry the K. father of the now Lord K. was
' crowned K. of England, had all the foreſaid chaces, warens, & liberties,
' as appurtenances to the honor & barony of Lewes. And ſay, that the
' ſame E. William occupied & uſurped nothing over the foreſaid lord
' K. Henry (father of the now Lord K.) nor this E. over this K. They
' ſay alſo, that in the town of Alberton (ſo much of it as is of the fee of
' William de Brews; & in like manner at Lyndefend, ſo much of it as is
' of the archbiſhop of Canterburys fee) the foreſaid E. hath not, nor
' claims to have, chace or waren. And it was found by the foreſaid
' jurats, that the foreſaid William E. Warenn, made uſe of all the
' foreſaid chaces & warens, in the foreſaid towns, before ever the fore-

ª Ex eodem Rot. ſupra dicto.

' ſaid

' faid lord Henry the K. father of the now lord K. was crowned;
' excepting the fees of William de Brews in Alberton, and of the
' Archbp. in Lyndefend. And that the forefaid E. William hath oc-
' cupied nothing over the forefaid K. Henry father of the now Lord
' K. nor this E. over the now Lord K. Whereupon it was adjudged
' that the Lord K. feife nothing by his writ for the prefent. And
' the forefaid E. was thereof &c. without being charged to appear on
' any other day: faving the action of the Lord K. when he fhall be

Mar. 20.
9. E. 1. ' minded to fpeak thereof. In the 9. of E. 1. [a] on the feaft of S. Cuth-
' bert [Mar. 20.] the archbifhop of York fent letters to the prior of
' Durham, fignifying that he intended to vifit him & the chapter of
' Durham on the morrow of S. John Baptift then next enfuing, &c. as
' archbifhop & metropolitan. Immediately upon thefe things the bifhop
' of Durham was confulted, who anfwered, that the prior was not oblig-
' ed to reply to the letter that had been fent, equally becaufe he that
' fent it had no jurifdiction over the prior & chapter of Durham,
' & alfo becaufe he enjoyned him on virtue of his obedience to fig-
' nifie what he had done on receipt of the faid letters, unto which
' obedience neither the prior nor chapter was bound, fince the metro-
' politan cannot have any jurifdiction over his fuffragans people, ex-
' cept in fome particular cafes, of which this was none. The bifhop
' therefore fetting out for Rome, the prior & chapter frequently re-
' quefted of the archbifhop, that he would put off his vifitation to a
' more convenient feafon; &, he not agreeing to it, appealed againft
' him: firft, becaufe every metropolitan, according to a canon of the
' council of Lyons, ought firft to vifit his own church, & chapter, &
' diocefe, before he vifit his fuffragan; which he had not done. Alfo
' becaufe the bifhop of Durham being abroad about the affairs of his
' church, could not at prefent be vifited: & he not being vifited, they
' ought not to be vifited, fince all vifitation ought to begin at the
' head. Laftly, becaufe the prior & chapter of Durham have hitherto
' enjoyed this privilege, that no archbifhop ever yet vifited them as
' metropolitan.' More of this prefently.

    VI. The fame year, [b] [c] Cicely, relict of Sampfon de Burley, in her free
' widowhood, gave the abbat and monks of Burg, all the right which
' fhe had in the third part of an acre of land, which William de
' Wodeford, facrift of that church, bought of her deceafed huf-
' band. This Cicely, as I take it, was mother of Roger de Burley.
' ' Roger de Burley [but when I find not] by his charter, gave his
' lords, the abbat & monks of Burg, a yearly rent of 12 fhillings,
' one culture of arable land at Pilfgate, three acres of arable at Bur-
' ley, & one rod of meadow at Pilfgate. Witneffes, Sir Gervafe de
' Bernak, Sir Peter de la Mare, Sir Geoffry de Suthorp, Sir Geoffry

---

a Roberti de Grayftanes hift. Dunelm. p.
44.
b Ex antiqui Regiftri ecclefiæ S. Petri de
Burgo penes nobiliffimum ducem de Monte
acuto. p. 295.
c Ex ejufdem Regiftri p. 33.

' Rufcel,

' Ruſcel, Sir John de Helpeſton, knights.   [a] The ſaid Roger de Burle
' died on the feaſt of the Epiphany [Jan. 6. 128 9. Ed. 1.] & was
' buried at Burg in the monks church yard, and the ſacriſt had two
' horſes for his mortuary.   Moreover, within the Octaves of the ſaid
' Epiphany, died Mary his wife, & the ſacriſt had a cow for her mor-
' tuary.   [b] Notwithſtanding all that the prior & convent of Durham
' as above, could ſay againſt it, on the morrow of S. John Baptiſt,
' the archbiſhop of York came to Durham; but when he went to en-
' ter at the north gate, was repulſed by the ſoldiers of the biſhopbric.
' Where the provocation (as before premiſed) being recited before him,
' he excommunicated the biſhop, prior, & heads of the chapter, &
' interdicted the chapter: & peremptorily cited them to appear on
' the Wedneſday next after the feaſt of the exaltation of the holy
' croſs then next enſuing in the church & chapter houſe of Durham,
' to undergo archiepiſcopal viſitation, & make ſatisfaction for the con-
' tempt, &c.   On the day appointed, came to Durham to hold this
' viſitation G. ſubdean of York & maſter Robert Pykering, the arch-
' biſhops commiſſaries; but when they arrived on the new bridge,
' certain perſons laying hold of their horſes bridles they were driven
' back, & ſo turned into S. Nicholas's church without the walls.   There
' the monks renewed their appeal, & offered many articles againſt the
' archbiſhop, alledging that he for ſeveral reaſons had incurred the ſen-
' tence of excommunication.   But thoſe notwithſtanding, the forenam-
' ed commiſſaries cauſed the biſhop & prior to be called, &, upon their
' not appearing, pronounced ſentence of excommunication againſt
' them: putting the church under an interdict.   But the prior &
' chapter procured the letters apoſtolic of pope Martin the 4. directed
' to the abbat of Waltham, & to the dean & chancellor of Lincoln,
' or any two of them, to determine the buſineſs.   Upon this, on
' the morrow of S. Matthias, in S. Maries church by the bridge
' at Stanford, the forenamed abbat & the ſubdelegates of the chan-
' cellor of Lincoln (the dean being rejected, as ſuſpected of partia-
' lity; & the archbiſhop being called, & not appearing by himſelf or
' proctor) nulled the ſentence of excommunication againſt the prior
' &c. & the interdict; releaſing the prior himſelf & the heads of the
' chapter *ad cautelam:* pronouncing the archbiſhop contumacious, &
' condemning him to pay the prior & chapter 300. l. for their charges
' & damages; & ordering him to be cited to the ſame place on the
' wedneſday next after the octaves of the holy Trinity.'   This buſineſs
was afterwards much canvaſſed & diſputed by the parties; but, as
nothing elſe relating to it was tranſacted at Stanford, it lies out of my
province to purſue it.   However a great deal more of it may be ſeen
in my author [c]; of which I ſhall only add, that the archbiſhop, who
began this troubleſom affair, was at length forced to go to Rome to

a Id. p. 312.   744, 745.
b Roberti de Grayſtanes, hiſt. Dunelm. p.   c Cap. 13. & 15. ejuſdem.

ſolicit

folicit the popes favor about it; where he at laſt died in 1283. then yet over head & ears engaged in it.

VII. About this time [a] ' on the marriage of lady Iſabel, daughter ' of John E. Warenn [lord of Stanford] to John de Baliol, a great ' baron of the north, K. Edward gave the ſaid E. Warenn full three ' years reſpite for payment of the cc. marks *per annum*, accepted of ' by K. H the 3. for the fine ſet upon him for aſſaulting Lord Zouch ' & his ſon. However the enquiries on the plea *de quo waranto* were now again revived againſt the ſaid earl, whereupon the jurats for the wa- pentake of Neſſe [b] ' (touching thoſe who do not ſuffer the bailifs of ' the lord K. to enter their lands to make diſtreſs for the debt of ' the lord K. & other things) ſay, that John de Warenn E. of Surrey, doth ' not permit the bailifs of the lord K. to enter into his town of Staun- ' ford, to make ſeiſin or diſtreſſes for the debt of the lord K. & claims ' to have return of writs, & other liberties, to wit, aſſiſe of bread ' & beer, gallows, and other liberties, & we know not by what wa- ' rant. Therefore the ſherif was commanded to cauſe him to appear ' within 15 days after the Feaſt of St. John the Baptiſt, to ſhew his ' warant. And he was again preſented before the inquiſition, for that ' the bailif of Neſſe was wont to make, as well in the borough of ' Staunford as without, all executions of writs & amercements, 'till ' Tho. de Boulton, ſometime bailif of the Lord K. that is now, whilſt ' the borough was in his hands, would not ſuffer the bailifs of the lord ' K. to enter the foreſaid borough, & this for 16 years laſt paſt.' In the octaves of Trinity term the ſame year, the ſaid [c] ' John de Warenn ' E. of Surrey, having been ſummoned to anſwer the Lord K. touching ' a plea by what warant he claims to have his coroners, priſon, mer- ' cat, fair, tronage [toll of wool] peſage [cuſtom for weighing wares] ' & a certain toll called thurtol [thorough toll; toll for going thro' the town] ' in Staunford & Graham, without licenſe or will of ' him the lord K. And the E. comes, & as to coroners & priſon in ' the town of Graham, ſays, that he claims nothing but within the ' liberties only. He claims alſo mercat, fair, weyſt, gallows, & thur- ' tol in the ſame town, for that the now Lord K. by a like grant, ' held the town aforeſaid, & lord Henry the K. his father, & alſo they ' who formerly held the town aforeſaid for a great many years paſt, ' had all the foreſaid particulars. And, as to the town of Staun- ' ford, ſays, that he claims tronage by the grant of Lord Henry the ' K. father of the now lord K. who, on that account, granted him ' his charter. And, as to priſon, ſays, that that priſon is the Kings ' priſon, & that he hath the hereditary keeping thereof. And as to ' coroners, mercat, fair, weyſt, gallows, & thurtol, ſaith, that the now

a Baron. Vol. I. p. 79. a.
b Ex placit. coronæ apud Lincoln. anno 9. Edw. 1.
c Ex placit. de libertatibus & quo waranto,

coram J. de Vallibus & ſociis ſuis, juſtitiariis itinerantibus, apud Lincoln. in Octabis S. Trinitatis, anno R. Ed. nono. rot. 16. or dorſ.

' lord

' lord K. whilft he held the town of Staunford, had thofe liberties
' entire; who afterwards feoffed him the E. in that town, to hold
' as freely & entirely as the fame lord K. (then commonly called Lord
' Edward) held it on the day of making of the charter of feof-
' ment to the fame E. therefore made. And faith, that lord Henry the
' K. father of the now Lord K. & E. William, whilft they fucceffively
' held the forefaid town, enjoyed the liberties aforefaid entire. And
' Gilbert de Thornton, who fues for the lord K. as to mercat, fair,
' weyft, & gallows which he claims in Graham, demands judgment,
' whether a late feifin can be a fufficient warant to the fame E. for
' thefe things which merely belong to the crown of the lord K. And,
' as to prifon in the town of Staunford, concerning which the fame E.
' anfwers nothing, fave only that he claims the keeping thereof, &
' touching which keeping there is here no plea or defence made; de-
' fires judgment for the lord K. againft him the E. as one unable to
' make good his claim. And as to coroners, mercat, fair, weyft, &
' gallows, which he claims of old in the town of Staunford, defires
' judgment thereof (as the forefaid liberties may belong more efpeci-
' ally unto the crown of the lord K.) if a late feifin can be in
' thefe particulars a fufficient warant to the fame E. And, as to thur-
' tol in either town, the fame Gilbert demands judgment thereof, as
' the fame E. does not fhew from what perfons, merchandifes, or in
' what places, nor what, or how much toll of this fort he may take;
' And, becaufe the fame E. does not now produce his charter for tro-
' nage. [In the end] at the inftance of him the E. was given him a
' day here in the morrow of the clofe of Eafter to fhew his charter,
' & hear his judgment concerning all the bovefaid particulars; faving
' neverthelefs to the fame E. the liberty of making fuch farther reply
' as to him fhall feem proper. And upon this came one John de
' Creyfacre, fteward of H. E. of Lincoln, & faith exprefly, that there
' is no prifon, nor ought to be any, in this county, fave the prifon
' of Lincoln only; the keeping whereof is the right & inheritance
' of Marg. wife of the forefaid E. Afterwards, at the forefaid day,
' was given him a farther day, viz. 'till the Oftaves of the holy Tri-
' nity, to anfwer before the lord K. wherever he fhall be, in form
' aforefaid.

VIII. In 1281. a' Sir John de Oketon & Alice his wife, prefented   1281.
' William de Empingham clerc to the church of little Caftreton in
' Rutland, & recovered their prefentation to the faid Church from
' the prior *de novo loco* [or Newfted] by Stanford.' On the 6. of
Oft. 1281. 9. Ed. 1. The bifhop of Lincolns official being at Stanford, Oft. 6
directed his letters to the dean of that place, requiring him to cite   1281.
Sir Peter de Burley to appear before him the official at Northampton, 9. E. 1
on the Wednefday next after the feaft of all fouls, to fhew caufe why

a Wrights Rutland, p. 37.

he refufed to pay a mortuary, demanded of him, for fome of his family lately deceafed, by the convent of Burg; & to pay the charges of their fuit thereupon for his refufal. In his faid letters the faid official thus expreffes himfelf[a]. ' The official of the lord bifhop of ' Lincoln, to the difcreet man the dean of Stanford, health in the ' author of health. Whereas, in a caufe moved before us (touch-' ing a certain mortuary) between the religious men the abbat & ' convent of Burg actors of the one part, & Peter de Burley on the ' other part, &c. we have thought fit the faid Peter (for payment of ' the mortuary demanded by the forefaid religious, and for the expences ' which the fame religious have been at in the faid caufe) be fined to ' the fame religious in the fum of . . . leaving the charging of their ' expences to them. To you, by firmly enjoining, we command, that ' ye cite the faid Peter peremptorily to appear before us on the Wed-' nefday next after the commemoration of all fouls in the church of ' all faints at Northampton, to fee & hear the taxation aforefaid, & ' that ye compell him to make payment of the forefaid mortuary to ' the forewrit religious (as the tenents of the military fees, of the ' fame religious have been ufed to pay) by cenfure ecclefiaftical. Alfo that ' ye acquaint us, at the faid day & place, by your letters patents (con-' taining a feries of thefe) what ye fhall thereupon act. Given at ' Staunford, the day before the nones of Oct. 1281.' In obedience to this letter of the official, the dean of Stanford excommunicated the faid Peter de Burley, who thereupon fubmitted & paid the fore-faid mortuary demanded by the abbat & monks of Burg: which done, the dean made a return of the officials letter, and his own proceedings, after the following manner. [b]' To the man of reverend difcretion, ' the official of the bifhop of Lincoln, his humble & devoted the dean ' of Staunford, greeting, with all obedience. I have received your ' commands in thefe words. [Then recites them as above, & pro-ceeds] ' The which your commands I have reverently & fully exe-' cuted, alfo him, as to payment of the faid mortuary to be made to ' the religious aforewritten (as the tenents of the military fees of the ' fame religious have been ufed to pay) by cenfure ecclefiaftical have ' compelled. In witnefs whereof, I have put to the feal of the deanery ' of Staunford. Given at Staunford, the monday next after the feaft ' of SS. Simon & Jude, in the year abovefaid. Henry de Hanna, warden of the white friers at Stanford, [c]' was now rechofen provin-' cial of his order, & governed 1 8 years more. [d] For being in France, ' he was made provincial throughout the kingdoms of France, Scotland, ' Ireland, & Germany; & fpread his order far & near with incredible ' induftry.

IX. If we may believe my author[e], ' K. Ed. the 1. now bore fo great

a Ex regiftri penes Nob. Ducem de Monte acuto fupra citati, p. 317.
   b id. ib.

c Balæi Cent. 10. p. 59.
d Pits in vita.
e Baron Vol. I p. 79. a.

' a refpect

' a respect unto John E. Warenn [lord of Stanford] that by his charter
' dated the 7. of Oct. in the 10. year of his reign, for the more tranqui-
' lity & advantage of himself & his heirs, & of the whole realm (as
' the preamble imports) he granted to him and his heirs the castle of
' Dynas-Bran, which was in his possession at the beginning of his
' wars in Wales, & all the land of Bromfield, with the appurtenances
' which Griffin & Lewelin, Sons of Madoc Vaughan, either by them-
' selves or their guardians then held, excepting to the said K. & his
' heirs, the castle and land of Hope, with the appurtenances.   ª This year
' also, on assessing the scutage of Rothelan [castle in Wales] for the
' service of K. Edward against Lewelin prince of Wales, & other of
' the Welch, then in rebellion ; this E. was charged for eleven ᵇ knights
' fees, viz. six of his own inheritance, & five for Stanford & Graham
' in Com. Linc. [he] being personally in that service.   ᶜ But Leweline
' surprised the castles of Flint & Rudlan, with the person of the lord
' Clifford sent justiciar into those parts, & in a great battel overthrew
' the earls of Northumberland & Surrey, with the slaughter of sir
' William Lindsey, sir Richard Tanny, & many others.   ᵈ In the 11.   11. E. 1.
' Edw. 1. Griffin Vaughan, son to Griffin Vaughan of Bromfield, granted
' to John E. Warenn [lord of Stanford] all his land of Yale in North-
' Wales, which he had as his purparty of the inheritance of Griffin his
' father. But concerning this land of Yale so granted by Griffin
' Vaughan, as here noted ; as also of Bromfield, which this E. after-
' wards possessed, let us hear how Dr. Powel reporteth he came by
' them. Griffith ap Madoc (saith he ᵉ) took part with K. H. the 3. &
' Ed. 1. against the prince of North-Wales. And therefore for fear
' of the prince, he was fain to lie in his castle of Dinas Bran, which
' standeth on the top of a very steep hill, to the which there is no
' way but one to come. He died, his children being within age,
' whereupon shortly ensued the destruction of two of them. For the
' said K. Edw. the 1. gave the wardship of Madoc (who had for his
' part the lordship of Bromfield & Yale, & the castle of Dinas Bran,
' with reversion of Mallor Saesnec, after his mothers decease, who had
' the same to her joynture) to John E. Warenn [Lord of Stanford]
' & granted the wardship of Lewelin (to whose part the lordship of
' Chirke & Nanheudwy came) to Roger Mortimer. These guardians,
' forgetting the service done by the father of the wards to the K. so
' guarded their wards with small regard, that they never returned to
' their possessions. And shortly after, the said guardians did obtain
' the said lands to themselves, by charter of the King.   ᶠ This John
' E. Warenn [lord of Stanford] began to build Holt Castle, & Wil-
' liam his son finished the same.   ᵍ John Stanford, an English francis

a Bar. ut supra.   e Hist. Wales, p. 194.
b Bar. ut supra.   f Bar. Vol. 1. p. 79. b.
c Bakers Chron. p. 95 b.   g Antiq. English Francis. p. 98.
d Bar. Vol. 1. p. 79. b.

                                          ' can

' can was, about this time advanced to be archbishop of Dublin &
' lord lieutenant of Ireland.

X. The nuns of St. Michael by Stanford being fallen into great
poverty, Oliver Sutton bishop of Lincoln appropriated the 3ᵈ part
of the church of Corebi in Linc. (the patronage whereof was given them
by Sir Gilbert Pecche) to their use, reserving only part of the altarage
of the said part to the vicar, as had been before done on appropriation
of the two other 3ᵈ parts by his predecessor Hugh the 2ᵈ. On which
occasion bishop Sutton thus expresses himself. ᵃ ' To all, unto the
' knowledge of whom the present writing shall come, Oliver, by divine
' permission, the humble minister of the church of Lincoln, health
' in God thro' whom all health is derived and increased. As alienati-
' ons & appropriations of parochial churches to religious persons (for the
' fruits & profits of the same to be converted to their particular uses)
' are detested by all the prelates of the church of Christ, especially since,
' except in cases of manifest poverty & other great necessity, they are
' by a very late law universally forbid; so, by assent of the very
' words, if an evidence of poverty, & a just cause concurring, may
' accidentally give occasion for any appropriation of this sort to be
' made; we hold it both convenient in law, as well as agreeable to
' piety, that it should be done. We therefore, at their incessant ap-
' plication, favourably inclining to the pious intreaties & tearful cries
' of our beloved daughters in Christ the prioress & nuns of the mo-
' nastery of St. Michael without Stanford, of our diocese, wherewith
' they continually weary us (whose estate, thro' their too great pover-
' ty, which almost extends to the misery of extreme want, touched
' with a pious compassion, we are compelled to condole) & alike re-
' membring it to be written by the judicious, that it is a natural fault
' for that to be neglected by all which is possessed in common, as he
' who holds but a part may think he hath nothing; and which is true
' that a community among divers does but more often, as it is written,
' occasion discords & disturbances; whence it necessarily follows, that
' just as great as the division of things is, just as much is the odious
' renewal of such dissentions: have therefore thought fit, that the third
' part of the church of Corebi in the deanery of Weltesse (of which
                                                        ' third

ᵃ Universis, ad quorum notitiam pervenerit presens scriptum, Oliverus, permissione
divina, Lincolniensis ecclesie humilis minister, salutem in Deo per quem salus omnis
pervenit & augetur. Sicut alienationes &
appropriationes parochialium ecclesiarum re-
ligiosis personis, de fructibus & proventibus
earundem in usus suos proprios converten-
dis, omnibus prelatis ecclesie Christi *opido*
[sic in MS.] sunt exose; presertim, cum
nisi in manifeste paupertatis & juste cause
casibus, sint de jure novissimo generaliter
interdicte; sic, assensu verborum, si paupertatis evidentia & justa causa concurrens, ap-

propriationem aliquam hujusmodi casualiter
commoveat faciendam, id fieri tam jure
conveniens quam pietati consonum arbitra-
mur. Nos igitur dilectarum in Christo fili-
arum Priorisse & monialium monasterii S.
Michaelis extra Stanford, nostre ditionis
(quarum statum, propter nimiam ipsarum
paupertatem, que fere accidit in miseriam
extreme egestatis, pie compassionis affectu
cogimur condolere) piis supplicationibus &
vocibus lachrymosis, quibus continue nos
lacessunt, inclinati favorabiliter nimio tractu;
& a peritis scriptum esse pariter animadver-
tentes, naturale vitium esse negligi ab omni-
                                                   bus

' third part the right of patronage, by a legal collation of Sir Gil-
' bert Pecche Kt. to thofe poor fifters is now known to belong; &
' two parts of all which church the fame nuns by grant of the bifhop,
' long time ago, to their proper ufe have had, and have) to the fame
' poor nuns (for confolidation of the Church it felf, & for ceafing of
' difcord moved as well in neceffity as before in epifcopal piety) with
' confent of the chapter of our church of Lincoln, by tenor of the pre-
' fents, be henceforth given unto their proper ufe, & with all its
' fruits & profits, to them & their fucceffors for ever freely granted.
' We appoint moreover, that the altarage of the part mentioned be
' according to the modus & conditions of an ordination of the vicar-
' age in the church abovefaid out of the pietaxaty of the lord, & af-
' fign it to the fame for an augmentation to the vicars for the time
' being continually for the future. Saving always nevertheless all
' epifcopal dues, & the dignity of our church of Lincoln. In witnefs
' whereof our feal is to thefe prefents appendent. Given at Thorne,
' the 2d of the ides of November, in the year of our lord 1284, &
' of our pontificate the fifth.'   I cannot difmifs this deed without fetting down here a remark made thereupon by a right reverend prelate.
' Some of our Englifh bifhops, faith his lordfhip [a], were now fo fenfi-
' ble of the iniquity and fhame of this practice of appropriations,
' that they dar'd no longer venture on it without apologie, & con-
' feffion of their doing ill.   For thus, within our own diocefe, when
' Oliver bifhop of Lincoln appropriated the church of Corbi to the
' nuns of Stanford, he was forced to make this acknowledgment;
' That alienations & appropriations of parochial churches, by converting
' the fruits & profits of them to the ufe of religious perfons, were
' abfolutely odious to all the prelates of the church, & had been for-
' bidden by a late law, nor could be tolerable but in cafes of mani-
' feft poverty & other great neceffity.

XI. But to proceed, fee the juftice of Gods judgments! He who
was formerly cruel to another mans children, by a fad accident now
lofes his own fon.   ' For [b] William Warenn [fon & heir of John E. of

---

bus quod communiter poffidetur, ut qui tenet pro parte exiftimet fe nihil habere; quod-
que verum, communio inter plures difcordie, ficut fcriptum eft, multo multoties eft
fomentum; ex quo neceffario fequitur, quod
quantum eft rerum divifio, odiofa tantum
eft ipfarum redintegratio : Tertiam partem
ecclefie de Corebi in decanatu de Weltteffa
(cujus tertie partis jus patronatus, ex legi-
tima collatione D. Gilberti Pecche militis,
ad ipfas pauperes nunc nofcitur pertinere,
cujufque totius ecclefie duas partes eedem
moniales, ex conceffione pontificali, a lon-
giffimis retro temporibus, in ufus proprios
habuerunt, & habent) eifdem pauperibus
monialibus (pro confolidatione ipfius ecclefie, & feceffione difcordie, tam in necef-
fitate quam pietate fuadente ante pontificali)
de confenfu capituli ecclefie noftre Linc.

Tenore prefentium, duximus concedendam
ex nunc in ufus proprios, & cum omnibus
fructibus & proventibus fuis, fibi & fuccefforibus fuis, perpetuis temporibus libere concedendam. Ordinamus infuper alteragium
memorate partis juxta modos & conditiones
ordinationis vicarii in ecclefia fupradicta ex
Domini pietaxate, & affignamus eidem in
augmentum vicariis qui pro tempore fuerint
ufq; quaq; pro futuris. Salvis femper tamen omnibus epifcopalibus confuetudinibus,
& ecclefie noftre Linc. dignitate. In cujus
rei Teft. figillum noftrum prefentibus eft
appenfum. Dat. apud Thorne, 2 Idus Novembris, A. D. 1284. & Pontif. noftri quinto. Ex codicum MS. Dodfworthianorum
Vol. 59. Fol. 165, &c.

a Bp. Kennets Par. Ant. p. 435.
b Stow. p. 311.

2

' Surrey

' Surrey & lord of Stanford] in a turneament at Croyden, was by the
' challenger intercepted, and cruelly flain.' Thus [a] ' this William
' died in the life time of the E. his father, on the 18. of the Kal. of

Dec. 15. 1286. 15. E. 1. ' Jan. [to wit the 15. of Dec.] 1286. 15. Ed. 1. leaving Joan his
' lady great with child of John his fon & heir, & was buried before
' the high altar in the abbey of Lewes. Joan relict of the faid Wil-
' liam, was daughter of Robert de Vere E. of Oxford. The faid Wil-
' liam had with her the manors of Medmenham in Bucks, Crawmerfh
' in Oxfordshire, and Befton in Norfolk in frank-marriage. As alfo
' the manors of Pritelwell, Tiburne, Wulfhamftone, Nechamfted, &
' Ginges; and lands of ten pound *per annum* in Ceftreham. [b] On the

2 May. 1287. ' 2. of May 1287, all the Jewes in England were apprehended, by precept
' from the K. being then at Bourdeaux, for what caufe it was not known,
' and they redeemed themfelves for 12000 *l.* of filver. [c] It is reported,
' that the commons graunted the K. the fifte parte of their movables,
' to have the Jewes banifhed out of the land; but the Jewes gave
' the K. greate fummes whereby they tarried yet a while longer.
' [d] John, fon of William (fon of John E. Warenn) was born on the

June 30. Mar. 24. 1287-8. 16. E. 1. ' 2[d] of the Kalends of July, to wit, June 30. 1287. 15. Ed. 1.' This
child fo born was afterwards lord of Stanford. It being the cuftom,
time out of mind, that the lord of Stanford for the time being, from
mid-lent Sunday to Eafter in the fair time, had the profit of all ftalls
belonging to his own tenents & abutting on the ftreets, in fuch places
as mid-lent fair is wont to be kept, & ufed to let them, for that feafon at his pleafure, to foreign merchants & tradefmen, one Nicholas
Fraunton, who had fuch a ftall in Stanford, refufed to empty the fame
in order for E. Warenns bailifs to let it to fome foreigner as had been accuftomed; whereupon Robert Shirelock & Clement de Burley the faid
Earls bailifs, affifted by Alexander Lucas, Hugh de Tykencoate, Ralph
de Erlfthorpe, & Hugh Bunting, publickly broke open his faid ftall, and
cleared it for that purpofe. On occafion whereof a fuit afterwards commenced between the faid Nicholas Fraunton & the earls bailifs; of which
more prefently. In 1288. [e] ' began a new taxation of the value of all
' churches, the tenths whereof were granted to K. Edw. by his holinefs,
' as an aid toward his expedition to the holy land; which, that they
' might be gathered to the full extent, the pope appointed two princi-
' pal collectors, Richard bifhop of Winchefter & Oliver bifhop of Lin-
' coln, who in every diocefe were to appoint their deputies & affift-
' ants. In this diocefe the delegated collectors were the abbat of Ofe-
' ney by Oxford, & the prior of St. Catherines by Lincoln. The in-
' quifition began this year, but the return was not fully made till
' 1292.

a Bar. Vol. 1. p. 80. b.
b Stow, p. 311.
c Holingfhed, p. 795. b.

d Bar. Vol. 1. p. 80. b.
e Bp. Kennets Par. Ant. p. 312.
Pat. 13 E. 1. m. 15

XII. On

XII. On the 10. of June 1289. 17. E. 1. Oliver bishop of Lincoln, June 10. under his episcopal seal, set forth a particular what the vicarage of St. 1289. Martins confisted of; whereby it appears, that the vicar was to pay two 17. E. 1 marcs a year to his patronesses the nuns of St. Michael, conditionally that if the chappel of Burgele, in the same his parish, ought to have service done in it, the said nuns should be at the charge of it. Also that the vicar was only to pay finodals; and the nuns the arch-deacons procurations and all other dues. The bishops letter runs thus. a 'To all ' unto whom the present letter shall come, Oliver by divine permission ' bishop of Lincoln, [greeting] in the savior of all. We make known ' to your univerfality by these presents, that the regiftry of the ordina- ' tion of vicarages lying in our diocese, being examined, thus, among ' other things, is found to be contained in the same. The vicarage in ' the church of St. Martin Staunforde, which is [the vicarage] of the ' priorefs and convent of St. Michael, Staunford, confifts in the whole ' altarage of the said church, by paying thence yearly to the said nuns ' two marcs; so nevertheless, that if the chappel of Burgele in the same ' his parish ought to have divine service, the said nuns shall support the ' charge of that chappel; also the vicar shall pay only finodals, and the ' said nuns shall pay the archdeacons procurations, & shall fuftain all ' other charges. In witnefs whereof our seal is to the presents appen- ' dent. Given at Edclesberge, the 4ᵗʰ of the nones of June 1289.

XIII. On the 22 of Jan. 12$\frac{88}{99}$. 18. E. 1. Robert Shirelock & Clement Jan. 22, de Burley E. Warenns bailiffs, with all their abettors aforesaid, b ' were 12$\frac{88}{99}$. ' attached to answer Nicholas de Fraunton, touching a plea, why they 18. E. 1. ' lately by force and arms broke open the house of him Nicholas at ' Staunford, and his goods & chattels to the value of 40 *l.* there found, ' took and carried away, & other enormities &c. to the grievous lofs, ' &c. & againft the kings peace, &c. whence he complains, that on ' the thurfday in the vigils of the annunciation in the 16 of the ' now K. they did to him the things aforesaid, and his goods & ' chattels, to wit, silver in pence, gold rings, & gold ᶜfirmacles, silver ' spoons, one forcer, one cup of mazer, one cup of silver, cloaths, ' linnen & woolen, & other goods & chattels to the value, &c. there ' found, took and carried away, whence he says, he hath been made ' worfe & is endamaged to the value of 40 *l.* & therefore brings his ' suit, &c. And the forefaid Alexander & others have come and de- ' fended the force and injury, when, &c. & the forefaid Alexander ' [Lucas] Hugh Bunting, Hugh de Tykencote, and Ralph [de Erlefthorpe] ' say, they are in nothing culpable, & touching this matter put them- ' felves upon their proper, &c. And the forefaid Robert & Clement say ' by themfelves, that whilft the forefaid town was in the hands of the

a Ex regiftri prioratus S. Michaelis juxta Stanford penes Galf. Minfhul Gen. Anno 1657. Fol. 4. b. & Mon. Ang. Tomi 2. Pagina 881. a.

b Ex placitis coram D. Rege apud Weft-monaft. in Octabis S. Hilarii, Anno R. R. E. 1. xviij°.

c Firmacula.

ᶜ lord

' lord K. & before, time out of mind, there was a custom in the same
' town, that all they who have stalls & shops in the same ought to
' open them in the fair time, & let them out to foreign merchants
' & others, to sell their wares in the same, the which state the same lord
' the K. hath granted to E. Warenn.   And say, that they, as being the
' bailiffs of him the E. went to the foresaid Nicholas, and demanded
' that they might let out that stall to the merchants aforesaid,
' who utterly protested against it ; for which they, as bailifs of him
' the E. opened the stall of him Nicholas, as to them the bailifs hath been
' lawful by the custom used in those parts [of the town] at the fair
' time, as is aforesaid ; nor have they taken or carried away any thing
' of the goods of him Nicholas found in the same, &c. & touching this
' put themselves upon their proper, &c.   And Nicholas saith, that he
' holds the foresaid stall of the lord K. *in capite* by serjeantry, & not
' of him the E.   And saith moreover, that the foresaid E. by no
' customs used in those parts of any tenements or tenents of the lord
' K. *in capite, &c.*   ought to have entrance, or them let out to
' any body against the will of him Nicholas, &c. but of the tenents
' holding of him the E. only.   And touching this puts himself upon
' his proper, &c. and Robert & Clement in like manner, &c. before the
' K. from that day three weeks, where-ever he shall be, &c. unless justice
' be done them before. And afterwards in the quindisme of St. Hillary,
' in the 19. of the K. now, came the jurats and parties in like manner.
' And the jurats say, upon their oath, that Alexander Lucas, Hugh
' Bunting, & Hugh de Tykencote, & Ralph [de Erlesthorpe] are in
' nothing blameable.   And, as to Robert Shirelock & Clement de Bur-
' ley, say, that they are the bailifs of E. Warenn.   And say, that the
' E. who now is, & his ancestors, & all they who have been lords
' of the foresaid town of Staunford, have used such a privilege, that
' from mid-lent till Easter, in the time of the fair, they ought to have,
' & have been accustomed to have, the profits of the stalls abutting
' on the streets, in the places where the fair hath been accustomed to
' be held.   And say, that the custom of the town is such, that if they
' who are owners of the stalls shall have shut up those stalls (after they
' shall have been required to open them) & have refused it, it is law-
' ful for the bailifs of the E. to break or set open those stalls, even
' tho' the owner of the same consent not, so that the foresaid E. may
' do therein his pleasure, & receive the profits of the same for the time
' aforesaid.   And because the foresaid Alexander and the others are in
' nothing culpable, according to the verdict of the jurats, it is determi-
' ned that the foresaid Nicholas take nothing by his writ, but be . . . .
' for his false clamor, &c. & the foresaid Alexander & others thence
' without a day, &c.' —About this time, if not earlier, ' Thomas son of
' Peter Marche of Staunford gave to . . . . . . one half acre of land
' lying in Wirthop meadows, between the meadow of Walter, west, &
' the meadow of William, east ; & heading upon the cross called may-

' denes

' denes croſs, ſouth, & on the bank of the Welland, north. B. H.' Perhaps the ſiſters who gave name to maiden-lane in Stanford, & as the
tradition goes, built great S. Michaels church, likewiſe erected this croſs:
but where it ſtood I am yet to ſeek.—— About this time alſo, if not
earlier, ' Henry Morin of Stanford gave to Samſon ſon of Roger Cokla . . .
' of Stanford, one houſe in Hovenſty, ſituate between the houſe of
' Nigel Madding north, & a houſe ſometime Robert Lennes of the
' other part; to have and to hold, &c. by paying therefore yearly to the
' lord of the fee (to wit, Henry Gangy) or his aſſigns, 12 d. at the
' two terms of the year, &c. B. H.'

XIV. The ſame year, ᵃ ' to purge England (whither K. E. the 1. was
' now returned from France) from ſuch corruptions and oppreſſions,
' as it groaned under, and not neglecting therein his own particular
' gaine, the K. baniſhed the Jews out of the realme, confiſcating all
' their goods, leaving them (as they by their cruel uſuries had eaten
' his people to the bones) nothing but mony to bear their charges.
' ᵇ The number of Jews now expulſed was 15060 perſons, whoſe
' houſes being ſold, the K. made a mighty maſſe of money.   William
' the conqueror, as Leland obſervesᶜ, firſt gave them leave to come
' over from Roan.   Whence in a little time they ſpread themſelves
' all over the kingdom, planting their ſynagogues in the beſt ſort of
' towns wherein they accurately taught the doctrine of their rabbins.
[But what is remarkable] ' as the number of Jews in Britain increaſed
' infinitely, equally with them increaſed uſury, & a ſordid love of riches.
' For ſome little time the Engliſh bore with their avarice, but at length
' when K. Richard the 1. came to the crown, they were ſeverely hand-
' led. Afterwards in the reign of this K. Edw. ſirnamed Longſhanks, all
' their riches were confiſcated to the kings treaſury, and their perſons
' baniſhed.   Then their ſynagogues at Huntingdon & Stanford being
' profaned, all the furniture, with the noble libraries belonging to them,
' were ſold by outcry.   At which time one Gregory de Huntingdon, a
' monk of Ramſey, being both a neighbour and full of mony, as ſoon
' as he heard of this auction, made haſt to the ſale, & giving the price
' ſet upon them, for his braſs (as he eaſily might at ſuch a time) got
' books worth gold, and returned to Ramſey overjoyed with the pur-
' chaſe.   This Gregory, before theſe things happened, had been very
' diligent in the ſtudy of the [learned] languages, & particularly the
' Hebrew; only he before wanted a ſufficient plenty of books to per-
' fect him in rudiments of ſo celebrated a ſtudy; wherewith this acci-
' dent compleatly ſupplied him. And what does he afterwards but night
' and day apply himſelf to theſe Hebrew copies, 'till out of theſe
' fountains he hath drawn a more perfect knowledge of the tongue.
' To his fellow monks he left of his own writing many choice anno-
' tations, which poſterity may read with a learned joy.   The catalogue

a Speed. p. 650. 651.   b Stow. p. 313.   c Comment. p, 321.

' of

' of Ramſey library makes large & honorable mention of the Hebrew
' books which he very induſtriouſly procured for that monaſtery.'   But
to return.   Mr. Holingſhed, ſpeaking of this expulſion of the Jews,
differs in ſome things from my authors above, beſides which his account
contains ſome circumſtances not elſewhere to be met with.   His relation runs thus.   a ' All their goodes not movable were confiſcate,
' with their tallies and obligations; but all other theyr goodes that
' were movable, togither with their coyne of gold and ſilver, the K.
' licenſed them to have and conveigh with them.   A ſort of the richeſt
' of them, being ſhipped with their treaſure in a mightie talle ſhippe
' which they had hired, when the ſame was under ſayle and gote downe
' the Thames towards the mouth of the river beyonde Quinborowe,
' the maſter mariner bethought him of a wile, and cauſed his menne
' to caſte ancre, & ſo rode at the ſame, till the ſhippe, by ebbing of
' the ſtreame, remayned on the drie landes.   The maſter herewith en-
' tiſed the Jews forth with him to walke aland for their recreation,
' and at length, when he underſtoode the tide to be comming in, he
' gote him backe to the ſhippe, whither he was drawne up by a corde.
' The Jewes made not ſo muche haſt as he did, bycauſe they were not
' ware of the daunger.   But when they perceyved how the matter
' ſtoode, they cried to him for helpe: but he tolde them that they
' ought to crie rather to Moyſes, by whoſe conduct their fathers paſſed
' through the red ſea, & therefore, if they would call to him, he
' was able ynough to helpe them out of thoſe raging flouds whiche
' nowe came in upon them: they cried indeede, but no ſuccour ap-
' peared; & ſo they were ſwallowed up in the water.   The maſter re-
' turned with the ſhippe, & told the K. howe he had uſed the matter,
' & had both thanks & rewarde, as ſome have written; where[as]
' other affirme, & more truly as ſhould ſeeme, that divers of thoſe
' mariners whiche dealte ſo wickedly againſt the Jewes, were hanged
' for their wicked practiſe, & ſo receyved a juſt rewarde of their frau-
' dulente & miſchievous dealing.'——About this time, if not earlier,
' Philip Gangy of Staunford clerc, gave to Hugh Child burgeſs of
' Staunford, the yearly rent of twelve pence, with the appurtenances,
' to wit, reliefs, eſchaets, &c. to be received of thoſe houſes which
' Simon ſon of the ſaid Hugh held of him in the lane called Ovenſty.
' B. H.——Not far from High-Dike, ſaith Mr. Butcher, upon the north
' ſide of the town of Stanford near unto York high way, and about
' twelve-ſcore from the town gate called Clement gate, *ſtands* [ſaith
he, in his account printed 1646. p. 27. *ſtood* in the MS. copy of his
intended 2d. Edition which ends 1659. p. 40. which laſt, by the by,
ſhews when it was demoliſhed] ' an antient croſſe of free-ſtone of a
' very curious fabric, having many ſcutcheons inſculped in the ſtone
' about it, as the armes of Caſtile and Leon quartered, being the pa-

a p. 799. a. b.

2   ' ternal

' ternal coat of the K. of Spain, and divers other hatchments belong-
' ing to that crowne, which envious time hath fo defaced, that only
' the ruins appear to my eye, and therefore are not to be defcribed by
' my pen.   This croffe, continues he, was called Queens Crofs, and
' erected by K. Edw. the firft in memory of Eleanor his wife ; who
' (as the ftory goes) when her husband was wounded with an inveno-
' med [arrow, in the printed account; dart, in the MS. but in both
he is miftaken, for as hath been fhewn ᵃ it was a dagger] ' with her
' mouth fucked the poyfon out, and fo healed her lord, when all his chi-
' rurgeons and phyficians had left the wound for mortal.' So Butcher.
But tho' the ftory of her fucking the poyfon out of her husbands wounds
be falfe, yet this princefs was indeed a great example of conjugal affection,
and therefore was this at Stanford, and other croffes elfewhere, erected
to her memory, by K. Edw. her husband, to exprefs his abundant forrow for the lofs of her.   ' ᵇ For in this 19. of Edw. 1. Q. Eleanor (the
' K. being then on his way towardes the bordures of Scotland) ᶜ was
' taken with a grievous ficknefs, and departed this life at Herdby, a
' Towne neer unto Lincoln (on the 9. of Nov. Butcher.   28. Nov.
' Stow.   29. Nov. Holingfhed, and Speed.   10 Dec. [iv. Idus Dec.]
' Walfingham) ᵈ whereupon the K. having now loft the jewel which
' he moft efteemed, ᵉ returned to convey the corps towards London,
' which he did with great forrow; for he bewailed the loffe of her all
' the daies of his life.   Her bowels were buried at Lincolne, & a tombe
' erected there, with the armes of Caftile thereupon, in our lady chappel.
' And in every place in which the body of the Q. was ftaied in bring-
' ing up to London, the K. caufed a ftately croffe to be erected, ᶠ of
' cunning workmanfhip, ᵍ every one of them being garnifhed with the
' image of the fame Q. alfo with his armes and hers.'   The croffes
erected were, 1. at Herdby.   2. Lincoln.   3. Grantham.   4. Stanford.
5. Gedington   6. Northampton.   7. Stony Stratford.   8. Dunftable.
9. Woborne.   10. St. Albans.   11. Waltham.   12. Weft-Cheape.
13. Charing-Crofs.   ' ʰ Thus her body was brought to Weftminfter,
' and there buried the 17. of December.   ⁱ Thefe croffes were thus fet
' up, to the end, that, according to the devotion of thofe times, all fuch
' as paffed by might be moved to pray for her foul.'   Some of thefe
croffes do yet remain & teftifie both the grief & magnificence of the
husband, as well as the mutual loves of him & the lady.   That at
Stanford is indeed utterly perifhed.   However the remains of what was
left in 1646. (when Mr. Butcher printed his Book) would not, I fuppofe, have fo fuddenly difappeared, as by his MS. I find they did, had
not thofe falvages in the great rebellion, more envious than time, fwept

a See the relation at large, Anno 1271.   e Stow, ut fupra
above.   f Hol.
  b Hol. Vol. II. p. 799. b.   g Stow.
  c Stow, p. 113.   h id.
  d Hol. ut fupra.   i Walfingham fub anno 1291.

away the very foundations of it.   But the cry of fuperftition hunts
down fuch things as thefe a great deal fafter than age can difpatch them.
As to queen Eleanor I fhall only add, Mr. Butcher fays (& pretends
to quote a book of Peterborough for it) that fhe founded a nunnery at
Stanford.   If fo, that nunnery could not be (as he thinks) the nunnery of S. Michael, fince that nunnery (as I have fhewn) was founded
in 1156. by William Walterville abbat of Burg; nor yet (I think) that
other nunnery at Wirthorp, afterwards united to S. Michael; but as
Mr. Speed (in his draught of Stanford) fets down the fite of a nunnery clofe by the black friers without Stanford, that, if any, muft be
the nunnery of Q. Eleanors foundation.   However, both of that nunnery fo marked down by Speed, & of this faid to have been erected by
Q. Eleanor, I as yet find not a tittle farther.

XV. ‘ a Alice, wife of John E. Warenn [lord of Stanford] fifter by
‘ the mothers fide to K. Henry the 3d. departed this life the 5. of the
‘ ides of Feb. an. 1290. (19. E. 1.) & was buried under a marble
‘ ftone, before the high altar in the abby church of Lewes, whereon
‘ the figure of a dragon, with a branch in his mouth, was graven. b This
‘ 19. E. 1. died alfo Gilbert Peche abovementioned, baron of Brunne,
‘ a benefactor to the nuns of St. Michael by Stanford.   About this time,
‘ or fome time before, Emma, daughter of Walter de S. Eadmundo,
‘ late burgefs of Staunford, gave to Walter of Staunford the phyfician,
‘ an houfe of hers ftanding in great S. Michaels parifh, viz. in the fouth
‘ head of the lane called Feldovenefty; between her tenement north
‘ & fouth, & near a tenement of Roger de Offington weft, & the fore-
‘ faid lane eaft. B. H.   In 1291. Emma, wife of Bartholomew de S.
‘ Feriolo, gave to Walter the phyfician of Stanford, a houfe ftanding
‘ in Colgate, &c. For corroboration of this covenant, Ralph, then rector
‘ of St. Marys at the bridge, was made furety for the above Emma. B. H.
This Emma, wife of Bartholomew de S. Feriolo, was the fame with
the above Emma, daughter of Walter de S. Eadmundo.   ‘ Richard, fon
‘ of Richard le Ferun of Stanford, clerc, gave [but when I find not]
‘ to Walter of Stanford the phyfician, one little empty place lying
‘ near the lane called Ovenefty in great S. Michaels parifh, between
‘ a place of Symon Child, north, and a houfe of Bartholomew the
‘ clerc, fouth. B. H.’

XVI. Under this 20. E. 1. the Oxford antiquary Mr. Anthony Wood
places the beginning of the modern fchools at Stanford.   Thefe are
his words.   ‘‘ That we may trace this more antient univerfity of Stan-
‘ ford [antient if oppofed to their opinion who think there was no
univerfity here before the Oxford men removed hither in 1333. &
1334.] ‘ let us examine its firft original, as far at leaft as can be
‘ difcovered by antient regifters; rejecting in the mean while the au-

Feb. 9.
1290.
19. E. 1.

20. E. 1.

a Baron. Vol. 1. p. 80. a.   c fub anno 1334
b id. p. 677. a.

‘ thority

' thority of thofe writers, who refer its inftitution to Bladud, 870
' years before the birth of our Saviour. And why fhould we not be
' of opinion that it was begun by Mr. Robert Lutterel, who ftudying
' for a time at Oxford, became afterwards rector of Ernham in this
' county? For in the 20th of Edw. 1. he made over the manor which
' he held in St. Peters parifh in Stanford, to the prior & convent of
' Sempringham, devoting it equally to the increafe of the faid convent,
' and fupport of fuch as fhould here ftudy divinity & philofophy; And
' alfo for the maintenance, either of a regular, or fecular, clerc, who
' fhould celebrate mafs within the chappel of the Bleffed Virgin in
' the faid manor. From this gift therefore of the faid Mr. Robert
' Lutterel (which I find confirmed on the 29. of Nov. 1303. by
' John d'Alderby bp. of Lincoln) I do not at all doubt began thefe
' fchools at Stanford, which the Oxonians (frequenting the place) find-
' ing to become famous, efpecially, as it is probable, the northern men,
' they removed to it; not at all driven thither by any difturbances in
' their own univerfity, but chiefly allured by the newnefs of the place,
' and other inducements.' Now when Mr. Wood fays, ' why fhould
' we not believe this univerfity was begun by mafter Robert Lutterel?'
Without intending any rudenefs to the judgment of fo eminent an
antiquary, I cannot help replying, why fhould we? That Robert Lutterel built a fort of a college here, and endowed it, as he affirms, I am
fo far from denying, that I fhall hereafter more largely illuftrate. But
I only ask, & it is as fair a queftion, whether he might not as probably
follow the example fet him by fome other perfon, as be the firft example to others? Since he had fo much refpect for the monks of S.
Gilbert, as to provide for the academical inftruction of the novices of
their order; if there were no univerfity here before, one would think
either Cambridge or Oxford (where they might be fure of good tutors)
would have been more convenient for fuch a purpofe. But that there
was an univerfity already begun here, and that the neighbouring youth
found as bright an education in it, as either of the other univerfities
of the kingdom afforded, before ever Mr. Lutterel founded, or thought
of founding, a houfe of learning in this town; a confideration of the
following particulars, I think, will make appear. That the Carmes
had a monaftery here, is as evident, as that the Gilbertine monks had
a place here called Sempringham hall. Alfo that the Carmes monaftery
at Stanford was founded by K. H. the 3. before Mr. Lutterel founded
Sempringham hall, is, I think, plain from what hath been elfewhere faid.
That the Carmes had alfo fchools here, & taught the neighbouring
youth is likewife notorious. Robert Lutterel, as Mr. Wood himfelf
acknowledges, founded Sempringham hall in this place this 20. of E. 1.
(feven or eight years before Henry de Hanna died, & above 40 after
he was firft elected Provincial) fo that he grants this univerfity was begun in the time of Henry de Hanna, tho' not by him. However, as
both the Carmes, & monks of Sempringham were, with other reli-

gious orders, indisputably patrons of this infant university (if begun in these times) I cannot but look on the Carmes (as being of older standing here than the monks of Sempringham) of the two, to be the most probable beginners of it. For let any person of judgment consider who was the fittest for such a work? Robert Lutterel, a private person, of a noble family indeed, but himself only rector of Irnham in Lincolnshire? Or Henry de Hanna, a man of great learning and figure, being provincial of the whole order of mount Carmel in England? Of as much diligence, for he spread his order far & near with incredible industry; And of interest and power equal to both, having procured so many noble monasteries to be erected for his brethren: Particularly one by the K. himself in this very place? From what hath been offered, to me then it seems almost certain, that Henry de Hanna (if it was not begun before his time) was the beginner of academical education & of the university it self at Stanford. For nothing could conduce more to the reputation of himself, or his order; And consequently to the spreading of it. And certainly no man was, at that time, better fitted for such a purpose, than he who had already succeeded in several other great undertakings. What confirms all this is, that the Carmelite fathers (as I shall hereafter shew) were all along the chief professors and tutors of the youth in this university. The Carmelites then, by reading lectures in philosophy and divinity, obtaining great renown, the monks of Sempringham, & other monasteries and abbies which lay near Stanford, sent first, it is probable, a few of their most towardly youth to be instructed by them at that place. But the number of these youth increasing every day, thro' their tutors reputation; the white friers, and other monasteries, at Stanford, grew too narrow for their reception. From this want of room, the patrons, abbats, & priors of such neighbouring cloisters as sent their youth to Stanford, were first obliged to hire, and afterwards build houses or inns, for reception of their people at Stanford; where they might both improve their knowledge, & perform their novitiate under inspection of an old monk or two, whom, it is like, they generally sent with them from their own monasteries to Stanford; both to inspect their private conduct, & likewise see they attended the public lectures, with all proper diligence and application; & perhaps also to read to them & others in their own houses. Such to me, it is most probable, was the beginning of this university; nor could Mr. Lutterel desire a greater encouragement than this for granting his manor in S. Peters parish for maintenance of the Gilbertine youth, to follow their studies in this then rising & very hopeful university. In which example he was seconded at least, if not preceded, by the abbats of Peterborough & Valdey; &, if we may believe tradition, those of Croyland, Thorney, & several other neighbouring convents.

XVII. In 1292. was compleated the general taxation of church dignities

nities and benefices. It was divided into two parts: The first called the taxation of the temporalities of the clergy; the second of their spiritualities. In the taxation of the temporalities of the clergy, occur these particulars.

	l.	*s.*	*d.*
' [a] The abbat of Valdey has in the deanry of Staunford——	1	4	00
' The abbat of Swynesheued in the same ——— ———	1	3	4
' The abbat of Crouland in the same ——— ——— ——	3	15	0
' The abbat of Burg in the same —— —— —— ——	14	5	10
' The abbat of Brunne in the same [b] ——— ——— ——	10	00	00

' The prior of S. Leonard without Staunford has,

' in the Deanery of Hoylland —— ——— ———	3	2	00
' in the D. of Nesse ——— ——— ——— ——	00	15	00
' in the D. of Staunford ——— ——— ——— ——	7	17	6
' in the D. of Aslackhow ——— —— ——— —	8	7	5
' in the D. of Manlake —— ——— ——— —	3	3	00
' in the D. of Lafford in Roteland, under the ' prior of Durhams name —— ——— ———	32	2	00
' in the D. of Manlake, under the same priors ' name —— ——— ——— ——— ——	1	13	9

' The prior of Newsted without Staunford, has,

' in the Deanery of Staunford ——— ——— ———	9	3	00
' in the D. of Boteleshawe ——— ——— ———	1	14	00
' in the D. of Roteland ——— ——— ———	5	19	11
' in the D. of Colyngham ——— ——— ——	10	00	00
' in the D. of Nesse —— ——— ——— ——	12	00	00

' The abbat of [c] Croxton has in the D. of Staunford ——— ——	1	11	4
' The prior of Broke in the same ——— ——— ——	2	13	4
' The abbat of Thorney in the same ——— ——— ——	00	18	00¼
' The prior of Fynnesheued in the same ——— ——	3	15	00
' The abbat of Crokesden in the same —— ——— —	00	17	10
' The abbat of Pipwell [d] in the same ——— ——	00	18	8
' The prior of Huntyndon in the churches of Staunford[e]	00	15	10
' The nuns of S. Michael without Staunford, have in temp. ' & spirit. in one place with another in the diocese ' of Lincoln, altogether —— ——— —— ———	66	13	4

' [f] In the taxation of the spirituality, of the deanery of Staunford,

' The church of S. John, besides a pension ——— ——— —	11	6	8
' A pension of the prior of S. Fremund in the same ch. ——	00	13	4
' A pension of the prior of Durham in S. Mary Bynwerk ' church, not to be taxed —— ——— —— ———	1	00	00

a Extract. e perantiquo valore penes Rich. Rawlinson L. L. D. Oct. 3. 1726.

b Brunne, 40. s. Tiberius, C. X. fol. 95. b.

c Croxton. 21. s. 4. d. id fol. 98. b.

d Pipwel. 46. s. 8. id. fol. 103.

e Huntyndon 12. s. id. p. 105.

f E. codicis MS. in bib. Cott. sub imagine Tib. C. X. fol. 122. b.

' S. Peters

	l.	*s.*	*d.*
' S. Peters church, befides a penfion ———— ———— ————	9	13	4
' A penfion of the mother church of Linc. in the fame——	1	00	00
' A penfion of the abbat of Crouland in great S. Michaels } ' church, not to be taxed ———— ———— ————	1	00	00
' S. Maries church at the bridge, befides a penfion ————	6	00	00
' A penfion of the prior of Durham in the fame ———— ————	2	00	00
' A penfion of the prior of St. Fremunds in S. Georges } ' church not to be taxed ———— ———— ————	10	13	4
' A penfion of the fame prior in S. Michael Cornftal } ' church not to be taxed ———— ———— ————	00	14	00
' A penfion of the fame prior in S. Pauls church not to be } ' taxed ———— ———— ————	00	13	4
' A penfion of the prior of Belver in the church of the } ' holy Trinity, not to be taxed ———— ———— ————	00	6	00
' A penfion of the Sacrift of Burg in S. Martins church } ' taxed elfewhere ———— ———— ————	00	10	00
' The vicarage of the fame, befides a penfion elfewhere } ' taxed ———— ———— ————	4	13	4
' The vicarage of all Saints in the mercat place, befides a } ' penfion elfewhere taxed ———— ———— ————	5	6	8

XVIII. [a] ' On that great competition betwixt Robert de Brufe & John
' de Baillol, for the crown of Scotland (circa 21. E. 1.) John E. Warenn
' [lord of Stanford] joined with that magnificent prelate Anthony Beke,
' bp. of Durham, in maintenance of Baillols title.' And good reafon,
for Baillol had married his daughter. [b] ' Joan (relict of William de
' Warenne flain in a tourneament at Croydon) departed this life on the
' 11. of the kal. of December [being the 21. of Nov.] 1293. 21. E. 1.
' & lieth buried with her husband before the high altar at Lewes, un-
1293. ' der a high tomb.——In 1293. Bartholomew de S. Feriolo, burgefs of
' Stanford, gave to Walter of Stanford the phyfician, an houfe in great
' S. Michaels parifh, being the fame which Emma (daughter of Walter
' de S. Eadmundo) his wife gave the faid Walter the phyfician in the
' 19. E. 1. before her marriage. Witneffes, Alexander Lucas, Geoffery
' de Cottifmore, &c. burgeffes of Stanford. B. H. [c] ' Maurice fon of
' Thomas 2. lord Berkley, being of a military difpofition in his very
' youth, was in the feveral tourneaments held at Worcefter, Dunftable,
' Stanford, Blithe & Winchefter.' The faid Maurice was now in his
23.E.1. youth, & as it fhould feem by my author, all thofe tourneaments were
1295. held before this 23. E. 1. ' In 1295. (faith our old antiquary Mr. Butcher)
' [d] general chapters were held at Stanford called *itere minorum :* perhaps he means *itinera minorum.* But the hiftory of Englifh Francifcans,
printed in 1726. fpeaks of no chapters of that order held at Stanford :

a Baron. Vol. I. p. 79. b: c Baron. Vol. 1. p. 355. a.
b id. p. 80. b.   d printed Book, p. 23.

So I know not what to make of this paffage. ᵃ‘ The Carmelites this
‘ year came to Cambridge & builded them a new church in Milneftreet,
‘ & then a frier of that Houfe, named Humfrey, obtained licenfe of
‘ W. de Luda bp. of Ely there to begin a reading of divinity ; & fo he
‘ read folemnly in his fchooles of that houfe.   At the fame time alfo
‘ the chanons of Sempelingham were diligent in lectures and difputa-
‘ tions.   Thefe had their being at S. Edmundes chappel : manie houfes
‘ were deftroyed in Cambridge for fetting up thefe colleges, & of the
‘ Auguftines.’   It is remarkable, that as all thefe orders were the chief
of thofe who now read lectures at Cambridge, they were alfo the
chief of thofe who now read lectures at Stanford.

    XIX. In this 23. E. 1. ‘ ᵇ John E. Waren [lord of Stanford] had
‘ the cuftody of the caftle of Bamburgh committed to his charge.’ ᶜ The K.
called a parliament to meet at Weftminfter the fame year & the burgeffes,
elected to reprefent the town of Stanford therein, were Nicholas de
Burton & Clement de Melton.   This is the firft time Stanford (or indeed any other place) ever returned members.   Upon which occafion
Mr. Willis writes thus.   ‘ ᵈ I believe you may have heard that I pub-
‘ lifhed 2 vols. of boroughs, & fo may expect me to fay fomething on
‘ this matter, as being my more immediate province.   And fo I take
‘ liberty to inform you, that on the very firft demand & return of
‘ burgeffes to parliament (wherein all boroughs were liable to return
‘ in E. the 1. reign) Stanford began fending at the firft, &c.’   The fame
year ᵉ ‘ the K. caufed all the monafteries in England to be fearched, &
‘ the money found in them to be brought up to London.   He alfo
‘ feifed into his hands all their lay-fees ; becaufe they refufed to pay
‘ him fuch a tax as he demanded.   Then ᶠ the lord chiefe juftice,
‘ fitting on the benche, fpake openly thefe words.   You Sirs, that be
‘ attorneys of my lords the archbifhops, bps, abbats, priors, & all other
‘ the clergie, declare unto your mafters & tell them, that from hence-
‘ forth there fhall no juftice be done them in the kyngs courte, for any
‘ maner of thyng, altho’ never fo heynous wrong be done them.   Where-
‘ upon the abbats & priors were glad to follow the court, and fued to
‘ redeem their goodes, with giving a 4ᵗʰ part thereof.   The cleargie
‘ fuffered many injuries in this feafon ; for religious men were fpoyled
‘ & robbed in the kynges highway, & could not have reftitution ’till
‘ they had redeemed the kyngs protection ; fo that when they rode
‘ forth any whither, they were glad to apparel themfelves in lay gar-
‘ ments, to pafs in fafety.’   In the 24. E. 1. ‘ ᵍ John E. Warenn [lord   24.E.1,
‘ of Stanford] being fent with a power into Scotland (together with
‘ William de Beauchamp E. of Warwick) for recovery of the caftle of
‘ Dunbar (then treacheroufly delivered up by fome of that garrifon)

a Stow, p. 315.
b Bar. Vol. I. p. 79. b.
c Ex literis B. Willis Arm. mihi miffis
Mar. 7. 1719-20.

d id. ib.
e Stow, p. 317.
f Hol. p. 824. a. b.
g Bar. Vol. I. p. 79. b.

                                        ‘ encounter’d

' encounter'd the Scottish army which came to relieve the same, with
' so much courage, [a] that he obtained a victory of great importance,
' the chase holding about 8 miles, in which the slaughter was not small :
' [b] no less than 10000 of the Scots being slain, & the castle thereupon
' rendered to the K.' Soon after, K. Edw. over-ran Scotland, John
Baillol resigned to him all his right to the crown of that kingdom,
& ' [c] John E. Warenn was made warden or governor thereof.' In

1296. 1296. ' [d] a marriage was concluded (betwixte lord Edw[d] the kings
' eldest sonne, & ladie Philippa daughter to Guy E. of Flanders) by
' Henry bishop of Lincoln & Erle Warenn [lord of Stanford] they be-
25.E.1. ' ing sent over ambassadors for the same.' In the 25. F. 1. ' . . . .
' Chyld, burgess of Stanford, gave to William de Saham, apothecary,
' a tenement in great S. Michaels parish, in the lane called Ovenefty :
' between a tenement of Hugh Hod north, & a tenement of Walter
' the physician south. B. H.'

May.   XX. In 1297. 25. E. 1. ' [e] about May beganne a rebellion in Scot-
1297. ' land by the setting on of William Waleys; the E. of Surrey [lord
' of Stanford] being then in England.   Whereupon the K. appointed
' that the said E. should have the leading of all such men of warre
' as might be levied beyond Trent, to represse the Scottish rebels. [f] Af-
' ter that the E. of Surrey was come to the English campe, bicause
' William Waleys ceassed not to assemble more people, the English-
' men doubting of some treason, resolved to give battle : but whylest
' they were in mind thus to do, the bp. of Glascow & William Douglass
' submitted themselves, & so were committed to warde. [g] About the
Aug. ' end of Aug. the E. of Surrey, when he saw the Scotishmen would
' not perform promise touchyng delivery of pledges, & that Waleys
' still moved the people to rebellion, assembled his army, & with the
' same entred Scotland.   [h] This march of E. Warenn into Scotland oc-
' casioned so great a terror to that people, that they sought peace of
' him, & gave hostages for their future peaceable demeanour.   But this
' fair shew of peace proved no other than a contrivance to entrap the
' English.   For the Scots hereupon gathering their whole strength to-
' gether about Striveling, thereupon enticed our E. to march thither.
' [i] Then the lord steward of Scotlande, & also the E. of Lenox came
' unto hym, requiring him to staye 'till they myght have leisure to see
' if they could bring the Scots to the kyngs peace : but when they
Sep.10. ' could not do it, they returned the 10. of Sep. promising to bring to
' the aid of the E. of Surrey, on the morrow after, xl. horsemen.   On
' which day two friers preachers were sent to the Scots to move them
' to the kings peace.   But their answer was, that they were not come
' to have peace, but to try the matter by battel.   The English armye

a Speed, p. 654. a.   f id. p. 827. b.
b Bar. ut supra.   g id. p. 828. b.
c Hol. p. 823.   h Bar. Vol. I. p. 79. b.
d id. p. 816, 817.   i Hol. p. 829. a. b.
e Hol. p. 826. a. b.

                                                    ' without

' without good advice, throughe the pride of Lord Hugh Creſſingham
' preaſed to the bridge, & haſtyng to paſſe the ſame, the Scottyſhe-
' menne came upon them, ere one halfe could get over, & ſo, fiercely
' aſſayling them, the Engliſh were beaten back & ſlayne downe.   For
' the Scots after they ſaw ſo many of the Engliſh to have paſſed the
' bridge as they thought themſelves able to diſtreſſe, made downe to
' the bridge foot, & with a number of their ſpearemen afoote, cloſed
' it up that no more ſhould come over to the ayd of their fellows, nor
' thoſe that were already paſſed, ſhould return again.   Yet a right va-
' liaunt Kt. one Sr. Marmaduke Thweng (one of the firſt that went
' over) after he and his companie had driven down one wing of their
' adverſaries, & had followed them in chaſe a good way, at length
' perceyving theyr company behynde diſtreſſed by the Scots, retourned
' with thoſe few that were about hym, purpoſyng to repaſſe the bridge,
' & ruſhed in among the Scots that ſtood afore him with ſuch violence,
' that he paſſed thorough them, making waye for himſelf & his folkes
' by great manhood ; ſaving one of his nephews alſo which was ſet
' afoote & wounded, after his horſe had bin killed under him.   At
' length the diſcomfiture was ſuche, & the Scottes preaſſed ſo earneſtly
' to winne the bridge alſo of thoſe Engliſhmen which were not yet
' paſſed, that the E. of Surrey commanded to break that end of the
' bridge, where they ſtoode at defence to keepe backe the Scots, for
' elſe had there fewe of the Engliſh eſcaped.   There were ſlayne (as
' ſome have written) to the number of 6000 men, & among other
' Sr. Hugh Creſſingham, whoſe ſkinne (as hath bene reported) the
' Scotts ſtripped off his dead carcaſe, for the malice they bare towardes
' him.   This diſcomfiture chaunced the 11. of Sept.   The E. of Sur- Sept. 11.
' rey [lord of Stanford] leaving in the caſtel of Striveling the ſaid
' Sr. Marmaduke Thweng, promiſed hym to come to his ayde at all
' times, when neede ſhould be, within ten weekes ſpace [after notice]
' & herewith taking his horſe, rode in ſuch haſt to Barwike, that af-
' ter his coming thither, his ſteede being ſet up in the ſtable of the
' friers minors, never after taſted meate, but dyed.   After this the ſaid
' E. making no long abode in Barwicke, rode up to London to Pr.
' Edward, & left the towne of Barwike as a prey to the Scottiſhmen.

XXI. On Sept. 29. 1297. 25. E. 1. William de Wodeford, lord abbat Sept. 29.
of Burg, viſiting the nunnery of St. Michael by Stanford, as patron &   1297.
ordinary of the ſaid houſe, abſolved Alexandra de Langtoft & Cecilia   25. E. 1.
Fleming, two nuns of the ſame, from the ſentence of the greater excommunication, which (for I know not what faults) they had incurred.   From the ſame ſentence he alſo then releaſed Margery Arketel,
another nun of the ſame houſe, whoſe crime it ſeems was being a
little rough with one Emma daughter of Matthew de Eſton, admitted
into the ſiſterhood.   The ſaid abbat, in his letters of abſolution, thus
expreſſes himſelf.   ª 'Be it known by theſe preſents to all ſons of holy

a Ex Codicis MS. in Bib. Cott. ſub Imagine Veſpat. E. XXII. folio 33.

' mother

‘ mother church whom it concerns, that we William, by divine per-
‘ miſſion, abbat of Burg, exerciſing the accuſtomed office of viſitation
‘ in the priory of the bleſſed Michael without Staunford, according to
‘ exigence of law and the rule of St. Bennet, abſolve our beloved daugh-
‘ ters in Chriſt, Alexandra de Langtoft, Cecilia Fleming, & Margery
‘ Arketel of Staunford, nuns of the ſaid priory, from the ſentence of
‘ the greater excommunication, wherein (the ſaid Alexandra & Cecilia,
‘ for their faults; & Margery, for laying violent hands on Emma D.
‘ of Matthew de Eſton, admitted to the eſtate of a nun) had ſtood
‘ bound.   In witneſs whereof to the preſents we have put to our ſeal.
‘ Given in the chapter of the ſaid priory, on the day of St. Michael
‘ the archangel, 1297.   ªK. Edw. [then in Flanders] hearing of the
‘ overthrow of John E. Warenn [as above related] commaunded the
‘ lords of England by his letters to bee ready to aſſiſt the ſaid E. Warenn
‘ (his cuſtos or guardian of Scotland) with their forces in the octaves

Feb.
129⁷⁄₈.

‘ of S. Hilary [129⁷⁄₈.] at Yorke, and alſo to proclaim ſuch of the
‘ Scotiſh lords as came not thither, enemies of the ſtate; ᵇ who yet
‘ came not, but contrarily had beſieged the caſtell of Rokesburghe.
‘ Whereupon the E. of Surrey [lord of Stanford] haſted thytherwardes,
‘ ſo that William Waleys & the Scotiſhmenne whiche laye there at
‘ the ſiege, reyſed the ſame and departed.   The E. of Surrey coming to
‘ Rokesburgh, & relieving them that kept it with ſuch things as they
‘ wanted, paſſed foorth to Kelſow, & came afterwards to Barwike,
‘ which the Scottiſhmenne had left voyde.   Here came letters from K.
‘ Edw. ſignifying that he had taken truce with the French K. & ment
‘ ſhortely to retourne, & therefore commaunded them not to make any
‘ farther enterpriſe than defending of the frontiers & the recovery of
‘ Barwike, til his comming over.   Hereupon was a great part of the
‘ army diſcharged, and ſuche only remained in Barwike as might ſuf-

26. E.1.

‘ fice for defence thereof.   In the beginning of the 26. of E. 1. W.
‘ de Saham, apothecary of Stanford, gave to Walter the phyſician one
‘ void place, ſituate in great St. Michaels pariſh in the lane there called
‘ Feldovenſty, between a tenement of Hugh Hods north, & a tenement
‘ of the ſaid Walters ſouth. B. H.   ᶜThe K. being returned, removed
‘ the barons of the exchequer, & the juſtices of the bench to York,
‘ calling a parliament thither.   ᵈThe perſons elected to repreſent the
‘ town of Stanford in this parliament at York, were Clement de Mel-
‘ ton & Robert de Pontfract.——Matilda prioreſs of the church of St.
‘ Michael nigh Staunford, & the nuns there, with aſſent of their prior
‘ Sr. W. de Stob.... gave in exchange to Walter the phyſician of
‘ Staunford two pieces of arable land lying in the north field of Stan-
‘ ford, whereof one piece lay between the land of Symon de Morchote
‘ eaſt, & the land of the prior of St. Leonard weſt, & abutted on the

a Speed, p. 655. b.   c Hol. p. 832. a.
b Hol. p. 831, 832.   d From Mr. Willis Letter to me as above.

‘ land

' land of the lord E. Warenne , &c. for a certain houſe ſituate in
' St. Martins pariſh, to wit, in Webſtereſgate, between a tenement of
' their own north, & a tenement of Henry Faderman ſouth ; & for one
' half acre of arable land with the meadow adjoining in the fee of the
' abbat of Burg, which lay between their own land weſt, & the land of
' Robert de Pontfract eaſt, & abutted on Kilinereſhenge north, &c. B. H.
' ª The E. of Hereford and the E. Marſchal, preſent with their retinues
' in the kings armie, now aſſembled at Rokesborough, on ſuſpition
' conceyved of that they had hearde, thought it not ſufficient to have
· the kyngs letters patentes, touching confirmation of the two charters,
' & other articles ſigned by him whileſt he was out of the realme, &
' therefore required that he would now within his own lande confirme
' the ſame againe.   Hereupon John E. Warenne [lord of Stanford]
' & others undertooke for the K. that, after he had ſubdued his ene-
' mies, & ſhould be again returned into the realme, he ſhould ſatisfie
' them in that behalfe.

XXII. ᶦ ᵇOn the 25. of July 1298. William de Woodford abbat of July.25.
' Burg, received Johanna daughter of Sir Walran Mortimer, Kt. to the 1298.
' habit of religion to be taken upon her in the monaſtery of St. Michael 26.E.1.
' without Stanford.   Given at Burg in the abbats hall near his cham-
' ber, in preſence of the monks, brother Gilbert de Aylington, brother
' Robert the younger of Staunford, Sir William de Wineleſthorp the
' capellan, Thomas de London, John his brother, & Robert de Hotoſts.
' And the abbat wrote to the prior of the nuns, that he ſhould confer
' the habit of religion on the foreſaid Johanna.   Now ᶜnuns are uſually
' conſecrated by the biſhop or prior, who covereth them with a veil,
' the abbeſs, on pain of excommunication, not daring to attempt it.
' Formerly 25, but now 12 years of age are thought ſufficient for them
' to take upon them their vow.   On the day of their admiſſion they
' are dreſſed in their richeſt apparel, preſented to the biſhop with mu-
' ſic playing, & tapers burning before them, & all other imaginable
' pomp & ſplendor.   But when they arrive at the altar, they are there
' ſtripped of all their glorious cloaths, & 'tis almoſt impoſſible to ima-
' gine, what haſt ſome of theſe young creatures make to put on them-
' ſelves the habit of a nun.   That done the biſhop puts on the veil,
' and generally expreſſes himſelf in theſe words. *Audi, Filia*, &c.' which
are ſo well tranſlated by our old deſpiſed Engliſh poet, John Hopkins ᵈ,
that I beg leave to inſert them.

    ' *O daughter, take good heed,*
     ' *Incline and give good ear ;*
   ' *Thou muſt forget thy kindred all,*
     ' *And fathers houſe moſt dear.*

a Hol. p. 832. b.
b Ex Codicis MS. in Bib. Cott. ſub imagine Veſp. E. XXII. fol. 7.
c Extracted out of a book entitled Monaſt.

Conventions: by J. S. Lond. 1686. 12. p.
22, &c.
d Pſ. 45. 11, 12.

              ' *Then*

' *Then shall the king desire*
' *Thy beauty fair & trim;*
' *For why? He is the lord thy God,*
' *And thou must worship him.*

' to which the people saying, Amen; the veil is cast over her, & the
' religious women & virgins present salute and embrace her. After
' which the bishop praying for & blessing her she is conducted to her cell.'
From celibacy next of matrimony. For about this time, if not earlier (as
near as I can guess by the autograph in my hands) Gerald de Normanville
in Rutland, on his daughters marriage with Geoffry de Mar, gave her
for her fortune an hundred shillings of rent at Empingham, & before
a great number of witnesses, as they went to celebrate the nuptials, at
S. Peters church door in Stanford, by the following instrument there
read aloud, proclaimed both his consent to the marriage, & the particulars of her dowry.   a ' Gerald de Normanville, to all his men & friends,
' as well present as future, greeting. Know all, as well present as fu-
' ture, that I Gerald de Normanville have granted & given to Geoffry
' de Mar, with Mary my daughter, in franc marriage, an hundred shil-
' lings of rent in the town of Empingham; to wit, in one mill 7 1. s.
' in three men, 9. s. in Alan, 3. s. in William son of Ponne 3. s. in
' Ralf by the water 3. s. & one carrucate of land with a toft and its
' proper appurtenances, 20. s. Witness Jurdan de Humarus that I have
' given to the same Geoffry, Mary my daughter, with my assent, at
' the door of the church of S. Peter of Stanford, the abbat of . . . .
' min, Gregory, & Geoffry the canon, Richard de Pec, Geoffry de
' Normanville, Hugh de Mare, & Geoffry his brother; William de
' Choenneres, John de Normanville, Matthew his brother, William de
' Monin, Hugh de Baenburc, Geoffry de Normanville, & Simon his
' brother; Hugh de la Mere, & Robert of Wyrcestre, Reynald son of
' Martin, with Herebert his brother; Gilbert son of Wacc, Simon his
' brother; Richard son of Turold, Hugh & Henry his sons, Alan son
' of Noel.'

Apr.
1299.
27. E. 1. XXIII. In Ap. 1299. 27. E. 1. Master Hugh de Clisseby (vicar of All
Saints in the mercat) being warden of the hospital of S. John the Baptist & S. Thomas of Canterbury at the bridge foot; that house was,
thro' his mismanagement, reduced to so much poverty, that he petitioned

a Geraldus de Normanvilla, omnibus hominibus & amicis suis tam presentibus quam
futuris, salutem. Sciant omnes, tam presen-
tes quam futuri, quod ego Geraldus de Normanville, concessi & dedi Galifrido de Mara,
cum Maria filia mea, in liberum matrimoni-
um, centum solidatas de reditu in villa de
Empingham, scil. in uno molendino lx. xi.
fol. in tribus hominibus ix. fol. scil. in Alano,
iii. fol. Willielmo filio Ponne iii. fol. Radulfo juxta aquam iii. fol. & unam carrucatam terre cum tofto & pertinentiis suis
propriis xx. fol. Teste Jurdano de Hu-
marus quod dedi Galifrido eidem Mariam filiam meam, assensu meo, ad hostium S.
Petri de Stanford, abbate de . . . . mina,
Gregorio & Galifrido canonico, Ricardo
de Pec, Gauf. de Normanvilla, Hugone
de Mara, & Gaufrido fratre ejus, Willielmo de Choenneres, Johanne de Normanvilla, & Matheo fratre ejus, Willielmo de
Monina, Hugone de Baenburc, Gaufrido de
Normanvilla & Simone fratre ejus, Hugone
de Lamere, & Roberto de Wyreceftria, Reginaldo filio Martini & Herberto fratre ejus,
Gilberto filio Wacc, Simone fratre ejus,
Ricardo filio Turoldi, Hugone & Henrico
filiis suis, Alano filio Noel.

William

William de Wodeford lord abbat of Burg & patron of the fame, for
liberty to refign ; who, thereupon, accepted his faid refignation, & then
committed the care and cuftody of the faid hofpital to Sir Robert rector
of Northburg, 'till fuch time as, with Gods bleffing, the houfe fhould
arrive at a more flourifhing eftate, & he, the abbat, on maturer confideration, appoint what was elfe to be done.   But hear the abbat himfelf.   ᵃ ' To all the faithful of Chrift who fhall infpect the prefent
' letters, William by divine permiffion abbat of Burg, everlafting health
' in the Lord.   Ye fhall underftand that we, at the earneft fuit of mafter
' Hugh of St. Martins, warden of the hofpital of St. Thomas the martyr
' by Staunford bridge, made to us by letter & an efpecial meffenger
' (the wardenfhip of the faid hofpital, committed to him by our pre-
' deceffor, by the actual inability of him defiring to refign, being de-
' folate) have committed & delivered to our beloved in Chrift, Sir
' Robert rector of the church of Northburg, the care & cuftody of the
' faid hofpital, with its rights & appurtenances, 'till by the counfel of the
' forenamed mafter Hugh, thro' the bleffing of God its moft high guar-
' dian, it fhall arrive at a more flourifhing eftate, & we think fit
' to ordain other more advifedly touching the wardenfhip of the fore-
' written hofpital.   In witnefs whereof we have to the prefents put
' to our feal.   Given at Burg, the 7. of the ides of April, 1299.' Sir
Robert rector of Northburg, held that employ about four months, &   Aug.
then the forefaid abbat, to prevent quarrels between them, & fancy-   1299.
ing perhaps the forefaid Hugh would amend his behavior, reftored   27.E.1,
him to his former poft.   At what time the abbat appointed fome of
his own officers to re-deliver the books, jewels, & other effects belonging to that hofpital (which, to prevent embezzlement, he had
formerly feifed into his own hands) to the forefaid Mr. Hugh, who
thereupon gave this acquittance for the fame.   ᵇ ' To all the fons of
' holy mother church, who fhall fee or hear thefe letters, Hugh de
' Cliffeby mafter of the hofpital of St. Thomas the martyr near Staun-
' ford bridge, eternal health in the Lord.   Your univerfality fhall un-
' derftand that I have received from the religious man lord William
' by divine permiffion abbat of Burg, my lord, by the hands of mafter
' Geoffry de Makefeye the clerc, all my books, jewels, & all the uten-
' fils, brafen & wooden, & other fmall matters in the chamber & my
' chefts being, and alfo in the hall, cellar, kitchen, & bake houfe, in
' cuftody of the officers of the faid lord abbat left, & by them found
' in the apartments aforefaid in the hofpital aforefaid ; & them all
' acknowledge to be to me fully reftored : the forenamed lord abbat
' & other his officers the deputed keepers of thefe things, from all
' action for the fame hereafter to be made on the occafion aforefaid,
' by tenor of the prefents declaring by the prefents quit.   In witnefs
' whereof to the prefents my feal is appendent.   And for greater evi-

a Ex codicis MS. in Bib. Cotton. fub   b id. fol. 30.
imagine Vefp. E. XXII. fol. 41.

' dence

' dence I have procured the feal of the deanery of the Naffe of Burg
' to be put to the prefents. Given at Staunford the Tuefday next
' after the feaft of St. Peter *ad vincula*, in the 27. E. 1.——The fame
' year Emma wife of Bartholomew de S. Feriolo gave to Walter the
' phyfician all her right & claim in thofe houfes ftanding in great St.
' Michaels parifh Stanford, near the lane called Feldovenefty eaft, be-
' tween a tenement of the faid Walter in Colgate, & her tenement
' contiguous to the fame tenement fouth, & a curtilage [a garden or
backfide] ' of the fame Walters north. B. H.' The fame Emma now
' gave to the fame Walter her houfes in Colgate, built in great S.
' Michaels parifh, between the houfes of the faid Walter eaft & north,
' & a tenement of Roger de Offington weft, & the kings high-way
' fouth. B. H. ª Sir Richard de Stanford was the fame year prefented
' by the K. to the church of Fisketon.' The great Henry de Hanna,
warden of the white friers at Stanford, & provincial of his order, in
England, ' ᵇ died [full of years] in the monaftery of the Carmes there,
' where he had fpent a good deal of his time, & on the 4. of the

Nov. 28.
1299.
27. E. 1.

' kalends of Dec. [to wit, Nov. 28.] was buried in the choir of that
' conventual church' [with all the folemnity due to a perfon of his
high rank & merit.] As he chofe to live & refide here, fo no doubt
but he himfelf appointed this for the place of his interment. For had
he not ordered his body to be fo difpofed of, certainly the friers of
feveral other houfes would have put in their claims for the remains
of fo great a prelate. For all thofe monafteries abovementionedᶜ,
being founded when he was provincial, & chiefly by his procurement,
muft needs have a great refpect for him. ᵈ ' He wrote (directed chiefly
' to his brethren) one book of epiftles, beginning, *dilectis in Chrifto*
' *Filiis*, &c. Another about ordering of convents. A third of fer-
' mons on feveral fubjects. And fome other pieces.'——' Ralph de Ca-
' fterton bought of John Stykeling his houfes in S. Peters parifh at
' Stanford ftanding between the lane called Punt-del'-arch-fty, eaft;
' & John Punt-delarches houfe, weft; & that houfe, &c. which is
' nearer to the hall of him Ralph in the forefaid lane, &c. for 15.
' marcs of filver, paid him in his neceffity. B. H. Alfo John Braban
' bought of Richard Baldefwel merchant, his right in a certain rent
' of x. s. due from fome houfes there. B. H. Likewife John, fon of
' John Gilbert, barber in Stanford, gave his houfes in S. Peters parifh
' to the forefaid John Braban. Witneffes, Robert the burfar, &c.
' B. H. ᵉ John E. Warenn [lord of Stanford] was now made go-
' vernor of Hope caftle in the county of Derby.

Ap. 14.
1300.
28. E. 1.

XXIV. Not long after the forementioned Mr. Hugh de Cliffeby was
re-admitted warden of St. Thomas hofpital, died William de Wode-

---

a Prefentatio extat in codicis MS. Cot. fub
imagine Vefp. E. XXII. fol. 45.

b In coenobio Stanfordienfi vita functus
eft, fepultufque in choro ibidem, quarto Kal.
Decembris, anno MCCXCIX. Ex Johannis

Balæi Heliad. MS. Harley.
c Anno 1256.
d Pits, in vita.
e Bar. Vol. I. p. 80. a.

ford

ford abbat of Burg, & was fucceeded by Godfrey de Croyland. Now whether William de Wodeford befriended the faid mafter Hugh by ufing him more mildly than he ought to have done; or whether his death emboldened, & made him act as if he thought he could deal yet better with a new patron, I cannot tell; but certain it is, if ever he forfook them (which is much to be queftioned) the faid mafter Hugh now went on in his old courfes; & in particular (tho' he was the chantry prieft, as well as warden, of the houfe) took little care to celebrate divine fervice, as he was obliged, in the chapel; gave none, or very inconfiderable alms to the poor & ftrangers paffing by the hofpital door; & whereas one Robert Wodefoul a convert ufually had a chamber & falary allowed him in the houfe (whofe bufinefs it was, under the faid mafter Hugh, to adminifter relief to the fick & poor) fubftracted from him half a marc yearly of the very mony allowed for his falary. Alfo he retrenched the lamps & other lights commonly maintained in the chapel & other places of the houfe. Befides which, he either fold, gave away, or fuffered himfelf to be tricked out of divers valuable relics belonging to the hofpital. And what likewife was very fcandalous, let the chapel it felf lie in a moft flovenly condition; &, as there were in the houfe divers apartments for accommodation of the fick & poor ftrangers, locked them almoft all up, & made ftore-rooms of them for his own goods & effects. The new abbat of Burg being at length made acquainted with thefe things, immediately refolved on a vifitation of the hofpital, in perfon; that, being on the fpot, he might, with his own eyes, fee what condition the chapel & houfe were in, & at the fame time hear what was alledged by the faid Robert Wodefoul & others againft the faid mafter Hugh, & what he himfelf had to fay in his own defence. Whereupon, when he came thither, all thefe matters abovementioned were proved by the oaths of divers perfons, & fo little had the faid mafter Hugh to offer in his own vindication, that every thing being but too plainly made out, the faid abbat forthwith depofed him from any farther exercife of his office. Being thus a fecond time depofed, the faid mafter Hugh humbly applying himfelf to John Dalderby lord bifhop of Lincoln elect, Jofceline archdeacon of Stow, & Sir John de Scaleby, at length obtained letters fupplicatory from them in his behalf directed to the faid lord abbat of Burg; who paying much regard to the letters of thofe worthy perfons, & being alfo fomewhat mollified by the faid mafter Hughs repeated promifes of amendment, at length agreed once more to admit him to his old poft, but propofed, he fhould firft take an oath, in cafe he was fo reftored, to fubmit to fuch reformation in every particular relating either to himfelf, or the hofpital, as he the faid abbat (& patron thereof) fhould award. Accordingly on the 14. of April, the faid mafter Hugh, repairing to Burg, there, in prefence of the faid abbat & divers other perfons, took his oath as aforefaid, & withal, by a particular inftrument under his own feal, made his fub-

miffion,

miſſion, confeſſing his offences, & yielding to be corrected in every thing as the ſaid lord abbat ſhould adjudge ; which letter of ſubmiſſi-on is thus worded. ᵃ ' To all the ſons of holy mother church who
' ſhall ſee or hear theſe letters, Hugh of St. Martins Staunford, ever-
' laſting health in the lord.   Your univerſality ſhall underſtand, that
' whereas lately my lord Godefry by divine permiſſion abbat of Burg,
' the hoſpital of the bleſſed Thomas the martyr at Stanford (to the
' wardenſhip whereof by the predeceſſor of the ſame [abbat] in the
' monaſtery of Burg, I was under a certain form, graciouſly deputed)
' by his officers eſpecially commiſſioned & the perſons in the ſame
' hoſpital abiding, according to the duty of his office, had viſited, &
' certain notorious deficiences in the wonted chantry & accuſtomed
' exhibition of alms to the poor & ſtrangers there uſed to be allowed ;
' as alſo in the ſuſtentation of Robert Wodefoul a convert in the
' ſaid hoſpital abiding (the ſame being for a certain ſeaſon withdrawn)
' by inquiſition of the faithful had moſt abundantly found : Being
' ready to obey my lord & his juriſdiction in all things ; correction
' & reformation of all my exceſſes touching the defects whatſoever my
' perſon, as alſo of the perſons & things the wardenſhip of the ſaid
' hoſpital any ways concerning to undergo with obedience & re-
' ceive ; my own eſtate, & the wardenſhip of the ſaid hoſpital, & of
' the things pertaining unto it, to the ordering & power of my lord
' abbat aforeſaid I do purely & abſolutely commit : my ſelf & all things
' to the ſaid hoſpital belonging, to the ordering, diffinition, & decree
' of the ſame [lord abbat] entirely yielding.   The ordering, reforma-
' tion, & injunction of whom, by virtue of my oath corporally taken,
' I promiſe that I will inviolably, during my wardenſhip in the hoſ-
' pital aforeſaid, take upon me readily, & obſerve, under pain of de-
' poſition & removal from the wardenſhip of the hoſpital above-
' written.   In witneſs whereof, I have put to my ſeal.   Given at
' Burg, on Eaſter eve, 1300. In preſence of the lord abbat, the ma-
' ſters Thomas de Freſton, & Geoffry de Makeſeye, John de Undele,
' Robert de Thorpe, Bernard de Caſtre, & Richard the clerc.' Beſides thoſe perſons here named, Sir Hugh Wake & Sir Robert de Bavent (tho' their names are omitted above) were preſent at ſealing of the ſaid letter of ſubmiſſion.   The ſaid maſter Hugh being thus tied down & obliged to performance of every article, the abbat then decreed, I. That he ſhould keep up all the rights & liberties of the houſe. II. That all the income, whether revenues belonging to the houſe, or offerings given to it, ſhould be divided into three parts. One for a chantry prieſt to celebrate in the chapel, & do all other prieſt-ly offices neceſſary for the ſick & poor ſtrangers ; & to buy lights, veſt-ments, & other ornaments.   Which office of the chantry prieſt the abbat enjoyned the ſaid maſter Hugh to perform himſelf.   Another

---

a Ex ejuſdem codicis **MS.** ſupracitati folio 51

part to be paid Robert Wodefoul abovementioned to provide neceffaries for the fick & poor. Who was alfo to have competent fatisfaction for the arrears due to him from the faid mafter Hugh. And
a third, for fupport of the wardens family. Thus the faid mafter
Hugh (tho' not fatisfied with the fame) had almoft two whole parts in
three of all the revenues allotted to himfelf. III. That all fuch perfons, whether beggars or ftrangers, as wafted the goods of the houfe,
or by forging tales raifed difputes between the faid mafter Hugh & the
tenents of E. Warenn & the lord abbat of Burg, and his other neighbours, fhould for the future be debarred from partaking of any alms.
IV. That the lamps & other lights which ufed to burn in the chapel
& other places of the hofpital, fhould be well maintained & kept up.
V. That the reliques of the faints fhould be recovered with the utmoft
care. VI. That the chapel & all places appointed for the fervice of God,
or reception of the poor, fhould be kept perfectly clean & neat. In fhort,
every defect fo thoroughly amended, that the faithful, obferving it, might
be thereby moved to continue their former offerings. VII. That
all difputes between the faid mafter Hugh & Sir Robert rector of
Northburg, & other officers & tenents of the abbat, be amicably
determined by the abbat himfelf, or a profecution made before a
competent judge: & thofe enemies of the faid mafter Hugh who will
not fubmit to one or other of thefe courfes, the abbat will, by a
fine, compel to be quiet. Laftly, That if the faid mafter Hugh do
not in every article conform to the premifes his place be *ipfo facto*
void, & the abbat to appoint another warden. This decree concluded with a claufe profeffing the readinefs of the faid mafter Hugh to
fubmit to the fame in whole, or in part; which being read, the faid
lord abbat caufed him to put his feal to it, & then, by a particular inftrument, under his own feal, admitted him a 3d. time to his place.
I fhall now give you both the decree & admiffion at large. The firft
opens it felf with this preamble. [a] Memorandum, that on Eafter eve
' 1300. came to lord Godefry, by divine permiffion abbat of Burg at
' Burg, mafter Hugh of St. Martins Staunford, from the wardenfhip
' of the hofpital of the bleffed Thomas the martyr (for many & no-
' torious defaults, fubftractions of the chantery & of the alms to the
' poor & ftrangers by antient cuftom in the faid hofpital wont to be
' allowed) by the forefaid abbat (folemn inquifition being firft made,
' & certain articles requiring his defpofition & removal by the fame
' inquifition in prefence of the fame mafter capellan being found)
' for his difobedience & obftinacy removed, juftice fo requiring; bring-
' ing the fupplicatory letters of the venerable man mafter John de
' Alderby elect of the church of Lincoln, mafter Goceline archdea-
' con of Stowe, & Sir John de Scaleby, which being reverently re-
' ceived, & the contents of the fame underftood; the forenamed ma-
' fter Hugh, to the favor, ordination, diffinition, & decree of the

a id. ib.
9 L   ' faid

' said lord abbat, himself & all the said hospitals & his concerns, free-
' ly & absolutely, by virtue of his oath corporally taken, hath submit-
' ted, in presence of the lords Hugh Wake & Robert de Bavent Kts.
' & others there present (as by the form of the same submission will,
' to him who inspects it, appear.) At length the forenamed abbat,
' in an intuition of charity, as also in respect of the letters of the
' venerable lord of Lincoln elect & others, to the wardenship of the
' same hospital (saving to himself & the church of Burg the rights &
' liberties in the said hospital antiently obtained, viz. of appointing
' & making a warden, without requiring the assent of any superior
' whatsoever, as also of removing him upon just occasion) under the
' conditions & forms, in the ordination, diffinition & decree of the
' said abbat, beneath written, for term of his life hath admitted
' him. First of all, for the honor & glory of almighty God, & of
' the glorious virgin his mother, & the blessed Thomas the proto-
' martyr, we ordain, diffine, & decree to be inviolably observed, that
' the hospital of the blessed Thomas the martyr upon Staunford bridge,
' with all its rights & liberties, by the warden of the same hospital,
' to the utmost power of the warden & without diminution, be kept
' & preserved. Also, that all the goods to the warden of the said
' hospital in the name of the same hospital accruing out of the lands
' & rents, as also obventions from the devotion of the faithful &
' industry of the warden arising, be divided into three parts & di-
' stributed, by equal portions, as in the earliest time of the foundation
' of the said hospital, & afterwards by custom of the place, we have
' learned truly to have been observed. To wit, that one part be al-
' lowed for support of a continual chantery by a fit priest, in the
' said hospital residing, celebrating divine service, & ministring the sa-
' cramentals to the sick & strangers ; & for buying & support of
' the light, vestments, & other ornaments necessary for ministration
' of divine worship in the hospital aforesaid : which by you, master
' Hugh, warden of the said hospital, year by year we command to
' be done, & to you enjoyn under the pain in the letter of your sub-
' mission contained. That another part of the foresaid goods, for
' support of the alms to be administred to the sick in the house abid-
' ing, as also to poor strangers thither resorting (as far as one third
' part will go) be paid to Robert Wodefoul for the meet support
' thereof, as the form of his agreement requires, in the chamber to
' him antiently allotted, to be paid without molestation. To whom,
' for arrears (to wit, for the annual payment of half a marc by you,
' master Hugh, withdrawn, tho' due to the forenamed Robert) we or-
' dain & command competent satisfaction to be made. The third
' part of the goods remaining wholly for support of the wardens ne-
' cessary & honest family. We ordain moreover & diffine, that sus-
' pected persons, squanderers of the goods of the said hospital, stirring
' contentions between you the forenamed Hugh & your neighbours,

                                                              ' as

' as alfo the tenents of E. Warenn & our tenents, thro' forged lies &
' falfe detractions, be ftroke out of the faid hofpital, & a participation
' of the goods of the fame; nor for the future relieved in any fort
' with the goods of the hofpital aforefaid, whether they be beggars
' or ftrangers. The fupport of the light in the faid hofpital as well
' in lamps as in other [veffels] due & accuftomed being fully reftor-
' ed; which, for reverence of the faints in the faid hofpital, before
' the time of your fubftraction, was honourably afforded; & the reliques
' of the faints in the faid hofpital by you afore time therein found,
' & by your fimplicity, or the malice of others, afterwards removed;
' we command to be recalled & reftored with all the due care & di-
' ligence that you poffibly can. Unto thefe things we ordain & de-
' cree, that every the places in the faid hofpital, for divine worfhip
' & reception of the poor & fick of old time fet apart, be kept per-
' fectly clear, & not ufed for ftore-rooms of other things. But let
' there be a thorough reformation made by you the warden, in our
' ftead, in the perfons & affairs of the faid hofpital; that the affec-
' tions of the faithful may be drawn unto example of the antient re-
' lief afforded; & things difperfed called back, with a fafe keeping of
' what are got together. Truly, unlawful ftirs about contentions &
' controverfies hinder perfect charity, as alfo confume the goods in-
' trufted to be kept, by heat of rancor & greedinefs of revenge; &
' brawls & contentions arife, the reft inflaming & impofing on by
' anger of the provoked. [& thus we fhall fee] the revival of your
' languid eftate turned into its old, or worfe, condition; & fo, which
' God forbid, the laft things fhall be worfe than the firft. Minding
' therefore for you & others, under our diftrict abiding, by our pre-
' fent ordination & diffinition, in an intuition of right & charity, to
' make all things eafie, & to the utmoft of our power extirpate the
' leaft poffible occafion of difagreement; we ordain, decree, & diffine,
' that the matters in difpute between you mafter Hugh & Sir Robert
' rector of the church of Northburg, & other our officers & tenents
' whomfoever, of whatever condition they be, under the . . . . or
' diftrict of our lordly power abiding, before whatfover judges dif-
' puted, from thefe prefents furceafe, & be, by us with an amicable
' difcifion, without the clamor fo frequent in courts of law, fetting
' afide all favor, impartially determined; that if your forenamed ad-
' verfaries fhall not have a mind to fubmit before us, to law & equity,
' or to a profecution made before a competent judge, we may
' caufe an opportune aid to be paid. We retain moreover to our
' felves full power of adding to the premifes, & if it fhall be ne-
' ceffary, of changing, declaring, interpreting, correcting, fubftracting,
' fupplying what of them we pleafe, or of ordaining & diffining a new
' as often & when to us it fhall feem expedient. Saving in all things,
' to us & our monaftery, the rights & liberties touching the difpofal of
' the perfons & things in the faid hofpital abiding, as alfo the rents &

' fervices

' fervices due & accuſtomed, & the payments perſonal & real, & all ſub-
' jections.   Unto the bovewritten we ordain & diffine, that if you
' maſter Hugh, againſt the form of your oath taken, to the premiſes
' in our ordination & diffinition contained, or to any of them (which
' be far from you) ſhall be the leaſt diſobedient (by oppoſing the pre-
' miſes, ordination, or diffinition in whole, or in part) from that
' inſtant, from the wardenſhip of the ſaid hoſpital, & alſo benefit of
' all the goods & obventions of the ſame, by authority of the pre-
' ſent ordination & decree, & of your oath taken, we decree you re-
' moved; with power to us of providing another warden, & of in-
' ducting the ſame into corporal poſſeſſion of the ſame hoſpital & of
' the goods being in the ſame, & to our ſucceſſors remaining ſaved
' & free.   In witneſs whereof to this preſent ordination, diffinition, &
' decree, we have put to our ſeal.   Given at Burg in the Feaſt of SS.
' Tyburtius & Valerian, 1300.   And I Hugh of S. Martins, the bove-
' written reformations, ordinations, diffinitions, & decree, willingly
' & reverently, in whole & in part, have undertaken; & to the pre-
' miſes, & each of them, to the utmoſt of my power, by virtue of my
' oath before corporally taken, do promiſe to be obedient.   In witneſs of
' which my deed to theſe preſents I have put to my ſeal.'   The admiſſion.   ' [a] To all the ſons of holy mother church, who ſhall ſee or
' hear theſe preſent letters, Godefry, by divine permiſſion abbat of Burg,
' greeting in the Lord.   Ye ſhall underſtand that we have graciouſly
' committed to maſter Hugh, vicar of the church of All-ſaints in the
' mercat place at Staunford, the care & adminiſtration of the hoſpital
' of S. Thomas on Staunford bridge, & of all things to the ſaid hoſ-
' pital belonging, to the perpetual intuition of his charity.   So that
' the charges for hoſpitality incumbent, wont, by law & the cuſtom
' of the place, to be allowed, he faithfully acknowledge & ſuſtain,
' according to the form of our ordination & diffinition, which he hath
' willingly taken upon him, under pain of depoſition & removal from
' the wardenſhip before ſaid, as by the form of ſubmiſſion & ordina-
' tion more fully will appear.   Saving, to us & our ſucceſſors power
' of viſiting & correcting the exceſſes of the warden & others in the
' ſaid hoſpital abiding, & other the rights & liberties to us & our mona-
' ſtary of Burg belonging.   In witneſs whereof to the preſents we
' have put to our ſeal.   Given at Burg in the Feaſt of the Saints
' Tyburt & Valerian.'   The foreſaid Godefry de Croyland, lord abbat

July. 14.
1300.
28. E. 1. of Burg, intending, as patron of the houſe, to viſit the nuns of St.
Michael by Stanford on Wedneſday the 20th of July 1300. that none
might pretend ignorance of his coming, gave notice of the ſame to
the prior & prioreſs, by this letter dated the 14 of the ſame month. [b]
' Godefry, by divine permiſſion abbat of Burg, to his beloved in Chriſt
' the prior of S. Michaels without Staunford, & the prioreſs of the

' ſame

' fame place, greeting & found increafe of religion.   Becaufe, for
' certain reafons (the fupreme difpofer affifting) we are difpofed on
' the next Wednefday, being the Feaft of S. Margaret the virgin, to
' exercife our office of vifitation in your priory ; concerning which
' by our letters we would have you to be forewarned, that your fol-
' licitude, thro' ignorance or diffimulation in the cure to you commit-
' ted may prevent all matter of pretended excufe : By tenor of thefe
' letters, for the reafon aforewritten, we fignifie our coming to your
' knowledge, & by you command it to be made known to them
' whom it concerns.   Given at Ketering, the Thurfday next before
' the feaft of S. Kenelm the K. & martyr, in the year of our Lord 1300.'
The fame year Thomas de Pappele bound himfelf to pay the fum of
ten marcs at 4 terms in his obligation mentioned to William Watervyle, procurator of the friers minors in Staunford, for the marriage [por-
tion] of his fifter Johanna [then, as I fuppofe, betrothed or married
to the faid Wm. Watervyle.] The original is now in my hands, & may
be thus tranflated.   ' To all the faithful of Chrift, who fhall fee or
' hear this prefent writing, Thomas de Pappele, greeting.   Your uni-
' verfality fhall underftand that I am bound & firmly obliged to Wil-
' liam de Watervyle of Aldwyncle, procurator of the friers minors
' at Staunford, for the marriage portion of Johanna my fifter, in ten
' marcs of the Efterlings, to be paid to the fame Wm. de Watervyle,
' or his certain attorney bringing this writing to me in my houfe at
' Pappele, at the four terms underwritten, within two years follow-
' ing; to wit, at the feaft of Eafter in the 29. of K. Edw. (the firft term
' then beginning) forty fhillings ; & at the feaft of S. Michael in the
' year abovementioned, two marcs ; & at the feaft of Eafter in the year
' next following, forty fhillings ; & at the feaft of S. Michael in the
' fame year, two marcs) without any farther delay.   And if it happen
' (which God forbid) that in payment of the faid mony at any of the
' terms I be wanting, I will, & in good faith grant, for me & my
' heirs, that the forefaid Wm. de Watervyle, or his certain attorney,
' may have full power, liberty, & licenfe, none gainfaying or letting,
' my tenements, arable lands, profits & rents, with all my other goods,
' moveable & immoveable, to feife, & peaceably poffefs, & poffeffed
' hold, 'till to the forenamed William de Watervyle, or his certain
' attorney, as well for the damages & expences (if they fhall make or
' fuftain any about getting the forefaid mony) as well as for the mony
' it felf, it fhall be moft fully fatisfied.   About the demand of which
' damages & expences let credit be given to the forenamed Wm. de
' Watervyle, or his certain attorney, or any other perfon of honeft fame
' . . . .   Moreover me corporally & my heirs & alfo my
' executors . . . . . ftatute of the lord the K. & all the goods mine &
' ours, moveable & immoveable, as was aforefaid, wherefoever within the
' rod & without they fhall be found, to be diftreined & kept by the
' marfhals & ftewards of the lord K. & alfo by the balifs of the lord

' abbat

‘ abbat of Burg, or by whomſoever the officers of the place in the ju-
‘ riſdiction or bailiwic of whom they ſhall be found, if all & every
‘ the foreſaid particulars at the terms aforeſaid, & according to form
‘ I ſhall not fully obſerve; renouncing alſo for me & my heirs &
‘ my executors, all aid of law canon & civil, all letters asked & to
‘ be asked, exceptions, cavillations, cuſtoms, liberties, privilege of the
‘ croſs, & moſt eſpecially the royal prohibition, & all other things
‘ which againſt this writing or deed are able to be objected, which
‘ are able to profit me, or my heirs, or my executors, or be an hin-
‘ drance to the foreſaid Wm. de Watervyle, or his certain attorney.
‘ I exclude moreover, from my heirs & my executors, poſſeſſion &
‘ adminiſtration of all my goods, ſo that no execution of my will, or
‘ alienation, or diſtribution, or impairing of my goods, be made, till to
‘ the foreſaid Wm. de Watervyle, or his certain attorney, of every
‘ the things aforeſaid as is before noted, it ſhall be moſt fully ſatis-
‘ fied. And for greater ſecurity to be made of this thing, to this pre-
‘ ſent writing obligatory for a ſign teſtimonial my ſeal is appendent,
‘ together with the ſeals of my pledges, that is to ſay of Robert de
‘ la Camayle of Ayſton, John de la More of Apethorpe, & Andrew
‘ de Bynedon, of whom every one obliges himſelf to be principal deb-
‘ tor in the ſolid terms abovewritten, if the ſaid Thomas in the fore-
‘ ſaid payment of 10 marcs at the terms appointed (which God for-
‘ bid) ſhall be wanting. Given at Ayſton, the ſunday next after the
‘ feaſt of S. Michael, in the 28. of K. Edward.’ The ſeals are wanting, &
the deed it ſelf, in ſome places, mutilated. ‘ In 1300. ſaith our old
‘ antiquary Mr. Butcher,[a] general chapters called *itere minorum,* were
‘ again held at Stanford.’ Which if we muſt not read *itinera minorum,* as I have elſewhere ſaid, I know not what to make of.

28. E. 1. XXVI. In this 28. E. 1. 1300. [b]‘ The K. ſummoned a parliament
1300.   ‘ to meet at Lincoln, & the perſons elected to repreſent the borough
‘ of Stanford in it, were John de Fal & Wm. de Downdale.’ Authors differ much both concerning the time when, & place where,
this parliament was held. As firſt. Some ſay it was held in 1300.
firſt at London, & afterwards at Stanford. Of this opinion is Speed.
‘ In 1300. (ſaith he[c]) the K. (whom wars had together made renowned
‘ & aged) graciouſly & wiſely yielded to confirme ſuch graunts of laws
‘ & liberties, as the earles & barons (the pretended conſervators of the
‘ peoples intereſt) did declare were by his promiſe to be confirmed to
‘ them at his returne from Scotland : & which hee accordingly did,
‘ in a parliament holden at London, upon prorogation, *in Quindena*
‘ *Paſchæ*; where, for their fuller ſatisfaction, hee (as ſaith Walſing-
‘ ham) left out this clauſe in the end, *ſaving the right of our crowne.*
‘ And what, at this time was wanting, hee made up afterward in a
‘ parliament at Stanford. But ſecondly. Others aſſert this parlia-

a MS. in my hands, p. 30.   b From Mr. Willis's letter, to me.   c p. 656.

2

‘ ment

' ment was held in 1301. at Stanford.   Of this opinion is Kniton.[a]
Thirdly.   Others write this parliament was held in 1301. at Stanford,
or Lincoln.   Of this opinion is Stow.   ' In 1301, faith he, [b] K. Edw.
' kept his Chriftmas at Northampton, & after held his parliament at
' Stanford, fome fay at Lincolne.'   Laftly, others maintaine this parliament was held in 1302. at Stanford.   Of this opinion is Walfingham.   For under the year 1302. he fays, [c] ' In thefe days the K. held
' a parliament at Stanford, to which the earls & barons came with
' horfe & armor for the purpofe, as was reported, that they might fully
' extort from him the hitherto delayed execution of the charter of
' the foreft.   And the K. hearkening to their reprefentations [as well
he might when they came in fuch numbers & were even ready to draw
upon him] ' in all things condefcended to oblige them.'

XXVII. On the death of Henry de Hanna (warden of the white
friers at Stanford & provincial of his order in England) Wm. Lidlington a Carme of Stanford, was elected provincial of that order in England ; this was done, as I take it, in a general chapter of the brotherhood held at Stanford in 1300.   Lidlingtons being elected provincial is by Bale in one place [d] put down under 1299. immediately after the death of Henry de Hanna.   But (as fome time muft be allowed
for notice, & to affemble the brethren) I rather chufe to follow him
when he corrects himfelf, & in another place fays, ' [e] the next year Wm.
' Ludlington, an Oxford divine, a man learned & eloquent, took up-
' on him the government of his order in England.'   And indeed if we
reobferve that Henry de Hanna was buried but Nov. 28. 1299.   Lidlington could not well be elected before 1300.   Bale adds, ' [f] that in
' Lidlingtons time one, & but one, chapter, of the Carmes was ce-
' lebrated at Stanford.'   Now that chapter, as I guefs, was in 1300.
when he was elected provincial.   As he was certainly provincial, I can
hardly queftion but he was alfo chofen warden of this houfe upon
Hanna's deceafe.   That his merit, refidence, & burial there, make almoft evident.   ' This Wm. Lidlington, faith Pits, [g] being either a Lin-
' colnfhire man, or (as others will have it) born fomewhere about Roy-
' fton in Cambridgefhire, was a Carmelite of Stanford, & S. T. P. of
' Oxford.   A celebrated perfon for his erudition, piety, prudence, &
' the reputation of every virtue.   After, by a diligent preaching of
' the word, he had raifed much fruit, & acquired great fame among
' all, he was elected provincial of his order in England, & ftrenuoufly
' maintained that poft above 14 years.   Leland [h] calls him William
' Lullendune, pronounces he was a Lincolnfhire man, & a perfon of
' the greateft fame : It will be worth the while therefore, fays he, to

a Col. 2528.
b p. 320.
c p. 80.
d Cent. 10. p. 69.
e Sequenti anno, regimen in Anglia fuf-
cepit Guilhelmus Ludlington, Oxon. theologus, vir eruditus & eloquens — Heliades.
MS. Harley.
   f unum tantummodo capitulum Stan-
fordie celebraffe memorant. ib.
   g in vita.
   h Comment. p. 341.

' know by what steps he afcended to it.   Then tells us, that he o_
' pened to himfelf the way to immortal fame, at what time he went
' to ftudy at Oxford.   And ftill increafed it by his continual induftry ;
' for he fpared for no pains, till he got both the name & [what is] the
' higheft ornament of a divine, [the degree of a profeffor]

Feb. 12.   XXVIII. ' a The juftice of the Englifh armies againft the Scots, being
1 30 4/7.   ' now impugned by the papal letters, comprehending fundry argu-
29. E.   ' ments on behalf of that nation, K. Edw. in a parliament at Lincolne
' publifhed their contents, & by confent of the whole reprefentative
' body of the realme, returned a copious defence of his whole pro-
' ceedings, with proteftation firft, that he did not exhibit any thing
' as in forme of judgment or trial of his caufe, but for fatisfaction of
' his holy fatherhoods confcience, & not otherwife.   But, whereas the
' pope had required the K. to ftand to his decifion for matter of claim,
' he writes, that thereunto he would make no anfwere, as having left
' that point to the earls, peers of his land.   That the refolution of
' thefe worthy pillars, in the cafe of their countries crowne & digni-
' ties may be imitated in their following pofterities, & celebrated in
' our everlafting remembrances we hold it fit here to record their an-
' fwer : b whiche beginneth thus.   To our mofte holy father in Chrifte,
' Boniface by Gods providence high byfhoppe of the holy Romaine & uni-
' verfal churche, his devoute fons, John E. Warenn [lord of Stanford & an
' hundred more in my authors named at large] with al humble fubmif-
' fion.   The holy mother churche, by whofe minifterie the catholik
' fee is governed : in hir deedes (as we throughly beleeve) proceed-
' eth with that ripeneffe in judgment, that fhe will be hurtful to none,
' but like a mother would every mans right be kept unbroken, afwel
' in another, as in hir felf.   Whereas therefore in a general parlia-
' ment called at Lincolne of late, by our mofte dreade lord Edward,
' &c. the fame our lord caufed certain letters receyved from you to bee
' reade openly & to be declared ferioufly afore us, about certaine bu-
' fineffe touching the condition & ftate of the realme of Scotlande :
' we did not a little mufe & marvel with ourfelves, hearing the mean-
' ings concerning the fame fo wondrous & ftrange as the like we have
' not heard at any time before.   For we know, moft holy father, &
' it is wel knowne within this realme of England (as alfo not un_
' knowen to other perfons befides) that from the firft beginninge of
' the realme of Englande, the certain & direct government of the
' realme of Scotlande in all temporal caufes from tyme to tyme be-
' longed to the kings of the fame realme of England & realme of
' Scotland, afwel in times both of the Britains as alfo Englifhemen :
' yea rather the fame realme of Scotlande of olde tyme was in fee to
' the auncetours of our forefaid lordes kynges of Englande, yea & to
' himfelf.   Furthermore, the kynges of Scottes & the realme have not

a Speed. p. 657. b.   b Hol. p. 836, 837, 838.
2   ' bene

' bene under any other than the kynges of Englande, & the kynges of
' Englande have [not] aunfwered, nor ought to anfwere for their rights
' in the forefaid realme, or for any his temporalities, before any judge
' ecclefiaftical or fecular; by reafon of the free preheminence of the ftate
' of hys royal dignity & cuftome kepte wythout breache at all tymes.
' Wherefore, after treatie had, & diligent deliberation of the contents
' in your forefaid letters, this was the common agreeing with one
' minde, & fhall be without faile in tyme to come by Gods grace; that
' our forefaide lorde the K. oughte by no means to aunfwere in judge-
' mente in any cafe, or bring his forefaide rights into doubte,
' nor ought to fend any proctours or meffengers to your prefence,
' fpecially feeing that the premifes tend manifeftly to the difenherit-
' ing of the right of the crowne of England, & the plaine overthrowe
' of the ftate of the faide realme, & alfo hurte of the liberties, cu-
' ftomes, & lawes of our fathers : For keping & defence of whiche,
' we are bounde by the dutie of the othe made, & we will mayn-
' taine them wyth all power, & will defende them (by Gods helpe)
' wyth all ftrengthe ; and further will not fuffer our forefayd lorde
' the K. to doe, or by anie meanes attempte, the premifes beyng
' fo unaccouftomed, unwont, & not hearde of afore. Wherefore we
' reverently & humbly befeeche your holineffe, that yee would fuffer
' the fame our lorde K. of England (who among other princes of the
' worlde fheweth himfelf catholic & devoute to the Romifhe churche)
' quietly to enjoy his rights, liberties, cuftomes, & lawes aforefaide,
' without all empairing, & trouble; & let them continue untouched
' In witneffe whereof, we have fette our feales to thefe prefentes, afwel
' for us, as for the whole communaltie of the forefaide realme. Dated
' at Lincolne, the 12 of Feb. in the year of our Lord 1301. & 29. of
' K. Edw.' This inftrument fhews both the time when, & place where
the parliament abovementioned was really held. However it might
be adjourned to Stanford, or London, or both. I fhall only obferve,
that John E. Warren & lord of Stanford is the firft perfon whofe
name is inferted in the preamble of the faid inftrument (after whom
follows Thomas E. of Lancafter, &c.) which fhews that our E. gave
place to none, the royal family only excepted. 'The fame year
' [a] the faid E. Warenn was fent with Guy de Beauchamp E. of War-
' wick, & others, to treat with agents from the K. of France, upon
' articles of peace betwixt K. Edward & the Scots. —— Letitia, Daughter
' of Hugh Hod late burgefs of Stanford, gave to Nicholas Hod bur-
' gefs of Stanford, one fhop ftanding in great St. Michaels Parifh in
' the Lane called Feldovenfty. B. H.'

XXIX. In the *Monafticon Anglicanum,* I read, ' [b] Ifabella de Roos,
' wife of Robert de Roos lies at New-fted by Stanford, & died in the
' year M.CCCI. In Mr. Lelands Itinerary I read the fame [viz. that

a Bar. Vol. 1. p. 80. a.   b T. I. p. 328.

she was buried at New-sted] ' but that she died in 1303 [a]. In Mr. Burtons account of the monuments at Bottesford in Leicestershire, I find this inscription. [b] ' Here lies lord Robert de Roos, whose heart was ' buried at Kirham in 1285. & lady Isabella his wife, whose heart lies at ' Noim [Newsted] by Stanford, she died 1301.' The mistake in the year I believe is Mr. Lelands or his printers. But from these accounts it may be questioned whether her body, or heart only, was buried at Newsted. Be that as it will, at the dissolution of monasteries all the bodies of the Roos's buried at the priories of Newsted, Kirkham, Croxton, & Belvoir, as I have been informed, were by the piety of the then lord Roos removed to Bottesford.—— There having been a suit in the kings court between Cecilia relict of Richard Plukets late of Staunford & Christiana her daughter, of the one part, complainants; & Godfrey lord abbat of Burg of the other part, defendant; about a messuage, three rods of land, & a rent of four shillings with the appurtenances in Stanford, claimed by the foresaid Cecilia as her joynture or part of the same, & claimable by the foresaid Christiana as heiress of her said mother; they now released to the foresaid abbat of Burg all their right in the said premises by particular instruments; whereof that of the mother runs thus. ' [c] All shall understand ' that whereas a plea was moved in the court of the lord K. between Ceci ' lia who was the wife of Richard Plukets complainant, & lord God ' frey abbat of Burg defendent, by a writ touching her joynture; the ' said Cecilia, in her free widowhood, hath released, & by the pre ' sent writing, quit claimed the whole right & claim which she had, ' or in any manner hath been able to have, by name of dowry, in ' all the messuages, lands, rents, & tenements, which at any time ' were [the lands &c.] of Richard her husband, in the town of Staun ' ford. So to wit that neither the foresaid Cecilia, nor any other ' in her name, in the foresaid messuages, lands, rents, & tenements, ' shall hereafter be able to demand or claim, in the name of dowry, ' for ever. In witness whereof the said Cecilia to this writing ' of quit claim hath put to her seal. Witnesses, Nicholas de Burton ' of Staunford, John de Warmington of the same, Eustace Malerbe of ' the same, Clement de Melton of the same, Henry Faderman of ' the same, Bernard de Bonde of the same, Peter de Burlee, Simon ' the butler of Burg, Adam le almoner of the same, Bernard de Castre, ' & others. Given at Burg the Saturday next before the circumci ' sion of our Lord, in the 30 of K. Edw.' The instrument of Christiana (daughter of the said Cecilia) is thus expressed. ' [d] All shall understand, ' that whereas a plea was moved in the court of the lord K. between ' Christiana (daughter of Richard Plukets) complainant, & lord God ' frey, abbat of Burg defendent, touching one messuage, three rods of ' land, & a rent of four shillings with the appurtenances in the town

a Itin. Vol. 8. p. 55.   Vesp. E. XXII. fol. 7. b.
b p. 50.   d id. ib.
c Ex Codicis MS. in Bib. Cot. sub imagine

‘ of Staunford, by a writ of intrusion; the said Christiana, for her
‘ self & heirs whomsoever, hath granted, released, & by the present writ-
‘ ing quit claimed to the foresaid lord Godfrey the abbat, all the right
‘ & claim which she had, or in any manner hath been able to have in
‘ the foresaid messuages, three rods of land, four shillings of rent,
‘ & all other messuages, lands, meadows, & rents whatsoever in the
‘ town of Staunforde aforesaid, which, by right of inheritance, or
‘ any other title, to her or her heirs could be able to accrue. So to
‘ wit, that neither the foresaid Christiana, nor her heirs, nor any
‘ other in her name, or of her heirs, any thing of right or claim in
‘ the foresaid messuages, lands, & rent, & all other tenements in
‘ the town of Staunford whatsoever, as afore is said, shall ever be able
‘ to demand or claim. In witness whereof she hath put to her seal,
‘ &c.’ The day, year, & witnesses as above. It is a very true observation of Mr. Burtons, ‘ ª that antiently the chiefest men, either abiding
‘ at, or near, any place, were chosen to be witnesses to deeds, to give
‘ strength & confirmation to the passing thereof: which thing was ob-
‘ served almost in the meanest conveyances.’ Thus, of the witnesses
to the two last recited deeds, Nicholas de Burton of Staunford was
lord of Tolethorpe in Rutland within two miles of Staunford & also one
of those who represented this borough in the parliament of 23.E.1.Eustace
Malerb was one of those who represented the town of Stanford in
the parliament at York the 15. E. 2. Clement de Melton was the other
representative of the same borough in the parliament at Westminster
23. E. 1. & one of those who represented it again at York 26. E. 1. above.
Peter de Burlee was lord of the manor there, &c.

XXX. In the 30. E. 1. ‘ ᵇ The K. called a parliament to meet at
‘ London, & the persons elected to represent the borough of Stan-
‘ ford at that assembly, were John Lessal & Roger le Ring. —— About
‘ this time, or before, Roger le Porter of Stanford, sold to Richard
‘ le Clerc (son of Richard le Ferun late of Stanford) one place in
‘ great S. Michaels parish, in the street called Ovensty, between the
‘ other place of the same Richard south, & the houses of Simon Child
‘ north. Also he gave him the whole court, or place, between
‘ his hall in the street called Ovensty, in great S. Michaels parish, south,
‘ & his cellar, & the gallery over it in the same street, north, as far
‘ as the gable end of the same gallery. B. H.’—— On the 9. Ap. 1302. Ap.
30. E. 1.’ Godfrey abbat of Burg & the convent of that place, pre- 1302.
sented Stephen de Burg a monk of their own monastery, to the priory 30. E. 1.
of S. Michael by Staunford, & sent him to John Dalderby bishop of
Lincoln with the following letter, for institution. ᶜ‘ To the reve-
‘ rend father in Christ lord John, by the grace of God, bishop of Lin-
‘ coln, his humble & devoted sons in Christ, Godefry, by gift of the

---

a Leicest. p.   c Ex codicis MS. in Bib. Cott. sub imagine
b From Mr. Willis’s letter to me. as   Vesp. E. XXII. fol. 54. b.
above.

'same grace, abbat of Burg, & the convent of the same place, greeting
'with all the reverence & obedience due & devoted.   To your holy fa-
'therhood we present our beloved son in Christ, brother Stephen de
'Burg our monk, the bearer of the presents, to the vacant priory of
'the nuns of S. Michael without Staunford, which belongs to our
'presentation; humbly & devoutly beseeching, that ye would admit
'him to the same priory, & institute him in the same; the cure,
'if it please you, of the rehearsed priory to the same committing.
'Saving, to us & our successors, the jurisdiction in the same accord-
'ing to manner accustomed, & the obedience before canonically paid.
'In witness whereof to the presents we have put to our seals.   Given
'in our chapter the fifth of the Ides of April, in the year of our Lord,
'1302—— About this time, Richard, son of Roger le Porter of Staun-
'ford, gave to Reginald Smereman of Staunford, his house standing
'in Colgate in great S. Michaels parish, between the lane leading to
'the mercat east, & the house of Bartholomew the preacher west. B. H.

26 Jan.   XXXI. On the 26. Jan. 130⅞. 31. E. 1. Godfrey, lord abbat of Burg,
130⅞. intending to visit the nuns of S. Michael the wednesday next after
31. E. 1. candlemass following, gave notice of the same to the prior & prioress of
that house, by the ensuing letter.   ' ᵃ Godfrey, by divine permission,
'abbat of Burg, to his beloved in Christ, the prior of S. Michaels with-
'out Staunford, & the prioress & convent of the same place, the health
'which hath flowed from the bowels of a Saviour.   Intending, out
'of affection, to exercise the wonted office of visitation which is in-
'cumbent on us to perform in your priory; to you we command that on
'the wednesday next after the purification of the blessed virgin Mary,
'in your conventual church of St. Michael, you, & all & every the
'rest of your congregation, who, by us, of right or custom, to be
'visited are bound, submissively appear to us, ready wholsomely
'to undergo our visitation in Christ Jesu for long times to profit you.
'Given at Eye, on Saturday the morrow of the conversion of St. Paul,
'in the year 1302.'   There being about this time some waste or mismanagement of the revenues belonging to the said nunnery of St Michael, the said abbat appointed brother T. de Sarum a monk of Burg,
warden of the temporalities of the said house, reserving however to
the prior & prioress the spiritual disposal in all things concerning the
same. His letter for that purpose is thus expressed.   ' ᵇ To all the sons
'of holy mother church who shall see or hear these letters, Godefry
'by divine permission abbat of Burg, greeting.   To your knowledge
'we would have it evidently come, that whereas the wardenship of the
'house of the nuns of S. Michael without Staunford, to the abbat
'& convent of Burg, in spirituals & temporals from time of old hath
'appertained, & now pertains in law & in fact; we with an earnest desire
'wishing to preserve the same wardenship, for the increase of its holy

a Ex codicis MS. in Bib. Cott. sub imag. Vesp. E. XXII. fol. 57. b.   b id. fol. 78. b.

'religion,

' religion, have appointed & ordained our beloved confrater, brother
' T. de Sarum, fpecial warden, in temporals only of the fame houfe;
' granting to the fame full & free power of ordaining & appointing,
' as well within the houfe aforefaid as without, in all temporal mat-
' ters whatfoever, as to the faid houfe he fhall fee profitable
' referving neverthelefs, to the prior & priorefs of the houfe above-
' faid, the fpiritual difpofal in all things the faid houfe concerning.

XXXIII. Wm. Lidlington, with many others, as Pits tells us, ' [a] was
' fummoned to a general chapter at Narbonne in France, by mafter
' Gerard of Bononia, provincial general of the whole order, where
' in 1303. Lidlington refifting as much as he was able, the Englifh
' Carmelites were divided into two provinces. However Lidlington,
' being joined by fome others, would not fubmit to the decree, but
' wrote againft it.' Among thofe who fided with Lidlington in this
difpute, Godfrey de Cornwal was one, who was a very learned man, &
could never be brought to confent to the divifion. [b] John Burley was
another, of whom prefently. ' And in fhort eight more perfons, as Bale
' notes, who were prefent at that affembly, were as much difpleafed at
' it; all which refifted ftoutly againft the decrees of that fynod, & by
' publifhing divers books & libels brought no little fcandal to the
' church & trouble to both parties, which pope Clement the fifth at
' length grievoufly refented. Wherepon excommunications were iffued
' out againft them, & Lidlington being fent for to Paris by the chief pro-
' vincial Gerard, to terrifie others underwent a penance of 40 days,
' & was detained there for fome time with his accomplices in banifh-
' ment.' Being thus overborn by authority of his fuperiors, faith
Pits, ' Lidlington at laft gave over the difpute, matters were com-
' pofed, & he & Gerard reconciled. After which, as Bale adds, in
' all their lectures & public difputations Lidlington behaved himfelf
' with a great deal of bravery.' At this time flourifhed the two Burleys,
John & Walter. ' John Burley, as Bale afferts, [c] was born in the
' weftern parts of England.' But I rather, as his name & place of
abode lead me to think, believe he was born at Burley by Stanford.
Be that as it will, as the fame author acquaints us, ' he was brought
' up a fcholar from his very cradle, & adorned the monaftery of the
' Carmes at Stanford with his profound learning. When the difpute
' about dividing the Englifh Carmelites into two provinces arofe be-
' tween Gerard of Bononia general of the whole order, & William
' Lidlington provincial of the fame in England, this Burley, as hath been
' obferved, took Lidlingtons part, & would not agree to the divifion;
' altho' both of them were at laft forced to yield to the juft authority
' of the provincial general. But, as Pits fays, [d] let us fee what [John]
' Burley added of his own to the commonwealth of learning. As I

a p. 412.   c in vita.
b Videfis Leland de fcript. Brit. p. 354.   d in vita.
Bale p. 388. & Pits ut fupra.

' gather,

' gather, faith he, from Leland & others, he wrote, upon Porphyry,
' Ariſtotle, Gilbert, & Peter Lombard, no leſs than 37 pieces.'
Here Pits ſays, Leland mentions ſome of John Burleys works; but in
truth Leland ſpeaks only a little of the man, nothing at all of what
he wrote. This then is one of the many proofs which might be advanced to ſhew, that, tho' Pits often pretends to have ſeen Leland, he
really never did. ' Walter Burley, ſaith Leland, [a] muſt (if ever any
' of the diſciples of Scotus was reckoned a ſcholar) be accounted one,
' & will deſervedly poſſeſs a great character at home, ſince, at Paris it
' ſelf, he was eſteemed the ſharpeſt diſputant of the age. My chief
' witneſs for this aſſertion (ſays he) ſhall be Herman Schedel of Norim-
' berg, who, not without an honourable mention of him, does reve-
' rence to Burleys ſharp arguments. As for this Burley himſelf, he
' ſtudied [firſt] in Merton Coll. at Oxford, where, by public ſuffrage
' of the univerſity, he was raiſed to the higheſt claſs of divines; as
' he was alſo at Paris. This Burley, as Pits ſaith, [b] was a man of a moſt
' ſharp wit, & the prime philoſopher of his time. He was once fellow-
' ſcholar with Occham at Paris, under the ſame maſter, Scotus. But
' he afterwards in England became a moſt eager oppoſer of his ſaid
' maſter. The writings he left behind him ſufficiently teſtifie the won-
' derful felicity of his ſubtle wit & knowledge in philoſophy. He wrote
' on the maſter of the ſentences, ſeveral other ſubjects, & almoſt all
' Ariſtotles works, above 130 pieces. Mr. Stevens ſays, [c] the authors
' that write of Walter Burley conceal his order; but I, with probabi-
' lity, judge him to have been a frier minor, as well becauſe he was
' Scotus's diſciple at Paris, where few but minors reſorted to the
' ſchools of that order, as becauſe all the reſt of Scotus's ſcholars there
' named by Wadding were of the ſaid order.' Here I might add, it
is as probable Walter Burley was a Carme of the ſame houſe at Stanford, with his nameſake, perhaps brother, John. But Fuller is againſt us
both, & tells us poſitively, that ' [d] Walter Burley was a ſecular prieſt, &
' called *doctor approbatus*; Occham, *doctor ſingularis*; & their maſter
' Duns, *doctor ſubtilis*.' Another tells us, that Walter Burley was not
called *doctor approbatus*, but the *plain & perſpicuous doctor*; [e] & that
he was a grey frier.

XXXIV. Robert Lutterel having, as before related, [f] given the prior
& convent of Sempringham a manor of his in S. Peters pariſh in Stanford, to maintain young ſtudents in divinity & philoſophy there, & a
capellan to celebrate divine offices in S. Maries chapel therein alſo ſituate; John Dalderby biſhop of Lincoln (altho' there had been for
many ages before a conſtant chantery in the ſaid chapel) now granted
the ſaid ſcholars & capellan licenſe to celebrate in the ſame, conditionally that no font, or bell-tower, ſhould be erected, nor any pro-

---

a Comment. p. 354.
b in vita.
c Addit. Vol. to the Monaſt. I. p. 105, 106.

d Church Hiſt. p. 94.
e Antiq. of the Engliſh Franciſ. p. 151.
f See anno 1292. above. b.

ceffion, act of folemnity, or facrament, adminiftred there, but that, upon all thofe occafions, they fhould repair to the parifh church, & that the offerings due thence, to the rector of S. Peters, fhould be punctually paid, & the faid church in all things faved harmlefs. And if any thing were attempted againft the form of his conceffion, then the fame to be void. The faid grant is thus expreffed. ‘ᵃ John, by ‘ divine permiffion bp. of Lincoln, to his beloved in Chrift, the prior ‘ & convent of Sempingham, greeting. Whereas mafter Robert Lutte- ‘ rel, hath given you the manor which he had in the parifh of S. Peter ‘ Stanford, in an intuition of charity, willing, that the fcholars, for ‘ augmenting the number of your convent, ftudying in divinity or phi- ‘ lofophy in the fame manor, & one fecular or regular capellan to ‘ celebrate divine offices in the chapel of the bleffed Mary, within ‘ the faid manor fituate, ye fhould for ever fuftain : We, commending ‘ his pious deed & propofal (altho’ in the faid chapel for many ages ‘ paft there hath been a chantry had, as we have learned, conftantly) ‘ neverthelefs for greater corroboration of the mind of mafter Robert ‘ aforefaid, & for the folace & quiet of the ftudents, grant you fpe- ‘ cial licenfe, as far as in us lies, for ever to caufe divine offices to ‘ be celebrated in the chapel aforefaid, without prejudice of the parifh ‘ church of S. Peter Stanford (within whofe parifh it is fituate) & of ‘ other the churches neighbouring ; fo neverthelefs that neither bap- ‘ tifmal font, nor bell-tower be erected ; nor any proceffion, or act ‘ of any fort of folemnity done ; nor the facraments in any manner ‘ there adminiftred ; & the oblations due thence to the rector of the ‘ parifh church abovefaid paid ; the faid church harmlefs in all things ‘ kept ; & the honor due to it in no fort rafhly withdrawn. And if ‘ any thing be attempted againft the form of this grant, let the fame ‘ conceffion be altogether of no moment. In witnefs whereof our ‘ feal is to the prefents appendent. Given at Buchden, the 3d. of the ‘ Ides of November, in the year of our Lord 1303.’ Upon mafter Robert Lutterels gift, as above confirmed, the prior & convent of Sem- pingham, by an inftrument under the feal of the above John Daldreby lord bifhop of Lincoln, acknowledged their obligations to the faid mafter Lutterel, for this & other his benefactions, to wit, for main- tenance of a chantry prieft at Irnham, another at S. Marys chapel in Stanford, & a third at Sempingham ; & promifed to keep a number of fcholars to ftudy divinity & philofophy at Stanford, upon Mr. Lut- terels foundation, for increafe of their convent. But take it in their own words. ‘ᵇ To all the faithful of Chrift, &c. the prior & convent ‘ of Sempingham, greeting. Know ye that we, with affent of the ve- ‘ nerable father lord Philip, mafter of our order, are in the word of ‘ verity bound to our moft beloved mafter & friend, mafter Robert Lut-

a Ex Regiftri Johannis Daldreby epif.   b Ex ejufdem Regiftri, fol 8. b. & dicti
Linc. folio 8. a. & Mon. Ang. T. 2. p. 792. b.   Mon. Ang. T. 2 p. 792. b.

‘ terel,

' terel, rector of the church of Irnham, & to his heirs for ever, for the
' lands & tenements which he hath given us in the towns of Keten,
' Cotifmore, & Caftreton, in the county of Ruteland, & in Stanford
' in the county of Lincoln, for maintenance of three capellanes to
' celebrate for the health of his foul, & in the underwritten form; to
' wit, for maintenance of one fecular capellan in the parifh church of
' S. Andrew at Irnham.   And of one other capellan to celebrate for
' ever, for the foul of the faid mafter Robert Lutterel, & the fouls of
' the fcholars ftudying at Stanford, in the chapel of the bleffed Mary,
' lying within the manor of Stanford ; which we have by gift of
' the forefaid mafter Robert.   And for maintenance of one other ca-
' pellan to celebrate for ever the mafs of the bleffed Mary in the
' conventual church of Sempingham. We alfo by thefe prefents for us &
' our fucceffors grant & acknowledge our felves bound to the forefaid
' mafter Robert Lutterel & his heirs, for maintenance of the fcholars, for
' increafe of our convent, ftudying divinity & philofophy at fitting times,
' at Staunford.   Sealed with the feal of John lord bifhop of Lincoln.
' Witneffes, lord Robert de Fligefthorp, Philip de Paunton, Theobald
' de Neurile, John de Folville, Roger Morteyn, Ralph of the Holy
' Land ; Geoffry de Brunne, Kts. &c.   Mr. Forfter fpeaking of Sempringham hall at Staunford writes thus.   '[a] Sempringham in the parifh
' of S. Peters was founded by Robert Lutterel rector of Irnham, who
' gave lands & tenements in the towns of Keten, Cotifmore & Caftre-
' ton in Rutland, & a large houfe & lands in Stanford, to maintain three
' chaplains to fay mafs for his foul, one in the parifh church of S.
' Andrew at Irnham ; another in the chapel of S. Mary Bennewerk
' at Stanford, & the 3d. in the conventual church at Sempringham :
' & all the reft he gave for fupport of a fchool at Stanford, wherein
' the youth were taught divinity & philofophy, to the increafe of the
' number of the convent at Sempringham.   The bifhop of Lincoln in
' 1303. did allow them the ufe of the chapel of S. Mary Bennewerk
' for divine fervice : The front of the houfe is ftill ftanding, & carries
' in it the appearance of a collegiate building.'   This account of Mr.
Forfters is already publifhed by Mr. Stevens in his 1ft additional vol.
to the Monafticon, but is full of miftakes, which are here therefore neceffary to be corrected.   Firft then, S. Mary Bennewerks was not a
private chapel in S. Peters parifh, as Mr. Forfter fuggefts, but a parifh
church, & had its own proper rector & parifh diftinct from S. Peters.
But II. when S. Mary Bennewerk church was deftroyed by the northern
men in 1461. the parifh was annexed to S. Peters.   And then III. one
of the town gates called before weft-gate, was foon after called S.
Peters gate.   And IV. a ftreet running up from Peter-hill to weft-gate,
& called before that time le Gannoc, was alfo not long after the union
of thofe parifhes called S. Peters ftreet.   V. St. Mary Bennewerk church

a Letter to Mr. Stevens, MS. in my hands, p. 12.

4

ftood

stood just within west-gate, & the place where it stood is yet called Bennewerk churchyard. VI. exactly before Bennewerk churchyard is an old house 'the front of the house carrying in it, as Mr. Forster ' rightly says, the appearance of a collegiate building.' VII. this house when Stanford was an university, I do certainly believe was a college or hall belonging to some of the students there; & is the most entire piece of antiquity of this kind, we have now left. VIII. the very situation of this house, shews it was not the house Mr. Lutterel gave the monks of Sempringham, his house being situate in S. Peters parish; whereas this abutts upon S. Mary Bennewerk churchyard. And indeed, IX. Sempringham hall (as I have been often assured by the late Mr. Richard Walburg) was not near the place where Bennewerk church stood, but that house in the middle of the street called le Gannoc, where Mr. Ald. Feast some time ago dwelt, was the very spot where it was situate. X. There therefore we must place S. Maries chapel, a chantry, founded indeed by whom I know not; but, as bishop Dalderby himself tells us, long before Mr. Lutterel built Sempringham hall close by it. XI. This chapel & St. Mary Bennewerk church, being both long ago destroyed, they are often taken for one & the same by them who knew not their distinct situations & uses. Thus Mr. Forster joyns them together in his account above; & thus, Bennewerk churchyard, by them who know not that there was also a chapel in the same street, dedicated to the same blessed virgin with that church, is sometimes called chapel close, & Bennewerk chapel yard, & sometimes Bennewerk churchyard: those names being confounded, or carelesly used for want of better information.

XXXIV. On Dec. 25. 1303. Godfrey lord abbat of Burg gave to Wm. Poncyn of Stanford the wardenship of S. Giles hospital for life, conditionally that he should three times a week supply the chantry in S. Giles chapel, keep up the buildings of the house, & maintain all other charges of the said hospital as of old time accustomed. His grant to the said Wm. Poncyn is thus expressed. a 'To all the faithful of Christ ' who shall see or hear this present writing, Godfrey by divine permis-' sion, abbat of Burg, greeting in the Lord. Ye shall understand that ' we have granted & delivered to William Poncyn in Staunford, the war-' denship of the hospital of the blessed Giles without Staunford, for ' term of his life; together with the edifices, lands, & rents, & ' all other the profits to the said hospital belonging, or out of the ' pious devotion of the faithful arising; so to wit, that he shall sup-' ply the chantry in the chapel of the blessed Giles three times a week, ' & also repair & sustain the edifices there erected, & support the rest of ' the charges on the said hospital incumbent, as of old accustomed. ' Saving to us & our successors the rights & liberties in the same hos-' pital, which, unto us & the monastery of Burg, by right & custom,

(margin) Dec. 25. 1303. 32. E. 1.

a Ex codicis MS. in Bib. Cotton. sub imagine Vesp. E. XXII. fol. 77. b.

' are

' are known to belong. In witnefs whereof to the prefents our feal is
' appendent. Given at Burg on the feaft of the Lords nativity, in the
' year 1303.' In this 32. E. 1. ' ᵃ John E. Waren [lord of Stanford]
' was again employed into Scotland in the kings fervice. Augnes
' . . . . . . of Staunford, gave to Augnes an houfe ftanding in the
' lane called Punchelardfty in S. Peters parifh, Stanford, between a
' tenement of John Braban north, & the caftle dike fouth. B. H.' Gilbert de Caftreton burgefs of Stanford, was now one of the receivers
of the kings tax, as alfo of his cuftoms on wool, &c. tranfported into the parts of Holland, Zealand, & Brabant. This Gilbert was undoubtedly a man of good wealth & fortune. Of whom more below. ᵇ

Sep. 27.   XXXV. ' ᶜ John E. Warenn [lord of Stanford] died at Kenington near
32. E. 1. ' London, upon the fifth of the kalends of October, having continued E.
' of Surrey no lefs than fifty four years, & was buried in the midft of
' the pavement in the quire of the abbey of Lewes, before the high
' altar with this epitaph upon his tomb.

> ' *Vous qe paffer ov bouche clofe,*
> ' *Prier pur cely ke cy repofe:*
> ' *En vie come vous efti jadis fu,*
> ' *Et vous tiel, ferretz come je fu;*
> ' *Sire Johan Count de Garenne gift yey;*
> ' *Dieu de fa alme eit mercy.*
> ' *Ky pur fa alme prierra,*
> ' *Troiz mill jours de Pardon avera.*

' Certain it is that he was a perfon in high efteem with the K. as
' may be feen by that fpecial precept directed to the then bifhop elect of
' London; whereby, fignifying how pious, & before almighty God, a mer-
' ciful work it was to pray continually for the dead, that fo they might
' be the more eafily delivered from the burthen of their fins; & that
' this our E. (who had been a moft faithful & ufeful fubject & fervant
' to him & the whole realm) was then departed this life to his very
' great forrow: he required him that he fhould caufe his foul to be
' commended to the mercy of God, by all religious & ecclefiaftic per-
' fons throughout his whole diocefe of London. The like precept
' was directed by the K. to the archbp. of Cant. his whole province;
' as alfo to the abbats of S. Auguftines in Canterbury, Weftminfter,
' Waltham, S. Albans, S. Edmunds Bury, & Evefham. Moreover
' for indulgences to fuch who fhould pray for his foul, I farther find,
' that Robert, then archbp. of Cant. granted forty days. *Gilbert bp.*
' *of Chichefter* ᵈ, forty days. Thomas bifhop of Rochefter, thirty days.
' The bp. of Durham forty days. The bp. of Kaerleol forty days. The
' bp. of Lincoln forty days. The bifhop of Coventry & Lichfield
' forty days. And *John, bifhop of Chichefter* ᵈ, forty days. By his

---

a Bar. Vol. 1. p. 80. a.   c Baron. Vol. 1. p. 80. a. b.
b Mich. Term. 11. E. 2. 1317:   d Sic in Dug.

I

' wife he had iffue William flain at Croyden, & two daughters, Alianor
' & Ifabel; which Alianor was firft married to Henry lord Piercy, &
' afterwards to the fon of a Scottifh earl ; and Ifabel to John Baillol
' afterwards K. of Scotland.' The faid John E. Warenn [lord of Stan-
ford] was fucceeded in honor & eftate by his grandfon ' ᵃ John, fon
' of William aforefaid, but born after his death.——ᵇ In the 33. of E. 1.   33.E. 1.
' the K. called a parliament to meet at Weftminfter, & the perfons
' elected to reprefent the borough of Stanford in that affembly were
' John de Meldon & Hugh de Alveton, That parliament was fitting
in January 130⁴⁄₅. For ' ᶜ John the 2. E. Warenn [lord of Stanford]   Jan.
' having an offer made unto him by the K. in his chamber at Weft-   130⁴⁄₅.
' minfter in parliament, upon the monday next before the feaft of S.
' Edward the K. & martyr [which feaft is celebrated Jan. 5.]
' of Joan, daughter to Henry E. of Baar, gratefully accepted thereof
' (he being not then fully 21 years of age) & took her to wife. ᵈ The
' faid Johan was the kings niece by his daughter Elianor, whom the
' E. of Barre had married.' Upon the 20th of March the fame year
K. Edward by infpeximus confirmed the grants of K. H. 2. K. John &
K. H. 3. to the nuns of S. Michael by Stanford. The grant of the faid
K. E. 1. is thus worded. ' ᵉ Edward by the grace of God, K. of England,
' lord of Ireland, & D. of Aquitain, to the archbifhops, bifhops, ab-
' bats, priors, earls, barons, judges, fherifs, provofts, officers, & to all
' bailifs & his faithful fervants, greeting. We have infpected the charter of
' lord Henry of good memory, fometime K. of England, our progeni-
' tor, which he made to the nuns of S. Michael at Stanford, in thefe
' words [then recites it, as above 4. H. 2.] We have alfo infpected
' the charter of lord John of good memory, fometime K. of England,
' our grandfather, which he made to the forenamed nuns, in thefe
' words [then recites it as above, Anno 12. John.] We have more-
' over infpected the charter of lord Henry, of renowned memory, our
' father, which he made to the fame nuns, in thefe words [then recites
it as above, Anno 12.H. 3.] We alfo, the conceffions & confirmations
' aforefaid holding ratified & good, them, for us & our heirs, as far
' as in us lies, to the forenamed nuns & their fucceffors, do grant &
' confirm, as the charters aforefaid more refpectively atteft. Witneffes,
' the venerable fathers, Antony of Durham, Walter of Coventry &
' Lichfield,

a Bar. Vol. I. p. 80. b.
b Ex literis B. Willis arm.
c Bar. Vol. 1. 80. b.
d Stow p. 321.
e Edwardus D. G. rex Anglie, dominus
Hibernie, & dux Aquitanie, archiepifcopis,
epifcopis, abbatibus, prioribus, comitibus,
baronibus, juftitiariis, vice-comitibus, prepo-
fitis, miniftris, & omnibus ballivis & fidelibus fuis, falutem. Infpeximus cartam bone
memorie D. Henrici quondam regis Anglie,
progenitoris noftri, quam fecit monialibus S.
Michaelis de Stanford, in hec verba. Infpeximus etiam cartam bone memorie D.

Johannis quondam regis Anglie, avi noftri,
quam fecit prefatis monialibus, in hec verba.
Infpeximus infuper cartam celebris memorie
D. Henrici, quondam regis Anglie, patris
noftri, quam fecit eifdem monialibus, in hec
verba. Nos autem conceffiones & confir-
mationes predictas ratas habentes & gratas,
eas pro nobis & heredibus noftris, quantum
in nobis eft, prefatis monialibus & earum
fucceffibus, concedimus & confirmamus, ficut carte predicte rationabiliter teftantur.
Hiis teftibus, venerabilibus patribus A.
Dunelm. W. Covetrenfi & Lichfeldenfi,
J. Karleolenfi, epifcopis; Henrico Lacy

' Lichfield, John of Carlifle, bifhops; Henry Lacy E. of Lincoln;
' Thomas E. of Lancafter; Humfrey de Bohun E. of Hereford & Effex;
' Guy de Beauchamp E. of Warwick; Adomar de Valence; Hugh Spen-
' cer; Robert fon of Roger; Robert de la Warde fteward of our
' houfhold, & others.   Given by our hand at Weftm. the 21. day of
21 Mar. ' March, in the 33. year of our reign.' The fame year ' Hugh Pert
' of Bradecroft fold, to Beatricia late the wife of Jofeph le Ferrour
' burgefs of Staunford, his houfes in the village of Bradecroft, fituate
' between an houfe of the nuns of S. Michael weft, & a houfe of
' . . . . . eaft, as they extend themfelves from the kings high way north,
' & the milldam of Bradecroft fouth.   Witneffes, W. Edelyn of Brade-
' croft, Walter de Tinwel of the fame. B. H.   Hugh fon of Matilda,
' late wife of Aylrich of Bradecroft, fold his fhare *in furno* [or a public oven] ' in Bradecroft to William Scot of Bradecroft. Witneffes,
' W. Edelyn, Walter de Tinwel, &c. Given at Bradecroft, 33. E. 1.'
This oven, as I take it, was a place where the whole town of Stanford
were obliged to bake.   Leland fpeaking of the weft fuburb fays,
' ᵃmark here that in this fuburbe is a parcelle of grounde caullid Brede-
' croft, becaufe that bakers fold there brede in that part of the fuburbe.'
And I believe he might have added, as I have faid, that they were all
obliged to bake there; ovens being formerly appointed without great
towns to prevent the danger of fire. Thus about this time I find ᵇ' the ab-
' bat of Burg had an hundred fhillings [for his fhare, rent, or licenfe
to them who kept it] ' out of the public oven of the town of Burg.'
28 June. The K. by his writ, directed to Lambert de Thrikingham, & Thomas de
33. E. 1. Burnham appointed affeffors of the Kings tax due from the tenents of
John 1. late E. Warenn in the towns of Staunford & Graham)
making known that the abbat of Burg had complained againft them,
for unjuftly diftreining upon his tenents in the fame places for not paying the like tax with the tenents of the faid earl, which, as the abbat
afferted, they never before did after the following manner; thus inhibited
their proceedings. ' ᶜThe K. to his beloved & faithful Lambert de
' Trikingham & Thomas de Burnham, affigns for the men of the
' towns of Staunford & Graham who were tenents of John de
' Warenne late E. of Surrey deceafed, to be talliated for our relief,
' greeting.   The abbat of Burg hath fhewed to us, that you, certain
' his tenents in the towns aforefaid (among the forefaid tenents who
' were the faid earls) to be taxed, & for the tax of this fort us to be
' paid, have unlawfully caufed to be diftreined; whereas the fame his
' tenents, among the forenamed tenents of the faid E. ought not to

comite Lincolnie Thoma comite Lanc.   Weftm. viceffimo die martii, anno regni no-
Humfredo de Bohun comite Hereford &   ftri 33°. Ex carta de anno 33. E. 1. n. 54.
Effex; Guidone de Bellocampo comite War-   & rotulo patenti de anno 3. R. E. 4.
wyk; Adomaro de Valencia, Hugone le   a Itin. Vol 6. p. 29.
Defpencer, Roberto filio Rogeri; Roberto   b Walt. de Whyt. p. 141.
de la Warde, fenefchallo hofpicii noftri, &   c Ex codicis MS. in Bib. Cotton. fub
aliis.   Datum per manum noftram apud   imagine Vefp. E. XXII. fol. 80.

                                                          ' be

' be taxed, nor ever have been accuftomed to be taxed.   And becaufe
' to the faid abbat or his tenents aforefaid, we would not, on this part,
' have any injury to be done; to you, we command, that in affeffing of
' the tax of this fort upon thofe whom it fhall appear to you to be
' tenents of the faid abbat in the towns aforefaid, ye utterly fuper-
' fede, & the diftreignment, if ye have caufed any to be made on that
' occafion, to the fame make to be releafed without delay.   Witnefs
' Walter de Langton bifhop of Lichfield & Coventry; the 28. of June, 13. June
' 33. Edward.   Upon receipt of thefe writs, Lambert de Triking- 1305.
ham abovementioned, wrote to Euftace Mallerbe & Hugh de Hameldonn (under him & Thomas de Burnham aforefaid) affeffors of the
kings tax at Stanford, to forbear levying the fame on the abbat of
Burgs tenents there, as follows.   ' ᵃLambert de Trikingham to his
' friends *fui gratia* Euftace Mallerbe & Hugh de Hameldonn the af-
' fignes to colleƈt the tax of the lord K. at Staunford, greeting in the
' Lord.   Whereas the lord K. by his writ witneffes, that the tenents
' of the abbat of Burg in the town of Staunford, with the tenents of
' the fee of E. Warenn, ought not to be taxed, nor ever hitherto
' have been ufed to be taxed in the fame town; to you I command,
' on the part of the lord K. that, from levying of the tax on the
' tenents of the abbat aforefaid (whom to you it fhall appear to
' be affeffed in the town aforefaid) ye utterly fuperfede, according
' to the mandate of the lord the K. to me therefore direƈted.'   However, on July 8. 1305. 33. E. 1. the K. fent his mandate to the July 8.
fherif of Lincoln, acquainting him, that as he had taxed his demefnes 1305.
in England, he commanded, if the burgeffes of Staunford & Gran- 33. E. 1.
tham have been his, or his predeceffors the kings of England, old
demefnes, & hitherto ufed to be taxed, then he fhould caufe the abbat of Burg to have a reafonable tax of his tenents in thofe boroughs;
but hear the record.   ' ᵇEdward, by the grace of God K. of England,
' lord of Ireland, & D. of Aquitain, to the fherif of Lincoln, greeting.
' Whereas we have at prefent caufed our demefnes throughout England
· to be taxed, to you we command, that, if the burgeffes of Staunford
' beyond the bridge, & the burgeffes of Graham, were our antient de-
' mefnes, or of our progenitors late kings of England, & hitherto have
' been wont to be taxed; then you caufe our beloved in *Chrift* the
' abbat of Burg to have a reafonable tax of his tenents in the boroughs
' aforefaid.   Witnefs my felf at Canterbury, the 8. of July in the 33d.
' of our reign.'   Note, the K. here calls the borough of Staunford,
Staunford beyond the bridge, with refpeƈt to the place he dates from.
Upon receipt of this mandate, John de Nevil, fherif of Lincoln, wrote
to the bailifs of the liberties of the abbat of Burg, as follows. ' ᶜJohn
' de Nevil, fherif of Lincoln, to the bailifs of the abbat of Burg, greet-
' ing. I have received the mandate of the lord K. in thefe words.' Then
recites it as above, & proceeds, ' wherefore to you I command, that
' you diligently execute this mandate, & this omit not.

a Ex ejufdem codicis MS. fol. 80.   b id. fol. 114.   c id. ib.

34. E. 1.

XXXVI. ' ᵃ In the 34. of E. 1. the K. called a parliament to
' meet at Weſtminſter, & the perſons elected to repreſent the borough
' of Stanford in that aſſembly were, Gilbert de Cotiſmore & Clement
' de Melton. —— Beatricia, widow of Joſeph le Ferrour burgeſs of Stan-
' ford, ſold to William de Apethorpe likewiſe burgeſs of Stanford,
' her houſes with a croft & . . . . curtilages [back yards] ſituate in the
' village of Bradecroft between a tenement of the nuns of S. Michael
' weſt, &c. Witneſſes, Edelyn of Bradecroft, Hugh Pert of the ſame,
' &c. Given at Stanford 34. E. 1. B. H. . . . . . . Relict of Regi-
' nald Smereman of Staunford, gave to Walter the phyſician one
' ſhop ſtanding in great S. Michaels pariſh between a tenement of the
' foreſaid Walter, weſt, & the lane called Feldovenſty, eaſt. B. H. Ni-
' cholas de Flemang, ſon of John de Flemang, of the eaſt gate, late
' burgeſs of Stanford, now alſo ſold the houſes & lands of Clement
' de Melton, burgeſs of Stanford. B. H. ᵇ In the 6. year of Godefry
' de Croyland abbat of Burg, there happened a difference between
' him & the abbat of Thorney, about a certain highway from a place
' in the river Neen called Herlotesforth, unto the town of Eye. And
' at laſt this agreement was made, at the inſtance of Walter [Langton]
' biſhop of Coventry, then lord high treaſurer, & other friends of
' them both; viz. that the aforeſaid abbat & convent of Burg, of
' their own meer will & ſpecial benevolence, for cheriſhing of mu-
' tual love & charity between them, granted, for them & their ſuc-
' ceſſors, that the abbat & convent of Thorney & their ſervants,
' friends, or ſtrangers coming thither, might hereafter uſe that way
' *ad latitudinem* 15 *pedum,* with their carts, waggons, carriages, horſes,
' drift of cattel, to fairs or markets, without any diſturbance. Done
' at Stanford, the day after the feaſt of S. Tyburtius & Valerian, in
' the 34. of K. Edward. ᶜ At that great ſolemnity of making prince
' Edward Kt. at the feaſt of Pentecoſt An. 34. E. 1. John the 2.
' E. Warenn [lord of Stanford] then received the like honor : the
' whole number then knighted being no leſs than 267. ᵈ On Thurſ-
' day the morrow of S. Andrew the apoſtle, in the 35. year of K.
' Edward, & 8. of Godefry lord abbat of Burg, dame Mabilia le Venur

Dec. 1.
1306.
35. E. 1.

' prioreſs of S. Michael without Stanford, did fealty to lord Godefry
' the abbat aboveſaid, at Eye, for the tenements which ſhe claimed
' to hold of him, in preſence of the brethren Stephen de Burg (then
' prior of the ſaid houſe of S. Michael) Robert de Spaleinggs, & John
' de Witherington, monks; & the dames Mirielle de Miridicu, Eli-
' zabet de Colingham & other nuns, & maſter G. de Make[ſeye]
' John de Milton, Sir Richard de Oſeneie, Robert de Mithingesby,
' & others. ᵉ John the 2. E. Warenn [lord of Stanford] was with
' K. Edward in that his Scotch expedition wherein he died.' The
ſaid K. Edward the firſt died July 7. 1307. & was ſucceeded by his ſon
K. Ed. the ſecond.

a Ex literis B. Willis arm.   b Gunton. p. 318.   c Bar. Vol. I. p. 80. b.   d Ex
codicis MS. in Bib. Cotton. ſub imagine Veſp. E. XXII. fol. 50   e Bar. Vol. I. p. 80. b.

The end of the ninth book.

Academia tertia Anglicana;

OR, THE

ANTIQUARIAN ANNALS

of the TOWN of

STANFORD

IN

Lincoln, Rutland, *and* Northampton *Shires.*

BOOK. X.
Containing the reign of K. Edward the fecond.

I. AFTER the death of K. Edw. the 1ft. [a] 'K. Edw. the 2d fent 1307.
' for Peter Gavefton, & when he cam, caullid hym brother [1.] E. 2.
' & gave hym Walingford, otherwife affignid to Q. Ifabelle.
' [b] At the parliament holden about the 13 of Oct. 1307. at Northamp- Oct. 13.
' ton, a marriage was concluded betwixt the E. of Cornwal Peers de
' Gavefton, & the daughter of Gilbert de Clare E. of Gloucefter (whiche
' he had by his wife the countesse Joane de Acres the kings fifter)
' which marriage was folemnifed on alhallowen day next enfuing. 'On
' the wednefday after epiphany all the Kts. templars were fiefed & im- Jan. 10.
' prifoned, & their lands efcheated to the K. [d] The order of their 130.7.8.
' apprehenfion was on this wife. The K. directed his writtes unto 1. E. 2.
' al fherifs, that they fhould give fummonaunce to a certain number
' of fubftantial perfons, knyghts or others of good accompt, to be afore
' them at certayne places within their governments, on Sunday the
' morrow after Epiphanie, & the fherifs to be there in their owne
' perfons to execute that which in other writtes to them directed, &
' after to be fent, fhould be conteyned. Dat. 15. Dec. The 2d writ
' was fent by certaine chaplaynes, in which the fheriffs were com-
' manded upon the opening, forthwith to receive an othe to put in
' execution al that was therein contained, & not to difclofe the con-
' tents to any man till they had executed the fame; & to take the like
' othe of them whom by vertue of the firft they had fummoned to

---

a Lelands Collect. Vol. I. p. 461.   c Bp. Kennets par. Ant. p. 355.
b Holingfhed, p. 847. b.   d Hol. p. 848. a. b.

2   10 B   ' appear

‘ appear before them.   Another writ was alſo ſent by the ſame chap-
‘ laines, by which the ſherifs were commanded to attach by their
‘ bodies all the templars within their precincts, & to ſeiſe all their
‘ lands & goods to the kings hands, together with their writings, char-
‘ ters, &c. & farther, that the ſayd goodes & chattels ſhould be put
‘ in ſafe cuſtody ; & the perſons ſo ſieſed, kept, not in ſtreight pri-
‘ ſon, but in ſuch order as the ſheriff might be ſure to bring them forth
‘ upon command ; to be found in the mean time, according to their
‘ eſtate of their own goodes.   Soon after [a] the heirs of the donors
‘ & ſuch as had endowed the templars with lands, entred upon thoſe
‘ parts of their antient patrimonies, & detained them till they were
‘ by parliament transferred to the Kts. of Rhodes.

Jan. 11.   II. Jan. 11. 130⅛. 2. E. 2. [b] John Dalderby biſhop of Lincoln being
130⅛.   ‘ at Newſted abby by Stanford confirmed divers privileges of the church
2. E. 2.   ‘ of Burg. [c] In the ſame 2. E. 2. Thomas the 2. lord Berkley [& the reſt of
the peers] ‘had ſummons to be at Stanford well furniſhed with horſe &
‘ arms to march againſt the Scots. — John, ſon of Bartholomew de S.
‘ Feriolo in Staunford gave to Walter the phyſician, the houſes, &c.
‘ ſtanding in Colgate in great S. Michaels pariſh, between a tenement
‘ of the ſaid Walter eaſt, & a tenement of Walter Wiſeman weſt. B. H.
Now flouriſhed John Repingale.   ‘John Repingale, as Pits relates, [d] born
‘ of honeſt parents in Lincolnſhire, was a Carme among the white
‘ friers at Stanford, & D. D. of Cambridge.   A man flouriſhing under
‘ the encomiums of piety & erudition ; & one who by the ſtudy of vir-
‘ tue, ſought not his own advantage only, but likewiſe by his very
‘ learned ſermons, promoted the travel of many in the road of ſpiri-
‘ tual perfection.   Some are not wanting who affirm, that he, as a
‘ public profeſſor, for ſeveral years, read & explained the maſter of the
‘ ſentences, to a well frequented auditory, with good applauſe ; and
‘ that in all ſchool diſputes he was much eſteemed for the ſubtlety of
‘ his wit, the ſoundneſs of his learning, & the ripeneſs of his judg-
‘ ment.   John [Synwel] biſhop of Lincoln at this time had him in
‘ great eſteem, & took him to himſelf to be his confeſſor ; at the re-
‘ queſt of which prelate he publiſhed, eighty three ſermons for ſun-
‘ days, in one vol. Two & forty more, in another, for divers ſaints
‘ days.   A vol. of ſynodical diſcourſes.   And another on epiſcopal
‘ viſitation.’   Now alſo flouriſhed ‘William Whetely, whom Leland
‘ ſaith Pits, [e] ſirnames Boetianus, becauſe he took great pains in explain-
‘ ing the works of Boethius.   For in that age, ſays Bale, [e] as well as
‘ this of ours, the lucubrations of Boethius were had in great eſtima-
‘ tion.   It ſeemed good therefore to Whetely, to illuſtrate ſuch pieces
‘ of his as were then in requeſt, with proper notes for the uſe of
‘ younger ſtudents.   This Whetely, continues Pits, was a man ex-

a Speed. p. 669. b.   d in vita.
b Walt. Witleſ. p. 161.   e in vita.
c Baron. Vol. I. p. 354. b.

                                              ‘ cellently

' cellently skilled in all humane literature, & all liberal arts. For
' to thefe ftudies he a long while applied himfelf with the utmoft di-
' ligence at Oxford under the beft tutors in that univerfity, & made
' vaft progrefs. At length for his learning & virtues he was made
' paftor of the church of Yatisbery, where he neither forfook his ftu-
' dies, nor abftained, any more than he could help it, from his wont-
' ed fociety & converfation with learned men. As to his writings
' we find thefe following, either mentioned by approved authors,
' or batteling it as it were in old libraries with the moths & book-
' worms. I. Upon Boethius on the confolation of philofophy, 5
' books, beginning *philofophie fervias, ut inde contingat,* &c. *a. MS.*
' *in Pembroke hall library in* Cambridge. II. A comment upon ano-
' ther piece of Boethius *de difciplina fcholarium,* about the training
' of fcholars, in one book; a MS. in Pembroke library at Cambridge
' & Merton library in Oxford. It begins, *Hominum natura multiplici-*
' *ter eft,* &c.' Note, this is the book mentioned by Mr. Wood, which,
as you will prefently find, he fays was drawn up for the ufe of the mafters & fcholars of this univerfity of Stanford. The copy which
Mr. Wood faw, with a very remarkable note in the beginning of it
about Stanford, was that I fuppofe at Merton college in Oxford, Mr.
Wood himfelf being a member of that fociety. III. ' A comment up-
' on another book of Boethius, called his divifions, in one book. IV. Let-
' ters to divers perfons, & fome other pieces. He lived about the
' year 1310.' So far Pits. Now then let us hear what Mr. Wood
fays, about the beginning of our univerfity at Stanford, & in particular about this Wheteley & his forefaid book touching the government of fchools. ' If any man, faith he, a fhould here command
' me to fay how many years this univerfity flourifhed at Stanford,
' that I muft confefs will be very hard to determine. Efpecially fince
' it appears by divers authentic regifters, that this place flourifhed as
' a fchool of good letters, a many years before the prohibitions of
' Edw. the 3d. were divulged. For to pafs by William Lidlington,
' John Repingale, & Walter Hefton, celebrated writers in their feve-
' ral ages; William Wheteley (whom Leland firnames Boetianus) af-
' ter he had fpent fome years in ftudy at Oxford, came to Stanford,
' & erected fchools there one & twenty years before the faid place
' was interdicted, as appears by a few minutes at the end of his, the
' pretended, Boethius's book, *de Difciplina Scholarium,* to this pur-
' pofe. *Here endeth the book of* Boethius *touching the difcipline of*
' *fcholars, after this fort ordered & compiled by a certain mafter who*
' *governed the fchools at Stanford, in the year of our Lord,* 1309. &c.'
Note, Mr. Wood fhould have faid, five, & not one & twenty years,
before the fchools at Stanford were fupprefled; for 1309. is not 21,
but 25 years before 1334. when that bufinefs (tho' by miftaken, for it

a Antiq. Oxon. fub anno 1334.

10 C

was

was not 'till 1335.) is fuppofed to have been tranfacted. [a] 'And left
' any one fhould imagine the forefaid William Wheteley prefided
' over a common grammar fchool only, he may be fatisfied to the
' contrary by this infallible reafon. To wit, the difcipline of the
' fchools there treated of, is altogether academical. For otherwife in
' the faid commentaries, he had not fo largely expatiated on queftions
' phyfical & aftronomical; nor would he have intermixed the dif-
' courfe with univerfity cuftoms, relating to degrees, founding of
' lectures, & other matters pertaining to the actual government of
' fuch a place.' I fhall only add this account demonftrates the being of
an univerfity at Stanford in 1309. but does not at all prove it began
then; but that, as I have faid, we muft look higher.

July
1309.
3. E. 2.

III. [b] In 1309. a parliament was convened at Stanford to fupprefs
' the infolence of the Scots upon the death of K. Edwd. the 1ft, &
' appointed to be held on the Sunday after the feaft of S. James.
This pretence for calling a parliament was very plaufible: but, what
it enacted againft the Scots, I am as yet to feek. However as Mr. Leland acquaints us with what K. Edward then did at Stanford, I believe
we may from him learn one true reafon why this parliament was affembled: And he fays. [c] 'After that the K. had defetid the acte of
' the banifhemente of Pers Gaveston at Stanford, Gaveston began to
' contemne the nobles of Englande, & rayled of them, caulling Gil-
' bert de Clare counte of Gloucestre, cocolds byrde; & Syr Henry
' Lacy E. of Lincolne, *böele crenee* [burften belly] & Syr Gui counte
' of Warwike, *noer chien d'Arderne* [the black dog of Arden] & he
' caullid the gentil counte Thomas of Lancaftre the kings nephew,
' *Vielers porceo qui'l ert greles, & de bel entaile.*' Another writer,
fpeaking of different matters, touches alfo upon this parliament at Stanford. 'The prior of Coldingham [whofe houfe was a cell to Dur-
ham] 'rebelled (fays he [d]) againft the prior of Durham, & would not
' be obedient to him. For he faid, the bifhop hated him, becaufe he
' ftuck to prior Richard. Whereupon Wm. de Tanfeld the now prior
' of Durham went to the cell of Coldingham, where the prior of
' Coldingham fwore at firft that he would obey all his orders, but
' afterwards privily withdrew. Upon that prior William of Dur-
' ham appointed another prior in his place, & receiving then the homage
' & fealty of the tenents of Coldinghamfhire, profecuted the runa-
' way as far as the parliament at Stanford in his own perfon not with-
' out great expence, in 1309. about the feaft of S. James. For be-
' caufe he, the prior who fled, was known to the K. & courtiers, in
' as much as he had carried the banner of S. Cuthbert [of Durham]
' with the K. in the war of Scotland, he believed the K. would be
' willing to protect him againft the prior. But the prior of Durham

a Wood. ut fupra.   c Collect. Vol. 1. p. 461.
b From one of Mr. Willis's Letters to   d Roberti de Grayftanes Hift. Dunelm.
me.   in Angliæ facræ Vol. 1. p. 753, 754.

'coming

' coming thither, found the K. & thofe about him, favourable enough
' to him; & the other not there. For he was gone beyond fea to
' the court of Rome, & there expected the bifhops death. [a] After
' this Piers de Gavefton, not able to contain himfelf within any bounds
' of prudence or moderation, proclaimed a torneament to be kept
' nigh his caftle of Walingford, & thither brought fo many foreign
' men at arms, that he moft vilely infulted over all the Englifh lords
' who came to that folemnity, among whom was Thomas E. of Lan-
' cafter, the carls of Pembroke, Hereford, Warenn, &c. who were
' fo offended at the affronts put upon them, that they entred into a
' common confult for fatisfaction & revenge.' But to return. Thus
have you the true reafon why this parliament was affembled on the
kings part. Neither did his fubjects let it pafs without attempting
fomewhat to their advantage, as the king had done to his. For as a
certain author tells us, [b] perfonal citations to the court of Rome, or
' before judges delegated by the pope [being now become grievous]
' the Englifh magiftrates fpared no pains to ftop the abufe thereof;
' particularly the parliament which was held at Stanford in Aug 1309.
' ordered a vigorous letter to be written to the pope to complain of
' them.

 IV. In 1310. flourifhed Nicholas Stanford. ' Nicholas Stenoford,   1310
' fays Leland, [c] was furely very worthy of the title of an illuftrious
' writer: but the negligence of former ages has left his fame almoft un-
' known to ours. I cannot therefore but grieve at the very name of him,
' as finding my felf deftitute of proper notices to do him juftice. How-
' ever that the reader may not lofe all his expectation, I fhall here
' briefly relate what little I have met with about him. A few years
' ago, as I rode thro' Bedfordfhire, intent upon the finding of old au-
' thors, I came to Woburn, a monaftery of Bernardines, founded by
' Hugh Bulbec, fometime fherif of that county; but not meeting
' with thofe treafures of vellum & parchment which I expected, by rea-
' fon they were all confumed in a fire which happened a little be-
' fore my coming thither; I went thence to Wardon in the fame
' county, where was alfo a Bernardine convent, & a library excellent-
' ly ftored with antient copies; among which there offered it felf to
' me a book finely illuminated, called, moral obfervations upon the
' book of Genefis by Nicholas Stenoford. And, reader, let not the
' title, tho' no better, difpleafe you. For the book contained a judg-
' ment in divinity very ready & remarkable: nor did it want a mode-
' rate eloquence. In reading of it I could not truly but admire that
' a man of his age fhould write fo folidly, fmartly, & fignificantly.
Pits fays, ' [d] befides this, I meet with the title of only one other piece
' of his, called a vol. of fermons.' But adds, ' however, as you may

---

a Bp. Kennets Par. Ant. p. 357, 358.   c Comment. p. 343.
b Acta regia, No. 2. p. 135, 136.   d in vita.

' know

' know a lion by his nail, so by these you may gather, both how
' great & what sort of a doctor he was.   Leland thinks he flourished
' about 1310, This Nicholas, I guess, was a Ciftercian of the monaftery of that order at Stanford.

4. E. 2.   V. ª ' In the 4. of E. 2. John the 2d. E. Warenn [lord of Stanford]
' went again into Scotland, being in such favor with the K. that he
' obtained a free grant the same year of the castle & honor of Peke in
' Derbyshire, together with the whole forest of high Peke; to hold
' during his life, in as full & ample manner, as Wm. Peverell antient-
' ly enjoyed the same, before it came to the K. of England by eschaet.
' ᵇ In 1311. saith our old antiquary Mr. Butcher, general chapters call-
Aug.   ' ed *Itinera minorum* were again held at Stanford.   ' ᶜ In aug. 1311.
1311.   ' 5 E. 2. about the feast of the affumption, the K. having with him
5. E. 2.   ' Piers de Gaveston & the earles of Gloucefter & Warenn, came to
' Berwike, which towne he fortified, & marched forth into Scotland:
' but soon returned thither.   The K. lying still at Berwike, the earles
' of Gloucefter & Warenne, after the beginning of lent, rode into
' the forest of Selkyrke, & receyved the forefters & other inhabitants
' there to the kings peace.   ᵈ In the same 5. E. 2. on that high dif-
' content by the nobles against the new raifed minion Piers de Gave-
' fton, John the 2d. E. Warenn [lord of Stanford] with the E. of Pem-
' broke, befieged Piers in Scardeburg caftle; ᵉ who so wearied out
' the garrifon, that he was forced to furrender himfelf, on condition
' of ftanding to the judgment of the barons.   The K. when he heard
' this defired liberty to fpeak with him, & that his life might be fav-
' ed: The E. of Pembroke promifing under penalty of the lofs of all
' his lands to keep him 'till fuch difcourfe with the K. & then to deli-
' ver him to the barons.   To which the barons confenting, the E.
' brought him to Walingford caftle, & coming to Dadington in Com.
' Oxon. committed him to fome of his guards, while he went to lodge
' with his lady in an adjacent village.   The E. of Warwick having in-
' telligence of this flender guard, came that night, & took him away
' to his caftle of Warwick, where, after a confult, whether they fhould
' carry him to the K. or put him to death, this latter was refolved up-
' on, so they brought him out to a place called Blacklow, & there be-
' headed him, From thefe wars among thefe great barons, let us now
turn to a fray among the men of letters.   William Lullendune, warden of the white friers in Stanford, ' being fent by the chief Carmelite
' fathers of England about the common bufinefs of religion into France,
' there carried himfelf (faith Leland ᶠ) with so much prudence, gravity
' & ftrength of reafoning, that he drew many foreign fathers of the
' order, affembled there by decree, into great admiration of him.   And
' there therefore by the fuffrage of others, but efpecially of Gerard

a Baron. Vol. I. p. 80. b.   d Baron. Vol. I. p. 80. b.
b printed account. p. 23.   e Bp. Kennets par. antiq. p. 364.
c Holing. p. 850. a. b.   f p. 341. Com.

3   ' the

' the chief mafter of the whole order, was he immediately appointed
' provincial of three provinces, to wit, England, Cyprus, & the Holy
' Land. And to this honor was he promoted, as I have read, in the year
' after Chrift, 1312.' Note, Bale & Pits affirm it was at Genoa in 1309.
& not at Paris in 1312. as Leland fays, when he was chofe provincial. Leland goes on. 'Before thefe things happened, by what means
' I know not, a difpute arofe between him & the faid Gerard, head
' of all the Carmes; & things went fo far, that he was at laft forced,
' by a judgment given againft him, to fubmit to the more powerful Ge-
' rard. Which affair, as I confefs, a little obfcures his otherwife il-
' luftrious fame. For being, among other of his order, at Paris, he
' publickly, tho unwillingly enough, both faid & did what was ne-
' ceffary to fatisfie the injured Gerard.' This laft is a very dark paffage, but well explained by what hath been faid above [a]. ' [b] The
' favor of Gerard being at length regained, Lullendune returned
' home to his own country, where he afterwards lived to a great age
' in high efteem. He wrote, faith Pits, [c] a vol. of fermons, another
' of determinations, a 3d. of lectures in divinity, & a fourth againft the
' decree of the chapter of Narbonne. His commentaries upon S. Mat-
' thews gofpel are extant, as Leland tells us, & remain as abundant
' teftimonies of his nervous erudition.' He adds, 'Lullendune fre-
' quently confulted one Thomas Allen, a Cambridge divine, but a
' Carmelite of Ipfwic, who fometime profeffed divinity at Bruges,
' & publifhed no unlearned commentaries upon the Revelation of
' S. John.

VI. In the 6. E. 2. ' [d] John the 2. E. Warenn [lord of Stanford] ob-   6. E. 2.
' tained the kings charter for a weekly market every Tuefday at
' his manor of Rigate in Surrey. Alfo for another market at his manor
' of Cukefeld in Surrey, upon the monday; & a fair there yearly up-
' on the eve, day, & morrow after the feaft of the holy Trinity.
' Likewife for a market every Tuefday at Dychening in Suffex; & a
' fair yearly on the eve, day, & morrow after the feaft of S. Marga-
' ret the virgin. Moreover for a market every thurfday at his manor
' of Brighelmefton in Suffex. Alfo for a fair every year, upon the
' feaft day of S. Laurence at Hurft. For the like upon *Martinmas* day
' in winter at Weftmefton: & a third at Porteftade, upon the feaft
' day of S. Nicholas; all in Suffex. [e] In the 7. E. 2. the faid E. Wa-   7. E. 2.
' renn, with Thomas E. of Lancafter & fome other of the great earls,
' refufed to attend the K. in his Scotch expedition then made. The
other great earls who refufed to attend the K. were [f] 'the earls of
' Warwick & Arundel.' The reafon why they did fo was, [g] 'becaufe

a anno 1303. Lib. IX. p. 49.
b Lel. ut fupra.
c in vita.
d Baron. Vol. I. p. 18. a.

e Bar. Vol. I. p. 81. a.
f Bp. Kennets par. antiq. p. 366.
g id. ib.

' the K. delayed to put in execution the articles for redrefs of grie-
' vances, often petitioned for, & often granted.   Agnes, late the wife
8. E. 2. ' of Peter de Noufle of Bradecroft, releafed to Walter fon of Wal-
' ter de Tinwel of Bradecroft, &c. one piece of meadow lying in the
' crofts of Bradecroft, between the meadow of John Drayton eaft, &
' the water running from the fountain [*a fonte*] weft, & abutting on
' the kings highway north, & about the water of Weland, fouth.
' Given at Bradecroft, the Sunday next after the feaft of S. Hilary.
' 8. E. 2. B. H. Milicent, relict of Gilbert . . . . . late burgefs of
' Stanford, gave to Stephen de Sleford, butcher in Staunford, two
' rods of land in Sunderfoken in the county of Roteland.   Given at
' Staunford the Monday next before Hockeday. 8. E. 2. B. H. Nico-
' las de Burton, lord of Tolethorp was now witnefs to a deed re-
' lating to a houfe [the angel inne] in S. Maries parifh by the bridge.
' B. H.   John de Knotteflhalle gave to Henry de Afhwell, his houfes
' ftanding in the parifh of S. Michael Cornftal, Staunford, between a
' tenement of the prior of Newfted, eaft, & a tenement of Richard de
' Baldefwell, weft, as they extend themfelves from the kings highway
' north, as far as the wall of the town of Staunford, fouth. B. H.
24. Apr. ' [a]John E. Warenn [lord of Stanford] by his deed bearing date 24.
' Apr. 8. E. 2. did releafe & quit claim to the canons of Rigate, his
' right to nineteen fhillings four pence, one plow fhare & four horfe-
' fhoes yearly rent; which the prior & covent of Rigate had antient-
' ly paid his anceftors for certain lands in Rigate ; & granted to them &
' their fucceffors 46 s. 11 d. yearly rent, iffuing out of certain other lands
' there, for a chantry which the faid canons of Rigate & their fuccef-
' fors were obliged to maintain in his caftle of Rigate ; for the health
' of his foul, & the fouls of his anceftors & heirs : fo that one mafs
' fhould daily be celebrated therein for ever.

1315.   VII. In 1315. 9. E. 2.   ' [b] The faid John the 2. E. Warenn was
' excommunicated by the bifhop of Chichefter for adultery.   Where-
' upon the faid E. came to the bifhop with armed men, & four, more
' hafty than the reft, threatned the bifhop.   Whereupon the bifhops
' men fell on them, & tooke the E. & the reft, & imprifoned them.
June 30. ' ' [c] It is obfervable that this E. (having no iffue by his wife) did by
1315. ' a fpecial grant give the inheritance of all his lands to the K. & his
9. E. 2. ' heirs.   Which grant bears date at Weftminfter, upon Thurfday, the
' morrow after the feaft of S. Peter & Paul, 9. E. 2. the particulars
' whereof are therein expreft, viz. the caftle & town of Rigate, with
' the manors of Dorking, Bechefworth, & Kenington in Surrey; the
' caftle & town of Lewes ; the manors of Cokefeld, Cleyton,
' Dychening, Mething, Fethlam, Brightelmefton, Rottingden, Hounde-
' den, Northerft, Rademeld, Kymere, Middleton, Alington, Worth,
' Picoumb, in Suffex; the towns of Iford, Pydinghow, & Seford in

a Baron. Vol. I. p. 82. a.   b Stow. p. 336.   c Bar. Vol. I. p. 81. a.

' Effex ;

' Effex ; the caftles & towns of Coningesbragh & Sandale ; & the
' manors of Wakefield, Heitfield, Thorne, Soureby, Braithwel, Fifh-
' like, Dewsbury, & Halifax, in Yorkfhire ; the manors & towns
' of Stanford & Grantham , in Lincolnfhire ; alfo the caftles of
' Dinas-Bran & Laones, with the lands of Bromfield, Yale, & Wright-
' fham, in Wales.——Geoffry le Parchmener fold to Walter, fon of Wil-
' liam de Apethorp, his houfes ftanding in S. Peters parifh between a
' tenement of the faid Walter, eaft, & a tenement of Gilbert de Wy-
' mondham, weft, as they extend themfelves from the kings highway
' north as far as the caftle dyke fouth. B. H. ᵃ Some diflike being grown
' betwixt John E. Warenn [lord of Stanford] & Joan his wife, they
' were divorced on pretence of a former contract made by him with
' Maud de Nereford (a perfon of a great family in Norfolk) & he al-
' lowed unto the fame Joan 740 marks *per annum.*

VIII. ᶜᵇ In 1316. upon the feaft of S. Dennis died Richard Kellow   Oct. 9.
' bifhop of Durham, & was buried in the chapter houfe by the bifhops   1316.
' throne.   The K. who was then at York fent his almoner to Durham,   10. E. 2.
' & honoured his body with a prefent of fome pieces of cloth of
' gold. Likewife the great E. of Lancafter offered for him three pieces
' of rich cloth, embroidered with his own arms : whereof were made
' thofe veftments, in which (faith my author) mafs is celebrated when
' the convent is in albs.   The forenamed E. wrote letters on behalf of
' his clerc John Kynardflei, to get him elected bifhop ; declaring that
' if that was done, he would protect the bifhopric againft the Scots.
' The K. moved for Thomas Charleton, doctor of the civil laws, then
' keeper of his privy feal : But afterwards, being bewitched by the
' queen, for Lovis Beaumont, treafurer of Sarum ; for whom he was fo
' preffingly urgent, that there was hardly a monk in the houfe of any
' name, but he had the kings letters of requeft on his behalf as alfo
' the queens.   Befides thefe, the E. of Hereford made intereft for his
' clerc John Walwayn, doctor of the civil laws.   But the monks, hav-
' ing God more before their eyes than their intreaties, on the feaft of
' S. Leonard ᶜ (being the day appointed for it) having firft procured
' the kings licenfe to elect, by compromife elected Sir Henry de
' Stanford prior of Fynkhalle, a perfon in his manners altogether fin-
' cere, of fit age, a pleafant countenance, & fufficiently learned. The
' earls of Lancafter, Hereford, Penbroche, & many other nobles a-
' waited in the church for the iffue of the election : As did likewife
' Henry Beaumont with his brother & other friends.   And there were
' alfo fome who threatned to cut off Stanfords head if he were elected.
' However the K. being at York had freely enough admitted the elect,
' if it had not been for the queen.   But fhe hearing that the K.
' was inclined to do fo, fell down on her bare knees before him, fay-

---

a Baron. Vol. I. p. 82. b. *Pat g £2 n. 32*   c *Leonis* in Wharton, but it fhould be
b Ex Roberti de Grayftanes hift. Dunelm.   *Leonardi :* fee anno 1320. infra.
P. 757, 758.

' ing,

' ing, Sir, I never asked any thing of you for any of my friends; but,
' this once, if you love me, pray take order that my cofin Lovis Beau-
' mont may be bifhop of Durham.   The K. therefore, overcome by
' her intreaties, refufed to admit the elect, & wrote to Rome for Lovis.
' Upon this the elect finding that he could not prevail with the K. &
' that the chapter of York began to cool about his confirmation (that
' church being then vacant by the death of W. Grenfeld) took ad-
' vice concerning his own going to Rome.   For John the 22d. being
' newly created pope, he believed, that, notwithftanding all the
' kings intrigues, he might find favor with him.   Neverthelefs be-
' caufe he could not without juft caufe decline the court of York, &
' tranfport himfelf to Rome, it was determined by his counfel, that
' a certain prieft named Robert Karker, born in Nefs, fhould appeal
' both againft the election & elect.   This done the elect, attended by
' three other monks, went to Rome.   But before he could get thither,
' at the requefts of the kings & queens of France & England, the pope
' had granted the bifhopric to Lewis Beaumont.   However Beaumont
' had fo great a fum appointed him to be paid to the Roman court,
' that in fourteen years after he could fcarce creep out of debt.   As
' for our elect the pope conferred on him the firft [cell] that fhould be-
' come vacant in the collation of the prior & chapter, notwithftand-
' ing it fhould be fomething which had before ufed to be held by
' feculars: but he got nothing by that grant.   And thus, having been
' at great charges in his journey & at the court, he returned with an
' empty purfe, & lived afterwards at [S. Leonards] cell at Stanford
' to his dying day.   ᵃ The fame yeere the K. tooke of everie towne
' in Englande, a man to ferve in his warres in Scotlande, & foure
' markes towardes his charges, having no refpect to the greatnefs or
' littlenefs of anie towne, which feemed to be undifcreetlie doone
' ᵇ The fame year, John E. Warenn [lord of Stanford] obtained of K.
' Edw. the 2d. a grant of part of thofe great poffeffions which he had
' given to him before, viz. the caftle & town of Rigate, with divers
' other lordfhips in Surrey ; the caftle & town of Lewes, with many
' lordfhips in Suffex; the caftles of Dinas Bran & Leons ; as alfo the
' lands of Bromfield, Yale, & Wrighlefham in Wales, to himfelf for
' life ; with remainder to John de Warenn, fon of Maudde Nereford,
' & to the heirs male of his body ; & for want of fuch to Thomas
' de Warenn, another fon of the fame Maud, & the heirs male of his
' body ; & for lack of fuch iffue, to the right heirs of him the faid E.
' with remainder to the K. & his heirs.'   The fame year, ' Agnes re-
' lict of Symon Chyld of Staunford, gave to Henry the phyfician of
' Staunford, a void place of ground lying in great S. Michaels parifh
' in the ftreet called Feldovenefty, between a tenement of Richard de
' Brigeftoke north, & a tenement of the faid Henry the phyfician fouth.

a Stow. p. 336.   b Baron. Vol.I. p. 82. b.

Witneffes,

' Witnesses, Roger le Scanclerc, John le Long, Richard le Coupere,
' &c. burgesses of Staunford B. H.   [a] The same year John the 2d E.
' Warenn [lord of Stanford] was in another expedition for Scotland.
' [b] On Munday preceding Assention day, 1317. 10. E. 2d. Alice de Laci,   1317.
' wife of Thomas E. of Lancaster, being at Caneford in Dorset; was
' violently taken thence by a certain Kt. of the family of John E.
' Warenn, there being many in the conspiracy, &, as was said, by
' the kings consent. She was carried, in triumph & contempt of
' the E. her husband, to the said E. Warenn then at his castle of Ri-
' gate in Surrey.   But in their passage amongst the hedges & woods be-
' twixt Haulton & Farnham, those who were her conducters, discerning
' certain streamers & banners (which were no other than the priests
' & people then going in procession round the fields) were struck with
' a sudden terror, & thinking the E. or some of his retinue were
' coming to rescue the lady, & revenge the affront, they left her all
' alone, & fled away; but, when they saw their mistake, returned, &
' with them a person of very mean stature, lame & hunchbackt, called
' Richard de S. Martin, who, with wonderful impudence, challenged
' the countess, thus miserably ensnared, for his wife, pretending that he
' was formerly contracted, & confidently affirming that he had carnally
' known her, before she was married to the E. which she (the great-
' est & noblest inheritrix of her time) did openlie confesse. So as this lady,
' who thro' the whole course of her life had been reputed chast &
' honourable, on a sudden turn of fortune must be proclaimed, thro'
' the whole world, for a lewd & infamous woman.   This deformed
' elfe, the wretch who had thus got possession of her (having mightie
' seconds) grew so insolent as to presume, in his pretended wifes name,
' to claim in the kings court the earldoms of Lincoln & Salisbury,
' tho' with no effect.   Thus however the name & honor of Thomas
' the great E. was baffold.   [c] This occasioned the divorce betwixt the
' E. & his countess, which historians mention to have been sometime
' before his death.   And the said E. of Lancaster in a spirit of revenge
' demolisht E. Warenns castles of Sandal & Wakefeld, & wasted all
' his manors on the other side Trent.   [d] These earles had either of
' them a wife, but neither of them cared for them. This indignity above
' gave so much farther provocation to Thomas E. of Lancaster, that
' when the K. called a parliament in London to treat of the injuries
' done by the Scots, &c. he absented from it, as he had before done
' at Clarendon, for which he was publickly proclaimed an enemy to
' the K. & kingdom.   [e] Upon the 6. day of May 1317. 10. E. 2. Ro-   May 6.
' bert Darlington was presented by prior Geoffry de Burdon & the
' convent of Durham to the rectory of the church of the blessed vir-

a Baron. Vol. I. p. 81. a.   d Stow. p. 337, 338.
b Speed. p. 673. a. Baron. Vol. p. 106.   e Ex registri dicti abbatis secundi, partis
a.b. Bp. Kennets Par. Ant. p. 376.   primæ, pagina 5.
   c Bp. Kennet, ut supra.

' gin

‘ gin Mary at the bridge of Stanford. In trinity term, ᵃ the parfon
‘ of S. Peters in Staunford brought his action againſt the prior of
‘ Durham & others for taking & carrying away their corn at Staunford
‘ [without paying him tythe] but they avowed the taking it, as being
‘ tythes belonging to the church of S. Leonard without Staunford, &c.
‘ Whereupon there came jurats & pleas before the K. at Weſtminſter,
‘ in trinity term, the 10. of K. Edward the 2d.

1317.
11. E. 2.

    IX. ‘In 1317. 11. E. 2. ᵇ Sir Gilbert Middleton Kt. being offended
‘ that maſter Lewes Beaumont was preferred unto the biſhops ſee of
‘ Durham, & Henry of Stanforde put from it (who, as you have
‘ heard, was firſt elected, & after diſplaced by the kings ſute made un-
‘ to the pope) tooke the ſayd Lewes Beaumont, & his brother Henry
‘ on Wingleſdon moore in Yorkſhire, neer unto Darlington, leading
‘ the biſhop to Morpath, & his brother the lord Beaumont unto the
‘ caſtel of Mitforde, & ſo deteyned them as priſoners, till they had re-
‘ deemed their libertie with great ſummes. At the ſame time & place,
‘ the ſayd Sir Gilbert alſo robbed two cardinals (to wit, Gancellino
‘ the popes chancellour, & Lucas de Fliſco, that were ſent from pope
‘ John the xxii. to conſecrate the foreſayde Lewes Beaumont biſhop
‘ of Durham, & to entreate a peace betwixt Englande & Scotlande,
‘ & alſo to make an agreement betwixt the K. & the E. of Lancaſter)
‘ theſe were robbed of ſuch ſtuffe & treaſure as they brought with
‘ them, but yet eſcaped themſelves, & came to Durham. The ſaid
‘ Sir Gilbert did alſo many damages to the priory of Tinmouth, &
‘ many other. And therewith being advaunced in pride, proclaimed
‘ himſelf duke of Northumberlande; & joyning friendſhippe with
‘ the Scottiſhe K. Robert Bruce, cruelly deſtroyed the countie of Riche-
‘ mont. With ſuch trayterous partes William Felton, Thomas Heton,
‘ & Robert Hornecliffe, being not a little ſtirred, firſt wan by force
‘ the caſtle of Mytforde, & after apprehended Sir Gilbert Middleton
‘ with his companion Walter Selbie, & ſent them up to London,
‘ where ſhortly after they were drawne, hanged & quartered, in pre-
‘ ſence of the cardinals. ᶜ In this 11. E. 2. John the 2. E. Warenne
[lord of Stanford] ‘ was charged with 200 foot for his lands of Bromfield
‘ & Yale, to be ſent into Scotland for the kings ſervice.’ There
being ſome arrears of a tax granted the 32d. of E. the 1. now demanded of them who then aſſeſſed the ſame in the towns of Stanford
& Grantham; Thomas de Burg (rector of Deping) executor of Gilbert
Cheſtreton late burgeſs of Stanford, craved the ſame to be allowed the
heirs & executors of the ſaid Gilbert in a certain overplus of an accompt
which the ſaid Gilbert, & Elias Ruſſel citizen of London, had in their
accompt of the kings wools & cuſtoms. Whereupon the accompt roll
being ſearched it was found, that they had ſuch allowance. Alſo Adam,

---

a Ex placit coram rege apud Weſtm.   b Holingſhed p. 854. b. & Stow. p. 336.
Trin. x. R. E. 2.   c Bar. Vol. I. p. 81. a.

son of Elias Ruſſel aforeſaid, being preſent, proved that one moiety of the ſaid ſum ought to be allowed the heirs of the ſaid Gilbert; & the ſaid Thomas de Burg proved, that the other moiety of the ſaid ſum ought to be allowed the heirs of the ſaid Elias, in the debts which they owe the K. here.   All which being accordingly admitted, it was thus recorded. 'ᵃ Memorandum, that there being demanded ' in the pipe of Lincoln, of Gilbert de Ceſtreton 8 l. 17 s. 10 d. of ' his tax in the town of Stanford, aſſeſſed in the 32 d. of K. Edward ' father of the K. now.   And alſo of Philip, ſon of Thomas de Gran- ' tham, 17 l. 15 s. 10 d. of a like tax in the town of Grantham aſſeſſed ' the ſame year; comes now Thomas de Burg (parſon of the church ' of Deping) executor of the teſtament of the foreſaid Gilbert deceaſed, ' & craves the dues aforeſaid to be allowed to the heirs & executors ' of him Gilbert in a certain overplus of 223 l. 4 s. 8 d. which the ' ſame Gilbert & Elias Ruſſel have in their accompt of the wools of ' K. Edw. the father aforeſaid, ſent unto the parts of Holland, Seland, ' & Brabant, & there ſold, &c. aſſerting him Gilbert to be heir & ' executor of the ſaid Philip, &c.   And upon this, the rolls being ' ſearched &c. it was found in the 29. roll of the ſaid K. Edward, be- ' ing the accompt roll, that Elias Ruſſel citizen of London, & Gil- ' bert de Ceſtreton burgeſs of Stanford, receivers of the monies in ' keeping of Robert Segre exiſting, & alſo ariſing as well from wools ' & other matters of the ſaid father of the K. in the parts of Holand, ' Seland & Brabant exiſting, as from the wools of him K. Edw. from ' England as far as to the parts aforeſaid tranſmitted; & of the monies ' ariſing from the payments of the cuſtume of the wools aforeſaid; ' have of a ſurpluſage in their accompt, &c. 223 l. 4 s. 8 d.   And ' upon this Adam Ruſſel, ſon, heir, & executor of the teſtament of ' the foreſaid Elias being preſent, &c. proved the one moiety of the ' overplus aforeſaid ought to be allowed to the heirs & executors of ' the ſaid Gilbert, in the debts which they owe the K. here.   And ' the ſame Thomas de Burg, by himſelf & his co-executors, in like ' manner proved the other moiety of the ſame ſurpluſage ought to be ' allowed to the heirs & executors of the forenamed Elias, in the ' debts which they owe the K. here.   And therefore it is to be con- ' ſidered, that the foreſaid ſurpluſage is to be allowed to the heirs & ' executors of the foreſaid Elias & Gilbert, by an equal portion, in ' their debts aforeſaid.'   In the 12. E. 2. ' Robert the phyſitian of 12. E. 2. ' Staunford, gave to Alice late the wife of W. de Folkyngham clo- ' thier in the ſame; two cellars with the ſhop above erected, which ' are ſituate in the pariſh of S. Martins Staunford, between a tene- ' ment of Stephen de Sleford north, & a tenement of John de Fol- ' kingham ſouth, as it extends it ſelf from the kings highway weſt ' as far as a tenement of the ſaid Stephen eaſt, to be held of the

a Ex codicis MS. in Bib. Cott. ſub imagine Veſp. E. XXII. fol. 85. b.

' capital

' capital demefne of that fee, &c. Witneffes, Richard Berthi then
' bailif of the lord abbat of Burg, &c.' B. H.

X. In 1319. Was held a general chapter of all the Carmes in England, at the white friers in Stanford, to elect a provincial of that order. This points out the time of Lidlingtons death. Leland fays[a],
he was made provincial in 1312. & lived feveral years after. Bale,
that he [b] was promoted to that office over England in 1300. over Cyprus & the Holy Land in 1319. & Pits, that [c] he died in 1309. which
laft I believe is a miftake of himfelf or his printer for 1319, when Richard Bliton was elected provincial (as I think we may venture to fay)
upon Lidlingtons death. Richard Bliton, faith Leland, [d] a Carme, &
' celebrated frequenter of the Oxford fchools, at length received the
' laurel or degree of a profeffor. He was of Lincoln diocefe, fays
' Bale, [e] & tenth provincial of his order in England, fo made at Stan-
' ford in 1319. [f] Richard the 2d. fays Leland, [f] was for fome time a
' great admirer of his eloquent & nervous fermons. For which rea-
' fon he would accept of none but him out of many others to be
' his own confeffor. Pits fays, [f] he was confeffor to K. Edw. the 2d.
' & elected for the fame reafon by him, as Leland fays he was by
' K. Richard the 2d.' And here Pits is in the right, for Bliton died
many years before the faid K. Richard the 2d. was born.' Leland
tells us, ' he wrote a vol. of fermons, another of epiftles, & a third
' called his *reperto ium*.' This chapter at Stanford being called upon
his account, fo much I thought it would not be amifs here to fay of
him. As for Lidlington, both Bale & Pits agree with Leland, [g] ' that
' he died at Stanford, & was buried in the monaftery of the Carmes
' there.' Lidlington was fucceeded in his wardenfhip of the white
friers by Walter Hefton. ' Walter Hefton, faith Pits [g], was born at
' Stanford, a Carmelite there, & D. D. of Cambridge. A perfon fo
' univerfally beloved for the uprightnefs of his manners, & fo remar-
' ably knowing both in facred & profane difcipline, that he fometimes
' taught philofophy, & at other times divinity, as a mafter & profeffor
' in feveral monaftaries of his own order, & at length, for his pru-
' dence, & other virtues, was chofen prior of his own houfe at Stan-
' ford.' Hefton then, whilft he was yet a frier, read lectures in the
Carmelite fchools at Stanford. When he was chofen prior, if he did
not continue to read himfelf, no doubt but he caufed thofe lectures
to be kept up by others of that fociety. I fhall only add, his being
a Carme & reading lectures is another inftance corroborating my affertion, that the fathers of that order were the chief managers & fupport of our little univerfity.

12. E. 2.   XI. ' [h] In the 13. of E. 2. John the 2d. E. Warenn [lord of

a Com. p. 341.
b in vita.
c in vita.
d Com. p. 382.
e Decimus Angliæ provincialis fucceffit
Ricaraus Blytonus Lyncolnienfis diocefis,

anno domini 1319. Stanfordiæ conftitutus.
Heliades. Cap. 33. MS. Harley.
f ut fupra.
g in vita.
h Baron. Vol. I. p. 81. a.

Stanford] ' was again in the wars of Scotland.——Agatha de Reynham,
' relict of John de Knotifhale burgefs of Staunford, gave to John
' Blackman woolmerchant in Staunford one tenement in the parifh of
' St. Clement without Scoftgate, between the tenements of Richard
' Baldefwel on either part; which extends it felf from the kings high-
' way north as far as the Croft of W. Bunting late burgefs of Staun-
' ford fouth. B. H.   ᵃ Upon the feaft of S. Gregory [Mar. 12.] 1320. died   Mar.12.
' Sir Henry de Stanford, late prior of Finchale & bifhop of Durham   1320.
' elect & was buried in the choir of S. Leonards [church without
Stanford] ' before the high altar : after whofe death was feen a light
' fhining from heaven, in manner of a funbeam, over his grave.
' What is remarkable of this man is, that he was born on S. Leo-
' nards day, elected bifhop of Durham on S. Leonards day, & buried
' in S. Leonards church.'   In 1321. 15. E. 2.   ' ᵇ The K. fummoned   July
' a parliament to begin at Weftminfter three weeks after midfummer.   1321.
' The barons came in forcible wife unto this parliament, & conftrayn-   15.E.2.
' ed John the 2. E. Warenn [lord of Stanford] & other lords, & like-
' wife fome bifhops, thro' feare, to take an othe to joine with them
' in expulfing the Spencers out of the realme.'   ' Aug. 1. died God-   Aug. 1.
frey de Croyland, lord abbat of Burg, & Oct. 17. following the tem-   Oct. 17.
poralities of that abbey were by the kings efcheators, reftored to his
fucceffor Adam de Bootheby ᵈ; ' when the faid efcheators anfwered to
' him for five fhillings, part of the rent of certain tenents in Stan-
' forde due at the Mich. laft.   And for eleven fhillings & fixpence, the
' perquifits of a court with a fight of franc pledge held there at the
' fame Mich.—— And the jurats fay, that there are in Stanforde di-
' vers free tenents who pay yearly, at the four ufual feafons, 20 fhillings.
' And that there is there a certain court held every three weeks,
' worth, with the two fights of franc pledge belonging to *it*, 20 s.
' ᵉ John the 2. E. Warenn [lord of Stanford] was the fame year joyned in
' fpecial commiffion with Edm. E. of Kent (the kings brother) joynt-
' ly & feverally to purfue Thomas E. of Lancafter & his adherents;
' as alfo to befiege his caftle of Pomfret, & take it.   ᶠ The K. kept his
' Chriftmas at Cirencefter, John the 2. E. of Surrey [lord of Stan-   Dec.25.
' ford] & other great lordes coming thither to joyne their powers
' with his.   ᵍ On Mar. 16. 132⁵⁄₇. 15. E. 2. was fought the battel of   Mar.16.
' Burton wherein the barons were defeated, & utterly overthrowne,
' many of them being taken prifoners.   ʰ Before this battel the K.
' on deliberate advice taken how to paffe the river, ordeyned that the
' E. of Surrey wyth certayne armed men, fhould go over by a bridge
' that was a three miles diftant from Burton, that he might come
' upon the backes of the enemies, as they were fighting with thofe

a Ex Rob. de Grayftanes Hift. Dunelm.   e Baron. Vol. I. p. 81. a.
p. 758.   f Holingfhed. p. 863. b.
   b Holings. p. 860. b.   g Stow p. 340.
   c Whittlefey. p. 175.   h Hol. p. 865. a.
   d id. p. 216.

' that

' that fhulde affaile them a frounte. ᵃThe 3d. day after the appre-

' henfion of the barons (to wit, March 19.) the K. in perfon being
' fet in judgment at Pontfract, & with him the faid E. of Surrey
' [lord of Stanford] & other lords, the E. of Lancafter was brought
' before them, & had fentence pronounced againft him as an arch-
' traitor; neverthelefs, for reverence of his blood (he being the kings
' near kinfman) drawing & hanging were remitted, ᵇ & it was appoint-
' ed that he fhould only lofe his head. —— Whereupon faying, fhall
' I die without anfwer? a certain Gafcoign took him away, & put
' a pilled broken hood on his head, & fet him on a lean white jade,
' without a bridle; & then he added, K. of heaven have mercy on
' me, for the K. of earth *nous ad guerthi.*   And thus he was carried,
' fome throwing pellets of dirt at him (having a fryer-preacher for
' his confeffor) to an hill without the town; where he kneeled down
' towards the eaft, till one Hugin de Muftin caufed him to turn his
' face towards Scotland, & then a villain of London cut off his head.'
Pr. Edward was now about ten years of age. ' In his youth, as Mr.
' Speed tells us from Tho. Walfinghamᶜ, he was trained up at Ox-
' ford under the learned Walter Burley.'   Let us now then fuppofe
that prince with his faid tutor at Oxford.   Dr. Plot fpeaking of the
antiquity of Oxford, writesᵈ, ' I think it very confiderable what re-
' mains upon record in Magdalen coll. library, in an antient MS. of
' Walter Burleys, fellow of Merton (tutor to the famous K. Edw. the
' 3d. & defervedly ftiled *doctor profundus*) who, upon the problem
' *complexio rara quare fanior,* has thefe words concerning the healthy
' fituation of Oxford, & its felection by ftudents for the feat of the
' Mufes.   A healthy city muft be open to the north & eaft, & moun-
' tanous to the fouth & weft; by reafon of the purity of the two
' former quarters, in refpect of the latter: juft as Oxford is feated,
' which was felected by the philofophers that came from Greece.'
Here, if it might not be thought unfair to queftion the doctors exact
copying, I could almoft fancy, from the fituation thus defcribed, & the Greek philofophers here fpoken of, that Burley was rather
fpeaking of the fituation of Stanford, & the univerfity there, than that
of Oxford: For the defcription of the fituation fuits exactly.   And
Bladud they fay, brought with him Greek philofophers to Stanford,
but who brought any to Oxford I find not.   But I proceed.   In this
' ' ᵉA parliament was fummoned to meet at York, & the
' perfons elected to reprefent the borough of Stanford in that affem-
' bly, were Euftace Malherb & John Thirsby.'   It was the cuftome
of thefe times that each member of parliament had two manucaptors
or fureties for him, whofe names were entered with his, on the

ᵃ Speed. p. 675. a.   ᵈ Hift. Oxford. p. 330. 1. Edit.
ᵇ Bar. Vol. I. p. 781 b.   ᵉ Ex literis Cl. Willifii mihi datis
ᶜ p. 724. a.   Mar. 7. 1719-20.

                                                            return

return made to the writ for electing. Dr. Brady had feen the record where the members for Stanford & their manucaptors this 15. E. 2. were fo entered [a]; but does not name them.

XI. [b] ' The Kts. templars, who had caught up 9000 manors in this king-
' dom, being diffolved as above, in 1312. & all their lands efcheated
' to the K. in 1323. by act of parliament, all their late poffeffions
' in England were given to the kts. hofpitallers of S. John of Jerufa-
' lem;' left, being beftowed for pious ufes, they fhould be perverted to other purpofes, contrary to the will of the donors. Adam de
Boothby lord abbat of Burg intending to vifit the priory of S. Michael without Stanford on the Monday next before the feaft of S.
Luke, on the 6. of Oct. gave notice to the prior, priorefs, & convent   Oct. 6.
of that houfe to be ready on the faid day, in their conventual church,   1323.
to receive his faid vifitation.   Commanding alfo the prior to warn   17. E. 2.
the mafter or warden of S. Thomas of Canterburys hofpital by the
bridge, & the brethren of that houfe, to be ready in the chapel of
that hofpital ; as likewife the warden of S. Leonards hofpital, & the
brethren of that houfe, to be ready in the chapel of that hofpital ;
on the Wednefday next after the feaft of S. Luke, to undergo the like
vifitation.   His letter, giving notice of thefe things, is thus worded.
' [b] Adam by divine permiffion abbat of Burg, to his beloved in Chrift
' the prior of S. Michaels without Stanford, & to the priorefs & con-
' vent of the fame place, the health which hath flowed from the
' bowels of a favior.   Intending, in a pious affection, to exercife the
' wonted office of vifitation which is incumbent on us to perform in
' your monaftery; to you we command, that on the Monday next be-
' fore the feaft of the bleffed Luke the evangelift next enfuing, you,
' & all & every the reft of your congregation, who by us of right
' or cuftom be bound to be vifited, in your conventual church of S.
' Michael do humbly appear before us, & exhibit themfelves ready whol-
' fomely to undergo our vifitation in form of law to be beftowed
' on you.   For which things to be done, we from this inftant do
' peremptorily cite you. Moreover, to you the prior aforefaid, by virtue
' of your obedience, by firmly injoining we command, that ye cite,
' or caufe to be cited, the mafter or warden of the hofpital of the
' bleffed Thomas the martyr, at the bridge of Stanford ; as alfo the
' warden of the hofpital of S. Leonard, peremptorily to appear before
' us, on the Wednefday next after the approaching feaft of the blef-
' fed Luke the evangelift; to wit, the mafter of the hofpital of the
' bleffed Thomas, in the chapel of the faid hofpital ; & the forefaid
' mafter of the bleffed Leonard, in the chapel of the fame hofpital,
' together with the brethren of either hofpital ; actually to undergo
' our vifitation, in form canonical to be beftowed on the fame ; as al-

a See Bradys I. Vol. of Bor. p. 72, 73.   c Ex codicis MS. in Bib. Cotton. fub
b Bp Kennets par. ant. p. 390.   imagine Vefp. E. XXI. fol. 7.

' fo

' fo to give in to us, or our commiffaries on this part, as is meet,
' the accompt, or disburfements, of the adminiftration of the
' goods of either hofpital, as unto them is known to belong, accord-
' ing to the form of a ftatute for this purpofe fet forth; & farther to
' do & receive, as fhall be juft & agree with canonical appointments.
' And touching the day of the receipt of the prefents, & how ye
' fhall have executed our prefent mandate, ye may clearly & openly
' acquaint us at the faid day & place, by your letters patents contain-
' ing a feries of thefe matters. Given at Burg the 6. of Oct. 1323,
On receipt of this mandate the prior of S. Michaels, cited the priorefs,
nuns, brethren, fifters & converts of the faid houfe, to attend, on the
faid Monday next before the feaft of S. Luke; as alfo, in his abfence,
Sir Ralf de Stoke (rector of Lilleford) mafter or warden of S. Thomas
the martyrs; & Sir Walter de Bernak, warden of S. Giles's, hofpital, then prefent; together with the brethren & fifters of either houfe;
to be ready on the faid Wednefday next after the feaft of S. Luke;
to undergo their feveral & refpective vifitations as above: which
done, he certified his performance of the fame after the following

17. Oct. manner. ' ᵃ To the reverend father in Chrift, lord Adam, by the
' grace of God abbat of Burg, his humble minifter, if it pleafe him,
' of the monaftery of S. Michael without Stanford, greeting with all
' reverence, obedience equally, & honor. I have received your man-
' date, dated the 6. of October, in thefe words. Adam by divine per-
' miffion, &c. as above. By authority therefore of this your mandate,
' I have warned & peremptorily cited, all & every of my congrega-
' tion, to wit, the priorefs, & all the nuns, brethren, fifters, & con-
' verts, who, by right or cuftom, are obliged to be at your vifitation;
' that on the Monday next before the feaft of the bleffed Luke the
' evangelift next enfuing they exhibit themfelves in the conventual
' church of S. Michael without Stanford, ready wholfomely to un-
' dergo your vifitation in form of law, the fame by you to be impof-
' ed, & farther to do & receive as juftice fhall require. Moreover
' I have peremptorily cited Sir Ralph de Stoke (rector of the
' church of Lilleford) mafter or warden of the hofpital of the bleffed
' Thomas the martyr at Stanford bridge, in the faid chapel of S.
' Thomas the martyr, perfonally not found; alfo Sir Walter de Bernak,
' warden of the hofpital of S. Giles, in his chapel of the faid hof-
' pital of S. Giles, perfonally found; that on the Wednefday next af-
' ter the inftant feaft of the bleffed Luke the evangelift; they appear
' ready, to wit, the faid Sir Ralph the mafter or warden in the faid cha-
' pel of S. Thomas the martyr; & the faid Sir Walter in the cha-
' pel of the faid hofpital of S. Giles, together with the brethren & fi-
' fters of either hofpital, your vifitation, in form canonical on the fame
' to be beftowed, actually to undergo, & alfo to render in the ac-

' compts or disbursements of the administration of the goods of either
' hospital as unto them is known to belong according, to the form
' of a constitution in this case provided, to you or your commissaries
' on this part as is convenient; & farther to do & receive as shall
' be just & agreeable to canonical institutes.   And thus your present
' mandate, in every its articles, as bound, I have diligently & reve-
' rently executed.   And these things by the presents I signifie to your
' reverend fatherhood.   Given at Stanford the 16. of the Kal. of
' November, 1323.   Afterwards the foresaid lord abbat went perso-
' nally to the monastery of nuns aforesaid, by reason of his visitation
' there to be held.   And the prioress of the same house & the nuns
' of the same, unanimously, & with that reverence wherewith it be-
' came them, admitted him to hold there his office of visitation with-
' out contradiction.   The which lord abbat calling to him, brother
' Hugh de Stivecle [Stukely] & brother Robert de Tanser his bre-
' thren & fellow monks (by him taken & elected to assist him in
' the said business of visitation) touching the state of that monastery,
' the life & conversation of the prior & prioress, as also of the
' holy nuns of the same place & other the persons there abiding, as
' he ought ; &, of other necessary & accustomed articles that his visi-
' tation concerning, diligently enquired, by continuing the same Mon-
' day till the morrow being Tuesday ; which Tuesday being come,
' the same lord abbat personally unto the said place returning, toge-
' ther with his foresaid brethren to him associated & elected, the
' things found by him, & to be corrected & reformed, duly cor-
' rected & reformed for that time.   And because the said lord ab-
' bat, for certain reasons hindered, the office of his visitation, accord-
' ing to the form of his mandate abovesaid, in the foresaid hospitals
' of the blessed Thomas the martyr at Stanford bridge, & of the bles-
' sed Giles, at the day assigned to the masters of the same, could not
' be personally present at ; his place & power to the foresaid bro-
' ther Hugh de Stivecle his fellow - monk & master Philip de Kil-
' kenni clerc, he, under a certain form, committed, as follows. Adam
' by divine permission abbat of Burg S. Peter in the diocese of Lin-
' coln, to his beloved son brother Hugh de Stivecle monk in
' the same monastery, & to master Philip de Kilkenni clerc, health
' in the savior of all.   Of the industry of your circumspection
' we having full confidence; to exercise the office of visitation, as
' also to enquire, correct, punish & reform in all things whatsoever
' the state or government of the hospital of the blessed Thomas the
' martyr at Stanford bridge, as also the house of lepers of the blessed
' Giles without Stanford of our patronage ; as also for the accompts
' or disbursements in the administrations of either hospital, accord-
' ing to-the form of a new constitution in this case set forth, from
' the masters or wardens of the same, or their proctors for the same
' having sufficient power, to be received this instant Wednesday next

' after

' after the feaft of the bleffed Luke the evangelift, in the chapels of
' the fame hofpitals, & for other things to be done which in the
' premifes fhall be neceffary, or alfo opportune; to you we commit
' our place & ftead, with power of every fort of canonical cohertion.
' And, if both of you cannot be prefent in doing of thefe things,
Oct. 18. ' one of you touching thefe matters may take cognizance & execute.
1323. ' Farewel. Given at Tinewel, on the feaft of S. Luke the evangelift, 1323.
18. E. 2.   XII. [a] ' In the 18. of E. 2. John the 2 E. Warenn [lord of Stanford]
' was conftituted captain general conductor of thofe military men,
' who were fent into Gafcoign, with command to bring them unto
' Edm. E. of Kent, then lieutenant of that dutchy.   [b] Simon de Luffen-
' ham lord abbat of Croyland now refigned his abbacy, [whereup-
' on] [c] Matthew Broun the kings efchaetor in the counties of Lin-
' coln, Northampton, Cambridge & Roteland, feifed all the goods
' of the forefaid abby into the kings hands.' Now flourifhed John
Berwic. ' [d] John Bervic, faith Leland [e], was cotemporary with Wil-
' liam Ocham, & one who clofely trod in his fteps at Oxford. His
' lucubrations on Longobardus are commended among the learned
' Francifcans. He wrote alfo a little book *de formis*: & [f] was buried
Aug. 15. ' at Stanford.' Aug. 15. 1324. 18. E. 2. Geoffry fon of mafter Geoffry
1324. de Makefey dimifed to Walter de Skilington of Staunford a meffuage
18. E. 2. with part of a curtilage in S. Pauls parifh for twenty years (the meffuage dimifed to be pulled down, & rebuilt by the leffee) Witneffes, Euftace Malherbe, &c. Given at Staunford, the Sunday next after the feaft of the affumption, in the 18. of K. Edward fon of K. Edward. ' This deed, faith Mr. Madox, [g] has the
' nine firft letters of the alphabet cut thro' indentwife, & a fmall feal
' of red wax upon a parchment label.' In Nov. the 18. E. 2. the
abbat of Burg let his lands, tenements, meadows, rents, firms, & paftures in Staunford to William de Morcote, to hold during pleafure, at
the rent of 12 l. a year. And the faid William then entered thereon.

19. E. 2.   XIII. In the 19. E. 2. ' [h] Matilda . . . . . was lady of Burley, &
' owner of the manor there. She had a daughter of the fame name,
' & a fon named Peter. Which Peter alfo had a fon of his own name.
' The faid Peter the father when he came to be lord of Burley, af-
' terwards fold the manor of Burley to one Robert Wyks.' John the 2
E. Warenn, lord of Stanford (having made the K. his heir, & refigned
all his lands to him for that purpofe as above [i].) ' [k] in this 19. E. 2.
' the fame K. affigned unto him for life, the caftles & manors of Co-
' ningsburgh & Sandale; the manors of Wakefield, Souresby, Brathe-
' well, Fifhlake, Dewsbury, & Halifax, in Yorkfhire.' There having

a Baron. Vol. I. p. 81. a.   g Form. Ang. form. 235.
b Mr. Willis Hift. Abbies Vol. I. p. 78.   h From Sir Wm. Cecils diary of his
c Ex Hift. Croy. Cont. pag. 482.   own life; a MS. in Mr Strypes hands.
d Hift. Eng. Francif. p. 141.   i 30. June 9. E. 2.
e Com. de Script. Brit. p. 326.   k Baron. Vol. I p. 81. a.
f ıft. additional Vol. to the monaft. p. 132.

been lately a fray between Robert rector of S. John Baptifts church, John fon of John le Longs of Staunford, Adam de Burley capellan, & William de Edenham another capellan of the one party, & Peter le Orfever of the other part; the faid Peter brought an action of affualt & battery againft the faid Robert: whereupon the K. directed a mandamus to the bifhop of Lincoln to fee that the faid Robert fhould be forth coming to anfwer the faid Peter about the faid charge; which mandamus runs thus.   ' [a] We command that ye caufe ' to come before us in the octaves of the bleffed Mary, wherefoever ' he fhall be in England, Robert parfon of the church of S. John ' Staunford, your clerc; to anfwer to Peter le Orfever of Staunford; ' why he, together with John fon of John le Longs of Staunford, ' & Adam de Burley capellan, & Wm. de Edenham capellan, with ' force & arms, upon him, at Staunford, made an infult, & him beat, ' wounded, & evil intreated, to the great damage of him Peter, & ' againft our peace, &c. Given at Weftminfter, the 21. of Nov. in ' the 19. of our reign.

21. Nov. 19. E. 2.

XIV. On the 29. Aug. 1326. 20. E. 2. Letters were fent under the kings privy feal to fummon the prelates & peers to a council or treaty at Staunford, to be held there the 14. of October.   One of which letters was directed to Adam de Boothby lord abbat of Burg, & runs thus.   ' [b] Edward, by the grace of God K. of England & D. of Aquitain, to our dearly beloved in God the abbat of Burg, greeting. ' For as much as upon fome great & important bufineffes, touching ' us & the eftate of our realme, we are willing to have advice & ' treaty with you & certain other prelates & great men of our realm ' at Staunford, the Monday on the quindifm of S. Michael next en- ' fuing; we command, upon the faith & amity which you owe us, ' & hereby firmly enjoyn you, that, all other bufineffes fet afide, you ' appear before us, at the faid day & place, for the reafon aforefaid: ' And this in no wife to omit.   Given under our privy feal at Ram- ' fey, the 29. of Auguft, in the 20th year of our reign.' This fummons in the kings name, was fent by the queen, not to ferve her husband, but to bring about her own wicked purpofes.   Likewife on the 14. of Sept. following, the K. being then at Dorchefter, a letter was wrote in his name to the archbifhop of Canterbury, fignifying, that whereas he underftood the archbifhop had without his knowledge fummoned a convocation to meet at London, he the K. having

29. Aug. 1326. 20. E. 2.

Sept. 14.

a Ex regiftri cujufdam MS. apud Linc. fol. 80. b.

b Edward, par la grace de Dieu, roi dengletere, & ducs daquitain, a noftre cher en Dieu abbe de Burghe feint Piere, faluz. Pur coe q' fur aucunes groffes & chargeauntes bufoignes, touchantes nous & leftat de noftre realme, voloms aver un confeil & tretiz en vous & aucuns autres prelaz & graunz de noftre realme, a Staunford, le lundy en la quinzeine de feint Michael prochein avenir; vous maundoms, fur la foi & lamifte que vous nous devez, fermement enjoignaunz, que totes autres chofes leffez, ferez a nous, as ditz jour & lieu, par la caufe fuifdite: & coe en nule manere ne leffez. Don fouz noftre prive feal, a Romefi, le 29. jour de Auguft, lan de noftre regne 20[me]. Ex codicis MS. in Bib. Cott. fub imagine Vefp. E. XXI. fol. 11.

occafion

occasion at the same time to call a great council at Stanford, the archbishop should put off the convocation to some other time. ' ᵃAccordingly the archbishop put off the convocation to the day after the feast of all souls. But tho' in his mandate he recites the kings writ, yet he does not so far own his authority as to call it a command ; but says the K. earnestly requested him to do it : *nobis affectuose supplicavit.'* This my author puts down as an instance of the archbishops slighting the king. Whereas, if we consider that the K. was now a prisoner in the hands of the queens minions, perhaps it may then be found an instance of his respect for him. For see the design & issue of this goodly council. ' Q. Isabel, says Kniton,ᵇ caused many prelates, earls, barons, & nobles of the kingdom to assemble at Stanford in a great multitude ; where after diligent treaty had thereupon, it was unanimously deliberated & told the Q. that they could by no means permit her to go to the K. her husband, altho' she had offered her self readily & willingly to do so, if she might with safety.' A piece of so vile hypocrisie, as explained by her behaviour afterwards, that I want words to express it. ' Robert le Flemyng of Staunford gave to John de Christemnes, burgess of Staunford, two acres of arable land lying in Staunford fields, near the mill *that was* Eustace Malherbes, abutting on the land of the priory of S. Leonard east. B. H.' The mill here spoken of being mentioned, as the mill that *was* Eustace Malherbes, shews that he had either given away, or sold the said mill, or that he was dead ; most probably the last : because his name occurs no more in any other old evidences I have yet met with. On the verge of an arch in the north-wall behind the wainscoat of the seats in the now free-school, formerly S. Pauls church, is this inscription.

𝔥𝔦𝔠 𝔧𝔞𝔠𝔢𝔱 𝔈𝔲𝔰𝔱𝔞𝔠𝔥𝔦𝔲𝔰 𝔐𝔞𝔩𝔥𝔢𝔯𝔟𝔢, 𝔅𝔲𝔯𝔤𝔦𝔫𝔠𝔦𝔰 𝔖𝔱𝔞𝔲𝔫𝔟𝔬𝔯𝔡𝔦𝔢.

That is, Here lies Eustace Malherbe, burgess of Staunford.

' ᶜIn this reign the prior *de novo loco* [or Newsted] was lord of lit

Jan. 25. tle Castreton in Rutland. On the 25. of Jan. 20. E. 2. ᵈJohn the 2d. E. Warenn [lord of Stanford] was one of the witnesses to K. Edw. the 2ds. resignation of his crown & kingdom to his eldest sonne. ' ᵉThe day before K. Edwards deposal, his son (afterwards Edw. the 3d.) was married at York to Philippa daughter of Wm. E. of Hainault.' And now having nothing more to say about this unfortunate prince (the rest of his story being out of my province) I shall only add a little farther account of Walter Burley, & John Rodington both then living at Stanford, & so pass to the next reign. I have before given the character of Walter Burley by Leland & Pits, with a specimen of his learning from Dr. Plot : it remains that I now give some farther account of him as I find it delivered in Holingshed, much of it translat-

a Hodys hist. Convoc. p. 3. p. 177, 178.   d Stow. p. 348.
b Col. 2767.   e Gunton p. 43.
c Wrights Rutland, p. 36.

ed from Bale. ' Walter Burley, faith he, [a] a doctor of divinitie, in
' his youth was brought up, not onelie in Martin college in Oxford,
' but alfo in the univerfities & fchooles abroade beyond the feas, in
' Fraunce & Germanye; & afterwards, for his wifedome, good demea-
' nour & learnynge, reteyned wyth the byfhoppe of Ulmes in Suaben-
' land, a region in hyghe Germanye; amongft other treatifes whiche
' he compiled (being manye, & namely of natural philofophie) he
' wrote a commentarie on the ethickes of Ariftotle, & dedicated the
' fame unto the faid bifhoppe; a worke which hath bin highly efteem-
' ed, not only in the univerfities of Italy, Germany & Fraunce, but
' alfo heere in our univerfities of England. To conclude, fuch was the
' fame of this doctor Burley, that when the lady Philip, daughter
' to the E. of Heynault, fhould come over into England to be mar-
' ried to K. Edwarde, this doctor Burley was reteyned by her, & ap-
' pointed to be hir almoigner; & fo continued in great eftimation.
Of which Burley yet many things hereafter. ' John Rodington, faith
' Pits, [b] was born in Lincolnfhire, & a Francifcan in the grey friers
' at Stanford [warden, I fuppofe.] He was one who fhined among thofe
' of his own age with the titles of virtue & erudition. He learned
' philofophy & divinity at Oxford, but arrived to the perfection of
' them both at Paris. In England he was for fome years provincial
' of his order, & ftifly maintained that the bleffed virgin was con-
' ceived in original fin. He did not much fet by a polite Latin ftile,
' but contented himfelf with the language of the fchools (fuch as they
' ufed in the times he lived) accounting a folid knowledge of things
' a much more valuable qualification, than a vain ornament of words.'
Of whom alfo more hereafter.

XV. Here I beg leave to note, that in all the accounts of thofe
learned men whofe characters are, above & hereafter, given in thefe
collections from Leland, Bale, & Pits, nothing is omitted relating to
any of them, but fome repetitions which three people who write upon the fame fubject muft needs run into; or tedious catalogues of
books, now not to be met with; or, if to be met with, now not
much regarded; or fuch reflections as Bale a proteftant, & Pits & a Ro-
manift (both very furious men in their feveral ways) are fometimes
too unmercifully pleafed to heap upon each others party. Concerning
the laft of whom it is certain (as I have elfewhere now & then hinted) that he never faw Leland, tho' he pretends to quote him in almoft every page, but that on the contrary he almoft conftantly followed Bale. I fubfcribe therefore to Mr. Whartons cenfure of him.
' As to Pits, faith that excellent perfon, [c] his intolerable arrogance de-
' ferves cenfuring. For he brags that he drew his principal materials
' out of Lelands collections, & that he thought the centuries of Bale
' fcarce worth his regard. Whereas, to me it abundantly appears,

' he had never feen Lelands work; but that, what Bale not ungrate‑
' fully compiled out of Leland, he hath moſt ungratefully copied
' out of Bale.' With this take alſo the learned Dr. Halls account of
them all three. ' 'Greatly to me they always feem to have deſerved
' of the commonwealth of letters who have commended to poſterity
' the lives & writings of illuſtrious & learned men. Among theſe, if
' not the firſt (for Boſton had gone before) yet the chief, of our
' countrymen, was John Leland the antiquary; for he, being provided
' with plenty of materials for this ſort of knowledge, begun to write
' four Books of the illuſtrious perſonages of this nation; but, ſnatched
' away by ſudden death, could neither publiſh, or indeed perfect them.
' This work, after the authors much to be lamented deceaſe, fell into
' the hands of John Bale, a Suffolk man, who tranſplanted it, ſullied
' with ſcandal & interpolated, into his own centuries. Him followed
' John Pits a plagiary, if ever any man was one, the moſt confident;
' who, tho' he never had a ſight of Leland, yet often praiſes him moſt
' outragiouſly.' So much of Leland, Bale, & Pits, as biographers;
concerning Leland, as a topographer, I beg leave to add, that this book
of mine being one of the firſt pieces of local antiquities wrote ſince the
publiſhing of his Itinerary & Collectanea (all which I carefully read
over with this one view) owes much of its beauty to divers curious
hints & notices in thoſe excellent collections. And, in farther juſtice
to his merit, no man, I think, ought to ſet about any undertaking of
this kind, without a thorough peruſal of thoſe excellent & moſt uſe‑
ful pieces. But I haſten to the next reign.

c in Præfat. ad Joh. Lelandi comment. de Scrip. Brit.

The end of the tenth book.

Academia tertia Anglicana;

OR, THE

ANTIQUARIAN ANNALS

of the TOWN of

STANFORD

IN

Lincoln, Rutland, *and* Northampton *Shires,*

BOOK XI.
Containing the reign of K. Edward the third.

'[a]**K**ING Edward the 3. was crowned at Weftminfter on the
'purification of our lady. And bycaufe he was but 14, it
'was decreed that xij. of the greateft lords [whereof John the
'2. E. Warenn, lord of Stanford, was one] fhould have the govern-
'ment till he came to more perfite years. [b]'Soon after K. Edw. the 3.
'being at Stanford, there granted an affignment to Sir Thomas Barclay &
'Sir John Maltravers, for fubfifting K. Edward the 2[d]. his father, then
'a prifoner in Berkley caftle; which affignment bares date at Stan-
'ford Ap. 24. 1327.' [c]'John 2. E. Warenn [lord of Stanford] was
'in that expedition now made into Scotland. Robert the Smith in
'Staunford gave to John Chriftemnes burgefs of Staunford all the te-
'nement which is in S. Clements Parifh without Scoftgate, between
'a tenement of Richard Pyth eaft, & a tenement of the forefaid John
'Chriftemnes weft, & extends it felf from the ftreet called Scoftgate
'fouth, as far as a tenement of the faid John Chriftemnes north .B. H.
'[d]On the Sunday next before the feaft of S. James the apoftle 2. E. 3.
'dame Mabilla priorefs of S. Michael without Stanford, did fealty to
'lord Adam abbat of Burg (for the lands & tenements which fhe
'claimed to hold of him in the counties of Lincoln, Northampton,
'& elfewhere) in the abbats chamber at Burg, in prefence of the bre-
'thren Nicholas de Pafton, & Henry de Botheby, monks of Burg; the

Feb. 2.
I. E. 3.

Ap. 24.
1327.

July,
2. E. 3

---

a Hol. p. 885. a.
b Acta regia N°. 3. p. 185.
c Bar. Vol. I. p. 81. b.

d Ex Codicis MS. in Bib. Cott. fub Imagine
Vefp. E. XXI. Fol. 39. b.

'fon

' fon of Warin fteward of the liberties of the forefaid lord abbat,
' Robert de Lufwyk clerc, & others.' ' Robert, fon and heir of Si-
' mon Peert of Bradecroft, fold to Henry le Knocker of Stanford, a
' meffuage with a public oven in the fame erected; & a curtilage ad-
' joining with the appurtenances fituate in Bradecroft; as it extends it
' felf from the kings highway fouth, as far as the arable land of W.
' Edelyn & Simon de Braffingburg north.   Given at Bradecroft the
' thurfday after Lammas day, 2. E. 3. B. H.'   Adam de Bootheby lord
abbat of Burg, a ' in the 7. year of his abbatfhip expended in prefents
' which he made the K. then at Oundle & Stanforde 34. l. 7. s. & 4. d.°
Matthew Brown the kings efchaetor, having as above 18. E. 2. feifed
the lands belonging to Croyland abby, upon the refignation of Simon
late abbat thereof; b ' the venerable father abbat Henry his fucceffor
' petitioned the K. that he would gracioufly be pleafed to allow them
' out of the income of the forefaid houfe what was antiently affigned
' for the time of the faid vacancy, for fupport of the prior of the faid
' monaftery, & of the convent, & of the corrodiars & fervants of the
' fame houfe, & for cloaths, fhoes, linen, & other neceffaries for the
' monks, & alfo for lights to be found in the churches in time of divine
' fervice.   Hereupon the K. directed his writ to the treafurer & ba-
' rons of his exchequer, to fearch the rolls & remembrances of the
' faid exchequer, to find by the efchaetors accompts, what was wont
' to be allowed the *cuftodes* of the faid abby, in the time of its va-
' cancy, for maintenance of the prior & convent, as above.   Where-
' upon, the forefaid remembrances being examined, they certified, that
' they had found a twofold vacation of the faid abby, but declared that
' they found no allowance at all for maintenance of the prior & con-
' vent, &c.   However the K. thinking it to be juft & agreeable to
' reafon, that the forefaid prior & convent, corrodiars & officers fhould
' be maintained out of the revenues of the houfe, during the vacati-
' on of the fame, & in like manner that the lights fhould be kept
' up for the worfhip of God; directed in his mandates to William
' Broukeloufby clerk, remembrancer of his exchequer, to enquire upon
' the oath of honeft & lawful men, how many monks, corrodiars, alfo
' how many fervants & neceffary officers were found in the abby afore-
' faid, during the whole time of the forefaid vacation.   Whereupon
' an inquifition was taken at Stanford before the forefaid William in
' the 2ᵈ. of K. Edw. the 3. by the oath of eighteen jurats, affirm-
' ing, that there had been in the abby of Croyland continually for
' the whole time of the vacation beforefaid, forty & one monks, fif-
' teen corrodiars, & fix and thirty fervants & neceffary officers, whom
' they particularly fet down by name.   Moreover when the K. had
' been certified about the forenamed inquifition by the faid remembran-

a Ex Hiftor. Coenobii Burgenfis Cont. per   etiam Gunton p. 44.
anony. edit. a Jof. Sparke 1724. p. 226. vide   b Ex Hift. Croyl. Contin. Pag. 482.

' cer,

' cer, he sent letters to the treasurer & barons of his exchequer afore-
' said, how that they should allow Matthew the eschaetor in his accompt
' for the time of the vacancy of the abby aforesaid, for the prior six pence
' a day, for every one of the monks three pence, in like manner for
' every one of the corrodiars three pence ; & for an officer or servant
' two pence : commanding also strictly to the eschaetor aforenamed, that
' he should pay the sum assigned to the foresaid monks.   And all these
' things being paid the abby was worth to the K. every week, 8 l. 1 s. 6 d.
' neat mony. Alice, relict of W. Folkyngham clothier, gave to Cecily her
' daughter, & John & Peter her sons, her house in S. Martins Parish. B. H.

II. ' Simon de Brassingburg of Bradecroft & Alice his wife sold to   Feb.
' Henry le Knocker of Stanford leather-dresser, one house with their   3. E. 3.
' meadows in Bradecroft, which house extends it self from the kings
' high-way south, as far as the garden of the foresaid Henry north.
' Given at Bradecroft, *die martis in festo S. Valentini martyris*, 3. E. 3.
B. H.   The same year the K. granted to Peter de Burley, liberty of
free-warenn in all his demesne lands not within the bounds of
the forest ; his charter is thus worded.   a ' Edward, &c. let all know,
' that I have granted, &c. to Peter de Burley & his heirs, free-warenn
' in all their demesne lands at Burlee by Stanford in the county of
' Northampton ; so long nevertheless as those lands be not with-
' in the bounds of the forest, so that no entry, &c. upon our forest.
' Witnesses, H. of Winton, R. of London, J. of Norwych, bishops ;
' Gilbert de Clare E. of Gloucester & his son ; Pagan the steward of
' our houshold.   b ' Certaine men to try what friends they had in
' England, craftily devised that Edw. the 2ᵈ. was alive in the castle of
' Corfe, & therefore used many nights to make shewes & masking
' with dancing upon the towres & walles of the castle, which being
' perceived by people of the country, it was thought there had been
' some great K. to whom they did these great solemnities ; whence it
' came to pass, that the E. of Kent [Edmund of Woodstock] sent thi-
' ther a fryer preacher, to try the truth of the matter, who (as it was
' thought) having corrupted the porter of the castle with rewardes, was
' let in, where he lay all day in the porters lodge very close : & when
' night was come, was willed to put on the habit of a lay man, &
' then brought into the hall, where he saw (as he thought) Edw. the
' father of the K. sitting royally at supper, with great majesty.   This
' fryer being thus persuaded, returned to the E. & reported, as he thought,
' what he saw : whereupon the E. said with an oath, that he would
' endeavour by all the means he could to deliver his brother from pri-

a Edwardus &c. Sciant &c. quod ego concessi &c. Petro de Burle & heredibus suis,
quod habeant liberam warennam in omnibus
dominicis terris suis de Burlee juxta Stanford
in com. Northampt. dum tamen terre ille
non sint infra metas foreste, ita quod nullus
introitus, &c. super forestam nostram. Hiis

testibus, H. Winton ; R. London ; J. Nor-
wyc ; episcopis ; Gilberto de Clare comite
Glocestrie & filio, Pagano senefchallo Hosp.
nostri. Dat. 3. E. 3.   Ex Gul. D. Burghley
Diario Codice MS. penes Rev. Virum Johannem Strype.

b Stow. p. 355.

' son.

' fon.' If K. Henry the 3. was not, this Edmund of Woodſtock abovementioned, ſirnamed Plantagenet & E. of Kent, was, I reckon, founder of the grey fryers college at Stanford: or if not he, certainly
ſome of his family, his anceſtor.   Be that as it will; his daughter
Joan, called the fair maid of Kent, & mother of K. Richard the 2ᵈ.
(with her 2ᵈ. husband Thomas Holland K. of the garter & E. of
Kent) was buried in the church belonging to the ſaid grey friers monaſtery at Stanford : of whoſe burials there more hereafter.   The abbat of Burg was now forced to ſue one of his tenents for ſome matters which he rented of him at Stanford.   For ſaith the record,

Nov.
3. E. 3.
1329.

' William de Morcote was ſummoned to anſwer the abbat of Burg,
' touching a plea, to pay him four & twenty pounds, which he owes
' him, & unjuſtly detains, &c.   And whence the ſame abbat ſaith,
' that when the ſame William (on the thurſday next after the feaſt of
' S. Matthew the apoſtle, in the 18ᵗʰ. of K. Edw. father of the lord
' the K. now) had received of the ſaid abbat the bailiſhip of the
' cuſtody of his liberty, of his lands, tenements, meadows, rents, farms,
' & paſtures in Staunford, during the ſaid abbats pleaſure to be held
' unto firm, by paying thence yearly to the ſaid abbat twelve pounds
' of ſilver, to wit, at the feaſts of Eaſter & S. Michael by equal por-
' tions: the ſaid William the bailiſhip aforeſaid, for the two years
' next following, by virtue of the reception aforeſaid, held, whereby
' to the ſaid abbat in the foreſaid twenty four pounds he was bound.
' The ſame abbat hath often required the ſaid William to pay the
' ſaid mony for the lands aforeſaid, & the ſaid William hath not
' paid it him, but as yet hath refuſed to pay, whence he [the abbat]
' ſaith he is made worſe & endamaged to the value of an hundred
' ſhillings.   And therefore he brings his ſuit, &c. & produces a cer-
' tain writing, which atteſts the foreſaid debt & reception.   And Wil-
' liam came & owned, that he is bound to the ſaid abbat in the fore-
' ſaid twenty and four pounds.   Therefore it was allowed that the
' foreſaid abbat ſhould recover againſt him the debt aforeſaid, & his
' damages aforeſaid.   And the foreſaid William in pity, &c. & the
' ſame abbat remitted the damage ——— & the foreſaid writing was can-
' celled.'   Theſe pleadings were at Northampton, before Geoffry le
Scrop, Lambert de Trikingham, John de Cantebrigg, John Randolf,
John de Radenhale, & Thomas de Louthe the juſtices itinerantes there,
the monday next after the feaſt of All Saints, in the 3ᵈ. year of K.
E. the 3.   At the ſame time divers bridges & highways in this neighbourhood being gone to decay, broken down, or otherwiſe out of
repair, ' The jurats touching bridges & highways, ſay, that the bridge
' of Walcotforth, where is a common paſſage of men, foot, horſe,
' & carriages, from the town of Oundle to Staunford is thrown down
' & broke, ſo that in the winter ſeaſon hardly any body, without dan-
' ger of loſing his life, hath been able to paſs there; & that the peo-
' ple of Fodryngey & Naſſington ought to repair & maintain that bridge.

                                                    ' Therefore

' Therefore it is commanded the fherif to caufe to come before him
' fix honeft & lawful men of the towns aforefaid to fhew, &c. & the
' fame towns of Fodrynghey & Naffington in pity becaufe they have
' not before repaired, &c.   They fay alfo that the bridge of Bereford,
' where is a common way from Keteringe towards Staunford, is thrown
' down & broke to the very great danger of all paffengers; & the
' people of the towns of Bereford, Getyngton, & Newton Great &
' Little, ought to repair that bridge.   In the 4. E. 3. [a] at the earneft   4. E. 3.
' requeft of fome, the K. held a parliament at Winchefter, where,
' by procurement of the old Q. & Roger Mortimer, the E. of Kent
' & many other noble men & religious perfons, to wit, the pro-
' vincials of the white fryers & of the blacking preaching fryers &
' friar Richard Wilton, were accufed of confpiracie, touching (as it
' was faid) the deliverie of the kings father.   Which matter altho'
' it| were but devifed fantafie & a meere lie, yet the faid E. for cer-
' tain confeffions which he made, & for certain letters which were
' found about him, was there beheaded.   The other, to wit, the
' provincials of the Predicants & Carmelites, were banifhed; but
' the bifhop of London [Stephen Gravefend] was fet at libertie ;
' Robert de Taunton prieft, & fome certaine Carmelite fryers &
' predicants were condemed to perpetual prifon.' —— The fame year
E. Warenns farmers of the tolls & cuftoms at Staunford demanding
thirtol of carrs, horfes, & wagons paffing thro' Wyrthorp, Bernak,
& Wytering, all in the abbat of Burgs liberty, & not in the earls,
were thereupon prefented, and fined for the fame.   For faith the record. [b] ' The jurats of the hundred of the Neffe of Burg, touch-
' ing them who have taken unlawful *tolls*, &c. fay, that Thomas
' Rowe of Staunford and Thomas fon of Robert de Brotherhoufe are
' farmers of the E. of Warenn of Staunford, of the cuftoms & tolls
' to the forefaid town of Staunford belonging; by reafon of which
' farm they do come into this county, at Wyrthorp, Bernack, & Wyter-
' ing, & there take Turghftol of the carrs, horfes & carriages thro' the
' fame towns paffing, they know not by what warant.   Therefore it is
' commanded the fherif, &c.   Afterwards the fherif returned, that they
' were not to be found, but have voluntarily withdrawn themfelves.
' Wherefore they in pity, &c. & they were fined by the juftices each of
' them at half a marc. —— John the 1. E. Warenn lord of Stanford (having
granted the burgeffes of Stanford liberty to chufe themfelves an alderman *pur lour common governeur & juftifyer*, &c. which *alderman* fhould
be fworne before the E. or his fteward [c])   [d] ' K. Edw. the 3[d]. by
' his charter now confirmed the fayd grant of the faid John E Warenne

---

a Stow. p. 356.
b Ex placitis coram jufticiariis predictis
apud Northamptoniam itinerantibus.
  c See 4. E. 1. above.
  d Out of a MS. in my hands entitled,

' an abftract of feveral charters concerning
' the borough of Stanford; dated 11. June
' 1677. article the 4th. [which refers this to]
♪ 4. E. 3. pat. 2. m. 25.

' to the burgeffes of Stanford in fee.——[a] About this time Peter Sutton,
' a learned Francifcan of the grey fryers college in Oxford, was buried
' at Stanford.——Adam de Bootheby lord abbat of Burg, [b] in his eleventh
' year expended in prefents fent to the K. &. Q. at Walmisforde &
' Staunforde, 42. pounds.' The day the K. was at Stanford was Ap. 13.
   1332. for it appears '[c] that the K. then confirmed a former charter in
' favor of foreign merchants trading into England, which confirma-
Ap. 13. ' tion bares date at Stanford the faid 13. of April 1332.——In 1332.
1332. ' faith Bale[d], died John Burley (the Carme) at Stanford.' See an
5. E. 3. account of his character & works above[e]. Pits fays[f], ' he died an old man
' at Stanford, & was buried there among thofe of his own order in
' 1333' And Leland that, [g] ' he died at Stenoford, an emporium, or
7. E. 3. ' great mercat town in Lincolnfhire ; & was there buried.'——' In the 7. E. 3.
' Henry de Empyngham capellan of Staunford, gave to Richard de Pappele
' fifhmonger of Staunford one acre of arable land above the fee of the
' abbat of Burg, between the lands of the nuns of S. Michael on ei-
' ther fide, & abutting on the kings high-way north & on Burle-lound
' fouth. —— As alfo, three rods of arable land lying above the fee of the
' lord abbat of Burg, between the land of Thomas de Chefterton fouth, &
' the land of the hofpital of S. Giles north, & abutting on Burlefyk weft,
' & on the land of the nuns of S. Michael eaft. B. H.——[h] About this time
' Richard de Weryngton was rector of S. John Baptifts church at Staunford.
' [i] In this 7. of E. 3. the Scots making an infurrection againft Edw. Baillol
' their K. in regard he had done homage to the K. of England for that
' realm ; John the 2. E. Warenn [lord of Staunford] affifted Baillol in
' wafting a great part of that country ; & merited fo well of him for the
' many eminent fervices he had done, & the charges he had fuftained in
' that war ; that Baillol (with confent of the nobles then with him)
' gave him the earldom of Stratherne, forfeited by rebellion of Mali-
' fius E. of that county.——[k] John Foffour prior of S. Leonards without
' Stanford, was one of the compromifers, who (being at Durham) fome
' time within the ides of Oct. 1333. elected Robert de Grayftanes bi-
' fhop of that fee.' This John Foffour was afterwards himfelf prior of
   Durham.   He was fucceeded at S. Leonards by Robert de Hexham.

      III. I am now arrived at the beginning of thofe times, when the
   removing of the Oxford fcholars to Stanford made fo much noife, &
   in the end was the ruin of thefe hitherto quiet, well-governed, &
Nov. flourifhing fchools. For ' in Nov. 1333. faith Mr. Stow[l], divers ma-
1333. ' fters & fchollers of Oxford withdrew themfelves to Stanford without
' licenfe of the K. obtained on that behalf: whereat the K. being of-

a Stephens I. addit. Vol. to the Mon. p.   g Com. p. 355.
97. hift. Englifh Franc. p. 146.   h Ex regiftro quodam MS. apud Linc.
   b Ex hift. coenobii Burg. Cont. per ano-   Fol. 176. b.
nymum, p. 230.   i Baron. Vol. I. p. 81. b.
   c Rymers Foedera Vol. IV. p. 516.   k Ex ejufdem Roberti de Grayftanes hift.
   d in vita.   Dunelm. p. 762.
      Lib. IX. Parag. XXXIII.   l p. 360.
   f in vita.

                                                 ' fended,

Brazen-nose College Gate at Stanford.

' fended, did by proclamation utterly forbid & fuppreffed it.   For this remove in Nov. 1333.   Mr. Stow (in the margin of his book) quotes Avesbury.   And yet in that authors hiftory of Edw. the 3. publifhed by Mr. Hearne, I dont find the leaft tittle about it.   However, to be as particular in this affair, as all the evidence, I have yet met with, will enable me.   Thofe Oxford fcholars, who removed hither in November 1333. were not banifhed hence, as fome may think from Mr. Stow, by the kings proclamation in 1333. but on the contrary, followed by others of the fame univerfity, in May, 1334.   Thofe again, by others in June; & thofe again by others in July, the fame year.   For, faith the Oxford antiquary, Mr. Anthony Wood [a], ' I come now to the maf-
' ters & fcholars removing in the months of May, June & July, 1334.
' in great companies from Oxford to Stanford in Lincolnfhire, & there
' either beginning, or what feems more probable, reftoring an univer-
' fity.'   That they did not now begin this univerfity is evident from Mr. Woods own affertions & teftimonies elfewhere fet down [b].   Alfo that they did not now reftore this univerfity, will evidently appear by a confideration of all fuch matters relating to it, as I fhall here in-fert.   ' For their leaving Oxford, faith Mr. Wood [c], befides what
' other colors or excufes they could give it, they pretended certain
' differences arifen there among themfelves.   But whatever was the
' reafon, now was fulfilled the prophecy which Merlin, the Britifh
' Apollo, had, feveral ages before, declared would come to pafs:

' 𝕿𝖍𝖆𝖙 𝖋𝖙𝖚𝖔𝖎𝖔𝖚𝖘 𝖙𝖍𝖗𝖔𝖓𝖌 𝖜𝖍𝖎𝖈𝖍 Oxen-ford 𝖉𝖔𝖙𝖍 𝖈𝖍𝖊𝖗𝖎𝖋𝖍,

' 𝕴𝖓 𝕿𝖎𝖒𝖊 𝖙𝖔 𝖈𝖔𝖒𝖊 𝖙𝖍𝖊 Stony-ford 𝖋𝖍𝖆𝖑𝖑 𝖓𝖔𝖚𝖗𝖎𝖋𝖍.

' Camden indeed, & our Oxford antiquary Brian Twine, would have
' the original of the univerfity, or rather fchool at Stanford, attributed
' to fome differences broke out among the northern & fouthern ftudents
' at Oxford: affirming, that the former loft the victory, whereupon
' they immediately removed to Stanford, & taught there.   But no time
' do they put down when thefe things happened.'   Camden does not fay indeed what month or year thefe things happened in; but then tells us they chanced in Edw. the 3[ds]. time.   His words may be thus rendered.   [d] ' In the reign of Edw. the 3. was begun here an univer-
' fity & profeffion of good letters, which the people of the town ac-
' count their chiefeft glory.   For at what time there broke out great dif-
' turbances at Oxford between the northern & fouthern ftudents, a
' great number of ftudents came hither; but foon after returning to
' Oxford, as quickly put an end, as they gave a beginning, to this
' rifing univerfity.   After which it was provided by oath, that no
' Oxford man fhould publickly profefs at Stanford.'   By the way, as one monument of this univerfity at Stanford, I infert here a fculpture of Brazen-nofe college gate.   As to the college it felf, I fhall dif-courfe of that by & by.   Mr. Selden, fpeaking of the differences be-

---

a Antiq. Ox. fub anno 1334.   c Ant. Oxon. ut fupra.
b Videfis fub annis 1290. 1309. fupra.   d in Corit.

tween the northern & southern scholars at Oxford, tells us, [a] that
' White of Basingstoke otherwise guesses at the cause of this dif-
' ference, making it the Pelagian heresie, & of more antient time, but
' erronously. Unto this, saith he, refer that supposed prophecy of
' Merlin.

' *Doctrine studium quod nunc viget ad* vada boum,
' *Ante finem secli celebrabitur ad* vada saxi.

' Richard White of Basingstoke (saith Mr. Wood [b]) who was of New
' college, with whom agrees Londinensis, relates, that the university
' of Cambridge being infected with the Pelagian heresie many [of the
scholars] ' fled to Chester, & there erected a school or university of
' about 200 Philosophers. Afterwards they removed to Stanford, &
' the poison of that heresie spreading it self among them there like-
' wise, not a few of the Oxford scholars, allured with the novelty of
' the opinion, came over to the same place, & joyned them. But
' White sets down no time for this remove.' I have already given an
account of the suppression of a supposed university at Stanford for
the Pelagian heresie, &c. about the year 605 [c]. However if ever the
university of Cambridge was infected with that heresie, & any of her
sons removed on that account to Chester, & thence to Stanford, it
must surely be long after the year 605. & probably (for the reasons
above alledged [d]) the 46. H. 3. was the very year. As for the Oxford mens
removing hither in 1333, & 1334. Mr. Wood, after having told us what
Camden says above, & himself concurring partly with White & partly
with Camden about that flight, as before touched, goes on. ' I do
' not believe the account of these mens leaving Oxford for peace sake,
' on the occasions by them set down, is in the least to be rejected ;
' altho' neither any charters of our university, or other antient writ-
' ing which I know of, agree with the relation. For this is certain,
' there were animosities among the scholars at this very time. This is
' evident by what appears in the complaints drawn against Merton col-
' lege in particular by the church of Durham, wherein is set forth,
' that the said college, to keep up a more perfect friendship with the
' rest of the university, refused to chuse the northern students into their
' fellowships, on the same level with the southern.' Here I believe
Mr. Wood has hit upon one good reason for this remove, many of
the Oxford men, who now made the most eminent figure at Stanford,
being of Merton college. What confirms this is, that as the monks of
Durham were complainants, there is no place whither they would sooner
carry their novices & students than to Stanford, where they had such
a noble priory of their own as S. Leonards ready to receive them, &
where their very next neighbours were the white friers, the fathers
of which order took so much pains in reading lectures in this little
academy. Besides, Stanford, as it is so much nearer Durham than

---

a Notes on Polyolb. p. 256
b sub anno 1334.

c Lib. I. Parag. XXXIX.
d See Lib. VIII. Par. XXIX. supra.

3

Oxford, was, upon this account likewise, abundantly more convenient for the reſt of their friends there.   However as Mr. Wood ſays, [a] ' Whe-
' ther the Oxford men betook themſelves to Stanford on account of
' ſome private contentions among themſelves at home; or, whether it
' happened thro' the deſire they were poſſeſſed with, of thereby ful-
' filling what Merlin had before ſo long ago predicted (for as much
' as, in the Kings letters, they are ſaid to have laid hold of theſe
' colors, or occaſions for their remove) there they ſtayed not a few
' months, reading lectures, holding diſputations, & receiving under
' their diſcipline & care much youth from the neighbouring parts.
' At length the univerſity of Oxford, not unwiſely conſidering what a
' great diſadvantage this would be to their univerſity, unleſs timely
' prevented; humbly beſought the K. that he would put an end to
' this new univerſity, & diſſolve it, by compelling the ſtudents to re-
' turn to their mother, Oxford.   In thoſe letters, as Londinenſis tells
' us more at large [b], Robert Stratford, then chancellor of the univer-
' ſity of Oxford (& afterwards of England) & the congregation of maſters
' beſought the K. that he would vouchſafe to write to pope Benedict
' the 12. by all means to prohibit the hurtful & peſtiferous & ſo new
' concourſe of their ſcholars to Stanford under pretence of holding
' ſchools there, the ſame being both a hindrance to their univerſity in
' particular, as well as a general nurſery to the diviſions of the whole
' kingdom.   Which concourſe, certain of their univerſity (whom it
' had raiſed from the duſt to be men, & adorned with many honors,
' having raſhly divided themſelves from the body of their mother, &
' not ſo contented) had begun, & thereby did allure & draw over many
' others from all parts to joyn them.'   I dont find the K. wrote to the
pope about this affair.   His letter to John de Trehampton ſherif of Lincoln rather argues that he took that matter into his own hands : which letter is thus worded.   [c] ' The K. to the high ſherif of Lincoln,
' greeting.   Whereas it is given us to underſtand, that divers maſters
' & ſcholars of our univerſity of Oxford, under color of certain diſ-
' ſenſions, in the univerſity aforeſaid, lately (as is ſaid) ariſen, & other
' excuſes pretended, themſelves, from the ſame univerſity withdrawing,
' do preſume to ſettle at the town of Staunford, & there to hold ſtudy,
' & exerciſe ſcholaſtic acts, our aſſent or licenſe not in the leaſt ob-
' tained; which, if it ſhould be ſuffered, would manifeſtly turn, not
' only to the contempt & diſhonor of us, but alſo to the diſperſion
' of our univerſity aforeſaid; we not being minded, that ſchools or
' ſtudies ſhould in any ſort be any where held within our kingdom,
' ſave than in places where there are now univerſities; to you, firmly
' injoyning, command, that, unto the foreſaid town of Staunford
' you perſonally repair, & there, & elſewhere, within your juriſdiction,

Aug. 2.

---

a ſub anno 1334.   c Rymers Foedera. Vol. p.
b p. 269, 270.

' where

' where you fhall fee it expedient, on our part caufe it to be publick.
' ly proclaimed & forbidden, that none, under confifcation of all their
' goods, elfewhere, than in our univerfities aforefaid, in any fort pre-
' fume to hold ftudies, or exercife fcholaftic acts; and that forthwith,
' under your feal you diftinctly & openly fignifie unto us, in our court of
' Chancery, the names of them, whom, after proclamation & inhibition as
' aforefaid, you fhall find doing the contrary. For we will, as it be-
' comes us, that fpeedy juftice be adminiftred to all & every, who
' touching violences or injuries, at the faid town of Oxford done, be-
' fore our juftices there for this purpofe efpecially deputed, fhall be
' willing to make known their complaints. Witnefs the K. at Wynde-
' for, the fecond day of Auguft. By the K. & council. A like writ,
' *mutatis mutandis*, was directed to the major & bailifs of the kings
' town of Oxford, attefted as above, & done alfo by the K. & coun-
' cil.' Mr. Wood, (without taking notice of the kings letters of the
2ᵈ. of Auguft, as above) goes on. ' Whereupon by his letters bear-

Aug. 11. ' ing date the 11ᵗʰ. of Auguft, & directed to the major & bailifs
' of Oxford, the K. required them to make publick proclamation in
' the town of Oxford, that it was his princely will & pleafure that
' the mafters & fcholars refiding at Stanford, & exercifing univerfity
' difcipline there, fhould return to Oxford, on pain of having their
' goods confifcated for their neglect. Thefe things being done, & the
' fcholars not yet returning, the high fherif of Lincolnfhire, being
' again thereunto required by a 2ᵈ. letter from the K. went to Stan-
' ford, & there proclaimed, that whoever did not immediately re-
' turn to Oxford, fhould have all his books & effects directly confif-
' cated. Upon this, many of them returned, altho' not a few ftayed
' almoft the whole year out at Stanford; both ftudying themfelves, &
' inftructing their auditors, in the liberal arts after the manner of an
' univerfity.

IV. The order of time now leads me to fpeak of fome other matters.
Particularly, Richard Bliton (fometime provincial of the Englifh Carmes,
to which office he was elected at Stanford in 1319.) died, as Pits fays[a],
in 1334. But Bale affirms[a], that he lived till 1361. under which year
fee more of him. ' Thomas, fon of Robert de Stapelford, gave to
' Richard de Hawville of Staunford, the weftern moiety of one mef-
' fuage fituate on Cleymont, between a tenement of Hugh le Rede
' weft, & the other moiety on the eaft part; together with the rever-
' fion of the other moiety. Witnefses, Richard de Tyddifwel, Roger
' le Skanclerc, burgefses of Staunford, & others. Given at Staunford

Nov. 29. ' the 8. of K. E. the 3ᵈ. B. H.' Nov. 29. died brother Thomas de
Stanford, warden of S. Michaels priory without Stanford; on whofe
death Adam de Boothby lord abbat of Burg & the convent of that
place, prefented brother William de Gretford, one of their own monks,

a in vita.

2

to that poft.   But, the bifhop of Lincoln Henry Burwafh being out of
the kingdom, his officers acted with great caution, &, as it fhould feem,
would not admit the faid William de Gretford, 'till they had firft
enquired into the faid abbat & convents title ; in order to which Jan. 9. Jan. 9.
John Longefper de Ragehill archdeacon of *Stow* & the bifhops vicar
general, wrote to mafter archdeacon of Lincolns official, acquainting
him that the abbat & convent of Burg had prefented the faid William,
& commanded him therefore to enquire whether the faid wardenfhip
was really vacant, & where, when, & how it became fo ; as alfo into
the character of the faid William, & other matters : whofe letter may
be thus englifhed.   a ' John Longefper de Ragehill, archdeacon of Stow,
' vicar general of the venerable father lord Henry by the grace of
' God Bp. of Lincoln (himfelf being in parts remote) to our beloved
' in Chrift the official of mafter archdeacon of Lincoln, health in the
' author of health.   Adam abbat of Burg & the convent of the fame
' place, do prefent to the faid venerable father, brother William de
' Gretford their fellow-monk, to the wardenfhip of the priory of the
' nuns of S. Michael without Stanford in the diocefe of Lincoln, va-
' cant, as is faid.   Wherefore to you we command, how that as well
' about the vacancy of the faid wardenfhip (to wit, whether it be va-
' cant, & if fo, where, when, & how it hath come to be vacant) as of
' the prefenters & perfon laft prefented unto the fame, as alfo about
' the perfon of [William now] prefented, and in what, or which or-
' ders he hath been admitted, & touching other articles accuftomed, in
' a full chapter of the place to be celebrated, calling thofe who ought
' to be called, ye make diligent inquifition.   And of the days of the
' receipt of the prefents, & of the inquifition on this part made, &
' what ye fhall act in the premiffes, the faid father, us, or our
' commiffary (when on the part of the faid prefented ye fhall be
' about this matter lawfully required) ye fhall certifie by your let-
' ters fealed, a feries of thefe things, & of the inquifition aforefaid,
' together with the number & names of the inquifitors more at large
' containing.   Given at Lincoln, under the feal of the faid venerable fa-
' ther, which we have at hand, the 5th of the ides of January, 1334.'
On Jan. 11. the abbat & convent of Burg prefented, by a fecond in- Jan. 11.
ftrument as I take it, William de Gretford abovementioned to the
priory of S. Michael without Stanford; which prefentation is thus
worded.   b ' To the reverend father in Chrift, lord Henry by the
' grace of God bifhop of Lincoln, his humble & devoted in Chrift,
' Adam by gift of the fame grace abbat of Burg & the convent
' of the fame place, greeting, & with all reverence the obedience due
' & devoted.   To your reverend fatherhood we prefent brother Wil-
' liam de Gretford our fellow-monk to the wardenfhip of the priory
' of the nuns of S. Michael without Stanford, vacant, & unto our

a Ex Codicis MS. in Bib. Cott. fub Imagine Vefp. E. XXI. Fol. 61.   b id. ib.

' prefentation

' prefentation belonging; humbly fupplicating & devoutly how that
' him brother William unto the faid wardenfhip ye would pleafe to
' admit & inftitute in the fame, the cure, if it pleafe you, of the
' priory remembred to the fame committing; faving to us & our fuc-
' ceffors the jurifdiction in the fame according to the manner accuf-
' tomed, & obedience firft canonically paid.   In witnefs whereof to
' the prefents we have put to our feals.   Given at Burg the 3ᵈ of
' the ides of Jan. 1334.'   Upon the fame 11ᵗʰ of January John Longefper above-mentioned, the bifhop of Lincolns vicar general, by an inftrument under the faid bifhops feal, made Simon de Iflep the faid bifhops official, his proctor to inftitute the forefaid William de Gretford
into the wardenfhip of the faid priory of S. Michael; he the faid Simon
de Iflep forbearing neverthelefs from fo doing, 'till after return of an
inquifition by the faid John Longefper appointed to be made at Stanford by the dean & chapter of that place, touching the articles above
ordered to be enquired into, & no juft caufe then appearing to ftay
inftitution.   His letter to the faid Simon de Iflep is thus expreffed.
' ᵃ To the reverend man, mafter Simon de Iflep, official of Lincoln,
' John Longefper, vicar general of the venerable father lord Henry by
' the grace of God bifhop of Lincoln (himfelf being in remote parts)
' health in the author of health.   Adam abbat of Burg & the con-
' vent of the fame place, have prefented to the faid venerable father,
' William de Gretford their fellow-monk, to the wardenfhip of the
' houfe of S. Michael without Stanford in the diocefe of Lincoln, va-
' cant, as is faid.   And whereas touching the vacation of the faid war-
' denfhip, after the accuftomed manner, we had commanded to be
' enquired, to receive certificate of this fort of inquifition, & examine
' the fame, & (if by inquifition of this fort, ye fhall find, touching
' canonical inftitutes or other reafonable caufe, which may require to
' let him, altogether nothing to object to the fame prefented) to ad-
' mit the fame brother William, or his proctor in his name, unto the
' wardenfhip aforefaid, & the warden (faving, in all things, the epifco-
' pal dues & dignity of the church of Lincoln; likewife to the prio-
' refs of the houfe aforefaid thofe things which to her of old belong-
' ed) canonically to inftitute in the fame, & the reft all & every the
' things to be done & difpatched which in the faid bufinefs fhall be
' neceffary, or alfo opportune, or of old have been accuftomed to be
' done, to you our office & place we commit, with power of cano-
' nical coercion.   Given at Lincoln, under the feal of the faid father,
' which we have at hand, the 3ᵈ of the ides of January, 1334.'   Mafter archdeacon of Lincolns official, on receipt of the bifhop of Lincolns
vicar generals mandate requiring him fo to do, fent his injunction to
the dean of Stanford to call a chapter of his clergy, & certifie, by inquifition of the fame, how matters ftood with relation to the patro-

ᵃ id. fol. 62.

nage

nage of the wardenſhip of the priory of S. Michael; the return of
which inquiſition is, in my author, thus entred. [a] ‘ Memorandum,
‘ that the mandate aforeſaid was, by the official of maſter archdeacon
‘ of Lincoln, directed to the dean of Stanford, who (after the common
‘ greeting premiſed) certified in theſe words. Therefore, by virtue of Jan. 18.
‘ this mandate, in the church of S. Martin at Stanford, in a full chapter
‘ of the place, calling thoſe who ought to be called, according to law
‘ touching the vacancy of the ſaid wardenſhip & other articles aboveſaid,
‘ I have made diligent inquiſition; to wit, by Sir Thomas rector of the
‘ church of S. Paul, & maſter Roger rector of the church of S. Peter, &
‘ Robert Guſtard rector of the church of the bleſſed Mary near the bridge,
‘ Sir Peter vicar of the church of S. Martin, & Sir William vicar of
‘ All Saints in the mercat place at Stanford, & Sir Robert vicar of the
‘ church of S. Andrew at Stanford. And the inquiſition ſays, that the
‘ ſaid wardenſhip is vacant, & began to be vacant on the eve of S.
‘ Andrew the apoſtle laſt paſt, by the death of brother Thomas de Stan-
‘ ford a monk of Burg the warden, the which Thomas, on the ſaid
‘ day, in the ſaid priory, departed this life. The religious men the
‘ abbat of Burg & the convent of the ſame place, are the true patrons
‘ & true preſenters to the ſaid wardenſhip, & the laſt time preſented
‘ the ſaid Thomas a monk of Burg unto the ſame. Moreover the
‘ ſaid perſon to the ſame preſented is a man, a religious monk of Burg
‘ aforeſaid, & is a man of good life & honeſt converſation, & is or-
‘ dained in three holy orders. And the ſaid wardenſhip is not diſput-
‘ ed, nor penſioned. All which to you I ſignifie by my letters cloſed
‘ with the ſeal of my office munited. Given at Stanford the 15. of
‘ the Kalends of Feb. in the year of our Lord abovementioned.’ The
next day, to wit Jan. 19. the ſaid William de Gretford having his way Jan. 19.
thus perfectly cleared for him thro’ the dean of Stanfords above-written
teſtimonial, by the following inſtrument appointed maſter John Trivet
clerc his proctor to be inſtituted & inducted for him. [b] ‘ Be it known
‘ to all by theſe preſents, that I brother William de Gretforde, monk
‘ of Burg, of the order of S. Benedict, & dioceſe of Lincoln, to the
‘ wardenſhip of the priory of the nuns of S. Michael without Stan-
‘ ford, to the venerable father lord Henry by the grace of God bi-
‘ ſhop of Lincoln, by the venerable & religious man lord Adam by
‘ divine permiſſion of the ſaid monaſtery abbat & the convent of the
‘ ſame place, preſented; the diſcreet man maſter John Trivet clerc,
‘ my true & lawful proctor, alſo agent of the buſineſs & eſpecial meſ-
‘ ſenger, do make, ordain, & appoint by the preſents: giving & grant-
‘ ing to him full & free power, alſo mandate eſpecial & final, of pro-
‘ ſecuting the foreſaid preſentation (as premiſed) of me made, before
‘ the foreſaid venerable father, or his commiſſary on this part deputed
‘ or to be deputed, for me & in my name; & of demanding, receiv-

a id fol. 63.   b id. fol. 61.

‘ ing,

' ing, & taking canonical inftitution, as alfo induction into the cor-
' poral poffeffion of the wardenfhip aforefaid, with all its rights &
' appurtenances whatfoever; & of taking the oath of obedience & any
' other whatfoever lawful oath on my foul, in proxy as above; alfo
' of doing, exercifing, & difpatching all other & fingular the things,
' which in the premiffes, & in any of the premiffes, fhall be necefla-
' ry or likewife convenient; alfo thofe things which are required for
' final difpatch of the forefaid bufinefs, & which I my felf ought to
' do, if I had been perfonally prefent; & (if the mandates fo require)
' to hold efpecial, ratified, obligatory, & firm in all times, whatfoever
' by my proctor fhall be done & acted in the premiffes, or he doth
' alfo procure. In witnefs whereof I have procured the feal of the
' forefaid lord abbat to be put to thefe prefents. Given at Burg, the
Jan. 23. ' 14. of the Kalends of Feb. 1334.' Four days after, to wit Jan. 23.
the bifhop of Lincolns official inftituted the faid William de Gretford
(by his proctor I fuppofe) at Lincoln to the faid wardenfhip of the
priory of S. Michael; of whofe inftitution the inftrument may be thus
englifhed. a ' Simon de Iflep, official for the diocefe of Lincoln, com-
' miffary on this part to the venerable father lord Henry by the grace
' of God bifhop of Lincoln, to his beloved in Chrift brother William
' de Gretford, monk of Burg, of the order of S. Bennet, health in the
' author of health. To the wardenfhip of the houfe of S. Michael
' without Stanford, unto which, by the reverend & religious man lord
' Adam, by divine permiffion, abbat of the monaftery aforefaid, & the
' convent of the fame place, to the venerable father aforefaid, you
' ftand prefented; by authority of the fame father, to us on this part
' efpecially committed, we admit & inftitute you warden in the fame,
' to you more fully committing the care & adminiftration of the faid
' houfe, & of the goods of the fame; faving in all things the epifco-
' pal dues & dignity of the church of Lincoln; alfo to the priorefs
' of the houfe aforefaid thofe things which unto her do of old be-
' long. Given at Lincoln, the 10th of the Kal. of Feb. 1334.

V. The very next thing inferted in the Cotton MS. from whence
thefe laft matters were taken is a copy of the petition of the Oxford
fcholars now ftudying at Stanford, fetting forth the true reafons of
their remove, & praying the kings leave to continue here. I fhall only
premife, this petition hath no date; but William de Gretfords inftitution to the priory of S. Michael ftanding, as above, immediately before
it, & being dated the 10. of the Kal. of Feb. (that is to fay, Jan. 23.)
we may fuppofe, by that, & what other matters follow in thefe collections, that the faid petition was wrote upon, or foon after the faid
23. of January: which in Englifh take as follows. b ' To our lord

3   the

---

a id. fol 62.
b A noftre feignieur le Roy, & a fon con-
fail, prient les clers demorauntz en la ville
de Staunford, qe come per refoun de plu-
fours debatz, concels, & melles qels long
temps ont efte, & uncore font, en la univer-
fite de Oxenford, donc grantz damages, perils, morts, mordres, maihemes, & robberies
fovent

' the K. & to his council, pray the clerc's refiding in the town of
' Staunford, that, whereas, by reafon of many debates, counfels, &
' differences which long time have been, & ftill are in the univerfity
' of Oxenforde, whereby great damages, perils, deaths, murders, maims,
' & robberies oftentimes have happened, for which, in hopes of the
' good grace of our lord the K. they have retreated out of the faid
' town of Oxenford to the town of Staunford, to ftudy & profit more
' in quiet & in peace than they were wont to do, by permiffion of
' the noble man John E. of Waren; that it would pleafe our lord the
' K. to fuffer the faid clerc's for the future (which are his liege peo-
' ple) to continue in the faid town of Staunford under his protecti-
' on, as people of all manner of profeffions of what condition foever,
' of the liegeance of our lord the K. may remain in any lordfhip, by
' leave of the king.' ᵃ ' Thefe proceedings again alarmed the Oxonians,
' who forefaw, that, unlefs fome remedy was fpeedily found out, the
' number of thefe deferters, which was of late fo much reduced, would
' very probably in a little time increafe to as great a concourfe as ever;
' whereupon they again betook themfelves to the K. & the K. at their
' requeft, wrote to William Truffel to fee the faid fcholars drove out
' of Stanford.' Mr. Rymer gives us the kings letter to the faid Truffel at large, which in Englifh may be read as follows ᵇ. ' The K. to
' his beloved & faithful William Truffel greeting. Know ye that,
' whereas lately it being given us to underftand, that divers mafters
' & fcholars of our univerfity of Oxford, under color of certain dif-
' fentions, in the univerfity aforefaid, lately, as was faid, arifen, & other
' excufes pretended; themfelves, from the fame univerfity withdraw-
' ing, have prefumed at the town of Staunford to fettle, & there to
' hold ftudy, & exercife fcholaftic acts, our affent or licenfe not in
' the leaft required; we commanded our high fherif of Lincoln, that
' as well in the forefaid town of Staunford as elfewhere in his jurif-
' diction where he fhould fee it neceffary, on our part he fhould caufe
' it to be publickly proclaimed & forbid, that none, under confifca-
' tion of all their goods, elfewhere, than in places where be now uni-
' verfities, fhould in any fort prefume to hold ftudy or exercife fcho-
' laftic acts. And afterwards underftanding, that certain, as well ma-
' fters as fcholars, our proclamation & inhibition aforefaid not refpect-
' ing, but them more truly defpifing, ftudy, in the faid town of Staun-
' ford, after thofe our proclamation & inhibition, have held, & acts
' fcholaftic exercifed, in defiance & contempt of us, & alfo to the manifeft

Mar. 28.
8. E. 3

---

fovent foiz font avenuz par quoi en efpoir
de la bone grace noftre feigneur le Roy,
ils fe font retretz hors de la dite ville de Oxenford, vers la ville de Staunford, a eftudier
& proficer plus en quiete & en pees, qils ne
foleient faire par foeffraunce le noble homme
Johan counte de Garen, qil plefe a noftre
feignieur le Roy foeffrer le dites clers de puis,
quils fount ces liges gentz, a demorer en la

dite ville de Staunford fouch fa proteccioun
q gentz de touz maners de meftiers de quele
condicioun qil foient de la ligaunce noftre
feignieur le Roy puiffent demorer en chefqune
feignurie par conge du Roy. id. ib. b.
   a Wood, fub anno 1334.
   b Foedera, Vol. IV. p. 621. e clauf. 8. E. 3.
m. 17. dorf.

' difperfion

' difperfion of our univerfity of Oxford; we again commanded our
' high fherif aforefaid, firmly enjoyning, that unto the fame town of
' Staunford in his own proper perfon he fhould repair, & the faid ma-
' fters & fcholars there being on our part ftrictly prohibit, that they
' might not prefume to hold there any ftudy, or exercife any acts fcho-
' laftic, under confifcation of all their goods, to be confifcated to us.
' And that if he fhould find any, after our inhibition by himfelf fo
' made, doing the contrary; then their books, & other their goods,
' found in the town aforefaid, he fhould without delay caufe to be
' feifed into our hands, & them fafely & without any embezzlement
' to be kept, until otherwife thereof we fhould think good to
' be difpofed. Alfo it being now given us to underftand, that the ma-
' fters & fcholars, in the fame town of Staunford, after our procla-
' mation & inhibition aforefaid, have exercifed acts fcholaftic, & daily
' to exercife do not defift: And that the fame high fherif our man-
' date aforefaid, according to the force & form of the fame, hath
' not, as he ought, executed, whence we are, not without caufe very
' much incenfed & difturbed; we, not being minded, the premiffes fhould
' thus, under diffimulation, pafs unpunifhed, have affigned you, on
' our part, to make inhibition of this fort to the forenamed mafters
' & fcholars, in the forefaid town of Staunford abiding (to wit, that
' they prefume not to hold any ftudy, or exercife acts fcholaftic there,
' under confifcation abovefaid) & to fatisfie us diftinctly & openly,
' with all the fpeed wherewith it can be done, of the names of the
' mafters & fcholars, whom, after our inhibition aforefaid, to them
' by you made, ye fhall find doing the contrary, that for punifh-
' ment of the fame we may on this part caufe farther to be done,
' as with advice of our council we fhall fee expedient. And there-
' fore we command you, that unto the forefaid town of Staunford
' you perfonally repair, & all & every the premiffes do & fulfil, in
' form aforefaid. We have alfo commanded our high fherif aforefaid,
' that he affift, obey, & attend you in difpatching the premiffes. For
' we will that to all & every perfons or perfon, touching violences or
' injuries, to them at the faid town of Oxford done, before our juftices
' thither for this purpofe efpecially deputed, willing to make known
' their complaints, fpeedy juftice be done. In witnefs whereof, &c.
' Witnefs the K. at Notyngham, the 28. of march. By him the K. &
' council.—William Truffel & the high fherif, as Mr. Wood proceeds[a],
' did as they were commanded, & ftayed there 'till the univerfity men
' were turned out of town; but to very little purpofe: for as foon as
' they were likewife departed, the ftudents perfuaded by the burghers,
' flew back, & renewed their former difcipline for feveral months.
' Upon this, continues Mr. Wood[a], the K. perceiving he muft go ano-
' ther way to gain his point, directed a commiffion of enquiry to exa-

a fub anno 1334.

2   ' mine

' mine into the names of the faid fcholars at Staunford, which the
' commiffioners were alfo to remit to him, & to fee likewife their
' books & goods immediately feifed & confifcated to the kings ufe.'
' By the way. ᵃ About midfummer the K. came with his army to New-
' caftle upon Tine, whither came to him [Baillol] the K. of Scots. And
' there order was taken that the K. of England fhould paffe to Carleile,
' & on the xij. of July enter Scotland. And that the K. of Scots, the
' E. of Surrey [lord of Stanford] & others, with their retinues fhould
' go to Barwike, & there enter the fame day. And as it was appoint-
' ed fo it was put in practice. For both the Kings the fame day en-
' tring Scotland, paffed forward without refiftance, wafting & brenning
' all the countreys, on this fide & beyond the Scottifh fea.'——On wed-
' nefday after the feaft of S. James, faith Mr. Wood ᵇ, an inquifition
' was taken at Stanford before the forefaid William Truffel, & a lift
' brought in of all their names, who, after it had been fo often for-
' bid by the kings exprefs commands, had ftayed at Stanford, & exer-
' cifed univerfity difcipline there. Their names were, mafter William
' de Barnebey, mafter Thomas de Kendale, mafter Thomas de Hotofte,
' mafter John de Whitwell, mafter William de Robey, mafter Robert
' de Barton, mafter Hugh de Lincoln, mafter William de Donelfchawe,
' mafter Simon de Bekyngham, mafter Peter de Auleby, mafter John
' de Stockton, mafter Thomas de Efton, mafter Peter rector of S. Pe-
' ters in Stanford, mafter John de Bolton, mafter Thomas de la Mare,
' mafter John de Ramifton, mafter Robert Bernard, William le bat-
' chelaur, Sir John Blandolfe, rector of the church of Scottes by Gran-
' tham, Sir Henry, rector of Tinwell, Sir Robert of Bourle, vicar of
' S. Andrews in Stanford, Sir Henry vicar of All Saints, on the other
' fide of Stanford bridge [to wit, in Northamptonfhire] Sir Richard,
' rector of S. Georges in Stanford; William de Everwickes [York-
' fhire] Ralph de Acherche, Walter de Notyngham, John de Lincoln,
' Walter de Trekyngham, John de Kirbye-Beliers, Sir Thomas rector
' of Stanhope, John de Twyfelyngton, Hugh de Suttewel, Robert de
' Hefelbethe, John de Kelemerfhe, Philip, *obfonator eneafenfis*, manci-
' ple of Brafen-nofe, in Stanford, John de Schetlanger, John fon of
' Gilbert de Foderinghey, John fon of Geoffry de Bernake.' In all
feventeen mafters, one bachelaur, fix parifh priefts, & 14 other ftudents. There were more at firft, but it may be remembred, many of
them, as Mr. Wood tells us above, were before returned. Here is alfo
no mention of any perfons belonging to any monafteries in & about
Stanford, whereof not a few read & attended the lectures & difputations here at this time. Stanford was their home, & fo they could not
be commanded to return to Oxford. But as it was common in thefe
times for divers parifh priefts to refide at Oxford, fo here we find feveral even of this town remanded thither; in which cafe their cures,

July 12.
1335.
9. E. 3.

a Hol. p. 898. a.   b ut fupra.

                                                              I fuppofe,

I suppose, were supplied by their capellans.   But to proceed. ' These,
' saith Mr. Wood[a], who appear to be not much less than forty, were
' the chief; besides which were returned many other names of servants
' & scholars of the lower order, who, in like manner with the bove
' mentioned, were punished with loss of goods & imprisonment, & at
' length remanded to Oxford.   And whereas master H. de R. as appears
' by a letter directed to the chancellor & masters of Oxford, was found
' to be the chief ringleader & encourager of the scholars in dispersing
' themselves from Oxford, & removing to Stanford; besides, striking out
' his name, & confiscating his goods, he was punished with ecclesiasti-
' cal censures, & other grievous fines.'   This master H. de R. was undoubtedly a considerable person, & its pity therefore but we knew
the rest of his name as well as the two first letters.   Many complaints have been raised against the editor & translators of Mr. Woods
history of the university of Oxford.   Some by the author himself[b].
How justly I care not to say.   But here seems to be room for a very
great one.   For first the name of this remarkable person is not printed
(as it ought to have been, & I believe yet might be) at length (if a
sight could be had of the authors papers.)   Secondly, a false reference
is made in the notes, pointing out another place where we might have
expected his name should have been found at length, & no such passage, as referred to, occurs.   And thirdly, no notice is taken of this
blunder, or design (for which it is I cannot say, tho' I vehemently suspect the last) in the *errata* at the end of the book.   But to proceed.
Mr. Selden speaking of the university at Stanford, & rejecting the story
of Bladud, writes ' [c] of later time that profession of learning was there
[at Stanford] ' is frequent.   For, when thro' discording parts among
' the scholars (reigning Ed. III.) a division in Oxford was into the nor-
' therne & southerne faction, the northerne (before under Hen. III.
' also was the like to Northampton) made secession to Stamford, and
' there profest, until upon humble suite by Robert of Stratford, chan-
' celor of Oxford, the K. by edict, *& his own presence*, prohibited them.'
By this passage it should seem the K. himself was forced to come to Stanford about this business, but I no where else meet with such an assertion.   However it is probably very true.   For it appears by all accounts, that the scholars were with the utmost difficulty prevailed on
to return.   Besides confiscating their books & effects as above, ' likewise
' left there should ever be any danger (saith Mr. Wood) of such a de-
' sertion for the future, the university of Oxford passed a statute (which
' was also lately put into their new book of statutes printed there in
' 1634. Tit. 9. Sect. 6.) that whoever should take a degree at Oxford,
' among other articles, should bind himself by oath, neither to read
' himself, or be present at the reading of, any lectures in Stanford af-
' ter the manner of an university, seminary, or public college.'   Now,

a ut supra.   & his preface to the Antiq. Oxon.
b See his life of bishop Fell in his Athenæ,   c Notes on polyolb. p. 123.

2   tho'

tho' Mr. Wood is of opinion that the above prophecy of Merlin, was, at this remove, fully accomplished; yet, by insisting on this oath, & inserting it in the new edition of their statutes (which, if I mistake not, were revised by archbishop Laud) some members of that university did formerly (if none do now) seem to dissent from his judgment, & fearing it is not, by this cautionary oath contend to prevent it.   However all this had been probably to little purpose, if the university of Cambridge, to oblige the Oxonians, or perhaps seeing their own in their danger, had not also made a statute much to the same purpose with that above.   For, as Londinensis addresses the Oxonians [a], ' when you ' your selves alone were not able to cure this evil [the remove to Stanford] ' without the Cantabrigians assistance; they made a conspi- ' racy for your welfare, & in conferring degrees, by public consent ' & decree of the whole university, it hath been for many ages en- ' acted, for none either to take a degree, or read publickly out of ' Cambridge, elsewhere than at Oxford.   The words of which statute ' be these.   They shall also swear, that out of this university they will ' no where else in England, save at Oxford, commence in any faculty; ' or their readings solemnly resume; or consent, that any person, com- ' mencing elsewhere in England, here be had for a master in that fa- ' culty.'   Give me leave to add here, (from a pamphlet wrote by an unknown Gent. who was bred a dissenter, but afterwards became a minister of the church of England) this very singular passage.   ' I have ' almost in the crowd (says he [b]) forgot one thing very remarkable [among the teachers in dissenting academies] ' 'tis their *salvo* for their ' oath in the university, when they engage not to take pupils, read ' lectures, &c.   I have seen a MS. handed about amongst us in ex- ' plication of this oath, which those in this employment have been ' often accused for the breach of.   The main things I remember they ' insist on, are those words wherein they plead the force of the oath ' lies; that they are not to read lectures, &c. *tanquam in Academia*; ' that is, say they, in such a manner as is done in the university, tak- ' ing & giving degrees in opposition thereto, as was once attempted ' for some years at Stanford (mentioned in the oath) which they plead ' is a direction or key to the sense thereof.'   An equivocation so pretty, that I believe few Jesuits themselves can produce a finer.

VI. Come we now to the colleges.   ' As for what relates to the ' halls & inns at Stanford for reception of scholars, it appears (saith Mr. ' Wood [c]) that there were not a few.   Of which (saith he) the chief, ' & most antient, I believe, was that which belonged to the convent ' of Sempringham.'   Here I cannot concur with Mr. Wood, that Sem- pringham hall at Stanford was either the chief or most antient col-

a p. 357.
b Letter from a country divine to his friend in London concerning the education of dis- senters in their private academies, &c. 4°.

Lond. 1704. printed for R. Clavel & R. Knaplock. p. 8.
c ut supra.

lege

lege or inn of this little univerſity. The colleges, halls, or inns at Stanford (call them which you pleaſe) as far as I can gather, were of three ſorts: & under thoſe three ſorts, according to my notion, they may be all thus ranged in point of antiquity. I. General colleges, halls, or inns, opened to all comers, who inclined to ſtudy here at their own, or relations, expence. Of this ſort, I take it, was Brazen-noſe college, & perhaps ſome others whoſe names are now loſt. II. Colleges, halls, or inns, appropriated to particular orders of reli-gious; as Black-hall, to ſome particular order of black monks; & the Carmes ſchool, to the youth of that order; or at leaſt, to receive all thoſe of that & other orders, as alſo noble & gentlemens children, who were educated by the fathers of that ſociety. The grey, black, & Auſtin fryers, as I take it had likewiſe their particular ſchools at the ſame time for the ſame purpoſe; but of them hereafter: only note here, Black-hall could not well belong to the Dominicans, becauſe Black-hall was endowed; whereas the four orders of mendicants had very rarely any other lands, than the ſite of their monaſteries. Black-hall at Stan-ford probably therefore belonged to ſome order of black monks, but which I find not. III. The 3ᵈ. ſort of colleges, halls, or inns at Stan-ford were appropriated to divers great monaſteries, moſt of them in this neighbourhood, who ſent hither their novices to be educated. Of this ſort were, Peterburgh, Sempringham, & Vauldy. When I write thus I am not ignorant Mr. Reyner ſays, that[a] ' Glouceſter hall at ' Oxford & Buckingham hall at Cambridge, did belong to the [Bene- ' dictin] monks: & thither all the monaſteries [of that order] St. Al- ' bans & Durham excepted, which had ſeparately provided their own ' colleges [at Camb. & Oxon] for themſelves; were obliged to ſend ' their monks to ſtudy; & there is in the capitular acts a note ſeveral ' times to be met with of the fines which the heads have enjoyned ' to thoſe abbats who neglected this inſtitution.' Now both theſe in-ſtitutions notwithſtanding, as Peterburgh actually did, we may conclude other Benedictin houſes made as little ſcruple in ſending their novi-ces to Stanford, & building inns for their better reception to ſtudy there. It was but repreſenting the convenience of doing ſo, & a diſpenſation for it was eaſy enough to be procured at Rome. It ſeems probable therefore that Brazen-noſe college, & ſome others (whoſe names are now loſt, & whoſe foundations were not appropriated to any religious order in general, or monaſtery in particular) were the firſt colleges, halls, & inns belonging to this univerſity; &, being places of general recep-tion, were in all likelihood, erected for the ſcholars, who came hither from Cheſter & Cambridge. And could I find when that remove hap-pened, I ſhould not much doubt but that I had found the true time, where certainly to fix the firſt æra or beginning of this univerſity. In this matter it is not altogether impoſſible but the records of the

a De antiq. Benedict. in Ang. p. 217.

town

town of Stanford it felf would have afforded fome light, but, as Mr. Leland informs us, [a] ' the northerne men, in one of the three firfte ' K. Edwards days, dyd ille to the toune of Staunford, & brenned many ' writings of their antiquities & privileges.' And again. [b] ' The nor- ' therne men brent miche of Staunforde tounne. It was not fins fully ' reedified.' By the way Mr. Leland fhould rather have faid, in one of the four firft K. Edwards days; for this burning of Stanford happen- ed in 1461. The abovementioned places of general reception, grow- ing at length too narrow for all comers who promifcuoufly flocked from all parts to this univerfity; & feveral religious orders difliking perhaps that their youth fhould live in fuch a mixture of lay & fecu- lar, as well as religious, perfons; particular places, fuch as Black-hall, were afterwards erected by the heads of feveral orders for their own youth to refide in. The particular colleges, inns, & halls, called by the particular names of Peterburgh, Sempringham, & Vauldey, & other religious houfes, were I guefs erected fometime after both the former forts above fpecified; to wit, when the laft of thofe kinds of places of more general reception being equally thronged with the firft; & almoft as many inconveniencies found in the mixture of many perfons, tho' of the fame order, yet of different monafteries; the patrons & fathers of thofe monafteries from whence they came, thought it more con- venient, to prevent all difpute & feparate interefts common to more mixed focieties, to prepare yet more particular places of reception for thofe of their own houfes. Thus Leland, who almoft concurs with thefe fentiments. [c] ' And bycaufe that a great voice rennith that fome ' tyme readinges of liberalle fciences were at Staunford, the names of ' Peterborough haulle, Semplingham, & Vauldier, yet remain there; ' as places for thofe houfes of men of religion that put their fcholars ' thither to ftudy. Except a man wille fay, that thefe houfes other- ' wyfe cumming to them, kept theyr names.' Sempringham hall at Stanford was exprefly given by the founder Robert Lutterel, as I have elfewhere fhewn, for the novices of that monaftery at Sempringham to ftudy here. And fo I reckon were Peterborough, Vauldier, &c. this inftance in one, making all the reft very probable. And fo much of our colleges, halls, & inns in general.

VII. Come we next to treat of thofe places in particular; & here my method fhall be to difcourfe firft of thofe colleges, inns, halls, & fchools, in the town of Stanford, whofe names & fituations may be, both, afcertained; next of thofe whofe fituations & remains are now, or were lately extant; but whofe names themfelves are not yet to be recovered. And firft. ' There ftood in S. Pauls parifh, by the gate of ' that name (faith Mr. Wood [d]) a very antient ftructure yet called Bra- ' fen-nofe college; becaufe, he continues, it hath ftill temaining a larger

a Itin. Vol. 6. p. 29.
b Itin. Vol. 7. p. 10.

c Itin. Vol. 6. p. 30.
d ut fupra.

' gate, & in that a wicket or lesser door, to which is affixed a brasen
' head, which carries with it an iron ring, hanging at a hole in the nose;
' having a shew of great antiquity. This place was also furnished
' with a fair refectory, or hall; & at this day, in all writings & re-
' ceipts, preserveth its old name of Brazen-nose college.' Brazen-nose
college was pulled down by Mr. Burman in 1688. by order of the
corporation, proprietors of the fabric; & another large building erected with the materials; which, tho' not designed for that purpose at
first, is since made use of for a charity school. The gate of Brazen-
nose college stood formerly more backward than it does now; but,
when pulled down with the college, the corporation knowing the value of that piece of antiquity, ordered it to be set up again, tho' not
in the very same place where it stood before; yet as near as might be.
The fashion of it, I think, looks a good deal older than Edw. the
thirds time. I have talked with one Alexander Morris (now living
1725.) one of the workmen who pulled down the refectory or hall
abovementioned, who tells me, it was a strange wide place, with a
fire hearth in the middle; a description exactly agreeing with that of
our university halls. He adds, there were many little rooms & apartments about the rest of the house, with stone stairs leading up to them:
which, we may suppose, were the students lodgings. II. There was
another antient fabric, situate over against the south door of All Saints
church; which was pulled down about 20 years ago by Mr. White
a baker, then owner of it, & rebuilt. Mr. Wood takes no notice of
this place. The refectory belonging to this place was a fair large room;
& when I went to school at Stanford to Mr. Rollo, then curate of S.
Johns, we kept our school feast in this very refectory. I well remember there was a large window at the north end of that room like
a church window, with much painted glass in it : particularly, a cock
in two or more places. Mr. Richard Walburg hath often assured me
this was Peterborough hall. And I believe so, because the same figure
of a cock is now to be seen often repeated in S. Martins church windows on the other side of the Welland : which church was originally
in the abbats of Burgs patronage. All the shops on the west side of
the white meat mercat, I reckon were built where antiently part of
Peterborough hall was before erected. Mr. Forster mistook this for
Black-hall, which I am next to speak of. III. ' Near All Saints church
' (saith Mr. Wood) was lately standing an house of great antiquity
' called Black-hall, belonging to which there was a kitchen formerly
' standing, which, in its structure, shewed evident marks of antiquity.'
Black-hall stood north-west of All Saints church, hard by the steeple;
& was lately known by the name of the Talbot inn. The old fabric
was demolished soon after Peterborough hall abovementioned, & a
new house built with the materials. Black-hall, as I take it, was antiently endowed; there being lands in Stanford field yet known by the
name of Black-hall lea's, a particular which shews it could not belong

to

to the Dominicans; but was rather, as I have said, appropriated to some house of black monks.   IV. Sempringham-hall situate in S. Peters parish in Stanford, was endowed, & had its proper chapel, dedicated to the blessed Virgin Mary.   And as this college had its own particular chapel, it is also not unlike but that divers others had likewise theirs.   Mr. Forster mistakes another college standing just before Bennewerk churchyard, for Sempringham-hall: And also S. Mary Bennewerk church for the chapel of S. Mary granted to the students of Sempringham-hall by bishop Daldreby.   But I have been often assured by the late Mr. Richard Walburg, that so much of Sempringham-hall as now remains was of late years the habitation of the late Mr. Alderman Feast.   And this is far more probable than Mr. Forsters conjecture.   For S. Mary Bennewerk was it self a parish church & had its own rectors, presented by the conventual prior & chapter of Durham. But the chapel of S. Mary given by Robert Lutterel to the monks of Sempringham, was in S. Peters parish, & had no parochial privileges: by which chapel, & not by S. Mary Bennewerk church which had all those rights ('till burnt down in 1461. by the northern men & united afterwards to S. Peters) we must place Sempringham-hall.   For the late Mr. Feasts house might be always in S. Peters parish; but the house assigned for Sempringham - hall close by S. Mary Bennewerk church, could not possibly be in S. Peters parish whilst Bennewerk church was yet standing.   When Bennewerk church was yet standing, as I before observed, the gate called now S. Peters was called west-gate, & the street leading up to it from Peter-hill, le Gannoc.   Upon Peter-hill stood S. Peters church.   A little way from it in the Gannoc stands Mr. Feasts house; a good deal farther, just at the right hand side of west - gate stood Bennewerk church, within a *little close* now called Bennewerk churchyard.   Before which churchyard, next to the street, yet stands a long collegiate building which Mr. Forster mistakes for Sempringham-hall: of which collegiate building more presently. Having thus fixed the place where Sempringham-hall stood, next let it be noted, that several antique pieces of sculpture in stone, representing divers birds, beasts, fruits, flowers, &c. & now inserted in a new court wall belonging to the late Mr. Feasts house; were not (as divers may hereafter think) originally part of *Sempringham-hall*, but more truly dug up in the Austin friers (when the seal of Thomas Bishop of Elphin was discovered there) & for ornament removed hither by the foresaid Mr. Feast.   V. ' In S. Georges parish, saith Mr. Wood [a], *is a* ' mansion adjoining to the parsonage house, in which sometime since a ' tanner dwelt; which is believed to have been a college, but the name ' is unknown.'   Mrs. Jane Cecil, the lord treasurer Burghleys mother (as appears by the said L. Burghleys own Diary a MS. in Mr. Strypes hands) was joyntred, among other things, in the white friers school in

a Ant. Oxon. p. 16-

S. Georges parifh in Stanford.   Mr. Forfter fays, [a] ' a houfe ftanding
' full eaft of the parfonage houfe of S. Georges, was a fchool of Car-
' melites or white friers; tho' Mr. Wood could not tell any more of
' it than that it was a college, for want of records.'   This building
was pulled down by the E. of Exeter in 1720. or thereabouts.   I remember a great room there like a college hall.   This fchool being a
good diftance from the white friers, it feems their pupils met here
from all parts to hear their lectures.   And probably thefe were
not only the Carmelite fchools, but the public fchools of this little
univerfity.   However being called the white friers fchools it looks as
I have often intimated, that the fathers of that order were probably
the chief managers & directors of the univerfity it felf, as well as of this
fchool.   VI. ' Matters concerning the reft of the colleges, faith Mr.
' Wood [b], are not fo plain.   However it will not be amifs to fet
' down what dwellings antiquity, by the conftant report of all ages,
' hath afcribed to them.   In St. Maries ftreet, continues he, is a houfe,
' formerly known by the name of the old fwan, which a many think
' was formerly a college or hall for ftudents.'   Part of this college or
hall is now 1725. the houfe where Mr. Boniface Bywater the gunfmith
lives.   His fhop & the parlor behind it were antiently the refectory,
or college hall.   The wainfcot, cieling, high roof, & carved mouldings about it, fpeak its antiquity, as well as fitnefs for fuch an ufe.
His kitchen window is of the fame age, & has fome remains of painted glafs in it.   In the kitchen floor juft before the fire hearth, lies a
ftone whereon was formerly affixed a fmall brafs plate as on grave-ftones.
VII. ' Over againft S. Georges church, faith Mr. Wood [c], runs a long
' edifice quite the whole length of the ftreet, extreamly like our halls
[at Oxford] ' now drooping with age; which this plainly imitates,
' both in the archings of the gates, & the old fafhioned fhape of its
' windows.   This building, as I take it, was on the fouth fide of S.
Georges church; parted from the Carmelite fchools above mentioned
by the parfonage houfe.   That large houfe where Mr. Kirk now lives
was probably erected with fome of the old materials.   VIII. The laft
houfe of this kind which I will venture to pronounce fuch is that in
the Gannoc juft before Bennewerk churchyard, being the fame Mr.
Forfter took for Sempringham-hall.   ' The front of the houfe, he fays [d],
' is ftill ftanding, & carries in it the appearance of a collegiate build-
' ing.'   This laft is, on the outfide, the moft entire of all this fort of
ftructures in Stanford.   For an infide, that of Mr. Bywaters's is more
worth an antiquaries obfervation.   This laft ftanding fo near the Auftin
friers, leads me to quære if they did not teach here.   For the Auftin
friers were many of them very famous fcholars, & I need not tell an
Oxford man what is meant by keeping of Auguftines.   There were,

a Letter to Mr. Stephens, MS. in my   c Ant. Oxon. p. 168.
hands, p. 13.   d Letter to Mr. Stephens, MS. in my
   b ut fupra.   hands, p. 12.

                                                                    befides

befides thefe, undoubtedly feveral other houfes of this fort in Stanford, & it is not improbable but a public houfe in the high ftreet called the windmill inn, another in the fame ftreet lately pulled down by Mr. More (where was much gilding, & the arms of E. the 3. are yet preferved on the chimney-piece) a houfe in S. Martins abutting north on the George inn, & fome others, were of this kind. But the tradition being now worn out for what purpofe they were erected, it fhall fuffice only to mention them in the grofs. However let it be remembred that one of thefe places, which of them I can't fay, was called Vauldey-hall. For preferving the names of Peterborough, Sempringham, & Vauldey halls, it may be re-obferved we are indebted to Mr. Leland. Vauldier or Valdey hall at Stanford belonged to the abby de *valle Dei*, Valdey abby by Grimfthorpe. ‘ Valdey abby was ‘ dedicated, faith Mr. Burton, to the blefed Virgin, founded by Gilbert ‘ de Gaunt E. of Lincoln in K. Stephens time, at the requeft of pope ‘ Eugenius the 3ᵈ. & S. Bernard abbat of Clarevall, for Ciftertian monks.’ To this Valdey - hall at Stanford belonged Nicholas de Stanford; a Ciftercian of the Bernardin branch, a good fcholar, & living in 1310. Among all thefe colleges, halls, & inns, the fcholars who came from Oxford in 1333. & 1334. foundfufficient room for their reception & entertainment. And fo much for the colleges belonging to this little univerfity.

VIII. After this account of the univerfity & colleges, now a little of the mafters who taught & prefided there. Henry de Hanna (as I find in Pits) wrote a book called ‘ *ordinationes conventuum*, about the ordering of convents,’ & it is not at all improbable but that, among other things, it might treat of the fchools & academical exercifes, which were eftablifhed, if not by him, yet as moft evidently appears in his time & in his own monaftery at Stanford. Henry de Hanna died, as is before related, in December 1299. & was fucceeded in his great poft of the Englifh provincialfhip, by William Lidlington, a frier of the monaftery belonging to the fathers of that order at Stanford. This William Lidlington, it is probable, was one of the chief readers to the youth at the white friers fchool in the time of Henry de Hanna. For as Pits informs us, Lidlington wrote 2 books, one of determinations, & another of lectures in divinity. Compofitions proper only for an univerfity audience, or, at leaft, a very learned monaftery, fuch as this was. The next learned man, that I meet with, of this town, was Nicholas de Stanford (fo called from this place where he was born) but whether he had any fcholars affigned to his tuition in this univerfity, I find not. However it is probable he had, for he was a very learned perfon, & well qualified for fuch an office. The next, of any figure, is John Burley a Carmelite, contemporary with Lidlington. Bale fays, ‘ he adorned the monaftery of ‘ the Carmelites at Stanford with his learning. And Pits, that he ‘ fearched much into natural philofophy, & wrote many books upon

‘ the

‘ the fathers and fchoolmen.’ I do not find exprefs mention that he
taught in our univerfity, but, by this account, it is probable he was
appointed to read upon natural philofophy.   For, as he belonged to the
Carmelites, who were fo bufy in this affair, they would hardly let a man
of his parts lie ftill.   He lived not to fee the ruin of this little univerfity, but died a year or two before it was diffolved.   John Rodington, prior of the grey friers college in Stanford & provincial of the
Francifcan fathers in England, affumes the next place among the *Li-
terati* of this univerfity.   By him we may fee that the other monafteries of this town were then not without their worthies.   The next
is Walter Hefton, another Carmelite, born at Stanford, & ‘ he (as Pits
‘ pofitively affirms) taught philofophy both as a mafter & profeffor, &
‘ fometimes divinity.’   He was prior of the white friers at Stanford,
& at length provincial of his order.   The next is John Repingale another Carmelite. ‘ There are not wanting (faith Pits) who affirm that
‘ he, as a publick profeffor for feveral years, read & explained the ma-
‘ fter of the fentences to a well frequented auditory, with good ap-
‘ plaufe.’   And this was at Stanford.   I fhall only add, when the
univerfity of Stanford was diffolved, the Carmelite fathers preferved
their reputation to the laft, & were afterwards as celebrated for their
virtue, as they were before for their learning[a].

July 1.   IX. Johanna de Collingham, Beatrix de Eylefworth, & Emma Pe-
1336. verel of Pafton, defiring to profefs & take on them the vow & order
of nuns in the priory of S. Michael without Stanford (which profeffion was generally made before the lord abbat of Burg for the time
being, patron of the faid priory) William de Bootheby the new lord
abbat being otherwife engaged, appointed brother William de Gretford, prior of the faid nunnery, his deputy to receive the profeffion
of the faid ladies; whofe commiffion may be thus rendred. [b] ‘ Adam,
‘ by divine permiffion abbat of Burg, &c. to our beloved bro-
‘ ther William de Gretford, &c. greeting in the Saviour of all
‘ men.   For as much as to receive the profeffion of Johanna de
‘ Colingham, Beatrix de Eylefworth, as alfo of Emma Peverel of Pa-
‘ fton, fifters of the monaftery of S. Michael abovefaid, in the fame
‘ monaftery, according to the rule of the bleffed Benedict ready to
‘ be profeffed, upon this inftant Sunday next after the feaft of the
‘ tranflation of the bleffed Thomas the martyr, to be made in the
‘ faid monaftery of nuns) being diverfly hindred by certain arduous
‘ caufes we cannot be perfonally prefent : To you, of the induftry
‘ of whofe circumfpection, we impute full confidence in the lord;
‘ for to receive the profeffion of Johanna, Beatrix, & Emma, fifters of
‘ the monaftery of the bleffed Michael beforefaid, according to the rule
‘ of the bleffed Benedict, upon the Sunday abovefaid in the fame mo-
‘ naftery to be made, & for other matters to be done which in the

a fee anno 1348. below.   gine Vefp. E. XXI. fol. 64. b.
b Ex Codicis MS. in Bib. Cott. fub Ima-

3   ‘ bufinefs

The west Gate of the Carmes,
or white Friers College without Stanford.

' bufinefs of this profeffion fhall be neceffary, or alfo accuftomed, our
' place & ftead, as far as unto us belongs, by thefe prefents we do
' commit.   Given at Burg, the kalends of July, 1336.

X. ' [a]In the parliament held at London the 11. of E. the third, a- Mar.17.
' mongft other eminent perfons who were raifed to the like dignity, 11.E.3.
' upon advancing of Edward the black prince to the dukedom of
' Cornwal, William Bohun was created E. of Northampton, Mar. 17.
' fhortly after which he had a grant of the caftle, manor, & town of
' Stanford, with the Lordfhip of Grantham in Lincolnfhire (which
' John de Warenn, E. of Surrey, yet held for life.)   Likewife of the
' caftle & manor of Fodringhey in Northamptonfhire (which Mary,
' Countefs of S. Paul, then alfo held for life) & the caftle & manor
' of Okeham in Rutland.'   That grant, in part, runs thus.   ' [b]The
' king, unto the value of a thoufand librates of land a year, hath given
' to William de Bohun, E. of Northampton, the caftle, manor & town
' of Stanford; the manor & town of Grantham, &c. to hold to the E.
' & his heirs male under certain conditions there expreffed; by the fer-
' vice of one knights fee.   [c]This year alfo the faid William Bohun
' [lord of Stanford in reverfion] was joyned in commiffion with the
' bifhop of Lincoln & others, to treat with Philip K. of France, touch-
' ing the right of K. Edw. to that realm, with power to make de-
' claration of the fame.'   Upon occafion of this quarrel with France,
K. Edward the 3[d] about this time firft quartered the arms of France
& England.   I have before fhewn that K. Henry the 3[d] (& not K. E.
the 3[d]) was founder of the white friers coll. in Stanford.   What
led Mr. Burton to imagine K. E. the 3[d] was founder of that houfe,
was, perhaps, his feeing the arms of France & England as they now
ftand quartered & infculped in a ftone efcutcheon on the gatehoufe
of that friery; but that efcutcheon only proves that K. Edw. the 3[d]
might be a benefactor, or that the faid gate itfelf was erected about
this time.   However as the faid gate is all that is now left of that
once magnificent ftructure, I have here thought good to infert a draught
of it.   ' [d]In this 11. of K. Edw[d] 3. William Bohun abovementioned
[lord of Stanford in reverfion] ' was conftituted one of the kings com-
' miffioners to treat of peace with David Bruys, K. of Scotland.

XI. Dame Mabilla de Venour, priorefs of the nunnery of S. Michael Ap. 1.
without Stanford, being now grown very aged, & thereby incapable 1337.
of performing the wonted duties of her office, refigned that place, before Henry lord bifhop of Lincoln, at his manor of Lydington, who
there releafed her from the fame.   Whereupon fifter Margery de Coling-

---

a Baron, Vol. 1. p. 185. a.
b Rex, in valorem mille libratarum terre per annum, dedit Willielmo de Bohun, co-miti Northamptonienfi, caftrum, manerium, & villam de Stanford; manerium & villam de Grantham, &c. tenend. comiti & he-

redibus fuis mafculis, fub certis conditionibus ibidem expreffis; per fervitium unius feodi militis, &c. Cart. 11. E. 3. n. 48. & anno 14. art. 10.
c Bar. V. I. p. 185. a.
d Baronage, ut fupra.

ham, fub-priorefs of the faid houfe & the reft of that fifterhood, in a
petition to Adam Bootheby, lord abbat of Burg & the convent of that
place (after reciting the premifes) craved leave to elect a new priorefs;
which petition (taken indeed from a very indifferent copy) may be
thus put in Englifh. ' ᵃTo the reverend father in Chrift, and to the
' lord, lord Adam, by the grace of God abbat of Burg & the convent of
' the fame place, Margery de Colingham, fub-priorefs of the nuns of
' S. Michael of Stanford, and the humble convent of the fame place,
' with devout inclination, fend due reverence & obedience. Whereas
' dame Mabilla de Venour, late our priorefs, being broke with age by rea-
' fon of the infirmity of her body. & in the office wherein fhe prefided,
' thro' impotence no longer able to govern the convent aforefaid,
' for the reafons aforefaid hath made ceffion of her office, & from the
' honor of her government, by giving up the fame into the facred
' hands of the venerable father the lord, lord Henry, by the grace of
' God bifhop of Lincoln, the diocefan of the place, at the manor of
' Lydington of the faid fathers, on the day of making of the pre-
' fents, her felf, hath rendered, as fhe ought, impotent; and alfo where-
' as the venerable father aforefaid, weighing the infirmity of the fame
' priorefs, her, from the honor aforefaid, at the requeft of the fame
' (minding to the beft of his power for the indemnity of our mona-
' ftery beforehand to provide) hath effectually abfolved; to your holy
' paternity we humbly & devoutly requeft how that, whereas the pa-
' tronage of our monaftery is known to belong unto you, ye, in an
' intuition of divine charity, would grant us liberty of electing
' a priorefs, &, if it may pleafe you, to give us your affent & favor.
' In witnefs whereof to thefe prefents our common feal is appendent.
' Given in our chapter at Stanford, the fourth of the nones of April,
' 1337.' This petition being thus drawn & fealed, was immediately
delivered to Elen de Caldecot & Sara de Multon, two nuns of the faid
houfe, who, forthwith repairing to the abbat & convent of Burg,
prefented it as the joynt requeft of themfelves & fifterhood. Whereupon the faid abbat, in name of himfelf & that convent, by the following licenfe, gave leave to elect one of their own body. ' ᵇAdam,
' by divine permiffion abbat of Burg, to his beloved daughters in Chrift
' Margery de Colingham, fub-priorefs of the monaftery of the holy
' nuns of the bleffed Michael without Stanford, & to the holy con-
' vent of the fame place, greeting in the Saviour of all men. There
' coming unto us Elen de Caldecote & Sara de Multon, nuns of your
' monaftery abovefaid on your part, with letters patents fealed with the
' feal of your chapter, they have reported to us the vacancy of your
' houfe by ceffion of dame Mabilla le Venour, late priorefs of your
' houfe aforefaid, made, as afferted, before the venerable father lord

a Ex codicis MS. in Bib. Cot. fub imag.   b id. ib.
Vefp. E. XXI. fol. ult. b.

' Henry,

' Henry, by the grace of God bishop of Lincoln, diocesan of the same
' place; humbly & devoutly beseeching us, how that to you & them
' we would grant license of electing a prioress.   Now we considering
' the vacancy of your said monastery, if it happen, may diversly incur
' loss; with consent of our brethren, to your & their petition benignly
' consenting, as far as unto us belongs, do give power to you & them of
' electing a prioress out of your own body.   To you & the same nuns,
' our daughters, as far as we are able, firmly . . . . the rest,
with the leaf it self, is wanting.   However the issue of this matter is
touched in another part of the same MS. whereby we learn that the
foresaid dame Mabilla le Venour was succeeded in the said prioresship
by dame Mabilla de Ryby.   It being there regiftred, that ' [a] In the 11.
' of Edw. the 3. & the 16. of Adam [Bootheby lord] abbat of Burg,
' on monday in Easter week dame Mabilla de Ryby, prioress of Staun-
' ford, did fealty to the said lord abbat in his chamber, in the abby of
' Burg, before Sir Gervase de Wylford, master Walter de Warmington,
' Peter son of Warine, William Casse, & others.'   According to Bale [b],
the great doctor Walter Burley died in 1337. in the 63. year of his age.
I have elsewhere shewn how he was tutor to K. Ed. the 3. & lord almoner
to Q. Philippa, but must here add, ' [c] after Edw. prince of Wales (eldest
' sonne to K. Edw. commonly called the black prince) was borne, &
' able to learne his booke, the said doctor Burley amongst other, was
' commaunded to be one of his instructors, by reason whereof Sir Si-
' mon Burley, being sonne to Sir John Burley, near kinsman to the
' said doctor Burley, was afterwards admitted among other young gentle-
' men to be schoolefellow with the said prince.'   Of which Sir Simon
Burley many things hereafter.

   XII. ' [d] In the 11. of E. the 3. by a writ dated Ap. 23. a parlia- Ap. 23.
' ment was called at Stanford, & appointed to be held on the friday, 11.E.3.
' or morrow, after the feast of the ascension.'   What was done in this 1337.
parliament I find not, but the main design of its assembling was undoubtedly about the business of France; likewise the kings being at Stanford
this year upon the 25. of June, makes it highly probable that the said
parliament was at that time sitting, & the K. himself attending it.   On [e]
the said 25. of June, the said K. by his letters patents, bearing date at
Stanford, confirmed to God & the hospital of S. Mary at Newsted the
two several grants of the founder William de Albini the 3. as also the
grant of William de Albini the 4. to the same hospital.   His letters patents in confirmation of the said premises, may be thus englished.
' [e] The K. to all whom, &c. greeting.   The donation, concession, &
' confirmation, which William de Albini the 3. by his writing made
' to God & the hospital of the blessed Mary at the bridge of Wasse be-

a folio 4. b.   d Ex literis Cl. Willisii mihi missis.
b p. 413.   e Ex pat. 11. E. 3. part 2 memb. 20 &
c Hol. p. 1002. a.   Monast. Ang. Tomi II. p. 451. a.

                                                      ' tween

' tween Stanford & Offinton, & to the then brethren of the fame hof-
' pital, in free, pure, & perpetual alms, of the place in which the cha-
' pel of the bleffed Mary there is fituate, with the whole houfe adjacent;
' & of the whole mill of Offinton, with fuit as well of the demefne of
' him William, as of the fervants of his houfe & of his tenents, &
' with all other matters unto the faid mill pertaining; & of fixty & five
' acres of land & an half, & ten acres & an half of meadow, lying in
' divers places and cultures in Offington & Talington; & of the whole
' land within the Berwes, which Peter the chevalier held; & of the
' meadow by the mill, which is called Fowrpenholm; & of one toft
' which Gunwara Gogel fometime held in Offington; & of pafture for
' an hundred fheep in the faid town, & for fix beafts, & for fix cows,
' & for two bulls with the demefne beafts, cows, & bulls of him Wil-
' liam.   Alfo the donation, &c. which the fame William by his writ-
' ing made to the forenamed brethren in pure & perpetual alms, of
' three bovates of land in Offinton, with the meadow, & pafture, & all
' its appurtenances; & of a rent of three fhillings & three pence, with
' nine hens & three cocks, yearly to be received in Offington; & of
' a rent of forty fhillings in the town of Chafunt; & of a rent of
' five fhillings in the town of Bottleford, &c.   Moreover the conceffi-
' on & confirmation which William of Albini the fourth, by his char-
' ter made to the canons of the faid place, in free, pure, & perpetual
' alms, of all that *New Place* at the bridge of Offington, as it is en-
' clofed with a wall & a ditch, with the appurtenances; & of all the
' donations, lands, men, poffeffions, rents, & liberties, with all the ap-
' purtenances & eafements, within the town & without, by William his
' father, & by who or whomfoever the donors on the forefaid canons
' & their fucceffors collated; & of the free election of the prior of the
' church aforefaid, & of the faid houfe & all the rents & poffeffions
' of the fame, with all the appurtenances & liberties in the hand &
' cuftody of the canons of the fame, in the mean time, till they have
' a prior to remain; & of all the rents, expences, & goods of the fore-
' named houfe by them, for the ufe of the poor, & profit of the church
' aforefaid, to be expended, &c.   Holding ratified & good, them for
' us & our heirs, as far as in us lies, &c. we do confirm.   In witnefs
' whereof, &c. witnefs the K. at Staunford the 25. of June.'   I fhall
only add, that the prior of this houfe, *quatenus prior*, was always a
ftanding member of convocation, as archdeacons & other dignitaries
are now[a]: And fo likewife was the prior of S. Leonards[b].   On the 12.
of July following, I find the king here again.   On which day were
figned the conventions between him & the E. of Hainault.   ' ' By
' which conventions it appears that the faid earl, tho' he was his bro-
' ther in law, wou'd not engage with him [againft France] but on

a Hody's Hift. Convocat. p. 7.   b id. ib.   c Acta regia N° 4. p. 242.

' condition

' condition that Edw. fhould have the title of the emperors lieutenant or
' vicar. Dated at Stanford, the 12. of July, 1337. And this fhews
' the reafon, fays my author, why Edw. courted that dignity, which
' the pope reproach'd him for afterwards, as being beneath him.' From
Stanford K. Edward, as I conceive, went to Huntingdon; for in a letter
of one of our kings dated at that town the 12. of July (without any
year or kings name to afcertain the time & perfon it belongs to) the
K. writes to the alderman & bailifs of Stanford, acquainting them,
that, when he came to Stanford, he went thro' Pilfgate field (coming
then I fuppofe from Peterborough) &, it being ufual it feems that
whatever way the king rides to any place (tho' the fame was no public road before) for every body elfe to claim the fame liberty afterwards, & thenceforth to call any fuch new paffage the kings highway;
being followed to Huntingdon by divers of his own tenents, inhabitants of Pillefgate, who then & there reprefented the damage they
fhould fuftain by fuch a practice, the K. by his letters immediately commanded that his paffing that way fhould not be made a precedent for
other peoples fo doing, but did utterly forbid & difcharge them therefrom.   His letter, directed, ' to our dearly beloved the alderman, bai-
' lifs, & good people of our town of Stanford,' upon this occafion, is
thus worded.   ' ᵃ Dear & well-beloved friends, by the grievous com-
' plaint of our beloved lieges & tenents of the town of Pillefyate
' near our town of Staunford, we have underftood, that, in as much
' as, on Tuefday laft, we paffed thro' the middle of a meadow & a cer-
' tain pafture there called Pillefyate fneadow appertaining to the faid
' town of Pillefyate, you, & others of the country circumjacent, claim
' to have & ufe an high way royal to pafs thro' the middle of the
' faid meadow & pafture, to the great damage & diffeifin of our faid
' lieges & tenents, whereupon they have fupplicated for a remedy;
' fo we will, if it be fo, & we command & charge firmly, that you nei-
' ther make, nor ufe, nor fuffer to be made, nor ufed, by others of our
' faid town of Staunford, nor others whatfoever, no high road thro' the
' middle of the faid meadow & pafture; but that you forbear from it en-

a De par le Roy. Chiers & bon amez, par
la grevovfe compleinte de nos amez lieges
& tenantz de la ville de Pillefyate pres de
noftre ville de Staunford, nous avons en-
tendu, que par tant que Marfdy darein paffe
nous chinachafmes par my une pree & cer-
teine pafture illoeqces appellez Pillefyate mede,
appurtenaunte a la dicte ville de Pillefyate;
vous, & autres de la pays environ, claimez
davoir & ufer une haulte chemyne roiale de
paffer parmy les diz pree & pafture, a grand
dommage & difaife de noz ditz lieges & te-
nauntz, dont ils nous ount fuppliez de remedy; fi volons, fi ainfi foit, & vous mandons & chargeons fermement, que voufne
facez, ne ufez, ne fuffrez faire ne ufer par
autres de noftre dicte ville de Staunford, ne
autres que conques, nulle haulte chemyn

par my les diz pree & pafture; Ainz en cef-
fez outrement, & que benefacez overtement
proclamer en mefne noftre ville, que tous
autres dicelle noftre ville & de la pais envi-
roun, parcillement facent. Au fin que nos
ditz tenantz avoir pourront & pefible men
joir leure ditz prees & pafture, ainfi & par
manere come ils ont eus devant ces heures,
fanz diftourbance ou empechement de vous
ou dautres de quel eftat ou condicioun quils
foient, non obftant que nous y chinachafmes
par manere comme defs eft dit: Et ce en
nulle manere ne leffez. Donne foubz noftre
fignet, a Huntyngdon, le 12. jour de Jullet.
—— A noz chiers amez les alderman, baillifs, & bonnes gens de noftre ville de Stanford. Ex codicis MS. in bib. Cotton. fub
imagine Fauftinæ, B. III. folio 5.

' tirely,

' tirely, & that you caufe it to be openly proclaimed in our faid town,
' that all others of our faid town, & the country round it, do likewife;
' to the end that our faid tenents may have & peaceably enjoy the
' faid meadow & pafture, fo, & in the manner, as they have done be-
' fore thefe times, without difturbance or impeachment of you or others,
' of what eftate or condition foever they be, notwithftanding that we
' paffed that way in manner as is faid : And this in no manner fail ye.
' Given under our fignet at Huntyngdon, the 12. day of July.'

Oct. 7.   XIII. ' ª The K. now gave a commiffion to William Bohun E. of
1337. ' Northampton [& lord of Stanford in reverfion] with others, to de-
' mand the crown of France, & to take poffeffion of it in his name.
' This full power is dated the 7. of October, 1337. at Weftminfter.

Nov.   ' ᵇ About the feaft of S. Martin in winter, there came to London two
' cardinals, fente by the pope to treate for a peace betwixte the kings
' of England & Fraunce.   The duke of Cornwal, with the E. of Sur-
' rey [lord of Stanford] received them a mile without the citie.   ᶜ In
11.E.3. ' this 11. year, K. Edw. called a council of trade to meet at Weft-
' minfter, & Robert de Pakinton, Thomas de Ravele, & William de
' Apethorp, were fent up from Stanford, as being fome of the moft
' confiderable tradefmen then living there, to be prefent at that affem-
Dec. 24. ' bly. —— Emma, relict of Richard de Baldefwel of Staunford, gave to
11.E.3. ' W. fon of Robert de Dyngele of Ingethorp, one grange with a garden
' adjoyning without the gates of Scoftegate fituate between a tenement
' belonging to the mafs of the bleffed virgin celebrated in the church of
' All-Saints in the mercat at Staunford, eaft ; & extending it felf from the
' kings, highway north as far as the arable land of Sir William de Burton,
' Kt. fouth. Witneffes, Thomas de Rauele, alderman of Staunford, & Ro-
' bert le Moigne of Staunford; the 24. of Dec. 11. E. 3. B.H.'   The
fouth chancel of All-Saints church is the chapel of S. Mary here fpoken
of.   In this chapel was a daily fervice performed by a particular prieft,
for whofe maintainance were given divers lands in & about Stanford,
but by whom I find not.   ' ᵈ Sir William de Burton, Kt. temp. E. 3.
' his chief feat was at Tollthorp [not Totthorp as in my author] in
' Rutland.   He bare a cheveron between three owles argent, crowned
' or ; the creft, out of an high cappe fable, an owles head argent, crow-
' ned or : this coat ftandeth very antient in Okeham church in Rut-
' land, & in many other churches in that fhire.'   Thomas de Rauele
abovementioned is the firft alderman of Stanford I yet meet with, by
name : However there were aldermen of Stanford long before, tho'
12.E.3. their names be now loft.   ' Adam de Normantoun, rector of the
' church of the bleffed Mary de Bynwerk, gave to Richard de Rothwel
' of Stanford & Agnes his wife, his meffuage fituate in the parifh of

a acta regia, p. 244.   mar. 7. 1719-20.
b Hol. p. 901. b.   d Burtons Leic. p. 108.
c Ex literis Br. Willis Arm. mihi miffis

' the

‘ the bleſſed Mary de Bynewerk aforeſaid,   between a tenement of
‘ Richard Randolf eaſt,   & the ſtreet which leads down to the river
‘ Welland weſt.’ B. H.   ‘ ᵃ In this 12. of E. the 3. William de Bohun ⌈lord
of Stanford in reverſion⌉ ‘ having married Eliz. the 3. of the ſiſters &
‘ coheirs of Sir Giles de Badleſmere (an eminent baron) then 28 years
‘ of age,   had an aſſignation of her purparty of thoſe lands, which, by
‘ inheritance, deſcended to her,   upon the death of her ſaid brother,
‘ viz. the manor of Tonge in Kent ; as alſo divers lands in Snodſhurſt
‘ & Greenwich in that county ;   the manors of Lachlegh *in Eſſex* ;
‘ Hameldon in Rutland ;   & Ideſhale in Shropſhire.   In which year he
‘ went with Henry E. of Lancaſter,   & others,   into Flanders ;   the K.
‘ alſo being at that time there, with a great army, in order to his claim
‘ of the crown of France.   And was one of the marſhals in the 3.
‘ battalia of K. Edwards army,   drawn up at Vironfoſſe againſt the
‘ French.

XIV. ‘ Richard de Bekyngham was now rector of great S. Michaels
‘ church in Stanford. B. H.’   ‘ ᵇ In this 13. of E. 3. John E. Warenn   13.E.3.
⌈lord of Stanford⌉ ‘ was conſtituted the chief perſon for arraying all
‘ the men at arms in Surrey & Suſſex, & for cuſtody of the ſea-coaſts.’
‘ ᶜ Sir Thomas Holland ⌈afterwards buried at Stanford⌉ was in the ex-
‘ pedition now made into Flanders.’   ‘ ᵈ William de Bohun ⌈lord of   14.E.3.
Stanford in reverſion⌉ ‘ in this 14. E. 3. was in that famous naval fight
‘ before Sluyſe in Flanders,   betwixt the K. of England & the French.
‘ And the ſame year obtained a grant of the manors of Eſtwood &
‘ Reylegh, with the honor of Reylegh, & hundred of Rochford *in Eſſex,*
‘ to himſelf & the heirs male of his body.   And being before the end
‘ of that year again beyond ſea, had an aſſignation of 4546 l. 17 s. 6d. ¼.
‘ part of a larger ſum due to him for his ſervice in the wars of France.’
‘ Reymund de Nottingham of Staunford, apothecary,   gave to Amice
‘ his daughter, one ſhop with a loft, &c. ſituate byhindebak, between a te-
‘ nement of John lord Warenn ſouth, & a tenement of the late Henry
‘ Bronds north, & annexed to the ſhop of Nicholas de Eſton eaſt. B. H.’
‘ Henry de Carleton of Staunford gave to John Mazoun, all his tenements
‘ there, whereof one is ſituate in the pariſh of the bleſſed Mary . . . . be-
‘ tween a tenement of Walran de Baſton weſt,   & the ſtreet called
‘ Corewenſty eaſt: Another tenement is ſituate between a tenement of
‘ the lord abbat of Croyland north, & the town wall of Staunford ſouth
‘ in the ſame pariſh: And one tenement ſtanding in the ſame pariſh,
‘ between a tenement of John de Pekebriggs weſt,   & a tenement of
‘ the late Henry de Silton. B. H.’   ‘ Walter le Halver, burgeſs of
‘ Staunford, gave to John his eldeſt ſon, two meſſuages, joyntly ſituate
‘ in S. Andrews pariſh near the way called Claymond, & the one piece

a Bar. Vol. 1. p. 185. a.   c Bar. Vol. 2. p. 74. a.
b Bar. Vol. 1. p. 81. b.   d Bar. Vol. 1. p. 185. a. b.

' of land adjacent, with one dovecoat ſtanding in the ſame, which were
' formerly Peter de Wermyngtons; & with one ſpring on the weſt part
' of the ſaid meſſuages: all which are ſituate between a meſſuage of
' Margaret who was the wife of Hugh de Thurleby eaſt, & a meſſuage
' of the ſaid Walter Weſt, & abutt upon the common way called Clay-
' mond ſouth, & upon the town wall of Staunford north. B. H.'   ' W.
' le Fleming alderman of Stanford was witneſs to a deed belonging to

No.30. ' Browns hoſpital, dated Nov. . . this 14. E. 3. B. H.'   ' ª In the night
1340. ' of the feaſt of S. Andrew, K. Edwarde came on lande at the tower
14.E.3. ' aboute cockes crowe, & with him the E. of Northampton [lord of
' Stanford in reverſion] & other lords.'   ' W. le Flemyng ald. of Staun-
15.E.3. ' ford was alſo witneſs to another deed bearing date the ſunday in the
' feaſt of S. Botolph the abbat, in the 15. of K. Edw. 3. over Eng-
' land, & of his reign over France the 2. B. H.'   The feaſt of S. Botolph
is celebrated, Mar. 23.

5. June   XV. ' ᵇ 15. E. 3. 5. June 1341. Q. Philippa was delivered of a ſonne
1341. ' at the town of Langley [in Hertfordſhire] the which was named Ed-
' mond, & ſurnamed Langley of the place where hee was thus born.
' ᶜ He was baptiſed by Michael then abbat of S. Albans.'   This Edmond
de Langley was afterwards lord of Stanford.   ' ᵈ Tourney was this year
' beſieged by K. Edw. & with him was William E. of Northampton
[lord of Standford in reverſion] ' ᵉ Thomas lord Holland [afterwards
buried here] ' & other great perſons.'   ' ᶠ Likewiſe in regard of more
' mony ſtill owing to William E. of Northampton by the K. for his
' ſervice in the wars; for want whereof he could not pay thoſe debts
' to his creditors which he had contracted by reaſon of the ſaid wars;
' he this year obtained licenſe to tranſport 80 ſacks of his own wool
' into Flanders.   And the ſame year had a farther aſſignation of ſuch
' lands as were of the inheritance of Eliſabeth his wife, viz. the manors
' of Erith, Langport, & Rumney in Kent: Drayton in Suſſex: two
' parts of the manor of Finmere in Oxfordſhire: a houſe near Algate
' in London, & the ſouth part of the manor of Thaxſted in Eſſex.   In
' this year alſo he was one of the great lords preſent at that famous feaſt &
' juſting, which K. Edw. then made for love of the counteſs of Salisbury
' as it was reported. So likewiſe in the Scotch expedition then made. And
' had likewiſe a grant of the caſtle & manor of Okeham, to himſelf & heirs
' male, wherein he had only but term of life before.——William in the
' Waulles gave to Robert de Scotelthorp, one meſſuage ſituate in the
' pariſh of All-Saints in the mercat, between a tenement of the prior
' of Fynneſheued of the one part, & a tenement of Emma de Baldeſwel
' of the other; & likewiſe one ſhop, with a loft, &c. ſituate between a
' ſhop of the late William del Cley [or Clev] of the one part, & the

a Hol. p. 912. b.   d Fabian 215. a.
b Hol. p. 916. b.   e Bar. Vol. II. p. 74. a.
c Bar. Vol. 2. p. 154. a   f Bar. Vol. 1. p. 185. b.

' kings

'kings high way called Woll-rowe of the other. B. H.' ' John Black-
' man of Staunford the elder, gave to John Cokerel, one houfe built
' within his meffuage which ftands without the gates of Scoftegate, be-
' tween the tenements of the forefaid John Cokerell . . . . . & a te-
' nement of W. de Skelton north; & extends it felf from the kings
' highway eaft as far as the land of Sir W. de Burton, Kt. weft. The
' which houfe, faith he, extends it felf from a certain chamber to the
' hall of my meffuage aforefaid annexed north, as far as my garden fouth.
' B. H.'

XVI. ' a In the 16. E. 3. the K. amongft other letters to divers of his 16.E.3.
' nobles, fent to John E. Warenn [lord of Stanford] to provide 40
' men at arms, & an hundred archers for his fervice in France; re-
' quefting him to be at London in perfon on the octaves of S. Hillary,
' there to treat & agree with his council touching the wages for thofe
' foldiers in that expedition.' ' b The fame year William Bohun [lord
of Stanford in reverfion] ' was made the kings lieutenant & capt. ge-
' neral in Britanny, with power to receive fealty & homage from the
' people there, on behalf of K. Edw. as K. of France.' ' c There be
' that write, how lord Walter de Manny, tooke a truce with the French
' to endure 'till Alhallowentide, with condition the K. of England were
' contented therewith; but the K. liked not thereof & fo fent over the
' erles of Northampton & Devon, &c. with 500 men of armes, & a
' 1000 archers, which taking fhip, the vigil of the affumption of our
' lady, fayled towards Britaine.' ' d Thence the E. of Northampton
[lord of Stanford in reverfion] ' fent letters to the K. fignifying how
' that within the octaves of the affumption they arrived on the coaft
' of Britaine neere the towne & caftle of Breft, in whyche the dutchefs
' of Britaine with hir children were of the enemies befieged, both by
' fea & land; but that perceiving the Englifh fleet, the French packed
' away. Afterwards the E. landing, & chufing a plot of ground con-
' venient for his purpofe, fought, flew, & took of them at leaft ccc.
' men of armes. The E. loft not any noble man in this fight, except
' onely the lord Edward Spencer.' ' e Afterwards the K. arriving in
' Britaine thofe that were there under the E. of Northampton, &c. fought
' with the French near Morleis, where a few Englifh, unneth [i. e.
' fcarcely] v. c. difcomfited a mighty power of French, efteemed to
' be above L. thoufand: of whom, fome they flew, & fome they tooke.'
' f In this fame 16. E. 3. Thomas lord Holland [afterwards buried at
Stanford] ' was fent, with Sir John d'Arvel to Bayon, with cc. men at
' arms, & cccc. archers to defend the frontiers.' ' g William Bohun
[lord of Stanford in reverfion] ' had another licenfe to tranfport 200
' facks of wool, each fack containing 26 ftone; & each ftone 14 pound.

a Bar. V. 1. p. 81. b.
b Bar. Vol. 2. p. 185. b
c Hol. p. 917. b.
d id. p. 918 a b.

e Hol. p. 919.
f Bar. Vol. 2. p. 74. b.
g Bar. Vol. 1. p. 185. b.

' And

' And was at the making of that famous league betwixt the K. of
' France & K. Edw. wherein the Spaniard & divers others were included;
' & by oath did undertake for K. Edwards observance thereof. ª The
' commissioners on both sides took their oaths for their respective masters,
' Jan. 19. 1343. 16. E. 3.

XVII. ' ᵇ In this 17. E. 3. William de Bohun [lord of Stanford in re-
version] ' was one of those who attended Henry E. of Lancaster in his
' expedition into Scotland, for raising the siege of Loughmabon castle
' by the Scots; which being effected, he [Bohun] was constituted go-
' vernor thereof. In the same year he was again in Britany in the kings
' service.' ' ᶜ Thomas lord Holland [afterwards buried at Stanford]
' was this year again in the wars of France. —— There now lived one
' Robert de Ashbourn of Staunford, a merchant. B. H.' ' W. Man of
' Tallington gave to John, son of Nicholas de Okeham, goldsmith of
' Staunford, one shop, with a loft, &c. situate in the street called By-
' hyndeback. B. H.' From this John the goldsmith, as I take it, goldsmiths lane in Stanford & goldsmiths grange in Leicestershire, were so
called. 'Tis certain the goldsmiths of Stanford & goldsmiths grange in
Leic. were patrons of divers churches in Stanford. ' Robert son &
' heir of John de Folkyngham of Staunford, gave to Sir Thomas de
' Bernack, parson of the church of Stretton upon the Fosse, one mes-
' suage in Staunford, upon the fee of the lord abbat of Burg, situ-
' ate between a tenement of W. Wynd's south, & a tenement of the
' late Walter de Hallestead north, as it extends it self from the kings
' highway west, as far as S. Martins croft east. B. H.' ' ᵈ Sir William Bur-
' ton of Tolthorpe sate justice of the kings bench from this 17. to the
' 36. of E. the 3.

XVIII. ' ᵉ Betwixt Candlemas & Lent, K. Edw. held a solemn feast at
' Windsor, in the end whereof, he devised the order of the garter.'
Thomas lord Holland [afterwards buried at Stanford] was one of those
Knts. then first made. They were in all 26. companions, whose pictures,
with the sovereigns K. E. & patrons S. George, were all of them afterwards set up in the chancel windows of S. Georges church at Stanford,
at the charge of William Bridges, Esq; made first garter king of arms by
K. H. 5. & buried afterwards in the said S. Georges church at Stanford,
& a great benefactor to the same. There is now in the hands of that
excellent antiquary John Anstis, Esq; garter principal K. of arms, a
curious book of drawings in folio, wherein the said Knts. are all depicted in colors as they were at first set up, saith the title of that book,
in S. Georges church at Stanford. I had once a sight of it by the favor
of the now proprietor. If I remember right Mr. Anstis told me that
book was once Mr. Ashmoles. Be that as it will, the figures of the
first Knts. of the garter as etched by Hollar on a brass plate, printed

a Hol. p. 920 b.
b Baron. Vol. I. p. 185. b.
c Bar. Vol. II. p. 74. a.

d Burtons Leic. p. 108.
e Hol. p. 923. a.

3   On

on a large fheet in Mr. Afhmoles hiftory of the garter, were all copied
from this book.   It coft Mr. Anftis five guinea's. —— Mr. Stow, from
Tho. de la Moor, places the battle of Morlais mentioned anno 16.
above, under this 18. year of K. Ed. the 3. where he gives this remarkable account of it & the E. of Northamptons valor.   ' [a] K. Edw. in
' fuccor of John duke of Britain & of his wife & children, who then
' remained in the kings cuftody, fent the earls of Northampton & Ox-
' ford, Hugh Spencer & Richard Talbot, Knts. & mafter William Kil-
' lesbie, clerc, every one having under them many men of arms & archers,
' into Britayne, who entred thereinto in defpight of all which refifted
' them, making many conflicts.   They took as well walled townes as
' others, with divers caftles, both by affault & furrender, by which they
' had the whole countrey under fubjection, conquering 'till they came
' to the towne of Morleis, where Charles de Bloys met them with a
' great army.   Therefore in the champaine ground nigh to Morleis,
' the two armies made great & moft ftout battle, wherein the worthinefs
' of both did well appear.   For the chief captain Charles de Bloys &
' William de Bohun [lord of Stanford in reverfion] fought fo long
' with hand ftrokes in the field that day, that no man but a liar could
' give more praife to the one than the other.   Three times being
' wearied on both fides, they withdrew themfelves to take breath,
' & then fell to it again with fpeare & fhield, & fword & target.   But,
' in the end, the right worthy & ftout Charles de Blois, his men fleeing
' away, was alfo forced to flie himfelf: whereupon, after many flain on
' both fides, the victory fell to the Englifh.

XIX. ' Peter fon of Cecily, daughter of Alice fometime wife of W. de   19.E.3
' Folkyngham clothier, gave two cellars, with a loft, &c. [as above
defcribed 12. E. 2.] ' to John Young of Eafton. B. H.'   ' Thomas de
' Bernack, fometime parfon of Stretton on the Foffe, afterwards vicar
' of Sutirton in Holland, gave to John le Young of Efton, a meffuage
' in Staunford upon the abbat of Burgs fee [as above defcribed, 12. E. 2.]
' together with another meffuage called Swal . . . . . Stede, fituate
' between a tenement of W. Wynd north, & a tenement fometime W.
' Lyfteres fouth, as it extends it felf from the kings highway weft as far
' as S. Martins croft eaft. B. H.'   ' [b] About this feafon the duke of Britain
' having with him the erles of Northampton & Oxford, Sir William de
' Killesby one of the kings fecretaries, & many other barons & knights,
' paffed over into Britain, againft the lord Charles de Blois, where they
' tarried a long time, & did little good to make anye accompte of, by
' reafon that the duke, in whofe quarrel they came into thofe parts,
' fhortly after his arrival there, departed this life, & fo they returned
' home.'   However whilft they yet tarried there, the K. faith Fabian [c],
' fente the E. of Derby with a ftrong armie into Guyan, for to ayde the

[a] P. 374.   [b] Hol. p. 925. b. l. ult.   [c] Fab. p. 219. b.

E.

‘ E. of Northampton [lord of Stanford in reverſion] whom the K. be-
‘ fore had left there at Burdeaux, to ſtrengthen that countrey againſt the
‘ French.   ᵃ In this 19. E. 3. Thomas lord Holland [Kt. of the garter,
& afterwards buried at Stanford] ‘ obtained a grant from the K. of 40 l.
‘ *per annum*, payable out of the ferme of the priory of Hayling, during
‘ the wars with France; until proviſion of lands of that value ſhould
‘ be made for him.   ᵇ Alſo Joan counteſs of Warenn, wife to John
‘ E. of Surrey [lord of Stanford] being to go beyond ſea upon ſome
‘ ſpecial employment for the K. had protection for all her lands here
‘ in England, which were aſſigned for her ſupport, with the ſtock there-
‘ upon; for the better defence & ſafeguard of them in her abſence.’ My
author goes on. ‘ But ſoon after this ſhe died.’ Not ſo tho’. For he
afterwards tells us, in the next page of his book, that ſhe did not die
’till 1361. 35. E. 3. ᶜ And there he is right. The reaſon why this
great lady thus went abroad, was not about the kings buſineſs, as my author ſurmiſes, but becauſe her husband was (for what reaſon I know
not) grown weary of her, &, as ſoon as her back was turned, married
another wife, one Iſabel de Houland. ‘ ᵈ About S. Nicholas-tide the
‘ erles of Darby & Northampton won the towne & caſtle of Begaret
‘ in Gaſcoyne, & ſlew there the E. of Valentynoys, chief captain there-
‘ of, & tooke there a noble man, called the E. of the Iſles, with many
‘ other rich priſoners.

20. E. 3.   XX. ᵉ Aboute Aprill, the ſayde erles wanne a ſtrong towne called
‘ the Riall. Whereof hearing Philip de Valoys, he in all haſt, ſent his ſon
‘ Jhon duke of Normandye, to withſtand & give battayl to the ſayd
‘ erles. But when the ſaid duke was nere unto the Engliſh, he had
‘ ſuch tidings of their ſtrength, that he retourned unto his father. For
‘ which his father with him was grevouſlee diſcontented, in ſo muche to
‘ avoyde his diſpleaſure, he tourned into Gaſcoyne, & layed ſiege unto
‘ the caſtle of Aguillon, & there remained till Auguſt, without getting
‘ of it any advantage, & then returned to his father.’ ‘ ᶠ The E. of
‘ Northampton [lord of Stanford in reverſion] & the other lords in
‘ Brytaine committed certaine caſtles wonne by them in Brytaine, to
‘ the ſafe keeping of faithful captains & ſouldiers, & then returned
20. May ‘ into England.’ ‘ ᵍ By indenture bearing date at Weſtm. 20. May 20.
1346. ‘ E. 3. 1346. John E. Warenn [lord of Stanford] ſettled upon Maud de
‘ Nereford his concubine, for term of her life, the caſtles, towns, &
‘ manors of Koningsburg & Sandale; with the manors of Wakefield,
‘ Hatfield, Soureſby, Brethwel, Fiſhlake, Dewſberry, & Hallifax; &
‘ after her deceaſe upon John & Thomas his ſons by her, & the heirs
‘ male of their bodies, with remainder to his right heirs. Unto which
‘ indenture his ſeal was affixed; whereupon, on one ſide is expreſſed his

a Bar. Vol. II. p. 74. a.   d Fab. part 2. p. 219. b.
b Bar. Vol. I. p. 81. b.   e id. p. 220. a. b.
c confer. Bar. Vol. I. p. 82. b. cum ejuſd.   f Stow, p. 377.
p. 81. b.   g Bar. Vol. I. p. 82. b.

‘ effigies

' effigies in a gown & fitting in a chair, holding a hawk in his left hand,
' with this circumfcription, viz. *Sigillum Johannis Comitis Warennie*
' *& Strathernie, &* ᵃ *Comitis Palatii.* And on the other fide, on horfe-
' back, with his fword in his right hand, & in his left his fhield of arms,
' with this circumfcription, *Sigillum Johannis Comitis Warennie & Sur-*
' *reye, Domini de Bromfield & Yale.* Which John his fon, by the be-
' fore fpecified Maud de Nereford bore for his arms, chequy, or & azure,
' a canton gules, with a lion rampant ermine thereon (the proper coat
' of Nereford) from whom the Warenns of Poynton in Chefhire de-
' rive their defcent. The forefaid John E. Warenn [& lord of Stanford]
' ᵇ by an indenture betwixt the king & him, bearing date at Chautune,
' the 2. of June, 20. E. 3. agreed, that the K. fhould thenceforth pro- June 2,
' tect & defend him againft all perfons whatfoever, natives or ftrangers,
' in all quarrels & caufes, which might in reafon concern him : as alfo,
' that he fhould fupport him in peaceable poffeffion of all his lands,
' whereof he was at that time feifed, either in England or Wales. And
' that, if God fhould pleafe to fend him an heir by Ifabel de Houland,
' then his wife, fhould the fame heir be male or female, it fhould be
' joyned in marriage to fome one of the blood royal, unto whom the
' K. fhould think fitteft : fo that the whole inheritance of this E.
' with the name & arms of Warenne, fhould be preferved by the
' blood royal, in the blood of him the faid E. And, in cafe he fhould
' depart this life without any fuch iffue, begotten on the body of
' her the faid Ifabel, that then all his caftles, manors, lands, & tene-
' ments in Surrey, Suffex, & Wales, fhould remain to the K. to be be-
' ftowed on fome one of his own fons (whom he fhould think fit) on
' condition, that, in the perfon of fuch fon & his heirs, the name, ho-
' nor, & arms of Warenne, fhould be for ever maintained & kept.
' And moreover, it was farther agreed, that if the faid Ifabel fhould, by
' law of the realm, be endowed of thofe lands & tenements, lying in
' the counties of Surrey, Suffex, & Wales before fpecified, whereof he
' was at that time poffeffed ; that then fhe fhould be only endowed of
' thofe manors, lands, & tenements, referving the caftles to the K. & to
' fuch of his fons on whom the K. fhould think fit to beftow them ;
' fhe having a reafonable affignation otherwife in lieu of them. ᶜ In
' July the K. fayled into Normandie, & the E. of Northampton [lord July,
of Stanford in reverfion] ' was one of the chiefe captains that went over
' with him : ᵈ the faid E. being then with the K. to raife the fiege of
' Aguillon. ᵉ After the departure of Jhon duke of Normandie from
' the fiege of Aguillon [now raifed] the E. of Northampton with his
' compaignie, gat a ftrong towne called in French la Roche Darien, the
' rock of Arien.' Holingfhed tells us from Froifart, that when K. Edw.

a This *Comes Palatii* was the fame, or   c Hol. p. 929. a. b.
fomething like the *mayor du palais* in France.   d Bar. Vol. I. p. 185. b.
   b Bar. ut fupra.   e Fabian, part 2. p. 220. b.

came to Caen ᵃ ' the conftable of France & E. of Tankervile, ment to
' have kept their defences on the walles, gate, bridge, & river, & to
' have left the fuburbs, bycaufe not clofed but by the river: but they
' of the towne faid they would fight the K.   When the conftable faw
' their good wills, he was content, & fo forth they went: but when
' they faw the Englifh approach in good order, & the archers ready to
' fhoote, they fled, & the Englifh flue many, & entred the towne with
' them.   The conftable & E. of Tankervile, took a tower to fave them-
' felves, but perceyving the place to be of no force, fubmitted them-
' felves to Sir Thomas Holland.'   Holingfhed himfelf afterwards con-
tradicts this ftory, & fays, ' whatfoever Froiffart doth report, it is to be
' proved the E. of Tankerville was taken by one Legh; to whom for
' that, & his other manlike prowes fhewed elfewhere in this journey,
' K. Edw. gave a lordfhip in Chefhire called Hanley.'   However, admitting Tho. lord Holland did not take the E. of Tankerville, yet he
actually tooke the conftable; whofe name was Raufe E. of Ewe &
Guines.   At the battle of Creffi ' ᵇ K. Edward ordeyned three battles:
' in the firft, was the prince of Wales, & with him ᶜ in the van, lord
' Thomas Holland [afterwards buried at Stanford] &c. In the 2. the
' E. of Northampton [lord of Stanford in reverfion] &c. In the 3.
' was the K. &c.   ᵈ The firft battel, whereof the prince was ruler, had
' the archers ftanding in maner of an herfe, & the men of armes in the
' bottom of the battel.   The E. of Northampton, with the fecond
' battel, was on a wing in good order redy to comfort the princes battel,
' if need were.   ᵉ This [battel of Creffi] was a perillous battaile & fore
' foughten: there were few taken to mercie, for the Englifh had fo de-
' termined.   Certain French & Almaines perforce opened the archers
' of the princes battaile, & came to fight with the men of armes hand
' to hand.   Then the fecond battaile of Englifhe came to fuccour the
' princes, & not before it was time; for they of that battayle had as
' then ynough to do: in fo much as the E. of Northampton & others
' fent to the K. where he ftood aloft on a windmill hill to advaunce for-
' ward, & come to theyr ayde, they being as then fore layd to of their
' enemies.   The K. hereupon demaunded if his fon were flain, or felled
' to the earth! No, fayde the Knt. that brought the meffage, but he is
' fore matched.   Well, faid the K. returne to him & them that fent
' you, & fay that they fend no more to me, fo long as my fon is alive;
' for I will that this jorney be his, with the honor thereof.   ᶠThe mef-
' fenger returned, & tho' he brought not men to their fuccor: yet this
' anfwer greatly encouraged them to do their beft, being half abafhed
' in that they had fo fent to the K. for ayde.'   And thus was the victo-
' ry atchieved.   ' ᵍ On the morrow before funrife there marched to-

a Hol. p. 930. b.   e id. p. 934. b.
b id. p. 932. b.   f Speed, p. 706. b.
c Bar. Vol. II. p. 74. a.   g Hol. p. 937. a
d Hol. p. 933. b.

‘ wards the Englifh another great hoft, mightie & ftrong of the French
‘ menne : but the E. of Northampton [lord of Stanford in reverfion] &
‘ the E. of Norfolk iffued out againft them in three battayles, & after
‘ long & terrible fight difcomfited them ; where they took of knights &
‘ efquiers a great number, & flue above 2000. purfuing the chace three
‘ leagues from the place.’   Thefe gentlemen, as another author tells
‘ us [a], knew nothing of the defeat of their friends the day before, but
depending on their getting the victory, came now to rifle the Englifh.
‘ [b] Alfo the E. of Northampton fetched a booty out of Arthoys, & as
‘ he returned tooke Terrouane.’   ‘ [c] Thus before, in, & after that
‘ memorable fight, the E. of Northampton [lord of Stanford in rever-
fion] ‘ approved himfelf a right valiant & expert commander.’   ‘ [d] The
‘ day before the feaft of the affumption the K. came to Poiffe, where, Aug.16.
‘ whiles the bridge was repairing,there came a great number of Frenchmen
‘ at armes & other foldiers to hinder the fame. But the E. of Northampton
‘ iffued out, & flue of them more than a 1000, & the reft fled.   [e] After
‘ that the K. marched toward Graund Vylliers, & while he was there en-
‘ camped, his vauntgard was difcried by the K. of Bohemes men at armes.
‘ Whereupon our men iffued out in great haft, & joyned battaile with
‘ them, but were enforced to retire.   Notwithftanding the E. of North-
‘ ampton iffued out, & refcued the horfemen with the other foldiers,
‘ fo that few or none of them were either taken or flain, faving only
‘ Thomas Talbot, but had again the enemy in chace within two leagues
‘ of Amiens, of whom we took eight, & flew twelve : the reft being
‘ well horfed, tooke into the towne.’   Sometime after the fame year
‘ [f] came two cardinals from pope Clement, to treate of a peace betwixte
‘ the two kings, whereupon commiffioners were appointed, of whom
‘ the E. of Northampton [lord of Stanford in reverfion] was one for the
‘ K. of England.

  XXI. ‘ [g] In Hilary term, 21. E. 3. was a pleading before the K. about 21.E.3.
‘ matters relating to the church of S. Peter in Stanford, & the gild of
‘ S. Peter there, & the alderman of the fame.’   I have yet feen no
more of this matter, fave this fhort memorandum.   ‘ [h] John Fiffor,
‘ one of the vicars choral of Linc. who pronounced the fentence of
‘ excommunication made by the pope againft Roger de Cloun incum-
‘ bent of S. Peters in Staunford was pardoned in Hilary term 21.
‘ E. 3. before the K.’   Which being taken out of the fame roll, I make
no doubt relates to the fame affair.   ‘ John fon of Walter le Halver
‘ fold the meffuages, &c. given him as above 14. E. 3. by his father,

a Speed, p. 707. b.
b Hol. p. 937. b.
c Bar. Vol. I. p. 186. a.
d Hol. p. 936. a. b.
e id. ib. b. a.
f Hol. p. 942. b.
g Extract. de placitis coram rege, termino
Hil. 21. E. 3. de ecclefia S. Petri, & de

gilda S. Petri & aldermanno ejufdem gilde,
Rot. 93.

  h Johannes Fiffor vicarius in choro Linc.
qui pronunciavit fententiam excommunica-
tionis per papam factam contra Rogerum de
Cloun incumbentem in ecclefia B. Petri de
Staunford pardonatur Hilar. 21. E. 3. coram rege, rot. 93.

‘ to Richard de Hauville burgefs of Staunford. B. H.   In this 2 1. E. 3.
‘ Thomas lord Holland [afterwards buried at Stanford] in confiderati-
‘ on of four thoufand florens, fold his prifoner the E. of Ewe [taken
as above at Caen] ‘ unto K. Edw.’   ‘ a John the 2. E. Warenne [lord
of Stanford] ‘ the laft E. of that noble & antient family, by his teftament
‘ dated at his caftle of Conesburgh in *Com. Ebor.* (where he ftiles him-
‘ felf John E. of Warenne, Surrey, & Strathern, lord of Bromfield &
‘ Yale) bequeathed his body to be buried in the church of S. Pancrace
‘ at Lewes; & (having given to Joan de Bafing his daughter, a filver
‘ cup, to his daughter Katherine ten marcs; as alfo to Ifabel, another
‘ of his daughters, then a nun at Sempringham, twenty marcs; & to
‘ Ifabel de Houland his wife, a ring with a ruby) departed this
‘ life without any lawful iffue the morrow preceding the Kalends

June 30. ‘ of July [that is, June the 30.] ann. 1347. 21. E. 3. being the 61. year
1347. ‘ of his age: & lieth buried alone under a raifed tomb, near the high
21.E.3. ‘ altar, in the abby of Lewes; leaving Alice his fifter, wife to Edmund
‘ E. of Arundel, his next heir in blood.   The lands, whereof the in-
‘ quifitions taken after his death, do report him to die feifed, were as
‘ followeth: the manor of Tiburne in Middlefex: the manors of Gran-
‘ tham, Stanford, & Paunton magna, in Lincolns: the caftle & towne
‘ of Lewes, with the lordfhips of Cokefield, Clenton, Brighelmeftone,
‘ Rottingden, Hounderden, Northefs, Radmeld, Kymer, Middleton,
‘ Alington, Worth, Pycombe, Pydingho, & Seford; in Suffex.   The
‘ caftle & towne of Rigate, with the manors of Dorking & Bechefworth
‘ in Surrey.   The manors of Troubrigge, Winterbourne, & Ambref-
‘ bury, in Wilts, for term of life, by the kings grant.   The caftle of
‘ Acre & manor of Beftone in Norfolk.   The manor of Gymingham,
‘ & advowfon of the abby of Marham.   The manor of Middlewold,
‘ the hundreds of Malhow & Brother-crofs in Norf.   The manor of
‘ Medmenham in Bucks. The manors of Caneford & Slapewike in Dor-
‘ fet, for term of life, with remainder to Thomas E. of Lancafter & his
‘ heirs.   The manors of Coningsburgh, Haitfield, & Wakefield in
‘ Yorkfhire.   The manors of Henftrig & Charleton in Somerfet.   The
‘ manor of Bokeland, in right of Joan his wife.   The manor of Wauton
‘ in Surrey, alfo for term of life, of the inheritance of John de Breaufe.’
William de Bohun E. of Northampton, as hath been fhewn, had a grant
of the caftle, manor, & town of Stanford in reverfion after the death
of the faid E. of Warenne.   And ‘ b in this 21. E. 3. Edmund de Lang-
‘ ley [the next lord of Stanford after the forefaid William Bohun] ‘ be-
‘ ing then but fix years of age, had a grant from the K. his father, in
‘ fpecial taile, of all the caftles, manors, & lands beyond Trent, for-
‘ merly belonging to John de Warenne, late E. of Surrey: but, in
‘ regard of his minority, Q Philippa, his mother, received the profits

a Bar. Vol. I. p. 82. a.   b Bar. Vol. II. p. 154. a.

                                                    ‘ of

' of them, for the maintenance & education of him, & other her
' younger children.' K. Edw. being the latter end of this year at the
fiege of Calais, ' ᵃ the Norman pirates took 15 of his fhips, in one of
' which Sir William Borton, Kt. [the fame, I fuppofe, who lived at
Tolthorpe by Stanford] ' as he was failing into England, was taken pri-
' foner. ᵃ At this fiege the E. of Northampton [lord of Stanford]
' made a rampire wherewith he kept away & beat back fuch fmall boats
' as the Bolloners were wont to victual Caleis with along the feafide,
' when the fhips could not be fuffered to pafs along the fea; & after-
' wards when the admiral of France came with his fhips of war to
' fight againft our Englifh fhips that lay at the fiege, thinking, whilft
' they were fighting, the fmall boats fhould pafs to Caleis with victu-
' als; the faid E. of Northampton meeting with him, valiantly put him
' to flight. ᵃ This fiege dured from the feaft of the nativity of our lady
[Sept. 8.] ' all the whole winter, with a great part of the fummer, ftill
' waxing ftronger. ᵇ In this 21. E. 3. Thomas lord Holland [afterwards
buried at Stanford] ' being again in France, was at the faid fiege of
' Calais. ᶜ Edmund Langley abovementioned had alfo about this time
' a grant from his father K. Edward the 3. of the caftle & manor of Fo-
' theringhay, affigned him for an inheritance or appennage, as it was then
' called.'

XXII. John Rodington, warden of the grey friers in Stanford, & a   1348.
man of good learning & figure, ' died, as Pits fays ᵈ, in 1348. at Bed-
' ford.' ' At this time, as Bale relates ᵉ, divers moft excellent foldiers
' of the equeftrian rank, ftroke with admiration at the holy lives of fe-
' veral white friers then living, became Carmelites, of which number Sir
' Geoffry Suthorpe, who entered himfelf into their monaftery at Stan-
' ford, was one.' At this time flourifhed John de Ultricuria.. ' John
' de Ultricuria, faith Pits ᶠ, was, I believe, an Englifhman, a perfon of
' great & ready wit, but that wit unfettled, rafh, & dangerous. He
' fometime wrote certain propofitions, which were firft condemned at
' Rome, & afterwards publickly recalled by himfelf in Oxford, where
' he ftudied in 1348. He wrote alfo fome fcholaftic pieces.' You will
hereafter find this John de Ultricuria at the great council held at
Stanford in 1392. which is the reafon why thus much relating to him
is here inferted. ' ᵍ Robert de Hextildefham, or Hexham, was at this
' time prefented, by John Foffor, prior of the conventual church of
' Durham & the chapter there, to the priory of S. Leonard by Stanford.'
The fiege of Caleis yet continuing, ' ʰ on Monday next before the feaft

a Stow. p. 382.
b Bar. Vol. II. p. 74. a.
c Britt. ant. & nova. Vol. 3. p. 473. b.
d in vita.
e Hiis temporibus [circa ann. 1348.] propter quorundam fratrum fanctitatem, quamplures equeftris ordinis ftrenuiffimi milites — Carmeli religioni fe donabant, & ex

hiis erant —— in domo Stanfordienfi, Galfridus Suthorpe. Ex Joh. Balæi Heliad. cap. 37. MS. Harley.
f in vita.
g Ex regiftri dicti Johannis prioris Dunelm. 2. partis 1. fol. 132. b.
h Stow, p. 382, 383.

22.E.3. ' of S. James [22. E. 3. 1348.] the French K. came with a great power
' to remove it.   Alſo the emperor (promiſing by othe to remove
' it by war or peace, or at leaſt victual the beſieged) came with
' his armie, & lodged ſcarce a mile from the Engliſh camp, re-
' queſting a treatie.   His ambaſſadors parleyed with the D. of Lancaſter,
' the E. of Northampton [lord of Stanford] & the E. of Huntingdon,
' but could not obtain their conſent ; ſo returned.   Mean ſeaſon the be-
' ſieged made known their ſtate to the French K. by ſigns & tokens.   For,
' at his firſt coming, they ſet up his ancient on the chief tower of the
' caſtle, alſo banners of the dukes & earles of France, & a little after
' the ſhutting in of the evening, made a great light on the top of one of
' the higheſt towers towards the French army, & a great ſhout & noiſe
' with trumpets & drummes.   The ſecond night they made the like,
' but ſomewhat leſſe.   The third night a very ſmall fire, giving forth
' therewith a ſorrowful voice, ſignifying thereby that their ſtrength
' touching the keeping of the town, was quite ſpent.   The ſame night
' they took in all their flags & antients, except their ſtandart.   The 2.
' of Auguſt, making fire in his tents, the French K. fled, whoſe taile the
' D. of Lancaſter & E. of Northampton cutting off, they ſlewe & tooke
' many of them.   When they of Caleis perceived this, they tooke their
' ſtandart downe, &, with great ſorrow, caſt it from the tower,
' into the ditch : & on the Saturday following ſurrendred.   [a] In this
' 22. E. 3. the ſaid E. of Northampton [lord of Stanford] in conſi-
' deration that K. Edw. did, at his requeſt, grant to Humph. de Bohun
' his brother E. of Hereford, the inheritance of the lordſhips of Upha-
' ven & Send in Wiltſhire (whereof Edw. his other brother had a grant
' to himſelf & the heirs male of his body, but died without iſſue) remit-
' ted to the ſaid K. two thouſand marcs of the mony due to him for
' his ſervice in Britany.'   Richard Parſons of Northwytham in Lincolnſ.
& Alice his wife ſold now a meſſuage with a croft, &c. there to John
Folerid & Iſabel his wife : which meſſuage & croft, &c. as I take it,
came afterwards to Browns hoſpital in Stanford :   I ſhall here therefore
inſert the deed of ſale.   ' [b] Let preſent & future people know that I
' Richard Parſuns of Northwytham & Alice my wife, have given, gran-
' ted, & by this our preſent charter confirmed, to John Folerid of the
' ſame & Iſabel his wife, for a certain ſum of mony to us before hand
' paid, one meſſuage with a croft adjacent & other their appurtenances
' in the town of Northwytham aforeſaid, between a tenement of Tho-
' mas Barnard ſouth & a tenement of Thomas de Scolthorp north, as
' it extends it ſelf from the kings highway eaſt as far as the field of the
' town aforeſaid weſt ; & an acre of arable land with the appurtenances
' lying at the weſtern head of the meſſuage aforeſaid, between the
' meſſuage aforeſaid, & a tenement of Thomas Barnard eaſt, & the road

a Bar. Vol. I. p. 186. a.   mus eleemoſynariæ Gul. Brown apud
b Ex autographo penes gardianum do-   Stanford.

                                                                      ' which

'which leads to Grantham weſt: to have & to hold the foreſaid meſ_
'ſuage, &c. to the foreſaid John Folerid & Iſabell his wife, &c. of the
'capital lord of that fee, by the ſervices thence due, & of right ac-
'cuſtomed: well, & in peace, freely, & quietly, & hereditarily for ever,
'&c. In witneſs whereof to this preſent charter we have put to our ſeals.
'Witneſſes, Geoffry Dyme of Northwytham, John Wache of the ſame,
'Thomas Barnard of the ſame, William de Gretvile lord of Gunby,
'Thoma Eſton, Roger Corby of Colſterworth; & others. Given at
'Northwytham the Sunday next after the feaſt of the ſaints Dennis, &
'his companions [Ruſticus & Elutherius] ' in the 22. of Edw. the 3.'

XXIII. ' John de Apethorpe of Staunford, granted to Reymund le 29.E.3.
'Knokker of the ſame, one place with the appurtenances in Bradecroft,
'as it extends from the kings highway ſouth, as far as the garden of the
'ſame Reymund north. Given at Stanford the ſunday next after the feaſt
'of the purification. B. H.' ' ᵃ William E. of Northampton [lord of
Stanford] ' was again conſtituted one of the kings commiſſioners to
'treat with the commiſſioners of the K. of France, upon a truce betwixt
'K. Edward & him. ᵇ The French would not agree to a final peace, un-
'leſs Caleis were reſtored, which would not be graunted: ſo the truce,
'taken for a year, was ſo continued.' At this time a great peſtilence
raged in England, whereof died ſeveral nuns in a little nunnery at great
Wirthorp on the hill, & all the reſt (one only excepted) fled & left the
houſe. ' W. Apethorp, burgeſs of Staunford, gave to John Knot capel-
'lan, four meſſuages & one cottage, & 17 acres of arable land, & one
'acre of meadow: whereof three meſſuages are together ſituate upon
'Cleymount, between a tenement of the abbat of Croylands eaſt, & a
'tenement of Robert de Wykes weſt; & the other meſſuage is ſituate
'in the ſtreet called Behyndeback, between a tenement of the lord
'abbat of Thorney north, & a tenement belonging to the maſs of
'the bleſſed Mary in the mercat Staunford ſouth. And the cottage lies
'between a tenement belonging to the maſs of the bleſſed Mary near
'the bridge caſt, & a tenement of W. de Melton weſt. And of the land two
'acres abutt on the land of the nuns of S. Michael &c. north, & the land
'ſometime belonging to the caſtle of Staunford ſouth; & two acres abutt
'on the land belonging to the chapel of S. Thomas the martyr north.
'B. H.' The three firſt tenements above deſcribed were ſituate where
now ſtands the chapel & alms-houſe of Mr. William Brown. The
houſe adjoyning to the eaſt end of the chapel is that formerly the
abbat of Croylands. Cleymount is that ſtreet or part of the town
where the ſaid hoſpital & mercat croſs ſtands. The ſtreet called Behyndeback is now called the white meat mercat. The maſs of the B. Virgin
in the mercat (as hath been ſaid) was celebrated in the ſouth chancel
of All-Saints church in the mercat. The maſs of S. Mary by the
bridge was ſome chantery in S. Marys church by the bridge. S. Thomas

ᵃ Bar. Vol. I. p. 186. a.   ᵇ Stow, p. 386.

the martyrs chappel was on the other fide of the bridge where now ftands the lord Burghleys hofpital.

24.E.3. XXIV. ' ᵃ It is faid by fome, that Sir Tho. Holland [afterwards bu-ried at Stanford] ' was fteward of the houfhold to William de Montacute ' E. of Salisbury, & married his miftrefs ; viz. Joan wife to that E. ' daughter of Edmund, & fifter & heir to John [Plantagenet] E. of ' Kent. But herein there is a miftake : for, by his petition to pope ' Clement the 6. reprefenting, that the faid E. of Salisbury had a pur- ' pofe to have wedded her, had not a precontract with her, by him, ' been formerly made, & carnal knowledge enfued: Alfo, that never- ' thelefs, the fame E. taking advantage of his abfence in foreign parts, ' made a fecond contract with her, & unjuftly with-held her: his ho- ' linefs, on full hearing of the caufe, gave fentence for him ; where- ' upon he accordingly enjoyed her : the E. of Salisbury acquiefcing ' therein, as it feems, by his aftermarriage with another woman. ' ᵇ In this 24. E. 3. William E. of Northampton [lord of Stanford] ' was made warden of the Marches in Scotland. ᶜThe fame year he ' was with K. Edw. a fhip-board at Winchelfea, where, on the feaft of ' the decollation of S. John the baptift, the K. obtained a glorious victo- ' ry over the Spanifh navy: the particulars whereof may be feen in my ' author.' Walter Hefton, befides being prior of the white friers at Stanford, if we may believe Bale ᵈ, ' was head of feveral other mona- ' fteries of his brethren in England.' Nay Leland afferts, that he was at laft ' ᵉ provincial of his order in this nation.' As for his works, Pits tells us ᶠ, ' he publifhed a treatife of queftions upon Ariftotles book ' concerning the foul, another of certain propofitions, & feveral more. ' At length, as the fame author adds, he furrendred up his fpirit to God at ' Stanford, & was there committed to his grave about the year of our Lord ' 1350.' —— Alfo fpeaking of the famous John Repingale, Pits writes ᵍ, ' it is faid he died at Stanford, & received burial in his own monaftery ' there in 1350.' Now that he died, & was buried there, I believe. But this is a grofs miftake in point of time. For the faid John Repingale was alive in 1359. when he, with the prior of S. Leonards by Stanford, were by his patron John Synwel bifhop of Lincoln, appointed his proxies to admit the new priorefs of S. Michaels nunnery by Stanford & give her poffeffion. See the inftrument it felf whereby they were fo empowered under that year. ' ʰ On the 16. of Jan. 1357. 24. E. 3. ' the lord abbat & convent of Burg exhibited a particular of their pri- ' vileges & annual penfions in this neighbourhood before John Syn- ' wel bifhop of Lincoln at his vifitation then held: &, among other ' matters, a penfion of three fhillings from the church of Efton, half a ' marc from the church of Tinwell, & ten fhillings from the church of

a Bar. Vol. II. p. 74. a.
b id. Vol. I. p. 186. a.
c Stow, p. 391.
d in vita.

e in vita.
f in vita.
g in vita.
h Ex regiftri Synwel folio 1.

' S.

' S. Martin in Stanford, were allowed of & confirmed by the said
' bishop at Buckden.

XXV. ' ª In the 25. E. 3. William de Bohun E. of Northampton [lord 25. E. 3
of Stanford] ' was one of the commissioners appointed to treat with the
' great men of Scotland, for enlargment of David Brus, & making a
' final peace betwixt England & Scotland. ᵇ In the 26. E. 3. the 26. E. 3.
' said William, together with John de Vere E. of Oxford, was in
' commission for arraying of soldiers in the counties of Essex &
' Hartford, to oppose the French then threatning an invasion; &
' was himself charged with the providing of 30. men at arms with
' lances, in respect of his lordship of Melenith in Wales. ᶜ Thomas
' lord Holland [afterwards buried at Stanford] the same year obtained
' a grant of one hundred marcs *per annum,* out of the ferme of the
' city of Exeter, for the better support of Joane his wife abovementi-
' oned, during her life.----Richard de Waltham was at this time parson of
' Colines-weston, now Colyweston, by Stanford. B. H.' ' W. de
' Steandeby, alderman of Stanford, was witness to a deed bearing date
' the Friday in Whitsun-week 26. E. 3. B. H.' Sir Nicholas Crophul, June 29.
Knt. & Margery his wife, daughter of Sir Robert de Hausted, Knt. de- 1352.
ceased, were, as it should seem, by the Bp. of Lincolns deputation to
the prior of S. Leonards by Stanford & others, for that purpose, about
this time divorced. About which, the said bishop writes thus. ' ᵈ John,
' by divine permission, bishop of Lincoln, to his beloved sons the prior
' of S. Leonards by Staunford, & to the masters John de Belver & Wil-
' liam de Spaldwic of our diocese skilled in the law; health, grace, &
' benediction. We, in your faithfulness & prudence very much con-
' fiding, to proceed, know, appoint, & diffine in a cause of divorce
' between Sir Nicholas de Crophul, Kt. actor of the one part, & Mar-
' gery daughter of Sir Robert de Hausted, Kt. deceased, whom the same
' Nicholas *de facto* holds for his wife [of the other part] to you, by
' virtue of these presents our place do commit to be canonically execu-
' ted. Given at Lafford the 3. of the Kal. of July [that is, June 29.]
' 1352. & of our consecration the 5. ᵉ At a visitation held at . . . . in
' 1352. in the 6. year of the consecration of the said bishop, the abbat
' & convent of Croyland produced their instruments, &c. whereby it
' appear'd that that abby received twenty shillings yearly from the
' church of S. Michael in Stanford.' The church here mentioned is
great S. Michaels. ' ᶠ Joan de Baars, the first wife of John the 2. E.

a Bar. Vol. I. p. 186. a.
b id. ib.
c id. Vol. II. p. 74. a.
d Johannes, permissione divina, Linc. episcopus, dilectis filiis priori S. Leonardi juxta Staunford ac magistris Johanni de Belvero & Willielmo de Spaldwic nostre diocesis jurisperitis, salutem, gratiam & bene-dictionem. De vestris fidelitate & pru-dentia plurimum confidentes, ad procedend. cognoscend. statuend. & diffiend. in causa divortii inter D. Nicholaum de Crophul mi-litem ex parte una, & Margeriam filiam D. Roberti de Hausted militis defuncti, quam idem Nicholaus de facto tenet pro uxore, vobis, tenore presentium vices nostras com-mittimus canonice exequend. Datum apud Lafford 3º. Kalend. Julii, A. D. 1352. & consecrationis nostre 5º. Ex registri Syn-wel fol. 6.
e id. ib.
f Bar. Vol. I. p. 82. b.

' Warenne

‘ Warrenne late owner of Stanford, being now beyond fea, had licenſe
‘ to continue there till the 15. of S. Michael this year.’

27.E.3.   XXVI. On the 21. of Jan. 135¾. 27. E. 3. John Synwel biſhop of
Lincoln made frier Roger de S. Lis, D. D. of the black friers college at
Stanford, confeſſor of that fraternity for the year enſuing, with power
to abſolve in epiſcopal caſes, as, in his ſaid licenſe (which was in part
as follows) are more particularly mentioned. ‘ ª John biſhop of Lin-
‘ coln to his beloved ſon frier Roger de S. Lis, profeſſor of divinity,
‘ of the order of friers predicants of the convent of Staunford, greet-
‘ ing, &c.   In your diſcretion & the ſerenity of zeal which you are
‘ known to have for procuring the good of ſouls, greatly confiding ;
‘ to confeſs all perſons in our juriſdiction within the bounds of the
‘ ſaid convent (when they think fit to be confeſſed to you) & in our
‘ ſtead to give them abſolution of their ſins, &c. in the underwritten
‘ epiſcopal caſes; to wit, in adulteries, inceſts, breaches of vows, de-
‘ flowering of virgins, ſodomies, laying violent hands upon clercs,
‘ blaſphemies againſt God or his ſaints, &c. we grant you a faculty to
‘ continue for one year only.   Given at Bardeney the 2. of the Kal.
‘ of Feb. 1352. & of our confecration the 6.   ᵇ This year Thomas
‘ lord Holland having iſſue by Joan his wife [both the ſaid Thomas &
Joan being afterwards buried in the grey friers church at Stanford] ‘ &
‘ doing his homage to the K. had livery of the lands of her inheri-
‘ tance.   Shortly after which, the ſame year, he obtained licenſe for
‘ a mercat upon the Wedneſday every week at his manor of Butter-
‘ crambe, in Yorkſhire; as alſo for a fair yearly, on the eve, day, &
‘ morrow of S. Botolph.’   ᶜ The ſaid Tho. lord Holland had ſummons
‘ to parliament among the barons of this realm from this 27. to the 31.
‘ of E. 3. incluſive.’   As the late learned Greek profeſſor of Cambridge
Mr. Joſhua Barnes acquaints us, ‘ ᵈ a parliament being ſummoned on
‘ the 15. of July to meet at Weſtminſter the 23. of Sept. following,
‘ Sir William Shareſhal the chief juſtice told them, that the K. had
‘ ſummoned that parliament for removing the ſtaple from beyond the
‘ ſeas into this realm.   Whereupon the commons petitioned that the
‘ ſtaple might be appointed at Worceſter, Nottingham, Hull, S. Bo-
‘ tolphs [i. e. Boſton] Stanford, Lyn, Ipſwich, & Canterbury. The K.
‘ anſwered, *One* ſhall be at Canterbury, & *that only*, in honor of S.
‘ Thomas.’   But he afterwards altered his mind.   For, ſaith Mr. Stow,

a Johannes, epiſcopus Linc. dilecto filio, fratri Rogero de S. Licio, S. T. P. ordinis fratrum predicatorum de conventu Staunford, &c. ſalutem.   De tua diſcretione & ſerenitate zeli quas ad ſalutem animarum procurand. habere, &c. ut omnes ſubditos noſtros, infra loca limitationis dicti conventus (quum tibi volunt confiteri) &c. & peccatorum ſuorum, &c. abſolutionem, vice noſtra, &c. valeas exigere, in caſibus epiſcopalibus infra ſcriptis, viz. in adulteriis, in-

ceſtibus, tranſgreſſionibus votorum, deflorationibus virginum, ſodomiis, manuum injectarum in clericos, blaſphemie in Deum vel ejus ſanctos, &c. facultatem tibi concedimus, per unum tantum annum duraturam.   Datum apud Bardenay 2. Kal. Feb. A. D. 1352. & conſecrationis noſtre 6°. Ex ejuſdem Joh. Reg. fol. 39.
   b Bar. Vol. II. p. 74. b.
   c id. ib.
   d Hiſt. Edw. 3. p. 431.

‘ ª the

' ᵃ the morrow after S. Mathies day began a parliament, wherein
' it was ordained, that the ftaple of wool before kept in Flaunders
' at Bridges, fhould from thenceforth be holden in divers parts of Eng-
' land, Wales, & Ireland, as at Newcaftle, Yorke, Lincolne, Canter-
' burie, Norwich, Weftminfter, Chichefter, Winchefter, Excefter,
' Briftow, & Carmarden.' ' ᵇ The E. of Northampton [lord of Stanford]
' went irto Scotland with a great companie of armed men & archers,
' where he rode thro' the marches & enforced the caftle of Loghmaban,
' & other fortreffes to yield; & took the Scots that were laid in am-
' bufhes. He alfo held a treatie of peace with the Scots, who gladly
' would have redeemed their K. [David Bruce yet a prifoner in England]
' & made a perpetual peace with the Englifh; but yet, fo as the K. of
' Scots fhould not hold his land of the K. of England.'—' W. de
' Steandby, burgefs of Staunford, gave to Robert de Wylingham,
' one meffuage fituate in the abbat of Burgs liberty, in S. Martins, in
' the ftreet called le Hyegate, between a tenement of John Young of
' Efton north, & a tenement of . . . . . Malerbe fouth, as it extends
' from the kings highway weft, as far as the land of *Sir* William de
' Birthorp [I fancy it fhould be Wirthorp] eaft. Witneffes, W. de Schy-
' lington, alderman of Staunford, &c. B. H.'

XXVII. Befides the nunnery of S. Michael at little Wirthorp by 28.E.3.
Stanford, there was alfo formerly another fmall convent of nuns at
great Wirthorp on the hill; of which laft Edmund of Woodftock E. of
Kent, or fome other perfon of the royal family & E. of that county, was
moft probably founder. But how the fame was endowed, other than
that the parifh church of the faid town of great Wirthorp on the hill was
very early appropriated thereto, I find not. Where note, the faid parifh church of great Wirthorp on the hill is not to be taken for the
conventual church of S. Michael aforefaid at little Wirthorp by Stanford, but diftinct from the fame, & fo continued 'till that little nunnery
at Wirthorp on the hill (to which the faid parifh church was firft appropriated) falling to decay (for want of fufficient revenues to fupport it) was
united to the priory of S. Michael by Stanford; by which union, the
appropriation of the faid parifh church of Wirthorp on the hill was,
as it were, carried along with the houfe to which it formerly appertained, & thereby alfo appropriated to the faid priory of S. Michael at
little Wirthorp by Stanford, conditionally neverthelefs that the priorefs
& convent of the faid houfe of S. Michael fhould conftantly find a
capellan to officiate in the fame, & adminifter the facraments & other
requifites to the parifhioners. This happened the 28. of E. 3. at what 28.E.3.
time, & after, the faid parifh church of great Wirthorp on the hill was
actually ftanding; exactly how long it afterwards remained, I know not;
but guefs it continued 'till the fuppreffion of religious houfes, there being even then a fmall village there; now reduced to a few houfes. As

ᵃ p. 398.   ᵇ id. ib.

for the other revenues belonging to the forefaid nunnery at great Wirthorp, the whole I believe never amounted to a great deal, but furely
at laft funk very low, when in fo early an age as this 28. of E. the 3.
what was left fufficed only to maintain a fingle nun. In the great peftilence 1349. (as I have already touched) fome nuns of this houfe died,
& the reft, all but one, fled. Upon the 11. of March 135¼. 28. E. 3.
Thomas lord Holland & Joanna his wife, daughter of Edm. of Woodftock E. of Kent (being now patrons of that deferted houfe) procured
therefore the kings licenfe for the ordinary to unite the faid nunnery
of Wirthorp on the hill to the forefaid convent of S. Michael at little
Wirthorp by Stanford, & to remove thither the one nun abovementioned who was left there deferted by her priorefs & fifterhood. Thereby alfo the faid K. gave leave for the faid Thomas lord Holland & lady
Joan his wife to make over the whole poffeffions of the faid priory of
Wirthorp on the hill, with the appropriation of the parifh church there
& their feveral rights in the fame, to the faid priory of S. Michael, with
power to the priorefs & convent thereof, any thing in the ftatute of
mortmane notwithftanding, to receive & hold the fame to them &
their fucceffors, referving only to the abbats of Croyland & Burg, lords
of the fees there, the due & accuftomed fervices. Take now the faid
K. Edw. the thirds licenfe for uniting the nunnery of Wirthorp to
the nunnery of S. Michael by Stanford, which is as follows. ' ªThe
' K. to all whom, &c. Know ye, that whereas our beloved & trufty
' Thomas de Holland, & Johann his wife, our moft dear cofen, pa-
' trons of the houfe of nuns of Wyrthorp in the diocefe of Lincoln,
' as is faid; have befought us, that (whereas the faid houfe is very
' meanly endowed, & what thro' the peftilence which hath lately raged,
' as well as other misfortunes, reduced to fo great poverty, that all the
' nuns of the faid houfe, one only excepted, thro' mere neceffity have
' gone & difperfed themfelves, whereby a miferable ftop is there put to
' religion; & whereas the faid houfe hath not fufficient means of its
' own to recover it from thefe misfortunes) we would grant leave for
' the diocefan of the place, with confent of thofe whom it concerns,
' regularly to annex the faid houfe, with all its rights & poffeffions to
' the priory of the nuns of S. Michael by Stanford, of the faid diocefe;
' that they being fo annexed & united, the worfhip of almighty God
' may be more honorably performed, & they better enabled to fupport
' the charges on them incumbent: We, to the forefaid requeft, fince
' it is both reafonable & pious, being willing to agree, have gracioufly
' granted & given leave, for us & our heirs, as far as in us lies, that the
' bifhop of the place aforefaid, may have power to annex & unite the
' faid houfe of Wyrthorp, with all its rights & poffeffions, alfo with the
' church of Wyrthorp, to the faid houfe appropriated, to the forefaid
' priory of S. Michael; & to tranflate the forementioned remaining

a Ex pat. 28. E. 3. par. 1. m. 16. & Mon. Ang. tom. I. p. 489.

3   ' nun

' nun to the said priory of S. Michael, there under a regular habit to
' abide.   Moreover we have granted & given leave, for us & our heirs,
' as far as in us lies, to the forenamed Thomas & Johan, that they may
' have power to give & confer, that which to them belongs of the said
' house of Wyrthorp & other the things & possessions of the same,
' with the appurtenances aforenamed, to the prioress & nuns of the
' said priory of S. Michael: And, to the same prioress & nuns of the
' same priory of S. Michael, that they, annexion & union of this sort
' being made, the foresaid house of Wyrthorp, with the said church ap-
' propriate, & with all the rights & possessions abovesaid, also with
' the appurtenances whatsoever, may be able to receive ; & to hold the
' same house, with the church so annexed & united, to them & their
' successors for ever, according to an ordination on this part to be
' lawfully made.   By virtue of these presents, we have moreover gran-
' ted our special license for so doing, the statute of lands & tenements
' not to be put unto mortmain notwithstanding : forbidding that the
' foresaid Thomas & Johan, or the heirs of her Johan, or any whom it
' concerns; or the forenamed prioress & nuns of S. Michael, or the
' successors of the same, on account of the premises, by us, or our
' heirs, or any our servants whatsoever, be therefore occasionally mo-
' lested, or in any sort aggrieved.   Saving always to the chief lords
' of the fees aforesaid, the services thence due & accustomed.   Witness
' the K. at Westm. &c. the 11. of March.'   Poverty was always a pretence both for union of monasteries & appropriation of churches to
them.   And indeed, if we may believe what is asserted in the preamble of the kings letters above, the house of nuns at Wyrthorp on
the hill was now reduced to the utmost distress.   Nor was the nunnery of S. Michael by Stanford (to which last it was proposed that other
should be united) at this time without complaint of great wants & necessities.   For, by the bishops act of union (which follows) it appears,
that the prioress & sisters of that house as much coveted such an union,
as the one nun who was left alone in the other convent of great Wirthorp on the hill.   A vast burden of debts, a very small income, the extraordinary charges they were at to support themselves in the last great
pestilence, & the irreparable lowness of estate whereunto they were now
reduced, as well as the near neighbourhood of these houses, being some
of the motives which they of that convent of S. Michael made use of,
in a petition of theirs to the bishop of Lincoln, the better to persuade
him to comply with this act of necessity, the union of the two houses.
Soon after receipt whereof, the said bishop inclining to grant what they
desired (besides what they had each said for themselves & one another)
alledged in particular for the priory of S. Michael, that it was now &
always a place of remarkable discipline & good religion ; &, as for the
poverty of both houses, that he had made a strict enquiry, & had reason to believe the same was but too true.   Wherefore having seen

the kings licenfe as above, & read the founders letter, both exprefly concurring, he tells us, he had thereupon treated with his chapter, & they likewife confenting, willingly proceeded to unite the faid priories, & finifh an affair wherein all the parties appeared to be fo well agreed. It feems neverthelefs, by his faid letters of union, tho' there was now, as hath been faid, but one nun left in the houfe of Wirthorp on the hill, yet was there, befides her, a now actual priorefs of the fame fomewhere elfe in being (fled, I fuppofe, to fome other monaftery for relief) without whofe confent, refignation, or death, the faid union could not proceed. How long both houfes waited for the removal of this impediment I know not; but, as foon as fhe died, refigned, or was removed, then, & not before, the bifhop gave leave for the priorefs of S. Michael, by her felf or proxy, to enter upon the premifes at Wirthorp on the hill, without taking out any farther licenfe from himfelf, or any other perfon, for fo doing: faving only to himfelf & his church of Lincoln their accuftomed dues, & providing likewife, that the priorefs & convent of S. Michael fhould ever after find a capellan to perform all religious offices in the church & parifh of Wirthorp on the hill; & the parifhioners thus provided for, that then the revenues of the faid church fhould be applied for relief of fuch nuns as were fick in the infirmary of the faid houfe, & to buy in provifions for the cook, & for no other purpofes. But hear his inftrument. ' ᵃ To all the fons of holy mother church, efpecially thofe
' unto whom thefe prefent letters fhall come, John, by divine permif-
' fion, bifhop of Lincoln, greeting in the favior of all. Our beloved
' daughters in Chrift, the priorefs & convent of the priory of S. Mi-
' chael by *Staunford*, of the order of S. Benedict, of our diocefe, by
' their petition have fhewed us, that they are loaded with fo great a
' burden of debts, alfo that the rents & profits of the faid priory are of
' late, fince the laft general peftilence, reduced to an irrecoverable fte-
' rility, fo that they do not, in thefe days, fuffice for maintenance of
' the fame priorefs & convent, the hofpitality which ought to be kept,
' & other the charges incumbent upon them to be fupported; nor can
' well be hoped to fuffice for the fame purpofes hereafter, unlefs it be
' fupplied them out of fome other means of relief. Whence they did
' moft humbly befeech us, that the priory of Wirthorpe, of our dio-
' cefe, to them & to the houfe of the fame lying near (which alfo is
' already

ᵃ Univerfis Sancte matris ecclefie filiis, prefertim ad quos prefentes litere pervenerint, Johannes, permiffione divina Lincolnienfis epifcopus, falutem in omnium falvatore. Sua, nobis, dilecte in Chrifto filie prioriffa & conventus prioratus S. Michaelis juxta Staunford, ordinis S. Benedicti, noftre diocefis, petitione monftrarunt, quod ipfe tanto debitorum onere funt depreffe, ac redditus & proventus dicti prioratus ad irreparabilem fterilitatem, poft ultimam generalem hominum peftilentiam, moderno tempore funt redacti, quod ad earundem prioriffe & conventus fuftentationem, hofpitalitatemq; tenendam, & alia eis incumbentia onera fupportanda non fufficiunt hiis diebus, nec fperantur verifimile fufficere in futurum, nifi eis de aliquo alio fubventionis remedio fuccurratur. Unde nobis humillime fupplicabant, ut prioratum de Wirthorp, noftre diocefis, eis & domus earundem vicinum (ad tantam inopiam jam redactum,
4   quod

' already reduced to fo great want, that the profits of the fame do not
' fuffice to provide neceffaries for one fingle nun) together with the
' parifh church of the fame place, unto the faid priory of Wirthorp
' of old notorioufly belonging; in which priory, after the faid pefti-
' lence, only one nun was left remaining; we, for the caufes premifed,
' would vouchfafe to unite & annex to them & the fucceffors of them,
' & to the priory of S. Michael aforefaid (wherein the favor of holy
' religion was wont, & is now found, in all perfons thereunto be-
' longing, to fhoot forth) unto the proper ufes of them, with all their
' rights & appurtenances, for ever to be poffeffed. We therefore
' (touching thefe things having made diligent enquiry, whereby we
' find all the forefaid particulars to be true; & having had with our
' chapter about thefe affairs a due & folemn treaty; & there having
' been fhewed to us a fpecial licenfe of our lord the K. granted to them
' for this purpofe; alfo the confent of the noble man Thomas de Holand,
' Kt. who married the heirefs & daughter of the E. of Kent, fometime
' patron of the faid priory of Wirthorp, to do fo by their letters ex-
' prefly concurring) the fame priory of Wirthorp, with the parifh
' church of the fame place, to the faid priory of Wirthorp of old an-
' nexed, together with all other the rights & appurtenances, to the fore-
' named priorefs & convent of S. Michael, & to the fucceffors of them,
' alfo to the priory of them abovefaid, for the reafons premifed
' (the truth whereof we have, according to form of law, fufficient
' grounds to believe, other folemnities of the law whatfoever on this
' part requifit being alfo obferved, & the right of every body faved) we
' do annex, unite, & incorporate, & unto their proper ufes grant for
' ever to be poffeffed. Willing & exprefly granting, that, fo foon
' as the faid priory of Wirthorp, by the death, refignation, or removal
' of the priorefs of the fame, or after any other manner, fhall become va-
' cant, it be from thenceforth lawful for the faid priorefs & convent of
                                                          ' S. Mi-

quod ad unius monialis neceffaria miniftran-
da non fufficiunt proventus ejufdem) una
cum ecclefia parochiali ejufdem loci, ad
dictum prioratum de Wirthorp ab antiquo
notorie pertinente; in quo prioratu, poft
dictam peftilentiam, unica duntaxat monialis
remanfit fuperftes; ex caufis premiffis, eis &
earum fuccefforibus, ac prioratui S. Michaelis
predicto (in quo odor facre religionis fole-
bat, & nunc invenitur, in omnibus pullu-
lare) unire & annectere dignaremur, in
earum ufus proprios, cum iuis juribus &
pertinentiis univerfis, perpetuo poffidendum.
Nos igitur (fuper hiis premiffa diligenti in-
quifitione, per quam invenimus predicta
omnia veritatem continere; habitoq; cum
capitulo noftro fuper hiis tractatu debito &
folempni; oftenfaq; nobis D. noftri regis
fuper hoc eis conceffa licentia fpeciali; ac
confenfu nobilis viri Thoma de Holand militis, qui heredem & filiam comitis Cantie,
quondam dicti prioratus de Wirthorp patroni,

duxit in uxorem, ad hoc per fuas literas expreffe accedente) eundem prioratum de Wirthorp, cum ecclefia parochiali ejufdem loci,
dicto prioratui de Wirthorp ab antiquo an-
nexa, una cum aliis fuis juribus & pertinentiis univerfis, prefatis prioriffe & conventui S. Michaelis, & earum fuccefforibus,
ac ipfarum prioratui fupradicto, ex caufis
premiffis (de quarum veritate eft nobis, in
forma juris, fufficiens facta fides, obferva-
tis quoq; aliis juris folempnitatibus quibufcunq; in hac parte requifitis, falvo jure cu-
jufcunq;) unimus, annectimus, & incorpo-
ramus, & in proprios ufus concedimus perpetuo poffidendum. Volentes & expreffe
concedentes quod quam cito dictum prioratum de Wirthorp, per mortem, ceffionem,
feu amotionem prioriffe ejufdem, vel alio
quovis modo, vacare contigerit, ex tunc
liceat dictis prioriffe & conventui S. Michaelis, per fe vel procuratorem fuum, corporalem poffeffionem dicti prioratus de
                                    Wirthorp,

‘ S. Michael, by themfelves or their proctor, freely to enter & take corpo-
‘ ral poffeffion of the faid priory of Wirthorp, & of all & every the rights
‘ & appurtenances thereof, our licenfe, or licenfe of any other perfon, on
‘ that behalf not in the leaft required. Saving neverthelefs, to us & our
‘ fucceffors, all rights & cuftoms epifcopal, & the dignity of our church
‘ of Lincoln. We will moreover & ordain, that all the fruits, rents,
‘ & profits of the faid priory of Wirthorp, & of the parifh church of
‘ the fame, be converted unto the common ufes of the infirmary,
‘ alfo for neceffaries for the cook of the nuns of the priory of S. Mi-
‘ chael aforefaid, & not unto other ufes. And the faid priorefs &
‘ convent of S. Michael fhall find one capellan, in the parifh church of
‘ Wirthorp, daily celebrating the divine offices; and, to the parifhioners
‘ of the fame, by day & by night, when they fhall need, the facraments
‘ of the church duly miniftring: and fhall fupport all other the charges
‘ of the fame church accuftomed & due. In witnefs & confirmation of
‘ all which, we have commanded the prefent procefs to be made, &
‘ caufed it to be fortified with the appenfion of our feal. Done & given
‘ at Kibworth the 3. of the ides of June [that is, June 11.] 1354. &
‘ of our confecration the 7.’ ‘ In this 28. of Edw. 3. Thomas lord
‘ Holland being made lieutenant & captain general in the dukedom of
‘ Britany, & parts of Poictou adjacent; as alfo in all other places ap-
‘ pertaining to John duke of Britany then in minority; had, for his
‘ fupport in that fervice, an affignation of the whole revenues of that
‘ dukedom. ᵇ The fame year William E. of Northampton [lord of
Stanford] ‘ was again appointed one of the commiffioners to meet
‘ with the nobles of Scotland, to treat with them touching the deli-
‘ very of David Bruys (called K. of Scots) ftill prifoner in England.

29.E.3.   XXIX. ‘ ᶜ Thomas lord Holland remained this year alfo, upon the
‘ occafions above, in Normandy. ᵈ William E. of Northampton [lord
of Stanford] ‘ was this year likewife in the kings fervice in Scotland.
‘ And the fame year upon K. Edwards paffing over to Calais, attended
‘ him thither; as alfo thence to S. Omers, expecting the K. of France,
‘ in thofe parts with his army, but finding him not there, wafted the
‘ country adjacent. Henry Engayne lived now at Efton *fupra montem*

Wirthorp, jurium & pertinentium ipfius omnium & fingulorum, libere ingredi & ap-
prehendere, noftra, aut alterius, licentia fuper hoc minime requifita. Salvis tamen,
nobis & fucefforibus noftris, omnibus juribus & confuetudinibus epifcopalibus, &
noftre Linc. ecclefie dignitate. Volumus
infuper & ordinamus, quod omnes fructus,
redditus, & proventus dictorum prioratus
de Wirthorp & ecclefie parochialis ejufdem,
in ufus communes infirmarie, ac neceffa-
riorum coque monialium prioratus S. Michaelis predicti, & non in ufus alios, con-
vertantur. Et invenient dicta prioriffa &
conventus S. Michaelis unum capellanum
in ecclefia parochiali de Wirthorp, divina

officia quotidie celebrantem, & parochianis
ejufdem, die & nocte, cum indigerint, fa-
cramenta ecclefiaftica debite miniftrantem.
Et omnia alia onera ejufdem ecclefie con-
fueta & debita fupportabunt. In quorum
omnium teftimonium atq; fidem, prefentem
proceffum fieri mandavimus, ac figilli noftri appenfione fecimus communiri. Actum
& datum apud Kibworth iij. idus Junii,
anno Dom. milefimo ccc. quinquagefimo
quarto, & confecrationis noftre feptimo.
Ex regift. Synwel.
a Bar. Vol. II. p. 74. b.
b Id. Vol. I. p. 186. a.
c Bar. Vol. II. as above.
d Id. Vol. I. as above.

‘ by

' by Stanford. B. H.'   In Sept. 1355. 29. E. 3. Sir Geoffry de la Mar   Sept.
knight, & dame Johan his wife, granted a leafe of the kings mills at
Stanford for ten years, at the rent of 40 s. a year to John Savage of
Stanford.   One of the original indentures is now in my hands.   Witneffes, Richard Perfonrie, William, Her . . . Thomas, Geoffry, Henry
Deynes, & others.   Given at Empyngham the Monday in the feaft of S.
Matthew the apoftle, 29. E. 3.   ' ᵃ Sir John Wingfield, Knt. attend-
' ing upon the black prince in the wars in Gafcoigne, wrote thence two
' letters to Sir Richard Stafford, Knt. the one dated the Tuefday next
' before Chriftmas, the other Jan. the 21. following; giving an account   Jan. 21.
' of the faid princes proceedings there; both which letters may be feen
' at large in Robert of Avesbury & Holingfhed.'

XXX.   ' ᵇ Upon the 24. of March 135⁵⁄₆. John Synwel Bp. of Lincoln,   Mar. 24.
' wrote to mafter William de Askeby canon of Lincoln, with the cler-   135⁵⁄₆.
' gy of all the archdeaconries in his diocefe, to appear, by their arch-   30. E. 3.
' deacons, in great S. Michaels church at Staunford, & there elect two
' fufficient & proper perfons to be fent as their proctors to a provinci-
' al council to be held at S. Brides church in London.   Given at
' Lydyngton, &c.'   ' ᶜ In this 30. of K. Edw. the 3. Thomas lord
' Holland [afterwards buried at Stanford] was conftituted governor of
' the ifles of Garnefey, Jerfey, Serke, & Aureney.   ᵈ The fame year
' William E. of Northampton [lord of Stanford] was again conftitu-
' ted a commiffioner to treat with the nobility & commons of Scotland,
' for enlargement of David de Brus, ftill a prifoner; & for a final peace
' betwixt both kingdoms.   ᵉ Elizabeth (daughter of Bartholomew de
' Badlefmere, one of the coheirs to Giles her brother, & widow to
' Edmund de Mortimer) now wife of the forefaid William E. of Nor-
' thampton [lord of Stanford] with her faid husbands leave, made her
' teftament, May 31. 1356. 30. E. 3. & bequeathed her body to be   May 31.
' buried in the quire of the friers preachers at London, & gave to that   1356.
' church C. marks fterling; as alfo a crofs made of the wood of the
' very crofs of our Savior, which fhe ufually carried about her, where-
' in was contained one of the thorns of his crown.   Moreover, two
' fair altar cloths of one fuit, two of cloth of gold, one chalice, one
' miffal, one grail, & one filver bell; likewife 31 ells of linen cloth
' for making of albes, one pulpitary, one portfory, & an holy water
' pot of filver.   To the friers preachers at Oxford C. marks, two
' whole veftments, with two whole copes thereto appertaining, two
' cloths of gold of one fuit, & a chalice.   To the friers preachers of
' Cambridge L. pounds.   To thofe of Chelmsford XX. pounds; & of
' Exeter XX. pounds.   And likewife CL. marks to be diftributed to
' feveral other convents of the fame order, in fuch fort as frere David
' de Stirington fhould think beft for her fouls health.   To the grey

a Holingfhed p. 952. a. &c.   d Id. Vol. I. p. 186. a.
b Ex Reg. Synwel, fol. 60. b.   e id. ib. b.
c Bar. Vol. II. p. 74. b.

' friers

' friers in London V. marks.   To the Carmelites V. marks.   To the
' Auguſtines V. marks.   And to the church of Rochford, one pair of
' veſtments, which ſhe uſed on holidays in her own chapel. The chief-
' eſt of her other legacies being theſe, viz. to the E. of Hereford a
' tablet of gold, with the form of the crucifix thereon; to Humphrey
' her ſon, a cup of ſilver gilt, with two baſins & one ewer of ſilver; to
' Eliſabeth her daughter, a bed of red worſted embroidered; to her
' ſiſter the counteſs of Oxford, a black horſe & an ouch, to her ſiſter
' Roos, a ſet of beads of gold & jet, with a firmaile —— The ſaid
' Eliſabeth lieth buried in the old church of the black friers, near Lud-

Sep. 19. ' gate.' ' ª Sept. 19. 1356. was fought the battel of Poictiers, wherein
' was taken priſoner by the black prince, John K. of France.' ' ᵇ Upon

Dec. 1. ' the firſt of Dec. 1356. Thomas de Darlington, rector of S. Marys by
' Stanford bridge exchanged that rectory with Henry de Thorpe for the
' rectory of Digtoft.

31.E.3.   XXXI. ' ᶜ Thomas lord Holland [afterwards buried at Stanford] con-
32.E.3. ' tinued yet in Brittany.   He alſo continued there the next year.
' ᵈ The ſame year William E. of Northampton [lord of Stanford] was
' again in Gaſcoign.' ' John de Cheſter, alderman of Stanford, was
' witneſs to a deed belonging to Browns hoſpital, bearing date the
' Monday next after the feaſt of the annunciation; this 32. E. 3. B. H.
' The ſame year W. Mous of Stanford ſold to W. Everard a garden,
' with the appurtenances, in Bradecroft. B. H.   A deed of the ſame date
' mentions a wooden croſs then ſtanding in Staunford field in the coun-
' ty of Roteland. B. H.   Thomas de Bernak was now rector of S. Peters
' in Stanford. B. H.' ' Nicholas de Eſton of Staunford gave to John
' Savage, baker, one meſſuage ſituate in the racoun rowe in great S.
' Michaels pariſh, between a tenement of John Templer ſouth, & a
' tenement of W. de Apethorp north, as it extends it ſelf from the
' kings highway eaſt, as far as a tenement of Richard de Lincoln weſt.
' B. H. ᵉ Henry de Thorpe abovementioned, rector of S. Maries by

July 19. ' the bridge, upon the 19. of July 1358. exchanged that rectory with
1358. ' Stephen Kynneſman, for the rectory of Qwynton.'   This Stephen
Kynneſman was a very rambling man.   ' ᶠ Thomas lord Holland [bu-
ried afterwards at Stanford] ' was this year made governor of the caſtle
' & fort of S. Saviour le Viſcont.   Likewiſe of all the caſtles which
' did belong to Sir Geoffry de Harecourt, in France.   ᵍ John K. of
' France, taken priſoner as above at the battel of Poictiers, was now
' removed from the caſtle of Hertford to the caſtle of Somerton in
' Lincolnſhire, & guarded thither by Sir William Colville (in place of
' the lord Robert Coleville, that could not travayle himſelf by reaſon

a Fabian. p. 213. a.
b Ex regiſt. Joh. Foſſor prioris Dunelm.
   fol. 183. b.
c Bar. Vol. II. p. 74. b.
d Bar. Vol. I. p. 186. a.

e Ex regiſt. Joh. Foſſor prioris Dunelm.
   fol. 154. b.
f Bar, Vol. II. p. 74. b.
g Holing. p. 964. a.

' of

' of ſickneſs) & others.   ª Ap. 8. 1359. Stephen Kynneſman abovemen-   Ap. 8.
' tioned, rector of S. Maries by Stanford bridge, exchanged the ſaid   1359.
' rectory with Ralf de Lameſly for the vicarage of Rihal, in Rutland
within two miles of Stanford.   There the ſaid Stephen Kynneſman
ſtayed not two months, but ' ᵇ June 6. 1359. exchanged the ſaid vi-   June 6.
' carage of Rihal, with Andrew Harbour of Stanford, for the rectory
' of Hethyr.'   The priory of the nuns of S. Michael being about this
time vacant, the ſiſterhood elected dame Agnes de Brakenbergh for
their prioreſs, whereupon John Synwel biſhop of Lincoln wrote as
follows to the prior of S. Leonards by Stanford & John Repingale,
D. D. to confirm & admit her.   ' ᶜ John, by divine permiſſion biſhop
' of Lincoln, to his beloved ſon the prior of S. Leonards by Staunford,
' alſo to frier John de Repingale, profeſſor of divinity, greeting, &c.
' Whereas our beloved daughter in Chriſt ſiſter Agnes de Brakenbergh,
' a nun of the houſe of S. Michael by Staunford, hath been elected prio-
' reſs of the ſame houſe now vacant, for confirmation of whoſe electi-
' on the foreſaid convent of the ſame houſe hath been earneſt with
' us, &c. to you we give power to confirm & in corporal poſſeſſion
' admit her, &c.   Given at Lydyngton the 3. of the ides of June 1359.
' & of our conſecration the 12.'   Sept. 3. enſuing the ſaid biſhop gave   Sept. 3.
leave to Sir Gervaſe de Wylleford, rector of Bernak by Stanford, to chuſe
a maſter to teach reading, muſic, & grammar there, in the underwritten
form.   ' ᵈ John, by divine permiſſion biſhop of Lincoln, to his beloved
' ſon Sir Gervaſe de Willeford, rector of the church of Bernak, of our
' dioceſe, greeting, grace, & benediction.   Whereas it is the office of
' a prudent paſtor of the church to his utmoſt power to enlarge the num-
' ber of ſtudents, particularly of clercs, which ſince the laſt peſtilence
' is every where diminiſhed, & that learning may not be denied to the ig-
' norant : alſo whereas we have been firſt given to underſtand that you are
' ready to cheriſh & favor poor boys & others in your large pariſh un-
' der diſcipline of a maſter in reading, ſinging, & grammar, for increaſe

---

a Ex regiſt. Joh. Foſſor prioris Dunelm.
fol. 159.
   b id. fol. 161. a.
   c Johannes permiſſione divina epiſcopus
Linc. dilecto filio priori S. Leonardi juxta
Staunford, ac fratri Johanni de Repyngale.
S. T. P. ſalutem, &c.   Cum dilecta in
chriſto filia, ſoror Agnes de Brakenbergh
monialis domus S. Michaelis juxta Staunford in prioriſſam ejuſdem domus vacantis
ſit electa, pro cujus electionis confirmati-
one predictus conventus ejuſdem domus
penes nos inſtitit, vobis, &c. ad confir-
mand. & in corporalem poſſeſſionem, &c.
Datum apud Lydington tertio idus Junii
anno Dom. 1359. & conſecrationis noſtre
12°. Ex Regiſtri Synwel folio 112. b.
   d Johannes permiſſione divina Linc. epiſcopus, dilecto filio domino Gervaſio de
Willeford, rectori eccleſie de Bernak,
noſtre dioceſis, ſalutem, gratiam & bene-

dictionem.   Cum ſit officium prudentis pa-
ſtoris eccleſie mundum ſtudentium, in eo
precipue clericorum . . . . qui poſt ultimam
hominum peſtilentiam ubiq; diminutus pro
viribus ampliare, & doctrina non ſit ignoran-
tibus deneganda ; ac cum primum propo-
ſitum intellexerimus te velle alere & favere
in tua parochia prolibata pueros inopes &
alios ſub virga magiſtrali in lectura, can-
tu, & grammatica facultate, ad augmentum
cultus divini : Nos, pio propoſito tuo hujus
favorabiliter annuentes, ut, magiſtrum lite-
ratum & idoneum in eadem parochia tua
qui pueros, &c. recte informet, poſſis eligere,
licentiam tibi ipſam (antea noſtram) eligen-
di & conſtituendi, & eidem ipſos pueros in
dictis . . . . informandi, tenore preſentium
concedimus, &c. Datum apud Lafford, 3°.
non. Sept. A. D. 1359. & conf. noſtre 12°.
Ex regiſtri Synwel fol. 135. b.

---

3   ' of

' of divine worſhip : we, to your pious deſign of this ſort favorably
' conſenting, do grant you licenſe (formerly our privilege) to elect a
' maſter lettered & fit in the ſame your pariſh, who boys, &c. may
' rightly inſtruct ; & to the ſame maſter, by virtue of theſe preſents,
' we grant leave to teach in the ſaid . . . Given at Lafford the 3. of
' Sept. 1359. & of our conſecration the 12.'   ' ª William E. of Nor-
' thampton [lord of Stanford] was now with K. Edward in France.

34.E.3.   XXXII. ' ᵇ Stephen Kynneſman abovementioned rector of Hethyr,
' on the 4. of March 13⁵⁹⁄₆₀. exchanged the ſaid rectory with Thomas
' Daun for the rectory of Tinwel in Rutland, within a mile of Stanford.'
There the ſaid Stephen Kynneſman ſtayed not long, but, what is very
ſurprizing, in leſs than two years more you will find him got back again
to his firſt church, S. Maries by the bridge at Stanford.   Thomas
Daun was likewiſe a perſon as quick in his removes as Mr. Kynneſman.   ' ᶜ In this 34. of K. Edw. the 3. Thomas lord Holland
[afterwards buried at Stanford] ' aſſumed the title of E. of Kent, in
' right of his wife as it ſeems : for it does not appear that he had ever
' any creation to that dignity.   And the ſame year, being conſtituted
' the kings lieutenant & captain general in France & Normandy, was,
' by indenture, reteined to ſerve him in that capacity, for one quarter
' of the year, with ſixty men at armes ; whereof one to be a banneret,
' ten knights, & 120 archers on horſeback : all at the kings charges.'
' ᵈ A treatie for peace between the kings of England & France was this
' year appointed to be holden on Good Friday in the Malederie of Lon-
' gigemew, where William E. of Northampton [lord of Stanford] &
' others appeared for K. Edw. but their treatie came to none effect.
May 1. ' ᵉ Upon May-day another treatie for the ſame purpoſe was appointed
' to be holden at Bretignie (little more than a mile diſtant from Chartres)
' where the ſaid E. & other commiſſioners on both ſides appeared, by
' whom a peace was at length concluded.'   The ſaid E. of Northampton
[lord of Stanford] ' as hath been ſhewn, ᶠ was a perſon of great action
' in his time, eſpecially in military affairs.'   But the wars were ended,
& he had got his full ſhare in the glory ; a peace was alſo made, ſoon
after which (as if he had now no more buſineſs in this world) he
Sep.16. ' ᶠ departed this life upon the 16. day of Sept. 1360. 34. E. 3. & was
1360.   ' buried in the abby of Walden on the north ſide of the presbytery ;
' leaving iſſue by Eliſabeth his wife one only ſon, viz. Humphrey, then
' 19. years of age ; & one daughter called Eliſabeth, married to Richard
' ſon & heir to Edmund E. of Arundel.   ᵍ Thomas Daun rector of S.
' Maries by Stanford bridge, upon the 4. day of Nov. 1360. exchanged
' that rectory with John capellan of Buckworth, for the vicarage of

a Hol. p. 964. b.   e id. p. 966. a.
b Ex regiſtri Joh. Foſſor prioris Dunelm.   f Bar. Vol. I. p. 186. a.
folio 161. b.   g Ex reg. Joh. Foſſor prioris Dunelm.
  c Bar. Vol. II. p. 74. b.   folio 165.
  d Hol. p. 965. b.

' All-Saints

' All-Saints in Wynwic.'   ' ᵃ Upon the 28. of December died [our 28.Dec,
other great soldier] ' Thomas Holland, E. of Kent; being then seised
' of the manor of Donyngton in Leicestershire, in right of the before
' specified Joane his wife, now surviving; as also of the manors of
' Cotingham, Witheton, Buttercrambe, Kirkby-Moresheved, with
' certain lands in Farndale, Gillingmore, Brauncedale, & Fademore;
' of the manors of Aton, Hemelington, & Cropton, with certain lands
' in Middelton & Haretoft, all in Yorks; of the manors of Gretham,
' Thorle, Brocelby, Beseby, with the Soke, & other its appurtenances
' in Beseby, Hawardeby, Walde-Newton, Gunnerby, Alwaldeby, Aske-
' by, Fenby, Briggesse, & North-Cotes, in Lincolns; of the ferme of
' the royaltie of the manor of Derteford, & of the manor of Wyk-
' ham, with the hundreds of Wacheleston, & Lutlefeld in Kent.   He
' likewise died seised of the manor of Talworth in Surrey; Lammersh
' with the hundred of Berestaple in Essex; Bishey in Hertfords; Kere-
' seye & Leyham in Sussex; Torpell, Upton, & Eston in Northamp-
' tons; Ryale in Roteland; Chesterfield in Derbys; & of one hundred
' pounds yearly rent issuing out of the ferme of Wyche in Worcesters;
' also of the manor of little Broughton in Bucks; & Yokeshale in
' Staffords; leaving Thomas his son & heir ten years of age; likewise
' two other sons, Edmund, & John; & a daughter called Maud,
' married to Hugh, son of Hugh, Courtney E. of Devon.'   This
Thomas lord Holland E. of Kent [as may appear by collating
Dugdales Bar. Vol. II. p. 78. with p 94. of the same Vol.] was buried
in a chapel adjoining to the grey friers church at Stanford, where he
had undoubtedly a fair monument erected to his memory, but of that
& the church it self, are now no remains left.

XXXIII.   ' ᵇ The lady Joan widow of Thomas lord Holland above-
' mentioned, staid not long without another husband after his death:
' for it appears that the very next ensuing year, she became the wife of   35.E.3,
' Edw. prince of Wales, commonly called the black prince.   ' And
' bicause the prince & shee, being within degrees of consanguinitie, were
' forbidden to marry, a dispensation was gotten from the pope to remove
' that lette.'   That she was so soon married again is not at all to be
wondered at; it had been a greater wonder if she had not.   For it may
be remembred, ' ᵈ she was the most admired lady of this age, & ᵉ for
' her exquisit beauty stiled, the fair maid of Kent.'   She had no doubt
therefore suitors in abundance, & when the black prince, so named,
' ᶠ not of his color, but of his dreaded acts in battel,' ᵍ who passionately
' loved her,' appeared amongst them, he was not to be resisted.   This
her sudden marriage then is not to be taken as a slight put upon her late
husband: but a match that was not to be refused.   As for her dead spouse

a Bar. Vol II. p. 74. b.
b Bar. Vol. II. p. 75. a.
c Hol. p. 968. a.
d Speed, p. 724. b.

e Hist. Rich. 2. by a person of Qual. 8°.
Lond. 1681. p. 1.
f Speed, p. 688. b.
g Speed, p. 725. a.

she had the highest respect for his memory, & when she came to die her self, ordered therefore her remains to be deposited by his at Stanford. But of that hereafter ᵃ. ' ᵇ In this year 1361. 35. E. 3. Joan ' de Baars, the divorced relict of John the 2. E. Warenn [sometime lord of Stanford] ' departed this world, but dying beyond the seas, ' was not buried in England. ᶜ This year Thomas de Spofford vicar ' of S. Andrews in Stanford, & others, entayled the lands of Robert ' Wyks, lord of Burley to the children of the said Robert successively. The said Robert Wyks, but when I find not, bought the manor of ' Burley by Stanford of Peter de Burley sometime lord of the same. The ' said Robert Wyks married Katherine . . . . . . by whom he had issue ' Edmund, Nicholas, & Thomas : which Thomas was lord of Burley, ' & had a numerous issue. ᵈ Simon Islep archbishop of Canterbury [having seen the remove of the Oxford scholars to Stanford] ' fearing the ' same might again, one time or another, come to pass, in the statutes ' of his hall, which he this year founded at Oxford (called whilst it ' stood by it self Canterbury hall, but afterwards made a part of Christ-' Church) provided, as the very words of his said statute express, that, ' if the place of the university of Oxford should happen to be changed [shifted any where else, suppose to Stanford, or where you please] ' then it should be lawful for his scholars, with consent of the arch-' bishop for the time being, also to transplant themselves, in the same ' form as they were founded, with all the goods which should then happen ' to belong to the house, wheresoever else it should seem good.' Richard Bliton, sometime provincial of the Carmes (to which office he was elected in 1319. at Stanford) died, as Pits says, ' ᵉ in 1334.' But Bale (who I believe is in the right) affirms ᶠ, ' that he lived to a very de-

July 31. ' crepit old age, & was buried at Lincoln, the last of July, 1361.
1361. ' ᵍ John capellan of Buckworth & rector of the church of the blessed vir-' gin Mary by Stanford bridge, in less than a year exchanged the same ' with its old rambling incumbent Stephen Kynnesman for the rectory ' of Tinwel in Rutland ; to which church of S. Mary at Stanford, by ' vertue of the said exchange, the said Stephen Kynnesman was ' again presented by John Fossor prior of Durham, & the convent of the
Sep. 4. ' same place, Sept. 4. 1361.

XXXIV. ' ʰ Edmund, fifth son of Edw. the 3. sirnamed Edmund of Lan-
Nov. 13. ' gele in the 36. of the said Ed. the 3ᵈ. the parliament then sitting, tho'
36. E. 3. ' he was at that time in Ireland, was created E. of Cambridge, his patent
1362. ' bearing date 13. Nov. And in 37. E. 3. obtained a grant in fee, of
37. E. 3. ' the castle, manor, & town of Stanford ; as also of the manor of

---

a 7. Aug. 1385.
b Bar. Vol. I. p. 82. b.
c From Sir William Cecils diary of his own Life, &c. a MS. in Mr. Strypes hands.
d Londinens. p. 358.
e in vita.
f — vixit ad ætatem usq; decrepitam, &

in Lyncoln. cœnobio sepulturam accepit, ultimo die Julii, incarnati verbi anno 1361. Heliades MS. Harley. cap. 33.

g Ex registri dicti Joh. Foss. prioris Dunelm. p. 168.

h Bar. Vol. II. p. 154. a.

' Grantham :

' Grantham : both in Lincolnſhire.   In the 38. E. 3. it appears, that 38.E.3.
' he ſhould have married Margaret, heir to the E. of Flanders; but, for
' nearneſs of blood, the pope being ſent to, for his diſpenſation therein;
' & Charles the 5. then K. of France, craftily hindering it ; ſhe be-
' came the wife of Philip duke of Burgundy, brother to that king.
' Notwithſtanding which it appears that in the 39. E. 3. Sir Nicholas de 39.E.3.
' Tamworth, Knt. & John Wyn, Eſq; were ſent, by K. Edw. to all
' the nobles, & other his friends, beyond the ſeas; to ſollicit their help,
' for expelling thoſe ſtrangers, who had invaded the counties of Bur-
' gundy, Nevers, & Reth, of right belonging to the counteſs of Flan-
' ders & her ſon ; which were to return unto this Edm. & to the
' dutcheſs of Burgundy (daughter to the ſame E. of Flanders) in regard
' of their matrimonial contract, made betwixt them : as the record ap-
' parently doth manifeſt.'   ' ᵃ William de Coſſeby, rector of S. Mary Mar.23.
' Bennewerk church in Stanford reſigned, & William Botelford was
' Mar. 23. 136⁴⁄₇. 39. E. 3. by prior John Foſſor & the convent of Dur-
' ham, preſented to the ſame.   Robert de Claxton was by the ſaid 40.E.3.
' prior & convent of Durham preſented to the then vacant priory of S.
' Leonards by Stanford, in 1366. ᵇ The 3. of April 40. E. 3. 1366. the Apr. 3.
' princeſs Joan, the black princes wife, was delivered at Bourdeaux of her 1366.
' ſecond ſon by the ſame prince; which 2ᵈ. ſon was called Richard of
' Bourdeaux, from the place where he was born, & afterwards K. of
' England by the name of K. Richard the 2ᵈ.   Of which Richard,
' ſaith a nameleſs author ᶜ, if he were afterwards ſo unhappy, as not al-
' together to inherit his grandfather K. Edw. the thirds prudence, & his
' father the black princes ſpirit & conduct, yet it cannot be denied, but
' he retained ſomething of his mothers handſomeneſs, being afterwards
' celebrated for the goodlieſt perſonage, & moſt amiable countenance of
' any K. that had been before him ſince the conqueſt.   ᵈ When this Ri-
' chard of Bourdeaux was born, the black prince, for ſpecial truſt &
' confidence whiche he had in Sir Simon Burley, committed the go-
' vernaunce & education of hys ſonne the ſaide Richard unto him,
' whereby hee was ever after highly in favore wyth the ſayde Rycharde,
' & no leſſe advaunced by him, when afterwardes he came to enjoy
' the crowne of this realme.'   ' W. ſon of Thomas Lymbrenner of
' Staunford gave to W. de Flete of Staunford, one garden beneath the
' abbat of Burgs liberty, &c. as it lies between a tenement of W.
' Sadeler of Staunford weſt, & the way which leads to Burle eaſt ; & abutts
' upon Borough-gate [or rather, Burley-gate] north. B. H.   Which gar-
' den, but when my notes ſay not, the ſaid W. de Flete gave to W.
' Rouland of Staunford. B. H.

XXXV. ' ᵉ This year peace being made with France, Edm. Langley E. 42.E.3.
' of Cambridge [lord of Stanford] was one of thoſe, who, on the behalf

a Ex regiſtri 2. dicti Prioris partis 2. fol. 36.   perſon of qual. p. 1.
b Stow, p. 421.   d Holing. p. 1002. a.
c Hiſt. K. Rich. 3. 8°, Lond. 1681. by a   e Bar. Vol. II. p. 154. a.

                                                  ' of

‘ of the K. his father, made oath for performance of the articles
‘ then agreed on. —— William fon of John de Aepthorpe gave to Ro-
‘ bert de Aepthorpe one tenement in Weft-gate, in the ftreet called le
‘ Gannok; which tenement is fituate between a tenement of the fore-
‘ faid Robert eaft, & a tenement of the prior of Sempyngham weft, &
‘ extends it felf from the kings highway north as far as a tenement of
‘ the faid prior fouth. B. H.’   ‘ Henry Brond of Staunford gave to Alan
‘ Capper of the fame one fhop with a loft, &c. which lies in the
‘ ftreet called Behyndebak, fituate between a fchop of Johan, who was
‘ the wife of Reimund Spycer fouth, & a fchop of Robert Greffinghale
‘ north, & extends it felf from the kings highway weft to a tenement

48 .E.3. ‘ of Richard de Ardern eaft. B. H.   ᵃ This year Edmund E. of Cambridge
[lord of Stanford] ‘ being fent with the E. of Pembroke, & others, in aid
‘ of the black prince (then in Normandy) was at the fiege of Bourdelf.
‘ ᵇ The faid earles of Cambridge & Pembroke won Burdille, by rea-
‘ fon of a fally that they within made forth, & paffed fo far from
‘ their fortreffe, that the Englifh men got betwixt them & home.
‘ ᶜ From Bourdelf they marched to the caftle of Roche fur yone.   ᵈ Si-
‘ mon Lefley, rector of S. Maries church by Stanford bridge, exchanged
‘ the fame with William Langare for fome other preferment: which
‘ William, upon that exchange, was by prior John Foffor. & the chap-

July 31. ‘ ter of Durham, prefented to the vicarage [fo it is now called] of S.
1369. ‘ Maries by the bridge, 31. July 1369.’   An old deed, dated this
year, mentions —— ‘ an acre of land at the Thwertdykes between the
‘ green Foffe weft, & abutting upon the Tunge north. B. H.’   The
green Foffe is that part of the old Roman road which runs up from
the north-weft corner of the Auftin friers wall, acrofs the field into the
north road: & now called Green Bank; for the fame reafon it was formerly called Green-Foffe: to wit, becaufe then & now little frequented
by travellers.

XXXVI. ‘ ᵉ Among the fouldiers (alfo called companions) which
‘ ferved the black prince this feafon in Normandy, were three cap-
‘ tains, right hardie & verie expert men of warre, Ortigo, Bernard de
‘ Wiske, & Bernarde de la Sale.   Thefe three, then in Lymofin, hear-
‘ ing that the D. of Bourbons mother (mother alfo to the Fr. Q.)
‘ lay within the caftle of Belle-perche in Burbonnois, with a fmall
‘ companie aboute hir, rode thither in one day & a night, fo that in
‘ the morning they approached the caftle, fcaled it, & toke it, with
‘ the ladie within it: & though they were after befieged in the fame
‘ caftle by the D. of Burbon & other French, yet they defended it till
‘ the E. of Cambridge [lord of Stanford] & E. of Pembroke came
‘ with 1500. fpears, & 3000 other men of warre, & offred the French
‘ battaile, lodging afore them 15. dayes; & when they perceived that

a Bar. Vol. II p. 74. b.   d Ex reg. 2. dicti Prioris fol. 36.
b Hol. p. 978. a.   e Hol. p. 979. a.
c Bar. ut fupra.

                                                        ‘ the

' the French would not iſſue out of the Baſtide (in which they lay) to
' give battaile; the ſaid earles cauſed all them within the caſtle to come
' forth, & to bring with them the dutcheſs of Burbon, whom they led
' away in ſight of her ſonne, leaving the caſtle voyd & free for him to
' enjoy. ᵃ After this, the E. of Cambridge joined with his brother, the
' D. of Lancaſter, at Begerath, to keep the frontiers againſt the
' French.

XXXVII. ' ᵇ The black prince laid ſiege to Limoges. There were 44.E.3.
' with hym at the laying of this ſiege, the E. of Cambridge [lord of
Stanford] ' Sir Simon Burley, & others. Robert Griffinhale gave to
' Richard Baroun of Willeſthorpe two ſhops in Staunford, ſtanding in
' the pariſh of All-Saints in the mercat, between a tenement of Henry
' Brond ſouth, & a tenement of Walter de Baldeſwel north, as they
' extend themſelves from the way called Behindebak weſt, to the kings
' high way on the other part eaſt. B. H. W. de Styandeby ald. of
' Stanford, was witneſs to a deed dated this 44. E. 3. B. H.' Alice,
daughter of Richard Cokerel of Staunford now gave a general releaſe
to the executors of John Young the elder of Eſton by Staunford, after
the following manner. ' ᶜ All ſhall know by the preſents that I Alice
' daughter of Richard Cokerel of Staunford have remitted, releaſed,
' & altogether for me, my heirs & executors, for ever quit claimed &
' . . . . . to the executor of the will of John Yonge the elder of
' Eſton by Staunford, all manner the actions general & demands which
' againſt the foreſaid executor I have, have had, or in any manner ſhall
' be able to have, by reaſon of any debt, accompt, tranſgreſſion, or
' of any action of others, from the beginning of the world to the
' day of the certification of the preſents: ſo to wit, that neither I the
' foreſaid, nor any for me, or in my name, any thing of right or
' claim againſt the foreſaid executor . . . . to require or challenge ſhall
' be ever able, but from all action are for ever excluded by the pre-
' ſents. In witneſs whereof to this preſent writing of acquictance I
' have put to my ſeal. Given at Eſton by Staunford, the Sunday next
' after the epiphany, in the 44. of E. 3.' The ſeal repreſents the virgin Mary & our Savior ſitting in two niches; the Virgin on the right
hand, but ſitting ſideways, looking towards our Savior: our Savior
ſitting forwards with a globe in his left hand, but ſomewhat inclining
towards the Virgin, as if diſcourſing with her. Under both an arch,
with a perſon breaſt high, praying to them. The inſcription not legible. ' Richard Ellington parſon of Eſton by Staunford, John Tyler, 45.E.3.
' & Roger Clerk of the ſame capellanes, delivered to John Young three
' meſſuages in Staunford beneath the abbat of Burgs liberty, &c. B. H.'
This John Young, I ſuppoſe, was ſon of John abovementioned. ' John
' Savage gave to W. Brid of Staunford his meſſuage in the racoun rowe,

a Bar. Vol. II. p. 74. b.   b Hol. p. 990. b.   c Ex ipſo autographo penes me.

' ſtanding between a tenement of John Templer, &c.' as above 32. E.
3. Mr. Forſter puts down two aldermen of Staunford for this 45. E.
3. to wit, Edward Styandeby & W. Styandeby. They were perhaps
brothers, & ſucceſſively aldermen of this town.

46.E.3.   XXXVIII. Sir William Dugdale places the taking of Limoges by the
black prince, under the 46. of Edw. the 3. ' where, he ſays, ᵃ Ed-
' mund Langle E. of Cambridge [lord of Stanford] with the E. of
' Pembroke, & Sir Guiſchard de Angle, entred & did much ſlaughter.
' After which the ſaid Edmund of Langle attended the K. in that expe-
' dition deſigned for the reſcuing of Thouars: but therein, being croſ-
' ſed by contrary windes, nothing was attempted.' Mr. Forſter
puts down two aldermen for this 46. of E. 3. to wit, W. de Styandeby & Jo. de la Panterie. B. H. ' The ſame year Gilbert Jakes gave
' to Thomas de S. Ives one empty place in the Gannok, as it lies be-
' tween a tenement of the foreſaid Gilbert eaſt, & a tenement of the
' prior of Sempyngham, &c. B. H. ᵇ Before the end of this year Ed-
' mund E. of Cambridge returned into England with John D. of Lan-
' caſter his brother; at which time they brought with them the two
' daughters of Don Pedro K. of Caſtile, viz. Conſtance, & Iſabel:
' which Iſabel ſhortly became the ſaid E. of Cambridges wife. ᶜIn
47.E.3. ' the 47. E. 3. the foreſaid Edm. E. of Cambridge [lord of Stanford]
' was retained by indenture to ſerve the K. for one whole year, in
' his fleet at ſea, with 250 men at armes, 250 archers; 30 knights &
48.E.3. ' 220 eſquires. ᶜ In the 48. E. 3. the ſaid Edm. E. of Cambridge
[lord of Stanford] ' was joyned in commiſſion (by the K. his father)
' with John D. of Brittany, in the lieutenancy of France & all other
' foreign parts. Whereupon he ſailed into Brittany, & had the town
' of S. Mathews on the ſea-coaſt, with the caſtles of Breſt & Orrey
' render'd to him. After which they beſieged Kemperle, wherein moſt
' of the chief men of Brittany at that time were: & had taken it, but
' that a certain knight brought them news of a truce betwixt England
' & France: with command from K. Edw. that they ſhould leave the
' ſiege, & return home ſpeedily.——John Brown was alderman of Stan-
49.E.3. ' ford 48. & 49. E. 3. B. H. ᵈ Sir William Burton, Kt. ſometime lord
' chief juſtice of the kings bench, died this 49. E. 3. as appears by
' an inquiſition taken after his death. He had iſſue by Elianor his
' wife Sir Thomas de Burton, Knt. ᵉ Edward the black prince of
June 8. ' Wales died at Canterburie on Trinitie Sunday, June 8. 49. E. 3. &
' was buried at Chriſt-Church there.' By his death the famous princeſs,
Joan his wife (afterwards buried at Stanford) again became a widow,
50.E.3. & ſo continued to her death. ' ᶠ In the 50. E. 3. Sir Thomas de
' Burton, Kt. [ſon of Sir William abovementioned] did by his deed,

a Bar. Vol. II. p. 154. b.   d Burtons Leiceſt. p. 108.
b Bar. ut ſupra.   e Speed, p 725. a.
c id. ib.   f Wrights Rutland p. 57.

' dated

' dated on the Saturday next after the feaſt of S. Martin the biſhop,
' convey unto John Brown of Stanford, Eſq; all his lands, tene-
' ments, rents, & ſervices in the village of little Caſtreton, with the
' reverſion of the patronage of the church there.   ᵃ In this 50. of E.
' 3. Edm. E. of Cambridge [lord of Stanford] was made conſtable
' of Dover caſtle, & warden of the Cinque-ports.   The ſame year
' Adomar Malherbe of Staunford gave to Sir Richard vicar of the
' church of All-Saints beyond Staunford bridge, & to Sir John Bond
' capellan, one garden within the abbat of Burgs liberty, lying be-
' tween a tenement of Robert de Burlee north, & a garden of John
' Spycer ſouth, as it abutts on the kings highway weſt. B. H.   By a
' papal proviſion dated July 2. 1376. 50. E. 3. John Swaſam, S. T. P.   July 2.
' a white frier of Lyn, educated at Cambridge, as Mr. Willis ob-   1376.
' ſerves ᵇ, was advanced to the ſee of Bangor, from that of Cloyne
' in Ireland.   This John Suafam, ſays Leland ᶜ, flouriſhed when the
' Viclifian ſectariſts waged a fierce, outragious, & bloody war againſt
' the orthodox fathers.   For which reaſon Suafam thought it his
' duty to drive away the wolves from the flock of Chriſt as far as
' poſſibly he could.   The main care remaining was, to have it
' done quickly by ſome advantageous method : But in that he
' was not long to ſeek.   For being a zealous man & fortified with the
' evangelic armor, he ruſhed into the midſt of his enemies : ſtabbing
' as it were ſome with his learned pen, & bearing others down
' with the thunder of his ſacred eloquence.   His books are yet ex-
' ſtant, & are moſt faithful witneſſes of an unconquerable virtue ;
' whereof one is profeſſedly againſt the Viclifians, & the other enti-
' tled a collection of ſermons.   Theſe holy labors were not long
' after followed with their honor ; Suafam *being at length appointed*
' biſhop of Bangor.'   What Leland calls unconquerable virtue, Bale
' pronounces ᵈ, a fanatic ſpirit, & adding that he was made biſhop of
' Bangor by Pope Gregory the 11. for his diligence in writing againſt
' the Wiclevites ; thus antichriſt, ſays he, is wont to reward her fol-
' lowers.'   You will find biſhop Suafam very buſie at the council of
prelates at Stanford in 1392. for which reaſon this ſhort account of
him, is here premiſed.   ' ᵉ On Friday the 20. of Feb. John of Gaunt   20. Feb.
' D. of Lancaſter [having his houſe beſet by the Londoners for tak-   51. E. 3.
ing part with Wiclif the day before at S. Pauls] ' fled to the
' manor of Kenington beſides Lambeth, where at that time the prin-
' ceſſe [Joan, afterwards buried at Stanford] was, with the yong
' prince [afterwards Rich. 2.] before whom he made his complaint.
' The princeſſe, having heard his talke, comforted him, & promiſed
' that ſhe would make a final end of all thoſe matters.   Which

a Bar. ut ſupra.   d p. 514.
b Hiſt. church of Bangor, p. 81.   c Stow, p. 433, 434.
c Comment. p. 389.

' princeſſe, deſirous to make peace, ſent unto London Sir Simon
' Burley & two other knights to perſuade them to peace, who an-
' ſwer'd, they would doe, for her honor, whatſoever ſhe had com-
' manded. [a] On the 21. of June 1377. died king Edward the third,'
& was ſucceeded by his grandſon K. Richard the ſecond.   I ſhall only
add, William de Bohun, Edmund Langley, & Edward lord Spencer, all
of them ſo often mentioned in the courſe of theſe collections, were all
knights of the garter, & ſo made by the foreſaid king Edward the third [b].

a id. p. 438.   b Heylins Hiſt. S. George, p. 320, 321.

The end of the eleventh book.

THE
ANTIQUARIAN ANNALS
of the TOWN of
STANFORD
IN
Lincoln, Rutland, *and* Northampton *Shires.*

BOOK XII.
Containing the reign of K. Richard the second.

I. **K**ING Edward the 3. departing this life the 21. day of June _{22. June} 1377. ' ᵃ the morrow after there were fent to London _{1377.} ' from K. Rich. Sir Simon Burley & others to bring the _{1. R. 2.} ' newes of his affured death. On the 15. of July, ᵇ being Wednefday, _{July 15.} ' K. Rich. was crowned, at which time Sir Simon Burley bare the ' fword before him. ᶜ At this coronation Sir John Burley, Kt. the ' kings chamberlain, Cuftos of Nottingham caftle, was, for terme of ' life, by patent, made keeper of the foreft of Sherwood. And Simon ' Burley, Kt. his brother, was made conftable of Windlefor caftle, ' Wigmore, Guilford, & the manor of Kenington; & alfo mafter of ' the kings falcons at the Mues, near Charing-crofs by Weftminfter. ' This Sir Simon Burley had his houfe in London in Thame ftreete, ' between Baynardes caftle & Pauls wharfe; which houfe fometime ' belonged to the abby of Fifcampe, &, by reafon of the wars in ' France, came to the kings hands. ᵈ The fame year Edmund E. of ' Cambridge [lord of Stanford] was again retained to ferve the K. in ' his fleet at fea, for a quarter of that year, with 100 men at arms, & ' 100 archers; whereof himfelf, & one baneret to be part of the num- ' ber; twelve knights, & the reft efquires. Froifard faith, that, upon ' appearance of the French, near the coaft of England, about that ' time, this Edmund, & Thomas of Woodftoke his brother, were at ' Dover in the head of an 100000 men, with banners difplayed. ᵉ The ' K. by reafon of his yong yeres, was not yet able to governe; & thereupon ' Edmund E. of Cambridge [lord of Stanford] with other peeres were

a Hol. p. 1004. a.
  b id. b. but Mr. Rapin fays he was crowned the 16. July. Acta regia, num. 7. p. 23.
  c Stow, p. 442.
  d Baron. Vol. II. p. 154. b.
  e Hol. p. 1007. a.

12 B ' appointed

' appointed to have the adminiftration. [a] The fame year K. Rich. held
' a great council of war at Stanford to confult about an expedition
' into France. But it came to nothing in that unactive reign. [b] I find
' however, that the townfmen of Staunford & Leicefter were the fame
' year ordered, at their own proper cofts, to fit out a barge, called a
' Balleinger: defigned, I fuppofe, for one of the tranfports in that expedition. ' Thomas de Wadingtoun of Staunford, gave to John Broun
' of Staunford, W. de Melton parfon of the church of the holy Trinity
' at Staunford, Robert de Bury parfon of the church of S. Paul at Staun-
' ford, & to John Bonde of the fame capellan, one meffuage fituate
' in the parifh of S. Mary at the bridge, with one curtilage adjacent; to
' wit, between the lane called Cornwanfty eaft, & a meffuage of John
' Taverner weft, & abutting on the kings highway fouth, & on a te-
' nement of Margery Marchesfeld north, &c. Witneffes, John de la
' Panetrie, &c. B. H. John de Crouland of Staunford gave to John
' Bonde capellan, one meffuage with the appurtenances fituate in Staun-
' ford, within the abbat of Burgs liberty; to wit, Eft-by-the-water;
' the which meffuage is fituate betwen a tenement of the forefaid John
' de Crouland eaft, & the empty place called the Pyn-fold late John
' de Wyterings weft, & extends it felf from the kings highway fouth,
' to the bank called Weland north. B. H. Walter Baldefwel of Staun-
' ford gave to W. Hamerton one fhop, with one loft, &c. fituate in
' the parifh of All-Saints in the mercat, between a tenement of Ri-
' chard Ardern fouth, & a fhop fometime Richard Brafyers of Willef-
' thorpe north, & abutting on the kings highway called Behynde-the-
' bak, weft: which was the fhop of Alan Capper. B. H. Agnes wife
' of Alan Capper of Staunford gave to Peter Goldfmith of the fame,
' one fhop with a loft, &c.' as above in the laft deed. B. H. ' Alder-
' man of *Staunford* this 1. R. 2. John Broun. B. H. ' The wardfhip
' of Thomas (commonly called Thomas lord Defpencer of Glamorgan
' & Morganok [who had lands at Stanford in Lincolnfhire as well as at
Stanford in Berks] ' was this 1. R. 2. granted to Edmund E. of Cam-
' bridge [lord of Stanford] to the end he fhould marry his daughter, as
' he afterwards did.' There feems to be fome analogy between this
lord Spencers title, Morganok, & the ftreet called the Ganok in Stanford. Perhaps he had a houfe there which gave name to the ftreet.

2. R. 2.   II. ' [d] In the 2. of Richard the 2. Edmund E. of Camb. [lord of Stan-
ford] ' was again in the kings fleet at fea. [e] In the beginning of K.
' Richards reign, the pope fent a bull to the univerfity of Oxford, up-
' braiding them for fuffering & countenancing Wicklif & his doctrine,
' & charging them that they fhould no longer tolerate the fame. But
' the heads were fo well fatisfied with Wicklifs integrity, faith my au-

---

a Brit. ant. & nova, Vol. II. p. 1423.   Pat. 1. R. 2. par. 5. m. . . dorfo.
 b ——— Quod homines ville de Staunford   c Bar. Vol. I. p. 396. b.
& de Leicefter faciant unam bargeam, vo-   d Bar. Vol. II. p. 154. b.
catam a Balleinger, fumptibus fuis propriis. e Hift. Rich. 2. by a perfon of qual. p. 38.

' thor,

' thor, that they were at a ſtand, whether they ſhould receive the bull,
' or rejeſt it with contempt.   However the pope plyed the K. archbp. &
' bp. of London, with ſeveral letters to the ſame effeſt: So that at laſt
' Wicklif was again convened before them.   But on the day aſſigned
' for his examination, Sir Lewis Clifford came into their court, & in
' the name of the princeſs Joan, the kings mother [afterwards buried
at Stanford] ' peremptorily commanded them to proceed no farther
' in that affair : with which being terrified, they deſiſted their proſecu-
' tion, & he got out of their clutches.——John ſon of Agnes Hert of
' Staunford gave to John Trenchepayn one meſſuage ſituate in great S.
' Michaels pariſh . . . . in Colegate, in the lane called racones rowe,
' between a tenement of Richard Foreſter ſouth, & a tenement of W.
' Brid north, & abutting on the kings highway eaſt, & a tenement of
' him John Hert weſt. B. H.   Alderman of Staunford this 2. R. 2.
' Robert Prat. B. H.'

    III. ' John Trenchpayn gave to W. Makeſey of Staunford & W. 3. R. 2.
' Brid of Rihale, one meſſuage, &c.' as above in the laſt deed. B. H.
' W. Makeſey gave the meſſuage, &c. as above, to W. Brid aforeſaid,
' under this condition, that the ſaid W. Brid & his heirs, or his aſſigns,
' ſhould pay yearly for ever to the warden of the chantery of the
' church of S. Clement in Staunford, ſix ſhillings of ſilver. B. H. K. No. 24.
Richard confirmed to the nuns of S. Michael at Stanford, the ſeveral
grants of K. H. 2. K. John, K. H. 3. & K. E. 1.   The charter of K.
Richard the 2. is thus worded.   ' ª Richard, by the grace of God, K.
' of England & France, & lord of Ireland, to all, unto whom the pre-
' ſent letters ſhall come, greeting.   We have inſpeſted the *letters* pa-
' tents of lord Edward K. of England, our progenitor, &c. in theſe
' words. [Then recites, as above, 33. E. 1. 12. H. 3. 12. John, 4. H.
2.] ' We alſo, the conceſſions & confirmation aforeſaid *holding good*
' & ratified, them for us & our heirs, as far as in us lies, to the fore-
' named nuns & their ſucceſſors, do grant & confirm, as the letters afore-
' ſaid more reſpeſtively atteſt.   In witneſs whereof we have cauſed
' theſe our letters to be made patents.   Witneſs my ſelf at Northamp-
' ton, the fourth day of Nov. in the 3. year of our reign.——Alderman
' of Staunford this 3. R. 2. Henry Bukeden. B. H.'

    IV. ' ᵇ Whereas there was variance & open war now maintained be-
' twixt John K. of Caſtile & John K. of Portingale, the E. of Cambridge
[lord of Stanford] ' & others were ſent into Portingale, with 500 armed

---

a Richardus D. G. rex Anglie & Francie, & Dominus Hibernie, omnibus ad quos preſentes litere pervenerint, ſalutem. Inſpeximus literas patentes D. Edwardi quondam regis Anglie, progenitoris noſtri, in hec verba. Nos autem conceſſiones & confirmationem prediſtam, ratas habentes & gratas, eas pro nobis & heredibus noſtris, quantum in nobis eſt, prefatis monialibus & earum ſucceſſoribus concedimus & confirmamus, ſicut litere prediſte rationabiliter teſtantur. In cujus rei teſtimonium has literas noſtras fieri fecimus patentes. Teſte meipſo apud Northampton, viceſimo quarto die Novembris, anno regni noſtri 3°. Ex rot. pat. de anno

b Hol. p. 1024. a.

' men

'men & 500 archers, to aid the K. of Portingale, againſt the K. of Caſtile.
'It was ment that the D. of Lancaſter (who by his wife had a right to the
'crown of Caſtile) ſhould have followed his brother the E. of Cambridge
'with a great power, to trie what chaunce God would ſend him. But other
'incidents diſappointed him for the preſent.   ᵃ On Monday after Whit-
'ſuntide a Knt. of the kings houſe, named Sir Simon Burley, having
'in his companie two ſerjeantes at armes of the kings, came to Gravel-
'end, where he challenged one to be his bondman, for whom men
'of the town did gently intreat him to ſhew favor, but Sir Simon
'would not take leſs than 300 l. of ſilver for his manumiſſion, &
'therefore arreſted him, & ſent him to Rocheſter caſtle, whereupon the
'commons of Kent began to riſe; ſaying, that there were more kings than
'one, which they would not ſuffer, nor have any other but K. Richard.
'This tumult thus begun in Kent, by meane of Sir Simon Burley, was
'alſo increaſed by divers other actions in other places.'   This rebellion
is beſt known by the name of the chief captain of it, Wat Tyler.
'ᵇ When they entred the tower of London (where the K. lay, & was
'forced to admit them) they uſed themſelves moſt preſumptuouſly
'againſt the princeſs of Wales, mother to the K. [afterwards buried at
Stanford] 'for, thruſting into her chamber, they offred to kiſſe hir, &
'ſwaſht themſelves down upon hir bed, putting hir into ſuch feare,
'that ſhee fell into a ſowne, & being taken up & recovered, was had
'to the waterſide, & put into a barge, & conveyed to the place called
'the queenes wardrobe, or the tower royal, where ſhe remayned all
'that day & night following, as a woman halfe dead.   ᶜ The young
'K. after a fortunate concluſion given to thoſe helliſh uprores about
'his principal city, repaired, in good array, to the tower royal, or
'queens wardrobe aforeſaid, a palace then in the boſom of London.
'There the Q. mother had remained, in very great feare & grief, for the
'ſpace of three daies & two nights.   But the ſight of her ſonne, & re-
'lation of his good ſpeed, blotted out of her memory the ſorrows
'formerly ſuſtained.'   At this time Henry Spencer biſhop of Norwich
'ᵈ had advertiſements, at his manor of Burley neare to Okam in the par-
'tyes about Stanford, of the ſturre whiche the commons in Norfolk kept;'
& repairing thither, very gallantly ſuppreſſed them.   'ᵉ Edmund Langley
'E. of Cambridge [lord of Stanford] now alſo obtained a grant from
'the K. that whereas, by reaſon of his former ſervices, & in his voyage to
'Portugal, he had contracted divers debts, his executors ſhould therefore
'reteine the profits of all his lands, for one whole year after his death;
'as alſo receive that ſum of 500 marks, which had been granted by
'K. Edw. the third to be paid yearly unto him, & the heirs male of
'his body.   ᶠ The D. of Lancaſter being accuſed of treaſon by a Car-
'melite fryar, lord Thomas of Woodſtocke (the ſame who was after-

a Stow, p. 451, 452.   d Hol. p. 1031. b.
b Holing. p. 1028. a.   e Bar. Vol. II. p. 154. b.
c Speed, p. 735. a.   f Speed, p. 738. a. b.
                                                        'ward

' ward D. of Gloucefter) rufhed into the chamber where the K. was, &
' bound his words with a terrible oath, that he would kill any one liv-
' ing, who durft lay treafon to his brothers charge; neither did he ex-
' cept the K.   In which fpeeches, as piety & zeale for his brothers ho-
' nor & fafetie were not wanting, fo certainly duty to his prince was
' exceedingly forgotten.'   You will hereafter find why this is inferted.

V. Now flourifhed John Tiffington.   ' John Tiffington, faith Pits [a],   1381
' was a Francifcan, D. D. of Oxford, & profeffor of that faculty there,
' & at length provincial of his order in England to the time of his
' death.   Leland (& after him Willot fays) he was a pious & learned
' man, & of great authority with all men.   He was one of thofe doctors
' who in 1381. with William Berton, chancellor of Oxford, condemn-
' ed the herefie of John Wicklif at that place.'   Thus far Pits, from
Leland as he would perfuade us, tho' 'tis certain he never faw him.
Hear now Leland himfelf.   ' John Tiffendune, fays he [b], a man of
' great authority among the Francifcans, with a deal of courage, & no
' lefs judgment, ventured to pronounce his affertion about the real pre-
' fence in the facrament of the altar, before a numerous audience of
' learned perfons; & foon after put in writing & publifhed it.   This I
' certainly believe he did for no other reafon, but that he might as
' early as poffible, put a bridle upon fome little pretenders to fcience,
' ftudious at that time of the new [Wiclifean] opinion at Oxford.
' Nor did Tiffendunes moft beautiful ftate of the queftion, in my opi-
' nion, fall fhort of the moft judicious divines.   For it appears, the Ox-
' ford fenate in 1381. gave him, as being an infuperable affertor of the
' real prefence, a place in the firft rank of learned men in that univer-
' fity.'   Thus highly do Pits & Leland extol him.   Let Bale now fpeak,
& fee if he can pluck him down from that height to which the others
think they have raifed him.   ' Tiffington, fays he [c], thro' his Arifto-
' telian fpirit interpreted all the holy fcriptures egregioufly to the ad-
' vantage of antichrift.   He was one of thofe twelve firft unjuft cenfurers
' of Wiclifs doctrine, who, in a convocation of Rabins at Oxford under
' the chancelor Berton condemned that pious man, the reftorer of truth,
' for herefie.   Tiffington, as Pits adds [d], wrote feveral pieces againft
' Wiclif.   Particularly, a defence of the Euchariff, which I think, fays
' he, is the fame book with a MS. of that title which they have in Ben-
' net coll. library in Cambridge.   Alfo of the facrament of the altar.
' Of the facraments.   A defence of auricular confeffion.   Scholaftic
' controverfies.   And another piece againft Wiclifs creed, beginning,
' *Semel confeffus eft filius Dei.'*   You will find more of Tiffington in
the account of the great council at Stanford in 1392. whereat he was
prefent, & very bufie againft the Wiclevites.——' Richard Hawvel gave
' feveral meffuages in Stanford (which he bought of Walter le Halver 21.

a in vita.   c in vita.
b Com. p. 396, 397.   d in vita.

' E. 3·) to John his fon.   See 14. & 21. E. 3. above. B. H.   Ald.
' this 4. R. 2. Henry Bukeden, as before. B. H.'

5. R. 2.   VI. ' John Long, alderman of Stanford, was witnefs to a deed bear-
' ing date 5. R. 2. the Monday after the feaft of the affumption of our
' lady. B. H.' An old deed of that year fpeaks of —— ' one empty place,
' fituate in S. Mary Bynwerk parifh in Stanford, in the ftreet called the
' Gannoc: to wit, between the empty place of Robert Grymes eaft, &
' a tenement of the prior of Sempynghams weft, & abutting on the
' kings highway north, & a garden of the faid prior of Sempynghams
' fouth. B. H.   Which empty place Gilbert Jakes fometime after
' fold to Thomas de S. Ives. —— William Everard fold to W. Tho-
' mas of Staunford Parchemyner, one curtilage beneath his clofe
' with their appurtenances in Bradecroft between the land of lord
' Thomas le Defpencer, Knt. eaft, & a garden of Sir Reymund Knok-
' ker the capellan weft, abutting on the kings highway fouth, & on the
' land of Sir John Hawvell capellan, north. Witneffes, W. de Styandeby
' alderman of Staunford, &c. Given at Staunford the Thurfday next after
' the feaft of S. Mathew the apoftle. B. H. Inftead of Defpencer *militis,*
' in another deed is wrote Defpencer chr.' F. In the 6. R. 2. Sir Richard
6. R. 2. ' perpetual vicar of the church of All-Saints beyond Staunford bridge, &
' Sir John Bonde capellan, gave to John Spycer of Staunford, one gar-
' den within the abbat of Burgs liberty, lying betwen a tenement of
' Robert de Burlee north, & a garden of him John Spycer fouth, & abut-
' ting on the kings highway weft. B. H.   The fame year ᵃ K. Richard
' gave to Sir Simon Burghley his chamberlaine, the keeping of his fo-
' reft of Wolmore in Hants, for tearme of his life.   He alfo gave to
' John Burghley, Simon Burghley, Richard Burghley, Knts, & Bawd-
' wine de Radington, Efq; all the manor of Parrok nigh to Gravefend.
' ᵇ The E. of Cambridge [lord of Stanford] returned home from Por-
' tingale, whither, as ye have heard, he was fent, & promife made, that
' the D. of Lancafter fhould have followed him; but, by reafon of the
' late rebellion, & alfo for other confiderations, as the warres in Flan-
' ders betwixt the E. & them of Gaunt, it was not thought convenient
' that any men of warre fhuld go foorthe of the realme; & fo the K. of
' Portingale, not able of himfelf to go thro' with his enterprife, after
' fom fmal exploits atcheved by the Englifh & other of the E. of Cam-
' bridges companie, as the wynning of certain fortreffes belonging to the
' K. of Caftile, & that the two kings had layne in field the one againft
' the other by the fpace of xv. daies without battayle, the matter was
' taken up, & a peace concluded betwixt them, fore againft the mind
' of the E. of Cambridge, who did what in him lay, to have brought
' them to a fett field: but when there was no remedie, he bare it fo pa-
' tiently as he mighte, & returned home with his people, fore offend-
' ed (tho' he fayd little) againft the K. of Portingale, for that he delt

a Stow, p. 472.   b Hol. p. 1041. a.

2   ' otherwife

' otherwife in this matter than was looked for.   The E. had fianced
' his fonne which he had by the daughter of Peter late K. of Caftile,
' unto the K. of Portingales daughter, nowe in the time of his being
' there: but, altho' he was earneftly requefted of the faid king, he would
' not leave his fon behind him, but brought him backe with him again
' into England (together with his mother) doubting the flippery faith
' of thofe people.   ᵃ Ifabel, wife of the faid Edmund E. of Cambridge   6. Dec.
[lord of Stanford] ' by his authority & fpecial licenfe declared her tefta-   1382.
' ment 6. Dec. 1382. 6. R. 2. & thereby bequeathed her body to be bu-   6. R. 2
' ried, wherefoever her faid husband & the K. fhould appoint.   Ordain-
ᵗ ing, that upon the day of her death, an hundred trentals, & an hun-
' dred pfauters fhould be faid for her foul.   Likewife, that four priefts,
' or one at leaft, fhould fing for her by the fpace of four years.   More-
' over, that on the day of her burial, her beft horfe fhould be delivered
' for her mortuary.   She alfo bequeathed to the K. her heart of pearls.
' To the D. of Lancafter a tablet of jafpar, which the K. of Armonie
' gave her.   To Edward E. of Rutland her fon [afterwards lord of
Stanford] ' her crown, to remain to his heirs.   To Conftance le De-
' fpencer her daughter [wife of Thomas lord Defpencer abovemention-
ed] ' a fret of pearls.   And to the dutchefs of Gloucefter, her tablet
' of gold, with images; as alfo her pfauter, with the armes of Northamp-
' ton.   And to K. Richard, after her other legacies paid, all the re-
' mainder of her goods: with truft that he fhould allow unto Richard
' her younger fon, his godfon, 500 marks *per annum*.

VII. Now flourifhed Henry Crump.   ' Henry Crump, faith Bale ᵇ,   1382.
' was an Irifh man, but refided at Oxford in a monaftic habit & pro-
' feffion, being a Ciftercian, of the Bernardine branch.   There, after
ᵉ he had ftudied the inferior arts, he was made D. D. but publickly
ᶜ fufpended by the chancellor from keeping his act, for having the bold-
' nefs, after example of one Peter Stokes a Carme, to call the difci-
ᵉ ples of Wiclif, hereticks & Lollards, in the very chair.   For, to fpeak
ᵉ the truth, there was at that time chancellor one Robert Rygges, a
' very pious divine, who, with his proctors, was an encourager of
' Wiclif.   Crump therefore immediately pofted to London, & laid his
ᶜ cafe & complaints open before Wᵐ. Courtney archbp. of Canterbury
' & the kings council.   Whereupon the chancelor was fent for up in
' 1382. by order of the K. & council, but at the popes inftigation; &
' had in command from them injunctions to fearch for, & pro-
ᶜ fecute all fuch hereticks, as he fhould find in his jurifdiction.'   But
as bufie as Crump was in getting the Wiclivites cenfured, you will afterwards find him changing fides, & (for which reafon this account is
here given of him) himfelf condemned for a heretick in the council held
about fuppreffing them at Stanford in 1392.   Now alfo lived Thomas
Winterton.   ' Thomas Winterton, faith Pits ᶜ, a Lincolnfhire man &

ᵃ Baron. Vol. II. p. 155. b.   ᵇ p. 246.   ᶜ in vita;

' frier

' frier eremite of the order of S. Auftin in the monaftery of thofe fa-
' thers at Stanford, was an Oxford D. D. & provincial of his own order
' in England.   A perfon learned both in facred & profane letters above
' the common rank, & no unelegant preacher.'   Befides which, as Leland affures us [a], ' he was not the leaft of that number of divines who
' handled the fubtleties of the fchoolmen in that univerfity, whereof
' he was a member.'   ' On account of their common ftudies, equal
' age, & long education together, he had contracted, faith Pits [b], a
' great friendfhip with John Wiclif.   Neverthelefs when Wiclif began
' to divulge his opinions among the people, Winterton thought
' it his duty to admonifh his old friend, & if poffible to reclaim him.'
Speaking of thefe matters, Leland writes thus.   ' [c] Winterton feeing
' the antient rites of holy church run down by certain new opinions,
' & more efpecially the venerable doctrine of the real prefence in the
' facrament undermined by unbelieving people tainted with Wiclives
' unfound, & by all good men, for this reafon, defervedly detefted opi-
' nion; thought delays were no longer to be endured, but immediately
' fet himfelf to prevent the fpreading plague.   And to the end that he
' might fooner ftop, or rather indeed wholly remove, it; the beft way
' he thought was to demolifh Wiclif with his own weapons, & cut
' him down with arguments drawn from his own writings.   He publifh-
' ed therefore a piece called, *Euchariftie affertio*, or the real prefence
' maintained, in oppofition to John Wiclif, then reviving the dying
' embers of the antient hærefiarchs: which (as I faw it lately in S. Pauls
' library at London) I thought it my duty to give the author of fo holy
' a work his juft honor.'   Befides the abovementioned piece, Winterton wrote, as Pits tells us, II. ' *Abfolutio fua contra confeffionem*
' *Wiclefianam*, beginning, *ficut teftante Apoftolo ad Rom. &c.* a MS.
' in the lord Lumleys library.   III. Theological difputations.   IV. A
' courfe of fermons for the year.   And many other learned pieces;
' fhewing, in all of them, a wonderful zeal & an equal fcholarfhip. He
' flourifhed in 1382. under the fickle government of K. Rich. the 2.'
Whether Winterton lived till 1392. I cannot tell, but if he did, undoubtedly he made a great figure in the council held that year at the
white friers in Stanford.

VIII. ' Alderman, John Spycer. B. H.   W. de Botteford now oc-
' curs rector of S. Mary Bennewerke. B. H.   [d] This year on an inva-
' fion made by the Scots, Edmund E. of Cambridge [lord of Stanford]
' attended the K. in his expedition, then by him made northward.
' [e] The cuftody of Dover caftle void by the death of Robert Afhton,
' was appointed to Simon Burley.   [f] The K. likewife advaunced him
' highly to other great honors & promotions, infomuch that at the
' fame time hee was made Kt. of the garter, lorde chamberlaine, &

a Com. p. 403.   d Bar. Vol. II. p. 155. a.
b in vita.   e Stow, p. 475.
c ut fupra.   f Hol. p. 1072. a. b.

' alfo

' alfo one of the privye counfaile. ᵃ This perfon, by his ill practifes, in
' few years increafed his fmall patrimony of 20 marks, to an eftate of
' about 3000 marks *per annum*. And grew to that excefs of pride, that
' at a Chriftmas he would give liveries to a great number of knights,
' fquires, ᵇ yeomen, & others, as well of the kings court, as of his
' owne family; ᶜ beftowing therein fometimes 140, or 160, nay fome-
' times 220. broad cloths, & thefe of great price, as being embroidered
' with gold, & fome of fcarlet. ᵈ Another fays, he was an intolle-
' rable proud man, & a greate oppreffor of the poor, &c.' But a third
more handfomely ᵉ, ' indeede the fayde Sir Symon Burley was thought
' to beare himfelfe more loftie, by reafon of the kings favor, than was
' requifite; which procured hym envie of them that could not abyde
' others to bee in any condition theyr equalls in authoritie.' Inftead of
faying, ' this perfon by his ill practifes in few years increafed his fmall pa-
' trimony of 20. marks to an eftate of 3000 marks *per annum*, as above;'
' Mr. Stow more candidly leaves out *ill practifes*, & fays ᶠ, ' this man might,
' by inheritance, difpend 20 markes, by yeere, but *in few yeeres fo grew*
' *in fervice of the K.* that he attained to the value of 3000 markes of
' yearly revenues.' But note, Sir Simon Burghley & his anceftors, held
their lands & the lordfhip of Burghley by Stanford of the abbat of Burg
by knights fervice; & made always a greater figure (as may be feen
by accounts of their mortuaries paid the faid abbat of Burg, & other
paffages in thefe collections) than men of bare 20 marcs a year. As for Sir
Simon, ' ᵍ there was not anye thing now done concernyng the affayres
' apperteyning to the ftate without his counfaile, appointment & di-
' rection; wherein he fo much favored & leaned to the partie of the
' D. of Ireland (there being faythful friendfhip growne betwixt them)
' that he was fore envied, & greatly hated of diverfe of the reft of the
' nobility, efpecially of the kings uncle the D. of Gloucefter; who,
' upon malice that he bare to the man, not fo much for his owne de-
' meanour, as for his allies, & peradventure for defire of his rowmeths,
' more than of his life (looking to have had fuch offices & rowmeths
' which Sir Simon enjoyed, by the kinges gracious favor & grauntes
' thereof to him made, as the wardenfhip of the Cinque-ports, &c.)
' caufed him afterward anno 1388. to be accufed of diverfe offences
' againft the crowne, realme & churche.'

IX. ' ʰ In the 8. R. 2. the E. of Cambridge [lord of Stanford] was 8. R. 2.
' again reteined by the K. to ferve him in his Scotifh wars. ⁱ The fame
' year died Sir Thomas de Burton, Knt. [of Tolthorpe by Stanford]
' leaving iffue Thomas de Burton of the age of 16, at the death of the
' faid Sir Thomas.' In memory of this Sir Thomas, I reckon it is, that

a Hift. Rich. 2. by a perfon of qual. p. 136.
b Stow, p. 487.
c Hift. R. 2 ut fupra. p. 136.
d Stow, ut fupra.
e Hol. p. 1073. a.
f p. 487.
g Hol. p. 1072. a. b.
h Bar. Vol. II. p. 155. a.
i Burtons Leic. p. 108.

we fee in little Caftreton church by Stanford, graved in brafs about the verge of a graveftone, this infcription. ' a *Hic jacet dominus Tho-* ' *mas Burton miles, quondam Dominus de Tolthorp, ac ecclefie iftius pa-* ' *tronus, qui obiit* . . . . . *Et domina Margarita uxor ejus in finiftris:* ' *quorum animabus propitietur Deus, Amen.*' b Thro' certaine young ' men brought up with the K. there arofe now great diffention be- ' twixt him & the D. of Lancafter, who departed from the court, & ' went to his caftle of Pomfret which he had fortified. c By reafon ' hereof it was greatly doubted, leaft fome civil warre wold have bro- ' ken forth. But thro' the earneft labor of the kings mother [afterwards buried at Stanford] ' who, notwithftanding hir indifpofition of body ' to travel, by reafon of her corpulencie, rid to & fro betwixt them; an ' agreement was made betwixt hir fonne & the duke, to hir great com- ' fort & contentation of mind, & no leffe furetie of quietnefs to the ' whole realme.' All authors agree that this great ladie, once the ad- miration of her age, was now very corpulent. But Mr. Speed exceeds them all, & tells us, ' d fhe was now exceeding tender of complexion, ' & fcarce able to bear her owne bodies weight thro' corpulency.' Now flourifhed William Folville. ' William Folville, faith Pits e, a ' frier minor of the order of S. Francis, was a Lincolnfhire man, D. D. ' of Cambridge, a perfon of a religious life, & not uncelebrated for ' many titles of erudition. In his time the univerfity of Cambridge (re- ' fenting that the grey friers, above all other religious orders, admitted ' every where young perfons into their monafteries, & fome in a man- ' ner boys) made a ftatute that they fhould receive none under 18 years ' of age. Upon this Folville, as Bale fays f, among others, being offend- ' ed, & knowing that the firft provincial general of their order in Eng- ' land had obtained a privilege of pope Gregory the ninth, long be- ' fore this difpute happened, in their favor for that purpofe; &, as ' Pits fubjoyns, that this ftatute was made therefore againft their privi- ' lege; in the name of his order & defence of their right, wrote againft ' it a piece *pro induendis pueris*, or a defence of receiving children into ' the order of S. Francis; it begins, *Hec eft fententia fratrum minorum,* ' *&c.* He died, & was buried among thofe of his own order at Stan-

9. R. 2. ' ford, in 1384.'———Alderman of Stanford this 8. & 9. R. 2. John Brown. B. H. ' g Edmund Langley E. of Cambridge [lord of Stan- ford] ' for his fervice in the Scotch wars, & many other great fer- ' vices, having highly merited, was advanced to the dignity & title of ' duke of York (the parliament then fitting) his charter bearing date 6.

6. Aug. ' Aug. 9. R. 2. whereby he had alfo 100 l. a year granted to him out ' of the iffues of the county of York. And 40 l. *per annum* out of the ' cuftoms of wools, skins, & pelts in Kingfton fuper Hull, as alfo 500 l.

a Wrights Rutland, p. 37.   e in vita.
b Stow, p. 477.   f in vita.
c Hol. p. 1048. a.   g Bar. Vol. II. p. 155. a.
d p. 740. a.

                                                                    ' *per*

‘ *per annum* out of the port of London, until a 1000 l. yearly, in lands
‘ & rents, fhould be fettled upon him.   The ceremony of his creation,
‘ by cincture with the fword, & putting a cap on his head, with a circle
‘ of gold, being performed at Hofelow lodge in Tividale, where the
‘ K. then lay with his army.

   X. ‘ ᵃ Joan princefs of Wales & mother of K. Rich. the 2. by her
‘ teftament bearing date 7. Aug. 1385. 9. R. 2. at her caftle of Wa-   7. Aug,
‘ lingford, bequeathed her body to be buried in the chapel at Stanford,
‘ near to the grave of Tho. E. of Kent her firft husband ; & gave to
‘ her fon K. Rich. her new bed of red velvet, embroidered with
‘ oftrich-feathers of filver, & heads of leopards of gold, with boughs &
‘ leaves proceeding from their mouths.   Alfo to her fon Tho. E. of
‘ Kent, her bed of red camac, paled with red & rays of gold ; & to
‘ John Holland her other fon, one bed of red camac.’   The occafion
of her death was very melancholy & remarkable.   ‘ ᵇ Her fon John
‘ Holland attending the K. in his expedition now made towards Scot-
‘ land ; & bearing himfelf over much upon the K. by reafon of his
‘ near alliance in blood, upon fome words which happened betwixt
‘ him & Raphe, eldeft fon of the E. of Stafford (occafioned by a quar-
‘ rel betwixt their fervants in their paffage on the way) he there killed
‘ Raphe with his dagger.   ᶜ The caufe of their falling oute was aboute
‘ a Kt. of Boheme, called Sir Miles, that was come to fee the queene.
‘ This Kt. kepte companie moft an end with the lord. ᵈ Richarde Stafforde,
‘ & chauncing to be at wordes with twoo of Sir John Hollandes fer-
‘ vantes, there came twoo archers perteyning to the lord Stafford,
‘ which blamed them, that were fo aboute to myfufe the ftranger in
‘ wordes, as they tooke it.   The ftrife hereby grewe to that point in
‘ the ende, that one of the archers fhotte at one of *Sir John Hollandes*
‘ fervantes, & flewe him.   This mifhap being reported to Sir John
‘ Holland, fette him in fuche a furie (by reafon of the love which he
‘ had to his fervant) that immediately he rufhed foorth of his lodging
‘ to revenge his deathe, &, thro’ misfortune, meeting with the lord
‘ Stafforde, flewe him.   ᵉ The lord Ralph Stafford thus flain, was killed
‘ in the way as he went to the queene, whofe fervant of houfehold he
‘ was, & greatly in favor with her, & he was no leffe beloved of the K.
‘ as he that had beene brought up with him, & beene his playfellowe
‘ from his tender age.   ᶠ The E. of Stafford (his father, then with the
‘ K.) tooke this mifadventure right heavily, as reafon was, yet becaufe
‘ he would not trouble the hoft nor difappoint the journey whiche
‘ they had in hand, upon the kings promife that he would do upright
‘ juftice in the matter, as fhould be thought meet & convenient, he
‘ bare his grief fo patiently as he might ; fo that he wanne himfelf

a Bar. Vol. II. p. 94. a   d Sic, pro Raphe.
b id. p. 78. a.   e Stow, p. 478.
c Hol. p. 1049. a.   f Holing, as above.

                                    ‘ much

' much praife for his wifdom therein fhewed.   ᵃ This fact was done near
' York towards Bifhopfthorpe.   Sir John Holland thereupon fled to
' fanctuary at Beverly.   But the K. being highly incenfed thereat,
' caufed him to be indicted & outlawed for the fame, according to the
' law; & feized upon all his lands & offices.   ᵇ By his juftice herein
' he wanne the hearts of the faid E. of Stafford, the E. of Warwick,
' the lord Baffet, & other great men of Staffords kindred & friends.'
But thereby he alfo brake his own mothers heart.   ' ᶜ For it is alfo faid,
' that the princefs Joane his mother, hearing that the K. had vowed, he
' fhould, for this fact, fuffer according to law, fent earneftly to him,
' imploring his favor (fhe being, as hath been faid, mother to them
' both) & that upon return of the meffenger to Walingford, where
' fhe lay, finding that her requeft availed not, fhe fell into fuch grief,
' that fhe died within five days; whereupon her body being wrapt in
' cerecloth & put in lead, was kept 'till the kings return from Scot-
' land, to be buried in the grey friers at Stanford.'   For a mother who
deceafed upon fo fad an occafion ; a mother who was always dear, &
formerly fo furpaffingly beautiful ; what exequies he celebrated, what
alms he diftributed, what fervices he caufed to be fung, what monument he erected (unlefs the head & neck of a lady with her hair difheveled about her fhoulders, now fet in the weftern outwall of the grey

friars inclofure be a part of the laft) the houfe & church it felf being
now all gone, & the area of both converted into a garden, we know
not ? But doubtlefs they who faw the funeral at the kings return, or
the monument which he afterwards erected, & was here ftanding till
the diffolution of monafteries ; faw that all was magnificent, & agreeable to the grandeur of fo great a king.   Love, grief, pity, every
tender affection would allow him to do no lefs.   But to proceed. The
K. having thus loft his mother, thought lord Raphes death fufficiently
atoned, & that it was too much for his brother alfo to die for what
his innocent mother had already expired.   Relenting therefore, he immediately pardoned him.   The E. of Stafford alfo was fatisfied, & likewife forgave him ᵈ.   ' ᵉ In this 9th. yeere the D. of Lancafter with a great

a Bar. as above p. 78. a.
b Speed, p. 741. a.
c Bar. p. 78. b.
d See Bar. Vol. II. p. 78. b.
e Hol. p. 1051. a. b.

' power

' power of men of warre went into Spain ; at which time Sir Richard
' Burghley was one of the marfhals of his army.——Joan, fometime wife
' of Simon Cokerel, gave to Walter Mace, two acres of arable land
' lying together in little Burlee fields, between the land of the late
' Gilbert de Chefterton weft, and the land of the late W. Wych eaft,
' & abutting on the land of the Fir[m] of S. Peter north, & the
' kings high way fouth. B. H.'

XI. ' ªThe D. of Lancafters foldiers in Spain died very faft, among
' whom deceafed Sir Rycharde Burley, Kt. of the Garter, who hadde
' bene as it were high marfhal of the armye.' Notwithftanding Edmund
Langley E. of Cambridge, lord of Stanford, was, as above, raifed to
be D. of York ' ᵇ he foon after adhered to the D. of Gloucefter ;
' as alfo to thofe others who oppofed the D. of Ireland. And in
' that parliament of the 10. R. 2. wherein the great lords were fo   10. R. 2.
' powerful, was one of them [thirteen] that had licenfe & authority
' to inquire into all abufes in government and grievances whatfoever,
' from the death of K. Edw. the 3ᵈ. 'till that very time. ᶜWhere-
' upon Nov. 19. the K. iffued forth his commiffion under the great   Nov. 19.
' feal, confirming the faid lords in fuch power. ——Joan, late. wife of
' Simon Cokerel of Staunford gave to W. Stacy, one fhop with a
' loft above erected, & one acre & half of arable land ; which fhop
' is fituate behynde-the-back in the parifh of All Saints in the mercat,
' &c. between a fhop of the late Richard Arderns north, & a fhop
' of John Longs fouth. And the acre & half of land lie together at
' Pertes croffe, between the way called Tynwell-gate north, & the
' parfon of S. Peters land fouth. B. H. ᵈ Sir Simon Burley Kt. was
' now one of the perfons which were in the publick envie for their
' overfwaying grace with the king, ᵉ The E. of Arundel now alfo took
' a hundred Flemifh veffels laden with wine & fent them into England.
' ᶠThis made wine fo plentiful in England that it was fold for 13 *s.*
' & 4 *d.* the tunne. ᵍ For this, & other gallant acts, Sir Simon Burley
' & others yet about the K. feemed rather to envie the E. of Arundels
' good name, than commend hym. ——Gilbert Jakes of Stanford quit-
' ted to W. Styandeby of the fame all claim to two acres of meadow,
' lying together in Brodeing, between John Longs meadow north, &
' the Holm near Efton mill-holme fouth, & abutting upon Eftholm
' weft. Witneffes, Thomas Cok, alderman of Staunford, &c. dated
' the Saturday next after the feaft of S. Thomas the apoftle, 10 R. 2.
' B. H.

XII. ' ʰ In the 11. R. 2. the D. of Ireland fled into Holland, but the D.   11. R. 2
' of Baviere bare fuch good will to the D. of York [lord of Stanford]
' & the Dukes of Lancafter & Gloucefter, that he commanded the D. of

a Holing. p. 1052. b.   e Hol. p. 1057. b.
b Baron. Vol. II. p. 155. a.   f id. p. 1058. a.
c Hift. Rich. 2. by a perfon of Qual. p. 88.   g id. ib. b.
d Speed p. 746. a.   h id. p. 1068. a.

' Ireland

'Ireland to depart his country. [a] The K. altho' fore againft his will,
'wanting power to withftand the [D. of Gloucefter, & other] lords,
'condefcended to do what they would have him, & commaunded Sir
'Simon Burley, and other fufpected perfons of his court & family to
'be awarded to prifon, to anfwer at the next parliament. [b] Aug.

Aug. 25. '25. the K. with the duke of Ireland [& other his favorites] being at
'Nottingham, fent thither for all the judges of England. [c] Who be-
'ing come into the councel chamber, it was propounded, whether the
'ftatutes made in a late parliament at Weftm. were not derogatory to
'the kings dignity & prerogative; & they were not to be punifhed who
'procured them, & did as much as in them lay to hinder the K.
'from exercifing his royal prerogative.' The perfons here ftroke at
were the D. of Gloucefter & other twelve abovementioned (whereof the
D. of York, lord of Stanford was alfo one.) One of thefe judges was
named William Burghe. But the author laft quoted calls him William
Burleigh: which looks as if he was a brother, or kinfman of Sir Si-
mons. Certain it is Sir Simon had a brother now living called William Burgley; but I think he was not the judge here fpoken of. As
for William Burgh, or Burleigh the judge, he & all his brethren, '[d] be-
'ing terrified with the fear of prefent death, anfwer'd, thofe perfons
'ought to fuffer death as traytors.' But foon after thofe thirteen

Feb. 3. lords growing too ftrong for the king & his party, '[d] the morrow
'after the purification of our lady the parliament began, which was
'named the parliament that wrought wonders. The K. would gladly
'have proroged the time of this parliament, if by any means he might.
'[e] The firft day of the feffion all the judges were arrefted as they fat in
'judgment on the bench; & moft of them fent to the tower: [f] Wil-
'liam Burgh, or Burleigh being one. Alfo the D. of Gloucefter
'caufed Sir Simon Burley to be accufed of divers offences againft the
'crowne, realme, & church, namely, I. for that he had (as they fur-
'mifed) fpoyled & wafted the kings treafure, & witholden the pay of
'the foldiers & men of warre. II. That the D. of Ireland & he had
'gathered great fummes of money, conveyed the fame to Dover, &
'from thence fent it in the night by fea into Germanie. III. The
'archbifhop forfooth & the monks charged him, that he foughte meanes
'to remove the fhrine of Thomas Becket from Canterburie unto Dover,
'under a colour of feare, leaft the French being affembled in Flaunders
'to invade England, fhould lande in Kent, & fpoyle it: whereas in-
'deede (as they furmifed) he ment to fend it over the feas unto the K.
'of Boheme. [g] Among other flaunderous tales that were fpredde a-
'broade of him, one was that he confented to the delivering of Dover

a Stow, p. 485.
b Hift. Rich. 2. by a perfon qual. p. 99.
c True relation of that memorable parliament 10. R. 2. which wrought wonders.
Lond. 1641. 4°. p. 10.

d Hol. p. 1070. b.
e Speed, p. 749. a.
f Hol. p. 1072. b.
g id. p. 1073. a.

'caftle

' caftle to the French for money. ª On the 6. of March William Burleigh, Mar. 6.
' & the reft of the barons of the exchequer, were called to anfwer for
' their confpiracy at Nottingham againft the commiffioners, & found
' guilty. ᵇ On the 12. of March being thurfday, Sir Simon Burley was Mar. 12.
' brought into the parliament houfe, where his accufations were read.
' From this day almoft till the afcention of our Lord, the parliament
' houfe was only taken up with the tryal of the faid Sir Simon Bur-
' leugh.   There he had very fevere ufage, to wit ᶜ no clearke allow-
' ed him to [help to] make uppe his account; & fo was found in ar-
' rearages 250000 franks.   And altho', for one part thereof, he de-
' maunded allowance of money, which he had defreyd & layde out in
' Almaine & in Boheme, about the kings marriage; and, for the refi-
' due, defired dais of payment; yet he could obteyne neyther.   ᵈ And
' as to the delivery of Dover caftle to the French, it was a thing not
' like to be true.   And fo alfo no doubt many things that he was
' charged with, by common report among the people, were nothing
' true at all; altho' happily the fubftance of thofe things might be true
' in fome refpect.   ᵉ However three of the appellants (viz. the D. of
' Gloucefter, & the earles of Arundel & Warwike) with the whole
' houfe of commons, urged that execution might be performed ac-
' cording to law: & on the other fide, the K. & Q. the earles of
' Derby & Nottingham, & the prior of S. John his uncle, with the major
' part of the upper houfe, did labour to fave him.   In particular, ᶠ the
' E. of Darbie did what he coulde to fave his life [& went fo far, that]
' by reafon thereof, great diffention rofe betwixt the fayd E. & the D.
' of Gloucefter.'   Nay, as you will hereafter find, the Q. her felf
vouchfafed to kneel to the D. of Gloucefter to beg his life.   I have
alfo read, but where my notes fay not, that fhe continued on her
knees a full hour, but was refufed her requeft, & churlifhly bid to
pray for her felf, & leave Burley to juftice.   ' ᵍ For the D. being a
' fore & a right fevere manne, myght not by any meanes be re-
' moved from his opinion and purpofe, if he once refolved upon any
' matter.   ʰ Now becaufe the commons were tired with fo long de-
' lays & excufes in the parliament; & fearing, as it was moft like,
' that all their pains would be to little or no purpofe, they humbly
' craved leave of the K. to goe to their habitations.   There was
' alfo fome muttering amongft the common people, & it was
' reported to the parliament, that the commons did rife in di-
' verfe parts of the realme, but efpecially about Kent, in favour
' of the faid Sir Simon Burley; which when they heard, thofe
' that before fpeak & ftood for him, now flew cleane from him, &,

a True relation of the memorable parl.   e True relation &c. p. 31.
p. 21.   f Hol. p. 1072. a.
  b id. p. 31.   g id. ib.
  c Hol. p. 1072. b,   h True acct. &c. p. 32.
  d id. p. 1073. a.

' by

May. 5. ' by joynt confent, on the 5. day of May, fentence was pronounced
' againft the faid Sir Symon, that hee fhould be drawne from the
' tower to Tyborne ; & then to be hanged 'till hee were dead, &
' then to have his head ftrooke from his body.   But becaufe hee was
' knight of the garter, a gallant courtier, powerfull, & once a favou-
' rite of the kings, & much refpected of all the court, the K. [he fhould
fay, the D. of Gloucefter] ' of his fpecial grace was pleafed to miti-
' gate his doome —— that he fhould only be led to tower-hill, & ther
' be beheaded.   ᵃ Hereupon he was firft committed to the tower, & be-
' fore the K. or his other friendes coulde procure his deliverance, was,
' without lawe or juftice, ᵇ with his hands bound behind him, led
' thro' the city of London, & had his head ftricken off, upon the

May 15. ' tower hill, on the 15. day of May, 1388.   This barbarous execu-
1388.   tion was done ' ᶜ by commaundment of the D. of Gloucefter, & other
' of his faction, quite contrarie to the kings will or knowledge, info-
' much that when he underftoode it, he fpake many fore wordes a-
' gaynft the duke, affirming, that hee was a wicked man, & worthie
' to be kept fhorter, fithe under a color of doing juftice, hee went
' aboute to deftroy every good & honeft man.   The K. was alfo of-
' fended with the D. of York [lord of Stanford] for his brothers pre-
' fumptuous doings ; tho' the fayde D. of Yorke (beeing verily a man
' of a gentle nature) wifhed that the ftate of the common-wealth might
' have beene returned without loffe of any mans lyfe, or other cruel
' dealing.   But the D. of Gloucefter, & diverfe other of the nobilitie,
' the leffe that they paffed for the kings threatening fpeeche, fo muche
' more were they readie to punifh all thofe whome they tooke to be
' theyr enemies.   ᵈ To pleafe him the better, now at this parliament,
' the faid Sir Simon Burleys lands were given to the K. a great part
' whereof he afterwards difpofed of to divers men, as he thought ex-
' pedient.'   Thus fell the great Sir Simon Burley, fo beloved at the
very day of his death, that he had many of the commons, the majo-
rity of the upper houfe, as I may fay two kings (Rich. 2. & the E. of
Derby afterwards H. 4.) to beg his life, & even a queen to kneel for
it, but all too little to fave it.   ' ᵉ The faid Sir Simon de Burleighs
' body, he being a Kt. Banneret, & of the garter, a great & gallant
' courtier, lyeth honourably buried and intombed in Pauls church.
' ᶠ Being thus cruelly beheaded, fo greatly to the offence of the K. &
' thofe that were his truftie counfailers, thereupon the K. caufed the
' D. of Ireland the fooner to affemble an armie againft the faid D.
' of Gloucefter & his accomplices, thereby to reftraine their prefump-
' tuous proceedings.'   The faid D. of Gloucefter apprehending his own
danger, & having the kings perfon as yet in his power, therefore ᵍ

a Hol. p. 1072. b.   e True account &c. p. 34.
b Stow. p. 487.   f Hol. ut fupra.
c Hol. ut fupra.   g Hift. Rich. 2. by a perfon of qual. p.
d Hol. p. 1073. a.   298.

' caufed

' caufed the faid K. in prefence of the duke of York [lord of Stan-
' ford] & very many other lords, in the faid D. of Yorks chapel at
' Langley, to fwear before the venerable facrament of the lords body,
' there placed upon the altar, that thence-forwards he would never en-
' damage, trouble, or grieve him the faid D. of Gloucefter, for any of
' his deeds which are faid to have been committed againft the per-
' fon of him the faid King; but chearfully & totally forgive him all
' his offence if any were.' But how unable even the moft folemn
oaths are to tie up fome perfons from revenging fuch great injuries
as thefe are, when they have it in their power, we may learn from the
example of this K. Rich. the 2d. who at laft caufed the faid D. of Gloucefter (tho' his own uncle) to be privately made away, chiefly for re-
fentment, if we may believe an author hereafter quoted, of his dear
friend Sir Simon Burleys death. But of thofe things below [a]. Here
I had almoft forgot to obferve what became of William Burghe, or
Burleigh the judge. Let it be remembred then, ' [b] that the faid Wil-
' liam Burleigh, & the other five juftices, who ftood condemned with
' him, were fent into Ireland, there to remaine for tearme of
' life; the faid William Burleigh being confined to the city of Dub-
' lin, with liberty of two miles for his recreation, & 40. l. a year dur_
' ing life for his maintenance.' One William Burgle (but I believe
not the William abovementioned, yet a) brother of Simon Burgle
(but whether this Simon Burley aforenamed I queftion, his charter
feeming ancienter than Richard the 2ds. time) for the foul of his faid
brother Simon in particular, became a benefactor to the nuns of S.
Michael by Stanford; whofe donation is thus expreffed. ' [c] Be it
' known both to prefent as well as future people, that I William de
' Burgle, have given, & granted, & by this my charter confirmed, in
' pure & perpetual alms, to the church of bleffed Michael of Stain-
' ford & to the holy nuns there ferving God *fub Lūda,* for the foul
' of Simon my brother, & for the fouls of my anceftors. The fore-
' faid church fhall forever poffefs the donation of this alms, freely &
' quietly, from all fervice & exaction fecular. Moreover I have made
' this donation in the chapter of the forenamed church, before Sir
' Reginald, & the convent of the fame place, & many others. Wit-
' neffes, Walt. S. Rob. S. Geoffry S. Richard de Armeft[une] Henry
' de Lugville, Reginald his fon, Afceline brother of William, Geoffry
' de la Mar, Pain Palm[er.]' The feal reprefents an armed knight on

a Anno 21. R. 2.

b True account, &c. p. 34.

c Notum fit tam prefentibus quam futuris, quod ego Willielmus de Burgleia dedi, & conceffi, & hac mea carta confirmavi, in puram & perpetuam eleemofinam, ecclefie B. Michaelis de Stainford & fanctimonialibus ibidem Deo fervientientibus fubLūda,
pro anima Simonis fratris mei, & pro animabus antecefforum meorum. Predicta ec-

clefia, hujus eleemofine donationem, libere,
& quiete, ab omni fervicio & exactione feculari, inperpetuum poffidebit. Hanc donationem vero in capitulo prenominate ecclefie, coram domino Reginaldo & conventu
ejufdem loci, & multis aliis, feci. His t.
Halt. S. Rob. S. Galf. S. Ricard. de Armeft.
Henrico de Lugvilla, Reginald. filio ejus, Af-
celino fratre Willielmi, Galf. de la Mar.
Pagano Palm.

horfeback.

horfeback. I know not what to make of the words *fub Lūda* in this charter; befides which in the whole there is likewife a ftudied obfcurity,
that I know not how to explain. All that I can therefore farther fay, is,
that the original is now in the E. of Exeters cuftody, from whence, with
my own hand, I carefully tranfcribed the copy inferted word for word
on the other fide, as it ftands in the fame; to which if any one require farther fatisfaction, I beg leave to refer.   ' Several perfons now gave to Sir
' John Machon warden of the chantery of S. Clement Staunford,
' one meffuage & one empty place with the appurtenances in the
' town of Staunford, whereof the meffuage aforefaid is fituate in S.
' Peters parifh Staunford; to wit, between a tenement of the gild of
' the bleffed Mary at Staunford weft, & S. Peters church eaft, & abutting
' on the kings highway north, & a tenement of Jo. Tyler fouth. And
' the faid empty place lies between a tenement of John Chefter weft,
' & the ftreet called felverftrete eaft, abutting on the kings highway
' fouth, & a tenement of the faid John Chefter north.   Given at Staun-
' ford the Sunday next after the feaft of S. Barnabas the apoftle, 11.
' R. 2. Witneffes, John Longe alderman of Staunford, &c. B. H.

Sept. 9.   XIII. ' ᵃ The ninth of September a parliament began at Cambridge,
12. R. 2. ' in which were divers ftatutes ordeined.'   At that time, as it feems,
under a pretence of their being nurferies of confpiracies & treafons a-
gainft the government, there was a defign of fuppreffing thofe ancient
focieties in moft towns called the gilds or fraternities of fuch or fuch a
faint as the parifh church was dedicated to, or the feveral brother-
hoods had chofe for their refpective patrons.   For this purpofe the K.
fent out the following mandate, or writ of enquiry.   ' ᵇ The K. for
' certain honeft & juft caufes, before him in the parliament held at
' Cambridge, propofed & declared, commandeth to every the fherifs

a Stow. p. 489.

b. Rex, certis de caufis honeftis & ratio-
nabilibus, coram fe, in parliamento apud
Cantabrigiam tento, propofitis & declaratis,
precepit fingulis vice-comitibus per Angliam,
quod ftatim, vifis prefentibus, in plenis co-
mitiis fuis, ac etiam in omnibus civitatibus,
burgis, villis, &c. & aliis locis, ubi melius
expedire viderint, publice proclamari face-
rent, quod omnes & finguli magiftri & cuftodes gildarum & fraternitatum quarumcunq;
infra ballivas fuas, certificent ipfum & confilium fuum, in cancellaria fua, in fcriptis
plenarie, viz. de modo, & forma, & auto-
ritate fundationis, & inceptionis, & continu-
ationis, & regiminis gildarum & fraternitatum predictarum. Ac de modo & forma fa-
crorum, congregationum, conviviorum, &
affemblearum fratrum & fororum. Ac omnium aliorum de gildis & fraternitatibus hu-
jufmodi exiftentibus. Necnon de libertatibus, privilegiis, ftatutis, ordinationibus, ufibus,
& confuetudinibus gildarum & fraternitatum
eorundem. Ac infuper de omnibus terris, tenementis, redditibus, & poffeffionibus, mortificatis & non mortificatis. Ac de bonis & catallis
quibufcunq; ad predictas gildas & fraterni-

tates pertinentibus, in quorumcunq; manibus exiftunt. Ac de vero valore annuo terrarum, tenementorum, reddituum ac poffef-
fionum. Ac de vero pretio bonorum & ca-
tallorum predictorum, &c. Ac omnium
aliorum articulorum & circumftanciarum,
dictas gildas & fraternitates qualitercunque
concernentium five tangentium; fub pena
forisfacture & omiffionis perpetue omnium
terrarum, tenementorum, bonorum, &c. er-
ga regem & heredes fuos. Et quod dicti
magiftri & cuftodes, cartas & literas patentes, fi quas habent, &c. predictas gildas &
fraternitates tangentes, coram rege & dicto
confilio fuo deferant, fub pena revocationis
& adnullationis perpetue cartarum & literarum predictarum, ac omnium libertatum,
immunitatum, privilegiorum, & conceffio-
num & cartis & literis predictis contento-
rum; facturi ulterius & recepturi quod per
regem & dictum confilium fuum, vigore
& auctoritate parliamenti, ordinari & decerni
contigerit in premiffis, &c. Tefte rege apud
Weftmon. 1. die Novemb. anno 12ᵒ. regni
fui. Ex codicis MS. in Bib. Cott. fub imagine Cleopat. E. II. fol. 189.

3

' through

‘ through England, that immediately, on fight of the prefents, in
‘ their own full courts, & alfo in all cities, boroughs, towns, & o-
‘ ther places where they fhall fee it to be more expedient, they
‘ caufe it to be publickly proclaimed, that all & every the mafters &
‘ wardens of the gilds & fraternities whatfoever within their bailiwic's,
‘ fhall certifie him & his counfil, in his chancery, fully in writing &c.
‘ to wit, of the manner, & form, & authority of the foundation &
‘ beginning, & continuance, & government of the gilds & fraterni-
‘ ties aforefaid. Alfo of the manner & form of the devotions, con-
‘ gregations, banquets, & affemblies of the brethren & fifters. And
‘ of all other matters concerning the gilds & fraternities of this fort
‘ being. Alfo of the liberties, privileges, ftatutes, orders, ufes, &
‘ cuftoms of the gilds & fraternities of the fame. And moreover of
‘ all the lands, tenements, rents, & poffeffions, in mortmane & not
‘ in mortmane. Alfo of the goods & chattels whatfoever to the
‘ forefaid gilds & fraternites, belonging, in the hands of whomfoever
‘ they be. Alfo of the true yearly value of the lands, tenements, rents,
‘ & poffeffions. Alfo of the true price of the goods & chattels aforefaid.
‘ Alfo of all other articles & circumftances the faid gilds & fraterni-
‘ ties any ways concerning or touching; under the pain of forfeiture
‘ & lofing for ever of all the lands, tenements, goods, &c. unto the
‘ king and his heirs. And that the faid mafters and wardens bring be-
‘ fore the king & his faid counfil the charters & letters patents (if
‘ any fuch they have) the forefaid gilds & fraternities concerning,
‘ under penalty of revocation & perpetual annulling of the charters
‘ & letters aforefaid, alfo of all the liberties, immunities, privileges,
‘ & conceffions, both in the charters & letters aforefaid contained;
‘ to do farther & receive as by the K. & his faid counfil, by virtue
‘ & authority of parliament, fhall happen to be ordained & decreed
‘ in the premifes. Witnefs the K. at Weftm. the 1. of Nov. in the Nov. 1.
‘ 12. year of his reign.’ After this record, the MS. from whence it
is taken, goes on. ‘ By vertue hereof proclamation was made in all
‘ the fhires of England, & thereupon certificates fent into the chan-
‘ cery accordingly from all quarters of the realm, & remain yet to
‘ feen amongft the ª queens records. By the particular view whereof
‘ the lamentable blindnefs of that time, & the fuperftitious zeal of
‘ the common people, utterly void of true faith & underftanding
‘ may appear, as likewife by the teftimonies of fome of the faid cer-
‘ tificates.’ The copier then proceeds to exhibit fome of the faid returns, & among others (as one of the moft grievous & fcandalous inftances of this kind) fets down the cuftom of the gild of S. Martin
in Stanford, which I fhall here tranfcribe. ‘ ᵇ In honor of God &
S. Martin,

---

a This fhews this collection was made
in queen Eliz. time, foon after the fuppreffion of thofe gilds, chanteries, & fraternities, by the greedy minifters of her brother K.

Edw. the 6. And perhaps it was firft gathered to color that defign.
b In honore Dei & S. Martini, ab antiquo tempore, ordinata fuit quedam gilda in
eccefia

' S. Martin, from old time hath been ordained a certain gild in the
' church of S. Martin at Staunford, under fuch like form; to wit, that
' the brethren & fifters of the forefaid gild fhould have a certain ca-
' pellan celebrating in the church aforefaid, in honor of S. Martin,
' for the brethren & fifters aforefaid, & for all their benefactors,
' & fhould find a certain light in the fame church, in honor of S.
' Martin. And it is, & was, the cuftom of the fraternity aforefaid,
' time out of mind, that, on the feaft of S. Martin aforefaid, the bre-
' thren have a certain bull; the which bull fhould be ufed & fold
' unto the profit of the fraternity aforefaid. And that, on the fame
' feaft, the aforefaid brethren & fifters may affemble to a drinking, &
' there pray for their brethren & fifters, & all their benefactors, &c.
' And every brother & fifter fhall give, at the feaft of S. Michael, for
' fupport of all the forefaid particulars, one bufhel of corn, &c.' By
this account it appears that the brethren & fifters of S. Martins gild
had always a bull-running on Martinmafs day; a diverfion for which
the good people of Stanford have a particular fondnefs. The brethren & fifters of the gild of S. Martin feem to have been the parifhioners of S. Martins parifh. The ufual place where they affembled to
prayers was in S. Martins church. But for their drinking & banquet
on S. Martins day, they had a particular room in the faid parifh called S. Martins gild-hall. I do not find, for all this ftrict enquiry, that
any gilds were diffolved in K. Richard the 2ds. time. But in K. Edward the 6. time they were all fuppreffed at once. When, it is probable, this mixture of bull-running, tipling, & popery, practifed by the
brethren & fifters of S. Martins gild at Stanford, was made ufe of as
one pretence to fupprefs all the reft.——' Henry de Herdeby now occurs
' rector of great S. Michaels. B. H.'

XIV. ' ª The wars between the D. of Lancafter & don John K. of
' Caftile had been fharp & tedious, but the end was now acceptable.
' That K. was a prince of no evil confcience, &, feeing therefore the
' right which the D. urged, fought & obtained a firm peace. The con-
' ditions were, that lord Henrie the kings fon, fhould marry lady
' Katherine the dukes daughter by Conftance daughter of Peter late K.
' of Caftile. And, that in default of iffue between the young couple,
' the crowne fhould come to Edmund D. of York [lord of Stanford]
' who had married the other daughter of K. Peter.' It is obferved,
that in all the troubles between K. Richard & his lords, ' ᵇ the wif-

ecclefia S. Martini de Staunford, fub tali forma; viz. quod fratres & forores predicte gilde haberent quendam capellanum cele-brantem in ecclefia predicta, in honore S. Martini, pro fratribus & fororibus predictis, & pro omnibus benefactoribus fuis; & in-venirent certum lumen in eadem ecclefia, in honore S. Martini. Et eft, & fuit, confuetu-do fraternitatis predicte, a tempore cujus memoria non exftat, quod in fefto S. Mar-tini predicti, fratres habeant quendam tau-

rum, qui quidem taurus huteretur & ven-deretur ad proficuum fraternitatis predicte. Et quod, in eodem fefto, predicti fratres & forores conveniant ad potandum, & ibi orent pro fratribus & fororibus fuis, & omnibus benefactoribus fuis, &c. Et quilibet frater & foror dabit, in fefto S. Michaelis, ad fup-portationem omnium predictorum, unum *bufhel* ordei. port. &c. id. ib.

a Speed. p. 670. b.
b id. p. 751. a.

                  ' dom

' dom & moderation of the said D. of York was such, that he is not
' so much as once named among the factious.' So Speed; but other
authors before cited, do not altogether so clearly acquit him of that
charge. This year a court marshal was held at Stanford, but on what
occasion I find not. In the continuation of Ingulf & Peter Blesens,
it is thus touched. ' ª Various threats were now daily squibbed out
' by the Depyngers against the abbat of Croyland, for an inquisition
' by him made in order for a perambulation in the parts of Holland
' & Kesteven, to determine the bounds & limits of his own monastery.
' And so, by means of Thomas Holland E. of Kent & his officers,
' many hardships were heaped on the abbat at his manors which lay
' at the greatest distance from him. These Depyngers began first to
' molest the said abbat, by their bills containing divers charges, all
' heavy, but false enough, exhibited against him in a court marshal
' of the kings, now held at Stanford. Also in ᵇ this 13. R. 2. or there-
' abouts, a great council was held at Staunford, about making peace
' with the French. ᶜ Edward eldest son of Edmund D. of York [lord
of Stanford] ' was created E. of Rutland 25. Feb. 13. R. 2. but to 25. Feb.
' enjoy that title no longer than his fathers life; having therewithall
' a grant of the castle, town, & lordship of Okeham in Rut. with the
' shriefalty of that county, sometime belonging to Wm. Bohun E. of
' Northampton [lord of Stanford] in part of satisfaction of 800
' marks per annum intended to him.' This Edward, after his fathers
death, was himself lord of Stanford. Alderman of Stanford, 13. R.
2. John de Sowresby. B. H.' ' Walter Baldeswel, gave Thomas Storin
' of Staunford chapman, one shop, with a loft above erected, situate
' behinde-the-bake in All-saints parish in the mercat, between a shop
' of the late Richard Ardern north, & a shop of John Longs south.
' Witnesses, Richard Forster, &c. Dated the Thursday next after the
' feast of S. James the apostle, 13. R. 2. B. H.

XV. ' ᵈ In the 14. R. 2. in part of satisfaction for the sum of a 14. R. 2.
' 1000. l. by year, promised to him, upon his advancement to the
' dukedom of York; Edmund Langle [lord of Stanford] obtained a
' grant of the manor of Hychen, then valued at 100. l. a year. As
' also of the manor of Somerford Keyns of 40. marks a year; & of
' the manor of Wendover of 84. l. a year; all in Bucks. ᵉThe same
' year Edward E. of Rutland [eldest son of the said D. of York, &
after him also lord of Stanford] ' was constituted lord admiral of
' the kings whole fleet to the northwards. ——Alderman of Stanford,
' 14. R. 2. Henry Bukeden. B. H. John Fulsham of Staunford gave
' to Richard de Depyng, one garden in the abbat of Burgs liberty
' in the Hyegate, between a garden of the nuns of S. Michael south,
' & a garden of the late Sir W. Hastmel the capellan north; as it

a p. 485.
b Lelandi collect. to. 1. p. 186.   d Bar. vol. II. p. 155. a.
c Bar. vol. II. p. 156. a.   e id. p. 156. a

'extends it felf on the kings highway eaft. B. H.' Now flourifhed Ralph de Spalding. ' Ralf Spalding, faith Bale, [a] was educated in the ' moft delightful monaftery which the brotherhood of mount Car- ' mel had formerly at Stanford in Lincolnfhire. Pits tells us, [b] he ' was a D. D. & head profeffor of that faculty at Cambridge, & no ' contemptible divine or philofopher, unlefs that he was over curious ' in inventing new hypothefes, rafh in divulging, & fo very ftubborn ' in maintaining them, that at length he fell into fufpition of herefie, & ' favoured fomewhat of Wiclif. However, faith he, I never as yet expref- ' ly read that either the author, or any of his works were condemned. ' A little piece of his, called, a fubtle difcuffion of the fophifms of ' Ariftotle, as Leland obferves, [c] was once in requeft. He wrote alfo, ' as Pits adds, a vol. of fermons, & another of determinations on fe- ' veral fcriptures; & dying, was buried in the monaftery of his own ' order at Stanford. Bale fays, he flourifhed in 1390. & at laft died ' at Stanford.' Now alfo lived Wm. Stenoford. ' The Auftin friers, ' faith Leland [d], pronounce Wm. de Stenoford theirs, a celebrated ' man as well for his fame as learning. He was cotemporary with ' Valdey the Auftin frier.' Wm. Egumond, according to Bale, [e] is the fame perfon whom Leland calls Wm. de Stenoford. ' Wm. ' Egumond, faith Pits, [f] was a frier hermit of the order of S. Auftin, ' in the monaftery belonging to thofe fathers at Stanford. A man ' who always joyned the ftudies of piety & learning together, & ' proceeding in both with an equal pace, arrived to the utmoft per- ' fection of each; being at the fame time a fmart philofopher, a pro- ' found divine, an eloquent preacher, fervent, & very artful in per- ' fuading. After he had finifhed his ftudies in the Englifh univerfities, ' he was created D. D. & at length being made profeffor, taught a ' great while with much honor. After this going to Rome, he ' was, by the fovereign pontif, made bifhop of Piffinenfis, & or- ' dained fuffragan to Henry Belfort bifhop of Lincoln. He put in ' writing, a vol. of fermons, another of fcholaftic replications, & fe- ' veral other pieces; flourifhing in 1390.' Now alfo lived John Val_ dey. Pits tells us, [g] that ' John Valdey (as Jofeph Pamphilus affirms ' from Thomas Colby) born at York of honeft parents, was a frier ' hermit of the order of S. Auftin, & D. D. of Oxford, where he ' ftudied fo feverely, that he gained not only the chief laurel to him_ ' felf, but much honor to his order, & great glory to his country. ' For he was an ingenious & induftrious man; learned & eloquent; ' no mean preacher, pious, prudent, grave, modeft, temperate, chaft, ' of fo great authority among the religious of his own order, that ' they conferred upon him the greateft honor they had to beftow, &

a in vita.
b in vita.
c Comment. p. 384.
d Comment. p. 343.

e in vita.
f in vita.
g in vita.

' voted

‘ voted him their provincial.   And indeed he was wonderfully beloved by every body, clergy & laity; fo that upon the death of Alex-
‘ ander Nevil archbifhop of York, he was chofe, tho’ never confirmed,
‘ to fucceed him.   For the pope gave that archbifhoprick to Thomas
‘ Arundel, & tranflated Valdey to the archbifhoprick of Dublin.’ More
of this John Valdey under the next year.   Here by the way, note,
‘ this John Valdey, as Bale faith ᵃ, had a brother named Robert.   Ro-
‘ bert Valdey, faith Leland, ᵇ was likewife an Auftin frier, a celebrated
‘ fcholar, & D. D. on whom, by the bounty of feveral kings, were confer-
‘ red many very great preferments; as the bifhopbrick of Adurenfis, the
‘ archbifhopbrick of Dublin, bifhopbrick of Chichefter, & archbifhop-
‘ brick of York; to which laft honor he was collated in 1397.’
Bifhop Godwin fpeaking of this Robert, as archbifhop of York, mentions
his being bifhop Adurenfis, but knows not what place is meant by that
name.   But Pits fays, *primus factus eft Epifcopus Adurenfis in Vafconia,
rectius forfan Cadurcenfis in Aquitania, deinde Dublinienfis*, &c.

XVI. ‘ ᶜK. Richard with Q. Anne his wife, four bifhops, as many   15. R. 2.
‘ earles, the D. of Yorke [lord of Stanford] many lords, & fifteen
‘ ladies, held a royal chriftmaffe at Langley [the D. of Yorks] neere
‘ S. Albons.   ᵈEdward E. of Rutland [afterwards lord of Stanford]
‘ was this year in the wars of France.   As alfo in commiffion, with
‘ John of Gant D. of Lancafter & others, to treat of peace with the
‘ French.   In this year likewife he was made juftice of all the forefts
‘ fouth of Trent; & conftable of the tower of London, for life, after
‘ the death of Thomas E. of Kent.   And was [ᵉ as was alfo his father Edmund D. of York & lord of Stanford] ‘ with John D. of Lan-
‘ cafter, at the treaty for peace then held at Amiens in France in ᵉmid-
‘ lent.——In 1392. as I find in Leland ᶠ, was a council at Stanford.’ And   1392.
true, for there was not one, but two great councils, about very different matters, held this year, &, as I take it, both at the very fame
time of the year, at Stanford.   One was a council about civil affairs,
to wit, how the Londoners fhould be dealt with, who had refufed
to lend the K. a thoufand pounds, & alfo abufed a foreigner, who,
on their refufal, had offered to furnifh him with it; as alfo whether
war or peace fhould be made with France. The other a council a-
bout religious affairs, & in particular the fuppreffion of Henry Crumpe
a great difciple of Wiclifs.

XVII. But to be particular. ‘ The K. about this feafon, fays Holingfhed ᵍ,
‘ fent to the Londoners, requefting to borrow of them the fumme of one
‘ thoufand poundes, which they uncourteoufly refufed to lende; & more-
‘ over fell upon an Italian or Lombarde (as they tearmed him) whom they
‘ beate, & neare hande flue; bycaufe hee offered to lende the K. that

a p. 499.
b Comment. p. 394.
c Stow, p. 492.
d Bar. vol. II. p. 156. a.

e id. p. 155. a.
f Collect. To. III. p. 383.
g Hol. ut fupra.

‘ money.

' money.   ª Which when the K. heard, he was marveloufly angred,
' & ᵇ foon after figned an order for the courts of juftice at Weftmin-
' fter, to remove to York; which order is dated at Stanford, March

Mar. 13. ' 13. 1392. Alfo calling together almoft all the nobles of the

May 25. ' land to Stanford on the five & twentieth day of May, he opened
' to them the malitioufneffe of the Londoners, & complayned of
' theyr prefumption. The which noblemen gave counfell, that theyr
' infolencie fhould be with fpeede repreffed, & their pride abated.
' ᶜ The citizens of London in thofe dayes, as fhould appeare, ufing
' their authoritie to the uttermoft, had devifed & fet forthe diverfe
' orders & conftitutions to abridge the libertie of foreyners, that came
' to the citie to utter their commodities. Religious men that wrote
' the doings of that age, feemed alfo to find fault with them, for that
' they favoured Wiclifes opinions, & therefore charge them with in-
' fidelitie, & maynteyning, I know not how, of lollards & heretiks.
' But howfoever the matter went they fell into the kings heavie dif-
' pleafure. By the kings judgment therefore was the major of Lon-
' don & the fheriffs, with other the beft citizens, arrefted to appear at

June 11. ' Nottingham; where, on the 11. of June, John Hinde major was
' depofed, & fent to Windfor-caftle; the fheriffs were alfo depofed &
' fent, the one to the caftle of Walingford, the other to the caftle of
' Odiham; & the other citizens to other prifons, till the K. with his
' councell had determined what fhould be done with them. And there
' it was determined, that from thenceforth the Londoners fhould not
' choofe nor have any major, but that the K. fhould appoint one of
' his Kts. to be ruler of the citie; their privileges were revoked, their
' liberties difanulled, & their lawes abrogated.'

   XVIII. But to proceed. As to other matters debated in this council, ' I find, upon the morrow of the holy Trinity in 1392. faith Kniton,
' ᵈ the K. held a great council at Stanford, to debate about affairs with
' relation to the French. In this council he affembled all the old
' foldiery of the kingdom, on purpofe that he might fooner put in
' execution that which he fhould be advifed to do by the counfel of
' thofe old & experienced captains.' So Holingfhed. ' ᵉ After the re-
' turne of the D. of Lancafter, & other the ambaffadors that had bene
' at Amiens, a councell of the lordes & chiefe eftates of the realme
' was called at Stanford, to the which, as if it had bin to a parlia-
' ment, there came forth of every good town certaine perfons ap-
' pointed to deliberate & take advice in fo weightie a matter, as ey-
' ther to conclude upon peace, or elfe upon warre. But in the ende
' they brought little or nothing to paffe, faving that they agreed to
' have the truce to endure for a twelvemonth longer. Both the kings

a Stow, p. 492.   d col. 2740.
b Acta regia. Nº. 7. p. 27.   e p. 1080. a. b.
c Hol. ut fupra.

                                                    ' fware

' fware to obferve the fame, afore fuch as were appointed to fee
' theyr othes receyved.   About the fame time came the duke of Guel-
' derland into this realme, being the kings coufin, a right valiant
' & hardie gentleman.   He was honourably received & welcomed of
' the K. & his uncles, the dukes of Lancafter & Gloucefter.   This
' D. of Guelderland counfailed the K. not to conclude peace, eyther
' with the French or Scots ; except upon fuch conditions as might
' be knowne to be both profitable & honourable to him & his realme :
' promifing, that if he had occafion to make war againft eyther of
' thofe two nations, he woulde be readie to ferve hym wyth a con-
' venient power of men at armes of his country.   After he had bin
' here a time, & highly feafted & banquetted, as wel by the K. as o-
' ther great eftates of the realme, he returned home not without
' diverfe riche giftes.'   So much concerning the council about civil
affairs, proceed we next to that about religious.

XIX. ' In the reigne of K. Rich. the 2. anno 1392. there was a
' meeting at Stamford, faith Mr. Butcher [a], called *Confilium Stamfordi-*
' *enfe Prælatorum*, at which meeting K. Richard himfelf was pre-
' fent, by command of pope Boniface the 9. about the fuppreffing
' of Wicliffes opinions.'   As Mr. Butcher feldom quotes his authors
for what he fays, & does not here ; it was long before I could meet
with any farther account of this affair ; but at laft, when I came to
fearch Leland, Bale, & Pits about the ftate of learning in our univerfity & monafteries, I found divers hints & little paffages relating to
this council, difperfed among the writings of thofe authors, which I
have collected into a body, & fhall now prefent my reader with.
' Wiclif himfelf, faith Bale [b], had been, in fome fort, already con-
' demned by the nniverfity of Oxford, in 1381.'   But that not availing,
this council of Stanford was called for the utter fuppreffion of his followers ; among whom Crump, a Ciftercian monk of Ireland, having
been a very buifie man in maintaining his opinions, was particularly
arraigned & condemned at this affembly.   ' For, as Bale adds, [c] Crump,
' who had been one of Wiclifs perfecutors, for a little expofing the
' beggarlinefs of his brethren the monks & friers, together with the
' confeffions he made himfelf, was himfelf at laft charged with herefie by
' the bifhops.'   Now this was done in this council at Stanford in 1392.
where the K. himfelf was prefent, & with him many divines & prelates from all parts of the kingdom.   There were five perfons at this
affembly remarkably buifie.   Befides whom undoubtedly feveral others
were employed, fome to open the difpute, fome to reply to Crump, fome
to moderate, & fome to minute & take account of the debates.   The
names of thofe five I have met with, were John Suafam, John de Ultricuria, John Tiffington, John Langton & John Valdey.   I. ' John Sua-
' fam, as Bale fays, [d] was engaged in the great council of prelates at

a MS in my hands, p. 30.   c p. 246.
b p. 515.   d in vita.

' Stanford,

' Stanford, in 1392. when K. Richard, by command of pope Boni-
' face the ninth, condemned the Wiclevites. II. John de Ultricuria,
' as Pits says, [a] being an old man affisted in the council at Stanford,
' when K. Richard the 2[d]. was there with many famous divines. III.
' John Tiffington, as the same Pits tells us, [b] was at Stanford, in 1392.
' with K. Richard the 2[d]. & many bishops & doctors in a council there,
' where the heresie of Wiclif & his followers was publickly & so-
' lemnly condemned. And there, faith he, this apostolical, brave man
' gave plain demonstrations of his being (like another David) an ene-
' my to the enemies of God; as his remarkable performances a-
' gainst those perfidious sectaries abundantly witness. IV. John Lang-
' ton, faith Bale, [c] (when William Courtney archbishop of Canter-
' bury, & divers other prelates, assembled with K. Richard the 2. at
' a council held in the white friers at Stanford in 1392. condemned
' the heresies of Henry Crumpe a Cistercian monk of Ireland) was
' present there, & noting all that was done, collected a book of
' speeches on that occasion, & another of the arguments & answers
' which the said Crump made use of to defend himself with. V.
' John Valdey the Austin frier, faith Leland, [d] applied himself to let-
' ters both at home & abroad with the greatest industry; as thinking
' it might sometime or other happen he might thereby profit not him-
' self only, but his country; a fancy which did not at all deceive him.
' For in 1392. when a public council was held at Stenoford, no ob-
' scure town in Lincolnshire, Valdey so weakened, enervated, & brake
' the force of the Wiclevites, that he extirpated that heretical depra-
' vity out of many hearts. There is extant a piece which he wrote
' against Wiclif & his followers, a witness of so memorable a victory.
' We may easily gather Valdeys zeal for the catholic faith from this,
' faith Pits, [e] to wit, that in 1392. coming with the K. to the council at
' Stanford, he carried himself boldly against the Wiclevites, & solidly con-
' futed their errors.' Crump then had enough to do to deal with him. And
indeed as one observes from Fuller, '[f] the friers of this order of S. Austin
' were esteemed great & able disputants, & are still remembred for this
' excellency at Oxford, where the act performed by the candidates
' for their masters degree is called keeping of Austins.' However
Bale says, [g] ' John Valdey, tho' at first the occasion of many troubles
' to the Wiclevites, after he had tried what spirit they were of, treat-
' ed them more gently.' Pits says, Robert Waldey (brother of John)
wrote also a piece against the Wiclevites: whence I am inclined to believe the said Robert likewise assisted at this council. By their names,
these two brothers seem to have some relation to the abby *de valle*

a p. 557. ' J. Ultricuria died, & was
' buried at York this same year.' id. ib.
b in vita.
c in vita.
d Com. p. 394.

e in vita.
f Britan. ant. & nova. vol. III. p. 213.
a. b.
g ut supra.

Dei,

Dei, Valdey near Grimfthorp within 7 miles of Stanford; perhaps they were born, or lived thereabouts. The Oxford antiquary Mr. Ant. Wood (as tranflated by the authors of the Britannia antiqua & nova [a]) gives us an account of Crump & this council at Stanford, fomewhat different than what hath been already touched; which, as it recapitulates things, fhall be here added for a conclufion. ' In 1391. K. ' Richard prohibited all fcholaftic exercifes [at Oxford] till 15 days ' after Eafter, upon a complaint made by the chancellor, of one Henry ' Crompe, for publickly defending & teaching Wicklifs doctrines, ' called Lollardy, in the fchools. This Henry Crompe was a Cifterci- ' an monk of Univerfity college, & being [firft] a zealous oppofer of ' Wicklifs doctrines, was one of the firft that fubfcribed the decree ' made in 1381. againft Wicklif & his abettors. But returning into ' Ireland his native country about this time [1391.] began to waver ' firft about the Romifh doctrines, & at length openly changed his ' mind; & both in teaching, writing, & difcourfe, laboured to per- ' fuade men to receive Wicklifs opinions. This, being noifed abroad, ' came to the ear of Wm. Andrew, then bifhop of Meath, who called ' him before him, admonifhed him again & again; but not being able ' to oblige him to alter his mind, he declared him an heretick, by ' which he came in danger of a profecution. Finding therefore, that ' he was not fafe in his own country, he returned to Oxford, & not ' only defended Wicklifes doctrines in his lectures, but expofed the ' Roman faith as much as he could. The chancellor complained of ' him to the K. for thefe actings, & Crompe was thereupon order- ' ed, by the kings letters, to appear before him & his council, & ' give an account of himfelf, which he accordingly did; & was or- ' dered to draw up his opinions, in order to a full confideration of ' them. He compriz'd them under ten articles or *heads,* which being ' propounded to a fynod of Carmelite friars met at Stanford in Lin- ' colnfhire, May 28. [1392.] were there condemned, & he was obliged ' to renounce them; which, having done, he returned to Oxford, ' & was there admitted to a regency. But notwithftanding his con- ' demnation & abjuration, he ftill perfifted in teaching & defending ' the fame doctrines, yet with fmall fuccefs. Becaufe men were a- ' fraid to embrace any notions from a perfon condemn'd for herefy. ' The chancellor obferving this, threatened Crompe with imprifon- ' ment, which tho' it was inflicted, yet he met almoft every day ' with fo many affronts & injuries, that he complained of them ' to the archbp. but, finding no relief that way, he waited upon him, ' & laid his notions before him (viz. the ten articles condemned at ' the fynod of Stanford) which the archbifhop, when he had well read ' & confidered the fame, was inclin'd to favour; & thereupon wrote ' his letters to Ralph Rudryth chancellor of Oxford, the abbat of Ofe-

---

a Vol. IV. p. 269. a.

' ney,

'ncy, & fome others, to examine & diligently infpect the faid ar-
'ticles, & tranfmit to him their opinion of them. But, what was
'done, in anfwer to the archbifhops order, we know not.' In this account of Mr. Woods this council of prelates at Stanford is called
only a fynod of Carmelite friers. But it was certainly a provincial
council, as is evident, by the popes letter to the K. & the king himfelf, the
archbp. of Canterbury, & many other bifhops & doctors, not only of the
white friers but all other orders, being there. Befides, what had the
white friers to do to condemn a Ciftertian? This council fat indeed
within the precincts of the white friers monaftery; & there I fuppofe
the K. then lay, as other of his fucceffors afterwards did, at their being here; the white friers college being both a royal foundation, & a
ftately fabric, & fo fitteft of any other at Stanford for his reception.
I fhall only obferve farther from Bale, that ' ᵃ Crompe wrote a vol. of
'fchool determinations, another piece againft the begging fryers, &
'a third in defence of the former, to anfwer the objections raifed
'againft it. And that returning into Ireland, he was by one Simon
'a Dominican (an Irifh bifhop) a long time detained prifoner for be-
'ing an heretic; what became of him afterwards I find not.'

XX. ' ᵇ John lord Clifford died in the flower of his youth, 18.
'Auguft 15. R. 2. ᶜ he was killed, but why, or after what manner, I
'find not by Richard E. of Cambridge, youngeft fon of Ed. D. of York
afterwards lord of Stanford. ' ᵈ In the 16. R. 2. licence was granted to
'found a chantery in the church of the holy Trinity without Stan-
'ford, & for fettling four cottages or houfes for a chantery prieft.
' ᵉ Something was alfo done this year for the alderman &c. of the
'gild of S. Mary by Stanford bridge.' But what, I have not the particulars. John Valdey abovementioned ' archbifhop of Dublin, to the
'credit & ornament of the catholic faith, & immortalizing of his own
'name, as Pits tells us, ᶠ wrote many things both in Englifh & Latin,
'directed chiefly to Thomas abbat of S. Albans.' So Leland. ' ᵍ Be-
'fides his book againft Wiclif & his difciples, John Valdey publifhed
'feveral fmall, but bright, expofitions of the Lords prayer, the *ave
'Maria*, & the apoftles creed.' Pits adds a larger catalogue of his
works, which if you pleafe, fee. ' Colby, faith the fame Pits, affirms
'that he died, & was buried among thofe of his own order at York,
'about the year 1393.' And with him agrees Bale. ' Alderman of
'Stanford this 16. R. 2. John de Apethorpe. B. H.'

XXI. ' ʰ In the 17. R. 2. Edmund D. of York [lord of Stanford]
'had a grant of the caftle of Moretagne, upon the river Gyronne in
'Aquitaine for life. ⁱ Edward E. Rutland [fon of the faid D. of

Left margin notes:
18. Aug
15. R. 2.

16. R. 2.

17. R. 2.

a partis 2. p. 246.
b Bar. vol. I. p. 341.
c Speed p. 863. b.
d Ex literis B. Willis arm. mihi miffis.
e Ex collectionibus MS. Petri le Neve
arm. Pro aldermannis, &c. Gilde B. Ma-

rie apud pontem de Staunford. Pat. 16. R.
2. p. 1. m. 29.
f p. 558.
g Com. p. 394.
h Bar. vol. II. p. 155. a.
i id. ib. p. 156. a.

York, & after him alfo lord of Stanford] ' the fame year had a grant
' of all the lands which Alianore wife of Raphe lord Baffet of Wel-
' don, held in dower; until Richard the fon & heir of the faid Raphe,
' fhould accomplifh his full age. And the fame year, about the fefti-
' val of our ladies nativity, attended the K. into Ireland. ᵃ Ifabell
' dutches of Yorke, & a lady noted for too great a fineneffe & deli-
' cacy, yet at her death fhewing much repentance & forrow for her
' love to thofe peftilent vanities, left this prefent life, the fame year.
' ᵇ It is faid this great lady having been fomewhat wanton in her
' younger years, at length became an hearty penitent, & departing this
' life an. 1394. 17. R. 2. was buried in the friers preachers at Lan-   1394
' gele. By her will [6. Dec. 1382. 6. R. 2. fupra] fhe bequeathed,
' after all her legacies paid, the remainder of her goods to K. Ri-
' chard, with truft that he fhould allow unto Richard her younger fon
' (his godfon) 500 marks a year for life. ᶜ Whereupon, out of the
' great refpect he bore to her, over & above that hundred pounds
' per annum which young Richard did receive, out of the iffues of
' the county of York; he gave him 233 l. 6 s. 8 d. for life, to be receiv-
' ed out of the exchequer, until he fhould fettle upon him lands or rents
' of 500 marks per annum value. [By the way] the 2ᵈ. wife of Edmund
' D. of York [lord of Stanford] was Joane, daughter & coheir to Ed-
' mund Holland E. of Kent; who, furviving him, married William
' lord Willoughby of Erefby; next Henry lord Scrope; & laftly, Hen-
' ry Bromflet, lord Vefci. His younger children were, Richard E. of
' Cambridge, & Conftance married to Thomas Spencer E. of Glou-
' cefter. Alderman of Stanford this 17. R. 2. John Spicer. B. H.'
Sarra Tanner of Staunford, now made her will, after this manner.
' I Sarra Tanner of Staunford &c. will, that John Brown & Maud
' his wife my daughter, have all the rents & tenements &c. in the
' parifhes of the B. Mary at the bridge & of S. George, to them &
' their heirs, &c. And that after the deceafe of the faid John, Maud,
' & their heirs &c. all the aforefaid &c. remain to the brethren &
' fifters of the gild of the B. Mary at the bridge & of Corpus Chrifti
' for ever. I will moreover that the forefaid John, Maud, & their
' heirs, have two meffuages fituate in Spalding with fix acres of mea-
' dow there. And that, after the deceafe of them, the forefaid two
' meffuages & fix acres of meadow remain to the brethren & fifters
' of the holy Trinity of Spaldying aforefaid for ever. Dated on Fri-
' day the feaft of the apoftles SS. Simon & Jude 1394. B. H.'
   XXII. ' ᵈ In the 18. R. 2. the E. of Rutland [afterwards lord of Stan- 18. R. 2.
ford] ' was retain'd to ferve the K. in another expedition into Ireland,
' for the one half of that year, with 50 men at armes, whereof ten
' to be knights; & 150 archers on horfeback.——Magot, relict of John
' Croyland of Staunford gave to John Bonde, rector of S. Maries at

ᵃ Speed p. 752. b. ᵇ Bar. vol. II. p. 155. b. ᶜ id. ib. ᵈ Bar. vol. II. p. 156. a.

       ' the

‘ the bridge, one meſſuage in All ſaints pariſh beyond Staunford bridge,
‘ in the abbat of Burgs liberty, between his own proper meſſuage
‘ eaſt, & a meſſuage of John Hawe weſt, as it abutts on the kings
‘ highway ſouth, & the water called Weland north. B. H. John
‘ Bonde, parſon of S. Maries at Staunford bridge gave to Thomas
‘ Catworth of Staunford ſkinner & Roger Palfreyman, one meſſuage, &c.
‘ ſituate in Staunford, in the abbat of Burgs liberty, to wit, eſt-be-the-
‘ water, between a tenement of John de Croulande eaſt, & a tenement
‘ of the abbat of Burgs weſt, and abutting on the kings highway ſouth,
‘ & the bank called Welond north. Which meſſuage was John de
‘ Croulandes. B. H. John Marchefeld gave to Henry Herdbi, one
‘ meſſuage ſtanding in Collegate in great S. Michaels pariſh Stanford,
‘ between a tenement of Thomas Barbur eaſt, & a tenement of the
‘ prior of Fynneſhede weſt, & abutting on the kings highway north,
‘ & a garden of John Brown, taverner of Staunford, ſouth. B. H.
This Henry Herdbi, as I take it, was now rector of great S. Michaels
pariſh. See anno 12. R. 3. above. — ‘ Wm. Rouland of Staunford
‘ gave to Thomas Barker of Staunford, one garden in the abbat of
‘ Burgs liberty, as it lies between a tenement of Thomas Corby weſt,
‘ & the way which leads towards Burle eaſt, & abutting towards Burle-
‘ gate north, & on the land of John Cheſter ſadeler, ſouth.’ B. H.
‘ Another deed of this year mentions one meſſuage ſtanding in S.
‘ Mary Bennewerke pariſh, between a tenement late Richard Ran-
‘ dolfes, &c. B. H. One Sir William [perhaps Botteford, ſee 39. E. 3.
& 7. R. 2. above] ‘ was now rector of S. Mary Bennewerk. B. H.
‘ John Long, alderman of Stanford, was witneſs to a deed dated on

Sept. 29. ‘ the feaſt of S. Michael 18. R. 2. B. H. Robert Lockſmith ald. of
‘ Stanford was witneſs to a deed dated on the feaſt of S. Edmund the
Nov. 20. ‘ K. & martyr [Nov. 20.] 18. R. 2. B. H. John Long alderman of
‘ Stanford was witneſs to another deed dated on the feaſt of S. Cle-
Nov. 23. ‘ ment [Nov. 23.] 18. R. 2. B. H. ª The D. of York [lord of Stan-
ford] ‘ guardian of England during the kings abſence, called a parlia-
‘ ment at London, eight days after twelfth-tide. ᵇ But this D. of
‘ Yorke was a man, rather coveting to lye in pleaſure, than to deale
‘ with muche buſineſſe, & the weightie affayrs of the realme. — Ro-
‘ bert Stolam, alderman of Stanford, was witneſs to a deed dated
‘ the Thurſday next before the feaſt of the purification, 18. R. 2. B. H.
‘ Frier John Tiſſington the Franciſcan [mentioned annis 1381. & 1392.
above] ‘ died, as Pits tells us, ᶜ in the monaſtery of his own order at
‘ London, & was buried there in 1395. ᵈ He was the 33ᵈ. provincial
‘ of his order.’

19. R. 2. XXIII. ‘ ᵉ In the 19. R. 2. the K. ſent the E. of Rutland [afterwards
lord of Stanford] ‘ & others on an ambaſſade to the French K. to

a Hiſt. Rich. 2. by a perſon of qual. p.   c in vita.
151.   d I. Addit vol to the monaſt. p. 90.
    b Hol. p. 1087. b.   e Hol. ut ſupra

‘ intreat

' intreat of a marriage betwixt him & lady Isabell daughter of the
' French K. They were joyfully received & so courteously entertain-
' ed, that all theyr expences were borne by the French K. & so, with
' hope to have their matter speed, they returned. ª The said E. of
' Rutland was afterwards one of the commissioners appointed, as proxie,
' to espouse the said lady Isabel eldest daughter of Charles the 6. K.
' of France on the part of K. Richard.' Edmond D. of York, & lord
of Stanford, now granted his letters of protection to the nuns of S.
Michael by Stanford, which may be thus englished. ' ᵇ Edmond, D.
' of York, E. of Cambridge, & lord of Tyndale, to our steward, bai-
' lifs, & officers of our town of Stanfford, greeting. For as much as
' we will the advancement & profit of our dear nuns of S. Michell
' without Stanfford, you we command, that when they shall have need
' of you, that you to them be aiding & counselling. And if any
' them do ill, or damage, or grievance, that you him cause to make
' amends to your power according to right, & them & their goods
' maintain undisturbed in their right to your power; & this fail not
' to do, in the manner which our predecessors de Warenne have done
' before these times. In witness of which things we have made them
' our letters patents. Done at Stanfford, the Wednesday after the
' feast of S. Michell, in the year of the reign of K. R. the 2. after
' the conquest, the nineteenth.' The original, with a curious impression of his seal, is now in the right honourable the E. of Exeters hands.

XXIV. ' ᶜ The K. in his 20. yere went over to Calice, with his 20. R. 2.
' uncles the dukes of York [lord of Stanford] & Gloucester, & a
' great many other lordes. Thyther came to hym the D. of Burgoigne,
' & they communed of peace. There was no enemy to the conclusi-
' on thereof, but the D. of Gloucester, who shewed well by his words,
' that he wished rather warre than peace, in so much that the K.
' stood in doubt, least he should procure some rebellion among his
' subjects, whom he knew not to favour greatly this new alliance.' As for
the D. of York, he staid not long abroad. For I find also, ' ᵈ this 20.
' R. 2. he was again made lieutenant for this realm in the kings ab-
' sence.' However his son Edward E. Rutland, afterwards lord of
Stanford, staid with the K. in France, ' ᵉ at which time, both kings
' having an enterview near Ghisnes, a peace was concluded betwixt

---

a Bar. vol. II. p. 156. a.

b Edmond duc Beverwyk, conte de Cantebrigg, & Seigneur de Tyndale, a nostre
senescall, balliss, & ministres de nostre ville
de Stanfford, saluz. Pour ce que nous
voulons le vauncement & le profit [de]
nostre chiers nonains de seint Michell de-
hors Stanfford, vous mandons, que quant
ils ancront mestier de vous, que vous lour
soiez eidant & conseillant; & sin ul lour face
mal, ne damage, ne grevaunce, que vous
le facez amender, a vostre poer, solont
droiture; & ens & lour biens, maigtegnez

ensement en droiture a vostre poer; & ce
ne lessez mie, en le manere que nostre
predecessours de Warenne ont setdenant
ces heures. En Tesmoigne de quele chose
lour avous set sere nostre letres patentes.
Donn a Stanfford, le mekerdi denant le
feste de seint Michell, l'an du regne le roy
Richard seconde puis. le conquest, disnesis-
me.

c Hol. p. 1088. b.

d Bar. vol. II. p 155. a.

e id. p. 156. a.

' thems

' them; & in memory thereof, a chapel, at both their cofts, appointed
' to be built in the place, & called our lady of peace.'   Sir Wm. Dugdale places this interview under the 19. R. 2. but it fhould be as here. His
accounts of Richard E. of Rutland for the three laft years are very much
tranfpofed & confufed, but are in this book rectified; as may be feen
by comparing them.   ª Alfo in this 20. R. 2. the faid E. of Rutland
[afterwards lord of Stanford] ' was conftituted governor of the ifles
' of Garnefey & Jerefey for life : & obtain'd the like grant of the
' ifle of Wiht, with the caftle of Caresbrooke ; as alfo of the whole
' dominion belonging to that caftle.   Moreover, about this time, he
' was conftituted warden of New-forreft in Hants, & of all the forefts
' fouth of Trent; conftable of Dover-caftle, & warden of the Cinque
' ports.   By which great trufts & benefits it is difcernable enough, that
' he was one of the principal perfons then in power with the K. &
' ftuck at nothing which might fatisfie his licentious humour ; for
' plain it is, that he was not only privy & confenting to that foul defign
' for murthering the kings uncle, the D. of Gloucefter, at Calais ; but fent
' one of his fervants viz. Cock of the chamber, to affift therein.'   But
of that black affair by & by ; at prefent of other matters leading to it.
' ᵇ The faid D. of Gloucefter, a moft fierce man, & of an headftrong
' wit , thinking thofe times wherein he had maftered the K. were
' nothing changed, tho' the K. was above 30 years old, forbare not
' roughly, not fo much to admonifh, as to check & fchoole, his fove-
' reign.   Particularly ᶜ in Feb. the K. holding a fumptuous feaft at Weft-
' minfter, many fouldiers newly come from Breft preaffed into the
' hall, & kept a roomthe together , whom, as the D. of Gloucefter
' beheld & underftood what they were, it grieved him not a little to
' remember how that towne was given up contrary to his minde &
' pleafure ; & therefore as the K. entred into his chaumber, with fewe
' about him, he could not forbeare, but breake forth, & fayde, fyr,
' fawe you not thofe felowes that fatte in fuche number this daye in
' the hall, at fuche a table? The K. aunfwered that he fawe them,
' & asked the duke what they were? To whom the D. faid, fyr, thefe be
' the fouldiers come from Breft, & as nowe have nothyng to take
' to, nor yet know how to fhifte for their lyvyngs ; & what is worfe, I
' am enfourmed, they have bin evill payde.   Then fayde the K. that is
' agaynft my wyll : for I would that they fhould have theyr due ; &
' if any have caufe to complayne, lette them fhewe the matter to the
' treafourer, & they fhall be reafonably anfwered ; & herewith com-
' maunded they fhould be appoynted to four villages about London,
' there to have meate, drink, & lodging upon his charges, tyll they
' were payde.   Thus as they fell into reafoning of this matter the
' duke fayde, fyr, your grace ought to win a ftrong holde by feate
' of warre, ere you felle or delyver any gotten with greate adven-
' ture by the manhood & policie of your noble anceftors.   To this

a id. ib.   b Speed p.   c Hol. p. 1090. b.

3   ' the

‘ the K. with changed countenance aunſwer’d, uncle, howe ſay you
‘ that? & the D. boldly without feare recited the ſame agayne, not
‘ chaunging one worde in any better ſorte.   Whereupon the K. be-
‘ ing more chafed, replied, thynke you that I am a merchant or verye
‘ foole, to ſelle my lande? by S. John Baptiſt, no.   But trouth is, oure
‘ couſin the D. of Britayne hath ſatisfied us of all ſuch ſummes of mo-
‘ ney as our progenitours lente unto him & his aunceſtours, upon
‘ gage of the ſayd towne; for whiche, reaſon & conſcience will no
‘ leſſe, the towne ſhould be reſtored.   ᵃ The E. of S. Paule [then in
England] ‘ hearing of this ſtout demeanour of the D. told the K. it
‘ was not to be ſuffered that a ſubject ſhould behave himſelf in ſuch
‘ ſort towards his prince.   The K. markyng his wordes, thought he
‘ gave him good & faithful counſel, & therupon determined to ſup-
‘ preſſe both the duke & his complices.   He alſo complayned of the
‘ duke to his brethren the dukes of Lancaſter & Yorke [lord of Stan-
ford] ‘ in that he ſhould ſtand againſt him in all things.   The dukes
‘ made anſwer, that they were not ignorant how theyr brother,
‘ as a man ſomtymes raſh in woordes, would ſpeak more than he
‘ could, or [if he could] would bring to effect, but the ſame
‘ proceeded of a faythful heart; for that it greeved him that the
‘ confines of the Engliſh dominions ſhould in any wyſe be diminiſh-
‘ ed: therefore his grace ought not to regard his wordes, ſith he
‘ ſhould take no hurt thereby : which perſuaſions quieted the K. for
‘ a time.   ᵇ There was now a final agreement made between Stephen
‘ Makeſeye of Staunford & . . . Grenham clerc, complainants of the
‘ one part : & John de Herlington of Yakeſley, defendent of the other
‘ part : touching the right of eight meſſuages, 54 acres of land, 18
‘ ſhillings of rent, &c. in Staunford; & of the advowſon of the chan-
‘ tery at the altar of S. Nicholas in the church of S. Clement in Staun-
‘ ford.—H. Herdbi of Staunford gave a meſſuage [deſcribed 18. R. 2.
above] ‘ to Richard Bulwike of Staunford. B. H.   Joan, late wife
‘ of Richard Baron gave to . . . . her ſon, two ſhops ſituate in All
‘ Saints pariſh in the mercat, between a tenement of Reginald Mercer
‘ ſouth, & a tenement of John Longe north, & extending themſelves
‘ from the way called behynde-bak weſt, to the kings highway of an-
‘ other part eaſt.   Witneſſes, Will. Stacey alderman of Stanford. Dat-   May 3.
‘ ed 3. May. 20. R. 2. B. H.

    XXV. ‘ ᶜ It is ſaid the D. of Glouceſter [the beginning of the 21.
R. 2.] ‘ with the archbp. of Canterbury, the earles of Arundel, War-   21. R. 2.
‘ wick, Marſhal & others, met at Arundel in Suſſex, where, after an
‘ oath of ſecrecy, they concluded to raiſe a power, to remove the

a id. p. 1091 a.
b Inter Stephanum Makeſeye de Staunford & . . . . . Grenham clericum, que-
rentes ; & Johannem de Herlington, de
Yakeſley defendentem ; 8. meſſuagiorum,
54. acrarum terre, 18. ſolidorum redditus,
&c. in Staunford ; & advocationis çantarie
ad altare S. Nicholai in eccleſia S. Clementis in Staunford. Vide fines coronæ Lincoln.
Anno 20. R. 2. Ex MS. collect. clar. antiquarii Petri le Neve arm. Norroy regis armorum.
    c Speed. p. 754. a.

‘ dukes

'dukes of Lancaster & Yorke [lord of Stanford] & such other as
'they thought best, from about the K. They are charged by some
'to have plotted the imprisonment of the K. & dukes, & the death
'of all other councellors. The blustring duke had breathed out dan-
'gerous words; as, that he would put the K. (of whose courage he
'spake contemptibly) into some prison, there to end his days, as
'himself thought best. His brethren [the dukes of Lancaster & York]
'hearing thereof, [a] fyrste reproving him for his too liberal talking,
'& perceyving that he set nothing by their words, were in doubt
'least, if they should remayne in the court still, he would upon a pre-
'sumptuous mind, in truste to be borne out by them, attempt some
'outragious enterprise. Wherefore they thought best to depart for
'a tyme into theyr countries, that, by their absence, hee might the
'sooner learne to stay himself for doubt of further displeasure. But
'it came to passe, their departure was the casting away of the duke.
'[b] The E. Marshal [Thomas Mowbray E. of Nottingham] discovered
'all their counsel to the K. The K. bad the E. take heede what he
'sayde, for, if it proved not true, he should repent it. But the E.
'aunswered, if the matter proved otherwise, he was contented to be
'drawn & quartered. [c] Hereupon the K. (his uncles of Lancaster &
'Yorke being gone from court) discovered himself to the said E. Mar-
'shal his greatest confident, what he had a mind to do, which, in
'short, was, to destroy the D. of Gloucester his own uncle.' About
the same time Edward E. of Rutland (afterwards lord of Stanford)
was, as it should seem, let into the secret; the said E. being, [d] 'up-
July 12. 'on the 12. of July this 21. R. 2. made constable of England.' These
things being done, '[e] the K. hereupon wente to London, where he
'dyned at his brother the E. of Huntingdons, in the streete behinde
'All-hallows church upon the bank of the Thames, whiche was a
'ryght fayre & stately house. After dinner, he gave his counsell to
'understand the matter, by whose advise it was agreed, that the K.
'should forthwith assemble what power he might, & streightways take
'horse. Hereupon at six in the afternoone, just when they used to
'go to supper, the K. mounted & rode his way: whereof the Lon-
'doners had great mervaile. After that the K. began to approache the
'dukes house at Plaschy in Essex (where he then lay) he commaund-
'ed his brother the E. of Huntington to ride afore, to know if the
'duke were at home? &, if he were, then to tell him that the K. was
'coming to speak with him. The E. amending his pace, came to
'the house, & asked if the D. were at home? And understanding by
'a gentlewoman, that both the D. & dutchess were in bed, be-
'sought hir to go to the duke, & shew him, that the K. was at hand
'to speake with him. And forthwith came the K. with a compe-

a Hol. page 1091. b.
b id. p. 1092. a.
c Bar. vol. II. p. 170. b.

d id. ib. p. 156. a.
e Hol. as above.

'tent

'tent number of men of armes, & a great companie of archers, rid-
'ing into the bafe court, his trumpets founding before him. The
'D. herewith came down into the bafe court, where the K. was,
'havyng none other apparell upon him, but his fhirt, & a cloke or
'mantel about his fhoulders, & with humble reverence, fayd, his
'grace was welcome: asking of the lords how it chanced they came
'fo early, & fent him no word of their coming? The K. heere-
'with courteously requefted him to goe & make him ready, & ap-
'pointe his horfe to be fadled, for that he muft needes ride with him
'a little waye, & conferre with him of bufyneffe. The D. went up
'againe, to put on his clothes, & the K. alighting, fell in talke
'with the ducheffe & hir ladies. The E. of Huntington & divers
'others followed the D. into the hall, & there ftayed for him, till he
'had put on his raiment. And within awhyle they came foorth a-
'gaine all together into the bafe courte, wher the K. was, devifing
'with the dutcheffe in pleafant talke, whome he willed now to re-
'turne to hir lodging againe, for he might ftay no longer; & fo
'tooke his horfe againe, & the D. likewife. And fhortly after that
'the K. & all his companie were gone forth of the gate of the bafe
'court, he commanded the E. Marfhal to apprehend the duke, which
'was incontinently doon.' Another author relates the arrefting of the
duke thus. The K. being refolved to deftroy him, [a] 'to that pur-
'pofe (as it were on hunting) rode to Havering atte Boure in Effex,
'(about 20 miles from London as alfo no lefs from Pleffy where
'the D. then lay and came to Pleffy about five of the clock, the
'D. having then newly fupt; who, hearing of his coming, with the
'dutchefs & her children, met him in the court. The K. being
'brought in, a table was fpread for his fupper. Whereat, being fet,
'he told the duke, that he would have him ride to London with him
'that night; faying, that the Londoners were to be before him on
'the morrow; as alfo his uncles of Lancafter & York [lord of Stan-
ford] 'with divers other nobles; & that he would be guided by their
'counfel: wifhing him to command his fteward to follow with his
'train. Hereupon the D. fufpecting no hurt, fo foon as the K. had
'fupp'd, got on horfeback, accompanied with no more than feven fer-
'vants taking the way to Boundelay, to fhun the common road to
'London: & riding faft, approached near Stratford on the Thames.
'Being got thus far, & coming near an ambufcado there laid, the K.
'rode away a great pace, & left him fomewhat behind. Whereupon
'the E. Marfhal with his band came galloping after, & overtaking him,
'faid, I arreft you in the kings name. The D. therefore difcerning
'he was betrayed, call'd out aloud to the king, but to no purpofe: for
'the K. rode on, & took no notice of it.' Another author fays the
K. himfelf arrefted the duke. '[b] Says the K. I arreft you. To whom

---

a Bar. vol. II. p. 170. b.   b Ex Joh. Lelandi collect. vol. II. p. 309.

'the

' the D. replied, deal favourably with me by faving my life.   Ay, fays
' the king, you fhall have the fame favor as you fhewed to Simon Bur-
' ley, when the queen fell on her knees to you; read that: giving
' him a fchedule of his accufation.   To whom the duke, as to that we
' fhall anfwer.   But the duke was delivered to the E. of Nottingham,
' who carried him to Calice to prifon.   ᵃ The fame evening that the
' K. departed from London towards Plafhye, to apprehende the D.
' of Gloucefter, the E. of Rutland [afterwards lord of Stanford] & the
' E. of Kent, were fent with a great number of men of arms to ar-
' reft the E. of Arundel, whiche was done.   The E. of Warwike
' was alfo taken, & committed to the tower.   There were alfo ap-
' prehended & committed to the tower, the fame time, the lord John
' Cobham, & Sir John Cheney Kts.   Shortly after the K. procured
' them to be indited at Nottingham, fuborneing fuche as fhould ap-
' peale them in the parliament, to wit, Edward E. of Rutland [after-
wards lord of Stanford] ' Thomas lord Spencer [who then alfo had
lands at Stanford] ' Thomas Mowbray E. Marfhal, Thomas Holland
' E. of Kent, John Holland E. of Huntingdon, Thomas Beaufort E.
' of Somerfet, John Montacute E. of Salisbury, & Wm. Scrope, lord
' chamberlaine.   Sir Wm. Dugdale fays, ᵇ Thomas lord Spencer, Ed-
' ward E. of Rutland, Thomas E. of Nottingham, &c. were then ar-
' refted at Nottingham, by the kings command, & charged with high-
' treafon, certain perfons being fuborned who were to profecute
' them in the enfuing parliament.'   But all this is falfe, & the contrary, as above & hereafter, true.   The duke of Gloucefter being, as
before related, fpirited away to Calice, there ' ᶜ with his own hand
' wrote an anfwer to the fchedule of his accufation.   But when that
' anfwer [was feen, &] did not pleafe the king, he commanded the E.
' of Nottingham, on pain of death, to make away with him.'   Upon
this the E. went to Calice, & there, ' ᵈ in September [it fhould be
Auguft] ' he & one John Colfox his efquire, went in the night to
' the chamber of one John Hall, a fervant of the faid E. Marfhals,
' then alfo at Calais;   whom Colfox, calling out of bed, command-
' ed to come forthwith to his lord.   When he came, the E. asked
' him, if he heard nothing of the D. of Gloucefter? he anfwered, he
' fuppofed him to be dead.   Whereupon the E. replied, no, he is
' not; but the K. hath given in charge, that he fhall be murdered;
' & himfelf, with the E. of Rutland [afterwards lord of Stanford] had
' fent certain of their efquires & yeomen, to be then there; & told
' the faid Hall, that he fhould likewife be prefent in his name.   Buₜ
' Hall faid, no; defiring he might lofe all he had, & depart, ratheᵣ
' than be prefent.   The E. replied, he fhould, or die for it: giving
' him a great knock on the pate.   Then the E. with Colfox & Hall,
' went to the church of Noftre-dame in Calais; where they found

a Hol. p. 1093. a.   c Ex Jo. Lel. collect. vol. II. ut fupra.
b Bar. vol. I. p. 396.   d Bar. vol. II. p. 171. a.

I   ' William

'William Hampſterley, & . . . Bradeſton (two eſquires of the ſaid
' earls) as alſo one William Serle, a yeoman of the chamber to the
' king; . . . . Fraunceys a yeoman of the chamber to the E. of Rut-
' land; William Rogers & William Denys, yeomen of the ſaid E.
' Marſhal; & another yeoman of the E. of Rutlands called Cock of
' the chamber. And there it was told Hall, that all the reſt had
' made oath, that they ſhould not diſcover any thing of their pur-
' poſe; cauſing him, in like manner to ſwear upon the Sacrament,
' in preſence of one Sir William a chaplain of S. George in that
' church of Noſtre-dame, that he ſhould keep counſel therein. After
' oath thus made, they went along with the E. to a certain hoſtel,
  called the princes inne; & being come thither, the E. ſent Colfox,
' Hampſterley, Bradeſton, Serle, Franceys, Rogers, Denys, Cock of
' the chamber, & Hall, into an houſe within that inne; & then de-
' parted from them with ſome unknown perſons. ª The E. then cal-
' led oute the duke at midnight, as if he ſhould have taken ſhippe
' to paſs over into England.' And ſo brought him to the princes
  inne. For ᵇ ' ſo ſoon as Colfox, &c. were come into that houſe,
' there entered one John Lovetoft, with divers other eſquires un-
' known; who brought with him the D. of Glouceſter, & deliver-
' ed him to Serle & Fraunceys in an inner room of the houſe, & ſaid,
' they would ſpeak with him: adding, it was the kings pleaſure, that
' he muſt ſuffer death. Whereunto he anſwered, if ſo, it is wel-
' come. Serle & Fraunceys forthwith appointed a prieſt to confeſs
' him, & that done, made him lie down upon a bed, & laying a
' featherbed upon him, held it about his mouth till he died: Roger,
' Denys, & Cock of the chamber holding down the ſides of it; &
' Colfox, Hamſterley, & Bradeſton, upon their knees all the while,
' weeping, & praying for his Soul: Hall keeping the door.' Thus
was the death of Simon Burley revenged upon the D. of Glouceſter.
' ᶜ And thus it is plain, that Edward E. of Rutland [afterwards lord
of Stanford] ' was not only privy & conſenting to that foul deſign
' of murthering his uncle the D. of Glouceſter at Calais; but ſent
' one [my author ſhould ſay two] of his own ſervants to aſſiſt there-
' in; which barbarous act was done, upon Saturday next after the
' feaſt of S. Bartholomew, the 21. R. 2. Wherefore, it may very well
' be thought, that, for his plotting & furtherance thereof, he eſteem-
' ed his own merit very great.

XXVI. The D. of Glouceſter being thus made away, ' ᵈ a parlia-
' ment was ſummoned to begin at Weſtminſter the 17. of Sept. &   17. Sept.
' writs directed to the lords [of the kings party] to bring with them
' a ſufficient number of armed men; for it was not known how the
' dukes of Lancaſter & York [lord of Stanford] would take his death,

a Hol. p. 1093. a.
b Bar. of Bucks
c id. vol. II. p. 156. a.
d Hol. p. 1093. b. 1094. a.

' And

' And furely the two dukes when they heard it, wift not what to fay
' to the matter, & beganne both to be forrowful for his death, &
' doubtful of their own ftates. Therefore they alfo affembled great
' numbers of their fervants, friends, & tenants, & commyng to London,
' were receyved into the city. For the Londoners were ryght forie
' for the dukes death. Here the dukes, & other fell in counfell:
' fome would that they fhould revenge it. But the dukes determin-
' ed, if the K. would amende his maners, to forget injuries paft. For
' there went meffengers betwixt the K. & them, whiche being men
' of honor, they were accorded; & the K. promifed to do nothing
' but by affent of the dukes.' Then it was I fuppofe, that ' [a] the D.
' of York [lord of Stanford] obtain'd a grant in fpecial tail of the
' manor of Sevenhampton, with the hundreds of Heyworth & Kirke-
' lade in Wilts, which lordfhips & hundreds John D. of Brittany
' & Joane his wife held, fo long as the caftle of Breft fhould be in
' poffeffion of the K. or his heirs. And the fame time had licenfe
' to raife one hundred men at arms, & 200 archers, to attend the K.
' at his next parliament. [b] When the tyme came that the parliament
' fhould be held, the lords repaired thither with great retinues; parti-
' cularly, the E. of Rutland [afterwards lord of Stanford] lord Tho-
' mas Spencer [who had likewife lands there] &c. the dukes of Lan-
' cafter & York were likewife there, giving attendance on the K. with
' like furniture of men of armes & archers. There was not half lodg-
' ing in the citie & fuburbs of London, for fuche companies as they
' brought with them. [c] In this parliament the act of atteynder of Sir
' Simon Burley was repealed. [d] Alfo, Sir John Bufhy accufed Thomas
' Arundel archbp. of Canterbury of threefold treafon. To wit, I.
' granting the government of the realm, when he was chancelor, to
' Thomas D. of Gloucefter. II. under pretence of that commiffion,
' ufurping royal authority. By which ufurpation, III. Sir Simon Bur-
' ley & Sir James Barnes, were traiteroufly murdered & put to death.
' Of which things, faid Bufhy, your commons demaund judgment
' worthy of fo high treafon, to be terribly pronounced by you; & be-
' caufe the archbifhop is a man of great confanguinitie, affinitie, power,
' & moft politike wit, & cruell nature, require he may be put into
' fafe cuftodie, until the final execution of his judgment. The K.
' anfwered, that, for the excellence of his dignity, he would take de-
' liberation till the next morrow. But all other put into the fame
' commiffion, he pronounced his faithful people. Then the duke of
' York [lord of Stanford] & Wickham bifhop of Winchefter, that
' were put into the fame, with teares fell downe on the ground be-
' fore the K. & gave him humble thanks for that grace & benefit be-
' ftowed on them. [e] Alfo on S. Mathewes day Edward E. of Rut-

a Bar. vol. II. p. 155. a.   d Stow. p. 510.
b Hol. p. 1094. a.   e id. p. 511.
c id. p. 1073. a.

2   ' land

‘ land [afterwards lord of Stanford] the lord Spencer [who had then
lands there] ‘ & others, in a fute of red gownes of filke, garded &
‘ bordered with white filke, & embroidered with letters of gold pro-
‘ poned the appeale by them to the K. at Nottingham, before touch-
‘ ed: in which they accufed Richard E. of Arundel &c. of treafon.
‘ ᵃ Then faid the K. [to the E. of Arundel] diddeſt not thou fay to
‘ mee in time of the parliament, in the Bathe behind the white-hall,
‘ that Sir Simon de Burley was worthie of death for many caufes ;
‘ & I aunfwered, that I knew no caufe of death in him, & yet thou
‘ & thy fellowes diddeſt trayteroufly put him to death. Then the D.
‘ of Lancaſter pronounced judgment, Richard, I John Steward of Eng-
‘ land, judge thee to bee a traytour, & I condemne thee, &c. Then
‘ was he led to the tower-hill, & there beheaded. ᵇ Alfo the arch-
‘ bifhop of Canterbury, his temporalities being confifcate, was banifh-
‘ ed the realme. ᶜ Sept. 28. 21. R. 2. Edward E. of Rutland [after- Sept. 28.
wards lord of Stanford] ‘ had a grant in tail fpecial, of the manor
‘ of Bruſtwyke in Holderneſſe, with the caſtle of Skypfe, & patron-
‘ age of the abby of Meaux, in Yorks. As alfo of the manor of
‘ Barwe, & patronage of Thornton abby in Linc. Likewife of all the
‘ manors, lands, &c. in Preſton, Burton-Pidfe, Bond, Bruſtwyke, E-
‘ fyngton, Kylnefee, Wythornefee, & Cleton, late Thomas D. of
‘ Glouceſters. Alfo of the town of Clone, in Salop, with the whole
‘ territory of Clone in the Marches of Wales ; & of the hundred of
‘ Poſſelow, thereunto annexed : late Richard E. of Arundels. The
‘ like grant he had then, of the manor of Flamſtede in Hertfords, with
‘ the chafe thereto belonging. And 29. Sept. was advanced to the Sept. 29.
‘ dignity of duke of Albemarle (late **Tho. E. of Warwicks** at-
‘ tainted) by which title he was, within 5 days enfuing, again made Oct. 4.
‘ conſtable of the tower of London. At the fame time, or thereabouts,
‘ ᵈ Thomas lord Spencer [who had lands at Stanford] was created E. of
‘ Glouceſter, by reafon of his defcent from Gilbert de Clare, fometime
‘ E. of that place. ᵈ And upon his creation, obtained a grant, to him-
‘ felf & his wife (Conſtance daughter of the D. of York) & to the
‘ heirs male of his own body, of the caſtle & manor of Elmley, the
‘ manors of Wickwane, Grafton, Flenorth, Albodely, Seintley, Cum-
‘ berton, & Elmley-Lovet, then in the crown ; by reafon of a judg-
‘ ment in parliament againſt Tho. Beauchamp E. of Warwick. ᵉ In 1398.
‘ K. Richard kept his chriſtmas at Litchfield, & then took his jour-
‘ ney towards Shrewsbury, where the parliament (lately prorogued) be-
‘ gan again. ᵉ There the lord Cobham was arraigned, for that he
‘ fat in judgment to judge Sir Simon Burley & Sir James Barnes, Kts.
‘ of the kings, in his abfence, & againſt his will. And upon this was
‘ convict, & judged to perpetual prifon in the iſle of Jerfey. ᶠ Moreover in

a id. p. 512.
b id. ib.
c Bar. vol. II. p. 156. b.

d Bar. vol. I. p. 396. 397.
e Stow, p. 514.
f Hol. p. 1098. a.

ᶢ this

‘ this parliament at Shrewsbury, the K. so wrought, that he obteined
‘ the whole power of both houses, to be graunted to Edmund D. of
‘ York, [lord of Stanford] Edward D. of Aumerle [afterwards lord also of the same place] ‘ & 13 other persons; or to seven of them.
‘ ᵃ In this parliament also Henry D. of Hereford, accused Thomas
‘ Mowbray (late E. of Nottingham, then) duke of Norfolk of trea-
‘ son. And presented a supplication to the K. wherein he appealed
‘ the D. of Norfolk in field of battel. ᵇ Whereupon the D. of Lan-
‘ caster his father, the D. of York his uncle, the D. of Aumarle his
‘ cosen, & the D. of Surry marshal of the realm, undertook, body for
‘ body, for the D. of Hereford.’ But the D. of Norfolk was committed to prison at Windsor, & at length a combat appointed between them at Coventry in Sept. following. ‘ ᶜ The same year the
‘ K. granted to Baldwin Harrington & Richard Furneys in fee, all the
‘ lands & tenements in Burle by Staunford in the counties of North-
‘ ampton & Lincoln, which lately belonged to Thomas de Arundel
‘ archbp. of Canterbury. . . . . Walter Smith of Extone gave to
‘ Richard Stake of Stanford, one messuage situate in All Saints parish
‘ in the mercat, between a tenement of the prior of Fyneshed of the
‘ one part, & a tenement of Robert Stoleham of the other part, &
‘ one shop with a loft, &c. in the same parish between a shop of
‘ Geoffry Bemfeld of the one part, & the kings highway called Wol-
‘ rowe of the other; & four acres, & three rods of land lying se-
‘ parated in Staunford fields, which were John Pursers by dimise of
‘ the lord of the town. B. H.

22. R. 2.   XXVII. ‘ ᵈ On the day appointed for the combat at Coventry be-
‘ tween the D. of Hereford & the D. of Norfolk, the D. of Albemarle
[afterwards lord of Stanford] ‘ was for the time made high constable,
‘ & came to the lists honourably attended with rich liveries, suitable
‘ to his greatness, his servants carrying tiptstaves for clearing the field.’
The two dukes also appeared, but were banished, without fighting.
‘ ᵉ The D. of Lancaster departed this life, & the K. seised into his
‘ hands all the goods that belonged to him; & all the rents & revenues
‘ which ought to have discended to the D. of Hereforde by lawful in-
‘ heritance; revoking his letters patents, by vertue whereof [tho' banished for a time] ‘ he might make his attorneis general to sue
‘ livery for hym, & hys homage be respited, wyth making reasonable
‘ fine: wherby it was evident that the K. ment his utter undoing.
‘ ᶠ The D. of York [lord of Stanford] was herewyth sore amoved.
‘ Hereupon he, with the D. of Aumarle his sonne [afterwards lord of

---

a Hol. p. 1098. b.
b id. p. 1099. a.
c Rex concessit Baldewino Harrington, & Richardo Furneys in feodo, omnes terras & tenementa in Burle juxta Staunford in comitatibus Northamptonie & Lincolnie, que nuper fuerunt Thome de Arundel, ar-

chiepiscopi Cantuariensis accinct. per servitium debit. Pat. 21. R. 2. p. 1. Ex MS. collect. Petri Le Neve arm.
d Hist. R. 2. by a person of qual. p. 168.
e Hol. p. 1102. a.
f id. ib. b.

I

Stanford] ' went to his houfe at Langley, rejoicing that nothing had
' mifhappened in the common-wealthe thro' his devife or confente.'
But there he ftaid not long, for the king, intending now to go to
Ireland, ' ª appointed for his lieftenant generall in hys abfence hys
' uncle the faid D. of York. ᵇ The fame year the faid duke [lord
of Stanford] ' was conftituted fteward of England; to hold the fame
' office, until Henry of Lancafter, earl [fo he is now called, not D.]
' of Hereford, or his heir fhould fue for it. By which the kings
' great truft & bounty towards him is fufficiently manifefted. ᶜ The
' fame year alfo his fon Ed. D. of Aumarle [afterwards lord of Stan-
ford] ' was conftituted general warden of the weft marches towards
' Scotland; & likewife join'd in commiffion with the Bp. of S. Afaph
' & others, to treat of peace with the Scots. Alfo retein'd by inden-
' ture, to ferve the K. in Ireland, for one whole year, with 140 men
' at armes, that is to fay, Kts. & efquires: & 200 archers on horfe-
' back, every 20 of the archers having one carpenter & one mafon.
' But, of that fhameful murder of the D. of Gloucefter, neither the
' K. nor he had much joy. For, the whole realm foon after being
' in no little difturbance, the K. retired into Ireland, this duke [fol-
lowing] ' & ᵈ Thomas E. of Glocefter [who then alfo had lands at
Stanford] ' attending him. Thither ᵉ in April the K. fet forward   April.
' with 200 fhips, & a puiffant power. —Alderman of Stanford 22.
' R. 2. John de Apethorp. B. H. Richard Stake, gave to John Smith
' of Staunford one meffuage, &c. fituate in All Saints parifh in the
' mercat, between a tenement of the prior of Fynefhed fouth, & a
' tenement of Robert Stoleham north. See the laft year above. B. H.
' John Spycer of Stanford gave to Stephen Manlyfter of Stanford, one
' meffuage with four acres of arable land lying in the town & fields
' of Stanford & Bernack; which meffuage is fituate in the abbat of
' Burgs liberty, between a meffuage of W. de Sybefton eaft, & a mef-
' fuage of John Palfreymans the younger weft, as it abutts on Martynf-
' croft fouth, & the kings highway north. B. H.

XXVIII. In the 23. R. 2. ᶠ ' K. Richard being at Kilkenny in Ire-   23. R. 2.
' land, ftayed there about 14 dayes, looking for the D. of Aumarle
[afterwards lord of Stanford] ' that was appointed to have met him,
' but he failed & came not.' By this, & what follows, it appears
that the faid D. of Aumarle went not over with K. Richard into
Ireland, as is above afferted from Dugdale: but followed him. For
faith my author, ' ᵍ not long after the D. of Aumarle with an hundred
' fayle arrived, of whofe coming the K. was ryght joyful, & altho'
' he had ufed no fmall negligence in that he came no fooner ac-
' cording to order before appointed, yet the K. (as he was of a gen-
' til nature) courteoufly accepted his excufe: whether he was in fault

a Hol. page 1103. a.   e Hol. ut fupra.
b Bar. vol. II. p. 155. a.   f Hol. p. 1103. b.
c id. ib. p. 156. b.   g Hol. p. 1104. b.
d id. vol. I. p. 397. a.

'or not, I have not to say: but verily he was greatly suspected,
'that he dealte not well in tarrying so long after his time assigned.
'John Spycer alderman of Staunford was witness to a deed bearing

Feb. 28. 'date Feb. 28. 23. R. 2. B. H. ª The lord governour Edmond D.
'of Yorke being advertised, that the D. of Lancaster [Hereford now
so called] 'kept the sea, & was readie to arrive, sent to the bishop
'of Chichester, the E. of Wilts, Bushy, Green, Bagot, & Russel, chief
'favourites of the kings privy council, to consult what was to be done
'in this exigency.   ᵇ The earl, Bushy, Bagot, & Greene, perceyving
'the commons would take part with Lancaster, left the D. of York,
'lord governour of the realme, & the bishop, to shift for themselves.'
'Nevertheless, ᶜ the D. of York [lord of Stanford] hearing that his
'nephew the D. of Lancaster was arrived & had gathered an armye,
'also assembled a puissant power; but all in vayne: not a man
'would thrust out an arrow against the D. of Lancaster. ᵈ The D.
'of Yorke therefore passing towards Wales to meete K. Rich. at hys
'commyng forth of Ireland, was receyved into Barkeley castle, &
'there remayned, 'til the D. of Lancaster came, & there communed
'with him. ᵉ There were arrested Sir Walter Burley & others, &
'committed to safe custodie. ᶠ The morrow after, the foresayd dukes
'with their power went towards Bristow.' By this it appears the D.
of York [lord of Stanford] now deserted K. Rich. & joined with the
D. of Lancaster. But this was because ' ᵍ the generality favouring
'Lancaster, he was loath to run the adventure of an improbable re-
'sistance. ʰ K. Rich. meant forthwith to have returned, to make re-
'sistance against the D. of Lancaster, but thro' persuasion of the D.
'of Aumarle [afterwards lord of Stanford] as was thought, stayed till
'he might have all his shippes & other provision, fully ready. ' Which
'fatal council it was K. Richards ill destiny to follow. Yet in the
'mean time he sent over the E. of Salisbury. ᵏ Eighteene days af-
'ter, he took the sea himself, together with the D. of Aumarle, &c. ˡ &
'landed in Wales; where, when he understood the forces assembled
'by the E. of Salisbury were disbanded, for want of his own coming
'sooner, he almost left off to be a man, & abandon'd himself to de-
'spair. ᵐ When the D. of Lancaster understood that K. Richard was
'returned, he left the D. of York [lord of Stanford] at Bristow, &
'came back to Berkley: & so on to Chester. ⁿ There came to him
'the D. of Aumarle [afterwards lord of Stanford] beseeching him to
'receive K. Richard into his favor. ᵒ Who also was with that duke at
'Flint castle, when he took K. Rich. thence. From Flint the un-

a id. p. 1105. a.
b Hist. R. 2. by a pers. of qual. p. 182.
c Hol. p. 1106. a.
d id. ib.
e Hol. p. 1106. b.
f id. ib.
g Hist. R. 2. p. 183.

h Hol. p. 1107. a.
i Hist. R. 2. p. 185.
k Hol. ut supra.
l Hist. R. 2. p. 186.
m Hol. p. 1108. a.
n id. ib.
o Bar. vol II. p. 156. b.

4   'fortunate

' fortunate K. Rich. was brought up to London, & committed to the
' tower.   After which ᵃ the D. of York [lord of Stanford] who but
' a little before had, as you have heard, been governor of the realm
' for the said K. Rich. but now Lancasters great director & best ora-
' cle, proposed it as very expedient, that K. Richard should volunta-
' rily resign, and also be solemnly deposed by the estates of the realm.
' ᵇ On the first Wednesday in October the parliament began in West-
' minster hall, which was hung & trimmed sumptuously, & a royal
' chaire set up, on purpose to choose a new king.   Where first sat
' the D. of Lancaster, then Edmond of Langley D. of York [lord of
Stanford] ' the D. of Aumarle [afterwards lord of the same place] &c.
' ᶜ There were not past four persons that were of K. Richards part,
' & they durst say nothing.   The archbishop asked each whom they
' would have for their king? Whether the D. of York? & they said,
' no: or his eldest son, the D. of Aumarle? & they said, no.   And so
' of divers other.   Then, staying a while, he asked, if they would
' have the D. of Lancaster? And they said, they would.'   I shall only add, ᵈ ' Thomas of Woodstock duke of Gloucester, Thomas Hol-
' land duke of Surrey, Thomas Mowbray duke of Norfolk, Edward
' Plantagenet duke of Aumerle, Sir Simon Burley, Sir Richard Bur-
' ley, & Sir John Burley [all of them so frequently mentioned in
the course of these collections] ' were all of them knights of the gar-
' ter, & so made by the unfortunate king Richard the second.'

a Hift. R. 2. p. 191.   c id. p. 523.
b Stow, p. 522.   d Heylins Hift. of S. George, p. 322.

The end of the twelfth book.

THE
ANTIQUARIAN ANNALS
of the TOWN of
STANFORD
IN
Lincoln, Rutland, *and* Northampton *Shires*.

BOOK XIII.
Containing the reigns of K. Henry the 4. & K. Henry the 5.

K. Henry the IV.

‘ ªI. KING Henry the fourth was crowned on Monday Oct. 13. Oct.13.
‘ 1399. being S. Edwards day. ᵇBefore the K. ſtode all 1399.
‘ the diner-while the duke of Amnarle [afterwards lord of ¹. H. 4.
Stanford] ‘ & other lords: ᶜ On Thurſday, Oct. 16. the parliament met Oct.16.
‘ again. ᵈ There a bill was read, made by Sir John Bagot, conteyn-
‘ ing, what great affection K. Richard bare to the duke of Aumarle ;
‘ inſomuch that he heard him ſay, that if he ſhuld renounce the go-
‘ vernment of the kingdom, he wiſhed to leave it to the ſaid duke,
‘ as to the moſt able man, for wiſdome & manhood of all other.’ For
this laſt article Holingſhed quotes Fabian, but I cannot find it in him.
The account he gives of Bagots charge againſt the duke of Amnarle,
as he calls him, is thus. ‘ ᵉ Furthermore he ſhewed, that there was
‘ no man of honour in thoſe days [to wit, when the D. of Glouceſter was murdered] ‘ more in favour with K. Richarde then
‘ was the D. of Amnarle. And that by his councell he toke the
‘ lordes, & wrought many other thinges after the ſaid dukes adviſe.
‘ Laſtly, that he hearde the duke of Amnarle ſay, unto Sir John
‘ Busſhey & to Sir Henry Grene, I had lever than xx. thouſand pound,
‘ that this man were deade. And when thei had asked him, whiche
‘ man ? he ſaid, the duke of Hereford [now K. Henry] not
‘ for dred that I have of his perſon, but for ſorowe & rumours
‘ that he is likely for to make within this realme. ᵉ After reading

ᵃ Hol. p. 1121. a.
b Fabian part 2. page 372. b.
c Hol. p. 1121. b.

d id. p. 1122. a.
e Fabian. p. 374. a, b.

13 B

‘ whereof,

' whereof, the faid duke of Amnarle [afterwards lord of Stanford]
' ftood up & faid, as touching fuche articles as in that bill were put
' in againft him, they were falfe & untrewe, & that he would prove
' upon his body, or otherwife as the king wold comand him.   ᵃ On the
Oct. 18. ' Saturday next [Oct. 18.] the lord Fitz-water rofe up, & fayd to the
' king, that whereas the D. of Aumarle excufeth himfelf of the D. of
' Gloucefters death, I fay, quoth he, that he was the very caufe of it:
' & fo appealed him of treafon, offring, by throwing downe his hoode
' as a gage, to prove it with his bodie.   There were xx. other lordes
' alfo that threw downe their hoodes, as pledges to prove the like mat-
' ter againft the duke of Aumarle.   ᵇ Then parties began to be taken
' among the lordes; in fo much that the D. of Surrei toke part with
' the D. of Aumarle, & fayed, that all that by hym was doen, was
' doen by conftrainte of Richarde then kyng, & he hymfelf & other
' confented parforce unto the fame.   ᶜ Moreover, whereas it was al-
' ledged that the D. of Aumarle [afterwards lord of Stanford] fhould
' fend two of his fervants unto Calais, to murther the duke of Glou-
' cefter, the fayd D. of Aumarle faid, that if the D. of Norfolk affirme
' it, he lyed falfely, & that he would prove with his bodie, throw-
' ing downe another hoode which he had borowed.'   A gallant action
indeed, to challenge a man whom he knew durft not appear! For the
D. of Norfolk was then not in England, being banifhed as above 22:
R. 2.   It follows indeed ' ᵈ the king licenfed the D. of Norfolk to
' returne, that he might arraigne his appeale.'   But the duke was not
fo unwife a man as to truft his greateft adverfary K. Henry, & fo never
Oct. 29. did return.   ᵉ On Wednefday, the morrow after SS. Simon & Jude,
' the duke of Aumarles appeale [whereby he & others, at Nottingham
& Weftm. in the 21. R. 2. above, impeached the E. of Arundel & others
of treafon] ' was founde [& read in parliament] to which he & the
' reft anfwered, that they never affented to that appeale of theyre owne
' free willes, but were compelled thereto by the king: & this they
' affirmed by their othes, & offred to prove it by what maner they
Nov. 3. ' fhould bee appoynted.   ᶠ On Monday following, being the morrow
' after all fouls, the D. of Aumarle [afterwards lord of Stanford] was
' judged to lofe his name of duke, together with the honors, titles,
' & dignities thereunto belonging.   ᵍ Thomas Spencer, E. of Glocefter
[who had then lands at Stanford] ' was at the fame time degraded
' from his honor.   ʰ And generally all the great ones of that faction were
' reduced to the fame eftate (for honor & fortune) in which they
' ftood, when firft the D. of Glocefter was arrefted.   The caftles, ho-
' nours, manors, & reft of the things which afterwards grew to them
' out of the ruine of that duke & his friends, or otherwife by the

a Hol. p. 1122. b.
b Fabian. p. 375. b.
c Hol. p. 1123. a.
d id. ib.

e Hol. p. 1124. a:
f id. ib. a. b.
g Bar. Vol. I. p. 397. a.
h Speed, p. 763. a b.

' late

' late kings gift, from the day of that arreft, were, by authority of
' this parliament, taken away, or put into the prefent kings mercy.
' It was likewife made unlawful for them to give liveries or badges
' to reteiners, or to keep any about them but neceffary fervants : they
' were alfo forbidden, under paine of high treafon, to goe about, by
' any way, to enable the late king againft this parliament, in which
' his depofition was enacted. Finally (what laide them open to infi-
' nite vexations) whereas, in the time of their late greatnefs, they, &
' theirs, were charged to have done & patronized manifold wrongs &
' oppreffions, all people were willed to come in, & declare their
' griefes, to the intent they might have redreffe.   With thefe punifh-
' ments of his adverfaries K. Henry contented himfelf, but not the
' Commons ; who inveighed againft the lords of the council, becaufe
' the faid Aumarle [afterwards lord of Stanford] & others were not
' put to death, as perfons who ftood deepe in the peoples hatred.
' ª After this came the lorde Fitzwater, & prayed to have day &
' place to arraigne his appeale agaynft [Aumarle now only called]
' erle of Rutland.   The K. fayd, he would fend for the D. of Nor-
' folke to returne, & then proceed in that matter.

II. After this the faid Edward E. of Rutland, & others, chiefly thofe
degraded with him, confpired to kill the king, & that was to be done,
as authors fay, one of thefe two ways.   Some fay, ' ᵇ it was devifed
' that they fhould take upon them folemn jufts to be enterprifed at Ox-
' ford, to which triumph K. Henrie fhould be defired to come, & when
' hee fhould be moft bufily regarding the martial paftime, he fodainely
' fhould be flaine.   ᶜ Others fay, they were acorded to make a mom-
' mynge to the kynge [on the twelfth night in Chriftmafs] & fo for
' to flee hym in the revelynge.'   Be the manner as it will.   ' ᵈ There-
' upon was an indenture made, in whiche eche ftood bound to other
' to do their whole endevour for accomplifhing their purpofed ex-
' ployte.   ᵉ After this the E. of Rutland departing to fee his father
' the D. of York [lord of Stanford] as he fat at dinner, had his coun-
' terpane of the indenture of the confederacie in his bofome.   The fa-
' ther efpying it, would needes fee what it was.   And tho' the fonne
' humbly denied to fhewe it, the father being more earneft, by force
' tooke it out of his bofome, & perceyving the contents, in a great
' rage, caufed his horfes to be fadled out of hande, & fpitefully re-
' proving his fonne of treafon (for whom he was become furetie &
' mainpernour for his good abearing in open parliament) incontinently
' mounted to ride to the king, to declare unto him the malicious in-
' tent of his fonne & his complices.   The E. of Rutlande feeing in
' what daunger he ftood, tooke his horfe, & rode another way to
' Windfor in poft, fo that he got thither before his father, & when

---

a Hol. p. 1125. a.   d Hol. p. 1126. b.
b Id. p. 1126. a.   e id. ib.
c Polychron. fol. 325. p. 1. col. a.

' he

' he was alighted at the caftle gate, caufed the gates to be fhutte,
' faying, that hee muft needs delyver the keys to the king.   When he
' came before the king he kneeled downe, befeeching him of mercie,
' & declaring the whole matter unto him, in order as every thing had
' paffed, obteyned pardon.   And therewith came his father, &, being
' let in, delivered the indenture which he had taken from his fonne
' unto the king, who thereby perceived his fonnes wordes to be
' true.

III. ' ᵃ Of what Thomas lord Spencer, late E. of Glouceſter [who
had now lands at Stanford] ' was, at this time, guilty, doth not direct-
' ly appear; but he feems to have been an adherent with the earls
' of Kent, Salisbury, & Huntingdon, who defigned the furprifal of K.
' Henry at Windfor.   For being confcious of his danger he refolved
' to flee, but was taken at Briſtoll, & [by the mobb] carried into
' the market place, & there beheaded, upon the 3ᵈ. day after S. Hilary,
' 1. H. 4. Being thus put to death, his body was buried in the midft
' of the quire at Tewksbury, under a lamp, which burned before the
' hoft.——Laurence Hawvile, vicar of All Saints beyond Staunford bridge,
' gave to John Everard & William Sybbeſton, two meſſuages lying
' in the abbat of Burgs liberty; whereof one was fituate eft-by-the-
' water, between a tenement of William Sybbeſton eaſt, & a tenement
' late Anice Browns weft, extending it felf to the kings high-way
' fouth, & the banks of the Welland north; the other, eft-by-the-
' water, between a tenement of John Croylands eaſt, & a tenement
' of the abbat of Burgs weft, abutting on the kings highway fouth,
' & on the bank of the Welland north. B. H.

25. Nov.   IV. ' ᵇ Edmond Langle [lord of Stanford] by his teftament bearing
1400.   ' date 25. Nov. 1400. 2. H. 4. wherein he calls himfelf duke of York,
2. H. 4.   ' earl of Cambridge, & lord of Tividale, bequeathed his body to be
' buried at Langele, near to the grave of Ifabell his firſt wife, appoint-
' ing that two priefts fhould be ordained by his executors, to perform
' divine fervice there every day for his foul, & the fouls of all his
' kindred.'   He died, as you will find, the next year.——' John Jakes,
' fon & heir of Gilbert Jakes of Staunford, fold to Robert Dufhoufe
' of Staunford mercer, a meſſuage with a dovecoat in Bradecroft in
' S. Peters parifh Staunford, &c.   Given at Staunford the Friday after
' the feaft of the conception [2. H. 4.] Witneffes John Longe, Alder-
' man of Staunford, &c. B. H.   ᶜ After the feaft of the Epiphanie a
' parliament was holden.   ᵈ In that parliament all Sir Simon Burleys
' lands ᵉ (except the lands given to the abbey of Grace by the tower
' of London, & to S. Stephens at Weftminfter, & to the white friers at
' Langle) ᶠ which then remayned ungraunted & unfold, were reftored
' to Sir John Burley knight, fon & heyre of Sir Roger Burley, bro-

a Bar. Vol. I. p. 397. a. b.   d id. p. 1073. a.
b Bar. Vol. II. p. 155. a.   e Stow. p. 529.
c Hol. p. 1132. b.   f Hol. p. 1073. a

' ther

‘ ther to the fayd Simon ; of whom (faith my author) lineally is difcend-
‘ ed Thomas Eyns efq ; fecretarie to the queens maj. counfaile in the
north parts.’ But to return. The E. of Rutland, afterwards lord of Staunford, being pardoned as before related, in this parliament ‘ ᵃ had refti-
‘ tution of his eftate.   ᵇ About the fame time the faid E. with divers
‘ others was fent over into Guifnes, where the D. of Burbon & others
‘ were ready to commune with them : & fo, affembling together at fundry
‘ times & places, the French required to have king Richards young
‘ queen Ifabell reftored to them, but the Englifh to have her married
‘ to Henry prince of Wales; but the French would in no wife con-
‘ difcend thereto.   The commiffioners then began to treat of peace,
‘ & at length renewed the truce for 26. years.   ᶜ The faid earl be-
‘ came now fo obfequious to K. Henry, that upon the 28. Aug. he   Aug. 28.
‘ was conftituted his lieutenant in the dutchy of Aquitane, bearing
‘ then the title of earl of Rutland & Corke.

V. An antient parchment roll, (once in Mr. Butchers, afterwards in   3. H. 4.
Mr. Forfters, & now in my hands) begins a lift of the aldermen
of Stanford thus.   ‘ Henry the 4. began his reigne, *anno Dom.* 1399.
‘ & in the third yeare of his reigne, was Garvis Wikes firft alderman
‘ of Stondford.——W. Rowland of Staunford then gave a garden (de-
‘ fcribed 40. E. 3. & 18. R. 2. above) to Agnes, wife of John Gilder efq ;
‘ B. H.   ᵈ Edmund Langley D. of York lord of Stanford departed
‘ this life 1 Aug. 3. H. 4. & was buried at Langley ; being then feifed   Aug. 1
‘ of the manor of Wendovre in Bucks ; of the caftle of Fodringheye
‘ with its members, viz.   Yarewell, Southwike, & Naffington in
‘ Northampt ; of the manors of Fafterne, Wotton, Winterborne, Tok-
‘ kenham, Compton-Baffet, Somerford-Keyns ; Cheleworth, with the
‘ cuftody of the foreft of Bradene & Sevenhampton , as alfo of the
‘ hundreds of Heyworth & Crikelade, in Wilts ; of the manors & towns
‘ of Staunford & Grantham in Linc ; of the caftle of Rifing in Norf ;
‘ of the caftle & manor of Anfty & manor of Hechen, in Hertf ; of
‘ the honor & manor of Reilegh, the manors of Thunderle, Eftwode,
‘ with the caftle & lordfhip of Hadlee, in Effex ; of the manors of
‘ Coningsburgh, Sandhale, Haitefeld, Thorney, Fifhlake, Holmefrithe,
‘ & Soureby ; likewife of the manor & lordfhip of Wakefeld, all in
‘ Yorks ; as alfo of the dominion of Tyndale, in Northumb ; leaving
‘ Edward E. of Rutland, his fon & heir, twenty fix years of age.
‘ ᵉ This Edmund Langle rebuilt Fothcringhay caftle & made the higheft
‘ fortification or keep thereof in form of an horfe-fetter, which fome-
‘ times alone, & at other times with a falcon in it, was the devife or
‘ imprefs of the family of York, his pofterity.

VI. Alderman 1402. Stephen Makefay ; bis : Roll. By the town-
books it appears that in Edward the fourths time, & long time after,

a Bar. Vol. II. p. 156. b.   d Bar. Vol. II. p. 155. b.
b Hol. p. 1132. b.   e Brit. ant. & nova. Vol. III. p. 473. b.
c Bar. Vol. II. p. 156. b.

the

the alderman of Stanford was always elected on the feaſt of S. Jerom
Sept 30. & I believe that was the cuſtom now.   For this Stephen
Makeſey ald. of Stanford was witneſs to a deed dated the Thurſday
next after the feaſt of S. Michael, 4. H. 4. & to another dated after
June 29. the ſame year, which brings him within leſs than three months
of S. Jerom again : ſo that I reckon his being alderman commenced
Sept. 30. 1402. & ended Sept. 29. 1403. & ſo on of his ſucceſſors.
' ᵃ In this 4. H. 4. Edward E. of Rutland being in Gaſcoigne, ſoon
' after his fathers death, had livery of all his lands with reſpite for
' his homage.——Robert Dufhouſe of Staunford mercer ſold to John in
' the pitt of the ſame place, a meſſuage with a dovecoat ſituate in
' Bradecroft in St. Peters pariſh.   Witneſſes, Stephen Makeſey, ald. of
' Staunford, &c. dated the Tueſday next after the feaſt of the apo-
' ſtles SS. Peter & Paul. B. H.

5. H. 4.   VII. Alderman, 1403. Robert Lockſmith. Roll.   ' Alderman 1404.
6. H. 4. ' Johan Stanby that is, Styandeby, or Steanby Roll. ' John Sta-
' bley was now rector of S. John Baptiſts church in Staunford. B. H.
' ᵇ Edward E. of Rutland lord of Stanford married Philippa, one
' of the daughters & heirs to John lord Mohun.   ' In this 6. yeare
' the Friday after S. Valentine, the E. of Marches ſonnes early in the
' morning were taken forth of Windſor caſtel, & conveyed away, it
' was not knowne whither at firſt, but ſuche ſearch was made, that
' ſhortly after they were broughte backe.   The ſmith that counter-
' feyted the keyes by which they, that conveyed them thence, got in-
' to the chamber where they were lodged, had firſt his hands cut off,
7. H. 4. ' & after his head.' Ald. 1405. Thomas Storme. Roll. ' ᵈ Edward E.
' of Rutland [lord of Stanford] in the parliament now held, was re-
' ſtored to his hereditary dignity of D. of York.   ' The ladie Spencer,
' ſiſter to the ſaid D. of York, & widow of lord Thomas Spencer, ex-
' ecuted at Briſtowe, as before ye have heard ; being apprehended &
' committed to cloſe priſon, accuſed hir brother the duke, as chiefe
' author in ſtealing away the E. of Marche his ſonnes.   And further,
' that the ſayde duke ment to have broken into the manor of Eltham
' the laſt Chriſtmaſſe, by ſcaling the walles in the night, the king be-
' ing there, to have murthered him.   For to prove hir accuſation true,
' ſhe offred, that if there were any knight or eſquire, that woulde take
' upon him to fight in hir quarrel, if he were overcome, ſhe would
' be contented to be burnt for it.   One of hir eſquires named Wil-
' liam Maidſtone, hearing what offer his ladie & miſtreſſe propound-
' ed, caſt downe his hoode, & proffered in hir cauſe the combate.
' The duke likewiſe caſt downe his hoode, readie by battaile to clear
' his innocencie.   Nevertheleſs the kings ſonne lord Thomas of Lan-
' caſter arreſted him, & put him under ſafe keeping in the tower, till

a Bar. Vol. II. p. 156. b.   d Bar. Vol. II. p. 156. b.
b id. ib.   e Hol. ut ſupra, b.
c Hol. p. 1145. a.

' it

' it were further knowen what order fhould be taken wyth him, &
' in the mean time were all his goodes confifcate. The fame time
' was Thomas Mowbray E. Marfhall accufed, as privie to the purpofe
' of the D. of Yorke; who confeffed indeede, that he knewe of the
' dukes purpofe, but in no wife gave his confente thereunto; & there-
' fore befought the king to be good & gracious lorde unto him, & fo
' obteyned pardon.

 VIII. Ald. 1406. Thomas Spicer. Roll.   ' ᵃ In the parliament which   8. H. 4.
' yet continued, the D. of Yorke [lord of Stanford] was reftored to
' his former libertie, eftate, & dignitie, whereas many fuppofed that
' he had bin dead long before that time in prifon —— John Palfreyman
' of Staunford gave to John Longe of the fame, one parcel of a gar-
' den lying in Cornftall in S. Georges parifh, which contains in length
' 1 5 virgates & an half by the kings ftandard, & in bredth 8 virgates :
' & lies between a garden of John Longe the elder weft, & his own
' garden eaft, & abutts on an orchat of the faid John Longe the elder
' fouth, & a garden of the fame John north. B. H.' Alderman 1407. Raphe   9. H. 4.
Harwood. Roll.   ' Laurence Hawvell capellan of Staunford [the
fame, or kinfman of the fame, mentioned, *anno* 1. H. 4. as vicar of
All Saints beyond the bridge] ' gave to Ralph Taylor of Staunford,
' one meffuage, fituate in the abbat of Burgs liberty, to wit, eaft-by-
' the-water ; between a tenement of Robert Staleham eaft, & a tene-
' ment of Richard Staunton of Burg weft ; & abutting on the kings
' highway fouth, & on the bank of Welond north : which was Richard
' Palfreymans a capellan of Staunford. B. H.   John Everard capellan of
' Staunford confirmed the bovefaid meffuage to the fame Ralph Taylor,
' which meffuage the forefaid John, & William Sibfton capellan, had
' by gift of Laurence Hawvell vicar of All Saints beyond Staunford
' bridge. B. H.

 IX. Ald. 1408. John Palfreman, bis : Roll.   ' Richard Paynton alias   10. H. 3.
' Ramfey of Staunford, gave to Godefry Gedney, one meffuage fituate
' in S. Georges parifh, between a garden of Th. Barker eaft, a mef-
' fuage of the abbat of Thorneys weft, & abutting on the town-wall
' fouth, & the kings highway north. B. H.   Ald. 1409. Raphe Brown.
Roll. ' William Bradecroft of Staunford fold to John Hawvell vicar   11. H. 4.
' of All Saints in the mercat, a piece of a meadow lying in the crofts
' of Bradecroft, between the meadow of John in the pitt eaft, & the
' meadow of John de Apethorpe weft, abutting on the mill holme
' fouth, & the kings highway north. Witneffes, John Palfreman, al-
' derman of Staunford, &c. dated on Friday the eve of S. Thomas the
' apoftle 11. H. 4. B. H.   Nicholas Hickfon of Withorp gave to John
' Brown draper of Staunford, two fhops with the appurtenances, fi-
' tuate in All Saints parifh in the mercat, between a tenement late
' Reginald Merceres fouth, & a tenement of John Longes north, as

' they extend themfelves from the way called behynde-bak weft, unto
' the kings highway of another part eaft : which fhops were Robert
12. H. 4. ' Barons of Willefthorp, a capellan. B. H.'　Alderman 1410. John Stacy.
Roll.　' Richard Bulwick of Staunford bocher, fold to John in the
' pitt of Staunford, & to Robert Parker of the fame, two gardens in
' Bradecroft, abutting on the kings highway fouth, &c.　Witneffes,
' Ralph Bond, alderman of Staunford, &c. dated the Tuefday next
13. H. 4. ' after the feaft of S. Matthias, 12. H. 4. B. H.'　Alderman 1411. Alexander Haine. Roll.　' ᵃ Edward duke of York [lord of Stanford] this
' yeere began the foundation of the college of Fodringhey in Nor-
' thamptonfhire, for a mafter, 12 priefts, eight clearkes, & 13 cho-
' rifters.'　All but the choir of that church is yet ftanding.　From it
we may gather what a beautiful ftructure the college was; the foundations whereof take up a great deal of gardening & other ground
on the fouth-weft point, & fouth fide of the church.　The fteeple is a
moft curious thing, being an octagon on a quadrangular tower, after the manner of Bofton in Lincolnfhire & Lowick in Northamptonfhire.　But to return.　' John Chandeler, alderman of Staunford, was
' witnefs to a deed dated the Wednefday next after the feaft of S.
Aug. 19. ' Thomas the apoftle. B. H.　ᵇ About the 19. of Auguft, K. Henry fent
' Edward D. of York [lord of Stanford] & many valiant men to help
14. H. 4. ' the D. of Orleance againft the D. of Burgoyne.'　Alderman 1412.
Robert Lockfmith. Roll.　King Henry the 4. deceafed upon the 20.
day of March 14$\frac{12}{13}$. being (as we fay at Stanford) our midlent-fair
Sunday; & was fucceeded by his eldeft fon,

King Henry the V.

1. H. 5.　X. Alderman 1413. Thomas Baffet. Roll.　Thomas prior of Beau-
June 3. vale in Nottinghamfhire, & the convent of that place, now granted
to John Grene of Grantham, William Affheby efq; John Purley, &
Roger Dalim capellan, & their heirs, the perpetual advowfon of S.
Pauls church in Stanford : whofe original deed, now in the hands of
the Rev. Mr. Samuel Rogers, vicar of All Saints in Stanford; may
be thus englifhed.　' Let prefent & future people know, that we
' Thomas prior of the houfe of the holy Trinity of Beauvale, of the
' Carthufian order, & the convent of the fame place in the county of
' Nottingham, with unanimous affent & confent, have given, grant-
' ed, & by this our prefent charter confirmed to John Grene of Gran-
' tham, William Affheby efq; John Purley, & Roger Dalim capellan,
' the advowfon, with our patronage, of the church of S. Paul in Staun-
' ford in the county of Lincoln, together with all & every its rights
' & appurtenances whatfoever to the forefaid advowfon & patronage
' any ways belonging, without an incumbent; to have & to hold the
' advowfon with our patronage of the church aforefaid, together with

' all & every its rights & appurtenances aforesaid, to the forenamed
' John, William, John, & Roger, & their assigns for ever. And we
' do will & grant, for us & our successors for ever, by these presents,
' that it be lawful for the forenamed John, William, John & Roger,
' their heirs & assigns, to the same church to present their clerc as
' oft as it shall become vacant for the future, without impediment,
' reclaim, or challenge of us, or our successors whomsoever, hereafter.
' In witness whereof to this present charter the common seal of our
' house is appendent.   Witnesses, Alexander Hyne alderman of Staun-
' ford, John Steneby, John Longe, William Lyttyl, John Allecok,
' & others. Given the 3. of June, 1. H. 5.' The seal is wanting.
' Ralph Tailour of Staunford, gave to Richard Freston, alias Freston,
' of Staunford, *Walker* a trade compounded of a dier & a fuller &
' John Corby, one messuage with one garden situate in All Saints
' parish beyond Staunford bridge, est be-the-water, within the abbat of
' Burgs liberty; to wit, between a messuage of Robert Stalam east, &
' a messuage of the foresaid abbat west, as it abutts on the bank of
' the Weland north, & on the way towards Burg south; which mes-
' suage with the garden was sometime L. Hawvilles, vicar of the foresaid
' church of All Saints. B. H.'   Mr. Forster says, he had seen Stanford
wrote with an m, Stamford, in a deed of this 1. H. 5. But I should
rather think it was Stainford, & the point of the i omitted, & so
he took it for an m.   Robert Stalam, alderman of *Stanford*, was
witness to a deed dated Friday the feast of the conception [Dec. 8.] Dec. 8.
B. H. This Robert Stalam is sometimes called Robert Locksmith;
Stalam I guess being his name, & Locksmith his profession.

XI. ' ᵃ Edward D. of York lord of Stanford in the 2. H. 5. was 2. H. 5.
' constituted justice of South Wales, & the same year made general
' warden of all the east marches towards Scotland.   ᵇ In a parliament
' held in May at Leicester, Richard the said D. of Yorks brother was May.
' made E. of Cambridge.——John de Apethorp gave to John de Apethorp
' one messuage in All Saints parish in the mercat, between a tenement
' of John de Apethorp deceased, & the lane called Mallory lane west.
' B. H.'   Robert Stalam alderman of Staunford was witness to a deed,
' dated on the eve of the Nativity of S. John Baptist. B. H.   Alderman June 23.
' 1414. John Brown, draper. Roll.   ᶜ A squier, called Sir John Brown, 1414.
' with 36. more in number, were now convicte of heresy & treason,
' & for the same hanged & brente in S. Gyles felde at London.'   How
this Brown was related to the Browns of Stanford, or if at all, I
know not. ' ᵈHenry Chicheley bishop of S. Davids being elected arch-
' bishop of Canterbury; upon the 16. of March in the presence of Mar. 16.
' Edward D. of York lord of Stanford & several other persons of the
' greatest quality, told the monks of Canterbury, that he could not

a Bar. Vol. II. p. 157.   d Ducks life of Chichele, Lond. 1709. 8°.
b Stow, p. 563.   p. 39.
c Fabian, part 2. p. 390. a.

' gratify

' gratify their defires, becaufe it was not lawful for him to lay down
' his bifhoprick of S. Davids, without leave from the pope. However
' that he was not wholly averfe to their offer, if the pope would
' confent.' The pope, being fent to, took this very kindly, & confirmed the election.

3. H. 3.   XII. The D. of Yorks brother, Richard E. of Cambridge, ' ᵃ being
' at Southampton with the king (then fhipping his army for France)
' having been corrupted by the French, joyned with Henry lord Scrope
' & others, in a confpiracie, to murther him there.   Which defign
' being difcovered; upon tryal by their peers, fentence of death was
' pronounced againft him & his confederates, who thereupon loft their
' heads, without the north-gate there.   Thus faith T. Walfingham.
' But others differ in their relation as to the true reafon of his inten-
' tion to murther K. Henry; & affirm, that his main defign was to
' raife Edmund Mortimer E. of March to the throne, as heir to Lio-
' nel D. of Clarence; not being ignorant of fome impediments in that
' earl for procreation of children; & that then, in time, the right would
' come to his own wife (fifter to the fame Edmund) & to her iffue,
' as afterwards it really did.   Which is moft likely to be true; what-
' ever hath been otherwife reported, of his acknowledging what he
' then did, to be in favor of the French king.   ᵇ It is remarkable that
' Mortimer himfelf was the very man who difcovered the confpiracy
Aug. 5. ' to the king.   ᶜ Upon the 5. of Aug. Edward D. of York [lord of
Stanford] ' in confideration of his vaft expences in building & en-
' dowing the collegiate church of Fotheringhay, & in fitting himfelf
' to ferve the king, in his prefent expedition (whereby he had con-
' tracted many debts; fo, that without the kings affiftance, he de-
' fpaired of perfecting that pious work) obtained licenfe to enfeoffe
' Henry de Beaufort bifhop of Winton & others, of the manors of
' Fafterne, Old-Wotton, Tokenham, Chelworth, Wynterborne, Comp-
' ton-Baffet, & Sevenhampton in Wilts; as alfo of the advowfon of
' the church of Tokenham, & burough of Wotton, with the hundreds
' of Heighworth & Cryklade, in the fame county; of the manor of
' Doghton, in Glouc; Anfty, with the advowfon of the church, in
' Hertf; Naffyngton & Yarewell, with the caftle & town of Fothe-
' ringhay, in Northampt; of the caftle & town of Stanford, with the
' town & foke of Grantham, in Linc; of the caftle & manor of Co-
' ningsburgh, & manors of Braiwel, Clifton, Hattefeld, Fifhlake &
' Thorney, in Yorks; with truft, that they fhould fee to the accomplifh-
Aug. 13. ' ment of that work.   ᵈ On the 13. of Auguft the faid D. tooke fhip-
Aug. 14. ' ping with the king & entred the fea, & on the 14. at night arrived
Aug. 16. ' at Kedicaux in Normandie.   ᵉ On the 16 of Auguft, the faid D. of
' York, high conftable of England, was at the fiege of Hereflete, &

a Bar. Vol. II. p. 159. b.   d Stow, p. 566.
b Acta regia, N°. 8. p. 133.   e id. p. 567.
c Bar. Vol. II. p. 157. a.

2

' lodged

' lodged with his band, on the same side the river that the king lay.
' [a] On the 17. of Aug. the said duke declared his testament, whereby Aug. 17.
' he bequeathed his body to be buried in the church parochial of that
' his college of Fotheringhay, in the midst of the quire, near the steps,
' under a flat marble; appointing that 50 marks, in half groats, should
' be given in dole, to such poor people as should come to his fu-
' neral.   To the lady Philippa his wife he bequeathed his bed with
' feathers & leopards, & all pertaining thereto; & directed, that in
' all masses & prayers to be made for him, mention should be made
' of K. Rich. the 2. K. Henry the 4. Edmund D. of York his father,
' the lady Isabell his mother; & all other persons departed this life,
' for whom he was in conscience obliged to pray, that God would
' have mercy on them.'   Alderman 1415. William Locksmith. Roll. 1415.
' [b] Oct. 22. the D. of York [lord of Stanford] who led the vant- Oct.22.
' garde of the kings armie in France, mounting up to the height of
' an hill with his people, sente oute skowts to discover the country,
' which upon their returne advertised hym, that a wonderful great
' armie of Frenchmen was at hand.'   The person whom the duke sent
out to view the enemy was, I suppose, David Gam, commander of a
company of Welch.   For I find he brought word back, ' [c] there were
' enow to be killed, enow to be taken prisoners, & enow to run
' away.   [d] The duke declared to the king what he had heard.   And
' the king thereupon caused the bataile (which he led himself) to stay,
' & incontinently rode forth to view his adversaries.   [e] Oct. 24. the Oct.24.
' night before the battel of Agencourt, the king, as it is said by ad-
' vice of the D. of York [lord of Stanford] gave commaundement
' thro' his host that every man should purvey him a stake sharp at
' both ends, to fix in the ground to keep off the enemies.'   On the
morrow, being ' [f] Friday, next preceding the festival of All Saints
' (which happened upon the 25. of Oct.) the said duke of York lost his Oct.25.
' life, tho' the English then obtained a glorious victory.   It is said,
' that he desired of king Henry that he might have the forward of the
' battel that day, & had it; & that by much heat & thronging, being
' a fat man, he was smothered to death.   [g] It is said also that K. Henry
' had but 9000 men, all tir'd, & obliged to fight naked from the waist
' downward, because of the distemper which hung upon them. [h] Where-
' as the French army consisted of 140000 at least! But to return.
' [i] The lands whereof the D. of York died seised were, the manors
' of Solyhull & Sheldone in Warw; the honor of Reyleghe, with the
' manors of Thunderle, Estwode, & hundred of Rochforde, in Essex;
' the manor of Ansty, in Hertf; the manor of Wendover & moietie
' of the manor of Horton, in Bucks; the manor of Whelnetham, in

a Bar. Vol. II. p. 157. a.   f Bar. Vol. II. p. 157. a.
b Holing. p. 1178. a.   g Acta regia, N°. 8. p. 134.
c Acta regia, N°. 8. p. 135.   h id. p. 135.
d Holing. ut supra.   i Bar. ut supra.
e Stow, p. 570.

                                                        ' Suff;

' Suff; the caſtle & manor of Stanford, the town & ſoke of Gran-
' tham, with the manors of Bondeby, Shillingthorpe, & lordſhip of
' Harlaſton, called Brewes-manor, in Linc; the manors of Yelvertoft,
' Naſſington, Yarwell, with the caſtle & manor of Fotheringhay, in
' Northampt; the manors of Doughton & Whittington, with the ma-
' nor & hundred of Bretone, juxta Briſtol, in Glouc; the manor,
' burough, & lordſhip of Avene, the manor & territory of Neuton-
' Notaſh, & manors of Dynas-powis, Sully, & Peterſton, in Wales;
' the caſtle & lordſhip of Ewyas-Lacy, in Heref; the iſle of Wiht &
' caſtle of Caresbroke, with the wardenſhip of New-foreſt; as alſo the
' manors of Thorle, Wetone, Aysſhele, & Mapul-Durwel, with the
' cuſtody of the foreſt of Bere, in Hants; the manors of Somerforde-
' Keynes, Faſterne, Wotton, Old Tokenham, Cheleſworthe, Winter-
' borne, Compton-Baſſet, Sevenhampton; the burough & hundred of
' Hyworth, the hundred of Crikkelade, with the manors of Winter-
' ſlowe, Sherſton, & Brodeton, in Wilts; the town & manor of Soureby,
' the caſtle & manor of Coningesburghe, with the manors of Brai-
' well, Clifton, Haitefeld, Fiſhlake, Thorne, & Hothome, in Yorks.
' But he left no iſſue, ſo that Richard his nephew (ſon to Richard E.
' of Cambridge his younger brother, beheaded as above at Southamp-
' ton) was found to be his next heir, & at this time three years of

Nov. 6. ' age.   a Upon the 6. of November K. Henry took ſhipping at Calais,
' & the ſame day landed at Dover, having with him the dead bodie

Dec. 1. ' of the late D of York [lord of Stanford.]   b Upon the 1. of De-
' cember the king cauſed the ſaid dukes exequies to be kept at London,
' with great ſolemnity; whereat were preſent divers biſhops & ab-
' bats, beſides a multitude of other perſons of great quality, both
' French & Engliſh.   c His corps was afterwards brought to Fothe-
' ringhay, & there interr'd, in the body of the quire, under a flat mar-
' ble, with his image (flat) in braſs upon it.   d There it remained 'till
' the 6. of Edw. 6. when, the choir of that church being pulled down
' by the duke of Northumberland, it was taken up, & expoſed to
' public view.   But afterwards Q. Eliz. being informed thereof, ſent
' a *mandamus* to have it reinterr'd in the church with the grave-ſtone
' over it.   e On the ſouth ſide of the altar of the ſaid church is a
' monument of free-ſtone, railed in with wooden rails coloured
' red, for the ſaid Edward D. of York, with his arms upon it; who,
' (as an inſcription, upon the wall above it, relates) was ſlain at Agen-
' court.' This monument was erected by Q. Eliſabeth; but is ſo plain
a thing that ſure her order about it was very ill performed.

4. H. 5.   XIII. Alderman, 1416. Johan Stonbe. Roll.   Alderman, 1417. Johan
5. H. 5.   Palfreeman. Roll.   ' f This yeare the king holding his parliament at

a Holing. p. 1183. a.   que Jacobi Holcot, vicarii de Fotheringhay.
b Bar. Vol. II. p. 157. b.   e Ex literis mihi miſſis May 29. 1725.
c id. ib. a.   f Fabian, p. 395, 396.
d Ex collect. MS. viri reverendi, docti-

' Weſtmynſter,

'Weſtmynſter; &, by autoritie of the ſame, Richarde, ſonne & heyre of
'the E. of Cambridge, which erle was put to death at Southampton,
'was created D. of Yorke.——In the 6.H.5. John Palfreyman & John Myl- 6. H. 5.
'ton bought a meſſuage in S. Georges pariſh, deſcribed as Godefry Ged-
'neys *anno* 10. H. 4. above. B. H. Ralph Taylour gave a meſſuage deſcrib-
'ed *anno* 9. H. 4. above to Roger Cliff of Staunford. B. H.   John Ward
'of Staunford bocher & Katherine Giffard gave to William Rawceby
'of Staunford capellan, & William Rippengale of Staunford, their
'ſhops with a loft, &c. together ſituate between the ſhops late John
'Clives eaſt, & a ſhop late Stephen de Slefords weſt, as they extend
'themſelves from the Butchers ſtreet ſouth unto Woolrow north:
'which ſhops they lately had by gift & feoffment of Richard Wal-
'lington clerc, & John Lindeſey capellan. B. H.'   To know theſe
ſtreets, note honey alley opens ſouth into the Butchers ſtreet, north
into Wool-row.   'John Stenby alderman of Stanford was witneſs to a
'deed dated the Monday next after S. John Baptiſt, & another the Thurſ-
'day next before SS. Simon & Jude. B. H.'   Alderman 1418. Alexander Marcer. Roll.   'Margaret relict of Richard Bulwike gave a
'meſſuage, deſcribed *annis* 18. R. 2. & 7. H. 5. above, to Thomas 7. H. 5.
'Baſſet, merchaunt. B. H.'   A deed of this year mentions 'eight acres
'of arable land lying at Lynghawe, between the land of the rector
'of the church of S. Peter, & the land belonging to the chapel of
'S. Thomas the martyr on the bridge ſouth, & abutting on Tynwell
'mere weſt. B. H.'   Alderman 1419. Johan Allcocke. Roll.   'John 8. H. 5.
'Trenchepayn gave to Thomas Baſſet of Staunford, two cellars with
'lofts, &c. in great S. Michaels pariſh ſituate together in the ſtreet
'called Coveneſty, between a tenement of his own which he then
'inhabited north, & a tenement of the prior of Fyneſhede ſouth. B. H.'
Alderman 1420. Andrew Draper. Roll.   ' [a] Feb. 24. queen Catherine, Feb.24,
'the French kings daughter, was crowned at Weſtminſter.   At din-
'ner, upon her lefte hand, nere to the bordes end, ſat the ducheſſe
'of Yorke.'   Ald. 1421. Tho. Baſſet. Roll.   Mr. Forſter left an old 9. H. 5.
note relating to ſome church in Stanford, which falls in here, but
is ſo very maimed & obſcure, that I know not well what to make of
it, only that it relates to the founders of ſome chantery, & their
obits.   But ſee it in his own words below [b].   ' [c] K. Henry the 5. [but
what year I find not] 'founded garter K. of arms of all Engliſhmen.'
The firſt garter, king of arms, was William Bruges eſq; a great bene-

a Fabian, p. 402. a.
b Anno 1421. regiſtratur, quod . . . .
. . . . . Idibus Martii, quibus rector iſtius
eccleſie ſervet obitum Henrici Sampſonis &
Alienore, fundatorum cujuſdam cantarie, &
Roberti Senkel junctoris (quondam rectoris
iſtius eccleſie) . . . . in capella B. Marie
  ⎰ cum duorum dierum
  ⎱ cum duo dies pullentibus
  ⎰ vel cum ſecundo pullentibus

& una die in quibuſlibet ſeptimanis dierum
                                    mentibus
cinerum piis melius Domme conſervetur.
Then a great chaſm, afterwards & poſte-
riorem . . . in perpetuum pro predictis; quorum animabus propitietur Deus, Amen.
  c Fabian, p. 402. b.

factor to S. Georges church in Stanford, & afterwards buried there.

Aug. 31. K. Henry the 5. died the 31. of Aug. 1422. & was succeeded by
1422. his son K. Henry the sixth.   To which I shall only add, ' ᵃ the lord
10. H. 5. ' Crumwell was one of the chief mourners as K. Henry the 5th.
' body was brought in state thro' France to be buried in England.

a Holing. p. 1218. a.

The end of the thirteenth book.

THE
ANTIQUARIAN ANNALS

of the TOWN of

STANFORD

IN

Lincoln, Rutland, *and* Northampton *Shires*.

BOOK XIV.

Containing the reign of K. Henry the VI.

ALDERMAN of Stanford 1422. 1. H. 6. John Brown; draper. Roll. ' Geoffry Walſh of Badyngton gave to John ' Badburgham of Bulwic, ſix meſſuages & 12 acres of ara-ble land lying ſeverally in the town & fields of Staunford, as well in the abbat of Burgs liberty, as in the demeſne of Edward late D. of York. Alſo two meſſuages together ſituate in S. Georges pariſh between Pekkes-hall-yarde north, & a grange belonging to the prior of S. Leonard ſouth, & abutting on a garden late W. Saltbys eaſt, & the kings highway weſt. And one meſſuage ſituate in Cornſtall, between a tenement of the rector of the church of S. Paul eaſt, & a tene-ment late Thomas Stormes weſt, as it abutts on the kings highway ſouth, & on a garden of Henry Cokk north. And one meſſuage in Cornſtall, ſituate between a tenement of the abbat of Thorney eaſt, & a tenement of lord Edward late D. of York weſt, as it abutts upon a garden of John Longe ſouth, & the kings highway north. John Smith of Staunford clerc gave to John Brown draper, two ſhops ſituate in All Saints pariſh in the mercat, whereof one is ſi-tuate in the Scobothes between a tenement of lord Edward late D. of York north, & a ſhop of the ſaid John Brown ſouth, & abutts on the kings highway eaſt. And the other ſhop is ſituate between a ſhop of John Alcocks north, & a ſhop of the foreſaid John Brown ſouth, & abutts on the way called behynde-the-bak weſt; which ſhops were John Longes of Staunford. Alſo one meſſuage in All Saints pariſh in the mercat, between a tenement of the prior of Finneſheuede ſouth, & a tenement of W. Stalehams north. Wit-neſſes, Thomas Baſſet alderman of Staunford, &c. dated 4. Mar. 1. H. 6. B. H.' Ald. 2. H. 6. 1423. Thomas Raffe. Roll. A deed

1. H. 6.

Mar. 4.
2. H. 6.
of 1423.

B

of this year mentions ' three acres of arable land lying in Deepdale
' between the land of the prior of S. Leonard weft, & the land of the
' rector of the church of the holy Trinity eaft; & two acres lying in
' the Kings-rife between the land belonging to the chantery in S.
' Clements church weft, & abutting on Bermergores. B. H.   [a] In 1424.
' died Roger Flower of Okeham, a perfon of great note, whofe cha-
' rities given by his will are a fignal monument of his piety, accor-
' ding to the times he lived in.'   Among other legacies he gave, ' to
' every order of friars at Stanford, fix marks.   And, to the prior &
' canons of Newfted near Stanford, xiij s. iiij. d.'   The reft may be
feen in my author.

3. H. 6.   II. Ald. 1424. Thomas Spicer. Roll.   ' [b] Upon the death of Ed-
1424.   ' mund Mortimer E. of March, Richard [Plantagenet, D. of York]
' was found to be his next heir, to wit, fon of Anne, fifter to the
' fame earl; & at this time fourteen years of age.   [c] This Richard
' was afterwards the fatal difturber of the realme of England, upon
' the pretence of Mortimers title to the crowne.'   The town of Stanford, as you will hereafter find, was almoft utterly ruined in his quarrel.   ' John Whitefide of Staunford gave to John Brown, one garden
' lying in Cornftall, Staunford, between the town-wall eaft, & a te-
' nement of John Stockton clerc weft, & abutting on the faid wall
' fouth, & the kings highway north; which garden was Thomas
' Barker of Staunford Corvifers. B. H.'   Another deed of this year
mentions, ' two acres lying together, & abutting on the headland of
' the rector of Bynnewerk church north. B. H.   [d] There lived now
' one William Ruffel, a grey frier; who fpread a many abfurd errors
' among the people.   Particularly in a fermon at Stanford in the dio-
' cefe of Lincoln, he very irreligioufly told them, it was lawful for
' a religious & monaftic perfon, *rem habere cum femina, nec coi-*
' *tum illum cum aliquo peccato conjunctum*; he maintained alfo, that
' no man was, by the law of God, obliged to pay any perfonal tythes
' to his parifh minifter; but at laft renounced thefe errors, which
' were condemned by both univerfities.'   The author of Chichele's
life, at this time archbifhop of Canterbury, fpeaking of a fynod or
April   convocation of the clergy, held at London in April 1425. writes
1425.   thus.   ' [e] One Robert Hoke & one Thomas Drayton, both priefts,
' one of the diocefe of Lincoln & the other of Canterbury, were
' brought before the fynod, & accus'd of herefy.   It was alledg'd againft
' them, that they would not kneel before the crucifix, & that they
' had in their poffeffion certain books, in which it was faid, that the
' prieft could not change the hoft in the facrament into the body of
' Chrift; that a monaftic life & auricular confeffion were the inven-
' tions of the devil, & that amongft chriftians all things ought to be

a Britannia ant. & nova, in Rutland, p.   c Speed, p. 830. b.
517. a. b.   d Ex Nich. Harpsfield hift. Wicleffiana.
   b Bar. Vol. II. p. 158. b.   e p. 118. &c.

' in

' in common.   But the sharpest accusation was brought against one
' William Russel of the order of minor friers, for teaching the
' people in his sermons, that personal tythes were not commanded
' by God, but that it was lawful for all christians to bestow them in
' charitable uses upon the poor, as they themselves pleased.   This ex-
' treamly troubled & perplexed the clergy, who feared, that if this opi-
' nion should spread it self among the people, they should lose this part
' of their income, by which the wealth of their order would be greatly
' diminished. Wherefore he was ordered, by the synod, on a day prefixed,
' to recant out of the pulpit at Pauls cross; but, before the time came, he
' fled out of England, whereupon he was pronounced contumacious by
' edicts set forth against him, & afterwards in open court proclaimed a
' heretic, & his opinion was adjudged to be impious by the decrees of both
' universities; which the university of Oxford presently signified by their
' letters to the archbishop & the synod, yet extant[a].   Shortly after
' the synod being inform'd that he was at Rome, sent messengers to
' apprehend him, & accuse him before the pope, who were allow'd a
' farthing in the pound out of all ecclesiastical preferments.   The ex-
' amination of this matter being referr'd by the pope to Branda car-
' dinal of Placenza, he was condemned to perpetual imprisonment,
' unless he repented of his error; but afterwards, escaping out of pri-
' son, he returned into England; &, having preached a sermon at
' Pauls cross, abjur'd his error with a formal oath.   The archbishop
' also by his mandate enjoin'd the Franciscans, that, as often as they
' preached to the people, they should teach them, that personal tythes
' were commanded to be paid both by the laws of God, & the con-
' stitutions of the holy fathers.

　　III. In the 4. H. 6. John Brown gave a garden, described the last 4. H. 6.
year above, to Henry Whitehened of Staunford, bocher. B. H.   Alderman 1425. John Palfreman. Roll.   ' [b] The K. caused a solemn feast 1425.
' to be kept on Whitsunday [at Leicester] on whiche day he created
' Richard Plantagenet, sonne & heire to the erle of Cambridge (whom
' his father at Southampton had put to death, as before ye have heard)
' D. of Yorke, not foreseeing that this preferment shoulde bee his de-
' struction, nor that hys seede shoulde of his generation be the ex-
' treame end, & finall confusion.'   Fabian says, K. Henry the 5. created
this Richard D. of York; & he I believe is in the right.   For there
being yet extant ' [c] a grant to Q. Catherine, the kings mother, of that
' palace in London which came to the king by the death of the E.
' of March, for her to live in during the minority of the D. of York,
' dated at Westm. Feb. the 26. 1425. that grant is a proof that the Feb. 26.
' D. of York had that title before the parliament of Leicester, be-
' cause it did not meet 'till above a year after the date of it.'   One
calls this creation ' [d] the fatal error of the council.'   Another, ' [e] the

a Liter acad. Oxon. in archiv. epist. 20.　　d Speed, p. 831. b.
b Hol. p. 1234. a.　　　　　　　　　　　　e Bp. Gibsons addit. to Camd. 1. Edit. p.
c Acta regia, N°. X. p. 265.　　　　　　　757.

' great,

‘ great, but unwary generofity of K. Henry the fixth.’ Be that as it will, thus was the faid Richard, now at leaft, if not before, ‘ ᵃ fully ‘ reftored, as fon of Richard brother of Edward late D. of York, &

May 4. ‘ cofin german to Edmund E. of March. ᵇ On the 4. of May, the D. ‘ of Bedford made divers knights at Leicefter, the D. of York [lord of Stanford] ‘ being at the head of them. And this, faith one ᶜ, I guefs ‘ was what gave occafion for the affertion, that this prince received ‘ the title of D. of York, in the parliament then affembled at Lei- ‘ cefter. ᵈ The fame year, the faid Richard D. of York (being then in ‘ warde to Joane countefs of Weftmoreland, by virtue of the laft ‘ will & teftament of Raphe E. of Weftmoreland, her late husband) ‘ had a grant of c. marks a year, over & above cc. marks a year, for- ‘ merly affigned for his maintainance; to be paid out of the lands ‘ of Edmund late E. of March, unto whom he was found to be next ‘ heir.

5. H. 6. IV. Alderman, 1426. Johan Whitfade. Roll. Ald. 1427. Johan
6. H. 6. Brown, draper. Roll. An old accompt of John Leche goldfmith of Stanford, churchwarden of S. Maries at the bridge this 6. Hen the 6. has thefe particulars. ‘ ᵉ Received of Sir Thomas Baffet, John ‘ Whytfide, John Leche, Robert Smyth, & other the parifhioners of ‘ the faid church, as appears in a certain roll of the monies granted ‘ by the faid parifhioners for maintaining the fabric of the forefaid ‘ church; 47 s. & 5ᵈ. (& there remains to be levied as appears by the ‘ faid roll 9 s. 10 d. ¼.)

	l.	*s.*	*d.*
‘ Expended in mending the bells	00	06	00
‘ Paid for . . . . & iron	00	01	02
‘ Wax bought to make two torches	00	15	04
‘ A chain	00	00	07
‘ Paid Thomas Harpmaker for making the fchafte	00	03	04
‘ And for making two torches	00	01	10
‘ Glue	00	00	11
‘ Red lead	00	00	02
‘ In charges for bringing the fchafte	00	00	08
‘ A bell-rope	00	00	08
‘ *Pro Nerfis* for the fchafte	00	00	01
‘ A little rope	00	00	02
‘ For . . . . . . plo . . . [plomber, perhaps]	00	03	04
‘ Cloth for the fchafte	00	00	11
‘ Writing	00	00	02
‘ Given the players	00	00	06
‘ For hanging the towel	00	00	04
‘ Thred for the canopy	00	00	01

a id. ib.
b Acta regia, Nº. X. p. 266.
c id. ib.
d Bar Vol. II. p. 158. b.

e Ex compoti lacerati ecclefiæ S. Petri de Burgo, in Bib. Cott. Vefp. A. XXIV. fol. 2. b.

‘ Mending

	l.	*s.*	*d.*
' Mending the books ————————————————	00	00	10
' For hanging the napary & towel ——————————	00	00	05
' Leather for the bell-ropes ————————————	00	00	02
' Victuals for Richard [the] carver & brother Rowsby ——	00	00	05
' Given to a certain carpenter, a carver, to inspect the rood-loft	00	00	06
[*Solut. vigario*] of John Whitside —————————	00	00	09
' Paid Thomas [the] glazier for mending the church-windows	00	05	00
' Paid John [the] roper for a bell-rope —————————	00	00	11
' Paid him for another rope—————————————	00	00	10
' Thred bought for the vestments ——————————	00	00	01
' Paid Agnes Yonge & others ————————————	00	00	10
' Paid Thomas Basse for a bawdryck ————————	00	00	06
' Paid Richard [the] carver ———————————————	01	10	00
' For a little bow for a bell ————————————	00	00	04
' Wax for the common light ————————————	00	04	00

Total 03 12 10

The two torches above were great wax candles, as I take it, made
to carry in procession, or to set on the high altar, or before the
rood, or some other image. The shaft, or spire, was an ornament
made to adorn the image, or shrine, of some saint. The mony given
the players, I guefs, was paid the wardens of the crafts or trades,
who, every year, acted the play of *corpus Christi* upon *corpus Christi*
day in the north-chancel of this church, called *corpus Christi* chapel;
or elsewhere in the town. In the Cotton library is a book entitled,
' ª *ludus corporis Christi; hoc est, dramata sacra, in quibus exhiben-*
' *tur historie veteris & novi testamenti, introductis quasi in scenam*
' *personis illic memoratis, quas secum invicem colloquentes pro ingenio*
' *fingit poeta.* The play of *corpus Christi;* that is, sacred representa-
' tions, wherein are exhibited the histories of the old & new testa-
' ment, the perfons therein mentioned being as it were brought up-
' on the stage, whom the poet, according to his fancy, introduces
' talking to one another.' One of these plays, presenting the fall of
man, may be seen in Mr. Stevens's first additional volume to the Monasticon ᵇ; to which they who have the curiosity to see what sort
of performances these were, may please to turn. Besides plays, there
were alfo solemn procesfions, upon the feast of *corpus Christi.* This
custom of procesfions upon *corpus Christi* day, as I take it, was brought
hither from Durham. My reafons are, I. In Mr. *Davies antient rites
& monuments of the church of Durham,* we read, ' ᶜ there was
' a goodly procesfion there, on the Thursday after Trinity Sunday,
' in honor of *corpus Christi* day, which was a principal feast.
' At that time the bayliff of the town did stand in the Tolbooth,
' & call all the occupations that were inhabitants within the

a Sub imagine Vesp. **D. VIII.**   b p. 138.   c p. 64.

' town,'

' town, every occupation in its degree, to bring forth their banners,
' with all their lights appertaining to their several banners, & to re-
' pair to the abbey church door. Every banner did stand arow in its
' degree from the abbey church door on the west side of the way, &
' on the east side all the torches pertaining to the said banners. There
' was also a goodly shrine in S. Nicholas church appointed to be car-
' ried the said day in procession, called *corpus Christi* shrine, all fine-
' ly gilt, & a goodly thing to behold; & on the height of the said
' shrine was a foursquare box of christal, wherein was inclosed the
' holy Sacrament of the altar. And it was carried the said day by
' four priests up to the palace green, the whole processions of all the
' churches in the said town going before it. And when it was come
' a little space within Windisholl-gate, it did stand still. Then was
' S. Cuthberts banner brought forth, with two goodly fair crosses to
' meet it; & the prior & convent, with the whole company of the
' choir, all in their best copes did meet the said shrine, falling down
' on their knees, & praying. The prior did fetch it, & then carry-
' ing it forward to the abbey church, the prior & convent with all
' the choir following it, it was set in the choir, & solemn service done
' before it, & *Te Deum* solemnly sung, & played on the organs, every
' man praising God. And all the banners of the occupations did fol-
' low the said shrine into the church, going round about S. Cuthberts
' feretory; their torches being lighted, & burning all the service time.
' Then was it carried thence, with the said procession of the town,
' back to the place whence it came, all the banners of the occupa-
' pations following it. And they set it again in the church; after
' which all having made their prayers to God, & being departed, the
' said shrine was carried into the revestry, where it remained till that
' time twelvemonth.' And such was the custom of Durham. II. That
we had much the same sort of processions on *corpus Christi* day at
Stanford, may be gathered from divers passages in the last will & testament of William Bruges esq; garter king at arms; inserted 28. H. 6.
below: by which will it appears that the parishioners of S. Maries by
Stanford bridge had a treasury, wherein were preserved divers jewels
& vestments appointed to be used on that occasion. Now III. that
these processions were introduced here from Durham seems probable, if we consider the many religious sent thence to S. Leonards
priory without Stanford, & to the two parishes of S. Maries within
Stanford; all, as hath been shewn, in the patronage of the prior & convent of Durham. Besides, this very church of S. Mary by the bridge,
stands in that part of Stanford antiently called S. Cuthberts fee. But,
be that as it will, this account of the procession at Durham, serves
well to illustrate that at Stanford. More of these processions below [a].
After these processions were over, the next thing, as I take it, was a

a anno 28. H. 6. infra.

                                           feast

feaſt held by the alderman & brethren of *corpus Chriſti* gild, in their gild hall yet ſtanding in the Monday mercat ſtreet.   That done, the plays, before ſpoken of, were exhibited to the populace.   I find alſo, that ' [a] before the ſuppreſſion of monaſteries, the city of Coventry ' was likewiſe very famous for the pageants that were played there ' on *corpus Chriſti* day, which occaſioning a very great concourſe of ' people to reſort to it from far & near, was of no ſmall benefit ' thereto ; which pageants being acted with mighty ſtate by the Fran- ' ciſcan friers, had theaters for the ſeveral ſcenes, very large & high, ' placed upon wheels, & drawn to all eminent parts of the city, for ' better advantage of the ſpectators.   Alſo the MS. abovementioned ' was called the play of *corpus Chriſti*, or *Coventry ſhew*, &c.'   Theſe plays exhibited on *corpus Chriſti* day at Stanford, by reaſon of the wars between the houſes of York & Lancaſter, wherein this town ſuf- fred greatly, were left off in the latter part of this kings reign, & the beſt part of his ſucceſſors ; but revived again 22. Edw. 4.   The ca- nopy mentioned in the above account was a common ſtate, ſet up, in theſe times, in all churches over the high altar ; under which in a pix, or little box of gold, ſilver, ivory, or chryſtal, hung the conſecrated hoſt, reſerved there to be carried to the ſick upon any emergency ; when it was taken down, & with the canopy over it, born by the clergy in proceſſion to the houſes of ſuch inhabitants as were dying, as they thought, & called for that ſacred *viaticum*.   By the above account it ſhould ſeem that many of the common ſort of people had, as yet, no ſirnames, but were rather known by the names of their ſeveral trades, as Richard the Carver, Thomas the Glaſier, John the Roper, &c. Brother Rowsby abovementioned was not a frier, but a ſecular prieſt. He attended the carver, as it ſhould ſeem, to overſee & direct him whilſt he was deſigning ſome new image or piece of ſculpture for the farther ornament of the church ; & therefore the church-warden ſpent 5 [d]. upon them ; money enough, in theſe days, to entertain any two men either at dinner or ſupper.   This William Rowceby made a ſtrange will, & died the 5. E. 4. being then parſon of S. Cle- ments.   The rood loft, inſpected, as above, by the carver ; was a gal- lery, in popiſh times, ſituate in every church between the nave & chan- cel.   It was called the rood-loft, from a great rood, or image of the crucifixion ſet up in the midſt of it ; beſides which, there were two other images, a Mary & a John (as the common people then called them) ſtanding by it, that of the bleſſed Virgin on the right, that of the beloved diſciple on the left, hand ſide of the rood.   In the ſame place was likewiſe a figure of the particular St. to whom the church was dedicated.   All theſe had generally a veil, or curtain, let down before them when ſervice was done ; but in ſervice time were lighted up with lamps & wax tapers.   In thoſe days men were fond of ſuch

[a] Addit. to the Monaſt. Vol. I. p 138, 139.

pageantries, but I now mention them, that my readers may better understand what I treat of.

7. H. 6. V. Alderman 1428. Robert Bendbow. Roll. Alderman 1429.
8. H. 6. Thomas Baffet. Roll. ' John Brygge, parfon of S. Clements, gave to
' Laurence Cheyne, &c. fix meffuages & twelve acres of arable land,
' as they lie in the town & fields of Staunford, as well in the abbat
' of Burgs liberty, as in the demefne of Edward late D. of York. B. H.
This Laurence Cheyne, or fome predeceffor of his, I reckon gave
name to Cheyne lane in Stanford. ' ᵃ In 1430. fines were levied be-
' tween Thomas Baffet of Staunford, John Chenercourt, & Margaret
' his wife complainants, & John Vowe of Whitwel defendant, of a
' meffuage & lands in S. Georges parifh in Staunford, the right of John
9. H. 6. ' Chenercourt.' Alderman 1430. Thomas Spycer. Roll. ' ᵇ The
' king intending to pafs over into France, to receive the diadem there-
' of: the conftablefhip of England, was, before his departure, affign-
' ed by patent, for tearme of life, to Richard D. of York [lord of
Stanford] ' which gave him a further feeling of greatneffe, & fecret-
' ly whetted his ambitious appetite upon this occafion. One John Up-
' ton of Feverfham in Kent notarie, accufed John Downe of the fame
' place gent. that he & his complices did imagine the kings death at
' his coronation. The combat was graunted, & in Smithfield [the D.
of York exercifing the office of high conftable] ' they fought in lifts.
' In the end the kings name was ufed to part & forgive them. It is
' a vice to fufpect too farre. The D. of Yorke, a moft fubtle man,
' feems never, in heart, to have been a true fubject to K. Henry ; yet
' no man faith, he was any author in this. Dugdale fays ᶜ, Richard
' D. of York was made conftable of England in the 8. H. 6. in the
' abfence of John D. of Bedford.' But he takes no notice it was for
term of life, & I believe is miftaken in the year. Stow feems to reconcile all this. ' ᵈ Richard D. of York was [firft] conftituted confta-
' ble of England in abfence of John D. of Bedford, regent of France,
' becaufe of a battel to be fought betweene Upton & Downe. He
' was [afterwards] confirmed conftable of England for terme of life,
' fo that he did no waies derogate John D of Bedford, that was be-
' yond the fea : [this confirmation was] dated the 20. of January 1430.
20. Jan. ' The 24. of January a battel was done in Smithfield, between Up-
1430. ' ton & Down. ᵉ Philippa [relict of Edward late D. of York, & now
wife of Robert Fitzwalter] ' by the title of dutchefs of York, & lady
' of the ifle of Wiht, declared her teftament at the caftle of Cares-
Mar. 11. ' broke, upon S. Gregories day [Mar. 11.] in 143⁷. 9. H. 6. whereby
' fhe bequeathed her body to be buried in the abby at Weftminfter,
' appointing, that, at every place where it fhould reft in the way thi-
' ther, her exequies fhould be performed with *dirige* over night, &,

a Ex collect. MS. Petri le Neve arm. c Bar. Vol. II. p. 158. b.
 Norroy regis armorum.   d p. 609.
  b Speed, p. 835. b.   e Bar. ut fupra, p. 157. b.

                      ' before

' before the removal thereof in the morning, a mass of *requiem*. Also,
' that being brought to Westminster, 24 poor men, cloathed in short
' gowns, with hoods of black, should each of them bear a torch, at
' the *dirige*, & at the mass of *requiem*, on the morrow; & each of
' them to have 20 d. in mony. Moreover, that her herse should be
' totally covered with black cloth, & a curious herse of wax, in a small
' proportion, placed upon it. And that upon the day of her funeral,
' six marks & forty pence should be distributed amongst a M. poor
' people; so that each might have a penny. She likewise ordained
' that a thousand *diriges* should be sung for her, upon one day; &
' the morrow after a thousand masses; & this to be done with all pos-
' sible speed that might be, after her decease, for the health of her
' soul, & all christian souls; for the performance whereof every priest
' to have four pence. She likewise bequeathed 20 l. to buy russet
' cloth, for c. poor men & women; each of them a short gown &
' hood. Also to two honest priests to sing mass, & to say the tren-
' tal of Gregorie, by the space of one whole year for her soul & all
' christian souls; & to 80 bedreyden men & women, 13 l. 6. s. 8 d.
' And departed this life shortly after.' Accordingly she was buried
in St. Nicholas chapel in Westminster abbey, where, ' [a] as you come
' out of that chapel, you may still perceive the remnants of an an-
' tient tomb, of free-stone, much decayed by age. Upon it is a sta-
' tue at full length, in a cumbent posture, of a lady in her robes,
' under a canopy of wood only, but curiously painted with azure,
' with stars of gold, & our Saviour on the cross, resting upon pil-
' lars of wainscoat, most excellently carved with spires, & coats of
' arms depicted thereon.——John Everard of Staunford capellan gave to
' W. Morewod, one messuage with a curtilage situate in Wollrowe
' between a tenement of John Browns draper cast; & . . . . . . of Tyn-
' wel west, & abutting on the kings highway south. B. H.   [b] April   Ap. 27.
' 27. the D. of York with the king took shipping at Dover, & landed
' the same day at Calcis.

VI. ' Alderman, 1431. John Long. Roll.   [c] In November Richard   10. H. 6.
' D. of York [& lord of Stanford] being at Roan with the king, went   Nov.
' thence with him to Pontoyse, & so to S. Denyse, to the intent for
' the king to make his entrie into Paris, there to be sacred.' After
their return from the coronation ' [d] a great counsaile was kept in
' the castel of Roane, where many doubts were moved, but few
' weightie things out of hand concluded.   [e] The D. of York [lord of
Stanford] ' & some others would have had large supplies of men &
' treasure levied, that K. Charles might no where have any rest. But
' this counsell was not followed, but another, in shew more frugal,
' which fed the evils, & redressed none. Present sparings do often-

a Ant. S. Peters West. by J. C. 8°. Lond.   c Hol. p. 1247. a.
1711. p. 69.   d id. p. 1249. b.
   b Stow, p. 609.   e Speed, p. 837. b.

' times

' times draw after them infinite waftes, & no husbandry proves fo ill
' as unfeafonable parfimonie.' However, ' ᵃ the French having reco-
' vered divers places in that realm, fo that there being little hope of
' better doings; it was refolved to defend Normandy, for the more
' fafegard of that province; & thought fit, that the faid D. of York
' fhould be fent to fecure the fea coafts; others being imployed to
1432. ' keep the garrifons.' Now flourifhed Nicholas Kenton. ' Nicholas
' Kenton, faith Leland ᵇ, belonged to the monaftery of the Carmelites
' at Stanford [was warden, I guefs, of that houfe] ' but ftudied divi-
' nity at Cambridge, where he was prefented with the degrees & other
' honors of that faculty. He was a man, faith Pits ᵇ, perfectly inftruct-
' ed in all kinds of learning & virtue, well acquainted with rhetoric
' & poetry, a fmart philofopher, & a celebrated divine. So eloquent,
' fays Bale ᵇ, that he frequently ufed to pray *extempore*, & that ele-
' gantly, & much longer, than was cuftomary in the age he lived.
' However in his epiftles he wrote many things, to Facius the provin-
' cial general, againft the new reform of his order, which he heard
' was attempted by Thomas Rhedon at Mantua about the year of our
' Lord 1432. which Thomas was afterwards burnt by Pope Eugenius
' the 4.' Bale here, & in what I fhall hereafter add from him, feems
to lay the burning of Rhedon upon Kentons writing againft him.

11. H. 6.   VII. Alderman 1432. John Page. Roll. ' ᶜ Though the inquifiti-
' ons after the death of Anne widow of Edmund E. of March, were
' not yet returned into Chancery; by the kings fpecial favour, Ri-
' chard D. of York [lord of Stanford] obtained livery of all the lands
' which fhe held in dower of his inheritance, doing his homage,
' notwithftanding he had not then made proof of his age. In this
' year alfo he had fpecial licenfe to be abfent from Ireland.' Alder-
12. H. 6. man 1433. Richard Lea. Roll. ' ᶜ Upon a great infurrection, made
' by the inhabitants of Normandy, Richard D. of York [lord of Stan-
ford] ' was fent with the D. of Somerfet, for reprefling thereof.'
' Laurence Cheyne efq; gave to Richard Cokke, Richard Lee, & John
' Halyday vicar of All Saints in Staunford mercat, fix meffuages &
' 12 acres of arable land in the town & territory of Staunford, as
' well in the abbat of Burgs liberty, as in the demefne of Edward late
' D. of York in the county of Linc. & Pillefgate in the county of
' Northampton. B. H.' Richard Cokk abovementioned was a Cor-
nyfer: but what trade or office that was I know not. ' Robert Browe
' gave to Richard Wilcoks of Staunford one meffuage in Staunford,
' in the abbat of Burgs liberty, in S. Martins parifh, in a certain ftreet
' called Eft-by-the-water, between a meffuage late Thomas Corbys
' weft, & the kings highway which leads to Burley eaft, & abutting
' on the kings highway north, & upon Martinscroft fouth: which
' meffuage was Agnes Meltons.' About this meffuage fee 14. H. 6.

Bar. Vol. II. p. 158, 159.   b in vita.   c Bar. Vol. II. p. 159. a.

2

below.

below. Alderman 1434. Laurence Melton. Roll.   Now died John 13. H. 6.
Langton, the white frier, who, as I before obferved, was very bufie
at the great council of religion held here in 1392. ' John Langton
' a Carme, faith Leland a, frequented the fchools at Oxford, & hath
' been defervedly reckoned among the top divines.   His common
' queftions were once in requeft, as likewife a little book wherein
' he confutes the heretical depravity of one Crump. b Befides the
' books abovementioned, he wrote another called *actus fuos ordinarios,*
' beginning, *cujuflibet rei creabilis idea.*   Langton, faith Pits c, hav-
' ing a zeal equal to his knowledge, took much pains, both in difput-
' ing with, & writing againft, the heretics of the age he lived in;
' & did much good.   For he ftrenuoufly defended the catholic faith,
' refifted ftoutly, & as happily vanquifhed many erroneous opinions.
' He wrote a hiftory of Englifh affairs, an examen of Henry Crump
' an Irifh heretic, another book of his errors, & fome other pieces.'
Bale fays, he died at London.   But Pits affirms, that ' being fent to
' the council at Bafil, he died, & was buried there, in 1434. d Upon   1434.
' the death of John D. of Bedford, regent of France, Richard D. of
' York [lord of Stanford] was joyned in commiffion with the D. of
' Sommerfet, in the government of that realm. e Sept. 24. 13. H. 6. Sept. 24.
' Henry Beaufort bifhop of Winchefter, & the other truftees of Ed-
' ward late D. of York [& lord of Stanford] articled with William
' Morwood to build the church of Fotheringhay.   The truftees to find
' lime, ftone, fand, timber, ropes, & carriage of them; [& he] to build
' the fame anfwerable to the choir for 300 l. to be paid at different
' times.   The length of the nave to be 80 feet.   The fide ifles to
' be made with windows like the choir; & the weft windows of the
' faid ifles to contain four lights each.   There to be fix buttreffes to
' each ifle: & the fteeple to be 80 feet high, & 20 broad or fquare;'
the height anfwering exactly to the length of the nave.   The hexagonal
tower was added afterwards by K. Edw. the 4. or his father; & is
about 20 feet more, anfwering, I fuppofe, in height to the length of the
choir or chancel, then ftanding. ' W. Morwood of Staunford [the fame,
I fuppofe, who undertook Fotheringhay church] ' gave to Thomas Baffet
' one meffuage fituate in great S. Michaels parifh, between a meffuage
' of the faid Thomas weft, & the lane called Cheyne lane eaft. B. H.

   VIII. Ald. 1435. William Brown. Roll. ' Richard Wilcoks fold 14. H. 6
' a meffuage which he had of Robert Browe, as above 12. H. 6. to
' Nicholas Ward of Staunford baker; & the faid Nicholas Ward fold
' the fame to Thomas Semark efq; & Thomas Gaffale of Withering,
' Wright. B. H. f Richard D. of York [lord of Staunford] was re-
' teined by indenture to ferve the king in his wars of France & Nor-
' mandy, for one whole year, with one baron, one banneret, feven

a Leland; Comment. p. 407.   d Bar. Vol. II. p. 159. a.
b Balæi Vol. II. p. 58.   e Monaft. Ang. Vol. III. p. 162. b.
c p. 624.   f Bar. Vol. II. p. 159. a.

' knights,

' knights, 490 men at arms, & 2200 archers.' Nay he was not only
reteined to ferve in the wars there, but, as Stow & Holingſhed report, appointed regent of France, by the Englifh parliament. For,
fay they, ' ᵃ altho' the D. of Yorke was worthy, both by birth &
' courage, for this honor & preferment, yet hee was fo difdeyned
' of Edmond D. of Sommerſet, being cofen to the king, that by all
' means poffible he fought his hindrance, as one glad of hys loffe, &
' forye for his well doing. By reafon whereof, ere the D. of York
' could get his difpatch, he was conftrayned to linger tyll Paris &
' divers other chief places were gotten by the French. The D. of
' York perceyving his evil will, openly diffembled that which he in-
' wardly minded; & thus eyther of them wrought things to the others
' difpleafure, till at length, by mortal warre, they were both confumed,
' wyth almoft all their whole lynes & offsprings.' The Normans continuing in rebellion, the D. of York (as yet hindred from going againft
them himfelf by his adverfary the D. of Somerfet) ' ᵇ fent the lord
' Scales & others, who fo afflicted thofe rebels, that they flew above
' 5000 perfons, & burnt all the towns & villages in the country.'
But this advantage was nothing in comparifon of what was loft in
other parts. ' ᶜ Nowe according to the old proverb (when the fteede
' is ftoln, fhut the ftable door) the D. of York, appointed at the laft par-
' liament to be regent of France (after Paris, S. Dennis, S. Germains
' & other towns were taken) was fent over into Normandy, with
' 8000 men. There he fet good orders, & did great juftice in the
' country. Howbeit he gat only, by long fiege, the towne & abby of
' Fefcamp, & did none other notable act during the time of his rule.

1ꝼ. H. 6.   IX. Ald. 1436. William Marwood. Roll. [Maſon] ' ᵈ The French
' K. befieged the ftrong town of Monftreau on Fault Yonne, whereof
' Thomas Gerard being capitayne, he fold the fame to him. The D. of
' York [lord of Stanford] about that time was difcharged of his office,
' & the E. of Warwike preferred to the fame. The D. of York would
' have gladly refcued the town, if his authoritie had not furceafed,
' & Warwike could not come in time, for the wind was contrarie.
' John Brown of Staunford, Draper, gave to William Brown his fon,
' all his entire fhop, lately four fhops together, fituate in All Saints
' parifh in the mercat, between a tenement of the D. of Yorks fouth,
' & a tenement of Margaret Sutton north, & abutting on the kings
' highway eaft, & on the way called behyndbak weft. The faid John
' Brown conftituted John Halyday [vicar of All Saints in the mercat]
' his attorney to deliver feifin of the fame to his faid fon: witneffes
' Richard Lee alderman of Staunford, &c. dated on the Tuefday next
' after the feaft of S. Matthias the apoftle, 15. H. 6. B. H.' This William Brown, fon of John, was the perfon, who, in the next reign, erected & moft plentifully endowed, the fair hofpital of S. Mary & All

a Hol. p. 1256. b. Stow, p. 616.   c id. p. 1258. b.
b Hol. ut fupra.   d id. p. 1262. a.

Saints

Saints in Stanford, now called the old beadhoufe. About this time,
by this bequeaft of his fhop, I reckon his father John Brown refigned
his bufinefs to him. Mr. William Brown, as Leland obferves, ' ᵃ was
' a marchant of a very wonderful richeneffe.' And true. He was by
trade a draper, as his father was ; what fpeaks his riches, is the laying of four fhops into one to hold his drapery. Befides, the little ftreet
called Wool-row, was chiefly taken up in ftore-houfes for his wool ;
he being a great dealer in that commodity, & a merchant of the
ftaple of Calice. Alfo his dwelling-houfe (ftanding at the weft end of
his hofpital, & now made two handfome dwellings, inhabited by Mr.
Denfhire & Mr. Wyche) was very fpacious, &, for the age he lived in,
magnificent above the common rank.

   X. Ald. 1437. Richard Lee. Roll.   ' ᵇ On the 6. of November the
' E. of Warwike, paffed the fea, after he had been feven times fhip-
' ped & unfhipped, & came to Roan ; & the D. of York [lord of Stan-
ford] ' returned into England.——John Warner of Brune gave to Wil-
' liam Rolftone of Staunford, one grange fituate in S. Clements parifh
' in the place called Skoftgate, without the north gate ; between a
' grange of the rector of S. Clements eaft, & the end of the town
' weft ; & abutting on the kings highway north, & a croft of Robert
' Burtons fouth. See 17. H. 6. below. B. H.' Alder. 1438. Laurence
Melton. Roll. ' ᶜ Mr. John Chenecourt, by his deed bearing date
' June 14. 17. H. 6. granted to William Gydding, Richard Lee, &
' John Briggs clerc, one meffuage, with the appurtenances, lying in S.
' Peters parifh, between an houfe of the gild of the bleffed Virgin
' Mary eaft, another of Simon Sclaters weft, the kings highway north,
' & another houfe of the forefaid Gild fouth ; to hold to them &
' their heirs for ever to the ufe of his will.——William Rolleftone of
' Staunford gave the grange abovementioned, which he had of John
' Warner the 16. H. 6. to William Brown, marchant. B. H.   Richard
' Barker, alias Tyler, of Burley, conftituted W. Ledys of Staunford
' taylor, his attorney, to deliver to John Smith of Burley *literatus*,
' full feifin of & in a tenement in Hyegate, in S. Martins parifh. B. H.'
A deed of this year mentions, ' an acre of arable land, having the
' land of the holy nuns eaft, & forty perches of land called litle-dale
' weft, & abutting on Empyngham way north, & Tynwel heath fouth ;
' which acre lies at Tynwel gallows. Alfo a place called Kings-rife
' in Stanford field, is mentioned in a deed of the fame date. B. H.'
By the name of Tynwell gallows in the firft of thefe fragments, it
looks as if the feffions for Rutland being now held at Bredcroft by
Stanford (as Mr. Leland tells us, they were in his time) execution
was done upon fuch malefactors as were condemned there at Tynwell
gallows. Mr. Leland, fpeaking of thefe things, writes thus. ' ᵈ Marke

16. H. 6.
Nov. 6.

17. H. 6.

June 14.

a Itin. Vol. VI. p. 29.
b Stow, p. 629.
c Ex autographo penes gardianos ecclefiæ
omnium SS. in foro, 1724.
d Itin. Vol. VI. p. 29.

' here,

' here, that in this [weſt] ſuburbe [of Stanford] is a parcelle of ground
' caullid Bredecroft, becauſe that bakers ſold there brede in that part
' of the ſuburbe; whither yett [temp. H. 8.] is recurſe oute of Ruthe-
' landſhire, & ther their ſeſſions be kept.   So that the ſhire ground
' of Rutheland cummith to this ſuburbe of Staunforde toune.'   Mr.
Leland might have added, that a good part of Stanford is in Rutland;
for, as I have ſhewed above, from the book of Doomsday, at the time
of the making of that ſurvey, S. Peters church in Stanford belonged
to the ſoke of Hameldun, & conſequently S. Peters pariſh at leaſt, if
not more of Stanford town, is in Rutland.   Mr. Leland adds, ' ᵃ the
' ſhire of Rutheland lyeth in a roundel, & lyeth partly upon Wiland
' water, from Staunford to the very bridge of Rockingham.'   The veſtigia of Bredcroft ſeſſions houſe, which tradition calls Bredcroft-hall,
may be traced about two furlongs before you come to the Waſh, acroſs
& cloſe by the northern bank of the new river.   And theſe veſtigia
I have reaſon to think were what Mr. Parry (whom I accidentally met
with, ſince the firſt book of theſe collections were printed off) took for
an encampment.

XI. Ald. 1439. William Morwode. Roll.   [Maſon] After the
death of the E. of Warwike, the D. of York, lord of Stanford, was
conſtituted lieutenant, & captain general for all France & Normandy.
July 2. ' ᵇ The letters patent for his reſuming the regency are dated July the
1440. ' 2ᵈ. 1440. at Weſtminſter.—John Smyth capellan gave to William
' Brown one meſſuage, ſituate in the ſtreet called Hyegate, &c. Witneſ-
' ſes, Richard Lee Ald. of Stanford, &c.   Given Mar. 29. 18. H. 6.
' B. H.' This John Smyth was the ſame with the next mentioned, John
Burley.   ' John Burley, vicar of Wotton by Wodeſtoke in Oxfordſhire,
' gave a tenement in Heygate, between a tenement of the nuns of
' S. Michael ſouth, & a tenement of John Young north, & abutting
' on the kings highway weſt, & on Martinscroft eaſt, to Robert
' Browe, &c. Witneſſes, Jo. Bolde major of Wodeſtoke, John Bryd
' valet of the crown, &c. B. H.'   This John Burley is the ſame, who
17. H. 6. above is called John Smyth of Burley *literatus.*   In
Apr. 7. ' an Engliſh deed, dated April 7. 18. H. 6. this John Smyth is called
18. H. 6. ' Syr John Smyth preeſt of Burley.   And John Brid abovementi-
' oned, parker or yeoman of the crown. B. H.   Richarde Cokke of
' Staunford dimiſed to farm to Richard Blogwyn, one tenement,
' with two ſhops annexed, ſituate in S. Maries pariſh by the bridge,
' called the aungel of the hope, & one grange with a garden in Corn-
' ſtal, for the yearly rent of viij. marcs.'   See the 33. H. 6. below.
B. H.   This tenement is now 1726. the Angel inne, & belongs to
May 15. Browns hoſpital, as doth the garden in Cornſtall.   ' ᶜ Upon the 15.
' May the D. of York [lord of Stanford] ſhipped at Portſmouth, &
' ſailed to Normandy.   ᵈ At his landing, the D. receyved advertiſe-
' ment of the ſiege of Pontoiſe by the French king.   Whereupon

a Itin. Vol. I. p. 19.   c Stow, p. 622.
b Aɛta regia, Nᵒ. X. p. 282.   d Hol. p. 1264, 1265.

4   ' he

' he came neer to that towne, & fent word to the French king, that
' thither he was come to give him battel, if he would come out of
' his baftiles.   But the king, by advice of his counfel, determined
' not to venture his perfon with men of fo bafe degree; but to keep
' his ground : bidding the lord regent to enter at his perill.   The D. per-
' ceyving the French king minded not to fight, purpofed to paffe over
' the river, to fight with him in his lodging.'   But when the D. was
got over, the French withdrew in the night.   ' ª Then the D. with
' his power entred the towne, & fent for new victual, & repaired the
' bulwarks.   And left behind a thoufand foldiers; &, intending once
' again to offer battel, removed to Poyffy, where he fet himfelf in
' order to fight.   But the French durft not encounter with the Eng-
' lifh power.   So the D. diflodged from Poyffi, & came to Maunte,
' & foone after to Roane.   ᵇ The third day after the duke's depar-
' ture, the French king fo fyerfly affailed Pontoyfe that he wan it by
' ftrength.

 XII. Ald. 1440. Richard Lee. Roll.   ' William Brown gave to John   19. H. 6.
' Brown the elder, one meffuage fituate in All Saints parifh in the
' mercat, between a tenement of the faid William Brown, late John
' Smiths fouth, & the vicarage of the fame church north, & abutting
' on the town-wall eaft, & the kings highway weft: which meffuage
' was W. Welden & W. Kelbys. B. H.'   Ald. 1441. Robert Brown,   20. H. 6.
glover. Roll.   ' ᶜ In the beginning of thys twentieth yeere, Richard
D. of York [lord of Stanford] yet regent of France & governour of
' Normandy, determined to invade the territories of his enimys, both
' by fundrye armyes, & in feveral places.   ᵈ Whereupon having an
' affignation of 20000 l. a year, for the defence of thofe parts, ᵉ he
' fent the lord Willoughby to deftroy the country of Amiens, lord
' Talbot to befiege Diepe, & himfelf fet forward into Anjow; and
' there deftroyed townes, & fpoiled the people, & with great prayes
' & prifoners returned into Normandy.—John Lyndefy clerc, gave to
' Robert Clerc & Ifabell his wife, a certaine toft, with a dovecoat in
' the fame, fituate in Bradecroft in S. Peters parifh, with a certain piece
' of meadow beneath the toft aforefaid, as it lies between the way
' wherein you go from Staunford to Broding, & a certain mill of
' Richard duke of York commonly called Bradecroft mills, &c. which
' toft, &c. was John Jakes's.   Witneffes, Robert Brown alderman of
' Staunford, &c.   Given at Staunford the Monday next after the
' feaft of the Nativity. 20. H. 6. B. H.   Robert Clerk & Ifabell his wife
' fold the premifes laft mentioned to John Chenercourt, John Bryg,
' Henry Burlee, Richard Lee, & Richard Cokk.   Witneffes, Robert
' Brown Ald. &c.   Given at Staunford on Saturday the morrow of
' the purification. 20. H. 6.   ᶠ Edward fon of Richard D. of York

a Hol. p. 1264, 1265.   d Bar. Vol. II. p. 159. a.
b Fabian, p. 437. a. b.   e Stow, p. 629.
c Hol. p. 1266. a.   f Hol. p. 1268. b.

Apr. 29. [lord of Stanford] ' was borne this yeare the 29. of April at Roan.'
This Edward was afterwards king by the name of Edward the fourth,
& a great friend to the town of Stanford. Mr. John Brown of Stanford, merchant of the staple of Calis, died July 26. 1442. & was buried at the upper end of the north isle of All Saints church in the
mercat. This we learn from an inscription on a plate of gilded brass
yet remaining, on the north wall; there affixed, in memory of the said
Mr. John Brown & his wife Margery, who died not till Nov. 22.
39. H. 6. under which year see the said inscription at large.

21. H. 6. 　XIII. Ald. 1442. William Storton. Roll. ' The deed whereby
' Robert Clerk & Isabell his wife, as above Feb. 3. 20 H. 6. sold
' John Chenercourt, John Bryg, Henry Burlee, Richard Lee, & Ri-
' chard Cokk, a certain toft with a dovecoat in Bradecroft, was en-
' rolled in the castle of Staunford upon the Tuesday next after the
' feast of S. Valentine this 21. H. 6. & there was paid 8ᵈ. in the court
15. Mar. ' for so doing. B. H.' Sir John Smyth of Burley, vicar of Wodestoke
144$\frac{2}{3}$. by Oxford, being troubled, in mind about a forgery of his, in pretending to sell an house at Stanford (which he had no right in) to Wil-
liam Lewys of Okeham, who thereupon sued the true owner William
Ledes of Stanford & put him to great trouble to make out his right;
came now before the chancellor of Oxfords commissary, & made open
confession of the juggle, & of the true right of William Ledes, earnestly desiring the said commissary to set forth & attest his said confession under the seal of his office for satisfaction of all men: which
he accordingly did as follows. ' ᵃ To all the faithful of Christ unto
' whom the present letters shall come, William Westkarre D. D. (of
' the venerable master master Henry Severe, also D. D. & chancellor
' of Oxford, commissary general in the said university) health in him
' who is the true health of all. For as much as the only begotten
' son of God, going forth from the highest heaven & descending
' to the lowest parts of the earth, hath offered witness to the truth,
' leaving us an example, in like manner, to afford testimony to the
' same; Hence we, upon the just desire & public confession of Syr
' John Smyth capellan, being desirous to certifie all whom it con-
' cerns, by these our letters do attest, that the said John Smyth ca-
' pellan, stirred, as he asserteth, by his own conscience, hath freely
' presented himself before us, by reason of a certain plea depending
' between William Lewys of Okeham demandant, & William Ledys
' of

ᵃ Universis Christi fidelibus, ad quos pre-
sentes litere pervenerint, Wilelmus Westkarre sacre theologie doctor, & venerabilis
domini magistri Henrici Seuere, sacre etiam
theologie doctoris, cancellarii universitatis
Oxon. commissarius in dicta universitate ge-
neralis, salutem in eo qui est omnium vera
salus. Quia unigenitus Dei filius egressus de
summo celo ad ima mundi descendens, testimonium veritati perhibuit, nobis relinquens

exemplum testimonium veritati consimili-
ter perhibere; hinc nos, super justam roga-
tionem & publicam confessionem domini
Johannis Smyth capellani, omnes quorum
interest certioare volentes, has nostras per literas attestamur, quod dictus Johannes Smyth
capellanus, ex conscientia sua motus, ut as-
seruit, obtulit se libere coram nobis, ob
quoddam placitum pendens inter Willielmum Lewys de Okham demandantem, &
Willielmum

' of Stanford occupier, touching one meſſuage with its appurtenances
' ſituate in the liberty of the abbat of Burg in Stanford aforeſaid, &
' openly confeſſed the meſſuage to be the right & free tenement of
' the forenamed William Ledys; & that he John Smyth never had
' right, title, or claim in the foreſaid meſſuage; & ſaith, the grant
' which he hath made to the foreſaid William Lewys of the meſſuage
' aforeſaid, by the charter & letter of attorney, which he contrived &
' ſealed with his own hand, to be altogether unjuſt, & by law inva-
' lid; alſo that on that occaſion, as he ſaith, the foreſaid William
' Lewys to have unjuſtly troubled the ſaid William Ledes.   In wit-
' neſs whereof, that this matter may manifeſtly appear to all men,
' at the inſtance & requeſt of the forenamed John Smyth capel-
' lan, we have cauſed theſe letters teſtimonial to be made patents, &
' ſealed with the ſeal of the office of the chancellorſhip of the uni-
' verſity of Oxford.   Given at Oxford, the 15. day of March, 1442.'
' The ſame year John Geffron & John Herby gave to Richard Blogwin
' of Staunford one meſſuage that was W. Knights, ſituate in great S.
' Michaels pariſh in the ſtreet called Colgate, between a tenement of
' Henry Sharps husbandman weſt, & the lane called Silverſtreet eaſt,
' & abutting on the kings highway ſouth, & on a tenement of the
' foreſaid Henry north.   Alſo one ſhop with a loft, &c. ſituate in All
' Saints pariſh, between a ſhop of John Brown ſouth, & the kings
' high-way north; abutting on a ſhop of lord Richard D. of York
' eaſt, & on the way called by-hind-bak weſt.   Dated 20. Mar. 21. H. 6.
' Richard Blogwin aforeſaid, by his deed bearing date the 1. day of
' May, the ſame year, ſold all the ſaid premiſes to Ralph lord Crum- May 1.
' well, Thomas Palmer, & W. Armſtone. B. H.   [a] Richard D. of York
[lord of Stanford] ' in this 21. H. 6. doing his homage (as ſon & heir
' to Anne, one of the daughters & heirs to Alianore, eldeſt ſiſter &
' coheir to Edmund, brother & heir to Thomas E. of Kent) had livery
' of his purparty of the lands of that inheritance.   The ſame year
' alſo he was employed with John E. of Shrewsbury & others, as
' embaſſador to treat of peace with the French.'   Now flouriſhed John
Upton.   ' John Upton, miſtakenly called by ſome foreigners Upſon,
' as Pits relates [b], was a Lincolnſhire man, a Carmelite in the mona-
' ſtery of that order at Stanford, D. D. of Oxford, & afterwards a

Willielmum Ledes de Stanford tenentem,
de uno meſſuagio cum ſuis pertinentiis, ſi-
tuato infra libertatem abbatis de Burgo S.
Petri, in Stanford predicta, & manifeſte con-
feſſus eſt, dictum meſſuagium eſſe jus & liberum tenementum prefati Willielmi Ledes;
& quod ipſe Johannes Smyth nunquam habuit jus, titulum, ſeu clameum in predicto
meſſuagio.   Et dicit, conceſſionem illam,
quam ipſe predicto Willielmo Lewys fecit
de meſſuagio predicto, per cartam & literam
attornati quas contrivit, & manu propria ſi-
gillavit, fore penitus injuſtam & de jure in-
validam; ac, ea occaſione, ut dicit, predictum Willielmum Lewys dictum Willielmum Ledes injuſte vexaſſe.   In cujus rei
teſt. ut hec materia omnibus manifeſte cla-
reat, has literas teſtimoniales, ad inſtanciam
& rogacionem prefati Johannis Smyth capellani, fieri fecimus patentes, ſigillo officii can-
cellariatus univerſitatis Oxon. ſigillatas.   Datum Oxonie, quintodecimo Die Marcii,
anno domini milleſimo, quadringenteſimo,
quadrageſimo ſecundo, & anno regni regis
Henrici ſexti poſt conqueſtum viceſimo primo.   Ex autographo penes me.
   a Bar. Vol. II. p. 159. a.
   b in vita.

                              ' London

' London preacher; where, as Bale obferves [a], for his fine fermons, he,
' (as alfo Pits continues [a],) at length became chaplain to the moft illu-
' ftrious Thomas duke of Clarence, by whom he was greatly efteem-
' ed, & made his ghoftly father. He is faid to have wrote many things,
' but I find only the title of one vol. of fermons. He died at Coven-
' try, in 1442.

22. H. 6.   XIV. Alderman 1443. Thomas Bulkfay. Roll. This family wrote
themfelves afterwards, Balguy. ' [b] Notwithftanding the impatience
' which the court of England difcovered for peace, the war was car-
' ried on during the years 1442. & 1443. under the conduct of the
' D. of York [lord of Stanford] regent in France for K. Hen. 6. The
' duke was a man of wifdom & valour, & fo throughly underftood
' the nature of the war, that if he had been but duly fupported, he
' would have given the French K. Charles a world of trouble : but,
' for the reafons already mentioned, he received very fmall affiftance
' from England.' In 1444. the Carmes, or white friers, held a general chapter, of their order, in S. Maries college at Stanford, where Nicholas Kenton was elected provincial of the Englifh brethren, by a
general fuffrage. ' Kenyngale the late provincial, faith Bale [c], refign-
' ing, as being called to higher imployments [being, as Leland tells us [d],
made the popes legate in caufes ecclefiaftical] ' the fathers of the or-
' der affembling in a council which they held in 1444. at Stanford,
' Nicholas Kenton, no ordinary doctor of Cambridge, was elected the
' 25. prefident of the Englifh fraternity. This was a man excellent-
' ly learned, being a divine, an orator, & an efpecial poet. In this of-
' fice, as Pits adds [d], he prefided 12 years. When he was provincial,
' as the fame author acquaints us, & vifited the monafteries of his
' order, one Edward Dinley a Carmelite of New-caftle, & a cele-
' brated preacher, was fo much in his favour, that he took him with
' him, & made him preach at feveral places upon that occafion.' Al-

23. H. 3. derman 1444. William Brown. Roll. ' [e] Richard D. of York [lord of
Stanford] ' being again abroad, as regent of France & Normandy, had a
' fpecial difpenfation to be abfent from Ireland.' A truce being taken
with the French, ' [f] during the tyme of the truce, the faid D. of
' York repaired into England, both to vifit his wife & children &
' friends, & alfo to confult what fhould be done, if the truce ended.
' [g] In this 23. of H. 6. Elizabeth relict of the late Richard Grey lord
' Codnovre, enfeoffed John D. of Somerfet & others, in all the lands
' of her inheritance ; to the intent that out of the revenues thereof,
' they fhould difcharge her debts, as alfo her funeral expences at

---

a in vita.

b Acta regia, N°. X p. 288.

c Confentientibus una patribus in fuo con-
cilio, quod Anno Dom. 1444. Stanfordiæ
celebrabant, cedenti ad altiora negotia Ke-
nyngalo, vicefimus quintus in præfecturam
ordinis fubrogatus eft Nicholaus Kentonus
Cantabrigienfis doctor non afpernendus. Fuit
homo ifte apprime eruditus, theologus, rhe-
tor, & poeta infignis. Heliades. MS. Harley.
cap. 47.

d in vita.

e Bar. Vol. II. p. 159. a.

f Hol. p. 1271. a.

g Bar. Vol. I. p. 711. l. penult.

' Aylesford

' Aylesford in Kent, where she appointed her self to be buried by her
' lord & husband; & to find a priest to sing there for the soul of her
' said husband, her self, & children for seven years; & to pay to the
' friers preachers at Stanford, ten pounds sterling, to pray for the
' souls of her self, her husband, & children, &c.' Alderman 1445. 24. H. 3.
John Page. Roll. Robert Wymbyssh having been for some time curator of S. John & St. Thomas's hospital, Richard abbat of Burg now
granted him a more full authority over the same, appointing him master & warden thereof. The commission, as not presenting him to the
diocesan for institution (which was the antient usage of the said abbats
predecessors, patrons of the house) nor yet intimating that he had, at any
time before, been so presented, is very singular : take it therefore in the
abbats own stile. ' ᵃ Richard, by divine permission abbat of Burg, to
' our beloved in Christ Robert Wymbyssh clerc, greeting in the com-
' mon Savior. Having knowledge of your probity & ingenuity of
' manners, we do confer on you the more full wardenship & govern-
' ment of the hospital of the blessed S. John the Baptist, & S. Thomas
' the martyr on Staunford bridge (unto our collation & appointment
' belonging) with all its rights & appurtenances, & do appoint you
' master & warden in the same; so nevertheless, that you keep up &,
' as usual, observe all the charges incumbent for hospitality. Sav-
' ing unto us & our monastery the liberties whatsoever due & ac-
' customed. As also & saved the annual pension to be paid John
' Combe on the 6. of May, during his life, assigned him by us with
' consent & assent of you the said Robert. In witness whereof we
' have caused our seal to be put to the presents. Given at Burg,
' the 14. of Feb. 1445.' It should seem that John Combe abovementioned was the last warden before this Robert Wymbyssh; which
John Combe being very aged, & so rendered incapable to look after
his trust, some mismanagements had happened in the affairs of the
house; whereupon Robert Wymbyssh had been appointed curator to
prevent the like inconveniences for the future, &, he acquitting himself well in that post, the old warden John Combe having a pension
reserved for his maintenance, had been prevailed upon to resign to
him. However, in less than a week after this the said abbat of Burg
granted the next turn of collating to this hospital, to William More,
Ralph Peynton, & Thomas Bysshe; provided that John Combe abovementioned was not dead before the date of his said grant. So that
whether Robert Wymbyssh ever held the wardenship of this hospital
with full power, as the grant before recited enabled him, or whether
he was not preferred to some better post, or dead, or what became of
him, I know not. Nevertheless take here likewise the abbats grant to
William More, &c. to collate upon the next vacancy. ' ᵇ Know all
' men by the presents, that we Richard, by divine permission abbat

---

ᵃ Ex registro dicti abbatis.   ᵇ id. ib.

' of Burg (fufficient deliberation upon this being premifed) have grant-
' ed to the reverend men William More, Ralph Peynton, clercs, &
' Thomas Bufhe, the next collation of the hofpital of the blefled S.
' John Baptift & S. Thomas the martyr on Staunford bridge in the
' diocefe of Lincoln, unto our collation belonging; to have & to hold
' unto the forefaid William, Ralph, & Thomas the collation of the
' faid hofpital for the firft turn of collation next after the date of
' the prefents.   Saving to us & our church of Burg abovefaid all
' things in the fame of old excepted.   So neverthelefs that if it do
' happen that John Combe deceafe (which God forbid) before colla-
' tion by the forefaid perfons, then this grant to be void.   In witnefs
' whereof we have caufed our feal to be put to the prefents.   Given

20. Feb. ' at Burg, the 20. of Feb. 1445.——John Folklyn of Cantebrig & John
1445.   ' Sybely of Staunford, clercs, gave to W. Hanford capellan, one te-
' nement & one acre of arable land, fituate in the town & fields of
' Staunford in the abbat of Burgs liberty; to wit, between a tene-
' ment of the faid abbat weft, & a tenement of John Sapcote (late
' W. Stalehams) eaft, & abutting on the kings highway fouth, & on
' the water of Wylond north; which was Henry Wardes of Staun-
' ford fadyler. B. H.'   This year a parliament was called, & ' ᵃ William
' Burley being fpeaker of the lower houfe, the D. of Somerfet was
' appointed to be regent of Normandy, & the D. of York [lord of
Stanford] ' difcharged of that office.   I have feen in a regifter booke
' belonging fometime to the abbey of S. Albans, fays John Stow ᵇ,
' that the D. of Yorke was eftablifhed regent of France after the de-
' ceafe of the D. of Bedford, to continue five yeres, which being ex-
' pired he returned home, & was joyfully received of the king with
' thanks for his fervice.   And further, that now when a new regent
' was to be chofen & fent over to fafeguard the countreys yet fubject
' to the Englifh, the faid D. of York was eftfoones (as a man moft meet
' to fupplie that roomth) appointed again regent with all his former
' allowances.   But the D. of Somerfet ftill maligning his advance-
' ment, likewife now fo wrought, that the kyng revoked his graunt
' made to the D. of York, & the D. of Somerfet obteyned it for
1446.   ' himfelf.'   Bale having, as I before obferved, laid the burning of
Rhedon of Mantua to the charge of the now provincial of the white
friers Nicholas Kenton; writing againft him, proceeds thus.   ' But Ken-
' ton, as he had ftirred up the coals out of England (to wit, at Rome)
' efcaped not utterly unpunifhed; for in England, Philip Norris &
' many other heretics, as Kenton calls them, about 1446. wrought
' much difturbance to his brethren.   Some alfo forfook their monaf-
' teries, & fome the plague deftroyed; fo that from one thoufand &
' fifty brethren, to his great forrow, they were reduced to fourfcore.

25. H. 6.   XV. Alderman 1446. Richard Lee. Roll.   ' William de Bradecroft

a Hol. p. 1271. a. b.   b Stow, p. 634.

' had

' had a daughter named Margery, who married one Drayton; after
' whose deceafe fhe gave a meadow there to her youngeft fon John
' Drayton, the 25. H. 6. B. H.' But perhaps it was not fo much the
mothers bequeft, as the cuftom of Borough Englifh, which entitled
the youngeft fon to that meadow. ' ᵃ Upon S. Andrews day, the Nov 30.
' D. of York [lord of Stanford] being with the king in S. Stephens
' chapel at Weftminfter, Lodovicus Cordona D. D. prefented the king
' with a golden rofe from the pope, expreffing the property & ap-
' plication of the fame, with the ceremony that is yearly ufed on
' Palme-Sunday, touching the fame rofe. ᵇ In Feb. the D. of Glou-
' cefter was murdered at Bury. Many great lords were drawn on to
' concurre for his ruine, not perceiving, that thereby they pluckt up
' the flood-gate, at which the D. of York entered, overwhelming all
' of them in a deluge of blood. ᶜ This year the faid D. of York [lord
of Stanford] ' obtained licenfe for a market every Wednefday at his
' manor of Beaudley in Worceft. & for a fair there yearly, upon the
' feaft of S. Agatha the virgin.——Mr. William Brown bought of Henry
' Burlee, &c. a toft, dovecoat, & piece of meadow, in Bradecroft.
' Witneffes, Richard Lee, Wright, Ald. of Stanford, &c. Given at
' Staunford 12. June. 25. H. 6. B. H.' Alderman 1447. Laurence 26. H. 6.
Melton, Roll. ' ᵈ Richard D. of York [lord of Stanford] by the er-
' ror of king Henry & the evil ftarres of our countrey, being of him-
' felf a great prince, & growne ftronger by affected popularity ᵉ, per-
' ceiving the king to be a ruler & not to rule, but the whole bur-
' then of the realm to reft in the ordinance of the queen & the D.
' of Suffolk, began fecretly to allure his friends of the nobilitie, &
' privily declared unto them his title unto the crowne, as likewife
' to certain governors of cities & townes; which attempt was fo po-
' litikely handled & fecretly kept, that his provifion was ready before
' his purpofe was opened.' What great towns engaged in this confpiracy on his behalf may be afterwards judged, by obferving which
of them were deftroyed by the Lancaftrians & northern men in their
journey to S. Albans in 1461 whereof our town of Stanford was
one. ' ᶠ Feb. 12. 1448. John Weftgate, clerc, was prefented by Ri- Feb. 12.
' chard lord abbat of Burg to the warden, or mafter-fhip of the hof- 1448.
' pital of S. John Baptift & S. Thomas of Canterbury on Stanford
' bridge.——John Apethorp of Staunford gave to W. Storeton one te-
' nement fituate in great S. Michaels parifh, in the ftreet called Ra-
' con-rowe, between a tenement of the forefaid William Storeton
' fouth, & a tenement of the forefaid John Apethorp north, & abut-
' ting on the common way called Racon-rowe eaft, & on a garden
' of Jo. Byllings weft. B. H. Richard Cokke of Staunford gave to
' W. Armeftone of the fame tyler, one fhop with a loft, &c. & one

a Stow, p. 635.   d Speed, p. 847. a.
b Speed, p. 846. a.   e Stow, p. 636.
c Bar. Vol. II. p. 159. a.   f Ex regiftro dicti abbatis.

ᵍ void

' void place fituate in All Saints parifh in the mercat, between a tene-
' ment late John Browns draper fouth, & a fhop late the fame Johns
' north; & abutting on the way called behyndbak weft, & on the fhop
' which John Sutton late of Staunford took & held of the lord of
' Staunford eaft.   And the faid void place is fituate in the fame ftreet
' called behyndbak, between a tenement late the forefaid John Browns
' north, & a void place of Peter Girdlers fouth, & abutts on a fhop late
' Elizabeth Mercers eaft, & on the ftreet aforefaid called behyndbak
' weft: which were John Palfreymans. B. H.'   A fragment of this year
mentions ' a tenement in S. Mary Bynnewerk parifh, between a tene-
' ment belonging to the chapter of Staunford, fome time John Ape-
' thorpes, eaft; & a garden of Robert Sherman, fometime the fore-
' faid John Apethorps weft, &c. B. H.   In this 26. H. 6. Richard
' D. of York [lord of Staunford] was conftituted lord lieutenant of
' Ireland for ten years. [a] For the peoples diffatisfaction with the
' court being grown to a very great height; they began to talk of the
' right which the D. of York had to the crown as heir male of the
' family of March.   This coming to the ears of the queen & the
' miniftry, they thought fit to fend the D. of York into Ireland, on
27. H. 6. ' pretence of appeafing fome diforders there.'   Alderman, 1448. John
Broun, [Roll.]   ' [b] About this time began a rebellion in Ireland, but
' Richard D. of York [lord of Stanford] being fent thither to appeafe
' the fame, fo affwaged the furie of the wilde & favage people
' there, that he wanne hym fuch favoure amongft them, as could never
28. H. 6. ' be feparated from hym & hys linage.'   Alderman 1449. William
Broun. Roll.   ' [c] The French king now befieged Caen, but did little
' hurt.   Sir Davy Hall as captane of the towne for his mafter the D.
' of York, owner therof, tooke upon him the chief charge.   One day
' a ftone, fhot into the town, fell between the dutchefs of Somerfet
' & her children, who, being amafed with this chance, befought her
' husband [then likewife in Caen] to have compaffion on his fmall
' infants, that they might be delivered out of the towne in fafetie.
' The duke, moved with the forrow of his wife, rendered the town.
' Upon which Sir Davy Hall departed to Cherbrough, & thence to Ire-
' land, to the D. of York his mafter, making relation to him of all
' thefe doings, which thing [& others before related] kindled fo great
' a rancour in the dukes heart, that he never left perfecuting the D. of
' Somerfet 'till he had brought him to his confufion.

Jan. 9.   XVI. ' [d] Jan. 9. 1450. Adam Molins bifhop of Chichefter, keeper
1450. ' of the kings privy feal, thro' procurement of Richard D. of York
[lord of Stanford] ' was, by fhipmen, flaine at Portfmouth.'   About
this time William Bruges efq; firft garter king of arms, rebuilt S.
Georges church, moftly at his own expence, &, as to the fhell, much
in the fame condition we now fee it.   This new church confifts of

a Acta regia, N°. X. p. 298.   c Stow, p. 637.
b Hol. p. 1275. b.   d id. ib.
3

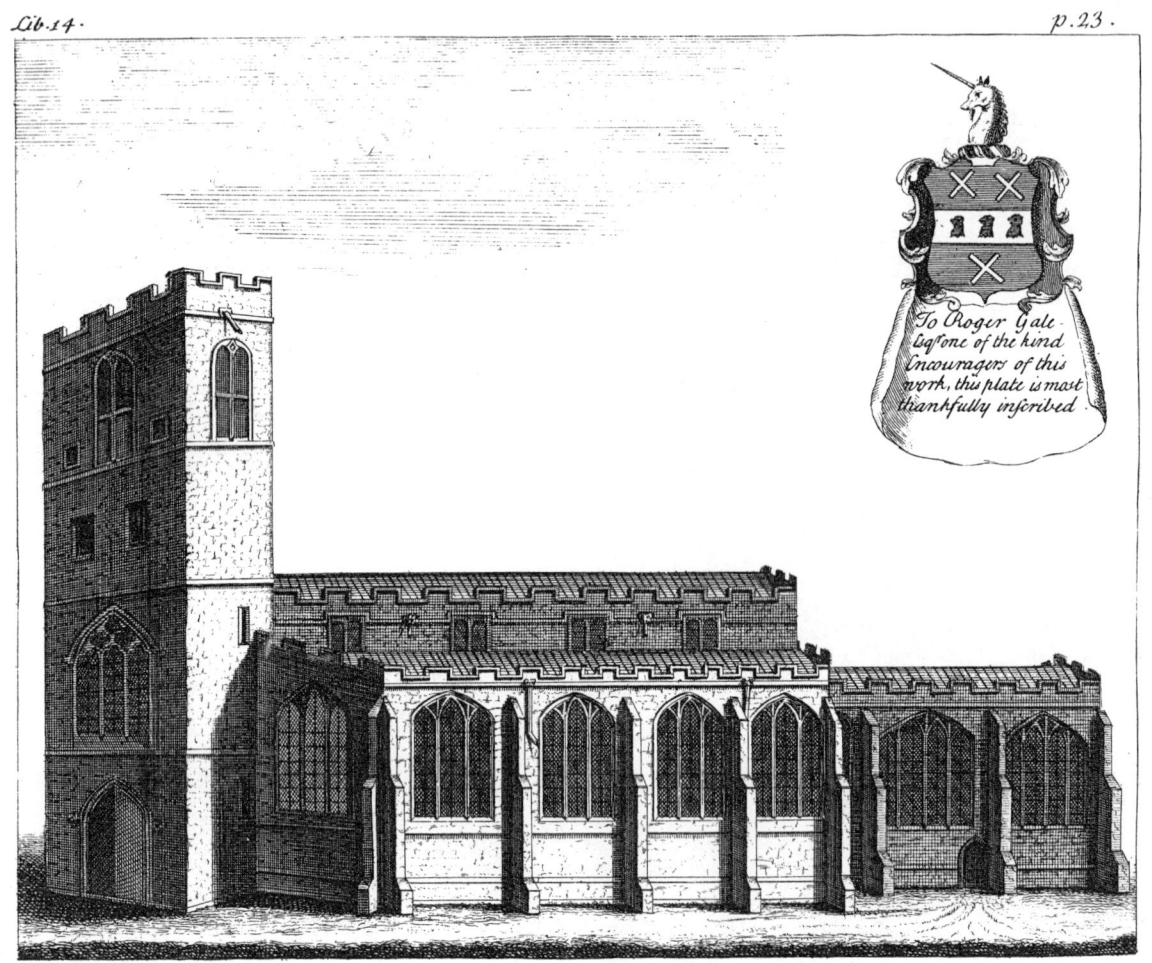

To Roger Gale Esq.re one of the kind Encouragers of this work, this plate is most thankfully inscribed

The South West Prospect of S.t GEORGES CHURCH in Stanford.

three small isles, & a chancel answering the nave or middle isle, all which are leaded. At the west end of the nave is a small tower wherein hang four small bells, all modern. It is a neat little church, & was formerly exceeding rich & full both of antiquities & jewels. The antiquities were, first, the pourtraits of S. George, patron of the garter, with the founder & knights of that order, all delineated, with their proper bearings & surcoats in the choir or chancel windows. These paintings were done at the charge of the foresaid Mr. Bruges. I have already set down the reason why I am of this opinion, under the 18. E. 3. above, so shall not need to repeat it here. The figures in the east window in the chancel, were I. The sovereign, K. Edw. the 3^d. II. Sir Edward the black prince; III. Sir Henry duke of Lancaster; all kneeling before the image of S. George. The figures in the windows on each side the choir, were IV. Sir Thomas Beauchamp E. of Warwic. V. The captain, Sir Peter de Bouche. VI. Sir Ralph Stafford E. of Stafford. VII. Sir William Montacute E. of Salisbury. VIII. Sir Roger Mortimer E. of March. IX. Sir John L'isle, lord L'isle. X. Sir John Beauchamp. XI. Sir Bartholomew Burgwash. XII. Sir John Mohun, lord Mohun. XIII. Sir Hugh Courteney. XIV. Sir Thomas Holland, E. of Kent. XV. Sir John Grey, lord Grey of Codnor. XVI. Sir Richard Fitz-Simon. XVII. Sir Miles Stapleton. XVIII. Sir Thomas Walle. XIX. Sir Hugh Wrottesly. XX. Sir Neele Loreng. XXI. Sir John Chandois, Kt. banneret. XXII. Sir James Audley. XXIII. Sir Otho Holland. XXIV. Sir Henry Esme. XXV. Sir Sanchio Dampredecourt. XXVI. Sir Walter Paveley. ' ^a It is re-' markable that of all these 25 knights companions, not one outliv-' ed the reign of the founder K. Edw. the 3^d. For there were 29 ' more installed at several times by that prince before he died. And ' the just number doth never exceed twenty six.' The figures of these knights, as painted in this church, were copied by Sir William Dugdale (foreseeing the late civil war & the great destruction of antient monuments which thereupon followed) into a curious book of draughts now, or late, in the lord viscount Hattons library. But I have not been able to procure a sight of it, as I was once told, by a curious person in these matters, I very easily might; on which presumption I ventured to promise my subscribers a plate of the same; but hope they will pardon the want of it, since it was what I much desired, but at last find, I cannot help them to. The other antiquities in this church were the arms, inscriptions, & figures in the windows, which as near as I can recover them, by the help of Mr. Hollis^b, Mr. Butcher^c, & a personal survey, were as follow. In the chancel. Ermyn, a cross pierced ermins; being the arms of William Bruges, esq; impaling, sable, a chevron between three wolves heads couped argent, collered, or. In the left hand light of the middle window of the north isle

a MS. in the hands of Mr. Thomas Daw-   b MS. in the hands of John Anstis, esq;
kins of Stanford.   c MS. penes me.

is the figure of S. Katherine, with a wheel in her hand; under her a man & woman in religious habits kneeling, with a label over them, inscribed, *Sancta Katherina, ora pro nobis.* In the right hand light of the same window is the figure of S. Margaret; under her two other persons in religious habits kneeling, with a label over them, inscribed, *Sancta Margareta, ora pro nobis.* At the bottom of all this window ran along an inscription, so much whereof as now remains, is, *orate pro bono statu Johis Johe mltis capyrn' et sue dul . . . . . suorum qui fenestram fieri fecerunt.* At the lower part of the east window in the same isle are the effigies of a man & woman in religious habits, kneeling; a label over the man is inscribed, *Christe, Marie fili, sis nobis clemens & propitius.* Over the woman, *Sancta dei genitrix, sis nobis auxiliatrix.* At the bottom of all, *orate pro animabus Alicie . . . . . Fox piscatoris, & Johanne consortis sue, qui istam fenestram fieri fecerunt.* In the east window of the south isle, sable, three dovecoats argent: being the coat of Sapcote. The same again impaled with argent, three turn-pikes, sable. At the bottom, *orate pro ai-abus Richardi Sapcote & Johanne uxoris ejus.* In other windows, or, a cheveron B. between three cinquefoyles gules. Or, two barrs gules, in chief three torteauxes; Wake. Gules, three waterbougets ermin; Roos. Or, three cheverons gules; Clare. Or, a plain crofs gules; Bigot. Checky, or & B. Warenn. Gules, a crofs patence argent. Or, a cheveron B. between three cinquefoyles, gules. Azure, a crofs moline, quarterly pierced, argent; Molineux. In the middle window of the south isle, a cheveron between three roses, Roscel; & a man in a religious habit, praying, under his picture, *frater Johannes Roscel.* All these antiquities I reckon were as old as the church it self. Some of the arms being theirs who were at the charge of painting the windows; others being, I believe, older; taken out of the windows when the old church was demolished, & put up again when the new church was erected. For what now remains of the old painted glafs here is some of it very antient, & some of it a good deal more modern. The jewels belonging to this church were many of them the gift of the beforementioned John Bruges esq; a most generous benefactor; who enriched it with many curious veffels of plate, costly images, & a variety of fine veftments, agreeable to the devotion of the times he lived in. What he gave, in his life, I know not; but no doubt his benefactions were then very confiderable: but what he gave at his death, let his will speak (a copy whereof his learned successor, the worthy now garter king of arms, John Anftis efq; was so kind as to oblige me with) & is as follows. '*In the name of the fader, son, & holy goft,* III '*persons in Trinite, & on sole God, Y William Bruges, otherwise cleped* '*garter kyng of armes, in my right & in my fresh mynde thrugh the* '*enspiracion of the holy goft, the thursday the* XXVI. *day of Feverer,* '*the yere of our Lord God* MCCCCXLIX. *& the yere of the reign of the*

L.

'*kyng Henry the sexte the* XXVI. *make this my present testament &* 2 '*last*

‘ *laſt will.   As for firſt & formoſt, Y bequethe my ſoule to the gret mercy*
‘ *of oure Lord God Jhu, that ſuffred payne & paſſion of his gret mercy,*
‘ *to bring my wretched ſoule from the carnal pyne & dampnation to*
‘ *the eternal blyſſe & redempcion, & to that gret mercy Y to be brought, Y*
‘ *beſeech our bleſſed lady, mayden & wyf, that ſhe, of her gret grace &*
‘ *goodneſſe, like & pleaſe to be mean & immediatrice.   And alſo Y beſeche*
‘ *al the glorious ſeyntes & ſeynteſſes in heven, that they, for thaire glo-*
‘ *rious martirdoms & goodneſſes, ... to almighty God,*
‘ *that ſo Y may finde, & have alſo, yf it be poſſible, my body to be*
‘ *brought & buryed in the chirch of ſaynt George within Staunford,*
‘ *there to be buried, in the myddes of the quere of the ſaid chirch.*
‘ *To the whych ſaid chirch Y bequeth a gret haly-water ſtoppe of ſilver,*
‘ *with a ſtaff benature, the ſaid benature, & ſtaff weyng* xx. *nobles*
‘ *in plate & more.* Item, *to the ſaid chirch I bequethe a peyre of cen-*
‘ *ſours of ſylver, with a ſhip of ſylver for frankincenſe, & I ſpone in*
‘ *the ſame ſhip, of ſylver.* Item, *I bequethe to the ſaid chirch a little*
‘ *handbell of ſylver, of the gretneſſe of a ſacryng-bell.* Item, *I bequethe*
‘ *to the ſame chirche, a little round cofyn of ſylver, cloſed in ſyngyng*
‘ *bred, & not the hoſte.* Item, *Y bequethe to the ſaid chirch, for*
‘ *ther ſolempne feſte dayes, to ſtande upon the high awter,* II *grete ba-*
‘ *ſyns of ſylver, &* II *high candleſticks of ſylver.* Item, *Y bequethe to*
‘ *the ſaid chirch, I coupe of ſylver, in the whych is one litel box of*
‘ *yvory, to put in the bleſſid ſacrament ; & to hang over the high awter.*
‘ *. . . . .* Item, *Y bequethe to the ſaid chirch, one gret chalice, over-*
‘ *gilt ; of the wight of* C s. *to ſerve for theyr ſolempne feſtes.* Item,
‘ *I bequethe to the ſaid chirch, ane hole ſute of veſtmyntes of ruſſet*
‘ *velvet.   One coope, cheſible diacones, for decones ; with the awbes &*
‘ *parures : And two caſe corporaſſes of the ſame ſute of veſtmyntes.*
‘ Item, *I bequethe to the ſaid chirch an other hole ſute of black vel-*
‘ *vet, I cheſible diacones, for decones, or frees of white clothe of gold*
‘ *powdred with garters, & two caſſe corporaſſes.* Item, *Y bequethe*
‘ *& ordeyne that the gret framd . . . . that Y have lying in the*
‘ *gret berne in my place at Kentiſhton* [*by London*] *be ſold to the moſt*
‘ *value, & the mony riſing therof to be beſtowed upon the compleſſhyng*
‘ *& endyng of the ſeyd chirch of Staunford ; that is to be underſtand,*
‘ *in coveryng with lede, glaſyng, & makyng of pleyn deſques, & of a*
‘ *pleyn rodelofte, & in puyng of the ſeyd chirch, nourt curiouſly, but*
‘ *pleynly ; & in paving of the hole chirch body & quere, with broad Ho-*
‘ *land tyle.* Item, *I bequethe to the ſeyd chirch of ſeynt George, a*
‘ *ſolempnitie of array for the feſt of* corpus Chriſti, *oon partie wrought*
‘ *in the plate, of ſylver, & over-gilt ; & that other in tymbre to be*
‘ *born betwen the decon & ſubdeacon : the tymbre is peynted, & over-*
‘ *gilt, with fyne gold.   And, for every ſign of the paſſion, an aungel*
‘ *berynge the ſign of the croſſe, & of the crowne of thorne ; another*
‘ *aungel beyryng the pillar & the ſcourges : another aungel beyryng the*
‘ *ſpere & the ſponges ; another aungel beyryng the remnant of the ſigns*
                                                                ‘ *of*

‘ *of the paſſion; and, in the middle of the feretorye, a gret round*
‘ *blak corver; & one peynted with gold & aſure, & peynted with*
‘ *ſterres of gold, in the middel of that round blok, for a gret coupe*
‘ *of ſylver, & overgilt, to ſtande on, upon a pynne of tre. And, in the*
‘ *ſeyd couple, a litel box of ſilver, & over-gilt; to put in the ſacrament.*
‘ *This gret coupe, & the litle together, firſt to be ſet upon the gret blok*
‘ *of tre, with a gret croun of & over-gilt, garniſhed with ſtones clepyd dub_*
‘ *lets, redde, blue, grene, & yellowe, garniſhed wyth counterfeyt perles*
‘ *made of ſilver; the croun of the wight of C. s. This croun fyrſt to*
‘ *be ſet upon the gret round blok of tre, & thanne upon the pynne*
‘ *ſtandyng in the ſeyd blok. The ſeyd coupe to be crouned withoute wyth*
‘ *a ſmall croune, ordeyned redy therefore.* Itcm, *I bequethe to the ſeyd*
‘ *feretorye, a tabernacle wele ywrought of ſylver & over-gilt, of the*
‘ *wight of one marc, or thereabouts, goyng wyth a byll to be ſet on*
‘ *high upon the coupe. And above, upon the poynt of the ſeyd taber-*
‘ *nacle, a litel croſſe of ſylver & over-gilt, goyng alſo by a vyce. All*
‘ *this plate that longeth to the feſte (that is to ſay of* corpus Chriſti)
‘ *yf myn executors ſamyn that yt ſhuld be in more ſure garde of the*
‘ *pariſſhors of the chirch of oure lady of Staunford; Y would yt ſhuld*
‘ *reſt & abyde in the garde of hem; & wythyn theire treſour. And*
‘ *atte daye of the feſt of* corpus Chriſti, *hit to follow the ſacrement*
‘ *of the ſeyd chirch of our lady, yf it pleſe the paryſſhors of the ſeyd*
‘ *chirch of our lady; onleſſe than they wol have yt ſerve for both.*
‘ Itcm, *Yordeyn & bequethe that the* II *chapelles of our lady & ſeynt*
‘ *George*[a], *wythyn the ſeyd chirch of ſeynt George be cloſid wyth oſtrich*
‘ *boarde, & clere ſtoryed, after ſuch quantite as the cloſure of pleyn*
‘ *borde there now conteineth. And to the ſeyd chappel of our lady, Y*
‘ *bequethe* II *images of our lady & ſeynt George, beyng in paynted*
‘ *ſtone, & in my chapel at Kentiſſhton. And to the ſame chappel of*
‘ *our lady of Staunford, Y bequethe my grete candleſtykes of laton, that*
‘ *ſtanden in my chapel at Kentiſhton.* Item, *Y bequethe to the*
‘ *ſeyd chappel of ſeynt George of Staunford, the ymage of the Trinite*
‘ *of ſtoon, ſtandyng in my chapel at Kentiſhton, wyth the braunche of*
‘ *laton, for* III *lights, accordyng thereto; yt to be ſett upon a foot*
‘ *of ſtone, higher than the heddes of the ymages of our lady & ſeynt*
‘ *George.* Item, *I bequethe the ſeyd ſmall candelſtykkes ſtandyng in*
‘ *my chapel at Kentiſhton, to the new chapel of oure lady now in mak-*
‘ *yng in the ſame town. And as for the ſeyd three ymages of ſtoon*
‘ *(that is to ſay, the ymages of the Trinite, our lady, & ſeynt George)*
‘ *Y woyl have made, for eiche of theym, a gret cofyn of elmyn borde;*
‘ *the ſeyd ymages to be nayled in faſt, ſtuffed with hey, & ſo carryed,*

a This church having neither north, or ſouth, chancels; theſe two chapels were therefore made of the upper parts of the north & ſouth iſles. The north chapel was parted from the reſt of the church by a ſcreen which went from the north-ſide of the chancel to the firſt pillar on the north ſide of the nave, & from that pillar by an- other ſcreen which ran acroſs to the wall of the ſaid north iſle. So that it took in a handſome ſquare corner, & two windows at the upper end of the ſaid north iſle. The ſouth chapel was exactly of the ſame com- paſs & proportion. Theſe ſcreens were taken down in 1719. when the church was repaired.

‘ *at*

' at my *coſte*, unto *Staunford*, & *ſet up in the ſeyd chirch of ſeynt*
' *George.*   Item, *the* II *leſs candelſtyks to be ſet upon the awter of our*
' *lady, in the ſeyd town of Staunford; & there to ſerve brennyng from*
' *the begynnyng of the goſpel, unto the tyme that the preſt have uſed,*
' *upon my coſt, as my goods, will ſuffyce to contynue yt .... every taper*
' *of halfe a pound wight; and every day a maſſe to be ſeyd of our lady.*
' Item, *I ordeyn & wol that the* II *greter candelſtyks, beyng in my*
' *ſeyd chappel at Staunford, ſerve in the chapel of our lady of Staunford;*
' *and that on ſtand upon the ground, afore the ymage of ſeynt George*
' *in the ſame chapel.   And, for eiche of theſe candelſtykkes, to be or-*
' *deyned a taper of waxe of* I *pound wight, &, ſo ſerved, to be light-*
' *ed atte dyvyne ſervyce at pryncipal feſt-days, & al other ſolempne*
' *feſtes, as, at matyns, pryme, maſſe, & the yeven ſongs.*   Item, *I be-*
' *quethe & ordeyne to the ſeyd chirch of St. George of Staunford, a*
' *little coffre, ſtandyng bounden wyth plate of yren, ful of veſtments;*
' *except on veſtment, yf yt be therein, & that ys of blak ſatyn ground,*
' *figured wyth rede velvet; the orfreyes wrought wyth the nedel wyth*
' *ymages.   The whych ſeyd veſtment Y wol yt ſerve for our lady chapel in*
' *Staunford only.*   Item, *I ordeyne & bequethe to the chapel of our lady*
' *in ſeynt Mary chirch at Sandewich, an half long gown of purple velvett*
' *furred wyth martrons, of that to be made a cheſible wyth the parures,*
' *& wyth the furre to be bouzt & ordeyned the orfreyes, lyke to the or-*
' *freyes of the ſingel veſtyment of blak ſatyn, lyned with rede velvet.   And*
' *yf the ſeyd furre of martrones wol not ſuffice to ordeyne the ſeyd*
' *orfreys, myn executors to put to ſuch mony as they may have of myne,*
' *to the percompliſſhing of the ſeyd orfreyes; & ſo endid to be dely-*
' *vered to the ſeyd chirch.*   Item, *I bequethe to the ſeyd chappel of our*
' *lady in ſeynt Mary chirch of Sandwich, the chalice of ſylver & over-*
' *gilt, that my wyf hath; & myne executors to make for the ſame cha-*
' *lice* II *ſmall nets of ſylver & over-gilt, of the pryce of* xx s. *& than*
' *my wyfe to ſend yt to the ſeyd chirch.   The reſidue of all my gooddes,*
' *after my dettes payd, Y geve & bequethe to Anneys my wyf, & of*
' *this my teſtament, Y make & ordeyne the ſame Anneys my wyf prin-*
' *cipal executrice, Thomas Haddon hir broder co-executor to her, & maſ-*
' *ter Clement Denſton clerk, overſeer of the ſame my teſtament; &*
' *that they ordeyne & dyſpoſe for my ſoule, as they ſhall ſeem beſt,*
' *to the pleſire of God, & to the proffite of my ſoule.   Yeven at London,*
' *the day & yere abovementioned* [a].   I ſhall only note, that Mr. Butcher
ſays, ' [b] there is belonging to S. Georges pariſh ſeven pounds a year,
' being a rent out of divers tenements in the ſame; but he adds, I
' cannot learne who gave the ſame to this church.'   Whence, for my
part, when I conſider the many benefactions of Mr. Bruges to this

---

a E. MSS. Aſhmoleanis a regiſtri Stafford. A. Epiſc. Cantuarienſis. p. 187. Pro-
batum coram domino archiepiſcopo apud
Lambith xii. Die Martii mccccxlix. &
commiſſa fuit adminiſtratio executoribus in
dicto teſtam. nominatis.

b MS penes me, p. 54.

church,

church, I cannot forbear thinking that thefe houfes were alfo part of his donations; & perhaps the rent of them was to buy wax candles for the ufes in his will mentioned. Matins, prime, mafs, & yeven fong being therein alfo mentioned (as alfo in divers other places of thefe collections) if I am right, it may be of fome ufe to obferve here, that, according to my notion, in antient times they went to prayers in many monafteries & churches every third hour night & day. Thofe hours had each of them particular names, & I believe may be thus afcertained. I. The fervice at our three a clock in the afternoon was called the fervice of the ninth hour; and fometimes, if I miftake not, the vigils: as, upon a feaft eve; the watching, fafting, & firft fervice beginning then. II. The fervice at our fix a clock in the afternoon, was called the vefpers or evening fong. III. The fervice at our nine of the clock at night, was called the *completorium*, or compline. IV. The fervice at our twelve of the clock in the night, was called the nocturns. V. The fervice at our three of the clock in the morning was called, the matins. VI. The fervice at our fix of the clock in the morning, was called the fervice of the firft hour, *hora prima*, prime. VII. The fervice at our nine of the clock in the morning, was called the fervice of the third hour, *hora tertia*; & at other times *High-mafs* time. VIII. The fervice at our twelve of the clock at noon, was called the fervice of the fixth hour, *hora fexta*; & again, if I miftake not, lands.

29. H. 6.   XVII. Alderman 1450. William Storeton. Roll. ' ª So great were ' the loffes in France (Burdeaux & Baion, the laft cities of Gafcoine, ' rendring to the French) that, with the D. of Somerfet, Richard D. ' of York [lord of Stanford] became neceffitated to quit the country, ' & went [again] into Ireland. ᵇ Thofe now who favoured the faid ' duke, & wifhed the crown upon his head, procured a commotion ' in Kent, under the infamous Jack Cade, who named himfelf Mor- ' timer, cofen to the D. of York. ᶜ A peftilent devife to found the ' affections of the multitude, & to proclaime the title to the crowne, ' which the D. (as heir of that family) afterwards challenged; for who ' would not ask, what fhould move him to ufe the name of Mortimer?' One of the faid Cades demands were, for the king ' ᵈ to take ' about his noble perfon the high & mighty prince the D. of York, ' lately exiled from his prefence.' But the rebels being fuppreffed,

H. 6. this ftorm blew over. Alderman 1451. Richard Blogwin. ' ᵉ The ' humours of the popular body in the laft commotion being not ob- ' fcurely difcovered, after Michaelmas Richard D. of York comes fo- ' dainly out of Ireland, & to begin his ufurped cenforfhip & dictature, ' apprehends John Sutton baron of Dudley, Reginald abbat of Glou- ' cefter, & John Gargrave keeper of the kings bench, & fent them to

a Bar. Vol. II. p. 159.   d Stow, p. 643.
b Stow, p. 639, 640.   e Speed, p. 851. Stow, p. 647.
c Speed, p. 849. b.

2   ' the

' the caftle of Ludlow.   ª And now bethinking with himfelf how to
' fet the crown upon his own head (being the lineal heir male to
' Edmund of Langley, fifth fon to Edward the third, & right heir
' to Leonel D. of Clarence third fon to the fame king, by Anne his
' mother, daughter to Roger Mortimer E. of March) he entred into
' confultation with Thomas Courtney E. of Devon, Edward Broke
' lord Cobham, & fome others, how he might effect it without any
' blemifh of difloyalty.   In regard therefore that Edward D. of Somer-
' fet was the chief prop to K. Henry, both in council & action, it
' was refolved in the firft place to take him off.   But keeping his
' main purpofe fecret, it was concluded, that he fhould raife what
' power he could, under pretence of removing certain evil counfel-
' lors, & to vindicate the peoples injuries thereby occafioned.   Of
' which evil counfellors the D. of Somerfet was the perfon only pointed
' at, in regard the vulgar fort had a bad opinion of him, for the lofs
' of Normandy.   ᵇ When the D. of York had thus framed his founda-
' tion of his long intended enterprife, he affembled a great hoft to
' the number 10000. men in the Marches of Wales, publifhing his
' letters as followeth ; Forafmuch as I Richard D. of York am inform-
' ed, that the king my fovereigne lord, is my heavy lord, & greatly
' difpleafed with me, & hath me in miftruft by finifter information
' of mine enemies, whereas God knoweth, from whom nothing is
' hid, I am, have been, & ever will be his true liege man, & fo have
' I faid before this divers times, as well by mouth as by writing.   And
' for that this notice of the difpleafure of my faid fovereign lord is
' to me fo grievous, I have prayed the bifhop of Hereford & my co-
' fen the E. of Shrewsbury to come hither, & hear my declaration
' in this matter.   Wherein I have faid to them, that I am true liege
' man to the king my fovereigne lord, ever have been, & fhall be to
' my dying day.   And to the very proof that it is fo, I offer my felf
' to fwear that on the bleffed Sacrament, & receive it, the which I
' hope fhall be my falvation at the day of doom.   And fo for my
' fpecial comfort I have prayed the faid lords to report unto the kings
' highnes my faid offer, & that I be ready to do the fame oth in pre-
' fence of two or three lords, fuch as fhall pleafe the kings highnes
' to fend hither to accept it.   Written in my caftle of Ludlow, the
' 9 of Jan. 30. H. 6.   Jan. 9.

XVIII. It was alfo about this time that the following letters paffed
between the duke & the king.   ' ᶜ Pleafe it your highnes to conceive
' that fith my departing out of this your realme by your commaunde-
' ment, & being in your fervice in your land of Ireland, I have
' beene informed that divers language hath beene faid of me to your
' moft excellent eftate, which fhould found to my difhonour, & charge
' of my perfon : howbeit that I aye have been, & ever will be your

a Bar ut fupra.   b Stow, p. 649.   c Stow, p. 650.

' true

' true liege man & servant: & if there be any man that will or dare
' say the contrary, or charge me otherwise, I beseech your rightwisenes
' to call him before your high presence, & I will declare me for my
' discharge as a true knight ought to do, & if I do not, as I doubt
' not but I shall, I beseech you to punish me as the poorest man of
' your land.   And, if he be found untrue in his suggestion, I beseech
' you of your highnes that he be punished after his desert, in exam-
' ple of all other.   Please it your excellence to know, that as well
' before my departing out of this your realme, for to go into your
' land of Ireland in your full noble service, as sith, certaine persons
' have lien in await for to hearken upon me, as Sir John Talbot
' knight at Holt castle; Sir Thomas Stanley knight in Cheshire; Pul-
' ford at Chester; Elton at Worcester; Brooke at Gloucester; & Ri-
' chard, groome of your chamber, at Beaumarris; which had in charge
' (as I am informed) for to take & put me into your castel of Con-
' way, & to strike off the head of Sir William Oldhall knight, & to
' put in prison Sir William Devereux knight, & Sir Edmond Malso
' knight withouten enlarging, until the time that your highnes had
' appointed their deliverance.   *Item*, At such time as I was purposed
' to have arrived at your haven of Beaumarris, for to have come to
' your noble presence to declare me your true man & subject, as my
' ductie is, my landing was stopped by Henry Norres, Thomas Nor-
' res, William Bulkley, William Grust, & Bartholomew Bould, your
' officers in North-Wales, that I should not land there, nor have vic-
' tual or refreshing for me & my fellowship, so farre forth that Henry
' Norres (deputie to the chamberlain of North Wales) said unto me,
' that he had in commandement that I should in no wise have land-
' ing, refreshing, or lodging, for men or horse, nor other thing that
' might turne to my worship or ease, putting the blame upon William
' Say usher of your chamber, saying & affirming, that I am against your
' intent, & a traitour.   And moreover certaine letters were made &
' delivered unto Chester, Shrewsbury, & other places for to let mine
' entrie into the same.   *Item*, above all injuries abovesaid done unto
' me of malice without any cause, I being in your land of Ireland,
' in your honourable service, certain commissions were made & di-
' rected unto divers persons, which, for execution of the same, sat in
' divers places, & the juries impannelled & charged; to the which
' juries certain persons laboured instantly to have me indited of
' treason, to the intent to have undone me & mine issue, & cor-
' rupted my blood, as it is openly published.   Wherefore I beseech
' your majestie roial, of your righteousnes, to examine these matters,
' & thereupon to do such justice in my behalf as the cause requireth:
' for mine intent is fully to pursue to your highnes for the conclusion
' of these matters.   [a] The king stooped so much as to answer.   [b] Cosin,

a Speed, p. 852. b.   b Stow, p. 650.

2   ' we

' we have feen the bill that ye took us late, & alfo underftand the
' good humble obedience that ye in your felf fhew unto us, as well
' in word as deed; wherefore our intent is, the more haftily to eafe
' you of fuch things as were in your faid bill : howbeit, that, at our
' more leifure, we might aunfwere to your faid bill, yet we let you
' to wit, that for the caufes aforefaid, we will declare you now our
' intent in thefe matters : fith it is that a long time among the peo-
' ple hath beene upon you many ftraunge language, & in efpecial,
' anone after your difordinate & unlawful flaying of the B. of Chi-
' chefter, divers of the untrue fhipmen & other faid, in their man-
' ner, wordes againft our eftate, making manace to our owne perfon
' by your fayings, that ye fhould be fetched with many thoufands, &
' ye fhould take upon you that, which ye neither ought, nor as we
' doubt not, will not attempt; fo farre forth that it was faid to our
' perfon by divers, & efpecially we remember of one Wafnes. And
' alfo there were divers of fuch falfe people, that went on & had
' like language in divers townes of our land, which, by our fub-
' ject were taken & duly executed. Wherefore we fent to divers of
' our courts & places to hearken & take heed if any fuch matter
' coming were, &, if there had beene, for to refift it. But coming
' into our land our true fubject as ye did, our intent was not that
' ye, nor lefs of eftate of our fubjects, nor none of your fer-
' vants, fhould have been letted or warned, but in goodly wife
' received : howbeit that peradventure your fudden coming, with-
' out certain warning, caufed our fervants to do as they did, con-
' fidering the caufes abovefaid. And as to the enditement that
' ye fpoke of, we think verily & hold for certain, that there was
' none fuch. And if ye can truly prove that any perfon was there-
' abouts, the matter fhall be demeaned as the cafe fhall require, fo
' that he fhall know it is to our great difpleafure. Upon this, for
' the eafing of your heart in all fuch matters, we declare, repute, &
' admit you our true & faithful fubject & as our welbeloved cofen.
' ª The duke then advanceth his practife one ftep farther, & writes
' to the king.   ᵇ Pleafe it your highnes tenderly to confider, that
' great murmur & grutching is univerfally in this your realme, in that
' juftice is not duly miniftred to fuch as trefpafs againft your lawes,
' & in efpecial of them that be endited of treafon, & other being
' openly noifed of the fame ; whereby great inconveniences have fal-
' len & are like to fall, if by your highnes provifion be not made for
' due reformation & punifhment in this behalf. Wherefore I your
' humble fubject & true liege-man Richard D. of York, willing, as
' effectually as I can, the furetie & profperitie of your moft royal per-
' fon, & the welfare of this your noble realm, counfel & advertife
' your excellencie, for the tranquilitie among all other fubjects, to or-

a Speed, p. 852.   b Stow, p. 652.

14 K   ᶜ daine

' daine that true juftice be had againft all fuch that fo be endited or
' openly named, wherein I offer my felf to execute your com-
' maundement in the premifes, for the punifhing of fuch offenders
' & redrefs of the faid mifrules. And for the haftie execution heere-
' of, like it your highnes to addrefs letters of privie feal & writs to
' your officers & minifters, to take & arreft all fuch perfons, of what
' eftate or condition foever they be, & them to commit to the tower
' of London, & other your prifons, there to abide, without baile or
' mainprife, untill they be tried & determined after the courfe of your
' laws.' To which fecond letter the king replied. ' Cofin, as touch-
' ing your bill laft put up to us, we underftand well that ye, of good
' hart, counfel & advertife us to the fetting up of juftice, & to the
' fpeedie punifhing of fome perfons endited or noifed; offering your
' fervice to be readie at commaundement in the fame; for many
' caufes moving us, we have determined in our foule to ftablifh a
' fad & a fubftantial council, giving them more ample authority than
' ever we did afore this, in the which we have appointed you
' to be one. But fith it is not accuftomed, fure, nor expedient
' to take a conclufion by advife of one perfon, it is thought fit
' that the greateft & the beft, the rich & the poore, in libertie, ver-
' tue, & effect of your voices be equal: we have therefore determin-
' ed to fend for our chancellor & other lords of our council, yea &
' all other together, within fhort time, to commune thefe & other
' our great matters: in the which communication fuch conclufion,
' by the grace of God, fhall be taken, as fhall found to his pleafure,
' the weale of us & our land, as well in thefe matters as any other.

Feb.16.   XIX. ' ᵃ Feb. 16. K. Henry, with the D. of Somerfet & many other
' lords, tooke towards the Marches of Wales to oppofe the duke. But,
' when the duke had witting of the kings great power, he turned
' from the way taken by the kings hoft, & hafted towards London.
' And when he had knowledge from the city that he might not there
' be received, he went over Kingfton bridge, & fo into Kent, &
' there upon Brent-heath neer unto Dertford, he pight his field, ᵇ &
' encamped himfelf very ftrongly, environing his field with artillerie
' & trenches. The king, hereof advertifed, brought his armie with
' all diligence to Black-heath, & there pight his tents. Whilft both
' armies lay thus embatteld the K. fent the bifhop of Winchefter &
' others to the duke, to know the caufe of fo great a commotion.
' The duke aunfwered, that his coming was neither to damnifie the
' king in honor, nor in perfon, neither yet any good man; but to
' remove from him certaine evil difpofed perfons of his counfayle,
' bloodfuckers of the nobilitie, pollers of the clergie, & oppreffors
' of the poor; amongft whom he chiefly named the D. of Somerfet.
' When the bifhop & others were returned with this aunfwereᶜ, at
' length it was agreed by the king, that the D. of Somerfet fhould

a id. p. 649.   b Hol. p. 1283. a.   c Stow, p. 652.

' be

' be committed to ward, there to abide & anſwere ſuch articles as
' the D. of York would lay againſt him. Upon which promiſes ſo
' made by the king to the duke ; the duke (who ſaw that the people
' of Kent, & of other places, came not to him, as they had pro-
' miſed, & that they were not ſtrong enough ; for the kings part
' was much more than his) brake up his fielde on the firſt of March, Mar. 1.
' & yeelded himſelf to the king at Dartford, where, contrary to the
' promiſe before made, he found the D. of Somerſet chief about the
' king, ª going at large, & ſet at libertie ; whom he boldly accuſed of
' treaſon, briberie, oppreſſion, & many other crimes. The D. of
' Somerſet not only made anſwer to the D. of Yorks objeċtions, but
' alſo accuſed him of high treaſon, affirming that he with hys com-
' plices had conſulted together how to obteine the ſceptre & re-
' gal crowne of this realme. By mean of which wordes the king re-
' moved ſtreight to London, & the D. of York, as priſoner rode, be-
' fore him, & ſo was kept awhile. The king aſſembled together a
' great counſaile at Weſtminſter, to hear the accuſations of the two
' dukes, the one objeċting to the other many hainous & greevous
' crimes. But the duke of Somerſet (whiche nowe conceyved in his
' minde the thing that ſhortly followed) inceſſantly exhorted the coun-
' ſayle, that the D. of York [lord of Stanford] by compulſion or
' otherwiſe, might be driven to confeſſe his offence ; that ſo, being
' atteinted of treaſon, he might ſuffer execution, & his children
' be taken as adverſaries to their native countrey, to the intente, that
' by the loſſe of this onely prince & his ſequele, all civil war &
' inward diviſion might be depreſſed, beſeeching God, that ſo great
' an enemy ſto the king & his blood, might never eſcape puniſhment,
' nor continue long in life. The D. of Somerſet ſette forth this
' matter the more vehemently, bycauſe he knew perfeċtly that the
' D. of York dayly imagined with himſelf how to get the crowne,
' & to deſtroy both the king & him. But the neceſſitie of deſtinie
' cannot, by any mans deviſe, be either letted or interrupted. For
' many things, to common judgment, declared the D. of York inno-
' cent in this caſe. As firſt his free & voluntarie coming to the king,
' when he was partly of puiſſance able to have encountered with the
' kings whole power .And ſecondly, his humble ſubmiſſion & reaſonable
' requeſts, as well on his owne behalf, as for the poore Commons :
' which argued that he ſought for no ſoveraigntie. But theſe things
' he uſed to daſle mens eyes withal. While the counſayle treated of
' ſaving, or diſpatching, this dolorous duke, a rumor ſprang thro
' London, that Edward E. of Marche, ſonne & heir apparent to the
' ſaid duke, with a great army of March-men, was coming towards
' London : which tidings ſore appalled the queen & the whole coun-
' ſayle : ſo that the duke was ſet at full libertie, & on the 10ᵗʰ of March Mar: 10.

a Hol. p. 1283. b.

I   ª made

' made his fubmiffion, & tooke his oath to be true & faithful to K.
' Henry.   ᵃ But let us view the forme & words of that caution, upon
' which K. Henry (meafuring other mens hearts by his own) adven
' tured to repofe his life & kingdom; which are thefe. ᵇ I Ri-
' chard D. of York, confeffe & beknow that I am & ought to be
' humble fubject & liegeman to you my foveraigne lord K. Henry
' the fixt, & owe therefore to bear you faith & truth, as to my fo-
' vereigne liege lord, & fhall doe all dayes unto my lives end, & fhall
' not at any time, will or affent, that any thing be attempted or
' done againft your moft noble perfon ; but wherefoever I fhall have
' knowledge of any fuch thing imagined or purpofed, I fhall with all
' fpeed & diligence poffible, make that your highnes fhall have know-
' ledge thereof; & over that do all that fhall bee poffible to me, to
' the withftanding & let thereof, to the uttermoft of my life.   I fhall
' not any thing take upon me againft your royal eftate or obeyfance
' that is due thereto, nor fuffer any other man to do, as farre foorth
' as it fhall be in my power to let it ; And alfo fhall come at your
' commandment whenfoever I fhall be called by the fame, in hum-
' ble & obeifant wife; except I be letted by any ficknes or impo-
' tence of my perfon, or by fuch other caufe as fhall be thought by
' you my fovereign lord reafonable.   I fhall never hereafter take upon
' me to gather any rowt, or to make any affembly of your people,
' without your commaundement or licenfe, or in my lawful defence,
' in interpretation or declaration of which my lawful defence, I fhall
' report me at all times to your highnes; &, if the cafe require, to
' my peeres, nor any thing attempt againft any of your fubjects, of
' what eftate, degree, or condition they be.   But whenfoever I find
' my felf wronged & agreeved, I fhall fue humbly for remedie to your
' highnes, & proceede after the courfe of your lawes, & none other-
' wife, faving in mine own lawful defence in manner abovefayde;
' & otherwife to have your highnes as an humble & true fubject ought
' to have him to his foveraigne lord.   All thefe things abovefaid I
' promife you truly to obferve & keep, by the holy evangelifts con-
' tained in the booke that I lay my hand heere upon, & by the holy
' croffe that I heere touch, & by the bleffed Sacrament of our lords
' body that I fhall now with his mercy receive. And over, I agree me
' & will, that if I any time heereafter, as by the grace of our lord
' God I never fhall, any thing attempt, by way of feate or otherwife,
' againft your royal majeftie & obeifance that I owe thereto, or any
' thing take upon me otherwife than is above expreffed, I from that
' time foorth to be unabled, & held, & taken as an untrue & openly
' forfworne man, & unable to all manner of worfhip, eftate, & de-
' gree, be it fuch as I nowe occupie, or any other that might in any
' wife growe unto me heereafter.   And this I have heere promifed

---

ᵃ Speed, p. 853. a.   ᵇ Stow; p. 653.

ɪ

&

The South West Prospect of S.t Iohn Baptists Church in STANFORD.

To the very Learned and
R.t Rev.d Father in God
Rich.d L.d Bishop of Lincoln,
one of y.e kind Encouragers of
this work, This Plate is most
Humbly Inscribed.

The Screen between the North Isle and the North Chancel of
St John Baptists Church in Stanford.

To the Honourable   James Brudenell Esqr.
Master of ye Kings Jewell Office   one of the kind Encouragers of
this Work, This Plate is most   thankfully Inscribed.

' & sworne, proceedeth of mine own desire & free-will, & by no
' constraining or coaction. In witness of all which I Richard D. of
' York subscribe with mine own hand & seale. ª Thus the D. of
' Yorks submission & solemn oath, salved all for the present: so that,
' 'till he found a fit opportunity, he continued quiet.' And no longer,
' ᵇ for he little esteemed of his oath, as by the sequele may appear.

XX. About this time was rebuilt & finished the new church of
S. John the Baptist in Stanford. It consists of three isles, & as many
chancels answering them, all which are leaded.   At the bottom of
the north isle is the steeple; being a stone tower & a neat regular
piece of work. The bells (as appear by an old parish book, wherein the fourth & middle bells are often mentioned) were formerly
five; but are now but four. The first, second, & fourth are dated
1561. the third has no date. Upon the sanctes bell is, *cum voco
venite.* 1605. The chancels of this church are parted from the isles,
by three screens of excellent workmanship, all handsomely painted & gilded. For the parishioners spared for no cost in adorning
this church; as these screens, the windows, & roof of it, do all yet
attest. The last in particular being adorned with many angels at length
all vested like priests, & many other figures carved in wood & stone.
Let us then take a view of the windows, beginning at the lowest
window of the north isle.   At the bottom of the left hand light is the
picture of S. Oswald the king & martyr at length.   Over his effigies (in
two lesser lights framed out of the top of the greater) are the repre-
sentations of hope & faith.   In the middle great light of the same
window, is pourtrayed S. Edmund the king & martyr at length; &
over his picture (in two lesser lights framed out of the top of the
greater) two other figures, but without any names.   In the right hand
light of the same window is delineated S. Edward the king & martyr.   And, in two lesser lights above, the figures of charity & *sancta
sapientia.*   The figures of the three princes above, particularly the faces,
are well done.   Thence we proceed to the second window from the
bottom of the same isle.   In the left hand light of this window
(which is at present 1718. the most beautiful in the whole church, &
most of it entire ; & well deserving the charity of some well disposed person to keep it so, by wiring the outside) is depicted a man
laid out upon a bier with several others standing about the corps ; over
them is the figure of S. Tulpus: & over him, the pictures of S. Era-
sine & S Giles. Over the casement in the middle light of the same
window is the half figure of a nameless saint, sitting in a very con-
templative posture: over which appears, as near as I can guess, the
figure of our blessed Lord surrounded with a glory, & supported by two
angels in beautiful coaps, their wings eyed like a peacocks train.
Above all in the same light are the figures of S. Blase & another saint

ª Bar. Vol. II. p. 159. b.	ᵇ Stow, p. 654.

without

without a name. In the right hand light of the fame window is reprefented the martyrdom of S. Laurence, his body lying upon a gridiron, with a fire under it. Above that his effigies at large in a blew coap, emboffed with divers eyelets or circles, in every one of which are inferted the three facred letters IHS. Over him are the pourtraits of S Leonard & S. Peter de ... At the bottom of all this window runs an infcription, *orate pro animabus Johannis Marchaunt* .... He & his wife, I fuppofe, were at the charge of painting it. Pafs we next to the 3ᵈ window of the north ifle, where, in the left hand light, ftood formerly, in my remembrance, the picture of S. Thomas of Canterbury; but it is now defaced. However in the fame light above is yet left the figure of S. Martin. In the middle light ftands part of a figure without any name under it. Above it the entire pourtraits of S. Ambrofe & S. Auftin. At the bottom of the right hand light is a perfon kneeling in a religious habit, with a book upon a desk before him, over his head a label infcribed, *Sancte Wilhelme ora pro nobis*. Above the label a large figure infcribed, *Sanctus Wilhelmus*. Above that the pictures of S. Blafe & S. Nicholas. At the bottom of all this window is part of an infcription, ... *feneftram fieri fecerunt, anno dni millo. cccc°. lj°.* We now go on to the north window in the north chancel. In the left hand light whereof are reprefented S. Simon & S. Jude, depicted like children in the arms of their parents; who have likewife two other fmall children ftanding by their fides. Above thefe reprefentations, are Cleophas & Anna; & above them, two other figures, without any names. In the middle light are delineated Jofeph & Mary; above them Joachim & the bleffed virgin with the child Jefus, holding a little ftaff in his hand; over them S. ... & S. Peter. In the right hand light are the figures of Zebedee, the bleffed virgin, & the child Jefus. Abve them S. ... & S. Marie. Above them one Richard, a benefactor to this church, who being probably buried in a monkifh habit, according to the fafhion of the times, thought good to have his effigies here depicted in the fame manner. This is the fecond beft window in the church, & deferves to be preferved with more care, than I fear it is like to meet with. The next is the eaft window of the fame chancel, at the bottom of the left hand light whereof are the effigies of fix perfons, one in fcarlet with a black girdle, kneeling before a desk, the other five alfo in religious habits kneeling behind him. Over them is the pourtrait of S. John the Baptift; & above him are S. Luke & S. Mark. At the top of the middle light are the pictures of S. George & S. Chriftopher. In the right hand light are the reprefentations of three more perfons in religious habits, likewife kneeling. Over them, in a label, *O beata trinitas*. Over it the figure of S. John the divine at length. And in the two little pannels above, S. Matthew & S. John the Evangelift. By thefe pictures it fhould feem the painter would have S. John the divine, & S. John the evangelift to be

be

be two perfons ; an error in which he is followed by the gravers for modern common prayer books. At the bottom of all this window is wrote, *orate pro animabus Willielmi. . . . . & Agnetis confortis fue, qui iftam feneftram vitream fecerunt, an. dni* M.CCCC°. L°. *primo.* The nine perfons here pictured on their knees in religious habits were that perfon & his wife & children, who beautified this window.   Monkifh habits being commonly ufed, both to bury in, & alfo reprefent any benefactor ; fuch habits ferving to teftifie the donors refpect for a monaftic life, & perhaps that he was admitted a lay brother of fome religious order, & fo hoped to be entitled to a fhare of their prayers. In the north window of the choir, or middle chancel, are the pictures of the Virgin Mary & pope . . .   At the bottom of the left hand light is alfo the reprefentation of a church (what if we fhould fay the old church of S. John the Baptift, which ftood in this place before the fame was pulled down & rebuilt ?) & underneath it, *orate pro anima dni* . . . . . *ces* . . . . *quondam iftius ecclefie qui* . . . . In the pavement, juft under this window, lies a very antient ftone, with an infcription upon it, but not legible ; laid down it is like for the fame perfon, who was probably rector when this church was rebuilt, &, as fuch, at the fame time rebuilt this chancel, & glafed this window at his own charge.   In the left hand light of the great eaft window over the high altar (which window contains in all feven lights) is yet left fome part of the effigies of S. Matthias, but very much battered.   In the middle light ftood formerly, in my remembrance, a large figure of the crucifixion ; but now quite demolifhed.   In 1644. Mr. Salter, then rector of this church, was charged with popery for letting it ftand there.   In the feventh light is yet to be feen part of the figure of S. John the Baptift.   And now I am furveying this church, & fee the largenefs of this window, & the fcattered remains of painted glafs in almoft every one of the reft ; I cannot help wifhing fome charitable perfon would be at the pains & charge of removing the beft & moft entire pieces yet left in the other windows, & difpofing them in this ; which, being done by a careful hand, with a little wiring, would preferve them to many generations.   The next window affords nothing remarkable.   But in the two little pannels at the top of the left hand light of the eaft window, in the fouth chancel, are the figures of S. . . . & S. Elizabeth.   In the fame part of the middle light of the fame window, are the bleffed Virgin & our Saviour.   In the fame part of the right hand light, S. Agnes & S. Barbara.   The next window yields nothing remarkable. We go on then to the upper window of the fouth ifle, where, in the little pannels at the top of the 3^d light, are yet to be feen the effigies of S. Petronilla, S. Mary Magdalene, & S. Etheldreda.   The next window hath nothing curious.   We proceed therefore to the 3^d window of the fouth ifle, below the fcreen ; where, in the left hand light, is reprefented the figure of one of the three kings or wife-men

of

of the eaſt, who came to offer to our bleſſed Lord at his nativity. He is depicted crowned with a chalice in his hand & a label over him with this inſcription, *video ſtellam ejus in oriente fulgentem cum ſplendore.* Above in the ſame light ſtands the angel Gabriel with a label, containing his ſalutation of the bleſſed Virgin, *ave maria! gratia plena, dnus tecum, beata tu inter feminas.* By it ſtands the bleſſed Virgin her ſelf, with a label about her, containing her anſwer to the foreſaid ſalutation, *ecce ancillam domini, fiat mihi ſecundum verbum tuum.* In the left hand pannel, at the top of the middle light of the ſame window, is another figure of the bleſſed Virgin with our Lord on her knees ſitting in a ſtable; above, *gloria in excelſis.* The other little pannel at the top of this light, & the whole top of the next light are filled with repreſentations of ſeveral ſhepherds feeding their flocks, over the head of one of whom is wrote, *we have here a Lorde therwyth to playe,* over the ſecond, *and here a pype the ſoothe to ſay,* & over the third, *ſave us, Lord, as thou well may.*

31. H. 6. XXI. Alderman 1452. Thomas Gregory, Roll. 'W. Hanford capel-
           'lan gave a meſſuage (deſcribed 24. H. 6. above) to Richard Goldeſ-
Oct. 9.   'worth. Witneſs Thomas Gregory, Ald. &c. Oct. 9. 31. H. 6. Ri-
           'chard Goldeſworth gave the ſaid meſſuage to W. Storeton of Staun-
Dec.16.   'ford, baxter. Witneſs Tho' Gregory, ald. &c. Dec. 16. 31. H. 6.
32. H. 6. 'B. H.' Alderman 1453. John Broun. Roll. '[a] This year the D.
           'of York [lord of Stanford] began to ſtir again, [b] by reaſon whereof
           'the nobles as well as common people were into parties devided, to the
           'utter deſtruction of many a man, & to the great ruine & decay of
           'this region [in general, & of the town of Stanford in particular]
           'for while the one partie ſtudied to deſtroy the other, all care of the
           'common-wealth was ſet aſide, & juſtice & equitie clearly exiled.
           'Above all things the duke firſt ſought how to provoke the malice
           'of the people againſt the D. of Somerſet, imagining that he being
           'made away, his purpoſe ſhould ſhortly come to a good concluſion.
           'He alſo practiſed to bring the king into the hatred of the people,
           'for that he was not a man apt to the government of a realme,
           'wanting both wit & ſtomacke, ſufficient to ſupply the roomth which
           'he held. Many of the high eſtates, not liking the world, & diſ-
           'alowing the acts & doings both of king & counſaile, determined to
           'practiſe how things might come to ſome alteration. When the
           'duke underſtood their mindes, he chiefly entertayned & wanne the
           'favour of the two Nevilles, viz. [c] Richard E. of Salisbury the fa-
           'ther, & Richard E. of Warwick the ſon; his wife being ſiſter to the
           'E. of Salisbury. [d] Warwick, thro' a certain natural inclination &
           'practiſe, did ſo ſet forward a ſorte of good qualities which reſted
           'in him, with wittie & gentle demeanour towards all maner of per-
           'ſons, that he grewe into ſuch favour among the common people,

a Bar. as above.   c Bar. Vol. II. p. 160. a.
b Hol. p. 1286. a. b.   d Hol. p. 1286. b
2   'that

' that they judged him able to do all things, & that without him no-
' thing could be well done.   For whiche caufes his authoritie fo far
' foorth increafed, that which way he bowed, that way ranne the
' ftreame, & what part he tooke, that fyde got the game.'   This is
the Warwick fo well known in hiftory by the name of Warwick the
king-maker.

    XXII. Ald. 1454. Laurence Melton. Roll.   ' ᵃ When the D. of 33. H. 6.
' York [lord of Stanford] had faftened his chaine betwene thofe two
' ftrong pillars (the Nevils) he, with his frends, wrought fo effectu-
' ally that the D. of Somerfet was arrefted in the queens great chamber,
' & fent to the tower; where he kept his Chriftmafs without great
' folemnitie.   Againft whom, in open parliament, were laid divers
' articles of high treafon, as well for the loffe of Normandie, as
' for fome late mifchance which happened in Guyenne.   The king
' at that time was fick at Clarendon; by reafon whereof no
' determination proceeded in this caufe, but all was put in fufpence
' 'tyll the next affemblie of the parliament.   Whileft the K. was
' ficke, the D. of York bare all the rule, & governed as regent or
' viceroy, by authoritie committed to him by the lords affembled
' in counfel, to fee the prefervation & good government of the com-
' mon wealth, during the kings ficknefs, which was fo greevous that
' he lay fenfelefs, & was not able, for a time, either to go or ftand.'
Sir William Dugdale fays, ' ᵇ the king being defperately fick, the
' dukes ftrength & power did not a little increafe; which when he
' faw, he made his addrefs to the pope for abfolution from thofe fo-
' lemn oaths which he formerly made.'   And for this he cites Holingfhed.   But Holingfhed fays, ' ᶜ the D. [not only fent for, but what
is more] ' obteyned abfolution of the pope, to difcharge him of his
' oth before taken.   ᵈ Alfo the government of Calais was taken from
' the D. of Somerfet, & the D. of York feifed it into his own hands,
' or rather got a patent in the kings name invefting him with it.'
This when he was fick.   But when the king began to recover, ' ᵉupon
' the 4. March 33. H. 6. the D. of York refigned his truft for the cap- Mar. 4.
' tainfhip of Calais & the Marches thereof.   ᶠ For the K. under color
' of obferving a neutrality between the dukes of Somerfet & York
' who difputed for it, depriv'd the D. of York of it, & declar'd him-
' felf governor of the place.'   And had the king refted there, all had
perhaps been well.   ' ᵍ But when he had recovered ftrength again, &
' refumed his former princely government, eyther of his owne mynde,
' or by the queenes procurement, he caufed the duke of Somerfet to
' be fet at libertie; by which doing, great envie & difpleafure grew.
' And to aggravate more the malice of the D. of York & his

a id. ib.
b Bar. Vol. II. p. 160. a:
c Hol. p. 1287. a.
d Acta regia, Nº. X. p. 303.

e Bar. as above.
f Acta regia, Nº. X. p. 303, 304.
g Holing. as above.

' friends,

' friends, the queene, who then bare the chief rule, caufed the D.
' of Somerfet to be preferred to the chief captainefhip of Calais,
' wherewith not only the commons, but alfo many of the nobility,
' were greatly grieved & offended ; faying, that he had loft Normandie,
' & fo would he do Calaice.   The D. of York & his adherents (perceiv-
' ing that neither exhortation ferved, nor accufation prevayled againft
' the D. of Somerfet) determined to revenge their quarrel, & ob-
' teyne their purpofe by open warre.   And fo, he being in the
' Marches of Wales accompanied with his friends the earls of Salis-

April. ' bury & Warwick, affembled a power, [a] & then in April took his
' journey toward London, the kyng then beeyng there, with a great
' retinue of lordes.   Whereof when the queene & the lordes were
' advertifed, thei caft in their myndes that it was to none of their
' profites.   And for that they entended to have conveighed the king
' weftward, & not to have encountered the D. of York ([b] meaning
' to meet with him rather in the north parts than about London,
' where it was thought he had too many friends) [c] the king departed

May 20. ' upon the 20. of May from Weftminfter, & fo helde his journey
' towards S. Albones.   Then the D. of York, havyng knowledge of
' the kings departyng from London, coafted the countries, & came

May 23. ' unto the townes end of S. Albones upon the 23. of May, then bee-
' yng Thurfdaie before Whitfundaie.

   XXIII. ' [d] The D. of York [lord of Stanford] & many other knights
' & efquires, the kings enemies, affembled in a place called Key-fielde,
' befide S. Albons.   The K. pight his banner in a place called Gofe-
' lowe (fometimes alfo called Sandforth) in S. Peters ftreet, & commaund-
' ed in ftrong manner to keep the wards & barriers of the towne.
' And thus they abode from feven, till almoft ten of the clocke
' in the morning, without any ftroke fmitten on either part.   [e] How-
' ever the king, when he heard firft of the dukes approach, fente
' to him meffengers, as the D. of Buckingham & others, to under-
' ftand what he meant by his comming thus furnifhed after the man-
' ner of warre.   [f] The D. by advife of his counfel, fent unto the
' king thefe words following.   Pleafe it your excellent grace to
' take me Richard D. of York as your true liege-man & humble
' fubject, & to confider & tender, at the reverence of God & in
' the way of charitie, the true intent of my coming, & to be
' good & gracious fovereigne unto me, & all other your true liege-
' men, which, that with all their power & might will be readie to
' live & die with you in your right, & to do all things as fhall
' like your majeftie royal to command us, if it be to the wor-
' fhip of the crowne of England, & the welfare of this your no-
' ble realme.   Moreover, gracious lord, pleafe it unto your majeftie

a Fabian. p. 457, 458.   d Stow, p. 658.
b Hol. ut fupra.   e Hol. p. 1287. b.
c Fab. p. 458.   f Stow, p. 659.

                                          ' roial,

' roial, of your great goodnes & rightwifenefs, to encline your will
' to heare & feele the right wife part of us your true fubjects &
' liege-men. Firft, praying & befeeching to our foveraigne Chrift
' Jefus, of his high & mighty power, to give you the vertue of pru-
' dence, & (thro' the prayer of the glorious martyr S. Albon) very
' knowledge of our trothes, & the intent of our affembling at this
' time : for God that is in heaven knoweth our intent is rightful &
' true. And therefore we pray unto that mighty lord in thefe words,
' *Domine, fis clypeus defenfionis noftre.* Wherefore, gracious lord,
' pleafe it your majeftie royal, to deliver fuch as wee will accufe, &
' they to have like as they have deferved. And this done, you to
' be honourably worfhipped as our moft rightful king & true gover-
' nour. And if wee fhould now at this time be promifed (as afore
' this time is not unknown have been promifes broken, which have
' been full faithfully promifed, & thereupon great othes fworne) we
' will not now ceafe for any fuch promifes, or oth, 'till we have them
' which have deferved death : or elfe we to die therefore. The an-
' fwere. I K. Henry charge & commaund, that no manner of per-
' fon, of what condition foever he be, abide, but that they avoide
' the field, & not be fo hardie to make refiftance againft me in my
' own realme. For I fhall knowe what traytor dare bee fo bolde to
' arife any people in mine own land, where through I am in great
' difeafe & heavineffe. By that faith I owe unto S. Edward & the
' crowne of England, I fhall deftroy them every mothers fonne ; &
' eke they to be hanged, drawne, & quartered, that may be taken
' afterward of them in example to make all fuch traytours to beware,
' for to make any rifing of people within mine own land, & fo tray-
' teroufly to abide their king & governour. And for a conclufion,
' rather than they fhall have any lord that here is with me at this
' time, I fhall this day, for their fake, in this quarrel my felf live
' & die.

XXIV. ' The words of the D. of York [lord of Stanford] upon re-
' ceipt of the kings anfwer, to the gentlemen & others affembled
' with the duke. Sirs, the king our foveraigne lord will not be re-
' formed at our befeeching ne prayer, nor will not in any wife un-
' derftand, the intent wherefore we be here affembled & gathered,
' but is in full purpofe to deftroy us all ; & thereupon a great oth
' hath made, that there is none other way, but that hee, with all his
' power, will purfue us, & if we be taken, give us a fhameful death,
' leefing our livelihode & goods, & alfo our heirs fhamed for ever.
' Therefore, Sirs, now fith it will none otherwife bee, but that wee
' fhall utterly die, better it is to dye in the field, than cowardlie to
' be put to an utter rebuke & fhameful death, for the *Right* of Eng-
' land ftandeth in *Us.* Confidering alfo in what perill it ftandeth at
' this time, & for to redreffe the mifchief thereof, let every man
' helpe to his power this daye, &, in that quarrel to the crown of
                                                    ' England,

' England, quit us like men; praying that Lord which is eternal, to
' keep & fave us this day in our right, & that thorough the giftes
' of his holy grace we may be made ftrong to withftand the great, abo-
' minable, & horrible malice of them that purpofe to deftroy us &
' the realme of England, & put us to a fhameful death: pray we
' therefore unto that Lord to be our comfort & defender, faying,
' *domine, fis clypeus defenfionis noftre.'* The battel now drawing on,
' ᵃ & the king being in the place of Edmond Weftby, hundreder of
' the faid towne of S. Albons, he commaunded his hoft to flay all
' maner of lords, knights, fquires, gentlemen & yeomen, that might
' be taken on the dukes partie. This done, the lord Clifford .kept
' fo ftrongly the barriers of the fame towne, that the D. of York
[lord of Stanford] ' might in no wife, with all the power that he
' had, enter or break into the towne. The E. of Warwick knowing
' thereof, took his men together with him, & brake in by the garden
' fide, between the fign of the key & the exchequer in holywel-
' ftreet.' Another fays, ' ᵇ the place where they firft brake into the
' towne, was about the middle of S. Peters ftreet.' Be that as it will,
the E. of Warwicks men ' ᶜ anon as they were within the fayde towne,
' blewe uppe the trumpet, & cried with a loud voice, a Warwicke, a
' Warwicke! that marvayle it was to heare. And till that time the
' D. of York might never have entrie. But then the faid duke, with
' the earls of Warwick & Salisbury, with their hoft, between
' eleven & twelve at noone, break in, in three feveral places. And
' then with ftrong hand they brake uppe the barriers, & fought.
' ᵈ The fight, for a time, was right fharp & cruel; for the D. of So-
' merfet with the other lords of the kings party, coming to the
' fuccours of their companions that were put to the worfe, did what
' they could to beate backe the enemies. But the D. of York fent
' ever frefhe men to fuccour the wearie, & fupplye the places of them
' that were hurt; by which policie the kings army was finally brought
' to confufion, & all the chiefetaines of the fielde flaine & beaten
' downe. For there dyed under the figne of the caftel Edmond D.
' of Somerfet, who, as hath been reported, was warned long before
' to avoid all caftels. Befide him lay Henry E. of Northumberland,'
& many other great perfons, whofe names may be feen in my authors.
All his men being now either fled or flain, ' ᵉ the king withdrewe
' into a poore mans houfe to fave himfelf from the fhot of arrows
' that flewe about his ears as thick as fnowe; ᶠ with one of which
' he was already fhot into the neck. ᵍ The D. of York [lord of Stan-
ford] ' advertifed of the place, hafted thither, & comforted hym the
' beft he could, affuring him, now the common enemy the D. of So-

a id. p. 660.   e id. p. 1288. a.
b Hol. p. 1287. a.   f Stow, p. 661.
c Stow, ut fupra.   g Hol. ut fupra.
d Hol. ut fupra.

3

merfet

' merfet was difpatched, he had caufe rather to rejoyce than be forrie,
' fith his deftruction was the kings prefervation; &, for himfelf, he
' & all his, he undertooke, were & would remayne, his moft faithful
' people. After he hadde ufed fuch words, [a] the king defired them to
' ceafe their people, that there fhould be no more hurt done, & the
' duke, to obey his commaundement, caufed to be proclaimed, in the
' kings name, that all manner of people fhould ceafe their malice &
' not fmite a ftroke more: And fo ceafed the battel. [b] Then the D.
' brought the king out of that fimple houfe into which he was crept
' with all due reverence fhewed towards him, fyrft to the fhryne of
' S. Alban, & after to his chamber. The D. having got this victory
' remembred that he had publifhed how the only caufe of the warre
' was for advauncement of the common-wealth, & therefore would
' not touch the kings perfon after any violent fort, but with all ho-
' nor conveyed him to Weftminfter, to which place was fummoned
' a parliament, whyche began the 9. of July, [c] wherein the D. of July 9.
' York [lord of Stanford] was made protector of the realme, the E.
' of Salisburie lord chancellor, & the E. of Warwick captain of Calis.
' [d] The duke was appointed protector with this claufe, that he fhould
' enjoy all the prerogatives of the faid dignity, 'till the parliament
' fhould difcharge him of it. The new protector, relying altogether
' upon this claufe, liv'd in a ftate of perfect fecurity, leaving the king
' & queen at as full liberty as they could wifh.——Richard Cokk of
' Staunford, & John Halyday vicar of All Saints in the town afore-
' faid, gave to William Brown a meffuage fituate in the parifh of S.
' Mary at the bridge, between a tenement late Richard Lee's eaft,
' & a tenement belonging to the gild of *corpus Chrifti* & the bleffed
' Virgin, of the one part; & a tenement fometime W. Staceys of the
' other part weft: & abutting on the kings highway fouth, & a tene-
' ment of John Vowes north. Likewife a meffuage fituate in S. Georges
' parifh, in the place called Cornftall, between the tenements of John
' Capron of either part, & abutting on the kings highway fouth, &
' a garden of Henry Cokk north. B. H.

   XXV. Alderman 1455. John Gregory, Roll. ' [e] The kings name 34. H. 6.
' being now only made ufe of, & the power of rule wholly in the
' D. of York [lord of Stanford] thereat fome of the moft potent
' nobles ftarted not a little; of which number Henry Beaufort D. of
' Somerfet (whofe father had been flain at S. Albans) & Humphry
' Stafford D. of Buckingham (whofe eldeft fon alfo loft his life there
' in that quarrel) were the chief: who, confulting with the queen, caufed
' him to be difcharged of his protectorfhip, & Salisbury from his of-
' fice of chancellor.' And I fuppofe Warwick from being captain of
Calis. However they quickly ' [f] complied with the D. of York again,

a Stow, ut fup.
b Hol. p. 1288. b.
c id. p. 1289. a.
d Acta regia, N°. X. p. 304.
e Bar. Vol. II. p. 160. a.
f id. ib.

' for

Nov. 11. 'for in a parliament called Nov. 11. he had power given him to hold
'the captainſhip of Calis in the kings name.' A cunning projeƈt to
create a difference between him from whom that office was taken
& him to whom it was given. ' Richard Witham of Grantham clerc,
' gave to W. Dykeman of Staunford, one meſſuage between the work-
' houſe late Thomas Wyngs ſouth, & the kings high-way which leads
' towards the high croſs north, & abutting on the common road weſt,
' & a workhouſe late W. Bochers eaſt; which meſſuage was John Motts
' of Grantham, who had it of Robert Lowick of Staunford. Wit-
' neſſes, John Gregory, ald. &c. Dated. Ma. 3. 34. H. 6. B. H.' The high
croſs here ſpoken of was that now called the mercat croſs. Mr. Forſter ſays, a deed of this year, which he had ſeen, calls Stanford on the
ſouth ſide of the Welland, Stanford-Baron. Now it is pity but he had
given us the deed it ſelf: for, this being the firſt time I meet with that
name, ſome light why it was there ſo called, might perhaps have been
gathered from other circumſtances in the ſame writing. However all
Stanford on the ſouth ſide of the Welland was & is now reckoned
within the ſoke of Burg, or part of thoſe lands which the abbat of Burg
held *per baroniam.* So that whenever that part of Stanford which
lies on the ſouth ſide of the Welland was firſt called Stanford-Baron, I
gueſs it was ſo named to diſtinguiſh it from Stanford on the north
ſide of that river, always called *burgus regis,* the kings borough.

35 H. 6.   XXVI. Ald. 1456. John Page, Roll. ' ª The Scots entred Nor-
' thumberland, & burned certaine cottages & houſes; but hearing that
' the D. of York [lord of Stanford] was marching thitherwarde with
1456. ' a great armie, they with all haſt returned into Scotland.' Nicholas Kenton provincial of the white friers in England, having ſeen the
wain or decreaſe of his order, as above related 1446. continued
in his office about ten years longer, & then reſigned. But, before he
did ſo, if we may believe Pits, ſaw his brethren increaſed to a greater
number, than when he came firſt to the government of them. For
to purſue his ſtory ᵇ. ' When he began to decline & grow into years,
' being deſirous of contemplation, & weary of the troubles of his
' office, he requeſted to be diſcharged from the burden of the provin-
' cialate; the cares attending it being too heavy for his age. For he
' had now above 1500 brethren in his province, & had rather be left
' more at leiſure to ſay his prayers, & ſerve God, than attend the
' government of them; being at laſt more willing to obey himſelf,
' than preſide over others. Whereupon the brethren at length con-
' ſented to his requeſt, & choſe another.' The perſon they made
choice of, was Dinley: of whom I have elſewhere ſpoken ᶜ. A cata-
Mar. 6. logue of Kentons works may be ſeen in Pits & Leland. ' ᵈ March 6.
' Richard D. of York [lord of Stanford] was made lord lieutenant of
' Ireland.'

a Stow, p. 665.   b in vita.   c Lib. XIV. p. 18.   d Bar. Vol. II. p. 160. a.

XXVII. Alderman 1457. William Hikham. Roll.   ' ᵃ The queen 36. H. 6.
' fecretly thirfting the overthrow of York & his faction, & perceiv-
' ing fhe could attempt nothing againft him near London, becaufe
' the duke was had in more eftimation among the citizens, than either
' the king or her felf; caufed the king to make a progreffe into War-
' wickfhire for his recreation, & fo, with hauking & hunting, he came
' to Coventrie, where divers ways were ftudied to compaffe her defire:
' for accomplifhing whereof, the D. of York & the earls of Salisbury &
' Warwick were fent for to Coventrie by the kings letters, whither they
' reforted; but, being admonifhed by fecret friends what was intended,
' they, not faying farewel, departed: the duke to [his caftle of] Wig-
' more in the Marches of Wales, Salisbury to his caftle of Mydelham
' in the north, & Warwick to Calis.   Thus were they feparated in
' bodies, but not in mindes: having always meffengers going betwixt
' them to communicate their devices.——Richard Cokk of Staunford
' merchaunt gave to W. Gydding two acres of arable land lying to-
' gether in Staunford fields in Sunderfoken, whereof one acre & an
' half are called the headlandys & lye in the fields aforefaid, & divide
' the field of Staunford & the field of Tynwell towards the north &
' fouth.   W. Dykeman of Staunford, mercer, gave to W. Brown mar-
' chaunt, one meffuage in All Saints parifh in the mercat, between a
' fhop late Thomas Wengs fouth, & the ftreet called Wolle-rowe
' north, & abutting on the common road weft, & on the fhop &
' workhoufe of Robert Skynner, bocher, eaft; which was Richard
' Withams of Grantham clerc.   Witneffes, William Hikham, ald.
' &c. 26. Oct. 36. H. 6. B. H.   ᵇ K. Henry & his adherents perceiv- 26.Oct.
' ing the D. of York [lord of Stanford] lay ftill, returned to London,
' & to the intent that he would be the chief author of peace, pro-
' mifed fo to entertaine the duke & all his fautors, that all old grutches
' fhould be forgot & forgiven.   Whereupon divers grave perfons were
' fent to the duke & other great eftates of the realme, which, fince
' the battel of S. Albons, never met, commaunding them to refort
' to the king without delay.   At this commaund came to London
' Rychard D. of Yorke [lord of Stanford] with 400 men, & was lodged
' at Baynards caftel, being his own houfe.   After him came Salisbury
' with 500 men, & was lodged at his own houfe called the Herber.   The
' E. of Warwicke alfo came from Calais with 600 men in red jackets,
' embroidered with white ragged ftaves, & was lodged at the grey
' friars.   Thus were all thofe of the Yorkifh faction lodged within
' the citie, & thofe of the Lancaftrian without.   The lords which
' lodged within the citie held a dayly counfaile at the black friers.
' The other, in the chapter-houfe at Weftminfter.   At length by the
' travaile of the archbifhop of Canterbury & other prelates, both par-
' ties were perfuaded to come to a communication; &, after long
' debating of their grievances, accorded. Conditionally, I. That at the

a Stow, p. 665.   b Hol. p. 1291. b.

4.   ' cofts

‘ cofts of York, Warwick & Salisbury xlv. pounds a year fhould be
‘ affigned for fuffrages, obits, & alms for the fouls of Edmund late
‘ D. of Somerfet, &c. flain at S. Albons. II. That York fhould pay
‘ the dutches of .Somerfet & her fon 5000 marks, &c. Laftly, that
‘ all variaunce betwixt any of the perfons aforefaid, fhould be for
‘ ever determined. Given under the kings 'great feale at Weftmin-

Mar. 24. ‘ fter, the 24 [not 23. as in Dugd.] day of March, 36. H. 6.

XXVIII. For publifhing of this agreement, there was, on Ladie-day,
‘ a folemn proceffion to S. Pauls, at which the king was prefent
‘ in his habit royal, with his crowne on his head. Before him
‘ went, hand in hand, the D. of Somerfet & the E. of Salisburie;
‘ the D. of Exeter & the E. of Warwick; & fo one of one fac-
‘ tion & another of the other: &, behind the king, the D. of York
‘ & the queene with great familiaritie. [a] O religion! O honour!
‘ O finceritie! that your divine vertue fhould not have contayned
‘ thefe fpirits in the harmonie of fweet obedience! But, if you could
‘ not —— what alas fhould? England muft be more feverely fcourged,
‘ than that fo goodly a bleffing of publick reconciliation fhould con-
‘ tinue; whereby the proud tops of her nation (offenfive to God &
‘ men) being taken off, the way might be opened to other names
‘ or races, which as yet were nothing thought of. There is no rea-
‘ fon to doubt but that the D. of York (a man of deepe retirement
‘ in himfelfe) fecretly continued his purpofe for the crowne, not-
‘ withftanding all thefe his vernifhed pretences. And did only there-
‘ fore not, as now, put for it; becaufe he prefumed the time was in-
‘ commodious. Again the queene (true head & life of the contrary
‘ part) as well in regard of her felf, her husband, & young fonne,
‘ may in likelihood be thought to have laid downe any thing, rather
‘ than the wakefulneffe & jealoufie which former perils & the eni-
‘ mies prefent ftrength, might worthily keep alive in her. The thinne
‘ afhes therefore which covered thefe glowing coals, were, by an acci-
‘ dent which I fhall fet down under the next year, foon unrakt again
‘ & fet to blafe.

37. H. 6. XXIX. Alderman 1458. William Shorton, Roll. Storeton. B. H.
‘ [b] Not long after the diffimuled amitie, as above related, between
‘ the Yorkifts & Lancaftrians; a fray, either by chaunce or of purpofe,
‘ was made on a yeoman of the E. of Warwickes, by one of the
‘ kings fervaunts, in which the affaylant was fore hurt, but the erles
‘ man fled. The kings fervaunts feeing their fellow hurt & the of-
‘ fender efcaped, affembled together & watched the erle as he return-
‘ ed from the counfayle to hys barge, & fodainly fet on him, the
‘ yeomen with fwordes, & the blacke garde with fpittes & fireforks.
‘ After long fight & many of the erles men hurt, by help of friends,
‘ he tooke a wherry, & fo efcaped to London. The queen adver-
‘ tifed hereof, incontinently commaunded he fhould be apprehended

a Speed, p. 857. a.   b Holing. p. 1293. b.

‘ &

' & committed to the tower : [but they mift of him.]   However by
' this unhappy fray there arofe anon after fuch trouble & terrible
' war, that the whole realme was thereby difquieted.   For, after this
' difpleafure done to the earl, & the queens good-mind to him by
' his fecret friends revealed; he with all diligence tooke his journey
' to Warwicke, & after into Yorkfhire, where he found the D. of
' York & the E. of Salisbury, declaring unto them the affault made
' on him by the kings fervants, & the intended evil purpofe of the
' queen.   After which, fearyng to be difpoffeffed of his roumth at
' Calais, he with great fpeed embarked & fayled thither.——John fon
' of Richard Cokk fold to William Brown merchaunt, one meffuage
' in Staunford, fituate in the parifh of S. Mary at the bridge, called
' the Aungel, & one grange with a garden adjacent in Cornftal. B. H.
' Robert Young of Staunford gave to W. Tundur & W. Ole one garden
' lying in the abbat of Burgs liberty, in the ftreet called Webfter-
' gate; between a garden of W. Pope, fouth; & a tenement of the
' forefaid abbat, in part; & a garden of *corpus Chrifti* gild, in part,
' on the north : as it abutts on Webfter-gate aforefaid, eaft, & the land
' of the nuns of S. Michael there, weft. B. H.

   XXX. Alderman 1459. Thomas Gregory, Roll.   ' [a] After the E. of 38. H. 6.
' Warwicke was departed & gone to Calais, the D. of York & E. of
' Salisbury falling into confultation agreed, that the E. of Salisbury
' with a warlike company fhould march toward the king, & fignifie,
' by way of complaint, both the manifeft injurie done to his fon,
' & alfo the uncourteous breach of the late fworne agreement : in
' which fuit if he prevailed, he fhould not then let paffe the occa-
' fion given for revenge of difpleafures to him done by the queen.
' Upon this the earl removed from Middleham caftel, with four or
' five thoufand men, thro' Lancafhire towards London.   Mean feafon
' the queen ymagining the erle of Warwicke had kindled this fire to
' fet the crowne on the D. of Yorks head, appointed James Twychet
' lord Audley (bycaufe his power laye in thofe partes) to rayfe an
' hoft of men, & give battel to the earl, if he faw caufe & place
' convenient.   [b] The 21. of Sept. the E. of Salisbury having gather- Sept. 21.
' ed a well appointed army, took his way towards Ludlow, where
' the D. of York [lord of Stanford] lay, to the intent that they both
' together would have ridden to the king at Colfhull in Staffordfhire,
' to excufe themfelves of certain articles laid againft them by their
' enimies, as they faid.   [c] But the queen conftruing they meant no
' good to hir or her husband, requefted lord Awdley to apprehende
' the E. of Salisbury, if by any means he might.   The lord Awdley
' accordingly affembled above 10000 men, & knowing which way
' the earl kept, approached neare to him on Bloreheath near Dray-
' ton in Shropfhire.   Next morning the earl caufed his foldiers to

   a Holing. p. 1293. b.   b Stow, p. 670.   c Hol. p. 1294. a.

' fhoote

' ſhoote towards the lord Awdleys company, & then made a ſigne
' of retreyt.   Lord Awdley ſuppoſing his adverſaries fled in deed,
' cauſed his trumpets to blow up, & ſet forth his vawarde.   Salis-
' bury (which knewe the ſleights of war) ſodainely returned, & ſet
' upon him, & in concluſion ſlew him.   After this the duke of York
[lord of Stanford] ' perceyving that the deſtruction of himſelf & friends
' was intended, thought now no longer to linger his buſineſs, but
' with all diligence diſplay his banner.   And therefore ſending for
' the earl of Salisbury, after long communication, they determined to
' raiſe an armie, & either die or winne their purpoſe.   Hereupon
' were men forthwith aſſembled, friends ſent for, & a puiſſant army
' gathered, both of northern men & Welch men, which in good order
' came into the Marches of Wales adjoyning to Shropſhire, deter-
' mining there to abide their enemies, or meet them if occaſion ſerv-
' ed.   Thither came to the D. of York; from Calais the E. of War-
' wick, bringing from that towne a great number of expert men,
' whereof two were of great experience, one called Andrew Trollop,
' the other John Blont.   The king having advertiſement of the dukes
' doings & intent, ſent forth commiſſioners to levie a power in all
' parts where he thought to have any friends.   Many for love of him
' reſorted to his ſide, but more for fear of the queen, whoſe frowns
' was their undoing.   The king thereupon marching forward came to
' Worceſter, where he ſtayed a while, & at length ſent the biſhop of
' Salisbury to offer them a free pardon, if they would give over
' their enterpriſe.   ᵃ To whom they anſwered by the E. of Warwicke,
' that as concerning the pardon they durſt not truſt to it.   Becauſe,
' notwithſtanding ſuch pardons, thoſe that were about the king were
' unruly & cared not to break the kings commaundement.   Inſtanc-
' ing altho' every lord, being called to parliament, ought freely to
' come & go; yet the ſaid E. of Warwick at a certain counſel hol-
' den at Weſtminſter, was in danger of death.   The king receyving
' ſuch anſwer was nothing contented therewith, & therefore com-
' maunded his ſtandarts to be advaunced, but before he came where
' the lords were encamped, they wrote a letter to him; ᵇ proteſting,
' they meant no harme in the world againſt his perſon, as by their
' demeanours might well appear, who had ever withdrawne themſelves
' from place to place; an evident token that they ſought nothing
' but their owne ſafeguards & quietnes of the realme, with ſo much
' favor, as in good ſuretie they might come unto his preſence, to de-
' clare certaine things which in their opinions might be to the welth
' of the realme, & farther make anſwere to all things objected agaynſt
' them.   And now, ſayde they, we are here in the uttermoſt con-
' fines of the land, not upon any preſumptuous meaning, but rather
' in all lowlineſs to abide his graces coming, which, they beſought

a Stow, p. 671.   b Holing. p. 1296. b.

' God,

' God, might be favourable in their behalfes.' Stow [a] gives us a long
letter, much to the same purpofe, ' written at Ludlow the 13. day Oct.13.
' of October, & figned, R. Yorke, R. Warwicke, & R. Salisbury.
' [b] The king having received this letter, & conjecturyng that venome
' lay hid under fo foft fpeche, commaunded his armie again to march
' forth, & comming within half a mile of the adverfaries campe pro-
' claimed, that whoever of his adverfaries would give over his lewd
' enterprife, & repayre to his prefence for mercie, he would pardon
' him. This proclamation comming to the underftanding of the D.
' of Yorks hoft, a great number that were there came away to the
' king. Amongft other Andrew Trollop, perceyving that they fhould
' fight againft the king (whofe friend they efteemed before that time
' the E. of Warwicke ever to have bene) in the dead of the night
' before the day of battel, he & the other Califians, fecretly depart-
' ed from the duke & fubmitted themfelves to the king, admonifhing
' him of all things devifed to his deftruction. For the duke per-
' ceyving by his expert captains a way how to fet upon his enemies
' & eafily difcomfit them, thought, on the next morning, to have af-
' fayled the king ere they had been readie. But now being adver-
' tifed that Trollop was thus departed, & all his counfayle revealed by
' him; [c] they concluded to flee, & leave the field ftanding as they had
' been ftil abiding. [d] Whereupon the duke with his younger fon
' Edmond E. of Rutland fecretly fled into Wales, & fo paffed over
' into Ireland, where he was gladly received, all the Irifh offering to
' live & die with him. The E. of March, fon & heir apparent of the
' faid duke, with the earles of Salifburie & Warwicke, ftale away the
' fame night, & came into Devonfhire, where by meanes of John
' Denham efq; (high treafurer of England in the days of Hen. the 7.)
' they bought a fhip, & fayled to Calais, where they were let in at
' a pofterne, & joyfully welcomed by William Nevil lord Faucon-
' bridge (Warwicks uncle & Salifburies brother) who then had the
' towne in keeping.

XXXI. ' The king in the morning advertifed that the D. of York [lord
of Stanford] ' & his partakers were fled, caufed all his horfemen to fol-
' low them, but in vain: for they were got farre enough out of daunger.
' He then pardoned all the poore fouldiers, faving certain ringleaders,
' of which fome he punifhed & fined, & fome he hanged & quartered.
' After this he removed to Ludlow, & there broke up his hoft, & fpoyled
' the towne & caftle, & fent the dutches of York with her two young
' fons to be kept in warde. This done he proclaimed the lords tray-
' tors, confifcated their eftates, & committed the government of the
' north parts to the E. of Northumberland & the lord Clifford, his
' trufty friends. The E. of Warwick being now at Calais fayled thence
' into Ireland, to commune with the D. of York [lord of Stanford.]

a Stow, p. 672.   c Fab. p. 466. b.
b Hol. p. 1297. a.   d Hol. p. 1297. a.

' The

' The weather & wind were both so favourable to his purpose, that
' in less than a month he passed from Calais to Dublin & back again,
' During this time the king called a parliament at Coventrie which
' began the 20. of Sept. saith Holingshed [a], [but it should rather be
November, or December; the order of things as before related not
allowing to be held in September] ' in which the D. of York [lord
of Stanford] ' & his confederates were attainted. But when the king
' came to give his consente & the clerk of the parliament read that
' statute of attaindure, such was the kings modestie & zeale unto
' mercie, that he caused a proviso to be added, that it might be law-
' ful for him without authoritie of any other parliament to pardon,
' & restore them in all things, so that they would come in into him,
' & beseech him of grace.

XXXII. Some time after, ' [b] the earls at Calais sent to the commons
' of England, beginning thus. We the D. of York, the earls of March,
' Warwick & Salisbury, sewed to have come unto the king, to have
' declared afore him. I. The great oppression, extortion, robbery,
' murther, & other violences done to Gods church & his ministers against
' law. II. The poverty & misery our soveraigne lord standeth in,
' not having any livelode of the crowne whereof he may keep his
' household, which causeth the spoiling of his liege-men by the takers
' of his household, which livelode is in their hands. III. How that
' his laws be partially guided, oppression favoured, & justice exiled.
' So that no man dreadeth to offend. IV. That it will please his
' grace to live upon his own livelode, as his progenitors have here-
' tofore, & not suffer the destroyers of his land & subjects to live
' thereupon, & find his household upon his poore commons. V. How
' oft the commons have been charged with taxes, whereof the king
' hath had to his part not half, & other persons the rest to their
' own use, suffering all the possessions that the king had in France to
' be lost. VI. How they now begin a new imposition, that is to
' say, every township to find men for the kings guard: which, if con-
' tinued, will be the heaviest charge that ever grew. VII. Divers lords
' have caused the king to write letters to his Irish enemies to enter
' into conquest of the said land, which letters the same Irish sent
' unto me the said D. of York. VIII. The king, by excitation of
' the same lords, wrote other letters, that in no wise they should
' shew any favour to the towne of Calais, & that nothing of refresh-
' ing or defence should come out of England to the relief of it, that it
' might be lost. IX. It is deemed the same lords would put the rule
' of England, if they might, into the said enemies hands. X. How
' it hath been laboured to have destroyed & murthered the said D.
' of York, & the issue it pleased God to send him of the roiall blood,
' & also the earles of Warwick & Salisbury. XI. How the earls of

a Hol. p. 1297. a.   b Stow, p. 674.

' Shrewsbury

' Shrewsbury & Wilts, & the lord Beaumont, our mortal enimies,
' having the guiding of our fovereign lord, would not fuffer the
' kings grace to receive us, as he would have done into his prefence,
' dreading the charge that would have been laid upon them. XII. How
' they excited his highnes to hold his parliament at Coventry, where
' an act is made againft us the faid D. of York, &c. to the intent of
' our deftruction & of our iffue; that they might have our livelode
' & goods, as they have openly robbed & defpoyled all our placcs &
' tenements, & now proceed to hanging & drawing of men, & there-
' in fhew the largenefs of their violence & malice as vengeably as
' they can. We therefore, feeing all the faid mifchiefs, purpofe yet
' again to come to the prefence of our faid foveraign lord, &, in the
' name of the land, fue, in as lowly wife as we can, to his good grace,
' to have pitie on his true fubjects, & not fuffer the fame mifchiefs
' to raigne upon them: requiring you therein to affift us, &c. Mean
' time the E. of Wiltfhire, the lord Scales, & lord Hungerford went
' to Newbery, which longed to the D of York, & there made inqui-
' fition of all them that in any wife had favoured the faid duke,
' whereof fome were drawed, hanged, & quartered; & all the inha-
' bitants fpoiled of their goods.' In July Richard D. of York & lord
of Stanford being yet in Ireland, his fon Edward E. of March, affifted
by the earls of Salisbury & Warwick, fought with K. Henry at Northampton, & took him prifoner. Whereupon the tower of London
was delivered to the E. of March.

XXXIII. Alderman 1460. William Brown. Roll. Frier Nicholas 39. H. 6.
Kenton, feveral times mentioned in the courfe of thefe antiquities,
fometime provincial of the White Friers, ' died, as Leland tells us [a],
' at London Sept. 4. 1460.' But note, either Bale, or his printer, was Sept. 4.
miftaken in the year of this Kentons death, which his book fets down 1460.
in 1468. However Pits, as he never faw Leland, knew nothing of
the blunder, & fo very gravely follows Bale in the miftake, & with
his ufual affurance pronounces Kenton died in 1468. But to proceed. [b] The D. of York [lord of Stanford] being advertifed of what
' lately happened in England, now fayled from Dublin, & landed at
' the redde bank near Chefter; & from Chefter, by long journeys,
' came to London, which he entered the Friday before the feaft of
' S. Edward the confeffor, with a fword born naked before him,
' trumpets founding, & a great traine of men of armes, & other of
' his friends & fervaunts. At his coming to Weftminfter he entred
' the palace, & paffing directly thro' the great hall, ftayed not till he
' came to the houfe of peeres, & there ftept up to the throne, & lay-
' ing his hand upon the cloth of eftate, held his hand fo a good while;
' & afterwards withdrawing his hand, turned hys face towards the
' people, beholding their preffing together, & marking what coun-

a Comment. p. 459.   b Holing. p. 1300. a.

' tenance they made. Whileſt he ſtoode & behelde the people, ſup-
' poſing they rejoyced to ſee his preſence, the archbiſhop of Canter-
' burie came to him, &, after due ſalutations, asked him if he would
' come & ſee the king. Wyth whiche demaunde he ſeeming to take
' diſdaine, anſwered, I remember not that I know any within this
' realme, but that it beſeemeth him rather to come & ſee my per-
' ſon, than I to go & ſee his. The archbiſhop hearing his anſwere,
' went backe to the king, & declared what he had receyved of the
' dukes own mouth. ᵃ And now this D. of York [lord of Stanford]
' being yet in the parliament houſe, grew to that pitch of boldneſs,
' that he there publickly claimed the crowne againſt king Henry ᵇ.
' For at laſt he ſat down in the throne, & after a pauſe made, began
' thus. My ſingular good lordes, marvayle not that I approache unto
' this throne: for I ſit here, as in the place to mee by very juſtice
' lawfully belonging, & here I reſt, as to whom this chair of right
' apperteineth: not as hee which requireth of you favour, parcialitie,
' or bearing; but equal right, friendlye indifferencie, & true juſtice.
' For I being the partie greeved, cannot miniſter to my ſelf the me-
' decine that ſhould helpe me (as expert leches & chirurgians may)
' except you be to me both faithful ayders & true counſaylers. Nor
' yet this noble realme & our natural countrey ſhall be unbuckled
' from hir dayly fever, except I as principal phiſition & you as truſtie
' apothecaries, conſult togither in making the potion, & trie out the
' cleane pure ſtuffe from the corrupt & putrifyed drugges. For un-
' doubtedly the root & bottom of this long feſtered canker is not yet
' extirpate, nor the feeble foundation of this fallible buylding yet
' eſpied, which hath been & is the dayly deſtruction of the nobilitie,
' & the continual confuſion of the poore commonaltie. For all you
' know (or ſhould know) that the high & mightie prince K. Richard
' the 2. was the true undoubted heir to the valiant conqueror & re-
' nowned prince K. Edward the 3ᵈ. as ſon & heire to the hardie
' knight & couragious captaine Edward prince of Wales, eldeſt ſonne
' to the ſaid K. Edward; which king was not only in deede, but
' of all men reputed & taken for the true infallible heire to the wiſe
' & politique prince K. Henry the 3ᵈ. as ſonne & heire to K. Edward
' the 2ᵈ. ſonne & heire to K. Edward the firſt, the very heyre of the
' ſaid noble & vertuous K. Henry the 3ᵈ. Which K. Richard the 2.
' was lawfully & juſtly poſſeſſed of the crowne, 'till Henry of Derbie
' D. of Lancaſter & Hereford, ſon to John of Gaunt D. of Lancaſter,
' 4. ſon to the ſayd K. Edward the 3ᵈ. & younger brother to my
' noble aunceſter Lionel D. of Clarence, third ſon of the ſaid K.
' Edward, by force & violence; contrarie to his allegiance, & alſo to
' his homage to him both done & ſworne, rayſed warre againſt the
' ſaid K. Richard, & him apprehended & impriſoned, during whoſe

ᵃ Brit. p 757.   ᵇ Hol. p. 1300. b.

ᶜ captivity

' captivity he wrongfully ufurped the royal power, taking upon him
' the name of king; & not therewith fatisfied, compaffed & accom-
' plifhed the death & deftruction of his natural prince; after whofe
' execrable murther the right of the crown reverted to Roger Mor-
' timer E. of March, fon & heyr to ladie Philip onely child of the
' above Lionel D. of Clarence, to which Rogers daughter called Anne,
' my moft dear and welbeloved mother, I am the true and lineal heyre;
' which difcent all you cannot juftly gainfaye.   Then, if the title be
' mine, why am I put from it? If I be true heyr, why is my right
' withholden? If my claime be good, why have I not juftice? For
' furely learned men affirme, that lineal difcent, or ufurped poffeffi-
' on, can nothing prevaile, if continual clayme be lawfully made.
' For avoyding of which fcruple, Edmond E. of March my moft wel-
' beloved uncle, in the time of the firft ufurper, in deede, but not
' by right, called king Henry the 4. by his cofins the E. of Nor-
' thumberland & the lord Percy (he being then in captivitie with
' Owen Glendower) made his clayme, tho' to the deftruction of both
' thofe noble perfons.   Likewife my moft deareft lord & father, fo
' farre fet forth that right & tytle, that he loft his life at Southamp-
' ton, more by power than indifferent juftice.   Sithe whofe death
' I coming to my full age, have never defifted to purfue my title,
' which by means of unjuft detention, I cannot recover.   So that of
' force I am compelled to ufe power inftead of prayer, not for my
' private emolument, but to reftore peace, which ever fince the firft
' ungodly ufurpation of the forenamed Henry, untruly called K. Henry
' the 4. hath beene clearly banifhed.   What murthers have been per-
' petrated, what number of noble men deftroyed, fince that unfor-
' tunate day; is too lamentable & manifeft.   For altho' Henrie of
' Lancafter tooke upon him the crown, & was not much tickled
' by myne uncle the E. of March, then within age: yet was he never
' in furetie of himfelf, nor enjoyed any quietneffe in minde or bodie:
' For a corrupt confcience never feeleth reft, but looketh when the
' fword of vengeance will defcend & ftrike.   His fon alfo, called K.
' Henry the 5. obteyned notable victories & immortal praifes for his
' noble acts in France; yet God, for the offence of his parent, fo-
' dainly touched him, unbodying his foul in the flower of his youth,
' & in the glorie of his conqueft.   And altho' he had a fayre fonne
' & a young, apparent heyre, yet was this orphan fuch an one, as,
' preachers faye, God threatned to fend for a punifhment to his un-
' ruly & ungracious people; faying, by his prophet Efay, I fhall give
' you children to be your princes, & infants without wifdom fhall
' have the governance of you.   And the prophet lied not, if you
' note things.   For, after this Henry the 5. fucceeded his fonne, whom
' all we have called our natural prince, & obeyed as his heyre, in
' whofe wrongful reigne, I require you diligently to confider, with
' what great afflictions God hath fcourged this miferable ifle, yea

'with fo many plagues as no nation (the Egyptians excepted) were
'ever tormented with. I will not fpeak of murthers & oppreffi-
'ons which of late have been done among us. But I will ma-
'nifeft how the glory of this realme is by the negligence of this
'filly man & his unwife counfaile minifhed & difhonoured. Is not
'Normandie, which his father got, regained? Is not Aquitaine,
'cc. & odd years peaceably poffeffed by the kings of this realme,
'gotten out of our hands & feigniory? What fhould I fpeak of
'Anjou, Mayne, or the loffe of the ifle of France, with the rich
'citie of Paris? Alas it is too apparent, neither will I moleft you
'with the recital. But now in the midft of this affliction, & to
'make an end of the fame, God of his ineffable goodnefs, look-
'ing on this country with eies of pitie, hath fent me to reftore
'again his decayed kingdome to hys antient fame & old renowne,
'whereof here in open parliament, according to my juft & true
'title, I take poffeffion, not putting diffidence but firm hope in
'God, that by his ayde, & affiftance of you the peeres, I fhall
'maynteine the fame, to the glorie of him, honour of my blood,
'& to the publick wealth as well of you all here prefent, as of the
'poore commons of the kingdome. When the duke had made an
'end of his oration, the lordes fat as men ftryken into a certaine
'amazedneffe, neyther whifpering nor fpeaking forth a word, as tho'
'theyr mouthes had bene fowed up. The duke not very well con-
'tent with their ftrange filence, advifed them to confider thoroughly
'& ponder the whole effect of his wordes; & fo, neyther fully dif-
'pleafed, nor yet altogether pleafed, departed to his lodging in the
'kings palace.' Where when he came, ' [a] the king being there, he
'brake up the doores of the kings chamber, fo that the king giving
'him place, took another.

XXXIV. ' [b] The lordes forgot not the dukes demaund, & there-
'fore to take fome good direction therein, dyverfe as well fpiritual
'lords as temporal, wyth many fage perfons of the communaltie dayle
'affembled at the black fryers & other places, to commune of this
'matter of fo great importance. Duryng which time the duke would
'not, for any requeft made unto him, once vifit or fee the king;
'affirming that he was fubject to none but God: & that he was lorde
'& none other.' At length ' [c] it was anfwered him that the barons
'of the kingdom, & the duke himfelf had fworn allegiance to the
'king; that the kingdom by act of parliament was conferr'd & en-
'tail'd upon Hen. the 4. & his heirs; that the duke deriving his title
'from the duke of Clarence, never took the arms of the faid duke;
'& that Henry the 4. was poffeffed of the crown by the right he
'had from Henry the 3d. All this he eafily evaded by replying, that
'the faid oath fworn to the king being barely an humane conftitu-
'tion, was not binding, becaufe inconfiftent with truth & juftice,

a Stow, p. 679   b Holing. p. 1302. b.   c Camdens Brit. p. 757.

3

' which

' which are of divine appointment. That there had been no need
' of an act of parliament to fettle the crown in the line of Lan-
' cafter, neither would they have defired it, if they could have
' relied upon any juft title: And, as for the arms of the D. of
' Clarence, which in right belonged to him, he had, in prudence,
' declined ufing them, as he had declined challenging the kingdom,
' 'till that moment: & that the title derived from Henry the 3ᵈ.
' was a ridiculous pretext to cloak the injuftice, & exploded by
' every body. ᵃ After diligent deliberation, peace between the
' king & duke, on the vigil of Alhallow, was concluded as follow-
' eth. Firft, whereas the duke hath opened his claim in manner as
' above, the faid title notwithftanding, the faid duke tenderly defir-
' ing the reft & profperity of this land, & to fet apart all that might
' trouble the fame; & confidering the poffeffion of the faid K. Henry
' the 6. & that he hath been for his time named, taken, & reputed
' king; is contented that he be king during life, & for that time
' fhall take him for his foveraigne. II. The faid duke fhall bind him-
' felf by othe, never to procure or ftir any thing that may found to
' the abridgment of the natural life of K. Henry. III. The fonnes
' of the faid duke fhall make like oth. IV. The faid duke fhall be
' called & reputed henceforth very & rightful heir to the crown, &
' his heirs after him. V. The faid duke fhall have yeerely 5000
' markes to his owne ftate; 3500 marks for Edward his firft begot-
' ten fonne, & 1000 l. for Edmond his fecond fonne, for their yeare-
' ly fuftentation. VI. If any perfon imagine, or compaffe the death
' of the faid duke, that it be adjudged high treafon. VII. The lords
' fpiritual & temporal fhall fwear to repute & take the duke & his
' heirs as heirs of the crown, & to refift all them that would prefume
' the contrary. VIII. The faid duke & his fons fhall defend the faid
' lords againft all thofe that attempt any thing againft them by rea-
' fon of this agreement. IX. That this accord be notified by the
' kings letters patents, as it fhall be thought expedient by the faid
' duke, &c. ᵇ The agreement aforefaid being put in articles was en-
' groffed, fealed, & fworn by the parties, & alfo enacted in the high
' court of parliament. For joy whereof ᶜ the king with the duke, &
' many other lords then there prefent, came that night to Paules, &
' there hard evenfong, & on the morrowe, came thither againe to
' maffe, where the king rode in proceffion crouned with great roial-
' tie, & fo laie ftill in the bifhops palace, a feafon after. And upon
' the Saturday following, being the ninth day of November, the duke
' was proclaimed thro' the citee heire aparaunt to the croune, & all his
' progenie after hym. ᵈ It was ordained by the fame parliament that
' the faid Richard D. of York [lord of Stanford] fhould be cal-
' led prince of Wales, duke of Cornwall, earl of Chefter, & protec-

a Stow, p. 679, &c.   c Fabian, p. 470. a.
b id. p. 683.   d Stow, p. 683.

' tor of England.   After this the parliament kept at Coventrie the
' laft yeare, was declared a devilifh councel, celebrated for the
' deftruction of the nobilitie, & no lawful parliament. The D. of
' York well knowing that the queene would fpurne againft the con-
' clufions agreed in this parliament, caufed both hir & hir fonne to
' be fent for by the king; but fhe being a ftout woman, by the coun-
' fel of the dukes of Exeter & Somerfet, not only denied to come,
' but alfo affembled a great army, intending to take the king by force
' out of the lords hands.

Nov. 22.   XXXV. Margaret, relict of the late John Brown merchant of the
ftaple, died the 22. of November, & was buried at the upper end of
the north ifle of All Saints church in the mercat; foon after whofe
death, in memory of her & her faid husband, a plate of gilded brafs
was fixed in a wall near the place where they were buried, with this
infcription. *Orate pro animabus Johannis Brown mercatoris ftapule
Califie & Margerie uxoris ejus.   Qui quidem Johannes obiit* xxvi°.
die menfis Julii, an dni. MCCCCXLII. *& que quedam Margeria obiit*
xxij°. *die Novembris,* MCCCCLX. *quorum animabus propitietur Deus,
Amen.*   It appears by this epitaph, that Mrs. Margaret Brown continued a widow after her husbands death more than 18 years; & was
then laid by him, in the fame earth, if not in the fame grave.   Here
a word or two of this All Saints church in the mercat.   This church
confifts of three ifles; & two chancels, one anfwering the fouth ifle,
& the other the nave.   Adjoyning to the weft end of the north ifle
is the fteeple, a beautiful ftone fabric, embattelled at the tower, &
crocketed all the way up the fpire.   The whole is a very neat, well-
proportioned, & much admired thing; being indeed one of the principal ornaments of Stanford.   In it hang five bells, the biggeft about 1500
weight: which are thus infcribed.   I. *Hec nova campana Margaretta
eft nominata.*   II. *Nomen Magdalene campana fonat melodie.*   III. *In
multis annis refonet campana Johannis.*   IV. New caft, 1726.   V. *God
fave the king, Tobias Norris caft me,* 1674.   Befides which there is
fanctes bell.   The firft & third of thefe bells were given, as I guefs,
by the above Mr. John Brown, & Margaret his wife.   The new fteeple was built by John Brown their eldeft fon.   Mr. Butcher fays it
was erected by Mr. William Brown, who founded the hofpital; but
the tradition is otherwife.

XXXVI. ' [a] The D. of York protector, [b] having perfite knowledge
' of the queens doings, affigned the D. of Norfolk & the E. of War-
' wicke his truftie friends to be about the king, & he with the earls
' of Salisbury & Rutland, & a convenient number of men, departed
Dec. 2. ' out of London the 2. of December northward, & fent to the E. of
' March his eldeft fonne to follow him with all hys power. The D.
' came to his caftel of Sandal befide Wakefield, on Chriftmafs even,

a id. ib.   b Holing. p. 1303. b.

2   ' &

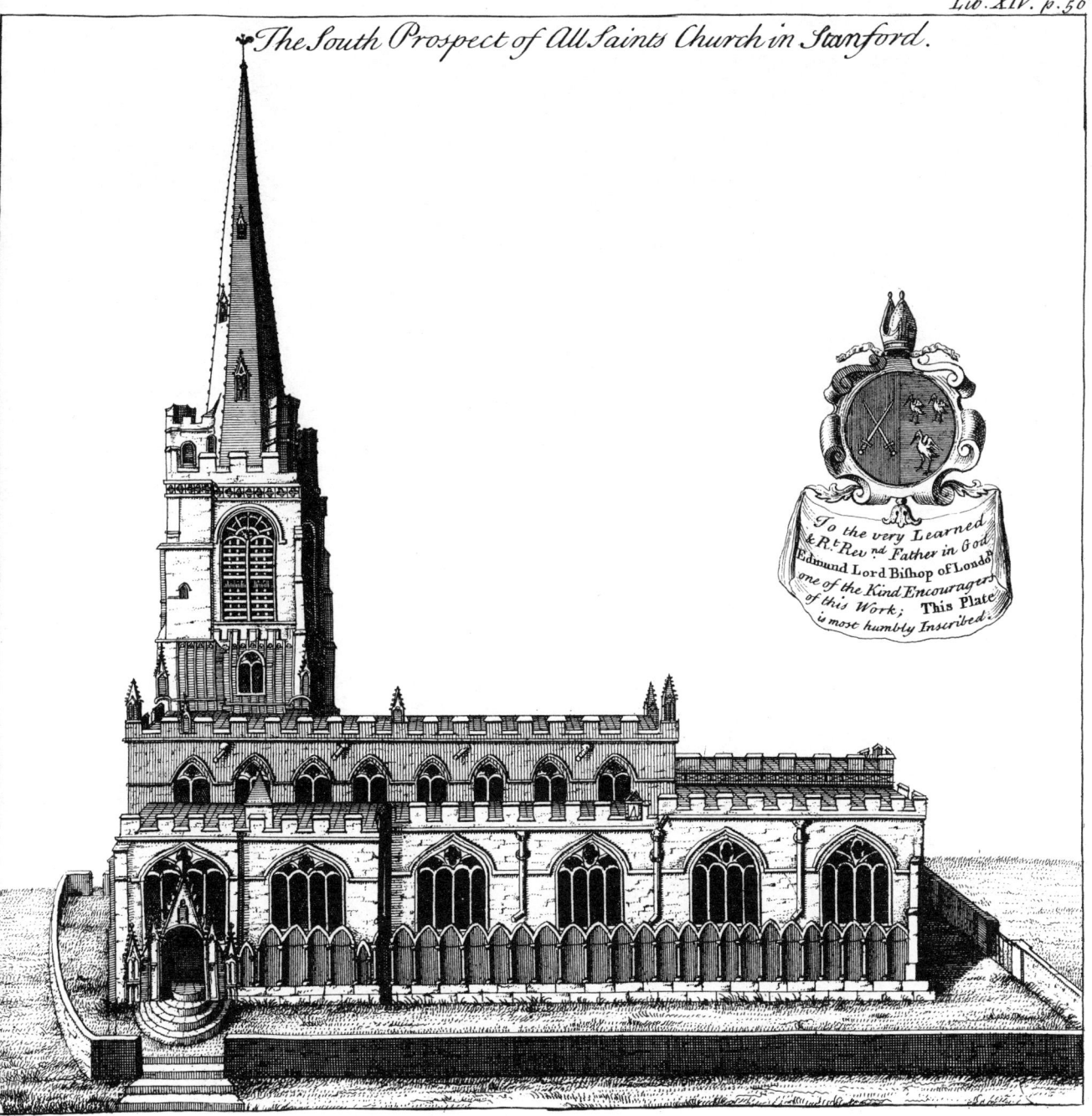

The South Prospect of All Saints Church in Stanford.

To the very Learned
& R.t Rev.nd Father in God
Edmund Lord Bishop of Londo̅
one of the Kind Encouragers
of this Work; This Plate
is most humbly Inscribed.

' & there begane to affemble his tenants & friends.   ᵃ There came to
' him under a colour of friendſhip the lord Nevill, brother to the E.
' of Weſtmorland, & required of him a commiſſion for him to raiſe
' the people for to chaſtiſe his rebels, as he ſaid ; but when he had
' raiſed 8000 men, he brought them to the lords of the countrie.
' ᵇ The queene advertiſed, thinkes it wiſdome to fight before the duke
' grow too ſtrong ; & thereupon marches forward, having an army of
' 18000 men, led by the dukes of Somerſet & Exceſter, the earles of De-
' von & Wilts, the lords Nevil, Clifford, Roſſe, & in effect all the nor-
' therne nobilite.   The hoſt (or ſo much thereof as they thought ne-
' ceſſarie to ſhew) preſents it ſelf before Sandall, ᶜ where they placed
' themſelves even before the caſtle gates, ᵈ to provoke & dare the duke
' to battel.   His bloud impatient of theſe braves, & ignorant perhaps
' that the enemy had ſo great a multitude, will needes fight, tho' the E.
' of Salisbury & Sir David Hall (an antient ſervant of his & a great ſoldier)
' gave him advice to ſtay till his ſonne the E. of March approached with
' ſuch Welchmen & Marchers as he had in great numbers aſſembled.
' But God would forbeare him no longer, but like a ſevere maſter
' means to take a preſent account : at which he found whether all the
' kingdoms of the earth are worth the leaſt ſinne, much leſſe a wilful
' perjurie.   The queene therefore addeth ſtratagem & wit to her force,
' to the intent he might not eſcape her hands ; whereupon the E. of
' Wilts upon one ſide of the hill, & the lord Clifford upon the other,
' lye in ambuſh to thruſt between him & the caſtell ; the dukes of So-
' merſet & Exceſter ſtand embattelled in the open field.   Their pol-
' licy had the wiſh'd ſucceſs, for the duke being not fully 5000 ſtrong
' iſſued out of the caſtle, ᵉ & came down the hill with his people in
' good order of array, & was ſuffred to paſſe on toward the maine
' battel.   But when he was in the plaine fielde betweene his caſtel
' & the towne of Wakefield, he was environed on every ſide, ᶠ like
' a fiſhe in a net, ſo that he manfully fighting was, within half an
' hour, ſlain, ᵍ his whole armie diſcomfited, & divers of his dear friends
' beaten downe with him.   There lay dead about him the lord Ha-
' rington, Sir Thomas Neville ſon to the E. of Salisbury, Sir Davy
' Hall, with ſundrie knights & others, in all about 2200, among which
' were the heirs of many ſouthern gentlemen of great account.   ʰ Some
' write that the duke was taken alive, & in deriſion cauſed to ſtande
' upon a molehill, on whoſe head they put a garlande (inſteade of a
' crowne) of ſegges or bulruſhes, & having ſo crowned him, they
' kneeled downe afore him in ſcorne ſaying, hail king without rule
' or heritage ! haile duke & prince without people or poſſeſſions !
' And at length having ſcorned him with theſe & divers other diſpite-
' ful words, they ſtroke off his head & preſented it to the queen.

a Stow, p. 684.   e Stow, ut ſupra.
b Speed, p. 863. a.   f Holing. ut ſupra.
c Stow, ut ſupra.   g Speed, ut ſupra. b.
d Speed, ut ſupra.   h Holing. ut ſupra.

                                                          ' In

' In this conflict the lord Clifford perceyving where the E. of Rut-
' land (the duke of Yorks second son) was conveyed out of the
' fielde by one of his fathers chaplains, schoolmaister to the same earl;
' followed him, & overtaking & understanding what he was, stabbed
' him to the heart with a dagger, as he kneeled before him. This
' earle was but a childe at this time of xij. years of age; but, neither
' his tender yeares, nor his dolorous countenance which he shewed,
' in holding up both his handes, & craving mercie & grace with his
' lamentable gesture (for hys speache was gone for feare) could
' plie the cruel heart of Clifford to take pitie on him; who thus
' slew him [a] in part of revenge for that the earles father (the D. of
' York) had slaine his. A deed neverthelefs which worthily blemish-
' ed the author. But who can promise any thing temperate of
' himself in the heat of martial furie? chiefly where it was refolved,
' not to leave any branch of York line standing: for so doth one
' make the lord Clifford to speak. [b] In this battel the said lord Clif-
' ford is reported to have made so great a slaughter with his own
' hands, that he was thenceforth called the Butcher. [c] The same lord
' Clifford not satisfied therewith, came afterwards to the place where
' the dead corpse of the D. of York lay, & caused his head to be
' stricken off, & set on it a crown of paper, & so fixed it on a poll,
' & presented it to the queene, lying not farre from the field, at
' which present great rejoycing was shewed. [d] Cruel joy is seldome
' fortunate. Cæsar wept over Pompeys head. But the queene (ig-
' norant how manifold causes of tears were reserved for her own
' share) makes her self merry with that ghastly & bloody spectacle.'
Thus died Richard D. of York [& lord of Stanford] who, as you have
heard, ' [e] endeavouring to anticipate his hopes, raised that pernicious
' war between his own house of York & that of Lancaster, distin-
' guished by the *white* & *red* roses. [f] Many deemed this miserable
' end chaunced to this duke of York, as a due punishment for break-
' ing his othe of allegiance to his sovereign lord K. Henry. But
' others helde him discharged thereof, bycause he obteyned a dispen-
' sation from the pope, by such suggestion as his procurator made unto
' him, whereby the same oth was adjudged voyd, as that which was
' receyved unadvisedly, to the prejudice of himself, & disinheriting of
' all his posteritie.' But the popes absolution is sure a poor pretence
for a man to think himself released from so sacred an engagement
as a most solemn oath, vowed to be observed; when likewise the cross
was touched, & the holy Sacrament it self received with it, to make
it, if possible, more binding. That violence was frequently offered
the D. of York whilst he lay quiet, was a good reason for him to
withdraw to save himself, & perhaps if then attacked to repel force

a Speed, p. 863. b.
b Bar. Vol. I. p. 343. a.
c Holing. p. 1304. a.

d Speed, ut supra.
e Britannia Camb. p. 758.
f Holing. p. 1304. a.

2

by force; but undoubtedly not enough to enable him utterly to difpence with his oath, & attack him whom he had engaged to live in peace with.

XXXVII. ' ᵃ After this victorie thus obtained by the queene, the
' earl of Salisburie & all the prifoners were fent to Pomfret & there
' beheaded; whofe heades, together with the D. of Yorkes, were con-
' veyed to Yorke, & there fet on polles over the gate of the citie,
' in defpite of them & their lynage. ᵇ Being thus flain & beheaded,
' the D. of Yorks corps was firft interred at Pontfract, but afterwards
' in the quire of the collegiate church at Fotheringhayᶜ, where he had
' afterwards a magnificent monument erected upon his grave; but it
' was thrown down & ruined together with the chancel of the church
' in K. Edward the 6. reign; but queen Elizabeth regretting that in-
' human fact, commanded a monument to be fet up in memory of
' him in the lower [he fhould fay, upper] ' end of the church,
' which is now ftanding: but fo fparing were they who had the
' charge of the work, that it is looked upon as mean & unworthy
' of fo great a prince, defcended from kings, & from whom the
' kings of England are defcended.' The now worthy vicar of Fotheringhay Mr. James Holcot fays, ' ᵈ the prefent monument of Richard
' D. of York flain at Wakefield, is erected on the north fide of the
' high wall of the nave of the church at the entring into that which
' was the quire, & over it, on the wall, is wrote, Here lieth the bo-
' dy of Richard D. of York, who was flain at Wakefield; and Cecilia
' his wife.' But note, Cecilia his wife died not till the 10. of Henry
the 7. 1495. Mr. Holcot adds, ' this monument, like that of Edward
' D. of York before defcribed, is of freeftone (I believe of Ketton
' ftone, or fuch like) without any infcription, & nothing but his coat
' of arms at large upon it; railed in with wooden rails, coloured
' red.' And now to fhut up his ftory. ' ᵉ Thus have we feen the
' tragique conclufion of this great dukes life: of whom (as I have
' read) it was faid by the late D. of Somerfet (his chiefeft opponent)
' that, if he had not learned to play the king by his regency in
' France, he had never forgot to obey, as a fubject, when he return-
' ed into England. ᶠ This battel (called the battel of Wakefield) was
' fought upon the laft day of December, of whofe weathers complexion,
' if their courages had participated, mifchiefe might have made her
' ftop here, which now is in her fwifteft courfe.

XXXVIII. ' ᵍ The E. of Marche, fo commonly called, but now af-
' ter the death of his father, in deede & in very right D. of Yorke
[& lord of Stanford] ' lying at Gloucefter, was wonderfully amazed,
' when the forrowful newes of thefe mifhappes came unto hym: but

a Holing. p. 1304. b.
b Bar. Vol. II. p. 161. b.
c Brit. ant. & nova. Vol. III. p. 473. b.
d Ex literis mihi datis May 29. 1725.

e Bar. Vol. II. p. 161. b.
f Speed, p. 863. b.
g Holing. p. 1304. b.

14 R ' after

'after comfort gyven hym by his faithful lovers & affured allies, he
remooved to Shrewsburie, declaring to the inhabitants of that &
'other townes, the murther of his father, the jeopardie of himfelf,
'& the prefent ruine of the common-wealth. ª This youthful & va-
'liant E. of Marches amiable prefence & carriage made him graci-
'ous with the people, & the rather for that he had the general good
'word of the women. Whereupon ᵇ the people on the Marches of
'Wales, for the favour which they bare to the Mortimers linage,
'more gladly offred him their ayde & affiftance than he could de-
'fire the fame: fo that he had incontinently a puiffant armie to the
'number of 23000, ready to go againft the queene & the murtherers
'of his father. But when he was fetting forward news was brought,
'that Jafper E. of Pembroke & James Butler E. of Ormond, had af-
'fembled together a great number of Welch & Irifh people to take
'him. He, being herewith quickened, retired back & met with his
'enemies in a fayre plaine near Mortimers croffe not far from Here-

Feb. 2. 'ford, on Candlemaffe day, at which tyme the fun (as fome write)
'appeared to him like three funs, & fuddenly joyned altogether into
'one: upon which fight he tooke fuch courage, that he fiercely fet-
'ting on his enimies put them to flight: & for this caufe men ima-
'gined that he gave the fun for his badge. Of his enemies were
'left dead on the ground 3800. ᶜ The fun of honour & fortune
'did thus begin to fhine, thro' clouds of bloud & miferie, upon Ed-
'ward, whom fhortly we are to behold K. of England.' But we
muft firft fee the deftruction of Stanford, which now draws on apace.

XXXIX. Befides the army defeated as above at Mortimers crofs,
if we reckon the victor army one, there were yet three more left
to ravage & prey upon the kingdom. One of thefe was at London
commanded by the great E. of Warwick, who had king Henry himfelf in keeping. Another was affembled in the north under Q. Margaret, refolved, as hath been intimated, to refcue her husband; &
the third was conducted by the E. of March. In thefe dangerous
times no body adventured, except in cafes of extreme neceffity, to
travel any where; nor then without a pafs from the commander of
that army which lay next to them; nor could they fo protected,
depend upon their fafety: wherefore as it is fomewhat curious, &
fhews the ftile of the times, I fhall give here a copy of one of thofe
letters of fafeguard, from the original now in my own hands. ' Ri-
'chard erle of Warrewyk & capitaine of Calais: to all oure frends,
'fervaunts, tenaunts, & welwillers; & to all other the king oure fo-
'verain lords fubjects, to whom this prefent oure writing fhal be
'fhewed, greeting. We, on the behalve of the king oure faid fou-
'verain lord charge & commaunde you, & in oure owne defire &
'pray, that ye in no wife vexe, trouble, hurte, fpoyle, or endomage

---

a Speed, as above.   b Holing, as above.   c Speed, p. 864. a

'in

'in body or goods unlawfully, John Andrew of Merton in the coun-
'tee of Oxonford, yoman, ne noon of his servaunts: But suffre him
'& theim plainly & peasibly to ride, goo, & come, & to abide in
'such place or places leeful as hee & they shall thenke best, upon
'such peynes as may fall thereof, yf ye attempte the contrairy, & as
'ye wol eschewe oure hevy lordship.   And that ye suffer him & his
'said servaunts yewysse this oure saufgarde without any vexation,
'letting, or unlawful impediment.   Yeven under oure signet at Lon-
'don the fourth day of ffeurer, the yere, of the reigne of the king Feb. 4.
'oure said souverain lord Henry the sext sithen the conquest, xxxix.'
The seal is wanting.   But to proceed.   ' [a] During this season the
'queene encouraged with her late victory at Wakefield, with a great
'number of people out of the north, marched toward London, in-
'tending to recover the company of the king her husband, & undo
'all that had been done in the last parliament.   These northern peo-
'ple, after they were once passed the river of Trent, spoiled & wasted
'the countrie afore them.   For Andrew Trollop grand captaine, & as
'it were leader of the battel, with a great armie of Scots, Welchmen,
'& other strangers, beside the northern men, destroyed the townes
'of Grantham, Stanford, Peterborough, Huntingdon, Roiston, Mel-
'leborne, & in a manner all the townes by the way unto S. Albans;
'sparing neither abbeies, priores, or parish churches, but bare away
'crosses, chalices, bookes, ornaments, & other things, whatsoever
'was worth the carriage, as tho' they had been Saracens & no
'christians.'   Speed says, ' [b] there came before them an evil fame
'of their behaviour to London, whose wealth looked pale knowing
'it self in danger.'   And well it might.   But hear what terrible apprehensions they who then lived in this neighbourhood were filled with
at their approach.   ' The duke of York, says the continuer of the
'history of Croyland [c], being slain, presently the northern men, see-
'ing that, he their hinderance once removed, there was no body
'who durst venture to resist their power; like a sort of a whirlwind,
'scouring back out of the north, sought to involve all England in
'the onset of their fury.   For on the very day of their victory, all
'the vagabonds & beggars of the neighbourhood, reckoning their
'own countrymen, who had defeated the duke, would be at peace
'with them, & do them no manner of harm; in an infinite multi-
'tude came pouring out of those parts, like so many mice breaking
'out of their holes, & fell to robbing & spoiling every where indif-
'ferently, without any respect of place or person.   For besides the
'prodigious great riches which they raked up for themselves from
'without, they likewise with a wild madness irreverently breaking
'even into, the churches & other sanctuaries of God, most wickedly
'took away chalices, books, vestments, nay the very pyxes made to

a Stow, p. 685.   b p. 864. a.   c p. 531.

'preserve

' preferve Chrifts body, fhaking out of them (oh impious!) the holy
' Sacrament it felf; & like defperate wretches cruelly murdered the
' priefts & other faithful of Chrift, in the very churches or churchyards,
' who in any manner offered to oppofe them. And thus in a grie-
' vous multitude paffing uncontrouled here & there thirty miles wide,
' & like locufts covering the whole face of the earth as far almoft as
' the walls of London, they every where took away all the good fur-
' niture they found, loading their horfes with it. Nay they came
' on with fuch an huge greedinefs of plunder, that they dug up again
' the pretious veffels which were buried in the earth for fear of them,
' & forced people, pain of death, to difcover their treafures, tho' hid
' in the moft fecret & cunning places. How much fear do you think
' we living in this ifland of Croyland were then filled with, when
' fuch unfortunate rumors every day daunted our ears, & what we know
' they have done to our neighbours, how dreaded we with great
' trembling that we fhould undergo the like? And what more efpe-
' cially gave us ground for thefe apprehenfions, was, that a many peo-
' ple living in the country about us, defirous to provide for the fafety
' of themfelves & their facred things, repaired in great numbers to
' this ifland as a fingular refuge. Whence, by bringing with them
' whatever they had in their treafures that was valuable, they did but
' render the place more fufpected to the enemy. Mean while our
' own pretious veftments are withdrawn, & our other jewels, &
' filver veffels, with our charters & muniments; & all of them moft
' fecretly inclofed in the walls. Moreover daily proceffions are cele-
' brated by the convent, & every night after mattin lauds, in the fpi-
' rit of humility & with a contrite foul, prayers & tears are moft
' devoutly poured out to implore the divine mercie by its interven-
' tion. Befides which, at all the gates of the monaftery, alfo in the
' adjacent village, both on the waters as well as land, watch & ward
' were continually kept. Alfo all the ftreams of water in the whirl-
' pools & pits furrounding the forefaid village, thro' which an entrance
' might any ways lie open, were ftopped with polls & pofts exceed-
' ing ftrong. Moreover the highways & our banks, whereby the foot
' road lies plain & open, were filled with things to block them up, &
' here & there trees laid acrofs in them which would have been no little
' impediment to them, who attempted to come to us. In this ftraight
' thus were we appointed, when it was fignified to us that fo ex-
' ecrable & wicked an army was got within fix miles of us. But
' bleffed be God, who delivered us not up for a prey unto their teeth!
' For, after the neighbouring countries had been given up to a
' miferable fpoil & plunder; our Croyland, like another little Segor,
' wherein we might be faved, by the divine mercy moft graci-
' oufly remained preferved.' Thus Croyland efcaped, but not thus
did Stanford. That town lay directly in their road, was rich, & what
was worfe, greatly affected to its then lords & proprietors the houfe

of

of York. It feverely felt therefore the fury of their mortal enemies
the Lancaftrians, in this mad journey of theirs towards London. For
this is the time, tho' he himfelf knew it not, which Leland fpeaks
of, when he fays, ' ᵃ the northern men brent miche of Staunforde
' tounne. It was not fince fully reedified.' And again. ' ᵇ The
' northerne men, in one of the three [he fhould rather fay, four] firft
' king Edwards days, dyd ille to the toune of Staunford, & brenned
' many writings of their antiquities & privileges.' This alfo is the
time, tho' he likewife knew it not exactly, when, as Mr. Camden,
fpeaking of the diffolution of our univerfity by K. Edward the third,
& what a lofs it was to the town, goes on, ' ᶜ neverthelefs this place
' flourifhed in trade, 'till the civil war falling out between the houfes
' of Lancafter & York, the northern foldiers, breaking into the town,
' deftroyed every thing with fire & fword: Nor could it ever after
' recover its antient dignity.' By this laft account it looks as if the
northern men met with fome ftop here. The town was walled, & the
inhabitants, it fhould feem, would not tamely fubmit to be plundered
without ftriking a ftroke. They fhut to their gates therefore, & kept
out their enemies, as long as they could; but at laft they broke in,
& then all went to wreck: by which means the town was at length
confumed by fire, & many of the inhabitants put to the fword. It
is very remarkable that almoft all thofe churches which ftood without
the town, or very near the walls, were now deftroyed, fince we meet
with little, if any, mention of them afterwards. Thus Bennewerk
church, which ftood by the weft gate, called now S. Peters gate,
was at this time certainly deftroyed: for a fragment of a deed dated
in the next reign, fpeaks of a houfe late in S. Mary Bennewerk, then
in S. Peters parifh. Cornftall church, which ftood fomewhere within
the walls in S. Georges parifh, was, I reckon, now alfo fwept away.
S. Thomas's church, but where fituate I find not, now alfo difappeared. S. Stephens & Trinity churches, both without the walls at the
eaft end of Stanford, were now likewife deftroyed, & the parifhes united,
firft to one another, afterwards to S. Pauls, & then to great S. Michaels. Laftly, All Saints church in Stanford-Baron, now vanifhes
with the reft, & the parifhes are reduced to Trinity without the walls,
S. Pauls, S. Andrews, great S. Michaels, S. Clements, All Saints, S.
Peters, S. Johns, S. Maries by the bridge, & S. Georges within the
walls: & S. Martins beyond the bridge; this laft confiderably damaged,
we may fuppofe, at this deplorable time, fince it was fo foon after rebuilt by bifhop Ruffel & other benefactors. Befides this deftruction
of churches, the town likewife, at this time, loft all its old records &
charters, whereby the place it felf, as well as this book, fuffers extreamly. Some indeed are retrieved in this collection, but nothing, to
what we might have expected, had not this great misfortune befallen

---

a Itin. Vol. 7. p. 10.   b Itin. Vol. 6. p. 29.   c In Corit

14 S   us.

us. After this grievous loſs therefore, I ſhall at preſent only add,
in general, with Mr. Leland, that ' ᵃ as much privilege is given to the
' town of Staunford, ſaving privilege for treaſon, as hath bene geven
' to any toune lightly in England.

XL. Let us now ſee what became of the northern men, who made
ſuch havoc at Stanford. ' ᵇ At length they came to Dunſtable, &
' ſo to S. Albons, & hearing that the dukes of Norfolk & Suffolk,
' & the earls of Warwick & Arundel, the lord Bonvile & other, whom
' the D. of York had left to governe the king in his abſence, had,
' by the kings aſſent, aſſembled a great hoſt, & were incamped with
' the king neere to the towne: thoſe northern lords & other that were
' with the queene, made forward, & entring S. Albons, meant to paſſe
' thro' the towne, & ſo to cope with their enemies; but finding a
' ſort of archers ranged neere to the great croſſe in the market-place
' to withſtand their paſſage, they were receyved with ſuche a ſtorme of
' arrowes, which came flying about their eares as thicke as haile, that
' they were quickly repulſed, & with loſſe driven to retire into the
' weſt end of the towne, ᶜ where by a lane that leadeth northwards
' up to S. Peters ſtreet, they made their entrie, & had there alſo a
' ſharp encounter agaynſt certaine bandes of the kings people ; but
' yet after great ſlaughter on both partes, they gote through, & upon
' the heathe that lyeth at the north end of the towne, called Barnard
' heath, ᵈ toward a little towne called Syndridge, in a place called no
' mans land, ᵉ they had a far greater conflicte with foure or five thou-
' ſand of the kings armie, that ſeemed as they had beene avaunt cou-
' rers, which gave the onſet ſo fiercely at the beginning, that the vic-
' tory reſted doubtful a certaine tyme ; ſo that if the eaſterne & ſoutherne
' men had continued as they began, the field had bin theirs; but, af-
' ter that they had ſtoode to it a pretty while, & perceyved none of
' their fellows from the great armie to come & aſſiſt them ; they
' began to faint, & turning their backes fledde amaine, over hedge &
' ditch, thro' thick & thinne, woodes & buſhes, ſeeking ſo to eſcape
' the hands of their cruel enemies that followed them with egre
' minds to make ſlaughter upon them ; namely, the northerne prickes,
' who nowe in the chaſe purſued moſt hotly, & bare down many,
' & more had done, if the night comming on, had not ſtayed the
' execution of their unmerciful willes. When the day was now cloſed
' & darkened with the ſhadow of night, thoſe that were about the
' king, being in number a 20000 perſons, hearing how evil their fel-
' lowes had ſped, began utterly to deſpaire of the victorie, & ſo fell
' without any long tarriaunce, to running away ; by reaſon whereof
' the nobles that were about the king, perceyving how the game went,
' & withall no comfort in the king, but rather a good wille & af-

a Itin. Vol. VI. p. 29.   d Stow, as above.
b Stow, p. 685.   e Hol. as above.
c Hol. p. 1305.

I

' ſection

' fection towards the contrarie part, they withdrew alſo. [a] The E. of
' Warwick went towards the E. of March, that was coming towards
' London out of Wales; [b] leaving the king, accompanied with the
' lord Bonville & Sir Thomas Kiriell of Kent, who, upon aſſurance
' of the kings promiſe, tarried with him & fled not. [c] This battel was
' fought on Shrove-Tueſday, the 17. of February, in which were Feb. 17.
' ſlain 1916. perſons. Now after the noble men & other were fled,
' & the king left in a manner alone, without any power of men to
' garde his perſon, he was counſelled by a ſquire called Thomas Hoo,
' a man well ſeene in the laws, to ſend ſome convenient meſſenger
' to the northern lords, advertiſing them that he would now gladly
' come unto them (whom he knew to be his friends, & had aſſem-
' bled for his ſervice) that he might remaine with them, as before
' he had under the governement of the ſoutherne lords. According-
' ly the king appointed the ſame ſquire to beare the meſſage, who
' firſt went & declared the ſame to the earl of Northumberland, &,
' returning, brought certaine lords with him, who conveyed the king,
' firſt into the lord Cliffords tent; then brought the queen & her
' ſonne prince Edward to his preſence, whom he joyfully received.
' The queen cauſed the king to dubbe her ſon knight, & this done,
' they went to the abby. The abbot made ſuit that order might be
' taken to reſtrain the northern men from ſpoiling the towne, & pro-
' clamation was forthwith made to that effect, but it availed not; for
' they maintained that the ſpoil of all things was granted them by
' covenaunt, after they were once paſſed the Trent: & ſo, not regard-
' ing any proclamation, they ſpared nothing that they could lay hands
' on. [d] Moreover the lord Bonvile & Sir Thomas Kiriel, notwith-
' ſtanding the kings aſſurance they ſhould have no bodily hurt, at the
' inſtance of the queen, were beheaded, at the queens departing
' from S. Albons. [e] The Queen having thus got the victorie, ſent to
' the maior of London for lenten ſtuffe to refreſhe her armie, who
' cauſed carts to be laden, & would have ſent them, but the commons
' would not ſuffer them to paſſe, but ſtaied them at Cripplegate.
' During which controverſie divers of the northern horſemen robbed
' in the ſuburbs of the citie, & would have entred at Cripplegate,
' but were repulſed by the commons & three of them ſlaine; where-
' upon the maior ſent the recorder to the kings counſil at Barnet, to
' excuſe the matter; & the dutches of Bedford, the lady Scales, with
' divers fathers of the ſpiritualtie, went to the queen to aſſwage her
' diſpleaſure againſt the citie. The queene therefore, at their requeſt,
' appointed certain lords & knights, with 400 tall perſons, to ride to
' the citie, & there view the demeanour of the people. But all theſe
' devices were ſhortly altered into another forme, becauſe true report

a Stow, as above.
b Holing. as above.
c Stow, as above.

d Stow, p. 686. Holing. p. 1305. b.
e Stow, p. 687.

' came,

' came, not only to the queene, but alſo to the citie, that the E. of
' March, having vanquiſhed the earls of Pembroke & Wilts, had
' met with the E. of Warwicke, after the laſt battel at S. Albons,
' at Chippingnorton by Cotſwolde, & that they, with both their
' powers, were coming towards London.   The queene therefore hav-
' ing little truſt in Eſſex, leſs in Kent, but leaſt of all in the Londo-
' ners, with her husband & ſon departed from S. Albons into the north
' countrie, where their refuge only conſiſted.   Nevertheleſs the dutches
' of York, having ſeen her husband & her 2ᵈ. ſon ſlaine, & not know-
' ing what ſhould ſucceede of her eldeſt, ſent her two youngeſt ſonnes
' to Utricht, where they were well received of Philip D. of Bur-
' goigne, & ſo remained 'till their brother had got the crowne.   The
' earles of Marche & Warwicke having knowledge that the king &
' queen were departed from S. Albons, rode ſtraight to London, en-
Feb.28. ' tring the citie the 28. of Februarie, where he was joyfully received;
' whoſe coming thither was no ſooner knowne, but the people re-
' ſorted to him out of Kent, Eſſex, & other parts in great numbers,
' to ſee, aid, & aſſiſt this luſtie prince, in whom the hope of all their
' joy conſiſted.   This prudent prince, minding to take time when time
' ſerved, called a great councell both of the lords temporal & ſpiri-
' tual, & declared to them the title & right he had to the crowne,
' rehearſing alſo the articles concluded betwixt K. Henry & his father
' by their writings ſigned & ſealed, & alſo confirmed by act of parlia-
' ment.   Which after the lords had conſidered, they determined, that,
' becauſe king Henrie was inſufficient of himſelf to rule the realme,
' he ſhould be deprived of all kingly honour, & incontinently was
' Edward E. of March, ſonne & heir to Richard D. of York [lord of
Stanford] ' named & elected king.'   I ſhall only add, that ſome time
in this laſt year of K. Henry the 6.   ' William Storeton of Stanford
' ſold to William Brown of the ſame place merchant, a tenement, &c.
' which he bought of Richard Goldeſworth: about which ſee the 24.
' & 31. H. 6. above. B. H.'   And here ends the reign, tho' not the life
of K. Henry the 6. & here likewiſe, as we have ſeen the ruin of Stanford under him, I ſhall put an end to theſe collections.   If I meet
with encouragement, perhaps I may hereafter attempt to ſhew how this
town revived under his ſucceſſor, & its great benefactor king Edward
the fourth, who (as Waller ſings)

' *Fierce, goodly, valiant, beautiful, & young,*
' *Thus rent the crown from vanquiſht Henrys head,*
' *Rais'd the white roſe, & trampled on the red.*

The end of the fourteenth book.

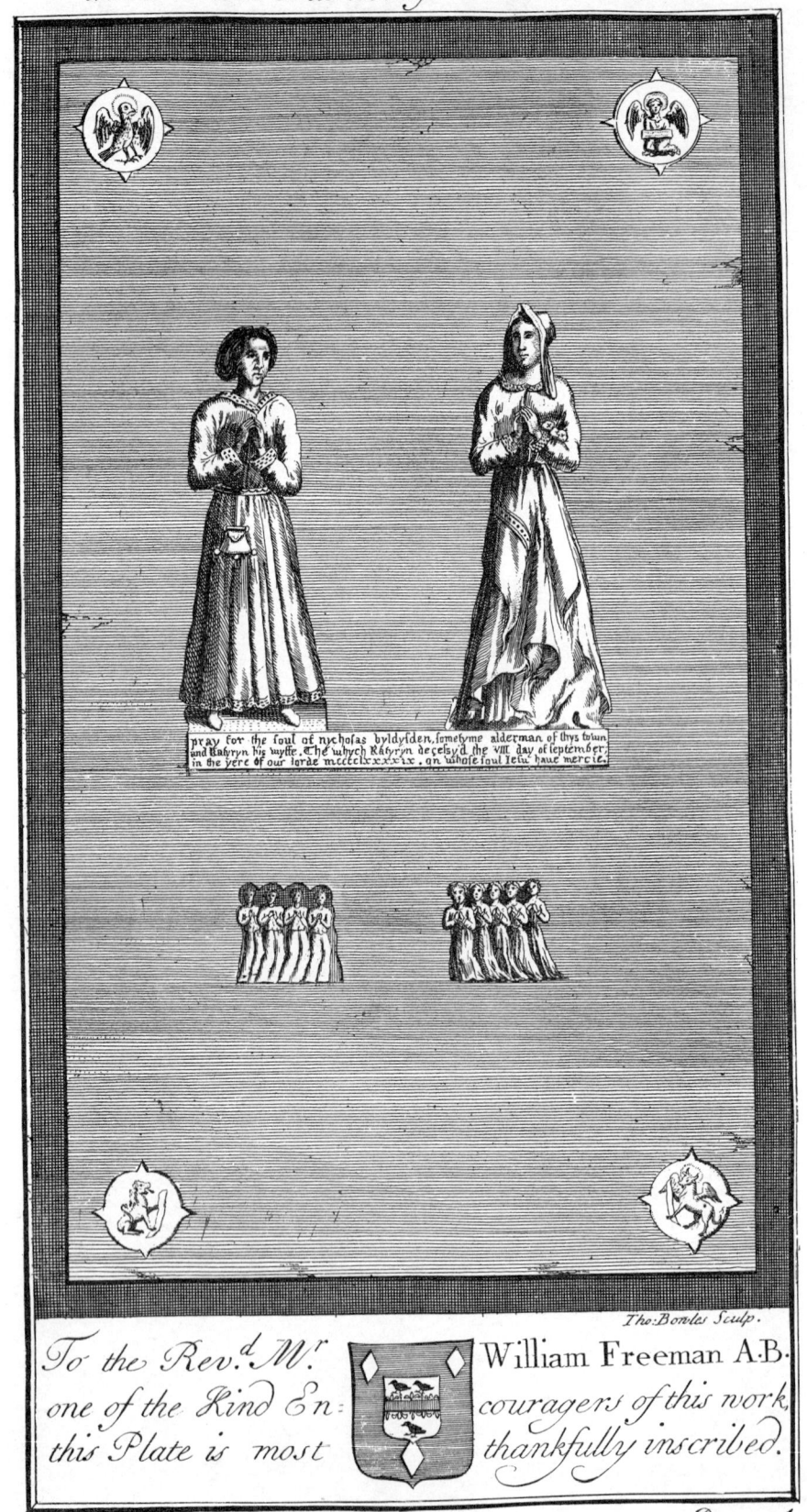

pray for the foul of nycholas byldyfden, fometyme alderman of thys toun
and katyryn his wyffe. The whych katyryn deceafyd the VIII day of feptember,
in the yere of our lorde mcccclxxxxix, on whofe foul Iefu haue mercie.

Tho: Bowles Sculp.

To the Revd Mr   William Freeman A.B.
one of the kind En=   couragers of this work,
this Plate is most   thankfully inscribed.

hic iacet magiſter henricus ſargeaunt quondam rector
totius eccle. qui obijt 14. die menſis iunij . an dñi .
M·CCCC·LXXXXVII. cuius anime ppicietur deus . AMEN

To Thomas Sargeant Esqr. Gentle =
man Porter of the Tower of London
one of the kind Encouragers of this work
this plate is most thankfully inscribed.

hic jacet margaretta Elmes filii Iohannis Elmes z Elizabetha uxoris
ejus de Kendale sup Comitati; que obiit prima die augusti; anno dni
M.CCCCLXXI cujus anime propihetur deus ....

Mrs Elmes's gravestone in St Maries
chappel in all Saints church

Sub hoc marmore
positæ sunt reliquiæ,
THOMÆ TRUESDALE de STAN-
FORD Generosi, plurimis noti, omnibus
chari, suis charissimi. In
Legum Anglicanarum usu & Curiarum praxi
apprime versatus, & peritia sua
honeste alios æq ac se ditavit.
Egenis, adhuc superstes, sæpe dedit;
cum moriebatur, semper .
In vico vicino Anglice Scotgate,
Hospitium statuit,
propriam domum sex pauperibus in perpetuo;
eandemq domum in agro Lincolniensi
ad Baston & Morton, cum fundis dotavit.
Fama ejus occulto, velut arbor,
ævo crescit, crescetq;
dignum laude virum
charitas (musa melior) vetat mori .
Si Gravitas, si Sobrietas, si mentis Honestas
Pulchrum homini nomen præbeat ipse tulit.
Obijt 23º. Octobris,
Anno 1700.

To Robert Meres Esq. The Rev.ᵈ Mr. Charles Titley,
Mr. William Barker, & Mr. Thomas Hurst,
the present Trustees of Mr. Truesdales Hospital, *this Plate*
representing The Founders Monument, *is*
most thankfully inscribed.

J. Sturt sculp.

The CLOSE.

FOR a conclusion of the present undertaking I beg leave to add, that in the south chancel of S. Johns church is a blue marble gravestone, for Mr. Nicholas Byldysden & Catherine his wife, with their effigies & other ornaments inlaid in brass. The figure whereof is here annexed [a].   [a] Plate A.

In the middle chancel of the same church is another blue marble grave-stone, laid down in memory of Mr. Henry Sargeaunt sometime rector of this parish, whose effigies, vested as when he used to sing mass, is likewise inlaid in brass-work, as represented in the draught [b]. [b] Plate B.

In S. Maries chapel in All Saints church is another blue marble stone, with the effigies of a woman likewise inlaid in brass-work, there placed in memory of Mrs. Margaret Elmes. The figure whereof is represented in the cut [c]. [c] Plate C.

In the same chapel, upon a very large blue marble stone, above the steps where the altar stood formerly, are beautifully pourtrayed in large plates of brass, with many curious ornaments & engravings, the effigies of Mr. William Brown (founder of the fine hospital called by his name) & his wife, cloathed in religious habits, according to the fashion of the times they lived in, [d] with inscriptions under them in wretch- [d] Plate D. ed Latin, but so very penitently expressed, that I was willing to try if I could give the English reader some notion of it by the following version.

Under him.

O King of kings, & Lord of lords, thy will
In yielding to the grave all must fulfil.
But as my flesh to earth, my sp'rite to thee,
On whom my hope depends, makes hast to flee;
Thou gracious Father, Son, & Holy Ghost,
Receive my soul, or I'm for ever lost.

Under her.

A many sins I've done, & much I'm griev'd,
Then let my cries for mercy be receiv'd.
Enter not into judgment with me, Lord;
Mercy I beg, thy mercy first afford.
Thou, who in pity didst our nature take,
Hear, & O save me for thy mercies sake.

In the same chapel is a neat monument of white marble set up against part of the east window, in memory of Mr. Thomas Truesdale [e], [e] Plate E. who (what is somewhat remarkable) lived in the same house where Mr. Brown lived, founded an hospital in the same town where Mr. Brown did, & was buried in the same chapel where Mr. Brown was buried. The inscription on Mr. Truesdales monument may be thus Englished.

14 T

Beneath

Beneath this marble
are depofited the remains
of Thomas Truefdale of Stanford, Gent.
known to very many, dear to all,
but moft dear to his friends.
In the ufe of the Englifh laws & practice of the Courts
excellently skill'd, by his knowledge wherein
he made others, as well as himfelf,
honeftly rich.
To the poor, whilft he was yet alive, he gave often;
when he died, always.
In a neighbouring ftreet called Scotgate,
he founded an hofpital,
a fit dwelling
for fix poor people for ever;
& endowed the fame with revenues
at Bafton & Morton in Lincolnfhire.
His Fame, like a Tree,
grows & fhall grow
to unknown time.
For Charity
(which furpaffes Poetry)
forbids that a perfon fo deferving praife
fhould ever be forgot.
If Gravity, if Sobriety, if a mind fincerely honeft,
can any of them procure a fair name,
this man hath made fure of it.
He died Oct. the 23.
in the year 1700.

Plate F.   In S. Martins church (the fculpture whereof is here given[f]) in the
second window from the bottom on the north fide, are a parcel of
Plate G. figures as reprefented in the next plate, [g] exhibiting, as I take it, the
poyfoning & burial of fome king or other great perfon, but who the
fame was, as we have no tradition to inform us, I muft leave to the
enquiries of the curious.

In the eaft window of the fouth chancel of the fame church, is a yet
more unaccountable piece of painting, being the figure of the devil (as
Plate H. drawn in the next plate[h]) holding a church fteeple in his claws, &, as
it fhould feem, attempting to eat it.   What fhould be the meaning
of this whimfical picture, is another thing I muft leave to a farther
enquiry.

In the upper windows of the middle ifle of the fame church, are
Plate I. divers efcutcheons of arms as reprefented in the next plate, [i] being the
coats of thofe perfons, who, as I take it, were at the charge of
the painted glafs in thofe windows reprefenting fundry prophets &
apoftles.

At

To the very Learned
and R.t Rev.d Father in God
White L.d Bishop of Peterborough
one of the kind encouragers
of this work, this plate is most
thankfully inscribed.

The North Prospect of S.t MARTINS CHURCH in Stanford Baron.

*Some remaining figures as depicted
in y:e 2:d window from the bottom in the north
isle of S:t Martins church, taken July 27. 1722.*

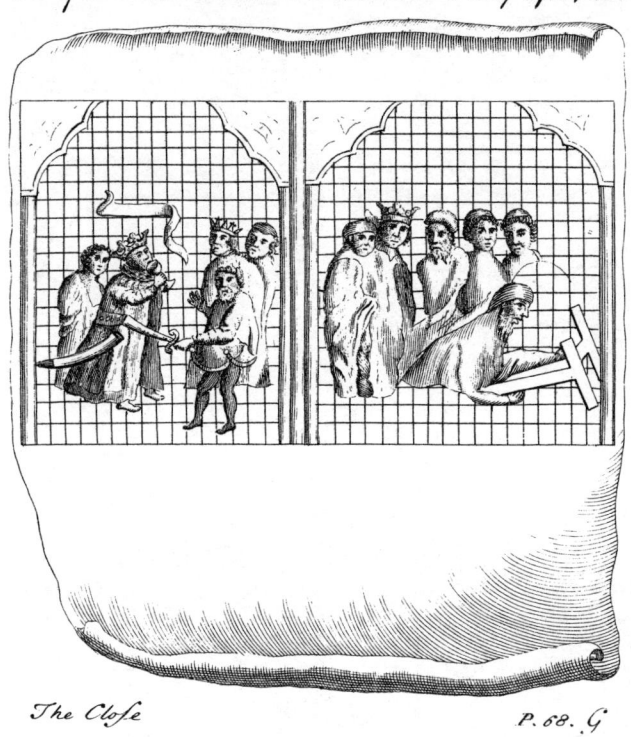

The Close

P. 68. G

Some remaining Figures in the East Window of the South Chancel of
S.MARTINS CHURCH IN STANFORD.

Ut ornate prodeant, Sculpſit, deditꝗ J. Sturt Calcographus. C.A.L.

Fourteen Coats in the upper Windows of ye Nave of St. Martins Church.

To that learned Antiquary Peter le Neve Esqr.
Norroy King of Arms, one of the kind Encourers
of this Work, this Plate is most thankfully Inscrib'd

The Monument of *Richard Cecil Esq.* & *Iane his Wife* & *their Three Daughters in S.t Martins Church at STANFORD.*

COR UNUM VIA UNA

IN HAPPY MEMORY OF RICHARD CECILE ESQ AND IAYNE HIS WIFE

To the R.t Hon.ble Brownlowe Earl of Exeter,
One of the kind Encouragers of this work, this
Plate is most thankfully inscribed.

P. Tillemans Antverpiensis delin.   *I. Sturt Sculp.*

At the upper end of the north chancel of the same church, stands a neat piece of work; [k] being a Cenotaph if we consider it as erected [k Plate K.] to the memory of Richard Cecil Esq; (father of the lord Treasurer Burghley) for, tho' the effigies of the said Richard is here set up, yet his body was not buried here, but at S. Margarets, Westminster : & a monument, if we consider it as erected to the memory of Jane, wife of the said Richard, her body lying buried in the vault under this chancel, just by her son the lord Treasurers cofin.

The Inscription.

In happy Memory of Richard Cecil, Esq; & Jane his wife.
The said Richard was of the Robes to K.
Hen. 8. & to K. E. 6. he deceased the 19. of May
1552. & is interr'd in S^t. Margarets
Church in Westminster. He was Sonne to David
Cecil of Stanford Esqr. High Sherif of the
County of Northampton in the 33. & 34.
Yeares of Kinge H. 8. & is buried in S^t.
George his Church in Stanford.

The said Jayne was Daughter & Heire of
W^{am}. Heckington of Bourne in the County
of Lincolne Esqr. She lived 87 Years,
whereof she continued a Widow 35
Yeares. She deceased the 10th. of March 1587.
She was a very grave, religious, vertuous,
& worthy Matron ; & delighted exceedingly
in the Works of Piety & Charity. She was
crowned wth. much Hono^r & Comfort, & (by
God his great Blessing) she lived to see
her Children, & her Childrens Children,
to the fourth & fift Generation, & that in a
plentifull & honourable succession,
being a happy Mother of that most Honor^{ble}.
S^r. W^m. Cecil Knight of the noble Order of
the Garter, Lo : Burghley, Lord high TRER$^.$.
of England, who lyeth here by her.

Margaret was first	Elizabeth was first	Anne marryed
married to Roger	marryed to Robert	to Thomas
Cave of Stanford	Wingfield of Upton	Whyte of
Esqr. of whom is	Esqr. of whom is	Tuxford Esqr.
descended Str Thomas	descended Ser	of whom is descend-
Cave ; & after to	Robert Wingfield	ed John Whyte
Ambrose Smith	of Upton Knight ;	Esqr.
of Bosworth	& after to Hugh	
Esqr.	Allington Esqr.	

Under

Under an arch, between the middle & north chancels of the same church, is erected a curious monument of Touch, Porphyry, & other [1] marble, set off with rich embellishments [1]; on the north side whereof is this inscription.

Deo optimo, maximo, & memoriæ sacrum.

Honoratiſſim. & longe clariſſim. D. Gulielm. Cecili⁹, Baro de Burghley, ſumm⁹ Angliæ Theſaurari⁹, Curiæ Pupillor. Præfect⁹, Georgiani ordinis Eques Auratus, Sereniſſimæ Eliſabethæ Angliæ, &c. Reginæ, a Sanctioribus conſiliis, & Academiæ Cantabrigienſis Cancellari⁹, ſub hoc tumulo ſecundum Chriſti adventum manet.

Qui, ob eximias animi dotes, primum a Secretis fuit Edwardo ſexto Angliæ Regi, deinde Reginæ Eliſabethæ; ſub qua, in maximis & graviſſimis hujus Regni cauſis ſpectat⁹ & imprimis probat⁹, veram religionem promovendo, Reipublicæ ſaluti & dignitati providendo, conſilio, æquitate, conſtantia, magniſq; in Remp. meritis, honores conſecutus ſummos, cum Naturæ & Gloriæ ſatis, Patriæ autem parum, vixiſſet;

Placide in Chriſto obdormivit.

On the north ſide.

Uxores habuit duas, Mariam, ſororem Johannis Cheeke Equitis aurati; e qua genuit filium unicum, Thomam nunc Baronem de Burghley; & Mildredam, filiam Antonii Cooke equitis aurati; quæ illi peperit Robertum Cecilium Equitem auratum, Reg. Eliſabethæ a Secretis, & Curiæ Pupillorum præfectum; Annam, enuptam Edwardo Comiti Oxoniæ; & Eliſabetham, Gulielmo Wentworth, filio primogenito Baronis Wentworth.

That is,

Sacred to God moſt good & great, & to memory.

The moſt honourable, & far renowned Lord, William Cecil, Baron of Burghley, Lord High Treaſurer of England, Preſident of the Court of Wards, Knight of the moſt noble order of the Garter, privy counſellor to the moſt ſerene Eliſabeth Queen of England, &c. & Chancellor of the Univerſity of Cambridge, under this Tomb awaits the ſecond coming of Chriſt:

Who, for the excellent endowments of his mind, was firſt made privy counſellor to Edward the ſixth, king of England; afterwards to Queen Eliſabeth: Under whom, being intruſted with the greateſt & moſt weighty affairs of this kingdom, & above all others approved; in promoting the true Religion, & providing for the ſafety & honour of the commonwealth; by his Pru-

The Monument of the R.t Hon.ble Will.m Lord Burghley, Lord
High Treasurer of England; in S.t Martins Church at Stanford.

To the Right Hon.ble Brownlow Earl of Exeter, one of
the kind Encouragers of this work, this Plate is most thankfully inscribed.

P. Tillemans Antverpiensis delin.

I. Sturt sculp.

THE
Monument of
JOHN EARL of EXETER
AND
ANNE HIS COUNTESS
in St Martins Church
at
STANFORD.

Monumentũ hoc pervenuſtum
Petrus Stephanus Monot Bi=
ſuntinus fecit Romæ.
MDCCIV.

To the
Right Honble
BROWNLOWE
EARL of EXETER
One of the kind Encoura=
gers of this Work, this
Plate is most
thankfully
inſcrib'd.

P. Tillemans Antverpienſis delin.   J. Sturt

dence, Honesty, Integrity, & great services to the nation, he obtained the highest honors : &, when he had lived long enough to nature, long enough to glory, but not long enough to his country, quietly fell asleep in Christ.

He had two wives: Mary, sister of Sir John Cheeke Knight, of whom he begat one son, Thomas, now Baron of Burghley; & Mildred, daughter of Sir Anthony Cooke Knight, who bore to him Sir Robert Cecil Knight, privy Counsellor to Queen Elisabeth, & President of the Court of Wards; Anne, married to Edward Earl of Oxford; & Elisabeth, to William Wentworth, eldest son of Baron Wentworth.

Against the north wall of the north chancel (below the monument of Richard Cecil Esq; & Jane his wife) is a most stately tomb of white & grey marble, erected for John Earl of Exeter & Anne his lady, daughter of William earl of Devon. A work, in its principal figures, surpassing almost any thing of the kind perhaps in the kingdom; for which reason I shall here add a brief description of it [m].   [m] Plate M.

Raised on a black marble step, stands a sort of an altar of white marble, on which supported by four lions paws, stands a second sort of an altar sloping inwards into a plain broad table, whereon is the inscription. Above are the figures of the Earl & his lady, in a cumbent posture, exquisitly done, all in one block of white marble, the earl leaning his right arm on a cushion of the same sort of marble, wrought with gilded embroidery, & thrown over an heap of books which appear under it.

In his habit he is represented like one of the old Romans; in his air, discoursing to his lady; whose Effigies (placed nearer the wall behind him, & raised somewhat higher than his; on purpose to be seen with the greater advantage over it) appears with a pen in her right, & an open book in her left, hand, rested upon her knee; as attending & ready to set down what her lord says.

Standing upon the lowest altar, on the right hand side of the tomb, is an exceeding large figure (all of one piece of white marble) representing a Minerva, with a a shield by her side, whereon is pourtrayed the Gorgons head; in her right hand, a spear; in her left, a Palladium.

On the left, over against this beautiful statue, is a mournful, but most delicate representation of the same fabulous divinity, now done as Goddess of arts & sciences; resting her right elbow on a thick book placed at the earls feet, & leaning her head upon her hand, as lamenting the loss of her patron. Her left hand, hanging down by her side, is crouded with an hammer, pencils & brushes, while, at her feet, appear, in an huddle, the compasses, rule, draughts, & other implements of art, all thrown by upon this sad occasion.

Behind & above the earl & his lady, the monument forms a third sort of an altar, at each end whereof is placed a large urn, with a gilded flame at the top.

In

In the middle of this third altar is a Void, over which (supported by two neat pieces of carving) a pyramid of grey marble ascends almost as high as the church roof. In the middle of the pyramid is a table of arms, Cecil, impaling Cavendish, done on a shield of white marble. Over all, for a finishing, is a large Cupid of white marble, holding in his hands a gilded snake, with the tail thrust into the mouth, as an Emblem of Eternity. I shall only add, that, for want of room, the Epitaph is close wrote upon the tomb, but, if the table would have given leave, it should have been thrown out, in the following manner.

H. S. E.
Johannes Cecil,
Baro de Burghley,
Exoniæ Comes,
Magni Burleii Abnepos
haudquaquam degener.
Egregiam enim indolem
optimis moribus,
optimis artibus,
excoluit.

Humanioribus literis bene instructus,
peregre,
plus vice simplici,
profectus est.
Et,
ab excultis Europæ regionibus,
multam, Antiquitatum,
Linguarum,
nec non & rerum civilium,
scientiam reportavit.
Cum nemo forte melius

vel Aulam ornare,
vel curare Res publicas
posset,
maluit tamen otium & secessum.
Itaque ruri suo vixit
eleganter, sumptuose, splendide ;
liberalibus studiis oblectatus,
Amicis comis & jucundus,
Egenis largus,
Legum, & Ecclesiæ Anglicanæ,
fortis semper Propugnator.

Suarum virtutum & peregrinationum,
immo fere & scientiarum,
sociam habuit uxorem
Annam,
ex prænobili domo de Cavendish,
Gulielmi Comitis Devoniæ Filiam;
Corporis forma,
& Animi ingenio,
& omnibus quæ foeminam decere possent
dotibus, insignem;
e qua quinque liberos suscepit:
foelix conjuge,
foelix & prole!
Sed, inter omnia, vitam
quæ faciunt beatiorem,
mortalitatis haud immemor,
dum, apud Italos,
præcipuæ artis opera
curiosus lustrabat,
hoc monumentum illic,
ubi exquisitissime fieri potuit,
sibi,
& charissimæ lecti sui,
& itinerum,
& curarum
omnium consorti,
F. F.

Obiit ille   *Obiit illa*
Aug. 29. 1700.   *Jun.* 18. 1709.

That is,

Here lies buried,
John Cecil,
Baron of Burghley,
Earl of Exeter,
Son of the great Burghleys great Grandson,
& in no wise unworthy of his renowned progenitor.
For he beautified an excellent Genius
with the best manners,
& the best arts.
Being well instructed in polite letters,
he went abroad
more than once;
And,
from the most refined parts of Europe,

2   brought

brought home much knowledge
of Antiquities,
Languages,
& civil affairs.
Yet, when no man perhaps could either better
adorn a court,
or manage the public buſineſs,
rather made choice of eaſe & retirement.
He lived therefore at his own country ſeat
elegantly, ſumptuouſly, ſplendidly;
delighted with all genteel ſtudies,
to his friends affable & pleaſant,
to the poor bountiful,
& of the laws, & church of England,
ever a ſtout champion.

He had for wife,
& the companion of his virtues,
& travels,
&, in a manner, of his ſtudies,
Anne,
of the right noble houſe of Cavendiſh,
daughter of William earl of Devon;
for the beauty of her body,
ingenuity of her mind,
& all thoſe accompliſhments
which can any ways adorn a lady,
famous;
Of whom he begat five children:
happy in his ſpouſe,
& happy in his offspring!
But,
among all the things
which make life more bleſſed,
being ever mindful of mortality,
when he was in Italy,
whilſt he thoroughly examined
& as curiouſly collected
the works of choiceſt art,
there he cauſed this monument to be made,
where it could be moſt exquiſitly done,
for himſelf,
& the moſt dear conſort of his bed,
& travels,
& of all his cares.

He died
Aug. 29. 1700.

She died
June 18. 1709.

FINIS.

(1)

The chief materials of this work are thus diftributed.

BOOK I.

From the fuppofed foundation of a Britifh·univerfity at Stanford, anno mundi 3100. before Chrift 863. to the fuppofed diffolution of the fame about 505 years after Chrift.

BOOK II.

From the ſuppoſed diſſolution of the Britiſh univerſity about the year of Chriſt 605. to the death of Vilfrid (biſhop of York, & founder of the Benedictin priory of S. Leonard by Stanford) who deceaſed in 709.

at

at Stanford became a cell to Lindisfarne, & so to Durham. Sir William Dugdale, Dr. Tanner, Mr. Burton, Reyner, & Mr. Steven's mistakes about this monastery, corrected. No town called Stanford in the bishoprick of Durham. Nor monastery at Stanford in Yorkshire, founded by Alchfrid or any body else. But S. Leonard's priory by Stanford in Lincolnshire, & two other churches there, all in the patronage of the cathedral priory of Durham. The manor and lands of S. Cuthberts fee at Stanford in Lincolnshire, belonging to Durham. The prior of Durham gives the abbat of Croyland a pension of 8 l. a year out of S. Leonards at Stanford in exchange for Coldingham.

XVI. Alchfrid's wife Cyniburga founds a nunnery at Castre seven miles from Stanford.

XVII. Peada begins to found the church & monastery of Medeshamstede, but is murdered by his wife, or, as others say, mother. The great antiquity of S. Leonards by Stanford. That monastery finished before Medeshamstede.

XVIII. Cells formerly used, for nurseries for young monks; or banishment of offenders; or retreat of great men who met with disappointments.

XIX. Milton's excellent verses in praise of a monastic life. Some account of the present remains of the priory church of S. Leonard.

XX. An. 660. Vilfrid's attestation of Q. Edilthryda's chastity. Gyrvii, who.

XXI. An. 662. bishop Lloyd's state of the controversie between the Scots & Romans about keeping Easter.

XXII. That controversie reviv'd. K. Osuiu sides with the Scots; Alchfrid with the Romans; takes Rippon, a monastery he had founded, from the Scots, & gives it to Vilfrid.

XXIII. An. 664. Vilfrid made priest. The council of Whitby about the quartadeciman controversie, canonical tonsure, &c. K. Osuiu & K. Alchfrid both there. K. Osuiu opens the synod. Colman speaks for the Scotch opinion; Vilfrid for the Roman; his unanswerable argument. Osuiu for fear of disobliging S. Peter brought over to the Romans. Egyptian day how computed. In the note, p. 18.

XXIV. Anonymous author censured.

XXV. Bp. Patrick on the power of the keys.

XXVI. Vulfere carries on his brother Peada's foundation of Medeshamstede. Abstract of his charter describing the bounds of the Soke of Burg. All Stanford on the south side of Welland, within that fee. That charter spurious, and why. To be a priest reckoned a greater honor than to be an abbat.

XXVII. K. Alchfrid's great respect for Vilfrid. Vilfrid consecrated bishop at Compeigne, but delaying to return, his enemies prevail with Osuiu to name Cedd to be consecrated in his place. Cedd's illegal ordination. Vilfrid returning, promotes divers Roman usages;

XXVIII. Lives privately at Rippon; then as a bishop in Mercia; supplies the want of an archbishop of Canterbury. An. 669. Theodore the new archbishop arrives; deposes Cedd, and restores Vilfrid. Vilfrid now bp. of York, and all K. Osuiu's dominions; in humility walks on foot to visit his diocese; Theodore the archbp. orders him to ride, and himself helps him on horseback. The slanders of the anonymous author before censured on Vilfrid, retorted.

XXIX. Vilfrid rebuilds York minster. An. 670. Osuiu dies. Vulfere translates the first place of the heptarchy from the Northumbers to the Mercians. His, and other princes, supposed favors to the monks of Lindisfarne, with relation to their cell of S. Leonard by Stanford.

XXX. Vilfrid builds a new church at Rippon; consecrates it before two kings; vanquishes the Picts with his prayers. An. 671. Edilthryda (K. Ecgfrids Q.) gets leave to withraw into a monastery; Vilfrid veils her; the K. repents; would have her again; is hinder'd by a miracle; hates Vilfrid. An. 673. Edilthryda founds a monastery for both sexes at Ely; made first abbess there by Vilfrid.

XXXI. The council of Hertford. Vilfrid there by his proxies, why not in person. Decrees of that council.

XXXII. An. 674. archbp. Theodore deposes Vynfrid bp. of the Mercians, and why. An. 675. Ecgfrid recovers Lindisse from Vulfere. Vilfrid dedicates a church at Hexham.

XXXIII. An. 678. Ermenburga (K. Ecgfrid's second wife) sets him against Vilfrid. He gets Theodore to depose him; who divides his diocese into three, & gives them to three new bps. of his own making. Mr. Wharton's account of this affair. The K. and Theodore unable to justifie their doings, persift in it. Vilfrid appeals to Rome. His prophetic speech to the K. and his lords, who laughed at the trick they had put upon him.

XXXIV. He retires to Q. Edilthryda at Ely; sets out for Rome; driven by an east wind into Friezland; converts the country; sets forward again; arrives in France; K. Dagobert offers him the best bishopric in his kingdom; which he refuses. Dagobert sends his own bishop Deodate, with him to Rome; well received on his way by the K. of Lombardy.

XXXV. An. 679. arrives at Rome. Archbp. Theodore sends one thither to make good his own proceedings. Pope Agatho calls a council to hear the business. Vilfrid cleared. Decree of that council about the number of dioceses in Britain.

XXXVI. An. 680. Another council at Rome. Vilfrid, by the Pope's order takes his place in it; & gives account of his faith, in opposition to certain hereticks con-

condemned there. The pope orders his confeſſion to be recorded.

XXXVII. Vilfrid procures a bull of divers privileges for the church of Medeſham-ſtede: extract of it.

XXXVIII. Vilfrid returns; is impriſon'd by K. Ecgfrid. Q. Ermenburga takes a caſket of reliques from him; is puniſhed for it. Vilfrid ſet at liberty; flies into Mercia. The council of Biſhops-Hatfield; The privileges granted to the church of Medeſhamſtede confirm'd there. The pope's bull about thoſe privileges forged.

XXXIX. Vilfrid expelled Mercia; flies to the K. of the Weſt Saxons; An. 681. expelled thence; preaches to the South Saxons; converts, & relieves them from famine. K. Edilualch gives him many lands. Vilfrid, for the number of his attendants, compared to Card. Wolſey; erects a monaſtery at Sealſey.

XL. An. 685. K. Ecgfrid ſlain; ſucceeded by Alchfrid. Archbp. Theodore begs Vilfrids pardon, and is reconciled. Theodore writes to K. Alchfrid, abbeſs Elfleda, & K. Ethelred, to be friends with Vilfrid. Ethelred reſtores him what he had loſt in Mercia. An. 686. Alchfrid reſtores him the biſhoprick of Hexham. Caedwall K. of the Weſt Saxons conquers Wight, and gives Vilfrid lands there; who gives them to his nephew.

XLI. An. 687. Alchfrid reſtores York & Rippon to Vilfrid; & removes the three biſhops put in by Theodore. An. 691. Alchfrid expells Vilfrid; the occaſions of this new quarrel. He flies to K. Ethelred; is by him made bp. of Lichfield; or as others ſay, Leiceſter. Mr. Wharton defended againſt an aſſertion of bp. Nicholſon. Vilfrid conſecrates Oſtfor bp. of Worceſter; &

XLII. An. 692. Suidbert biſhop of Frieſland. An. 695. Q. Edilthryda's body taken up at Ely ſixteen years after her burial; Vilfrid one of thoſe who atteſts it was uncorrupt. Bedes reaſon of it; & the authors. Account of the marquiſs of Dorſets body found uncorrupt 78 years after burial. Q. Edilthryda canoniſed, & called S. Audry.

XLIII. An. 703. Vilfrid ſummoned by K. Alchfrid & archbp. Berctuald to the council of Neſtrefield by Rippon; reparation promiſed, but more injuries intended. Their deſigns made known to Vilfrid by a friend. Their unreaſonable demands. All taken from him but Rippon. He again appeals to Rome; and flies to K. Ethelred; who condoles with him, and promiſes to keep

for him what he had in Mercia till he knew the pope's mind. Vilfrids enemies excomunicate him and his followers.

XLIV. An. 704. he arrives at Rome; as do his enemies from archbp. Berctuald. Vilfrid complains to the pope of the many injuries done him. Pope John enquires what his predeceſſors decreed about Vilfrid before.

XLV. Vilfrids former ſubſcription againſt the heretics in pope Agatho's time, to his honor now read before pope John. His old friend archdeacon Boniface yet alive.

XLVI. His accuſers charge againſt him; his ſpeech in his own defence.

XLVII. That ſpeech received with great applauſe; & Vilfrid again acquitted. Pope John writes to K. Ethelred & K. Alchfrid in Vilfrid's behalf.

XLVIII. Vilfrid coming back, falls ſick at Meaulx. In a trance ſees S. Michael who tells him he ſhall recover, & be reſtored to the beſt part of his poſſeſſions in Britain; but muſt four years after prepare to die. He recovers accordingly, & arrives in Britain.

XLIX. Upon reading the popes letter archbiſhop Berctuald & K. Ethelred (then an abbat) favor him. Ethelred recommends him to Cenred his own ſucceſſor. But K. Alchfrid will hear nothing of him. That prince falls ſick; repents his unkindneſs; and promiſes amendment; but dying, requires his ſucceſſor, for the good of his ſoul, to ſatisfie Vilfrid. An. 705. Vilfrid applies to Eadulf his ſucceſſor for reparation; but his companions are threatned with death. Eadulf expell'd, & ſucceeded by Oſred. Berctuald calls a ſynod of bps, & lays before the K. & them the Roman decree. The three new bps will not part with their bpbrics; but all agree to make peace with Vilfrid, by reſtoring him the monaſteries of Hexham & Rippon.

L. An. 707. Vilfrid falls ſick again; & again recovers. An. 708. diſpoſes of his treaſure; makes Tadbert abbat of Rippon; withdraws into Mercia, & why. An. 709. Ap. 24. dies in a little monaſtery at Oundle by Stanford. Some account of the chappel of that monaſtery now ſtanding. The death of Mr. Bridges, a great loſs to antiquities. Vilfrid carried from Oundle to be buried at Rippon. His epitaph.

LI. Removal afterwards to Canterbury. Enſhrined & at laſt buried there. Difference between Mat. Weſtminſter & Mr. Smith about the day of his death. Vilfrid canonized. His feſtival when.

BOOK

BOOK III.

From the death of bishop Vilfrid anno 709. to the coming in of William the conqueror, anno 1066.

I. OF the Danes. The Danes the worst scourge of this island. Their manner of spoiling any country.

II. In 870. they land in Lindsey; destroy Bardney abbey; proceed to Kesteven. Count Algar and the youth of Holland, joyn'd by a body of Croyland men under the monk Toly, oppose them: Morchar lord of Brunne, and Osgot sheriff of Lincoln, assist. At first beat the Danes; but (the Danes being afterwards reinforced) are defeated. A famous body of Stanford men in that battle, commanded by Harding of Rihale. The news of the overthrow carried to Croyland. Some of the monks fly; the rest stay; and are all murder'd but Turgar. The church plunder'd; and burnt. The monks of Medeshamstede murdered; and that church burnt. Ingulf's mistake about the Danes proceedings at Burg corrected; in the note, p. 5. The Croyland monks who fled return; bury their own dead; and them at Medeshamstede; erect a monument over the last; that monument now to be seen. Ingulf's mistake about it corrected; in the note, p. 7.

III. Stanford now destroyed by the Danes. Character of the Saxon K. Beorrhed. In 871. Beorrhed confiscates the lands belonging to Medeshamstede and Croyland abbies, near Stanford. Apology for his so doing. In 874. the Danes drive him out of England, and make Ceolwolph K. of Mercia.

IV. Stanford rebuilt and fortified by the Danes. Mr. Butcher's mistake about K. Alfred's building a stone bridge at Stanford. The misery of these times.

V. In 901. K. Alfred dies. In 907. Welmesford field, a mistake for Wodensfield. In 911. Edward the elder beats the Danes there. The Danes throw down Stanford castle, and withdraw.

VI. In 914. Elfleda, Countess of Mercia, rebuilds Stanford castle. The objection that she built a castle at Stafford, and not at Stanford, considered and reconciled. Description of the site of Stanford castle.

VII. The Danes retake Stanford castle, and fortifie it afresh. Mr. Moreton's account of the battle on the south side of Burghley park in 921. where the Danes were defeated by Edward the elder.

VIII. In 922. Edward the elder builds a castle on the south side of the river at Stanford; and reduces the castle, city, and country on the north side.

IX. Remarks on the several accounts of these matters;

X. And on the situation of this other castle; the true place where it stood.

XI. The death of Elfleda countess of Mercia. Her prodigious acts and character. The places she built. Huntingdons verses upon her.

XII. In 924. Edward the elder dies, succeeded by Athelstan. He gives the abbat of Medeshamstede privilege of a mint at Stanford.

XIII. Athelstan dies, succeeded by Edmund. He and Onlaf the Dane divide the kingdom between them. Stanford in Onlafs province; surrendred to the Danes. Stanford then capital of one of the five great Danish provinces. Stanfordshire contained divers counties.

XIV. In 942. Edmund takes the five cities from the Danes; of which five cities, some say Stanford, others Stafford, was one.

XV. The advocates for Stanford;

XVI. For Stafford;

XVII. Stanford asserted to be the place.

XVIII. In 947. Turketil, K. Edreds chancellor, gives Writhorp, &c. to Croyland.

XIX. In 970. Adelwold, K. Edgars chancellor, restores Medeshamstede, and calls it Burg. In 972. K. Edgar confirms the privileges of that foundation; particularly the mint at Stanford; appoints a mercat at Burg; and that there be no other between Stanford and Huntendune; repeats the bounds of the Soke. Stanford then a mercat town and royal borough.

XX. Adelwold in 1006. succeeded by Elfius. Kyniburga, Cynisuitha and Tibba, translated from Castre and Rihal to Burg.

XXI. In 1013. Suane arrives. Uhtred, the Northumbers, Lindifians, and Fifburgenses, all submit and give hostages to him. A mixture of Danes and Saxons then living at Stanford.

XXII. Suanes cruelties in the neighbourhood of Stanford; and death.

XXIII. In 1014. the Fifburgenses submit to Cnute. K. Ethelred falls upon them for so doing, and defeats Cnute. Cnute flies into Kent, and cuts off their hostages noses for submitting to Ethelred.

XXIV. The Clito Edmund reduces the five cities more perfectly to Ethelred. Cnute flies to Denmark. Turkil, a perfidious Dane in Ethelreds service, invites him back. He prepares to return. Edric revolts to him.

XXV. In 1016. Cnute plunders the country that was for Ethelred; and Uhtred and Edmund the country that was for Cnute.

15 C XXVI.

BOOK IV.

From the coming of William the conq. in 1066. to the death of king Stephen in 1154.

I. AN. 1066. Leofric abbat of Burg dies. That monaftery vaftly enriched by him. Brand elected; fent to Edgar Atheling to be confirm'd (thefe parts being for Edgar) the conqueror refents his applying to Edgar: he buys his peace. The families which came in with the conqueror and fettled hereabouts.

II. Circ. 1068. the Jews come firft into *England*; many of them fettle at Stanford. Hereward de Wake knighted by his uncle Brand abbat of Burg; manner of that ceremony. Nov. 27. 1669. Brand dies; fucceeded by Turold a Norman. All the monafteries in *England* rifled by the Normans. June 2. 1070. Hereward and Swane (a Danifh K.) plunder Burg. Ywar the prior carries off much riches to the abbat at Stanford. Abbat Turold marches from Stanford, with 160 Normans, againft Hereward. The Danes withdraw; carry off the fpoil; lofe part of it in a ftorm, and the reft by fire. Turold arrives at Burg, and the monks. Bp. Egelric excommunicates the Danes; finds a treafure, and builds Deping-bank. Hereward returns. Turold gives lands to certain kts to protect him from Hereward; but is taken prifoner by him; releafed on paying a great fine; he renews the war. Hereward returns and burns the town and monaftery. In 1071. Hereward and E. Morchar war againft the K. in the ifle of Ely. The K. builds Wisbech caftle to reftrain them; and they a fort, called Hereward, to fhelter themfelves. Morchar withdraws; and Hereward. Hereward takes Ivo Talbois prifoner; and, for his ranfom, is reftored to his own lands.

III. In 1076. a famous trial appointed to be heard at Stanford between Ingulf abbat of Croyland, and Afhford of Helpftone his bailif. The diftreffed condition of that monaftery by the villany of Afhford. The hearing of the caufe prevented by Afhfords horfe killing him. As his relations carry him towards Burg to be buried, a hurricane rifes; the bier broke in the ftorm, and his body tumbled into the dirt in a meadow which he would have cheated the monks of Croyland of. Ingulf returning from Stanford, finds them at that inftant with the body lying in the dirt; at fight of him they acknowledge Gods judgment, and reftore the land.

IV. In 1082. Wm. the conq. and Wm. bp. of Durham, refound S. Leonards priory: account of the noble church erected by them; furvey of its prefent remains. Hardfhip put upon the rectors of S. Mary Bennewerk, and S. Mary's church at Stanford bridge by their patrons the prior and monks of Durham. Bennewerk, what it fignifies.

V. An. 1086. 20. W. 1. Doomfday furvey; the commiffioners in thefe parts; chief articles of their enquiry; occafion of that furvey; friendfhip of the commiffioners to fome places; inquifition books where kept.

VI. Stanford in general how furveyed. Conjecture that Stanford was then a county town. What fort of a borough Stanford is, not now well known. The common notion of a borough. Danegeld, what.

VII. Stanford in Lincolnfhire, how furveyed: Sac, foc, and manfions, what.

VIII. Stanford in Rutland how furveyed. Portland the fame as Boroughland. A carucate, what. Rutland formerly part of Northampton, and Nottinghamfhires.

S. Pe-

S. Peters, and S. Mary Bennewerk pariſhes, in Rutland. As alſo Bradecroft and Broadheng. Stanford therefore certainly in three counties. A bovate, villain, bordarius, and tenent in demeſne, what.

IX. Stanford in Northamptonſhire, how ſurveyed. Method of Doomſday ſurvey. A hide, and virgate, what.

X. Burghley, how ſurveyed.

XI. Great Wirthorp, how ſurveyed. The abbat of Croyland anciently lord of great Wirthorp.

XII. The abbat of Burgh, anciently lord of little Wirthorp. That manor how ſurveyed. Socmen, who?

XIII. 1087. William Rufus diſtributes his fathers alms; viz. 100 l. to every borough; ten marc's to every principal church; ſix marc's to every ſecond rate church; and five ſhillings to every pariſh church.

XIV. Sept. 29. 1103. 3. H. 1. Council by Anſelm to put down married prieſts. Remarks on Anſelm and his *deploratio pro amiſſa virginitate.* Decreed that abbats ſhall not make any more knights; & that there be no more ſelling of men.

XV. In 1109. Joffrid abbat of Croyland ſends divers monks to Cotenham who preach, and ſet up ſchools at Cambridge; & others to Wridthorp by Stanford, who preach againſt the Jews. All of them beg contributions towards building their church lately conſumed by fire. The abbat gives the monks of Wridthorp power to confeſs the nuns, and neighbours; and aſſigns them his manor there. That the univerſity, or ſchools, at Stanford, was firſt ſet up by thoſe monks very probable; & that All Saints college at Wridthorp was then founded by abbat Joffrid: That college how valued at the ſuppreſſion.

XVI. Richneſs of Stanford at this time; part of Croyland built by mony raiſed there. Account of the Benedictin nunnery at great Wridthorp.

XVII. July 5. 1110. 10. H. 1. K. Henry at Stanford; confirms the charter of Manaſſer Arſic to the priory of Cogges. An. 1118. one Leofwine pretending a grant of 5 s. for the abbat of Burgs houſes at Stanford, adjudged to loſe it. An. 1125. the abbat of Burgs lands, at Stanford. An. 112$\frac{7}{8}$. the vile Character of Henry Peitow, abbat of Burg. A parcel of demons ſeen hunting between Stanford and Burg. Remarks on that fable.

XVIII. Circ. 1133. Martin de Vecti abbat of Burg builds S. Martins church at Stanford; aſſigns a penſion from it to the ſacriſty of Burg. All Saints the only pariſh on that ſide the water before S. Martins church was built; but then divided into two. Stanford, north of Welland, in the demeſne of K. Henry the 1. Stanford abby, a Ciſtercian monaſtery, firſt built.

XIX. An. 1140. a great meeting at Stanford to conclude a peace between K. Stephen, and Ranulph E. of Cheſter. The wars between them. They ſwear not to betray one another. Yet the K. ſeiſes the E. but lets him go.

XX. 17. Dec. 1145. pope Eugenius the third confirms, I. the abbat of Burgs lands, churches, mint, &c. at Stanford. II. 20. Dec. 1145. the fees of Roger de Torpel, Aſceline of Waterville, and Geoffry of Winceſter. And III. 17. Aug. 1147. the prior of Huntendunes tythe of Stanford mills.

XXI. An. 1149. K. Stephen at Stanford confirms, I. Weng to the monks of Thorney. II. Nortop to the monks of Burg. III. All their lands to the monks of Croyland. An. 1152. E. Ranulph poiſoned by William Peverell. An. 1153. Duke Henry at Stanford; beſieges it a third time; takes the town; and caſtle. K. Stephen adopts the duke.

BOOK V.

Containing the reign of K. Henry II.

I. An. 2. 1154-5. Wm. Waterville elected abbat of Burg; manner of his election. Hugh the ſpirit, a monk, why ſo called: note, p. 2. Some of Wm. Watervilles good deeds to his own church. Notes about the Dyves.

II. 2. H. 2. Stanford, with the caſtle and borough, granted to Rich. Humet. The abbat of Burg & Wm. Lanvalei's lands excepted out of that grant. Rich. Humets lands at Writtorp, Ketene, Dudinton, &c.

III. 1156. Wm. Waterville founds S. Michaels a Benedictin nunnery by Stanford; ſtocks it with nuns; gives them, I. the church of S. Michael, of his own erection for their conventual church. II. the revenues of S. Martins church at Stanford. And III. of S. Firmin at Thurlby. Sad accidents at pulling down the ruins of this priory church.

IV. The nuns recognition, confeſſing their ſubjection to the monaſtery of Burg; at large. The ſame more conciſe. K. Henry the 2. confirms the founders donations.

V. 5. 7. H. 2. Richard Humet ſherif of Rutland, accompts. 1162-3. Jan. 9. pope Alexander 2. confirms the abbat of Thorneys lands at Stanford. 1163. 9. H. 2. Rich. Humet takes Combert caſtle in Brittany; is ſherif of Rutland ſeveral years. 10. H. 2. Wm. Lanvalei witneſs to the kings

kings recognition of the peoples rights.
K. Henry befieging Bridgnorth caftle, Hubert St. Clere receives an arrow fhot at
the K. into his own body to fave him ;
in gratitude the K. caufes Wm. Lanvalei
to marry Huberts daughter. Wm. Lanvalei's eftate at Wakerley. Dugdales omif-
fions about him. Of his fon. Stows miftake about him.
VI. Feb. 3. 1170-1. Rich. Humet at the
defire of Wm. Coleville, appropriates S.
Andrews church at Stanford to the nuns
of S. Michael. Sir Wm. Dugdales miftake about a rent of x. marcs which, he
faith, this R. Humet gave the faid nuns ;
proved, from himfelf, to be the gift of
Wm. Humet fon of this Rich. Short account of Peter, dean of Stanford, rector
of S. Martins, & S. Andrews. Stanford-
hall. Ric. Humet guardian to Bertram
de Verdun.
VII. 1174. 21. H. 2. Rich. Humet witnefs to an agreement between the K. &
Wm. K. of Scotland. Brand de Foffato
& Siward build the hofpital of S. John
& S. Thomas of Canterbury at Stanford-
bridge, for relief of paffengers & other
poor. Rich. Humet & Bertram de Verdun give land to build a church on, &
for a churchyard there. Anketil de Mallory & Wm. Dive, the E. of Leicefters
conftables, furrender his caftles to the K.
Mallory lane in Stanford, whence fo called. Jeoffry bp. of Lincoln raifes an im-
menfe fum in his diocefe, & afterwards
returns it. K. Henry the fon fwears fealty
to K. Hen. the father at Mauns in Normandy before Rich. Humet.
VIII. 1175. Conclufion of the life of Wm.
Waterville abbat of Burg, & founder of
S. Michaels priory by Stanford. His

many good deeds at Burg. He purchafes
all the village on that fide the bridge at
Stanford ; and redeems fourteen houfes
on this fide : is depofed. And why.
IX. 1176. Bertram de Verdun founds Crokefden abby. This Bertram faid to be lord
of Staunford. How that affertion may
be admitted. He endows Crokefden, *inter alia*, with a tenement & mill at Stanfort. K. Henry the 2. confirms that grant.
Bertrams mother, who. Bertram made
one of the kings juftices itinerantes. A-
chard de Staunford, on the death of Gui-
do his fon, & heir, gives the nuns of S. Michael the church of All Saints in the mercat.
X. 1177. Burial places appointed for the
Jews, before obliged to carry their dead
to London. Bull of pope Alexand. 2.
receiving the hofpital of S. John & S.
Thomas at Stanford, under the protection
of S. Peter.
XI. 24. H. 2. Bertram de Verdun fent to
confer with the Spanifh ambaffadors. K.
Henry the 2. confirms the conftablefhip
of Normandy, the manor of Stanford,
with the caftle & borough, & all his fathers lands in England & Normandy ; to
Wm. Humet.
XII. May 2. 1182. 28. H. 2. Difpute between Wm. Humet & Akarius abbat of
Burg, about the abbats privileges at Stanford, how determined. Tol, Tem, Infangthef, & Utfangthef, what. More
days than one formerly kept in commemoration of great faints.
XIII. 30. H. 2. Wm. Humet has 50 l.
blanc firm in Stanford. Bertram de Verdun long time fherif of Warwic & Lei-
cefter-fhires ; 31. H. 2. hath the cuftody
of Chefter caftle.

BOOK VI.

Containing the reign of K. Richard I.

I. SEpt. 3. 1189. 1. R. 1. Murder of the
Jews at London. K. Rich. refolves
to relieve Jerufalem.
II. Dec. 5. 1182. 1. R. 1. K. Rich. confirms to the abbat of Burg the houfe of
the holy fepulchre, S. Giles hofpital, all
Stanford fouth of Welland, S. Martins
church, All Saints church on that fide the
bridge, the priory of S. Michael, & the
hofpital of S. John baptift & S. Thomas
of Canterbury. Account of S. Pulchers
foundation ; & of S. Giles hofpital. Reafon why all churches & hofpitals dedicated to S. Giles ftood without all fuch
towns as they were erected at.
III. Murder of the Jews at Lyn.
IV. Murder of the Jews at Mid-lent-fair at
Stanford ; one John a Chriftian murdered

at Northampton for lucre of the money
he got from the Jews at Stanford ; fimple
folks watch his fepulchre, & fancy him a
faint. A mefchaunt man, what.
V. Mar. 16. 1189-90. 1. R. 1. murder of
the Jews at York.
VI. 21. Ap. 1190. 1. R. 1. K. Rich. confirms to the mafter & brethren of S. John
bapt. & S. Thomas of Canterburys hofpital I. the place whereon it ftood. II. the
houfe & chapel founded by Siward. III.
the lands & achats given by Brand de
Foffato. IV. the meadow given by Wm.
Humet & Bertram de Verdun to build a
church on, & make a churchyard of :
account of the chapel & church there.
VII. Dugdales miftake about this hofpital.
Frater, how many ways to be tranflated.

VIII.

VIII. June 25. 1190. 1. R. 1. K. Richard confirms to Wm. Humet & his heirs the constableship of Normandy, & the manor & castel of Stanford. Jordan de Humez & Bertram de Verdun two of K. Richards sureties at the agreement between him & Tancred K. of Sicily. The admirals of K. Richards fleet.

IX. Hamon Peche senior gives the nuns of S. Michael, part of the tythes of Corebi. Account of Pain Peverell & his descendents. *Vetus feoffamentum*, what? in the notes, p. 11.

X. 21. Aug. 3. R. 1. Bertram de Verdun made constable of Acon. 4. R. 1. dies at Joppa, & is buried at Acon. The Jews get hold of Wm. de Burghels estate at Stanford, & the abbat of Burg lends him mony to redeem it. Odd tradition of the common people at Stanford about frier Bacon. What we are to understand by his brazen head.

XI. 2. Ap. 1194. Gerard de Camville accused of receiving thieves who had robbed the merchants going to Stanford fair, & of treason; his stout answer; he is fined.

XII. Aug. 22. 1194. 6. R. 1. Torneaments at Stanford. The reason of them. Laws to be observed by them who torney, their oath.

XIII. Wm. de Albini the 3d. with K. Richard in Normandy. The abbat & convent of Burg grant Master Reiner of Stanford tythe of four mens demesnes at Bernac:

Reiner grants them a pension of ten shillings a year out of it. Hubert the archbishop commends his so doing.

XIV. Account of Ascelina de Walterville & her family. She gives the nuns of St. Michael, I. a moiety of Upton chapel. II. two shares of one third part of the church of Corbi. III. the remaining third part of the foresaid third part of the church of Corbi. IV. four bovates of arable land at Corbi. V. another bovate there for a pittance.

XV. Account of Matildis de Diva & her family. She gives the nuns of S. Michael I. one third part of the church of Corbi. II. part of Upton chapel. III. tythe of all such wood as was, or should be, grubbed up in the lands belonging to her & her heirs.

XVI. Matildis de Diva gives Adelicia de Capeni a bovate of land at Corbi; who gives it to the nuns of S. Michael. Matildis de Diva confirms it.

XVII. 7. 8. 9. R. 1. Wm. de Albini the 3d, sherif of Warwick, Leicester, & Rutland. No man, after midlent fair at Stanford 9. R. 1. to sell any cloth but by prescribed measure. 10. R. 1. Wm. de Albini the 3d sherif of Rutland, Bucks, & Bedford; marries Agatha Trusbut. The lord Trusbuts arms. Wm. de Coleville gives a fine for his lands at Binebruc & Aburne; & grants some land at North Witham to Q. the monk.

BOOK VII.
Containing the reign of K. John.

I. 1. JOhn. Ranulf Blandevil E. of Chester forsakes his wife because the K. haunted her company, & marries Clemencia Dinant, Wm. de Humets niece. Wm. de Albini the 3d Sherif of Bucks & Bedford. Nov. 18. 1200. Hugh bp. of Lincoln dies. Miracles that happened as they carried his body from London to Lincoln, on the road, at Bicklefwade, & at Stanford.

II. 2. John. Wm. de Albini licensed to make a park at Stoke, & to hunt in Rockingham forest. The kings justices pretending to seise the cloth at Boston fair not made according to the prescribed measure of the 9. R. 1. raise a great sum of the merchants. 3. John. Baldwin Wac marries Agnes Daughter of Wm. Humet. K. John & his barons quarrel; he demands their castels; particularly Belvoir of Wm. Albini, who gives his son for a hostage, & so keeps it. Jan. 15. 4. John. the K. gives Wm. Albini the manor of Ouston, & C. s. of Soccage land at Wilberston & Stoke. Ranulph E. of Chester being suspected by K. John, Wm. Humet & R. constable of Chester, are bound for him. The borough of Stanford fined for a foolish pre-

sentment, & removing the mercat, & chosing mean jurats. Stephen de Lenne of Stanford fined for selling wine contrary to assise measure; as also Jordan de London. The borough fined again.

III. Luci wife of Wm. Humet gives the nuns of S. Michael half a marc of silver at Bredcroft, one half for a pittance, the other half to the infirmary.

IV. Walter de Cardonville having given the nuns of S. Michael a virgate of land at Draiton by Sudwic, & Lucy Humet having given the monastery of Sudwic a like quantity at Bradecrofd, those convents make an exchange.

V. Wm. Humet gives the Cystercian monks of Stanford ten marcs a year. He is made justice of England; advises the K. to go into Normandy. The country rise upon the K. & take him. The K. returns; Humet flies. 6. John, Wm. E. Warenn (the 5th of the name of Wm) obtains the castel & honor of Eye; & the manors of Graham & Stanford, till he recover his lands in Normandy, or the K. give him an equivalent. But that E. not to talliate the men of Stanford without the kings precept.

VI. 9. John the K. refusing to admit Step. Langton archbishop of Cant. the pope & he quarrel. Mar. 22. the bishops, by the popes order, interdict the kingdom. Wm. E. Warenn gives the town of Stanford five acres to make a burial place for excommunicate persons, & to build a chapel & hospital; probably S. Logars. The K. seises all the lands of the religious who refuse to officiate in the interdict; & shuts up their barns. Steph. the archbishop procures the conventual churches license to celebrate once a week. The K. orders all the clergy to go to the pope & require him to do the K. justice.

VII. Wm. E. Warenn gives a fine for the custody of Gilbert de Aquila's lands. The kingdom interdicted afresh; & the lords released of their allegiance by the pope. Manner of the interdict. The K. requires a new oath of allegiance of his nobles, pledges of them he suspected, & homage of all freeholders of 12 years of age; throws down the pales of his parks & forests that the deer may eat the corn of his rebellious subjects. All Stanford south of Welland then part of Rockingham forest.

VIII. 1210. K. John plagues the Jews. Wm. de Albini the 3ᵈ. one of his sureties that he shall observe the peace between him & the French king.

IX. 14. John. Wm. Lanvalei marries Alan Bassets daughter. 1213. Wm. E. Warenn one of the four who swore King John should give the pope satisfaction. And May 15. witness to his resigning the realm & crown to the pope, & at his doing homage. The castles of Bambury & Newcastle upon Tine with the bailiwic of Northumberland committed to him. The K. summons four men of every demesne town of the crown to appear the 4th of Aug. & enquire what satisfaction he should make the bishops. Aug. 25. the interdict released in part.

X. 29. June 1214 the interdict entirely released. Robert Lindsey abbat of Burg & the convent oblige themselves to pay the K. 1200 marcs to disforest part of the Nesse of Burg; who agrees to it. All Stanford south of Welland then disforested. Stupende-Stan without Stanford.

XI. 22. Nov. 1214. 16. John. K. John confirms Wm. Humets grant of ten marcs a year to the Ciftercian monks of Stanford. Sir Wm. Dugdales mistake about those monks corrected.

XII. K. Johns benefactions to the house of lepers, monks of S. Michael, hospital of S. Logar, monks of S. Leonard, & nuns of S. Michael. Some antiquities at Kings Cliffe.

XIII. Wm. Langvale gives the nuns of S. Michael, the church of S. Clement in Stanford.

XIV. Roger de Torpel confirms to the nuns of S. Michael, his mother Ascelina de Waltervilles gift of the third part of the church of Corby; & her donation of four bovates of arable land there. Torpel town where? Roger de Torpel, who?

XV. Hugh de Diva confirms his mother Mauds grant to the nuns of S. Michael of the third part of the church of Corby.

XVI. Ralph de Diva confirms his mother Mauds grant to those nuns of the third part of the church of Corby, & of the tythe of wood then, or afterwards, grubbed up in the lands belonging to her & her heirs, & of her part of Upton chapel: also her grant of a bovate of land at Corby to Adelicia de Capeni, which bovate the said Adelicia gave to the said nuns.

XVII. Wm. Albini & Wm. E. Warenn commissioners to conduct all persons to the king, to implore his favor, after releasing of the interdict. The northern barons assemble at Stanford against King John. Their pretence for so doing. The true causes; viz. K. Johns attempting to debauch Eustace de Vesci's lady; poysoning Robert Fitzwalters daughter; banishing the E. of Chester; his unreasonable avarice; refusing to observe the laws of K. Edward.

XVIII. The vast army the barons assembled at Stanford. The names of those barons.

XIX. The names of those barons who staid yet with the king. May 10. 1215. 17. John. The K. offers to treat with them. Wm. E. Warenn one of his pledges.

XX. June 15. by E. Warenns advice the K. grants them the great charter & charter of the forest. Wm. de Albini one of those twenty five who swore to observe those charters & to compel the king to do so likewise. Wm. E. Warenn one of the eight & thirty more sworn to assist those twenty five; sworn by proxy. The K. sends his writs for all men to observe those charters. And June 19. commands an enquiry into the evil practices of sherifs, foresters, &c. Wm. E. Warenn witness to K. Johns charter to the clergy.

XXI. The barons will not disarm. The K. discontented; sends to the pope to be released of his oath, & for more foreign soldiers. The male-practices of the barons. They appoint a tourneament at Stanford. That tourney much promoted by Wm. de Albini; but adjourned by the rest to Hounflow heath. The prize of tilting, a bear.

XXII. The pope threatens to excommunicate the barons. They send for Wm. de Albini. Treaty at Staines. The barons excommunicated. They divide the kingdom among themselves as so many justiaries. Wm. de Alb. justitiary of Lincolnshire.

XXIII. Wm. de Albini made governor of Rochester castel by the barons; besieged in it by the king; valor of the besieged.

XXIV. The extremities they were reduced to. Wm. de Albini gallantly refuses to let an expert bowman shoot the king.

XXV.

XXV. Nov. 30. they surrender. The K. threatens to hang all the nobles; but is hindered. The barons sent to prison. The pope excommunicates them.

XXVI. K. John summons Belvoir castel, & threatens, that if it were not delivered, Wm. de Albini should never eat more. The castel surrendred by his son. Wm. de Albini's manor of Offington given to Wm. E. Warenn.

XXVII. The barons excommunicated by name. They send for the French kings son Lewes to be king. June 14. 1216. he summons all the great men to do him homage, or depart the kingdom. Wm. E. Warenn desetrs K. John, who orders his castel of Pevensey to be demolish'd. Wm. de Albini submits to K. John, & pays a great fine for his liberty; which is raised by his wife. K. John in Suffolk; at Stanford; & at Lincoln, where he raises the siege of the castel. But Oct. 19. dies, not without suspicion of poyson; leaving his affairs in great confusion.

BOOK VIII.

Containing the reign of K. Henry the third.

I. OCT. 27. K. Johns son prince Henry elected king. Lewis the dolphin at Stanford. Wm. de Albini submits & gives hostages to K. Henry. The dolphin goes over to France. Wm. E. Warenn & others resent it, & desert him. Lewis returns. The rascally army he brought with him.

II. Wm. de Albini in great favor with K. Henry. 1217, Lovis defeated at Lincoln. Muleton castel given to Wm. de Albini. Coats of arms now first hereditary; & badges now first brought up.

III. 2. H. 3. Hamon Peche fines for his barony. Mar. 30. all Jews ordered to wear badges. 4. H. 3. Wm. E. Warenn sherif of Surrey. The austin friers at Stanford founded by one Flemyng. Lelands account of him.

IV. Ralph son of Achard de Stanford grants the abbat of Burg liberty to keep up the banks of his mill-dam at Stanford. His nephew Wm. son of Wm. de Berc confirms it.

V. 1220. Hugh late bishop of Lincoln canonized. 5. H. 3. Wm. E. Warenn sherif of Surrey. The manors of Graham & Stanford confirmed to him. A famous inquisition at Stanford. Wm. de Fortibus 2. E. of Albemarle fortifies Bitam & Fotheringhay castels. His message to the cities & boroughs. Bitam castel demolished by the K. Conjecture that this Wm. de Fortibus founded the black friers at Stanford. Wm. de Albini 3. obtains the wardship of Hugh Nevil.

VI. 1222. 7. H. 3. The prior of S. Leonards & dean of Stanford ordered by the pope to make inquisition about some lands belonging to the church of Burg. Hamon Peche levies scutage on his tenents.

VII. 1224. Faukes de Brent fortifies Bedford castel, & imprisons one of the kings justices. His castel taken, & wife committed to E. Warenn. Feb. 11. 9. H. 3. E. Warenn witness to *magna carta*. F. de Brent banished. E. Warren conducts him to the sea. The clergy ordered to renew their charters. Mar. 17. K. Henry confirms to the church of Burg all Stanford south of Welland, &c.

VIII. Hamon Peche gives the nuns of S. Michael part of Corbi. 10. H. 3. Hugh Wells bishop of Lincoln confirms to those nuns I. a third part of Corbi church given them by Matildis de Diva, & her son Hugh. II S. Martins, All Saints, S. Andrews, & S. Clements churches in Stanford; as also Thirlby church, & a 3^d part of Corbi, & the tythe of grubbed wood belonging to the Diva's. III. two other parts of Corbi given them by Maud de Diva, Ascelina de Walterville, & Hamon Peche.

IX. 1227. The barons meet Richard E. of Cornwal with an army at Stanford against his brother the K. E. Richard grants the nuns of S. Michael letters of protection. The Nesse of Burg again disforested.

X. 18. Nov. 12. H. 3. K. Henry gives the nuns of S. Michael a load of wood out of Clive Forest. Martin abbat of Burg frees those nuns from paying Landgavel for some lands at Stanford.

XI. 12. Apr. 1229. the deans of Rutland & Stanford decree matters about the priory of Lewis & the cells of Castelacre, & Bromholm.

XII. circa 1230. Sir Clement Heia rector of S. Michael Cornstal sells Hu. Bladelaw an house at Stanford; who sells it to the abbat of Thorney. Cornstal church & gate where. Great S. Michaels church at Stanford, described. Built crosswise. The oldest fabric of any now left there. Steeple & bells modern.

XIII. 15. H. 3. the bishop of Lincolns pension from S. Peters church in Stanford. The nuns of S. Michaels proctor at Rome having procured them some privileges disliked by the abbat of Burg, they beg pardon for his so doing.

XIV. The hospital & priory of S. Mary at Newsted founded by Wm. de Albini 3. The first endowment. The second.

XV. 1232. Randolf E. of Chester confirms the monks of Thorneys lands. Hubert de Burg committed to E. Warenns custody. Wm. E. Warenn gives a fine for his daughter Isabell to marry the E. Arundel. 1233. the pope orders monasteries to be visited. 19. H. 3. E. Warenn

4

has

has 50. l. blanc firm in Stanford. Jan. ..
1235-6. 20. H. 3. is cupbearer at the kings wedding. Churches in Linc. dioces ordered to be dedicated.

XVI. May 6. 1236. 20. H. 3. Wm. de Albini 3. dies; buried at Newſted; his benefaction to Belvoir priory: his wives and children. Agatha Trusbut his 2ᵈ wife buried at Newſted. Will. de Bever his ſon admitted to his lands. 1237. 21. H. 3. Wm. E. Warenn one of the three peers made the kings ſole council; & one of the 4. in whoſe hands a great tax is lodged. Nov. 20. He reſcues the legates ſervants at Ouſney, & impriſons divers Oxford ſcholars.

XVII. 1238. 23. H. 3. Richard of Stanford, elected abbat of Thorney, dies 2 days after. Simon Pierpoint, after a law ſuit, grants Wm. E. Warenn a charter of free Warenn. May 27. 1240. Wm. E. Warenn dies. His wives. He gives the nuns of S. Michael 40. s. per annum to keep an obit for Elias de Marnile. After his death the king ſeiſes Stanford.

XVIII. 25. H. 3. Hamon Peche dies in the Holy Land; gives the nuns of S. Michael the 9. part of Corbi, &c. his benefaction to the canons of Fineſhade.

XIX. Alice, relict of Aſceline de Walterville, lady of Maxra, gives the nuns of S. Michael a virgate of land, &c. at Aiſſele worth 8. s. a year for two anniverſaries (viz. her own, & her daughter Cecily's.) Wm. de Albini the 4. (her brother) confirms it; his remarkable ſeal. John Palmer obliges himſelf & heirs to pay the ſaid 8. s.

XX. 26. H. 3. Wm. de Aubeni 4. fines to be excuſed going into Gaſcoigne. Tuniburg caſtel committed to Maud relict of Wm. E. Warenn. Gilbert Peche does homage for his fathers lands. Walter abbat of Burg augments the rent of the infirmary there with 57. s. at Stanford. 27. H. 3. Wm. Albini 4. ſides with the K. againſt the E. of Pembroke; confirms his fathers foundation of Newſted, & gives them leave to chuſe their own prior. Account of the book of Doomſday kept at Newſted.

XXI. 29. H. 3. Thomas de Arches claims the advowſon of Sumordeby againſt the prioreſs of S. Michael. 30. H. 3. Maud (relict of Wm. late E. Warenn) appoints a deputy to act for her as marſhal of England; & has Strigoil caſtel. 1246. The archbp. of Cant. procures the popes grant for a years firſt fruits in his own dioceſe. Bp. Groſtheads ſtrict enquiry into the nobilities lives.

XXII. 1247. 31. H. 3. John E. Warenn marries Alice the Kings ſiſter. Wm. de Valence gets a grant of Rob. Pontdelarches lands. The archbp. ſuſpends them who won't pay him their firſt fruits. The coin changed. Wm. de Albini 4. his death, burial, wives, daughter. 32. H. 3. Maud (relict of Wm. late E. Warenn) dies. John E. Warenn at the parliament at London.

XXIII. 35. H. 3. The bps. oppoſe the archbps. exactions. Bp. Groſtheads manner

of viſiting his dioceſe. 1251. The bps. ſtop the archbps. viſiting. Groſtheads ſevere way of viſiting monaſteries & nunneries; he would enforce beneficed men to be prieſts, but is hindered; inſtitutes vicarages in appropriate churches.

XXIV. 37. H. 3. a quarrel between the archbp. & the elect of Winton. No. 8. 1253. Groſthead dies. The archbp. & bp. of Winton reconciled. John E. Warenn concerned in that quarrel.

XXV. 1254. John E. Warenn pays an aid on making the prince a knight. Henry Hanna flouriſhes at Brunham; elected the ſecond provincial of his order in England. This the perſon who began the ſchools at Stanford. The prince marries Alianora ſiſter of Alphonſo K. of Caſtile. The K. gives him Stanford, &c. on his marriage, & he jointures his wife in it, &c.

XXVI. 39. H. 3. John E. Warenn joyns with the K. in oppreſſing the people. Pr. Edw. mortages Stanford to William de Valence. 40. H. 3. John E. Warenn at Weſtm. where the archbp. excommunicates the infringers of magna carta; has the *tertium denarium* of Surrey. 1256. K. Henry 3. grants the burgeſſes of Stanford divers privileges. Aveſia counteſs of Warenn dies much lamented.

XXVII. 1257. 42. H. 3. Hen. Hanna begs Stockwel in Oxfordſhire of Rich. K. of the Romans, & turns it into a monaſtery of Carmes. The monks of . Leonards reſiſt the popes exactors; are excommunicated; & abſolved. Matthew Paris commends them. Speeds character of Mat. Paris. The abbat & convent of Burg lett their mill at Stanford to the prioreſs of S. Michael. John E. Warenn elected one of the arbitrators between the K. & the rebellious barons; at Oxford, refuſes the oath enjoined by that mad parliament; ſummoned to attend the K. againſt the Welch; July 5. 1258. guards Wm. de Valence to the ſea ſide.

XXVIII. Thomas ſon of Wm. de Fortibus 3. E. of Albemarle, buried in the black friers at Stanford. Account of that monaſtery & the church there. Difference between a monk & a frier. But four orders of mendicants allowed by the council of Lions. Their ſeveral ſorts of poverty. Miſtakes of Speed, & Mr. Stevens about the black friers at Stanford corrected.

XXIX. Feb. 1261-2. 46. H. 3. Several Cambridge men remove to Northampton, with the kings paſsport. John E. Warenn ſets his ſeal to the agreement between the K. & his barons; 47. H. 3. has Pevenſel caſtel intruſted to him; 1263. is elected one of their captains by the rebellious barons; but leaves them; &, upon the princes ſurpriſing Windſor, goes thither to him & the king.

XXX. Feb. 3. 1263-4. 48. H. 3. John E. Warenn joyns in ſubmitting to the award of Lovis betwixt the K. & barons. Friar John Stanford dies, at Linne. The Oxford men remove to Northampton; where they ſide with the barons againſt the K. who threatens to hang, but pardons them.

The

The abbat of Burgs bailif demands land-gavel of the priorefs of S. Michael; who pleads abbat Martins releafe, which is allowed; & the priory for ever difcharged paying it. John E. Warenns bailif levies mony of the abbat of Burg, on pretence of his fiding with the Barons. That earl is befieged at Rochefter. The kings of England & Almaine with their armies at Stanford. The abbat of Burgs great gifts to them, the prince, & divers nobles there. Valor of John E. Warenne at Rochefter. The king relieves him. May 12. 1264. 48. H. 3. Battel of Lewes, where the K. & prince were taken prifoners by S. Mountfort. John E. Warenn flies to Pemfey. All his lands, given by Mountfort to Gil. E. of Clare: He flies into France. The abbat of Burgs management in thefe troubles. He fetches provifion for his monaftery from Stanford.

XXXI. 1265. 49. H. 3. Warenn, Valence, &c. return. Warenn demands his lands. Mountforts anfwer. Warenn joyns the prince after his efcape at Ludlow. Mountfort fummons the kings tenents to go againft them. Battel of Evefham: Mountfort flain, & the K. releafed. The abbat of Burg pays John E. Warenn a fine to redeem his lands.

XXXII. Feb. 1. 1265-6. 50. H. 3. The king revokes his grant of the new univerfity at Northampton; & why. The white friers at Stanford founded. Arms on the gate. Fine fituation, church & fteeple. The kings of England always lay there. Burtons miftake about the founder corrected. The gate when built. The founder. The univerfity begun here by Henry Hanna; who refides at Stanford. The white friers college there full of learned men. Thofe learned men put in by Hen. Hanna & K. H. the 3. The white friers fchools at Stanford. Lord Burghleys mother joyntred in them. The K. connives at this univerfity begun by the Carmes of his own foundation. Their wifdom in fetting up fchools. Mr. Forfters miftakes about the houfe & founder corrected.

XXXIII. 1266. 50. H. 3. E. Warenn defeats the E. of Derby at Chefterfield; John Danville by his great valor efcapes;

many flain; the E. of Derby taken. 51. H. 3. Part of Stanford (hitherto part of Nottinghamfhire) now made part of Rutland. 1266-7. The K. fummons his tenents to go againft Danvil in the ifle of Ely. The E. of Gloucefter encourages Danvil. E. Warenn fent to admonifh Gloucefter. His reply. June 24. 1268. 53. H. 3. The K. prince, E. Warenn, &c. take the crofs upon them. Margery Carun & Emma de Oundle give the templars lands at Stanford.

XXXIV. John E. Warenn & the E. of Lincoln raife men againft each other. The K. takes up the quarrel. The judges decide againft Warenn. 1269. John E. Warenns letters of protection in behalf of the nuns of S. Michael; his odd feal.

XXXV. 1270. 54. H. 3. Quarrel between John E. Warenn & Alan Lord Zouche of Afhby in Weftm. hall; they fight; Ld. Zouch & his fon wounded. The E. flies to Rigate; refufes to take his trial. The prince fent to reduce him. He fubmits; is fined. Ld. Zouch dies of his wounds. Speed & Dugdales miftakes about this matter corrected.

XXXVI. 1271. 55. H. 3. Pr. Edw. wounded with a poifoned dagger in the holy Land by an affaffin. Miftake of Speed, Baker, & Butcher about the manner of his cure.

XXXVII. Defcription of S. Maries church & fteeple. The bells how infcribed. Note upon fancte's bells.

XXXVIII. Remarks on churches in general. Infides with pillars. Infides without pillars. Fronts. Fine fteeples at, & about Stanford. Odd church at Tickencoat. Difference between a Saxon & Norman church. To know what time of the year any church was built. Churches of the fame age always alike in fome things. The oldeft fort of churches. The feveral forts of fteeples obferved by the author. A fault of fome antiquaries touched. S Maries the mother church of Stanford. Compared to Rachel weeping for her children.

XXXIX. The grey friers at Stanford founded; the ruins & prefent ftate; in what cuftody.

BOOK IX.

Containing the reign of K. Edward the firft.

I. 1272. PRince Edw. in the holy Land 1. E. 1. when his father died; reafon of that expedition. John E. Warenn at K. Henrys funeral; fwears fealty to K. Edw. Jan. 31. 1272-3. Walter Burley, born. John E. Warenn & others covenant to defend the kings perfon & right. The K. makes S. Leonards & other monafteries take letters of protection. John E. Warenn claims Stainford in Yorkfhire.

II. Aug. 19. 2. E. 1. 500 great horfes turned loofe at the kings coronation by J. E. Warenn, &c. catch them who could. 3. E. 1. J. E. Warenn entertains the K. at Rigate, where the K. remits part of his fine about Ld. Zouches bufinefs. 4. E. 1. Inquifition about tolls at Stanford. E. Warenn gives the burgeffes of Stanford leave to chufe an alderman. Licenfe granted to found a chantery in S. Clements church. Rutland

15 E

land when difmembred from Northamptonfhire.

III. 6. E. 1. The K. orders the ftatute of *quo waranto* to be put in execution. E. Warenns ftout anfwer to the kings juftices thereupon. The proceedings ftopped a while. 1278. Emma de S. Medardo buried at Stanford.

IV. 1279. 7. E. 1. Roger de Colville frees the nuns of S. Michael of all fervices from a tenement of theirs at Wenton & Berk.

V. 25. June. John E. Warenn impleaded on the ftatute *de quo waranto.* The earls firft plea; &c. Nov. 19. 8. E. 1. his fecond plea. The jurats. Their report. The archbp. of York acquaints the prior of Durham he intends to vifit him as Metropolitan; the priors anfwer.

VI. 1280. Cecilia relict of Samfon Burley releafes her right to fome land bought of her husband by the abbat of Burg. Sir Roger Burley gives the abbat & monks of Burg a rent, &c. at Pilsgate & Burley. Jan. 6. 1280-1. Sir Roger Burley dies (his mortuary to the Monks of Burg) & his lady foon after (her mortuary.) The archbp. of York being hindered from vifiting the church of Durham excommunicates the bp. &c. The caufe is heard at Stanford before the popes delegates, & the archbp. worfted.

VII. Ifabel E. Warenns daughter married to John Baillol K. of Scots. 9. E. 1. K. Ed. refpites E. Warenns payment of his fine; but proceeds farther againft him on the ftatute *de quo waranto.* The King charges the earl that he will not let his bailifs enter Stanford; & enquires how he claims return of writs, affife of bread & beer, gallows, coroner, prifon, mercat, tronage, pefage, and thurtol in Stanford & Grantham. The earls reply.

VIII. 1281. Sir John de Oketon recovers the patronage of little Caftreton from the prior of Newfted. Oct. 6. the bp. of Lincolns official, by his letter to the dean of Stanford, cites Sir Peter de Burley to fhew caufe at Northampton, why he refus'd to pay a mortuary due to the abbat of Burg. The dean excommunicates Sir Peter; & he fubmits. The deans return to the official. Hen. Hanna rechofe provincial of the Carmes; fpreads his order.

IX. Oct. 7. 1282. 10. E. 1. The K. grants the caftel of Dynas Bran & other lands in Wales to John E. Warenn. His eftate at this time. He is in the Welch wars; & defeated by Leweline. 11. E. 1. Griffin Vaughan grants his land of Yale to E. Warenn. That E. & Roger Mortimer appointed guardians to Griffith ap Madocs children, defraud them. E. Warenn begins Holt caftel. John Stanford a Francifcan flourifhes.

X. Nov. 12. 1284. 12. E. 1. Oliver bp. of Lincoln appropriates the third part of Corebi church to the nuns of St. Michael. Bp. Kennets remark on that appropriation.

XI. Dec. 15. 1286. 15. E. 1. William fon of John E. Warenn flain in a torneament

at Croyden; leaving his wife great with child. His burial. Wife who. The lands he had with her. May 2. 1287. all the Jews in England apprehended by the kings order; redeem themfelves for a great fine. The commons move for them to be banifhed. June 30. 1287. John fon of Will. (fon of John E. Warenn) born. Mar. 24. 1287-8. 16. E. 1. Difpute between Nicholas Fraunton & E. Warenns bailifs about their letting his fhop at Midlent fair. 1288. The tenths granted to the K. by the pope & a new taxation made.

XII. June 10. 1289. 17. E. 1. Oliver bp. of Lincoln exemplifies a particular of the vicarage of S. Martin.

XIII. 22. Jan. 1289-90. Pleadings between E. Warenns bailifs & Nicholas Fraunton; the jurats report.

XIV. 1290. K. Edw. banifhes the Jews. Their fynagogues at Stanford & Huntingdon burnt. Their libraries there fold by out-cry. Gregory of Hunt. buys many books & carries them to Ramfey. Lelands account of Gregory. Many Jews miferably drowned by a bafe mariner. Q. Eleanors croffes as at Stanford & other places; & the nunnery fhe founded at Stanford.

XV. Feb. 9. 1290-1. 19 E. 1. Alice the Ks. fifter (E. Warenns wife) dies. As doth Gilbert Peche.

XVI. 20 E. 1. Mr. Woods enquiry about the beginning of the univerfity at Stanford. His affertion that Robert Lutterel founded it this year, examined, & rejected. Henry de Hanna afferted to be the perfon. Many other Carmes proceed to fupport it.

XVII. 1292. The new taxation of the clergy finifhed. A particular of their *temporalia* & *fpiritualia* fo taxed in Stanford.

XVIII. 21. E. 1. John E. Warenn aids his fon in law Baillol in Scotland. Joan relict of Wm. (fon of John E. Warenn) dies, buried at Lewes. 1293. Tourneaments about this time at Stanford. General chapters at Stanford called *itinera minorum.* The Carmes, monks of Sempringham, & Auftin friers read lectures at Cambridge & Stanford.

XIX. 23. E. 1. Bamburg caftel committed to E. Warenn. The firft parliament that ever was, called; the members for Stanford. 1695. The K. fearches monafteries for money. The chief juftices fpeech when he declared the clergy out of the kings protection. 24. E. 1. John E. Warenn kills 10000 Scots; recovers Dunbar caftel; made governor of Scotland; 1296. concludes a marriage between Pr. Edw. & the E. of Flanders daughter.

XX. May 1297. 25. E. 1. Wm. Waleys rebels in Scotland. E. Warenn ordered againft him. The Scots give hoftages; entice him to Sterling; defeat the Englifh, by Sir Hu. Creffinghams folly. Valor of Sr. Marm. Thweng. E. Warenn breaks down the bridge to fave his army. Sir Hu. Crefs. flain. E. Warenn rides his horfe to death in the flight. The Scots take Berwic.

XXI.

XXI. Sep. 29. 1297. Wm. Wodeford abbat of Burg vifits the nuns of Stanford, & abfolves feveral of them. K. Edw. orders his lords to affift E. Warenn to recover Scotland. That E. haftes thither; raifes the fiege of Roxborough; enters Berwic. Parliament at York; the members for Stanford. The priorefs & nuns of S. Michael exchange fome lands, &c. at Stanford with Walter the phyfician. John E. Warenn undertakes for the K. that he fhall grant the two great charters.

XXII. July 25. 1298. 26. E. 1. Johanna, lord Waleran Mortimers daughter, admitted a nun at Stanford; manner of that folemnity. Mary daughter of Gerald de Normanville & Geoffry de Mar married at S. Peters Stanford. Her fortune; & the ceremony.

XXIII. Ap. 1299. 27. E. 1. Hugh de Cliffeby, warden of S. Thomas hofpital, impoverifhes the houfe & refigns. The abbat of Burg appoints Sir Robert rector of Northburg to take care of that houfe; who does fo for a time. Hugh de Cliffeby, on promife of amendment, reftored. Nov. 28. 1299. Henry de Hanna dies; buried in the white friers; his works. E. Warenn made governor of Hope caftle.

XXIV. Apr. 14. 1300. 28. E. 1. Hu. de Cliffeby relapfing to his old courfes, neglects faying fervice & relieving the poor; withdraws Rob. Wodefouls fallary, retrenches the lamps, embezzles the reliques, lets the houfe lie in dirt, & makes ftore rooms of the lodgings for the fick. The new abbat of Burg vifits the houfe, & again depofes him. He applies to John D'alderby elect of Linc. & others to intercede for him; promifes amendment; his fubmiffion; the abbats decree: Hugh's readmiffion.

XXV. July 14. 1300. The abbat of Burg gives notice to the nuns that he intends to vifit them. Thomas Pappele bound to Wm. Watervylle procurator of the friers minors to pay him x. marc's for his daughters portion. General chapters at Stanford called *itinera minorum*.

XXVI. A parliament for confirming the charters of the foreft: The members for Stanford. Difference among authors about the time & place of this parliament. The barons affemble in arms & come to parliament at Stanford.

XXVII. A general chapter of the Carmes at Stanford. Wm. Lidlington elected provincial there. His great character.

XXVIII. Feb. 12. 1300-1. the pope meddling with K. Ed. proceedings in Scotland, John E. Warenn & the barons write a fharp letter to him. That E. treats about a peace with the Scots.

XXIX. Ifabella de Roos's heart buried at Newfted. The bodies of divers perfons buried there removed, at the diffolution of monafteries, to Bottesford in Leicefterfhire. Cecilia Plukets & her daught.

releafe their right to the abbat of Burg of fome land, &c. at Stanford. Mr. Burtons obfervation on witneffes to old deeds. The truth of it, by two inftances.

XXX. 30. E. 1. Parliament at London. The members for Stanford. Ap. 9. 1302. 30. E. 1. Stephen, a monk of Burg, prefented to the priory of S. Michael by Stanford.

XXXI. 26. Jan. 1302-3. 31. E. 1. The abbat of Burg gives notice that he intends to vifit the nuns; appoints T. de Sarum warden of their temporalities.

XXXII. 1303. Wm. Lidlington, at the chapter of Narbonne, differs with Gerard of Bononia provincial gen. of the Carmes, about dividing the Eng. Carmes into 2 provinces. Godfrey de Cornwal & John Burley fide with Lidlington. They are excommunicated by the pope. Lidlington does penance. He & Gerard reconciled. John Burley, a Carme at Stanford, his works & character. Walter Burley, his character & works.

XXXIII. No. 11. 1303. 31. E. 1. Bp. D'alderby confirms Robert Lutterels gift of a manor in S. Peters parifh to the monks of Sempringham for an houfe of Students, & allows them an old chapel there (called S. Maries chapel) for their college chapel. The prior of Sempringhams acknowledgment of Mr. Lutterels benefaction. Mr. Forfters miftakes about Sempringham hall, S. Mary Bennewerk church, & S. Maries chapel, all at Stanford, corrected.

XXXIV. Dec. 25. 1303. Wm. Poncyn made warden of S. Giles hofpital. John E. Warenn in Scotland; Gilb. Ceftreton receiver of the kings tax.

XXXV. Sept. 27. 32. E. 1. John E. Warenn dies. His epitaph. The K. orders prayers for his foul, & divers bps. grant indulgences on the fame account: fucceeded by his grandfon John. 33. E. 1. Parl. at Weft. the members for Stanford. John E. Warenn marries the kings niece. 20. Mar. the K. confirms the nuns liberties. 28. June. 33. E. 1. the K. (on the abbat of Burgs complaint) prohibits his affeffors from levying the fame tax on the abbats tenents in Stanford & Grantham, as they did on E. Warenns tenents. They write to their under officers to forbear. The K. fends his mandate to the fherif of Lincoln for the abbat to have a reafonable talliage of his own tenents at Stanford & Grantham.

XXXVI. 34. E. 1. a Parl. at Weftm. the members for Stanford. Ap. 15. 34. E. 1. Walter bp. of Coventry makes up a difference between the abbats of Thorney & Burg. Pr. Edw. & John E. Warenn knighted. Dec. 1. 35. E. 1. the priorefs of S. Mich. does fealty to the abbat of Burg. John. E. Warenn in Scotland with the K. when he died.

BOOK

BOOK X.

Containing the reign of K. Edward the 2.

I. 1. E. 2. KING Edw. sends for Pierce 1307. Gaveston; who marries the E. of Gloucesters daughter. The Templars arrested; manner of it.

II. Jan. 11. 1308-9. 2. E. 2. Bp. D'alderby at Newsted, confirms the privileges of the church of Burg. The Peers summoned to meet in arms at Stanford against the Scots. John Repingale, a Carme, reads lectures at Stanford. His character & works. Wm. Whetely, a secular, his character & works. 1309. Mr. Woods farther enquiry about the beginning of the university at Stanford. His account of Whetelys reading lectures there in 1309.

III. A parliament at Stanford to suppress the Scots; & repeal Gavestons banishment; he nick-names the great lords. The prior of Durham lays the prior of Coldinghams rebellion against himself before the parliament at Stanford. Gaveston proclaims a tourney at Walingford, & abuses the great lords there. The parliament at Stanford order letters to the pope to complain of citations to Rome, & the behaviour of his delegates.

IV. 1310. Nicholas Stanford, a Cystercian, his works & character.

V. 4. E. 2. John E. Warenn in Scotland; has a grant of Peke castel & forest. 1311. *Itinera minorum* at Stanford. John E. Warenn at Berwic; he receives the foresters of Selkyrk to the kings peace. 5. E. 2. E. Warenn &c. besiege P. Gaveston in Scarborow castel; take & carry him to Walingford; where the E. of Warwic surprises, & beheads him. 1312. William Lidlington, warden of the white friers, his character; chose provincial of England, Cyprus, & the holy Land. Farther account of his dispute with Gerard of Bononia. He is forced to submit. His works. Thomas Allen of Cambridge a person much consulted by him.

VI. 6. E. 2. John E. Warenn gets a charter for divers mercats & fairs at divers places in Sussex; 7. E. 2. refuses to attend the K. into Scotland; 8. E. 2. founds a chantry in Rigate castel.

VII. 1315. 9. E. 2. Is excommunicated by the bp. of Chichester for adultery; comes to the bps. with armed men. The bps. men imprison him. For want of heirs the E. gives the K. inheritance of Stanford & all his lands. He & his lady divorced.

VIII. 1316. 10. E. 2. Henry Stanford elected bp. of Durham. His election put by, & Lovis Beaumont thrust into his place. Stanford retires to S. Leonards by Stanford. The K. takes a man of every town for the Scotch wars; regrants part of E. Warenns lands back to him,

with remainder to his base children by Maud de Nereford. E. Warenn in Scotland. The E. of Lancasters lady seized by E. Warenns men, & carried to Rigate. Richard Dampmartin challenges her for his wife, asserting he had carnal knowledge of her; which she confesses; in her right claims the earldoms of Lincoln & Sarum. The E. of Lancaster divorced; demolishes E. Warenns castels in revenge. Neither of them care for their wives. Lancaster refusing to attend the parliament proclaimed a traitor. The rector of S. Peters sues the prior of Durham, &c. for carrying away their corn, without paying him tythe. They avow it, as tythe belonging to S. Leonards.

IX. 1317. 11. E. 2. Sir Gilb. Middleton offended that Hen. Stanford was put by from being bp. of Durham, takes Lovis Beaumont & his brother prisoners, & fines them; robs two cardinals sent to consecrate Lovis; proclaims himself D. of Northumberland, & joyns the Scotch; but is apprehended & hanged. John E. Warenn charged with 200 foot to be sent into the Scotch wars. Certain arrears of a tax granted 32. E. 1. being now demanded of their heirs who assessed the towns of Grantham & Stanford, they prove it was & ought to be allowed them in other accompts between them & the K.

X. 1319. Lidlington dies, &, at a general chapter of the Carmes at Stanford, Rich. Bliton is elected provincial of the English Carmes. His character. Lelands mistake about him corrected. Walter Heston elected prior of the Carmes at Stanford; his character; he reads lectures in the white friers school.

XI. 13. E. 2. John E. Warenn in the Scotch wars. Mar. 12. 1320. Henry Stanford, bp. of Durham elect, dies at S. Leonards; a light seen over his grave; remarkable things of him. 15. E. 2. The barons compel E. Warenn to swear he will joyn in expelling the Spencers. The abbat of Burgs estate at Stanford. John E. Warenn in commission to pursue & besiege the E. of Lancaster. E. Warenn at Cirencester. The battel of Burton. E. Warenn there. Lancaster taken, & beheaded. Walter Burley tutor to Pr. Edward. Burleys description of the situation of Oxford. Parl. at York; the representatives for Stanford; a note about their manucaptors.

XII. 1323. The templars lands given to the hospitallers. Oct. 6. 17. E. 2. the abbat of Burg acquaints the nuns he intends to visit; & injoyns the prior of S. Michaels to inform the masters of S. Thomas & S. Giles

S. Giles hofpital, that he alfo intends to vifit them. Oct. 17. the prior cites the parties to attend. Oct. 18. the abbat vifits the nuns in perfon; the hofpitals, by proxy. His commiffion to his proxies.

XIII. 18. E. 2. John E. Warenn appointed to conduct foldiers to the E. of Kent in Gafcoign. The abbat of Croyland refigns, & Matt. Brown the kings efcheator feifes his lands. John Berwic, a grey frier, buried at Stanford. Wm. Morcot farms the abbat of Burgs lands at Stanford.

XIV. 19. E. 2. Account of Matilda Burley & her children. The K. affigns John E. Warenn part of thofe lands, &c. before given the K. by that E. 21. Nov. Robert Rector of S. Johns & others fued by Peter le Orfever in an action of affault & battery.

XV. 29. Aug. 20. E. 2. a great council fummoned by the queen & the reft of the kings enemies at Stanford. Sept. 14. a letter fent in the kings name to the archbp. to put off the convocation, that the bps. &c. may come to the council at Stanford. The wicked advice then given the Queen. Euftace Malherbs epitaph in S. Pauls church. The prior of Newfted lord of little Caftreton. 25. Jan. John E. Warenn witnefs to K. Edwards refignation. Pr. Edw. married to the E. of Hainaults daughter Philippa. Walter Burley appointed her almoner. John Rodington a grey frier of Stanford; provincial of his order in England; his character, & works.

XVI. Some account of Leland, Bale, & Pits.

BOOK XI.

Containing the reign of K. Edw. the third.

I. 1. E. 3. JOHN E. Warenn one of the 12 governors in the Ks. minority. Ap. 24. 1327. K. Ed. 3. at Stanford affigns a maintenance for his father K. E. 2. John E. Warenn in Scotland. July. 2. E. 3. the priorefs of S. Michael does fealty to the abbat of Burg. The abbat of Burgs prefents to the K. at Stanford. The abbat of Croyland petitions the K. for maintenance for the monks, &c. in the vacation of the monaftery, who grants it; an inquifition at Stanford about it.

II. The K. grants Peter de Burley a charter of free Warenn. Strange fights at Corfe caftel. Edm. Plantagenet E. of Kent refolves to refcue his brother K. E. 2. whom he fancies alive in prifon there. Conjecture that this Edmund, or fome anceftor of his, founded the Grey friers at Stanford. Nov... 3. E. 3. Wm. Morcote impleaded for not paying the abbat of Burg his rent, & caft. Walcotforth & Bereford bridges by whom to be repaired. 4 E. 3. Edw. E. of Kent beheaded. The farmers of E. Warenns tolls at Stanford fined for taking toll in the abbat of Burgs liberty. K. Ed. confirms E. Warenns grant to the burgeffes of Stanford to chufe an ald. Peter Sutton, a grey frier of Oxford, buried at Stanford. The abbat of Burgs farther prefents to the K. at Stanford. Ap. 13. 5. E. 3. K. Ed. at Stanford confirms a charter in favor of foreign merchants. John Burley the Carme buried at Stanford. John E. Warenn affifts his fon in law Baillol, who makes him E. of Strathern. 1333. John Foffour prior of S. Leonards one of thofe who elected Rob. Grayftanes bp. of Durham.

III. Nov. 1333. 7. E. 3. fome Oxford men remove to Stanford. May, June, July. 1334. followed by others. Difference among themfelves one reafon why they left Oxford. Merlins prophecy about it fulfilled. Camden & Twines account. Selden & White of Bafingftokes account of the Camb. mens remove to Chefter & thence to Stanford. Mr. Woods account of the differences at Oxf. between the fouthern ftudents & the Durhamites of Merton coll. Many of the Stanford profeffors originally of Merton. Advantage of this remove to the Durhamites. Mr. Woods account of the univerfity & lectures at Stanford. The univerfity of Oxf. complain to the K. Londinenfis extract of that complaint. Aug. 2. the kings letter to the fherif of Lincoln, that the fchools at Stanfd. were fet up without his licenfe, & ordering him to proclaim a confifcation of their goods who prefume to hold exercife at Stanford. Aug. 11. a proclamation at Oxf. requiring the ftudents to return. Another at Stanford. Many return; & many ftay, read lectures, &c.

IV. Nov. 29. Thomas de Burg, warden of the nuns, dies. Wm. Gretford prefented to fucceed him. Jan. 9. the bp. of Lincolns vicar general directs the archdeacon of Lincolns official to enquire about the faid Wms. prefentation & character. Jan. 11. Wm. Gretford prefented afrefh. The bps. vicar general appoints the bps. official his proctor to inftitute Wm Gretford, if, after return of the dean & chapter of Stanfords inquifition, no juft caufe appear to hinder him. Mr. archdeacon of Lincolns official enjoyns the dean of Stanford to call a chapter, & certifie how matters ftand as to Gretfords affair. Jan. 18. the deans return. Jan. 19. Wm. Gretford appoints a proctor to be inftituted for him. Jan. 23. He is inftituted.

V. Petition of the Oxford fcholars fetting forth the reafons of their remove to Stanford, & praying to stay there. The university of Oxford petition the K. afresh. Mar. 28. 8. E. 3. He writes to William Truffel to see the Oxf. scholars drove out of Stanford. Truffel & the sherif expel them accordingly; but they return. July 12. E. Warenn at Berwic. The K. orders an account of the scholars names, & to seife their books, & banish them. The names of near forty persons so treated. Mr. H. de R. the ringleader grievously punished. Unfair dealing of the editor, or translators, of Woods Antiq. Oxon. The K. comes to Stanford about this business. Statute passed at Oxf. against professing at Stanford. And another at Cambridge. The use dissenting academies make of this business.

VI. Colleges at Stanford of three sorts; as, I. some places of general reception. II. others appropriated to particular orders. III. others to particular monasteries.

VII. Of Brazen-nose college, Peterborough hall, Black hall, Sempringham hall, the Carmes school, college in St. Maries street, another over against S. Georges church, another by S. Mary Bennewerk church, &c.

VIII. Of the masters who presided in the university & schools of Stanford.

IX. July 1. 10. E. 3. several nuns admitted at Stanford.

X. Mar. 17. 11. E. 3. Wm. Bohun created E. of Northampton has a grant of Stanford in reversion; sent into France to treat about K. Ed. right to that crown. K. Edw. now first quarters the arms of France & Eng. Those arms so quartered on the white friers gate. Wm. Bohun treats of peace with the Scots.

XI. Ap. 2. 1337. the prioress of S. Michael resigns; the nuns petition the abbat of Burg for leave to elect; which he grants. The new prioress does fealty to him. Walter Burley dies. Sir Simon Burley his nephew brought up with Ed. the black princes eldest son.

XII. Apr. 23. 11. E. 3. 1337. a parliament at Stanford. June 25. the K. there confirms two grants of the founder & one of Wm. de Albini the 4. to Newsted hospital. The priors of Newsted & S. Leonard always members of the Convocation. July 12. the K. at Stanford, a convention between him & the E. of Hainault signed there. The K. going thro' Pillesgate meadow, the people of Stanford, &c. thereabouts, claim the privilege of the road he took for an high way. The K. writes to the ald. & bailifs of Stanford to forbid it.

XIII. Oct. 7. 1337. Wm. Bohun one of those appointed to demand the crown of France. Nov. 11. E. Warenn one of those who receive the cardinals sent to make peace. A council of trade at Westm. three persons sent up from Stanfd. The south chancel in All Saints church antiently called S. Maries chapel; a particular endowment & priest there. Tho. de Ravele the first ald. of Stanford whose name can yet be recovered. 12. E. 3. Wm. Bohun marries;

goes into Flanders; one of the marshals of the kings army at Vironfosse.

XIV. 14. E. 3. John E. Warenn arrays the Surrey & Sussex men. Sir Tho. Holland in Flanders. Wm. Bohun in the Seafight at Sluyse; a grant of lands & mony to him; Nov. 30. 15. E. 3. he lands with the K. at the tower.

XV. 5. June Edm. Langley, afterwards Lord of Stanford, born. Wm Bohun & Tho. L. Holland at the siege of Tournay. Bohun has license to transport wool; & more lands given him; present at the justs the K. made for love of the countess of Salisbury; in the Scotch war; a grant of Okeham castle to him.

XVI. 16. E. 3. The K. sends to E. Warenn to provide soldiers against France. Wm. Bohun lieutenant of Britany; goes thither; raises the siege of Brest; beats the French twice. Tho. L. Holland at Bayonne. Bohun has another license to transport wool; present at making the league between the kings of Eng. & France; undertakes for K. Edw. & sworn.

XVII. 17. E. 3. Bohun in Scotland; raises the siege of Loughmabon castel; made governor of it; he is in Britany. Tho. L. Holland in France.

XVIII. 18. E. 3. The order of the garter instituted. Pictures of all the first Knts. formerly painted in S. Georges church windows at Stanford; & by whom. The original design of those paintings where. Mr. Ashmoles cut of the first Knights whence taken. E. of Northamptons valor at Morlais.

XIX. 19. E. 3. Bohun in Britain. Tho. L. Holland gets a grant of 40. l. a year out of the firm of Hayling priory. Joan countess of Warenn goes beyond sea. Bohun wins Begaret castel & takes several great prisoners.

XX. 20. E. 3. He wins Riall; the D. of Normandy afraid of him; he returns into England. 20. May. E. Warenn settles lands on his concubine & base issue. His seal, titles, & agreement with the K. about his lands & heirs. Bohun in Normandy; at Aguillon; takes la Roche Darien. Tho. L. Holland takes the constable of France. He & Bohun at the battel of Cressi. Bohun sends to the K. for help; is refused; but victorious. The next day beats another army; plunders Arthoys; kills divers at Poisse; rescues his friends in danger; treats about peace.

XXI. 21. E. 3. Pleading about S. Peters church, &c. Roger rect. of S. Peters excommunicated. Tho. L. Holland sells his prisoner the constable to the K. John E. Warenns will, death, burial & lands. Wm. Bohun next L. of Stanford. Many of E Warenns lands granted to Edm. Langley. Sir Wm. Burton taken prisoner by the French. Bohun at the siege of Calais; beats the French. Tho. L. Holland at that siege. Foderinghay granted to Edm. Langley.

XXII. 1348. Rodington, warden of the Grey friers, dies. The great reputation of the white friers at Stanford for religion. Sir Geoffry Sutherop enters that monastery. John de Ultricuria, a great scholar, his character. Calais surrendred : Bohun there. Agreement between the K. & him about some lands.

XXIII. Bohun treats of peace. All the nuns at little Wirthorp (but one) die of the plague.

XXIV. 24. E. 3. Dispute between Tho. L. Holland & the E. of Salisbury about the E. of Kents daughter, Hollands wife. Bohun warden of the Scotch marches ; at the sea-fight at Winchelsea. Walt. Heftons preferments, works, death, & burial at Stanfd. Pits mistake about John Repingale corrected. Jan. 16. 1350-1. the abbat of Burgs pensions at several places confirmed.

XXV. 25. E. 3. Bohun a commissioner to treat with the Scots; 26. E. 3. arrays soldiers to oppose the French invasion. Tho. L. Holland obtains c. marc's a year for his wifes better support. June 29. 1352. Sir Nicholas Crophul & his lady divorced. Abbat of Croylands pension in great S. Michaels church. E. Warenns lady licensed to continue beyond sea.

XXVI. 27. E. 3. Dr. Roger de S. Lis a frier predicant made confessor of that fraternity at Stanford. Tho. L. Holland does homage for his ladys lands; summoned to parliament. Parl. about removing the staple into England; Stanford proposed to be a staple town. Wm. de Bohun in Scotland takes several forts, & treats of peace.

XXVII. 28. E. 3. 1354. Account of the nunnery at great Wirthorp, & of the parish church there. That nunnery united to S. Michaels by Stanford. The kings license for that union. Poverty of both houses. Piety of the nuns of S. Michael. The bps. instrument of union.

XXVIII. Tho. L. Holland lieutenant of Britany. Wm. de Bohun commiss. to treat again about peace with the Scots.

XXIX. 29. E. 3. Holland yet in Normandy. Bohun in Scotland ; at Calais ; St. Omers. Sir Geoffry de la Mar & Johan his lady lease the kings mills at Stanford to John Savage. Sir John Wingfield with the black prince in France.

XXX. 24. Mar. 30. E. 3. Bp. of Lincoln summons his clergy to meet at Stanford, & chuse convocation men. Tho. L. Holland governor of Guernsey, &c. Wm. de Bohun again commiss. to make peace with the Scots. His ladys will. Sep. 19. 1356. Battel of Poictiers ; John K. of France taken prisoner.

XXXI. 31. E. 3. Tho. L. Holland yet in Britany. 32. E. 3. There still. Wm. de Bohun in Gascoign. A cross at Stanford in Rutland. 33. E. 3. Tho. L. Holland governor of S. Saviour le Viscount. John K. of France guarded to Somerton by Sir Wm. Coleville. Ap. 8. 1359. John Repingale & the prior of S. Leonards confirm the prioress of S. Michael. Sept. 3. the bp. grants the parson of Bernac leave to chuse a schoolmaster. Bohun in France.

XXXII. 34. E. 3. Tho. L. Holland assumes the title of E. of Kent; in the Fr. wars. Bohun treats of peace with the French; concludes it ; dies. Dec. 28. Tho. L. Holland dies ; his lands; buried at the grey friers.

XXXIII. 35. E. 3. The black prince marries Hollands widow. 1361. Joan (E. Warenns divorced wife) dies. Tho. Spofford vicar of S. Andrews entayls Robert Wykes lands on his children. Account of that family. Simon Islep founds a hall at Oxford with a proviso to remove it, if the university remove to Stanford or elsewhere. Richard Bliton dies.

XXXIV. Nov. 13. 36. E. 3. Edm. Langley created E. of Camb. 37. E. 3. has a grant of Stanford ; 38. E. 3. prevented from marrying the E. of Flanders heir ; 39. E. 3. claims her notwithstanding. 3. Apr. 40. E. 3. K. Rich. 2. born. Sir Simon Burley made his governor.

XXXV. 42. E. 3. Edm. Langley makes oath his father shall observe the peace with France. 43. E. 3. Edm. Langley at the siege of Bourdelf; takes it; at Roche sur yone.

XXXVI. Langley at Belle-perche ; carries off the dutchess of Bourbon ; at Begerath.

XXXVII. 44. E. 3. He & Sir S. Burley at Limoges.

XXXVIII. 46. E. 3. Edm. Langley at Limoges; & Thouars; returns; marries the K. of Castiles daughter; 47. E. 3. retained to serve the K. at sea; 48. E. 3. in commiss. of the lieutenancy of France; at S. Matthews ; Brest ; Orrery; Kemperle; returns. June 8. 49. E. 3. the black prince dies. 50. E. 3. Sir Tho. Burton sells his lands at Tolthorp to John Brown. Edm. Langley constable of Dover & warden of the cinque ports. John Suafam a great scholar; & enemy of the Wiclevites. 51. E. 3. John of Gaunt complains of the Londoners to the princess Joan. Sir Simon Burley sent to her to make peace. K. Edw. 3. dies.

BOOK XII.

Containing the reign of K. Richard the second.

I. 22. JUNE, 1377. 1. R. 1. Sir Simon Burley sent from K. Rich. to tell the city of K. Edw. death; 15. July. carries the sword at the Ks. Coronation. Sir John Burley, the kings chamberlain, custos of Nottingham castel, made keeper of Sherwood forest. Sir Simon Burley made constable conftable of Windfor, Wigmore, Guilford, & Kenington, & mafter of the Ks. falcons. His houfe in London where. Langley retained to ferve at fea; at Dover with a vaft army; one of the adminiftrators in the Ks. minority. K. Richard holds a council of war at Stanford; Stanford & Leicefter ordered to fit out a balleinger. The wardfhip of Tho. L. Spencer granted to Langley. The Gannoc a ftreet, whence fo called.

II. 2. R. 2. Langley at fea. The princefs Joan protects Wiclif.

III. 3 R. 2. Wm. Makefey gives 6 s. per annum to the warden of the chantry of S. Clements. Nov. 24. K. Rich. confirms the grants of H. 2. K. John. H. 3. & E. 1. to the nuns.

IV. 4. R. 2. Langley aids the K. of Caftile. S. Burley arrefts a man at Gravefend. The Kentifh men rife under Wat Tiler. Rudenefs of thofe rebels to the Q. mother. The K. comforts her. Spencer bp. of Norwich, leaves Burley on the hill, to fupprefs the Norf. rebels. The Ks. grant to Langley. Rafh behaviour of L. Thomas of Woodftock.

V. John Tiffington joyns to condemn Wiclif. Tiffingtons character.

VI. 6. R. 2. S. Burley made keeper of Woolmore foreft. The K. gives John, Simon, & Richard, Burley, knts & Bald. Radington efq. the manor of Parrok. Langley returns from Portugal. 6. Dec. 1382. his ladys will.

VII. Henry Cromp a Giftercian; his character; at firft a great enemy of the Wiclevites. Tho. Winterton, an auftin frier at Stanford; a great enemy of Wiclif. His works.

VIII. 7. R. 2. Langley goes with the K. againft the Scots. S. Burley made conftable of Dover; Kt. of the Garter; warden of the Cinque Ports; lord chamberlain; privy counfelor. His rife; rich liveries; pride; envied; originally not fo poor as reported; a great favourite; friend to the D. of Ireland; hated by the D. of Gloucefter.

IX. 8. R. 2. Langley in Scotland. Sir Tho. Burton dies; his epitaph. Difference between the K. & D. of Lancafter; reconciled by the Q. mother; her corpulency. Wm. Folville, warden of the grey friers; defends the grey friers receiving boys in their order, againft the univerfity of Cambridge; buried at Stanford. 9. R. 2. Langley created D. of York; grants to him.

X. 7. Aug. The princefs Joans will; melancholy occafion of her death; buried in the grey friers, Stanford. D. of Lancafter in Spain; Sir Rich. Burley one of the marfhals of his army there.

XI. 10. R. 2. Sir Rich. Burley dies in Spain. Langley adheres to the D. of Glouceft. againft the D. of Ireland; one of the 13 to enquire into abufes; Nov. 19. their commiff. confirmed. Sr. Sim. Burley now much envied. The E. of Arundels gallantry; envied by Burley.

XII. 11. R. 2. The D. of Ireland flies into Holland; by Yorks intereft commanded

to depart. Glouceft. compels the K. to award Burley to prifon, to anfwer next parliament. Aug. 25. the K. fends for the judges, queries if the ftatutes of the laft parliament be not derogatory to his dignity, & the procurers were not to be punifhed? This defign againft Glouc. York, & 12. others. Wm. Burghle one of the judges; who anfwer, they ought to die. Thofe lords too ftrong for the K. Feb. 3. hold the parliament; fend the judges to the tower; Glouc. arrefts Burley; & impeaches him. Mar. 6. the judges found guilty of confpiring againft the Lords. Mar. 12. Burley brought to the houfe; his accufation read; long trial; hard ufage; Glouc. &c. urge for his execution. Burleys great friends. The Q. kneels to beg his life; but cannot fave him. The Commons defire leave to depart. His deftruction haftened by a rumor. May 5. fentence pronounced: May 15. beheaded. The K. refents it highly againft Gloucefter & York. Burleys lands given the K. to pleafe him. Burleys burial. The K. orders the D. of Ireland to raife an army to revenge his death. Gloucefter forces the K. to take an oath he will never hurt him: but to no purpofe. Wm. Burle the judge & his companions banifh'd. Wm. Burle gives the nuns of S. Michael an odd benefaction for the foul of his brother Simon. June... benefactors to S. Clements chantery.

XIII. Sept. 9. 12. R. 2. parliament at Cambridge enquire into gilds, &c. the cuftom of S. Martins gild at Stanford.

XIV. 13. R. 2. Agreement between the D. of Lancaft. & K. of Caftile. Moderation of York; queftioned. Court marfhal; & great council, about making peace with the French, at Stanford. 25. Feb. the D. of Yorks fon Edw. created E. of Rutland.

XV. 14. R. 2. Grants to York. Rutland made admiral. Ralf. Spalding a white frier at Stanford, his character & writings. Wm. Stenoford or Egumond an Auftin frier at Stanford; his character & works. John & Robert Valdey two Auftin friers, their characters.

XVI. 15. R. 2. K. Richard keeps Chriftmafs at the D. of Yorks. Rutland in France; treats of peace; made juftice of the foreft fouth of Trent; conftable of the tower; he & his father at Amiens. 1392. two great councils at Stanford.

XVII. In the firft, the city of London grievoufly punifhed & why. Mar. 13. the K. at Stanford orders the courts of juftice to remove to York.

XVIII. A debate whether war or peace fhould be declared with France, all the old foldiers at this council, & commons from every borough. The D. of Guelderland for war, but nothing done.

XIX. The 2d council about religion; called by the K. at the popes requeft, to fupprefs the Wiclevites, particularly Cromp. The K. & bps. there. John Suafam, John de Ultricuria, John Tiffington, John

3   Langton,

Langton, & John Valdey, all very bufie at this council. Mr. Woods account of this council. This a provincial council, & not, as he fays, a council of white friers only. Held in the white friers, & why. Farther account of Crump.

XX. 18. Aug. 15. R. 2. John L. Clifford killed by Rich. E. of Camb. 16. R. 2. licence granted to found a chantery in Trinity church. John Valdeys works and death.

XXI. 17. R. 2. York has a grant of Moretaigne caftel. Alianor wife of Raphe lord Baffet of Weldon, her lands granted to Rutland. Rut. in Ireland. Ifab. dutchefs of York her character, death, will: K. Richards kindnefs to her younger fon. Yorks 2ᵈ wife, & younger children. Sara Tanners benefaction to Corpus Chrifti gild at Stanford, & Trinity gild in Spalding.

XXII. 18. R. 2. Rutland retained to ferve in Ireland. York guardian of England, calls a parliament; his character. John Tiffington dies.

XXIII. 19. R. 2. Rutland fent to treat about the Kings marriage to the French kings daughter; one of the proxies to efpoufe her. York grants his letters of protection to the nuns of Stanford.

XXIV. 20. R. 2. York with the K. at Calice; the K. afraid of Glouc. York lieutenant in the Kings abfence. Rutland in France with the K. Miftakes in Dugdale rectified. Rutland governor of Guernfey; &c. his character. Gloucefters roughnefs to the K. The E. of S. Pauls advice to the K. about Glouc. The K. refolves to deftroy him; complains of him to York & Lancafter. Their anfwer.

XXV. 21. R. 2. Glouc. & others confpire againft York, Lanc. & the King. Glouc. threatens the K. His brothers York & Lanc. rebuke & leave him. Moubray E. marfhal difcovers all to the K. who acquaints him with his refolution to deftroy Glouc. Rutland let into the fecret; July 12. made conftable of England. The K. dines in London; informs his council; rides to the dukes; diffembles with him: Moubray arrefts him. Another account. A third. Rutland & Kent arreft the E. of Arundel. Others arrefted; indited; impeached. Dugdales miftake about Thomas lord Spencer, &c. Glouc. writes an anfwer to his charge, which is difliked by the K. who orders Nottingham to make him away. Nottingham goes to Calice about it; contrives it; tells the D. he will

carry him to England; leads him to his murderers; he is fmothered.

XXVI. The K. fummons a parliament to meet the 17. Sept. & orders his friends to arm for fear of the dukes brothers; who alfo arm, but are reconciled to him. His grants to York. Simon Burleys atteinder repealed. Archbp. Arundel impeached for befriending Gloucefter, & contriving Burleys death. York & Wikham pardoned. Sep. 1. Rutland & others impeach the E. of Arundel, &c. The K. retorts Arundels former Speeches againft S. Burley upon him. He is condemned & beheaded. The archbp. banifhed. Sep. 28. grants to Rutland; who Sept. 29. is made D. of Aumarle; & Oct. 4. conftable of the Tower. Tho. L. Spencer created E. of Glouc. 1398. parliament of Shrewsbury. Cobham arraigned for fitting in judgment on S. Burley; & condemned to perpetual imprifonment. All the power of both houfes granted to York, Aumarle, & 13 more. Hereford impeaches & challenges Norfolk. York one of Herefords fureties. A combat appointed at Coventry. Archbp. Arundels lands at Burley by Stanford granted to Bald. Harrington & Rich. Furneys.

XXVII. 22. R. 2. Aumarle high Conftable at Coventry. The combatants appear, & are banifhed. The Kings feverity to Hereford on his fathers death. York troubled at it; withdraws; appointed lieutenant in the Kings abfence; and fteward of England. Aumarle made warden of the weft marches towards Scotland; in commiffion to treat of peace with the Scots; reteined to ferve in Ireland. The K. retires to Ireland.

XXVIII. 23. R. 2. K. Rich. ftays at Kilkenny for Aumarle, who difappoints him; but at laft arrives. York fummons the kings friends to advife what to do, the D. of Hereford being on the fea; they all defert York; who arms, but none will fight againft Hereford [now Lancafter.] York goes towards Wales to meet K. Richard. Lancafter meets York at Berkley. Sir Walter Burley arrefted. York & Lanc. at Briftol. K. Rich. delays in Ireland; he & Aumarle land in Wales. K. Richard in great defpair. Aumarle intercedes for him to Lancafter. K. Richard taken at Flint; brought to London. York now Lancafters oracle; propofes K. Rich. fhould refign. A Parliament to chufe a new king; Lancafter elected. Knts of the garter made by K. Richard.

BOOK XIII.

Containing the reigns of K. Hen. the IV. & K. Hen. the V.

I. OCT. 13. 1399. 1. H. 4. Aumarle* ftands before the kings table at his coronation. K. Richards great love for him. Bagot accufes him. His reply. Oct. 18. Ld. Fitzwalter & other charge

him with the D. of Glouceft. death. Parties for, & againft him. Aumarle challenges Norfolk then fled; that challenge ridiculous. Oct. 29. Aumarles charge againft Arundel, &c. found, &

read againſt himſelf. His anſwer. Nov. 3. adjudged to loſe the name, &c. of duke & only be called E. of Rutland. Spencer E. of Glouceſt. degraded; & all that faction. Their new acquired lands taken away; & all people allowed to accuſe them. Rutland hated by the commons. Fitzwalter renews his charge.

II. Rutland & others conſpire to kill the K. at a juſts at Oxford, & at a mumming at Windſor. Indentures for that purpoſe. Rutland dining with York he ſpies his counterpart in his boſom; will ſee it; upbraids him; rides to tell the K. Rutland gets there firſt; diſcovers all: pardoned.

III. Tho. L. Spencer flies; beheaded at Briſtol by the mob.

IV. 25. Nov. 1400. 2. H. 4. York makes his will. Simon Burleys lands reſtored to his nephew. Rutland reſtored to his eſtate; in Guiſnes to treat of prince Henrys marrying Q. Iſabel, & a peace; lieutenant of Aquitain.

V. 3. H. 4. An antient liſt of the aldermen of Stanford beginning this year. Aug. 1. York dies; his lands; building of Fotheringhay caſtle; & device.

VI. Alderman of Stanford when elected. 4. H. 4. Rutland has livery of his fathers lands.

VII. 6. H. 4. Rutland marries. The E. of Marches ſons eſcape out of Windſor caſtle. The ſmith who made the picklocks put to death. 7. H. 4. Rutland reſtored to his hereditary dignity of D. of York. His ſiſter accuſes him of ſtealing away the E. of Marches ſons, & of deſigning to murder the K. & offers, if any Kt. will fight in her defence, to be burnt if he be overcome. Wm. Maidſtone her ſquire undertakes the combat. York arreſted; ſent to the tower; his goods confiſcated. Moubray E. Marſhall accuſed as privy to Yorks purpoſe; confeſſes; & is pardoned.

VIII. 8. H. 4. York, when every body thought he was dead, brought out & reſtored to all.

IX. 13. H. 4. He begins Fotheringhay col-

lege (account of it & the church there) ſent to help the D. of Orleans againſt the D. of Burgundy.

Henry the V.

X. June 1. 1. H. 5. the prior & convent of Beauvale in Nott. grant John Grene, Wm. Aſſheby, John Purley, Roger Dalim, & their heirs the perpetual advowſon of S. Pauls church. Stanford wrote with an m.

XI. 2. H. 5. York juſtice of S. Wales, & warden of the Eaſt marches by Scotland. His brother Rich. made E. of Cambridge. Sir John Brown burnt for hereſie. Chichely bp. of S. Davids elected archbp. of Cant. will not accept without the popes leave.

XII. 3. H. 5. Rich E of Camb. conſpires to kill the King; beheaded; different accounts of his deſign. Aug. 5. York enfeoffs truſtees in his lands to carry on his college at Fotheringhay; Aug. 14. with the K. at Kedicaux in Normandy; Aug. 16. high conſtable of England; at the ſiege of Hereflete; makes his will; Oct. 22. diſcovers the French army. David Gams account of it. York acquaints the King with it; a ſubtle device of his; Oct. 25. he is ſlain at Agincourt. The prodigious difference between the Engliſh & French army. Yorks lands. Richard his nephew ſucceeds to them. Nov. 6. the K. returns, bringing with him Yorks dead body. Dec. 1. ſolemn exequies for him; buried at Fotheringhay. His body taken up 6. E. 6. & expoſed to view. Q. Eliz. orders him a monument.

XIII. 5. H. 5. Rich. E. Camb. his nephew created D. of York. 8. H. 5. The dutcheſs of York at the queens coronation ſits at the queens table. 9. H. 5. a fragment relating to the founders of ſome chantery & their obits at Stanford. K. Henry 5. firſt founded garter K. of arms. Wm. Bruges Eſq. the firſt in that office. Aug. 31. 1422. 10. H. 5. K. Hen. dies. The L. Crumwell one of the chief mourners when his body was brought in ſtate thro' France, to be buried at home.

BOOK XIV.

Containing the reign of K. Henry the ſixth.

I. a 1424. ROger Flowers legacies to the friars at Stanford, & to Newſted.

II. 3. H. 6. Rich. Plantagenet found to be Mortimers heir. Friar Ruſſels ſtrange ſermon at Stanford; proſecuted for it.

III. 4. H. 6. Rich. D. of York knighted at Leiceſter. Allowance for his maintenance.

IV. 6. H. 6. The churchwarden of S. Mary at the bridge, his accompt. The torches mentioned in it, what? The players, who? Play of *corpus Chriſti*. Proceſſions on *corpus Chriſti* day. Account of them at Durham. Treaſury of *corpus Chriſti* gild at Stan-

ford. Thoſe proceſſions brought hither from Durham. Feaſt & plays on *corpus Chriſti* day. Coventry very famous for them. Diſcontinued at Stanford. Canopy, what? Sirnames from trades. Rood, Mary & John, what?

V. 9. H. 6. York made conſtable; his ſuſpicious dealings. Philippa, relict of Edw. late D. of York, her will, & burial. York at Calis.

VI. 10. H. 6. York at Roan; Pontoyſe; S. Denis; council at Roan; his advice, ſent to ſecure the ſea-coaſt of Normandy. 1432. Nicholas Kenton a Carme flouriſhes at Stanford; his character; writes againſt Rhedon.

VII. 11. H. 6. York has livery of Anne Mortimers lands, & leave to be abſent from Ireland. 12. H. 6. he is ſent to repreſs a rebellion in Ireland. 13. H. 6. John Langton the Carme dies; his works. York & Somerſet joynt regents of France. The truſtees of Edw. late D. of York article with Wm. Horwood of Stanford to build Fotheringhay church.

VIII. 14. H. 6. York reteined to ſerve in France; appointed regent there; envied by Somerſet; ſends lord Scales into France who kills 5000 rebels; ſent over himſelf; his juſtice; takes Feſcamp.

IX. 15. H. 6. Monſtreau loſt; York diſcharged; vindicated. Some account of Mr. Wm. Brown, founder of Browns hoſpital.

X. 16. H. 6. York returns. Tynwel gallows. When the ſeſſions for Rutland were held at Stanford malefactors executed there. Lelands account of Bradecroft & the ſeſſions houſe there. Mr. Parrys encampment nothing but the *veſtigia* of this ſeſſions houſe.

XI. 18. H. 6. York regent of France & Normandy; ſails thither; offers the Fr. K. battel; raiſes the ſiege of Pontoiſe; departs; the French take it.

XII. 20. H. 6. York invades France. July 26. 1442. Mr. John Brown dies.

XIII. 21. H. 6. Sir John Smith vicar of Wodeſtock repairing to the chancellor of Oxford, confeſſes a forgery of his about an houſe at Stanford; the chancellors commiſſary atteſts the confeſſion. York has livery of his ſhare of the E. of Kents lands; embaſſador in France. John Upton a Carme, flouriſhes at Stanford.

XIV. 22. H. 6. York not well ſupported in France; the people begin to talk of his right to the crown. 1444. a general chapter of the Carmes at Stanford. Nicholas Kenton elected provincial there. His character. Edw. Dinley a great favourite of his. 23. H. 6. York the French regent diſpenſed with for being abſent from Ireland; returns to viſit his relations. Lady Eliz. Grey of Codnovres legacy to the black friers at Stanford. 24. H. 6. Robt. Wymbyſh curator of S. Thomas hoſpital; & warden. Grant of the next preſentation to Wm. More, Ralf Peyton, & Tho. Byſſhe. Wm. Burley ſpeaker of the houſe of commons. York diſcharged, & Somerſet made regent. Farther account of Kenton.

XV. 25. H. 6. York with the king who receives a gold roſe from the pope. The D. of Glouceſter murdered at Bury. York gets a mercat & fair for Beaudly. 26. H. 6. York attempts the crown; the great towns for him. John Weſtgate preſented warden to S. Thomas hoſpital. York made lieutenant of Ireland for ten years. 27. H. 6. gets the love of that nation. 28. H. 6. Sir David Hall his deputy at Caen. The dutcheſs of Somerſet

frighted by a canon ball perſuades her huſband to ſurrender Caen. Sir D. Hall complains of it to the D. of York.

XVI. Jan. 9. 1450. the bp. of Chicheſter murdered by Yorks procurement. Wm. Bruges eſq. rebuilds S. Georges church. Deſcription of it. Paintings & arms in the windows. Mr. Bruges will; & many benefactions to S. Georges church & to S. Mary & *corpus Chriſti* chapel & gild at Stanford; alſo to S. Mary's church at Sandwich. Hours of prayer how called.

XVII. 29. H. 6. Somerſet & York quit France. Jack Cades riſing in Yorks favor. 30 H. 6. York impriſons lord Dudley & others; conſults to get the crown; reſolves to deſtroy Somerſet; arms; pretends the K. is his enemy, but profeſſes loyalty.

XVIII. His letter to the K. The kings anſwer. Another of Yorks letters; the kings anſwer.

XIX. The K. retires to oppoſe him. York marches for London. He encamps at Brent-heath, & the K. at Black-heath. The bp. of Winton & others ſent to York to know why he arms. He complains of Somerſet. The K. promiſes Somerſet ſhall be committed. York ſubmits; finds Somerſet with the king, who accuſes him. The K. carries York priſoner to London. Somerſet adviſes the deſtruction of him & his family. York, by a rumor of his ſons being in arms, & ſwearing fealty to K. Henry, eſcapes.

XX. S. Johns church rebuilt. Deſcription. Bells. Screen. Roof. Figures in the windows.

XXI. 32. H. 6. York ſtirs again. Parties on both ſides. York provokes the people againſt Somerſet & the king. Many factious lords He gains the Nevils. Warwic the king-makers character.

XXII. 33. H. 6. Somerſet arreſted; articles againſt him. The K. ſick, & York governs; he ſends to the pope to be releaſed of his oath, who abſolves him; ſeiſes the captainſhip of Calis, reſigns it; the K. takes it himſelf. Somerſet ſet at liberty, & made captain of Calis. York reſolves upon war; appears with many followers at London. The K. withdraws to S. Albans; York follows him.

XXIII. The king ſends to know his meaning; Yorks anſwer; the kings ſharp reply.

XXIV. Yorks ſpeech to his followers. Firſt battel of S. Albans. Somerſet ſlain. The K. wounded. York comforts him; ſtays the battel; carries the K. to church; conveys him to Weſtminſter. A parliament. York made protector & Warwic capt. of Calis. York thinks himſelf in great ſecurity.

XXV. 34. H. 6. York diſcharged of his protectorate; made capt. of Calis by his enemies to divide him & Warwic. Stanford-Baron, the firſt time the name occurs. Conjecture why ſo called.

XXVI. 35. H. 6. the Scots invade Northumberland, but retire on Yorks approach.

Farther

Farther account of Nicholas Kenton the Carme. The great number of Carmes in his time. York lieutenant of Ireland.

XXVII. 36. H. 6. York sent for to Coventry by the queen; flies; K. Henry sends to him to be reconciled. York & his friends come to London with great numbers of followers. He & the K. agree. The conditions.

XXVIII. The K. & York go to S. Pauls in procession. All this but profession.

XXIX. 37. H. 6. Warwic in danger of his life; repairs to York; & sails to Calis.

XXX. 38. H. 6. Salisbury arms; marches thro' Lancashire. The queen appoints lord Audley to fight him. Audley defeated. York arms. Warwic, And. Trollop & John Blount come to him from Calis. The K. arms; marches to Worcester; offers them pardon; which is not accepted. York, &c. write to the king. The K. proclaims a pardon to them that will desert York. Trollop leaves him, & discovers their designs. York & his son Edmund fly into Ireland; his son Edward, Warwic, & Salisbury to Devon & thence to Calis.

XXXI. The soldiers pardoned. The dutchess of York & her two youngest sons sent to ward. The lords proclaimed traytors. Warwic sails into Ireland to confer with York. The kings lenity. The lords attcinted.

XXXII. Declaration of York, &c. complaining of grievances. Yorks friends at Newberry hanged & plundered. Edward E. of March fights K. Henry, & takes him. The tower delivered to March.

XXXIII. 39. H. 6. Friar Kenton dies. Pits corrected. York arrives; enters London in state; his behaviour in the parliament house; rough answer to the kings message; claims the crown. Amazement of the lords; they take time to consider. York turns the king out of his chamber.

XXXIV. The lords debate upon Yorks claim; their answer; & Yorks. Peace agreed; the articles. The king and York go again in procession to S. Pauls. York

proclaimed heir apparent, prince of Wales, &c. Parliament of Coventry declared void. York makes the K. send for the queen; who refuses to come; & arms.

XXXV. Mrs. Margaret Brown dies. Hers & her husbands epitaph. Description of All Saints church. Inscriptions on the bells. The steeple built by Mr. John Brown, son of the above John & Margaret.

XXXVI. York leaves the K. in his own friends hands, & departs to fight the queen; arrives at Sandale; lord Nevil deceives him; battel of Wakefield. York slain. Lord Clifford stabs Yorks second son in cold blood, in revenge of his father slain by York. Clifford called the butcher; cuts off Yorks head; presents it to the queen. Reflections on Yorks death, & the popes absolution.

XXXVII. Salisbury beheaded; his, & Yorks heads set upon York gates. Yorks body buried at Pontfract; removed to Fotheringhay. New monument erected for him by Q. Eliz. Conclusion of his story.

XXXVIII. Edward E. of March receives the sad news of his fathers death; a vast army joyns him. He beats his enemies at Mortimers cross.

XXXIX. Three several armies now in England at once. No travelling without a pass. Warwic's pass granted to John Andrews. The queen marches for London; her army commanded by Andrew Trollop. Many places destroyed by the northern men. The dismal apprehensions people had of this army at London, & Croyland. Stanford ruined by it. Leland & Camden explained. The churches & writings destroyed at Stanford. Privileges of Stanford.

XL. The second battel of S. Albans. The king, queen, & prince meet. March vanquishes the earls of Pembroke & Wilts; proceeds for London. The K. & Q. retreat into the north. March enters the city; is joyfully received; claims the crown; proclaimed King.

The

THE

SURVEY and ANTIQUITIE

of the TOWNE of

STAMFORD,

With its antient Foundation, Grants, Privileges,
& feveral Donations thereunto belonging :

Written by Richard Butcher, Gent. fome time towne-
clerke of the fame.

Caput & membra funt una perfona.   Tho. Aquinas.

London : Printed by Tho. Forcet, dwelling in Old Fifhftreet in Heydon Court, 1646.

Since continued by the author to 1660. & much enlarged, as being intended
to have been reprinted, firft by himfelf, and then by his Son ; but now firft
publifhed from two MS. copies, compared with each other ; wherein all
the additions may be feen at one view, as being here printed in *Italic.*

To which are added,

Two Letters about the Original & Antiquities of Stanford, by the late Reverend William
Forfter, A. M. fome time Reétor of S. Clement Danes ; the one to the Reverend Thomas
Tanner, D. D. author of the *Notitia Monaftica* ; the other to Mr. John Stevens author
of the two additional Vols. to the *Monafticon Anglicanum* ; now firft publifhed entire
from the Originals.

The whole (both Mr. Butchers book & Mr. Forfters letters) illuftrated with notes written
by the publifher.

In wood under a window in maiden lane.

London : Printed by J. BETTENHAM, for the Editor.

The Epiftle Dedicatory.

To all the worthy citizens of London, borne in the towne of Stamford in the county of Lincolne, that have been, or intend to be, benefactors to the fame ; & more efpecially to thofe two worthy brothers & members of that city, Mr. Robert Bullacke, & Mr. John Bullacke, who have not only beene pious benefactors to their faid native towne; but alfo liberall & indulgent incouragers to this prefent furvey thereof.

GENTLEMEN,

I Here prefent unto you, for a new-yeares guift, the furvey of your cradle places; a worke upon which I fixed my firft thoughts by the motion which fome of you by letter made unto others; who, eyther not at leifure, or not willing, or hindered by fome other impediment, I know not what, forbare the enterprife; which I perceiving (though the unfitteft of many others) have prefum'd to fet my pen on worke, rather then your defires fhould be altogether fruftrate, or that I fhould conceal what I know, have heard, or read of my native town. As it is homely, fo I hope it is harmelefs; if it appear not worthy of your applaufe, yet I hope it will no way appeare worthy of your difpleafures; take it therefore as it is meant, not as it might have been made better by me: for it is the beft that my poore invention, obfervation, or reading can afford, or the treafury of my note-book can render.

ª It had come to your views fome moneths before this, had not the troubles of thefe times hindered my intended fpeed; yet glad I am, I have finifhed it at the end of the old yeare, hoping it would have been publifhed at the beginning of the new. If it be thought ufeful for the publique, I defire for the publique good it may be publifhed; & that what errors have efcaped my pen, may by the corrector be amended, by the reader pardoned, & the whole fubftance of this furvey be by you kindly accepted, from him who is, & ever will be, a lover of you & your native place, whilft he is

Stamford, the 1. of Jan. 1646.   Your friend, RICHARD BUTCHER.

Viro doctrina & pietate in patriam eximio, RICHARD BUTCHER.

Πάντα καλῶς· qui librum edis, docteq; pieq;
    Arteq; pertingis, quo ftimulavit amor:
Qui negat alterutrum, non noverit ille, neceffe eft,
    Scribendi caufas (patria nempe tua eft)
Scribendive modum: parfifti nempe labori
    Tu nulli, pietas quo tua docta foret;
Nec fruftra fudaffe liquet: quod quilibet alter,
    Agnofcet mecum, qui tua fcripta leget.   B. H. Med. Doctor.

ROBERT BULLACKE, chirurgeon; in laudem authoris, & contra Zoilum.

WHEN firft I mov'd in the terreftrial fphere
    * Of your Sol's influence I doubted not, my dear
* Friend, of your love, your care, pains, and finceritie,
* Which Stamford muft cognize to all pofteritie.
Of this, our authors book, I fay but this,
For that is praife enough, that it is his;
Nor all the Mufes, nor Apollo's lays,
Can fing his worth; be his own lines his praife.
Againft the Zoilus, who's fraught with fpite,
I fend this old convoy on him to light;

ª This paragraph is omitted in the MS. of the intended fecond edition, & inftead of it is fubftituted this. ' I had once determined to have ftayed my pen from further proceeding with this furvey, ' for fome reafons not here to be expreft; but the importunity of fome, with the refpect I bare unto ' them, & their love hath more prevailed with me for a Second, than the hatred of others towards ' me, did make me repent the publifhing of the Firft.
    * * * Thefe three verfes are each of them a foot longer than they ought to be; but they ftand thus in all the copies I have yet feen.

Cum

Cum tua non edis, carpis mea carmina, Læli,
    Carpere vel noli noſtra, vel ede tua.
Sloth ſits and cenſures what th' induſtrious teach:
Foxes deſpiſe the grapes they cannot reach.

INTO the little volume of this book,
    With judgments eye, whoſo ſhall pleaſe to look,
Such various learning he therein ſhall find
As ſhall expreſs the authors glorious mind:
The ſcite of Stamford, in rhetorick ſtraine,
Set forth, demonſtrateth unto us plaine
His eloquence; his knowing antiquitie,
The ſubſtance of this book doth teſtifie.
Then, for his skill in antient hiſtory,
And likewiſe in the art of heraldry;
Such copious matter it to us affords,
As poſſibly can be declar'd in words:
His poetries, like golden veins, appear
Throughout the work, as ſcattered here and there:
This learned labour from his painful hands
Shall laſt whilſt Welland runs & Stamford ſtands.
                                                THO. SEAMER.

DARES and Homer long ago did write
    The Greeks & Trojans bloody diſmal fight.
Our author ſeldom dips his pen in blood;
Yet, by his ſtory, may be underſtood
How Stamford flouriſht both in art & trade,
And then again how ſhe was wretched made
By bloody Mars, who all her ſtately tow'rs
Earſt in a moment, fire and ſword devours;
Her various fortune here he lets us know,
Which, like the ocean, oft did ebb & flow;
And this into our memory freſh brings
World's frailty, viciſſitude of things.
In wealth & glory much ſhe once did thrive
What time ſhe was the ſacred Muſes hive;
And then her glory fell into decay
When as thoſe painful bees did flie away.
But now againe, methinks ſhe mends her ſtate,
By that which here our author doth relate.
Then, Stamford, love the man that honours thee,
Or much unworthy thou wilt ſeem to be
Of ſuch a towne-clerke, who, to thy great glory,
Sets forth herein thy true & antient ſtory.
                                                E. A.

* *To the worſhipfull Baldwin Hamy, doctor of Phyſick, the thankful addreſſe of*
        Richard Butcher, the writer of this ſurvey.

Worthy Sir,

THE *meer moral heathen long ſince left unto us a true monitory leſſon when he ſaid,* ingratum ſi dixeris, omnia dixeris. *That which he made but a moral precept, we chriſtians ought to make a divine law; that which, with him, was but a fault againſt good behaviour, we ought to make a ſin againſt chriſtian love & charity. As I would not offend againſt
duty, ſo would I not willingly ſin againſt love, in not returning a thankful retribution for favours received from your worthy ſelfe, who were pleaſed, in my firſt edition, largely to approve of that eſſay, which I then made of this ſubject, & now again do continue to write upon
the ſame with ſome additions, encouraged thereunto by your former favours & approbations.
Should I forget to thank you, for ſuch your favourable regard towards me, I ſhould forget
that I am my ſelf, & thereby be condemned of all other faults as well as of ingratitude. I have
therefore thought it my part at this time to addreſſe theſe my poor papers of my ſecond labour*

---

a This dedication was wrote by Mr. Butcher, when he himſelf had thoughts of publiſhing a
new edition.

to your learned view, desiring your kind acceptions of the same from him who desires to continue to be most respectful of you, & no longer to be, then so to continue. RICHARD BUTCHER.

[a] *To my worthy friend,* Mr. RICHARD BUTCHER.

TURNE o'er the leaves of th' authors book,
 And view his lines with serious look,
And you'l confess that Butchers pen
Hath made old Stamford young again.
My penns too young to write of thee
Whose subject is antiquity.
While Welland runs, or times remaine,
This book shall eccho forth thy fame.
Live Butcher ever; 'tis thy glory,
In spite of Oxford wee'l have story.

GEORGE HILL.

[b] *To his highly honoured friend* Mr. PHILIP JOHNSON *of Stamford in the county of Lincolne.*

Worthy Sir,

TO satisfy the many importunities of friends (in which number you are to be reckoned, & whose request, with me, was more prevalent than all the rest) I have adventured once more these papers to the press, for the which they were design'd long before my fathers death: And so much I am induced hereunto, that thereby I might take occasion publicquely to tell the world, how deeply I stand engaged unto you, requesting you to vouchsafe the acceptation & protection of the same. Indeed, by reason of the many courtesies, the author during his life received from you, & the many favours you have accumulated upon me, you may challenge the dedication thereof to your self as a due debt. Indeed, worthy Sir, I have held ingratitude to be a monster in nature, a solœcisme in law, a paradox in divinity, an ugly sin; if there be any sin against the holy Ghost, it is this, saith queen Elisabeth, in a letter of hers to the French king. Therefore I could do no less than dedicate this small piece to your selfe, as to one to whom I am much obliged. It is reported by the naturalists, the storke leaves one of her young ones where she hatches them; the elephant is said to turn up the first sprigge towards heaven, when he comes to feed; both certainely do this out of some instinct of gratitude. The unthankfull & evill are very aptly joined together, by our Saviour. And, ingratum si dixeris, omnia dixeris, was the saying of the antients. All therefore, dear sir, that I can do, by the way of retribution for your many free favours, is to make this publick acknowledgment under my hand, once more requesting you to receive it from him, who is, & ever will be, a lover of you while he is himself & able to subscribe his name, with the addition of
Your faithful servant, ROBERT BUTCHER.

[c] *On the worke of her dear & near relation* Mr. RICHARD BUTCHER, *written since his decease, anno dom.* 1665.

BRAVE Stamford, of thy quondam clerke be proud,
 Who hath with gifts & honours thee endow'd;
Since 'tis a maxim, that the preservation
Bears an equality to the creation.
On golden angels wings he did not rear,
Yet by his bonus genius did repair,
Thy antient structure that in rubbish lay,
Which time & war had almost worne away;
Nay it had quite annihilated been
Had not this skilful architect stept in,
Who div'd to Lethe's bottom, & brought forth
Such reliques as adorn'd its pristine worth.
Antiquity with ign'rance had combin'd
That our more moderne ages ne're should find
Who built, demolish'd, & re-edified
This famous towne, with many things beside,
As termes & etymologies, which he
Searcht out & made conspicuous to be.
The rights and privileges, with the sports
And donatives, he faithfully reports;

a This copy of verses was to have been published, if Mr. Butcher himself had reprinted his book.
b This dedication was wrote by Mr. Butchers son, when he proposed to reprint his fathers book.
c This & the next copy were intended to have been published when Mr. Butchers son proposed a new edition of his fathers book.

Nor

Nor from the pious donors ought detracts,
But yields them all the glory of their acts.
And thus, what Stamford was, it still remaines:
Upon record, by this grave authors pains.
Survey't not then with supercilious eye,
But pay due honour to his memory.

  Sleep, gentle soul, within thy quiet urne,
While learned hands thy book do over-turne.
To write thy worth my female hands too weak;
Let this small treatise thy large praises speak.　　　ELLEN BUTCHER.

To the memory of Mr. RICHARD BUTCHER.

STamford, let none despise thee, 'tis thy glory
  That thou canst truly boast of antient story.
Yet had not Butchers penn, in time, stept in,
Thy pristine glories had quite buried been
In deep oblivion: therefore share the praise;
Take thou the glory, & give him the bays.　　　JOHN DICKENSON.

Upon the honourable ensignes of *the towne of Stamford in the county of Lincolne, with the glory thereof, & how the same came to be atchieved, by the towne of Stamford.*

THE *coat of armes depicted on our shield*
  Was honourably won in Loose-coat-field.
The Norman bastard bastard beasts did bear,
And leopards twain upon his surcoat wear;
Which to the world did plainely signifie
His mongril birth & spurious progeny.
But when this bastard blood was quite out-worne,
And Englands kings were speech & birth her owne;
Our second Henry, by a rightful claime
(Matching Eleanor, heyre of Aquitaine)
A golden lyon passant, guly field,
For th' Aquitanian dutchy bore on's shield;
The blood being clear'd, the scutcheon perfect stood,
And thence three lyons in a field of blood;
For England two, & one for Aquitaine,
Field, colour, posture, all alike remaine.
  Fourth Edward, both in birth & blood as great
(A lyneal lyon, true Plantagenet)
Investing Stamford with a charter kind,
His owne paternal arms to it assign'd;
Impaling them to Warrens checkie coat,
Who formerly the towne of Stamford ought.
  No city, borough, towne, or corporation,
Within the circuit of this warlike nation;
Such noble arms do bear upon their shield,
As those atchiev'd in Stamfords Loose-coat-field.
  When as fourth Edward over England reign'd,
Their birth & blood four odious traytors stain'd;
Whose base rebellion he, their lawful king,
With Stamfords aid, did soon to ruin bring.
Warwick, Wells, Dymocke, de la Lande were they
Whose trayt'rous spirits scorned to obey
King Edwards scepter royall, 'till that he,
With all his force & valiant chivalry,
From Fotheringhay, a castle of renowne,
March'd, and arriv'd in safety at this towne;
And, with such strength as here he then did gaine,
A noble conquest bravely did obtain;
Wells, Dymocke, de la Lande, without a trial,
Then lost their heads under the standard roiall;
And next to honour Stamford for such aid,
His own paternall armes to it convey'd,
Joyn'd with earl Warrens shield of high renowne,
Who formerly was owner of this towne;
Adding, to former grants, immunities,
For helping him against his enemies.

THE

THE
SURVEY and ANTIQUITY
of the TOWNE of
STAMFORD.

CHAP. I. The several appellations, foundation, scituation, & forme of Stam- ford, with the erection & diffolution of the univerfity there. MS. p. 1.

IF we will believe Nicholas Matchiavell, he tells us pofitively (Hift. Flor. Lib. V.) *that all kingdoms, countreys, civil focieties, and commonwealths were at the firft founded by war, & by the fword of the foldier : it hath been therefore obferved, faith he, by wife men, that learning follows arms ; and, in all places, captains were before philofophers. For well govern'd armies having wonn victory, & that victory fettled in a quiet pofture, warlike mindes in policy then fettled the ftudy of good letters, religion, & laws, for the more firm eftablifhment of what they obtained by the fword. Æneas the Trojane, after Troy was taken and ruinated by the Greeks, by his fword gained the government of Italy, and there fettled his Trojan penates, according to the religion he brought from Troy. Brutus, the grandchild of Æneas, having accidentally flain his father Pofthumus Silvius, fled from Italy, & arriving here in this our ifland of Britaine, fubdued thofe giants, or giant-like people, which here then inhabited ; from whom, after many kings of Trojan flock, in a right line, defcended Bladud, who built Stamford, of which I am now about to write. At that time England was undivided into fhires or counties, & fo continued till the Saxon government, whofe king Allured, for the better adminiftration of juftice, divided the fame into counties, as it is this day.*

The towne of Stamford, alias Stantford, alias Stampford (for by fo many feveral names the fame is called in divers records) is fcituated upon the furtheft point weft in the county of Lincolne, on the confines of the counties of Rutland & Northampton ; the fame & Stamford-Baron adjoining, is placed in a very heathful, pleafant, & temperate ayre ; which in the forme thereof, doth frame the figure of a Roman T. It is watered on the fouth parts with the river

Welland, which *takes the name from the well making & fructifying the lands by which it paffeth,* [a] *&* hath the originall fpring in the county of Leicefter, towards the weft, not far from the towne of Harborow. From whence extending her ftreame, fhe divideth by her channel in the beginning of her courfe the counties of Leicefter & Northampton, & fo gliding with her filver current eaftward, in her journey proves a fruitful parent, making her felf the rich mother of green hewe & many feverall coloured flowers, which fhe brings forth upon the fruitfull meadows, enamelling the fame therewith all along as fhe paffeth ; dividing, before fhe come at Stamford, the counties of Rutland and Northampton ; & then, arriving there, with her [b] fragrant ftreame, fhe divideth the fame from the towne & parifh of Stamford-Baron, in the county of Northampton ; a place, tho' not fubject to the mace of Stamfords government, yet joyned to the fame in all taxes, fubfidies, fifteenes, or other payments to the ftate, amounting to a fifth part of a full mulct. And fo fubjugating her felf to paffe under the ftony yoake of a bridge of five arches, fhe holds on her conftant travell towards the eaft ; thence, making a feparation betwixt the counties of Lincolne & Northampton, till fhe comes to the towne of Crowlande, where fhe drowneth her felf and name in the fennes of Holland, and payes the tribute of her waves to the monarch Neptune, by delivering her waters towards [c] Lynne in the county of Norfolk, into the grand ocean.

[d] '*Ethelverdus, an author to whom In-* 'gulphus is an appendix, fpeaking of the fi- 'tuation of Stanford, hath thefe words, Stan- 'forda, hoc eft inter fluenta amnis Vueo- 'lod, & condenfo fylve que vulgo Ceoftef- 'ne nuncupatur [e].' *If the author of this fhould now rife from the dead, he would fwear*

---

a The reader will fmile at Mr. Butchers poor etymology of the Welland ; but he may find one in my annals Lib. I. Paragraph the IX. which, I hope, he will like better.　　b Fragrant is an odd epithet for a ftream ; but Mr. Butcher feeing there were fo many flowers produced by the Welland, perhaps fancied the river, as well as its banks, fmelt of them.　　c In the MS. Lyn, &c. is ftroke out, & Bofton put in.　　d This paragraph is not in fome MS. copies, particularly that old one which I have ; but in another copy I found the fame thruft into this place.　　e In Ethelwerd the paffage ftands thus——Ab occidentali profectus eft parte tunc [fcilicet, circa an. 897.] Anglorum Ethelnoth dux, adit in hoftes Euoraca urbe qui non parva territoria pandunt in Myrciorum regno loci in parte occidentali Stanforda, &c. ut fupra. Lib. 4. cap. 3. fol. 482. a. 10. edit. Lond.

2　　　　　　　　　　　　　　　　　　　　　　　　　　　　　　　　*this*

this is not the same town, for now there is not any thick wood within many miles of the north-side of Stamford.

This towne of Stamford is of great antiquity, & was built (as the tradition goes) 863. years before the incarnation of Chrift, by Bladud a king of the Brittaines, who, being himfelf a great Philofopher, endeavoured at this towne to plant the ftudy of philofophy, in emulation or imitation of the antient Athenian fchooles; & drawing hither the learnedft & graveft men of that fcience that were to be found in the whole world, it flourifhed in all manner of heathenifh learning 'till the time of K. Lucius, who was the firft that here embraced the Chriftian faith by the preaching of Fugatius & Damianus, fent hither by Eleutherius bifhop of Rome. And as before it was very famous through the world for the great proficiency of Ethnick learning, fo in that bleffed time when England was firft enlightened with the glorious beames of the gofpel, it much more flourifhed with learned, holy & religious men who very devoutly taught the foul-faving knowledge of Chrift; infomuch that in a fhort time (according to the devotion of thofe times) in & about Stamford, eight houfes of religion, thirteene parifh churches, & three chapels, all of them in, or neare the fame towne, were erected (as MS. p fhall hereafter in the proper place be more particularly named) the fame being furnifhed with the learnedft & graveft men of that age; the fame of whofe piety and learning caufed many of the chriftian princes & other great men neighbouring upon the ifles of Britaine, to fend their fonnes & friends hither to be taught and educated by thofe *fo* pious mafters, whereby it, in thofe days, attayned to the name & honour of an univerfity. But as no glory is permanent in this tranfitory life, fo, in time, the luftre of this bright fhining taper of fame began to wax dimme & to decline by the foggie & peftiferous myfts of herefie & errours; like mortal difeafes breeding in a body long inured with peace, health, & quietnefle, which caufed this Stamfordian univerfity to be diffolved by the decree and power of Gregory *the firft of that name* then bifhop of Rome, about the yeare after the incarnation of Chrift, 727. [a]

CHAP. II. Stanford ruinated by the Danes; re-edified, & the bridge over Welland built by Aliren [b] the fecond, king of Denmark; the caftle and walls built by Edmund Ironfide, a Saxon king; with the names of the gates; the names and ufes of the watch-towers; the fcituation of the caftle; the number of the ftreets and lanes; with the conduits, wells & *pumps* which water the fame; together with the churches & houfes of religion in & about the fame.

ABOUT the yeare after the incarnation of Chrift 116.[c] Canutus the heathen king of Denmark, invading England with a potent army, amongft other of his fpoyles & rapines layd waft the towne of Stamford; which, not long after, was by Aliren the fecond his fucceffour, re-edified, & a bridge of ftone built over the river of Welland, leading into Stamford-Baron. It remained without caftle or walls 'till the time of Edmund Ironfide, a Saxon king, about 200 years before the Norman conqueft [d]; who built the caftle, & compaffed the towne with a wall of ftone of an indifferent height, for the better defence againft the Danes invafion; garnifhing the fame with five ftrong & ftately watch-towers: two towards the waterfide, for the difcovery & defence againft the enemy towards the fouth; the one called Bees-fort, the other Holme-towes; the other three bulwarkes or watch-towers, are towards the eaft, north, & weft, for the difcovery and defence againft the enemy on thofe parts, called Carpe-tower, White-tower, & North-bulwarke.

The walls have in them five principal gates or entries. Peter-gate on the weft; St. Clements gate, on the north; Paul-gate & St. George's-gate, toward the eaft; & the bridge-gate towards the fouth. To thefe may be added a fixth ftanding North-Eaft, called the New-gate; but made long fince the antient gates were erected; all the reft appearing to have flippes of ftrong portculleffes, which New-gate wanteth. Befides there is towards the fouth two antient pofterne-gates, which feem as antient as the walls themfelves; the one joining to the Bridge-gate, the other not far from St. Georges gate, [e] leading into the Tenter-meadows.

But, as the length of time corrupteth not only manners & good government from the antient intent & integrity thereof, but alfo ftone walls from their true ufe and fufficiency; fo hath it brought to paffe in thefe more moderne times, that the manners of good & carefull government of majeftrates becoming corrupted, eyther by felf-feeking covetuoufnefs, or friendly partiality, have fo farre corrupted thefe very walls of ftone, that they

MS. p. 4.

a Here Mr. Butcher errs in his chronology moft egregioufly, for, if pope Gregory the firft ever interdicted any fuch univerfity here, it muft have been, not in 727, but about 605. And as to his fancy that there were fo many churches, chapels & monafteries here in the time of Lucius, fee my annals Lib. I. Paragraphs XXVIII. & XXIX. b There was no Danifh king named Aliren. He rather means Alured, or Alfred the Saxon.   c Sic, pro 1016.   d He fhould fay, about fifty years before the conqueft. But the whole paragraph hitherto is a jumble of blunders. If he would fpeak in any order, he fhould have told us firft what Aliren, next what Edmund Ironfide, & then what Canute did.   e MS. Georges *lane.*

                                                                have

have loft the true ufe and ftrength of them, contrary to the intent and wife meaning of the firft founders, by permitting the adjacent inhabitants within them to make backe-doors out of them : fo that one may fay, fo many tenements as border upon them, fo many new pofternes are made out of them; ferving for no other purpofe than for the letting in & out, at unlawful houres, nightwalkers & fufpected perfons, who fear to appeare in the prefence of a watch, or to be feene in the heart of a towne; or to come within the compaffe of the awfull eye of the publique majeftrate; things of no fmall & dangerous confequence in the times eyther of peace or warre, efpecially where they are permitted to the back-fides of victualing-houfes, as too many of them are. *But it* MS. p. 5. *feems the majeftrates of the times within fuch walled townes, feldome or never look into the ftatute of Winchefter made in the* 13. *year of king Edward the firft, where they fhall find their duty laid down before them as to this point, & their danger with the townes damage for neglecting the fame. But to return to the difcourfe of my further furvey.*

The caftle was fcituated, whilft it ftood, upon the fide of an hill (as indeed all the towne ftands upon the rifing of an hill) but the caftle hill appeares fomewhat artificiall, being caft up round & higher than the ordinary degree, ftanding well towards the middeft of the towne, & fomewhat fouthweft, facing the river with a very pleafant profpect.

Mr. Cambden makes mention of another caftle, fometime ftanding in Stanford Baron, built by Edward the elder a Saxon king, as a fortification againft the Danes; which was deftroyed in the warres betwixt king Stephen & Henry the fecond [a]. And indeed the very ruines thereof are now come to ruine, for no place there appeares to give evidence where it ftood; *only the book of Peterborough relates, that Elenor the wife of Edward the firft after the conqueft, in the place where the faid caftle ftood, erected an houfe of nunns, & endowed the fame with fair poffeffions; which being diffolved, amongft many others, in the time of Henry the eight, the fame came, in the days of Q. Elizabeth, into the poffeffion of William Cecil lord baron of Burghley; & at this day is turned into a farme, & part of the inheritance of his pofterity, in the houfe of Exeter.*

To manifeft the profitable & pleafant fci-tuation of this towne, the monks, friers, & nunnes of thofe fuperftitious times (like fo many rats, or mice, which make choyce to feede of the daintieft cheefe) made choyce of this place to build feveral receptacles; as one obferves of them

They plant themfelves in faireft plotts,
   For pafture, wood, & fpring;
No griefe, nor care, comes to their lots;
   When others figh, they fing.

For in, & about, this towne they had no leffe than eight feverall cells or monafteries; MS. p. 6. as namely, the gray-friers, the white-friers, the black-friers, the auguftine-friers, St. Leonards (being a cell belonging to the abbey of Durham) Newfted monaftery, the hermitage (being the place where now the 'fpittle houfe ftandeth) & a houfe of nunnes in Stamford-Baron [b].

Befides (as appears in the particular regifter of Geofrey abbot of Peterburrough, called the white book, & fometime belonging to the faid abbot, but now remaining in the cuftody of Chriftopher lord Hatton of Kirby in the county of Northampton) William abbot of the burrough of St. Peter, did found & endow a nunnery, called the nunnery of St. Michael of Stamford; together with the church of St. Michael there. And the faid abbot & covent were patrons of the faid church, & referv'd to themfelves, out of the nunnery aforefaid, halfe a marke yearly to be paid to them as a penfion, the next day after the feaft of St. Michael; to which the faid monaftery of St. Michael did acknowledge their fubjection & obedience. At laft this houfe of religion being diffolv'd by Henry the eight, the faid king became patron to the parifh of St. Michaels; fo that the faid lands belonging to the faid monaftery, with the patronage of the faid church, were, by Queen Elizabeth, granted to William Cecil, baron of Burghley; in whofe pofterity the fame ftill continues [c].

Here hath been likewife in former times (as I faid before) thirteene parifh churches, befides three chappels; namely, St. Maries, All Saints, St. Thomas, St. Michaels, Trinity, St. Johns, St. Pauls, St. Peters, St. Georges, St. Andrews, Clement church, St. Stephens, & St. Martins in Stamford-Baron [d]. Alfo Bennet chappel, St. Thomas chappel, & Magdaline chappell [e]. Thefe are now all reduced into five parifhes within the liberties, & St. Martins without;

a Duke Henry befieged the caftle of Stanford three times, & at laft took it in 1153. but I don't find any author, except Cambden, fays, he deftroyed the caftle of Stanford-Baron. The caftle he took, was, I rather think, Stanford caftle.

b There were alfo feveral other monafteries at Stanford, as may be feen in my collections, which Mr. Butcher knew nothing at all of.

c Here Mr. Butcher gives a tolerable account of the nunnery founded by William Walterville abbat of Burg; neverthelefs as the church belonging to that nunnery was dedicated to St. Michael, he thence imagines the parifh church of S. Michael now ftanding, was the conventual church belonging to thofe nuns. But there he errs. And as to the patronage of the parifh church of St. Michael now ftanding, that, I believe, before the reformation, belonged to the abbat of Croyland, & not to the abbat of Burg.

d There were alfo three other parifh churches at Stanford, to wit, S. Mary Bennewerk, St. Michael Cornftal, & All Saints beyond the bridge. As alfo a parifh church at great Wirthorp.

e There was alfo S. Marys chapel in the Gannoc.

namely,

MS. p. 7. namely, St. Maries, All Saints, St. Michaels, St. Johns, & St. Georges. And yet none of all these fix parishes (excepting All Saints) hath fo much maintenance belonging to any of them as will competently maintain a minifter in them; a thing which may feem very ftrange, when fixteene feveral benefices are reduced to the number of five or fix! But I conceive the reafon to be heere as it is in the univerfity of Cambridge, which hath in it (as I take it) fifteen parifh churches, & yet not any of them of any competent maintenance. Becaufe the fellowes of the feverall colleges do officiate in thofe feverall cures for the better exercife & practice of their miniftery; as having their chiefeft maintenance from the colleges. Even fo the monks of the feverall monafteries in this place (whileft thofe monafteries ftood) did officiate in the feverall parifhes here, having their principall maintenance from the monafteries; which being diffolved, moft of thefe parifhes became united (efpecially thofe that had any livelihood *belonging* unto them) for the fupport of the future miniftery; & thofe that had meerely nothing were totally ruinated.

This town hath in it to the number of eleven indifferent faire ftreets, & ten fmall ftreets or lanes, well replenifhed with houfes *& well furnifhed with inhabitants.* But in former times (as appears by the ruines of many antient buildings) it was much more populous than now it is; the reafon of which hereafter appeareth in the proper place. The names of the ftreets & lanes are as followeth. Peter-hill-ftreet, St. Maries ftreet, Pauls ftreet, St. Michaels ftreet, St. Georges ftreet, Clement-hill [a] (where the Friday market crofs ftands) Clips-hill, St. Maries market ftreet, All-hallowes gate, the bridge ftreet, the market ftreet, Clement lane [b], Star lane, Goldfmiths lane, Mannerly lane [c], Chenie lane [d], St. Thomas lane, St. Johns lane, MS. p. 8. St. Maries lane, Caftle dike, & pillory-nooke, where the white meat market is kept.

The towne is watered by two common conduits, namely St. Michaels & Pauls conduits. Befides *which* it hath four common wheel-wells belonging thereunto; *namely*, All-hallowes well, St. Georges well, Poule well, & Clement well. *And of late, for the better watering of the faid towne, there are two new pumps erected, the one in St. Johns parifh, & the other in St. Michaels.* The *aforefaid* conduits are fed by pipes of lead, which defcend from a fpring called the conduit head, being twelve fcore or thereabouts, without the walls, upon the north eaft of the town in the common field; & hath the land next adjoining to it, for the benefit both of the fpring & conduits.

Chap. III. The antiquities, antient priviledges, *honours,* and antient owners of the town of Stamford.

THE *arch-deacon of Huntingdon reckons this towne amungft the antient cities of England. For, writing of the warrs that were between Edmond Ironfide a Saxon king & the Danes here in England, he fets forth the fame in thefe words.* Edmundus rex ducens exercitum in illam partem Merce, que paganis diu fubdita fuerat, ufque ad latiffimum flumen Humbre, belli forte Dacos vicit, & quinque urbes victoriofus cepit, Lincolniam, Legeceftriam, & Stanfordiam, & Snotingham, & Derebi.

After this Ingulphus, an abbot of Crowland, reports, that here at Stamford were terms held (as now there are at Weftminfter) for writing concerning a fuit & difference between him the faid Ingulphus & one Af- MS. p. 9. *fordus, who had formerly been a bayliffe belonging to that abby, & had coufened the fame of a great eftate in lands & tenements, which he held from the faid monaftery, & claimed as his owne; he hath thefe words.* Sed fenioribus noftris femper contradicentibus, ille jura noftra fufflavit, & coram regiis juftitiariis fe palam verificaturum ipfa tenementa fua effe patrimonia, cum multa contentione, promifit; & fic de cenobio noftro proceffit. Nobis itaque in dictis tenementis calumpniam ponentibus, dies juridicus apud Stanfordiam datus eft. *And this was in the time of the conqueror; in which this Ingulphus lived.*

Mafter Cambden, in his learned Britannia in the county of Lincolne, defcribes the fcituation, ftructure, & general priviledges antiently ufed in this town, in thefe words, Stean̄poꝺ, e Saxo ftructili, unde & nomen, ædificatum. Oppidum frequens, & variis immunitatibus ornatum; muroque firmatum. Geldum, ut eft in libro cenfuali, pro duodecim hundredis & dimidio dedit, in exercitu, navigio, & Dane-geld. Ibique fuerunt fex cuftodie. With this in part agrees the book of Crowland, which makes mention of Stamford-fhire *being a county before the conqueft. Hovedens annals, fol.* 249. *a.* n. 10.

Moreover John Stow, in his chronicle p. 131. reports, that in the time of K. Athelftane before the conqueft, there was a mint for the coining of money in Stamford-Baron; fo that, without doubt, the limits of the jurifdiction & liberties of Stamford have been farre beyond what they now are.

As touching the antient owners of Stamford, I find, by an inquifition taken for the Wapentake of Neffe in the countie of Lincolne without date, [e] *by the oathes of Ralph de Wafprey, Ralph at head, William de Gretford, Ancente of the fame, Roger le Rus de Thurlby, Walter at the box of Upthorpe, Mat-* MS. p. 10. *thew of Creffington, Gilbert de Bedford, Robert Clarke of Langham, Roger the fon of William of Offington, William Ruffey of the*

---

a Clay-mont hill.   b Clay-mont lane; now the Ironmonger ftreet.   c Mallory lane.
d Cheyne lane.   e This inquifition was taken as I conceive in the 5. H. 3. See my annals
under that year.

same, and William of the same; who say upon their oathes, that the towne of Stamford is out of the barons or knights fees, & held in capite of the king. It was in the demesne of K. Henry the first. King John gave all which belonged to him in Stamford, to Richard de Humet, to hold the same by homage [a]. But the inquisition upon this record saith, that they know not that the said Richard did any service to the king for it; unless as he was constable to the king. After the death of Richard de Humet, William his sonn & heir held the same. But at the taking the inquisition, William earl Warenn held the same at will of K. John. The aforesaid William de Humet gave out of this lordship to Henry de Gray in service, one messuage in Stamford at ij. d. rent, which Stephen Basset surrendred to him: And this is alienated, saith the record. Richard Humet gave to David the sonn of Suren, seven acres of land, which Alexander his sonn held by service; but this is alienated from the demesne. But the inquisition knows not for what service the king [b] gave & alienated from the lordship of Stamford ten carucats & an half, & five acres of heirable land to the hospitall of lepers [c]; & two acres to the monks of St. Michael; & one acre & half to the hospital of St. Logar; & two acres to the monks of St. Leonards; in pure almes. In the town of Stamford beyond the bridge, saith the record, in the county of Northampton, the abbot of Peterburrow MS.p.11. holds ten yard lands & an half of the king, with part of the town of Stamford. But the inquisition cannot find by what service the said abbot held the said lands; & they say, the said abbot hath not given, or alienated, the same or any part thereof. Further the said inquisition saith, that beyond the bridge is a certain tenement, which, at the time of taking the said inquisition, was held of the king by Roger de Somery; which tenement Gervase de Barnack held of him. And the said Gervase received yearly of the tenants of the said tenement five shillings. But, they say, they are ignorant what service the said Roger did do to the king for that fee. And say, that nothing of it is alienated. In the towne of Stamford Nigrel de Lovetot held in capite of the king, one mill with a messuage; & the monks of Croxton [d] held the same of him for twenty shillings per annum. And they say, they know not by what service the said Nigrell held the same. Bertram de Verdon held one messuage with the appurtenances of the king in Stamford; which William the son of William held of him. And the said William received yearly one shilling & nine pence. But, they say, they know not by what service the said Bertram held the same. In the towne of Stamford Thomas the sonn of Eustace held of the king, eight messuages with the appurtenances which yield to him . . . . . . But they know not by what service they were held. David earle of Huntingdon, as of the honour of Huntingdon, [e] held of the king in

Stamford, one messuage with thappurtenances which Achard de Sproxton held of the earle. The said earle David held in Stamford a tenement of the burgesses of Stamford, which Sampson de Achard de Sproxton held in free burgage for one penny; rent yearly, five pounds, one shilling. William de Lannat holds in chief of the king in Stamford, fourteen messuages in free burgage; which yield unto him yearly the sum of nine shillings & one penny. But they know not what service the said William doth for the same; neither hath he given, or alienated the same, or any part thereof. The abbot of Thorney holds of the king in chief in Stamford ten messuages, which yield unto him yearly six shillings & eight pence: But the jury know not by what service he holds the same; & say, that he hath not alienated the same. The prior & monks of Durham hold certain lands & tenements in Stamford, which yield to them MS.p.12. yearly fourteen shillings & one penny. And, they say, they are held in free alms of the king, by charter which they have. The brethren of the hospital of St. John of Jerusalem hold in Stamford a certain messuage with the appurtenances, for which they receive yearly twelve shillings; which they held from time to time of K. Henry the elder, by the gift of the burrough, which they call Biggots Lombard. And they hold the same from king to king, by their charter which they have. William earle Warenn gave & granted in the lordship of Stamford to Tipler, one messuage with the appurtenances, in the possession of Hugh at Water, which yields yearly two pence half penny.

The antient owners of this towne have been many, but all holding from the crown in chief. The tower roll makes mention that K. John gave the castle & town of Stamford to William earle Warenn. For the pope having cursed K. John & interdicted all England, he gave the same to Lewis the dawphine sonn to Phillip K. of France; which Lewis made war with K. John, & had almost beaten him out of England. In which warr the aforesaid Humet, owner of this towne, sided with the French against his sovereigne. But the English at length gaining the upper hand, K. John confiscated all his subjects lands that had taken part against him. Among which he seised, & for requital of the pains & charges which the said earle Warenn had sustained on the kings behalfe, gave the castle & towne of Stamford to the said earle Warenn.

After the death of William earle Warenn, Henry the third seised the castle & towne, & gave the same to prince Edward his eldest sonn; who held them some time, & when he came to be king, gave the same back againe to John earle Warenn. John earle Warenn gave, amongst other things, the said castle & towne back againe to the king after his death. The said earle John died in the 21. yeare of Edward the third, seised of the seid castle & towne for life, the remain-

---

a This is a gross mistake. Richard de Humet was dead before K. John came to the crown, & it was K. Henry the 2. who gave Stanford to him.   b John.   c St. Giles hospital.
    d In Staffordshire.   e These words, as of the honour of Huntingdon, are not in some copies.

der

der to the king; as appeares by the inquisition upon the tower roll taken after the death of the said John, in the 21. year of the said K. Edward the third. Edward the third, after the death of the said John earle Warenn, gave the said castle & towne to William de Bohun earle of Northampton, & to his heires males; And, in default of such issue the remainder to the king.

The said William earle of Northampton died without heires males; whereupon the reversion of the said castle & towne did againe returne into the crowne, & so continued, 'till the first *yeare* of *king* Edward the fourth. In which said first yeare, by letters patents bearing date the first of June, the said

K. Edward the fourth granted the said town & castle to his mother Sisley dutches of York for terme of her life, the remainder to the king and his heirs. After the death of the said Sisley dutches of York, the same remained in the crowne 'till the time of queen Elisabeth, at what time William Cecell, then newly made lord Burghley, a man great in the state, & also lately become great in possessions in & about Stamford, being trusted by the townesmen for the obtaining of the fee-farm thereof for the use of the corporation, obtained the same for himselfe, in whose posterity it as yet remaineth, to the great disadvantage of the said towne. MS.p.

CHAP. IV. The antient government of Stamford. The first incorporating thereof by letters patents. The reason why the kings of this land have from time to time nourished & cherished corporations. The priviledges & immunities of Stamford by the new grants & late charters. The power given them there to make laws for the better regulating the same; & the lawes made particularly set downe.

THE government of Stamford was (long before their written charter) held & used amongst themselves by an antient prescription, which was called the aldermanry of the gild; as strong & as large (if not more strong) than now the same is settled by the charters of the first and fifteenth of Edward the fourth; who was first that did incorporate the town by letters patents. For it appeareth upon the tower roll in the 3d year of K. Edward the first, per veredictum duodecim minorum ville de Stanford (rotulo hundred. Lincoln) quod ibi fuerunt duodecim qui vocantur Legemani; qui sic vocabantur, quia ab antiquo fuerunt judices legum in eadem villa. Whereby it is manifest that in those days there were twelve men in Stamford which were called Legemani, because they were judges of the law, & had the law in their own hands, for the governement of this towne.

MS.p.14. Edward the fourth in the first yeare of his reigne, Anno Dom. 1461. by his charter, directed to George Chapman, the first incorporate Alderman, & others, both of the upper & lower bench, then called the Comburgesses & Capital-Burgesses (being then the first & second twelve, as they are more particularly named in the said charter; but since inlarged by a later charter, to the alderman & twelve Comburgesses, & to the number of twenty four capital burgesses) did incorporate the said town, both in name & deed, by the name of the alderman & burgesses of Stamford; & thereby gave, or rather confirmed unto the same, many great & profitable priviledges. As, to be freed from the sheriffes jurisdiction; & from being put on inquests out of the towne; to have the returne of all writs; to be freed from all lords lieutenants; or their deputies, in respect of taking of musters, as touching the militia of the said towne; making the

alderman for the time being the king's immediate lieutenant within his liberties & jurisdiction; & to be, within the same, the second man in the kingdome. To have one, or more, mace, or maces, of gold or silver, at his choyce, to be carried before him, for his greater honour and dignity. To have a common seale at armes; and, for the honour thereof, the same are allowed to be the armes of England, both in field, colour, & posture [a], without difference, impaled with the checkie-coat, or & azure, of earle Warenn, the antient lord (as hath been said) of this towne. *And that may be said for the honour of the same, as no other corporation in England can say so much, as being wonn, & given for their service, in the field, as here followeth. In the year 1469. Sir Robert Wells, Sir Thomas Dimmocke, & Sir Thomas de la Lande, taking part with Richard Nevil, the great earle of Warwick, against K. Edward the fourth; they raised a great armey in the county of Lincolne (the king at that time being in his castle at Fotheringhay in Northamptonshire) & assembled with a formidable force in the fields between the villages of Rihal & Tinwel in Rutland. The king, marching from Fotheringhay with all his power, entred into Stamford, where he dined; & the townesmen added to his party a considerable number of horse & foot, warlike men; which, being joined with the kings armie, gave the rebells battel under Stamford walls, & in the end totally routed them, & tooke Wells, Dimmocke, & de la Lande prisoners, who were forthwith beheaded under the standard royall. There the king, for the good service those of Stamford had done him in this battel, (as an atchievement by them gained in the field) besides the confirmation of their former priviledges, ordered, that, from henceforth, the towne should bear upon a surcoate the* MS.p.

---

a In colour, charge, & posture. MS.

banner

banner royall of England, that is, Mars, three lyons paſſant, gardant, in pale Sol; annexed to the banner of earle Warenn, checque, topaz & Saphire. This famous fight is called, in the ſtory of thoſe times, looſe-coat-fight. Becauſe the rebells being routed & flying, for their more ſpeedy paſſage, threw off their coates, which they left behind them as a prey to their purſuers. And *the king alſo granted to the towne* further to do & execute within the ſame & liberties thereof, ut ab antiquo uſi fuerunt, as of antient time they had been accuſtomed; which makes it evident that this charter is but a new confirmation of more antient priviledges.

The naturaliſts report, that the viperous brood are procreated by the deſtruction of both the parents; the male deſtroyed in the act of generation, the female at the time of bringing forth. Such a generation of vipers have, from time to time, unfortunately been gotten & brought forth in this towne; I meane men, who have been begotten into prime offices, by the votes & ſuffrages of others; by which very act they have proved the ruin of thoſe which begat them; &, being conceived in the womb of their offices, to make themſelves a birth to their better benefit & greater preferment, have torne out S.p.16. the bowells of this their nouriſhing mother, by purloyning from her her antient records, charters, & muniments; tending to the death & deſtruction of this corporation, only to advance their *owne* private deſignes, together with the deſignes of the townes C O M M O N ENEMY. Whereby our antient immunities appeare no otherwiſe, than ſcatteringly here & there, upon the tower roll; little better than mere circumſtances, yet pregnant evidences, of more antient priviledges. So that, at this day, we can ſhew none, under any authentic warrant, beyond the firſt yeare of the raigne of K. Edward the fourth. But, ſince the obtaining of this firſt charter, the ſame hath been confirmed by divers inſpeximus's from all the ſucceeding kings & queens that have been ſovereignes to the time of K. Charles that now is [a], & divers new grants added, as, the monday market, the three fayres of Simon & Jude, greengooſe-fayre, & St. James fayre. *The towne* having formerly but the friday market, & the great mid-lent mart, the profits of which only, belong to the lord; *but* theſe latter to the corporation. By a late inſpeximus, there is granted to the alderman & burgeſſes, to hold a court of plea's of all actions real, perſonall, or mixt, to the value of 40 *l.* And to hold ſeſſions & goale delivery for all criminal actions perpetrated & done within the liberty; high treaſon & pettit treaſon only excepted. *By the firſt charter of Edward the fourth, the alderman & burgeſſes may purchaſe lands; ſue & be ſued, by the name of the alderman & burgeſſes; & have granted unto them all fines & forfeitures in ſeſſions, & the goods of outlaws & felons. And, beſides theſe, many other immunities, to no great purpoſe here to be related.*

This towne hath (as many other antient boroughs of England have) a power to ſend up two burgeſſes to every parliament. So that they have not only a power to execute laws, but alſo a ſhare in making of lawes. And here is to be obſerved the reaſon, why the princes & policy of England have had a regard as it were to the fencing & hedging about of the cities & antient boroughs of this land with priviledges & immunities, for the ſtronger defence, preſervation, & main- MS.p.17. tenance of the ſame; & that for divers great & weighty ends & purpoſes. In the time of William the conqueror it was conſtituted [b] by the ſaid king, in theſe words. Item, nullum mercatum vel forum ſit, nec fieri permittatur, niſi in civitatibus regni noſtri, & in burgis clauſis & muro vallatis, & caſtellis, & locis tutiſſimis, ubi conſuetudines regni noſtri, & jus noſtrum commune, & dignitates corone noſtre, que conſtitute ſunt a bonis predeceſſoribus noſtris deperire non poſſint, nec defraudari, nec violari; ſed omnia rite, & per judicium & juſtitiam fieri debent. Et ideo caſtella, & burgi, & civitates ſunt & fundati & edificati, ſcilicet, ad tuitionem gentium & populorum regni, & ad defenſionem regni; & idcirco obſervari debent cum omni libertate, & integritate, & ratione. Lambert, fol. 121. So as by this it appeares, that cities & antient boroughs (as this towne is) were inſtituted for three purpoſes. I. the conſervation of the cuſtomes of the kingdome, & the common right & dignity of the crowne. II. for the defence of the nation & the people of the kingdome. And III. as for the defence of the kingdome, ſo for the converſation of the lawes thereof; by which lawes every man enjoyes his owne in peace. IV. For tuition & defence of the kings ſubjects, & for the keeping of the kings peace in time of ſuddaine uproares. And finally, for the defence of the realme againſt outward, & inward, hoſtility.

And indeed the graunts of kings & ſoveraigne princes, either to counties, cities, or townes corporate, make ſuch counties, cities, & townes corporate, as it were ſmall county palatines within themſelves, in giving them power for the better government of ſuch places, to have magiſtrates of their owne members; &, for their more ample authority & peculiar rule, to make lawes, conſtitutions & ordinances, to bind themſelves & every member within their juriſdiction. When the conqueror created Hugh Lupus earl of Cheſter, he made that ſhire a county palatine; upon which creation Henry Bradſhawe a monk of Cheſter, about the beginning of K. Henry the eights *reign* ſpeaking (in vita Werburg, cap. 16.) of the manner MS.p.18. of the conquerors graunt to the ſaid Hugh, hath theſe following verſes, which in part doe reſemble the free & large liberties & graunts to inferior corporations.

——The king gave him for his inheritance
The county of Cheſter, with thappurtenance;

---

a the late K. Charles, MS.　　　b inſtituted, MS.

Made a sure charter to him & his succession
By the sword of dignity, to hold it by might,
And to call a parliament to his will & fight;
To order his subjects after true justice,
As a prepotent prince, & statutes to devise.

This Hugh Lupus, for the better ayding of him in his government, & for the more compleating of him in his parliament, which should bee the fountaine of his laws to rule by, substituted & made under him these eight barons; that is to say,

1. Robertus filius Hugonis, Baro de Malpas.
2. Richardus de Vernon, Baro de Shipbrooke.
3. Willielmus Malbanc [a], Baro de Nantwich.
4. Willieimus filius Nigelli, Baro de Halton.
5. Hamo de Massey, Baro de Dunham.
6. Gilbertus de Venables, Baro de Kinderton.
7. Hugo filius Normandi [b], Baro de Hawarden.
8. Nicholas de Stockport [c], Baro de Stockport.

In like manner, as this earle & his barons assembled in the great hall of his castle of Chester, had the power to make lawes & constitutions for the government of that his county, so hath this lesser body aggregate (the survey of which I now write) a power within themselves, in their common hall *MS.p.19.* assembled, to make lawes as *their owne* peculiar & proper rules, for their better goverment. The said assembly being a little court of parliament if it be lawfull for me to compare small things with great; or, like a cosmographer, to frame a modell of the great world in one small skin of parchment; for, in this small modell, is a representation of the highest & greatest government. For here the alderman, as the chiefest magistrate, represents the person of the king; his brethren the comburgesses, sitting round about him, as so many peeres of the upper house. The capital-burgesses (which we here call the twenty four) being *senatores minorum gentium*, are the representative body of the whole towne, &, in their place, doe symbolize with the lower house of parliament. The recorder, being the mouth of the court, doth represent the speaker in this microcosme; the towne-clarke, the register or clarke of the same; the gilded mace-bearer, the serjeant at armes; & the jayler (being the arresting serjeant in the liberty) the knight of the black rod.

Now, in pursuance of that power given to this corporation for the making of good & wholsome lawes for the better government of the same, Richard Wolphe Gent. alderman of the said towne, at a common court, or hall, there held the 15. day of March, in the sixth yeare of the raigne of our soveraigne lord K. Charles that now is [d], with the advice & consent of the comburgesses & capital-burgesses, in the common hall assembled, did ordaine & constitute as followeth.

I. That no new habitation shall be erected in the said town, unless it be made fit for the dwelling of such person or persons as shall be cessed, or fit to be cessed, in the subsidie, at xx s. in land, or iij l. in goods, at the least (excepting hospitals & houses of correction) upon peyne to forfeit to the alderman & burgesses, or their successors, the summe of x s. for every moneth that such cottage or new building shall be used for habitation.

II. That no barnes, or other *out*-houses, *MS.p.20* shall be converted into *habitations or* tenements; & no antient tenement shall be divided into sundry habitations (except same so divided shall be made fit for the dwelling of subsidie men of xx. s. lands or iij. l. goods) the erector to forfeit ten shillings monethly, & the tenant v s. monethly, to the use aforesaid.

III. That such who take in inmates, shall forfeit x s. monthly, to the use aforesaid.

IV. That none shall let, or assigne, any tenement, to any one not assessed, or fit to be assessed at xx s. lands, or iij l. goods (except to free-men that have not discontinued from the towne with their families by the space of one yeare before) unlesse the landlord become bound with the tenant, or *some* one other sufficient surety in xl. l. *bond*, to save the towne harmlesse; upon peyne of v. l. forfeit for the contempt, & x s. monethly for the continuance by the landlord, & v s. monethly by the tenant, to the use aforesaid.

V. That these orders extend not to any that take in tenants of xx s. lands, or iij l. goods in the subsidy (except they be inmates.)

VI. That the alderman for the time being, with two of the next [e] comburgesses to the place (not being offenders) shall be judges whether such erections be meet for the habitation of such subsidy men?

VII. That the streets & lanes in the said towne be cleansed every Saturday by the adjacent inhabitants; or the parties delinquent to forfeit for every offence vi. d. & the constables, in that precinct, to forfeit, for not presenting every *such* offence at the next sessions after the same is committed ij. s. & vj. d. to the use aforesaid.

VIII. That no alderman shall presume to *MS.p.21.* make any a free-man out of the towne-hall, unlesse the same be granted in the open-hall, & the fine for such freedome there assessed; upon peyne to forfeit v. l. to the use aforesaid.

IX. That no tradesman whatsoever (except free-men by birth or service) shall presume to open any shop, or to sell any wares, untill they have agreed for their freedome; upon peyne of forfeiting x. s. for every month they shall so do, to the use aforesaid.

X. That all the conduits, common wells,

a Sir Pierce Malbanc, Britannia antiqua & nova, vol. 1. p. 278. b.   b Eustace Crew de Rouhalt. id. ib.   c Warenn de Pointon. id. ib.   d the late K. Charles, MS.   e nearest, MS.

& pumps

& pumps about the said towne, shall, from time to time, be repaired at the towne charge; upon pain of forfeiture of vj. s. & viij. d. apeece by the two chamberlains, to the use aforesaid.

XI. That so many of the comburgesses or capitall burgesses as shall be dwelling within the parish where the alderman, or his deputy, for the time being, shall dwell (having no lawfull excuse to the contrary) shall attend upon the said alderman, or his deputy, to, & from, his parish church, upon every Lords day, both before noone & after noone, if there be any sermon at the said church; upon peyne for every one offending to forfeit for every offence the sum of iv. d. to the use aforesaid.

XII. That all such as have built upon the town-walls, or upon the rampier thereof, or made any doores or gates out of the said walls, within the space of xl. yeares before these ordinances, shall take leases from the towne, of the said passages; or shall forfeit xij. d. for every moneth they shall continue the same without leases, to the use aforesaid.

MS.p.22. XIII. That the pindar of the said towne shall impound, & take i. d. for every beast that he finds in the towne-streets, & in the liberties thereof; not put before the common heard.

XIV. That all the forfeitures aforesaid shall be paid to the chamberlaines for the time being, who, in default of payment, shall leavie & recover the same by action or actions of debt, or by distresse of the goods & chattels of the offenders. Which distresse being taken, shall be impounded, untill the penalty, for which it was taken, be fully payd. Or else, for non-payment by the space of six days after the taking, & not in the mean time repleavied, the same to be appraized by two indifferent persons to be chosen by the alderman for the time being, & by the chamberlaines sold for the satisfaction of the said penalties, & the overplus to be delivered to the owner, or owners, of the said goods.

XV. That the severall summes hereafter to be paid, recovered, or levied by vertue of these ordinances, or any of them, shall be, from time to time, imployed to & for the good of the poore of the said towne of Stamford; & not otherwise.

These lawes, constitutions, & ordinances were, in the same yeare, viewed, approved of & confirmed under the hands & seals of Sir Richard Hutton Kt. then one of the justices of his majesties court of common pleas [a]; & Sir George Crooke Kt. one of his majesties justices of the court of kings-bench [b]; being the two judges of assize for the county of Lincolne (in which county the said corporation of Stamford standeth) & thereby made lawes, according to the forme of the Statute (19. H. 7. cap. 7.) in that case made & provided; & are sett up in the counsell-chamber of the said towne, fairely written in parchment, & fixed in a wooden frame.

But these lawes, how good soever in themselves, remaine but as so many lifelesse letters, for want of that quickening spirit, which the authority of the majestrate ought to put into them, by the just & impartiall execution of them. For, as in cases criminall, the death of the malefactor is the life of the law; so, in all offences of a lesse nature, the due punishment of the offender shews the instrument of the living law in the hand of the justicer. And therefore such magistrates as have good rules prescribed, but in regard either of negligence, idlenesse, or ignorance forbear to do their duties; are like to counterfeit mankins, set up on corne lands, only to fright away the birds. And the offender perceiving such a one what he is, is, by him, rather incouraged, than made afraid, to offend. Because, he knows, he may offend without controule; having for his governour but Æsops dead beame flung into the water, which every base frog, in contempt & derision, will hop & trample on. *So that we may, from hence, observe, that a majestrate without courage, is like a lion without a heart; & courage, without the fear of God, is but armed justice. Againe. If their persons, or parentage, be in contempt, how shall the people regard? Or, if they have not wisdom to rule, what are they else but an eye without sight, or, as if the day & night should be governed without sun & moon?* What shall I call such blockish justices? They are like round ciphers, which have neither the figures of justice, judgment, equity, courage, nor the fear of God before their eyes. Or, like the picture of St. George on horseback, threatning, with his sword, to kill the dragon, but never hitting him. Therefore, to finish the character of this sin-suffering beast, with this chapter, the poets definition fits him.

Mild magistrates are winters too to warme,
Which neither chill the weed, nor kill the
worm.   Du Bartas.

MS.p.23.

MS.p.24. CHAP. V. *The dignity & antiquity of the word & title Alderman described.*

NOW since this towne hath for her principal magistrate an alderman [c], I conceive it will not be amisse, nor out of order or method (before I set down the manner of election & inauguration of this prepotent officer) somewhat to vindicate the dignity & antiquity of the word alderman it self, with the large extent & antient power

a then one of the justices of the peace of the court of pleas. MS.   b one of the justices of the then court of kings-bench. MS.   c an alderman when Mr. Butcher wrote; but Stanford was since made a mayor town by King Charles the 2d.

2

thereof

thereof here in England, long before the Norman conqueſt; farre beyond that of major or any other name of magiſtrate at this time appointed, for the rule or government of a[ny] city or town incorporate; though the conceit & opinion of theſe more modern times ſeem to be otherwiſe. Sed non fuit ſic ab initio. And I am ſure the beſt antiquaries preferre an antient dignity, though by time neglected, before a new invented title, though never ſo much for the preſent adored. So likewiſe do the beſt heralds preferre an antient family (retaining the old vertue, though declined in eſtate) before a new & upſtart houſe, though never ſo much glittering for the preſent in wealth, pomp, & proſperity. For we know, that tho many times a black cloud interpoſeth it ſelf betwixt us & the ſunnes brightneſſe, yet the ſun ſtill remaineth to be the ſame, both in heat & ſplendor; though ſeeming darkened, cooled, & obſcured to dull conceits & thick capacities. So, though time & uſe, like an abſconding vail or curtain, drawes it ſelf betwixt us & the former antient luſtre & extent of government appropriate unto the name & dignity of the word alderman, yet the ſame ſtill remains, as at the firſt, glorious & ſplendid in it ſelf. For it is to be noted, that in all old Saxon titles, the word alderman or duke (as Selden obſerves) was one & the ſame. For authority whereof, he cites an inſtrument, made by Ethelred & Etheſſed (the aldermen, dukes, or lords of Mercia) to Werfred biſhop of Worceſter, in the year 904. for the profit & benefit of

MS.p.25.　that church. And (as the book of the church of Worceſter ſaith) the name of alderman is ſometimes expreſſed by ſub-regulus, & regulus; ſometimes by patricius, princeps, dux, comes, and conſul. Nor is it without example that they are called reges. Camb. Brit. p. 368. There was an old inſcription at the abby of Ramſey in antient time, of one Ailwin, who, being of the blood royal, was alderman of all England under K. Athelſtan, & founder of that abby, as there appeares, by the epitaph upon his tomb, in theſe words. Hic requieſcit Ailwinus incliti regis Eadgari cognatus, totius Anglie Aldermannus, & hujus ſacri cenobii miraculoſus fundator. Here lies Ailwin, kinſman of *the renowned* K. Eadgar, alderman of all England, & the miraculous founder of this ſacred cell[a]. Obiit anno Chriſti, 992. Cod. Ramſey in archivis ſcaccarii.

The word elderman (ſaith Hoveden, p. 607.) in Engliſh is the ſame with ſenior or ſenator in Latine. Not ſo much ſo called propter ſenectutem, ſed propter ſapientiam; not ſo much for their age as for their wiſdome. And divers others (as Polychron, Polidore Virgil, inter leges Molmutii) have it to the ſame purpoſe in other words, by way of notation obſerving, that thoſe whom the Saxons formerly called, & now we call, eldermen or earles, the Romans called ſenators. Et ſimiliter olim apud Britanos, temporibus Romanorum, in regno iſto Britanie, vocabantur Senatores; qui poſtea, temporibus Saxonum, vocabantur Aldermanni. Non propter etatem, ſed propter ſapientiam & dignitatem; cum quidem adoleſcentes, eſſent juriſperiti tamen & in hoc experti. *And likewiſe formerly among the Britons, when the Romans were here, they were called ſenators; who were afterwards, in the Saxon times called aldermen; not for their age, but wiſdom & dignity. For as much as ſome, tho young men, yet were underſtanding in the laws, & in this particular of good experience.* So that it appeares hereby, that the antiquity, dignity, & the extent of authority of the name or title, alderman, ſurpaſſeth that of major, provoſt, bayliffe, or warden; by which ſeveral titles given to the chief magiſtrates, divers cities & corporate townes are governed.

MS.p.26.　**CHAP. VI.** The manner of chuſing the alderman of Stamford, with other ſubordinate officers in that corporation; by which meanes the ſaid body is from time to time kept in life & being.

IN the next place followes in order the originall grant, & preſent practice according to that grant, in the election & chooſing of this prime magiſtrate & the other ſubordinate officers under him. For, as I ſaid before, K. Edward the fourth, in the firſt year of his raigne, directed his letters patents to George Chapman & others, by the name of the alderman & comburgeſſes of Stamford; & to twelve more of an inferior rank, by the name of the capitall burgeſſes of Stamford; which ſecond twelve have been, by a later charter, augmented to the number of twenty four: ſo as K. Edward the fourth, creating this body by his princely power, by his wiſdome & policy gave rules & directions to the ſame, how it ſhould, from time to time, be preſerved in a perpetuall life & being, by a continued ſucceſſion. And therefore, when any of the firſt number do deceaſe, or leave their place, the alderman with the reſt of his company, do elect & chooſe, out of the ſecond number, ſuch a meet & able man as they think fit for the ſupply of the *place* vacant. The ſaid election being made in the private councell chamber, by the alderman & thoſe with him of the firſt number, & this by the major number of voyces: the alderman having in this, as in all other voices, a double, or caſting voice. And when any of the ſecond number happen to deceaſe or to be diſplaced,

---

a 'This Ailwin was called Healf-coning, that is Half-king, from his great authority & favour with the king.' Camd. Bp. Gibſons firſt edit. p. 422. And from this paſſage I ſuppoſe was that Mr. Butcher ſays above, ' nor is it without example that they are called reges.'

both companies joining together, by the major number of voyces, choofe, out of the body of the whole towne, fuch a difcreet, able, & fufficient man, as fhall be thought convenient to fupply the then vacant place.

MS.p.27.   Both companies thus compleatly furnifhed, being congregated in their common hall, upon the firft thurfday after the feaft of St. Bartholomew the apoftle, every year, do elect two out of the firft number (who have neither of them been alderman by the fpace of two years then paft) to the end that one of thefe two, the firft thurfday in the cleane week [a] next after the feaft of St. Michael the archangell then following, may, by the major fuffrages of both companies, be chofen alderman for the year then to come. Which party thus elected, is brought & prefented, by his predeceffor, to the Steward of the court leete, in the open courte, after proclamation made, in folemn manner, to that purpofe: The ceremony of which day is as followeth.

The former alderman, attended by the firft and fecond companies; the firft company in their robes of purple faced with foynes (fuch as the fecond robe of London is) and the fecond company in their decent gownes of black, fit for fuch an affembly; do repayre to the houfe of the new elected alderman, where, after a fhort banquet, they all do paffe in order to the caftle yard, where the *court* leet is kept; & there being prefented (as is aforefaid) he is folemnly fworn by the fteward of the leete; firft taking the oath of fupremacy and allegiance [b], next the oath of juftice of the peace & alderman of the corporation; & having a tippet of black velvet taken from the neck of his predeceffor, & by the hands of his faid predeceffor put upon his; he then is feated on the right hand of the fteward, where he fits till the charge be given. And then, attended by the feverall companies, they go to the church

of St. Mary in Stamford, where they heare a Sermon. Which being finifhed, the new alderman paffeth to his houfe, with his two MS.p.28, maces (the one of gold [c], the other of filver) borne before him; & attended by the feverall companies as is aforefaid, with the lowd mufick of the towne playing before them. And, in divers places as they paffe, the fchollars of the free-grammar-fchoole do pronounce before them feverall orations in Greek & Latine. After which the alderman at his own houfe for the moft part, & at his own coft & charges, doth make a great feaft to the towne, & to as many of the gentry of the country, as, upon folemn invitation, think good to be prefent.

This folemnity being finifhed, prefently after he keeps his firft court (which is called a hall) where he fweares all his firft company to be faithfull unto him, & truly to counfell him in the execution of his office. And likewife he then fwears the fecond company to be ayding & affifting unto him, in all things that appertain to the aldermanry, during the time of his office. At the hall he likewife takes an oath of the town clark, for the true execution of his office. And likewife he then fweares the coroner of the town for the year to come, who is, by cuftom, the fame party that was alderman the year before. Alfo he then fweares the two chamberlaines, & ten or twelve conftables at *the* leaft; fearchers for the corne, flefh, & fifh markets. Sealers & fearchers of leather are at this time likewife fworne; & all other inferior officers, as, the bayliffe of the liberty, the fergeant of the mace, *& all* fuch as are needfull & neceffary for the ayd & fupport of the townes government, are, at this hall, chofen & fworn, well & faithfully to perform & execute their feverall offices, during the yeere then next following.

MS.p.29. C H A P. VII.   Memorable things happening at feveral times, in & about Stamford.

MR. Cambden, out of *Henry* Huntingdon, reports, that when the whole nations of the Picts & Scots had invaded the northe*rne parts* of England, & were come fouthwards as farre as Stamford, that Hengift (who was, as I take it, the firft Saxon king that here reigned) came againft them with his Saxons with fuch unwearied great ftrength & fortitude, that hee there fo ftopped the journey of thefe barbarous invaders, that moft of them were flain & taken; the reft, which were put to flight, were drowned in the waters.

I have read in the ftory of Ingulphus, that at what time the Danes invaded England, had burnt the abbey of Crowland, & put

to the fword all the monks in the fame, & *were* marching towards Stamford, the then baron of Eafingdine, with the men of Stamford, gave them battell neare unto the faid towne & beat them backe for that time; though afterwards they returned to the deftruction of the fame, as formerly hath been related [d].

The aforefaid Huntingdon makes mention of another battle that was held here between Harold K. of Norway & Harold K. of England, when as the Englifh King moft valiantly, at Stamford-bridge, gave battel to the Norwegians; & that it being a fierce fight, continued from morning till noon with great flaughter on both fides; when as a certain

---

a The week here meant is not the week on any day whereof the feaft of St. Michael falls (tho' it happen before Thurfday) but the next week after it.   b the oath, which formerly was the oath of fupremacy and allegiance. MS.   c The corporation of Stanford have three maces, but none of them of gold. And why Mr. Butcher fhould think one of them was of that metal, I can't imagine; they being all but filver gilt.   d About this paffage fee my annals, fub anno 870.

valiant Norwegian, who had almost foil'd the English throughout the whole battell, returning to go into his shipp (where note that the river was then navigable) was stroaken with a dart, so that he forthwith dyed ; whereby the Norwegians were discomfited.

In the year of· Christ 1153. K. Stephen holding the castle of Stamford against Henry Fitz-Empress, that is, Henry the second ; the said castle was besieged & wonne by the said Henry.

In 1189. all the Jews that then repaired to the midlent-mart at Stamford from all parts, were spoiled of their goods & murthered.

In 1227. there was a great meeting at Stamford of divers lords, about plotting of the rebellion against K. Henry the third, called the barons warres.

In 1293, 1300, & 1311. general chapters called itinere [a] minorum were held at Stamford.

MS.p.30.   In 1334. by reason of a bloody difference happening betwixt the southerne & northerne students in the university of Oxford ; part of that university (being the whole northerne faction) removed it self to Stamford. Whereby was accomplished a former antient prophecy, which followeth in these words,

Hoc magnum studium quod nunc est ad vada boum,

Tempore futuro celebrabitur ad vada saxi.

As Ox*en*ford, where learning now doth flourish ;

In time to come the Stony-ford shall nourish.

Mr. Cambden, in his learned Britannia, confirms this faction at Oxford, & the setling for a time of the northerne students here at Stamford. For saith he, regnante Edwardo tertio, coepta hic academia & bonarum literarum professio (quod suæ gloriæ imprimis ducunt cives) Cum enim Oxoniæ, inter studiosos boreales & australes, omnia litibus ferverent, magnus studiosorum numerus huc concessit. But here they staid not long. For, saith the same Cambden, paulo tamen post Oxoniæ reversi, academiæ huic orienti, ut initium, ita finem, cito posuerunt. Yet this separation occasioned that ever since that university, when any of their members are to take any degree, they give them an oath never to reade Logick in

MS.p.31. Stamford (strangely conceiving that either the foresaid prophecy is not yet fulfilled, or else that their policy can prevent the decree of eternity, when as we see that God when he pleaseth brings the same thing to passe, by the same means whereby fond man goes about to prevent it) For saith Cambden further, cautumq; deinceps in jurejurando ne quis Oxoniensis publice Stanfordiæ prælegeret. This towne of Stamford neverthelesse flourished for some time afterwards in trade & merchandise, untill the warrs unhappily happened betwixt the two families of Yorke & Lancaster. In which intestine strife the

northern souldiers breaking into the town, burnt the houses, & so farre destroyed all things here, that since the towne could never fully recover her antient dignity. For saith Cambden, speaking of the town after the removal of the Oxford students, nihilominus illa mercemoniis floruit, donec ardente inter familiam Lancastrensem & Eboracensem civili bello, boreales milites irrumpentes, cædibus & incendiis omnia miscuerint. Nec inde vero dignitatem pristinam plane recuperare potuit.

In 1392. there was a meeting at Stamford, called consilium Stanfordiense prælatorum ; at which meeting K. Richard himself was present, by the command of pope Boniface the ninth, about the suppressing of Wicklifes opinions.

King Edward the fourth came to Stamford in 1462. the year after he had incorporated the town by letters patents.

In 1469. *Sir Robert* Wells, *Sir Thomas* Dimmocke, & *Sir Thomas* de la Lande, were executed at Stamford for treason *& rebellion* Thomas Royston then being alderman.

The castle of Stamford was overthrown & demolished in the time of *king* Richard the third ; *&* the materials thereof taken away to repair the White-friers in Stamford.

King Henry the eight came to Stamford at his progresse into Lincolnshire in 1532. where he was royally welcomed *& feasted* by Henry Lacy Gent. their alderman ; as his predecessor Edward the fourth was before received by John Brown esq; *the* then alderman.

The town-house, or common hall, over the bridge gate in Stamford was newly built by John Haughton alderman in 1558.

In 1565. Q. Elisabeth passed through Stamford, & dyned in the White-friers, in her progresse into Lincolnshire ; Godfrey Dawson then being alderman.   MS.p.32.

In 1594. Robert Medowes then being alderman, a great tumult was raised at the inne called the bull in Stamford, by Molineux of Nottinghamshire, & Terwil [b] of Lincolnshire of the one side, & one Rookwood [c] a gentleman of Suffolke of the other party. The occasion began upon a trifle. A foot-boy drying himself in the evening by the kitchen fire (where his master Rookwoods [c] supper was making ready) Molineux & Terwil [d] sitting at a table & drinking neer to the fire, took exceptions against the boy & beat him, because he did not stand uncovered before them. The boy making complaint thereof to other of his masters servants then in the house, divers of them came down to revenge the boys wrong, &, with naked swords, so affronted the foresaid gentlemen, that at length *all of them*, gentlemen & servants, on both sides became ingaged.

Flumina magna vides parvis de fontibus orta.

---

a Itinere, in the printed copy ; itere, in the MS. perhaps it should be itinera fratrum minorum.
b Thorold, MS.   c Rockwood, MS.   e Thorold, MS.

And

And a great ſtream of blood might have iſſued from this ſmall originall, had not the ſame been wiſely prevented by the valour & diſcretion of that honourable ſouldier Peregrine lord Willoughby of Grimſthorp [a], who (living then in Stamford, & hearing that the ſaid alderman, though he uſed his beſt indeavour for appeaſing of the ſaid ſtirre, could not prevail) armed himſelf & his followers, & mounted upon his warlike courſer, entered into the midſt of the throng, &, like a right valiant perſon & wiſe commander, pacified the uproare before any mortall wound was given; ſo ſerving her majeſty by procuring [b] of her peace, & ſaving the lives of many, who otherwiſe were in danger to have periſhed in that tumult, *or at the gallows*; & by his wiſdome & diſcretion, before he parted from them, made them all friends.

MS. p. 33.

In 1633. King Charles [c] lay in Stamford-Baron one night (as he paſſed into Scotland there to receive the crown of that kingdom) & then paſſed through the corporation of Stamford in ſtate; John Atton the then alderman bearing the mace before him: the ſaid alderman & all the firſt company *being* mounted on horſeback, and riding in their robes upon their foot-clothes.

In 1634. *the ſaid* K. Charles & his queen, in their progreſſe northward, lodged two nights at the earle of Weſtmorelands at Apethorpe five miles from Stamford. But when they removed from thence, they paſſed in ſtate through this town; Edward Camocke, then alderman, bearing the mace before them.

In April 1641. by the means of *a* great raine & *wind*, the wind then being full weſt, the river of Welland ſo farre ſwelled above the banks, that the flood ſo farre prevailed, as it went over the north end of Stamford bridge & flowed up St. Maries hill, the midway to St. Maries church; drowning the lower roomes & cellars on both ſides the ſtreets. And on the ſouth ſide *of the bridge* it drowned the lower roomes of the new-bead-houſe, & both the yard & the lower roomes of the inne called the George, inſomuch that ſome horſes were then & there drowned in the ſtables, & the walls & roofe over one of the ſtables, thrown down by the violence of the water; the flood being ſo high all over the yard, that a horſe might have ſwom therein. It drowned all the lower roomes of the houſes that ſtand in the water-ſtreet of Stamford-Baron. Yet, though this flood did riſe ſo high upon the ſudden on the eaſt & weſt of the river Welland, flowing over all the lower roomes by which it paſſed, & carrying down the ſtreame both cattell, timber, & all that lay within the compaſſe thereof (thanks be to God) I could never hear of man, woman, or child that periſhed thereby.

The new goale, or ſerjeantes houſe for the bayliffe of the liberty to inhabit & keepe debtors & priſoners of the beſt rank out of the common goale or dungeon, a moſt neceſſary ſtructure (which was formerly wanting) alſo convenient upper roomes for lodgings, & a ſtately dining roome adjoyning to the common-hall, for the alderman to keep his ſeſſions dinner in, & for other publick entertainments; was begun & perfected by the care & diligence of Francis Dalby, Gent: in 1658.

The laſt, moſt moderne & memorable thing that ever happened in this towne, or in this nation for ought I know, is not to be omitted, but to be regiſtred to poſterity, as proceeding from him who is God to all eternity.

MS. p. 34.

[d] There was, ſtill is, & a long time hath been (as an apprentice, journeyman & inhabitant) in this towne, one Samuel Wallis, a ſhoemaker; who, from his youth, was much weakned with ſickneſs [e]; & as he grew into years, ſo his infirmity grew upon him, & he was a long time waſted with a lingring conſumption, which was attended with a continual lameneſs through his limbs. And, being poore, & not able to uſe any meanes for his recovery, he gave himſelf over as altogether incurable. In this weak & deſperate condition, continuing, & lying upon his bed all alone (his wife being abroad tending a ſicke perſon) upon the 30th of May 1658. in the afternoon (being the feaſt of Pentecoſt) one knockt at his doore, which he opening, there ſtood before him an old man of mean ſtature [f], comely, & of a grave aſpect. Wallis demanded, what he would have? I come, ſaid he, to crave a cup of your ſmall beer. The other told him it was ſmall both in quantity & quality; but, ſuch as it was, he was welcome to it: and wiſhed him to come in. Wallis, as well as he was able, fetched him a cup of ſmall beer; which, being brought, he ſet it upon the table. For, ſaith he, as to my drink it is of the water of Chriſt Jeſus. But I perceive, quoth he to Wallis, you are ſick & weak & lame? To which Wallis anſwered, he had been ſo a long time. What means have you uſed for your recovery, ſayes the old man? To whom Wallis replied, he was poor, & not able to be at the charge of a phyſitian. Why then, ſaith the other, God hath ſent you a phyſitian I therefore, in the firſt place, adviſe you to ſerve God. And, for the means of your recovery, you have, in your garden, red ſage. Take three leaves of that ſage every morning, & ſteep them in this drink which you bring to me. Drink of the ſame for the ſpace of nine days together, & believe in God; & you ſhall recover both in health & limbs. But beware of drinking any ſtrong beer, ale, or wine. And, when you find your ſelf able & ſtrong to walk abroad, go to ſome friends houſe three or four miles from the towne, & there ſtay for ſome ſhort time to take the freſh air: But, in any caſe, ſerve God, & believe in

a Eresby, MS.   b preſerving, MS.   c the late K. Charles of bleſſed memory MS.
d This whole paragraph is wanting in ſome copies.   e A miſtake; his caſe, as Wallis himſelf afterwards tells us, was not a weakneſs or ſickneſs from his youth; but an accidental ſurfeit which turned firſt to a fever, & then brought on a conſumption.   f Another miſtake; for Wallis himſelf, as you will by & by find, affirms he was a proper, tall, old man.

     him.

him. This he said, & then departed; his habit being a violet short cloth coat, under which was a suit of the same; white woollen stockings, & cleane black shoes. The wayes & weather were very foul & dirty. Yet no spot of dirt was seene upon him. Wallis's house being neare a gate called St. Pauls gate, he saw this old man go through the gate; but never after beheld him. Wallis then applied himself to that course which the old man had directed. And within the space of a week or less, recovered his perfect health both in body & limbs, in a more firme manner than all his life before; & so continues. But, as he was further directed, having his limbs & health restored, he went to a friends house three or four miles from Stamford, & travelled more ably & stronger than the party that accompanied him. At last certain of his friends coming to him, to behold & heare of this miraculous cure; he forgot himself, & contrary to the old mans directions, drank a small quantity of strong ale; whereupon his speech was immediately taken away from him, so that he continued dumb for the space of twenty four hours. But at length, by the same mercy that he was healed, his speech returned. After this he went home, & now followes his calling, serves his God, & lives in perfect health both in body & limbs. And (though he had, by meanes of his long infirmity, discontinued from his trade a long time, yet) after the old man departed from him, he found, among his bed-clothes, a new awl (never before used) with which he at this day getts his living.

MS. p. 35. Since I set downe the former relation, touching the miraculous cure of the aforesaid Samuel Wallis (which was as well as I could call things to memory as reported to me at the instant when the same was first done) I find there is some difference between the same, & what I have since received from the person & under the hand-writing of the said Wallis himself. I have therefore thought good in this place, to transcribe it in his own phrase & language, & subscribed by himself.

[a] Upon Whitsunday, which was in the year of our Lord God 1658. about six of the clock in the afternoone, after evening sermon, I being newly up, &, as I sat by the fire, reading in that little book called Abrahams suit for Sodom, about halfe an hour; so it was that the woman that kept me was gone forth, & had shut the doores upon me [b]. In the mean time, whilst I was reading in the book, I heard one rapp at the doore. I thought it to be a stranger, because it was sabbath day. So I was constrained to go to the door my self; & I took my stick in my hand, & by the

wall with my other hand, as well as the Lord God did enable me, I went to the door. There I beheld a proper, tall, grave, old man [c]. Thus he said, friend, I pray thee give an old pilgrime a cup of small beere. And I said, Sir, I pray you come in, & welcome. And he said, I am no Sir, therefore call me not Sir; but come in I must, for I cannot pass by thy door before I come in. And I said, come in I pray you, and welcome: For I thought he could not passe by my door untill he had dranke, he was so drye: So we both came in together, & left the door open. So as well as the Lord God did enable me, with my stick in one hand & the wall in my other hand, I went & drew him a cup of small beer [d], & gave it him in his hand, & satt me downe. And he walked twice or thrice to & fro; & then he drank, & walked againe as before, & drank againe. And so he did likewise three times, before he had drank it all [c]. Then he set the cup in the window by me. All this while he said nothing to me, nor I to him. Then I thought he would have been goeing; but he was not. He walked twice or thrice as he did before. And, when he came almost at me, he said, friend, thou art not well? I said, no, truly, Sir, I MS. have not beene well this many years. He said, what is thy disease? I said, a deep consumption, Sir; our doctors say past cure. He said, there they said well: But what have they given thee for it? I said, Sir, truly nothing. For indeed I am a very poor man, & not able to follow doctors councell. Therefore I do commit my selfe to the almighty God; what his will is, I am content with it. He said, in that thou sayest very well. Then I will tell thee what thou shalt doe, & by the helpe & power of almighty God above, thou shalt be well (do but remember my words, & observe to doe them; but however thou dost, above all things fear God, & serve him) To morrow, when thou risest up, go into thy garden, & get there two leaves of red sage & one of bloodworte; & put these three leaves into a cup of thy small beer, & let them lie in it three dayes. Drink as often as need requires; &, when the cup is empty, fill it again. But this remember, that thou lett the leaves lye in still untill the fourth day in the morning; then cast them away, & put in thereto the fourth day in the morning three more fresh leaves. I pray thee remember my words, & observe, & do them, but however thou dost, above all things fear God, & serve him. The fourth day in the morning is the first day of the three againe. And so continue thus doeing every fourth day

---

a The famous presbyterian divine Mr. Samuel Clerk, Minister of St. Benet Fink, in his examples, Lond. 1671. fol. vol. 2. p. 18. has inserted, 'a true & faithful relation of one Samuel 'Wallace, &c. whereof he gave this account, with much affection & sensiblenes of the lords 'mercy & goodness to him, upon April 7. 1659.' Which account in Mr. Clerk is much the same with this in **Mr. Butcher.** I shall not therefore tire the reader with a repetition of it in Mr. Clerks words, but only where any material difference, or enlargement, occurs, set down the same at the foot of the page.   b There being no body in the house then with him, & his wife gone into the country to seek relief of some friends; finding himself a little lightsome, he crept to the fire-side. And as he was reading, &c. Clerk.   c a proper, grave, old man. Clerk.   d in a little jug-pot. Clerk.   e who took it by the bottom, & drank a little, & then walked, &c. Clerk.

in the morning, for the space of twelve dayes together; neither more, nor less. I pray thee remember my wordes, & observe, & doe them; but howsoever thou dost, above all things, fear God, & serve him. And for the space of these twelve days, thou must drink noe strong beer or ale. But afterwards thou mayest; a little, to suffice a *nature. And thou shalt see, through Gods great goodness &* .p.36. *mercy unto thee, before these twelve days be past, thy disease to be cured, & thy body* b *altered. I doubted the truth of these things, that they could do me small good. I said, Sir, be these good for all consumptions? He said, I tell thee remember my words, & observe to do them. But howsoever thou dost, above all things, fear God, & serve him. Then he said, friend, this is not all; thou must change the aire too for thy health. And I said, what mean you by saying that I must change the aire? He said, you must goe three, four, five miles, or more* c; *the further, the better. And there you must continue in the fresh aire by the space of one month. And thou must goe as speedily as thou possibly canst doe;* d *or else a very grievous fit of sickness will follow very suddenly; yet, through Gods great goodness & mercy unto thee* e, *thou mayest avoid this likewise. And thou shalt see, through Gods great goodness & mercy unto thee, & that before the month be up & within these twelve dayes* f, *that the cloaths which thou now wearest, thou shalt not be able to wear with ease* g. *I said, Sir, but if it may please the almighty God so far to enable me as to goe into our owne fields two or three times a day, will not that serve? He said, I tell thee it will not. For this aire, where the infection was taken, is not so properly good to cure the same disease. Therefore I pray thee remember my words, & observe, & doe them; but however thou dost, above all things, fear God, & serve him. I said, Sir, I had thoughts to be let blood, as weak a creature as I am? He said, no, friend; by no means possibly. For thou'lt see the great goodness of*

God unto thee, & that before the month be up, & within these twelve dayes, thy blood shall be as good as ever thou hadst it in thy life. But this observe, thy joynts will be weak as long as thou livest. I pray thee remember my words, & observe to doe them; but however thou doest, above all things, fear God, & serve him : So, friend, I must be going. So when I saw that he was a going MS.p.37. *indeed, I thought he might as well be an hungry as dry. So I said, Sir, if it please you to eat any bread & butter, or bread & cheese, you shall be very wellcome. For truly I am a very poor man, & have no other food in the house. For, if I had, you should have it, & wellcome. But he said, no, friend; I will not eat any thing: the Lord Christ is sufficient for me. Very seldome doe I drink any beer neither, but that which comes from the rocke* h. *So, friend, the Lord God of heaven be with thee. I said likewise, God in heaven be with you.* i *My condition was such at that time that the skin clave to my bones for want of flesh. It was parcht & dry; with a yellow skin & white scurf, upon it. Upon the fourth day* k *afterwards (when I was rising out of my bed) the aforesaid white scurfe came off of my bosome, & I wondred what it was? I rubb'd my hand upon my body, & the more I rubb'd my hand there, the more it came off. So that day, & that night, it all came off. The next morning, when I arose, I lookt upon my body : The yellow skin was dryed, which no body ever saw but I; & the same was broke into little scales, but a little bigger than the white scurfe was. So the yellow skin & white scurfe came both off together in three days time; & under them was a young tender skin all over my body, like as a young child born of his mother. And so, blessed be God, I grew every day in flesh more & more, untill that my cloaths (as the old man said unto me) were so little that I could not weare them with ease. And, blessed be God, I do continue both in*

a Strengthen nature, Clerk.　　b the frame of thy body, Clerk.　　c or if it be twenty miles off, Clerk.　　d after the twelve days are over, Clerk.　　e by doing this, Clerk.　　f ended, Clerk.　　g thy body will be grown so much, Clerk.

h I heard my own father once speak of this story to some Stanford neighbours, with this remarkable circumstance, that the old man should tell Wallis, that he almost never drank any thing but water, & that the water he drank was sometimes the water of St. Thomas's well. That well, said my father, was the well you know in such a place. I heard him describe the place, but being then very young, can only remember it was somewhere without Stanford on the east, not far from the Uffington road. I have since enquired of several persons, but they can none of them tell of any such well.　　i ' When Wallace saw him go out of doors, ' he went to shut them after him. But the old man returned half way into the entry again, ' & said, friend, I pray thee remember what I have said unto thee, & do it; but above all things, ' whatsoever thou dost, fear God, & serve him. And so they parted.' Clerk. ' Wallace adds, ' that he saw him pass along the street, some half a score yards from his door; & so he went ' in. But he was not seen by any body else, though some neighbours were standing at their doors ' opposite to the said Wallaces house.' Clerk. Now whereas Wallis here says no body saw the old man but himself, I understand him speaking to the best of his knowledge. For I was told by the Reverend Mr. Samuel Rogers now [1726] vicar of All Saints, in Stanford; that he once heard his father the late Mr. John Rogers affirm, that he heard the late lady Cust (who lived to a very great age) say, that she [being then a maiden, &] living at the black friers in Stanford when these things happened, walking forth to take the air [on Whitsunday evening, & returning homewards] met a venerable, comely old man, in his person & dress exactly the same as described by Wallis. Which is not impossible; only the day being rainy from morning to night, it is much any young lady should be abroad in the wet.　　k ' Within ' four days after Wallace had made use of the leaves aforementioned, there arose a scurfe upon his ' body, &, when that came off, under it a new skin, like that of a sucking child.' Clerk.

　　　　　　　　　　　　　　　　　　　　health

health & strength from day to day [a]. *The habit of the old man was as followeth* [b]. *His hatt was fashionable. His hair of his head was white, curl'd up to his hatt. His beard was white & broad. But a little hair upon both sides his cheeks; & of a fine ruddy complexion. His band but a little turn'd from his coller. His coat was of a purple couler,* MS.p.38. *button'd down to his waste. His britches of the same couler & cloth; all new to see to. His britches had no trimming at the knees. His stockens was very white; whether linnen, or jersey, I know not. His shooes was black, tyed with the same colour'd strings that his suit was. His hand was pure white. No gloves that I know of; nor cuffs that I saw. He had a white stick in his hand. The day was rainy, from morning untill night* [c]; *but he had not one spott of dirt upon his shooes or stockings, that I could perceive; or raine upon his cloaths.*

By me, Samuel Wallis.

[d] *It is a farther memorable thing here to sett downe the uncharitable censures of those that call themselves ministers of the gospell, as touching this occasion. Some say, that this old man was a witch; others, that he was a divell changed into an angell of light. (As if the divell would advise any man to serve God, & to trust in him!) disclaiminge all miracles as being ceased, & (as if God was limited) never considering the infinite mercy of the Omnipotent, in shewing himselfe miraculously in this atheisticall age, in which men think there is neither God nor divell, heaven nor hell, angell nor spirit, day of resurrection or day of judgment or account, which, if they did suppose, they would never dare to doe what is done dayly amongst us. And those ministers that shall deny the visible hand of God in this action, rather teach impiety than christianity. When our Saviour healed the leper, he commanded him to tell no man, but bad him goe & shew himselfe to the priests. Whereby it seems this sinn of infidelity hath been a sin of antiquity, as well formerly a-* MS.p.39. *mongst the Jewish priests (whom Christ desired to convert by his miracles) as now a-mongst the Christian, who believe not in the mercy or power of God, any further than what they, for gain, make godliness. To be shorte, the best we can think of such ministers as these, is to account of them at the best to be but as the Pharisees amongst the Jews, who said, that Christ cast out divells through Beelzebub the prince of the divells* [e].

CHAP. VIII. Such antient & more moderne monuments as are to be seen in & about Stamford & Stamford-Baron; as well without as within the said towne.

FROM the memorable things & accidents which have happened in this towne, I come now to write of the antient & more modern monuments, of & in the same.

There is an antient dike appeareth here & there in divers places betwixt Stamford & Lincolne; &, being obscured by ruinating time [f]; some miles from Stamford, some part of it appeares againe upon the north side of the towne betwixt Stamford & Brigcasterton, & comes almost to the town wall toward Peter-gate. But afterwards it appeares no more southward (for as much as I could ever perceive.) This is vulgarly called the high dike. But Cambden, in his Britannia, calls it, via militaris Romanorum; & brings it to Stamford in the same place I have here related it. *Licet nonnulla,* faith he, *antiquitatis indicia hic supersint, trajectumque, olim fuisse, via militaris Romanorum, quæ statim te ex oppido in Boream proficiscentem excipit, satis declaret: Gausennas tamen, quas non procul hic statuit Antoninus, fuisse fidem non faciunt.*

a ' By the end of the twelve days he was as heathful & strong as ever he was ; only this he says, ' that when he came to sit down, his knees would smite together ; so that he still found a ' weakness in his joynts, as was foretold him. He said also, that one day within the time pre-' scribed, by the solicitation of some friends, he drank a little strong drink, & immediately his ' speech was taken from him for the space of twenty four hours.' Clerk. b ' As for ' the description of this old mans person & habit, thus he related it. He was tall & antient. ' His hair as white as wool, &c. He wore a fashionable hat, & a little narrow band. His coat ' & hose [that is, his breeches] were both of a purple colour; his stockings pure white, &c.' Clerk. c ' as many remember'd.' Clerk. d Here Mr. Butcher begins a defence of Wallis to clear him from the charge of an impostor, an imputation from which it seems he was not altogether free. To acquit him wherefrom, Mr. Butcher was one of the properest persons in the world, himself then living in the town, knowing Wallis, &, by what he here says, shewing himself fully convinced of his innocence. And indeed I never heard that Wallis ever made this matter a pretence for asking alms, or drawing money, from them who came to see him, & to hear the circumstances of it from his own mouth ; which, in my opinion, very much helps to clear him. e If some ministers would not believe, there were others who had a different sense of this matter. For Mr. Clerk concludes, ' this [affair] being noised ' abroad, divers ministers met together at Stanford, to consider & consult about it ; &, for ma-' ny reasons, were induced to believe, that this cure was wrought by the ministry of a good an-' gel.' To which I shall only add here, there is yet another relation of this business under Wallis's own hand which Mr. Forster met with, & inserted in the close of his letter about the antiquities of Stanford to Mr. John Stephens, which other relation, containing divers passages not to be found in any of those here given, shall be inserted in its proper place, with such farther observations as I have met with. f being absconded by the ruins of time. MS.

Not

Sʳ David Philip's Monument in
Sᵗ Maries Church Stanford.

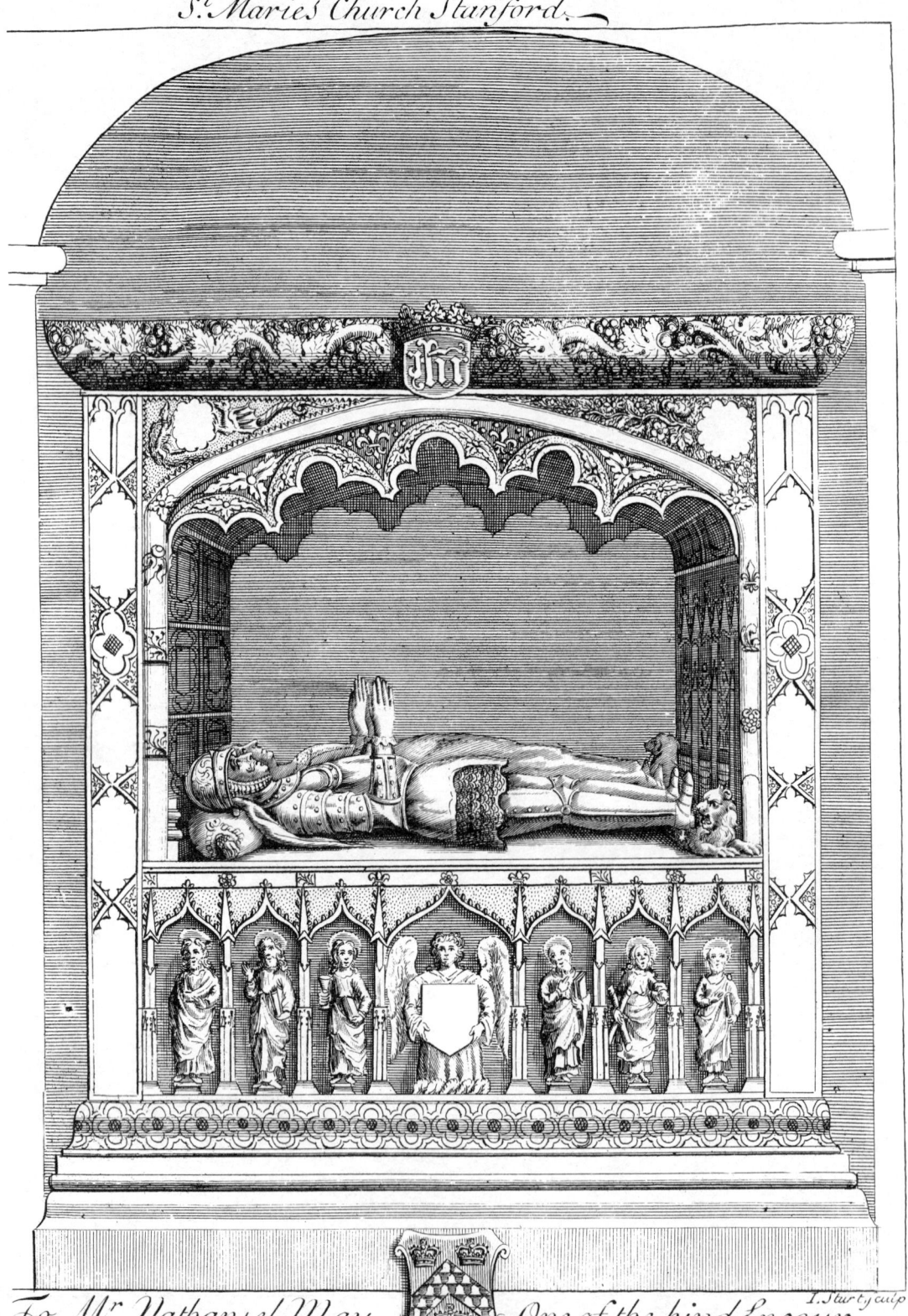

I. Sturt sculp.

To Mʳ Nathaniel May,   One of the kind Encour-
=agers of this work, this   Plate is most thankfully inscrib'd.

An Antient Monument in the North Wall of Corpus Christi Chappel in St. Maries Church.

Sturt sculp

To Mr. Thomas Richardson L.P.

One of the kind Encouragers of this Work, this

Plate is most thankfully inscribed.

Fletcher, page 17. B.

MS.p.40. Not farre from hence upon the north side of the town neer unto York highway, & about twelve score from the towngate which is called Clementgate, stands [a] an antient crosse of free stone of a very curious fabrick, having many antient scutcheons of armes insculped in the stone about it; as, the armes of Castile & Leon, quartered; being the paternall coat of the king of Spain; & divers other hatchments belonging to that crowne, which envious time hath so defaced, that only the ruins appear to my eye, & *are* therefore not to be *particularly* described by my pen. This crofs is called Queens crofs, & was erected in this place by K. Edward the first about the year 1293. The occasion of this erection was in memory of Elenor daughter to Ferdinand the third of that name king of Castile, & wife of the said K. Edward the first; a most religious, chast, & virtuous lady, who (as the story goes) when her husband was wounded with an invenom'd arrow at the warres in Palestine, with her own mouth suck'd the poyson out of the wound, & so healed her lord, when all his chyrurgions & physitians had left the wound for mortall. This Queen falling sick at Herdeby beyond Lincolne, there dyed the ninth of November 1290. & her corpes being brought from thence to be buried at Westminster, in every place where the same rested by the way *as it passed thither*, K. Edward the first, shortly after, caused, in memory of her, a sumptuous crofs of stone to be erected neer the place; some of which are standing & remaining (if not lately destroyed) till this day, as *namely* at Lincolne, Grantham, Stamford, Waltham, & Charing-crofse near unto Westminster which yet appeareth [b].

Of the reliques or footsteps of learning which do here shew themselves, are only two remaining. Namely, Brazen-nose-college, in the dissolved parish of St. Paule; & Black-Hall, part of which is now a bakehouse, in the possession of John Blithe in the parish of All Saints. When these were possessed with students it is not certaine, otherwise than by MS.p.41. *conjecture, to have been at what time the northerne men departed from Oxford, from those of the South, in the time of K. Edward the third; who did not continue here long, but were recalled back again to Oxford by the said king, as in the chapter last before I have declared.*

In St. Maryes *church.*

At the upper end of the middle quire, stands a monument, more curious for the workmanship, than for the matter whereof it is framed. Having no superscription nor

armes *about it*, to denote unto us who the party was that it was made for. *It appears to be some great person & his lady.* He lyeth in armour, cap of pee. The tradition is that he was a knight who went by the name of Sir Daniel [c] Philips, a great man for Henry earle of Richmond in the battle *of Bosworth* against the usurping tyrant Richard the third. But I suppose he was one of a higher rank, & of the blood royall. For, at his feet, there is a lyon couchant, &, round about the tombe, roses (the culler not *to be* perceived) supported by a grayhound & a dragon; being hatchments of honour appertaining to the crowne of England. *The portcullis, an hatchment belonging to the house of Somerset, which was a branch of the blood royall, appeareth also on the tomb.*

At the upper end of the middle quire, in the glasse window, did stand (before they were lately defaced) three scutcheons of armes. The first, gules, a fesse betwixt six crofse croslets de or; being the coat armor of Beauchamp sometime earle of Warwick. Likewise another coat, viz. argent, a fefse, between three crescents gules: which is the coat of Oagle of Pinchback in the county of Lincolne; from which family, as to me appeares, the Oagles, barons of the north, are descended; because these Oagles of Lincolnshire bear the paternall coat without difference. The third is, azure, a crofse fitched, between two eagles wings, or. In the middle window on the south side of the said church (before the same was defaced) stood the coat armour of Shelton of Norfolke, viz. Azure, a crofse or.

Upon the north side of the golden quire [d] of this church, in the wall of the same, is a monument *of a knight* lying in armor MS.p.42. cap a pe. But having neither scutchion nor superscription, saving, that in the glafse window neer to the same, there sometimes (& but lately) stood a shield of armes, sable, three lyons paws cupped & erected argent, armed gules; which coat belongs to the name of Usher, & this makes me to conceive that this party was of that family [e].

In the midst of the flore of the said golden quire, lies buried, under a fair stone of blew marble (plated very curiously with brafse work) William Hickman [f], sometime alderman of Stamford, who, at his own cost & charges, did gild over the roof of the said quire. The full pourtraiture both of him & his wife in brafse, did lately lie fixed upon the same stone.

At the upper, or east, end of the same gilded quire, there hangs upon the wall a table of armes, dedicated —— To the memory of

a Stood, MS. this shews the said crofs was destroyed between 1646. & 1660.   b which lately appeared, MS.   c David, MS. & this was his right name. He founded a chantry in this church.   d It was called the golden quire, from the gilded roof. e Here instead of, *but having neither scutcheon,* &c. to the end of the paragraph; the MS. leaves all this out, & substitutes ' his surcoat is a cheveron engrailed between three lyons paws ' couped & erected; whether Ushers, or some near unto the same, I will not determine.' Whence I am of opinion that the said coat, tho' now not to be seen either in the window or on the monument, was formerly to be seen on both.   f Hickham, MS. & this was his right name. The brafs work is now all torn up.

Frances,

Frances, the wife of Robert Slow, of this parish, Gent. second daughter of Sir John Burrel of Dowseby in this county, Kt. who departed this life the 31. of July, 1654.— *the armes above this inscription are, argent, a fesse gules, between three . . . . . charged with a cinquefoyne ermine, between two martlets spectant from the sinister to the dexter, or; by the name of Slow. Impaled to argent, a saltier gules, between four burr leaves slipped proper; upon a chief azure, a lyons head erased, langued gules, between two pickaxes or; by the name of Burrell.*

In St. Georges *church,*

In the upper window of the quire, are pourtrayed, kneeling (as in St. Georges chappell at Windsor) before the picture of that Saint, *K.* Edward the third, his queen, the prince of Wales, & Henry duke of Lancaster; all in their robes of the order of the garter. And in the windowes on each side *of* the said quire, are pourtrayed (according to the first institution) the first knights of that order that were made, kneeling in their garter robes, with their surcoats of armes: which order of *knighthood* was founded by the said *K.* Edward the third. The names of these first knights are *here* sett downe MS.p.43. in order *following.* Edward the third, *king.* Edward, prince of Wales. Henry Duke of Lancaster. Thomas earle of Warwicke. Captaine de Bouche. Raphe earle of Stafford. William de Monte-acuto earle of Salisbury. Roger de Mortimer, earle of March. John de Insula. Bartholomew Burwarsh. John de Bello-campo. John de Mohun. Hugh Courtney. Thomas Holland. John Grey. Richard Fitz-Symon. Miles Stapleton. Thomas Walle. Hugh Wrothesley. Nigellus Loring. John Chandois. John Audley [a]. Otho Holland. Henry Eme. Zachetus Dabridgcourt. William Paganell.

In the windowes of the said church in sundry places appear the coat armour of divers antient & noble families. *As,* there is the coat of earle Warenn the antient lord & owner of Stamford, checkie, or & azure. There is likewise the armes of Sapcoate, who bears, sable, a pidgeon coat erected argent. The armes of le Grosse, being, or, a cheveron betwixt three roses gules; is likewise placed in the lower window of the said church towards the south. There is likewise, in another window on the same side, the coat armour of Molineux of Haughton in the county of Nottingham, who bears azure, a crosse moline, quarter pierced, argent. *Likewise the coat of Baldwin Lord*

Wake, or, three torteauxes in chief, a fess gules. Which several monuments of armes were here placed [b], either in regard the bearers of them were benefactors to this church, or had lands & possessions in the same parish.

In All Saints *church,*

I observe not any monument of stone worth the noting [c], & very few monuments of armes in the windows. The armes of the town of Stamford, gules, three lyons passant or; impaled to *the coat of* earle Warenn, checky, or & azure; stand on the north side of the lowest window west. On the south side of the same window stand the armes of the merchants of the staple *of Calais* being, nebile of six pieces [d], argent & sable; a chief azure, charged with a lyon passant argent. My conjecture, *as* touching MS.p.44. the placing of these armes in this window is, that the said window was first built at the joynt charge of the towne & of William Brown, who was (as hereafter shall appeare) a great benefactor to this church; & a merchant of the staple. *Without the south porch of All Saints church, stands erected a tomb of free-stone, built by the author of this survey, under which lyes interr'd the body of Dorothy his late most virtuous wife, who dyed the 18. of Aug. 1653* [e]. For the parishes of

St. Johns & St. Michaels,

I doe not observe any monuments worth the noting, neither in the quires, bodies, or windowes of the said churches [f].

In St. Martins *church* in Stamford-Baron,

There is, at the upper end of the middle quire, a stately Mausolean monument, built in the memory of William Cecell lord Burghley, *&* lord treasurer of England; standing just over the vault in which his body lies interr'd [g].

Upon the north side of the north quire of the said church, against the wall, is erected a reasonable faire monument, in the memory of Richard Cecel esquire & Jane his wife (the father & mother of the said William lord Burghley.) *But* though the statue of the said Richard there stands, yet his body lies buried in St Margarets church in Westminster [h]. But the body of the said Jane lies in the vault by her said son William lord Burghley.

Both in the uppermost window of the quire of this church, & in many of the windowes & *elsewhere in the* stonework of the same, stands the paternall coat of Trigg, viz. Azure, two chevernels, or, betwixt three roses argent [i]. Whereby it seemes that the

---

a James Audley, MS.   b ' Which, with several other monuments of arms, were here ' placed, &c.' MS. There were indeed more; & it is a great pity Mr. Butcher did not take more notice of them.   c There were divers monuments of stone worth the noting here in Mr. Butchers time.   d Wavey of six bars, MS.   e This monument is long since quite destroyed.   f St. Johns church has yet some old monuments, & the windows (more entire in Mr. Butchers time) are yet full of curiosities. St. Michaels church has been almost covered on the floor with inscriptions & brass effigies, but they are now all torn up; tho' probably divers remained in Mr. Butchers time, if he would have been at the pains to have taken notice of them.   g His body can hardly be said to be interr'd; it standing in a stone cofin in the vault indeed, but altogether above the area or floor of it.   h If Mr. Butcher would have read the inscription he would have found he was buried in St. Georges church in Stanford.   i This is not the coat of Trigg, but of John Russel bishop of Lincolne.

ancestors

MS.p.45. anceſtors of that family have been good benefactors, as well to the windows as to the reſt of the fabrick of this church. *The fruits of the piety & charity of this family ſhew themſelves in many other reſpects, as well as here, in this place.*

There is in the ſame windowes, the coat armor of the Vincents, who were the antient lords of Barneck neer Stamford; being, azure, three grey hounds heads cupped, *two & one* or. Alſo the armes *of the right reverend father in God* Mathew Parker ſometime archbiſhop of Canterbury; being verte, three cunneyes argent, *two & one*, impaled to the armes of the archbiſhopbrick [a]. There is in the ſame windowes an antient coat of armes, attributed, by ſome heralds, to be born by Egbert a Saxon king; the field is Jupiter, a croſſe patence ſol. Which demonſtrateth the antiquity of this church [b], & the charity of the pious benefactors to the ſame.

But glaſs & ſtone in time decay,
Yet vertues fame ſhall laſt alway.

CHAP. IX. The names & pious deeds of ſuch as have been benefactors to Stamford, either to the corporation in generall, or to particular pariſhes in the ſame, with the ſeverall uſes of thoſe good deeds deſcribed.

IT now followes, that I here ſett downe the names of ſuch as have, from time to time, been benefactors to the ſaid towne of Stamford; generally, or particularly.

And, in the firſt place, I cannot but acknowledge that the lord & giver of all good gifts, the almighty God of heaven & earth, MS.p.46. hath not only inſpired many worthy & religious perſons, who, by their charity & almes-deeds, have, from time to time, & till the end of time, given allowance, either to the generall, or particular, members thereof; but alſo by his provident care (whereby all things doe ſubſiſt) with a preventing knowledge did poſſeſſe the firſt founders of this towne with ſuch a foreſight, that, for the better preſervation thereof to all poſterity, they ſcituated it in ſuch a place, that the moſt ſkilfull engineers, which, in theſe civill warrs, [c] have ſurveyed the ſame on both ſides, nor the plots or practices of thoſe who without judgment would have garriſoned it, could never find the way to make it a towne tenable either for offence or defence; which yet hitherto hath cauſed the ſame (though much weakened by the free quartering of paſſing & repaſſing of *troops & companies*) not to ſuffer ſuch miſerable ſpoiles as other neighbour cities & townes have undergone, by the taking & retaking of them on both ſides [d], to the utter ruine & deſtruction of the harmleſſe inhabitants. In which regard it were impiety in me, if I ſhould not acknowledge our great & good

God to be the prime & beſt benefactor to us at Stamford.

William earle Warenn, one of the antient lords of this towne, in the time of K. John, gave & granted to this towne, one place of buriall, containing five acres, without the eaſt gate [e] *of Stamford, to bury the dead bodies of excommunicated perſons, & to build there a chappell & houſe for poor brethren* [f]. *He alſo built & largely endowed the Auguſtine fryers* [g], *with the wall of this towne* [h], *& (as is conceived) moſt of the other monaſteries in & about the ſame* [i].

Nicholas de Farnham biſhop of Durham in the year 1247, *founded & endowed the priory of St. Leonards near Stamford, & dedicated it unto St. Cuthbert* [k], *& ordered it ſhould be a cell appertaining to the abby of Durham, endowing the ſame with a mannour & divers lands & tenements in & a-* MS.p.47. *bout Stamford; all, or moſt part, of which, are now parcell of the lands & inheritance of the earls of Exeter.*

K. Edward the fourth, *in the firſt year of his reigne,* upon the incorporating of this towne, gave the lands of Gowen Southerope, *being one ſhopp, thirty acres of land, three acres of meadow, & four acres of paſture,* which were confiſcated to the crowne *in the time of K. Edward the third,* to the alderman & burgeſſes of Stamford for ever.

William Brown, merchant of the ſtaple MS.p.48. & ſometime alderman of Stamford, erected

a The armes he took for archbiſhop Parkers were the armes of Rotheram archbiſhop of York. They are not three conies, but three bucks tripping.   b This church was rebuilt in Edward the fourths time, by the foreſaid biſhop Ruſſell & others. So that, as to the arms of Egbert ever being here, it is a meer fancy.   c in the late civil wars. MS.   d every ſide. MS.   e S. Pauls gate.   f What chapel & houſe this was I know not; except it were St. Logars abovementioned.   g The Auſtin friers were founded by one Fleming. But neither the Auſtin friers at Stanford, nor any other friery any where elſe, could, by the rule of their order, be endowed with any more lands, than the meer ſite of their monaſteries.   h William earle Warenn might poſſibly repair the walls of Stanford, probably ruined in the barons wars, when K. John gave him William de Albini's manor of Uffington for the better defence of his caſtle of Stanford.   i But I dont find that he founded any monaſtery in & about Stanford, except the hoſpital & chapel abovementioned in the time of the interdict.

k S. Leonards was founded, many hundred years before Nicholas de Farnham was born, by S. Vilfrid the elder biſhop of York. By the ſaid founder it was dedicated to St. Leonard, & made a cell to Durham. Whence, tho' we cannot ſay, with Mr. Butcher, that it was dedicated to St. Cuthbert, yet we may very well allow it was devoted to that Saint. Alſo Farnham might at this time procure the privileges of the houſe to be confirmed.

in 1493. the old beadhouse [a] there, called Browns beadhouse; incorporating the same of a warden, confrater, twelve poor old men, & one woman [b] for a nurse [c] unto them. *He* gave to the same the mannor of Swayfield, seven miles from Stamford, worth 400 l. per annum, besides divers great farmes, messuages, lands, & tenements (in Stamford, Pilsgate, Easton, North Luffenham, & other places) of good value. A very pious & liberall guift, though (the more is the pity) as many of the like nature are much abused by the avarice & misimployment of the governors thereof.

William Ratcliffe esquire, having been alderman of Stamford foure times, in 1530. gave all his messuages, lands, & tenements in Stamford, for the perpetual maintenance of a free-grammar-schoole in that towne. Which land, as it stands for the present improved, yeelds to the head schoolmaster & usher 30 l. per annum, or thereabouts. For the augmentation of which stipend, William Cecell late lord Burleigh, gave (or pretended to give) 4 l. per annum to the said schoole for ever, issuing out of a depopulated towne neare Stamford called Pickworth. But, in regard the heires of the said lord Burleigh (when they let the last leases of the said mannor of Pickworth for the better advancement of the fines) pretended to the tenants that they should hold their farms tythe-free; but no sooner were their leases made, sealed & delivered, when as the said heire presented a chaplaine of his owne to the parsonage thereof (the same having neither towne nor church standing, only the ruines of both appearing) so that the parson making good the title & tythes from the tenants, they have ever since refused to pay the said four pounds per annum, to the use of the said schoole.

The late most pious & gracious prince K. Edward the sixth gave the lands & tenements formerly belonging to the dissolved gild or fraternity of Corpus Christi in Stamford, to the alderman, & burgesses, & their successors for ever, which are worth to the town at present 160 l. per annum; being the greatest & chiefest revenue the town hath at this time in lands.

Mrs. Jane Cecell widow, in 1561. at her own coste & charges, leaded & paved the Fryday market crosse in Stamford.

In 1570. the north end of the town-bridge in Stamford, being born down by the violence of a great flood, was reedified at the cost & charges of William Cecell then lord Burghley. And good reason. For he & his heires do raise 100 l. per annum for the tollage of the said bridge; & out of the fayres & markets of Stamford.

Francis Trigge clerk, in 1585. gave 4 l. per annum for ever, to buy barley to make bread for the poor of Stamford.

George Trigge, Gent. in 1586. gave 400 l.

in money, to be lent out for ever upon good security, to poore young tradesmen & artificers of Stamford without interest.

MS. p. 49.

In 1588. The foresaid Mrs. Jane Cecell, by her last Will & testament, gave 50 l. to be lent out for ever without interest, to poor tradesmen & artificers in Stamford & Stamford-Baron; the same to be disposed of by certain feoffees nominated in her said will.

William lord Burghley in 1597. erected an hospitall at the south end of Stamford bridge (in a place where formerly stood a religious house [d], the lands & tenements whereof he obtained of queen Elisabeth) & gave a perpetual annuity to the said hospitall, issuing out of Cliffe-park near Stamford; for the maintenance of a warden & twelve poor men. The warden receiving 3 s. & 4 d. & each poor man 2 s. 4 d. weekly; with a yearly allowance of wood, & blew cloth to make each of them a gown. And the said lord Burghley did appoint the alderman of Stamford for the time being to have the nomination of foure of the said poor men, when any of the said places shall happen to fall void.

Richard Snowden clarke & parson of St. Johns in Stamford, by his last will in 1604. gave certain lands & tenements in Stamford for ever (after the decease of his wife) for seaven poore widowes of the age of 60 years & upwards. The profits whereof do afford each widow 7 d. a weeke, & a house to dwell in. And by the said will it is appointed, that the aldermen of Stamford for the time being, shall appoint them to their places when any of them shall fall void.

Jane Kesby, late of Stamford, widdow, the same year, by her last will, gave 8 l. for ever to be put forth to interest, & the profits thereof to go to the use of the poor of Stamford.

Sir Robert Wingfield, late of Upton in the county of Northampton knight (being one of the comburgesses of Stamford, & likewise one of the burgesses of the parliament *for the same towne*) the same yeere, obtained of K. James the pardon & remittance of two fifteenes [e] for Stamford & Stamford-Baron, amounting to the summe of 84 l. 8 s. 4 d. The same Sir Robert Wingfield in 1605. obtained pardon & remittance of the said K. James, for Stamford & Stamford-Baron, of six entire fifteenes [e], amounting to the summe of 254 l. 6 s.

In 1609. the right honourable Thomas late earle of Exeter, a right pious & charitable person, a man (as we of Stamford may say) fixed in his generation, as our Saviour Christ was in his passion, betwixt two, &c. gave a perpetuall annuity of 41 l. 1 s. 8 d. per annum, issuing out of certain lands *in*

---

a Bead-houses are so called, for that formerly the poor there used daily to say so many pater nosters, or other prayers, for the souls of the founders; at the end of every which prayer they used to drop a bead. A practice yet in use in the Roman church.   b two women. MS.
c nurses. MS.   d The hospitall of SS. John the Baptist & Thomas of Canterbury.
e Fifteenths.

the manor of *Deping* in Lincolnſhire, for the putting forth of poor children *to be apprentizes* (ſuch as ſhould be borne in the towne of Stamford) & towards other charitable uſes. Beſides, the towne *of Stamford* did often receive from him (whilſt it was bleſſed with his life) many great & beneficiall favours.

Hugh Allington, late of Tinwell in the county of Rutland eſquire, by his laſt will gave 40 l. for ever, to be lent to the poor artificers in Stamford & Stamford-Baron, without intereſt, by certain feoffees named in his ſaid will.

MS.p.50. Roger Manors *late* of Uffington in the county of Lincolne eſquire, by his laſt will, gave to the uſe of the poor of Stamford 20 l. for ever, to be put forth to intereſt; the profits whereof to be beſtowed in coles amongſt the ſaid poor yearly; by the diſcretion of the alderman for the time being.

The reverend & pious prelate Robert Johnſon late of North-Luffenham in the county of Rutland, B. D. archdeacon of Leiceſter, amongſt other his pious works to Stamford whilſt he lived, gave a bible of the largeſt ſize to paſſe from alderman to alderman, & to be laid on the aldermans cuſhion before him in the church every lords day, or at other times when he goeth to church.

Anthony Acham, Gent. by his laſt will gave 5 l. per annum for ever, to the uſe of the poor in Stamford.

Mr. Edward Wells gave a houſe which yields 3 l. 10 s. per annum, & three acres of land, to be pay'd to a petty ſchool-maſter in Stamford, to teach poor free mens children of that town to reade Engliſh.

In 1638. William Bevil, late of Cheſterton in the county of Huntingdon eſquire, by his laſt will gave to the uſe of the poore of Stamford 80 l. the intereſt whereof to be diſtributed amongſt the ſaid poor by the diſcretion of the alderman for the time being.

In 1647. David earle of Exeter, & Eliſabeth his beloved counteſs, gave between them 100 *l.* (to wit, 50 *l. apiece*) *the intereſt thereof for ever to buy bread for the poor of Stamford & Stamford-Baron.*

In 1655. *John Weaver eſquire, one of the comburgeſſes of Stamford & one of the burgeſſes repreſenting that borough in parliament, gave* 100 *l. for ever, to be lent out gratis to twenty of the pooreſt tradeſmen, artificers, & free-men of this corporation. To witt, to ten of them being tradeſmen* 6 *l.* 13 *s.* 4 *d. apiece; & to tenn of them being artificers* MS.p.51. 3 *l.* 6 *s.* 8 *d. He alſo gave twelve bibles to be kept at St. Maryes church at Stamford, & to be diſpoſed of by the clarke of the ſaid pariſh to ſuch ſtrangers as ſhould frequent the lecture there* [a]. *Alſo he gave a fair cuſhion*

to be laid before the alderman in his ſeat at church.

The right worſhipfull Sir Chriſtopher Clappham knight (now captain of the troop of volunteers in Stamford, *a Gent. of very high & antient extraction, a freeman & inhabitant of this towne, & a good benefactor to the ſame) when he was made free in* 1658. *gave to this towne* (to paſs from alderman to alderman) *a very large ſilver cupp; the armes of the towne inſculped on the one ſide, & on the other ſide his owne paternall coat of armes, viz. argent, a bend azure, charged with ſix flower de luvis's or, two, two, & two. The ſaid cupp is in weight thirty five ounces. As for the donor, he is a perſon liberall in hoſpitality, charitable to the poor, & loving to all. A forward & firm ſupporter of the towne liberties & immunities, & as great an adverſary againſt the diſturbers of the ſame. Yet, in point of reſpect & thankfulneſs he hath been uſed by us, as the Romans uſed Camillus & Coriolanus, or as the Athenians uſed Ariſtides & Themiſtocles.*

Benefactors to St. Maries *pariſh.*

William Hickham, alderman of Stamford in 1467. at his own coſt & charges built the gilded quire [b] on the north ſide of the chancell of the church. And both he & his wife lye buried under a fair ſtone of blew marble, as aforeſaid, in the midſt of the floor of the ſaid quire.

Mr. John Leiſe, one of the Comburgeſſes of Stamford, & late an inhabitant of this pariſh, gave twenty pound, the intereſt whereof to be for the repayers of the ſaid church.

Mr. John Weſt (citizen & butcher of MS.p.52. London, born in this pariſh) gave 4 l. to the ſaid pariſh, the intereſt of which is yearly to be beſtowed upon the poor of the ſame [c].

Mr. Richard Baniſter, late of the ſame pariſh, Gent. erected [d] at his owne *coſts & charges* in the ſouth quire, a publick library, & gave ſome books to the ſame, as Galens works, & ſome other bookes both of phyſick & chyrurgery. And at his death gave 10 l. [e] in money, the intereſt of which ſumme is yeerely to be beſtowed in books for the increaſe of the ſaid library, ſuch as the miniſter of that his pariſh ſhall think moſt fit.

Mr. Robert [f] Bullack, ſometime of this pariſh, was a good benefactor to the ſame, in ſetting the poor children (not onely of this pariſh, but of the towne in generall) at work to the knitting of Jerſey.

Robert Bullack [g], citizen of London, chyrurgeon, gave 3 l. to be added to the four pound his uncle John Weſt gave, for the uſe of the poor. The intereſt to buy

---

a This was when John Vicars was lecturer.
north chancel, & gilded the cieling of it.
book, was given in 1626. d He
tition to take in the ſouth chancel.
but I believe it ſhould be as above, Robert.

b He only built a new roof over the
c This mony, as appears by the pariſh
erected nothing but a few ordinary ſhelves & a partition
e This money is now loſt. f John. MS.
g Son, I ſuppoſe, of him above.

bread

bread the fabath afore & after Chriftide [a], yeerly for ever ; to be diftributed in the church to needfull poore, by the officers [b] of the faid parifh.

John Bullack *citizen* of London, butcher, gave 3 l. to make the forefaid feven pounds, ten pounds. And the intereft of the faid 10 l. to be given monthly *in bread* or at the difcretion of the elders [c] or churchwardens. *He was also a good benefactor to the fame parifh, (whilft he lived in it) in fetting the poor children (not only of this parifh, but of the towne & country about it) to work in knitting & fpinning of Jerfey ftockings.*

The aforefaid Robert Bullack [d], by his deed dated the 24. of July 1655. gave to the faid parifh of St. Mary in Stamford, the fumme of 50 l. for ever. To the end that the poor of the faid parifh, fhould have, out of the profits of the faid fumme, the value of two fhillings & fix pence weekly, during the fpace of twenty weeks yearly. The faid twenty four weeks to begin the firft Saturday after the feaft of St. Michael the archangell, & thence to continue for twenty four weeks following as aforefaid. The faid bread to be diftributed amongft the faid poor, according to the difcretion of the churchwardens & overfeers of the poor of the faid parifh.

Mr. Edward Robinfon, citizen & white-baker of London, gave 11 l. 6 s. 8 d. to the faid parifh, during the terme of certain yeers yet to come [e], in a leafe which he had at the time of his death, of the inne called the white horfe in Fetter-lane, London ; part of which faid fumme is to buy bookes for the faid library, & the reft to be for the repairing & adorning of the faid church.

One Mr. Greene, who lately [f] fojourned in this parifh, & here dyed, gave very liberally towards the building of a very faire pulpit [g] in this church, & towards a rich velvet pulpit cloth for the fame [h]. *And to add to this good work* Mr. John Marfhall, citizen & white-baker of London, gave 3 l. & Mr. Thomas Harrifon citizen & vintner of London gave 2 l. The faid mafter Harrifon gave likewife, for the ufe of the faid parifh, two pewter flagons (very fayre ones) for communion wine, & a pewter peece to carry the bread from communicant to communicant. Likewife he gave to the faid parifh, a gilt alcumy bafon to gather collections in the church, for the poor.

There is 6 s. 8 d. per annum, paid to St. Maries for the repayers of the church ; being the annual rent of a fhop in Stamford-Baron ; but who gave the fame to this church I cannot find.

MS.p.53.

To All Saints *parifh.*

William Brown, marchant of the ftaple, two hundred yeares or thereabouts now paft [i], at his own proper cofts built the fteeple [k] belonging to this church, being a very curious & excellent fabrick. Likewife he built a great part of the church it felf *& founded an almeshoufe in this parifh* [l], as I have formerly noted, for a warden, twelve poor men, & two matrons to look unto them. He endowed the faid almeshoufe with very large revenues, though the poor thereof receive but 2 s. 4 d. a week, out of five or fix hundred pounds a year, given for their maintenance. And both he & his wife lye buried in a chappel proper to his family, on the north fide of the faid church towards the quire [m].

The forefaid Mr. John Marfhall, citizen & white baker of London, gave 10 l. to this parifh, the intereft of which fumme to be given to the ufe of the poore of this parifh. Alfo the faid Mr. Marfhall gave twenty marks per annum for a weekly lecture in this parifh ; which, for a time was maintained ; but the lecture ceafing, the mony was, & ftill is detained [n].

Mr. John Denham gave 5 l. to this parifh, the intereft whereof yeerly to be to the ufe of the poor of the fame.

Mr. Robert Warner gave 5 l. to the faid parifh, the intereft to be to the ufe of the poor thereof.

William Fifher, late of Bourne in the county of Lincolne, Gent. gave fix pence a weeke for ever, to be given in bread, for the ufe of the poore of this parifh.

Mrs. Winifred Brown, wife & executrix of John Brown late of this parifh efquire, gave 10 l. the intereft of which fumme to be to the ufe of the poor of this parifh.

The lady Jane Buck gave the fumme of 20 l. to this parifh, the intereft of which is yeerely to be diftributed to the poor of the fame.

To St. Georges *parifh.*

Mrs. Jane Cecell widdow, mother to William lord Bur**gh**ley, gave 151. for ever, the intereft of which to be to the ufe of the poor of this parifh. MS.p.54.

John Chirme, late of Stamford-Baron, Gent. gave 20 s. per annum for ever to the ufe of the poor of this parifh, the fame to be payd to them every quarter.

The forefaid William Fifher gave to this parifh 12 d. a week for ever, to be diftributed to the poor of the fame in bread.

There is belonging to this parifh 7 l. per annum, being the rent of divers tenements in the fame ; but I cannot learne who gave the fame to this church.

---

a Sabath, Chriftide. Thefe were the phrafes of the times in 1646. in the MS, they are altered again to Sunday, Chriftmafs.   b Thefe officers are, in the next paragraph, called elders.
c Elders, omitted in the MS.   d Robert the fon, I guefs.   e 60 years to commence from 1623. Parifh book.   f about 1645.   g If it was the pulpit now ftanding, it never was a very extraordinary one.   h This pulpit cloth is now gone.   i Above two hundred years fince. MS.   k The tradition is, that not he, but his brother John Brown Efq; built the faid fteeple.   l Browns Hofpital is in St. Michaels parifh.   m Mr. John Brown was buried in the place here mentioned. Mr. William Brown was buried in the fouth chancell.
n Thefe words, which for a time, &c. are omitted in the MS. the lecture being fince reftored.

William Cave Efq. now living at the black-Fryers [a], in the fame parifh, gave 40 s. per annum for ever to the faid parifh, to provide bread & wine for a communion to be *ad*ministred upon the firft lords day of every month in the yeare.

To St. Johns *parish.*

The forefaid lady Buck gave 20 l. to this parifh, the intereft whereof to be yeerly diftributed amongft the poore of the fame.

There was a tenement given to the parfon of this parifh & his fucceffors for ever by Mr. George Trigge, upon this condition, that the faid parfon & his fucceffors fhould yeerly diftribute to the poore of this parifh the fumme of 20 s. *As for*

St. Michaels,

I cannot learne that there was ever any benefactor, either to the church, or to the poore of this parifh [b].

To St. Martins in Stamford-Baron,

The lady Dorothy Cecell gave lands for ever, of the yeerly value of 12 l. 5 s. 8 d. for the ufes following. That is to fay, part thereof to be payd to the putting forth of poore children of the faid parifh to be apprentizes. Another part to be weekly allowed to fome honeft perfon, who fhall teach the poore children of this parifh to read Englifh. Another part thereof for the

buying of wooll, flax, & hemp to fet both young & old poor people of this parifh to worke. Another part thereof to be allowed to fome honeft perfon to teach the faid poor people to work. And alfo twenty fhillings to be yearly allowed, out of the profits of the faid land, to the vicar & churchwardens of this parifh, for them to joyn with the over-feers of the poor, to fee the faid poor kept at work. And that the overplus, if any be, fhall be beftowed weekly upon the poorer fort, who (though endeavouring themfelves) are not able to find themfelves by their labours. *MS.p.55.*

The forefaid lady Bucke gave 20 l. to this parifh, the intereft of the fame to bee yeerly diftributed among the poore of the faid parifh.

Jane Sallet, fpinfter, lately deceafed (& borne in this parifh) gave a rent of 11 s. 8 d. per annum for ever, to be paid to the churchwardens, upon Monday in Eafter week, that is to fay, 6 s. 8 d. (part thereof) for one fermon to be preached on the fame day in this parifh church, & 5 s. (the remainder of the faid fumme) to be diftributed, by 4 d. a piece, to fifteen poor people of this parifh.

Lord fend us mercy, truth, & peace,
That benefactors may increafe;
That, when a new [c] editions made,
More pious people I may adde.

Chap. X. *A relation of fuch as are, & have been, not only evil-doers, but evill-fayers in & againft this towne* [d].

*T*HERE is neither perfon nor body, take it either naturall or politick, but hath malicious & faithlefs evill-willers, as well as faithfull friends & good benefactors. Therefore having already fett downe particularly fuch, as, by their gifts & deeds of charity, have, from time to time, done good to this corporation; I have thought it not to deviate from my theme in hand, in a more generall manner, to declare & expreffe the malefactors of the fame.

MS.p.56. We may fuffer wrong from our enemies, either evill deeds or evill words, either fpiritually or temporally; in both which kinds this towne hath been, & is, a great patient. Breeding & feeding fuch viperous members in the fame, as have, & ftill endeavour, to gnaw out her bowels, with the envious teeth of fuch malice, diftraction, & divifion, as reflects not only upon the temporall, but alfo upon the fpirituall parts thereof.

The vulgar demonftrate the divell by his cloven foot. Which, though a vulgar demonftration, yet is not to be accounted amongft vulgar errors. For in the fame is couched a good pithie & morall meaning. Setting forth thereby faction, fedition, difcord, confufion & divifion; of which foule enormities the divell himfelf is the founder & author.

Hiftory's afford us many & various examples of empires, kingdoms, cittyes, & corporations that have been undone, made defolate, & deftroyed, by fuch whelps of the divells kennell; & that (which is none of the fmalleft of our judgments) thofe men which profefs themfelves preachers of the gofpell of peace, have been feeds-men of fedition, faction, & divifion amongft us, & the fource from which the nature of thefe humours & all other things which difturb the government of all civil focieties, do take their nutriment. This was it which held Rome difunited, & this (if I may compare fmall things with great) is that which continues Stamford divided.

To omit thofe that have abufed their truft, in deceiving the corporation of the chiefeft flower in the garland of fuch a fociety (I mean the royalty & fee farme thereof [e].) And alfo to omit thofe that, whilft they reprefented the whole body, have tyrannifed over many of the particular members, by falfe fuggeftions & feigned informations. And likewife thofe that have endeavoured to rob the towne of fuch things as their pious anceftors have given unto it; I will only here infift upon thofe, who, not only by evill-doings, but alfo by factious fayings, have made a breach

---

a Now deceafed, but fometime living at the black-fryers. MS. indeed many benefactors to either, but I have met with fome to both.

b There were not

d There is not a tittle of this chapter in either of the printed copies. paragraph of Mr. Butchers third chapter above.

c third edition. MS.

e See the laft

& diviſion amongſt the members of this body.

MS.p.57. About the year 1624. this towne was well eſtabliſhed, ſettled, & diſpoſed to peace & unity in it ſelfe, & ſo might have ſtill continued to this day, had it not been for ſome majeſtrates, who, out of vain-glouriouſneſſe & to have their golden mace borne before them to church (more for a proud oſtentation to the people, than any humility to the ſceptre) brought into the church of St. Maryes in this towne, a preacher, young in years, & a preacher of as young & new doctrine; by which, in a ſhort time, he made ſedition an act of religion, by ſetting a diviſion between man & wife, father & child, maſter & ſervant. So that from a former neighbourly love & converſation, the people came to be divided into faction & vexation one againſt another; thoſe of the moſt ſeeming ſort of holy men, rejoycing at the ruine & deſtruction of thoſe of contrary judgments; paſſing uncharitable cenſures upon events, & boldly (if not blaſphemouſly) expounding the actions of the moſt high [a].

This wicked ſeed thus ſowne, the unhappy cropp thereof doth daily ſpring up amongſt us; & that by a worſe & more corrupted increaſe of naughtineſs, than was the ſeed of naughtineſs that ſowed it. For theſe more moderne miniſters, or miniſhers (as I may call them) abuſed (if not the word) the ſacraments (like Lucians dogg) forbearing to miniſter the ſame to any that would gladly receive, but to thoſe they call their gathered congregations; yet to thoſe, not according to the forme of our Saviour, nor the inſtitution of the primitive church. Likewiſe, ſeeking more their own vain-glory than the true glory of God, they oppoſe their betters from preaching, or officiating, within the precincts of this corporation; leaſt it ſhould happen, that contraria juxta ſe oppoſita magis

eluceſcerent [b], ieaſt others knowledge ſhould betray their ignorance. And though theſe men want much of the Jeſuits learning, yet in the practice of their lives, by their imitation of them, they would ſeem to be their apes. For the popes in Rome, the cardinals in their conclaves, & the Jeſuits in their colledges (or any where elſe in all the world) meddle not ſo much in the affaires of temporall goverment, as theſe men doe in great townes & corporations, into which, through all England, they ſtrive to intrude, in chuſing knights & burgeſſes for the parliament; MS.p.58. in directing majeſtrates & juſtices of the peace in their ſeſſions & goale deliveries; in procuring reprieves & pardons for condemned malefactors whom they favour; & in getting hangmen for ſuch as they hate. And are not aſhamed to affirme, that let a miniſter ſay, or doe, what he pleaſeth, yet the lay power ought not to puniſh any authority upon him. So that I wonder what the popiſh clergy can ſay, or doe, more than theſe men!

I have heard of a skilfull fowler, who, to bring the innocent birds into his ſnare, framed a device with a pole. He made divers holes in it, in which he placed many twiggs in the forme of a buſh, which he dawbed all over with bird-lime, &, at the lower part of this buſh, he placed a living owle. The birds, according to their nature, in admiration of this ſo ſtrange a creature, in great numbers flock to this buſh, & are taken in theſe lime-twiggs, & deſtroyed by the fowler. The fowler is the divell, who hath placed in a platt (not proper for ſuch) the owles of falſe prophets, hatched in the neſt of ſelfe-intereſt. To the admiration of ſuch monſters, ſilly & ignorant chriſtians reſort, & are taken in the lyme-twiggs of confuſed ambition, ſchiſmaticall & erroneous opinions, to the ruine & deſtruction of their ſouls for ever.

CHAP. XI. The antient & publick ſports of Stamford.

AS touching the antient & publike ſports uſed at this town they are not many; in all but two: & too many by one. The one a ſport ſavouring *both* of manhood & gentry; a concourſe of noblemen & gentlemen, meeting together in mirth, peace, & MS p.59. amity, for the exerciſe of their ſwift running horſes *kept for the race* every thurſday [c] in March. The prize they run for is a gilt & ſilver cup with a cover, to the value

of ſeven or eight pounds, provided by the care of the alderman for the time being. But the money is rayſed out of the intereſt of a ſtock formerly made up by the nobility & gentry who are neighbours or wellwiſhers to the towne.

The ſecond ſport, though more antient than the former, yet more beaſtlike than any: it is their bull-running. A ſport of no pleaſure, except to ſuch as take a

a This chapter would appear to the reader, as it long did to me, very unintelligible, were I not to inform him that ſome ten years ago, as I was turning over a parcel of old papers at a friends houſe at Stanford, I there met with five & twenty ſheets of paper, the firſt four containing divers ſtrange poyntes of doctrine delivered in St. Maries church in Stanford by John Vicars, clerk, as they were ſent up to the kings attorney general in 1629. the reſt the examination of witneſſes (of which witneſſes our author Mr. Butcher is one) upon the ſaid articles. They are all in MS. & every article ſigned by the ſeveral perſons there depoſing with their own proper hands. When I come my ſelf to write of ſuch things as happened in 1629. I ſhall there give the ſum of this monſtrous charge, whereby the reader will ſee how much reaſon Mr. Butcher had to expreſs himſelf as he does, & how juſtly the character of the young miniſter here given in every particular agrees with the behaviour of the ſaid Mr. Vicars; which may alſo ſerve as one inſtance more of that ſtrange ſpirit which afterwards ſpread it ſelf thro' the whole nation, and overturned all that was ſacred.   b Contraries are beſt diſtinguiſht by their contraries.

c the laſt Thurſday. MS.

pleaſure

pleasure in beastliness & mischief. It is performed just the day six weeks before Christmass. The butchers of the towne, at their own charge, against the time, provide the wildest bull they can get. This bull, over night, is had into some stable or barne belonging to the alderman. The next morning proclamation is made by the common bell-man of the town, round about the same, that each one shut up their shops, doors, & gates, & that none, upon payne of imprisonment, offer to do any violence to strangers. For the preventing whereof (the towne being a great thorough-fare, & then being term-time) a guard is appointed for the passing of travellers through the same, without *any hurt or molestation. And that none have any iron upon their bull-clubs, or other staffes which they pursue the bull with.* Which proclamation made, & the *shops &* gates all shut up, the bull is turned out of the aldermans house, & then hivie, skivie; tag, & rag; men, women, & children of all sorts & sizes, with all the dogs in the town, promiscuously run after him, with their bull-clubs spattering dirt in each others faces, that one would think them to be so many furies started out of hell for the punishment of Cerberus, as when Theseus & Pirithous conquered that place (as MS.p.60. Ovid describes it)

> A ragged troupe of boyes & girles
> Doe pellow him with stones;
> With clubs, with whips, & many nips,
> They part his skin from bones.

And (which is the greater shame) I have seen both senatores majorum gentium & matrones de eodem gradu, following this bulling business.

I can say no more of it, but, only to set forth the antiquity thereof. As the tradition goes, William earle Warenn the first lord [a] of this town in the time of K. John,

standing upon his castle walls in Stamford, viewing the fair prospect of the river & meadowes under the same, saw two bulls fighting for a cow. A butcher of the towne, the owner of one of these bulls, with a great mastiffe dog accidentally coming by, set his dog upon his owne bull; who forced the same bull up into the towne, which no sooner was come within the same, but all the butchers dogs, both great & small, followed in the pursuit of the bull, which (by this time made starke mad with the noise of the people, & the fiercenesse of the dogs) ran over man, woman, & child that stood in the way. This caused all the butchers & others in the town to rise up as it were in a tumult, making such a hideous noise that the sound thereof came into the castle into the eares of earle Warenn, who presently thereupon mounted on horseback, & rid into the town to see the businesse; which then appearing (to his humour very delightfull) he gave all those meadowes in which the two bulls were at first found fighting (which we now call the castle meadowes) MS.p.61. perpetually as a common to the butchers of the town (after the first grasse is eaten) to keepe their cattle in, till the time of slaughter: upon this condition, that as upon that day on which this sport first began (which was, as I said before, the day six weekes before Christmass) the butchers of the towne should, from time to time, yearely for ever, find a mad bull for the continuance of that sport. An ominous thing to the towne! for some of the same (of his succession, though not of his descent) have since, upon their hornes of greatnesse, tossed the best of the burgesses out of their gownes. And why? Because the burgesses were not foxes; otherwise they would not have suffered themselves to have been so abused by such bulls, whose eares were longer than their hornes. And so much for the sports of Stamford.

CHAP. XII [b]. *A list of the names & succession of the aldermen of the gild [c] in Stamford (before the time of the first incorporateing of the same by letters patents) in order, according to the year of our Lord in which each of them governed.*

THERE is no doubt, & it is past all question, that all the antient cittyes & boroughs in England, which have their respective voices in parliament, have had, from the first foundation of them, appointed by the founders, rulers & governours of their owne inhabitants; which, from yeare to yeare, they chose amongst themselves: so that time brought in custome, & that custome, in time, grew to a prescription.

The Brittaines (the first that planted in this island, & that laid the first foundations of all the antient citties & burroughs in the same, & reduced it to a civill government) gave laws to those of their then new plantation, which continued to be used in those cittyes & great townes, all the time of the Brittish rule, & run, in the same form of MS.p.62. prescription, through the times of the Romans, Saxons, Danes, & Normans; which severall conquerours permitted to the said places, the usage & customes of their antient lawes, government & governours. Yea London itselfe, at the entrance of the Normans, was

---

[a] Being lord. MS.   b There is not a tittle of this chapter in either of the printed copies.   c There were divers gilds in Stanford, each of which gilds was governed by its own alderman. But I dont find that the alderman of any of those gilds ever governed the town of Stanford, *quatenus* alderman of that gild; tho' sometimes perhaps it might happen that one & the same man was, at the same, time alderman of Stanford & also alderman of some gild there.

ruled

ruled by a prescriptive power, by the name of portgraveshipp, unto which the conquerour added a confirmation, by way of charter, in these words.

William king greeteth William bishopp & Godfrey portgrave, & all the burgesses within London, French & English. And I grant that they be all of their law-worth, that they were in Edwardes dayes the king. And I will that each child be his fathers heir. And I will not suffer any man to do you wrong. And God keep you.

Afterwards divers successive kings of this land granted to sundry cities & great townes in England, new privileges & immunities, but alwayes with a reference to the confirmation of their uses & practices of more antient times, as I have formerly observed in the first charter that K. Edward the fourth granted to Stamford, concluding those his new grants with these generall words, ut ab antiquo usi fuerunt.

I have formerly noted how this towne was governed by a prescriptive magistrate (long before K. Edward the fourths charter) whom we here called the alderman of the gild. But records being ill kept, & rebellious & troublesome times happening (by which meanes the towne was consumed by fire, & consequently many of the antient records lost & imbezzeled) the names of many of these antient magistrates do not appear; yet neverthelesse by the discovery of George Hill, Gent. (my very good friend & steward of this towne) by a roll in his hands [a], appears to the number of sixty of those aldermen, which successively ruled this towne by

MS.p.63. *prescription, before the charter of K. Edward the fourth made to George Chapman, &c. whose names & times of government here in order follow.*

[b] *Henry the fourth began his reign Sep. 29. 1399. & in 1401. the third year of his raigne was*

Garvis Wykes, first alderman of Stondford [c]
1402 *Stephen Maxey, Bis.*
1403 *Robart Lockesmith*
1404 *Johan Standby*
1405 *Thomas Storme*
1406 *Thomas Spicer*
1407 *Raphe Harwood*

1408 *Johan Palfreeman, Bis.*
1409 *Raphe Browne*
1410 *Johan Stacy*
1411 *Alexander Hains*
1412 *Robart Locksmith*
1413 *Thomas Basset*
1414 *Johan Browne, draper*
1415 *William Locksmyth*
1416 *Johan Stonbe*
1417 *Johan Palfreeman*
1418 *Alexander Marcer*
1419 *Johan Allcocke*
1420 *Andrew Draper.*
1421 *Thomas Basset*
1422 *Johan Browne, draper*
1423 *Thomas Raffe*
1424 *Thomas Spicer*
1425 *Johan Palfreeman*
1426 *Johan Whitesade*
1427 *Johan Browne, draper*
1428 *Robert Bendbore*
1429 *Thomas Basset*
1430 *Thomas Spicer*
1431 *Johan Longe*
1432 *Johan Page*
1433 *Richard Lee*
1434 *Laurans Melton*
1435 *William Browne 1.*
1436 *William Marwood*
1437 *Richard Lee*
1438 *Luwrans Melton*
1439 *William Morwood*
1440 *Richard Lee 2.*
1441 *Robert Browne, glover.*
1442 *William Storton*
1443 *Thomas Bulksaye*
1444 *William Browne*
1445 *Johan Page*
1446 *Richard Lee*
1447 *Laurance Melton*
1448 *Johan Browne*
1449 *William Browne 2.*
1450 *William Storton*
1451 *Richard Blogwin*
1452 *Thomas Gregory*
1453 *Johan Browne*
1454 *Laurance Melton*
1455 *Johan Gregory*
1456 *Johan Page*
1457 *William Hickame*
1458 *William Storton*
1459 *Thomas Gregory*
1460 *William Browne*

a This roll came afterwards into Mr. Forsters hands, & is now in mine.

b All the copies I have seen of Mr. Butchers MS. being very faulty, I here chuse to follow the roll it self.

c If Mr. Butcher had regarded the roll with any care he would not have called them aldermen of the gild, whom the roll it self here calls aldermen of Stondford. Garvis Wykes is here called, first alderman of Stondford, as I suppose he was first alderman by some charter granted by K. Henry the fourth. For that there were aldermen of Stanford long before the 3. of H. 4. will appear by the course of my collections. Also it is as evident that this roll it self once reached higher, the holes of the needle wherewith another piece was formerly stitched to the top of it, being now plainly to be seen. Besides, after the name of Stephen Maxey, the next alderman is added, *bis*; which shews he was alderman of Stondford once before. And so it seems was Johan Palfreeman who has the same word *bis* after his name, the first time it is mentioned. This roll reaches down to the end of the year 1628. & the first sixty names here mentioned I believe were copied from some old town-book now lost. For the name John, always written Johan, almost demonstrates it was copied or extracted from some account wrote in Latin, as a part of the town books antiently were, & now are.

CHAP.

MS.p.64. **CHAP. XIII.** A Lift of the names & fucceffion of the aldermen of Stamford (fince the time of the firft incorporating of that towne by *K. Edward the fourths* letters patents) in order, according to the yeare of our Lord in which each of them governed.

1. 1461 George Chapman, *firft alderman of the corporation of Stamford* [a].
1462 Johan Browne, Efq;
1. 1463 John Gregory
1. 1464 William Hickame
not. not. not. [b]
1. 1465 Robert Hance, *fecond aldermaine.*
1. 1466 William Browne, Efq.
2. 1467 William Hickame
2. 1468 George Chapman
1469 Thomas Kefteven
2. 1470 William Browne, Efq.
2. 1471 Johan Gregory
2. 1472 Robert Hance
1473 Johan Neylle
1474 Alexander Tyard
1475 Johan Gibbes
1. 1476 Johan Diccane, Efq.
1. 1477 Henry Cooke, *efquire, fervant to K. Edward the fourth; the which king gave the firft charter to the towne of Stamford* [c].
1478 Robert Skynar
3. 1479 William Hickame
3. 1480 George Chapman
3. 1481 Robert Hance
1. 1482 Chriftopher Browne, Efq.
2. 1483 Johan Dickane, *bis, ut patet in lib.* [c] Efq;
1484 David Malpafe
1485 John Stede
1486 Thomas Kefteven
2. 1487 Henry Rooke [d], Efq. *died alderman & in his ftead . . . .* [e]
1488 Johan Frebarne
1. 1489 Thomas Philip
1490 William Gaywood
2. 1491 Chriftopher Broune, Efq. } *not in the*
1. 1492 Nicolas Bilfeden, } *bookes* [f].
3. 1493 Johan Diccans, Efq.
1. 1494 Thomas Edward, Efq.
1. 1495 William Ratliffe, Efq.
1496 John Clepole
1497 Richard Cannell
1498 Robert Craine
2. 1499 Thomas Philip
1500 Geffry Hampton
2. 1501 Nicolas Bilfedon
3. 1502 Chriftopher Broune, Efq.
2. 1503 William Ratliffe Efq.
1. 1504 David Cecyll, Efq.
1505 Nicolas Trigge, Gent.
1. 1506 Thomas Lacie, Gent.
1. 1507 Johan Cab
1. 1508 Johan Hargrave
1509 Johan Tyard
1510 Richard Waftlen, Efq.

1511 Robert Martindale
3. 1512 William Ratliffe Efq.
1. 1513 Johan Ley, Gent.
1514 William Rankell
2. 1515 David Cecill, Efq.
2. 1516 Johan Cobe
1517 Water Feyrday [g]
1. 1518 Moris Johnfon
1. 1519 Thomas Croffe
1520 Johan Thomas, *the duke of Buckingham beheaded.*
2. 1521 Johan Hargrave, Efq.
1. 1522 Henry Lacy, Gent.
4. 1523 William Ratcliffe, Efq.
4. 1524 Johan Ley, Gent.
1. 1525 Andrew Gant, *Canne, in Butcher.*
1526 Edward Browne, Efq.
3. 1527 David Cecill, Efq.
2. 1528 Moris Johnfon
3. 1529 Johan Hargrave, Efq.
2. 1530 Thomas Croffe
3. 1531 Johan Ley, Gent.
2. 1532 Henry Lacy, Gent.   MS.p.65.
1. 1533 Thomas Watfon
1534 Richard Ingham
1. 1535 Roger Beylle
1536 Thomas Gedney, *a rebellion in Lincolnfhire* [h].
1537 Robert Haver, *another in Yorfhire* [h].
2. 1538 Andrew Game, *Canne, in Butcher.*
3. 1539 Moris Johnfon
3. 1540 Henry Lacy, Gent.
2. 1541 Thomas Watfon
1542 Johan Fenton
1. 1543 Johan Allen
2. 1544 Roger Beile
1545 William Button
1546 Robert Winwicke
1. 1547 Nicolas Willis
1548 Henry Ley, Gent. *a rebellion in Denfhire & in Norfolk* [h].
1549 William Myles
3. 1550 Thomas Watfon, *a fweating ficknefs* [h].
1551 Andrew Scarre
1552 Johan Fenton, *here entred Q. Mary* [h].
1. 1553 William Campinet, *Wyats rebellion* [h].
1. 1554 Raphe Harroppe
1555 Henry Tampian
2. 1556 Nicolas Willes, *draper.*
1557 Francis Thorneffe, *inholder.*
1. 1558 Johan Houghton, Gent.
1559 Johan Ridalle, *glover.*
1560 William Bagoole, *dyer.*
1. 1561 Henry Hinman
1562 Thomas Beyle
2. 1563 Raphe Berrope, *inholder.*
2. 1564 William Campinet, *draper.*

a So in the roll which I chufe to follow.   b Thus in the roll.   c Roll.
d Cooke. Butcher.   e Roll.   f Roll. There are divers empty leaves in the town books for thefe three years, & no entries of the aldermens names, or any other officer, or bufinefs for that time.   g Water Feyrday is omitted in Mr. Butchers copy, print & MS. but it was an overfight of him or his tranfcribers.   h So in the roll.

1. 1565 Godfre Dawson, *butcher.*
2. 1566 Johan Haughton, *gent.*
   1567 Gregory Burton, *baker.*
   1568 Alexander Anthony, *mercer.*
1. 1569 Reynold Harrison, *mercer, a commotion in the north.* [a].
2. 1570 Henry Hinman
   1571 John Backehouse, *draper.*
   1572 Richard Barton, *butcher.*
   1573 William Lacy, *gent.*
   1574 Johan Hawkings
3. 1575 Johan Haughton
3. 1576 William Campinet, *draper.*
2. 1577 Godfrey Dawson, butcher.
1. 1578 John Elmes, *gent.*
   1579 Richard Evelie
   1580 John Wimbleby, *mercer.*
2. 1581 Reynold Harrison
4. 1582 Johan Houghton
1. 1583 Richard Sute, *atturney.*
1. 1584 Robert Medowes, *mercer.*
1. 1585 William Clarke, *glasier.*
   1586 Laurence Wilseby
1. 1587 Toby Loveday, *glover.*
   1588 Anthony Gunstone, *appothecarie.*
   1589 Robert Langton, *shoomaker.*
1. 1590 Robert Ramsdale, *mercer.*
2. 1591 ⎱ Richard Sute, *an atturney in the law.*
3. 1592 ⎰
   1593 William Watson, *bruer.*
2. 1594 Robert Medowes, *mercer.*
   1595 Cuthbert Grenebirie, *butcher; who died before the yeare was expired, & in his place was elected Mr. William Clarke glasier, by a particular, but not by a generall consent; namely, by the comburgesses, but not by the commoners: & so hee held the place untill the yeare was expired, & then was hee elected by a generall consent for the yeare following* [b].
2. 1596 William Clearke, *glasier.*
2. 1597 Lionel Featherston, *inholder.*
   1598 Nicolas Lamb, draper, *elected by the greatestpart of the burgesses, but not of the comburgesses, whereby grew great contention amongst them, with no small expences in . . . . . .* [b].
2. 1599 John Elmes, gent. *In this year some base people had raised some notorious scandalls against Meadows & Ramsden, two of the comburgesses; but those things coming to be examined by commissioners, appointed for that purpose, to witt, Mr. Allington, Mr. Wingfield, Mr. Lambert, & Mr. William Bodenham; & they appearing to be falsely accused, & those things maliciously suggested, the two comburgesses were cleared, & the wicked detractors punished* [b].
3. 1600 Robert Medowes. *The 23. of February in this yeare, the earles of Essex, Southampton, & Rutland,*

were proclaimed traitors, at the market cross in Stamford [c].

2. 1601 Toby Loveday, *glover.*   MS.p.66.
1. 1602 William Saulter, *an atturney. K. James entred March 24* [d]. *This year K. James, at his first coming into England, was attended into this towne by the alderman & his breethren on horseback, in their purple gownes; each one riding on his foot cloth, & the second company every man in his gowne* [e].
   1603 Reignald Waters, *physitian, in whose time there was great mortality, through a great plague which then was in Stamford* [e]. *The plague began in Stamford the 10. of October, by the space of one year & upward, in which time died of it 713* [f].
2. 1604 William Saulter, *atturney. Towards the end of his yeare an assesment was made for the river* [g].
3. 1605 William Clarke, *glasier.*
   1606 John Loveday, *glover.*
2. 1607 Robert Ramsdale, *mercer.*
1. 1608 John Browne, *gent.*
2. 1609 Lionel Featherstone, *inholder.*
1. 1610 Thomas Jackson
1. 1611 Robert Whatton
   1612 Francis Cole
   1613 Robert Fawcett
3. 1614 Toby Loveday
   1615 Thomas Watson, *gent. Summersets fall* [h].
   1616 Toby Aslocke. *In his time the new river began* [i].
1. 1617 Edmund Corker, *in his time . . . .* [i].
3. 1618 William Saulter, *atturney. Q. Anne died* [i].
2. 1619 John Browne, gent.
2. 1620 Thomas Geason
2. 1621 Thomas Jackson
2. 1622 Robert Whatton. *Prince Charles returned out of Spaine* [i].
1. 1623 Peter Fulwood
1. 1624 Henry Rastell, gent. *K. James died* [i].
   1625 Vincent Hall. *A troublesome parliament* [i].
   1626 Henry Death, gent.
2. 1627 Nicolas Lambe, *draper, in his yeare . . . . . .* [i].
2. 1628 Peter Fulwood [k].
2. 1629 Edmond Corker
1. 1630 Richard Wolphe
   1631 Vincent Hall
   1632 John Atton
1. 1633 Edward Cammocke
   1634 Thomas Palmer
1. 1635 Abraham Falkener
   1636 Henry Eldred
2. 1637 Henry Rastell, gent.
   1638 Richard Wolphe
   1639 Leonard Cole
1. 1640 Jeremy Cole

a So in the roll.   b Roll.
e Butchers MS.   f Roll.
i Roll.   k Here ends the roll

c Butchers MS   d Roll.
g Butchers MS.   h Roll.

1641 Richard Langton, gent. *In this year the plague began in this towne, & in half a year there died of it, 5 or 600.*
1. 1642 Robert Cammocke
2. 1643 Edward Cammocke
1644 Vincent Hall
1. 1645 Richard Dannalte [a].
1646 *Robert Fawcett*
1647 *John Bullock*
2. 1648 *Jeremy Cole*

2. 1649 *Robert Cammocke*
1. 1650 *James Langton*
1. 1651 *John Palmer*
1652 *Abraham Faulkner*
1653 *Edward Johnson*
1654 *Robert Wilson*
2. 1655 *Richard Danalt*
1656 *Thomas Norris*
1657 *Francis Dalby*
2. 1658 *John Palmer*
2. 1659 *James Langton* [b].

MS.p.67.

CHAP. XIV. The names of such Lincolnshire men as have born the honourable office of lord majors of the city of London, since the time of the Norman conquest till 1633 [c].

And here *it* is to be noted, that no one county in England can say so much as this county, in regard of the number of lord majors of London which have descended out of the same, as hereafter appeareth.

IT will be no great digression, nor much from the purpose, if I now walke a little out of Stamford into the county of Lincolne (in which this towne standeth) and, since I have, in their order & succession, set downe the names of the prime majestrates, as they have successively borne office in this towne; give me leave, in the next place, to set forth such as this county of Lincolne hath, from time to time, sent up to London, who have borne the head office in that mighty city. It is true this county hath received backe, as it were by way of exchange, two families of gentry which are descended from *the lord* majors of London, & have planted their posterity in this county. *For* in the first place, I find the family of the Granthams, which are descended from John Grantham, Grocer, major of London in the 3. yeare of the raigne of K. Edward the 3. (which was anno dom. 1328) & ever since settled in this county of Lincolne, as appeares by the armes of that *Sir John* Grantham, borne by the Granthams of this county at this day [d]. The next family which London hath lent to this county, to garnish the same with the flowers of her gentry, is the illustrious family of the Askewes [e] of Lincolnshire, which are descended from Sir Christopher Askew, draper (the sonn of John Askew of Edmunton in the county of Middlesex) being *lord* major of London in 1534. (being in the 26. yeare of the

raigne of King Henry the 8.) as appeares by the same coat armour, borne by the Askewes of Lincolnshire at this day.

It is true, this towne of Stamford hath never been so fortunate as to have any major of London descended out of the same. But for what this place hath been defective in, the county hath given a larger supply than any one county of England, having sent up tenne majors, besides other aldermen & sheriffes, to that city. As, I. in 1470. (which was in the 10. yeare of K. Edward the 4.) Sir John Stockdon [f], mercer (the sonne of Richard Stockdon of Bratoft in the county of Lincolne) was major of London, at what time the bastard Falconbridge assaulted the city at Algate & at the bridgegate; who, for his valour in the defence of the same, with eleven [g] of his brethren the aldermen, & Ursewicke the then recorder of London, were then knighted in the field by the said K. Edward the fourth. II. Sir Nicholas Alwin, mercer (sonne to Richard Alwin of Spalding in the county of Lincolne) was major of London in 1500. (in the 15. yeare of K. Henry the 7.) Hee gave xij. d. apiece to 3000 poore people in & about Spalding; & to as many more in & about London. III. William Remington, fishmonger (sonne of Robert Remington of Boston in the county of Lincolne) was major of London in 1501. which was in the 16. yeare of K. Henry the 7. IV. William

MS.p.68.
MS.p.69.

a Here ends the list published in Mr. Butchers printed book 1646. b And here ends the list as continued in Mr. Butchers MS. which, by the way, fixes the time whereto he continued not this list only, but his whole book in general. After the restoration Stanford was made a Mayor town. A more correct list of these magistrates from the 1. Ed. 4. to this time shall be hereafter published in the continuation of these annals, as I extracted them my self from the corporation books. So that it is needless here to trouble the reader any more either with the mistakes of the roll or of Mr. Butcher. To which I shall only add, that all the disputes & quarrels so darkly hinted at above, in 1595. 1598. & 1599. from some short memorandums on the roll & in Mr. Butchers MS. shall be related at large from authentic evidences under those years in the continuation of my annals, which I therefore crave leave to refer to; it being impossible to throw the substance of so many & great disputes into the compass of a few notes at the bottom of a page. c Till the time of the second edition of this survey. MS.

d The very name of Grantham shews that this was originally a Lincolnshire family, so that Mr. Butcher has made the city of London a complement of sending that family to the county of Lincolne, which in truth it fetched from it. e Ayscoughs MS. f Stockden, MS. g many more of his brethren, MS.

Foreman

Foreman [a], haberdafher (fonne to William Foreman [a] of Gainfborough in the county of Lincolne) was major of London in 1539. (which was in the 31. yeare of King Henry the 8.) V. Sir Henry Hubberthorne [b], marchant-taylor (fonne to Chriftopher Hubberthorne of Wadingfworth in the county of Lincolne) was major of London, in 1546. (which was in the laft yeare of King Henry 8.) VI. Henry Ancoles [c], fifhmonger (fonne of William Ancoles of Aftrap in the county of Lincolne) was major of London in 1549. (which was in the 2. yeare of K. Edward the 6.) VII. Sir John Langley, goldfmith (fonne to Robert Langley of Althorpe [d]) in the county of Lincolne) was major of London in 1577.

(which was in the 19. yeare of Q. Elizabeth. VIII. Sir Nicholas Mofeley, clothworker (fonne to Edward Mofeley of Hough in the county of Lincolne) was major of London in 1600. (which was the 42. yeare of Q. Elizabeth.) IX. Sir George Bowles, grocer (fonne of Thomas Bowles of Newbold in the county of Leicefter; defcended from the Bowles of Lincolnfhire, as by his coat of armes, agreeable with thofe, appeareth) was major of London in 1618. (which was in the 16 yeare of K. James.) X. Sir Nicholas Raynton [e], haberdafher (fonne of Robert Raynton of Highington in the county of Lincolne) was major of London in 1633. (which was in the 9. yeare of K. Charles *the firft*.)

MS.p.70.

CHAP. XV. *An appendix to this furvey & antiquity of the towne of Stamford, ferving as an illuftration of what I have here formerly written [f].*

BLADUD, *who built Stamford, & made it an univerfity, reigned in England in the yeare of the worlds creation 3066. He (comeing from Athens before the birth of Chrift 863. yeares) then built this towne; &, to compleat the fame as an univerfity, he placed here four philofophers, which he brought with him from Athens. This univerfity continued three hundred years after the coming of our Saviour, & did flourifh with many fchollars; but haveing fo continued by the fpace of 1163. yeares, was diffolved by the bifhopp of Rome, for the herefie of Arrius (as formerly I have noted.) But divers monafteries being then, & fince, erected in & about the towne [g], the fame were replenifhed with learned monks who taught the liberall fciences, & fo ftill retained fome fhew of learning, as likewife I have elfewhere declared.*

Merlin a Brittifh hiftorian, writeing of Stamford, faith, that Bladud brought four philofophers from Athens, & placed them in MS.p.71. *a pleafant foile at Stamford, & made fchooles for them there, to teach the feven liberall*

fciences, which flourifhed with many fcholars.

Cambden, in his Brittania, faith, that this towne was an univerfity in the time of K. Edward the third. But give me leave to add, that the fame was but of a fhort continuance, & happened upon a difcontentment amongft the ftudents at Oxford, & was prefently removed by the kings proclamation, as I have formerly fet downe [h]. And the faid Mr. Cambden would farther prove, that this was no univerfity before the time of the faid K. Edward the third, yet his owne author is againft him [i]. For, in the ftory of K. Edward the third, it is faid [k], that the ftudents in Oxford fled to Stamford in November 1333. & returned to Oxford before 1334. as they were commanded by the kings proclamation.

Alfo the foundation of Brazen-nofe Colledge, & other houfes that were colledges here do plainly prove that it could not be in fo fhort a time that they could build colleges; or that thofe ftudents, or any other, fhould do, it being forbid by the kings proclamation [l].

a Forman, MS.　　b Hoberthorne, MS.　　c Amcoates, MS. d Afthorpe aforefaid, MS.　　e Royfton, MS.　　f There is not a tittle of this chapter in the printed copies.　　g There were divers monafteries at Stamford fince the fuppofed diffolution of this univerfity by pope Gregory about the year of Chrift 605. but none I believe then. See my annals, book I. paragraphs the xxviii. & xxix.　　h The Oxford men came hither in Edward the thirds time, but there were fchools at Stanford above twenty years before they came. Of which fchools Mr. Butcher knew nothing, but fancied that fome imaginary colleges, founded, as he thought, at Stanford, in the time of the fuppofed Britifh univerfity there, remained till the faid K. Edward the thirds time, & were then occupied by the Oxford men. i Mr. Camden quotes no body himfelf, nor Mr. Butcher for him; but I guefs Mr. Butcher here means Stow.　　k Stows words are ‘ This yeere [1333] in the moneth of No- ‘ vember divers mafters & fchollers of Oxford withdrew themfelves to Stamford, minding there to ‘ have begunne an univefity, without licenfe obtained of the king in that behalfe: whereat the ‘ king being offended, did by proclamation utterly forbid & fuppreffe it.’ Chron. Lond. 1492. 4°. p. 360. Where note, tho’ Mr. Stow fays they came in November 1333. yet he does not affirm (as Mr. Butcher would perfuade us he does) that they returned before 1334. No; he only (being willing to put all he had to fay of this matter of the Oxford mens remove together) adds at the fame time, ‘ whereat the king being offended, did by proclamation utterly forbid, & ‘ fuppreffed it,’ but this was not till 1335.　　l The time the Oxford men ftaid was too fhort for them to build much in; which proves indeed that the colleges at Stanford were built before they came hither, but not, as I before intimated, that thofe fchools were the remains of the Britons here, erected in, or before. Auftins time.

3

And it is evident that Brazen-nofe colledge in Oxford was founded in the time of K. Henry the feventh (according to the patterne of the more antient Brazen-nofe in Stamford) by William Smith doctor of the civil law [a].

Alfo the very flying of the fludents in Edward the thirds time, doth make all this appeare very plainely. For whither fhould fchollars fly, when they betake themfelves to flight, but to a place that is fitting to receive them? And no place could be more fitt to receive them than Stamford, the fame being furnifhed with colledges fo many years before [b].

Hereby it plainly appeares that Stamford could not be an univerfity without the kings licenfe. Which argues that it was planted & incorporated before that time, as both Stow & Grafton in their chronicles do make it appear [c].

The towne of Stamford, as appeares by the book of doomefday, in the exchequer, gave guild or tribute to 1250 foldiers in the time of K. Edward the confeffor & had it in fix wards.

K. Henry the fecond gave the whole towne, or fo much of it as was in the kings demeafnes, to Richard de Humett, the king only referving the fees of the knights & barons, as I have formerly written.

I conclude this relation; & wifh, that fome of power & greatnefs would rather help to reftore the ruins of this place, or at leaft not ruinate it any more, by enriching themfelves with the fpoyles thereof, & by encroaching & invading upon the priviledges & liberties of the fame.

The CONCLUSION.

Thus have I at length brought this furvey to the wifhed end, according to my poore abilitie.

*BY various changes, & great change of things,
Which rule & fand, built to experience,
    brings;*
Through times of trouble, prifonment, & all
Diftractions which can wretched man befall;
I have at length (through my creators ayd)
The towne of Stamford ferioufly furvey'd,
And by the paine of my now wearied pen,
It lies apparent to the view of men
Who firft the building of the fame contriv'd,
And (when, in time, it grew more longer liv'd)
With what difafters it was then turmoyl'd,
By hereticks undone, by Danes much fackt & fpoyl'd.
Yet at the length her ruines were redreft,
By kings & friends; her enemies fuppreft:
In ftrength & ftate, with walls & caftle proud,
With grants & priviledges great endow'd,
She flourifh'd under governours difcreet
Till the whole land with civil warres did meet;
When Yorke & Lancafter their fwords out
    drewe,
And, like mad lyons keene, their kindred flew.
The northerne foulders all with rage incenft,
With quenchlefs flames then Stamfords glory
    quencht.
Who never fince her towring creft could raife
To former greatneffe, as in former dayes;
Though our fourth Edward by his charter kind
Did fhew his princely love, his royall mind
For Stamfords good; & his pofterity
Confirm'd, & added what was neceffary.
Yet, what's the caufe as yet I cannot tell,
Great oddes there is 'twixt us, & being well.
God fend the kingdome better for to fare,
And then, I hope, Stamford will have a fhare
In that well-being. Let us all repent,
Then God, no doubt, in mercy will relent,
And make our cities & our townes to fhine
Againe in glory, earthly & divine:
    Heav'n grant the fame; &, till the dooming
        day,
    May they & Stamford reft in joy alway.

a The remains of brazen-nofe college, & of all the other colleges in Stanford, carry no face of antiquity higher, if fo high, as Henry the firfts time.   b What thefe colleges were which the Oxford men found built to their hands in Edward the thirds time may be feen related at large in my annals, to which I muft here beg leave to refer.   c All that Stow elfewhere fays of this univerfity of Stanford is, ' Bladud, the fonne of Rudhudibrafs, who had ' long ftudied at Athens brought with him foure philofophers, to keep fchoole in Brytaine: for the ' which he builded Stamford, & made it an univerfity, wherein he had great number of fchollers ftu-' dying in all the feven liberall fciences; which univerfity dured to the comming of St. Auguftine, at ' which time the bifhop of Rome interdicted it for herefies that fell among the Saxons & Brytaines ' togither mixte, fo faith Harding. Stow p. 15.' All that Grafton fays of this univerfity, is, ' John ' Harding in the firft book & twenty fifth chapter of his ftory fheweth, that the fchool or univerfity ' of Stamford was forbidden by Auftin the monk, like as other univerfities of this realme were, under ' pretence that they maintained the Arrian & Pelagian herefies. The which his prohibition was the ' caufe of the decay of the fame univerfities; & therefore long after his time there was no common ' profeffion of learning, but in the great monafteries & abbies. Chron, p. 46.' Here it may be obferved that Stow fays pofitively the Oxford men attempted to found an univerfity at Stanford without the kings licenfe; & that neither he nor Mr. Grafton, tho' they affert it was planted by Bladud, fay any thing of its being licenfed or incorporated by him or any other prince. That being a ftretch of Mr. Butchers own. Except we fhould fay, that Bladuds planting, implies a licenfe & incorporation; & there I believe we fhall hit his meaning. But all this amounts to nothing. For he muft firft prove that there was fuch a man as Bladud, next that he granted fuch a licenfe, & laftly, that it was more than once confirmed by divers other princes. Or elfe what will all this avail to make out his affertion, that Stanford could not be an univerfity without the kings licenfe?

Two letters about the original & antiquities of the town of Stanford, by the late reverend William Forster, A. M. rector of St. Clement Danes; now first published at large from the original copies, with remarks by the editor.

The first letter, to the Revd. Thomas Tanner D. D. author of the *Notitia Monastica*; from Dr. Tanners copy, wrote by Mr. Forsters own hand.

SIR,

MS. p. 1. UPON my being Benefic'd in the parish of St. Michaells in Stamford, Lincolnshire, a particular friend & parishioner of mine [a], put into my hands Mr. Butchers survey & antiquities of this town, soliciting me to revise the book, and correct some scurrilous and false reflections in it made upon the great treasurer Burghley & his noble family, living near us; [b] & to put out a new edition of it [c]. My studies had hitherto lain another way, which made me very unwilling to undertake a thing of that nature, as being altogether unqualify'd for it; however I resolved to run over the book, to see what information it would give me of a place which the divine providence had been pleased to settle me in. But upon reading it over the author seem'd, even to me who am a perfect stranger to antiquity, to be a very credulous & injudicious person: his foundation of this town & university by King Bladud, 863 years before Christ's incarnation, is a strain even beyond Jeoffry himselfe.

Whereupon, with those few helps I have, I apply'd my selfe to find out the truth, if I could; &, after that little search I have hitherto been able to make, what I think is nearest the truth, I have made bold to communicate to You, to beg your Judgment in the matter: which I should never have had the confidence to have done, had I not mett with your usefull book, the *Notitia Monastica*; whereby I was soon sensible of your unwearied diligence & the great pleasure you take in the searches after our antiquities. For which reason I could not but promise my selfe your pardon for this more than ordinary Trouble and Boldness; & that You would Encourage one that is a hearty Well Wisher to the same delightfull study, & assist him in the Inquiries into the Antiquities of a place of some note & Antiquity, tho' vastly short of that Romantick Age which Mr. Butcher (I suppose from Harding, or from Stow rather) hath made it.

And, after the best search I have yet been able to make, I cannot but conclude, that this town of Stamford is of pure Saxon original.

For had it been a British Citty, especially such a One as is represented in the Survey, how coms it to pass that Nennius takes no notice of it in the Catalogue of his British Cities? & no Roman author that I know of mentions any town or citty in this place. The Itinerary is quite silent; and Ptolemy in his Geography of Britain makes mention but of two citties of the Coritani, Lindum and Ragæ or Ratæ, which last Mr. Cambden supposes to be Leicester; and certainly so exact a man as Ptolemy would not have omitted so noted a place as this is reported to have been.

So that from the silence of all Ancient Authors, who have written concerning this Island, I think wee may reasonably conclude, that either there was no town at all here before the Saxons, or at least a very Inconsiderable one, not worth the taking notice of. For had it been enobled with such a famous university, that was replenish'd with the Gravest and Learnedst Philosophers that were to be found in the whole world, as the surveyer writes, and flourish'd in such a manner even 'till pope Gregory the great suppress'd it; it is not to be imagined that it should be pass'd over by All Writers, nor so much as mention'd either by Tacitus or Any other that treated of the Roman affairs here in Britain; nor afterwards by Gildas, or Bede, when it would have lain so naturally in the way of the Ecclesiasticall History of this last [d].

But besides, the Description, that Cæsar & Strabo give us, of the British Towns before the Coming of the Romans, does not agree at all with the politeness of the Græcian Breeding and Building. Nor can this story I think be reconciled with what Mr. Cambden hath collected out of Cæsar, Tacitus, Strabo, &c. concerning the Manners of the Britains, when the Romans first arriv'd among them. Not to mention what Tacitus

---

a This person I guess was the late Mr. Richard Walburg. b I never met with Mr. Forsters answers to any part of Mr. Butchers reflections on the lord treasurer, &c. otherwise they should have been here given. c Mr. Forster at first intended to follow Mr. Butchers method, but afterwards drew up so many different schemes that I can't tell which he proposed to write after. d Here, in another copy, Mr. Forster adds, 'Sir John Price when he ' endeavours to prove Learning here before the Romans coming hither, makes no mention of this ' university, which, had there been then such a place, would have been an effectuall argument to ' prove his assertion' —— But Sir John Prices silence does not prove there was no British university at Stamford, but rather tacitly argues that he thought there was none.

17 B sayes

sayes in the life of Agricola, how that in the second year of his Leivetenancy here, He began to instruct the Britains in the Roman learning & Civility (who before liv'd rude & scatter'd) and caused the noblemens sons to be instructed in the liberall sciences. What? were they to be instructed in the Libe-Arts & Sciences at this time of day, when King Bladud had founded so famous an University in this town, & furnish'd it with Greek Philosophers for that end, & which flourish'd in all manner of heathenish Learning (& I dare say Agricola's Liberal Sciences were not Christian Learning) till the time of King Lucius? Tacitus and the Surveyer clash beyond hopes of reconciliation here[a]. And if learning did so flourish in this place, it is very strange that none of the Writeings of those learned Worthies should remain, at least be mention'd by others; & extreamly unkind they were to this island that not one of them should deliver down to posterity somthing of a history of it before the Roman conquest. And more ungratefull still to leave no account of their own famous university. Nay Gildas when he wrote (if I understand him right) seems to make a doubt whither Any of the Britains had even then writt any thing in relation to their own country; its certain he never saw it, if they had.

MS. p. 2.

But what I think puts the matter beyond dispute is, that there are no remains in this place, either of Britains, or Romans, or Greeks either; no encampments, no pavements, &c. no coins dug up, or found amongst us, but what are Saxon, or since the Norman conquest. Now had this Town been of so great note & so Ancient as is pretended, it had very hard fate beyond all other places, not to shew the least footsteps of its Quondam Inhabitants & Greatness, which almost every litle Roman station at this day is able to do.

The learned Mr. Gibson in his Additions to Essex in the Britannia tells us, that it is an observation made by antiquaries, that the Saxon Kings & Nobles seated themselves upon the forsaken camps & stations of the Romans, & made new names by adding their Ceaster, Burgh, &c. to a part of the Roman name. But Stanford being purely Saxon, wee may probably argue from thence, that this town was neither of British nor Roman Originall, because wee find no footsteps of its former name in the present. And its scarce to be supposed that the Saxons should wholly extinguish the old name in this place only, & that too contrary to their custome, when wee see that they retayn'd part of the old name in towns of far less note, than they would have us believe this to have been; if they did, a hard fate still attended poor Stamford.

The Roman way that went from Castor near Peterborow to Gaussennæ, and thence to Lincoln, does cross, from south to north,

at the West End of this town, and is the only remain of Antiquity beyond the Saxon times that wee have; but it does not at all prove that a great town was therefore in this place either before or during the Roman government here; seeing there are no other remains of Antiquity to induce us to believe so; & they may as well argue that there was one continued town all along that Roman way to Lincoln; for every spot of ground it passes by, has an equall & the same pretence to have an ancient town upon it.

But where this Roman bank crosses the Welland, as it does at the South West point of Stamford close to the town, there is a gravelly or *stoney-ford*, from whence I doubt not but Stamford took this its first & only name in the Saxon Language.

And these reasons, till I am better inform'd, do induce me to think that this town is no older than the Saxon age, & that from them it had its originall.

But now to fix the time of its birth is I fear (to me I am sure it is) impossible, from the want of letters among our first Saxon ancestours. And besides, the accidentall & small beginnings of some places at first, makes em below the taking notice of; & so, tho' they may afterwards by degrees rise to be of great note, yet their originall meanness renders the finding out the exact time of their foundation impracticable. And truly the Saxons had something else to mind at first, it being their business first to win the country from the Britains, & then to maintain it against them; they [the Britains] strugling hard for it under Vortimer, Aurelius Ambrosius, &c. Wherefore, seeing wee can have only conjectures to goe upon, without indulging idle fancies, I shall make bold to offer my thoughts to your correction & exact judgment in these matters. And my opinion as to its first Rise is this: I do verily believe that Mr. Cambden is much in the right, when He sayes, that it rose out of the ruines of that Roman station which was at Brig-Casterton, two litle miles to the north west of us; and this I think was done very early in the Saxon times, soon after their settlement in these parts of the island. My reasons are these.

1. Henry Huntington, &c. tells us, that the Scotts & Picts in the ravages they made upon the Britains being come as far as Stamford, were there first mett, & encounter'd with by the Saxons, and totally overthrown. Whereupon Vortigern, as a requitall, gave Hengist lands in Lincolnshire to sustain him & his souldiers, as Matt. West. Ran. Higden, &c. inform us. *Agros plurimos*, saith John Fordun; and Dr. Gale in his third appendix to Nennius, ch. 64. agrees to this relation. And so far as I am able to gather from the History of those times, the Saxons seem to have had possession of this county, in whole or in part, all along from that time or immediately after: for severall of the

MS. p. 3.

---

a Here Mr. Forster adds in another copy, 'Sure the Monk or the man, who forged this story, had never read Tacitus, knew very little history, or hardly ever hoped to be believed.'

battels

battels fought between the Britains & the Saxons (thofe efpecially mentioned to be under Arthur) Dr. Gale thinks were undoubtedly in this county, in order to drive the Saxons out of it.

After Hengifts firft fuccefs againft the Scots, &c. we find he prevail'd with Vortigern, that He might fend his Brother & his Son to fecure the northern parts of Britain againft the invaders; & why might not fome of them fetle fouth of Humber? However, when the Saxons began to quarrel with the Britains, I doubt not but thefe northern Auxiliaries then drew fouthward to be ready to affift Hengift, & did then take up their Habitations in our County, & began to fortify themfelves in it.

For tho' feverall of the battels attributed to Arthur are faid to have been fought in Lincolnfhire [a], as I hinted before, yet Dr. Gale in his notes on Nennius fayes, they were fought during the fpace of 40 yeares & upwards under Vormiter, Ambrofius, & other Generalls, as well as Arthur. And truly, by the beft accounts that I can perceive of Arthur, his Command feems to have extended only over Cornwall, & it may be Devonfhire, or fome parts thereabouts, and, if the ftory of his wife Guenhere being ftolen & defiled by one Meluas be true, &c. as the learned Stillingfleet relates it, Orig. Brit. p. 339. [b] it by no means anfwers the character of fuch a Mighty Prince, as Jeoffry has reprefented him. And tho' I doubt not but He might be a brave, warlike perfon; yet I can not think that He ever Oppofed, or was ingaged, againft the whole Saxon power, or ever came nigh our County of Lincoln: but, that He might have feverall Ingagements with the Weft Saxons, and with good fuccefs too, it is highly probable; and he might perhaps drive them out of fome places, which They had fetled themfelves in; which Actions, to his great Difadvantage, have been foolifhly magnify'd into Incredible Exploits & Idle Stories. And by what Obfervation I can make in thofe old Hiftorians I have read, I cannot perceive that any Thing of Moment happen'd hereabouts, between the Britains & the Saxons, after the Death of Ambrofius. Wherefore I am apt to think, that foon after the Death of Vortimer & Ambrofius (the laft of whom is fuppofed to dye about the year 501.) the Saxons had quiet poffeffion of Lincolnfhire. For, from that time, the South and Weft feem to have been the only Scene of Action; the Power of the Natives finking very faft, & They retiring apace towards thofe places, whereunto afterwards they were wholly Confin'd. And add to this, how that frefh forces out of thofe northern parts of Germany were daily powring in upon the poor Britains, and their Towns being but thinly inhabited (as Gildas obferves) after that unmerciful Deftruction which Hengift & his Saxons had firft made of them, I can not but think, that if any Britains were left in thefe parts, that they did foon after the year 501. quietly fubmit to the Saxon power [here] as they had done in the Northumbrian Country. 'Stow tells us, that Erchenwine firft fet up the Kingdom of the Eaft Saxons, An. 527. but that he held it as feodatary to the Kings of Kent, who were as yet Sovereigns of the whole Country from Thames to Humber; if fo, then all the Britifh power muft be loft in thefe parts. And if it be matter of fact that Huntington relates, ad annum 517. how that many Angles or Saxons came that year, & took poffeffion of the Eaft Angles & Mercia, it is no fmall Confirmation of my affertion. Mr. Tyrrel fayes, that Mr. Twine had feen a copy of Mat. Weftm. which places this coming of the Angles ad ann. 527. ten years later than Hen. Hunt. but, which of the years foever it was that They came, they feem to have found but very litle refiftance from the Natives, but carried all before them, there being no memorable Oppofition recorded that was made againft them: which fhews that the Britifh ftrength was extream weak in thefe parts then. And from this time the neareft action to us that happen'd between the Britains & Saxons was that which the Saxon chronicle places under the year 571. of Cuthwulfe King of the Weft Saxons ingageing and beating the Britains at Bedford, and takeing from them four Towns, viz. Leighton in Bedfordfhire (as, I believe Mr. Gibfon does rightly place it) & Ailsbury in Bucks, & Benfington & Einfham in Oxfordfhire; all which places, as they are at a confiderable diftance from us, fo they all tend towards the weft: The poor Britains ftill retiring towards their Narrow & Laft Habitation, whereinto they feem to be almoft totally driven about the year 577. as fome will have it; tho' the Britifh Hiftory will not have them wholly confin'd to Wales and Cornwall till Cadwaladers time, who dy'd at Rome An. 688. Hift. Wales p. 16. edit. 1584.

MS. p. 4.

---

a In another copy Mr. Forfter adds 'Nennius, fpeaking of Arthurs battels againft the Saxons fays, that the firft was at the mouth of the River Glen. Upon which words Dr. Gale has this 'note. Some will have it Glen in Devonfhire, but it feems rather to be Glen in Lincolnfhire, where 'Glemford now is. Vortigern gave Hengift Lincolnfhire, out of which the Britains endeavoured 'to drive the Saxons in the following wars under Aurelius, Vortiger, & Arthur.' Notes upon Nennius. p. 131.　　　b In another copy Mr. Forfter adds 'See the fame in archbifhop 'Ufhers antiquit. Brit. p. 274. Archbifhop Ufher makes Uther Pendragon to be brother to Ambrofius 'Aurelianus, & fucceed him in the kingdom; & to be the father of Arthur. ib. p. 244. Arthur 'began to reign the 10. year of Cerdic, who erected the Weft Saxon kingdom, ib. p. 250. & died in the year 542. ib. p. 274.　　　c In another copy Mr. Forfter adds 'I believe this part of 'the kingdom was but very thinly inhabited by the Britains at the coming hither of the Saxons, by 'reafon of thofe frequent inroads of the Scots & Picts, which they made as far as this town.'

More-

Moreover anno 585. the Mercian Kingdom is said to begin under Creda, whereof the County of Lincoln was a member. Now it is to be supposed that the Britains were totally brought under in this country, & also that It was tolerably well fill'd with Saxons before they would give it the name of a Kingdom. And that it was then well peopled there is good reason to think by those great actions which Penda *soon after* [a] was able to perform. And if Staffordshire, & those other Counties of the Mercian Kingdom, which lye to the South and West of us, & out of which the Britains were the last dispossest, & which also border'd upon that litle remnant that was left the Britains, were so early replenish'd with Angles or Saxons; wee may with greater reason suppose, that these parts which lye at so much greater distance from those territories which remain'd to the natives, were more early under the Saxon yoke.

So that I can not but think, that after the death of Ambrosius, the Saxons gott firm footing in this country; & what with their fresh & continuall supplies out of Germany, & their numerous issue here (which the northern Nations are noted for) they were grown very powerfull in these parts, & had in the space of eighty years (which was between the death of Ambrosius & the erecting the Mercian Kingdom) over-run & conquer'd the severall provinces which constituted that large Kingdom, & extended to the very Borders of those small Remains which were left to the unhappy Natives.

Henry Huntingdon, in the prologue to his 5th book, has these words, *Saxones pro viribus paulatim terram bello capessentes, captam obtinebant, obtentam edificabant, edificatam legibus regebant.* Which shews, that as fast as they gott footing, they fix'd & setled themselves into towns & government. And if there is reason to suppose (as I think there is) that they were so early masters of these parts of Lincolnshire, & that where they came they seated themselves upon the British & Roman Towns and Stations, then Gaussennæ, we may conjecture, was very early possest by them, and its name chang'd to Castreton, from whence I suppose them to have flitted presently to this place, as perhaps finding Gaussennæ ruin'd & demolish'd by the Scots & Picts, as Cambden relates out of Huntington; and so chose rather to erect a new town here, than repair an old demolish'd one, & that too the sooner out of respect it may be to their first encounter & success in this place against the Scots [b]. Or else, their numbers increasing very fast, & so making it necessary to build new towns

& habitations, they might pitch upon this for its pleasant & delightful Situation, lying on the south side of a hill, gently declining to a handsom navigable River, whereby it became not onely pleasant but also usefull; makeing a good frontier Garison against the Britains, that should attack them from the south. And probably this last might be the chief reason of their removeing from Gaussennæ hither, it being so much the more convenient for a frontier towards the south; & then this must be done very early, upon their first setling in this country, which is my next reason for placeing the begining of this town so early in the Saxon Times, viz. from its being a frontier Garison against the Britains.

II. That this was a fortify'd town at the time of the Danish invasion, it seems to me pretty certain; for almost the first mention we have of it is in Ingulphus, who sayes, of those Stamfordians whom Harding of Ryhal led out against the Danes An. 870. at the ingagement with them in this Kestiven division of Lincolnshire, that They were *Bellicosi nimium*, very warlike people, as it were train'd up to it. That it was a Garrison of the Danes An. 922. the Saxon chronicle informs us, when it sayes, that King Edward came against it with his army, & order'd a castle or fort to be built on the south side of the river (that was exactly where the Roman way crosses the ford) & then all the people in the City on the north side, or as Florence reads it, all the people that kept the castle on the north side the River, yielded to Him & beg'd his protection. And whereas it is called by the Saxon Annals *Byrigh*; by Hen. Hunt. *Civitas*; & by Florence, *Arx*, it shews it then to be a fortify'd & wal'd town; [c] & that it was so before the Danish invasion I do verily believe, both from the abovemention'd Character, which Ingulphus gives of its Inhabitants that fought the Danes under Harding of Ryhal, anno 870. & also because after that fight the Danes do not seem to have setled in these parts, but only pass'd thro' 'em like free booters, Burning and Robbing whereever they came; till part of them over-ran all the Northumbrian country & made themselves Masters of it; & the Rest of em having murder'd King Edmund possess'd themselves of his territories, from whence they infested Mercia, Kent, & the South & West Saxons. But there is not the least appearance of their being in this place till Ann. 922. when it is said the people in the City on the north Side the River yielded to King Edward upon his building a fort on the south side. Now it is not said that they were Danes that submitted, but they might be Rebellious

MS. p. 5.

d Penda came not to the crown of Mercia 'till the year 626. which is 31 years after 585. too long a time I think to be comprehended in these words, *soon after.* b Here Mr. Forstet seems to suspect himself, & therefore in another copy adds 'tho' finding no memoriall of that 'action in the name of this town, which we might well expect, I do not much depend upon this 'reason for their setling here.' c Here Mr. Forster in another copy adds, '& so 'it continued a garison town during all the Danish wars, & afterwards in the wars between K. 'Stephen & the Empress Maud, & Those of the Barons, & between the Houses of York & Lancaster; '& some of its old Walls are still standing & entire.'

2   subjects;

subjects; [a] yet it is probable that at that time there might be a Danish Garison here; but it does not follow that therefore they first fortify'd the Town; but only had possess'd themselves of it & put a Garison into it, which now surrendered to K. Edward: & truly to build a castle here, & to Wall so large a Town, as it would be a work of some time, so wee might reasonably expect to have it mention'd (had it been done now by the Danes) as well as their building forts at Beamfleet, Apuldre, & Temsford, &c. and I don't see by the History of these Times, that the Danes could have either a sufficient Body of men, or Time, to spare to compleat such a work in this place; K. Alfred in the latter part of his reign, and K. Edward, generally gaining upon them. And whereas the Saxon Annalls call Stamford at this time Byrig, the expression looks as if it had been formerly known by that Title, & was not a new upstart wal'd Citty.

Now if it was a fortify'd place before the Danish invasion, it must be made so (in all probability) on one of these two Occasions; either by the Saxons against the Britains, or afterward by the Mercian Kings against their neighbour Saxons. That it was not fortify'd upon this last occasion, I think, for this reason; because that after the Mercian Kingdom was Erected, this Town lay almost at the farthest end of it; [b] not only at a great Distance from the Royall Seat of the Kings, but also from the frontiers of the other Saxon Governments. The greatest part of their county of Lincoln on one Side, & the counties of Nottingham, part of Leicester, & all Rutland on the other side, lay between Stamford & the Northumbrian Kingdom. And the woody and deep county of Huntingdon, & boggy & unpassable fenns parted us from the East Angles; which were the two nearest of the Saxon Kingdoms to this Town. So that there was no occasion to fortify this town against them, nor would it have been of any use so to do, so far as I can see: for lying so far from the Borders or Frontiers, it could not serve to stop or hinder any sudden invasion of the neighbouring princes; & before the enemy could march thus far, the field army must in all probability be totally routed and dispersed; & then, as it would be to no purpose, so I do not find that the Inland Towns, during the Heptarchy, used to make any resistance, but commonly follow'd the fate of the Army in the field, & the Royall Seat & frontier Towns. And this appears from the instance of this very Mercian kingdom; for when Penda was slain,

& his Army overthrown by Oswi the Northumbrian King; all the Mercian territories were immediately at the disposall of the Conquerour, who permitted Peada his son in Law to govern the Mercians south of Trent, but still as Tributary to him. And the next year, upon Peada's death, Oswy seized the Mercian Kingdom again & annex'd it to his own Territories, till Wulphere with his nobles rescued it out of his hands three years after. And Stamford being so very remote from the Royall Seat of the Mercian Kings, & from that part of the country from whence they march'd to attack their Enemies, or Where their Enemies attack'd Them; there is nothing memorable mention'd to have happen'd at, or near, this Town, it being so far out of the way of action. All which seems to confirm, that this was not made at first a Garison by the Mercian Kings against their Saxon neighbours. And if so, then wee have good reason to think that it was at first fortify'd against the Britains, & very commodious it was for that purpose, being situate on a good River, & by secureing the ford, they effectually stopt the march of the Britains into Lincolnshire on this side [c].

And if it was a Garison against the Britains, it must be made so at the first coming of the Saxons here, during their Contests with the Britains in these parts, & while they were in fear & under apprehension of Insults from them, & before the British power & strength was quite broken here. For after the Britains were driven to a great distance hence into the south and west, & that large provinces conquer'd from them, with strong Armies, lay between this Town & Them; I do not see that this place would be then of any more consequence against the Britains, than it was, after the erecting of the Mercian Kingdom, against the Rest of the principalities that compos'd the Heptarchy; tho' the Saxons might be thenceforward still increasing the Bigness & Strength of the Town for the worst & a turn of affairs. Now if these Conjectural premisses be true, we may I think from thence conclude, that this town was founded about the year 501. or soon after, if not before it. To which let me add `MS. p. 6.`

III. That the first time we have any mention made of Stamford, it is spoke of as a considerable place. The first notice taken of it that I have been able to observe is in that charter recorded in the Saxon chronicle under the year 656. pretended to be granted by K. Wulphere to the abby of Medeshamstede; where Stamford is made one of the

---

a They were certainly Danes, who submitted, & not rebellious subjects.   b Here wants some amendment, for first Mr. Forster says, *this town lay almost at the farthest end of the Mercian kingdom,* & then presently, that it lay *at a great distance from the frontiers of the other Saxon governments:* either of which assertions is a contradiction to the other.   c The Welland is fordable at so many places both above & below Stanford, that, unless those places be all likewise secured, secureing the pass or ford at Stanford is doing almost nothing against an army which is bent to get over it. Besides, the Britons, if they came out of Wales, need never have march'd to Stanford, much less passed the Stony-ford there, to get into Lincolnshire. If they came out of Cornwall indeed, then, supposing all the other passes of the river made safe, we may say with Mr. Forster, 'by securing the ford they effectually stopt the march of the Britains into Lincolnshire on this side. '

boundary's

boundary's of the Land, which that King gave to the said Abby. Now if this charter was true & genuine, & could be depended upon; we have abundant proof of the being of a Town here at that time, & very likely for a good space before [a]. For that Charter represents the Country hereabouts well inhabited & the Saxon towns pretty thick, which we can not imagine was done all in an instant, but successively, & was a Work of time, and multiply'd as their numbers increas'd.

I have not observ'd Stamford to be mention'd again till Ingulphus speaking of the forementioned Ingagement with the Danes in this County, which the Saxon chronicle places under the year 870. sayes, that Hardingus de Ryhal cum omnibus Stanfordensibus, eo quod omnes juvenes erant, & nimium bellicosi &c. which intimates that a good Body of men were muster'd out of Stamford, & that consequently it was then a great place. Hen. Hunt. in the war between Edmund Ironside & the Danes, calls it an Antient Citty; the Saxon chronicle, as I noted before, calls it a Citty at that time. And it was reckon'd one of the five great Cities of the Mercian Kingdom, [b] whose Inhabitants (perhaps Danish as well as Saxon [c]) were called, by way of Eminency Fifburgenses, the Inhabitants of the five Citties. Hen. Hunt. ad ann. 1013. Sax. Chron. ad eundem ann. Mr. Gibson in voce Fifburg. & new edition of Cambden in Northumberland, col. 865. in notis ad imum paginæ.

It appears by K. Edgars charter to the Abby of Peterborow, that there was a market then at Stamford; for He there granting a market to Burgh sayes, there shall not be any other market between Stamford and Huntingdon, which implyes that there was a market then at both those places. By that Charter he also grants to the Abbat a mint in this town; but whether the mint was first then sett up here, or whether it was erected here before by K. Athelstan, who (as we learn from his laws) order'd one to be sett up in every great Town & now given by King Edgar to that Abby, I will not take upon me to determine, tho' this last is the likelyest to be true [d]. However from hence it seems that Stamford was then grown almost to full maturity, & therefore wee must look a Great Way back to discover its Infancy & first Originall, for it is not probable that it should grow up all of a sudden to be thus Considerable. And truly its Bigness, its Fortifications & Castle, its number of Churches, &c. do seem to intimate that it was at first

design'd for more than an Ordinary Common Village.

These, Sir, are the reasons that induce me to think that Stamford cannot date its Originall beyond the Saxon Setlement here; & that it sprung up with Them, & is altogether, or near upon, as Old as their fixing in this country. But How Conclusive They may be in themselves, or what weight they may have with so great a Master of our Antiquities as You must be acknowledg'd to be, I can not tell, but if I might hope for such a Favour, it would be a great satisfaction to me to hear your Opinion herein; for I value my own Judgment as nothing, being so poor a novice in Inquiries of this nature; & withall Living in a place where there are no Helps or Advantages to be had in Order thereto; few Books to be procur'd without a better purse than I am master of; fewer men that know any thing of these matters to consult with for direction; and still fewer MSS. to open a clearer view to us.

And since, Sir, I have proceeded thus far MS. p. 7, to trouble You, give me leave to add a line or two in relation to the University said to have been in this Town. If wee take the word University as a Law Term implying a legall Society incorporated for the profession of Learning, which the Civilians say none but the supreme Authority of a Nation can do (as Stillingfleet Orig. Brit. p. 207. tells us) then I don't think that there ever was such a thing here. But that there were Schooles here for the Education of Youth, of Novices especially for the neighbouring Monasteries, You have sufficiently shewn from Leland in the preface to your Notitia Monastica. And that there were such schools here before your Oxonians came hither in Edward the thirds time, I am apt to think. For why should They all agree to come to this rather than any other place, had there not been some schools of Learning here before, & a sort of an Academy already instituted, whereby there was a kind of invitation to 'em to come hither? & the considerable setlement & number of the Students Houses when they were dislodg'd hence by publique Authority, does not look like the Work of so few months as the Oxonians were suffer'd to stay here.

Wherefore I believe your Learned Antiquary Mr. Anthony Wood has fixt this matter right in dateing the Commencement of our studies here from the Donation of Robert Lutterel Rector of Irnham, who, in the 20. of Edward the first, gave a Farm situate in the Parish of St. Peter in Stamford, for instructing Novices here to in-

---

a This charter of King Wulphere is spurious, the reasons why I think it so may be seen in my collections Book II. Paragraph the XXVI. However there is good proof that there was a town called Stanford, standing where our Stanford now stands, in the year 449. if not long time before. See my collections, Book I. Paragraphs the XXX, &c.   b Not of the Mercian, but of the Danish kingdom. See my collections, Book III. Paragraph the XIII.   c The inhabitants of the five Cities were chiefly Danes; all the Saxons among them being either servants, or such as by intermarriages were become Danes in affection, religion, & every thing else, but descent.

d Athelstan first granted that privilege of a mint to the abbat of Medeshamstede, & afterwards Edgar confirmed it.

crease

creafe the number of the Convent of Sempringham, &c. Except wee fhould venture a litle Higher, & fuppofe the Originall of thefe Schools to be laid by thofe Monks of Croyland that Joffridus the Abbat fent to Worthorpe after the Burning of their Monaftery in Hen. the firfts time, & that They did not only preach here, but Taught the Youth alfo, as Pet. Blefens. tells us that fome of the Monks of the fame monaftery who were fent at the fame time to Cottenham did at Cambridge, viz. read Logick, Philofophy, & Rhetorick ; & on Sundayes & Saints-dayes preached to the People, & had great numbers of Scholars. This, Sir, is a bare conjecture of mine, & for that reafon I dare lay no ftrefs upon it ; but humbly Beg of you to inform me whither Leland, or any other MSS. you have mett with, do give a clearer Light & fuller Account of thefe Schools of Learning at Stamford, than what Mr. Wood, or any other has yet publifh'd ? particularly whither Leland fayes any thing more about Peterborow Haulle, Semplingham, & Vauldey, the names of which he faid remain'd in his time at Stamford, as you have acquainted us in your preface to the Notitia Monaftica [a].

I will wrack your patience, Sir, but with one word more, & that is in Relation to the Religious Houfes that were in & about this Town. I find the names of more in the Monafticon than you have mentioned in your Notitia ; & wee feem to have the Ruines, & Common Tradition informs us of more than the Monafticon has taken notice of. And if You can direct me where to meet with a more exact Account of their number, Founders, &c. than is hitherto publifhed, I fhall acknowledge the Favour. You mention, in the Notitia, two MSS. that promife more than is yet printed.

And now, Sir, if I might prefume, I would fuggeft to You one thing which I believe is a Slip in your Notitia Monaftica,

concerning a Religious Houfe here with us. Under the Title of Lincolnfhire, numb. 58. p. 131. You mention Newftede juxta Stamford, a Priory of Gilbertines, dedicated to St. Leonard, &c. Now the Houfe at Newftede was founded by William de Albiney, & They were Canons of St. Auftin, & dedicated to the Bleffed Virgin. Monaft. Vol. 2. p. 444. Whereas that which was dedicated to St. Leonard (and which ftill retains the name of St. Leonards, as the other does of Newftede, & are about a furlong diftance from each other) is the fame which You mention under the Title of Durham, numb. 15. p. 59. & was a Cell to Durham, & is now converted into a farm houfe; the chapell (as I take it, becaufe it ftands eaft & weft) is ftill remaining, & now profan'd into the ufe of a Barn; & the Revenue which belong'd to it is now enjoy'd by the E. of Exeter, & is a fmall mannour within the larger mannour of Stamford, and commonly known by the name of Cuthberts fee, no doubt becaufe it formerly belong'd to the church of Durham, which was under the patronage of St. Cuthbert.

I have nothing, Sir, to add now, but over & over again to beg your pardon for this extraordinary Trouble, & that too from an abfolute ftranger to you, at which I cannot but Blufh as often as I reflect upon it. I have only your Goodnefs & your Love to thefe Studies to depend upon for an excufe & Forgivenefs; in Confidence of which I have ventur'd to direct This to You, & to fubfcribe my felfe with the greateft Sincerity,

Sir,
Your moft humble &
affectionate fervant

W. FORSTER.

Stamford, May 12.
1702.

[a] To this letter of Mr. Forfters, Dr. Tanner cannot now tell whether he fent any, or what, anfwer; for, if he fent any, he kept no copy of it; neither could I find any copy, or traces of any fuch anfwer among Mr. Forfters papers which afterwards came to hand. However, as to Leland, I can anfwer, that having, by the favour of my learned friend Mr. Thomas Baker, had the perufal of all the nine Vols. of his Itinerary, & likewife of all the fix Vols. of his Collectanea; & having his Commentarii de Scriptoribus Britannicis my felf: there is not one particular, in all thofe books, relating to Stanford, but what is tranfcribed & inferted in its proper place in my collections.

The

Mr. Forſters Letter to Mr. John Stevens, author of the two additional volumes to the Monaſticon Anglicanum; from a MS. copy, wrote out by Mr. Forſters Son.

S I R,

MS. p. 1.   I Have ſent you a ſhort account, ſuch as my head would give me leave [a], of our antient churches, religious houſes, & colleges; whereby it may eaſily be perceived what We have been.

[b] Stanford in Lincolnſhire is a Saxon town, & perhaps one of the firſt founded here by that nation. For after the Death of Vortimer & Aurelius Ambroſius the Britiſh Generals (the laſt of whom is ſuppos'd to die about 501.) the Saxons had quiet poſſeſſion of the Country hereabouts; from which time the ſouth & the weſt were the conſtant ſcene of action, the power of the Brittains ſinking very faſt, & they retireing apace towards thoſe places, whereunto afterwards they were wholly confin'd. Henry Huntington, in the wars between Edmond Ironſide & the Danes, calls it an antient Citty. The Saxon chronicle calls it, a citty at that time; & it was reckon'd one of the five great citties of the Mercian Kingdom, whoſe Inhabitants were called by way of eminency Fifburgenſes, the Inhabitants of the five Citties. Wherefore wee muſt looke a great way back to diſcover its Infancy, for it is not probable that it ſhould grow up to be thus conſiderable of a ſudden. But to look higher up for its originall than the Saxon time, is vain; nor have we the leaſt authority for it either from Hiſtory or Antiquitys: for here are no remains either of Brittains or Romans; no Encampments, no pavements, no coins dug up, nor any other mark whatever, to ſhew that it is older than the Saxon dayes. It is obſerv'd by Antiquaries, that the Saxon Kings & Nobles ſeated themſelves upon the forſaken Camps & Sta-

MS. p. 2.   tions of the Romans, & made new names by their Ceaſter, Burgh, &c. added to a part of the old Roman, as we have an inſtance in Caſterton near us. But it does not appear from any of our old Hiſtorians or other Records, that this town was known by any other name, than that which it now bears. The Roman way that goes from Caſtor near Peterborough to Lincoln croſſes the River Weland the South Weſt corner of this Town, where there is a ſtony ford at the bottom of a place which they call Nuns Lane, from whence I make no doubt it took its firſt & only name in the Saxon language Stcanꝼonꝺ; but this no way proves that a great town was therefore here, either before, or during the Roman government; ſeeing, as I ſaid before, there are no other remains of Antiquity or Hiſtory to induce us to believe it, as I ſhall ſufficiently make appear, if it pleaſes God to reſtore me to that ſtate of health, whereby I may be able to finiſh the Antiquities of this town.

We have good reaſon to ſuppoſe that this Town was built very early by the Saxons; eſpecially if we may believe Henry Huntington, who informs us, that the Scots & Picts having burnt the Roman ſtation of Gauſſennæ two miles north of us, were here firſt met, & defeated by the Saxons [c]; in memory therefore of their firſt ſucceſs, which prov'd ſo extraordinary beneficiall to them, as to make them Lords of that Land, which they were at firſt hir'd as common mercenaries to defend from thoſe northern enemies; they erected this Town.

Stanford has formerly been much larger without the walls than it is now, & contain'd in it ſixteen pariſh churches or chapells, beſides thoſe of the religious houſes; thirteen in Stanford, & three over the Bridge in Stanford Baron. The names were theſe; St. Marys near the bridge, St. Johns, St. Clements, All Saints in the market place, St. Peters, the chapel of St. Mary Bynwerk or Benewerk [d] juſt within Peter Gate (the place where it ſtood is now called the chapell cloſe [e]) the chapell of Breadcroft without the weſt end of the town in the pariſh of St. Peters [f], St. Michaels, St. Andrews, Trinity, St. Pauls, St. Georges, & St. Stephens, juſt out of Pauls gate; & on the other ſide the water St. Martins, & all Saints within the liberty of the abbat of Peterborough, & the chapell of Burgele (now Burgeley) in the pariſh of St. Martins, where the Prioreſs of St. Michael was obliged to find a miniſter [g]. But by an Act of Parliament 1. Ed. 6. the ordinary, the Alderman, & two more Juſtices of Peace were impowr'd to leſſen   MS. p. 3.

---

a This Letter is without date, but is the laſt thing Mr. Forſter ever wrote about the antiquities of Stanford; his head being ever after diſordered by an inveterate palſie.   b This paragraph is almoſt wholly extracted from his letter to Dr. Tanner.   c Henry of Huntington ſays not a word of their burning the Roman ſtation of Gauſennæ two miles north of us; his words are, *Saxones inierunt autem certamen contra Pictos & Scottos qui jam venerunt uſque ad Stanfordiam, &c.* p. 178. a. 10. edit. Lond.   d St. Mary Bennewerk was not a chapel, but a pariſh church & a rectory.   e More truly is it called in ſeveral old writings I have ſeen, not chapel cloſe, but Bennewerk church yard.   f Breadcroft chapel could not be in St. Peters Pariſh, if in any it muſt be in St. Mary Bennewerks; but I rather think it was in neither, but a parochial chapel of it ſelf.   g Here Mr. Forſter has left out St. Thomas's church, St. Michael Cornſtal church, St. Benets chapel, St. Mary Magdalenes chapel (over againſt St. Martins church) St. Marys chapel by Sempringham hall; & ſeveral others.

the number of them [a], which they did [b], & re-
duc'd them to five in Stanford, & one over
the Bridge, according to an old divifion of the
town into wards [c], allowing a church to each
ward; & fo left ftanding, St. Maries near the
bridge, St. Johns, All Saints, St. Michaels &
St. Georges in Stanford, & St. Martins, over
the bridge; all the reft were taken down, except St. Pauls, which they referv'd for a
fchool-houfe. For William Ratcliffe Efq,
(having been four times Alderman of Stamford) An. Dom. 1530. founded there a free
grammar fchool, & liberally endow'd it
with Meffuages, Lands & Tenements, fituated in Stanford aforefaid, to a confiderable value, which at prefent are let up upon
Leafe, & the referv'd rents to the fchool-
mafter amount to upwards of fixty pounds
per annum.

Now tho' the number of the churches
were thus leffen'd, yet there is but one good
living in the Town, which is All Saints,
having the rectory of St. Peter annext to it,
which hath the Tythes of far the greateft
part of the fields about Stanford; moft of
the reft are now under a kind of confolidation, two of them making a fcanty maintenance for one perfon; tho' my Lord Treafurer Burghley did generoufly give the great
Tythes to the vicaridge of St. Martins.

Befides thefe Churches, there were eight
or nine Religious Houfes; which, becaufe,
Sir, the Monafticon does not take notice of
MS. p. 4. them all, & Speed & our other Hiftorians
give Lame accounts of them, I fhall add
fomething of them, to fupply the defect of
the one, & the miftakes of the other.

On the Eaft of Stanford there is the Priory of Newftead, or *de novo loco*, fituated
upon the River Wafs, in the parifh of Uffington [d], founded by William de Albini
the third (who was buried here in the chapell; as were alfo his wife and his fon William the fourth [e]) dedicated to the bleffed virgin Mary, & the Canons to live after the
Rule of St. Auftin; valued at the diffolution
at 37 l. 6 s. 0 d. Dug. 42 l. 1 s. 3 d. Speed.
I have nothing elfe to add of this Pryory,
but what is in the Monafticon.

A little way from hence, nearer Stanford,
there was a houfe of Benedictin monks dedicated to St. Leonard, & belong'd to the
church of Durham. I cannot find by whom,
or when, it was founded [f]; but it was pretty well endow'd, having the mannor of
Cuthberts Fee in Stanford in part of its poffeffions. It had the advowfon of St. Maries
rectory near the Bridge [g], which I fuppofe
then had fome revenue belonging to it, tho'
now it has nothing left but a fmall houfe.
Part of the chapell to this religious houfe is
ftanding, & makes a venerable appearance [h],
tho' it now ferves for no better ufe than a
farmers barn. Thus thofe facred places are
profan'd. The Monafticon fetts the value at
the diffolution at 25 l. 1 s. 2 d. ob. but Reyner makes it 36 l. & Speed 36 l. 17 s.

Directly north of this Cell ftood a houfe
of the Francifcans, commonly called Grey
Friars or Minorites, but when, or by whom,
founded, I have not been able to find, nor
any other particulars concerning the fame,
befides what follow. In the town coffer of
Stanford is preferv'd this memoriall. That
in the 48 year of K. Edward the third, William de Stone guardian of the Friers minors
& the convent of the fame in Staunford,
did make an exchange of a fountain at
Stacyes-mylne, called Eftwellfheued, with
the town of Staunford (John Brown being
then Alderman) for another Fountain lying,
in what is now called Emblens clofe, juft
oppofite to them, whereby the water was
conveyed to them in leaden pipes, at an eafie
charge. This was a pretty neat fpring fince I
can remember, but now fallen in & deftroyed. The other, about a bowfhot from the
town, now ferves the leaden conduit in St.
Pauls ftreet with Water; & that water which
runs from it fupplies the ftone conduit in the
Butchers row near St. Michaels church;
there being Land in the field left for the fupport of it for ever.

A little to the fouth weft of this, the Dominicans, called the black or preaching fryars,
had feated themfelves; their convent took
up a large parcel of ground, & feems to have
been a confiderable ftructure; but who found-

---

a The number of churches at Stanford was firft reduced by the northern men in 1461. who broke
into the town, & burnt feveral of them, which were never after rebuilt. They were again reduced by
the diffolution of monafteries in 1538. & again by this act 1. E. 6.   b 7. E. 6. when, & not
before, they put the act of the 1. E. 6. in execution.   c Stanford, burgus regis, dedit
geldum T. R. E. pro 12 hundret & dimidio, in exercitu, navigio, & Danegelt. Ibi funt fex cuftodie,
quinque in Lincolfcyre, & fexta in Hantunfcyre, que eft ultra pontem. Ex libro de Domefday.
   d All religious houfes, as I take it, were extra-parochial.   e William de Albini the fourth,
was not buried here, but at Belvoir, & his heart at Croxton. See Dug Bar. Vol. I. p. 115. b.   f It
was founded anno 658. by S. Vilfrid the elder, afterwards Bifhop of York. See his life in my Collections
Book the II.   g The prior & chapter of the conventual church of Durham, & not the prior of
St. Leonards at Stanford, were patrons of the church of St. Mary at the bridge. They were alfo patrons of St. Mary Bennewerk.   h Several years ago I caufed a plate of this chapel to be engraved, by Mr. John Langton of this town, at my own expence. A print from which plate I gave
Mr. Forfter, who, with this letter about the antiquities of Stanford, gave the faid print to Mr. Stevens,
which Mr. Stevens therefore (in his firft additional Vol. to the Monafticon p. 226. b.) writes thus ——
' For what relates to this town of Stanford, & the cut of St. Leonards chapel, we are obliged to the Re-
' verend Mr. William Forfter Rector of St. Clements Danes, who was pleafed to favour us with his
' MS. Collections.' Having thus got a copy of my plate, but not the plate it felf, Mr. Stevens caufed
the faid profpect of St. Leonards chapel to be re-engraved, larger, but exactly like mine, & fo inferted
it in his faid firft Volume, for which he thinks himfelf obliged to Mr. Forfter, tho' he was in truth
more indebted to me. But this he knew not. See the plate I thus got engraved in my collections,
Lib. IV. p. 8.

ed it

MS. p. 5. ed it & when is uncertain : there is a houſe built upon the ruines of it, & belongs to Savil Cuſt Eſq.

Juſt at the eaſt end of the convent of Franciſcans, there was ſituated a large houſe of Carmelites or white fryars, dedicated to the bleſſed virgin Mary ; it was founded by the black princes wife [a], where ſhe was alſo interr'd [b] : it ſeems to have been a large & noble ſtructure for thoſe dayes ; the gate of the outward wall leading to it, is ſtill ſtanding, having three niches where three ſtatues ſeem to have ſtood, & over them three coats of arms ; that, in the middle, was the arms of England & France quarter'd [c] ; but the two others on each ſide of it are ſo defaced, that we cannnot gueſs what they were. This convent was confirm'd by Edward the third, who lodg'd here, & in probability held a great councill (Bradys Hiſt. Vol. II. p. 216.) in this place, when he was at Stanford, & here gave confirmation to the priory of Newſtede the 25 day of June [d].

Theſe religious houſes before mentioned are all ſituated on the eaſt end of Stanford :

at the weſt end whereof, as ſoon as you are out of Peter gate, on the left hand, there ſtood a convent of Auſtin fryars, which, if anſwerable to the circumference of incloſed ground, was a very large one, being above a quarter of a mile in length ; one Flemming (Lel. Collect. Vol. 6. p. 29.) a very rich man of Stanford, was the founder of it ; the care of finiſhing it was committed to the archdeacon of Richmond ; but no mention of any date or other particulars.

[e] ' The [Auſtin] friery without St. Peters ' Gate, on the left hand, has doubtleſs been ' a moſt noble Fabrick, as appears by the ' remaining ruins which have been careful- ' ly inſpected. The weſt front appears to ' have been 80 yards long. The ſouth ' front 10 yards long. The chapel ſtand- ' ing on the north ſide, may eaſily be ' diſcern'd to have been 40 yards long & ' 20 yards wide [f] ; & the end of the chapel, ' weſtward, ſeems to have rang'd along the ' the cloyſters, which are of the ſame length ' & breadth with the chapel [g]. In which ' place lately digging to make a ſaw-pit,

---

a It was founded by K. Henry the third.   b She was not buried in the white friers, but in the Grey Friers at Stanford.   c Not England & France, but France & England.

d See an account of the parliament at Stanford. Ap. 23. 11. Edw. 3. 1337. when the King was there, in my collections under that year. Alſo his confirmation to the hoſpital of S. Mary of Newſted, June 25. the ſame year.   e This whole paragraph was wrote by Mr. Richard Walburg, who gave me a copy of it under his own hand, which I gave to Mr. Forſter, who gave it to Mr. Stevens, who printed it in his ſecond additional Vol. to the Monaſticon, p. 228. Mr. Walburgs copy is now again in my hands, return'd by Mr. Forſters Son. Mr. Forſter however did not know by whom, or when, it was wrote ; for I never told him. For which reaſon, & becauſe Mr. Walburg writes in the preſent tenſe, the eaſt front *is* 80 yards, the whole *is* an entire ſquare, &c. inſtead of the preterperfect (as he ſhould have done) Mr. Stephens at firſt ventures to write ; ' the ruins of it now ' ſtanding are venerable, & give a good Idea of its former Grandeur, of which the following is an ex- ' act account from the MS. collections of the Reverend Mr. Forſter ' —— then tranſcribes this paragraph, as wrote by Mr. Walburg, verbatim as here given ; but concludes it thus, ' this account of theſe ' ruins I tranſcribed from the old MS. above quoted, & they might be ſtanding when the ſame was ' written. But I am aſſured by the aforeſaid Mr. Forſter, now reſiding at Stanford, that there are no ſuch ' remains now, nor any thing but ſome heaps of rubbiſh '; which is indeed true.   f This deſcription is rather florid & imaginary, than true & real. For there were, to my certain knowledge, no ruins ſtanding when Mr. Walburg took this account ; only here & there ſome little riſings in the ground, by which it might, in ſome places, be juſt diſcern'd where the foundation walls of the houſe went ; but thoſe riſings very little more than what we now ſee. Beſides for a chapel to be but forty yards long, & yet twenty yards wide, is a very odd proportion.   g And for the cloyſters to be as broad as the chapel (that is twenty yards wide) is what I believe was never yet heard of in any old monaſtery. The above digging at the Auſtin-Friers was in Feb. 1711. 12. when Mr. Richard Feaſt, who then rented the ſite of that houſe of the late earl of Exeter, procured leave to dig for ſtone out of the ruins, in order to build a barn there ; at which time, beſides what ſtone ſufficed for the ſaid barn, he alſo took up as much other ſtone, as built a little court wall in his yard at Sempringham hall on St. Peters hill, where he then lived. Many of the ſtones which he brought to Sempringham hall & fixed in the wall there, were curiouſly carved, repreſenting divers birds, beaſts, fruits, & flowers ; which carved ſtones, it is probable, were fixed in the centre or joinings of the arching over head in the cloiſter, which, we may ſuppoſe, ran quite round the inſide of the court. At the ſame time one of the workmen picked up among the rubbiſh two antient ſeals ; one of them, as I remember by an impreſs of it which I once had (tho' both it & the ſeal it ſelf are now again loſt) repreſenting the buſt, or face & neck parts, of a bearded man, & inſcribed around the border, *Sigillum Hugonis capellani.* This ſeal was about as broad as a Q. Eliz. ſhilling. The other a much more remarkable & beautiful ſeal, was purchaſed, of the labourer who found it, by John Maddiſon Eſq. the figure whereof is here inſerted, as drawn from an impreſſion of it, given me by the late Mr. Richard Walburg. Another impreſſion of this ſeal I ſome time ago ſent the learned & revd. White lord biſhop of Burg S. Peters, who thereupon wrote thus to me. ' I thank you for the impreſs of the ſeal. In Sir James ' Wares catalogue of Iriſh Biſhops are mentioned ſeveral of the ſee of Elphin of the name of Tho- ' mas. As I. Thomas O Connor, dean of Achonry, conſecrated 1246. & tranſlated to Tuam 1259. ' II. Thomas Mac Ferral, Mac Dermot, abbat of Buelly, who died biſhop of Elphin in 1265. a ' benefactor to the temple & church of S. Paul in London. III. Thomas Barret, archdeacon of Enach- ' dun, conſecrated in 1372. who died in 1404. IV. Thomas Cheſter born at London, died at Killia- ' than, in June 1584. This laſt is out of the queſtion —— Mar. 6. 1719. 20. ' Moſt are of opinion that this ſeal belonged to Thomas O Connor. But as biſhop Barrets name ſounds Engliſh, I rather fancy it was his ; & that he lay here in his travels & then loſt it. But theſe are meer conjectures.

' were

Sigillum dñi thome dei
gracia elphinenſis epī.

To
Samuel Gale Esqr.
one of the kind Encouragers
of this work.
this plate is most thankfully
inscribed

To that Curious and
Communicative Antiquary
Brown Willis of Whaddon
Hall in y County of Bucks
Esq: this Plate in Gratitude
for his Favor and many
Encouragements of this work
is most thankfully Inscrib'd.

The South West Prospect of M.ʳ W.ᵐ Browns Hospital.

M.ʳ Forsters Leiters . p. 11.

' were found the skulls & bones of men.
' The chapel feems to range even with, &
' joyn to the eaft front, as the cloyfters do
' to the weft. The eaft front is alfo 80 yards;
' fo that the whole is an entire fquare, & in
" the middle thereof very plainly appears a
' curious & compleat court, being exactly 30
' yards every way. The ftone pillars & win-
' dows, which have been dug up in the ruins,
' render the ftructure very magnificent; &
' fome of the rooms, whether for convenien-
' cy or curiofity, have been paved with a fine
' fort of glaz'd tiles of different colours,
' two inches thick, & nine Inches fquare;
' a whole load of them was found, as they
' lay on a pav'd floor, & more might have
' been taken up, but that they were fpoil'd,
' & fo not thought worth while. On the
' weft front, at a fmall diftance, there yet
' appears to have been a very curious gar-
' den, as by the degrees, which both in
' length, breadth, & afcent, were very care-
' fully, exactly, & proportionably made; &
' the South front, by the rifing of the ground,
' affures us it was approached to by a noble
' & gradual afcent; the whole being envi-
' ron'd by a ftone wall, near half a mile a-
' bout. The fituation as fweet, pleafant &
' delightfull, as if nature here wanted no
' affiftance from art. The South & Weft
' Profpects made agreeable by the filver
' ftream of the River Welland & its moft
' rich & fragrant meadows. A little beyond
' the North-Weft end of this Friery is a long
' Hedge, commonly call'd Pewterers-Hedge,
' where, according to Tradition, was for-
' merly a ftreet, inhabited by Pewterers [a],
' for which we have no other authority; &
' at the weft end of this [friery,] very fairly
' appears the Roman High-Way. About
' a quarter of a mile weft of this friery,
' ftood a fmall village called Breadcroft,
' which fome are of opinion receiv'd its
' name from the feveral Bakers inhabiting
' the fame, as appears by fome old wri-
' tings in the evidence room, of Mr.
' William Browns Hofpital in Stanford; &
' nigh Breadcroft was lately found, by a
' perfon at plow, a large ftone Coffin, which
' may be ftill feen in a Clofe called Rock's
' Clofe, without St. Clements gate; & is
' us'd as a trough to water horfes.

Directly oppofite to this [friery] on the
fouth fide of the river in Stanford-Baron
Northamptonfhire, in the parifh of St. Martins, was a convent of nuns [b], founded by
MS. p. 6. William [Waterville] Abbot of Peterborough, upon the Roman way, for forty religious, in the reign of Hen. 2. & dedicated
to St. Michael; & it was directly under the
protection of the Abby of Peterborough.

About half a mile off, at Wyrthorpe [c] in the
faid parifh [d], there was another convent for
nuns, which, thro' a peftilence & other accidents, was fo ruin'd, that there was but one
nun left in it; whereupon Thomas Holland &
Joanna [his wife] petitioned K. Edward the
3. that it might be united to St. Michaels a-
bove faid, which the King by letter gave
the Bifhop of Lincoln (in whofe Diocefs it
then was) leave to perform.

I have nothing to add of this convent
of St. Michael, but what is in the Monafticon; at the diffolution it was valued
at 65 l. 19 s. 9 d.

In the fame parifh [of St. Martin] at the
foot of the bridge, Brand de Foffato, Ri-
cardus de Humez conftabularius, & Ber-
tramnus de Verdun, founded & endowed a
religious houfe, dedicated to St. John [the
Baptift] & Thomas [Becket] the Martyr,
for the reception of poor ftrangers frequently paffing that road. K. Richard the 1. confirmed this donation. It was valued at the
diffolution at 18 l. 16 s. 0 d. ¼. The houfe
of Mr. Death feems to be a part of the old
ftructure [e].

More fouthward in Stamford-Baron, before you enter the town, there was another
houfe dedicated to St. Egidius, with a chapel & feveral lands in the field, for all difeafed
poor perfons that travel'd that way. This
is all we can tell of it; now two or three
poor houfes ftand there called the fpital.

In the market place in Stanford, William Brown merchant of the Staple of Calais, & fometime Alderman of Stanford, e-
rected a very fine building for a Beadhoufe,
dedicated . . . . . [f] with an handfome chapel for
divine fervice, for ten poor men & two women, & two chaplains of the fecular clergy
(for Mr. Brown had no good opinion of MS. p. 7.
the Regulars) This place was firft incorporated by K. Edward the 4. & in the 11. of Henry the 7. they were again, by an infpeximus,
incorporated by the name of the Almshoufe
of Will. Brown, confifting of a Warden,
Confrater, & twelve poor. And thus it
ftood 'till the reign of K. James the 1. when
fome perfons, defiring to engrofs the revenue, fuggefted that it was abus'd to fuperftitious ufes, in hopes to get a grant of it;
but the truth being laid before the King,
he was fo far from liftening to the fuggeftions of thofe ill defigning perfons, that he
was pleas'd to confirm it, & gave them a
new charter, calling it by the name of the
beadhoufe of Will. Brown, for a warden,
confrater, & twelve poor, of the foundation of K. James; by vertue of which they enjoy the liberal foundation of the founder; &
may they ever do it.

a It is more likely the pewterers kept their ftalls there at Midlent fair. For formely a great part of
that fair was held without the town.   b This convent was not in St. Martins parifh,
but extra-parochial, & called little Wyrthorp.   c Great Wyrthorp.   d Not
in St. Martins parifh.   e Mr. Dethes houfe could not be a part of the old ftructure; tho'
I believe it was either a college or a religious houfe, perhaps St. Pulchers. As for the hofpital of St.
John & St. Thomas it ftood next the bridge; next to it ftood the abbat of Croylands houfe, next to it
Mr. Dethes. So that it is very unlikely that part of this hofpital fhould ftand on one fide of the
abbat of Croylands houfe (now the George inne) & part of it on the other.   f To St. Mary
& All Saints.

3

When

When any place in this Beadhouse falls void, whether of the chaplains, or of the poor; then the vicar of All Saints & the Dean of Stanford fill up the[a] vacancy; but if they do it not in a fortnights time, then the mayor of Stanford may do it in a fortnights time; which if he fails in, then the heirs of the founder shall do it in the like time; but if they fail, the bishop of Lincoln has a fortnights time to fill them up; but he not doing it, it shall return to the vicar of all Saints & the Dean of Stanford [b] again for a fortnight; & so on, *toties quoties*, 'till the vacancy is fill'd.

Mr. Brown gave them the manor of Swafield & North-Witham; with divers farms, messuages, lands, & tenements in Stanford, Pilsgate, Easton, North-Luffenham & other places, which being let upon the lease, the reserv'd rent affords to the poor 2 s. & 4 d. per week each of them, to the Warden 24 l. & to the confrater 20 l. per annum; they have woods of their own which supply the house with fuel for the whole year; the poor have new gowns of blew cloth every two years; the warden has a convenient habitation to dwell in, who has the government of the house, looks after the estate, & lets the leases. The Confrater reads prayers twice a day, except when there are prayers at All Saints church, which the poor are obliged to attend[c]; The vicar of All Saints audits the accounts every year; & the bishop of Lincoln is the Visitor.

Stanford is the head of a rural Deanery, & there has always been a Dean nominated by the bishop of Lincoln as often as it has become vacant, in order to fill up the vacancies in the above-mentioned Bead-house.

There was also one John Brown, merchant of the staple of Calais, brother, or very near Relation of the aforemention'd Will. Brown[c], who built the beautiful steeple of All Saints church, at his own charge[d].

William lord Burghley, ann. dom. 1597. erected an hospital at the south end of Stanford Bridge, upon part of the place where formerly stood the religious house dedicated to St. John [Baptist] & Thomas the martyr; & endow'd it with lands & tenements, & a perpetual annuity out of Cliff Park near Stanford, for the maintenance of a Warden & twelve poor men; the Warden receiving 3 s. & 4 d. & each poor man 2 s. & 4 d. per week, with a yearly allowance of wood, & blew cloth to make each of them a gown.

Mr. Thomas Truesdale Gent. & Attorney at Law, was, in his life time, a constant & liberal benefactor to the poor; &, at his death (which was 23. Oct. 1700.) left, by his last will, a house in Scotgate, for six poor men for ever, & endow'd it with lands at Baston & Moreton, whereby the poor have 2 s. 6 d. each per week, new gowns, & a chaldron of coals for fuel yearly[e].

As to the University, if wee will listen to Hardings chronicle, we must look a prodigious way back for the beginning of it; even to K. Bladud, seven or eight hundred years before Christ: for thus he sings,

Bladud his sonne soone after him did succede,
And reigned after then full xx. yere;
Cair Bladud, so that now is Bath I rede,
He made anone the hot Bathes there infere.
When at Athenes he had studied clere,
He brought withe him iiii. Philosophiers wise,
Schole to hold in Britayn & exercise,
Stanforde he made, that Stanforde hight this day,
In which he made an Universitie,
His Philosophiers, as Merlyn doth saye,
Had scholers fele of great habilitee,
Studyng ever alwayes in unitee,
In all the seven liberal science,
For to purchace wysedome & sapience.

Now this was above 100. years before Thales, who first brought philosophy out of the East into Greece. But such stories we leave to them, who are lovers of such Romantick Tales.

[f] If you take the word University as a law term, implying a legal society, incorporated for the profession of learning, which, as the Civilians say, none but the supream authority can do, then there never was such a thing as an university here. But that there were *Scholæ illustres* for the education of novices for the neighbouring monasteries, sufficiently appears from Leland (Collect. Vol. 6. p. 30.[g]) who tells us, that the names of Peterburgh haul, Sempringham & Vauldey remain'd at this time at Stanford, as places for those houses of men of religion that sent their schollars thither to study. And moreover he tells us, that in the age next the conquest, the monks had their colleges founded & liberally endow'd for the education of their novices[h].

Now why may not we suppose the original of these schools to have been laid by those monks of Croyland, that Joffridus the Abbot sent to Wyrthorpe in Henry the firsts time, after that monastery was burnt; & that they did not only preach here, but

MS. p. 8.

MS. p. 9

MS. p. 10.

---

a If Mr. Forster had cast his eye upon the fifth statute of the founder he would have seen, that every vacancy was to have been filled by the vicar of All Saints in the mercat & the dean of Stanford in a fortnight; or the heirs of the said William Brown in another fortnight; or the alderman of Stanford & the abbat of Croyland in another fortnight; or the bishop of Lincoln in another fortnight; & so on, according to the order here specified.   b The dean of Stanford was formerly a person of great power, & the clergy of Stanford, religious & secular, were his chapter; which makes him something more than a meer rural dean.   c He was Mr. William Browns elder brother.   d Mr. Butcher says Mr. Will. Brown built that steeple. The inscription on Mr. John Browns monument says, he was *hujus ecclesie benefactor*. e Mr. Forster gives no account here of the Calice, S. Logars, & Mr. Snowdens hospitals. f This paragraph is mostly taken from his letter to Dr. Tanner.   g It should be Itin. Vol. 6. p. 3.   h I don't remember this last passage is in Leland any where.

taught

The Seal of Mr Browns hospital.

To Charles Bale, M.D. one of
the kind Encouragers of this work,
this Plate is most gratefully inscribed.

The North Prospect of the Lord Burghley's Hospital in Stanford Baron.

Mr Forster's Letters

P. 42. B.

St Martin's Church Steeple

The great Common.

The Welland

taught the youth likewise, as, Pet. Blefens tells us, fome of the monks of that monaftery, who were fent at the fame time to Cottenham, did at Cambridge ? viz. read Logick, Philofophy, &c.

However let this pafs as meer conjecture; yet it is certain that Robert Lutterel Rector of Irnham did, in the 20. of Ed. 1. found a fchool for the ufe of Sempringham convent; fo that it is plain there was one, & very probably more feminaries for Learning inftituted here, before the Oxonians came hither in the time of Edward the 3. (which Mr. Cambden fuppofes to have given birth to the univerfity of Stanford) for it is not likely that they would fix upon this place for their retreat, & be fo unwilling to leave it as they were, except there had been fome fchools of learning here before, for their reception; & fome fort of Academy already inftituted.

ᵃ ' Whatever was the occafion of their ' coming hither; whether contefts between ' the northern & fouthern ftudents; or whe- ' ther, according to Mr. Wood, that the ' Prophecy of Merlin might be fulfill'd, ' tho' perhaps it was made after this bufi- ' nefs was over) which fays,

' Doctrine ftudium quod nunc viget ad Va- da Boum,
' Tempore venturo celebrabitur ad Vada Saxi.

MS.p.11. ' Of which our admirable Spencer thus fings ' in his marriage of the Rivers, Thames & ' Medway,

' And after him the fatal Wellant went,
' That, if old fawes prove true (which God forbid)
' Shall drowne all Holland with his excre- ment,
' And fhall fee Stanford, tho' now homely hid,
' Then fhine in Learning more than ever did
' Cambridge or Oxford, Englands goodly beams.

' Whatever the caufe was, in 1334. dur- ' ing the months of May, June, & July, ' they flock'd in great numbers to Stanford, ' & there went on with their Academical ' ftudies. But, upon complaint of the univer- ' fity of Oxford to the king, his majefty, in ' Auguft, by proclamation, commanded the ' High Sheriff of Lincolnfhire to difperfe ' them; but they took no notice of it. ' Whereupon the king, by a fecond procla- ' mation in November, commanded the ' High Sheriff to go to Stanford himfelf, ' which he did, & gave notice, that if they ' did not immediately return back to Ox- ' ford, their goods & books fhould all be ' confifcated, Upon this fome return'd, ' but others ftaid at Stanford; whereupon

' Oxford complained again to the king; ' whereupon his majefty, by a third pro- ' clamation, commanded the High She- ' riff to drive the remaining ftudents by force ' out of Stanford; which ftill had not the de- ' fired effect, 'till the King gave Power to ' fome perfons, to take the names of the ' ftudents at Stanford, & fend 'em to him, ' having firft feis'd upon their books & o- ' ther effects, & brought them into the kings ' treafury; therefore upon wednefday next ' after the feaft of S. James, there was an ' inquifition made before William Truffell, ' & twelve men upon oath joyntly gave ' in their names who had taught univerfity ' Learning, after they had been forbidden by ' the king; which [perfons fo teaching] ' were thefe. Magifter Gulielmus de Bar- ' nabey. Magifter Thomas de Kendale. ' Magifter Thomas de Hotofte. Magifter ' Johannes de Whitwell. Magifter Guli- ' elmus de Robey. Magifter Robertus de ' Barton. Magifter Hugo de Lincolne. Ma- ' gifter Gulielmus de Donelfhaw. Magifter ' Simon de Beckingham. Magifter Petrus ' de Aulebey. Magifter Johannes de Stock- ' ton. Magifter Thomas de Efton. Ma- ' gifter Petrus Rector S. Petri in Stanfordia. ' Magifter Johannes de Bolton. Magifter ' Thomas de la Mare. Magifter Johannes ' de Ramifton. Magifter Robertus Bernard. ' Gulielmus le Bachelaure. Dominus Jo- ' hannes Blandolfe Rector ecclefie de Scot- ' tes prope Granthamam. Dominus Hen- ' ricus Rector Tinwellenfis. Dominus Ro- ' bertus de Bourle, vicarius S. Andree in ' Stanfordia. Dominus Henricus, vicarius ' omnium SS. ultra pontem Stanfordianum. ' Dominus Richardus Rector S. Georgii MS.p.12 ' in Stanfordia. Gulielmus de Everwickes. ' Radulphus de Acherche. Gualterus de ' Notyngham. Johannes de Kirbie-Beliers. ' Dominus Thomas Rector de Stanhope. ' Johannes de Twyfelyngton. Hugo de ' Suttewel. Robertus de Hefelbethe. Jo- ' hannes de Kelmcrfhe. Philippus obfona- ' tor eneafenfis in Stanfordia. Johannes de ' Schetlanger. Johannes filius Gilberti de ' Foderinghey. Johannes filius Galfridi de ' Bernake. And this put an end to the Oxo- ' nians ftudy here; &, for fear the like acci- ' dent fhould ever happen again, the univer- ' fity made a ftatute, that no Oxford man ' fhould profefs in Stanford.

The names of our Colleges that we have any mention of, are thefe. I. Sempringham hall, in the parifh of St. Peter, was founded by Robert Lutteril Rector of Irnham, who gave lands & tenements in the towns of Ketten, Cotifmore, & Cafterton in the county of Rutland, & a large houfe & lands in Stanford, to maintain three chaplains to fay mafs for his foul, one in the parifh church of S. Andrew at Irnham, another in the chapel of S. Mary Benwerk ᵇ at Stanford, & the third

---

a All this account of the univerfity is copied, tranflated, & extracted from Mr. Woods Antiquitates Oxon. fub anno 1334. The fame, much enlarged, from other authors, may be feen in my collecti- ons, under the years 1333, 1334, & 1335.   b Robert Lutterel gave the monks of Sem- pringham a manor of his in S. Peters parifh, within which manor was a fmall chapel, with a chante-

third in the conventual church at Sempringham; & all the rest he gave for the support of a school at Stanford, wherein the youth were taught Divinity & Philosophy, to the increase of the number of the convent at Sempringham. The Bishop of Lincoln in 1303. did allow them the use of the chapel of St. Mary Bennewerk ᵃ for divine service. The front of the house is still standing, & carries with it the appearance of an old collegiate building ᵇ. II. Over against All Saints church in the market place there stands an antient building called formerly Black-hall ᶜ. Mr. Wood says, there was a kitchen there that gave very evident marks of antiquity. I know not what the kitchen might be, but the shape of the windows & a room used for a parlour did most plainly shew it not to be of common use. It is now the dwelling house of Mr. White a Baker. III. In S. Maries street there is an inne called the old Swan, which common fame will have to have been a college. IV. That there was a college here called Brazen-Nose is certain. The old Gate, with the Brazen-nose, with a ring thro' it, is still remaining there; that there was a refectory or hall here in Mr. Woods time, is plain ; but that is pull'd down, & a new house built, which now is appropriated to the poor children of the charity school; by whom it was built, or to what convent it belong'd, we have no records left to shew. But it was here in Edward the thirds time; for one of those that were return'd by the jury for keeping up university exercises, after they had been enjoin'd the contrary by the king, was Philip the obsonator or manciple of Brazen-nose in Stamford. Thus it is certain that this could not borrow the title of Brazen-nose from Oxford, but rather Oxford from this ᵈ. ' Because, as we have seen, this of Stamford ' is as old as K. Edward the third, and per- ' haps older. Whereas Brazen-nose in Ox- ' ford was founded but in K. Henry the 7ᵗʰˢ. ' time by William Smith bishop of Lincoln ' & Richard Sutton. Now it is probable ' that the bishop, in visiting his diocess, did ' meet with this college of Brazen-nose in ' Stamford, & so called his own college af- ' ter it.' V. An house standing full east of the parsonage house, of St. Georges, was a school of Carmelites or white Friers, tho' Mr. Wood could not tell any more of it than that it was a college, for want of

MS.p.13.

records. VI. There runs along the south side of S. Georges church the length of the street, a building very like the old Halls in Oxford; while it stood entire, the arch'd doors & windows, after the antient form, plainly shew'd it to have been a house of Learning ᵉ.

I shall conclude all with a remarkabe story of a poor man who was miraculously cur'd of a consumption ; the story is certainly true, & there are several alive now that knew the man. The relation was wrote by his own hand, which I rather set down in his words, to avoid all suspition of falsehood or mistake. It is as follows.

ᶠ ' First of all this my sickness was a sur- ' fit taken by carrying in of two loade of ' wood into my own yarde upon our green- ' goose faire day ; it was in the yeare of our ' Lord 1645. & the day was very hot; so ' I tooke in hand for to carry it in my self. ' And when I found my self very hott, & ' weary, & dry, I went into the house, & ' dranke, &, all unbrased, I layd me down ' upon the grasse. And, when I felt my self ' somewhat coole, I went & carryed in a- ' gain; & so likewise when I found my self ' weary, hott, & dry, I went into the house, ' & dranke, & lay me downe upon the ' grasse : And thus I did at the least a half ' dozen times before I had carryed it all in. ' At the last when I had carryed it all in, ' I thought my self to be very well, but on- ' ly I was very hott. But in that night I ' fell very sick, so that many said, I should ' not live. So I continued very bad. But ' at length it turned to a feaver, & the ex- ' tremity of the feaver brought me to a ' deep consumption. Yet I wrought of my ' trade for the space of four years a little; ' & then I grew so weak, that I could not ' maintain my trade no longer. Then I ' taught children for to read & wright; & ' thus I did for the space of seven years, ' until I founded [swooned] as I taught ' them. Then my neighbours came in, & ' tooke me up for dead, & layed me upon ' my bed; yet the Lord being merciful un- ' to me, he gave me life & breath again ; ' & I lay in bed for the space of two whole ' years, except the time of my bed making, ' sometime about an hour when I found ' my self in my best case : this was my first ' fall in my sickness.

ry belonging to it, dedicated to the blessed virgin Mary ; but not called S. Mary Bennewerk. Bennewerk is thrust in by Mr. Forster without any manner of warrant. St. Mary Bennewerk was a parish church standing in the same street with this S. Marys chapel, & that led him into the mistake. For he thought that chapel & S. Mary Bennewerk were one & the same, whereas they were distinct.

a Here he thrusts Bennewerk in again without any authority for so doing. See the bishop of Lincolns license in my collections under the year 1303. Bennewerk is not to be found in it. The chapel of S. Mary there spoken of, was a small thing that was not privileged with so much as a font or a belfry, either of which S. Mary Bennewerk, being a rectory, could not want. b Here Mr. Forster takes an old college, which stood before S. Mary Bennewerk church, for Sempringham Hall, which stood where Mr. alderman Feast lately dwelt. c This is a mistake for Peterborough Hall. Black-hall stood at the north west end of All Saints church, where is now, or was lately, the sign of the Talbot. d What else he here says of Brazen-nose college, is taken almost word for word from Mr. Butcher. e There is a large account of these, & divers other colleges, in my collections. f This whole paragraph is very curious, & I think not to be met with in any other accounts of Wallis which I have yet seen. Whence Mr. Forster copied it, I find not.

' Upon

' Upon Whifon-Sunday, about fix a clock
' in the afternoon after evening fermon, be-
' ing but newly up, the woman, that keept
' me, had made me a fire, & was gone forth,
' & had fhut to the doores. And as I came
' from my bed by the way in the window,
' there I tooke a paire of fpectacles, & a
' little booke (the booke is called, Abrahams
' fute for Sodom) & I read about the fpace
' of halfe a hour; then I hard one rap at
' the dore; fo I fuppofed it for to be a ftranger,
' becaufe they came not in, & being that
' it was the fabbath day. So, being that the
' doores was fhut, I was conftrained for to
' go my felf. So I laide down the booke.
' So I tooke my ftick in my hand, &, by
' the wall with my other hand, I went to
' the doore; which I had not been fo far
' of two years before. And, when I had
' opened the doore, there I did behold a
MS. p. 14. ' fine, proper, tall, grave, old man. He faid,
' friend, I pray thee give an old pilgrim a
' cup of thy fmall beer. I faid, Sir, I pray
' you come in. He faid, friend, call me not
' Sir, for I am no Sir; but come in I muft,
' for I cannot pafs thy dore, before I doe
' come in. I faid, Sir, I pray you, come
' in & wellcom; for indeed I had thought
' he had been fo dry, that he could not
' pafs the doore before he had drunk: there-
' fore thus did I expect. So we both came
' in together, & left the doors both open.
' So as well as the Lord God did inable
' me, with my ftick in one hand, & by the
' wall with my other, I went & drew him
' a cup of fmall beer; & I gave it him in
' his hand, & full glad was I to fit me down.
' So hee walked twice or thrice to & fro,
' & then dranke; & thus did he walk to
' & fro three times, before that he had drank
' it all off. And then he came, & fet the cup
' in the window by me. Then I thought
' that he had been going, but he was not.
' So he walk'd to & fro as he did before.
' All this while he faid nothing to me, nor
' I to him. Then, when he came almoft at
' me, he faid, friend, thou art not well. I
' faid, no truly, Sir, I have not been well
' thefe many years. He faid, what is thy
' difeafe? I faid, in a deep confumption,
' Sir, & our Doctors faie I am paft cure.
' He faid, in that they fay very well. But
' what have they given thee for it? I faid, tru-
' ly, Sir, nothing; for I am a very poor
' man, & unable to follow Doctors advice;
' fo I willingly commit my felf into the
' hands of the almighty God: whatever his
' will is I am very well content. In that,
' faid he, thou faieft very well; but I will
' tell thee what to do by the help & power
' of the Almighty God above; I pray thee
' remember my words, & obferve them, &
' do it : But, whatfoever thou doeft, above
' all things, fear God & ferve him——To
' morrow, when thou rifeft, go into thy
' garden, & there gather two red fage leaves
' & one Bloudwort leaf, & put thofe three
' leaves into a cup of fmall beer, & let

' them lye in the cup the fpace of three
' dayes together; drinke as oft as need re-
' quires; &, when thou haft drunke it all off,
' fill the cup againe. But obferve this thing,
' that thou let the leaves remaine ftill in the
' cup; but the fourth day in the morning caft
' them away, & put in three more frefh.
' The fourth day is the firft of the three a-
' gain. And thus do every fourth day in
' the morning for 12 daies together, neither
' more nor lefs. Therefore I pray thee re-
' member my words, & obferve them, &
' do it; but, howfoever thou doeft, above
' all things fear God & ferve him. And for
' the fpace of thefe 12 dayes, thou muft
' drink neither Ale nor ftrong beer; yet af-
' terwards thou maift, a little; & thou fhalt
' fee, through the goodnefs & mercy of God
' unto thee, that before thefe 12 dayes be   MS. p. 15.
' forth, that thy difeafe will be cur'd, & thy
' body alter'd. I thought thofe things were
' very fmall to cure my difeafe, & faid, Sir,
' are thefe things good for all confumpti-
' ons? He faid, I tell thee, I tell thee, I
' pray thee remember what I fay unto thee;
' & obferve, & do it : but, howfoever thou
' doeft, above all things fear God & ferve
' him. But, faid he, this is not all; for
' thou muft change the air for thy health.
' And I faid, Sir, what do you mean by
' changing the air? And he faid, thou muft go
' the fpace of three, four, or five miles off
' but if it be twenty miles off the better; &
' there thou muft continue in the frefh air,
' for the fpace of a whole month. I, be-
' ing unwilling to do that, faid, Sir, if it may
' pleafe God to enable me fo as to go into
' our own air twice or thrice a day, will not
' that ferve? He faid, I tell thee, it will not ;
' for that air where this infection was taken,
' is not properly good to cure this difeafe.
' Therefore I pray thee remember my words
' which I fay unto thee, & obferve them, &
' do it; but howfoever thou doeft, above
' all things fear God & ferve him. And
' thou muft go as fpeedily forth as thou
' poffibly canft, or elfe a very grievous fit
' of ficknefs will overtake thee very fudden-
' ly; yet, through Gods great goodnefs &
' mercy unto thee, this by doing thou
' mayft avoid it. And againe thou fhalt fee,
' through Gods great goodnefs & mercy un-
' to thee, that before thy month [a] and thefe
' 12 days be forth, that thofe cloaths
' thou now weareft will be too little for
' thee, that thou canft not wear them with
' eafe. I pray thee remember what I fay
' unto thee, & obferve my words, & do it;
' but, howfoever thou doeft, above all things
' fear God & ferve him. In remembrance
' of words before fpoken concerning my
' being let blood, which none of a long
' time before would advife me to; I put
' this queftion to him. Sir, faid I, I had
' thought to have been let blood, as weak a
' creature as I am. But he faid, no, no,
' friend, by no means; for thou fhalt fee,
' through the great goodnefs & mercy

[a] The month that he was to go into the country for the benefit of the air.

' of

MS.p.16. ‘ of God towards thee, that before thy
‘ month & theſe 12 days be forth, that thy
‘ blood will be as good as ever it was in all
‘ thy life; & thou will't be as healthful &
‘ as ſound as ever thou was in all thy life;
‘ but this thing remember, obſerve that thy
‘ ioynts will be weak as long as thou liveſt.
‘ Now friend, ſaid he, I muſt be going. So
‘ when I ſaw him turn his face towards the
‘ door, I remembred & thought with my ſelf,
‘ that, becauſe he had drank, he might be as
‘ well hungry as dry. Therefore, Sir, ſaid
‘ I, doth it pleaſe you to eat any bread &
‘ cheeſe, or butter? you ſhall be very wel-
‘ come. He ſaid, no, no, friend, I will not
‘ eat any thing; the Lord Chriſt is ſufficient
‘ for me: & very ſeldom do I drink any
‘ beer, only what comes from the rock :
‘ ſo the Lord God in heaven be with thee.
‘ Then I roſe up, & took my ſtick in one
‘ hand, & by the wall with the other, went
‘ to ſhut the door after him: So when I was
‘ at the houſe door, he was at the ſtreet door
‘ but not gone forth. So he return'd
‘ back again half way in the entry towards
‘ me, & I ſtood ſtill at the houſe door. And
‘ thus he ſaid, friend, thou haſt heard what
‘ I have ſaid unto thee, I pray thee remem-
‘ ber my words, & obſerve them, & do it ;
‘ but, I ſay unto thee, howſoever thou doſt,
‘ above all things fear God & ſerve him.
‘ And ſo he departed from me.
‘ At that time this was my condition.
‘ My ſkin cleav'd to my bones for want of
‘ fleſh; my body being parcht & dry, with a
‘ yellow ſkin all over, & a white ſcurf up-
‘ on it, for want of moiſture. So the fifth
‘ day in the morning, when I roſe, being
‘ ſomewhat lightſome, the white ſcurf flew
‘ forth out of my boſome, & I wonder'd
‘ what it was. So I rub'd my hand upon
‘ my body, & the more I rub'd, the more
‘ ſcurf came off; ſo I regarded it not much,
‘ but the next morning I look'd upon my
‘ body, & the ſcurf was almoſt all off, &

‘ the yellow ſkin was crack'd in ſmall
‘ ſcales lik the ſcurf, & as I thought ſome-
‘ what looſe. But in the ſpace of three
‘ daies it all came off, & there was a new
‘ ſkin all over my body, as young & tender
‘ as the ſkin of a new born child. So bleſ-
‘ ſed be the Lord, my fleſh came upon me
‘ more & more, 'till my cloaths were ſo
‘ little that I could not wear them with
‘ eaſe; according as he had ſaid.
‘ Thus was his habit. His hat was faſhi-
‘ onable, & ſuch as men now wear. The
‘ hair of his head was as white as wool,
‘ curl'd up round & buſhy, cloſe unto his
‘ hatt. The hair of his beard was as white;
‘ broad, but not very long. He had a little
‘ hair on both ſides of his cheeks. He was
‘ very fair, with a fine, ruddy complection ;
‘ & very tall of ſtature. His band was but a
‘ little turn'd from his collar. His coat was
‘ of a purple colour; no trimming at his
‘ knees. He had no gloves or ruffles; but
‘ a ſmall white ſtick in his hand, & his
‘ hand was of a very pure white. His ſhoes
‘ were black & plain; ty'd with ſtrings of
‘ a purple colour, ſuitable to his cloaths ;
‘ but, whether ribbon, or inkle, I know not.
‘ And his ſtockings were pure white; whe-
‘ ther linnen, or jerſey, I cannot tell. All
‘ that he wore to me ſeem'd quite new.
‘ That day, it is well known, was rain all
‘ day long from morning to night; it rain'd
‘ when he came in, & likewiſe when he
‘ went forth ; yet I could not perceive any
‘ foulneſs upon his ſhoes, ſpot upon his
‘ ſtockings, or any wett upon his cloaths.
‘ I Samuel Wallis, upon whom this great
‘ and powerful work of Almighty God
‘ was wrought, wrote this with my
‘ own hand [a]. I am,
Sir,
Your moſt affectionate &
humble ſervant

W. FORSTER.

a See a farther account of this matter in Mr. Butchers p. 13, &c. above. Now (notwithſtanding all that is there ſaid by Mr. Butcher & others, & here by Mr. Forſter) ſhould I ſay, I think this relati- on of Wallis is true, ſome would perhaps reply, then I could believe any thing. Or again, ſhould I ſeem to doubt it, as many, it is like, would pronounce me a Sceptic, & one who had no faith. I ſhall not therefore trouble the reader with any thing ſo little to the purpoſe as my own ſentiments, but only add, there are none of this mans relations, that I know of, now left in the town, they being remov'd, as I am told, to Kettering. Nor, as far as I can find, is there any perſon now alive who knew him, tho' ſeveral whoſe fathers did. Particularly the Reverend Mr. John Clarke (Curate of Dudding- ton in Northamptonſhire, ſome three miles off) whoſe father knew the man, & hath often (as he tells me) told his ſaid ſon many of the foreſaid particulars, as he had them from Wallis himſelf, with this addition, that the ſaid Wallis was always reckoned a man of a very honeſt character. The late moſt Reverend John Sharp archbiſhop of York, riding thro' Stanford, & ſeeing an old man, one Alex- ander Morris, in the ſtreet, cauſed his coach to ſtop, & (as the ſaid Alexander Morris himſelf told me) asked him ſeveral queſtions about this Samuel Wallis, & whether he believed this relation concerning him was true? who replied, that, as far as he could find, every body that knew him thought ſo. But after all, how ſhall we reconcile this ſtory with the following paſſage in Mr. Aubreys miſcellanies 8vo, Lond. 1696. p. 69. ‘ An. 165 . . At . . . . . in the Moorlands, in Staffordſhire, lived a poor old ‘ man, who had been a long time lame. One ſunday in the afternoon, he, being alone, one knock'd ‘ at his door: he bade him open it, & come in. The ſtranger deſir'd a cup of beer. The lame man ‘ deſir'd him to take a diſh, & draw ſome; for he was not able to do it himſelf. The ſtranger ask'd the ‘ poor old man, how long he had been ill? The poor man told him. Said the ſtranger, I can cure ‘ you. Take two or three balm leaves ſteep'd in your beer for a fortnight or three weeks ; & you ‘ will be reſtor'd to your health: but conſtantly & zealouſly ſerve God. The poor man did ſo, & ‘ became perfectly well. This ſtranger was in a purple ſhag gown, ſuch as was not ſeen or known in ‘ thoſe parts: & no body in the ſtreet (after Even ſong) did ſee any one in ſuch a colour'd habit. Dr. ‘ Gilbert Sheldon (ſince Archbiſhop of Canterbury) was then in the Moorlands, & juſtified the truth of this to Elias Afhmole Efq; from whom I had this account; and he hath inferted it in fome of his memoirs, which were in the Mufæum, at Oxford? I anfwer, Mr. Aubrey having heard this ftory from Mr. Afhmole, a many years, as it fhould feem, before he put it into writing, might eafily miftake the place, the illnefs, and the leaves. As for Mr. Afhmoles having it confirm'd to him by archbifhop Sheldon, Mr. Aubrey might again miftake Mr. Afhmoles informer. For as Mr. Afhmole was, I believe, acquainted with Mr. Butcher, and, as I conceive, wrote that copy of verfes before his printed book fign'd E. A. it is very probable that he had the ftory from him; &, if his papers which Mr. Aubrey mentions, be in being, I fancy any body, who fhall think it worth their while to confult them, will find it fo. But of this enough.

F I N I S.

E R R A T A.

LIB. I. p.7. l.23. read *Peallan*. l. 24. *Peallano*. p. 15. l. 22. for near, read, at. Lib. II. p.7. l.8. read, obferved that Eddius, as publifhed by the learned Dr. Gale. p.14. l. 13. read, for that K. Ecgfrid. p.37. l. 11. for Parag. XIII. & XIV. read Parag. XV. Lib. III. p. 17. l.4. read, S. Ofwald. l. 15. read, *parans*. Lib. IV. p. 1. read, de la Land. p. 17 l. penult. read, fame time. p. 22. l. 39. read, tells us, this is no ftory, for. Lib. V. the firft note in p. 5. relates to Waltervilles firft charter in p. 4. Lib. VII. p. 8. l. 20. read, no where. Lib. VIII. p. 14. l.41. read, into that fee. p. 16. l. 17. read, Erlefhage. p. 18. l. 7. read, conceffion &c. p. 28. l. 16. read, *teftæm*. p. 56. l. 25. read, dimifed. l. 29. dimife. p. 41. l. 13. read, being a rent. Lib. IX. p. 5. l. 29. after *hands*: begin Parag. V. p. 19. l. 39. read, the rudiments. p. 40. l. 38. after Valerian. begin Parag. XXV. p. 49. read, Parag. XXXII. p. 50. read, Par. XXXIII. Lib. X. p. 3. l. ult. read, miftake. p. 4 l. 12. read, but for that. p. 9. l. 2. 3. read, Fifh-lake. p. 10. l. 36. read, Maud de. p. 17. read, Par. XII. p. 20. read, Par. XIII. XIV. p. 21. read Par. XV. p. 23. read, Par. XVI. Lib. XI. p. 21. l. 29. read, main thing. p. 26. l. 28. read, dropping. p. 38. l. 34. read, Bruges. p. 56. l. 19. after *the* 7. begin Parag. XXVIII. p. 64. l. 18. read Leffey. p. 68. dele Edw. L. Spencer, & read, Wm. de Bohun & Edm. Langhley, both of them. Lib. XII. p. 24. margin, read, Mar. 13. May 25. Lib. XIII. p. 13. l. 1. dele, &, l. 7. read, Rowceby. Lib. XIV. p. 21. after meadow. l. 5. begin Parag. XV. p. 25. l. 30. read, the orfrees. p. 28. l. 23. read, lauds. p. 56. l. 33. read, a fanctes bell. Table. p. 11. col. b. l. 5. read, deferts. p. 14. col. b. l. 27. dele, as. ib. l. 55. read, 1295. Butcher. p. 3. col. a. l. 19. read, thefe. p. 6. col. a. l. 30. read, was the firft. p. 10. col. a. l. 21. read, feemingly. l. ult. read, was it. l. 18. dele the note h. Forfter. p. 9. 11. 13. 15. in the running title, read to Mr. John Stevens. p. 11. col. a, l. 25. read affures us. It. p. 15. col. b. l. 50. read, by doing this.

N. B. By an Overfight there are 7 & 8 pages to the XI. Book.

INDEX

This index has been compiled by members of the Stamford Survey Group (especially by Mrs M. M. Baile) over a number of years. Every attempt has been made to remove the inconsistencies inevitable in such a group project.

REFERENCES
Roman numerals indicate the book in which a reference may be found; this is followed by arabic numerals indicating the pages in that book. Ded. indicates the Dedication which forms an introduction to the work. Pre. indicates the Preface. B indicates the revised *Survey* of Richard Butcher; and F the two *Letters* of the Revd. William Forster, printed at the end of the book; these have separate paginations.

ABBREVIATIONS

abb	abbey, abbot	e	earl
ald	alderman	K	King
abp	archbishop	n	note
bp	bishop	Q	queen
ch	church	s	son
d	duke	St	saint
dtr	daughter	w	wife

PERSONAL AND PLACE NAMES
The index has usually retained the spelling forms in Peck, with cross references where persons and places are clearly identified. Where names are uncertain they have been left unidentified. The form of name used for Peck's scholarly references is generally that given in the *British Museum Catalogue of Printed Books*. Where place names have been clearly identified they have been located by their traditional counties; but since 1974 the old counties of Huntingdon and Rutland have formed part of the enlarged counties of Cambridge and Leicester. Some places formerly in Northamptonshire are now also part of Cambridgeshire. Bath and Bristol are now part of the new county of Avon.

ILLUSTRATIONS
Illustrations have not been indexed as individual plates are often wanting in copies of the book. A complete list of the illustrations is included in the preliminary pages of this edition.

i